SEVENTH EDITION

STRATEGIC MANAGEMENT

CONCEPTS & CASES

FRED R. DAVID

Francis Marion University

Prentice Hall
Upper Saddle River, New Jersey 07458

Acquisitions Editor: David Shafer
Associate Editor: Shane Gemza
Editorial Assistant: Shannon Sims
Editor-in-Chief: Natalie Anderson
Marketing Manager: Tami Wederbrand
Production Editor: Lynne Breitfeller
Production Coordinator: Tara Ruggerio
Managing Editor: Dee Josephson
Manufacturing Supervisor: Arnold Vila
Senior Designer: Jill Little
Design Director: Pat Smythe
Cover Design: Michael Fruhbeis
Composition/Project Management: TSI Graphics, Inc.
Cover Art/Photo: Mehau Kulyk, Photo Researchers, Inc.

Copyright © 1999, 1997, 1995, 1993, 1991 by Prentice-Hall, Inc.
Upper Saddle River, New Jersey 07458

Library of Congress Cataloging-in-Publication Data
David, Fred R.
    Strategic management / Fred R. David. — 7th ed.
        p.   cm.
    Includes bibliographical references and index.
    ISBN 0-13-080785-0
        1. Strategic planning—Case studies.   2. Strategic planning.
    I. Title.
    HD30.28.D385   1998   98-47066
    658.4′012—dc21   CIP

Printed in the United States of America

10 9 8 7 6 5 4 3

ISBN 0-13-080785-0

Prentice-Hall International (UK) Limited, London
Prentice-Hall of Australia Pty. Limited, Sydney
Prentice-Hall Canada Inc., Toronto
Prentice-Hall Hispanoamericana, S.A., Mexico
Prentice-Hall of India Private Limited, New Delhi
Prentice-Hall of Japan, Inc., Tokyo
Pearson Education Asia Pte. Ltd., Singapore
Editora Prentice-Hall do Brasil, Ltda., Rio de Janeiro

To:
Joy, Forest, Byron, and Meredith—my wife and children—
for their encouragement and love.

Brief Contents

Contents

Preface

The business world today is much different than it was just two years ago when the previous edition of this text was introduced. Internet use has skyrocketed, China peacefully annexed Hong Kong, Europe agreed on a common currency, Southeast Asian stock markets crashed, thousands of firms globalized, and thousands more merged. Downsizing, rightsizing, reengineering and countless divestitures, acquisitions, and liquidations permanently altered the corporate landscape. Hundreds of new strategic management articles appeared in journals, magazines, and newspapers and altered strategic thinking. Changes made in this edition are aimed squarely at illustrating the effect that our rapidly changing world has on strategic management theory and practice.

Our mission in preparing the seventh edition of *Strategic Management* was "to create the most current, well written business policy textbook on the market—a book that is exciting and valuable to both students and professors." To achieve this mission, significant improvements have been on every page and to every piece of the teaching package. The time basis for all cases included in this edition is 1997–1998, representing the most up-to-date compilation of cases ever assembled in a business policy text. New strategic management research and practice from this era are incorporated throughout the chapters. Hundreds of new examples appear throughout the text. The Cohesion Case on Hershey Foods and the Experiential Exercises are fully updated.

Scores of reviewers and I believe you will find this edition to be the best ever, and now the best business policy textbook available, for communicating both the excitement and value of strategic management. Now published in four different languages—English, Chinese, Spanish, and German—this text is perhaps the most widely used strategic planning book in the world.

SPECIAL NOTE TO PROFESSORS

This textbook meets all AACSB guidelines for the business policy and strategic management course at both the graduate and undergraduate level. Previous editions of this text have been used at more than 500 colleges and universities. Prentice Hall maintains a separate Web site for this text at www.prenhall.com/davidsm. The author maintains the Strategic Management Club Online at www.strategyclub.com. Membership is free to professors and $29 for students.

Although structure of this edition parallels the last, great improvements have been made in readability, currentness, and coverage. In keeping with the mission "to become the most current, well written business policy textbook on the market," every page has undergone rethinking and rewriting to streamline, update, and improve the caliber of presentation.

A net result of this activity is that every chapter is shorter in length. The most current concepts and practices in strategic management are presented in a style that is clear, focused, and relevant. Changes in this edition add up to the biggest revision ever made on this popular text.

CHAPTER THEMES

The following three themes permeate all chapters in this edition, and contribute significantly to making this text timely, informative, exciting, and valuable.

1. *Global Factors Affect Virtually All Strategic Decisions*

   The Global theme is enhanced in this edition because doing business globally has become a necessity rather than a luxury in most industries. Growing interdependence among countries and companies worldwide is evidenced by stock markets around the world dramatically affecting volatility of each other. But doing business globally is more risky and complex than ever. The dynamics of political, economic, and cultural differences across countries directly affect strategic management decisions.

2. *Information Technology Is a Vital Strategic Management Tool*

   The Information Technology theme is more deeply integrated in response to accelerating strategic use of computer technology to gather, analyze, send, and receive information. Unlike several years ago, most college students now surf the Web, send e-mail, and use the Internet. Since the last edition, literally thousands of companies have established world wide web home pages and are conducting commerce internationally on the Internet. Important U.S. government documents are now available over the Internet and updated monthly. Using monthly rather than annually updated information makes a tremendous difference in strategic decision making.

3. *Preserving the Natural Environment Is a Vital Strategic Issue*

Unique to strategic management texts, the Natural Environment theme is strengthened in this edition in order to promote the need for firms to conduct operations in an environmentally sound manner, or face increasingly stiff penalties and criticism. Smog in Southeast Asia has killed thousands of people and El Niño devastates coastal areas worldwide. Numerous countries globally have enacted laws to curtail firms from polluting streams, rivers, the air, land, and sea. The strategic efforts of both companies and countries to preserve the natural environment are described. Respect for the natural environment has become an important concern for consumers, companies, society, and the AACSB.

TIME-TESTED FEATURES

This edition continues many of the special *time-tested features* and content that have made this text so successful over the last decade. Trademarks of this text strengthened in this edition are as follows:

Chapters: Time-Tested Features

◆ The text meets AACSB guidelines which support a practitioner orientation rather than a theory/research approach. This text aims to support that effort by taking a skills-oriented approach to developing a mission statement, performing an external audit, conducting an internal assessment, and formulating, implementing, and evaluating strategies.

◆ The author's writing style is concise, conversational, interesting, logical, lively, and supported by numerous current examples throughout.

◆ A simple, integrative strategic-management model appears in all chapters and on the inside front cover of the text.

◆ A fully updated Hershey Foods Cohesion Case appears after chapter 1 and is revisited at the end of each chapter. The Hershey case allows students to apply strategic-management concepts and techniques to a real organization as chapter material is covered. This integrative (cohesive) approach readies students for case analysis. Hershey encourages professors and students to call 1-800-468-1714 for additional information or visit their home page at www.hersheys.com.

◆ End-of-chapter Experiential Exercises effectively apply concepts and techniques in a challenging, meaningful, and enjoyable manner. Eighteen exercises apply text material to the Cohesion Case; ten apply textual material to a college or university; another ten send students into the business world to explore important strategy topics. The exercises are relevant, interesting, and contemporary.

◆ Pedagogy, including Notable Quotes and Objectives to open each chapter, and Key Terms, Current Readings, Discussion Questions, and Experiential Exercises close each chapter.

◆ Excellent coverage of business ethics aimed at more than meeting AACSB standards.

◆ Excellent coverage of strategy implementation issues such as corporate culture, organizational structure, marketing concepts, and financial tools and techniques.

◆ A systematic, analytical approach presented in chapter 6, including matrices such as the TOWS, BCG, IE, GRAND, SPACE, and QSPM.

◆ The chapter material is again published in four color.

◆ "Take It to the Net" Internet exercises available online at www.prenhall.com/davidsm.

◆ The Web site www.prenhall.com/davidsm provides chapter and case updates and support materials.

◆ A paperback version of only the Concepts is available.

◆ An outstanding ancillary package, including:

   ◆ A comprehensive *Instructor's Manual.*

   ◆ An elaborate *Case Solutions Manual* with a complete set of matrices.

   ◆ An extensive transparency package available in PowerPoint format.

   ◆ Seventeen corporate case videos.

   ◆ A computerized test bank.

   ◆ A companion Web site for students and professors at www.prenhall.com/davidsm.

Cases: Time-Tested Features

◆ The 1997–1998 time frame for cases offers the most current set in any business policy text on the market.

◆ The cases focuses on well known firms as well as smaller organizations making strategic changes. All cases are undisguised and most are exclusively written for this text to reflect current strategic-management problems and practices.

◆ The cases feature a great mix of small business, international, and not-for-profit firms organized conveniently by industry.

◆ All cases have been class tested to ensure that they are interesting, challenging, and effective for illustrating strategic-management concepts.

◆ An excellent Industry Note precedes each set of cases.

◆ Almost all cases provide complete financial information about the firm and an organizational chart.

◆ Customized inclusion of cases to comprise a tailored text is available to meet the special needs of some professors.

◆ A paperback version of only the cases is available.

◆ A special matrix provided here in the Preface compares all cases in the text on important criteria such as topics covered, size of firm, complexity of case, etc.

NEW TO THIS EDITION

In addition to the special time-tested trademarks described above, this edition includes some exciting new features designed to position this text as the clear leader and best choice for teaching business policy and strategic management:

Cases: New Features

◆ Twelve brand new, 1997/1998 cases focusing on companies in the news appear exclusively for the first time in this text:

Dayton Hudson
Harrah's Entertainment
Southwest Airlines
H.J. Heinz
Apple Computer
America Online
Swisher International Group
Grace Lutheran Church
Central United Methodist Church
RailTex
Riverbanks Zoo
Revlon

◆ Twenty-three fully-updated 1997/1998 cases from the last edition:

The Limited, Inc.
Wal-Mart Stores
Circus Circus Enterprises
Banc One
Citicorp
Audubon Zoo
DM&E Railroad
Greyhound Lines
Carnival Corporation
Elkins Lake Baptist Church
Classic Car Club of America
Harley-Davidson
Winnebago Industries
Avon Products
UST, Inc.
Campbell Soup
Pilgrim's Pride
Boeing
Stryker
Biomet
Playboy Enterprises
Nike
E.L. Nickell

◆ Three church cases are included in this edition as more and more churches embrace strategic planning—one Baptist church case, on Methodist church, and one Lutheran church.

◆ A new, comprehensive 1997 Industry Note precedes each set of cases.

◆ A new mix of cases include 11 small business cases, 22 international cases, and six not-for-profit cases.

◆ A new Hershey Foods Cohesion Case is fully updated from the previous edition.

Chapters: New Features

◆ A new Global Perspective boxed insert is integrated into each chapter to support the expanded global nature of the text.

◆ A new Information Technology boxed insert is appropriately integrated into each chapter to portray the increasing reliance upon information technology by both large and small firms.

◆ A new Natural Environment boxed insert appears in each chapter to show increasing strategic relevance of this issue to business.

◆ New topics covered more extensively in the chapters include reengineering, downsizing, rightsizing, restructuring, culture, and use of the Internet for strategic purposes.

◆ New company examples are provided in every chapter.

◆ New research is integrated into every chapter with new current readings at the end of each chapter.

◆ New Web site addresses (over 100) are provided throughout the chapters.

◆ Chapter 10 on International Strategic Management Issues has been completely overhauled and greatly improved.

◆ Chapter 4 on Conducting an External Strategic Management Audit has been shortened and strengthened with new Internet sources of information replacing lists of library sources.

ANCILLARY MATERIALS

◆ *Case Solutions Manual.* Provides a comprehensive teacher's note for all 35 cases. The teacher's notes feature detailed analyses, classroom discussion questions with answers, an external and internal assessment, specific recommendations, strategy-implementation material, analytical matracies and an epilogue for each case.

◆ *Instructor's Manual.* Provides lecture notes, teaching tips, answers to all end-of-chapter Experiential Exercises and Review Questions, additional Experiential Exercises not in the text, a glossary with definitions of all end-of-chapter key terms and concepts, sample course syllabi, and a test bank of 1,364 questions with answers.

◆ *Seventeen Corporate Case Video Segments.* To accompany the Cohesion Case, a 21-minute color video prepared by Hershey Foods Corporation is available to adopters free of charge. Shown near the beginning of the course, the Hershey Foods video can arouse students' interest in studying the Cohesion Case and completing Experiential Exercises that apply chapter material to this case. In addition, a collection of sixteen other case video segments are available free of charge. The segments average 15 minutes each and were professionally prepared by firms used in cases in this text. Videos are provided to accompany the following cases: The Limited, Winnebago Industries, Playboy Enterprises, Banc One, Audubon Zoo, Nike, and Pilgrim's Pride.

◆ *Transparency Masters.* A total of 50 color transparency acetates are available with this text. Half of the transparencies are from exhibits and figures in the text, while the other half are from sources outside the text.

◆ *Printed and Computerized Test Bank.* The test bank for this text includes 737 True/False questions, 425 multiple choice questions, and 202 essay questions for the text chapters. Sample comprehensive tests for chapters 1–5 and chapters 6–10 are also given, and answers to all objective questions are provided. The test questions given in the instructor's manual are also available on computerized test software to facilitate preparing and grading tests.

◆ *PowerPoint Case Solutions Manual Diskette.* Each case is accompanied by a set of PowerPoint slides to assist in class discussion and analysis.

◆ *Companion Web site on PHLIP (Prentice Hall learning on the Internet Partnership):*

—*Interactive Study Guide:* Includes multiple choice and true/false questions for every chapter of the text. Graded by our server, the immediate feedback includes additional help and page references to the text.

—*Current Events Articles and Exercises:* are added bi-monthly, to illustrate how management concepts impact the real world.

—*Management Internet Resources:* include helpful sites linked to the relevant sections of the text.

—*Study Hall and Writing Center:* feature student-orientated links to virtual libraries, dictionaries, on-line tutors and more.

—*Faculty Resource Center:* includes sample syllabi, PowerPoint presentations, using the Internet, and faculty chat rooms.

—*On-Line Course Syllabus Building:* allows the instructor to create a custom on-line syllabus.

SPECIAL NOTE TO STUDENTS

Welcome to business policy. This is a challenging and exciting course that will allow you to function as the owner or chief executive officer of different organizations. Your major task in this course will be to make strategic decisions and to justify those decisions through oral and written communication. Strategic decisions determine the future direction and competitive position of an enterprise for a long time. Decisions to expand geographically or to diversify are examples of strategic decisions.

Strategic decision making occurs in all types and sizes of organizations, from General Motors to a small hardware store. Many people's lives and jobs are affected by strategic decisions, so the stakes are very high. An organization's very survival is often at stake. The overall importance of strategic decisions makes this course especially exciting and challenging. You will be called upon in business policy to demonstrate how your strategic decisions could be successfully implemented.

In this course you can look forward to making strategic decisions both as an individual and as a member of a team. No matter how hard employees work, an organization is in real trouble if strategic decisions are not made effectively. Doing the right things (effectiveness) is more important than doing things right (efficiency). For example, Kodak was prosperous in the early 1990s, but ineffective strategies led to billion dollar losses in the late 1990s.

You will have the opportunity in this course to make actual strategic decisions, perhaps for the first time in your academic career. Do not hesitate to take a stand and defend specific strategies that you determine to be the best. The rationale for your strategic decisions will be more important than the actual decision, because no one knows for sure what the best strategy is for a particular organization at a given point in time. This fact accents the subjective, contingency nature of the strategic-management process. Use the concepts and tools presented in this text, coupled with your own intuition, to recommend strategies that you can defend as being most appropriate for the organizations that you study. You will also need to integrate knowledge acquired in previous business courses. For this reason, business policy is often called a capstone course; you may want to keep this book for your personal library.

This text is practitioner-oriented and applications-oriented. It presents strategic-management concepts that will enable you to formulate, implement, and evaluate strategies in all kinds of profit and nonprofit organizations. The end-of-chapter Experiential Exercises allow you to apply what you've read in each chapter to the Hershey Foods Cohesion Case and to your own university.

Consider joining the Strategic Management Club Online at www.strategyclub.com. The templates and links there will save you time in performing analyses and will make your work look professional. Work hard in policy this term and have fun. Good luck!

ACKNOWLEDGMENTS

Many persons have contributed time, energy, ideas, and suggestions for improving this text over four editions. The strength of this text is largely attributed to the collective wisdom, work, and experiences of business policy professors, strategic-management researchers, students, and practitioners. Names of particular individuals whose published research is referenced in the fourth edition of this text are listed alphabetically in the Name Index. To all individuals involved in making this text so popular and successful, I am indebted and thankful.

Many special persons and reviewers contributed valuable material and suggestions for this edition. I would like to thank my colleagues and friends at Auburn University, Mississippi State University, East Carolina University, and Francis Marion University. These are universities where I have served on the management faculty. Scores of students and professors at these schools shaped development of this text.

Individuals who develop cases for the North American Case Research Association Meeting, the Midwest Society for Case Research Meeting, the Eastern Casewriters Association Meeting, the European Case Research Association Meeting, and Harvard Case Services are vitally important for continued progress in the field of strategic management. From a research perspective, writing business policy cases represents a valuable scholarly activity among faculty. Extensive research is required to structure business policy cases in a way that exposes strategic issues, decisions, and behavior. Pedagogically, business policy cases are essential for students in learning how to apply concepts, evaluate situations, formulate strategies, and resolve implementation problems. Without a continuous stream of up-to-date business policy cases, the strategic-management course and discipline would lose much of its energy and excitement.

The following individuals wrote cases that were selected for inclusion in this text. These persons helped develop the most current compilation of cases ever assembled in a business policy text:

Claire Anderson, Old Dominion University
Jill Austin, Middle Tennessee State University
Robert Barrett, Francis Marion University
Henry Beam, Western Michigan University

Art Boyette, Francis Marion University
Lynn Brumfield, Middle Tennessee State University
Donald Bumpass, Sam Houston State University
Jim Camerius, Northern Michigan University
Thomas Carey, Western Michigan University
Carol Cumber, South Dakota State University
Satish Deshpande, Western Michigan University
Ronald Earl, Sam Houston State University
Caroline Fisher, Loyola University New Orleans
Jack Goebel, Francis Marion University
Christie Haney, Sam Houston State University
James Harbin, East Texas State University
Marilyn Helms, University of Tennessee at Chattanooga
Mike Keeffe, Southwest Texas State University
Kay Lawrimore, Francis Marion University
Ted Legatski, Sam Houston State University
Dean Lewis, Sam Houston State University
Charles Manz, Arizona State University
John Marcis, Francis Marion University
Bill Middlebrook, Southwest Texas State University
Kent Nassen, Iowa State University
Shelby Nickell, CEO of EL Nickell Company
Melodie Phillips, Middle Tennessee State University
Tyra Phipps, Frostburg State University
J. Porciello, Bentley College
Paul Reed, Sam Houston State University
John Ross, Southwest Texas State University
Richard Scamehorn, Ohio University
Peter Schoderbek, University of Iowa
Amit Shah, Frostburg State University
Frank Shipper, Arizona State University
Charles Shrader, Iowa State University
Matthew Sonfield, Hofstra University
David Stanton, Stanton Consulting
Charles Sterrett, Frostburg State University
Carolyn Stokes, Francis Marion University
Sharese Whitecotton, Sam Houston State University

Scores of Prentice Hall employees and salespersons have worked diligently behind the scenes to make this text a leader in the business policy market. I appreciate the continued hard work of all those persons.

I also want to thank you, the reader, for investing time and effort reading and studying this text. As we approach the twenty-first century together, this book will help you formulate, implement, and evaluate strategies for organizations with which you become associated. I hope you come to share my enthusiasm for the rich subject area of strategic management and for the systematic learning approach taken in this text.

Finally, I want to welcome and invite your suggestions, ideas, thoughts, and comments and questions regarding any part of this test or the ancillary materials. Please call me at 843-661-1431/1419, fax me at 843-661-1432, e-mail me at Fdavid@Fmarion.edu, or write me at the School of Business, Francis Marion University, Florence, South Carolina 29501. I appreciate and need your input to continually improve this text in future editions. Drawing my attention to specific errors or deficiencies in coverage or exposition will especially be appreciated.

Thank you for using this text.

HOW TO LOCATE THE CASE COMPANIES

	STOCK SYMBOL	STOCK EXCH	TELEPHONE NUMBER	HEADQUARTERS ADDRESS	WEB PAGE ADDRESS
1. The Limited, Inc.	LTD	NY	614-479-7000	3 Limited Parkway Columbus, Ohio 43230	www.limited.com
2. Wal-Mart Stores, Inc.	WMT	NY	501-273-4000	Wal-Mart Stores Bentonville, Arkansas 72716	www.wal-mart.com
3. Dayton Hudson Corp.	DH	NY	612-370-6948	777 Nicollet Mall Minneapolis, Minnesota 55402	www.dhc.com
4. Circus Circus Enterprises	CIR	NY	707-734-0410	2880 Las Vegas Blvd. S. Las Vegas, NV 89109	www.circuscircus.org
5. Harrah's Entertainment	HET	NY	901-762-8600	1023 Cherry Road Memphis, TN 38117	www.harrahs.com
6. Banc One Corp.	ONE	NY	614-248-5944 800-573-4048	100 E. Broad St. Columbus, OH 43271	ww.bankone.com
7. Citicorp	CCI	NY	212-559-1000 800-248-4636	349 Park Ave., 2nd Fl. New York, NY 10043	www.citicorp.com
8. Audubon Zoo	N/A	N/A	504-861-2537	New Orleans, LA	www.auduboninstitute.org
9. Riverbanks Zoo	N/A	N/A	803-779-8717	Riverbanks Society PO Box 1060 Columbia, SC 29202	www.riverbanks.org
10. DM&E Railroad	N/A	N/A	—	Brookings, SD	www.dmerail.com
11. RailTex, Inc.	RTEX	NASDAQ	210-841-7600	4040 Broadway, #200 San Antonio, TX 78209	www.railtex.com
12. Greyhound Lines, Inc.	BUS	AMEX	214-789-7000	15110 N. Dallas Pkwy., #600 Dallas, TX 75248	www.greyhound.com
13. Carnival Corp.	CCL	NY	800-438-6744 305-599-2600	3655 N.W. 87th Miami, FL 33178	www.carnival.com
14. Southwest Airlines Co.	LUV	NY	214-792-4000	P.O. Box 3661 Dallas, TX 75235	www.iflyswa.com
15. Central United Methodist Church	N/A		803-662-3218	225 W. Cheves St. Florence, SC 29501	N/A
16. Elkins Lake Baptist Church	N/A		409-295-7694	Huntsville, Texas	N/A
17. Grace Lutheran Church	N/A		—	Waterford, SD	N/A
18. The Classic Car Club of America, Inc.	N/A		847-390-0443	1645 Des Plaines River Rd. Suite 7 Des Plaines, IL 60018	www.classiccarclub.org
19. Harley-Davidson, Inc.	HDI	NY	414-342-4680	3700 W. Juneau Ave. Milwaukee, WI 53208	www.harley-davidson.com

20. Winnebago Industries, Inc.			515-582-03535	605 W. Crystal Lake Rd.	www.winnebagoind.com
	WAGO	NY		Forest City, Iowa 50436	
21. Avon Products, Inc.	AVP	NY	212-546-6015	9 W. 57th Street	www.avon.com
				New York, NY 10019	
22. Revlon, Inc.	REV	NY	212-527-4000	625 Madison Ave.	www.revlon.com
				New York, NT 10022	
23. UST, Inc.	UST	NY	203-661-1100	100 W. Putnam	N/A
				Greenwich, CONN 06830	
24. Swisher International Group, Inc.			203-656-8000	20 Thorndale Circle	N/A
	SWR	NY		Darien, CONN 06820	
25. Campbell Soup Co.	CPB	NY	609-342-4800	Campbell Place	www.campbellsoup.com
				Camden, NJ 08103	
26. Pilgrim's Pride Corp.	CHX	NY	903-855-1000	110 South Texas St.	www.pilgrimspride.com
				Pittsburg, Texas 75686	
27. H.J. Heinz Co.	HNZ	NY	412-456-5700	600 Grant Street	N/A
				Pittsburg, PA 15219	
28. The Boeing Co.	BA	NY	206-655-2121	7755 E. Marginal Way S.	www.boeing.com
				Seattle, WA 98108	
29. Apple Computer, Inc.	AAPL	NASDAQ	408-996-1010	1 Infinite Loop	www.apple.com
			800-776-2333	Cupertino, CA 95014	
30. America Online, Inc.	AQL	NY	703-448-8700	22000 American Online Way	www.aol.com
			800-827-6364	Dulles, VA 20166	
31. Stryker Corp.	STRY	NASDAQ	616-385-2600	2775 Fairfield Rd.	www.stryker.com
				Kalamazoo, MI 49002	www.endostrykercorp.com
32. Biomet, Inc.	BMET	NASDAQ	219-267-6639	Airport Industrial Pk.	www.biomet.com
				Warsaw, Indiana 46581	
33. Playboy Enterprises, Inc.	PLA	NY	312-751-800	680 N. Lake Shore Dr.	www.playboy.com
				Chicago, IL 60611	
34. Nike, Inc.	NKE	NY	503-671-6453	1 Bowerman Dr.	www.nike.com
				Beaverton, OR 97005	
35. E.L. Nickell Co.	N/A	N/A	616-435-2475	PO Box 97	N/A
				Constantine, MI	

How to Analyze a Business Policy Case

OBJECTIVES

After studying this chapter, you should be able to do the following:

1. Describe the case method for learning strategic-management concepts.

2. Identify the steps in preparing a comprehensive written case analysis.

3. Describe how to give an effective oral case analysis presentation.

4. Discuss fifty tips for doing case analysis.

NOTABLE QUOTES

The essential fact that makes the case method an educational experience of the greatest power is that it makes the student an active rather than a passive participant.—WALLACE B. DONHAM

The great aim of education is not knowledge, but action.—HERBERT SPENCER

Two heads are better than one.—UNKNOWN AUTHOR

Good writers do not turn in their first draft. Ask someone else to read your written case analysis, and read it out loud to yourself. That way, you can find rough areas to clear up.—LAWRENCE JAUCH

One reaction frequently heard is, "I don't have enough information." In reality, strategists never have enough information because some information is not available and some is too costly.—WILLIAM GLUECK

I keep six honest serving men. They taught me all I know. Their names are What, Why, When, How, Where, and Who.—RUDYARD KIPLING

Don't recommend anything you would not be prepared to do yourself if you were in the decision maker's shoes.—A.J. STRICKLAND III

A picture is worth a thousand words.—UNKNOWN AUTHOR

The purpose of this section is to help you analyze business policy cases. Guidelines for preparing written and oral case analyses are given, and suggestions for preparing cases for class discussion are presented. Steps to follow in preparing case analyses are provided. Guidelines for making an oral presentation are described.

What Is a Business Policy Case?

A *business policy case* describes an organization's external and internal condition and raises issues concerning the firm's mission, strategies, objectives, and policies. Most of the information in a business policy case is established fact, but some information may be opinions, judgments, and beliefs. Business-policy cases are more comprehensive than those you may have studied in other courses. They generally include a description of related management, marketing, finance/accounting, production/operations, R&D, computer information systems, and natural environment issues. A business policy case puts the reader on the scene of the action by describing a firm's situation at some point in time. Business policy cases are written to give you practice applying strategic-management concepts. The case method for studying strategic management is often called *learning by doing*.

Guidelines for Preparing Case Analyses

The Need for Practicality   There is no such thing as a complete case, and no case ever gives you all the information you need to conduct analyses and make recommendations. Likewise, in the business world, strategists never have all the information they need to make decisions: information may be unavailable, too costly to obtain, or may take too much time to obtain. So, in preparing business policy cases, do what strategists do every day—make reasonable assumptions about unknowns, state assumptions clearly, perform appropriate analyses, and make decisions. *Be practical.* For example, in performing a pro forma financial analysis, make reasonable assumptions, state them appropriately, and proceed to show what impact your recommendations are expected to have on the organization's financial position. Avoid saying, "I don't have enough information." You can always supplement the information provided in a case with research in your college library. Library research is required in case analyses.

The Need for Justification   The most important part of analyzing cases is not what strategies you recommend, but rather how you support your decisions and how you propose that they be implemented. There is no single best solution or one right answer to a case, so give ample justification for your recommendations. This is important. In the business world, strategists usually do not know if their decisions are right until resources have been allocated and consumed. Then it is often too late to reverse the decisions. This cold fact accents the need for careful integration of intuition and analysis in preparing business policy case analyses.

The Need for Realism   Avoid recommending a course of action beyond an organization's means. *Be realistic.* No organization can possibly pursue all the strategies that could potentially benefit the firm. Estimate how much capital will be required to implement what you recommended. Determine whether debt, stock, or a combination of debt and stock could be used to obtain the capital. Make sure your recommendations are feasible. Do not prepare a case analysis that omits all arguments and information not supportive of your recommendations. Rather, present the major advantages and disadvantages of several feasible alternatives. Try not to exaggerate, stereotype, prejudge, or overdramatize. Strive to demonstrate that your interpretation of the evidence is reasonable and objective.

THE NEED FOR SPECIFICITY   Do not make broad generalizations such as "The company should pursue a market penetration strategy." *Be specific* by telling what, why, when, how, where, and who. Failure to use specifics is the single major shortcoming of most oral and written case analyses. For example, in an internal audit say, "The firm's current ratio fell from 2.2 in 1998 to 1.3 in 1999, and this is considered to be a major weakness," instead of, "The firm's financial condition is bad." Rather than concluding from a SPACE Matrix that a firm should be defensive, be more specific, saying, "The firm should consider closing three plants, laying off 280 employees, and divesting itself of its chemical division, for a net savings of $20.2 million in 1998." Use ratios, percentages, numbers, and dollar estimates. Businesspeople dislike generalities and vagueness.

THE NEED FOR ORIGINALITY   Do not necessarily recommend the course of action that the firm plans to take or actually undertook, even if those actions resulted in improved revenues and earnings. The aim of case analysis is for you to consider all the facts and information relevant to the organization at the time, generate feasible alternative strategies, choose among those alternatives, and defend your recommendations. Put yourself back in time to the point when strategic decisions were being made by the firm's strategists. Based on information available then, what would you have done? Support your position with charts, graphs, ratios, analyses, and the like—not a revelation from the library. You can become a good strategist by thinking through situations, making management assessments, and proposing plans yourself. *Be original.* Compare and contrast what you recommend versus what the company plans to do or did.

THE NEED TO CONTRIBUTE   Strategy formulation, implementation, and evaluation decisions are commonly made by a group of individuals rather than by a single person. Therefore, your professor may divide the class into three- or four-person teams to prepare written or oral case analyses. Members of a strategic-management team, in class or in the business world, differ on their aversion to risk, their concern for short-run versus long-run benefits, their attitudes toward social responsibility, and their views concerning globalization. There are no perfect people, so there are no perfect strategists. Be open-minded to others' views. *Be a good listener and a good contributor.*

PREPARING A CASE FOR CLASS DISCUSSION

Your professor may ask you to prepare a case for class discussion. Preparing a case for class discussion means that you need to read the case before class, make notes regarding the organization's external opportunities/threats and internal strengths/weaknesses, perform appropriate analyses, and come to class prepared to offer and defend some specific recommendations.

THE CASE METHOD VERSUS LECTURE APPROACH   The case method of teaching is radically different from the traditional lecture approach, in which little or no preparation is needed by students before class. The *case method* involves a classroom situation in which students do most of the talking; your professor facilitates discussion by asking questions and encouraging student interaction regarding ideas, analyses, and recommendations. Be prepared for a discussion along the lines of, "What would you do, why would you do it, when would you do it, and how would you do it?" Prepare answers to the following types of questions:

- ◆ What are the firm's most important external opportunities and threats?
- ◆ What are the organization's major strengths and weaknesses?
- ◆ How would you describe the organization's financial condition?
- ◆ What are the firm's existing strategies and objectives?
- ◆ Who are the firm's competitors and what are their strategies?
- ◆ What objectives and strategies do you recommend for this organization? Explain your reasoning. How does what you recommend compare to what the company plans?
- ◆ How could the organization best implement what you recommend? What implementation problems do you envision? How could the firm avoid or solve those problems?

THE CROSS-EXAMINATION   Do not hesitate to take a stand on the issues and to support your position with objective analyses and outside research. Strive to apply strategic-management concepts and tools in preparing your case for class discussion. Seek defensible arguments and positions. Support opinions and judgments with facts, reasons, and evidence. Crunch the numbers before class! Be willing to describe your recommendations to the class without fear of disapproval. Respect the ideas of others, but be willing to go against the majority opinion when you can justify a better position.

Business policy case analysis gives you the opportunity to learn more about yourself, your colleagues, strategic management, and the decision-making process in organizations. The rewards of this experience will depend upon the effort you put forth, so do a good job. Discussing business policy cases in class is exciting and challenging. Expect views counter to those you present. Different students will place emphasis on different aspects of an organization's situation and submit different recommendations for scrutiny and rebuttal. Cross-examination discussions commonly arise, just as they occur in a real business organization. Avoid being a silent observer.

PREPARING A WRITTEN CASE ANALYSIS

In addition to asking you to prepare a case for class discussion, your professor may ask you to prepare a written case analysis. Preparing a written case analysis is similar to preparing a case for class discussion, except written reports are generally more structured and more detailed. There is no ironclad procedure for preparing a written case analysis because cases differ in focus; the type, size, and complexity of the organizations being analyzed also vary.

When writing a strategic-management report or case analysis, avoid using jargon, vague or redundant words, acronyms, abbreviations, sexist language, and ethnic or racial slurs, and watch your spelling. Use short sentences and paragraphs and simple words and phrases. Use quite a few subheadings. Arrange issues and ideas from the most important to the least important. Arrange recommendations from the least controversial to the most controversial. Use the active voice rather than the passive voice for all verbs; for example, say, "Our team recommends that the company diversify," rather than, "It is recommended by our team to diversify." Use many examples to add specificity and clarity. Tables, figures, pie charts, bar charts, time lines, and other kinds of exhibits help communicate important points and ideas. Sometimes a picture *is* worth a thousand words.

THE EXECUTIVE SUMMARY   Your professor may ask you to focus the written case analysis on a particular aspect of the strategic-management process, such as (1) to identify and evaluate the organization's existing mission, objectives, and strategies; or (2) to propose and defend specific recommendations for the company; or (3) to develop an industry analysis by describing the competitors, products, selling techniques, and market conditions in a given industry. These types of written reports are sometimes called *executive summaries*. An executive summary usually ranges from three to five pages of text in length, plus exhibits.

THE COMPREHENSIVE WRITTEN ANALYSIS   Your professor may ask you to prepare a *comprehensive written analysis*. This assignment requires you to apply the entire strategic-management process to the particular organization. When preparing a comprehensive written analysis, picture yourself as a consultant who has been asked by a company to conduct a study of its external and internal environment and make specific recommendations for its future. Prepare exhibits to support your recommendations. Highlight exhibits with some discussion in the paper. Comprehensive written analyses are usually about ten pages in length, plus exhibits.

STEPS IN PREPARING A COMPREHENSIVE WRITTEN ANALYSIS   In preparing a comprehensive written analysis, you could follow the steps outlined here, which correlate to the stages in the strategic-management process and the chapters in this text.

Step 1 Identify the firm's existing mission, objectives, and strategies.

Step 2 Develop a mission statement for the organization.

Step 3 Identify the organization's external opportunities and threats.

Step 4 Construct a Competitive Profile Matrix.

Step 5 Construct an EFE Matrix.

Step 6 Identify the organization's internal strengths and weaknesses.

Step 7 Construct an IFE Matrix.

Step 8 Prepare a TOWS Matrix, SPACE Matrix, BCG Matrix, IE Matrix, Grand Strategy Matrix, and QSPM as appropriate. Give advantages and disadvantages of alternative strategies.

Step 9 Recommend specific strategies and long-term objectives. Show how much your recommendations will cost. Itemize these costs clearly for each projected year. Compare your recommendations to actual strategies planned by the company.

Step 10 Specify how your recommendations can be implemented and what results you can expect. Prepare forecasted ratios and pro forma financial statements. Present a timetable or agenda for action.

Step 11 Recommend specific annual objectives and policies.

Step 12 Recommend procedures for strategy review and evaluation.

MAKING AN ORAL PRESENTATION

Your professor may ask you to prepare a business policy case analysis, individually or as a group, and present your analysis to the class. Oral presentations are usually graded on two parts: content and delivery. *Content* refers to the quality, quantity, correctness, and appropriateness of analyses presented, including such dimensions as logical flow through the presentation, coverage of major issues, use of specifics, avoidance of generalities, absence of mistakes, and feasibility of recommendations. *Delivery* includes such dimensions as audience attentiveness, clarity of visual aids, appropriate dress, persuasiveness of arguments, tone of voice, eye contact, and posture. Great ideas are of no value unless others can be convinced of their merit through clear communication. The guidelines presented here can help you make an effective oral presentation.

ORGANIZING THE PRESENTATION Begin your presentation by introducing yourself and giving a clear outline of topics to be covered. If a team is presenting, specify the sequence of speakers and the areas each person will address. At the beginning of an oral presentation, try to capture your audience's interest and attention. You could do this by displaying some products made by the company, telling an interesting short story about the company, or sharing an experience that you had related to the company, its products, or its services. You could develop or obtain a video to show at the beginning of class; you could visit a local distributor of the firm's products and tape a personal interview with the business owner or manager. A light or humorous introduction can be effective at the beginning of a presentation.

Be sure the setting of your presentation is well organized, with chairs, flip charts, a transparency projector, and whatever else you plan to use. Arrive at least 15 minutes early at the classroom to organize the setting, and be sure your materials are ready to go. Make sure everyone can see your visual aids well.

CONTROLLING YOUR VOICE An effective rate of speaking ranges from 100 to 125 words per minute. Practice your presentation out loud to determine if you are going too fast. Individuals commonly speak too fast when nervous. Breathe deeply before and during the presentation to help yourself slow down. Have a cup of water available; pausing to take a drink will wet your throat, give you time to collect your thoughts, control your nervousness, slow you down, and signal to the audience a change in topic.

Avoid a monotone by placing emphasis on different words or sentences. Speak loudly and clearly, but don't shout. Silence can be used effectively to break a monotone voice. Stop at the end of each sentence, rather than running sentences together with *and* or *uh*.

MANAGING BODY LANGUAGE Be sure not to fold your arms, lean on the podium, put your hands in your pockets, or put your hands behind you. Keep a straight posture, with one foot slightly in front of the other. Do not turn your back to the audience, which is not only rude but which also prevents your voice from projecting well. Avoid using too many hand gestures. On occasion leave the podium or table and walk toward your audience, but do not walk around too much. Never block the audience's view of your visual aids.

Maintain good eye contact throughout the presentation. This is the best way to persuade your audience. There is nothing more reassuring to a speaker than to see members of the audience nod in agreement or smile. Try to look everyone in the eye at least once during your presentation, but focus more on individuals who look interested than on persons who seem bored. Use humor and smiles as appropriate throughout your presentation to stay in touch with your audience. A presentation should never be dull!

SPEAKING FROM NOTES Be sure not to read to your audience, because reading puts people to sleep. Perhaps worse than reading is memorizing. Do not try to memorize anything. Rather, practice using notes unobtrusively. Make sure your notes are written clearly so you will not flounder trying to read your own writing. Include only main ideas on your note cards. Keep note cards on a podium or table if possible so that you won't drop them or get them out of order; walking with note cards tends to be distracting.

CONSTRUCTING VISUAL AIDS   Make sure your visual aids are legible to individuals in the back of the room. Use color to highlight special items. Avoid putting complete sentences on visual aids; rather, use short phrases and then elaborate on issues orally as you make your presentation. Generally, there should be no more than four to six lines of text on each visual aid. Use clear headings and subheadings. Be careful about spelling and grammar; use a consistent style of lettering. Use masking tape or an easel for posters—do not hold posters in your hand. Transparencies and handouts are excellent aids; however, be careful not to use too many handouts or your audience may concentrate on them instead of you during the presentation.

ANSWERING QUESTIONS   It is best to field questions at the end of your presentation, rather than during the presentation itself. Encourage questions and take your time to respond to each one. Answering questions can be persuasive because it involves you with the audience. If a team is giving the presentation, the audience should direct questions to a specific person. During the question and answer period, be polite, confident, and courteous. Avoid verbose responses. Do not get defensive with your answers, even if a hostile or confrontational question is asked. Staying calm during potentially disruptive situations such as a cross-examination reflects self-confidence, maturity, poise, and command of the particular company and its industry. Stand up throughout the question and answer period.

FIFTY TIPS FOR SUCCESS IN CASE ANALYSIS

Business policy students who have used this text over six editions offer you the following fifty tips for success in doing case analysis:

1. View your case analysis and presentation as a product that must have some competitive factor to differentiate it favorably from the case analyses of other students.

2. Prepare your case analysis far enough in advance of the due date to allow time for reflection and practice. Do not procrastinate.

3. Develop a mind-set of "why," continually questioning your own and others' assumptions and assertions.

4. The best ideas are lost if not communicated to the reader, so as ideas develop, think of their most appropriate presentation.

5. Maintain a positive attitude about the class, working *with* problems rather than against them.

6. Keep in tune with your professor and understand his or her values and expectations.

7. Since business policy is a capstone course, seek the help of professors in other specialty areas as needed.

8. Other students will have strengths in functional areas that will complement your weaknesses, so develop a cooperative spirit that moderates competitiveness in group work.

9. Read your case frequently as work progresses so you don't overlook details.

10. When preparing a case analysis as a group, divide into separate teams to work on the external analysis and internal analysis. Each team should write its section as if it were to go into the paper; then give each group member a copy.

11. At the end of each group session, assign each member of the group a task to be completed for the next meeting.

12. Have a good sense of humor.

13. Capitalize on the strengths of each member of the group; volunteer your services in your areas of strength.

14. Set goals for yourself and your team; budget your time to attain them.

15. Become friends with the library.

16. Foster attitudes that encourage group participation and interaction. Do not be hasty to judge group members.

17. Be creative and innovative throughout the case analysis process.

18. Be prepared to work. There will be times when you will have to do more than your share. Accept it, and do what you have to do to move the team forward.

19. Think of your case analysis as if it were really happening; do not reduce case analysis to a mechanical process.

20. To uncover flaws in your analysis and to prepare the group for questions during an oral presentation, assign one person in the group to actively play the devil's advocate.

21. Do not schedule excessively long group meetings; two-hour sessions are about right.

22. A goal of case analysis is to improve your ability to think clearly in ambiguous and confusing situations; do not get frustrated that there is no single best answer.

23. Push your ideas hard enough to get them listened to, but then let up; listen to others and try to follow their lines of thinking; follow the flow of group discussion, recognizing when you need to get back on track; do not repeat yourself or others unless clarity or progress demands repetition.

24. Do not confuse symptoms with causes; do not develop conclusions and solutions prematurely; recognize that information may be misleading, conflicting, or wrong.

25. Work hard to develop the ability to formulate reasonable, consistent, and creative plans; put yourself in the strategist's position.

26. Develop confidence in using quantitative tools for analysis. They are not inherently difficult; it is just practice and familiarity you need.

27. Develop a case-writing style that is direct, assertive, and convincing; be concise, precise, fluent, and correct.

28. Have fun when at all possible. It is frustrating at times, but enjoy it while you can; it may be several years before you are playing CEO again.

29. Acquire a professional typist and proofreader. Do not perform either task alone.

30. Strive for excellence in writing and technical preparation of your case. Prepare nice charts, tables, diagrams, and graphs. Use color and unique pictures. No messy exhibits!

31. In group cases do not allow personality differences to interfere. When they occur, they must be understood for what they are and put aside.

32. Do not forget that the objective is to learn; explore areas with which you are not familiar.

33. Pay attention to detail.

34. Think through alternative implications fully and realistically. The consequences of decisions are not always apparent. They often affect many different aspects of a firm's operations.

35. Get things written down (drafts) as soon as possible.

36. Read everything that other group members write, and comment on it in writing. This allows group input into all aspects of case preparation.

37. Provide answers to such fundamental questions as what, when, where, why, and how.

38. Adaptation and flexibility are keys to success; be creative and innovative.

39. Do not merely recite ratios or present figures. Rather, develop ideas and conclusions concerning the possible trends. Show the importance of these figures to the corporation.

40. Support reasoning and judgment with factual data whenever possible.

41. Neatness is a real plus; your case analysis should look professional.

42. Your analysis should be as detailed and specific as possible.

43. A picture speaks a thousand words, and a creative picture gets you an A in many classes.

44. Let someone else read and critique your paper several days before you turn it in.

45. Emphasize the Strategy Selection and Strategy Implementation sections. A common mistake is to spend too much time on the external or internal analysis parts of your paper. Always remember that the meat of the paper or presentation is the strategy selection and implementation sections.

46. Make special efforts to get to know your group members. This leads to more openness in the group and allows for more interchange of ideas. Put in the time and effort necessary to develop these relationships.

47. Be constructively critical of your group members' work. Do not dominate group discussions. Be a good listener and contributor.

48. Learn from past mistakes and deficiencies. Improve upon weak aspects of other case presentations.

59. Learn from the positive approaches and accomplishments of classmates.

50. Be considerate, dependable, reliable, and trustworthy.

CURRENT READINGS

Fielen, John. "Clear Writing Is Not Enough." *Management Review* (April 1989): 49–53.

Holcombe, M., and J. Stein. *Presentation for Decision Makers* (Belmont, Calif.: Lifetime Learning Publications, 1983).

_____ *Writing for Decision Makers* (Belmont, Calif.: Lifetime Learning Publications, 1981).

Jeffries, J., and J. Bates. *The Executive's Guide to Meetings, Conferences, and Audiovisual Presentations* (New York: McGraw-Hill, 1983).

Shurter, R., J. P. Williamson, and W. Broehl. *Business Research and Report Writing* (New York: McGraw-Hill, 1965).

Strunk, W., and E. B. White. *The Elements of Style* (New York: Macmillan, 1978).

Zall, P., and L. Franc. *Practical Writing in Business and Industry* (North Scituate, Mass.: Duxbury Press, 1978).

Instructions for Using the Strategy Formulator Software

The *Strategy Formulator* software that accompanies this text is user-friendly programs that run on any IBM or IBM-compatible machine with at least one floppy disk drive and 512K (or greater) memory. A copy can be found in the back of your instructors Case Solution Manual or downloaded from the Web site that accompanies this text: www.prenhall.com/davidsm. Step-by-step instructions for using this software are provided in this section. *Strategy Formulator* will greatly reduce the time it takes you to prepare quantitative, professional exhibits to support your oral case presentations and written case assignments.

The *Strategy Formulator* program generates strategy-formulation matrices that are widely used among organizations. The matrices are described in chapters 4, 5, and 6 of the text. You will want to use *Strategy Formulator* in analyzing all business policy cases. No prior experience with computers is needed to use this software, which is DOS-based.

MAKING A BACKUP COPY OF THE DISKETTES It is a good idea to make a working copy of the *Strategy Formulator* diskettes. Keep the original copies in a safe place as a backup. The operating system manual that came with your computer contains instructions on how to make backup copies. Follow instructions in your computer manual for creating a subdirectory, (or folder) and copy the original diskette to that subdirectory (or folder).

THE *STRATEGY FORMULATOR* SOFTWARE

Strategy Formulator is an innovative program that enables managers and students to formulate strategies for organizations. This personal computer software program incorporates the most modern strategic planning techniques in a simple way. The simplicity of *Strategy Formulator* enables this software to facilitate the process of strategic planning by promoting communication, understanding, creativity, and forward thinking among users.

Strategy Formulator is not a spreadsheet or database program; it is a structured brainstorming tool that enhances participation in strategy formulation. The software begins with development of an organizational mission statement as described in chapter 3. Then, the software guides you through an internal strategic planning audit of the company, followed by an external audit of the firm as described in chapters 4 and 5. Next, the software generates alternative strategies for the firm, using analytical tools discussed in chapter 6.

Strategy Formulator enables students or managers to create an organizational mission statement, identify key internal strengths and weaknesses as well as key external opportunities and threats, and then generate, evaluate, and prioritize alternative strategies that the firm could pursue. Individuals can work through the software independently and then meet to discuss particular strategies.

Strategy Formulator runs on any IBM-compatible personal computer system that has a high density (HD) disk drive. It includes numerous help screens and examples and offers clear printouts. No documentation manual is needed with *Strategy Formulator.* Simply boot DOS, type SF, and follow directions.

Strategy Formulator gives you hands-on experience using actual strategic planning software and facilitates business policy case analysis. This new software is similar to the CheckMATE strategic planning software that is widely used among organizations worldwide. (For additional information about CheckMATE, contact the author at Strategic Planning Systems, P.O. Box 13065, Florence, SC 29504; Phone 843-669-6960; Fax 843-673-9460, e-mail strategy29@aol.com) CheckMATE is Windows-based and costs $195.

THE STRUCTURE AND FUNCTION OF *STRATEGY FORMULATOR* The first and second screens that appear in the *Strategy Formulator* software are given in Figures 1 and 2. Note from the first screen that the F1, F2, and F3 keys are the Save key, Load key, and Print key, respectively. Note that the second screen gives an outline or flowchart of the *Strategy Formulator* program. This second screen is a main menu that returns throughout the program; you simply highlight the particular area you wish to work on and hit Enter to begin that part of the program.

FIGURE 1
THE FIRST SCREEN

***Strategy Formulator* Software**

The *Strategy Formulator* program provides a systematic approach for managers to devise strategies their organizations could pursue. *Strategy Formulator* incorporates the most modern strategic planning techniques in a simple way.

The recommended approach for using *Strategy Formulator* is for managers to work through the software independently and then meet together to discuss the results and develop a single set of joint recommendations. This approach to strategic planning facilitates communication, forward thinking, understanding, commitment, and performance. The help key (F1) is available at all times throughout the *Formulator* program to give you more information. Press the F1 key now to obtain information about the Save key (F2), Load key (F3), Print key (F4), and Escape key.

Press the Return key on the highlighted topic on the menu to activate the various parts of the program.

FIGURE 2
THE SECOND SCREEN

The Structure and Function of *Strategy Formulator*

    I. Create a Mission Statement
   II. Identify Key Internal Strengths and Weaknesses
  III. Identify Key External Opportunities and Threats
  IV. Generate Alternative Strategies Using:
        IE Analysis
        TOWS Analysis
        SPACE Analysis
        GRAND Analysis
   V. Refine Alternative Strategies
  VI. Select Strategies to Pursue
       Other functions:
         Load Data from Disk
         Save Data to Disk
         Print
         Quit Program

GETTING STARTED Run the *Strategy Formulator* software by typing SF at the DOS prompt or double click on the SF.EXE program from Windows Explorer.

Read the first screen. Hit the F1 key just to get familiar with the Help routine. Hit the Escape key to return to the main menu. Hit Enter to go to the second screen. Note from the second screen that you may simply highlight the Create a Mission Statement line and hit Enter to begin work on developing a mission statement—which is the first activity in formulating strategies. Hit Enter again when you are ready to return to the main menu. You may hit the F1 key anytime in the program for help. The Program Mechanics Help, as shown in Figure 3, will appear on the screen if you hit the F1 key twice.

After completing the mission statement, highlight the next line, Identify Key Internal Strengths and Weaknesses. Hit Enter and begin development of a list of the company's key strengths and weaknesses. When you have completed this work, return to the main menu. Continue working sequentially in this manner through the program.

THE SAVE AND LOAD ROUTINES It is easy to save and load your work in the *Strategy Formulator* program. The Help Screens (F1 key) associated with the Save and Load routines are given in Figures 4 and 5.

THE PRINT ROUTINE The *Strategy Formulator* software generates nine planning reports that can be printed separately or together, (as indicated on a print screen as shown in Figure 6) that appears near the end of the program.

Simply highlight the reports you desire to be printed, and hit Enter to begin printing your work. You could highlight Print All Reports to print all of your work. If you press the F1 key, the screen shown in Figure 7 appears.

FIGURE 3
THE PROGRAM MECHANICS HELP SCREEN

- Movement between screens within a module is accomplished by pressing the UP and DOWN arrows. This is true both within the Help facility and within the main program.
- If you wish to delete to the left of the cursor, you should press the BACKSPACE key. If you wish to delete to the right of the cursor, you should press the DELETE key.
- If you wish to insert text, place the cursor where you wish to begin the insertion and press the INSERT key. When the insert mode is in operation, the cursor changes its size and the word "Insert" appears in the bottom right corner of the screen. Insert is turned off again either by pressing the INSERT key or by moving to another answer.
- You can access the HELP facility at any time by pressing the F1 key. From the Help facility, you can return to the screen you were working on by pressing the ESCAPE key.
- You can SAVE all of your work at any time by pressing the F2 key.
- You can LOAD all of your work at any time by pressing the F3 key.
- You can PRINT all or part of your work at any time by pressing the F4 key.
- You can return to the menu at any time by pressing the ESCAPE key.

FIGURE 4
THE SAVE ROUTINE HELP SCREEN

The Save routine is where the information that has been entered into the system is saved for later use.

The Drive is the disk drive where the data is saved.

The Path is the logical place on the drive where the information is saved. You should either read up on this in the DOS manual or go with the default. The default is the drive and path where the program is located.

The File Name is the name that is given to the information that is saved. This name is used later to retrieve the information. It is eight characters long.

The Directory List will give you a list of files that already exist. If you save over a file (use the same name), the contents of that file are lost. It is a good idea to save your files in two places so that there will be a backup if the primary file is lost. To do this, put a floppy disk in the drive and change the disk drive letter to the letter corresponding to the drive you are using. Usually the letter is A; sometimes it is B.

FIGURE 5
THE LOAD ROUTINE HELP SCREEN

The Load routine is where the information that has been saved on the disk is brought back into the system.

The Drive is the disk drive where the data is saved.

The Path is the logical place on the drive where the information is saved. For more information on this, you should read the DOS manual.

The File Name is the name that is given to the information that is saved. This name is used to retrieve the information. It is eight characters long.

The Directory List will give you a list of files that exist on the disk and path that are listed on the screen. The name must show up on the directory in order for the information to be read.

FIGURE 6
***STRATEGY FORMULATOR* PRINT REPORTS**

Print ALL Reports	TOWS Analysis Report
Mission Statement Report	SPACE Analysis Report
Internal Analysis Report	GRAND Analysis Report
External Analysis Report	Alternative Strategies Report
E Analysis Report	Selected Strategies Report

FIGURE 7
THE PRINT ROUTINE HELP SCREEN

The Print routine is accessed by hitting the F4 key or the print option on the main menu.

Within the print menu, select the report you wish by pressing the up and down arrow keys. You can print all reports or individual ones.

If there is a "printer off line" error, you should locate the on-line button on your printer and press it. This should put your printer on-line.

If there is a "printer paper out" error, you should load paper into your printer. This should correct this problem.

If you wish to bypass the program's printer error detection features for any reason, press the "D" (for disable) key. This is usually not needed, but if the user has nonstandard software or hardware, it may be necessary.

PART 1

OVERVIEW OF STRATEGIC MANAGEMENT

CHAPTER 1

The Nature of Strategic Management

CHAPTER OUTLINE

- ◆ WHAT IS STRATEGIC MANAGEMENT?
- ◆ KEY TERMS IN STRATEGIC MANAGEMENT
- ◆ THE STRATEGIC-MANAGEMENT MODEL
- ◆ BENEFITS OF STRATEGIC MANAGEMENT
- ◆ BUSINESS ETHICS AND STRATEGIC MANAGEMENT
- ◆ COMPARING BUSINESS AND MILITARY STRATEGY
- ◆ THE COHESION CASE AND EXPERIENTIAL EXERCISES

- ◆ THE COHESION CASE: HERSHEY FOODS CORPORATION—1998

- ■ EXPERIENTIAL EXERCISE 1A
  Strategy Analysis for Hershey Foods
- ■ EXPERIENTIAL EXERCISE 1B
  Developing a Code of Business Ethics for Hershey Foods
- ■ EXPERIENTIAL EXERCISE 1C
  The Ethics of Spying on Competitors
- ■ EXPERIENTIAL EXERCISE 1D
  Strategic Planning for My University
- ■ EXPERIENTIAL EXERCISE 1E
  Strategic Planning at a Local Company

CHAPTER OBJECTIVES

After studying this chapter, you should be able to do the following:

1. Describe the strategic-management process.
2. Explain the need for integrating analysis and intuition in strategic management.
3. Define and give examples of key terms in strategic management.
4. Discuss the nature of strategy formulation, implementation, and evaluation activities.
5. Describe the benefits of good strategic management.
6. Explain why good ethics is good business in strategic management.

NOTABLE QUOTES

If we know where we are and something about how we got there, we might see where we are trending—and if the outcomes which lie naturally in our course are unacceptable, to make timely change. —ABRAHAM LINCOLN

*W*ithout a strategy, an organization is like a ship without a rudder, going around in circles. It's like a tramp; it has no place to go.—JOEL ROSS AND MICHAEL KAMI

*P*lans are less important than planning.—DALE MCCONKEY

*T*he formulation of strategy can develop competitive advantage only to the extent that the process can give meaning to workers in the trenches.—DAVID HURST

*M*ost of us fear change. Even when our minds say change is normal, our stomachs quiver at the prospect. But for strategists and managers today, there is no choice but to change.—ROBERT WATERMAN, JR.

*I*f business is not based on ethical grounds, it is of no benefit to society, and will, like all other unethical combinations, pass into oblivion.—C. MAX KILLAN

*I*f a man take no thought about what is distant, he will find sorrow near at hand. He who will not worry about what is far off will soon find something worse than worry.—CONFUCIUS

*I*t is human nature to make decisions based on emotion, rather than fact. But nothing could be more illogical.—TOSHIBA CORPORATION

*N*o business can do everything. Even if it has the money, it will never have enough good people. It has to set priorities. The worst thing to do is a little bit of everything. This makes sure that nothing is being accomplished. It is better to pick the wrong priority than none at all.—PETER DRUCKER

*E*xecutives, consultants, and B-school professors all agree that strategic planning is now the single most important management issue and will remain so for the next five years. Strategy has become a part of the main agenda at lots of organizations today. Strategic planning is back with a vengeance. —JOHN BYRNE

This chapter provides an overview of strategic management. It introduces a practical, integrative model of the strategic-management process and defines basic activities and terms in strategic management and discusses the importance of business ethics.

This chapter initiates several themes that permeate all chapters of this text. First, *global considerations impact virtually all strategic decisions!* The boundaries of countries no longer can define the limits of our imaginations. To see and appreciate the world from the perspective of others has become a matter of survival for businesses. The underpinnings of strategic management hinge upon managers' gaining an understanding of competitors, markets, prices, suppliers, distributors, governments, creditors, shareholders, and customers worldwide. The price and quality of a firm's products and services must be competitive on a worldwide basis, not just a local basis. A Global Perspective is provided in all chapters of this text to emphasize the importance of global factors in strategic management.

A second theme is that *information technology has become a vital strategic-management tool.* An increasing number of companies are gaining competitive advantage by using the Internet for communication with suppliers, customers, creditors, partners, shareholders, clients, and competitors who may be dispersed globally. On-line services allow firms to sell products, advertise, purchase supplies, bypass intermediaries, track inventory, eliminate paperwork, and share information. In total, *electronic commerce* is minimizing the expense and cumbersomeness of time, distance, and space in doing business, which yields better customer service, greater efficiency, improved products, and higher profitability. Acquiring up-to-date information as a basis for decisions is a key benefit offered a firm operating on-line.

The Internet and personal computers are changing the way we organize our lives; inhabit our homes; and relate to and interact with family, friends, neighbors, and even ourselves. Personal-computer penetration of U.S. households topped 52 percent in 1998. More than 72 percent of U.S. households with an annual income above $40,000 have personal computers. Less than half of these households use the Internet, but the percentage is increasing rapidly. Estimates are that more than $100 billion of goods will be bought annually over the Internet in the United States by the year 2000. An Information Technology Perspective is included in each chapter to illustrate how electronic commerce impacts the strategic-management process.

A third theme is that *the natural environment has become an important strategic issue.* With the demise of communism and the end of the cold war, perhaps there is now no greater threat to business and society than the continuous exploitation and decimation of our natural environment. Mark Starik at George Washington University says, "Halting and reversing worldwide ecological destruction and deterioration . . . is a strategic issue that needs immediate and substantive attention by all businesses and managers." A Natural Environment Perspective is provided in all chapters to illustrate how firms are addressing environmental concerns.

WHAT IS STRATEGIC MANAGEMENT?

Once there were two company presidents who competed in the same industry. These two presidents decided to go on a camping trip to discuss a possible merger. They hiked deep into the woods. Suddenly, they came upon a grizzly bear that rose up on its hind legs and snarled. Instantly, the first president took off his knapsack and got out a pair of jogging shoes. The second president said, "Hey, you can't outrun that bear." The first president responded, "Maybe I can't outrun that bear, but I surely can outrun you!" This story captures the notion of strategic management.

DEFINING STRATEGIC MANAGEMENT　*Strategic management* can be defined as the art and science of formulating, implementing, and evaluating cross-functional decisions that enable an organization to achieve its objectives. As this definition implies, strategic management focuses on integrating management, marketing, finance/accounting, production/operations, research and development, and computer information systems to achieve organizational success. The term *strategic management* is used at many colleges and universities as the subtitle for the capstone course in business administration, Business Policy, which integrates material from all business courses. Consider joining the Strategic Management Club Online at www.strategyclub.com that offers many benefits for business policy students.

STAGES OF STRATEGIC MANAGEMENT　The *strategic-management process* consists of three stages: strategy formulation, strategy implementation, and strategy evaluation. *Strategy formulation* includes developing a business mission, identifying an organization's external opportunities and threats, determining internal strengths and weaknesses, establishing long-term objectives, generating alternative strategies, and choosing particular strategies to pursue. Strategy-formulation issues include deciding what new businesses to enter, what businesses to abandon, how to allocate resources, whether to expand operations or diversify, whether to enter international markets, whether to merge or form a joint venture, and how to avoid a hostile takeover.

Because no organization has unlimited resources, strategists must decide which alternative strategies will benefit the firm most. Strategy-formulation decisions commit an organization to specific products, markets, resources, and technologies over an extended period of time. Strategies determine long-term competitive advantages. For better or worse, strategic decisions have major multifunctional consequences and enduring effects on an organization. Top managers have the best perspective to understand fully the ramifications of formulation decisions; they have the authority to commit the resources necessary for implementation.

Strategy implementation requires a firm to establish annual objectives, devise policies, motivate employees, and allocate resources so that formulated strategies can be executed; strategy implementation includes developing a strategy-supportive culture, creating an effective organizational structure, redirecting marketing efforts, preparing budgets, developing and utilizing information systems, and linking employee compensation to organizational performance.

Strategy implementation often is called the action stage of strategic management. Implementing strategy means mobilizing employees and managers to put formulated strategies into action. Often considered to be the most difficult stage in strategic management, strategy implementation requires personal discipline, commitment, and sacrifice. Successful strategy implementation hinges upon managers' ability to motivate employees, which is more an art than a science. Strategies formulated but not implemented serve no useful purpose.

Interpersonal skills are especially critical for successful strategy implementation. Strategy-implementation activities affect all employees and managers in an organization. Every division and department must decide on answers to questions such as "What must we do to implement our part of the organization's strategy?" and "How best can we get the job done?" The challenge of implementation is to stimulate managers and employees throughout an organization to work with pride and enthusiasm toward achieving stated objectives.

Strategy evaluation is the final stage in strategic management. Managers desperately need to know when particular strategies are not working well; strategy evaluation is the primary means for obtaining this information. All strategies are subject to future modification because external and internal factors are constantly changing. Three fundamental strategy-evaluation activities are (1) reviewing external and internal factors that are the bases for current strategies, (2) measuring performance, and (3) taking corrective actions. Strategy evaluation is needed because success today is no guarantee of success tomorrow! Success always creates new and different problems; complacent organizations experience demise.

Strategy formulation, implementation, and evaluation activities occur at three hierarchical levels in a large organization: corporate, divisional or strategic business unit, and functional. By fostering communication and interaction among managers and employees across hierarchical levels, strategic management helps a firm function as a competitive team. Most small businesses and some large businesses do not have divisions or strategic business units; they have only the corporate and functional levels. Nevertheless, managers and employees at these two levels should be actively involved in strategic-management activities.

Peter Drucker says the prime task of strategic management is thinking through the overall mission of a business:

> . . . that is, of asking the question, "What is our Business?" This leads to the setting of objectives, the development of strategies, and the making of today's decisions for tomorrow's results. This clearly must be done by a part of the organization that can see the entire business; that can balance objectives and the needs of today against the needs of tomorrow; and that can allocate resources of men and money to key results.[1]

INTEGRATING INTUITION AND ANALYSIS The strategic-management process can be described as an objective, logical, systematic approach for making major decisions in an organization. It attempts to organize qualitative and quantitative information in a way that allows effective decisions to be made under conditions of uncertainty. Yet, strategic management is not a pure science that lends itself to a nice, neat, one-two-three approach.

Based on past experiences, judgment, and feelings, *intuition* is essential to making good strategic decisions. Intuition is particularly useful for making decisions in situations of great uncertainty or little precedent. It is also helpful when highly interrelated variables exist, when there is immense pressure to be right, or when it is necessary to choose from several plausible alternatives.[2] These situations describe the very nature and heart of strategic management.

Some managers and owners of businesses profess to have extraordinary abilities for using intuition alone in devising brilliant strategies. For example, Will Durant, who organized General Motors Corporation, was described by Alfred Sloan as "a man who would proceed on a course of action guided solely, as far as I could tell, by some intuitive flash of brilliance. He never felt obliged to make an engineering hunt for the facts. Yet at times, he was astoundingly correct in his judgment."[3] Albert Einstein acknowledged the importance of intuition when he said, "I believe in intuition and inspiration. At times I feel certain that I am right while not knowing the reason. Imagination is more important than knowledge, because knowledge is limited, whereas imagination embraces the entire world."[4]

Although some organizations today may survive and prosper because they have intuitive geniuses managing them, most are not so fortunate. Most organizations can benefit from strategic management, which is based upon integrating intuition and analysis in decision making. Choosing an intuitive or analytic approach to decision making is not an either-or proposition. Managers at all levels in an organization should inject their intuition and judgment into strategic-management analyses. Analytical thinking and intuitive thinking complement each other.

Operating from the I've-already-made-up-my-mind-don't-bother-me-with-the-facts mode is not management by intuition; it is management by ignorance.[5] Drucker says, "I believe in intuition only if you discipline it. 'Hunch' artists, who make a diagnosis but don't check it out with the facts, are the ones in medicine who kill people, and in management kill businesses."[6] As Henderson notes:

> The accelerating rate of change today is producing a business world in which customary managerial habits in organizations are increasingly inadequate. Experience alone was an adequate guide when changes could be made in small increments. But intuitive and experience-based management philosophies are grossly inadequate when decisions are strategic and have major, irreversible consequences.[7]

In a sense, the strategic-management process is an attempt to duplicate what goes on in the mind of a brilliant, intuitive person who knows the business and hinge it with analysis.

ADAPTING TO CHANGE   The strategic-management process is based on the belief that organizations should continually monitor internal and external events and trends so that timely changes can be made as needed. The rate and magnitude of changes that affect organizations are increasing dramatically. Consider, for example, Windows 98, Internet commerce, laser medicine, laser weapons, the aging population, and merger mania. To survive, all organizations must be capable of astutely identifying and adapting to change. The strategic-management process is aimed at allowing organizations to adapt effectively to change over the long run.

> In today's business environment, more than any preceding era, the only constant is change. Successful organizations effectively manage change, continuously adapting their bureaucracies, strategies, systems, products, and cultures to survive the shocks and prosper from the forces that decimate the competition.[8]

Information technology and globalization are external changes that are transforming business and society today. On a political map, the boundaries between countries may be clear, but on a competitive map showing the real flow of financial and industrial activity, the boundaries have largely disappeared.[9] Speedy flow of information has eaten away at national boundaries so that people worldwide readily see for themselves how other people live. People are traveling abroad more; 10 million Japanese travel abroad annually. People are emigrating more; Germans to England and Mexicans to the United States are examples. As the Global Perspective indicates, U.S. firms are challenged by competitors in many industries. We are becoming a borderless world with global citizens, global competitors, global customers, global suppliers, and global distributors!

The need to adapt to change leads organizations to key strategic-management questions, such as, What kind of business should we become? Are we in the right fields? Should we reshape our business? What new competitors are entering our industry? What strategies should we pursue? How are our customers changing? Are new technologies being developed that could put us out of business?

KEY TERMS IN STRATEGIC MANAGEMENT

Before we go any further in discussing strategic management, we should define eight key terms: strategists, mission statements, external opportunities and threats, internal strengths and weaknesses, long-term objectives, strategies, annual objectives, and policies.

GLOBAL PERSPECTIVE
Do U.S. Firms Dominate All Industries?

The Wall Street Journal's annual ranking of the world's largest companies reveals that U.S. firm's are being challenged in many industries. The world's 10 largest insurance companies, banks, and electronics firms, for example, are listed below in rank order. Note that Japanese firms dominate these three industries.

INSURANCE FIRMS	BANKS	ELECTRONICS FIRMS
Nippon Life, Japan	Bank of Tokyo-Mitsubishi, Japan	General Electric U.S.
Zenkyoren, Japan	Deutsche Bank, Germany	Hitachi, Japan
Dai-Ichi Mutual Life, Japan	Sumitomo Bank, Japan	Matsushita Electronic, Japan
Axa, France	Dai-Ichi Kangyo Bank, Japan	Siemens, Germany
Allianz Holding, Germany	Fuji Bank, Japan	Sony, Japan
Sumitomo Life, Japan	Sanwa Bank, Japan	Toshiba, Japan
Metropolitan Life, U.S.	ABN Amro Holdings, Netherlands	NEC, Japan
Compagnie UAP, France	Sakura Bank, Japan	Philips Electronics, Netherlands
Internationale Nederlanden Group, Netherlands	Industrial & Commercial Bank, China	ABB Asea Brown Boveri, Switzerland
Prudential Insurance, U.S.	HSBC Holdings, U.K.	Mitsubishi Electric, Japan

Source: Adapted from Urban Lehner, "The Global Giants," The Wall Street Journal (September 18, 1997): R. 25.

STRATEGISTS *Strategists* are individuals who are most responsible for the success or failure of an organization. Strategists have various job titles, such as chief executive officer, president, owner, chair of the board, executive director, chancellor, dean, or entrepreneur. Jonas, Fry, and Srivastva contend that strategists' three principal responsibilities in organizations are creating a context for change, building commitment and ownership, and balancing stability and innovation.[10]

Strategists are expected to change in ways outlined in Table 1–1. For example, strategists in the 2000s will provide more visionary leadership, better link compensation to performance, communicate more frequently with employees, and emphasize business ethics more.

Strategists differ as much as organizations themselves, and these differences must be considered in the formulation, implementation, and evaluation of strategies. Some strategists will not consider some types of strategies due to their personal philosophies. Strategists differ in their attitudes, values, ethics, willingness to take risks, concern for social responsibility, concern for profitability, concern for short-run versus long-run aims, and management style. The founder of Hershey Foods, Milton Hershey, built the company to manage an orphanage. From corporate profits Hershey Foods today cares for over 1,000 boys and girls in its School for Orphans.

Some strategists agree with Ralph Nader, who proclaims that organizations have tremendous social obligations. Others agree with Milton Friedman, an economist, who maintains that organizations have no obligation to do any more for society than is legally required. Most strategists agree that the first social responsibility of any business must be to make enough profit to cover the costs of the future, because if this is not achieved, no other social responsibility can be met. Strategists should examine social problems in terms of potential costs and benefits to the firm, and address social issues that could benefit the firm most.

TABLE 1–1

What Traits CEOs Have—and Will Need: Percent Describing Traits or Talents Dominant in the CEO in 1989 and Important for the CEO in 2000

PERSONAL BEHAVIOR	1989	2000	KNOWLEDGE AND SKILLS	1989	2000
Conveys Strong Sense of Vision	75	98	Strategy Formulation	68	78
Links Compensation to Performance	66	91	Human Resource Management	41	53
Communicates Frequently with Employees	59	89	International Economics and Politics	10	19
Emphasizes Ethics	74	85	Science and Technology	11	15
Plans for Management Succession	56	85	Computer Literacy	3	7
Communicates Frequently with Customers	41	78	Marketing and Sales	50	48
Reassigns or Terminates Unsatisfactory Employees	34	71	Negotiation	34	24
Rewards Loyalty	48	44	Accounting and Finance	33	24
Makes All Major Decisions	39	21	Handling Media and Public Speaking	16	13
Behaves Conservatively	32	13	Production	21	9

Note: This information is based on a Columbia University survey of 1,500 senior executives, 870 of them CEOs, in 20 countries.
Source: Lester Korn, "How the Next CEO Will Be Different." *Fortune* (May 22, 1989): 157.

MISSION STATEMENTS *Mission statements* are "enduring statements of purpose that distinguish one business from other similar firms. A mission statement identifies the scope of a firm's operations in product and market terms."[11] It addresses the basic question that faces all strategists: "What is our business?" A clear mission statement describes the values and priorities of an organization. Developing a business mission compels strategists to think about the nature and scope of present operations and to assess the potential attractiveness of future markets and activities. A mission statement broadly charts the future direction of an organization.

Research suggests that about 60 percent of all organizations have developed a formal mission statement and that high-performing firms have more well-developed mission statements than low-performing firms.[12] Note that the mission statement of Adolph Coors Company below should, but does not, reveal that Coors is in the brewery business:

> We are a highly successful, innovative company of stand alone and self-sustaining businesses. We are leaders in technology, quality products and services that provide recognizably superior customer satisfaction. We are growth and profit oriented, developing new businesses from internally generated technology and synergistic acquisitions. Our business is known for quality relationships which are honest, ethical, and caring. Our employees grow personally as the company grows. Our work life is exciting, challenging and rewarding in a friendly atmosphere of teamwork and mutual respect. We are socially responsible and strive for the betterment of society.[13]

EXTERNAL OPPORTUNITIES AND THREATS *External opportunities* and *external threats* refer to economic, social, cultural, demographic, environmental, political, legal, governmental, technological, and competitive trends and events that could significantly benefit or harm an organization in the future. Opportunities and threats are largely beyond the control of a single organization, thus the term *external*. The computer revolution, biotechnology, population shifts, changing work values and attitudes, space exploration, recyclable packages, and increased competition from foreign companies are examples of opportunities or threats for companies. These types of changes are creating a different type of consumer and consequently a need for different types of products, services, and strategies. As indicated in the Information Technology Perspective, adding phone lines in underdeveloped countries is an opportunity for many companies.

Other opportunities and threats may include the passage of a law, the introduction of a new product by a competitor, a national catastrophe, or the declining value of the dollar.

A competitor's strength could be a threat. Unrest in Eastern Europe, rising interest rates, or the war against drugs could represent an opportunity or a threat.

A basic tenet of strategic management is that firms need to formulate strategies to take advantage of external opportunities and to avoid or reduce the impact of external threats. For this reason, identifying, monitoring, and evaluating external opportunities and threats is essential for success. This process of conducting research and gathering and assimilating external information is sometimes called *environmental scanning* or industry analysis.

INTERNAL STRENGTHS AND WEAKNESSES *Internal strengths* and *internal weaknesses* are an organization's controllable activities that are performed especially well or poorly. They arise in the management, marketing, finance/accounting, production/operations, research and development, and computer information systems activities of a business. Identifying and evaluating organizational strengths and weaknesses in the functional areas of a business is an essential strategic-management activity. Organizations strive to pursue strategies that capitalize on internal strengths and improve on internal weaknesses.

Strengths and weaknesses are determined relative to competitors. *Relative* deficiency or superiority is important information. Also, strengths and weaknesses can be determined by elements of being rather than performance. For example, a strength may involve ownership of natural resources or an historic reputation for quality. Strengths and weaknesses may be determined relative to a firm's own objectives. For example, high levels of inventory turnover may not be a strength to a firm that seeks never to stock-out.

Internal factors can be determined in a number of ways that include computing ratios, measuring performance, and comparing to past periods and industry averages. Various types of surveys also can be developed and administered to examine internal factors such as employee morale, production efficiency, advertising effectiveness, and customer loyalty. Robert H. Short, chief executive officer of Portland General Corporation, described his firm's strategy in terms of strengths and weaknesses:

> First and foremost we are an energy company for the people of Oregon. Indeed, energy is our fundamental strength, and we intend to pursue growth aggressively in this business. To build on our strengths, however, we must mitigate or eliminate our weaknesses. I am proud of the way Portland General is drawing on its strengths to build for another century of success.[14]

LONG-TERM OBJECTIVES *Objectives* can be defined as specific results that an organization seeks to achieve in pursuing its basic mission. *Long-term* means more than one year. Objectives are essential for organizational success because they state direction; aid in evaluation; create synergy; reveal priorities; focus coordination; and provide a basis for effective planning, organizing, motivating, and controlling activities. Objectives should be challenging, measurable, consistent, reasonable, and clear. In a multidimensional firm, objectives should be established for the overall company and for each division. Minnesota Power's long-term objectives are to achieve a 13 percent return on equity (ROE) in their core electric utility, 14 percent ROE on water resource operations, and 15 percent ROE on support businesses. Minnesota Power also strives to stay in the top 25 percent of electric utilities in the United States in terms of common stock's market-to-book ratio and to maintain an annual growth in earnings per share of 5 percent.

STRATEGIES *Strategies* are the means by which long-term objectives will be achieved. Business strategies may include geographic expansion, diversification, acquisition, product development, market penetration, retrenchment, divestiture, liquidation, and joint venture. Strategies currently being pursued by E*Trade and Promus Hotels are described in Table 1–2.

INFORMATION TECHNOLOGY

Developing Countries Want to Call Home

In 1996 only 15 percent of the world's population has 71 percent of the world's phones. More than 50 percent of the world's people have never even used a phone. Over two-thirds of households around the world have no telephone. Cambodia has about the fewest phones of any country, only 0.06 phone lines per 100 inhabitants. The United States has close to 60 phone lines per 100 inhabitants. There are 47 countries with less than 1 phone line per 100 people.

Developing countries now realize they cannot develop their own economies or compete in world markets without phones. They must be able to communicate to survive. So, third-world countries are quickly adding phone lines. Underdeveloped countries are increasing their number of phone lines by an average 11.7 percent a year for the next 5 years (compared to 3.7 percent for the world's 24 highest-income countries). For example, China will install 100 million phones between 1996 and 1999.

An integral component of any computer system is the telephone. A phone is essential for using a modem and a fax machine. As indicated in the following table, there is explosive telephone growth in many developing countries. Analysts expect computer growth in these countries to follow on the heels of the phone growth. Implications of these two trends for all kinds of companies is immense.

Recognize that when countries add phones, their people become potential consumers of many new products and services. The addition of phones thus opens whole new markets. For example, Brazil has the ninth-largest economy in the world and 150 million people, but a phone-line density of only 6.8 per 100 inhabitants. (About 721,000 Brazilians have cellular phones in 1996, but that number is expected to reach 6 million by 1998.) The situation in Indonesia, a nation of 190 million, is similar. In Africa there are only 0.8 phone lines per 100 people.

MCI, Sprint, AT&T, Motorola, Nynex, BellSouth, U.S. West, Northern Telecom, and Bell Atlantic are competing aggressively with foreign phone companies to service developing countries. Note that the dollar infrastructure investment required to install phone lines in a country is huge.

Source: Adapted from Catherine Arnst, "The Last Frontier," Business Week (September 18, 1995): 98–114.

COUNTRY	1992 PHONE LINES PER 100 PEOPLE	2000 PHONE LINES PER 100 PEOPLE	1992–2000 INVESTMENT FOR PHONES (AS EXPRESSED IN MILLION $U.S.)
China	0.98	3.50	$53.3
Thailand	3.10	9.35	6.6
India	0.77	1.52	13.7
Hungary	12.54	23.80	1.6
Poland	10.28	16.62	4.0
Russia	15.28	24.50	23.3
Chile	8.92	19.71	2.8
Brazil	6.83	9.49	10.2
Mexico	7.54	12.49	9.4
USA	56.49	65.92	55.8

Source: Adapted from Catherine Arnst, "The Last Frontier," Business Week (September 18, 1995): 106.

ANNUAL OBJECTIVES *Annual objectives* are short-term milestones that organizations must achieve to reach long-term objectives. Like long-term objectives, annual objectives should be measurable, quantitative, challenging, realistic, consistent, and prioritized. They should be established at the corporate, divisional, and functional levels in a large organization. Annual objectives should be stated in terms of management, marketing, finance/accounting, production/operations, research and development, and information systems accomplishments. A set of annual objectives is needed for each long-term objective. Annual objectives are especially important in strategy implementation, whereas long-term objectives are particularly important in strategy formulation. Annual objectives represent the basis for allocating resources.

TABLE 1–2
Two Organizations'
Strategies in 1998

E*TRADE (www.etrade.com)

Headquartered in Palo Alto, California, tiny E*Trade now accounts for 13 percent of all on-line stock trades, tied with Fidelity and behind only Schwab's 35 percent market share. E*Trade's strategy is to become a "great financial company for the twenty-first century." E*Trade has about 230,000 accounts and is opening more than 600 new ones daily—and with only 475 employees total. The average age of an E*Trader is 38 versus 45 for Schwab's average customer. E*Trade's primary strategies are market penetration; spending heavily on advertising; and product development by offering stocks first, mutual funds next, then bonds, then IRAs, and then credit cards. E*Trade's business of on-line stock trading is growing by the hour.

PROMUS HOTELS (www.promus-inc.com)

Headquartered in Memphis, Tennessee, Promus Hotels aggressively is pursuing horizontal integration. With the acquisition of Doubletree and Red Lion hotels in 1997, Promus became the third-largest hotel chain in the United States behind Holiday Inn and Marriott. Promus already owns Embassy Suites, Hampton Inns, and Homewood Suites hotels. (Consolidation in the hotel industry is gaining momentum. Marriott recently acquired Renaissance Hotels, Cendant acquired both Ramada and Best Western, and in the largest lodging merger of 1997, Starwood Motels acquired ITT Corporation for $10.2 billion.) Promus now has over $5 billion in annual revenues.

Source: Lister, Harry, "Patriat Gains," *Lodging* (January 1998): 9.

Campbell Soup Corporation has an annual objective to achieve 20 percent growth in earnings, a 20 percent ROE, and a 20 percent return on invested cash. The company calls this ERC, for earnings, returns, and cash.

The Tribune Company (the nation's fifth-largest publisher of newspapers and owner of the Chicago Cubs baseball team) is another firm that has clear annual objectives. Stanton Cook, president and chief executive officer of Tribune, emphasizes annual objectives. Tribune strives to have an 18 percent annual ROE (net income divided by average stockholders' investment) and a 30 percent debt to total capital ratio.

POLICIES *Policies* are the means by which annual objectives will be achieved. Policies include guidelines, rules, and procedures established to support efforts to achieve stated objectives. Policies are guides to decision making and address repetitive or recurring situations.

Policies are most often stated in terms of management, marketing, finance/accounting, production/operations, research and development, and computer information systems activities. Policies can be established at the corporate level and apply to an entire organization, at the divisional level and apply to a single division, or at the functional level and apply to particular operational activities or departments. Policies, like annual objectives, are especially important in strategy implementation because they outline an organization's expectations of its employees and managers. Policies allow consistency and coordination within and between organizational departments.

Substantial research suggests that a healthier workforce can more effectively and efficiently implement strategies. The National Center for Health Promotion estimates that more than 80 percent of all American corporations have No Smoking policies. No Smoking policies are usually derived from annual objectives that seek to reduce corporate medical costs associated with absenteeism and to provide a healthy workplace. Pullman Company in Garden Grove, California, charges smokers $10 more each month for health insurance than it charges nonsmokers.

THE STRATEGIC-MANAGEMENT MODEL

The strategic-management process best can be studied and applied using a model. Every model represents some kind of process. The framework illustrated in Figure 1–1 is a widely accepted, comprehensive model of the strategic-management process.[15] This model does not guarantee success, but it does represent a clear and practical approach for formulating, implementing, and evaluating strategies. Relationships among major components of the strategic-management process are shown in the model, which appears in all subsequent chapters with appropriate areas shaped to show the particular focus of each chapter.

Identifying an organization's existing mission, objectives, and strategies is the logical starting point for strategic management because a firm's present situation and condition may preclude certain strategies and may even dictate a particular course of action. Every organization has a mission, objectives, and strategy, even if these elements are not consciously designed, written, or communicated. The answer to where an organization is going can be determined largely by where the organization has been!

The strategic-management process is dynamic and continuous. A change in any one of the major components in the model can necessitate a change in any or all of the other components. For instance, a shift in the economy could represent a major opportunity and require a change in long-term objectives and strategies; a failure to accomplish annual objectives could require a change in policy; or a major competitor's change in strategy could require a change in the firm's mission. Therefore, strategy formulation, implementation, and evaluation activities should be performed on a continual basis, not just at the end of the year or semiannually. The strategic-management process never really ends.

The strategic-management process is not as cleanly divided and neatly performed in practice as the strategic-management model suggests. Strategists do not go through the process in lockstep fashion. Generally, there is give-and-take among hierarchical levels of an organization. Many organizations conduct formal meetings semiannually to discuss and update the firm's mission, opportunities/threats, strengths/weaknesses, strategies, objectives, policies, and performance. These meetings are commonly held off-premises and called *retreats*. The rationale for periodically conducting strategic-management meetings away from the work site is to encourage more creativity and candor among participants. Good communication and feedback are needed throughout the strategic-management process.

As shown in Figure 1–2, a number of different forces affect the formality of strategic management in organizations. Size of organization is a key factor; smaller firms are less formal in performing strategic-management tasks. Other variables that affect formality are management styles, complexity of environment, complexity of the production process, nature of problems, and purpose of the planning system.

BENEFITS OF STRATEGIC MANAGEMENT

Strategic management allows an organization to be more proactive than reactive in shaping its own future; it allows an organization to initiate and influence (rather than just respond to) activities, and thus to exert control over its own destiny. Small business owners, chief executive officers, presidents, and managers of many for-profit and nonprofit organizations have recognized and realized the benefits of strategic management.

FIGURE 1–1
A Comprehensive Strategic-Management Model

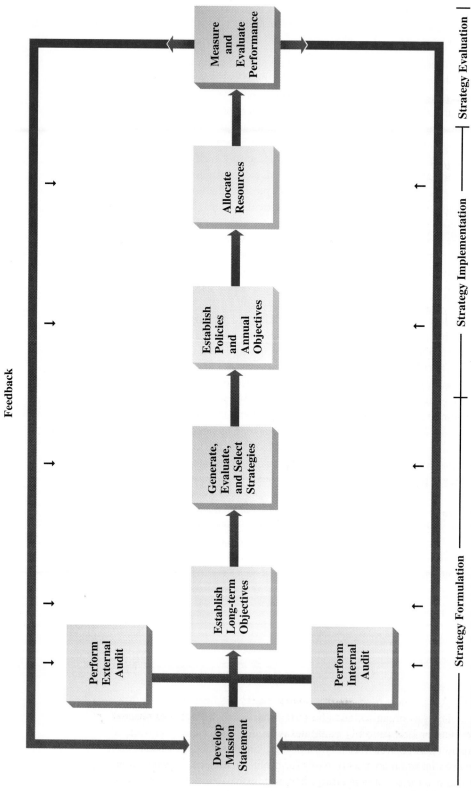

Source: Fred R. David, "How Companies Define Their Mission," *Long Range Planning* 22, no. 3 (June 1988): 40.

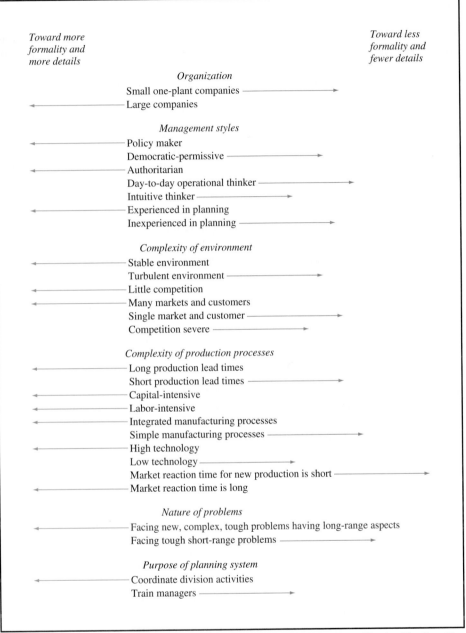

Source: Reprinted with permission of the Free Press, a Division of Macmillan, Inc., from *Strategic Planning: What Every Manager Must Know* by George A. Steiner (New York: Free Press, 1979): 54. Copyright 1979 by the Free Press.

Historically, the principal benefit of strategic management has been to help organizations make better strategies through the use of a more systematic, logical, and rational approach to strategic choice. This certainly continues to be a major benefit of strategic management, but research studies now indicate that the process, rather than the decision or document, is the more important contribution of strategic management.[16] *Communication is a key to successful strategic management.* Through involvement in the process, managers and employees become committed to supporting the organization. Dialogue and participation are essential ingredients. The chief executive officer of Rockwell International explains, "We believe that fundamental to effective strategic management is fully informed employees at all organizational levels. We expect every business segment to inform every employee about the business objectives, the direction of the business, the progress towards achieving objectives, and our customers, competitors and product plans."

The manner in which strategic management is carried out is thus exceptionally important. A major aim of the process is to achieve understanding and commitment from all managers and employees. Understanding may be the most important benefit of strategic management, followed by commitment. When managers and employees understand what the organization is doing and why, they often feel a part of the firm and become committed to assisting it. This is especially true when employees also understand linkages between their own compensation and organizational performance. Managers and employees become surprisingly creative and innovative when they understand and support the firm's mission, objectives, and strategies. A great benefit of strategic management, then, is the opportunity that the process provides to empower individuals. *Empowerment* is the act of strengthening employees' sense of effectiveness by encouraging and rewarding them to participate in decision making and exercise initiative and imagination. *The Wall Street Journal* reports that 40 percent of U.S. manufacturers have adopted empowerment, usually through creation of self-directed work teams.[17]

More and more organizations are decentralizing the strategic-management process, recognizing that planning must involve lower-level managers and employees. The notion of centralized staff planning is being replaced in organizations by decentralized line-manager planning. The process is a learning, helping, educating, and supporting activity, not merely a paper-shuffling activity among top executives. Strategic-management dialogue is more important than a nicely bound strategic-management document.[18] The worst thing strategists can do is develop strategic plans themselves and then present them to operating managers to execute. Through involvement in the process, line managers become "owners" of the strategy. Ownership of strategies by the people who have to execute them is a key to success!

Although making good strategic decisions is the major responsibility of an organization's owner or chief executive officer, managers and employees both must also be involved in strategy formulation, implementation, and evaluation activities. Participation is a key to gaining commitment for needed changes.

An increasing number of corporations and institutions are using strategic management to make effective decisions. Over 75 percent of all companies now use strategic-management techniques, compared to less than 25 percent in 1979.[19] But strategic management is not a guarantee for success; it can be dysfunctional if conducted haphazardly. The benefits of strategic management to Rockwell International Corporation, Columbia Gas System Service Corporation, and Ogden Corporation are evidenced in Table 1–3.

William Dearden of Hershey Foods Corporation attributes his company's success to strategic management: "Planning for the long-term future has been entrenched as a way of life at Hershey, and we certainly plan to strengthen and rely on the process going forward."[20]

FINANCIAL BENEFITS   Research indicates that organizations using strategic-management concepts are more profitable and successful than those that do not. For example, a longitudinal study of 101 retail, service, and manufacturing firms over a 3-year period concluded that businesses using strategic-management concepts showed significant improvement in sales, profitability, and productivity compared to firms without systematic planning activities; another study reported that up to 80 percent of the improvement possible in a firm's profitability is achieved through changes in a company's strategic direction: Cook and Ferris reported that the practices of high-performing firms reflect a more strategic orientation and longer-term focus.[21] High-performing firms tend to do systematic planning to prepare

TABLE 1–3
**Top Managers Discuss
Strategic Management in
Their Firms**

ROCKWELL INTERNATIONAL CORPORATION (www.rockwell.com)

We expect every business segment head to be responsible for the strategic direction of the business and the business team to be very knowledgeable about their business in the worldwide marketplace, to know where they are taking the business long term; and how they are going to position the business vis-à-vis worldwide competition, as well as the marketplace as a whole. We also expect every business to make full use of the corporation's resources in developing functionally integrated implementation strategies that will beat the best of the competition. We will distinguish ourselves as a strategically managed worldwide company through the care and thoroughness with which our strategic management is linked to operational decision making. (Donald Beall, chief executive officer of Rockwell International, *Internal Report*, 1990.)

COLUMBIA GAS SYSTEM SERVICE CORPORATION (www.columbiaenergy.com)

Headquartered in Wilmington, Delaware, Columbia Gas System's Strategic Plan forms the basis of all other planning activities—marketing plans, capital programs, financial plans, and so forth. Strategic management goes far beyond operational planning that has been traditional throughout Columbia. We are not just looking at projections of how much gas we'll need and where it will come from. The first part of our Strategic Plan is the Mission Statement, which sets the direction for the company. All operating units have their own mission statements, defining their business and their corporate reason for existing. These in turn are followed by long-term objectives which are broad statements of what the company intends to do, followed by annual objectives which for the most part are quantified. (James D. Little, executive vice president of Columbia Gas System, *Columbia Today,* Winter 1985–86, p. 2.)

OGDEN CORPORATION (www.ogdencorp.com)

The best long-run results come from good strategic decisions, which ensure doing the right things (effectiveness), and the combination of design, technology, and automation, which ensure doing things right (efficiency). To predict . . . without the ability to adapt is simply to foresee one's own end! The strategic objectives Ogden has achieved have enabled the adaptation necessary to cope with the changing economic environment for the balance of this century. We are describing a classic example of evolution; in this case, corporate evolution. To survive, both organisms and corporations must adapt to new circumstances. (Ralph Ablon, chair of the board, Ogden Corporation.)

for future fluctuations in their external and internal environments. Firms with planning systems more closely resembling strategic-management theory generally exhibit superior long-term financial performance relative to their industry.

High-performing firms seem to make more informed decisions with good anticipation of both short- and long-term consequences. On the other hand, firms that perform poorly often engage in activities that are shortsighted and do not reflect good forecasting of future conditions. Michael Allen found that strategic management demonstrated impressive power by dramatically improving the performance of a number of major companies that had implemented it, including General Electric, American Express, Allied Corporation, Dun & Bradstreet, and Pitney Bowes.[22] Strategists of low-performing organizations are often preoccupied with solving internal problems and meeting paperwork deadlines. They typically underestimate their competitors' strengths and overestimate their own firm's strengths. They often attribute weak performance to uncontrollable factors such as poor economy, technological change, or foreign competition.

Dun & Bradstreet reports that more than 100,000 businesses in the United States fail annually. Business failures include bankruptcies, foreclosures, liquidations, and court-mandated receiverships. Although many factors besides a lack of effective strategic management can lead to business failure, the planning concepts and tools described in this text can yield substantial financial benefits for any organization. An excellent Web site for businesses engaged in strategic planning is www.checkmateplan.com.

NONFINANCIAL BENEFITS Besides helping firms avoid financial demise, strategic management offers other tangible benefits, such as an enhanced awareness of external threats, an improved understanding of competitors' strategies, increased employee productivity, reduced resistance to change, and a clearer understanding of performance-reward relationships. Strategic management enhances the problem-prevention capabilities of organizations because it promotes interaction among managers at all divisional and functional levels. Interaction can enable firms to turn on their managers and employees by nurturing them, sharing organizational objectives with them, empowering them to help improve the product or service, and recognizing their contributions. According to Tom Peters, the difference between a turned-on and a turned-off worker is not 5 percent or 10 percent, but 100 percent to 200 percent.[23]

In addition to empowering managers and employees, strategic management often brings order and discipline to an otherwise floundering firm. It can be the beginning of an efficient and effective managerial system. Strategic management may renew confidence in the current business strategy or point to the need for corrective actions. The strategic-management process provides a basis for identifying and rationalizing the need for change to all managers and employees of a firm; it helps them view change as an opportunity rather than a threat.

Greenley stated that strategic management offers the following benefits:

1. It allows for identification, prioritization, and exploitation of opportunities.
2. It provides an objective view of management problems.
3. It represents a framework for improved coordination and control of activities.
4. It minimizes the effects of adverse conditions and changes.
5. It allows major decisions to better support established objectives.
6. It allows more effective allocation of time and resources to identified opportunities.
7. It allows fewer resources and less time to be devoted to correcting erroneous or ad hoc decisions.
8. It creates a framework for internal communication among personnel.
9. It helps to integrate the behavior of individuals into a total effort.
10. It provides a basis for the clarification of individual responsibilities.
11. It gives encouragement to forward thinking.
12. It provides a cooperative, integrated, and enthusiastic approach to tackling problems and opportunities.
13. It encourages a favorable attitude toward change.
14. It gives a degree of discipline and formality to the management of a business.[24]

BUSINESS ETHICS AND STRATEGIC MANAGEMENT

Business ethics can be defined as principles of conduct within organizations that guide decision making and behavior. Good business ethics is a prerequisite for good strategic management; good ethics is just good business!

A rising tide of consciousness about the importance of business ethics is sweeping America and the world. Strategists are the individuals primarily responsible for ensuring that high ethical principles are espoused and practiced in an organization. All strategy formulation, implementation, and evaluation decisions have ethical ramifications.

Newspapers and business magazines daily report legal and moral breaches of ethical conduct by both public and private organizations. As the Natural Environment Perspective indicates, firms increasingly view cooperation with environmental groups as more effective than confrontation. Harming the natural environment is unethical, illegal, and costly; as more countries and companies realize this fact, export opportunities for pollution control equipment abound.

A new wave of ethics issues related to product safety, employee health, sexual harassment, AIDS in the workplace, smoking, acid rain, affirmative action, waste disposal, foreign business practices, cover-ups, takeover tactics, conflicts of interest, employee privacy, inappropriate gifts, security of company records, and layoffs has accented the need for strategists to develop a clear code of business ethics. United Technologies Corporation has issued a 21-page Code of Ethics and named a new vice president of business ethics. Baxter Travenol Laboratories, IBM, Caterpillar Tractor, Chemical Bank, Exxon, Dow Corning, and Celanese are firms that have a formal code of business ethics. Note how clearly BellSouth's *code of business ethics* in Table 1–4 outlines the standards of behavior expected of all managers and employees. A code of business ethics can provide a basis on which policies can be devised to guide daily behavior and decisions at the work site.

Merely having a code of ethics, however, is not sufficient to ensure ethical business behavior. A code of ethics can be viewed as a public relations gimmick, a set of platitudes, or window dressing. To ensure that the code is read, understood, believed, and remembered, organizations need to conduct periodic ethics workshops to sensitize people to workplace circumstances in which ethics issues may arise.[25]

Internet privacy is an emerging ethical issue of immense proportions. There is a national push for industry assurances that children have parental permission before giving out their names, ages, and other private details to companies that run Web sites. Privacy advocates increasingly argue for new government regulations to enforce protection of young users.

Netscape recently revealed a flaw in its browsing software that allows some Web site operators to access the personal computers of users. This flaw was corrected quickly but is indicative of privacy problems that plague the Internet.

Millions of computer users are worried about privacy on the Internet and want the U.S. government to pass laws about how data can be collected and used. Advertisers, marketers, companies, and people with various reasons to snoop on other people now can discover easily on the Internet others' buying preferences, hobbies, incomes, medical data, social security numbers, addresses, previous addresses, sexual preferences, credit card purchases, traffic tickets, divorce settlements, and much more. Many Internet users are ready for what they call "some law and order" in cyberspace.

Consumers using the Internet sacrifice privacy and anonymity. People today are being laid off and rejected for jobs without ever knowing the reason, sometimes due to something someone discovered on the Internet. America Online sold its subscriber list of over 11 million people and even cross-referenced that information with data from Donnelley Marketing and other companies. Privacy is important, but some people contend that access to reliable information is at least as important.

The U.S. Supreme Court's 1997 decision to strike down the Communications Decency Act paved the way for even less regulation and even less privacy on the Internet. Justice John Paul Stevens stated that "the interest in encouraging freedom of expression in a democratic society outweighs any theoretical but unproved benefit of censorship. Government regulation of the content of speech is more likely to interfere with the free exchange of ideas than to encourage it. The Internet is not as invasive as radio or television. Users seldom encounter content by accident." With the ruling, telecommunications executives and free-speech advocates were elated, but many consumers, parents, and privacy advocates were disappointed.

TABLE 1–4
BellSouth's Code of Conduct

COUNT ON US!

We are committed to the highest ethical standards because we want people to know they can count on us. This commitment flows naturally from our responsibilities to our customers, our owners, our vendors and suppliers, our families, the communities where we live and work, and to each other. Trust is at the heart of these connections, and trust can only be built on honest and dependability—on ethical conduct.

OUR CUSTOMERS CAN COUNT ON US

We believe our first responsibility is to the people who count on us for their telecommunications needs—in the office, on the road, at home, wherever they might be. All else hinges on this. We will deal with customers straightforwardly and honestly. They will know they can depend not only on our products and services, but on our word and our character. We will promise only what we can deliver. When we err, we will make things right.

OUR OWNERS CAN COUNT ON US

We will provide the highest quality at a reasonable price. As we do so, we will earn a fair return on our owners' investment. Our aim is to increase the value of their investment over the years.

OUR VENDORS AND SUPPLIERS CAN COUNT ON US

Vendors and suppliers must know we will be fair. BellSouth's interests will dictate our decisions about what products and services to buy; our decisions will be based on factors such as quality, price, service, and reliability.

OUR FAMILIES CAN COUNT ON US

We want our families to be proud of our character as individuals in the jobs we do and proud that we work for a company known for its integrity. We seek a healthy balance between our work and our family life.

OUR COMMUNITIES CAN COUNT ON US

Beyond the quality, day-to-day service they expect from us in telecommunications, the cities and towns where we operate can also count on us for help in civic, charitable, and other community activities.

WE CAN COUNT ON EACH OTHER

We take pride in the quality of our collective efforts as BellSouth; we take pride in the integrity of our company. A company's reputation is built on what its people do every day. BellSouth's reputation was built on the honesty of hundreds of thousands of people over the years, and we recognize that we can diminish that reputation in one single instant. We also know, however, that we can reinforce it every day. And since you and I inherited a company with a reputation for honesty and integrity, we are obligated to pass the heritage on to the women and men who follow us.

   We will be even-handed with everyone around us—in scheduling work, in assigning jobs, in awarding incentives and promotions, and in the way we treat one another generally.

   Each of us expects to be heard and we in turn pledge to listen. We want honesty and openness—about mistakes as well as successes.

   We will speak out when we see ethical lapses. We expect that no one will ask us to do anything wrong. Likewise, we will not ask anyone else to do anything wrong.

   Satisfying the letter of the law is not enough. Ours is a higher standard. BellSouth's obligations are for the long term—not just for this quarter or this year. These obligations demand this pledge of us on professional, industry and personal ethics: We will build on BellSouth's heritage of integrity so that people will have an abiding trust in the company and our employees; they will know they can count on us. This is our pledge.

Source: BellSouth Corporation, *Internal Report,* 1993.

NATURAL ENVIRONMENT

Is Cooperation Better Than Confrontation?

More U.S. firms today actively seek out environmental groups and the Environmental Protection Agency (EPA) to engage proactively in dialogue aimed at setting environmental standards for the firm and industry. The old, reactive, command-and-control approach to environmental affairs no longer is considered the most effective. Ciba-Geigy, Monsanto, Exxon, Amoco, and General Motors are just a few among thousands of firms that today actively engage trade associations; regulatory bodies; and state, national, and foreign legislatures in setting industry natural environment standards. Companies find that many environmentalists are highly competent technologically and operationally. Dialogue thus often results in new processes that significantly improve corporate efficiency as well as environmental effectiveness.

Benefits of this activity far exceed public relations.

Before a firm engages an environmental group in discussions, the following seven recommendations can pave the way for success:

- Be sincere in wanting their input.
- Be willing to accept some advice.
- Be part of the issue, so you have credibility.
- Look at the larger interests, see the big picture.
- Staff the meeting with decision makers.
- Have a good corporate reputation.
- Reach out on other issues, also.

When organizations today face criminal charges for polluting the environment, firms increasingly are turning on their managers and employees to win leniency for themselves. Employee firings and demotions are becoming common in pollution-related legal suits. Managers being recently fired at Darling International, Inc., and Niagara Mohawk Power Corporation for being indirectly responsible for their firms' polluting water exemplifies this corporate trend. Therefore, managers and employees today must be careful not to ignore, conceal, or disregard a pollution problem or they may find themselves personally liable.

Source: Adapted from Gail Dutton, "Green Partnerships," Management Review (January 1996): 24–28. Also, Dean Starkman, "Pollution Case Highlights Trend to Let Employees Take the Rap," The Wall Street Journal, (October 9, 1997): B10.

Given the global nature of the Internet, any U.S. government regulations to inhibit free flow of information will not carry much weight anyway in places such as Moldova, home of a phone-porn scam. But perhaps the United States at least should set a standard for Internet rules and regulations that other countries could consider adopting.

An ethics "culture" needs to permeate organizations! To help create an ethics culture, Citicorp developed a business ethics board game that is played by 40,000 employees in 45 countries. Called *The Work Ethic*, this game asks players business ethics questions, such as how to deal with a customer who offers you football tickets in exchange for a new, backdated IRA. Diana Robertson at the Wharton School believes the game is effective because it is interactive. Many organizations, such as Prime Computer and Kmart, have developed a code-of-conduct manual outlining ethical expectations and giving examples of situations that commonly arise in their businesses. Harris Corporation's managers and employees are warned that failing to report an ethical violation by others could bring discharge.

One reason strategists' salaries are high compared to those of other individuals in an organization is that strategists must take the moral risks of the firm. Strategists are responsible for developing, communicating, and enforcing the code of business ethics for their organizations. Although primary responsibility for ensuring ethical behavior rests with a firm's strategists, an integral part of the responsibility of all managers is to provide ethics leadership by constant example and demonstration. Managers hold positions that enable them to influence and educate many people. This makes managers responsible for the development and implementation of ethical decision making. Gellerman and Drucker respectively offer some good advice for managers:

All managers risk giving too much because of what their companies demand from them. But the same superiors who keep pressing you to do more, or to do it better, or faster, or less expensively, will turn on you should you cross that fuzzy line between right and wrong. They will blame you for exceeding instructions or for ignoring their warnings. The smartest managers already know that the best answer to the question "How far is too far?" is don't try to find out.[26]

A man (or woman) might know too little, perform poorly, lack judgment and ability, and yet not do too much damage as a manager. But if that person lacks character and integrity—no matter how knowledgeable, how brilliant, how successful—he destroys. He destroys people, the most valuable resource of the enterprise. He destroys spirit. And he destroys performance. This is particularly true of the people at the head of an enterprise. For the spirit of an organization is created from the top. If an organization is great in spirit, it is because the spirit of its top people is great. If it decays, it does so because the top rots. As the proverb has it, "Trees die from the top." No one should ever become a strategist unless he or she is willing to have his or her character serve as the model for subordinates.[27]

According to John Akers, ethics and competitiveness are inseparable.[28] No society anywhere in the world can compete very long or successfully with people stealing from one another or not trusting one another, with every bit of information requiring notarized confirmation, with every disagreement ending up in litigation, or with government having to regulate businesses to keep them honest. Akers stated that being unethical is a recipe for headaches, inefficiency, and waste. History has proven that the greater the trust and confidence of people in the ethics of an institution or society, the greater its economic strength. Business relationships are built mostly on mutual trust and reputation. Short-term decisions based on greed and questionable ethics will preclude the necessary self-respect to gain the trust of others. More and more firms believe that ethics training and an ethics culture create strategic advantage.

Some business actions *always* considered to be unethical include misleading advertising or labeling, causing environmental harm, poor product or service safety, padding expense accounts, insider trading, dumping banned or flawed products in foreign markets, lack of equal opportunities for women and minorities, overpricing, hostile takeovers, moving jobs overseas, and using nonunion labor in a union shop.[29] Recent research also suggests that Japanese firms are perceived by consumers to be more ethical than American firms.[30]

Ethics training programs should include messages from the CEO emphasizing ethical business practices, development and discussion of codes of ethics, and procedures for discussing and reporting unethical behavior. Firms can align ethical and strategic decision making by incorporating ethical considerations into long-term planning, integrating ethical decision making into the performance appraisal process, encouraging whistle-blowing or the reporting of unethical practices, and monitoring departmental and corporate performance regarding ethical issues.

In a final analysis, ethical standards come out of history and heritage. Our fathers and mothers and brothers and sisters of the past left to us an ethical foundation to build upon. Even the legendary football coach Vince Lombardi knew that some things were worth more than winning, and he required his players to have three kinds of loyalty: to God, to their families, and to the Green Bay Packers, "in that order."

COMPARING BUSINESS AND MILITARY STRATEGY

A strong military heritage underlies the study of strategic management. Terms such as *objectives, mission, strengths,* and *weaknesses* first were formulated to address problems on the battlefield. In many respects, business strategy is like military strategy, and military strategists have learned much over the centuries that can benefit business strategists today. Both business and military organizations try to use their own strengths to exploit competitors' weaknesses. If an organization's overall strategy is wrong (ineffective), then all the efficiency in the world may not be enough to allow success. Business or military success is generally not the happy result of accidental strategies. Rather, success is the product of continuous attention to changing external and internal conditions and the formulation and implementation of insightful adaptations to those conditions. The element of surprise provides great competitive advantages in both military and business strategy; information systems that provide data on opponents' or competitors' strategies and resources are also vitally important.

Of course, a fundamental difference between military and business strategy is that business strategy is formulated, implemented, and evaluated with an assumption of *competition,* whereas military strategy is based on an assumption of *conflict.* Nonetheless, military conflict and business competition are so similar that many strategic-management techniques apply equally to both. Business strategists have access to valuable insights that military thinkers have refined over time. Superior strategy formulation and implementation can overcome an opponent's superiority in numbers and resources.

Both business and military organizations must adapt to change and constantly improve to be successful. Too often, firms do not change their strategies when their environment and competitive conditions dictate the need to change. Gluck offered a classic military example of this:

> When Napoleon won it was because his opponents were committed to the strategy, tactics, and organization of earlier wars. When he lost—against Wellington, the Russians, and the Spaniards—it was because he, in turn, used tried-and-true strategies against enemies who thought afresh, who were developing the strategies not of the last war, but of the next.[31]

CONCLUSION

All firms have a strategy, even if it is informal, unstructured, and sporadic. All organizations are heading somewhere, but unfortunately some organizations do not know where. The old saying "If you do not know where you are going, then any road will lead you there!" accents the need for organizations to use strategic-management concepts and techniques. The strategic-management process is becoming more widely used by small firms, large companies, nonprofit institutions, governmental organizations, and multinational conglomerates alike. The process of empowering managers and employees has almost limitless benefits.

Organizations should take a proactive rather than a reactive approach in their industry, and should strive to influence, anticipate, and initiate rather than just respond to events. The strategic-management process embodies this approach to decision making. It represents a logical, systematic, and objective approach for determining an enterprise's future direction. The stakes are generally too high for strategists to use intuition alone in choosing among alternative courses of action. Successful strategists take the time to think about their businesses, where they are with the businesses, and what they want to be as organizations, and then implement programs and policies to get from where they are to where they want to be in a reasonable period of time.

It is a known and accepted fact that people and organizations that plan ahead are much more likely to become what they want to become than those who do not plan at all. A good strategist plans and controls his or her plans, while a bad strategist never plans and then tries to control people! This textbook is devoted to providing you with the tools necessary to be a good strategist.

TAKE IT TO THE NET

We invite you to visit the DAVID page on the Prentice Hall Web site at
www.prenhall.com/davidsm
for this chapter's World Wide Web exercises.

KEY TERMS AND CONCEPTS

Annual Objectives	(p. 11)	Internal Strengths (p. 9)	Strategic-Management Model (p. 13)
Business Ethics	(p. 18)	Internal Weaknesses (p. 9)	Strategic-Management Process (p. 5)
Code of Business Ethics	(p. 19)	Intuition (p. 6)	Strategies (p. 11)
Electronic Commerce	(p. 4)	Long-Term Objectives (p. 10)	Strategists (p. 8)
Empowerment	(p. 16)	Mission Statements (p. 9)	Strategy Evaluation (p. 5)
Environmental Scanning	(p. 10)	Policies (p. 12)	Strategy Formulation (p. 5)
External Opportunities	(p. 9)	Strategic Management (p. 4)	Strategy Implementation (p. 5)
External Threats	(p. 9)		

ISSUES FOR REVIEW AND DISCUSSION

1. Explain why Business Policy often is called a "capstone course."

2. Read one of the suggested readings at the end of this chapter. Prepare a 1-page written summary that includes your personal thoughts on the subject.

3. What aspect of strategy formulation do you think requires the most time? Why?

4. Why is strategy implementation often considered the most difficult stage in the strategic-management process?

5. Why is it so important to integrate intuition and analysis in strategic management?

6. Explain the importance of a formal mission statement.

7. Discuss relationships among objectives, strategies, and policies.

8. Why do you think some chief executive officers fail to use a strategic-management approach to decision making?

9. Discuss the importance of feedback in the strategic-management model.

10. How can strategists best ensure that strategies will be effectively implemented?

11. Give an example of a recent political development that changed the overall strategy of an organization.

12. Who are the major competitors of your college or university? What are their strengths and weaknesses? What are their strategies? How successful are these institutions compared to your college?

13. If you owned a small business, would you develop a code of business conduct? If yes, what variables would you include? If no, how would you ensure that ethical business standards were being followed by your employees?

14. Would strategic-management concepts and techniques benefit foreign businesses as much as domestic firms? Justify your answer.

15. What do you believe are some potential pitfalls or risks in using a strategic-management approach to decision making?

16. In your opinion, what is the single major benefit of using a strategic-management approach to decision making? Justify your answer.

17. Compare business strategy and military strategy.

18. What do you feel is the relationship between personal ethics and business ethics? Are they, or should they be, the same?

NOTES

1. Peter Drucker, *Management: Tasks, Responsibilities, and Practices* (New York: Harper & Row, 1974): 611.

2. Weston Agor, "How Top Executives Use Their Intuition to Make Important Decisions," *Business Horizons* 29, no. 1 (January–February 1986): 6. Also, see Andrew Campbell, "Brief Case: Strategy and Intuition—A Conversation with Henry Mintzberg," *Long Range Planning* 24, no. 2. (April 1991): 108–10.

3. Alfred Sloan, Jr., *Adventures of the White Collar Man* (New York: Doubleday, 1941): 104.

4. Quoted in Eugene Raudsepp, "Can You Trust Your Hunches?" *Management Review* 49, no. 4 (April 1960): 7.

5. Stephen Harper, "Intuition: What Separates Executives from Managers," *Business Horizons* 31, no. 5 (September–October 1988): 16.

6. Ron Nelson, "How to Be a Manager," *Success* (July–August 1985): 69.

7. Bruce Henderson, *Henderson on Corporate Strategy* (Boston: Abt Books, 1979): 6.

8. Robert Waterman, Jr., *The Renewal Factor: How the Best Get and Keep the Competitive Edge* (New York: Bantam, 1987). See also *Business Week* (September 14, 1987): 100. Also, see *Academy of Management Executive* 3, no. 2 (May 1989): 115.

9. Kenichi Ohmae, "Managing in a Borderless World," *Harvard Business Review* 67, no. 3 (May–June 1989): 153.

10. Harry Jonas III, Ronald Fry, and Suresh Srivasta. "The Office of the CEO: Understanding the Executive Experience." *Academy of Management Executive* 4, no. 3 (August 1990): 36.

11. John Pearce II and Fred David, "The Bottom Line on Corporate Mission Statements," *Academy of Management Executive* 1, no. 2 (May 1987): 109.

12. Ibid., 112. See also John A. Pearce and Fred R. David, "Corporate Mission Statements: The Bottom Line," *Academy of Management Executive* 1, no. 2 (May 1987): 109; and Fred R. David. "How Companies Define Their Mission." *Long Range Planning* 22, no. 1 (February 1989): 90.

13. Adolph Coors Company, *Annual Report* (1988): 1.

14. Portland General Corporation, *Annual Report* (1986): 2, 3.

15. Fred R. David, "How Companies Define Their Mission." *Long Range Planning* 22, no. 1 (February 1989): 91.

16. Ann Langley, "The Roles of Formal Strategic Planning," *Long Range Planning* 21, no. 3 (June 1988): 40.

17. Timothy Aepel, "Not All Workers Find Idea of Empowerment as Neat as It Sounds," *The Wall Street Journal* (September 8, 1997): A1.

18. Bernard Reimann, "Getting Value from Strategic Planning," *Planning Review* 16, no. 3 (May–June 1988): 42.

19. Michael Allen, "Strategic Management Hits Its Stride," *Planning Review* 13, no. 5 (September–October 1985): 6.

20. Hershey Foods Corporation, *Annual Report* (1983): 3.

21. Richard Robinson, Jr., "The Importance of Outsiders in Small Firm Strategic Planning," *Academy of Management Journal* 25, no. 1 (March 1982): 80. Also, S. Schoeffler, Robert Buzzell, and Donald Heany. "Impact of Strategic Planning on Profit Performance," *Harvard Business Review* (March 1974): 137; Lawrence Rhyne, "The Relationship of Strategic Planning to Financial Performance," *Strategic Management Journal* 7 (1986): 432; and Deborah Cook and Gerald Ferris, "Strategic Human Resource Management and Firm Effectiveness in Industries Experiencing Decline," *Human Resource Management* 25, no. 3 (Fall 1986): 454.

22. Allen, 6.

23. Tom Peters, "Passion for Excellence," Public Broadcasting System videotape, 1987.

24. Gordon Greenley, "Does Strategic Planning Improve Company Performance?" *Long Range Planning* 19, no. 2 (April 1986): 106.

25. Saul Gellerman, "Managing Ethics from the Top Down," *Sloan Management Review* (Winter 1989): 77.

26. Saul Gellerman, "Why 'Good' Managers Make Bad Ethical Choices," *Harvard Business Review* 64, no. 4 (July–August 1986): 88.

27. Drucker, 462, 463.

28. John Akers, "Ethics and Competitiveness—Putting First Things First," *Sloan Management Review* (Winter 1989): 69–71.

29. Gene Laczniak, Marvin Berkowitz, Russell Brooker, and James Hale, "The Ethics of Business: Improving or Deteriorating?" *Business Horizons* 38, no. 1 (January–February 1995): 43.

30. Ibid, p. 42.

31. Frederick Gluck, "Taking the Mystique Out of Planning," *Across the Board* (July–August 1985): 59.

CURRENT READINGS

Arnesen, David W., C. Patrick Fleenor, and Rex S. Toh. "The Ethical Dimensions of Airline Frequent Flier Programs." *Business Horizons* 40, no. 1 (January–February): 47–56.

Azzone, Giovanni, Umberto Bertelé, and Giuliano Noci. "At Last We Are Creating Environmental Strategies Which Work." *Long Range Planning* 30, no. 4 (August 1997): 562–571.

Barnett, W. P. and R. A. Burgelman. "Evolutionary Perspectives on Strategy." *Strategic Management Journal* 17, Special Issue (Summer 1996): 5–20.

Barry, David and Michael Elmes. "Strategy Retold: Toward a Narrative View of Strategic Discourse." *Academy of Management Review* 22, no. 2 (April 1997): 429–452.

Bauerschmidt, A. "Speaking of Strategy." *Strategic Management Journal* 17, no. 8 (October 1996): 665–668.

Boeker, Warren. "Strategic Change: The Influence of Managerial Characteristics and Organizational Growth." *Academy of Management Journal* 40, no. 1 (February 1997): 152–170.

Bonn, Ingrid and Chris Christodoulou. "From Strategic Planning to Strategic Management." *Long Range Planning* 29, no. 4 (August 1996): 543–551.

Bowman, Cliff and Andrew Kakabadse. "Top Management Ownership of the Strategy Problem." *Long Range Planning* 30, no. 2 (April 1997): 197–208.

Burgelman, R. A. "A Process Model of Strategic Business Exit: Implications for an Evolutionary Perspective on Strategy." *Strategic Management Journal* 17, Special Issue (Summer 1996): 193–214.

Cannella, Albert A., Jr. "Contrasting Perspectives on Strategic Leaders: Toward a More Realistic View of Top Managers." *Journal of Management* 23, no. 3 (1997): 213–238.

Chakravarthy, Bala. "A New Strategy Framework for Coping with Turbulence." *Sloan Management Review* 38, no. 2 (Winter 1997): 69–82.

Cravens, David W., Gordon Greenley, Nigel F. Piercy, and Stanley Slater. "Integrating Contemporary Strategic Management Perspectives." *Long Range Planning* 30, no. 4 (August 1997): 493–503.

Daily, Catherine M. and Jonathan L. Johnson. "Sources of CEO Power and Firm Financial Performance: A Longitudinal Assessment." *Journal of Management* 23, no. 2 (1997): 97–118.

Dean, James W., Jr., and Mark P. Sharfman. "Does Decision Process Matter? A Study of Strategic Decision-Making Effectiveness." *Academy of Management Journal* 39, no. 2 (April 1996): 368–396.

Donaldson, Thomas. "Values in Tension: Ethics Away From Home." *Harvard Business Review* (September–October 1996): 48–139.

Duening, Tom. "Our Turbulent Times? The Case for Evolutionary Organizational Change." *Business Horizons* 40, no. 1 (January–February 1997): 2–8.

Epstein, Marc J. "You've Got a Great Environmental Strategy—Now What?" *Business Horizons* 39, no. 5 (September–October 1996): 53–59.

Farjoun, M. and L. Lai. "Similarity Judgments in Strategy Formulation: Role, Process and Implications." *Strategic Management Journal* 18, no. 4 (April 1997): 255–274.

Farkas, Charles M. and Suzy Wetlauffer. "The Ways Chief Executive Officers Lead." *Harvard Business Review* (May–June 1996): 110–124.

Gaddis, Paul O. "Strategy Under Attack." *Long Range Planning* 30, no. 1 (February 1997): 38–45.

Gellerman, Saul W. and Robert J. Potter. "The Ultimate Strategic Question." *Business Horizons* 39, no. 2 (March–April 1996): 5–10.

Ginsberg, Ari. "Strategy at the Leading Edge—'New Age' Strategic Planning: Bridging Theory and Practice." *Long Range Planning* 30, no. 1 (February 1997): 125–128.

Hamel, Gary. "Strategy As Revolution." *Harvard Business Review* (July–August 1996): 69–83.

Hart, Stuart L. "Beyond Greening: Strategies for a Sustainable World." *Harvard Business Review* (January–February 1997): 66–77.

Hartman, Cathy L. and Edwin R. Stafford. "Green Alliances: Building New Business with Environmental Groups." *Long Range Planning* 30, no. 2 (April 1997): 184–196.

Hosmer, L. T. "Response to 'Do Good Ethics Always Make for Good Business?'" *Strategic Management Journal* 17, no. 6 (June 1996): 501–511.

Iaquinto, A. L. and J. W. Fredrickson. "Top Management Team Agreement About the Strategic Decision Process: A Test of Some of Its Determinants and Consequences." *Strategic Management Journal* 18, no. 1 (January 1997): 63–76.

Inkpen, A. C. "The Seeking of Strategy Where It Is Not: Towards a Theory of Strategy Absence: A Reply to Bauerschmidt." *Strategic Management Journal* 17, no. 8 (October 1996): 669–679.

Liebeskind, J. P. "Knowledge, Strategy, and the Theory of the Firm." *Strategic Management Journal* 17, Special Issue (Winter 1996): 93–108.

Markides, Constantinos. "Strategic Innovation." *Sloan Management Review* 38, no. 3 (Spring 1997): 9–24.

Miller, Danny, Theresa K. Lant, Frances J. Milliken, and Helaine J. Korn. "The Evolution of Strategic Simplicity: Exploring Two Models of Organizational Adaptation." *Journal of Management* 22, no. 6 (1996): 863–888.

Near, Janet P. and Marcia P. Miceli. "Whistle-Blowing: Myth and Reality." *Journal of Management* 22, no. 3 (1996): 507–517.

Nehrt, C. "Timing and Intensity Effects of Environmental Investments." *Strategic Management Journal* 17, no. 7 (July 1996): 535–548.

Porter, Michael E. "What is Strategy?" *Harvard Business Review* (November–December 1996): 61–80.

Rajagopalan, Nandini and Deepak K. Datta. "CEO Characteristics: Does Industry Matter?" *Academy of Management Journal* 39, no. 1 (February 1996): 197–207.

Ross, Jeanne W., Cynthia M. Beath, and Dale L. Goodhue. "Develop Long-Term Competitiveness Through IT Assets." *Sloan Management Review* 38, no. 1 (Fall 1996): 31–42.

Russo, Michael V. and Paul A. Fouts. "A Resource-Based Perspective on Corporate Environmental Performance and Profitability." *Academy of Management Journal* 40, no. 3 (June 1997): 534–559.

Schwab, B. "A Note on Ethics and Strategy: Do Good Ethics Always Make for Good Business?" *Strategic Management Journal* 17, no. 6 (June 1996): 499–500.

Sahlman, William A. "How to Write a Great Business Plan." *Harvard Business Review* (July–August 1997): 98–109.

Stafford, Edwin R. and Cathy L. Hartman. "Green Alliances: Strategic Relations between Businesses and Environmental Groups." *Business Horizons* 39, no. 2 (March–April 1996): 50–59.

Teece, D. J., Pisano, G., and A. Shuen. "Dynamic Capabilities and Strategic Management." *Strategic Management Journal* 18, no. 7 (August 1997): 509–534.

Tushman, Michael L. and Charles A. O'Reilly III. "The Ambidextrous Organization: Managing Evolutionary and Revolutionary Change." *California Management Review* 38, no. 4 (Summer 1996): 8–30.

Whittington, Richard. "Strategy at the Leading Edge—Strategy as Practice." *Long Range Planning* 29, no. 5 (October 1996): 733–735.

THE COHESION CASE AND EXPERIENTIAL EXERCISES

Two special features of this text are introduced here: (1) the Cohesion Case and (2) the Experiential Exercises. As strategic-management concepts and techniques are introduced in this text, they are applied to the Cohesion Case through Experiential Exercises. The Cohesion Case enters on Hershey Foods Corporation in 1998. As the term *cohesion* implies, the Hershey Foods case and related exercises integrate material presented throughout the text. At least one exercise at the end of each chapter applies textual material to the Hershey Foods case. The Cohesion Case and Experiential Exercises thus work together to give students practice applying strategic-management concepts and tools as they are presented in the text. In this way, students become prepared to perform case analyses as the policy course progresses.

Based in Hershey, Pennsylvania, and a leading manufacturer of candy and pasta, Hershey Foods was selected as the Cohesion Case for several important reasons. First, Hershey is a multinational corporation, so global issues can be discussed in class. Second, Hershey is a multidivisional organization, thus allowing strategic-management concepts to be applied at the corporate, divisional, and functional levels. Third, Hershey is undergoing extensive strategic changes. Fourth, you probably have eaten Hershey candy and pasta; this familiarity will help you learn this business. Fifth, Hershey is an exemplary organization in terms of business ethics and social responsibility; a significant part of Hershey's profits go toward operating the Milton Hershey School for Orphaned Children. Finally, Hershey is very cooperative with students and professors who call to obtain additional information about the company.

Some Experiential Exercises in the text do not relate specifically to the Cohesion Case. At least one exercise at the end of each chapter applies strategic-management concepts to your university. As a student nearing graduation, you are quite knowledgeable about your university. Apply concepts learned in this course to assist your institution. More colleges and universities are instituting strategic management.

After reading the text and applying concepts and tools to the Cohesion Case through Experiential Exercises, you should be well prepared to analyze business policy cases. The objectives of the case method are as follows:

1. to give you experience applying strategic-management concepts and techniques to different organizations
2. to give you experience applying and integrating the knowledge you have gained in prior courses and work experience
3. to give you decision-making experience in real organizations
4. to improve your understanding of relationships among the functional areas of business and the strategic-management process
5. to improve your self-confidence; because there is no one right answer to a case, you will gain experience justifying and defending your own ideas, analyses, and recommendations
6. to improve your oral and written communication skills
7. to sharpen your analytical and intuitive skills

THE COHESION CASE
Fred R. David
Francis Marion University

HERSHEY FOODS CORPORATION—1998
www.hersheys.com

What is your favorite candy bar? Mr. Goodbar, Reese's, Kit Kat, Big Block, Whatcha-macallit, Allsorts, Rolo, Krackel, BarNone, Mounds, Almond Joy, 5th Avenue, Snickers, or Baby Ruth? Did you know that all of these are made by Hershey Foods (except Snickers made by M&M Mars and Baby Ruth made by Nestlé)? Mars and Nestlé are Hershey's two major competitors. Hershey can be phoned toll-free at 1-800-HERSHEY or phoned at 717-534-4900.

Have you ever been to Hershey, Pennsylvania, the home of Hershey Foods Corporation? It is known as "Chocolate Town, USA." The air in the city actually smells like chocolate. There you can walk down Chocolate Avenue, see sidewalks lit with lights in the shape of Hershey Kisses, visit the Hershey Zoo, and see the Chocolate Kiss Tower in Hershey Park. Hershey's Chocolate World is America's most popular corporate visitors' center with more than 2 million guests annually.[1] Admission is free. Even the White House in Washington, D.C., only attracts about 1.5 million visitors annually. Calendar 1998 was the twenty-fifth birthday of the Hershey's Chocolate World and celebrations went on there daily.

Hershey grew from a one-product, one-plant operation in 1894 to a nearly $4 billion company producing an array of quality chocolate, nonchocolate, pasta, and grocery products in 1998. Hershey entered 1998 as the largest candy maker in the United States with about a 34.1 percent market share, just ahead of M&M Mars. Hershey is also the largest pasta manufacturer in the United States with a 27.0 percent market share, just ahead of Borden.

But Hershey does have problems. Hershey's international sales have declined drastically and at year-end 1997 made up only 4.46 percent of total revenues. Hershey remains inexperienced, ineffective, and uncommitted in markets outside the United States, Mexico, and Canada, even though the candy and pasta industries are globalized. Mars, Borden, Nestlé, and other competitors have a growing and effective presence in international markets. In contrast, Hershey recently divested its two main European businesses, Gubor in Germany and Sperlari in Italy, and divested its Canadian Planter's business. Hershey also recently divested its OZF Jamin confectionery and grocery operations in the Netherlands and Belgium and divested Petybon S.A., its pasta and biscuit manufacturer in Brazil.

Hershey's candy and pasta market shares declined slightly in 1997 and long-term debt nearly increased 57 percent to $1.029 billion. Analysts question whether Hershey can continue to survive as a domestic producer of candy and pasta, while its competitors gain economies of scale and experience in world markets. Shareholders are becoming concerned, too. Hershey needs a clear strategic plan to guide future operations and decisions.

HISTORY

Milton Hershey's love for candy making began with a childhood apprenticeship under candy maker Joe Royer of Lancaster, Pennsylvania. Mr. Hershey was eager to own a candy-making business. After numerous attempts and even bankruptcy, he finally gained success in the caramel business. Upon seeing the first chocolate-making equipment at the Chicago Exhibition in 1893, Mr. Hershey envisioned endless opportunities for the chocolate industry.

By 1901, the chocolate industry in America was growing rapidly. Hershey's sales reached $662,000 that year, creating the need for a new factory. Mr. Hershey moved his company to Derry Church, Pennsylvania, a town that was renamed Hershey in 1906. The new Hershey factory provided a means of mass producing a single chocolate product. In 1909, the Milton Hershey School for Orphans was founded. Mr. and Mrs. Hershey could not have children, so for years the Hershey Chocolate Company operated mainly to provide funds for the orphanage. Hershey's sales reached $5 million in 1911.

In 1927, the Hershey Chocolate Company was incorporated under the laws of the state of Delaware and listed on the New York Stock Exchange. That same year, 20 percent of Hershey's stock was sold to the public. Between 1930 and 1960, Hershey went through rapid growth; the name "Hershey" became a household word. The legendary Milton Hershey died in 1945.

In the 1960s, Hershey acquired the H. B. Reese Candy Company, which makes Reese's Peanut Butter Cups, Reese's Pieces, and Reese's Peanut Butter Chips. Hershey also acquired San Giorgio Macaroni and Delmonico Foods, both pasta manufacturers. In 1968, Hershey Chocolate Corporation changed its name to Hershey Foods Corporation. Between 1976 and 1984, William Dearden served as Hershey's chief executive officer. An orphan who grew up in the Milton Hershey School for Orphans, Dearden diversified the company to reduce its dependence on fluctuating cocoa and sugar prices.

In the 1970s, Hershey acquired Y&S Candy Corporation, a manufacturer of licorice-type products, such as Y&S Twizzlers, Nibs, and Bassett's Allsorts. Hershey purchased a pasta company named Procino-Rossi and the Skinner Macaroni Company. During the 1980s, Hershey acquired both A. B. Marabou of Sweden and the Dietrich Corporation, maker of Luden's Throat Drops, Luden's Mellomints, Queen Anne Chocolate-Covered Cherries, and 5th Avenue candy bars. Hershey also acquired the Canadian confectionery (chocolate and nonchocolate candy), as well as the snack nut operations of Nabisco Brands Ltd., which gave them candies such as Oh Henry!, Eatmore, Cherry Blossom, Glosettes, Lowney, Life Savers, Breath Savers, Planter's nuts, Beaver nuts, Chipits chocolate chips, Moirs boxed chocolates, Care*Free gum, and Bubble Yum gum. Hershey acquired Peter Paul/Cadbury's U.S. candy operations, which gave them Mounds, Almond Joy, York Peppermint Pattie, Cadbury Dairy Milk, Cadbury Fruit & Nut, Cadbury Caramello, and Cadbury Creme Eggs. Hershey received rights to market the Peter Paul products worldwide.

In the 1990s, Hershey acquired Ronzoni Foods Corporation from Kraft General Foods Corporation for $80 million. The purchase included the dry pasta, pasta sauce, and cheese businesses of Ronzoni Foods and strengthened Hershey's position as a branded pasta supplier in the United States. Hershey purchased Nacional de Dulces (NDD) and renamed it Hershey Mexico; today, it produces, imports, and markets chocolate products for the Mexican market under the Hershey brand name. In 1996, Hershey acquired Leaf North America to gain market share leadership in North America in nonchocolate confectionery candies.

MISSION STATEMENT

Hershey Foods's mission statement as of the mid-1990s is given below:

> Hershey Foods Corporation's mission is to become a major diversified food company and a leading company in every aspect of our business as:
>
> The number-one confectionery company in North America, moving toward worldwide confectionery market share leadership.
>
> A respected and valued supplier of high-quality, branded consumer food products in North America and selected international markets.[2]

Hershey's mission statement later was modified and reads as follows:

> to be a focused food company in North America and selected international markets and a leader in every aspect of our business. Our goal is to enhance our number one position in the North American confectionery market, be the leader in U.S. pasta and chocolate-related grocery products, and to build leadership positions in selected international markets.[3]

Note that the current statement is shorter and backs off from aspiring to be a world leader in the confectionery industry. It also lacks a number of components generally included in a good mission statement.

HERSHEY CHOCOLATE NORTH AMERICA

This division combines Hershey's Mexican, Canadian, and U.S. confectionery operations and generated 77.6 percent of total company 1997 sales. Sales and profits of this division increased 15 percent and 11 percent respectively in 1997. Most of the volume gains came from the Leaf acquisition and new products as the base business revenues were flat. U.S. market share decreased from 34.2 percent in 1996 to 34.1 percent in 1997. U.S. confectionery market share information for the six leading competitors is given in Case Figure 1–1.

Hershey's U.S. confectionery manufacturing operations are located in:

Hershey, PA
Oakdale, CA
Stuarts Draft, VA
Reading, PA
Hazelton, PA
Lancaster, PA
Naugatuck, CT
Memphis, TN
Denver, CO
Robinson, IL
New Brunswick, NJ

The Leaf facilities and Henry Heide's confectionery operations are located in the last four cities cited above. Canadian operations are located in Smith Falls, Ontario; Montreal, Quebec; and Dartmouth, Nova Scotia. Mexican operations are located in Guadalajara, Mexico.

Hershey Chocolate North America produces an extensive line of chocolate and non-chocolate products sold in the form of single bars, bagged goods, and boxed items. Hershey introduced its first full-line boxed chocolate named Pot of Gold in late 1996. Its products are marketed under more than 60 brand names, and sold in over 2 million retail outlets in the United States, including grocery wholesalers, chain stores, mass merchandisers, drug stores, vending companies, wholesale clubs, convenience stores, and food distributors. Sales to Wal-Mart Stores account for 12 percent of Hershey's total revenues.

The U.S. confectionery market is growing only 2 percent annually in sales volume. The nonchocolate segment, which accounts for about one-third of the overall sweets market, is growing at 5 percent annually, while the chocolate segment is growing at 1 percent. Hershey has only 4 percent of the nonchocolate confectionery market, and the leader is RJR Nabisco with 18 percent. RJR's Life Savers and Gummy Life Savers compete with Hershey's Amazin' Fruit Gummy Bears. The "other" category for 1997 includes Tootsie Roll/Charms (2.9%), Favorite Brands (3.7%), and Russell Stover (7.0%).

HERSHEY INTERNATIONAL

This division is a big trouble spot for Hershey. Hershey exports confectionery and grocery products to over 60 countries outside of North America although these sales represent less than 5 percent of Hershey's sales. All company business outside of North America, including confectionery, grocery, and pasta, is handled under this division. Hershey's International sales declined from $330 million in 1996 to only $192 million in 1997.

Europeans have the highest per capita chocolate consumption rates in the world, but Hershey has no plans to overtake or even threaten Nestlé or Mars in Europe. In the Far East, Hershey has signed licensing agreements with Selecta Dairy Products to manufacture Hershey's ice cream products in the Philippines and with Kuang Chuan Dairy in Taiwan to manufacture Hershey's beverages. Hershey introduced its products into Russia, the Philippines, and Taiwan in 1994. Overall, however, Hershey is not planning sustained efforts anywhere outside the United States.

HERSHEY PASTA AND GROCERY

Hershey consolidated its pasta and grocery divisions in late 1996, a move widely criticized by analysts. Hershey's pasta sales declined nearly 3 percent in 1997 while grocery sales increased 7.9 percent. For 1997, Hershey's pasta sales declined to $400 million from $412 million the prior year, while grocery sales increased to $370 million from $343 million.

CASE FIGURE 1–1
U.S. Confectionery Market Share Percentages

COMPANY	1997	1996	1995
Hershey	34.1	34.2	34.0
Mars	22.3	26.3	26.1
Nestlé	7.9	9.1	8.9
Brach & Brock	4.6	7.4	8.6
Leaf	NA	3.8	3.8
RJR Nabisco	3.5	3.4	3.3
Other	27.6	15.8	15.3

Source: Credit Suisse First Boston Corporation, *Investment Report* (March 2, 1998): 10.

In terms of pasta market share, Hershey had a 27.0 percent share at year-end 1997, versus 27.2 percent for 1996. This compares to Borden (20.1 percent versus 24.5 percent), Private Label (17.1 percent versus 15.2 percent), and CPC (9.8 percent versus 11.0 percent). The Italian pasta maker Barrilla and other foreign firms continue to take market share away from Hershey through heavy promotional and merchandising activity.

The pasta and grocery divisions contributed 17.9 percent of Hershey's 1997 total company sales as indicated in Case Figure 1–2. Pasta imports in the United States are increasing much more rapidly than pasta consumption. The flood of low-priced imported pasta into the United States is coming primarily from Italy and Turkey. This is a major external threat for Hershey. United States pasta market share data is given in Case Figure 1–3.

Hershey first expanded its business into pasta with its 1996 acquisition of San Giorgio Macaroni in Lebanon, Pennsylvania. Hershey owns pasta facilities in Louisville, Kentucky; Auburn, New York; Omaha, Nebraska; Philadelphia, Pennsylvania; and Excelsior Springs, Missouri. Hershey's pasta brands include San Giorgio, Skinner, Delmonico, P&R, Light 'n Fluffy, American Beauty, Perfection, Pastamania, and Ronzoni. Sales of these brands surpass Borden's Creamette brand. Hershey's main pasta manufacturing facility is in Winchester, Virginia. Hershey manufactures and distributes pasta throughout the United States, but does no exporting of pasta and has no plans to build pasta facilities anywhere outside the United States.

CASE FIGURE 1–2
Hershey Foods Sales and Profit (EBIT) Data By Segment (in millions of dollars)

DIVISION SALES	1997		1996		1995	
Hershey Chocolate North America	$3,340	77.64%	$2,904	72.80%	$2,595	70.31%
International	192	4.46%	330	8.27%	335	9.08%
Grocery	370	8.60%	343	8.60%	341	9.24%
Pasta	400	9.30%	412	10.66%	420	11.37%
Total	$4,302	100.00%	$3,989	100.00%	$3,691	100.00%
DIVISION PROFITS (EBIT)						
Hershey Chocolate North America	$548	87.13%	$494	87.59%	$440	86.27%
International	6	.95%	7	1.24%	3	.58%
Grocery	37	5.88%	31	5.50%	33	6.47%
Pasta	38	6.04%	32	5.67%	34	6.67%
Total	$629	100.00%	$564	100.00%	$510	100.00%

Source: www.freeedgar.com.

CASE FIGURE 1–3
U.S. Pasta Market Share Percentages

COMPANY	1997	1996	1995
Hershey	27.0	27.2	27.0
Borden	20.1	24.5	26.0
Private labels	17.1	15.2	15.2
CPC International	9.8	11.0	11.4
Imports	NA	10.7	9.9
Quaker Oats	NA	2.9	2.9
Archer Daniels	NA	1.0	1.1
Other	NA	6.5	6.5

Source: Merrill Lynch Capital, *Investment Report* (January 29, 1998): 8.

HERSHEY'S OPERATIONS

SOCIAL RESPONSIBILITY

Hershey Foods Corporation is committed to the values of its founder, Milton S. Hershey—that is, the highest standards of quality, honesty, fairness, integrity, and respect. The firm makes annual contributions of cash, products, and services to a variety of national and local charitable organizations. Hershey is the sole sponsor of the Hershey National Track and Field Youth Program. Hershey also makes contributions to the Children's Miracle Network, a national program benefiting children's hospitals across the United States.

The corporation operates the Milton Hershey School, whose mission is to provide all costs and full-time care and education for disadvantaged children, primarily orphans. The school currently cares for over 1,000 boys and girls in grades kindergarten through 12. The Hershey School Trust owns over 75 percent of all Hershey Corporation's common stock.

CORPORATE STRUCTURE

Hershey in 1997 reorganized its corporate structure, changing from a four-division structure (Hershey Chocolate North America, Hershey Grocery, Hershey International, and Hershey Pasta Group) to a three-division structure (Hershey Chocolate North America, Hershey Pasta and Grocery, and Hershey International). Hershey's current organizational chart is shown in Case Figure 1–4.

FINANCE

Hershey annually spends about $26 million on research and development. Hershey's recent financial statements are given in Case Figures 1–5 and 1–6.

CASE FIGURE 1–4
Hershey's Chain of Command

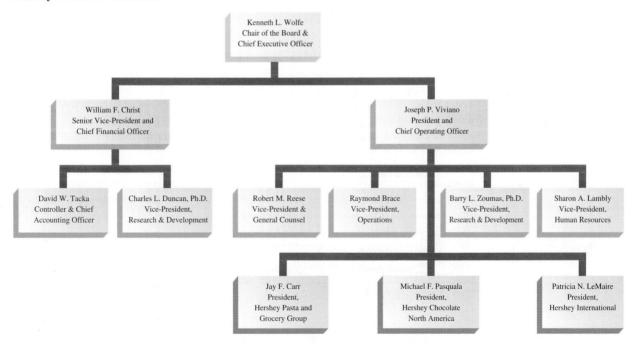

Source: Hershey Foods, *Annual Report* (1997): 40.

CASE FIGURE 1–5

Hershey Foods Corporation
CONSOLIDATED STATEMENTS OF INCOME
In thousands of dollars except per share amounts

FOR THE YEARS ENDED DECEMBER 31,	1997	1996	1995	1994
NET SALES	$4,302,236	$3,989,308	$3,690,667	$3,606,271
COSTS AND EXPENSES:				
Cost of sales	2,488,896	2,302,089	2,126,274	2,097,556
Selling, marketing and administrative	1,183,130	1,124,087	1,053,758	1,034,115
Total costs and expenses	3,672,026	3,426,178	3,180,032	3,131,671
RESTRUCTURING CREDIT (CHARGE)	—	—	151	(106,105)
LOSS ON DISPOSAL OF BUSINESSES	—	(35,352)	—	—
INCOME BEFORE INTEREST AND INCOME TAXES	630,210	527,780	510,786	368,495
Interest expense, net	76,255	48,043	44,833	35,357
INCOME BEFORE INCOME TAXES	553,955	479,737	465,953	333,138
Provision for income taxes	217,704	206,551	184,034	148,919
NET INCOME	$ 336,251	$ 273,186	$ 281,919	$ 184,219
NET INCOME PER SHARE	$ 2.25	$ 1.77	$ 1.70	$ 1.06
CASH DIVIDENDS PAID PER SHARE:				
Common Stock	$ .8400	$ .7600	$ .6850	$ .6250
Class B Common Stock	.7600	.6850	.6200	.5675

Source: Hershey Foods, *Annual Report* (1997): 34.

MARKETING

Per capita candy sales in the United States increased by 7.1 percent over the last 5 years. Americans spend over $21 billion a year on sweets. Upscale candy items such as Mars's Dove Promises are selling well. People are eating more ethnic foods today than 10 years ago, which means they are eating more garlic and flavorings; breath freshener–type candies are selling well in response to this trend.

Hershey's expenditures on advertising and promotion have increased annually as shown in Case Figure 1–7.

Conventional wisdom in the candy industry is that a person rarely selects the same brand of candy bar twice in a row; consequently, product variety is crucial to success. Marketing issues relative to health, nutrition, and weight consciousness are important. The media Hershey uses most for advertising are network television, followed by syndicated television, spot television, magazines, network radio, and spot radio.

Confectionery sales generally are lowest during the second quarter of the year and highest during the third and fourth quarters, due mainly to the holiday seasons. Hershey generates about 20 percent of annual sales during the second quarter and 30 percent of annual sales during the fourth quarter.

CASE FIGURE 1–6
Hershey Foods Corporation
CONSOLIDATED BALANCE SHEETS
In thousands of dollars

DECEMBER 31,	1997	1996	1995
ASSETS			
CURRENT ASSETS:			
Cash and cash equivalents	54,237	61,422	32,346
Accounts receivable—trade	360,831	294,606	326,024
Inventories	505,525	474,978	397,570
Deferred income taxes	84,024	94,464	84,785
Prepaid expenses and other	30,197	60,759	81,598
Total current assets	1,034,814	986,229	922,323
PROPERTY, PLANT AND EQUIPMENT, NET	1,648,237	1,601,895	1,436,009
INTANGIBLES RESULTING FROM BUSINESS ACQUISITIONS	551,849	565,962	428,714
OTHER ASSETS	56,336	30,710	43,577
Total assets	3,291,236	3,184,796	2,830,623
LIABILITIES AND STOCKHOLDERS' EQUITY			
CURRENT LIABILITIES:			
Accounts payable	146,932	134,213	127,067
Accrued liabilities	371,545	357,828	308,123
Accrued income taxes	19,692	10,254	15,514
Short-term debt	232,451	299,469	413,268
Current portion of long-term debt	25,095	15,510	383
Total current liabilities	795,715	817,274	864,355
LONG-TERM DEBT	$1,029,136	655,289	357,034
OTHER LONG-TERM LIABILITIES	346,500	327,209	333,814
DEFERRED INCOME TAXES	267,079	224,003	192,461
Total liabilities	2,438,430	2,023,775	1,747,664
STOCKHOLDERS' EQUITY:			
Preferred Stock, shares issued: none in 1997, 1996, and 1995	—	—	—
Common Stock, shares issued: 149,484,964 in 1997;			
149,471,964 in 1996; and 74,733,982 on a pre-split basis in 1995	149,485	149,472	74,734
Class B Common Stock, shares issued: 30,465,908 in 1997;			
30,478,908 in 1996; and 15,241,454 on a pre-split basis in 1995	30,465	30,478	15,241
Additional paid-in capital	33,852	42,432	47,732
Cumulative foreign currency translation adjustments	(42,243)	(32,875)	(29,240)
Unearned ESOP compensation	(28,741)	(31,935)	(35,128)
Retained earnings	1,977,849	1,763,144	1,694,696
Treasury—Common Stock shares, at cost: 37,018,566 in 1997;			
27,009,316 in 1996; and 12,709,553 on a pre-split basis in 1995	(1,267,861)	(759,695)	(685,076)
Total stockholders' equity	852,806	1,161,021	1,082,959
Total liabilities and stockholders' equity	3,291,236	3,184,796	2,830,623

Source: www.freeedgar.com.

CASE FIGURE 1–7
Hershey's Expenditures on Advertising and Promotion (in millions of dollars)

YEAR	$ ADVERTISING	$ PROMOTION	$ TOTAL
1992	137	398	535
1993	130	444	574
1994	120	419	539
1995	159	403	562
1996	174	429	603
1997	—	—	650

Source: www.freeedgar.com.

GLOBAL ISSUES

The chocolate/cocoa products industry is SIC 2066 and candy/confectionery is SIC 2064. The main distribution channels for chocolate are grocery, drug, and department stores as well as vending machines. Almost all of these distributors are local, regional, or national; only a few are multinational. Although chocolate producers have not yet developed globally uniform marketing programs, the situation is changing. European unification extended grocery and department store channels of distribution. For example, Safeway, a U.S. grocery chain, now operates stores in Canada, Britain, Germany, and Saudi Arabia. As global channels of distribution become more available for chocolate manufacturers, global marketing uniformity will become more prevalent in the industry. Global cultural convergence is accelerating the need for global marketing uniformity in the confectionery industry. Hershey's competitors are taking advantage of this globalization trend.

The confectionery industry is characterized by high manufacturing economies of scale. Hershey's main chocolate factory, for example, occupies more than 2 million square feet, is highly automated, and contains a great deal of heavy equipment, vats, and containers. It is the largest chocolate plant in the world. High manufacturing costs in any industry encourages global market expansion, globally standardized products, and globally centralized production.

The confectionery industry also is characterized by high transportation costs for moving milk and sugar, the primary raw materials. This fact motivates companies such as Hershey to locate near their sources of supply. Because milk can be obtained in large volumes in many countries, chocolate producers have many options in locating plants. Also, producing chocolate is not labor-intensive, nor does it require highly skilled labor.

Product development costs in the confectionery industry are relatively low because the process mostly involves mixing different combinations of the same ingredients. Whenever product development costs are low in an industry, firms are spurred to globalize existing brands rather than develop new ones for different countries.

Industry analysts expect the candy industry to continue to grow. Consumption of chocolate, according to industry analysts, is closely related to national income, although the Far East is an exception to this rule. Candy consumption varies in the major markets of the developed nations. Americans consume about 22 pounds of candy annually per person and Europeans consume about 27 pounds of candy per person annually.

Chocolate accounts for about 54 percent of all candy consumed. Northern Europeans consume almost twice as much chocolate per capita as Americans. Among European countries, Switzerland, Norway, and the United Kingdom citizens consume the most chocolate, whereas Finland, Yugoslavia, and Italy citizens consume the least. The Japanese consume very little chocolate—about 1.4 kilos per capita. Throughout Asia and Southern Europe, there is a preference for types of sweets other than chocolate, partly because of the high incidence of lactose intolerance (difficulty in digesting dairy products) in those populations.

Many consumers worldwide are becoming weight-conscious and health-oriented. Numerous organizations and individuals discourage candy consumption and promote the need for exercise and nutrition. The teenage customer base that historically has consumed so much chocolate is shrinking in the United States and most other countries. These persons are being replaced by older, wealthier consumers who prefer more sophisticated chocolates. In countries where birth rates and numbers of youth are still growing, disposable income tends to be low, which is a barrier to market entry for candy makers.

The most important raw material used in production of Hershey's products is cocoa beans. This commodity is imported from West Africa, South America, and Far Eastern equatorial regions. West Africa grows approximately 60 percent of the world's crop. Cocoa beans exhibit wide fluctuations in price, flavor, and quality, due to (a) weather and other conditions affecting crop size; (b) consuming countries' demand requirements; (c) producing countries' sales policies; (d) speculative influences; and (e) international economics and currency movements.

Hershey purchases roughly 180,000 tons of cocoa per year, representing about 15 percent of the company's total cost of goods sold. Hershey purchases and sells cocoa futures contracts. Hershey maintains West African and Brazilian crop-forecasting operations and continually monitors economic and political factors affecting market conditions. Cocoa prices rose moderately in both 1996 and 1997.

Hershey's second most important raw material is sugar. Sugar is subject to price supports under domestic farm legislation. Due to import quotas and duties, sugar prices paid by U.S. users are substantially higher than prices on the world market. The average wholesale list price for refined sugar has remained stable at $0.30 per pound over recent years.

Other raw materials that Hershey Corporation purchases in substantial quantities include semolina milled from durum wheat, milk, peanuts, almonds, and coconut. The prices of milk and peanuts are affected by federal marketing orders and subsidy programs of the U.S. Department of Agriculture. Raising and lowering price supports on milk and peanuts greatly affect the cost of Hershey's raw materials. Market prices of peanuts and almonds generally are determined in the latter months of each year, after harvest.

Tariffs imposed by different countries can greatly impede or promote globalization within an industry. For example, U.S. tariffs on chocolate are very low, ranging from 35 cents per pound for mass-produced chocolate to about $2.50 for some premium brands. Even a 10-cent difference in price among competing brands makes a big difference to consumers.

Nationalistic tariffs as they impact candy are falling but still are high enough to be a concern. Japan, Korea, and Taiwan, for example, have reduced their tariffs on imported chocolate from 20 percent to 10 percent. Europe is retaining its 12 percent tariff on chocolate imports from outside Europe. The United States has a 5 percent tariff on solid chocolate products and a 7 percent tariff on all other chocolate confectionery products. Technology standards across countries are similar to tariffs in that they vary and can impact global strategy plans. Japan, for example, prohibits the sale of chocolates that contain the additives BHT and TBHQ, which are approved by the U.S. Food & Drug Administration.

COMPETITORS

Some of Hershey's competitors do much of their business outside North America. For example, Cadbury-Schweppes obtains 50 percent from international sales and Mars obtains

50 percent, while Hershey obtains the least (10 percent). Hershey's two major candy competitors are Mars and Nestlé.

MARS

Mars is present in Europe, Asia, Mexico, Russia, and Japan. Mars gained 12 percent of the market in Mexico only 1 year after entering that market. Analysts estimate Mars's worldwide sales and profits to be over $7 billion and $1 billion respectively. Mars was successful introducing its Bounty chocolate candy from Europe into the United States without test marketing. Mars uses uniform marketing globally. The company's M&M candies slogan, "It melts in your mouth, not in your hands," is used worldwide. In contrast, Hershey's successful BarNone candy is named Temptation in Canada.

Mars is controlled by the Mars family through two brothers, John and Forrest, Jr. A marketing executive at Mars recently said, "Being Number 2 doesn't sit well with the brothers, and that's the biggest motivator." Mars is one of the world's largest private, closely held companies. It is a secretive company, unwilling to divulge financial information or corporate strategies. Recently, Mars has not been performing well and there are reports of high turnover in their executive and sales staff.

Unlike Hershey, Mars historically has relied on extensive marketing and advertising expenditures rather than on product innovation to gain market share. Mars has been repackaging, restyling, and reformulating its leading brands, including Snickers, M&M's, Milky Way, and 3 Musketeers, and is supplementing that strategy with extensive product development. New Mars products include Bounty, Balisto, and PB Max. It also successfully developed and marketed frozen Snickers ice cream bars. The product was so successful that it dislodged Eskimo Pie and Original Klondike from the number-one ice cream snack slot without any assistance from promotional advertising. Mars has world-class production facilities in Hackettstown, New Jersey; from that plant it ships products worldwide. Mars also has manufacturing plants in Mexico and several European locations.

NESTLÉ

With annual sales of $7.3 billion in the United States and the recent acquisition of Carnation, Nestlé is the largest food company in the world (see Case Figure 1–7). Nestlé's U.S. operations are headquartered in Glendale, California (818-549-6000). With corporate headquarters in Vevey, Switzerland (021-924-2111), Nestlé is a major competitor in Europe, the Far East, and South America. Nestlé sells products in over 360 countries on five continents, including many in the Third World. It is the world's largest instant-coffee manufacturer, with Nescafé as the dominant product. Nestlé also produces and markets chocolate and malt drinks, and is the world's largest producer of milk powder and condensed milk.

Nestlé's chocolate and confectionery products carry some popular brand names including Callier, Crunch, and Yes. With the acquisition of Rowntree, additional notable brands were added to the product line, including Smarties, After Eight, and Quality Street. Nestlé's Perugina division produces Baci. Through the RJR Nabisco acquisition, Nestlé acquired Curtiss Brand, a U.S. confectionery producer with such products as Baby Ruth and Butterfinger. Based in Switzerland, Nestlé is the world leader in many food categories, including candy. Almost 98 percent of Nestlé's revenues come from international sales. Nestlé manufactures chocolate in 23 countries, particularly in Switzerland and Latin America. Each factory is highly automated and employs an average of 250 people.

Another major product concentration for Nestlé is frozen foods and other refrigerated products. Findus in Europe and Stouffer in the United States represent the bulk of Nestlé's frozen food sales with well-known brands such as Lean Cuisine. Nestlé also manufactures a fast-developing range of fresh pasta and sauces in Europe and the United States under the name Contadina.

CONCLUSION

A major strategic issue facing Hershey today is where, when, and how to best expand internationally. Perhaps Hershey should expand into the Far East because currencies of those countries are depressed. China and India are huge untapped markets. Malaysia, Indonesia, Vietnam, and Thailand also are untapped. Should Hershey wait for Mars and Nestlé to gain a foothold in those countries?

Some analysts contend that Hershey International as a separate division producing and selling diverse products is an ineffective structural design. Critics also contend that Hershey's merging its pasta and grocery operations was a mistake. Can you recommend an improved organizational design for Hershey?

Should Hershey acquire firms in other foreign countries? Analysis is needed to identify and value specific acquisition candidates. In developing an overall strategic plan, what recommendations would you present to Hershey CEO Kenneth Wolfe? What relative emphasis should Hershey place on chocolate versus pasta in 1999 through 2001? Should Hershey diversify more into nonchocolate candies because that segment is growing most rapidly? Should Hershey build a new manufacturing plant in Asia or in Europe?

Design a global marketing strategy that could enable Hershey to boost exports of both chocolate and pasta. Should Hershey increase its debt further or dilute ownership of its stock further to raise the capital needed to implement your recommended strategies? Develop pro forma financial statements to fully assess and evaluate the impact of your proposed strategies.

NOTES

1. www.hersheys.com.
2. Hershey Foods, *Annual Report* (1994): 1.
3. Hershey Foods, *Annual Report* (1997): 1.

EXPERIENTIAL EXERCISES

Experiential Exercise 1A

STRATEGY ANALYSIS FOR HERSHEY FOODS

PURPOSE

The purpose of this exercise is to give you experience identifying an organization's opportunities, threats, strengths, and weaknesses. This information is vital to generating and selecting among alternative strategies.

INSTRUCTIONS

Step 1 Identify what you consider to be Hershey's major opportunities, threats, strengths, and weaknesses. On a separate sheet of paper, list these key factors under separate headings. State each factor in specific terms.

Step 2 Through class discussion, compare your lists of external and internal factors to those developed by other students. From the discussion, add to your lists of factors. Keep this information for use in later exercises.

Experiential Exercise 1B

DEVELOPING A CODE OF BUSINESS ETHICS FOR HERSHEY FOODS

PURPOSE

This exercise can give you practice developing a code of business ethics. In 1989, research was conducted to examine codes of business ethics from large manufacturing and service firms in the United States. The 28 variables listed below were found to be included in a sample of more than 80 codes of business ethics. The variables are presented in order of how frequently they occurred. Thus the first variable, "Conduct business in compliance with all laws," was most often included in the sample documents; "Firearms at work are prohibited" was least often included.

1. Conduct business in compliance with all laws.
2. Payments for unlawful purposes are prohibited.
3. Avoid outside activities that impair duties.
4. Comply with all antitrust and trade regulations.
5. Comply with accounting rules and controls.
6. Bribes are prohibited.
7. Maintain confidentiality of records.
8. Participate in community and political activities.
9. Provide products and services of the highest quality.
10. Exhibit standards of personal integrity and conduct.
11. Do not propagate false or misleading information.

12. Perform assigned duties to the best of your ability.
13. Conserve resources and protect the environment.
14. Comply with safety, health, and security regulations.
15. Racial, ethnic, religious, and sexual harassment at work is prohibited.
16. Report unethical and illegal activities to your manager.
17. Convey true claims in product advertisements.
18. Make decisions without regard for personal gain.
19. Do not use company property for personal benefit.
20. Demonstrate courtesy, respect, honesty, and fairness.
21. Illegal drugs and alcohol at work are prohibited.
22. Manage personal finances well.
23. Employees are personally accountable for company funds.
24. Exhibit good attendance and punctuality.
25. Follow directives of supervisors.
26. Do not use abusive language.
27. Dress in businesslike attire.
28. Firearms at work are prohibited.[1]

INSTRUCTIONS

Step 1 On a separate sheet of paper, write a code of business ethics for Hershey. Include as many variables listed above as you believe appropriate to Hershey's business. Limit your document to 100 words or less.

Step 2 Read your code of ethics to the class. Comment on why you did or did not include certain variables.

Step 3 Explain why having a code of ethics is not sufficient for ensuring ethical behavior in an organization. What else does it take?

NOTES

1. Donald Robin, Michael Giallourakis, Fred R. David, and Thomas E. Moritz. "A Different Look at Codes of Ethics," *Business Horizons* 32, no. 1 (January– February 1989): 66–73.

Experiential Exercise 1C

THE ETHICS OF SPYING ON COMPETITORS

PURPOSE

This exercise gives you an opportunity to discuss ethical and legal issues in class as related to methods being used by many companies to spy on competing firms. Gathering and using information about competitors is an area of strategic management that Japanese firms do more proficiently than American firms.

INSTRUCTIONS

On a separate sheet of paper, number from 1 to 18. For the 18 spying activities listed below, indicate whether or not you believe the activity is Ethical or Unethical and Legal or Illegal. Place either an *E* for ethical or *U* for unethical, and either an *L* for legal or an *I* for illegal for each activity. Compare your answers to your classmates' and discuss any differences.

1. Buying competitors' garbage.
2. Dissecting competitors' products.
3. Taking competitors' plant tours anonymously.
4. Counting tractor-trailer trucks leaving competitors' loading bays.
5. Studying aerial photographs of competitors' facilities.
6. Analyzing competitors' labor contracts.
7. Analyzing competitors' help wanted ads.
8. Quizzing customers and buyers about the sales of competitors' products.
9. Infiltrating customers' and competitors' business operations.
10. Quizzing suppliers about competitors' level of manufacturing.
11. Using customers to buy out phony bids.
12. Encouraging key customers to reveal competitive information.
13. Quizzing competitors' former employees.
14. Interviewing consultants who may have worked with competitors.
15. Hiring key managers away from competitors.
16. Conducting phony job interviews to get competitors' employees to reveal information.
17. Sending engineers to trade meetings to quiz competitors' technical employees.
18. Quizzing potential employees who worked for or with competitors.

Experiential Exercise 1D

STRATEGIC PLANNING FOR MY UNIVERSITY

PURPOSE

External and internal factors are the underlying bases of strategies formulated and implemented by organizations. Your college or university faces numerous external opportunities/threats and has many internal strengths/weaknesses. The purpose of this exercise is to illustrate the process of identifying critical external and internal factors.

External influences include trends in the following areas: economic, social, cultural, demographic, environmental, technological, political, legal, governmental, and competitive. External factors could include declining numbers of high school graduates; population shifts; community relations; increased competitiveness among colleges and universities; rising number of adults returning to college; decreased support from local, state, and federal agencies; and increasing number of foreign students attending American colleges.

Internal factors of a college or university include faculty, students, staff, alumni, athletic programs, physical plant, grounds and maintenance, student housing, administration, fund raising, academic programs, food services, parking, placement, clubs, fraternities, sororities, and public relations.

INSTRUCTIONS

Step 1 On a separate sheet of paper, make four headings: External Opportunities, External Threats, Internal Strengths, and Internal Weaknesses.

Step 2 As related to your college or university, list five factors under each of the four headings.

Step 3 Discuss the factors as a class. Write the factors on the board.

Step 4 What new things did you learn about your university from the class discussion? How could this type of discussion benefit an organization?

Experiential Exercise 1E

STRATEGIC PLANNING AT A LOCAL COMPANY

PURPOSE

This activity is aimed at giving you practical knowledge about how organizations in your city or town are doing strategic planning. This exercise also will give you experience interacting on a professional basis with local business leaders.

INSTRUCTIONS

Step 1 Use the telephone to contact several business owners or top managers. Find an organization that does strategic planning. Make an appointment to visit with the strategist (president, chief executive officer, or owner) of that business.

Step 2 Seek answers to the following questions during the interview:
   a. How does your firm formally conduct strategic planning? Who is involved in the process?
   b. Does your firm have a written mission statement? How was the statement developed? When was the statement last changed?
   c. What are the benefits of engaging in strategic planning?
   d. What are the major costs or problems in doing strategic planning in your business?
   e. Do you anticipate making any changes in the strategic planning process at your company? If yes, please explain.

Step 3 Report your findings to the class.

Strategies in Action

CHAPTER OUTLINE

CHAPTER OBJECTIVES

After studying this chapter, you should be able to do the following:

1. Identify 16 types of business strategies.

2. Identify numerous examples of organizations pursuing different types of strategies.

3. Discuss guidelines when generic strategies are most appropriate to pursue.

4. Discuss Porter's generic strategies.

5. Describe strategic management in nonprofit, governmental, and small organizations.

Alice said, "Would you please tell me which way to go from here?" The cat said, "That depends on where you want to get to."—LEWIS CARROLL

Tomorrow always arrives. It is always different. And even the mightiest company is in trouble if it has not worked on the future. Being surprised by what happens is a risk that even the largest and richest company cannot afford, and even the smallest business need not run.—PETER DRUCKER

Planning. Doing things today to make us better tomorrow. Because the future belongs to those who make the hard decisions today.—EATON CORPORATION

By taking over companies and breaking them up, corporate raiders thrive on failed corporate strategies. Fueled by junk bond financing and growing acceptability, raiders can expose any company to takeover, no matter how large or blue chip.—MICHAEL PORTER

When organizations reach a fork in the road, forces are in motion that will, if not halted, drive a planning process towards the end-state of a self-perpetuating bureaucracy.—R. T. LENZ

One big problem with American business is that when it gets into trouble, it redoubles its effort. It's like digging for gold. If you dig down twenty feet and haven't found it, one of the strategies you could use is to dig twice as deep. But if the gold is twenty feet to the side, you could dig a long time and not find it.—EDWARD DE BONO

If you don't invest for the long term, there is no short term.—GEORGE DAVID

Innovate or evaporate. Particularly in technology-driven businesses, nothing quite recedes like success.—BILL SAPORITO

The demise of strategic planning has been exaggerated. The process has simply moved from corporate staff down to operating managers.—BERNARD REIMANN

Hundreds of companies today, including Sears, IBM, Searle, and Hewlett-Packard, have embraced strategic planning fully in their quest for higher revenues and profits. Kent Nelson, chair of UPS, explains why his company has created a new strategic planning department: "Because we're making bigger bets on investments in technology, we can't afford to spend a whole lot of money in one direction and then find out 5 years later it was the wrong direction."[1]

This chapter brings strategic management to life with many contemporary examples. Sixteen types of strategies are defined and exemplified, including Michael Porter's generic strategies: cost leadership, differentiation, and focus. Guidelines are presented for determining when different types of strategies are most appropriate to pursue. An overview of strategic management in nonprofit organizations, governmental agencies, and small firms is provided.

TYPES OF STRATEGIES

The model illustrated in Figure 2–1 provides a conceptual basis for applying strategic management. Defined and exemplified in Table 2–1, alternative strategies that an enterprise could pursue can be categorized into 13 actions—forward integration, backward integration, horizontal integration, market penetration, market development, product development, concentric diversification, conglomerate diversification, horizontal diversification, joint venture, retrenchment, divestiture, and liquidation—and a combination strategy. Each alternative strategy has countless variations. For example, market penetration can include adding salespersons, increasing advertising expenditures, couponing, and using similar actions to increase market share in a given geographic area.

INTEGRATION STRATEGIES

Forward integration, backward integration, and horizontal integration are sometimes collectively referred to as *vertical integration* strategies. Vertical integration strategies allow a firm to gain control over distributors, suppliers, and/or competitors.

FORWARD INTEGRATION *Forward integration* involves gaining ownership or increased control over distributors or retailers. One company that is betting a large part of its future on forward integration is Boeing. It recently engaged in negotiations with American, Delta, and Continental Airlines whereby those airlines purchase Boeing jets exclusively. The airlines like Boeing's forward integration strategy because it gets them a better price on new jets and saves maintenance and training costs. Boeing's major competitor, Europe's Airbus, vehemently opposes exclusivity pacts.

Another example of forward integration strategy underway today is in the computer industry where Packard Bell has begun to sell personal computers directly to business customers, hoping to emulate the success of Dell Computer Corp. Packard Bell's new strategy aimed at cutting inventory while attracting new customers is, however, angering many current retailers. Dell's build-to-order approach eliminates reseller markups, hastens inventory turnover, and allows the firm to quickly take advantage of falling component prices. Compaq, too, is instituting a new forward integration, build-to-order strategy.

FIGURE 2–1
A Comprehensive Strategic-Management Model

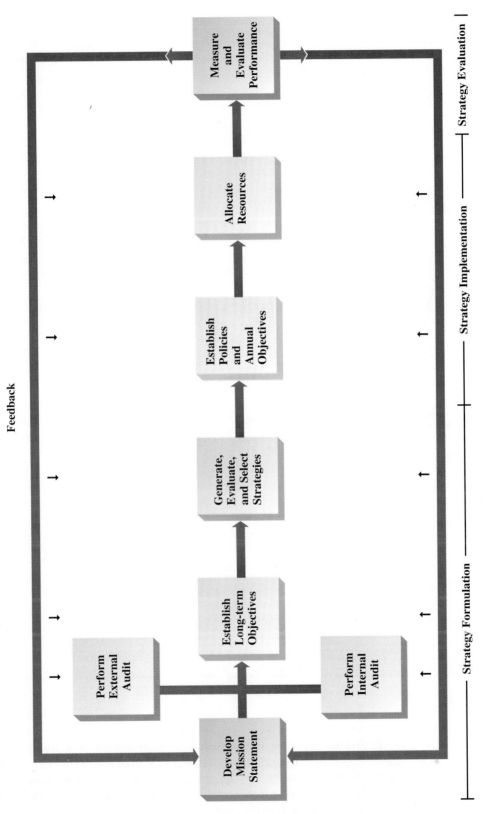

TABLE 2–1
**Alternative Strategies
Defined and Exemplified**

STRATEGY	DEFINITION	EXAMPLE
Forward Integration	Gaining ownership or increased control over distributors or retailers	AT&T opened 45 retail stores, named AT&T Wireless Services, in 1997
Backward Integration	Seeking ownership or increased control of a firm's suppliers	Motel-8 acquired a furniture manufacturer.
Horizontal Integration	Seeking ownership or increased control over competitors	First Union Bank acquired First Fidelity Bancorp.
Market Penetration	Seeking increased market share for present products or services in present markets through greater marketing efforts	Johnson Insurance doubled its number of agents in Mexico.
Market Development	Introducing present products or services into new geographic area	Anheuser-Busch acquired Mexico's largest brewer, Grupo Modelo SA.
Product Development	Seeking increased sales by improving present products or services or developing new ones	Ford developed stand-alone service centers away from dealer locations.
Concentric Diversification	Adding new, but related, products or services	Walt Disney Co. built high-tech arcades for families and teens that feature interactive games and motion-simulator rides, some based on Disney characters. Disney's first arcade, occupying 100,000 square feet in Orlando, Florida, opened in 1998.
Conglomerate Diversification	Adding new, unrelated products or services	Britain's Misys, a banking and insurance firm, acquired Medic Computer Systems, a health care software firm.
Horizontal Diversification	Adding new, unrelated products or services for present customers	First Union acquired Wheat First Butcher Singer.
Joint Venture	Two or more sponsoring firms forming a separate organization for cooperative purposes	Lucent Technologies and Philips Electronics NV formed Philips Consumer Communications to make and sell telephones.
Retrenchment	Regrouping through cost and asset reduction to reverse declining sales and profit	Wells Fargo Bank cut 12,600 jobs during 1996 and 1997.
Divestiture	Selling a division or part of an organization	Raytheon sold its Amana appliance unit for $750 million to Goodman Holding.
Liquidation	Selling all of a company's assets, in parts, for their tangible worth	Ribol sold all its assets and ceases business.

An effective means of implementing forward integration is *franchising*. Approximately 2,000 companies in about 50 different industries in the United States use franchising to distribute their products or services. Businesses can expand rapidly by franchising because costs and opportunities are spread among many individuals. Total sales by franchises in the United States are about $1 trillion annually.

BACKWARD INTEGRATION   Both manufacturers and retailers purchase need materials from suppliers. *Backward integration* is a strategy of seeking ownership or increased control of a firm's suppliers. This strategy can be especially appropriate when a firm's current suppliers are unreliable, too costly, or cannot meet the firm's needs.

When you buy a box of Pampers diapers at Wal-Mart, a scanner at the store's checkout counter instantly zaps an order to Procter & Gamble Company. In contrast, in most hospitals, reordering supplies is a logistics nightmare. Inefficiency due to lack of control of suppliers in the health care industry is, however, rapidly changing as many giant health care purchasers, such as the Defense Department and Columbia/HCA Healthcare Corporation, move to require electronic bar codes on every supply item purchased. This allows instant tracking and reordering without invoices and paperwork. Of the estimated $83 billion spent annually on hospital supplies, industry reports indicate that $11 billion can be eliminated through more effective backward integration.

Some industries in the United States (such as the automotive and aluminum industries) are reducing their historical pursuit of backward integration. Instead of owning their suppliers, companies negotiate with several outside suppliers. Ford and Chrysler buy over half of their components parts from outside suppliers such as TRW, Eaton, General Electric, and Johnson Controls. Deintegration makes sense in industries that have global sources of supply. *Outsourcing*, whereby companies use outside suppliers, shop around, play one seller against another, and go with the best deal, is becoming widely practiced. US Airways recently outsourced its internal reservations system, being performed by 875 of its own workers, to Sabre Group Holdings. Sabre agreed to offer jobs to all displaced US Airways workers, but this business deal still surprised analysts because 82 percent of Sabre is owned by American Airlines.

Global competition also is spurring firms to reduce their number of suppliers and to demand higher levels of service and quality from those they keep. Although traditionally relying on many suppliers to ensure uninterrupted supplies and low prices, American firms now are following the lead of Japanese firms, which have far fewer suppliers and closer, long-term relationships with those few. "Keeping track of so many suppliers is onerous," says Mark Shimelonis of Xerox.

HORIZONTAL INTEGRATION   *Horizontal integration* refers to a strategy of seeking ownership of or increased control over a firm's competitors. One of the most significant trends in strategic management today is the increased use of horizontal integration as a growth strategy. Mergers, acquisitions, and takeovers among competitors allow for increased economies of scale and enhanced transfer of resources and competencies. Kenneth Davidson makes the following observation about horizontal integration:

> The trend towards horizontal integration seems to reflect strategists' misgivings about their ability to operate many unrelated businesses. Mergers between direct competitors are more likely to create efficiencies than mergers between unrelated businesses, both because there is a greater potential for eliminating duplicate facilities and because the management of the acquiring firm is more likely to understand the business of the target.[2]

Horizontal integration has become the most favored growth strategy in many industries. For example, Compaq Computer recently acquired Tandem Computers for $3 billion. Already the world's largest maker of PCs, Compaq received from Tandem advanced computers used by telephone companies and stock exchanges as well as a new 4,000-member sales force with access to hundreds of big companies. Prior to the acquisition, Compaq computers were sold mainly by retailers. Another recent example of horizontal integration occurred when North Carolina–based Wachovia Bank acquired Central Fidelity Banks in Virginia for $2.3 billion, moving Wachovia ahead of NationsBank as the largest bank in Virginia.

INTENSIVE STRATEGIES

Market penetration, market development, and product development are sometimes referred to as *intensive strategies* because they require intensive efforts to improve a firm's competitive position with existing products.

MARKET PENETRATION   A *market-penetration* strategy seeks to increase market share for present products or services in present markets through greater marketing efforts. This strategy is widely used alone and in combination with other strategies. Market penetration includes increasing the number of salespersons, increasing advertising expenditures, offering extensive sales promotion items, or increasing publicity efforts. Procter & Gamble is an example of this, spending heavily on advertising to increase market share of Venezia, its upscale perfume. Its advertising campaign includes full-page ads with scent strips in glossy magazines. Microsoft's multimillion-dollar advertising campaign to promote the new Windows 98 software is another example, as is the increasing use of e-mail for advertising by all kinds of companies. Note in the Information Technology Perspective that more than 100 million users of e-mail are projected within the United States by the year 2000.

MARKET DEVELOPMENT   *Market development* involves introducing present products or services into new geographic areas. The climate for international market development is becoming more favorable. In many industries, such as airlines, it is going to be hard to maintain a competitive edge by staying close to home. U.S. exports reached a

INFORMATION TECHNOLOGY

How Pervasive Is Technology in U.S. Households?

PERCENTAGE PENETRATION OF TECHNOLOGY INTO U.S. HOUSEHOLDS (1997)

Color TV	98	Home CD player	49	Computer with CD-ROM	21
Radio	98	Personal computer	40	Modem or fax/modem	19
Corded phone	96	Computer printer	38	Direct-view satellite dish	10
VCR	89	Cellular phone	34	Fax machine	9
Cordless phone	66	Pager	28		
Telephone answering device	65	Camcorder	26		

Source: Consumer Electronics Manufacturers Association

PAST AND PROJECTED CONSUMER USE OF E-MAIL IN THE UNITED STATES

YEAR	USERS (MILLIONS)	MESSAGES/DAY (MILLIONS)	MESSAGES/DAY/PERSON
1996	40	100	2.5
1997	55	150	2.7
1998	75	225	3.0
1999	95	313	3.3
2000	115	402	3.5
2001	135	500	3.7
2005	170	5,000	29.4

Source: Forrestor Research, Inc.

record $78.4 billion in June 1997, which was 10.6 percent more than in June 1996, and increases continue. Foreigners are increasingly eager to buy U.S. products and services, even though the value of the U.S. dollar rose 9.4 percent in 1997 compared to currencies of 19 other major countries. The rising value of the dollar makes U.S. products and services more expensive in overseas markets.

Wal-Mart is an example firm that aggressively is pursuing a market development strategy. Wal-Mart recently purchased Cifra SA in Mexico for $1.2 billion, marking the company's first major entry into international markets. Less than 5 percent of Wal-Mart's more than 2,500 stores are located outside the United States, but the giant retailer plans to increase its foreign operations and stores significantly in the near future.

PRODUCT DEVELOPMENT *Product development* is a strategy that seeks increased sales by improving or modifying present products or services. Product development usually entails large research and development expenditures. An example firm betting its future on a product development strategy is NetMedia, which launched a new feature on its Web site called Net Saver Alert that provides airline and hotel discount deals continuously. Just go to www.ltravel.com, click on last-minute deals, fill out the form, and give your e-mail address. In another bold product development strategy, Canadian cigarette maker Imperial Tobacco introduced Mercer, a "natural cigarette without additives." R. J. Reynolds recently introduced Salem Preferred, a low-smoke cigarette, into Japan. As indicated in the Natural Environment Perspective, a decreasing number of firms appear to be actively developing green products—in response to an alarming decline in consumer interest in such efforts.

NATURAL ENVIRONMENT

Is Consumer Concern for Environmental Matters Declining?

Americans are not as vigilant about environmentally driven purchases as they used to be, partly because they feel businesses are making changes. There is a declining willingness among consumers to spend extra money on green products. The only natural environment activity that has gained support in recent years has been recycling, but even this activity may be waning as supply/demand/price relationships hinder company and community efforts.

The national recycling rate for all products in the United States reached 27 percent in 1995, up from only 7 percent in 1970. Many states such as Indiana, California, Colorado, and New York have a goal to recycle 50 percent of their trash by the year 2000. But prices for recycled materials have dropped dramatically since 1996, so the costs of recycling in the eyes of many consumers and businesses now exceed the benefits. For example, old cardboard boxes fetched about $200/ton in

1995, but only $65/ton in 1997. Washington, D.C., recently scrapped its recycling program due to high costs that included more trucks and more workers to pick up separated trash. Many communities find that it costs four times as much to collect and process recyclables as it does to dump trash in landfills. More trucks and more sorting plants also add to pollution. Professors at Carnegie Mellon University recently concluded that recycling benefits the environment, but at too high a cost.

Other environmental activities such as avoiding restaurants using Styrofoam, avoiding ecologically irresponsible companies, buying refillable packages, buying products made of recycled materials, using biodegradable soaps, avoiding aerosols, and reading labels for environmental impacts have less support today than in 1990. The percentage of American adults who care nothing at all about the natural environment has risen from 28 percent in

1990 to 37 percent today. Research suggests that consumers' buying habits are increasingly determined by past experience, price, brand recognition, others' recommendations, and convenience rather than environmental impact. Although Americans do not shop with environmental purpose as they once did, they have internalized deep concerns for the welfare of earth's living plants and animals. Indirect, displaced, and often hidden costs, such as pain and suffering associated with pollution, far exceed direct costs such as cleanup and equipment.

Source: Adapted from Tibbett Speer, "Growing the Green Market," American Demographics, (August 1997): 45–50; and Laura Litvan, "Has Recycling Reached Its Limit?" Investors Business Daily (August 6, 1997): 1.

Large expenditures in product development are a major reason why automotive and computer firms, such as General Motors, Ford, IBM, and Apple, do not own their distributors or dealers. Tandy is the only computer company that owns its distributors, which are Radio Shack stores. By the year 2000, GM plans to launch new car models monthly. The end of the fall new-car season is almost here.

DIVERSIFICATION STRATEGIES

There are three general types of *diversification strategies*: concentric, horizontal, and conglomerate. Overall, diversification strategies are becoming less popular as organizations are finding it more difficult to manage diverse business activities. In the 1960s and 1970s, the trend was to diversify so as not to be dependent on any single industry, but the 1980s saw a general reversal of that thinking. Diversification is now on the retreat. Michael Porter of the Harvard Business School says, "Management found they couldn't manage the beast." Hence, businesses are selling, or closing, less profitable divisions in order to focus on core businesses.

There are, however, a few companies today that pride themselves on being a conglomerate, from small firms such as Pentair Inc. and Blount International to huge companies such as Textron, Allied Signal, Emerson Electric and, of course, the reigning monarch of the conglomerate world, General Electric. Conglomerates prove that focus and diversity are not always mutually exclusive. Even Walt Disney Company competes in hotels, merchandising, television, and theme parks, but makes a case that all its businesses are entertainment-related.

Peters and Waterman's advice to firms is to "stick to the knitting" and not to stray too far from the firm's basic areas of competence. However, diversification is still an appropriate and successful strategy sometimes. For example, Philip Morris derives 60 percent of its profits from sales of Marlboro cigarettes. Hamish Maxwell, Philip Morris's CEO, says, "We want to become a consumer-products company." Diversification makes sense for Philip Morris because cigarette consumption is declining, product liability suits are a risk, and some investors reject tobacco stocks on principle. In a diversification move, Philip Morris spent $12.9 billion in a hostile takeover of Kraft General Foods, the world's second-largest food producer behind Nestlé.

CONCENTRIC DIVERSIFICATION   Adding new, but related, products or services is widely called *concentric diversification*. An example of this strategy is the recent acquisition of Baltimore-based brokerage Alexander Brown by Bankers Trust New York for $1.6 billion, representing the largest purchase ever of a brokerage firm by a commercial bank. This is part of a growing merger trend between banks, brokerage companies, and insurance firms in response to deregulation of the financial services industry. Banks can now derive up to 25 percent of securities-related revenue from underwriting, versus 10 percent in the mid-1990s. Less than halfway through calendar 1997, more than $75 billion in financial services mergers and acquisitions were consummated in the United States—a record pace.

HORIZONTAL DIVERSIFICATION   Adding new, unrelated products or services for present customers is called *horizontal diversification*. This strategy is not as risky as conglomerate diversification because a firm already should be familiar with its present customers. For example, beverage behemoths Pepsi and Coca-Cola recently entered the $3.6 billion bottled water market controlled mainly by Perrier, which makes Arrowhead, Poland Spring, and Great Bear brands of water. Pepsi introduced Aquafina, its first domestic bottled water. Bottled water is the nation's fastest-growing beverage category, growing 8 percent per year, more than twice that of carbonated drinks. Small, 16-ounce bottles of water are growing 30 percent per year. A few years ago, Pepsi and Coca-Cola entered the bottled tea market and quickly emerged as the top two firms with their Lipton and Nestea brands respectively, overtaking Snapple.

CONGLOMERATE DIVERSIFICATION   Adding new, unrelated products or services is called *conglomerate diversification*. Some firms pursue conglomerate diversification based in part on an expectation of profits from breaking up acquired firms and selling divisions piecemeal. Richard West, dean of New York University's School of Business, says, "The stock market is rewarding deconglomerations, saying company assets are worth more separately than together. There is a kind of antisynergy, the whole being worth less than the parts."

Supermarkets beginning to sell gasoline is a recent conglomerate diversification strategy. Albertson's had 12 stores selling gas in late 1997, Food Lion had 10 stores selling gas, and Kroger had 2 stores selling gas. U.S. West pursued a diversification strategy. U.S. West, a telecommunications firm, now owns operations in industries such as cable TV, equipment financing, advertising services, real estate development, cellular telephones, and publishing. Based in Denver, U.S. West recently purchased Financial Security Assurance for $345 million, further diversifying into financial services.

General Electric is an example of a firm that is highly diversified. GE makes locomotives, lightbulbs, power plants, and refrigerators; GE manages more credit cards than American Express; GE owns more commercial aircraft than American Airlines.

DEFENSIVE STRATEGIES

In addition to integrative, intensive, and diversification strategies, organizations also could pursue joint venture, retrenchment, divestiture, or liquidation.

JOINT VENTURE   *Joint venture* is a popular strategy that occurs when two or more companies form a temporary partnership or consortium for the purpose of capitalizing on some opportunity. This strategy can be considered defensive only because the firm is not undertaking the project alone. Often, the two or more sponsoring firms form a separate organization and have shared equity ownership in the new entity. Other types of *cooperative arrangements* include research and development partnerships, cross-distribution agreements, cross-licensing agreements, cross-manufacturing agreements, and joint-bidding consortia.

Joint ventures and cooperative arrangements are being used increasingly because they allow companies to improve communications and networking, to globalize operations, and to minimize risk. Lucent Technologies and the Dutch consumer electronics giant Philips Electronics recently created a joint venture firm named Philips Consumer Communications, which today is the largest telephone maker in the world with annual revenue over $2.5 billion. The new venture combined Lucent's research and manufacturing skills with Phillips's experience in consumer marketing overseas. Kathryn Rudie Harrigan, professor of strategic management at Columbia University, summarizes the trend toward increased joint venturing:

> In today's global business environment of scarce resources, rapid rates of technological change, and rising capital requirements, the important question is no longer "Shall we form a joint venture?" Now the question is "Which joint ventures and cooperative arrangements are most appropriate for our needs and expectations?" followed by "How do we manage these ventures most effectively?"[3]

Cooperative agreements even between competitors are becoming popular. For example, Canon supplies photocopies to Kodak, France's Thomson and Japan's FVC manufacture videocassette recorders, Siemens and Fujitsu work together, and General Motors and Toyota assemble automobiles. Italian automaker Piat SpA and Russia's Gorky Automobile Factory recently formed a joint venture to produce 150,000 cars annually for the Russian market. Gorky is Russia's largest and most successful automaker. For collaboration between competitors to succeed, both firms must contribute something distinctive, such as technology, distribution, basic research, or manufacturing capacity. But a major risk is that unintended transfers of important skills or technology may occur at organizational levels below where the deal was signed.[4] Information not covered in the formal agreement often gets traded in day-to-day interactions and dealings of engineers, marketers, and product developers. American firms often give away too much information to foreign firms when operating under cooperative agreements! Tighter formal agreements are needed, and Western companies must become better learners since leadership in many industries has shifted to the Far East and Europe.

RETRENCHMENT   *Retrenchment* occurs when an organization regroups through cost and asset reduction to reverse declining sales and profits. Sometimes called a turnaround or reorganizational strategy, retrenchment is designed to fortify an organization's basic distinctive competence. During retrenchment, strategists work with limited resources and face pressure from shareholders, employees, and the media. Retrenchment can entail selling off land and buildings to raise needed cash, pruning product lines, closing marginal businesses, closing obsolete factories, automating processes, reducing the number of employees, and instituting expense control systems.

Wal-Mart implemented a retrenchment strategy in 1998 when the retailer closed 48 of its 61 Bud's Discount City Outlets with plans to close the other 13 soon. Most Bud's Outlets were losing money. International Paper also announced a retrenchment strategy cutting 9,000 jobs, more than 10 percent of its workforce, and eliminating certain production operations. Kodak recently laid off 200 senior and middle managers and trimmed 10 percent of its administrative staff.

In some cases, *bankruptcy* can be an effective type of retrenchment strategy. Bankruptcy can allow a firm to avoid major debt obligations and to void union contracts. Levitz Furniture, the home-furniture retailer in the United States behind Helig-Myers, filed for bankruptcy in late 1997. Levitz is closing 21 of its 129 stores as part of the restructuring.

Corporate America appears to be gearing for continued large layoffs of managers and employees. Corporate downsizing in the United States is evidenced in Table 2–2.

There are five major types of bankruptcy: Chapter 7, Chapter 9, Chapter 11, Chapter 12, and Chapter 13.

Chapter 7 bankruptcy is a liquidation procedure used only when a corporation sees no hope of being able to operate successfully or to obtain the necessary creditor agreement. All the organization's assets are sold in parts for their tangible worth.

Chapter 9 bankruptcy applies to municipalities. The most recent municipality successfully declaring bankruptcy is Bridgeport, the largest city in Connecticut. Some states do not allow municipalities to declare bankruptcy.

Chapter 11 bankruptcy allows organizations to reorganize and come back after filing a petition for protection. Declaring Chapter 11 bankruptcy allowed the Manville Corporation and Continental Products to gain protection from liability suits filed over their manufacturing of asbestos products. Million-dollar judgments against these companies would have required liquidation, so bankruptcy was a good strategy for these two firms. Similarly, Wang Laboratories recently emerged from Chapter 11 with one of the strongest balance sheets in the computer industry.

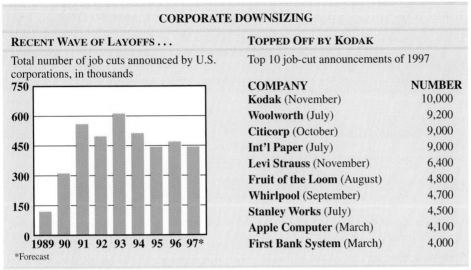

TABLE 2–2
Corporate Downsizing in the United States

CORPORATE DOWNSIZING

RECENT WAVE OF LAYOFFS . . .	TOPPED OFF BY KODAK	
Total number of job cuts announced by U.S. corporations, in thousands	Top 10 job-cut announcements of 1997	
	COMPANY	**NUMBER**
	Kodak (November)	10,000
	Woolworth (July)	9,200
	Citicorp (October)	9,000
	Int'l Paper (July)	9,000
	Levi Strauss (November)	6,400
	Fruit of the Loom (August)	4,800
	Whirlpool (September)	4,700
	Stanley Works (July)	4,500
	Apple Computer (March)	4,100
*Forecast	**First Bank System** (March)	4,000

Source: Adapted from Fred Bleakley, "New Round of Layoffs May Be Beginning," *The Wall Street Journal* (November 13, 1997): A2.

Chapter 12 bankruptcy was created by the Family Farmer Bankruptcy Act of 1986. This law became effective in 1987 and provides special relief to family farmers with debt equal to or less than $1.5 million.

Chapter 13 bankruptcy is a reorganization plan similar to Chapter 11 but available only to small businesses owned by individuals with unsecured debts of less than $100,000 and secured debts of less than $350,000. The Chapter 13 debtor is allowed to operate the business while a plan is being developed to provide for the successful operation of the business in the future.

Personal bankruptcies in the United States exceeded 1.1 million in 1996, a 29 percent increase over 1995. Tennessee, Georgia, and Alabama had the highest personal bankruptcies in the nation with 9.0, 7.3, and 7.2 bankruptcies per 1,000 people respectively, while Maine, Vermont, and Alaska had the fewest personal bankruptcies with 2.3, 2.1, and 1.7 bankruptcies per 1,000 people respectively. The national average is 4.2 personal bankruptcies per 1,000 people.

DIVESTITURE Selling a division or part of an organization is called *divestiture*. Divestiture often is used to raise capital for further strategic acquisitions or investments. Divestiture can be part of an overall retrenchment strategy to rid an organization of businesses that are unprofitable, that require too much capital, or that do not fit well with the firm's other activities. For example, Columbia/HCA Healthcare Corporation continues to divest all of its operations that are not related to hospitals, including ValueRX and Value Health. Headquartered in Nashville, Tennessee, Columbia is the subject of a massive federal investigation into possible Medicare fraud.

Divestiture has become a very popular strategy as firms try to focus on their core strengths, lessening their level of diversification. A few divestitures consummated in 1998 are given in Table 2–3.

LIQUIDATION Selling all of a company's assets, in parts, for their tangible worth is called *liquidation*. Liquidation is a recognition of defeat and consequently can be an emotionally difficult strategy. However, it may be better to cease operating than to continue losing large sums of money.

Thousands of small businesses in the United States liquidate annually without ever making the news. It is tough to start and successfully operate a small business. In China

TABLE 2–3
Some Divestitures in 1998

PARENT COMPANY	DIVESTED BUSINESS	ACQUIRING COMPANY
Simon & Schuster	Education divisions	Pearson (British firm)
Merck	A pharmaceutical division	Dupont
Dow Jones & Co.	Telerate	Bridge Information Systems
Black & Decker	Sports equipment division	(to be announced)
General Motors	Seating business	Lear
Xerox	Crum & Forster	Fairfax Financial
Limited	Henri Bendel	(to be announced)
Philips Electronics	PolyGram	(to be announced)
TRW	Odyssey satellite system	ICO Global Communications
Softbank (Japanese firm)	Ziff-Davis (*PC Magazine* and *PC Week*)	(to be announced)
Pennzoil	Jiffy Lube	(to be announced)

and Russia, thousands of government-owned businesses liquidate annually as those countries try to privatize and consolidate industries.

COMBINATION   Many, if not most, organizations pursue a combination of two or more strategies simultaneously, but a *combination strategy* can be exceptionally risky if carried too far. No organization can afford to pursue all the strategies that might benefit the firm. Difficult decisions must be made. Priorities must be established. Organizations, like individuals, have limited resources. Both organizations and individuals must choose among alternative strategies and avoid excessive indebtedness.

Organizations cannot do too many things well because resources and talents get spread thin and competitors gain advantage. In large diversified companies, a combination strategy is commonly employed when different divisions pursue different strategies. Also, organizations struggling to survive may employ a combination of several defensive strategies, such as divestiture, liquidation, and retrenchment, simultaneously.

GUIDELINES FOR PURSUING STRATEGIES

Table 2–4 reveals situations, conditions, and guidelines for when various alternative strategies are most appropriate to pursue. For example, note that a market development strategy is generally most appropriate when new channels of distribution are available that are reliable, inexpensive, and of good quality; when an organization is very successful at what it does; when new untapped or unsaturated markets exist; when an organization has the needed capital and human resources to manage expanded operations; when an organization has excess production capacity; and when an organization's basic industry is rapidly becoming global in scope.

TABLE 2–4
Guidelines for Situations When Particular Strategies Are Most Effective

FORWARD INTEGRATION

- When an organization's present distributors are especially expensive, or unreliable, or incapable of meeting the firm's distribution needs
- When the availability of quality distributors is so limited as to offer a competitive advantage to those firms that integrate forward
- When an organization competes in an industry that is growing and is expected to continue to grow markedly; this is a factor because forward integration reduces an organization's ability to diversify if its basic industry falters

continued

TABLE 2–4 *continued*

- When an organization has both the capital and human resources needed to manage the new business of distributing its own products
- When the advantages of stable production are particularly high; this is a consideration because an organization can increase the predictability of the demand for its output through forward integration
- When present distributors or retailers have high profit margins; this situation suggests that a company profitably could distribute its own products and price them more competitively by integrating forward

BACKWARD INTEGRATION

- When an organization's present suppliers are especially expensive, or unreliable, or incapable of meeting the firm's needs for parts, components, assemblies, or raw materials
- When the number of suppliers is small and the number of competitors is large
- When an organization competes in an industry that is growing rapidly; this is a factor because integrative-type strategies (forward, backward, and horizontal) reduce an organization's ability to diversify in a declining industry
- When an organization has both capital and human resources to manage the new business of supplying its own raw materials
- When the advantages of stable prices are particularly important; this is a factor because an organization can stabilize the cost of its raw materials and the associated price of its product through backward integration
- When present supplies have high profit margins, which suggests that the business of supplying products or services in the given industry is a worthwhile venture
- When an organization needs to acquire a needed resource quickly

HORIZONTAL INTEGRATION

- When an organization can gain monopolistic characteristics in a particular area or region without being challenged by the federal government for "tending substantially" to reduce competition
- When an organization competes in a growing industry
- When increased economies of scale provide major competitive advantages
- When an organization has both the capital and human talent needed to successfully manage an expanded organization
- When competitors are faltering due to a lack of managerial expertise or a need for particular resources that an organization possesses; note that horizontal integration would not be appropriate if competitors are doing poorly because overall industry sales are declining

MARKET PENETRATION

- When current markets are not saturated with a particular product or service
- When the usage rate of present customers could be increased significantly
- When the market shares of major competitors have been declining while total industry sales have been increasing
- When the correlation between dollar sales and dollar marketing expenditures historically has been high
- When increased economies of scale provide major competitive advantages

MARKET DEVELOPMENT

- When new channels of distribution are available that are reliable, inexpensive, and of good quality
- When an organization is very successful at what it does
- When new untapped or unsaturated markets exist
- When an organization has the needed capital and human resources to manage expanded operations
- When an organization has excess production capacity
- When an organization's basic industry rapidly is becoming global in scope

PRODUCT DEVELOPMENT

- When an organization has successful products that are in the maturity stage of the product life cycle; the idea here is to attract satisfied customers to try new (improved) products as a result of their positive experience with the organization's present products or services
- When an organization competes in an industry that is characterized by rapid technological developments
- When major competitors offer better-quality products at comparable prices

continued

TABLE 2–4   *continued*

- When an organization competes in a high-growth industry
- When an organization has especially strong research and development capabilities

CONCENTRIC DIVERSIFICATION

- When an organization competes in a no-growth or a slow-growth industry
- When adding new, but related, products significantly would enhance the sales of current products
- When new, but related, products could be offered at highly competitive prices
- When new, but related, products have seasonal sales levels that counterbalance an organization's existing peaks and valleys
- When an organization's products are currently in the decline stage of the product life cycle
- When an organization has a strong management team

CONGLOMERATE DIVERSIFICATION

- When an organization's basic industry is experiencing declining annual sales and profits
- When an organization has the capital and managerial talent needed to compete successfully in a new industry
- When an organization has the opportunity to purchase an unrelated business that is an attractive investment opportunity
- When there exists financial synergy between the acquired and acquiring firm; note that a key difference between concentric and conglomerate diversification is that the former should be based on some commonality in markets, products, or technology, whereas the latter should be based more on profit considerations
- When existing markets for an organization's present products are saturated
- When antitrust action could be charged against an organization that historically has concentrated on a single industry

HORIZONTAL DIVERSIFICATION

- When revenues derived from an organization's current products or services would increase significantly by adding the new, unrelated products
- When an organization competes in a highly competitive and/or a no-growth industry, as indicated by low industry profit margins and returns
- When an organization's present channels of distribution can be used to market the new products to current customers
- When the new products have countercyclical sales patterns compared to an organization's present products

JOINT VENTURE

- When a privately owned organization is forming a joint venture with a publicly owned organization; there are some advantages of being privately held, such as close ownership; there are some advantages of being publicly held, such as access to stock issuances as a source of capital. Sometimes, the unique advantages of being privately and publicly held can be synergistically combined in a joint venture
- When a domestic organization is forming a joint venture with a foreign company; a joint venture can provide a domestic company with the opportunity for obtaining local management in a foreign country, thereby reducing risks such as expropriation and harassment by host country officials
- When the distinctive competencies of two or more firms complement each other especially well
- When some project is potentially very profitable, but requires overwhelming resources and risks; the Alaskan pipeline is an example
- When two or more smaller firms have trouble competing with a large firm
- When there exists a need to introduce a new technology quickly

RETRENCHMENT

- When an organization has a clearly distinctive competence, but has failed to meet its objectives and goals consistently over time
- When an organization is one of the weaker competitors in a given industry
- When an organization is plagued by inefficiency, low profitability, poor employee morale, and pressure from stockholders to improve performance
- When an organization has failed to capitalize on external opportunities, minimize external threats, take advantage of internal strengths, and overcome internal weaknesses over time; that is, when the organization's strategic managers have failed (and possibly will be replaced by more competent individuals)
- When an organization has grown so large so quickly that major internal reorganization is needed

continued

TABLE 2–4   *continued*

DIVESTITURE

- When an organization has pursued a retrenchment strategy and it failed to accomplish needed improvements
- When a division needs more resources to be competitive than the company can provide
- When a division is responsible for an organization's overall poor performance
- When a division is a misfit with the rest of an organization; this can result from radically different markets, customers, managers, employees, values, or needs
- When a large amount of cash is needed quickly and cannot be obtained reasonably from other sources
- When government antitrust action threatens an organization

LIQUIDATION

- When an organization has pursued both a retrenchment strategy and a divestiture strategy, and neither has been successful
- When an organization's only alternative is bankruptcy; liquidation represents an orderly and planned means of obtaining the greatest possible cash for an organization's assets. A company can legally declare bankruptcy first and then liquidate various divisions to raise needed capital
- When the stockholders of a firm can minimize their losses by selling the organization's assets

Source: Adapted from F. R. David, "How Do We Choose Among Alternative Growth Strategies?" *Managerial Planning* 33, no. 4 (January–February 1985): 14–17, 22.

MERGERS AND LEVERAGED BUYOUTS

Acquisition and merger are two commonly used ways to pursue strategies. An *acquisition* occurs when a large organization purchases (acquires) a smaller firm, or vice versa. A *merger* occurs when two organizations of about equal size unite to form one enterprise. When an acquisition or merger is not desired by both parties, it can be called a *takeover* or *hostile takeover*. Regarding merger-mania restructuring in the United States, *Business Week* offered the following conclusion:

> It is clear now that restructurings are driven by a lot more than tax considerations, low stock prices, raiders' desire for a quick buck, and aggressive merger merchants on Wall Street. . . . Restructuring continues because U.S. industry needs it. Deregulation in industries from financial services to energy, from communications to transportation, has exposed managerial complacency and inefficient practices caused by years of shelter from market forces. . . . Plenty of companies have simply recognized that if they want to compete globally, they must slim down, toughen up, and focus on a narrower range of businesses.[5]

Among mergers, acquisitions, and takeovers in recent years, same-industry combinations have predominated. A general market consolidation is occurring in many industries, especially banking, insurance, defense, and health care, but also pharmaceuticals, food, airlines, accounting, publishing, computers, retailing, financial services, and biotechnology.

Even labor unions are trying to merge. The United Automobile Workers, the International Association of Machinists and Aerospace Workers, and the United Steelworkers of America are engaged in merger talks. Due to mergers, the AFL-CIO today is composed of only 78 unions, and that number is expected to drop to fewer than 50 by 1999. Unions represent only about 14.5 percent of the U.S. workforce today, down from 35 percent in the 1960s.

In 1997, Travelers brokerage subsidiary Smith Barney acquired Saloman Inc. for $9 billion to create the third-largest investment house behind industry leader Merrill Lynch and recently formed Morgan Stanley Dean Witter.

Table 2–5 shows some mergers and acquisitions completed in 1997. There are many reasons for mergers and acquisitions, including the following:

TABLE 2–5
**Some Examples of
Mergers and Acquisitions
Completed in 1997**

ACQUIRING FIRM	ACQUIRED FIRM
Dean Witter Discover	Morgan Stanley
First Bank Systems	U.S. Bancorp
Banc One	First USA
Washington Mutual Savings	Great Western Financial
Household International	Transamerica Con. Fin.
American General	USLIFE
Bankers Trust New York	Alexander Brown
Marsh & McLennan	Johnson & Higgins
First Maryland	Dauphin Deposit
Associated Bank	First Financial
Safeco	American States

Reasons to merge

- ◆ To provide improved capacity utilization
- ◆ To make better use of existing sales force
- ◆ To reduce managerial staff
- ◆ To gain economies of scale
- ◆ To smooth out seasonal trends in sales
- ◆ To gain access to new suppliers, distributors, customers, products, and creditors
- ◆ To gain new technology
- ◆ To reduce tax obligations

The volume of mergers completed annually worldwide is growing dramatically and exceeds $1 trillion annually. There are more than 10,000 mergers annually in the United States that total more than $700 billion. Six U.S. mergers in 1996 topped $10 billion each, while over 100 topped $1 billion. For the first 6 months of 1997, nearly 5,000 deals valued at $366 billion were announced versus $314 billion in the year-ago period, a 16 percent increase. The largest merger ever was the 1998 WorldCom acquisition of MCI for $30 billion, exceeding the Bell Atlantic acquisition of Nynex for $25.6 billion.

Globally, merger activity rose to $692 billion in the first half of 1997, up 18 percent from $588 billion in that period for 1996. The three most active industries for mergers are hotels/casinos, brokerages/banks, and oil/gas firms.

The proliferation of mergers is fueled by companies' drive for market share, efficiency, and pricing power as well as by globalization, the need for greater economies of scale, reduced regulation and antitrust concerns, and the stock market rewarding merger activity with higher stock prices.

Mergers do not always give quick results. Of sixty $500 million-plus deals between 1992 and 1995, fifty-five percent of buyers saw their stock underperform their industry average. Many mergers fail because the acquired company is not integrated effectively into the parent firm. For example, when PacifiCare Health Systems acquired rival FHP International Corporation, the former's stock plunged 27 percent. PacifiCare had trouble integrating FHP's computer system, culture, and operations. Similarly, shares of United HealthCare dropped 30 percent after the giant Minnesota HMO acquired MetraHealth Companies recently.

LEVERAGED BUYOUTS (LBOs)   A *leveraged buyout* (LBO) occurs when a corporation's shareholders are bought out (hence *buyout*) by the company's management and other private investors using borrowed funds (hence *leveraged*).[6] Besides trying to avoid a hostile takeover, other reasons for initiating an LBO are senior management decisions that particular divisions do not fit into an overall corporate strategy or must be sold to raise cash, or receipt of an attractive offering price. An LBO takes a corporation private.

Borg-Warner, Owen-Illinois, and Jim Walter are companies that experienced leveraged buyouts. Under this arrangement, the debt is paid back later through funds from operations and the sale of assets. Many banks, insurance companies, and other financial institutions are in the buyout business, sometimes called *merchant banking*.

Merchant bankers usually sell companies acquired in leveraged buyouts in pieces and at high profits. In the most profitable leveraged buyout ever recorded, Kohlberg, Kravis, Roberts and Company acquired RJR Nabisco for $25 billion and then began selling divisions separately at premiums. RJR's divestitures included selling its fresh-fruit business for $875 million to Polly Peck, a London-based food company, and its Del Monte canned food business for about $1.48 billion to another leveraged buyout group led by Citicorp Venture Capital.

MICHAEL PORTER'S GENERIC STRATEGIES

Probably the three most widely read books on competitive analysis in the 1980s were Michael Porter's (www.hbs.edu/bios/mporter.) *Competitive Strategy* (Free Press, 1980), *Competitive Advantage* (Free Press, 1985), and *Competitive Advantage of Nations* (Free Press, 1989). According to Porter, strategies allow organizations to gain competitive advantage from three different bases: cost leadership, differentiation, and focus. Porter calls these bases *generic strategies*. *Cost leadership* emphasizes producing standardized products at very low per-unit cost for consumers who are price-sensitive. *Differentiation* is a strategy aimed at producing products and services considered unique industrywide and directed at consumers who are relatively price-insensitive. *Focus* means producing products and services that fulfill the needs of small groups of consumers.

Porter's strategies imply different organizational arrangements, control procedures, and incentive systems. Larger firms with greater access to resources typically compete on a cost leadership and/or differentiation basis, whereas smaller firms often compete on a focus basis.

Porter stresses the need for strategists to perform cost-benefit analyses to evaluate "sharing opportunities" among a firm's existing and potential business units. Sharing activities and resources enhances competitive advantage by lowering costs or raising differentiation. In addition to prompting sharing, Porter stresses the need for firms to "transfer" skills and expertise among autonomous business units effectively in order to gain competitive advantage. Depending upon factors such as type of industry, size of firm, and nature of competition, various strategies could yield advantages in cost leadership, differentiation, and focus.

COST LEADERSHIP STRATEGIES   A primary reason for pursuing forward, backward, and horizontal integration strategies is to gain cost leadership benefits. But cost leadership generally must be pursued in conjunction with differentiation. A number of cost elements affect the relative attractiveness of generic strategies, including economies or diseconomies of scale achieved, learning and experience curve effects, the percentage of capacity utilization achieved, and linkages with suppliers and distributors. Other cost elements to consider in choosing among alternative strategies include the potential for sharing costs and knowledge within the organization, R&D costs associated with new product development or modification of existing products, labor costs, tax rates, energy costs, and shipping costs.

Striving to be the low-cost producer in an industry can be especially effective when the market is composed of many price-sensitive buyers, when there are few ways to achieve product differentiation, when buyers do not care much about differences from brand to brand, or when there are a large number of buyers with significant bargaining power. The basic idea is to underprice competitors and thereby gain market share and sales, driving some competitors out of the market entirely.

A successful cost leadership strategy usually permeates the entire firm, as evidenced by high efficiency, low overhead, limited perks, intolerance of waste, intensive screening of budget requests, wide spans of control, rewards linked to cost containment, and broad employee participation in cost control efforts. Some risks of pursuing cost leadership are that competitors may imitate the strategy, thus driving overall industry profits down; technological breakthroughs in the industry may make the strategy ineffective; or buyer interest may swing to other differentiating features besides price. Several example firms that are well known for their low-cost leadership strategies are Wal-Mart, BIC, McDonald's, Black and Decker, Lincoln Electric, and Briggs and Stratton.

DIFFERENTIATION STRATEGIES   Different strategies offer different degrees of differentiation. Differentiation does not guarantee competitive advantage, especially if standard products sufficiently meet customer needs or if rapid imitation by competitors is possible. Durable products protected by barriers to quick copying by competitors are best. Successful differentiation can mean greater product flexibility, greater compatibility, lower costs, improved service, less maintenance, greater convenience, or more features. Product development is an example of a strategy that offers the advantages of differentiation.

A differentiation strategy should be pursued only after careful study of buyers' needs and preferences to determine the feasibility of incorporating one or more differentiating features into a unique product that features the desired attributes. A successful differentiation strategy allows a firm to charge a higher price for its product and to gain customer loyalty because consumers may become strongly attached to the differentiation features. Special features to differentiate one's product can include superior service, spare parts availability, engineering design, product performance, useful life, gas mileage, or ease of use.

A risk of pursuing a differentiation strategy is that the unique product may not be valued highly enough by customers to justify the higher price. When this happens, a cost leadership strategy easily will defeat a differentiation strategy. Another risk of pursuing a differentiation strategy is that competitors may develop ways to copy the differentiating features quickly. Firms thus must find durable sources of uniqueness that cannot be imitated quickly or cheaply by rival firms.

Common organizational requirements for a successful differentiation strategy include strong coordination among the R&D and marketing functions and substantial amenities to attract scientists and creative people. Firms pursuing a differentiation strategy include Dr. Pepper, Jenn-Air, The Limited, BMW, Grady-White, Ralph Lauren, Maytag, and Cross.

FOCUS STRATEGIES   A successful focus strategy depends upon an industry segment that is of sufficient size, has good growth potential, and is not crucial to the success of other major competitors. Strategies such as market penetration and market development offer substantial focusing advantages. Midsize and large firms effectively can pursue focus-based strategies only in conjunction with differentiation or cost leadership–based strategies. All firms in essence follow a differentiated strategy. Because only one firm can differentiate itself with the lowest cost, the remaining firms in the industry must find other ways to differentiate their products.

Focus strategies are most effective when consumers have distinctive preferences or requirements and when rival firms are not attempting to specialize in the same target segment. Firms pursuing a focus strategy include Midas, Red Lobster, Federal Express, Sprint, MCI, Coors, and Schwinn.

Risks of pursuing a focus strategy include the possibility that numerous competitors recognize the successful focus strategy and copy the strategy, or that consumer preferences drift toward the product attributes desired by the market as a whole. An organization using a focus strategy may concentrate on a particular group of customers, geographic markets, or product line segments in order to serve a well-defined but narrow market better than competitors who serve a broader market.

THE VALUE CHAIN   According to Porter, the business of a firm can best be described as a *value chain* in which total revenues minus total costs of all activities undertaken to develop and market a product or service yields value. All firms in a given industry have a similar value chain, which includes activities such as obtaining raw materials, designing products, building manufacturing facilities, developing cooperative agreements, and providing customer service. A firm will be profitable as long as total revenues exceed the total costs incurred in creating and delivering the product or service. Firms should strive to understand not only their own value chain operations, but also their competitors', suppliers', and distributors' value chains.

THE COMPETITIVE ADVANTAGE OF NATIONS   Some countries around the world, such as Brazil, offer abundant natural resources, while others, such as Mexico, offer cheap labor. Others, such as Japan, offer a high commitment to education, while still others, such as the United States, offer innovativeness and entrepreneurship. Countries differ in what they have to offer businesses, and firms increasingly are relocating various parts of their value chain operations to take advantage of what different countries have to offer.

Porter reveals in his most recent book that some countries seem to have a disproportionate share of successful firms in particular industries. Examples are the United States in entertainment, Italy in ceramic tile, Sweden in trucks, Japan in banking, Switzerland in candy, and Germany in cars. Porter attributes these differences to four decisive elements: (1) availability of strengths in certain narrow, technical fields; (2) high demand in the home country; (3) related and supporting industries in the home country; and (4) strong domestic rivals.[7] Local rivalry, for example, often stimulates growth in local distributors and suppliers. Organizations should strive to pursue strategies that effectively enable the firm to capitalize

---

GLOBAL PERSPECTIVE
How Extensively Is the Internet Used in Europe?

A lack of personal computers in most households, high connection costs, and currency obstacles have caused the Internet to be used only sparingly in Europe for sales and marketing applications. In France, for example, 20-year-old Minitels are small videotext consoles that link one-quarter of all households and businesses but do not offer access to the Internet. European businesses that do use the Internet for commerce only provide information about their products and services, with no mechanism for actually purchasing goods.

In 1997 in all of Europe, only about 9 million businesses and households logged onto the Internet and consummated only about $500 million in commerce. This number is expected to climb to more than 35 million users by the year 2000 and total over $3 billion in commerce, for two big reasons:

1. Deregulation of Europe's telecommunications industry in scheduled for 1998. Currently, Europeans who log onto the Internet pay 50 percent more than Americans to sign on and, in addition, have to pay 30 cents per minute of connection. These costs should fall in 1998, thus spurring growth of the Internet.

2. Introduction of a single European currency in scheduled for January 1, 1999.

The euro or common coinage for all of Europe will make it much easier to engage in commerce using the Internet because so many different currencies in Europe now make electronic commerce unwieldly and cumbersome. A single currency would spur growth of the Internet.

Source: Adapted from Jack Gee, "Parlez-Vous Internet," Industry Week (April 21, 1997): 78–82.

on the relative strengths of various nations. According to Porter, comparative differences among nations result in the following generalizations for strategic management: devaluation is bad for competitiveness; relaxing antitrust is bad; relaxing product safety and environmental regulations is bad; deregulation is good; promoting interfirm cooperation is bad; orderly marketing agreements are bad; and increasing defense contracts is bad.

The United States is far ahead of rest of the world in use of the Internet for commerce. As indicated in the Global Perspective, Europe lags considerably behind the United States in this regard.

STRATEGIC MANAGEMENT IN NONPROFIT AND GOVERNMENT ORGANIZATIONS

The strategic-management process is being used effectively by countless nonprofit and governmental organizations, such as the Girl Scouts and Boy Scouts, the Red Cross, chambers of commerce, educational institutions, medical institutions, public utilities, libraries, government agencies, and churches. The nonprofit sector, surprisingly, is by far America's largest employer, with 80 million Americans giving on average nearly 5 hours each week to one or more nonprofit organizations. Many nonprofit and governmental organizations outperform private firms and corporations on innovativeness, motivation, productivity, and strategic management. For example, the Salvation Army in Florida is able to rehabilitate 80 percent of persons convicted of their first offense. The Daisy Scouts, a Girl Scout program for 5-year-olds, has grown rapidly to more than 100,000 strong after being initiated only a few years ago.

Compared to for-profit firms, nonprofit and governmental organizations often function as a monopoly, produce a product or service that offers little or no measurability of performance, and are totally dependent on outside financing. Especially for these organizations, strategic management provides an excellent vehicle for developing and justifying requests for needed financial support.

EDUCATIONAL INSTITUTIONS Educational institutions are using strategic-management techniques and concepts more frequently. Richard Cyert, president of Carnegie-Mellon University, says, "I believe we do a far better job of strategic management than any company I know." Population shifts nationally from the Northeast and Midwest to the Southeast and West are but one factor causing trauma for educational institutions that have not planned for changing enrollments. Ivy League schools in the Northeast are recruiting more heavily in the Southeast and West. This trend represents a significant change in the competitive climate for attracting the best high school graduates each year.

Schools of business in colleges and universities increasingly are developing and offering custom courses for individual companies. At Northwestern University's Kellogg School, for example, custom courses for companies such as Ernst & Young and Johnson & Johnson now make up 40 percent of all executive education offerings. Custom courses account for 59 percent of executive education offerings at the University of Pennsylvania's Wharton School. "In the past, schools felt they were teaching the truth, and everyone would come kneel at their feet," says Nancy Hartigan at Kellogg. "Now companies are much more selective. Schools have to become more responsive to what organizations want." To become accredited by the American Association of Collegiate Schools of Business (AACSB), an elaborate strategic plan must be prepared by the applying school.

MEDICAL ORGANIZATIONS The $200 billion American hospital industry is experiencing declining margins, excess capacity, bureaucratic overburdening, poorly planned and executed diversification strategies, soaring health care costs, reduced federal support, and high administrator turnover. The seriousness of this problem is accented by a 20 percent annual decline in inpatient use nationwide. Declining occupancy rates, deregulation, and accelerating growth of health maintenance organizations, preferred provider organizations, urgent care centers, outpatient surgery centers, diagnostic centers, specialized clinics, and group practices are other major threats facing hospitals today. Many private and state-supported medical institutions are in financial trouble as a result of traditionally taking a reactive rather than a proactive approach in dealing with their industry.

Hospitals—originally intended to be warehouses for people dying of tuberculosis, smallpox, cancer, pneumonia, and infectious diseases—are creating new strategies today as advances in the diagnosis and treatment of chronic diseases are undercutting that earlier mission. Hospitals are beginning to bring services to the patient as much as bringing the patient to the hospital; in 20 years, health care will be concentrated in the home and in the residential community, not on the hospital campus. Chronic care will require day treatment facilities, electronic monitoring at home, user-friendly ambulatory services, decentralized service networks, and laboratory testing. A successful hospital strategy for the future will require renewed and deepened collaboration with physicians, who are central to hospitals' well-being, and a reallocation of resources from acute to chronic care in home and community settings.

Current strategies being pursued by many hospitals include creating home health services, establishing nursing homes, and forming rehabilitation centers. Backward integration strategies that some hospitals are pursuing include acquiring ambulance services, waste disposal services, and diagnostic services. The Stuart Circle Hospital in Richmond, Virginia, is using newspaper, radio, and outdoor advertising as part of a market penetration strategy. Archbold Memorial Hospital in Thomasville, Georgia, is pursuing a product development strategy by creating an outpatient mental health service, a nurse midwife service, and a substance abuse center. The Children's Memorial Hospital in Chicago has developed a new program called Pediatric Excellence that provides nursing care at home for medically fragile children. This strategy could be considered concentric diversification, as could the strategies of building fitness centers and diet centers. Desert Hospital in Palm Springs, California, has moved its noninvasive cardiac catheterization services out of the hospital and into a joint venture arrangement with physicians.

The 10 most successful hospital strategies today are providing freestanding outpatient surgery centers, freestanding outpatient diagnostic centers, physical rehabilitation centers, home health services, cardiac rehabilitation centers, preferred provider services, industrial medicine services, women's medicine services, skilled nursing units, and psychiatric services.[8]

Due largely to costs, hospitals increasingly are contracting with outside companies to perform services such as providing 24-hour emergency room and life-support systems. Psicor in San Diego, for example, leases equipment and provides technicians for open-heart surgery in 80 hospitals across the country. At least 1,000 hospitals nationwide have contracted with firms such as Coastal Emergency Services in Durham, North Carolina, to provide emergency room services.

GOVERNMENTAL AGENCIES AND DEPARTMENTS   Federal, state, county, and municipal agencies and departments, such as police departments, chambers of commerce, forestry associations, and health departments, are responsible for formulating, implementing, and evaluating strategies that use taxpayers' dollars in the most cost-effective way to provide services and programs. Strategic-management concepts increasingly are being used to enable governmental organizations to be more effective and efficient.

But strategists in governmental organizations operate with less strategic autonomy than their counterparts in private firms. Public enterprises generally cannot diversify into unrelated businesses or merge with other firms. Governmental strategists usually enjoy little freedom in altering the organizations' missions or redirecting objectives. Legislators and politicians often have direct or indirect control over major decisions and resources. Strategic issues get discussed and debated in the media and legislatures. Issues become politicized, resulting in fewer strategic choice alternatives. There is more predictability in the management of public sector enterprises.

On the surface, it may seem that strategic management is not applicable to government organizations, but the opposite is true. Government agencies and departments are finding that their employees get excited about the opportunity to participate in the strategic-management process and thereby have an effect on the organization's mission, objectives, strategies, and policies. In addition, government agencies are using a strategic-management approach to develop and substantiate formal requests for additional funding.

STRATEGIC MANAGEMENT IN SMALL FIRMS

Strategic management is vital for large firms' success, but what about small firms? The strategic-management process is just as vital for small companies. From their inception, all organizations have a strategy, even if the strategy just evolves from day-to-day operations. Even if conducted informally or by a single owner/entrepreneur, the strategic-management process significantly can enhance small firms' growth and prosperity. Recent data clearly show that an ever-increasing number of men and women in the United States are starting their own businesses. This means more individuals are becoming strategists. Widespread corporate layoffs have contributed to an explosion in small businesses and new ideas. For example, although less than 1 percent of the 900,000 auto mechanics in the United States are women, Janet Brown of Newport News, Virginia, recently opened and is successfully operating the Women's Auto Clinic, which features women mechanics.

Numerous magazine and journal articles have focused on applying strategic-management concepts to small businesses.[9] A major conclusion of these articles is that a lack of strategic-management knowledge is a serious obstacle for many small business owners. Other problems often encountered in applying strategic-management concepts to small businesses are a lack of both sufficient capital to exploit external opportunities and a day-to-day cognitive frame of reference. Recent research also indicates that strategic management in small firms is more informal than in large firms, but small firms that engage in strategic management outperform those that do not. The CheckMATE strategic planning software at www.checkmateplan.com offers a version especially for small businesses.

CONCLUSION

The main appeal of any managerial approach is the expectation that it will enhance organizational performance. This is especially true of strategic management. Through involvement in strategic-management activities, managers and employees achieve a better understanding of an organization's priorities and operations. Strategic management allows organizations to be efficient, but more importantly, it allows them to be effective. Although strategic management does not guarantee organizational success, the process allows proactive rather than reactive decision making. Strategic management may represent a radical change in philosophy for some organizations, so strategists must be trained to anticipate and constructively respond to questions and issues as they arise. The 16 strategies discussed in this chapter can represent a new beginning for many firms, especially if managers and employees in the organization understand and support the plan for action.

We invite you to visit the DAVID page on the Prentice Hall Web site at
www.prenhall.com/davidsm
for this chapter's World Wide Web exercise.

KEY TERMS AND CONCEPTS

Acquisition	(p. 59)	Focus	(p. 62)	Market Development	(p. 50)
Backward Integration	(p. 49)	Forward Integration	(p. 46)	Market Penetration	(p. 50)
Bankruptcy	(p. 54)	Franchising	(p. 48)	Merchant Banking	(p. 61)
Combination Strategy	(p. 56)	Generic Strategies	(p. 61)	Merger	(p. 59)
Concentric Diversification	(p. 52)	Horizontal Diversification	(p. 52)	Outsourcing	(p. 49)
Conglomerate Diversification	(p. 53)	Horizontal Integration	(p. 49)	Product Development	(p. 51)
Cooperative Arrangements	(p. 53)	Integration Strategies	(p. 46)	Retrenchment	(p. 54)
Cost Leadership	(p. 61)	Intensive Strategies	(p. 50)	Takeover	(p. 59)
Differentiation	(p. 62)	Joint Venture	(p. 53)	Value Chain	(p. 63)
Diversification Strategies	(p. 52)	Leveraged Buyout	(p. 60)	Vertical Integration	(p. 46)
Divestiture	(p. 55)	Liquidation	(p. 55)		

ISSUES FOR REVIEW AND DISCUSSION

1. How does strategy formulation differ for a small versus a large organization? for a for-profit versus a nonprofit organization?

2. Give recent examples of market penetration, market development, and product development.

3. Give recent examples of forward integration, backward integration, and horizontal integration.

4. Give recent examples of concentric diversification, horizontal diversification, and conglomerate diversification.

5. Give recent examples of joint venture, retrenchment, divestiture, and liquidation.

6. Read one of the suggested readings at the end of this chapter. Prepare a 5-minute oral report on the topic.

7. Do you think hostile takeovers are unethical? Why or why not?

8. What are the major advantages and disadvantages of diversification?

9. What are the major advantages and disadvantages of an integrative strategy?

10. How does strategic management differ in profit and nonprofit organizations?

11. Why is it not advisable to pursue too many strategies at once?

12. Explain Porter's value chain concept.

13. Describe the mechanics of a leveraged buyout.

14. What are the implications of Porter's "competitive advantage of nations" research?

15. Visit the CheckMATE Strategic Planning software Web site at www.checkmateplan.com and discuss the benefits offered.

NOTES

1. John Byrne, "Strategic Planning—It's Back," *Business Week* (August 26, 1996): 46.

2. Kenneth Davidson, "Do Megamergers Make Sense?" *Journal of Business Strategy* 7, no. 3 (Winter 1987): 45.

3. Kathryn Rudie Harrigan, "Joint Ventures: Linking for a Leap Forward," *Planning Review* 14, no. 4 (July–August 1986):10.

4. Gary Hamel, Yves Doz, and C. K. Prahalad, "Collaborate with Your Competitors—and Win," *Harvard Business Review* 67, no. 1 (January–February 1989): 133.

5. "Why Nothing Seems to Make a Dent in Dealmaking," *Business Week* (July 20, 1987): 75.

6. Dan Dalton, "The Ubiquitous Leveraged Buyout (LBO): Management Buyout or Management Sellout?" *Business Horizons* 32, no. 4 (July–August 1989): 36.

7. Bernard Reimann, "Selected Highlights of the 1988 Strategic Management Society Conference," *Planning Review* (January–February 1989): 26–7. See also Michael Porter, *Competitive Advantage of Nations* (New York: Free Press, 1989).

8. *Hospital*, May 5, 1991: 16.

9. Some of these articles are P. H. Thurston, "Should Smaller Companies Make Formal Plans?" *Harvard Business Review* 61, no. 5 (September–October 1983): 162–88; R. Robinson, J. Pearce, G. Vozikis, and T. Mescon, "The Relationship Between Stage of Development and Small Firm Planning and Performance," *Journal of Small Business Management* 22, no. 2 (April 1984): 45–52; L. Nagel, "Strategy Formulation for the Smaller Firm: A Practical Approach," *Long Range Planning* 14, no. 4 (August 1981): 115–20; P. G. Holland and W. Boulton, "Balancing the 'Family' and the 'Business' in Family Business," *Business Horizons* 27, no. 2 (March–April 1984): 16–21; F. R. David, "Computer-Assisted Strategic Planning for Small Businesses," *Journal of Systems Management* 36, no. 7 (July 1985): 24–33.

CURRENT READINGS

Anand, J. and H. Singh. "Asset Redeployment, Acquisitions and Corporate Strategy in Declining Industries." *Strategic Management Journal* 18, Special Issue (Summer 1997): 99–118.

Argyres, N. "Evidence on the Role of Firm Capabilities in Vertical Integration Decisions." *Strategic Management Journal* 17, no. 2 (February 1996): 129–150.

Barkdoll, Gerald and Morris R. Bosin. "Targeted Planning: A Paradigm for the Public Service." *Long Range Planning* 30, no. 4 (August 1997): 529–539.

Bergh, D. D. and G. F. Holbein. "Assessment and Redirection of Longitudinal Analysis: Demonstration with a Study of the Diversification and Divestiture Relationship." *Strategic Management Journal* 18, no. 7 (August 1997): 557–572.

Busija, E. C., H. M. O'Neill, and C. P. Zeithaml. "Diversification Strategy, Entry Mode, and Performance: Evidence of Choice and Constraints." *Strategic Management Journal* 18, no. 4 (April 1997): 321–328.

Byrd, John, Kent Hickman, and Hugh Hunter. "Diversification: A Broader Perspective." *Business Horizons* 40, no. 2 (March–April 1997): 40–44.

Castrogiovanni, Gary J. "Pre-Start-up Planning and the Survival of New Small Businesses: Theoretical Linkages." *Journal of Management* 22, no. 6 (1996): 801–822.

Chang, S. J. "An Evolutionary Perspective on Diversification and Corporate Restructuring Entry, Exit, and Economic Performance During 1981–89." *Strategic Management Journal* 17, no. 8 (October 1996): 587–612.

Dailey, C. M. "Governance Patterns in Bankruptcy Reorganizations." *Strategic Management Journal* 17, no. 5 (May 1996): 355–376.

Dooley, R. S., D. M. Fowler, and A. Miller. "The Benefits of Strategic Homogeneity and Strategic Heterogeneity: Theoretical and Empirical Evidence Resolving Past Differences." *Strategic Management Journal* 17, no. 4 (April 1996): 293–306.

Fiegenbaum, A., J. M. Shaver, and B. Yeung. "Which Firms Expand to the Middle East: The Experience of American Multinationals." *Strategic Management Journal* 18, no. 2 (February 1997): 141–148.

Flanagan, David J. "Announcements of Purely Related and Purely Unrelated Mergers and Shareholder Returns: Reconciling the Relatedness Paradox." *Journal of Management* 22, no. 6 (1996): 823–836.

Goldsmith, Stephen. "Can Business Really Do Business With Government?" *Harvard Business Review* (May–June 1997): 110–122.

Gunz, Hugh P. and R. Michael Jalland. "Managerial Careers and Business Strategies." *Academy of Management Review* 21, no. 3 (July 1996): 718–756.

Hennart, J. F. and S. Reddy. "The Choice between Mergers/Acquisitions and Joint Ventures: The Case of Japanese Investors in the United States." *Strategic Management Journal* 18, no. 1 (January 1997): 1–12.

Hopkins, W. E. and S. A. Hopkins. "Strategic Planning–Financial Performance Relationships in Banks: A Causal Examination." *Strategic Management Journal* 18, no. 8 (September 1997): 635–652.

Inkpen, Andrew C. and Paul W. Beamish. "Knowledge, Bargaining Power, and the Instability of International Joint Ventures." *Academy of Management Review* 22, no. 1 (January 1997): 177–202.

Jennings, David. "Outsourcing Opportunities for Financial Services." *Long Range Planning* 29, no. 3 (June 1996): 393–404.

Kabir, R., D. Cantrijn, and A. Jeunink. "Takeover Defenses, Ownership Structure and Stock Returns in the Netherlands: An

Empirical Analysis." *Strategic Management Journal* 18, no. 2 (February 1997): 97–110.

Khanna, Tarun and Krishna Palepu. "Why Focused Strategies May Be Wrong for Emerging Markets." *Harvard Business Review* (July–August 1997): 41–54.

Krishnan, H. A., A. Miller, and W. Q. Judge. "Diversification and Top Management Team Complementarity: Is Performance Improved by Merging Similar or Dissimilar Teams?" *Strategic Management Journal* 18, no. 5 (May 1997): 361–374.

Khurana, Anil and Stephen R. Rosenthal. "Integrating the Fuzzy Front End of New Product Development." *Sloan Management Review* 38, no. 2 (Winter 1997): 103–113.

Liedtka, Jeanne M. "Collaboration Across Lines of Business for Competitive Advantage." *Academy of Management Executive* 10, no. 2 (May 1996): 20–37.

Lubatkin, Hemant Merchant and Narasimhan Srinivasan. "Merger Strategies and Shareholder Value During Times of Relaxed Antitrust Enforcement: The Case of Large Mergers During the 1980s." *Journal of Management* 23, no. 1 (1997): 61–84.

Milofsky, Carl. "Review of 'Strategic Management for Nonprofit Organizations: Theory and Cases.'" *Academy of Management Review* 22, no. 2 (April 1997): 568–570.

Moulton, Wilbur N., Howard Thomas, and Mark Pruett. "Business Failure Pathways: Environmental Stress and Organizational Response." *Journal of Management* 22, no. 4 (1996): 571–596.

Pearce, Robert J. "Toward Understanding Joint Venture Performance and Survival: A Bargaining and Influence Approach to Transaction Cost Theory." *Academy of Management Review* 22, no. 1 (January 1997): 203–225.

Ramaswamy, Kannah. "The Performance Impact of Strategic Similarity in Horizontal Mergers: Evidence from the U.S. Banking Industry." *Academy of Management Journal* 40, no. 3 (June 1997): 697–715.

Rowe, W. G. and P. M. Wright. "Related and Unrelated Diversification and Their Effect on Human Resource Management Controls." *Strategic Management Journal* 18, no. 4 (April 1997): 329–339.

Saunders, Carol, Mary Gebelt, and Quing Hu. "Achieving Success in Information Systems Outsourcing." *California Management Review* 39, no. 2 (Winter 1997): 63–79.

Experiential Exercise 2A

WHAT HAPPENED AT HERSHEY FOODS IN 1998?

PURPOSE

In performing business policy case analysis, you will need to find epilogue information about the respective companies to determine what strategies actually were employed since the time of the case. Comparing *what actually happened* with *what you would have recommended and expected to happen* is an important part of business policy case analysis. Do not recommend what the firm actually did, unless in-depth analysis of the situation at the time reveals those strategies to have been best among all feasible alternatives. This exercise gives you experience conducting library research to determine what strategies Hershey, Mars, and Nestlé pursued in 1998.

INSTRUCTIONS

Step 1 Look up Hershey Foods Corporation, Mars, and Nestlé Corporation on the Internet. Find some recent articles about firms in the confectionery industry. Scan Moody's, Dun & Bradstreet, and Standard & Poor's publications for information. Check the Edgar files at www.sec.gov and Hoover's on-line at www.hoovers.com.

Step 2 Summarize your findings in a three-page report titled "Strategies of Hershey Foods in 1998." Include information about Mars and Nestlé. Also include your personal reaction to Hershey's strategies in terms of their attractiveness.

Experiential Exercise 2B

EXAMINING STRATEGY ARTICLES

PURPOSE

Strategy articles can be found weekly in journals, magazines, and newspapers. By reading and studying strategy articles, you can gain a better understanding of the strategic-management process. Several of the best journals in which to find corporate strategy articles are *Planning Review, Long Range Planning, Journal of Business Strategy,* and *Strategic Management Journal.* These journals are devoted to reporting the results of empirical research in strategic management. They apply strategic-management concepts to specific organizations and industries. They introduce new strategic-management techniques and provide short case studies on selected firms.

Other good journals in which to find strategic-management articles are *Harvard Business Review, Sloan Management Review, Business Horizons, California Management Review, Academy of Management Review, Academy of Management Journal, Academy of Management Executive, Journal of Management,* and *Journal of Small Business Management.*

In addition to journals, many magazines regularly publish articles that focus on business strategies. Several of the best magazines in which to find applied strategy articles are *Dun's Business Month, Fortune, Forbes, Business Week, Inc. Magazine,* and *Industry Week.* Newspapers such as *USA Today, The Wall Street Journal, The New York Times,* and *Barrons* cover strategy events when they occur—for example, a joint venture announcement, a bankruptcy declaration, a new advertising campaign start, acquisition of a company, divestiture of a division, a chief executive officer's hiring or firing, or a hostile takeover attempt.

In combination, journal, magazine, and newspaper articles can make the business policy course more exciting. They allow current strategies of profit and nonprofit organizations to be identified and studied.

INSTRUCTIONS

Step 1 Go to your college library and find a recent journal article that focuses on a strategic-management topic. Select your article from one of the journals listed above, not from a magazine. Copy the article and bring it to class.

Step 2 Give a three-minute oral report summarizing the most important information in your article. Include comments giving your personal reaction to the article. Pass your article around in class.

Experiential Exercise 2c

CLASSIFYING 1998 STRATEGIES

PURPOSE

This exercise can improve your understanding of various strategies by giving you experience classifying strategies. This skill will help you use the strategy-formulation tools presented later. Consider the following strategies announced in 1998 by various firms:

1. Aetna Inc., a huge insurance firm, bought New York Life Insurance Company's health insurance division (NYL Care).
2. Toyota developed a tree that absorbs smog.
3. Merrill Lynch purchased a large European private bank.
4. Pfizer developed and marketed Viagra.
5. Enron withdrew from doing business in California.
6. National Semiconductor laid off 10 percent of its employees.
7. Microsoft developed and marketed Windows 98.
8. CVS, formally Revco, purchased Arbor Drugs.
9. Bethlehem Steel purchased Lukens Steel.
10. Pacific Gas & Electric began selling services outside California.
11. Procter & Gamble began selling Pringles made with Olestra .
12. American Online completed its acquisition of CompuServe.
13. Boeing cut production of 747s from 5 planes to 3.5 a month.
14. General Motors expanded production in Mexico from 300,000 to 600,000 vehicles annually.
15. Digital Equipment merged with Compaq Computer.

16. Japan's NEC acquired 49 percent of Packard Bell.
17. Crescent Real Estate Equities acquired Station Casinos.
18. Apple Computer closed its Claris software unit.
19. J.C. Penney closed 75 stores and cut 4,900 jobs.
20. Dutch retailer Royal Ahold acquired Giant Food.

INSTRUCTIONS

Step 1 On a separate sheet of paper, number from 1 to 20. These numbers correspond to the strategies described above.

Step 2 What type of strategy best describes the 20 actions cited above? Indicate your answers.

Step 3 Exchange papers with a classmate and grade each other's paper as your instructor gives the right answers.

Experiential Exercise 2D

STRATEGIC MANAGEMENT AT THE DYNAMIC COMPUTER COMPANY

PURPOSE

This exercise can give you experience choosing among alternative growth strategies for a specific company. Remember that organizations cannot pursue all the strategies that potentially may benefit the firm. Difficult decisions have to be made to eliminate some options. Use the guidelines given in Table 2–4 to complete this exercise.

BACKGROUND

Dynamic Computer, Inc. (DCI) is a highly regarded personal computer manufacturer based in central California. DCI designs, develops, produces, markets, and services personal computer systems for individuals' needs in business, education, science, engineering, and the home. The company's main product is the Dynamic II personal computer system, complete with optional accessories and software. The company recently announced a new system, the Dynamic III, that is aimed at large business firms. It is much more expensive than the Dynamic II. Dynamic's computer systems are distributed in the United States and Canada by 1,000 independent retail stores and internationally through 21 independent distributors, who resell to 850 foreign retail outlets. Approximately 700 of the retail outlets in the United States and Canada are authorized service centers for Dynamic products, but none of the outlets sell Dynamic products exclusively. Many of these outlets are not marketing Dynamic's products effectively.

TABLE 2D–1 Selected Financial Information for DCI	1997	1998	1999
Sales	$ 13,000,000	$ 12,000,000	$ 10,000,000
New Income	3,000,000	1,000,000	500,000
Total Assets	180,000,000	200,000,000	250,000,000
Market Share	15%	12%	10%

The American computer industry grew at an inflation-adjusted, compound annual rate of about 20 percent from 1958 through the late 1980s. For the 1990s, real annual growth in the computer industry is expected to have averaged about 18 percent a year. The outlook for personal computers continues to be positive. However, this market is highly competitive and is characterized by rapid technological advances in both hardware and software. Margins on software are nearly double operating margins on hardware. New firms are entering the industry at an increasing rate, and this has resulted in a decline in Dynamic's sales, earnings, and market share in recent years. Many computer companies expect software sales and services to represent 50 percent of their total revenues by 2000. Dynamic is concerned about its future direction and competitiveness. Selected financial information for Dynamic is given in Table 2D–1.

INSTRUCTIONS

The owners of DCI have indicated a willingness to explore a number of alternative growth strategies for the future. They have hired you as a consultant to assist them in making strategic decisions regarding the future allocation of resources. The feeling is that to sustain growth, the company must make some critical decisions. Dynamic is financially capable of investing in several projects. The owners wish to use their resources wisely to produce the highest possible return on investment in the future. They are considering five alternative strategies:

1. Market penetration—establish a nationwide sales force to market Dynamic products to large firms that do not buy through independent retailers.

2. Product development—develop an easier-to-use computer for small business firms.

3. Forward integration—offer major new incentives to distributors who sell and service Dynamic products.

4. Backward integration—purchase a major outside supplier of software.

5. Conglomerate diversification—acquire Toys Unlimited, a large and successful toy manufacturer.

Based on the strategy guidelines given in Chapter 2, your task is to offer specific recommendations to the strategists of DCI. Follow these steps:

Step 1 Across the top of a separate sheet of paper, set up five columns, with the following headings:

| Individual Percentage Allocations | Group Percentage Allocations | Expert Percentage Allocations | The Absolute Difference Between Columns 1 and 3 | The Absolute Difference Between Columns 2 and 3 |

Down the left side of your paper, number from 1 to 5. These numbers correspond to the five strategies listed above.

Step 2 Take 10 minutes to determine how you would allocate DCI's resources among the five alternative strategies. Record your answers by placing individual percentage values for strategies 1 through 5 under column 1. Your only constraint is that the total resources allocated must equal 100 percent. Distribute resources in the manner you think will offer the greatest future return on investment and profitability.

Step 3 Join with two other students in class. Develop a set of group percentage allocations and record these values for strategies 1 through 5 under column 2. Do not change your individual percentage allocations once discussion begins in your group.

Step 4 As your teacher reveals the right answer and supporting rationale, record these values for strategies 1 through 5 under column 3.

Step 5 For each row, subtract column 3 values from column 1 values and record the absolute difference (ignore negatives) in column 4. Then, sum the column 4 values.

Step 6 For each row, subtract column 3 values from column 2 values and record the absolute difference (ignore negatives) in column 5. Then, sum the column 5 values.

Step 7 If the sum of column 4 values exceeds the sum of column 5 values, then your group allocation of DCI's resources was better than your individual allocation. However, if the sum of column 4 values is less than the sum of column 5 values, you were a better strategist than your group on this exercise.

Strategic-management research indicates that group strategic decisions are almost always better than individual strategic decisions. Did you do better than your group?

Experiential Exercise 2E

HOW RISKY ARE VARIOUS ALTERNATIVE STRATEGIES?

PURPOSE

This exercise focuses on how risky various alternative strategies are for organizations to pursue. Different degrees of risk are based largely on varying degrees of *externality*, defined as movement away from present business into new markets and products. In general, the greater the degree of externality, the greater the probability of loss resulting from unexpected events. High-risk strategies generally are less attractive than low-risk strategies.

INSTRUCTIONS

Step 1 On a separate sheet of paper, number vertically from 1 to 10. Think of 1 as "most risky," 2 as "next most risky," and so forth to 10, "least risky."

Step 2 Write the following strategies beside the appropriate number to indicate how risky you believe the strategy is to pursue: horizontal integration, horizontal diversification, liquidation, forward integration, backward integration, product development, market development, market penetration, joint venture, and conglomerate diversification.

Step 3 Grade your paper as your teacher gives you the right answers and supporting rationale. Each correct answer is worth 10 points.

This exercise is based on a commonly accepted and published classification of strategies given in James Belohlav and Karen Giddens-Emig, "Selecting a Master Strategy," *Journal of Business Strategy* 7, no. 3 (Winter 1987): 77.

Experiential Exercise 2F

DEVELOPING ALTERNATIVE STRATEGIES FOR MY UNIVERSITY

PURPOSE

It is important for representatives from all areas of a college or university to identify and discuss alternative strategies that could benefit faculty, students, alumni, staff, and other constituencies. As you complete this exercise, notice the learning and understanding that occurs as people express differences of opinions. Recall that *the process of planning is more important than the document.*

INSTRUCTIONS

Step 1 Recall or locate the external opportunity/threat and internal strength/weakness factors that you identified as part of Experiential Exercise 1D. If you did not do that exercise, discuss now as a class important external and internal factors facing your college or university.

Step 2 Identify and put on the chalkboard alternative strategies that you feel could benefit your college or university. Your proposed actions should allow the institution to capitalize on particular strengths, improve upon certain weaknesses, avoid external threats, and/or take advantage of particular external opportunities. List at least 20 possible strategies on the board. Number the strategies as they are written on the board.

Step 3 On a separate sheet of paper, number from 1 to the total number of strategies listed on the board. Everyone in class individually should rate the strategies identified, using a 1 to 3 scale, where 1 = *I do not support implementation*, 2 = *I am neutral about implementation*, and 3 = *I strongly support implementation*. In rating the strategies, recognize that your institution cannot do everything desired or potentially beneficial.

Step 4 Go to the board and record your ratings in a row beside the respective strategies. Everyone in class should do this, going to the board perhaps by rows in the class.

Step 5 Sum the ratings for each strategy so that a prioritized list of recommended strategies is obtained. This prioritized list reflects the collective wisdom of your class. Strategies with the highest score are deemed best.

Step 6 Discuss how this process could enable organizations to achieve understanding and commitment from individuals.

Step 7 Share your class results with a university administrator and ask for comments regarding the process and top strategies recommended.

PART 2

STRATEGY FORMULATION

The Business Mission

CHAPTER OUTLINE

CHAPTER OBJECTIVES

After studying this chapter, you should be able to do the following:

1. Describe the nature and role of mission statements in strategic management.

2. Discuss why the process of developing a mission statement is as important as the resulting document.

3. Identify the components of mission statements.

4. Discuss how a clear mission statement can benefit other strategic-management activities.

5. Evaluate mission statements of different organizations.

6. Write good mission statements.

NOTABLE QUOTES

A business is not defined by its name, statutes, or articles of incorporation. It is defined by the business mission. Only a clear definition of the mission and purpose of the organization makes possible clear and realistic business objectives.—PETER DRUCKER

A corporate vision can focus, direct, motivate, unify, and even excite a business into superior performance. The job of a strategist is to identify and project a clear vision.—JOHN KEANE

Where there is no vision, the people perish.—PROVERBS 29:18

Customers are first, employees second, shareholders third, and the community fourth. That's the credo at H. B. Fuller, the century-old adhesives maker in St. Paul.—PATRICIA SELLERS

What is especially difficult is getting different departments working together in the best interest of customers. Yet managers at all levels are the critical link to aligning the entire organization toward the customer.—RICHARD WHITELEY

For strategists, there's a trade-off between the breadth and detail of information needed. It's a bit like an eagle hunting for a rabbit. The eagle has to be high enough to scan a wide area in order to enlarge his chances of seeing prey, but he has to be low enough to see the detail—the movement and features that will allow him to recognize his target. Continually making this trade-off is the job of a strategist—it simply can't be delegated.—FREDERICK GLUCK

The best laid schemes of mice and men often go awry.—ROBERT BURNS (paraphrased)

A strategist's job is to see the company not as it is . . . but as it can become.—JOHN W. TEETS, CHAIRMAN OF GREYHOUND, INC.

That business mission is so rarely given adequate thought is perhaps the most important single cause of business frustration.—PETER DRUCKER

This chapter focuses on the concepts and tools needed to evaluate and write business mission statements. A practical framework for developing mission statements is provided. Actual mission statements from large and small organizations and for-profit and nonprofit enterprises are presented and critically examined. The process of creating a mission statement is discussed.

WHAT IS OUR BUSINESS?

Current thought on mission statements is based largely on guidelines set forth in the mid-1970s by Peter Drucker (www.cgs.edu/faculty/druckerp.html), often called "the father of modern management" for his pioneering studies at General Motors Corporation and for his 22 books and hundreds of articles. *Harvard Business Review* calls Drucker, now in his 80s, "the preeminent management thinker of our time."

Drucker says asking the question "What is our business?" is synonymous with asking the question "What is our mission?" An enduring statement of purpose that distinguishes one organization from other similar enterprises, the *mission statement* is a declaration of an organization's "reason for being." It answers the pivotal question, "What is our business?" A clear mission statement is essential for effectively establishing objectives and formulating strategies.

Sometimes called a *creed statement*, a statement of purpose, a statement of philosophy, a statement of beliefs, a statement of business principles, a vision statement, or a statement "defining our business," a mission statement reveals the long-term vision of an organization in terms of what it wants to be and whom it wants to serve. All organizations have a reason for being, even if strategists have not consciously transformed this into writing. As illustrated in Figure 3–1, a carefully prepared statement of mission is widely recognized by both practitioners and academicians as the first step in strategic management.

> A business mission is the foundation for priorities, strategies, plans, and work assignments. It is the starting point for the design of managerial jobs and, above all, for the design of managerial structures. Nothing may seem simpler or more obvious than to know what a company's business is. A steel mill makes steel, a railroad runs trains to carry freight and passengers, an insurance company underwrites fire risks, and a bank lends money. Actually, "What is our business?" is almost always a difficult question and the right answer is usually anything but obvious. The answer to this question is the first responsibility of strategists. Only strategists can make sure that this question receives the attention it deserves and that the answer makes sense and enables the business to plot its course and set its objectives.[1]

We can perhaps best understand a business mission by focusing on a business when it is first started. In the beginning, a new business is simply a collection of ideas. Starting a new business rests on a set of beliefs that the new organization can offer some product or service, to some customers, in some geographic area, using some type of technology, at a profitable price. A new business owner typically believes that the management philosophy of the new enterprise will result in a favorable public image and that this concept of the business can be communicated to, and will be adopted by, important constituencies. When the set of beliefs about a business at its inception is put into writing, the resulting document mirrors the same basic ideas that underlie the mission statement. As a business grows, owners or managers find it necessary to revise the founding set of beliefs, but those original ideas usually are reflected in the revised statement of mission.

Business mission statements often can be found in the front of annual reports. Mission statements often are displayed throughout a firm's premises, and they are distributed

FIGURE 3–1
A Comprehensive Strategic-Management Model

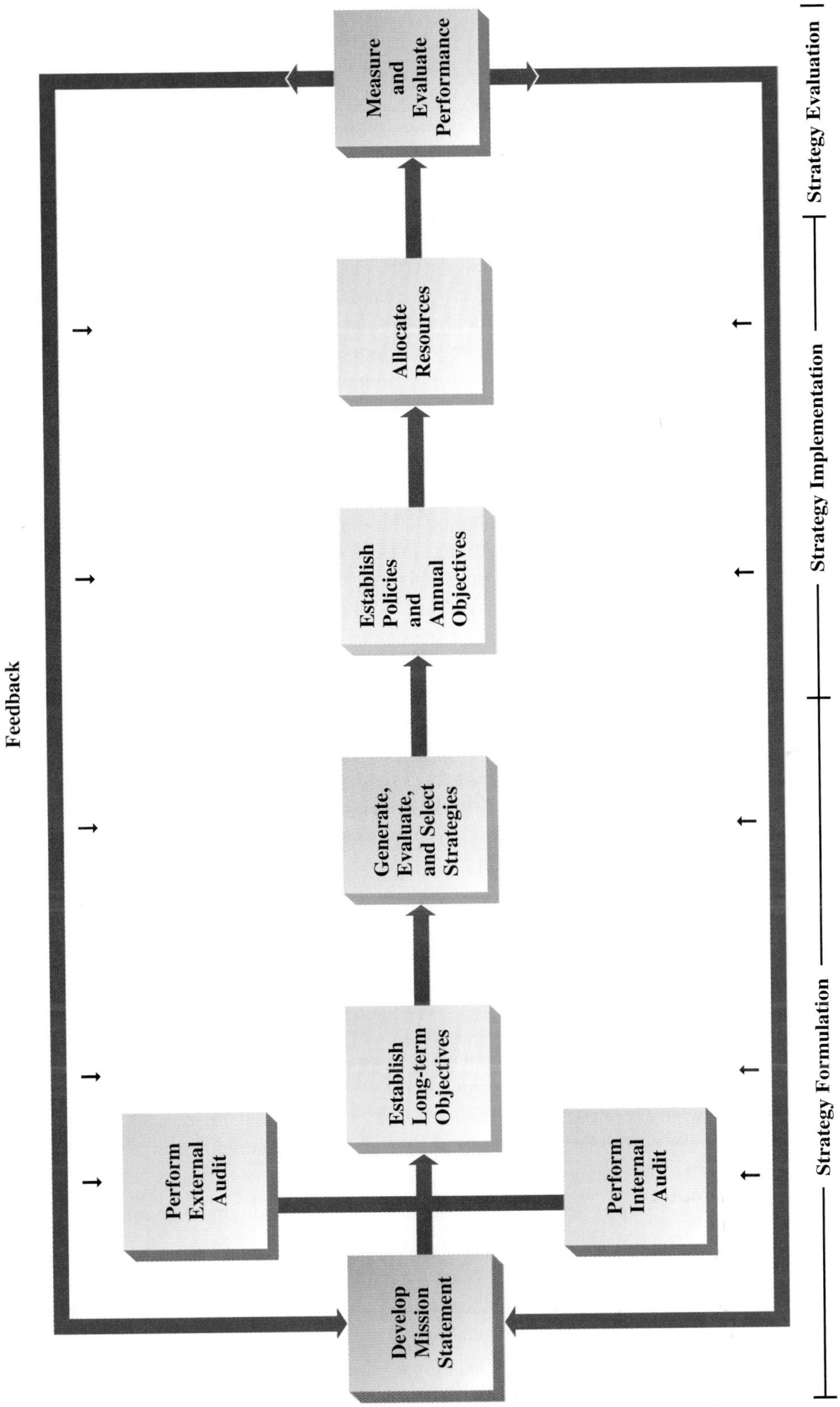

Develop Mission Statement

Perform External Audit

Perform Internal Audit

Establish Long-term Objectives

Generate, Evaluate, and Select Strategies

Establish Policies and Annual Objectives

Allocate Resources

Measure and Evaluate Performance

Feedback

Strategy Formulation

Strategy Implementation

Strategy Evaluation

with company information sent to constituencies. The mission statement is a part of numerous internal reports, such as loan requests, supplier agreements, labor relations contracts, business plans, and customer service agreements. Barnett Bank's current mission statement is as follows:

> Barnett's mission is to create value for its owners, customers, and employees by creating and capitalizing on market leadership positions to sell and service a broad range of high quality, profitable financial services. Our sales emphasis will be full service to consumers and businesses in our communities and advisory and processing services to others. We will operate at the lowest possible cost consistent with maintaining high service quality and market leadership.[2]

A good mission statement describes an organization's purpose, customers, products or services, markets, philosophy, and basic technology. According to Vern McGinnis, a mission statement should (1) define what the organization is and what the organization aspires to be, (2) be limited enough to exclude some ventures and broad enough to allow for creative growth, (3) distinguish a given organization from all others, (4) serve as a framework for evaluating both current and prospective activities, and (5) be stated in terms sufficiently clear to be widely understood throughout the organization.[3]

Some strategists spend almost every moment of every day on administrative and tactical concerns, and strategists who rush quickly to establish objectives and implement strategies often overlook developing a mission statement. This problem is widespread even among large organizations. Approximately 40 percent of large corporations in America have not yet developed a formal mission statement, including Walt Disney Company, Grumman Corporation, and Wal-Mart. However, about 60 percent do have a formal mission document.[4] An increasing number of organizations are developing formal mission statements.

Some companies develop mission statements simply because they feel it is fashionable, rather than out of any real commitment. However, as will be described in this chapter, firms that develop and systematically revisit their mission, treat it as a living document, and consider it to be an integral part of the firm's culture realize great benefits. Johnson & Johnson (J&J) is an example firm. J&J managers meet regularly with employees to review, reword, and reaffirm the firm's mission. The entire J&J workforce recognizes the value that top management places on this exercise, and these employees respond accordingly.

THE IMPORTANCE OF A CLEAR MISSION

The importance of a mission statement to effective strategic management is well documented in the literature. A recent study comparing mission statements of Fortune 500 firms performing well and firms performing poorly concluded that high performers have more comprehensive mission statements than low performers.[5] King and Cleland recommend that organizations carefully develop a written mission statement for the following reasons:

1. To ensure unanimity of purpose within the organization.
2. To provide a basis, or standard, for allocating organizational resources.
3. To establish a general tone or organizational climate.
4. To serve as a focal point for individuals to identify with the organization's purpose and direction, and to deter those who cannot from participating further in the organization's activities.
5. To facilitate the translation of objectives into a work structure involving the assignment of tasks to responsible elements within the organization.

6. To specify organizational purposes and the translation of these purposes into objectives in such a way that cost, time, and performance parameters can be assessed and controlled.[6]

Reuben Mark, CEO of Colgate, maintains that a clear mission increasingly must make sense internationally. Colgate's mission can be summarized in five words: "We can be the best." Mark's thoughts on a mission statement are as follows:

> When it comes to rallying everyone to the corporate banner, it's essential to push one vision globally rather than trying to drive home different messages in different cultures. The trick is to keep the vision simple but elevated: "We make the world's fastest computers" or "Telephone service for everyone." You're never going to get anyone to charge the machine guns only for financial objectives. It's got to be something that makes them feel better, feel a part of something.[7]

VISION VERSUS MISSION   Some organizations develop both a mission statement and a vision statement. Whereas the mission statement answers the question "What is our business?" the *vision statement* answers the question "What do we want to become?" Two example companies that have both a mission and vision statement are Amoco Corporation and Harley-Davidson Corporation, as given in Table 3–1.

It can be argued that profit, not mission or vision, is the primary corporate motivator. But profit alone is not enough to motivate people.[8] Profit is perceived negatively by some employees in companies. Employees may see profit as something that they earn and management then uses and even gives away—to shareholders. Although this perception is undesired and disturbing to management, it clearly indicates that both profit and vision are needed to effectively motivate a workforce.

When employees and managers together shape or fashion the vision or mission for a firm, the resultant document can reflect the personal visions that managers and employees have in their hearts and minds about their own futures. Shared vision creates a commonality of interests that can lift workers out of the monotony of daily work and put them into a new world of opportunity and challenge.

THE PROCESS OF DEVELOPING A MISSION STATEMENT   As indicated in the strategic-management model, a clear mission statement is needed before alternative strategies can be formulated and implemented. It is important to involve as many managers as possible in the process of developing a mission statement, because through involvement, people become committed to an organization. Mark's comment about machine guns accents the need for a good mission statement.

A widely used approach to developing a mission statement is first to select several articles about mission statements and ask all managers to read these as background information. Then ask managers themselves to prepare a mission statement for the organization. A facilitator, or committee of top managers, then should merge these statements into a single document and distribute this draft mission statement to all managers. A request for modifications, additions, and deletions is needed next, along with a meeting to revise the document. To the extent that all managers have input into and support the final mission statement document, organizations can more easily obtain managers' support for other strategy formulation, implementation, and evaluation activities. Thus the process of developing a mission statement represents a great opportunity for strategists to obtain needed support from all managers in the firm.

During the process of developing a mission statement, some organizations use discussion groups of managers to develop and modify the mission statement. Some organizations hire an outside consultant or facilitator to manage the process and help draft the language. Sometimes an outside person with expertise in developing mission statements and unbiased views can manage the process more effectively than an internal group or

TABLE 3–1
Two Companies' Mission and Vision Statements

AMOCO CORPORATION (www.amoco.com)

MISSION STATEMENT

Amoco is a worldwide integrated petroleum and chemical company. We find and develop petroleum resources and provide quality products and services for our customers. We conduct our business responsibly to achieve a superior financial return balanced with our long-term growth, benefiting shareholders and fulfilling our commitment to the community and the environment.

VISION STATEMENT

Amoco will be a global business enterprise, recognized throughout the world as preeminent by employees, customers, competitors, investors and the public. We will be the standard by which other businesses measure their performance. Our hallmarks will be the innovation, initiative and teamwork of our people and our ability to anticipate and effectively respond to change and to create opportunity.

HARLEY-DAVIDSON (www.harley-davidson.com)

MISSION STATEMENT

Stay true to the things that make a Harley-Davidson a Harley-Davidson. Keep the heritage alive. From the people in the front office to the craftsmen on our factory floor, that is what we do. And it's why each new generation of Harley-Davidson motorcycles, well refined, contains the best of the ones before it. We have a passion for our product few companies understand. But when you see the result, it all becomes clear. We're not just building motorcycles. We're carrying on a legend. Ask anyone who's ever owned a Harley-Davidson. It gets in your blood. Becomes a part of your life. And once it does, it never leaves. It's something you can't compare with anything else. We know because we've been there. That's why, for 90 years, we've remained firm in our commitment to building the kind of motorcycles that deserve the intense loyalty that Harley-Davidson enjoys. The styling is still pure. The engines still rumble. It's also why you'll see us at major rallies and rides throughout the year, listening and talking to our customers. Staying close to riders and to the sport is how we've kept alive the things that make a Harley-Davidson a Harley-Davidson. Our approach has always been different. But again, so has owning a Harley-Davidson. We wouldn't have it any other way.

VISION STATEMENT

Harley-Davidson, Inc. is an action oriented, international company—a leader in its commitment to continuously improve the quality of profitable relationships with stakeholders (customers, employees, suppliers, shareholders, governments, and society). Harley-Davidson believes the key to success is to balance stakeholders' interests through the empowerment of all employees to focus on value-added activities.

Our Vision is our corporate conscience and helps us to eliminate short-term thinking, such as cashing in on demand for our motorcycles by giving quantity precedence over quality or cutting corners in recreational or commercial vehicles to save a few dollars per unit. It also encourages every employee in our organization to be acutely aware of his or her role in satisfying our stakeholders.

Equally important to our Vision, we live by a Code of Business Conduct that is driven by a value system which promotes honesty, integrity, and personal growth in all our dealings with stakeholders. Our values are the rules by which we operate: Tell the truth; be fair; keep your promises; respect the individual; and encourage intellectual curiosity.

In addition, we never lose sight of the issues we feel must be addressed in order to be successful in the 1990s: Quality, participation, productivity, and cash flow. As a shareholder, you should expect no less from us.

---

committee of managers. Decisions on how best to communicate the mission to all managers, employees, and external constituencies of an organization are needed when the document is in final form. Some organizations even develop a videotape to explain the mission statement and how it was developed.

A recent article by Campbell and Yeung emphasizes that the process of developing a mission statement should create an "emotional bond" and "sense of mission" between the organization and its employees.[9] Commitment to a company's strategy and intellectual agreement on the strategies to be pursued do not necessarily translate into an emotional bond; hence strategies that have been formulated may not be implemented. These researchers stress that an emotional bond comes when an individual personally identifies with the underlying values and behavior of a firm, thus turning intellectual agreement and commitment to strategy into a sense of mission. Campbell and Yeung also differentiate between the terms vision and mission, saying vision is "a possible and desirable future state of an organization" that includes specific goals, whereas mission is more associated with behavior and with the present.

THE NATURE OF A BUSINESS MISSION

A DECLARATION OF ATTITUDE A mission statement is a declaration of attitude and outlook more than a statement of specific details. It usually is broad in scope for at least two major reasons. First, a good mission statement allows for the generation and consideration of a range of feasible alternative objectives and strategies without unduly stifling management creativity. Excess specificity would limit the potential of creative growth for the organization. On the other hand, an overly general statement that does not exclude any strategy alternatives could be dysfunctional. Apple Computer's mission statement, for example, should not open the possibility for diversification into pesticides, or Ford Motor Company's into food processing. As indicated in the Global Perspective, French mission statements are more general than British mission statements.

Second, a mission statement needs to be broad to effectively reconcile differences among and appeal to an organization's diverse *stakeholders*, the individuals and groups of persons who have a special stake or claim on the company. Stakeholders include employees; managers; stockholders; boards of directors; customers; suppliers; distributors; creditors; governments (local, state, federal, and foreign); unions; competitors; environmental groups; and the general public. Stakeholders affect and are affected by an organization's strategies, yet the claims and concerns of diverse constituencies vary and often conflict. For example, the general public is especially interested in social responsibility, whereas stockholders are more interested in profitability. Claims on any business literally may

GLOBAL PERSPECTIVE
British versus French Mission Statements

Researchers recently studied the mission statements of British and French firms. Results are summarized here.

Researchers found that a highly participative (French) approach to developing a mission statement is more effective in gaining employee commitment than a less participative (British) approach. Differences between British and French statements are rooted in or attributed to different cultural, social, and economic factors in the two countries. For example, in Britain the predominance of equity financing has led to companies frequently being bought and sold like commodities. In contrast, the traditions of family ownership are stronger in France, providing a sense of community and a better basis for development of shared mission statements.

Source: Adapted from "Sharing the Vision: Company Mission Statements in Britain and France," Long Range Planning (February 1994): 84–94.

CHARACTERISTICS OF DOCUMENT	BRITAIN	FRANCE
Length	Short	Long
Specificity	Specific	General
Emphasis	Financial goals	Value to society
Architects	Top managers	All managers and employees
Durability	A year or less	Several years
Focus	Internal	Internal and external

NATURAL ENVIRONMENT
Is Your Firm Environmentally Proactive?

Conducting business in a way that preserves the natural environment is more than just good public relations; it is good business. Preserving the environment is a permanent part of doing business, for the following reasons:

1. Consumer demand for environmentally safe products and packages is high.

2. Public opinion demanding that firms conduct business in ways that preserve the natural environment is strong.

3. Environmental advocacy groups now have over 20 million Americans as members.

4. Federal and state environmental regulations are changing rapidly and becoming more complex.

5. More lenders are examining the environmental liabilities of businesses seeking loans.

6. Many consumers, suppliers, distributors, and investors shun doing business with environmentally weak firms.

7. Liability suits and fines against firms having environment problems are on the rise.

More firms are becoming environmentally proactive, which means they are taking the initiative to develop and implement strategies that preserve the environment while enhancing their efficiency and effectiveness. The old undesirable alternative is to be environmentally reactive—waiting until environmental pressures are thrust upon a firm by law or consumer pressure. A reactive environmental policy often leads to high cleanup costs, numerous liability suits, loss in market share, reduced customer loyalty, and higher medical costs. In contrast, a proactive policy views environmental pressures as opportunities, and includes such actions as developing green products and packages, conserving energy, reducing waste, recycling, and creating a corporate culture that is environmentally sensitive.

A proactive policy forces a company to innovate and upgrade processes; this leads to reduced waste, improved efficiency, better quality, and greater profits. Successful firms today assess "the profit in preserving the environment" in decisions ranging from developing a mission statement to determining plant location, manufacturing technology, product design, packaging, and consumer relations. A proactive environmental policy is simply good business.

Source: Adapted from "The Profit in Preserving America," Forbes (November 11, 1991): 181–189.

number in the thousands, and often include clean air, jobs, taxes, investment opportunities, career opportunities, equal employment opportunities, employee benefits, salaries, wages, clean water, and community services. All stakeholders' claims on an organization cannot be pursued with equal emphasis. A good mission statement indicates the relative attention that an organization will devote to meeting the claims of various stakeholders. More firms are becoming environmentally proactive in response to the concerns of stakeholders.

Reaching the fine balance between specificity and generality is difficult to achieve, but is well worth the effort. George Steiner offers the following insight on the need for a mission statement to be broad in scope:

> Most business statements of mission are expressed at high levels of abstraction. Vagueness nevertheless has its virtues. Mission statements are not designed to express concrete ends, but rather to provide motivation, general direction, an image, a tone, and a philosophy to guide the enterprise. An excess of detail could prove counterproductive since concrete specification could be the base for rallying opposition. Precision might stifle creativity in the formulation of an acceptable mission or purpose. Once an aim is cast in concrete, it creates a rigidity in an organization and resists change. Vagueness leaves room for other managers to fill in the details, perhaps even to modify general patterns. Vagueness permits more flexibility in adapting to changing environments and internal operations. It facilitates flexibility in implementation.[10]

An effective mission statement arouses positive feelings and emotions about an organization; it is inspiring in the sense that it motivates readers to action. An effective mission statement generates the impression that a firm is successful, has direction, and is worthy of time, support, and investment.

It reflects judgments about future growth directions and strategies based upon forward-looking external and internal analyses. A business mission should provide useful criteria for selecting among alternative strategies. A clear mission statement provides a basis for generating and screening strategic options. The statement of mission should be dynamic in orientation, allowing judgments about the most promising growth directions and those considered less promising.

A RESOLUTION OF DIVERGENT VIEWS What are the reasons some strategists are reluctant to develop a statement of their business mission? First, the question "What is our business?" can create controversy. Raising the question often reveals differences among strategists in the organization. Individuals who have worked together for a long time and who think they know each other suddenly may realize that they are in fundamental disagreement. For example, in a college or university, divergent views regarding the relative importance of teaching, research, and service often are expressed during the mission statement development process. Negotiation, compromise, and eventual agreement on important issues are needed before focusing on more specific strategy formulation activities.

> "What is our mission?" is a genuine decision; and a genuine decision must be based on divergent views to have a chance to be a right and effective decision. Developing a business mission is always a choice between alternatives, each of which rests on different assumptions regarding the reality of the business and its environment. It is always a high-risk decision. A change in mission always leads to changes in objectives, strategies, organization, and behavior. The mission decision is far too important to be made by acclamation. Developing a business mission is a big step toward management effectiveness. Hidden or half-understood disagreements on the definition of a business mission underlie many of the personality problems, communication problems, and irritations that tend to divide a top-management group. Establishing a mission should never be made on plausibility alone, should never be made fast, and should never be made painlessly.[11]

Considerable disagreement among an organization's strategists over basic purpose and mission can cause trouble if not resolved. For example, unresolved disagreement over the business mission was one of the reasons for W. T. Grant's bankruptcy and eventual liquidation. As one executive reported,

> There was a lot of dissension within the company whether we should go the Kmart route or go after the Montgomery Ward and J. C. Penney position. Ed Staley and Lou Lustenberger (two top executives) were at loggerheads over the issue, with the upshot being we took a position between the two and that consequently stood for nothing.[12]

Too often, strategists develop a statement of business mission only when their organization is in trouble. Of course, it is needed then. Developing and communicating a clear mission during troubled times indeed may have spectacular results and even may reverse decline. However, to wait until an organization is in trouble to develop a mission statement is a gamble that characterizes irresponsible management! According to Drucker, the most important time to ask seriously, "What is our business?" is when a company has been successful:

> Success always obsoletes the very behavior that achieved it, always creates new realities, and always creates new and different problems. Only the fairy story ends, "They lived happily ever after." It is never popular to argue with success or to rock the boat. The ancient Greeks knew that the penalty of success can be severe. The management that does not ask, "What is our mission?" when the company is successful is, in effect, smug, lazy, and arrogant. It will not be long before success will turn into failure. Sooner or later, even the most successful answer to the question, "What is our business?" becomes obsolete.[13]

A CUSTOMER ORIENTATION A good mission statement reflects the anticipations of customers. Rather than developing a product and then trying to find a market, the operating philosophy of organizations should be to identify customers' needs and then provide a product or service to fulfill those needs. Good mission statements identify the utility of a firm's products to its customers. This is why AT&T's mission statement focuses on communication rather than telephones, Exxon's mission statement focuses on energy rather than oil and gas, Union Pacific's mission statement focuses on transportation rather than railroads, and Universal Studios's mission statement focuses on entertainment instead of movies. The following utility statements are relevant in developing a mission statement:

> Do not offer me things.
> Do not offer me clothes. Offer me attractive looks.
> Do not offer me shoes. Offer me comfort for my feet and the pleasure of walking.
> Do not offer me a house. Offer me security, comfort, and a place that is clean and happy.
> Do not offer me books. Offer me hours of pleasure and the benefit of knowledge.
> Do not offer me records. Offer me leisure and the sound of music.
> Do not offer me tools. Offer me the benefit and the pleasure of making beautiful things.
> Do not offer me furniture. Offer me comfort and the quietness of a cozy place.
> Do not offer me things. Offer me ideas, emotions, ambience, feelings, and benefits.
> Please, do not offer me things.

A major reason for developing a business mission is to attract customers who give meaning to an organization. The Information Technology Perspective reveals the top reasons why customers do not purchase products and services over the Internet. A classic description of the purpose of a business reveals the relative importance of customers in a statement of mission:

> It is the customer who determines what a business is. It is the customer alone whose willingness to pay for a good or service converts economic resources into wealth and things into goods. What a business thinks it produces is not of first importance, especially not to the future of the business and to its success. What the customer thinks he/she is buying, what he/she considers value, is decisive—it determines what a business is, what it produces, and whether it

INFORMATION TECHNOLOGY

Why People Don't Make Purchases Over the Internet

1. Don't trust payment method/security	19.5%
2. No need	14.4%
3. Don't know how	9.3%
4. Prefer store shopping	9.1%
5. Don't have credit card	6.9%
6. Privacy issues	6.7%
7. Nothing worth buying	5.1%

As with automated teller machines (ATMs) of the 1980s and electricity of the 1880s, people are wary of new, complex technology. This is true with the Internet today. Although computer hackers can steal your credit card number if given to purchase goods over the Internet, the fact is that giving your credit card number over the telephone or to a waitress is more risky in terms of it being stolen, used illegally, or intercepted than typing a credit card number into a secure, established Internet site. Although 10 percent of Americans use the Internet regularly today, this percentage is growing dramatically. Sophisticated encryption methods to shield transactions and software to safeguard security are getting better daily, which is spurring more purchases.

Internet businesses actually will have a much harder time calming fears of consumers regarding privacy than about credit card security. Internet sites can regularly monitor your mouse and thus determine what Web pages you call up. Through cross-referencing, they then can determine what type of consumer you are in terms of buying habits. Web site owners can sell this information to advertisers and marketers just as America Online attempted to do recently until its customers threatened boycotts. Internet privacy and security are two key concerns for businesses and individuals today.

Source: Adapted from "Privacy, Security Fears Hinder Acceptance of Internet," USA Today (August 13, 1997): 2B.

will prosper. And what the customer buys and considers value is never a product. It is always utility, meaning what a product or service does for him or her. The customer is the foundation of a business and keeps it in existence.[14]

A DECLARATION OF SOCIAL POLICY   The words *social policy* embrace managerial philosophy and thinking at the highest levels of an organization. For this reason, social policy affects the development of a business mission statement. Social issues mandate that strategists consider not only what the organization owes its various stakeholders but also what responsibilities the firm has to consumers, environmentalists, minorities, communities, and other groups. After decades of debate on the topic of social responsibility, many firms still struggle to determine appropriate social policies.

The issue of social responsibility arises when a company establishes its business mission. The impact of society on business and vice versa is becoming more pronounced each year. Social policies directly affect a firm's customers, products and services, markets, technology, profitability, self-concept, and public image. An organization's social policy should be integrated into all strategic-management activities, including the development of a mission statement. Corporate social policy should be designed and articulated during strategy formulation, set and administered during strategy implementation, and reaffirmed or changed during strategy evaluation.[15] The emerging view of social responsibility holds that social issues should be attended to both directly and indirectly in determining strategies.

Firms should strive to engage in social activities that have economic benefits. For example, Merck & Company recently developed the drug ivermectin for treating river blindness, a disease caused by a fly-borne parasitic worm endemic in poor, tropical areas of Africa, the Middle East, and Latin America. In an unprecedented gesture that reflected its corporate commitment to social responsibility, Merck then made ivermectin available at no cost to medical personnel throughout the world. Merck's action highlights the dilemma of orphan drugs, which offer pharmaceutical companies no economic incentive for development and distribution.

Despite differences in approaches, most American companies try to assure outsiders that they conduct business in a socially responsible way. The mission statement is an effective instrument for conveying this message. The Norton Company, for example, concludes its mission statement by saying:

> In order to fulfill this mission, Norton will continue to demonstrate a sense of responsibility to the public interest and to earn the respect and loyalty of its customers, employees, shareholders, and suppliers, and the communities in which it does business.[16]

COMPONENTS OF A MISSION STATEMENT

Mission statements can and do vary in length, content, format, and specificity. Most practitioners and academicians of strategic management consider an effective statement to exhibit nine characteristics or components. Because a mission statement is often the most visible and public part of the strategic-management process, it is important that it includes all of these essential components. Components and corresponding questions that a mission statement should answer are given here.

1. *Customers*: Who are the firm's customers?
2. *Products or services*: What are the firm's major products or services?
3. *Markets*: Geographically, where does the firm compete?
4. *Technology*: Is the firm technologically current?

5. *Concern for survival, growth, and profitability*: Is the firm committed to growth and financial soundness?

6. *Philosophy*: What are the basic beliefs, values, aspirations, and ethical priorities of the firm?

7. *Self-concept*: What is the firm's distinctive competence or major competitive advantage?

8. *Concern for public image*: Is the firm responsive to social, community, and environmental concerns?

9. *Concern for employees*: Are employees a valuable asset of the firm?

Excerpts from the mission statements of different organizations are provided in Table 3–2 to exemplify the nine essential components.

WRITING AND EVALUATING MISSION STATEMENTS

Perhaps the best way to develop a skill for writing and evaluating mission statements is to study actual company missions. Therefore, 11 mission statements are presented in Table 3–3. These statements are then evaluated in Table 3–4 based on the nine criteria presented in the previous section.

There is no one best mission statement for a particular organization, so good judgment is required in evaluating mission statements. In Table 3–4, a *Yes* indicates that the given mission statement answers satisfactorily the question posed in Table 3–3 for the respective evaluative criteria. For example, the *Yes* under customers for the Chase Manhattan mission statement means this statement answers "Who are our customers?" Notice that Chase Manhattan's customers are "individuals, industries, communities, and countries." A *No* would mean a particular mission statement does not answer or answers unsatisfactorily the key question associated with one of the nine evaluative criteria. For example, note that the Apple Computer, AT&T, BellSouth, and Corning mission statements do not identify the organizations' customers. To determine whether a particular statement satisfactorily includes a given component, ask yourself the following question: "If I were responsible for writing a mission statement for this organization, would I have communicated this component better?" If your answer is yes, then record a *No* in the evaluation matrix. Generally, simple inclusion of the word *customers* or *employees* or *technology* is not adequately informative or inspiring in a statement.

Table 3–4 indicates that the Bancorp Hawaii and Chase Manhattan mission statements are the "best" and the Corning mission statement is the "worst" of the examples. Overall, the example mission statements are weakest in the areas of technology; philosophy; and concern for survival, growth, and profitability. The statements are strongest in the areas of products or services, markets, and self-concept.

Let's focus specifically for a moment on the Apple Computer mission statement. Note that the statement does not include coverage of the customer component, which could be individuals, businesses, educational institutions, and governmental agencies. Apple's statement does include the products/services component in saying that Apple provides "exceptional personal computing products and innovative customer services." The statement includes coverage of the market component in saying that Apple helps "people around the world" and includes the technology component in saying that the company finds "innovative ways to use computing technology." No mention of concern for survival, growth, and profitability is given in the statement. Nor is coverage of the philosophy, concern for public image, or concern for employees components. The Apple mission statement includes

TABLE 3–2
Examples of the Nine Essential Components of a Mission Statement

1. CUSTOMERS

We believe our first responsibility is to the doctors, nurses, and patients, to mothers and all others who use our products and services. (Johnson & Johnson)

2. PRODUCTS OR SERVICES

AMAX's principal products are molybdenum, coal, iron ore, copper, lead, zinc, petroleum and natural gas, potash, phosphates, nickel, tungsten, silver, gold, and magnesium. (AMAX)

Standard Oil Company (Indiana) is in business to find and produce crude oil, natural gas, and natural gas liquids; to manufacture high-quality products useful to society from these raw materials; and to distribute and market those products and to provide dependable related services to the consuming public at reasonable prices. (Standard Oil Company)

3. MARKETS

We are dedicated to the total success of Corning Glass Works as a worldwide competitor. (Corning Glass Works)

Our emphasis is on North American markets, although global opportunities will be explored. (Blockway)

4. TECHNOLOGY

Control Data is in the business of applying micro-electronics and computer technology in two general areas: computer-related hardware; and computing-enhancing services, which include computation, information, education, and finance. (Control Data)

The common technology in these areas is discrete particle coatings. (Nashua)

5. CONCERN FOR SURVIVAL, GROWTH, AND PROFITABILITY

In this respect, the company will conduct its operations prudently, and will provide the profits and growth which will assure Hoover's ultimate success. (Hoover Universal)

To serve the worldwide need for knowledge at a fair profit by gathering, evaluating, producing, and distributing valuable information in a way that benefits our customers, employees, authors, investors, and our society. (McGraw-Hill)

6. PHILOSOPHY

We believe human development to be the worthiest of the goals of civilization and independence to be the superior condition for nurturing growth in the capabilities of people. (Sun Company)

It's all part of the Mary Kay philosophy—a philosophy based on the golden rule. A spirit of sharing and caring where people give cheerfully of their time, knowledge, and experience. (Mary Kay Cosmetics)

7. SELF-CONCEPT

Crown Zellerbach is committed to leapfrogging competition within 1,000 days by unleashing the constructive and creative abilities and energies of each of its employees. (Crown Zellerbach)

8. CONCERN FOR PUBLIC IMAGE

To share the world's obligation for the protection of the environment. (Dow Chemical)

To contribute to the economic strength of society and function as a good corporate citizen on a local, state, and national basis in all countries in which we do business. (Pfizer)

9. CONCERN FOR EMPLOYEES

To recruit, develop, motivate, reward, and retain personnel of exceptional ability, character, and dedication by providing good working conditions, superior leadership, compensation on the basis of performance, an attractive benefit program, opportunity for growth, and a high degree of employment security. (The Wachovia Corporation)

To compensate its employees with remuneration and fringe benefits competitive with other employment opportunities in its geographical area and commensurate with their contributions toward efficient corporate operations. (Public Service Electric and Gas Company)

coverage of self-concept by mentioning education, which is a segment of the industry that Apple does especially well. Overall, the Apple statement includes only three of the nine essential mission statement components.

In multidivisional organizations, strategists should ensure that divisional units perform strategic-management tasks, including the development of a statement of mission.

TABLE 3–3
Mission Statements of Eleven Organizations

AMERICAN HOME PRODUCTS (www.ahp.com)

American Home Products Corporation makes a significant contribution to health care worldwide as a leader in researching, developing, manufacturing and marketing products that meet important health needs.

Our prescription drugs, nutritionals, over-the-counter medications, and medical devices, supplies and instrumentation benefit millions of people. We also produce and market well-known quality food brands in the United States and Canada.

We are focused on improving health care by finding and commercializing innovative, cost-effective therapies and technologies. Key to our efforts are efficient manufacturing, global distribution and marketing, and strict financial controls.

In 1992, American Home Products Corporation achieved record sales and earnings, and the company increased its dividend for the 41st consecutive year.

PFIZER, INC. (www.pfizer.com/main.html)

Pfizer, Inc. is a research-based, global health care company. Our principal mission is to apply scientific knowledge to help people around the world enjoy longer, healthier and more productive lives. The company has four business segments: health care, consumer health care, food science and animal health. We manufacture in 39 countries, and our products are available worldwide.

CHASE MANHATTAN CORPORATION (www.chase.com)

We provide financial services that enhance the well-being and success of individuals, industries, communities and countries around the world.

Through our shared commitment to those we serve, we will be the best financial services company in the world.

Customers will choose us first because we deliver the highest quality service and performance.

People will be proud and eager to work here.

Investors will buy our stock as a superior long-term investment.

To be the best for our customers, we are team players who show respect for our colleagues and commit to the highest standards of quality and professionalism.

Customer focus

Respect for each other

Teamwork

Quality

Professionalism

FOOD LION, INC. (www.foodlion.com)

The Food Lion team will work hard to use our *talents* and *resourcefulness* to satisfy every customer by providing Extra Low Prices on a wide variety of quality products in a *clean*, *convenient*, and *friendly* environment.

APPLE COMPUTER (www.apple.com)

It is Apple's mission to help transform the way customers work, learn and communicate by providing exceptional personal computing products and innovative customer services.

We will pioneer new directions and approaches, finding innovative ways to use computing technology to extend the bounds of human potential.

Apple will make a difference: our products, services and insights will help people around the world shape the ways business and education will be done in the 21st century.

AT&T (www.att.com)

We are dedicated to being the world's best at bringing people together—giving them easy access to each other and to the information and services they want—anytime, anywhere.

BANCORP HAWAII, INC. (www.boh.com/news/970220.html)

The mission of Bancorp Hawaii is to be the finest, most effective financial services organization in the state of Hawaii and the Pacific markets we serve.

As a family of companies built around an outstanding regional bank, we will sell and deliver a broad range of services that meet the needs of our customers at prices which are competitive and consistent with our profit goals.

Our basic business strategy is to identify, understand and then satisfy the financial needs and wants of consumers, businesses, and governments. We will be alert to changes which impact our businesses and exercise initiative to capitalize on new opportunities.

The geographic scope of our business will be expanded only to areas where our unique background, experience and capabilities will give us a competitive advantage and a reasonable opportunity for an adequate financial return. We will introduce only those new financial services which we can perform well.

continued

TABLE 3–3 *continued*

Two primary goals are to achieve significant reductions in noninterest expense through enhanced productivity and automation and to increase noninterest income by marketing fee-based services.

We want to conduct our business under conditions largely determined by ourselves and will, therefore, always maintain a strong financial position. Our goal is to consistently rank among the top 10 percent of our peer group in terms of financial performance. This will ensure that we will fulfill our responsibility to increase the value of our shareholders' investment.

We will maintain a stimulating work environment—one that encourages, recognizes, and rewards high achievers, at all levels of the organization.

We will always conduct ourselves with integrity and endeavor to be a good neighbor and a responsible corporate citizen.

BELLSOUTH CORPORATION (www.bellsouth.com)

BellSouth Corporation provides information services in local exchange and exchange access markets in its nine-state franchised territory. It also provides communications services and products such as advertising and publishing, mobile cellular telephone service, paging, and telecommunications and computer systems through its entities, in both the nine-state region and other major U.S. and international markets.

CORNING, INC. (www.corning.com)

Our purpose is to deliver superior, long-range economic benefits to our customers, our employees, our shareholders, and to the communities in which we operate. We accomplish this by living our corporate values.

NICHOLLS STATE UNIVERSITY (COLLEGE OF BUSINESS) (www.server.nich.edu/~nsu)

The principal mission of the College of Business is to prepare students to participate in society and the work force as educated individuals able to compete in a dynamic global economy. In order to enrich the learning process, the College also contributes to scholarship through applied research and instructional development. In addition to providing support to the employer community through the development of marketable skills in potential employees, the College also enhances the competitive capabilities of regional businesses by providing continuing education courses and consulting services through the Small Business Development Center (SBDC) and the individual efforts of faculty. The faculty advances the welfare of the University, the community, and academic and professional organizations through professional interactions.

SAM HOUSTON STATE UNIVERSITY (COLLEGE OF BUSINESS ADMINISTRATION) (www.shsu.edu)

The mission of the College of Business Administration is to support Sam Houston State University's mission by providing students with the educational experience in the field of business necessary to become productive citizens, to develop successful business-related careers and to provide interested students with the background necessary to pursue advanced studies in the field of business and related fields. The educational experience at the undergraduate and master's levels is designed to provide students with the intellectual flexibility to be successful in a dynamic business environment.

The highest priority of the College of Business Administration is teaching, primarily at the undergraduate level. In addition, the College encourages faculty professional development, scholarly productivity, and service to benefit all stakeholders: students, alumni, donors, regional businesses, and the State of Texas.

Each division should involve its own managers and employees in developing a mission statement consistent with and supportive of the corporative mission. Anchor Hocking is an example of a multinational organization that has developed an overall corporate mission statement and a statement for each of its eight divisions. Notice that the Nicholls State and Sam Houston State mission statements that are given in Table 3–3 are for those in situations at the College of Business rather than in the university at large.

An organization that fails to develop a comprehensive and inspiring mission statement loses the opportunity to present itself favorably to existing and potential stakeholders. All organizations need customers, employees, and managers, and most firms need creditors, suppliers, and distributors. The business mission statement is an effective vehicle for communicating with important internal and external stakeholders. The principal value of a mission statement as a tool of strategic management is derived from its specification of the ultimate aims of a firm:

It provides managers with a unity of direction that transcends individual, parochial, and transitory needs. It promotes a sense of shared expectations among all levels and generations of

TABLE 3–4

An Evaluation Matrix of Mission Statements

		EVALUATIVE CRITERIA			
COMPANY	CUSTOMERS	PRODUCTS/ SERVICES	MARKETS	CONCERN FOR SURVIVAL, GROWTH, AND PROFITABILITY	TECHNOLOGY
American Home Products	Yes	Yes	Yes	Yes	Yes
Pfizer, Inc.	Yes	Yes	Yes	No	No
Chase Manhattan Corporation	Yes	Yes	Yes	No	Yes
Food Lion, Inc.	Yes	No	No	No	No
Apple Computer	No	No	Yes	Yes	No
AT&T	No	No	Yes	No	No
Bancorp Hawaii, Inc.	Yes	Yes	Yes	No	Yes
BellSouth Corporation	No	Yes	Yes	No	No
Corning, Inc.	No	No	No	No	No
Nicholls State University	Yes	Yes	No	No	No
Sam Houston State University	Yes	Yes	Yes	No	No

COMPANY	PHILOSOPHY	SELF-CONCEPT	CONCERN FOR PUBLIC IMAGE	CONCERN FOR EMPLOYEES
American Home Products	No	Yes	No	No
Pfizer, Inc.	No	No	No	No
Chase Manhattan Corporation	Yes	Yes	Yes	Yes
Food Lion, Inc.	No	Yes	No	No
Apple Computer	No	Yes	No	No
AT&T	No	Yes	No	No
Bancorp Hawaii, Inc.	Yes	Yes	Yes	Yes
BellSouth Corporation	No	No	No	No
Corning, Inc.	Yes	No	Yes	Yes
Nicholls State University	No	Yes	Yes	Yes
Sam Houston State University	No	Yes	Yes	Yes

employees. It consolidates values over time and across individuals and interest groups. It projects a sense of worth and intent that can be identified and assimilated by company outsiders. Finally, it affirms the company's commitment to responsible action, which is symbiotic with its need to preserve and protect the essential claims of insiders for sustained survival, growth, and profitability of the firm.[17]

CONCLUSION

Every organization has a unique purpose and reason for being. This uniqueness should be reflected in a statement of mission. The nature of a business mission can represent either a competitive advantage or disadvantage for the firm. An organization achieves a heightened sense of purpose when strategists, managers, and employees develop and communicate a clear business mission. Drucker says developing a clear business mission is the "first responsibility of strategists." A good mission statement reveals an organization's customers, products or services, markets, technology, concern for survival, philosophy, self-concept, concern for public image, and concern for employees. These nine basic components serve as a practical framework for evaluating and writing mission statements. As the first step in strategic management, the mission statement provides direction for all planning activities.

A well-designed mission statement is essential for formulating, implementing, and evaluating strategy. Developing and communicating a clear business mission is one of the most commonly overlooked tasks in strategic management. Without a clear statement of mission, a firm's short-term actions can be counterproductive to long-term interests. A mission statement always should be subject to revision but, if carefully prepared, it will require major changes only infrequently. Organizations usually reexamine their mission statement annually. Effective mission statements stand the test of time.

A mission statement is an essential tool for strategists, a fact illustrated in a short story told by Porsche CEO Peter Schultz:

> Three people were at work on a construction site. All were doing the same job, but when each was asked what his job was, the answers varied. "Breaking rocks," the first replied, "Earning a living," responded the second. "Helping to build a cathedral," said the third. Few of us can build cathedrals. But to the extent we can see the cathedral in whatever cause we are following, the job seems more worthwhile. Good strategists and a clear mission help us find those cathedrals in what otherwise could be dismal issues and empty causes.[18]

We invite you to visit the DAVID page on the Prentice Hall Web site at
www.prenhall.com/davidsm
for this chapter's World Wide Web exercise.

KEY TERMS AND CONCEPTS

Concern for Employees	(p. 90)	Markets	(p. 89)	Self-Concept	(p. 90)
Concern for Public Image	(p. 90)	Mission Statement	(p. 80)	Social Policy	(p. 89)
Concern for Survival, Growth,		Mission Statement Components	(p. 89)	Stakeholders	(p. 85)
and Profitability	(p. 90)	Philosophy	(p. 90)	Technology	(p. 89)
Creed Statement	(p. 80)	Products or Services	(p. 89)	Vision Statement	(p. 83)
Customers	(p. 89)				

ISSUES FOR REVIEW AND DISCUSSION

1. Do local service stations need to have written mission statements? Why or why not?

2. Why do you think organizations that have a comprehensive mission tend to be high performers? Does having a comprehensive mission cause high performance?

3. Explain why a mission statement should not include strategies and objectives.

4. What is your college or university's self-concept? How would you state that in a mission statement?

5. Explain the principal value of a mission statement.

6. Why is it important for a mission statement to be reconciliatory?

7. In your opinion, what are the three most important components to include in writing a mission statement? Why?

8. How would the mission statements of a for-profit and a nonprofit organization differ?

9. Write a business mission statement for an organization of your choice.

10. Go to your nearest library and look in the annual reports of corporations. Find a mission statement, make a photocopy of the document, bring the copy to class, and evaluate the document.

11. Who are the major stakeholders of the bank that you do business with locally? What are the major claims of those stakeholders?

12. Select one of the current readings at the end of this chapter. Look up that article in your college library and give a 5-minute oral report to the class summarizing the article.

NOTES

1. Peter Drucker, *Management: Tasks, Responsibilities, and Practices* (New York: Harper & Row, 1974): 61.

2. Barnett Bank, Internal document (1993).

3. Vern McGinnis, "The Mission Statement: A Key Step in Strategic Planning," *Business* 31, no. 6 (November–December 1981): 41.

4. Fred David, "How Companies Define Their Mission," *Long Range Planning* 22, no. 1 (February 1989): 90–92. Also, see John Pearce II and Fred David, "Corporate Mission Statements: The Bottom Line," *Academy of Management Executive* 1, no. 2 (May 1987): 110.

5. Pearce and David, 110.

6. W. R. King and D. I. Cleland, *Strategic Planning and Policy* (New York: Van Nostrand Reinhold, 1979): 124.

7. Brian Dumaine, "What the Leaders of Tomorrow See," *Fortune* (July 3, 1989): 50.

8. Joseph Quigley, "Vision: How Leaders Develop It, Share It and Sustain It," *Business Horizons* (September–October 1994): 39.

9. Andrew Campbell and Sally Yeung, "Creating a Sense of Mission," *Long Range Planning* 24, no. 4 (August 1991): 17.

10. George Steiner, *Strategic Planning: What Every Manager Must Know* (New York: The Free Press, 1979): 160.

11. Drucker, 78, 79.

12. "How W. T. Grant Lost $175 Million Last Year," *Business Week* (February 25, 1975): 75.

13. Drucker, 88.

14. Drucker, 61.

15. Archie Carroll and Frank Hoy, "Integrating Corporate Social Policy into Strategic Management," *Journal of Business Strategy* 4, no. 3 (Winter 1984): 57.

16. The Norton Company, *Annual Report* (1981).

17. John Pearce II, "The Company Mission as a Strategic Tool," *Sloan Management Review* 23, no. 3 (Spring 1982): 74.

18. Robert Waterman, Jr., *The Renewal Factor: How the Best Get and Keep the Competitive Edge* (New York: Bantam, 1987). Also, *Business Week* (September 14, 1987): 120.

CURRENT READINGS

Baetz, Mark C. and Christopher K. Bart. "Developing Mission Statements Which Work." *Long Range Planning* 29, no. 4 (August 1996): 526–533.

Bartlett, Christopher A. and Sumantra Ghoshal. "Changing the Role of Top Management: Beyond Strategy to Purpose." *Harvard Business Review* (November–December 1994): 79–90.

Brabet, Julienne and Mary Klemm. "Sharing the Vision: Company Mission Statements in Britain and France." *Long Range Planning* (February 1994): 84–94.

Collins, James C. and Jerry I. Porras. "Building a Visionary Company." *California Management Review* 37, no. 2 (Winter 1995): 80–100.

Collins, James C. and Jerry I. Porras. "Building Your Company's Vision." *Harvard Business Review* (September–October 1996): 65–78.

Cummings, Stephen and John Davies. "Brief Case—Mission, Vision, Fusion." *Long Range Planning* 27, no. 6 (December 1994): 147–150.

Davies, Stuart W. and Keith W. Glaister. "Business School Mission Statements—The Bland Leading the Bland?" *Long Range Planning* 30, no. 4 (August 1997): 594–604.

Gratton, Lynda. "Implementing a Strategic Vision—Key Factors for Success." *Long Range Planning* 29, no. 3 (June 1996): 290–303.

Graves, Samuel B. and Sandra A. Waddock. "Institutional Owners and Corporate Social Performance." *Academy of Management Journal* 37, no. 4 (August 1994): 1034–1046.

Hemphill, Thomas A. "Legislating Corporate Social Responsibility." *Business Horizons* 40, no. 2 (March–April 1997): 53–63.

Larwood, Laurie, Cecilia M. Falbe, Mark P. Kriger, and Paul Miesing. "Structure and Meaning of Organizational Vision." *Academy of Management Journal* 38, no. 3 (June 1995): 740–769.

McTavish, Ron. "One More Time: What Business Are You In?" *Long Range Planning* 28, no. 2 (April 1995): 49–60.

Osborne, Richard L. "Strategic Values: The Corporate Performance Engine." *Business Horizons* 39, no. 5 (September–October 1996): 41–47.

Oswald, S. L., K. W. Mossholder, and S. G. Harris. "Vision Salience and Strategic Involvement: Implications for Psychological Attachment to Organization and Job." *Strategic Management Journal* 15, no. 6 (July 1994): 477–490.

Snyder, Neil H. and Michelle Graves. "The Editor's Chair/Leadership and Vision." *Business Horizons* 37, no. 1 (January–February 1994): 1–7.

Swanson, Diane L. "Addressing a Theoretical Problem by Reorienting the Corporate Social Performance Model." *Academy of Management Review* 20, no. 1 (January 1995): 43–64.

EVALUATING MISSION STATEMENTS

PURPOSE

A business mission statement is an integral part of strategic management. It provides direction for formulating, implementing, and evaluating strategic activities. This exercise will give you practice evaluating mission statements, a skill that is prerequisite to writing a good mission statement.

INSTRUCTIONS

Step 1 Your instructor will select some or all of the following mission statements to evaluate. On a separate sheet of paper, construct an evaluation matrix like the one presented in Table 3–4. Evaluate the mission statements based on the nine criteria presented in the chapter.

Step 2 Record a *yes* in appropriate cells of the evaluation matrix when the respective mission statement satisfactorily meets the desired criteria. Record a *no* in appropriate cells when the respective mission statement does not meet the stated criteria.

MISSION STATEMENTS

Carolina Power & Light Company (www.cplc.com) It is the mission of the Carolina Power & Light Company to provide the best service to present and future customers at the lowest rates consistent with fair compensation to employees, a fair return to those who have invested in the Company, safety for employees and the public, reasonable protection of the environment, and the development of technology to provide future service. Through the development and contribution of all employees, to the maximum of their potential, the Company will assure total quality performance that results in the highest achievable levels of customer satisfaction and recognition for excellence.

Stetson University (www.stetson.edu) The mission at Stetson University is to provide an excellent education in an intellectually challenging and collaborative learning community. We pursue excellence through superior teaching, close student-faculty interaction, creative and scholarly activity, and programs solidly grounded in liberal learning. We seek academically talented students with leadership potential and records of personal growth and community service. We prepare them for rewarding careers, selective graduate and professional programs, and a lifetime of learning. Building on Stetson's Christian tradition, we pursue truth in an open and caring environment that is socially and religiously diverse. The University encourages all members of its community to be morally sensitive and effective citizens committed to active forms of social responsibility.

CSX Corporation (www.csx.com) CSX is a transportation company committed to being a leader in railroad, inland water, and containerized distribution markets.

To attract the human and financial resources necessary to achieve this leadership position, CSX will support our three major constituencies:

> For our customers, we will work as a partner to provide excellent service and meet all agreed-upon commitments. For our employees, we will create a work environment that motivates and allows them to grow and develop and perform their jobs to the maximum of their capacity.

For our shareholders, we will meet our goals to provide them with sustainable superior returns.

University of North Carolina at Chapel Hill (www.unc.edu) The University of North Carolina at Chapel Hill has been built by the people of the state and has existed for two centuries as the nation's first state university. Through its excellent undergraduate programs, it has provided higher education to ten generations of students, many of whom have become leaders of the State and the nation. Since the nineteenth century it has offered distinguished graduate and professional programs.

The university is a research university. Fundamental to this designation is a faculty actively involved in research, scholarship, and creative work, whose teaching is transformed by discovery and whose service is informed by current knowledge.

The mission of the university is to serve all the people of the state, and indeed the nation, as a center for scholarship and creative endeavor. The university exists to expand the body of knowledge; to teach students at all levels in an environment of research, free inquiry, and personal responsibility; to improve the condition of human life through service and publication; and to enrich our culture.

To fulfill this mission, the university must

Acquire, discover, preserve, synthesize, and transmit knowledge.

Provide high quality undergraduate instruction to students within a community engaged in original inquiry and creative expression, while committed to intellectual freedom, to personal integrity and justice, and to those values that foster enlightened leadership for the state and the nation.

Provide graduate and professional programs of national distinction at the doctoral and other advanced levels to future generations of research scholars, educators, professionals, and informed citizens.

Extend knowledge-based services and other resources of the university to the citizens of North Carolina and their institutions to enhance the quality of life for all people in the State.

Address, as appropriate, regional, national, and international needs.

This mission imposes special responsibilities upon the faculty, students, staff, administration, trustees, and other governance structures and constituencies of the university in their service and decision-making on behalf of the university.

Federal Express (www.fedex.com) Federal Express is committed to our people-service-profit philosophy. We will produce outstanding financial returns by providing totally reliable, competitively superior global air-ground transportation of high-priority goods and documents that require rapid, time-certain delivery. Equally important, positive control of each package will be maintained utilizing real-time electronic tracking and tracing systems. A complete record of each shipment and delivery will be presented with our request for payment. We will be helpful, courteous, and professional to each other and the public. We will strive to have a satisfied customer at the end of each transaction.

Experiential Exercise 3B

WRITING A MISSION STATEMENT FOR HERSHEY FOODS

PURPOSE

There is no one best mission statement for a given organization. Analysts feel that the Hershey mission statement provided in the Cohesion Case can be improved. Writing a mission statement that includes desired components—and at the same time is inspiring and reconciliatory—requires careful thought. Mission statements should not be too lengthy; statements under 200 words are desirable.

INSTRUCTIONS

Step 1 Take 15 minutes to write a mission statement for Hershey Foods that does not exceed 200 words. Scan the case for needed details as you prepare your mission statement.

Step 2 Join with three other classmates to form a group of four people. Read each other's mission statements silently. As a group, select the best of your group's mission statements.

Step 3 Read that best mission statement to the class.

Experiential Exercise 3C

WRITING A MISSION STATEMENT FOR MY UNIVERSITY

PURPOSE

Most universities have a mission statement, as indicated by the examples provided in this chapter. The purpose of this exercise is to give you practice writing a mission statement for a nonprofit organization such as your own university.

INSTRUCTIONS

Step 1 Take 15 minutes to write a mission statement for your university. Your statement should not exceed 200 words.

Step 2 Read your mission statement to the class.

Step 3 Determine whether your institution has a mission statement. Look in the front of the college handbook. If your institution has a written statement, contact an appropriate administrator of the institution to inquire as to how and when the statement was prepared. Share this information with the class. Analyze your college's mission statement in light of concepts presented in this chapter.

Experiential Exercise 3D

CONDUCTING MISSION STATEMENT RESEARCH

PURPOSE

This exercise gives you the opportunity to study the nature and role of mission statements in strategic management.

INSTRUCTIONS

Step 1 Call various organizations in your city or county to identify firms that have developed a formal mission statement. Contact nonprofit organizations and government agencies in addition to small and large businesses. Ask to speak with the director, owner, or chief executive officer of one organization. Explain that you are studying mission statements in class and are conducting research as part of a class activity.

Step 2 Ask several executives the following four questions and record their answers.
   1. When did your organization first develop a formal mission statement? Who was primarily responsible for its development?

2. How long has your current mission statement existed? When was it last modified? Why was it modified at that point in time?
3. By what process is your firm's mission statement altered?
4. How is your mission statement used in the firm? How does it affect the firm's strategic-planning process?

Step 3 Provide an overview of your findings to the class.

Experiential Exercise 3E

ARE MISSION STATEMENTS ESOTERIC?

PURPOSE

Some large American corporations have publicly denounced the importance of having a clear mission. Louis Gerstner, CEO of IBM, recently said, "The last thing IBM needs now is a vision." Robert Eaton, CEO of Chrysler, recently said, "Internally we don't use the word vision (mission). I believe in quantifiable short-term results—things we can all relate to—as opposed to some esoteric thing no one can quantify." Bill Gates, CEO of Microsoft Corporation, recently said, "Being a visionary (concerned with mission) is trivial." Douglas Lavin of *The Wall Street Journal* recently said, "Vision (mission) may not exactly be dead in corporate America, but a surprising number of CEOs are casting aside their crystal balls to concentrate on the nuts-and-bolts of running their businesses in these leaner times; CEOs whose notion of vision (mission) is a sharp eye on the bottom line include Ronald Compton at Aetna Life & Casualty and John Smith, Jr., at General Motors."

This exercise is adapted from "Robert Eaton Thinks 'Vision' Is Overrated and He's Not Alone," *The Wall Street Journal* (Oct. 4, 1993): A1, A8.

INSTRUCTIONS

Step 1 Decide whether you agree or disagree with the CEO comments cited above. Do you agree with these persons that mission statements are esoteric or a matter for crystal balls? Discuss this issue with several local business executives.

Step 2 Write a 2-page essay explaining your personal views regarding the importance of mission statements.

Step 3 Summarize your views in a 1-minute presentation to the class.

The External Assessment

CHAPTER OBJECTIVES

After studying this chapter, you should be able to do the following:

1. Describe how to conduct an external strategic-management audit.

2. Discuss 10 major external forces that affect organizations: economic, social, cultural, demographic, environmental, political, governmental, legal, technological, and competitive.

3. Identify key sources of external information, including the Internet.

4. Discuss important forecasting tools used in strategic management.

5. Discuss the importance of monitoring external trends and events.

6. Explain how to develop an EFE Matrix.

7. Explain how to develop a Competitive Profile Matrix.

8. Discuss the importance of gathering competitive intelligence.

9. Describe the trend toward cooperation among competitors.

If you're not faster than your competitor, you're in a tenuous position, and if you're only half as fast, you're terminal.—GEORGE SALK

Positive trends in the environment breed complacency. That underscores a basic point: In change there is both opportunity and challenge.—CLIFTON GARVIN

The opportunities and threats existing in any situation always exceed the resources needed to exploit the opportunities or avoid the threats. Thus, strategy is essentially a problem of allocating resources. If strategy is to be successful, it must allocate superior resources against a decisive opportunity.—WILLIAM COHEN

Organizations pursue strategies that will disrupt the normal course of industry events and forge new industry conditions to the disadvantage of competitors.—IAN C. MACMILLAN

The idea is to concentrate our strength against our competitor's relative weakness.—BRUCE HENDERSON

There was a time in America when business was easier. We set the pace for the rest of the world. We were immune to serious foreign competition. Many of us were regulated therefore protected. No longer. Today's leaders must recreate themselves and their ways of doing business in order to stay on top and stay competitive.—ROBERT H. WATERMAN, JR.

Competitive strategy must grow out of a sophisticated understanding of the rules of competition that determine an industry's attractiveness.—MICHAEL PORTER

The main reason for Japan's industrial might is that Japan leads the world in devising ways of creating products derived from basic technologies. America is by no means lacking in technology. But it does lack the creativity to apply new technologies commercially. This is America's biggest problem. On the other hand, it is Japan's strongest point.—AKIO MORITA

*"W*ith the rise of the Internet, a broad shift is underway to a culture that values collaboration and community—attributes more hospitable to women. Ted Leonsis, president of AOL's content division, says the numbers prove this trend: AOL's female membership has grown from 18 percent to 45 percent in the past 2 years."[1]

This chapter examines the tools and concepts needed to conduct an external strategic-management audit (sometimes called *environmental scanning* or *industry analysis*). An *external audit* focuses on identifying and evaluating trends and events beyond the control of a single firm, such as increased foreign competition, population shifts to the Sunbelt, an aging society, information technology, and the computer revolution. An external audit reveals key opportunities and threats confronting an organization so that managers can formulate strategies to take advantage of the opportunities and avoid or reduce the impact of threats. This chapter presents a practical framework for gathering, assimilating, and analyzing external information.

THE NATURE OF AN EXTERNAL AUDIT

The purpose of an external audit is to develop a finite list of opportunities that could benefit a firm and threats that should be avoided. As the term *finite* suggests, the external audit is not aimed at developing an exhaustive list of every possible factor that could influence the business; rather, it is aimed at identifying key variables that offer actionable responses. Firms should be able to respond either offensively or defensively to the factors by formulating strategies that take advantage of external opportunities or that minimize the impact of potential threats. Figure 4–1 illustrates how the external audit fits into the strategic-management process.

KEY EXTERNAL FORCES *External forces* can be divided into five broad categories: (1) economic forces; (2) social, cultural, demographic, and environmental forces; (3) political, governmental, and legal forces; (4) technological forces; and (5) competitive forces. Relationships among these forces and an organization are depicted in Figure 4–2. External trends and events significantly affect all products, services, markets, and organizations in the world.

Changes in external forces translate into changes in consumer demand for both industrial and consumer products and services. External forces affect the types of products developed, the nature of positioning and market segmentation strategies, the types of services offered, and the choice of businesses to acquire or sell. External forces directly affect both suppliers and distributors. Identifying and evaluating external opportunities and threats enables organizations to develop a clear mission, to design strategies to achieve long-term objectives, and to develop policies to achieve annual objectives.

Some organizations survive solely because they recognize and take advantage of external opportunities. For example, Larson Company in Tucson, Arizona, has capitalized upon the growing concern for our natural environment by creating naturalistic environments for zoos, aquariums, shopping centers, amusement parks, and resort hotels. Larson's sales have grown dramatically to over $20 million annually. Larson contends that large, flashy nature exhibits are a big tourist draw. The new Mirage hotel and casino in Las Vegas, for example, attributes its success to the extensive use of artificial environments, ranging from a giant aquarium behind the registration desk to a 60-foot-high volcano outside the hotel.

The increasing complexity of business today is evidenced by more countries' developing the capacity and will to compete aggressively in world markets. Foreign businesses and countries are willing to learn, adapt, innovate, and invent to compete successfully in

FIGURE 4–1
A Comprehensive Strategic-Management Model

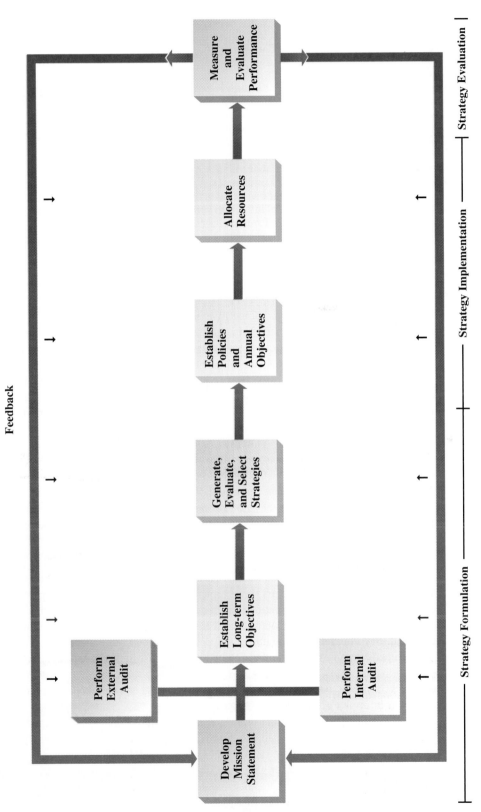

FIGURE 4–2

Relationships Between Key External Forces and an Organization

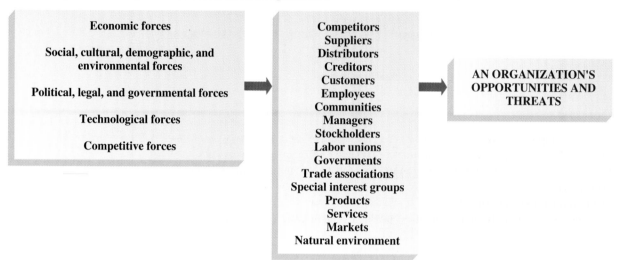

the marketplace. There are more competitive new technologies in Europe and the Far East today than ever before. American businesses can no longer beat foreign competitors with ease. For example, the world's four largest manufacturers of industrial and farm equipment are Mitsubishi of Japan, INI of Spain, Mannesmann of Germany, and BTR of Britain; the world's two largest jewelry and silverware companies are Citizen Watch and Seiko, both of Japan. In publishing and printing, no U.S. company ranks among the six largest; in textiles, no U.S. company ranks among the eight largest; in chemicals, only two U.S. firms (DuPont and Dow Chemical) rank in the top 12; in metals, only one U.S. firm (Alcoa) ranks among the largest 16 firms globally.

Most organizations practice some form of external analysis as part of their planning process. Nearly 75 percent of chief executive officers of the Fortune 500 companies reported that their firms performed external analysis and achieved numerous benefits from doing so.[2] Another 16 percent report that they do not have organized external analysis but probably should. Only 11 percent report that their firms do not conduct external audits and have no plans to begin.

THE PROCESS OF PERFORMING AN EXTERNAL AUDIT The process of performing an external audit must involve as many managers and employees as possible. As emphasized in earlier chapters, involvement in the strategic-management process can lead to understanding and commitment from organizational members. Individuals appreciate having the opportunity to contribute ideas and to gain a better understanding of their firm's industry, competitors, and markets.

To perform an external audit, a company first must gather competitive intelligence and information about social, cultural, demographic, environmental, economic, political, legal, governmental, and technological trends. Individuals can be asked to monitor various sources of information such as key magazines, trade journals, and newspapers. These persons can submit periodic scanning reports to a committee of managers charged with performing the external audit. This approach provides a continuous stream of timely strategic information and involves many individuals in the external-audit process. *On-line databases* provide another source for gathering strategic information, as do corporate, university, and public libraries. Suppliers, distributors, salespersons, customers, and competitors represent other sources of vital information.

Once information is gathered, it should be assimilated and evaluated. A meeting or series of meetings of up to 20 managers is needed to collectively identify the most important opportunities and threats facing the firm. Critical success factors should be listed on flip charts or a blackboard. A prioritized list of these factors could be obtained by requesting all managers to rank the factors identified, from 1 for the most important opportunity/threat to 20 for the least important opportunity/threat. *Critical success factors* can vary over time and by industry. Relationships with suppliers or distributors are often a critical success factor. Other variables commonly used include market share, breadth of competing products, world economies, foreign affiliates, proprietary and key account advantages, price competitiveness, technological advancements, population shifts, interest rates, and pollution abatement.

Freund emphasized that critical success factors should be (1) important to achieving long-term and annual objectives, (2) measurable, (3) relatively few in number, (4) applicable to all competing firms, and (5) hierarchical in the sense that some will pertain to the overall company and others will be more narrowly focused on functional or divisional areas.[3] A final list of the most important critical success factors should be communicated and distributed widely in the organization. Both opportunities and threats can be critical success factors.

INFORMATION TECHNOLOGY *Information technology (IT)* has become a powerful tool for conducting an external audit. The quantity and quality of industry and competitive information available to organizations has increased dramatically in recent years. Advanced computer technology, telecommunications, data access and storage devices, fax machines, on-line databases, graphics, and software represent efficient and effective vehicles for identifying and evaluating opportunities and threats. Effective use of the *Internet* as the information superhighway is becoming essential for business success.

The *World Wide Web* is a global network available via the Internet whereby an individual or firm can place information or advertisements for consumption by others around the world—or just within a corporation. Unlike other cyberspace services, Web pages can contain both text and nontext items, including sound clips, graphics, and even movies. Having a Web site in *cyberspace* can allow large savings in paper, copying, phone, and postage. The savings in advertising can be even higher. A Web browser such as Netscape Communications Navigator or America Online on a personal computer can allow anyone to look at what is stored on any Web server in the world.

Using the Internet can be the difference between formulation strategies based on up-to-date rather than out-of-date information. Consultants are readily available to provide assistance.

By the year 2000, millions of people and businesses will each own a small part of cyberspace; they will own their own Web site. Shouldn't your company have its own Web site and peruse the sites of competing companies, suppliers, distributors, and customers? The answer, increasingly, is *yes*. The proliferation of people and companies worldwide using the Web, however, is raising questions about invasion of privacy and breaches of security.

With both private and corporate connections to the Web proliferating, firms must take for granted that every computer on the planet can reach and interact with almost any other. Security and privacy are becoming more of a concern. Linking a firm's computer to cyberspace opens it to potentially millions of largely unidentified visitors, some of whom may have malicious, criminal, or otherwise unethical intent. Verification that senders or receivers on the Internet are who they say they are can be a challenge. A competitor could bombard your system with false messages and information.

The range of products and measures designed to enhance computer security is increasing daily. Software is now available that can generate a new password every few minutes, encrypt all outgoing messages with secret codes or keystrokes, or even block unwanted traffic arriving to your computer from the Internet. Yet, electronic commerce creates vast opportunities for tax evasion, money laundering, and other financial crimes. "There is potential for a serious challenge to the whole political and social order," says Nathaniel Borenstein. "I'm not that sanguine that the government has the control they think they do."

Information technology itself is changing the very nature of opportunities and threats by altering the life cycles of products, increasing the speed of distribution, creating new products and services, erasing limitations of traditional geographic markets, and changing the historical trade-off between production standardization and flexibility. IT is altering economies of scale, changing entry barriers, and redefining the relationship between industries and various suppliers, creditors, customers, and competitors. As an example, consider the airline industry's business travel market:

> Given the current rate of development in telecommunications and office technology, video conferences may become a major substitute for some business air travel soon. This would significantly affect the airline industry's business travel market. Strategists today must address a crucial question: What impact will IT have on our industry over the next five to ten years in terms of products and services, markets, and production economies?[4]

The era of the mainframe computer has given way to a proliferation of affordable microcomputers that are almost as powerful. This trend has created a new basis for competition in virtually all industries and generated new buyers, suppliers, products, and services. The microcomputer revolution especially represents an opportunity for innovative young companies. Entrenched industrial leaders face more competition than ever from small firms using advanced microcomputer technology.

To effectively capitalize on information technology, a number of organizations are establishing two new positions in their firms: *chief information officer (CIO)* and *chief technology officer (CTO)*. This trend reflects the growing importance of information technology in strategic management. A CIO and CTO work together to ensure that information needed to formulate, implement, and evaluate strategies is available where and when it is needed. These persons are responsible for developing, maintaining, and updating a company's information database. The CIO is more a manager, managing the overall external-audit process; the CTO is more a technician, focusing on technical issues such as data acquisition, data processing, decision support systems, and software and hardware acquisition.

ECONOMIC FORCES

In the late 1990s, the United States is benefiting from the best economic conditions in 50 years (U.S. Department of Commerce, www.doc.gov). A balanced federal government budget coupled with low inflation, low interest rates, and low unemployment benefit companies and consumers. Nine states now have no state income tax: Alaska, Florida, Nevada, New Hampshire, South Dakota, Tennessee, Texas, Washington, and Wyoming.

Increasing numbers of two-income households is an economic trend in America. As affluence increases, individuals place a premium on time. Improved customer service, immediate availability, trouble-free operation of products, and dependable maintenance and repair services are becoming more important. Americans today are more willing than ever to pay for good service if it limits inconvenience.

Economic factors have a direct impact on the potential attractiveness of various strategies. For example, if interest rates rise, then funds needed for capital expansion become more costly or unavailable. Also, as interest rates rise, discretionary income declines, and the demand for discretionary goods falls. As stock prices increase, the desirability of equity as a source of capital for market development increases. Also, as the market rises, consumer and business wealth expands. A summary of economic variables that often represent opportunities and threats for organizations is provided in Table 4–1.

Trends in the dollar's value have significant and unequal effects on companies in different industries and in different locations. For example, the pharmaceutical, tourism, entertainment, motor vehicle, aerospace, and forest products industries benefit greatly when the dollar falls against the yen, franc, and mark. Agricultural and petroleum industries are hurt by the dollar's rise against the currencies of Mexico, Brazil, Venezuela, and Australia. Generally, a strong or high dollar makes American goods more expensive on overseas markets. This worsens America's trade deficit. When the value of the dollar falls, tourism-oriented firms benefit because Americans do not travel abroad as much when the value of the dollar is low; rather, foreigners visit and vacation more in the United States. As indicated in the Global Perspective, more foreigners are visiting the United States to receive medical care. U.S. hospitals actively are marketing services to foreigners to capitalize on the rising economic level of many people in foreign countries.

A low value of the dollar means lower imports and higher exports; it helps U.S. companies' competitiveness in world markets. The years 1997 and 1998 have seen the U.S. dollar gaining against virtually every other currency. One benefit of this trend is that consumers pay less for imported goods such as cars and computer memory chips. Domestic firms that manufacture extensively outside the United States also benefit from the rising value of the dollar. If the U.S. budget deficit is cut further, the value of the dollar almost surely will continue to rise, to 150 yen perhaps.

Every business day, thousands of American workers learn that they will lose their jobs. More than 500,000 annual employee layoffs by U.S. firms in the 1990s has led to terms such as *downsizing, rightsizing,* and *decruiting* becoming common. European firms, too, are beginning to downsize. The U.S. and world economies face a sustained period of slow, low-inflationary expansion, global overcapacity, high unemployment, price wars, and increased competitiveness. Thousands of laid-off workers are being forced to become entrepreneurs to make a living. The United States is becoming more entrepreneurial every day.

TABLE 4–1
Key Economic Variables to Be Monitored

Shift to a service economy in the United States	Import/export factors
Availability of credit	Demand shifts for different categories of goods and services
Level of disposable income	Income differences by region and consumer groups
Propensity of people to spend	Price fluctuations
Interest rates	Exportation of labor and capital from the United States
Inflation rates	Monetary policies
Economies of scale	Fiscal policies
Money market rates	Tax rates
Federal government budget deficits	European Economic Community (ECC) policies
Gross domestic product trend	Organization of Petroleum Exporting Countries (OPEC) policies
Consumption patterns	Coalitions of Lesser Developed Countries (LDC) policies
Unemployment trends	
Worker productivity levels	
Value of the dollar in world markets	
Stock market trends	
Foreign countries' economic conditions	

SOCIAL, CULTURAL, DEMOGRAPHIC, AND ENVIRONMENTAL FORCES

Social, cultural, demographic, and environmental changes have a major impact upon virtually all products, services, markets, and customers. Small, large, for-profit and non-profit organizations in all industries are being staggered and challenged by the opportunities and threats arising from changes in social, cultural, demographic, and environmental variables. In every way, the United States is much different in 1999 than it was in 1989, and the year 2009 promises even greater changes.

The United States is getting older and less Caucasian, feeding generational and racial competition for jobs and government money. The gap between rich and poor is growing while the federal bureaucracy gets smaller. America's 76 million baby boomers plan to retire in 2011, and this has lawmakers and younger taxpayers deeply worried and concerned about who will pay their social security, medicare, and medicaid. Persons aged 65 and older in the United States will rise from 12.7 percent of the population to 18.5 percent between 1997 and 2025.

By the year 2075, the United States will have no racial or ethnic majority. This forecast is aggravating tensions over issues such as immigration and affirmative action. Hawaii and New Mexico already have no majority race or ethnic group and by the year 2000, neither will California.

In the year 2050, India is projected to have 1.53 billion people and to overtake China as the world's most populous nation. That year, the United States will have 394 million people. A list of the world's most populous countries is given on page 111.

Social, cultural, demographic, and environmental trends are shaping the way Americans live, work, produce, and consume. New trends are creating a different type of consumer and, consequently, a need for different products, different services, and different strategies. There are now more American households with people living alone or with unrelated people than there are households consisting of married couples with children. Census data suggest that Americans are not returning to traditional life-styles. Church membership fell substantially during the 1980s for nearly all religious denominations, except Southern Baptists and Mormons. It is interesting to note that Protestant churches in

RANK	COUNTRY	1996 POPULATION	RANK	COUNTRY	2025 POPULATION
1.	China	1,217.6	1.	China	1,492.0
2.	India	949.6	2.	India	1,384.6
3.	United States	265.2	3.	United States	335.1
4.	Indonesia	201.4	4.	Indonesia	276.5
5.	Brazil	160.5	5.	Nigeria	246.0
6.	Russia	147.7	6.	Pakistan	232.9
7.	Pakistan	133.5	7.	Brazil	202.3
8.	Japan	125.8	8.	Bangladesh	175.8
9.	Bangladesh	119.8	9.	Russia	153.1
10.	Nigeria	103.9	10.	Mexico	142.1

World's Most Populous Countries (*Estimated, in millions*)

the United States take in over $7 billion in donations annually. The eight largest U.S. church denominations are (in millions of members) Roman Catholic (60.3), Southern Baptist (15.7), National Baptist (11.7), United Methodist (8.5), Lutheran (5.2), Morman (4.7), Presbyterian (3.7), and Episcopalian (3.5).

Significant trends for the 1990s include consumers becoming more educated, the population aging, narcissism replacing the work ethic, minorities becoming more influential, people looking for local rather than federal solutions to problems, fixation on youth decreasing, more emphasis being placed on preserving the natural environment, and more women entering the workforce. The United States Census Bureau projects that the number of Hispanics will increase to 15 percent of the population by 2021, when they will become a larger minority group than African Americans in America. The percentage of African Americans in the U.S. population is expected to increase from 12 percent to 14 percent between 1996 and 2021. Many states currently have more than 500,000 Hispanics as registered voters, including California, New Mexico, Arizona, Texas, Florida, New York, Illinois, and New Jersey. The fastest-growing businesses in the United States are owned by women of color. From 1987 to 1996, the number of firms owned by African American, Asian, Latina, and Native American women increased by 153 percent to 1 million enterprises. Firms owned by women of color employ 1.7 million people and generate $184 billion in sales annually.

During the 1990s, the number of individuals aged 50 and over will increase 18.5 percent, to 76 million. In contrast, the number of Americans under age 50 will grow by just 3.5 percent. The number of babies born in the United States has declined annually since 1990 to a low of 3.7 million in 1998. The trend toward an older America is good news for restaurants, hotels, airlines, cruise lines, tours, resorts, theme parks, luxury products and services, recreational vehicles, home builders, furniture producers, computer manufacturers, travel services, pharmaceutical firms, automakers, and funeral homes. Older Americans are especially interested in health care, financial services, travel, crime prevention, and leisure. The world's longest-living people are the Japanese, with Japanese women living to 86.3 years and men living to 80.1 years on average.

The aging American population affects the strategic orientation of nearly all organizations. Apartment complexes for the elderly, with one meal a day, transportation, and utilities included in the rent, have increased to more than 200,000 units nationwide. Called *lifecare facilities*, these complexes are expected to increase in number to exceed 2 million by 2000. Some well-known companies building these facilities include Avon, Marriott, and Hyatt. By the year 2005, individuals aged 65 and older in the United States will rise to 13 percent of the total population; Japan's elderly population ratio will rise to 17 percent, and Germany's to 19 percent.

Americans are on the move in a population shift to the South and West (Sun Belt) and away from the Northeast and Midwest (Frost Belt). The Internal Revenue Service provides the Census Bureau with massive computer files of demographic data. By comparing individual address changes from year to year, the Census Bureau publishes extensive information about population shifts across the country. For example, Arizona will be the fastest-growing state during the 1990s as its population increases 23 percent. Nevada, New Mexico, and Florida are close behind with projected growth rates above 20 percent. Wyoming will remain the nation's least populated state and California the most populated state. Texas will replace New York as the most populous state. States incurring the greatest loss of people for the 1990s are North Dakota, Wyoming, Pennsylvania, Iowa, and West Virginia. This type of information can be essential for successful strategy formulation, including where to locate new plants and distribution centers and where to focus marketing efforts.

Americans are becoming less interested in fitness and exercise. Fitness participants declined in the United States by 3.5 percent annually in the 1990s. Makers of fitness products, such as Nike, Reebok International, and CML Group—which makes NordicTrack—are experiencing declines in sales growth. American Sports Data in Hartsdale, New York, reports that "the one American in five who exercises regularly is now outnumbered by three couch potatoes."

Mark Starik at George Washington University argues that with the thawing of the Cold War, no greater threat to business and society exists than the voracious, continuous decimation and degradation of our natural environment. The U.S. Clean Air Act went into effect in 1994. The U.S. Clean Water Act went into effect in 1984. As indicated in the Natural Environment Perspective, air and water pollution causes great anguish worldwide. A summary of important social, cultural, demographic, and environmental variables that represent opportunities or threats for virtually all organizations is given in Table 4–2.

TABLE 4–2
Key Social, Cultural, Demographic, and Environmental Variables

Childbearing rates	Attitudes toward retirement
Number of special interest groups	Attitudes toward leisure time
Number of marriages	Attitudes toward product quality
Number of divorces	Attitudes toward customer service
Number of births	Pollution control
Number of deaths	Attitudes toward foreign peoples
Immigration and emigration rates	Energy conservation
Social security programs	Social programs
Life expectancy rates	Number of churches
Per capita income	Number of church members
Location of retailing, manufacturing, and service businesses	Social responsibility
Attitudes toward business	Attitudes toward careers
Life-styles	Population changes by race, age, sex, and level of affluence
Traffic congestion	Attitudes toward authority
Inner-city environments	Population changes by city, county, state, region, and country
Average disposable income	Value placed on leisure time
Trust in government	Regional changes in tastes and preferences
Attitudes toward government	Number of women and minority workers
Attitudes toward work	Number of high school and college graduates by geographic area
Buying habits	Recycling
Ethical concerns	Waste management
Attitudes toward saving	Air pollution
Sex roles	Water pollution
Attitudes toward investing	Ozone depletion
Racial equality	Endangered species
Use of birth control	
Average level of education	
Government regulation	

NATURAL ENVIRONMENT
Is Your Business Polluting the Air or Water?

AIR

More than 1.5 billion people around the world live in urban areas with dangerous levels of air pollution. Alarmingly, cities are growing more rapidly than progress is being made to reverse this trend. Seven of the 10 worst cities for sulfur dioxide and carbon monoxide are in developing countries. These and other pollutants cause acute and chronic lung disease, heart disease, lung cancer, and lead-induced neurological damage in children. Lung cancer alone killed 989,000 people in 1996, and 1.32 million new cases of lung cancer were diagnosed that year. In the European Union countries, a 33 percent increase in female lung cancer cases is predicted by 2005. There is no effective treatment for lung cancer—only 10 percent of patients are alive 5 years after diagnosis. Polluted air knows no city, state, country, or continent boundaries.

The Environmental Protection Agency (EPA) wants to expand air pollution regulation in the United States to cover microscopic particles as tiny as 2.5 microns, down from the current standard of 10 microns. The EPA also wants to expand the allowable level of ozone from 0.12 parts per million cubic feet of air to 0.08 parts per million. The EPA says this will cut premature deaths in the United States by 20,000; cases of aggravated asthma by 250,000; cases of acute childhood respiratory problems by 250,000; bronchitis cases by 60,000; hospital admissions by 9,000; and cases of major breathing problems by 1.5 million. The total savings of these benefits would exceed $115 billion. Critics say the proposed new regulation will cost too much to U.S. companies and cities.

Source: Adapted from William Miller, "Clean-Air Contention," Industry Week (May 5, 1997): 14. Also, World Health Organization Report, 1997.

WATER

Is your business polluting the water? Contaminated water is blamed for as much as 80 percent of all disease in developing countries. Well over 1 billion people in the world still are without safe water to drink, bathe, cook, and clean. Less than 2 percent of the domestic and industrial wastewater generated in developing countries receives any kind of treatment. It just runs into rivers and groundwater resources, thus poisoning populations, the environment, and the planet. Unsafe drinking water is a prime cause of diarrhea, malaria, cancer, infant deformities, and infant mortality. A few statistics reveal the severity, harshness, and effect of water pollution.

- More than 5 million babies born in developing countries die annually in the first month of life, mainly due to polluted water.
- About 4 million babies are born with deformities annually.
- Diarrhea and dysentery kill 2.5 million people annually.
- Malaria kills 2.1 million people annually.

Industrial discharge, a major water problem even in the United States, contributes significantly to the dramatic rise in cancer both here and abroad. More than 10 million new cases of cancer are diagnosed annually and about 6.5 million people die of cancer annually. More than 1.2 billion of these deaths are due to stomach and colon cancer, two types often associated with poor water and eating habits. Besides deaths, the anguish, sickness, suffering, and expense inflicted upon people directly or indirectly due to contaminated water is immeasurably high even in the United States. Dangerous industrial chemicals are used here as fertilizers, pesticides, solvents, food additives, fuels, medicines, cosmetics, and in a wide range of manufacturing processes.

Source: Adapted from World Health Organization Report, 1997.

POLITICAL, GOVERNMENTAL, AND LEGAL FORCES

Federal, state, local, and foreign governments are major regulators, deregulators, subsidizers, employers, and customers of organizations. Political, governmental, and legal factors therefore can represent key opportunities or threats for both small and large organizations. For industries and firms that depend heavily on government contracts or subsidies, political forecasts can be the most important part of an external audit. Changes in patent laws, antitrust legislation, tax rates, and lobbying activities can affect firms significantly. The United States Justice Department offers excellent information at its Web site (www.justice2.usdoj.gov) on such topics.

In the world of biopolitics, Americans are still deeply divided over issues such as assisted suicide, genetic testing, genetic engineering, cloning, brain imaging technology, and even abortion. Such political issues have great ramifications for companies in many industries ranging from pharmaceuticals to computers.

The increasing global interdependence among economies, markets, governments, and organizations makes it imperative that firms consider the possible impact of political variables on the formulation and implementation of competitive strategies. A number of nationally known firms forecast political, governmental, and legal variables, including Frost & Sullivan, Probe International, and Arthur D. Little (ADL). ADL forecasts the political climate in foreign countries by examining five criteria: (1) social development, (2) technological advancement, (3) abundance of natural resources, (4) level of domestic tranquility, and (5) type of political system. ADL has found that political unrest follows whenever a country's development in any one of these areas gets too far ahead of the others. Ford, DuPont, Singer, and PepsiCo are among the many companies that use forecasts developed by outside firms to identify key political and governmental opportunities and threats.

Political forecasting can be especially critical and complex for multinational firms that depend on foreign countries for natural resources, facilities, distribution of products, special assistance, or customers. Strategists today must possess skills to deal more legalistically and politically than previous strategists, whose attention was directed more to economic and technical affairs of the firm. Strategists today are spending more time anticipating and influencing public policy actions. They spend more time meeting with government officials, attending hearings and government-sponsored conferences, giving public speeches, and meeting with trade groups, industry associations, and government agency directors. Before entering or expanding international operations, strategists need a good understanding of the political and decision-making processes in countries where their firm may conduct business. For example, republics that made up the former Soviet Union differ greatly in wealth, resources, language, and life-style.

To be considered legally intoxicated even varies considerably among countries. The maximum legal blood alcohol level (.01 percent equals one part alcohol to 10,000 parts blood) for driving in selected countries, with drinks per hour needed to reach it, are as follows:

	LIMIT	DRINKS
Sweden	.02%	2
Japan, France	.05%	3
United States (16 states), United Kingdom	.08%	4
Germany, Italy	.08%	4
United States (34 states, D.C.)	.10%	5

Note: A drink equals 1 oz. whiskey, 5 oz. wine, or 12 oz. beer.

Increasing global competition toward the year 2000 accents the need for accurate political, governmental, and legal forecasts. Many strategists will have to become familiar with political systems in Europe and Asia and with trading currency futures. East Asian countries already have become world leaders in labor-intensive industries. A world market has emerged from what previously was a multitude of distinct national markets, and the climate for international business today would be much more favorable than yesterday. Mass communication and high technology are creating similar patterns of consumption in diverse cultures worldwide! This means that many companies may find it difficult to survive by relying solely on domestic markets.

Government regulations or deregulations	Sino-American relationships
Changes in tax laws	Russian-American relationships
Special tariffs	European-American relationships
Political action committees	African-American relationships
Voter participation rates	Import-export regulations
Number, severity, and location of government protests	Government fiscal and monetary policy changes
Number of patents	Political conditions in foreign countries
Changes in patent laws	Special local, state, and federal laws
Environmental protection laws	Lobbying activities
Level of defense expenditures	Size of government budgets
Legislation on equal employment	World oil, currency, and labor markets
Level of government subsidies	Location and severity of terrorist activities
Antitrust legislation	Local, state, and national elections

TABLE 4–3
Some Political, Governmental, and Legal Variables

It is no exaggeration that in an industry that is, or is rapidly becoming, global, the riskiest possible posture is to remain a domestic competitor. The domestic competitor will watch as more aggressive companies use this growth to capture economies of scale and learning. The domestic competitor will then be faced with an attack on domestic markets using different (and possibly superior) technology, product design, manufacturing, marketing approaches, and economies of scale. A few examples suggest how extensive the phenomenon of world markets has already become. Hewlett-Packard's manufacturing chain reaches halfway around the globe, from well-paid, skilled engineers in California to low-wage assembly workers in Malaysia. General Electric has survived as a manufacturer of inexpensive audio products by centralizing its world production in Singapore.[5]

Local, state, and federal laws, regulatory agencies, and special interest groups can have a major impact on the strategies of small, large, for-profit, and nonprofit organizations. Many companies have altered or abandoned strategies in the past because of political or governmental actions. For example, many nuclear power projects have been halted and many steel plants shut down because of pressure from the Environmental Protection Agency (EPA). Other federal regulatory agencies include the Food and Drug Administration (FDA), the National Highway Traffic and Safety Administration (NHTSA), the Occupational Safety and Health Administration (OSHA), the Consumer Product Safety Commission (CPSC), the Federal Trade Commission (FTC), the Securities Exchange Commission (SEC), the Equal Employment Opportunity Commission (EEOC), the Federal Communications Commission (FCC), the Federal Maritime Commission (FMC), the Interstate Commerce Commission (ICC), the Federal Energy Regulatory Commission (FERC), the National Labor Relations Board (NLRB), and the Civil Aeronautics Board (CAB). A summary of political, governmental, and legal variables that can represent key opportunities or threats to organizations is provided in Table 4–3.

TECHNOLOGICAL FORCES

Revolutionary technological changes and discoveries such as superconductivity, computer engineering, thinking computers, robotics, unstaffed factories, miracle drugs, space communications, space manufacturing, lasers, cloning, satellite networks, fiber optics, biometrics, and electronic funds transfer are having a dramatic impact on organizations. Superconductivity advancements alone, which increase the power of electrical products by lowering resistance to current, are revolutionizing business operations, especially in the transportation, utility, health care, electrical, and computer industries.

Microprocesser-based equipment and process technologies, such as computer-aided design and manufacturing (CAD/CAM), direct numerical control (DNC), computer-centralized numerical control (CNC), flexible production centers (FPC), equipment and process technology (EPT), and computer-integrated manufacturing (CIM), are burgeoning.

Technological forces represent major opportunities and threats that must be considered in formulating strategies. Technological advancements dramatically can affect organizations' products, services, markets, suppliers, distributors, competitors, customers, manufacturing processes, marketing practices, and competitive position. Technological advancements can create new markets, result in a proliferation of new and improved products, change the relative competitive cost positions in an industry, and render existing products and services obsolete. Technological changes can reduce or eliminate cost barriers between businesses, create shorter production runs, create shortages in technical skills, and result in changing values and expectations of employees, managers, and customers. Technological advancements can create new *competitive advantages* that are more powerful than existing advantages. No company or industry today is insulated against emerging technological developments. In high-tech industries identification and evaluation of key technological opportunities and threats can be the most important part of the external strategic-management audit.

Organizations that traditionally have limited technology expenditures to what they can fund after meeting marketing and financial requirements urgently need a reversal in thinking. The pace of technological change is increasing and literally wiping out businesses every day. An emerging consensus holds that technology management is one of the key responsibilities of strategists. Firms should pursue strategies that take advantage of technological opportunities to achieve sustainable, competitive advantages in the marketplace.

> Technology-based issues will underlie nearly every important decision that strategists make. Crucial to those decisions will be the ability to approach technology planning analytically and strategically. . . . technology can be planned and managed using formal techniques similar to those used in business and capital investment planning. An effective technology strategy is built on a penetrating analysis of technology opportunities and threats, and an assessment of the relative importance of these factors to overall corporate strategy.[6]

In practice, critical decisions about technology too often are delegated to lower organizational levels or are made without an understanding of their strategic implications. Many strategists spend countless hours determining market share, positioning products in terms of features and price, forecasting sales and market size, and monitoring distributors; yet too often technology does not receive the same respect:

> The impact of this oversight is devastating. Firms not managing technology to ensure their futures may eventually find their futures managed by technology. Technology's impact reaches far beyond the "high-tech" companies. Although some industries may appear to be relatively technology-insensitive in terms of products and market requirements, they are not immune from the impact of technology; companies in smokestack as well as service industries must carefully monitor emerging technological opportunities and threats.[7]

Not all sectors of the economy are affected equally by technological developments. The communications, electronics, aeronautics, and pharmaceutical industries are much more volatile than the textile, forestry, and metals industries. For strategists in industries affected by rapid technological change, identifying and evaluating technological opportunities and threats can represent the most important part of an external audit.

Some technological advancements expected before the year 2000 in the computer and medical industry are computers that recognize handwriting; voice-controlled computers; gesture-controlled computers; color faxes; picture phones; and defeat of heart disease, AIDS, rheumatoid arthritis, multiple sclerosis, leukemia, and lung cancer. New technological advancements in the computer industry alone are revolutionizing the way businesses operate today.

COMPETITIVE FORCES

The top five U.S. competitors in four different industries are identified in Table 4–4. An important part of an external audit is identifying rival firms and determining their strengths, weaknesses, capabilities, opportunities, threats, objectives, and strategies.

Collecting and evaluating information on competitors is essential for successful strategy formulation. Identifying major competitors is not always easy because many firms have divisions that compete in different industries. Most multidivisional firms generally do not provide sales and profit information on a divisional basis for competitive reasons. Also, privately held firms do not publish any financial or marketing information.

Despite the problems mentioned above, information on leading competitors in particular industries can be found in publications such as *Moody's Manuals, Standard Corporation Descriptions, Value Line Investment Surveys, Ward's Business Directory, Dun's Business Rankings, Standard & Poor's Industry Surveys, Industry Week, Forbes, Fortune,*

TABLE 4–4

The Top Five U.S. Competitors in Four Different Industries in 1997

	1997 SALES IN $ MILLIONS	PERCENTAGE CHANGE FROM 1996	1997 PROFITS IN $ MILLIONS	PERCENTAGE CHANGE FROM 1996
AEROSPACE				
Boeing	45,800.0	+29	−178.0	NM
Lockheed Martin	28,069.0	+4	+1,300.0	−3
United Technologies	24,713.0	+5	+1,072.0	+18
Northrop Grumman	9,153.0	+6	+407.0	+54
General Dynamics	4,062.0	+13	+316.0	+17
FOREST PRODUCTS				
International Paper	20,115.0	0	−151.0	NM
Georgia-Pacific	12,968.0	+1	−86.0	NM
Kimberly-Clark	12,546.6	−5	+884.0	−37
Fort James	7,259.0	−6	+104.5	−68
Champion International	5,735.5	−2	−548.5	NM
COMPUTERS				
IBM	78,508.0	+3	+6,093.0	+12
Hewlett-Packard	42,895.0	+12	+3,119.0	+21
Compaq Computer	24,584.0	+23	+1,855.0	+41
Xerox	18,166.0	+5	+1,452.0	+20
Digital Equipment	13,062.2	−4	+274.8	NM
PUBLISHING				
Time Warner	13,294.0	+32	+301.0	NM
CBS	5,363.0	+29	−131.0	NM
Gannett	4,729.5	+7	+712.7	+14
McGraw-Hill	3,534.1	+15	+290.7	−41
Times Mirror	3,318.5	−2	+250.3	−21

Source: Adapted from Corporate Scoreboard, *Business Week* (March 2, 1998): 113–136.
NM: Not Measurable

Business Week, and *Inc.* In addition, the *Million Dollar Directory* lists key personnel, products, divisions, and SIC codes for over 160,000 U.S. public and private companies whose revenues exceed $500,000. *Standard & Poor's Register of Corporate Directors and Executives* and the *Directory of Corporate Affiliations* are other excellent sources of competitive information. However, many businesses use the Internet to obtain most of their information on competitors. The Internet is fast, thorough, accurate, and increasingly indispensable in this regard. Questions about competitors such as those presented in Table 4–5 are important to address in performing an external audit.

Competition in virtually all industries can be described as intense, and sometimes cutthroat. For example, when United Parcel Service (UPS) employees were on strike in 1997, competitors such as Federal Express, Greyhound, Roadway, and United Airlines lowered prices, doubled advertising efforts, and locked new customers into annual contracts in efforts to leave UPS customer-less when the strike ended. UPS still is struggling to regain its former market share. If a firm detects weakness in a competitor, no mercy at all is shown in capitalizing on its problems.

Seven characteristics describe the most competitive companies in America: (1) Market share matters; the 90th share point isn't as important as the 91st, and nothing is more dangerous than falling to 89; (2) Understand and remember precisely what business you are in; (3) Whether it's broke or not, fix it—make it better; not just products, but the whole company if necessary; (4) Innovate or evaporate; particularly in technology-driven businesses, nothing quite recedes like success; (5) Acquisition is essential to growth; the most successful purchases are in niches that add a technology or a related market; (6) People make a difference; tired of hearing it? Too bad; (7) There is no substitute for quality and no greater threat than failing to be cost-competitive on a global basis; these are complementary concepts, not mutually exclusive ones.[8]

COMPETITIVE INTELLIGENCE PROGRAMS   Senator William Cohen (R-Maine) says, "When France, Germany, Japan, and South Korea are included in a list of nations, we automatically assume that this must be a list of America allies—our military and political partners since the end of the World War II. Unfortunately, this is not only a list of America's trustworthy friends, it is a list of governments that have systematically practiced economic espionage against American companies in the past—and continue to do so to this day. France openly admits that it operates a special department devoted to obtaining confidential information about U.S. companies." Good competitive intelligence in business, as in the military, is one of the keys to success. The more information and knowledge a firm

TABLE 4–5
Key Questions About Competitors

1.	What are the major competitors' strengths?
2.	What are the major competitors' weaknesses?
3.	What are the major competitors' objectives and strategies?
4.	How will the major competitors most likely respond to current economic, social, cultural, demographic, environmental, political, governmental, legal, technological, and competitive trends affecting our industry?
5.	How vulnerable are the major competitors to our alternative company strategies?
6.	How vulnerable are our alternative strategies to successful counterattack by our major competitors?
7.	How are our products or services positioned relative to major competitors?
8.	To what extent are new firms entering and old firms leaving this industry?
9.	What key factors have resulted in our present competitive position in this industry?
10.	How have the sales and profit rankings of major competitors in the industry changed over recent years? Why have these rankings changed that way?
11.	What is the nature of supplier and distributor relationships in this industry?
12.	To what extent could substitute products or services be a threat to competitors in this industry?

can obtain about its competitors, the more likely it can formulate and implement effective strategies. Major competitors' weaknesses can represent external opportunities; major competitors' strengths may represent key threats.

Unfortunately, the majority of U.S. executives grew up in times when American firms dominated foreign competitors so much that gathering competitive intelligence seemed not worth the effort. Too many of these executives still cling to these attitudes, to the detriment of their organizations today. Even most MBA programs do not offer a course in competitive and business intelligence, thus reinforcing this attitude. As a consequence, three strong misperceptions about business intelligence prevail among American executives today:

1. Running an intelligence program requires lots of people, computers, and other resources.
2. Collecting intelligence about competitors violates antitrust laws; business intelligence equals espionage.
3. Intelligence gathering is an unethical business practice.[9]

All three of these perceptions are totally misguided. Any discussions with a competitor about price, market, or geography intentions could violate antitrust statutes, but this fact must not lure a firm into underestimating the need for and benefits of systematically collecting information about competitors for the purpose of enhancing a firm's effectiveness. The Internet has become an excellent medium for gathering competitive intelligence, as indicated in the Information Technology Perspective. Information gathering from employees, managers, suppliers, distributors, customers, creditors, and consultants also can make the difference between having superior or just average intelligence and overall competitiveness.

Firms need an effective *competitive intelligence (CI)* program. The three basic missions of a CI program are (1) to provide a general understanding of an industry and its

INFORMATION TECHNOLOGY

How Can the Internet Be Used to Gain Competitive Intelligence?

The Wall Street Journal recently asked corporate executives and consultants which Web sites are best for gaining competitive intelligence. The results are summarized here. At any given time on the Internet, thousands of people are talking about your company's products and competing products in newsgroups. You can eavesdrop on these discussions most easily using Deja News at www.dejanews.com; this site lets you search these discussions by keyword.

The best all-around starting point for conducting research on the Web is Yahoo! at www.yahoo.com. Unlike AltaVista and other search engines that use computers to automatically index every word at a Web site, Yahoo! is a true directory. So if you type Ford Motor Company into Yahoo!, you get a list of all Ford's

Web sites, whereas typing that name into any other search engine gets you a 12-page list of Web sites that have the name Ford in the title or on the first page. Yahoo! is speedy but not always completely up-to-date.

If you are desperately seeking something that a Yahoo! search does not find, the *WSJ* panelists prefer AltaVista at altavista.digital.com; Excite at www.excite.com; Hotbot at www.hotbot.com; Infoseek at www.infoseek.com; or Lycos at www.lycos.com. These engines are unbelievably thorough. To find a person, Four11 at www.four11.com and Switchboard at www.switchboard.com offer far greater power than a telephone call to directory assistance.

For information on competitors, the *WSJ* panelists prefer to use Hoover's Online at www.hoovers.com; Infospace

at www.infospace.com; and the Securities Exchange Commission's Edgar database at www.sec.gov. To make travel plans, schedule flights, purchase airline tickets, book hotel rooms, and reserve rental cars, the *WSJ* panelists prefer Expedia at www.expedia.com; Mapquest at www.mapquest.com; and Travelocity at www.travelocity.com. Accessing these sites is much easier and quicker than calling a travel agent.

Source: Adapted from Thomas Weber, "Watching the Web: Experts Pick Their Most Useful Sites," The Wall Street Journal, (August 28, 1997): B6.

competitors, (2) to identify areas in which competitors are vulnerable and to asseses the impact strategic actions would have on competitors, and (3) to identify potential moves that a competitor might make that would endanger a firm's position in the market.[10] Competitive information is equally applicable for strategy formulation, implementation, and evaluation decisions. An effective CI program allows all areas of a firm to access consistent and verifiable information in making decisions. All members of an organization, from the chief executive officer to custodians, are valuable intelligence agents and should feel a part of the CI process. Special characteristics of a successful CI program include flexibility, usefulness, timeliness, and cross-functional cooperation.

The increasing emphasis on *competitive analysis* in the United States is evidenced by corporations putting this function on their organizational charts under job titles such as Director of Competitive Analysis, Competitive Strategy Manager, Director of Information Services, or Associate Director of Competitive Assessment. The responsibilities of a *director of competitive analysis* include planning, collecting data, analyzing data, facilitating the process of gathering and analyzing data, disseminating intelligence on a timely basis, researching special issues, and recognizing what information is important and who needs to know. Competitive intelligence is not corporate espionage because 95 percent of the information a company needs to make strategic decisions is available and accessible to the public. Sources of competitive information include trade journals, want ads, newspaper articles, and government filings, as well as customers, suppliers, distributors, and competitors themselves.

Unethical tactics such as bribery, wire tapping, and computer break-ins should never be used to obtain information. Marriott and Motorola—two American companies that do a particularly good job of gathering competitive intelligence—agree that all the information you could wish for can be collected without resorting to unethical tactics. They keep their intelligence staffs small, usually under five people, and spend less than $200,000 per year on gathering competitive intelligence.

COOPERATION AMONG COMPETITORS   Strategies that stress cooperation among competitors are being used more. For example, Lockheed recently teamed up with British Aerospace PLC to compete against Boeing Company to develop the next-generation U.S. fighter jet. Lockheed's cooperative strategy with a profitable partner in the Airbus Industrie consortium encourages broader Lockheed-European collaboration as Europe's defense industry consolidates. The British firm offers Lockheed special expertise in the areas of short takeoff and vertical landing technologies, systems integration, and low-cost design and manufacturing.

In the oil industry, Shell Oil and Texaco recently combined their West Coast and Midwestern refining and marketing operations into a new company with $9 billion in assets. Mobil and Amoco are engaged in similar discussions about combining their entire U.S. refining and marketing operations. Marathon Oil and Ashland also are engaged in merger discussions.

The idea of joining forces with a competitor is not easily accepted by Americans, who often view cooperation and partnerships with skepticism and suspicion. Indeed, joint ventures and cooperative arrangements among competitors demand a certain amount of trust to combat paranoia about whether one firm will injure the other. However, multinational firms are becoming more globally cooperative, and increasing numbers of domestic firms are joining forces with competitive foreign firms to reap mutual benefits. Kathryn Harrigan at Columbia University says, "Within a decade, most companies will be members of teams that compete against each other."

American companies often enter alliances primarily to avoid investments, being more interested in reducing the costs and risks of entering new businesses or markets than in acquiring new skills. In contrast, *learning from the partner* is a major reason why Asian and European firms enter into cooperative agreements. American firms, too, should place learning high on the list of reasons to cooperate with competitors. American companies often form alliances with Asian firms to gain an understanding of their manufacturing excellence, but Asian competence in this area is not easily transferable. Manufacturing excellence is a complex system that includes employee training and involvement, integration with suppliers, statistical process controls, value engineering, and design. In contrast, American know-how in technology and related areas more easily can be imitated. American firms thus need to be careful not to give away more intelligence than they receive in cooperative agreements with rival Asian firms.

SOURCES OF EXTERNAL INFORMATION

A wealth of strategic information is available to organizations from both published and unpublished sources. Unpublished sources include customer surveys, market research, speeches at professional and shareholders' meetings, television programs, interviews, and conversations with stakeholders. Published sources of strategic information include periodicals, journals, reports, government documents, abstracts, books, directories, newspapers, and manuals. Computerization and the Internet have made it easier today for firms to gather, assimilate, and evaluate information.

INDEXES   A number of excellent indexes reveal the location of strategic information by subject, topic, source, author, company, and industry. Indexes can save managers considerable time and effort in identifying and evaluating opportunities and threats. A description of major indexes available for locating information is provided in Table 4–6.

TABLE 4–6
Major Indexes That Reference Economic, Social, Political, Technological, and Competitive Information

NAME OF INDEX	TYPE OF INFORMATION	DESCRIPTION
Applied Science & Technology Index	Technological	A subject index that covers more than 200 selected journals in the fields of aeronautics and space science, automation, chemistry, construction, earth sciences, electricity and electronics, engineering, industrial and mechanical arts, materials, mathematics, metallurgy, physics, telecommunication, transportation, and related subjects. *ASTI* is published monthly.
Business Periodicals Index	Economic Social Political Technological Competitive	This is probably the best known index for its overall subject coverage of selected periodicals in the following fields of business: accounting, advertising and public relations, automation, banking, communications, economics, finance and investments, insurance, labor, management, marketing, taxation, and also specific businesses, industries, and trades. This index also includes a review of books appearing in the journals it indexes, listed together under the heading "Book Reviews." *BPI* is published monthly.
Funk & Scott Index of Corporations & Industries	Competitive	This is the best index for current information on companies and industries. It covers a wide selection of business, industrial, and financial periodicals and also a few brokerage house reports. The yellow pages in the weeklies and the green pages in cumulated issues list articles (or data in articles) on all SIC (Standard Industrial Classification) industries; the white pages list articles on companies. Because many of the entries refer to very brief citations, it is important to note that major articles are designated by a black dot that precedes the abbreviated title of the journal. *F&S* is published weekly.
F&S Index International	Competitive Political	A companion of the index above, covering articles on foreign companies and industries that have appeared in some 1,000 foreign and domestic periodicals and other documents. It is arranged in three parts: (1) by SIC number or product; (2) by region and country; (3) by company. *F&SI* is published monthly.

continued

TABLE 4–6 *continued*

Public Affairs Information Service Bulletin	Social Political[a]	This is a selective listing in the areas of economic and social conditions, public administration, and international relations, published in English throughout the world. The important differences in this index are (1) it only selectively indexes journals to cover those articles pertinent to its subject coverage; (2) it covers not only periodical articles but also selected books, pamphlets, government publications, and reports of public and private agencies. There is a companion index called *Public Affairs Information Service: Foreign Language Index*. The *PAIS* is published weekly.
Readers' Guide to Periodical Literature	Economic Social Political Technological Competitive	A very popular author and subject index to periodicals published in the United States. The *RGPL* is published bimonthly.
Social Sciences Index	Social Economic Political	A subject and author index to articles in over 260 journals that cover the fields of anthropology, area studies, economics, environmental science, geography, law and criminology, medical sciences, political science, psychology, public administration, sociology, and related subjects. At the back of each issue is a listing by author of book reviews that appear in the indexed journals. The *SSI* is published quarterly.
New York Times Index	Economic Social Political Technological Competitive	This is an excellent and very detailed index of articles published by the *New York Times* newspaper. The index is arranged alphabetically and includes many helpful cross-references. The *NYTI* is published bimonthly.
Wall Street Journal/ Barron's Index	Economic Social Political Technological Competitive	A valuable index of *Wall Street Journal* and *Barron's* articles. Each issue is in two parts; corporate news and general news. The index includes a list of book reviews. The *WSJ/BI* is published monthly.

[a]"Social" includes cultural, demographic, and environmental information; "Political" includes governmental and legal information.
Source: Adapted from Lorna M. Daniells, *Business Information Sources* (Los Angeles: University of California Press, 1976), 14–17.

INTERNET Millions of people today use on-line services for both business and personal purposes. *America Online* and *Netscape* are leading commercial on-line services. These companies are expanding their menu of available services to include everything from on-line access to most major television networks, newspapers, and magazines to on-line interviewing of celebrities, and they offer access to the furthermost boundaries of the Internet. These companies harness the power of multimedia, combining sound, video, and graphics with text. Excellent sources of strategic management and case research information on the World Wide Web are provided in Table 4–7. Table 4–8 provides selected academic and consulting strategic planning Web sites.

The Internet offers consumers and businesses a widening range of services and information resources from all over the world. Interactive services offer users not only access to information worldwide but also the ability to communicate with the person or company that created the information. Historical barriers to personal and business success—time zones and diverse cultures—are being eliminated. The Internet is poised to become as important to our society by the end of this decade as television and newspapers.

TABLE 4–7

Excellent Internet Sources of Information

I. INVESTMENT RESEARCH

American Stock Exchange ⟶ www.amex.com
DBC Online ⟶ www.dbc.com
Hoover's Online ⟶ www.hoovers.com
InvestorGuide ⟶ www.investorguide.com
Wall Street Research Net ⟶ www.wsrn.com
Market Guide ⟶ www.marketguide.com
Money Search - Find It! ⟶ www.moneysearch.com
NASDAQ ⟶ www.nasdaq.com
New York Stock Exchange ⟶ www.nyse.com/public/home.html
PC Financial Network ⟶ www.dljdirect.com
Quote.Com ⟶ www.quote.com
Stock Smart ⟶ www.stocksmart.com
Wright Investors' Service on the World Wide Web ⟶ www.wisi.com
Zacks Investment Research ⟶ www.zacks.com/docs/Bob/hotlinks.htm

II. SEARCH ENGINES

Alta Vista ⟶ www.altavista.digital.com
Deja News ⟶ www.dejanews.com
DogPile ⟶ www.dogpile.com
Excite ⟶ www.excite.com
HotBot ⟶ www.hotbot.com
InfoSeek ⟶ www.infoseek.com
Lycos ⟶ www.lycos.com
Magellan Internet Guide ⟶ www.mckinley.com
Metacrawler ⟶ www.metacrawler.com
Starting Point ⟶ www.stpt.com
WebCrawler ⟶ webcrawler.com
Yahoo! ⟶ www.yahoo.com

III. DIRECTORIES

Argus Clearinghouse ⟶ www.clearinghouse.net
BigBook ⟶ www.bigbook.com
ComFind ⟶ www.comfind.com
U.S. Business Advisor ⟶ www.business.gov/business.html
Thomas Publishing Co. ⟶ www.thomaspublishing.com
Competitive Intelligence Guide ⟶ www.fuld.com

IV. NEWS, MAGAZINES, AND NEWSPAPERS

PR Newswire ⟶ www.prnewswire.com
American Demographics ⟶ www.marketingtools.com
Barron's Magazine ⟶ www.barrons.com
Business Week ⟶ www.businessweek.com
CNNfn ⟶ www.cnnfn.com/search
Financial Times ⟶ www.usa.ft.com
Forbes Magazine On-line ⟶ www.forbes.com
Fortune Magazine ⟶ www.fortune.com
USA Today ⟶ www.usatoday.com
Wall Street Journal ⟶ www.wsj.com
Washington Post Online ⟶ www.washingtonpost.com

V. U.S. GOVERNMENT

Better Business Bureau ⟶ www.bbb.org
Census Bureau ⟶ www.census.gov
Federal Trade Commission ⟶ www.ftc.gov
FreeEDGAR ⟶ www.freeedgar.com
Edgar-Online ⟶ www.edgar-online.com

continued

TABLE 4–7   *continued*

> General Printing Office ⟶ www.gpo.gov
> Internal Revenue Service ⟶ www.irs.ustreas.gov
> Library of Congress ⟶ www.loc.gov
> SEC's Edgar Database ⟶ www.sec.gov/edgarhp.htm
> Small Business Administration ⟶ www.sba.gov
> U.S. Department of Commerce ⟶ www.doc.gov
> U.S. Department of the Treasury ⟶ www.ustreas.gov
> Environmental Protection Agency ⟶ www.epa.gov
> National Aeronautics and Space Administration ⟶ www.hq.nasa.gov

TABLE 4–8
Important Strategic Planning Web Sites

I. ACADEMIC

1. *NEW MEXICO STATE UNIVERSITY—www.nmsu.edu/strategic/*
This site provides a full description of the strategic planning process at New Mexico State University, including a chart, reading material on strategic planning, and guidelines about how to do strategic planning. A great site for seeing strategic planning in action.

2. *STRATEGIC MANAGEMENT SOCIETY—www.virtual-indiana.com/sms/*
This is a not-for-profit professional society composed of nearly 2,000 academic, business, and consulting members from 45 countries. This group publishes the *Strategic Management Journal* and offers annual meetings and conferences. The Web site is well designed and outlines the society's services and resources.

3. *AMERICAN MANAGEMENT ASSOCIATION—www.amanet.org*
AMA provides educational forums worldwide for businesses to learn practical business skills. This Web site is comprehensive in providing access to all AMA seminars, videos, and courses worldwide, including strategic planning products. AMA publishes *Management Review*.

4. *ACADEMY OF MANAGEMENT ONLINE—www.aom.pace.edu*
This not-for-profit organization is the leading professional association for management research and education in the United States. Almost 10,000 members from businesses and universities around the world participate. About 2,500 of these members specify Business Policy and Strategy as their primary interest. This site provides a search engine to locate and contact all these members. Many links and personal Web pages are provided. This organization publishes *Academy of Management Executive*, *Academy of Management Review*, and *Academy of Management Journal*.

5. *STRATEGIC LEADERSHIP FORUM—www.slfnet.org*
This is an international organization of executives focusing on strategic management and planning. The Web site is outstanding. Many excellent strategic planning links are provided. The Forum publishes *Strategy and Leadership* (formerly *Planning Review*).

II. CONSULTANTS

1. *STRATEGIC PLANNING SYSTEMS—www.checkmateplan.com*
This site provides CheckMATE, the industry leader in strategic planning software worldwide. This software is Windows-based and easy to use. Twenty-three different industry versions are available. Also provided on this site is a strategic planning video and workbook, as well as free links to scores for other good sites for gathering strategic planning information.

2. *MIND TOOLS—www.mindtools.com/planpage.html*
This is an excellent Web site for providing strategic planning information. More than 30 pages of narrative about how and why to do strategic planning are provided. Planning templates are provided.

3. *PERFORMANCE STRATEGIES, INC.—www.perfstrat.com/articles/ptp.htm*
This Web site offers about 20 pages of excellent narrative about how and why to do strategic planning. A model of the planning process is provided, as well as excellent discussion of mission, benefits of planning, objectives, priorities, and timing.

continued

TABLE 4–8   *continued*

4. **PALO ALTO SOFTWARE—*www.bizplans.com***
    This Web site offers a model of the business planning process with excellent narrative as well as seven example business plans from real firms. This is one of the two best sites available for business planning information. (The other is the Small Business Administration Web site.)

5. **CENTER FOR STRATEGIC MANAGEMENT—*www.csmweb.com***
    This Web site describes strategic management training, seminars, and facilitation services. The site also provides excellent links to other strategic planning academic and government sites.

6. **BOSTON CONSULTING GROUP—*www.bcg.com***
    This perhaps is the best-known strategic planning consulting firm. The Web site offers some nice discussion of strategic planning but focuses mostly on getting a job with BCG rather than on strategic planning information.

7. **FULD & COMPANY—*www.fuld.cum***
    This Web site specializes in competitive intelligence. Nice links are provided regarding the importance of gathering information about competitors. This site offers audio answers to key questions about intelligence systems.

FORECASTING TOOLS AND TECHNIQUES

Forecasts are educated assumptions about future trends and events. Forecasting is a complex activity due to factors such as technological innovation, cultural changes, new products, improved services, stronger competitors, shifts in government priorities, changing social values, unstable economic conditions, and unforeseen events. Managers often must rely upon published forecasts to identify key external opportunities and threats effectively.

Many publications and sources on the Internet forecast external variables. Several published examples include *Industry Week*'s "Trends and Forecasts," *Business Week*'s "Investment Outlook," and Standard & Poor's *Industry Survey*. The reputation and continued success of these publications depend partly on accurate forecasts, so published sources of information can offer excellent projections.

Sometimes organizations must develop their own projections. Most organizations forecast (project) their own revenues and profits annually. Organizations sometimes forecast market share or customer loyalty in local areas. Because forecasting is so important in strategic management and because the ability to forecast (in contrast to the ability to use a forecast) is essential, selected forecasting tools are examined further here.

Forecasting tools can be broadly categorized into two groups: quantitative techniques and qualitative techniques. Quantitative forecasts are most appropriate when historical data are available and when the relationships among key variables are expected to remain the same in the future. The three basic types of quantitative forecasting techniques are econometric models, regression, and *trend extrapolation*. *Econometric models* are based on simultaneous systems of regression equations that forecast variables such as interest rates and money supply. With the advent of sophisticated computer software, econometric models have become the most widely used approach for forecasting economic variables.

All quantitative forecasts, regardless of statistical sophistication and complexity, are based on historical relationships among key variables. *Linear regression*, for example, is based on the assumption that the future will be just like the past—which, of course, it never is. As historical relationships become less stable, quantitative forecasts becomes less accurate.

Qualitative Approaches [handwritten note]

The six basic qualitative approaches to forecasting are (1) sales force estimates, (2) juries of executive opinion, (3) anticipatory surveys or market research, (4) scenario forecasts, (5) delphi forecasts, and (6) brainstorming. Qualitative or judgmental forecasts are particularly useful when historical data are not available or when constituent variables are expected to change significantly in the future.

Due to advancements in computer technology, quantitative forecasting techniques are usually cheaper and faster than qualitative methods. Quantitative techniques such as multiple regression can generate measures of error that allow a manager to estimate the degree of confidence associated with a given forecast. Forecasting tools must be used carefully or the results can be more misleading than helpful, but qualitative techniques require more intuitive judgment than do quantitative ones. Managers sometimes erroneously forecast what they would like to occur.

No forecast is perfect, and some forecasts are even wildly inaccurate. This fact accents the need for strategists to devote sufficient time and effort to study the underlying bases for published forecasts and to develop internal forecasts of their own. Key external opportunities and threats can be effectively identified only through good forecasts. Accurate forecasts can provide major competitive advantages for organizations. Forecasts are vital to the strategic-management process and to the success of organizations.

MAKING ASSUMPTIONS   Planning would be impossible without assumptions. McConkey defines assumptions as "best present estimates of the impact of major external factors, over which the manager has little if any control, but which may exert a significant impact on performance or the ability to achieve desired results.[11] Strategists are faced with countless variables and imponderables that can be neither controlled nor predicted with 100 percent accuracy.

By identifying future occurrences that could have a major effect on the firm and making reasonable assumptions about those factors, strategists can carry the strategic-management process forward. Assumptions are needed only for future trends and events that are most likely to have a significant effect on the company's business. Based on the best information at the time, assumptions serve as checkpoints on the validity of strategies. If future occurrences deviate significantly from assumptions, strategists know that corrective actions may be needed. Without reasonable assumptions, the strategy-formulation process could not proceed effectively. Firms that have the best information generally make the most accurate assumptions, which can lead to major competitive advantages.

COMPETITIVE ANALYSIS: PORTER'S FIVE-FORCES MODEL

As illustrated in Figure 4–3, *Porter's Five-Forces Model* of competitive analysis is a widely used approach for developing strategies in many industries. The intensity of competition among firms varies widely across industries. Table 4–9 reveals the average return on equity for firms in 24 different industries in 1996. Intensity of competition is highest in lower-return industries. According to Porter, the nature of competitiveness in a given industry can be viewed as a composite of five forces:

1. Rivalry among competitive firms
2. Potential entry of new competitors
3. Potential development of substitute products
4. Bargaining power of suppliers
5. Bargaining power of consumers

FIGURE 4–3
The Five-Forces Model of Competition

RIVALRY AMONG COMPETING FIRMS Rivalry among competing firms is usually the most powerful of the five competitive forces. The strategies pursued by one firm can be successful only to the extent that they provide competitive advantage over the strategies pursued by rival firms. Changes in strategy by one firm may be met with retaliatory countermoves, such as lowering prices, enhancing quality, adding features, providing services, extending warranties, and increasing advertising.

TABLE 4–9
Intensity of Competition Among Firms in Different Industries–1996 and 1997 Results Provided

INDUSTRY	1996/1997 AVERAGE RETURN ON EQUITY	1996/1997 AVERAGE EARNINGS PER SHARE
Consumer Products	26.5/27.7	2.25/1.90
Health Care	24.8/21.9	2.39/1.78
Telecommunications	23.1/18.1	2.59/2.25
Chemicals	22.3/18.8	2.96/2.31
Manufacturing	20.4/18.2	2.56/2.18
Conglomerates	20.4/20.6	3.07/2.05
Food	19.4/17.3	1.54/1.07
Automotive	19.3/23.6	3.96/5.16
Fuel	17.1/17.6	4.13/3.17
Office Equipment and Computers	16.8/19.7	1.59/1.55
Aerospace and Defense	16.8/11.7	2.44/1.77
Banks	15.7/16.3	4.16/3.59
Transportation	15.3/16.7	3.45/2.95
Nonbank Financial	15.1/16.0	3.19/3.35
Housing and Real Estate	14.9/20.1	1.64/2.03
Electrical and Electronics	14.3/15.8	2.11/2.21
Leisure Time Industries	13.7/11.4	1.82/1.48
Publishing and Broadcasting	12.0/4.9	1.35/0.54
Utilities and Power	11.4/10.1	2.10/1.87
Discount and Fashion Retailing	11.3/13.5	1.10/1.34
Paper and Forest Products	9.4/3.2	2.06/0.52
Containers and Packaging	9.0/6.5	1.25/0.70
Metals and Mining	8.5/12.2	1.26/1.82
Service Industries	8.3/10.9	0.79/0.98

Source: Adapted from "Corporate Scoreboard," *Business Week* (March 3, 1997): 95–115. Also, "Corporate Scoreboard," *Business Week* (March 2, 1998): 113–136.

The intensity of rivalry among competing firms tends to increase as the number of competitors increases, as competitors become more equal in size and capability, as demand for the industry's products declines, and as price cutting becomes common. Rivalry also increases when consumers can switch brands easily; when barriers to leaving the market are high; when fixed costs are high; when the product is perishable; when rival firms are diverse in strategies, origins, and culture; and when mergers and acquisitions are common in the industry. As rivalry among competing firms intensifies, industry profits decline, in some cases to the point where an industry becomes inherently unattractive.

POTENTIAL ENTRY OF NEW COMPETITORS Whenever new firms can easily enter a particular industry, the intensity of competitiveness among firms increases. Barriers to entry, however, can include the need to gain economies of scale quickly, the need to gain technology and specialized know-how, the lack of experience, strong customer loyalty, strong brand preferences, large capital requirements, lack of adequate distribution channels, government regulatory policies, tariffs, lack of access to raw materials, possession of patents, undesirable locations, counterattack by entrenched firms, and potential saturation of the market.

Despite numerous barriers to entry, new firms sometimes enter industries with higher-quality products, lower prices, and substantial marketing resources. Compaq's entering the personal computer market and Wal-Mart's entering the discount market are examples. The strategist's job, therefore, is to identify potential new firms entering the market, to monitor the new rival firms' strategies, to counterattack as needed, and to capitalize on existing strengths and opportunities.

POTENTIAL DEVELOPMENT OF SUBSTITUTE PRODUCTS In many industries, firms are in close competition with producers of substitute products in other industries. Examples are plastic container producers competing with glass, paperboard, and aluminum can producers, and acetaminophen manufacturers competing with other manufacturers of pain and headache remedies. The presence of substitute products puts a ceiling on the price that can be charged before the consumers will switch to the substitute product.

Competitive pressures arising from substitute products increase as the relative price of substitute products declines and as consumers' switching costs decrease. The competitive strength of substitute products is best measured by the inroads into market share those products obtain, as well as those firms' plans for increased capacity and market penetration.

BARGAINING POWER OF SUPPLIERS The bargaining power of suppliers affects the intensity of competition in an industry, especially when there is a large number of suppliers, when there are only a few good substitute raw materials, or when the cost of switching raw materials is especially costly. It often is in the best interest of both suppliers and producers to assist each other with reasonable prices, improved quality, development of new services, just-in-time deliveries, and reduced inventory costs, thus enhancing long-term profitability for all concerned.

Firms may pursue a backward integration strategy to gain control or ownership of suppliers. This strategy is especially effective when suppliers are unreliable, too costly, or not capable of meeting a firm's needs on a consistent basis. Firms generally can negotiate more favorable terms with suppliers when backward integration is a commonly used strategy among rival firms in an industry.

BARGAINING POWER OF CONSUMERS When customers are concentrated or large, or buy in volume, their bargaining power represents a major force affecting intensity of competition in an industry. Rival firms may offer extended warranties or special services to gain customer loyalty whenever the bargaining power of consumers is substantial. Bargaining power of consumers also is higher when the products being purchased are standard or undifferentiated. When this is the case, consumers often can negotiate selling price, warranty coverage, and accessory packages to a greater extent.

INDUSTRY ANALYSIS: THE EXTERNAL FACTOR EVALUATION (EFE) MATRIX

An *External Factor Evaluation (EFE) Matrix* allows strategists to summarize and evaluate economic, social, cultural, demographic, environmental, political, governmental, legal, technological, and competitive information. There are five steps in developing an EFE Matrix:

1. List key external factors as identified in the external-audit process. Include a total of from 10 to 20 factors, including both opportunities and threats affecting the firm and its industry. List the opportunities first and then the threats. Be as specific as possible, using percentages, ratios, and comparative numbers whenever possible.

2. Assign to each factor a weight that ranges from 0.0 (not important) to 1.0 (very important). The weight indicates the relative importance of that factor to being successful in the firm's industry. Opportunities often receive higher weights than threats, but threats too can receive high weights if they are especially severe or threatening. Appropriate weights can be determined by comparing successful with unsuccessful competitors or by discussing the factor and reaching a group consensus. The sum of all weights assigned to the factors must equal 1.0.

3. Assign a 1-to-4 rating to each critical success factor to indicate how effectively the firm's current strategies respond to the factor, where 4 = *the response is superior*, 3 = *the response is above average*, 2 = *the response is average,* and 1 = *the response is poor*. Ratings are based on effectiveness of the firm's strategies. Ratings are thus company-based, whereas the weights in Step 2 are industry-based.

4. Multiply each factor's weight by its rating to determine a weighted score.

5. Sum the weighted scores for each variable to determine the total weighted score for the organization.

Regardless of the number of key opportunities and threats included in an EFE Matrix, the highest possible total weighted score for an organization is 4.0 and the lowest possible total weighted score is 1.0. The average total weighted score is 2.5. A total weighted score of 4.0 indicates that an organization is responding in an outstanding way to existing opportunities and threats in its industry. In other words, the firm's strategies effectively take advantage of existing opportunities and minimize the potential adverse effect of external threats. A total score of 1.0 indicates that the firm's strategies are not capitalizing on opportunities or avoiding external threats.

An example of an EFE Matrix is provided in Table 4–10 for UST, Inc., the manufacturer of Skoal and Copenhagen smokeless tobacco. Note that the Clinton Administration was considered to be the most important factor affecting this industry, as indicated by the weight of 0.20. UST was not pursuing strategies that effectively capitalize on this opportunity, as indicated by the rating of 1.01. The total weighted score of 2.10 indicates that UST is below average in its effort to pursue strategies that capitalize on external opportunities and avoid threats. It is important to note here that a thorough understanding of the factors being used in the EFE Matrix is more important than the actual weights and ratings assigned.

TABLE 4–10
**An Example External
Factor Evaluation Matrix
for UST, Inc.**

KEY EXTERNAL FACTORS	WEIGHT	RATING	WEIGHTED SCORE
OPPORTUNITIES			
1. Global markets are practically untapped by smokeless tobacco market	.15	1	.15
2. Increased demand due to public banning of smoking	.05	3	.15
3. Astronomical Internet advertising growth	.05	1	.05
4. Pinkerton is leader in discount tobacco market	.15	4	.60
5. More social pressure to quit smoking, thus leading users to switch to alternatives	.10	3	.30
THREATS			
1. Legislation against the tobacco industry	.10	2	.20
2. Production limits on tobacco increases competition for production	.05	3	.15
3. Smokeless tobacco market is concentrated in southeast region of United States	.05	2	.10
4. Bad media exposure from the FDA	.10	2	.20
5. Clinton Administration	.20	1	.20
TOTAL	1.00		2.10

THE COMPETITIVE PROFILE MATRIX (CPM)

The *Competitive Profile Matrix (CPM)* identifies a firm's major competitors and their particular strengths and weaknesses in relation to a sample firm's strategic position. The weights and total weighted scores in both a CPM and EFE have the same meaning. However, the factors in a CPM include both internal and external issues; the ratings refer to strengths and weaknesses. There are some important differences between the EFE and CPM. First of all, the critical success factors in a CPM are broader; they do not include specific or factual data and even may focus on internal issues. The critical success factors in a CPM also are not grouped into opportunities and threats as they are in an EFE. In a CPM the ratings and total weighted scores for rival firms can be compared to the sample firm. This comparative analysis provides important internal strategic information.

A sample Competitive Profile Matrix is provided in Table 4–11. In this example, advertising and global expansion are the most important critical success factors, as indicated by a weight of 0.20. Avon's and L'Oreal's product quality are superior, as evidenced by a rating of 4; L'Oreal's "financial position" is good, as indicated by a rating of 3; Procter & Gamble is the weakest firm overall, as indicated by a total weighted score of 2.80.

TABLE 4–11
A Competitive Profile Matrix

CRITICAL SUCCESS FACTORS	WEIGHT	AVON		L'OREAL		PROCTER & GAMBLE	
		RATING	SCORE	RATING	SCORE	RATING	SCORE
Advertising	0.20	1	0.20	4	0.80	3	0.60
Product Quality	0.10	4	0.40	4	0.40	3	0.30
Price Competitiveness	0.10	3	0.30	3	0.30	4	0.40
Management	0.10	4	0.40	3	0.30	3	0.30
Financial Position	0.15	4	0.60	3	0.45	3	0.45
Customer Loyalty	0.10	4	0.40	4	0.40	2	0.20
Global Expansion	0.20	4	0.80	2	0.40	2	0.40
Market Share	0.05	1	0.05	4	0.20	3	0.15
TOTAL	1.00		3.15		3.25		2.80

Note: (1) The ratings values are as follows: 1 = major weakness, 2 = minor weakness, 3 = minor strength, 4 = major strength. (2) As indicated by the total weighted score of 2.8, Competitor 3 is weakest. (3) Only eight critical success factors are included for simplicity; this is too few in actuality.

A word on interpretation: Just because one firm receives a 3.2 rating and another receives a 2.8 rating in a Competitive Profile Matrix, it does not follow that the first firm is 20 percent better than the second. Numbers reveal the relative strength of firms, but their implied precision is an illusion. Numbers are not magic. The aim is not to arrive at a single number, but rather to assimilate and evaluate information in a meaningful way that aids in decision making.

CONCLUSION

Due to increasing turbulence in markets and industries around the world, the external audit has become an explicit and vital part of the strategic-management process. This chapter provides a framework for collecting and evaluating economic, social, cultural, demographic, environmental, political, governmental, legal, technological, and competitive information. Firms that do not mobilize and empower their managers and employees to identify, monitor, forecast, and evaluate key external forces may fail to anticipate emerging opportunities and threats and, consequently, may pursue ineffective strategies, miss opportunities, and invite organizational demise. Firms not taking advantage of the Internet are falling behind technologically.

A major responsibility of strategists is to ensure development of an effective external-audit system. This includes using information technology to devise a competitive intelligence system that works. The external-audit approach described in this chapter can be used effectively by any size or type of organization. Typically, the external-audit process is more informal in small firms, but the need to understand key trends and events is no less important for these firms. The EFE Matrix and five-forces model can help strategists evaluate the market and industry, but these tools must be accompanied by good intuitive judgment. Multinational firms especially need a systematic and effective external-audit system because external forces among foreign countries vary so greatly.

We invite you to visit the DAVID page on the Prentice Hall Web site at
www.prenhall.com/davidsm
for this chapter's World Wide Web exercises.

TAKE IT TO THE NET

KEY TERMS AND CONCEPTS

America Online	(p. 122)	Director of Competitive	(p. 120)
Chief Information Officer (CIO)	(p. 108)	Analysis	
Chief Technology Officer (CTO)	(p. 108)	Downsizing	(p. 109)
Competitive Advantages	(p. 116)	Econometric Models	(p. 125)
Competitive Analysis	(p. 120)	Environmental Scanning	(p. 104)
Competitive Intelligence (CI)	(p. 119)	External Audit	(p. 104)
Competitive Profile Matrix	(p. 130)	External Factor Evaluation	(p. 129)
(CPM)		(EFE) Matrix	
Critical Success Factors	(p. 107)	External Forces	(p. 104)
Cyberspace	(p. 107)	Industry Analysis	(p. 104)
Decruiting	(p. 109)	Information Technology (IT)	(p. 107)

Internet	(p. 107)
Learning from the Partner	(p. 120)
Linear Regression	(p. 125)
Lifecare Facilities	(p. 111)
Porter's Five-Forces Model	(p. 126)
Netscape	(p. 122)
On-Line Databases	(p. 107)
Rightsizing	(p. 109)
Trend Extrapolation	(p. 125)
World Wide Web	(p. 107)

ISSUES FOR REVIEW AND DISCUSSION

1. Explain how to conduct an external strategic-management audit.

2. Identify a recent economic, social, political, or technological trend that significantly affects financial institutions.

3. Discuss the following statement: Major opportunities and threats usually result from an interaction among key environmental trends rather than from a single external event or factor.

4. Identify two industries experiencing rapid technological changes and three industries that are experiencing little technological change. How does the need for technological forecasting differ in these industries? Why?

5. Use Porter's five-forces model to evaluate competitiveness within the U.S. banking industry.

6. What major forecasting techniques would you use to identify (1) economic opportunities and threats and (2) demographic opportunities and threats? Why are these techniques most appropriate?

7. How does the external audit affect other components of the strategic-management process?

8. As the owner of a small business, explain how you would organize a strategic-information scanning system. How would you organize such a system in a large organization?

9. Construct an EFE Matrix for an organization of your choice.

10. Make an appointment with a librarian at your university to learn how to use on-line databases. Report your findings in class.

11. Give some advantages and disadvantages of cooperative versus competitive strategies.

12. As strategist for a local bank, explain when you would use qualitative versus quantitative forecasts.

13. What is your forecast for interest rates and the stock market in the next several months? As the stock market moves up, do interest rates always move down? Why? What are the strategic implications of these trends?

14. Explain how information technology affects strategies of the organization where you worked most recently.

15. Let's say your boss develops an EFE Matrix that includes 62 factors. How would you suggest reducing the number of factors to 20?

16. Select one of the current readings at the end of this chapter. Prepare a 1-page written summary that includes your personal opinion of the article.

17. Discuss the ethics of gathering competitive intelligence.

18. Discuss the ethics of cooperating with rival firms.

19. Visit the SEC Web site at www.sec.gov and discuss the benefits of using information provided there.

NOTES

1. Paul Judge, "Is the Net Redefining Our Identity?" *Business Week*, (May 12, 1997): 102.

2. John Diffenbach, "Corporate Environmental Analysis in Large U.S. Corporations," *Long Range Planning* 16, no. 3 (June 1983): 109.

3. York Freund, "Critical Success Factors," *Planning Review* 16, no. 4 (July–August 1988): 20.

4. Gregory Parsons, "Information Technology: A New Competitive Weapon," *Sloan Management Review* 25, no. 1 (Fall 1983): 5.

5. Frederick Gluck, "Global Competition in the 1990s," *Journal of Business Strategy* (Spring 1983): 22, 24.

6. John Harris, Robert Shaw, Jr., and William Sommers, "The Strategic Management of Technology," *Planning Review* 11, no. 1 (January–February 1983): 28, 35.

7. Susan Levine and Michael Yalowitz, "Managing Technology: The Key to Successful Business Growth," *Management Review* 72, no. 9 (September 1983): 44.

8. Bill Saporito, "Companies That Compete Best," *Fortune* (May 22, 1989): 36.

9. Kenneth Sawka, "Demystifying Business Intelligence," *Management Review*, (October 1996): 49.

10. John Prescott and Daniel Smith, "The Largest Survey of 'Leading-Edge' Competitor Intelligence Managers," *Planning Review* 17, no. 3 (May–June 1989): 6–13.

11. Dale McConkey, "Planning in a Changing Environment," *Business Horizons* 31, no. 5 (September–October 1988): 67.

CURRENT READINGS

Baum, Joel A. C. and Helaine J. Korn. "Competitive Dynamics of Interfirm Rivalry." *Academy of Management Journal* 39, no. 2 (April 1996): 255–291.

Belohlav, James A. "The Evolving Competitive Paradigm." *Business Horizons* 39, no. 2 (March–April 1996): 11–19.

Brooks, Ian and Jon Reast. "Redesigning the Value Chain at Scania Trucks." *Long Range Planning* 29, no. 4 (August 1996): 514–525.

Cheng, Joseph and Idalene F. Kesner. "Organizational Slack and Response to Environmental Shifts: The Impact of Resource Allocation Patterns." *Journal of Management* 23, no. 1 (Spring 1997): 1–18.

Cheng, Ming-Jer. "Competitor Analysis and Interfirm Rivalry: Toward a Theoretical Integration." *Academy of Management Review* 21, no. 1 (January 1996): 100–134.

Doz, Y. L. "The Evolution of Cooperation in Strategic Alliances: Initial Conditions or Learning Processes?" *Strategic Management Journal* 17, Special Issue (Summer 1996): 55–84.

Elenkov, D. S. "Strategic Uncertainty and Environmental Scanning: The Case for Institutional Influences on Scanning Behavior." *Strategic Management Journal* 18, no. 4 (April 1997): 287–302.

Evans, Philip B. and Thomas S. Wurster. "Strategy and the New Economics of Information." *Harvard Business Review* (September–October 1997): 70–83.

Gleb, Betsy D. and Linda Hayes. "When Your Competitor Turns Obstructionist . . ." *Business Horizons* 40, no. 2 (March–April 1997): 33–39.

Goll, I. and A.M.A. Rasheed. "Rational Decision-Making and Firm Performance: The Moderating Role of Environment." *Strategic Management Journal* 18, no. 7 (August 1997): 583–593.

Gruca, Thomas S., Deepika Nath, and Ajay Mehra. "Exploiting Synergy for Competitive Advantage." *Long Range Planning* 30, no. 4 (August 1997): 605–611.

Harrison, Jeffrey S. and Caron H. St. John. "Managing and Partnering with External Stakeholders." *Academy of Management Executive* 10, no. 2 (May 1996): 46–60.

Jose, P. D. "Corporate Strategy and the Environment: A Portfolio Approach." *Long Range Planning* 29, no. 4 (August 1996): 462–472.

Lado, Augustine A., Nancy G. Boyd, and Susan C. Hanlon. "Competition, Cooperation, and the Search for Economic Rents: A Syncretic Model." *Academy of Management Review* 22, no. 1 (January 1997): 110–141.

McGahan, A. M. and M. E. Porter. "How Much Does Industry Matter, Really?" *Strategic Management Journal* 18, Special Issue (Summer 1997): 15–30.

Mowery, D. C., J. E. Oxley, and B. S. Silverman. "Strategic Alliances and Interfirm Knowledge Transfer." *Strategic Management Journal* 17, Special Issue (Winter 1996): 77–92.

Newman, Victor and Kazem Chaharbaghi. "Strategic Alliances in Fast-Moving Markets." *Long Range Planning* 29, no. 6 (December 1996): 850–856.

Pawar, Badrinarayan Shankar and Ramesh Sharda. "Obtaining Business Intelligence on the Internet." *Long Range Planning* 30, no. 1 (February 1997): 110–121.

Powell, T. C. and A. Kent-Micallef. "Information Technology as Competitive Advantage: The Role of Human, Business, and Technology Resources." *Strategic Management Journal* 18, no. 5 (May 1997): 375–406.

Price, Robert M. "Executive Forum: Technology and Strategic Advantage." *California Management Review* 38, no. 3 (Spring 1996): 38–56.

Randall, Doug. "Consumer Strategies for the Internet: Four Scenarios." *Long Range Planning* 30, no. 2 (April 1997): 157–168.

Spekman, Robert E., Lynn A. Isabella, Thomas C. MacAvoy, and Theodore Forbes III. "Creating Strategic Alliances Which Endure." *Long Range Planning* 29, no. 3 (June 1996): 346–357.

Stimpert, J. L. and Irene M. Duhaime. "Seeing the Big Picture: The Influence of Industry, Diversification, and Business Strategy on Performance." *Academy of Management Journal* 40, no. 3 (June 1997): 560–583.

Zahra, Shaker A. "Governance, Ownership, and Corporate Entrepreneurship: The Moderating Impact of Industry Technological Opportunities." *Academy of Management Journal* 39, no. 6 (December 1996): 1713–1735.

EXPERIENTIAL EXERCISES

DEVELOPING AN EFE MATRIX FOR HERSHEY FOODS

PURPOSE

This exercise will give you practice developing an EFE Matrix. An EFE Matrix summarizes the results of an external audit. This is an important tool widely used by strategists.

INSTRUCTIONS

Step 1 Join with two other students in class and jointly prepare an EFE Matrix for Hershey Foods. Refer back to the Cohesion Case and to Experiential Exercise 1A if needed to identify external opportunities and threats.

Step 2 All three-person teams participating in this exercise should record their EFE total weighted scores on the board. Put your initials after your score to identify it as your team's.

Step 3 Compare the total weighted scores. Which team's score came closest to the instructor's answer? Discuss reasons for variation in the scores reported on the board.

THE LIBRARY SEARCH

PURPOSE

This exercise will help you become familiar with important sources of external information available in your college library. A key part of preparing an external audit is examining published sources of information for relevant economic, social, cultural, demographic, environmental, political, governmental, legal, technological, and competitive trends and events. External opportunities and threats must be identified and evaluated before strategies can be formulated effectively.

INSTRUCTIONS

Step 1 Select a company or business located in your county. Go to your college library and conduct an external audit for this company. Find opportunities and threats in recent issues of the local newspaper. Also check magazines. Search for information using the Internet.

Step 2 On a separate sheet of paper, list 10 opportunities and 10 threats that face this company. Be specific in stating each factor by including percentages and numbers wherever possible.

Step 3 Include a bibliography to reveal where you found the information.

Step 4 Share your information with a manager of that company. Ask for his or her comments and additions.

Step 5 Write a three-page summary of your findings and submit it to your teacher.

Experiential Exercise 4C

DEVELOPING AN EFE MATRIX FOR MY UNIVERSITY

PURPOSE

More colleges and universities are embarking upon the strategic-management process. Institutions are consciously and systematically identifying and evaluating external opportunities and threats facing higher education in your state, the nation, and the world.

INSTRUCTIONS

Step 1 Join with two other individuals in class and jointly prepare an EFE Matrix for your institution.

Step 2 Go to the board and record your total weighted score in a column that includes the scores by all three-person teams participating. Put your initials after your score to identify it as your team's.

Step 3 Which team viewed your college's strategies most positively; which team viewed your college's strategies most negatively? Discuss the nature of the differences.

Experiential Exercise 4D

DEVELOPING A COMPETITIVE PROFILE MATRIX FOR HERSHEY FOODS

PURPOSE

Monitoring competitors' performance and strategies is a key aspect of an external audit. This exercise is designed to give you practice evaluating the competitive position of organizations in a given industry and assimilating that information in the form of a Competitive Profile Matrix.

INSTRUCTIONS

Step 1 Turn back to the Cohesion Case and review the section on competitors.

Step 2 On a separate sheet of paper, prepare a Competitive Profile Matrix that includes Hershey Foods, Nestlé, and Mars.

Step 3 Turn in your Competitive Profile Matrix for a classwork grade.

DEVELOPING A COMPETITIVE PROFILE MATRIX FOR MY UNIVERSITY

PURPOSE

Your college or university competes with all other educational institutions in the world, especially those in your own state. State funds, students, faculty, staff, endowments, gifts, and federal funds are areas of competitiveness. The purpose of this exercise is to give you practice thinking competitively about the business of education in your state.

INSTRUCTIONS

Step 1　Identify two colleges or universities in your state that compete directly with your institution for students. Interview several persons who are aware of particular strengths and weaknesses of those universities. Record information about the two competing universities.

Step 2　Prepare a Competitive Profile Matrix that includes your institution and the two competing institutions. Include the following factors in your analysis:

1. Tuition costs
2. Quality of faculty
3. Academic reputation
4. Average class size
5. Campus landscaping
6. Athletic programs
7. Quality of students
8. Graduate programs
9. Location of campus
10. Campus culture

Step 3　Submit your Competitive Profile Matrix to your instructor for evaluation.

The Internal Assessment

CHAPTER OUTLINE

- THE NATURE OF AN INTERNAL AUDIT
- RELATIONSHIPS AMONG THE FUNCTIONAL AREAS OF BUSINESS
- MANAGEMENT
- MARKETING
- FINANCE/ACCOUNTING
- PRODUCTION/OPERATIONS
- RESEARCH AND DEVELOPMENT
- COMPUTER INFORMATION SYSTEMS

- INTERNAL AUDIT CHECKLISTS
- THE INTERNAL FACTOR EVALUATION (IFE) MATRIX

- EXPERIENTIAL EXERCISE 5A
  Performing a Financial Ratio Analysis for Hershey Foods

- EXPERIENTIAL EXERCISE 5B
  Constructing an IFE Matrix for Hershey Foods

- EXPERIENTIAL EXERCISE 5C
  Constructing an IFE Matrix for My University

CHAPTER OBJECTIVES

After studying this chapter, you should be able to do the following:

1. Describe how to perform an internal strategic-management audit.

2. Discuss key interrelationships among the functional areas of business.

3. Identify the basic functions or activities that make up management, marketing, finance/accounting, production/operations, research and development, and computer information systems.

4. Explain how to determine and prioritize a firm's internal strengths and weaknesses.

5. Explain the importance of financial ratio analysis.

6. Discuss the nature and role of computer information systems in strategic management.

7. Develop an Internal Factor Evaluation (IFE) Matrix.

NOTABLE QUOTES

*L*ike a product or service, the planning process itself must be managed and shaped, if it is to serve executives as a vehicle for strategic decision-making.—ROBERT LENZ

*T*he difference between now and five years ago is that information systems had limited function. You weren't betting your company on it. Now you are.—WILLIAM GRUBER

*W*eak leadership can wreck the soundest strategy.—SUN ZI

A firm that continues to employ a previously successful strategy eventually and inevitably falls victim to a competitor.—WILLIAM COHEN

*I*t is the ability of an organization to move information and ideas from the bottom to the top and back again in continuous dialogue that the Japanese value above all things. As this dialogue is pursued, strategy evolves.—L. J. ROSENBERG AND C. D. SCHEWE

*A*n organization should approach all tasks with the idea that they can be accomplished in a superior fashion.—THOMAS WATSON, JR.

*W*orld-class information technologies are proving to be a significant strategic advantage, helping North American companies maintain and expand their position in the global marketplace.—Y. NAKAMURA

*B*y 2010, managers will have to handle greater cultural diversity. Managers will have to understand that employees don't think alike about such basics as "handling confrontation" or even what it means "to do a good day's work."—JEFFREY SONNENFELD

*T*here is no substitute for quality and no greater threat than failing to be cost-competitive on a global basis. These are complementary concepts, not mutually exclusive ones.—BILL SAPORITO

This chapter focuses on identifying and evaluating a firm's strengths and weaknesses in the functional areas of business, including management, marketing, finance/accounting, production/operations, research and development, and computer information systems. Relationships among these areas of business are examined. Strategic implications of important functional area concepts are examined. The process of performing an internal audit is described.

THE NATURE OF AN INTERNAL AUDIT

All organizations have strengths and weaknesses in the functional areas of business. No enterprise is equally strong or weak in all areas. Maytag, for example, is known for excellent production and product design, whereas Procter & Gamble is known for superb marketing. Internal strengths/weaknesses, coupled with external opportunities/threats and a clear statement of mission, provide the basis for establishing objectives and strategies. Objectives and strategies are established with the intention of capitalizing upon internal strengths and overcoming weaknesses! The internal-audit part of the strategic-management process is emphasized in Figure 5–1.

KEY INTERNAL FORCES   It is not possible in a business policy text to review in depth all the material presented in courses such as marketing, finance, accounting, management, computer information systems, and production/operations; there are many subareas within these functions, such as customer service, warranties, advertising, packaging, and pricing under marketing.

For different types of organizations, such as hospitals, universities, and government agencies, the functional business areas, of course, differ. In a hospital, for example, functional areas may include cardiology, hematology, nursing, maintenance, physician support, and receivables. Functional areas of a university can include athletic programs, placement services, housing, fund raising, academic research, counseling, and intramural programs. Within large organizations, each division has certain strengths and weaknesses. For example, AT&T is strong in communications and weak in computers.

A firm's strengths that cannot be easily matched or imitated by competitors are called *distinctive competencies*. Building competitive advantages involves taking advantage of distinctive competencies. For example, 3M exploits its distinctive competence in research and development by producing a wide range of innovative products. Strategies are designed in part to improve on a firm's weaknesses, turning them into strengths, and maybe even into distinctive competencies.

Some researchers emphasize the importance of the internal audit part of the strategic-management process by comparing it to the external audit. Robert Grant concluded that the internal audit is more important, saying:

> In a world where customer preferences are volatile, the identity of customers is changing, and the technologies for serving customer requirements are continually evolving, an externally focused orientation does not provide a secure foundation for formulating long-term strategy. When the external environment is in a state of flux, the firm's own resources and capabilities may be a much more stable basis on which to define its identity. Hence, a definition of a business in terms of what it is capable of doing may offer a more durable basis for strategy than a definition based upon the needs which the business seeks to satisfy.[1]

THE PROCESS OF PERFORMING AN INTERNAL AUDIT   The process of performing an *internal audit* closely parallels the process of performing an external audit. Representative managers and employees from throughout the firm need to be involved in

FIGURE 5-1
A Comprehensive Strategic-Management Model

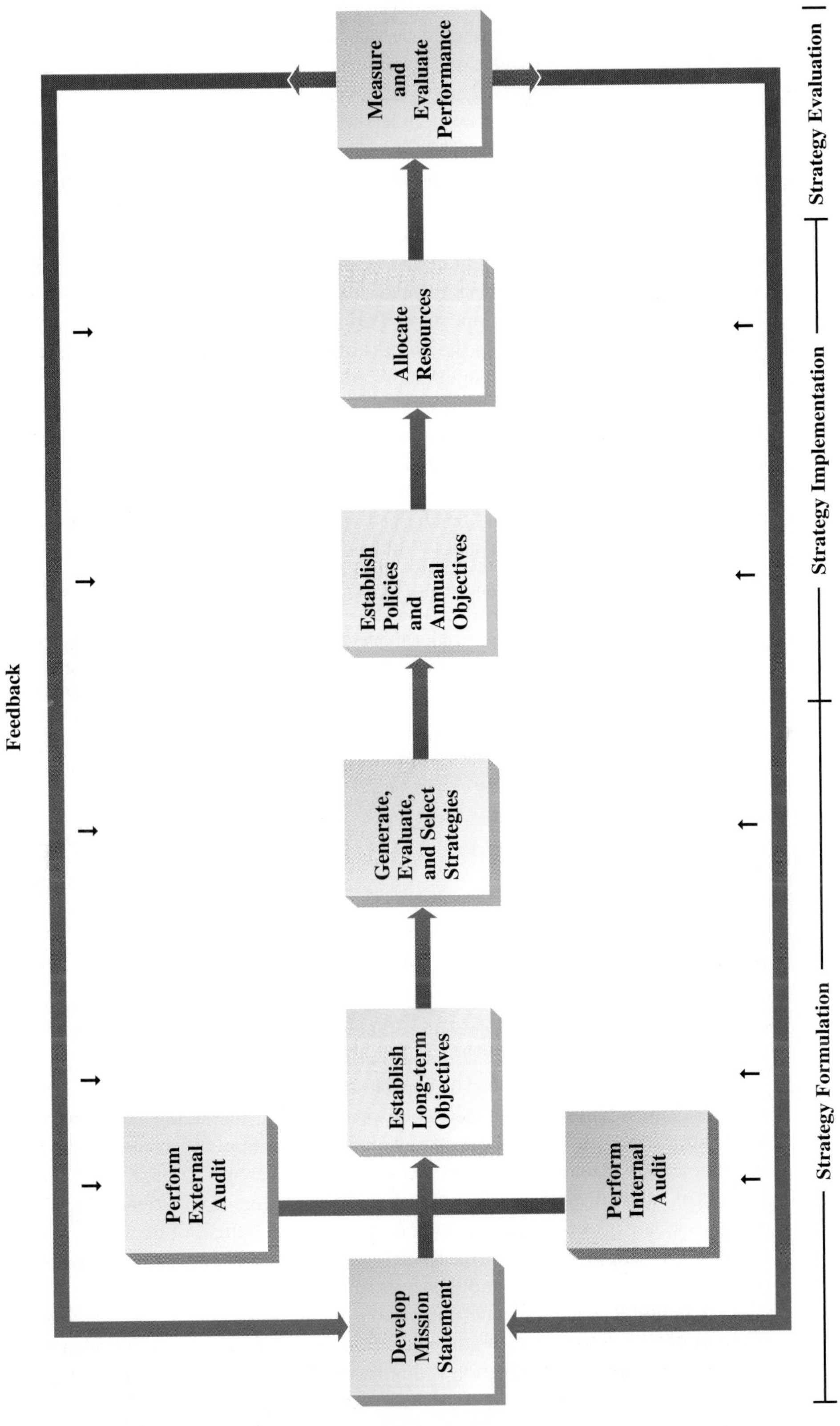

determining a firm's strengths and weaknesses. The internal audit requires gathering and assimilating information about the firm's management, marketing, finance/accounting, production/operations, research and development (R&D), and computer information systems operations. Key factors should be prioritized as described in Chapter 4 so that the firm's most important strengths and weaknesses can be determined collectively.

Compared to the external audit, the process of performing an internal audit provides more opportunity for participants to understand how their jobs, departments, and divisions fit into the whole organization. This is a great benefit because managers and employees perform better when they understand how their work affects other areas and activities of the firm. For example, when marketing and manufacturing managers jointly discuss issues related to internal strengths and weaknesses, they gain a better appreciation of issues, problems, concerns, and needs in all the functional areas. In organizations that do not use strategic management, marketing, finance, and manufacturing managers often do not interact with each other in significant ways. Performing an internal audit thus is an excellent vehicle or forum for improving the process of communication in the organization. "Communication" may be the most important word in management.

Performing an internal audit requires gathering, assimilating, and evaluating information about the firm's operations. Critical success factors, consisting of both strengths and weaknesses, can be identified and prioritized in the manner discussed in Chapter 4. According to William King, a task force of managers from different units of the organization, supported by staff, should be charged with determining the 10 to 20 most important strengths and weaknesses that should influence the future of the organization:

> The development of conclusions on the 10 to 20 most important organizational strengths and weaknesses can be, as any experienced manager knows, a difficult task, when it involves managers representing various organizational interests and points of view. Developing a 20-page list of strengths and weaknesses could be accomplished relatively easily, but a list of the 10 to 15 most important ones involves significant analysis and negotiation. This is true because of the judgments that are required and the impact which such a list will inevitably have as it is used in the formulation, implementation, and evaluation of strategies.[2]

RELATIONSHIPS AMONG THE FUNCTIONAL AREAS OF BUSINESS

Strategic management is a highly interactive process that requires effective coordination among management, marketing, finance/accounting, production/operations, R&D, and computer information systems managers. Although the strategic-management process is overseen by strategists, success requires that managers and employees from all functional areas work together to provide ideas and information. Financial managers, for example, may need to restrict the number of feasible options available to operations managers, or R&D managers may develop such good products that marketing managers need to set higher objectives. A key to organizational success is effective coordination and understanding among managers from all functional business areas! Through involvement in performing an internal strategic-management audit, managers from different departments and divisions of the firm come to understand the nature and effect of decisions in other functional business areas in their firm. Knowledge of these relationships is critical for effectively establishing objectives and strategies.

A failure to recognize and understand relationships among the functional areas of business can be detrimental to strategic management, and the number of those relationships that must be managed increases dramatically with a firm's size, diversity, geographic dispersion, and the number of products or services offered. Governmental and nonprofit enterprises traditionally have not placed sufficient emphasis on relationships among the business functions. For example, some state governments, utilities, universities, and hospitals only recently have begun to establish marketing objectives and policies that are consistent with their financial capabilities and limitations. Some firms place too great an emphasis on one function at the expense of others. Ansoff explained:

> During the first fifty years, successful firms focused their energies on optimizing the performance of one of the principal functions: production/operations, R&D, or marketing. Today, due to the growing complexity and dynamism of the environment, success increasingly depends on a judicious combination of several functional influences. This transition from a single function focus to a multifunction focus is essential for successful strategic management.[3]

Financial ratio analysis exemplifies the complexity of relationships among the functional areas of business. A declining return on investment or profit margin ratio could be the result of ineffective marketing, poor management policies, research and development errors, or a weak computer information system. The effectiveness of strategy formulation, implementation, and evaluation activities hinges upon a clear understanding of how major business functions affect one another. For strategies to succeed, a coordinated effort among all the functional areas of business is needed. In the case of planning, George wrote:

> We may conceptually separate planning for the purpose of theoretical discussion and analysis, but in practice, neither is it a distinct entity nor is it capable of being separated. The planning function is mixed with all other business functions and, like ink once mixed with water, it cannot be set apart. It is spread throughout and is a part of the whole of managing an organization.[4]

INTEGRATING STRATEGY AND CULTURE Relationships among a firm's functional business activities perhaps can be exemplified best by focusing on organizational culture, an internal phenomenon that permeates all departments and divisions of an organization. *Organizational culture* can be defined as "a pattern of behavior developed by an organization as it learns to cope with its problem of external adaptation and internal integration, that has worked well enough to be considered valid and to be taught to new members as the correct way to perceive, think, and feel."[5] This definition emphasizes the importance of matching external with internal factors in making strategic decisions.

Organizational culture captures the subtle, elusive, and largely unconscious forces that shape a workplace. Remarkably resistant to change, culture can represent a major strength or weakness for the firm. It can be an underlying reason for strengths or weaknesses in any of the major business functions.

Defined in Table 5–1, *cultural products* include values, beliefs, rites, rituals, ceremonies, myths, stories, legends, sagas, language, metaphors, symbols, heroes, and heroines. These products or dimensions are levers that strategists can use to influence and direct strategy formulation, implementation, and evaluation activities. An organization's culture compares to an individual's personality in the sense that no organization has the same culture and no individual has the same personality. Both culture and personality are fairly enduring and can be warm, aggressive, friendly, open, innovative, conservative, liberal, harsh, or likable.

Dimensions of organizational culture permeate all the functional areas of business. It is something of an art to uncover the basic values and beliefs that are buried deeply in an organization's rich collection of stories, language, heroes, and rituals, but cultural products can represent important strengths and weaknesses. Culture is an aspect of organizations that no longer can be taken for granted in performing an internal strategic-management audit because culture and strategy must work together.

The strategic-management process takes place largely within a particular organization's culture. Lorsch found that executives in successful companies are emotionally

TABLE 5–1
Cultural Products and Associated Definitions

Rites	Relatively elaborate, dramatic, planned sets of activities that consolidate various forms of cultural expressions into one event, carried out through social interactions, usually for the benefit of an audience
Ceremonial	A system of several rites connected with a single occasion or event
Ritual	A standardized, detailed set of techniques and behaviors that manage anxieties, but seldom produce intended, technical consequences of practical importance
Myth	A dramatic narrative of imagined events, usually used to explain origins or transformations of something. Also, an unquestioned belief about the practical benefits of certain techniques and behaviors that is not supported by facts
Saga	An historical narrative describing the unique accomplishments of a group and its leaders, usually in heroic terms
Legend	A handed-down narrative of some wonderful event that is based on history but has been embellished with fictional details
Story	A narrative based on true events, sometimes a combination of truth and fiction
Folktale	A completely fictional narrative
Symbol	Any object, act, event, quality, or relation that serves as a vehicle for conveying meaning, usually by representing another thing
Language	A particular form or manner in which members of a group use sounds and written signs to convey meanings to each other
Metaphors	Shorthand words used to capture a vision or to reinforce old or new values
Values	Life-directing attitudes that serve as behavioral guidelines
Belief	An understanding of a particular phenomenon
Heroes/Heroines	Individuals whom the organization has legitimized to model behavior for others

Source: Adapted from H.M. Trice and J.M. Beyer, "Studying Organizational Cultures Through Rites and Ceremonials," *Academy of Management Review* 9, no. 4 (October 1984): 655.

committed to the firm's culture, but he concluded that culture can inhibit strategic management in two basic ways. First, managers frequently miss the significance of changing external conditions because they are blinded by strongly held beliefs. Second, when a particular culture has been effective in the past, the natural response is to stick with it in the future, even during times of major strategic change.[6] An organization's culture must support the collective commitment of its people to a common purpose. It must foster competence and enthusiasm among managers and employees.

Organizational culture significantly affects business decisions and thus must be evaluated during an internal strategic-management audit. If strategies can capitalize on cultural strengths, such as a strong work ethic or highly ethical beliefs, then management often can implement changes swiftly and easily. However, if the firm's culture is not supportive, strategic changes may be ineffective or even counterproductive. A firm's culture can become antagonistic to new strategies, with the result being confusion and disorientation. An organization's culture should infuse individuals with enthusiasm for implementing strategies. Allarie and Firsirotu emphasized the need to understand culture:

> Culture provides an explanation for the insuperable difficulties a firm encounters when it attempts to shift its strategic direction. Not only has the "right" culture become the essence and foundation of corporate excellence, it is also claimed that success or failure of reforms hinges on management's sagacity and ability to change the firm's driving culture in time and in tune with required changes in strategies.[7]

The potential value of organizational culture has not been realized fully in the study of strategic management. Ignoring the effect that culture can have on relationships among the functional areas of business can result in barriers to communication, lack of coordination, and an inability to adapt to changing conditions. Some tension between culture and a firm's strategy is inevitable, but the tension should be monitored so that it does not reach a point at which relationships are severed and the culture becomes antagonistic. The resulting disarray among members of the organization would disrupt strategy formulation, implementation, and evaluation. On the other hand, a supportive organizational culture can make managing much easier.

Internal strengths and weaknesses associated with a firm's culture sometimes are overlooked due to the interfunctional nature of this phenomenon. It is important, therefore, for strategists to understand their firm as a sociocultural system. Success is often determined by linkages between a firm's culture and strategies. The challenge of strategic management today is to bring about the changes in organizational culture and individual mind-sets necessary to support the formulation, implementation, and evaluation of strategies. As indicated in the Global Perspective, this challenge becomes greater as a firm initiates or expands multinational operations. Note how managers in the Far East differ from U.S. and European managers in style and behavior.

OPERATING AS IF THE NATURAL ENVIRONMENT MATTERS Both employees and consumers are becoming especially resentful of firms that take from more than they give to the natural environment; likewise, people today are especially appreciative of firms that conduct operations in a way that mends rather than harms the environment.

The U.S. Justice Department recently issued new guidelines for companies to uncover environmental wrongdoing among their managers and employees without exposing

GLOBAL PERSPECTIVE

How Cultures of Countries Vary

There are two basic types of cultures in the world—high-context and low-context. High-context cultures are oral cultures in which what a person says in writing is *less important* than who a person is and what the social context is surrounding a business agreement. In low-context cultures, what a person says in writing is *more important* than who a person is and what the social context is surrounding a business agreement. The following diagram gives an arrangement of high-context and low-context cultures worldwide:

Chinese	High-Context Culture
Korean	↑
Japanese	
Vietnamese	
Arab	
Greek	
Spanish	
Italian	
English	
North American	
Scandinavian	↓
Swiss	
German	Low-Context Culture

There are numerous implications of the high-context/low-context culture analysis that should be considered in doing business globally. For example:

1. In high-context countries, casual conversations have a level of business significance far beyond the content being discussed. High-context foreign nationals want to know a lot about people personally and about their companies before making business commitments.

2. Businesspeople in high-context cultures expect a presentation to be in short, separate segments to allow time for questions and digestion of what has been presented. Frequent deviations from the major business topic are expected. High-context persons are not time- or efficiency-oriented and thus like to relax some during business meetings.

3. In high-context cultures, age, seniority, and experience are very important, so sending a young expert to conduct a meeting or close a sale would often be interpreted negatively.

4. A passive, impersonal style of communication is best with low-context cultures. Avoid exaggeration, hyperbole, superlatives, and egocentrism.

Source: Adapted from Ronald Dulek, John Fielden, and John Hill, "International Communication: An Executive Primer," Business Horizons (January–February 1991): 19–25. Also, Edward Hall, "How Cultures Collide," Psychology Today (July 1976): 67–74.

themselves to potential criminal liability. The new guidelines give nine hypothetical examples to illustrate the new legal requirements. The examples include Company A, which regularly conducts a comprehensive environmental audit, goes straight to the government as soon as something wrong is turned up, disciplines the responsible people in the company, and gives their names as well as all relevant documentation to the government. The Justice Department will prosecute but be lenient in this case. The extreme example is Company K, which tries to cover up an environmental violation and does not cooperate with the government or provide names. Its audit is narrow, and its compliance program is "no more than a collection of paper." No leniency is likely for this firm. United Technologies Corporation, for example, recently was a Company K and incurred a $5.3 million fine for abuses in handling and discharging hazardous wastes.

MANAGEMENT

The *functions of management* consist of five basic activities: planning, organizing, motivating, staffing, and controlling. An overview of these activities is provided in Table 5–2.

PLANNING   The only thing certain about the future of any organization is change, and *planning* is the essential bridge between the present and the future that increases the likelihood of achieving desired results. Planning is the cornerstone of effective strategy formulation. But even though it is considered the foundation of management, it is commonly the task that managers neglect most. Planning is essential for successful strategy implementation and

TABLE 5–2
The Basic Functions of Management

FUNCTION	DESCRIPTION	STAGE OF STRATEGIC-MANAGEMENT PROCESS WHEN MOST IMPORTANT
Planning	Planning consists of all those managerial activities related to preparing for the future. Specific tasks include forecasting, establishing objectives, devising strategies, developing policies, and setting goals.	Strategy Formulation
Organizing	Organizing includes all those managerial activities that result in a structure of task and authority relationships. Specific areas include organizational design, job specialization, job descriptions, job specifications, span of the control, unity of command, coordination, job design, and job analysis.	Strategy Implementation
Motivating	Motivating involves efforts directed toward shaping human behavior. Specific topics include leadership, communication, work groups, behavior modification, delegation of authority, job enrichment, job satisfaction, needs fulfillment, organizational change, employee morale, and managerial morale.	Strategy Implementation
Staffing	Staffing activities are centered on personnel or human resource management. Included are wage and salary administration, employee benefits, interviewing, hiring, firing, training, management development, employee safety, affirmative action, equal employment opportunity, union relations, career development, personnel research, discipline policies, grievance procedures, and public relations.	Strategy Implementation
Controlling	Controlling refers to all those managerial activities directed toward ensuring that actual results are consistent with planned results. Key areas of concern include quality control, financial control, sales control, inventory control, expense control, analysis of variances, rewards, and sanctions.	Strategy Evaluation

strategy evaluation, largely because organizing, motivating, staffing, and controlling activities are dependent upon good planning.

The process of planning must include involvement of managers and employees throughout an organization. As noted in Figure 5–2, the time horizon for planning decreases from two to five years for top-level to less than six months for lower-level managers. The important point is that all managers do planning and should involve subordinates in the process to facilitate employee understanding and commitment.

Planning can have a positive impact on organizational and individual performance. Planning allows an organization to identify and take advantage of external opportunities and minimize the impact of external threats. Planning is more than extrapolating from the past and present into the future. It also includes developing a mission, forecasting future events and trends, establishing objectives, and choosing strategies to pursue.

An organization can develop synergy through planning. *Synergy* exists when everyone pulls together as a team that knows what it wants to achieve; synergy is the 2 + 2 = 5 effect. By establishing and communicating clear objectives, employees and managers can work together toward desired results. Synergy can result in powerful competitive advantages. The strategic-management process itself is aimed at creating synergy in an organization.

FIGURE 5–2
The Three Levels of Planning

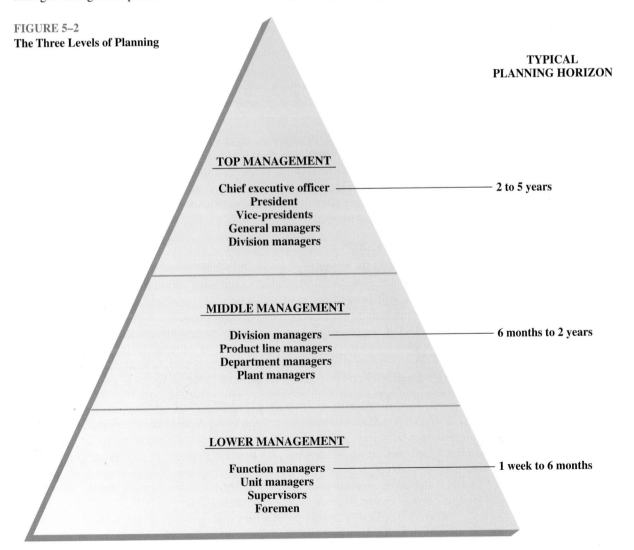

Planning allows a firm to adapt to changing markets and thus shape its own destiny. Strategic management can be viewed as a formal planning process that allows an organization to pursue proactive rather than reactive strategies. Successful organizations strive to control their own futures rather than merely react to external forces and events as they occur. Historically, organisms and organizations that have not adapted to changing conditions have become extinct. Swift adaptation is needed today more than ever before because changes in markets, economies, and competitors worldwide are accelerating.

ORGANIZING   The purpose of *organizing* is to achieve coordinated effort by defining task and authority relationships. Organizing means determining who does what and who reports to whom. There are countless examples in history of well-organized enterprises successfully competing against, and in some cases defeating, much stronger but less-organized firms. A well-organized firm generally has motivated managers and employees who are committed to seeing the organization succeed. Resources are allocated more effectively and used more efficiently in a well-organized firm than in a disorganized firm.

The organizing function of management can be viewed as consisting of three sequential activities: breaking tasks down into jobs (work specialization), combining jobs to form departments (departmentalization), and delegating authority. Breaking tasks down into jobs requires development of job descriptions and job specifications. These tools clarify for both managers and employees what particular jobs entail. In *Wealth of Nations* published in 1776, Adam Smith cited the advantages of work specialization in the manufacture of pins:

> One man draws the wire, another straightens it, a third cuts it, a fourth points it, a fifth grinds it at the top for receiving the head. Ten men working in this manner can produce 48,000 pins in a single day, but if they had all wrought separately and independently, each might at best produce twenty pins in a day.[8]

Combining jobs to form departments results in an organizational structure, span of control, and a chain of command. Changes in strategy often require changes in structure because new positions may be created, deleted, or merged. Organizational structure dictates how resources are allocated and how objectives are established in a firm. Allocating resources and establishing objectives geographically, for example, is much different from doing so by product or customer.

The most common forms of departmentalization are functional, divisional, strategic business unit, and matrix. These types of structure are discussed further in Chapter 7. Sears recently reorganized its 825 stores into six broad divisions: electronics and appliances, home fashions, home improvement products, men's and children's products, women's apparel, and automotive and recreational products.

Delegating authority is an important organizing activity, as evidenced in the old saying "You can tell how good a manager is by observing how his or her department functions when he or she isn't there." Employees today are more educated and more capable of participating in organizational decision making than ever before. In most cases, they expect to be delegated authority and responsibility, and to be held accountable for results. Delegation of authority is embedded in the strategic-management process.

MOTIVATING   *Motivating* can be defined as the process of influencing people to accomplish specific objectives.[9] Motivation explains why some people work hard and others do not. Objectives, strategies, and policies have little chance of succeeding if employees and managers are not motivated to implement strategies once they are formulated. The motivating function of management includes at least four major components: leadership, group dynamics, communication, and organizational change.

When managers and employees of a firm strive to achieve high levels of productivity, this indicates that the firm's strategists are good leaders. Good leaders establish rapport with subordinates, empathize with their needs and concerns, set a good example, and are trustworthy and fair. Leadership includes developing a vision of the firm's future and inspiring people to work hard to achieve that vision. Kirkpatrick and Locke reported that certain traits also characterize effective leaders: knowledge of the business, cognitive ability, self-confidence, honesty, integrity, and drive.[10]

Research suggests that democratic behavior on the part of leaders results in more positive attitudes toward change and higher productivity than does autocratic behavior. Drucker said:

> Leadership is not a magnetic personality. That can just as well be demagoguery. It is not "making friends and influencing people." That is flattery. Leadership is the lifting of a person's vision to higher sights, the raising of a person's performance to a higher standard, the building of a person's personality beyond its normal limitations.[11]

Group dynamics play a major role in employee morale and satisfaction. Informal groups or coalitions form in every organization. The norms of coalitions can range from being very positive to very negative toward management. It is important, therefore, that strategists identify the composition and nature of informal groups in an organization to facilitate strategy formulation, implementation, and evaluation. Leaders of informal groups are especially important in formulating and implementing strategy changes.

Communication, perhaps the most important word in management, is a major component in motivation. An organization's system of communication determines whether strategies can be implemented successfully. Good two-way communication is vital for gaining support for departmental and divisional objectives and policies. Top-down communication can encourage bottom-up communication. The strategic-management process becomes a lot easier when subordinates are encouraged to discuss their concerns, reveal their problems, provide recommendations, and give suggestions. A primary reason for instituting strategic management is to build and support effective communication networks throughout the firm.

> The manager of tomorrow must be able to get his people to commit themselves to the business, whether they are machine operators or junior vice-presidents. Ah, you say, participative management. Have a cigar. But just because most managers tug a forelock at the P word doesn't mean they know how to make it work. In the 1990s, throwing together a few quality circles won't suffice. The key issue will be empowerment, a term whose strength suggests the need to get beyond merely sharing a little information and a bit of decision making.[12]

STAFFING The management function of *staffing*, also called *personnel management* or *human resource management*, includes activities such as recruiting, interviewing, testing, selecting, orienting, training, developing, caring for, evaluating, rewarding, disciplining, promoting, transferring, demoting, and dismissing employees, and managing union relations. After the Teamsters strike at United Parcel Service, the rhetoric of labor activists implied a strong union revival in the United States. Facts, however, do not support the rhetoric. Unions in the Southeast United States held 32 percent fewer elections in 1996 than in 1990. Union membership as a percentage of the workforce in the Southeast continues to plummet, to 5.3 percent in 1996 from 8.1 percent in 1986. In the entire United States, there were 3,623 union elections in 1990 but only 2,792 in 1996. North and South Carolina still rank 49th and 50th among states in percentage of union members among all workers.

Staffing activities play a major role in strategy-implementation efforts, and for this reason human resource managers are becoming more actively involved in the strategic-management process. Strengths and weaknesses in the staffing area are important to identify.

The complexity and importance of human resource activities have increased to such a degree that all but the smallest organizations now need a full-time human resource manager.

Numerous court cases that directly affect staffing activities are decided each day. Organizations and individuals can be penalized severely for not following federal, state, and local laws and guidelines related to staffing.[13] Line managers simply cannot stay abreast of all the legal developments and requirements regarding staffing. The human resources department coordinates staffing decisions in the firm so that an organization as a whole meets legal requirements. This department also provides needed consistency in administering company rules, wages, and policies.

Human resources management is particularly challenging for international companies. For example, the inability of spouses and children to adapt to new surroundings has become a major staffing problem in overseas transfers. The problems include premature returns, job performance slumps, resignations, discharges, low morale, marital discord, and general discontent. Firms such as Ford Motor and Exxon have begun screening and interviewing spouses and children before assigning persons to overseas positions. 3M Corporation introduces children to peers in the target country and offers spouses educational benefits.

Strategists are becoming increasingly aware of how important human resources are to effective strategic management. Human resource managers are becoming more involved and more proactive in formulating and implementing strategies. They provide leadership for organizations that are restructuring or allowing employees to work at home as suggested in the Information Technology Perspective.

Waterman described staffing activities among successful companies:

> Successful (renewing) companies are busy taking out layers of management, cutting staff, and pushing decisions down. Nucor Corporation runs a successful, near billion-dollar steel enterprise from a headquarters office and complement of seven people in a Charlotte, N.C., shopping mall. At Dana Corporation, President Woody Morcott and others take extraordinary pride in the fact that today there are only five layers between the chief executive's office and the person on the factory floor. In the mid-1970s there were 14. . . Leaner organizations set the stage for success (renewal). They make each one of us more important. They empower the individual.[14]

INFORMATION TECHNOLOGY

The Officeless Office

In many firms information technology is doing away with the workplace and allowing employees to work at home or anywhere, anytime. The number of work-at-home employees and managers is expected to exceed 13 million by 1998 in the United States. "There is nothing I can do in an office that I can't do at home," says William Holtz, vice-president for global enterprise services with Northern Telecom. From his home in Philadelphia, Holtz supervises a staff of 1,000 in Nashville, Tennessee. Managers are moving away from the mindset of having to see their employees and watch them work.

The mobile concept of work allows employees to work the traditional 9-to-5 workday across any of the 24 time zones around the globe. Affordable desktop videoconferencing software developed by AT&T, Intel, Lotus, or Vivo Software allows employees to beam in whenever needed. Any manager or employee who travels a lot away from the office may be a good candidate for working at home rather than in an office provided by the firm. Salespersons and consultants are good examples, but any person whose job largely involves talking to others or handling information could easily operate at home with the proper computer system and software. The accounting firm Ernst & Young has reduced its office space requirements by 2 million square feet over the past three years by allowing employees to work at home.

Many people see the officeless office trend as leading to a resurgence of family togetherness in American society. Even the design of homes may change from having large open areas to having more private small areas conducive to getting work done.

Source: Adapted from Edward Baig, "Welcome to the Officeless Office," Business Week (June 26, 1995): 104.

CONTROLLING   The *controlling* function of management includes all those activities undertaken to ensure that actual operations conform to planned operations. All managers in an organization have controlling responsibilities, such as conducting performance evaluations and taking necessary action to minimize inefficiencies. The controlling function of management is particularly important for effective strategy evaluation. Controlling consists of four basic steps:

1. Establishing performance standards
2. Measuring individual and organizational performance
3. Comparing actual performance to planned performance standards
4. Taking corrective actions

Measuring individual performance is often conducted ineffectively or not at all in organizations. Some reasons for this shortcoming are that evaluation can create confrontations that most managers prefer to avoid, can take more time than most managers are willing to give, and can require skills that many managers lack. No single approach to measuring individual performance is without limitations. For this reason, an organization should examine various methods, such as the graphic rating scale, the behaviorally anchored rating scale, and the critical incident method, and then develop or select a performance appraisal approach that best suits the firm's needs. Increasingly, firms are striving to link organizational performance with managers' and employees' pay. This topic is discussed further in Chapter 7.

MARKETING

Marketing can be described as the process of defining, anticipating, creating, and fulfilling customers' needs and wants for products and services. Joel Evans and Barry Bergman suggested that there are nine basic *functions of marketing*: (1) customer analysis, (2) buying supplies, (3) selling products/services, (4) product and service planning, (5) pricing, (6) distribution, (7) marketing research, (8) opportunity analysis, and (9) social responsibility.[15] Understanding these functions helps strategists identify and evaluate marketing strengths and weaknesses.

CUSTOMER ANALYSIS   *Customer analysis*—the examination and evaluation of consumer needs, desires, and wants—involves administering customer surveys, analyzing consumer information, evaluating market positioning strategies, developing customer profiles, and determining optimal market segmentation strategies. The information generated by customer analysis can be essential in developing an effective mission statement. Customer profiles can reveal the demographic characteristics of an organization's customers. Buyers, sellers, distributors, salespeople, managers, wholesalers, retailers, suppliers, and creditors can all participate in gathering information to identify customers' needs and wants successfully. Successful organizations continually monitor present and potential customers' buying patterns.

BUYING SUPPLIES   The second function of marketing is buying supplies needed to produce and sell a product or service. *Buying* consists of evaluating alternative suppliers or vendors, selecting the best suppliers, arranging acceptable terms with suppliers, and procuring the supplies. The buying process can be complicated by such factors as price controls, recession, foreign trade restrictions, strikes, walkouts, and machine breakdowns. Even the weather can significantly disrupt procurement of needed supplies. Quite often, the question arises whether to make or buy needed supplies and services. Recall that backward integration, gaining control over suppliers, is a particularly attractive strategy when suppliers are unreliable, costly, or incapable of meeting company needs.

SELLING PRODUCTS/SERVICES Successful strategy implementation generally rests upon the ability of an organization to sell some product or service. *Selling* includes many marketing activities such as advertising, sales promotion, publicity, personal selling, sales force management, customer relations, and dealer relations. These activities are especially critical when a firm pursues a market penetration strategy. The effectiveness of various selling tools for consumer and industrial products varies. Personal selling is most important for industrial goods companies, and advertising is most important for consumer goods companies. Determining organizational strengths and weaknesses in the selling function of marketing is an important part of performing an internal strategic-management audit.

With regard to advertising products and services on the Internet, a new trend is to base advertising rates exclusively on sale rates. This new accountability contrasts sharply with traditional broadcast and print advertising that bases rates on the number of persons expected to see a given advertisement. The new cost-per-sale on-line advertising rates are possible because any Web site can monitor which user clicks on which advertisement and then can record whether that consumer actually buys the product. If there are no sales, then the advertisement is free.

Some mass retailers such as Amazon Books and CUC International are paying millions of dollars in sales commissions and advertising fees in exchange for prominent placement on high-traffic Web sites, search engines, and home pages of on-line service providers such as America Online.

Anheuser-Busch currently is being investigated by the U.S. Justice Department to determine whether the company's sales practices are a violation of antitrust laws. Anheuser has 45 percent of the U.S. beer market, followed by Miller's 22 percent, Coors's 10 percent, Stroh's' 8.3 percent, Import's 6.5 percent, and Pabst's 2.5 percent.[16]

PRODUCT AND SERVICE PLANNING *Product and service planning* includes activities such as test marketing; product and brand positioning; devising warranties; packaging; determining product options, product features, product style, and product quality; deleting old products; and providing for customer service. Product and service planning is particularly important when a company is pursuing product development or diversification.

One of the most effective product and service planning techniques is *test marketing*. Test markets allow an organization to test alternative marketing plans and to forecast future sales of new products. In conducting a test market project, an organization must decide how many cities to include, which cities to include, how long to run the test, what information to collect during the test, and what action to take after the test has been completed. Test marketing is used more frequently by consumer goods companies than by industrial goods companies. Test marketing can allow an organization to avoid substantial losses by revealing weak products and ineffective marketing approaches before large-scale production begins.

PRICING Five major stakeholders affect *pricing* decisions: consumers, governments, suppliers, distributors, and competitors. Sometimes an organization will pursue a forward integration strategy primarily to gain better control over prices charged to consumers. Governments can impose constraints on price fixing, price discrimination, minimum prices, unit pricing, price advertising, and price controls. For example, the Robinson-Patman Act prohibits manufacturers and wholesalers from discriminating in price among channel member purchasers (suppliers and distributors) if competition is injured.

Competing organizations must be careful not to coordinate discounts, credit terms, or condition of sale; not to discuss prices, markups, and costs at trade association meetings; and not to arrange to issue new price lists on the same date, to rotate low bids on contracts, or to uniformly restrict production to maintain high prices. Strategists should view price from both a short-run and a long-run perspective, because competitors can copy price changes with relative ease. Often a dominant firm will aggressively match all price cuts by competitors.

With regard to pricing, as the value of the dollar increases, which it has been doing steadily, U.S. multinational companies have a choice. They can raise prices in the local currency of a foreign country or risk losing sales and market share. Alternatively, multinational firms can keep prices steady and face reduced profit when their export revenue is reported in the United States in dollars.

DISTRIBUTION   *Distribution* includes warehousing, distribution channels, distribution coverage, retail site locations, sales territories, inventory levels and location, transportation carriers, wholesaling, and retailing. Most producers today do not sell their goods directly to consumers. Various marketing entities act as intermediaries; they bear a variety of names such as wholesalers, retailers, brokers, facilitators, agents, middlemen, vendors, or simply distributors.

Major cargo carriers in the United States, including trains, trucks, ships, and planes, are being swamped with business in the late 1990s. Union Pacific, the nation's largest railroad, has such a monumental backlog that the firm now ships goods by sea, through the Panama Canal. Freight in the United States has piled up at rail terminals, ship docks, and trucking centers. Trucks move 80 percent of consumer goods in the United States. There is a widespread shortage of both truck drivers and trucks in this country.

Distribution becomes especially important when a firm is striving to implement a market development or forward integration strategy. Some of the most complex and challenging decisions facing a firm concern product distribution. Intermediaries flourish in our economy because many producers lack the financial resources and expertise to carry out direct marketing. Manufacturers who could afford to sell directly to the public often can gain greater returns by expanding and improving their manufacturing operations. Even General Motors would find it very difficult to buy out its more than 18,000 independent dealers.

Successful organizations identify and evaluate alternative ways to reach their ultimate market. Possible approaches vary from direct selling to using just one or many wholesalers and retailers. Strengths and weaknesses of each channel alternative should be determined according to economic, control, and adaptive criteria. Organizations should consider the costs and benefits of various wholesaling and retailing options. They must consider the need to motivate and control channel members and the need to adapt to changes in the future. Once a marketing channel is chosen, an organization usually must adhere to it for an extended period of time.

MARKETING RESEARCH   *Marketing research* is the systematic gathering, recording, and analyzing of data about problems relating to the marketing of goods and services. Marketing research can uncover critical strengths and weaknesses, and marketing researchers employ numerous scales, instruments, procedures, concepts, and techniques to gather information. Recent market research regarding the top 10 selling brands of liquor and wine are provided in Table 5–3. Marketing research activities support all of the major business functions of an organization. Organizations that possess excellent marketing research skills have a definite strength in pursuing generic strategies.

> The President of PepsiCo says, "Looking at the competition is the company's best form of market research. The majority of our strategic successes are ideas that we borrow from the marketplace, usually from a small regional or local competitor. In each case, we spot a promising new idea, improve on it, and then out-execute our competitor."[17]

About 20,000 new products are introduced by U.S. companies annually, but 85 percent of these fail within three years. Many CEOs continue to trust their own best judgment

TABLE 5–3
Leading Liquor and Wind Brands

LEADING LIQUOR BRANDS
(IN THOUSANDS OF 9-LITER CASE SALES)

			CASE SALES	
BRAND	**MARKETER**	**TYPE**	**1995**	**1996**
Bacardi	Bacardi	Rum	6,120	6,050
Smirnoff	Heublein	Vodka	5,785	5,950
Seagram's	Seagram	Gin	3,840	3,625
Absolut	Carillon	Vodka	3,165	3,330
Jim Beam	Beam	Bourbon	3,260	3,080
Seagram's 7 Crown	Seagram	Whiskey	3,050	3,015
Jack Daniel's Black	Brown-Forman	Whiskey	3,000	3,010
Canadian Mist	Brown-Forman	Whiskey	2,960	2,885
Popov	Heublein	Vodka	3,000	2,805
E & J	E & J Gallo	Brandy	2,525	2,775

TOP 10 WINE BRANDS
(IN THOUSANDS OF 9-LITER CASE SALES)

			CASE SALES	
	BRAND	**COMPANY**	**1995**	**1996**
1.	Franzia	The Wine Group	13,000	15,800
2.	Carlo Rossi	E&J Gallo Winery	11,695	11,800
3.	Gallo Livingston Cellars	E&J Gallo Winery	11,230	11,150
4.	The Wine Cellars of Ernest & Julio Gallo	E&J Gallo Winery	9,300	9,500
5.	Almaden	Canandaigua Wine Co.	7,385	7,165
6.	Inglenook	Canandaigua Wine Co.	7,250	6,960
7.	Sutter Home	Sutter Home Winery	5,285	6,255
8.	Woodbridge	Robert Mondavi Winery	4,350	4,685
9.	Glen Ellen	Heublein Wines Group	3,350	3,475
10.	Vendange	Sebastiani Vineyards	2,465	3,200
	Total Top 10		75,310	79,990

Source: Adapted from IMPACT DATABANK.

over market research; this mind-set can be detrimental to a business. For example, the Greyhound Bus Company first pursued the African American market by placing advertising on African American radio stations. However, instead of creating a new commercial, Greyhound used its popular Country & Western music ad, which later was considered to have failed in that market.

OPPORTUNITY ANALYSIS The eighth function of marketing is *opportunity analysis*, which involves assessing the costs, benefits, and risks associated with marketing decisions. Three steps are required to perform a *cost/benefit analysis*: (1) compute the total costs associated with a decision, (2) estimate the total benefits from the decision, and (3) compare the total costs with the total benefits. As expected benefits exceed total costs, an opportunity becomes more attractive. Sometimes the variables included in a cost/benefit analysis cannot be quantified or even measured, but usually reasonable estimates can be made to allow the analysis to be performed. One key factor to be considered is risk. Cost/benefit analyses should also be performed when a company is evaluating alternative ways to be socially responsible.

SOCIAL RESPONSIBILITY The final function of marketing, according to Evans and Bergman, is to determine how best to meet the firm's social responsibility obligations. *Social responsibility* can include offering products and services that are safe and reasonably priced. Demands by special-interest groups on business organizations greatly increased during the 1980s. Arguments still rage today, though, about how socially responsible firms should be. A clear social policy can represent a major strength for organizations, whereas a poor social policy can be a weakness.

Some strategists view social responsibility as a focus that detracts from, or is counter to, their profit-minded pursuits. Although there may be some clearly distinct economic versus social concerns, there is a rather broad area in which economic and social concerns are consistent with one another. Many corporate activities are profitable, and at the same time are socially responsible. When a firm engages in social activities, it must do so in a way that receives economic advantages.

In perhaps the largest philanthropic gift ever by one individual, Ted Turner in 1997 donated $1 billion, one-third of his entire net worth, to United Nations charities. Turner, who owns 10 percent of Time Warner Inc., said, "I'm putting every rich person in the world on notice that they're going to be hearing from me about giving money. If you want to lead, you got to blow the horn and get out in front of the parade." Turner clearly believes firms should be highly socially responsible.

FINANCE/ACCOUNTING

Financial condition is often considered the single best measure of a firm's competitive position and overall attractiveness to investors. Determining an organization's financial strengths and weaknesses is essential to formulating strategies effectively. A firm's liquidity, leverage, working capital, profitability, asset utilization, cash flow, and equity can eliminate some strategies as being feasible alternatives. Financial factors often alter existing strategies and change implementation plans.

FINANCE/ACCOUNTING FUNCTIONS According to James Van Horne, the *functions of finance/accounting* comprise three decisions: the investment decision, the financing decision, and the dividend decision.[18] Financial ratio analysis is the most widely used method for determining an organization's strengths and weaknesses in the investment, financing, and dividend areas. Because the functional areas of business are so closely related, financial ratios can signal strengths or weaknesses in management, marketing, production, research and development, and computer information systems activities.

The *investment decision*, also called *capital budgeting*, is the allocation and reallocation of capital and resources to projects, products, assets, and divisions of an organization. Once strategies are formulated, capital budgeting decisions are required to implement strategies successfully. The *financing decision* concerns determining the best capital structure for the firm and includes examining various methods by which the firm can raise capital (for example, by issuing stock, increasing debt, selling assets, or using a combination of these approaches). The financing decision must consider both short-term and long-term needs for working capital. Two key financial ratios that indicate whether a firm's financing decisions have been effective are the debt-to-equity ratio and the debt-to-total-assets ratio.

Dividend decisions concern issues such as the percentage of earnings paid to stockholders, the stability of dividends paid over time, and the repurchase or issuance of stock. Dividend decisions determine the amount of funds that are retained in a firm compared to the amount paid out to stockholders. Three financial ratios that are helpful in evaluating a firm's dividend decisions are the earnings-per-share ratio, the dividends-per-share ratio, and the price-earnings ratio. The benefits of paying dividends to investors must be balanced against the benefits of retaining funds internally, and there is no set formula on how to balance this trade-off. For the reasons listed here, dividends are sometimes paid out even when funds could be better reinvested in the business or when the firm has to obtain outside sources of capital:

1. Paying cash dividends is customary. Failure to do so could be thought of as a stigma. A dividend change is considered a signal about the future.

2. Dividends represent a sales point for investment bankers. Some institutional investors can buy only dividend-paying stocks.

3. Shareholders often demand dividends, even in companies with great opportunities for reinvesting all available funds.

4. A myth exists that paying dividends will result in a higher stock price.

BASIC TYPES OF FINANCIAL RATIOS   Financial ratios are computed from an organization's income statement and balance sheet. Computing financial ratios is like taking a picture because the results reflect a situation at just one point in time. Comparing ratios over time and to industry averages is more likely to result in meaningful statistics that can be used to identify and evaluate strengths and weaknesses. Trend analysis, illustrated in Figure 5–3, is a useful technique that incorporates both the time and industry average dimensions of financial ratios. Note that the dotted lines reveal projected ratios. Some Web sites such as Wall Street Research Net at www.wsrn.com calculate financial ratios and provide data with charts. Four major sources of industry-average financial ratios follow:

1. Dun & Bradstreet's *Industry Norms and Key Business Ratios*—Fourteen different ratios are calculated in an industry-average format for 800 different types of businesses. The ratios are presented by Standard Industrial Classification (SIC) number and are grouped by annual sales into three size categories.

2. Robert Morris Associates' *Annual Statement Studies*—Sixteen different ratios are calculated in an industry-average format. Industries are referenced by SIC

FIGURE 5–3
A Financial Ratio Trend Analysis

Current ratio

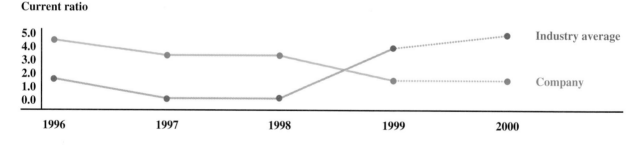

Profit margin (percent)

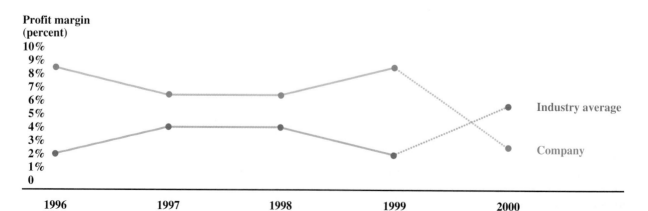

numbers published by the Bureau of the Census. The ratios are presented in four size categories by annual sales for all firms in the industry.

3. *Almanac of Business & Industrial Financial Ratios*—Twenty-two financial ratios and percentages are provided in an industry-average format for all major industries. The ratios and percentages are given for 12 different company-size categories for all firms in a given industry.

4. Federal Trade Commission Reports—The FTC publishes quarterly financial data, including ratios on manufacturing companies. FTC reports include analyses by industry group and asset size.

Table 5–4 provides a summary of key financial ratios showing how each ratio is calculated and what each ratio measures. However, all the ratios are not significant for all industries and companies. For example, accounts receivable turnover and average collection period are not very meaningful to a company that does primarily a cash receipts business. Key financial ratios can be classified into the following five types:

1. *Liquidity ratios* measure a firm's ability to meet maturing short-term obligations.
   Current ratio
   Quick (or acid-test) ratio

2. *Leverage ratios* measure the extent to which a firm has been financed by debt.
   Debt-to-total-assets ratio
   Debt-to-equity ratio
   Long-term debt-to-equity ratio
   Times-interest-earned (or coverage) ratio

3. *Activity ratios* measure how effectively a firm is using its resources.
   Inventory-turnover
   Fixed assets turnover
   Total assets turnover
   Accounts receivable turnover
   Average collection period

4. *Profitability ratios* measure management's overall effectiveness as shown by the returns generated on sales and investment.
   Gross profit margin
   Operating profit margin
   Net profit margin
   Return on total assets (ROA)
   Return on stockholders' equity (ROE)
   Earnings per share
   Price-earnings ratio

5. *Growth ratios* measure the firm's ability to maintain its economic position in the growth of the economy and industry.
   Sales
   Net income
   Earnings per share
   Dividends per share

Financial ratio analysis is not without some limitations. First of all, financial ratios are based on accounting data, and firms differ in their treatment of such items as depreciation, inventory valuation, research and development expenditures, pension plan costs, mergers, and taxes. Also, seasonal factors can influence comparative ratios. Therefore, conformity to industry composite ratios does not establish with certainty that a firm is performing normally or that it is well managed. Likewise, departures from industry averages

TABLE 5–4

A Summary of Key Financial Ratios

RATIO	HOW CALCULATED	WHAT IT MEASURES
LIQUIDITY RATIOS		
Current Ratio	$\dfrac{\text{Current assets}}{\text{Current liabilities}}$	The extent to which a firm can meet its short-term obligations
Quick Ratio	$\dfrac{\text{Current assets minus inventory}}{\text{Current liabilities}}$	The extent to which a firm can meet its short-term obligations without relying upon the sale of its inventories
LEVERAGE RATIOS		
Debt-to-Total-Assets Ratio	$\dfrac{\text{Total debt}}{\text{Total assets}}$	The percentage of total funds that are provided by creditors
Debt-to-Equity Ratio	$\dfrac{\text{Total debt}}{\text{Total stockholders' equity}}$	The percentage of total funds provided by creditors versus by owners
Long-Term Debt-to-Equity Ratio	$\dfrac{\text{Long-term debt}}{\text{Total stockholders' equity}}$	The balance between debt and equity in a firm's long-term capital structure
Times-Interest-Earned Ratio	$\dfrac{\text{Profits before interest and taxes}}{\text{Total interest charges}}$	The extent to which earnings can decline without the firm becoming unable to meet its annual interest costs
ACTIVITY RATIOS		
Inventory Turnover	$\dfrac{\text{Sales}}{\text{Inventory of finished goods}}$	Whether a firm holds excessive stocks of inventories and whether a firm is selling its inventories slowly compared to the industry average
Fixed Assets Turnover	$\dfrac{\text{Sales}}{\text{Fixed assets}}$	Sales productivity and plant and equipment utilization
Total Assets Turnover	$\dfrac{\text{Sales}}{\text{Total assets}}$	Whether a firm is generating a sufficient volume of business for the size of its asset investment
Accounts Receivable Turnover	$\dfrac{\text{Annual credit sales}}{\text{Accounts receivable}}$	The average length of time it takes a firm to collect credit sales (in percentage terms)
Average Collection Period	$\dfrac{\text{Accounts receivable}}{\text{Total credit sales/365 days}}$	The average length of time it takes a firm to collect on credit sales (in days)
PROFITABILITY RATIOS		
Gross Profit Margin	$\dfrac{\text{Sales minus cost of goods sold}}{\text{Sales}}$	The total margin available to cover operating expenses and yield a profit
Operating Profit Margin	$\dfrac{\text{Earnings before interest and taxes (EBIT)}}{\text{Sales}}$	Profitability without concern for taxes and interest
Net Profit Margin	$\dfrac{\text{Net income}}{\text{Sales}}$	After-tax profits per dollar of sales
Return on Total Assets (ROA)	$\dfrac{\text{Net income}}{\text{Total assets}}$	After-tax profits per dollar of assets; this ratio is also called return on investment (ROI)
Return on Stockholders' Equity (ROE)	$\dfrac{\text{Net income}}{\text{Total stockholders' equity}}$	After-tax profits per dollar of stockholders' investment in the firm
Earning Per Share (EPS)	$\dfrac{\text{Net income}}{\text{Number of shares of common stock outstanding}}$	Earnings available to the owners of common stock
Price-earning Ratio	$\dfrac{\text{Market price per share}}{\text{Earnings per share}}$	Attractiveness of firm on equity markets.
GROWTH RATIOS		
Sales	Annual percentage growth in total sales	Firm's growth rate in sales
Income	Annual percentage growth in profits	Firm's growth rate in profits
Earnings Per Share	Annual percentage growth in EPS	Firm's growth rate in EPS
Dividends Per Share	Annual percentage growth in dividends per share	Firm's growth rate in dividends per share

do not always indicate that a firm is doing especially well or badly. For example, a high inventory turnover ratio could indicate efficient inventory management and a strong working capital position, but it also could indicate a serious inventory shortage and a weak working capital position.

It is important to recognize that a firm's financial condition depends not only on the functions of finance, but also on many other factors that include (1) management, marketing, production/operations, research and development, and computer information systems decisions; (2) actions by competitors, suppliers, distributors, creditors, customers, and shareholders; and (3) economic, social, cultural, demographic, environmental, political, governmental, legal, and technological trends. Even natural environment liabilities can affect financial ratios, as indicated in the Natural Environment Perspective. So financial ratio analysis, like all other analytical tools, should be used wisely.

PRODUCTION/OPERATIONS

The *production/operations functions* of a business consists of all those activities that transform inputs into goods and services. Production/operations management deals with inputs, transformations, and outputs that vary across industries and markets. A manufacturing operation transforms or converts inputs such as raw materials, labor, capital, machines, and facilities into finished goods and services. As indicated in Table 5–5, Roger Schroeder suggested that production/operations management comprises five functions or decision areas: process, capacity, inventory, workforce, and quality.

Production/operations activities often represent the largest part of an organization's human and capital assets. In most industries, the major costs of producing a product or service are incurred within operations, so production/operations can have great value as a competitive weapon in a company's overall strategy. Strengths and weaknesses in the five functions of production can mean the success or failure of an enterprise.

Many production/operations managers are finding that cross-training of employees can help their firms respond to changing markets faster. Cross-training of workers can

NATURAL ENVIRONMENT

Environmental Liability on the Balance Sheet

Environmental liability may be the largest recognized or unrecognized liability on a company's balance sheet. More American firms are finding themselves liable for cleanup costs and damages stemming from waste disposal practices of the past, in some cases going back 100 years. Environmental liabilities associated with air and water pollution, habitat destruction, deforestation, and medical problems can be immense. For this reason, many financial institutions now inquire about environmental liabilities as part of their commercial lending proce-

dures. Firms such as American Insurance Company specialize in providing environmental liability insurance to companies.

Environmental Protection Agency (EPA) regulations take up more than 11,000 pages; they vary with location and size of firm and are added to daily. The complexity of these regulations can translate into liabilities for the environmentally reactive firm. Proactive firms, on the other hand, are adding a "green executive" and department to oversee management of environmental policies and practices of the firm. The responsi-

bility of green executives includes thinking through environmental regulations, marketing needs, public attitudes, consumer demands, and potential problems. Ideally, green executives should promote development of a corporate culture in which all managers and employees become "green," or environmentally sensitive. Such a culture would represent an internal strength to the firm.

TABLE 5–5
The Basic Functions of Production Management

FUNCTION	DESCRIPTION
1. Process	Process decisions concern the design of the physical production system. Specific decisions include choice of technology, facility layout, process flow analysis, facility location, line balancing, process control, and transportation analysis.
2. Capacity	Capacity decisions concern determination of optimal output levels for the organization—not too much and not too little. Specific decisions include forecasting, facilities planning, aggregate planning, scheduling, capacity planning, and queuing analysis.
3. Inventory	Inventory decisions involve managing the level of raw materials, work in process, and finished goods. Specific decisions include what to order, when to order, how much to order, and materials handling.
4. Workforce	Workforce decisions are concerned with managing the skilled, unskilled, clerical, and managerial employees. Specific decisions include job design, work measurement, job enrichment, work standards, and motivation techniques.
5. Quality	Quality decisions are aimed at ensuring that high-quality goods and services are produced. Specific decisions include quality control, sampling, testing, quality assurance, and cost control.

Source: Adapted from R. Schroeder, *Operations Management* (New York: McGraw-Hill Book Co., 1981): 12.

increase efficiency, quality, productivity, and job satisfaction. For example, at General Motors's Detroit Gear & Axle plant, costs related to product defects were reduced 400 percent in 2 years as a result of cross-training workers. A shortage of qualified labor in America is another reason cross-training is becoming a common management practice.

There is much reason for concern that many organizations have not taken sufficient account of the capabilities and limitations of the production/operations function in formulating strategies. Scholars contend that this neglect has had unfavorable consequences on corporate performance in America. As shown in Table 5–6, James Dilworth outlined several types of strategic decisions that a company might make with production/operations implications of those decisions. Production capabilities and policies can also greatly affect strategies:

> Given today's decision-making environment with shortages, inflation, technological booms, and government intervention, a company's production/operations capabilities and policies may not be able to fulfill the demands dictated by strategies. In fact, they may dictate corporate strategies. It is hard to imagine that an organization can formulate strategies today without first considering the constraints and limitations imposed by its existing production/operations structure.[19]

RESEARCH AND DEVELOPMENT

The fifth major area of internal operations that should be examined for specific strengths and weaknesses is research and development (R&D). Many firms today conduct no R&D, and yet many other companies depend on successful R&D activities for survival. Firms pursuing a product development strategy especially need to have a strong R&D orientation.

R&D expenditures overall for U.S. companies increased 5.6 percent in 1997. Microsoft increased its R&D expenditures 300 percent in 1997. IBM received more than 2,000 patents in 1997, up from 1,867 in 1996 and marking the fifth year in a row of leading all U.S. firms in number of patents received. Total R&D expenditures for all U.S. firms exceeded $200 billion for the first time in 1997.

TABLE 5–6
Impact of Strategy Elements on Production Management

POSSIBLE ELEMENTS OF STRATEGY	CONCOMITANT CONDITIONS THAT MAY AFFECT THE OPERATIONS FUNCTION AND ADVANTAGES AND DISADVANTAGES
1. Compete as low-cost provider of goods or services	Discourages competition Broadens market Requires longer production runs and fewer product changes Requires special-purpose equipment and facilities
2. Compete as high-quality provider	Often possible to obtain more profit per unit, and perhaps more total profit from a smaller volume of sales Requires more quality-assurance effort and higher operating cost Requires more precise equipment, which is more expensive Requires highly skilled workers, necessitating higher wages and greater training efforts
3. Stress customer service	Requires broader development of servicepeople and service parts and equipment Requires rapid response to customer needs or changes in customer tastes, rapid and accurate information system, careful coordination Requires a higher inventory investment
4. Provide rapid and frequent introduction of new products	Requires versatile equipment and people Has higher research and development costs Has high retraining costs and high tooling and changeover in manufacturing Provides lower volumes for each product and fewer opportunities for improvements due to the learning curve
5. Strive for absolute growth	Requires accepting some projects or products with lower marginal value, which reduces ROI Diverts talents to areas of weakness instead of concentrating on strengths
6. Seek vertical integration	Enables company to control more of the process May not have economies of scale at some stages of process May require high capital investment as well as technology and skills beyond those currently available within the organization
7. Maintain reserve capacity for flexibility	Provides ability to meet peak demands and quickly implement some contingency plans if forecasts are too low Requires capital investment in idle capacity Provides capability to grow during the lead time normally required for expansion
8. Consolidate processing (Centralize)	Can result in economies of scale Can locate near one major customer or supplier Vulnerability: one strike, fire, or flood can halt the entire operation
9. Disperse processing of service (Decentralize)	Can be near several market territories Requires more complex coordination network: perhaps expensive data transmission and duplication of some personnel and equipment at each location If each location produces one product in the line, then other products still must be transported to be available at all locations If each location specializes in a type of component for all products, the company is vulnerable to strike, fire, flood, etc. If each location provides total product line, then economies of scale may not be realized
10. Stress the use of mechanization, automation, robots	Requires high capital investment Reduces flexibility May affect labor relations Makes maintenance more crucial
11. Stress stability of employment	Serves the security needs of employees and may develop employee loyalty Helps to attract and retain highly skilled employees May require revisions of make-or-buy decisions, use of idle time, inventory, and subcontractors as demand fluctuates

Source: Production and Operations Management: Manufacturing and Nonmanufacturing, Second Edition, by J. Dilworth. Copyright © 1983 by Random House, Inc. Reprinted by permission of Random House, Inc.

Organizations invest in R&D because they believe that such investment will lead to superior product or services and give them competitive advantages. Research and development expenditures are directed at developing new products before competitors do, improving product quality, or improving manufacturing processes to reduce costs.[20]

One article on planning emphasized that effective management of the R&D function requires a strategic and operational partnership between R&D and the other vital business functions. A spirit of partnership and mutual trust between general and R&D managers is evident in the best-managed firms today. Managers in these firms jointly explore; assess; and decide the what, when, why, and how much of R&D. Priorities, costs, benefits, risks, and rewards associated with R&D activities are discussed openly and shared. The overall mission of R&D thus has become broad-based, including supporting existing businesses, helping launch new businesses, developing new products, improving product quality, improving manufacturing efficiency, and deepening or broadening the company's technological capabilities.[21]

The best-managed firms today seek to organize R&D activities in a way that breaks the isolation of R&D from the rest of the company and promotes a spirit of partnership between R&D managers and other managers in the firm. R&D decisions and plans must be integrated and coordinated across departments and divisions by sharing experiences and information. The strategic-management process facilitates this new cross-functional approach to managing the R&D function.

INTERNAL AND EXTERNAL R&D   Cost distributions among R&D activities vary by company and industry, but total R&D costs generally do not exceed manufacturing and marketing start-up costs. Four approaches to determining R&D budget allocations commonly are used: (1) financing as many project proposals as possible, (2) using a percentage-of-sales method, (3) budgeting about the same amount that competitors spend for R&D, or (4) deciding how many successful new products are needed and working backward to estimate the required R&D investment.

R&D in organizations can take two basic forms: (1) internal R&D, in which an organization operates its own R&D department, and/or (2) contract R&D, in which a firm hires independent researchers or independent agencies to develop specific products. Many companies use both approaches to develop new products. A widely used approach for obtaining outside R&D assistance is to pursue a joint venture with another firm. R&D strengths (capabilities) and weaknesses (limitations) play a major role in strategy formulation and strategy implementation.

Most firms have no choice but to continually develop new and improved products because of changing consumer needs and tastes, new technologies, shortened product life cycles, and increased domestic and foreign competition. A shortage of ideas for new products, increased global competition, increased market segmentation, strong special-interest groups, and increased government regulation are several factors making the successful development of new products more and more difficult, costly, and risky. In the pharmaceutical industry, for example, only one out of every 10,000 drugs created in the laboratory ends up on pharmacists' shelves. Scarpello, Boulton, and Hofer emphasized that different strategies require different R&D capabilities:

> The focus of R&D efforts can vary greatly depending on a firm's competitive strategy. Some corporations attempt to be market leaders and innovators of new products, while others are satisfied to be market followers and developers of currently available products. The basic skills required to support these strategies will vary, depending on whether R&D becomes the driving force behind competitive strategy. In cases where new product introduction is the driving force for strategy, R&D activities must be extensive. The R&D unit must then be able to advance scientific and technological knowledge, exploit that knowledge, and manage the risks associated with ideas, products, services, and production requirements.[22]

COMPUTER INFORMATION SYSTEMS

Information ties all business functions together and provides the basis for all managerial decisions. It is the cornerstone of all organizations. Information represents a major source of competitive advantage or disadvantage. Assessing a firm's internal strengths and weaknesses in information systems is a critical dimension of performing an internal audit. The company motto of Mitsui, a large Japanese trading company, is "Information is the lifeblood of the company." A satellite network connects Mitsui's 200 worldwide offices.

A computer information system's purpose is to improve the performance of an enterprise by improving the quality of managerial decisions. An effective information system thus collects, codes, stores, synthesizes, and presents information in such a manner that it answers important operating and strategic questions. The heart of an information system is a database containing the kinds of records and data important to managers.

A *computer information system* receives raw material from both the external and internal evaluation of an organization. It gathers data about marketing, finance, production, and personnel matters internally, and social, cultural, demographic, environmental, economic, political, government, legal, technological, and competitive factors externally. Data is integrated in ways needed to support managerial decision making.

There is a logical flow of material in a computer information system, whereby data is input to the system and transformed into output. Outputs include computer printouts, written reports, tables, charts, graphs, checks, purchase orders, invoices, inventory records, payroll accounts, and a variety of other documents. Payoffs from alternative strategies can be calculated and estimated. *Data* becomes *information* only when it is evaluated, filtered, condensed, analyzed, and organized for a specific purpose, problem, individual, or time.

An effective computer information system utilizes computer hardware, software, models for analysis, and a database. Some people equate information systems with the advent of the computer, but historians have traced recordkeeping and noncomputer data processing to Babylonian merchants living in 3500 B.C. Benefits of an effective information system include an improved understanding of business functions, improved communications, more informed decision making, analysis of problems, and improved control.

Because organizations are becoming more complex, decentralized, and globally dispersed, the function of information systems is growing in importance. Spurring this advance is the falling cost and increasing power of computers. There are costs and benefits associated with obtaining and evaluating information, just as with equipment and land. Like equipment, information can become obsolete and may need to be purged from the system. An effective information system is like a library, collecting, categorizing, and filing data for use by managers throughout the organization. Information systems are a major strategic resource, monitoring environment changes, identifying competitive threats, and assisting in the implementation, evaluation, and control of strategy.

We are truly in an information age. Firms whose information-system skills are weak are at a competitive disadvantage. On the other hand, strengths in information systems allow firms to establish distinctive competencies in other areas. Low-cost manufacturing and good customer service, for example, can depend on a good information system.

Watson and Rainer found that executive information systems provide managerial support in six key areas: electronic mail, access to external news, access to external databases, word processing, spreadsheets, and automated filing.[23] A good executive information system provides graphic, tabular, and textual information. Graphic capabilities are needed so current conditions and trends can be examined quickly; tables provide greater detail and enable variance analyses; textual information adds insight and interpretation to data.

STRATEGIC PLANNING SOFTWARE   The computer revolution today is being compared in magnitude to the industrial revolution. Computers are now common at the desks of almost every professional and administrative employee of industry, government, and academia. The proliferation of computers has aided strategic management because software products can be designed to enhance participation and to provide integration, uniformity, analysis, and economy. Strategic planning software can allow firms to tap the knowledge base of everyone in the firm. There are a number of commercially available software products designed to train and assist managers in strategic planning, including *Business Advantage, Business Simulator, SUCCESS, ANS-PLAN-A, Strategy!, CheckMATE, EXCEL, STRATPAC, SIMPLAN, REVEAL, COSMOS,* and *BASICS P-C.*[24]

Some strategic decision support systems, however, are too sophisticated, expensive, or restrictive to be used easily by managers in a firm. This is unfortunate because the strategic-management process must be a people process to be successful. People make the difference! Strategic planning software thus should be simple and unsophisticated. Simplicity allows wide participation among managers in a firm and participation is essential for effective strategy implementation.

One strategic planning software product that parallels this text and offers managers and executives a simple yet effective approach for developing organizational strategies is *CheckMATE.* This IBM-compatible, personal computer software performs planning analyses and generates strategies a firm could pursue. *CheckMATE,* a Windows-based program, incorporates the most modern strategic planning techniques. No previous experience with computers or knowledge of strategic planning is required of the user. *CheckMATE* thus promotes communication, understanding, creativity, and forward thinking among users.

CheckMATE is not a spreadsheet program or database; it is an expert system that carries a firm through strategy formulation and implementation. A major strength of the new *CheckMATE* strategic planning software is its simplicity and participative approach. The user is asked approptiate questions, responses are recorded, information is assimilated, and results are printed. Individuals can work through the software independently and then meet to develop joint recommendations for the firm.

The *CheckMATE* software utilizes the most modern strategic planning analytical matrices to generate alternative strategies firms could pursue. Specific analytical procedures included in the *CheckMATE* program are Strategic Position and Action Evaluation (SPACE) analysis, Threats-Opportunities-Weaknesses-Strengths (TOWS) analysis, Internal-External (IE) analysis, and Grand Strategy Matrix analysis. These widely used strategic planning analyses are described in Chapter 6.

Twenty-three customized industry applications of *CheckMATE* are available in a new Windows format. An individual license costs $195. More information about *CheckMATE* can be obtained at www.checkmateplan.com or 843-669-6960 (phone).

INTERNAL AUDIT CHECKLISTS

The checklists of questions provided in this section can be helpful in determining specific strengths and weaknesses in the functional area of business. An answer of *no* to any question could indicate a potential weakness, although the strategic significance and implications of negative answers, of course, will vary by organization, industry, and severity of the weakness. Positive or *yes* answers to the checklist questions suggest potential areas of strength. The questions provided in Table 5–7 are not all-inclusive, but they can facilitate internal audit efforts.

TABLE 5–7
Internal Audit Checklist of Questions

MANAGEMENT

1. Does the firm use strategic-management concepts?
2. Are company objectives and goals measurable and well communicated?
3. Do managers at all hierarchical levels plan effectively?
4. Do managers delegate authority well?
5. Is the organization's structure appropriate?
6. Are job descriptions and job specifications clear?
7. Is employee morale high?
8. Are employee turnover and absenteeism low?
9. Are organizational reward and control mechanisms effective?

MARKETING

1. Are markets segmented effectively?
2. Is the organization positioned well among competitors?
3. Has the firm's market share been increasing?
4. Are present channels of distribution reliable and cost-effective?
5. Does the firm have an effective sales organization?
6. Does the firm conduct market research?
7. Are product quality and customer service good?
8. Are the firm's products and services priced appropriately?
9. Does the firm have an effective promotion, advertising, and publicity strategy?
10. Are marketing planning and budgeting effective?
11. Do the firm's marketing managers have adequate experience and training?

FINANCE

1. Where is the firm financially strong and weak as indicated by financial ratio analyses?
2. Can the firm raise needed short-term capital?
3. Can the firm raise needed long-term capital through debt and/or equity?
4. Does the firm have sufficient working capital?
5. Are capital budgeting procedures effective?
6. Are dividend payout policies reasonable?
7. Does the firm have good relations with its investors and stockholders?
8. Are the firm's financial managers experienced and well trained?

PRODUCTION

1. Are suppliers of raw materials, parts, and subassemblies reliable and reasonable?
2. Are facilities, equipment, machinery, and offices in good condition?
3. Are inventory-control policies and procedures effective?
4. Are quality-control policies and procedures effective?
5. Are facilities, resources, and markets strategically located?
6. Does the firm have technological competencies?

RESEARCH AND DEVELOPMENT

1. Does the firm have R&D facilities? Are they adequate?
2. If outside R&D firms are used, are they cost-effective?
3. Are the organization's R&D personnel well qualified?
4. Are R&D resources allocated effectively?
5. Are management information and computer systems adequate?
6. Is communication between R&D and other organizational units effective?
7. Are present products technologically competitive?

COMPUTER INFORMATION SYSTEMS

1. Do all managers in the firm use the information system to make decisions?
2. Is there a chief information officer or director of information systems position in the firm?
3. Are data in the information system updated regularly?
4. Do managers from all functional areas of the firm contribute input to the information system?
5. Are there effective passwords for entry into the firm's information system?
6. Are strategists of the firm familiar with the information systems of rival firms?
7. Is the information system user-friendly?
8. Do all users of the information system understand the competitive advantages that information can provide firms?
9. Are computer training workshops provided for users of the information system?
10. Is the firm's information system continually being improved in content and user-friendliness?

THE INTERNAL FACTOR EVALUATION (IFE) MATRIX

A summary step in conducting an internal strategic-management audit is to construct an *Internal Factor Evaluation (IFE) Matrix*. This strategy-formulation tool summarizes and evaluates the major strengths and weaknesses in the functional areas of a business, and it also provides a basis for identifying and evaluating relationships among those areas. Intuitive judgments are required in developing an IFE Matrix, so the appearance of a scientific approach should not be interpreted to mean this is an all-powerful technique. A thorough understanding of the factors included is more important than the actual numbers. Similar to the EFE Matrix and Competitive Profile Matrix described in Chapter 4, an IFE Matrix can be developed in five steps:

1. List critical success factors as identified in the internal-audit process. Use a total of from 10 to 20 internal factors, including both strengths and weaknesses. List strengths first and then weaknesses. Be as specific as possible, using percentages, ratios, and comparative numbers.
2. Assign a weight that ranges from 0.0 (not important) to 1.0 (all-important) to each factor. The weight assigned to a given factor indicates the relative importance of the factor to being successful in the firm's industry. Regardless of whether a key factor is an internal strength or weakness, factors considered to have the greatest effect on organizational performance should be assigned the highest weights. The sum of all weights must equal 1.0.
3. Assign a 1-to-4 rating to each factor to indicate whether that factor represents a major weakness (rating = 1), a minor weakness (rating = 2), a minor strength (rating = 3), or a major strength (rating = 4). Ratings are thus company-based, whereas the weights in Step 2 are industry-based.
4. Multiply each factor's weight by its rating to determine a weighted score for each variable.
5. Sum the weighted scores for each variable to determine the total weighted score for the organization.

Regardless of how many factors are included in an IFE Matrix, the total weighted score can range from a low of 1.0 to a high of 4.0, with the average score being 2.5. Total weighted scores well below 2.5 characterize organizations that are weak internally, whereas scores significantly above 2.5 indicate a strong internal position. Like the EFE Matrix, an IFE Matrix should include from 10 to 20 key factors. The number of factors has no effect upon the range of total weighted scores because the weights always sum to 1.0.

When a key internal factor is both a strength and a weakness, the factor should be included twice in the IFE Matrix, and a weight and rating should be assigned to each statement. For example, the Playboy logo both helps and hurts Playboy Enterprises; the logo attracts customers to the *Playboy* magazine, but it keeps the Playboy cable channel out of many markets.

TABLE 5–8

A Sample Internal Factor Evaluation Matrix for Circus Circus Enterprises

KEY INTERNAL FACTORS	WEIGHT	RATING	WEIGHTED SCORE
INTERNAL STRENGTHS			
1. Largest casino company in the United States	.05	4	.20
2. Room occupancy rates over 95% in Las Vegas	.10	4	.40
3. Increasing free cash flows	.05	3	.15
4. Owns 1 mile on Las Vegas Strip	.15	4	.60
5. Strong management team	.05	3	.15
6. Buffets at most facilities	.05	3	.15
7. Minimal comps provided	.05	3	.15
8. Long-range planning	.05	4	.20
9. Reputation as family-friendly	.05	3	.15
10. Financial ratios	.05	3	.15
INTERNAL WEAKNESSES			
1. Most properties are located in Las Vegas	.05	1	.05
2. Little diversification	.05	2	.10
3. Family reputation, not high rollers	.05	2	.10
4. Laughlin properties	.10	1	.10
5. Recent loss of joint ventures	.10	1	.10
TOTAL	1.00		2.75

An example of an IFE Matrix for Circus Circus Enterprises is provided in Table 5–8. Note that the firm's major strengths are its size, occupancy rates, property, and long-range planning as indicated by the rating of 4. The major weaknesses are locations and recent joint venture. The total weighted score of 2.75 indicates that the firm is above average in its overall internal strength.

In multidivisional firms, each autonomous division or strategic business unit should construct an IFE Matrix. Divisional matrices then can be integrated to develop an overall corporate IFE Matrix.

CONCLUSION

Management, marketing, finance/accounting, production/operations, research and development, and computer information systems represent the core operations of most businesses. A strategic-management audit of a firm's internal operations is vital to organizational health. Many companies still prefer to be judged solely on their bottom-line performance. However, an increasing number of successful organizations are using the internal audit to gain competitive advantages over rival firms.

Systematic methodologies for performing strength-weakness assessments are not well developed in the strategic-management literature, but it is clear that strategists must identify and evaluate internal strengths and weaknesses in order to formulate and choose among alternative strategies effectively. The EFE Matrix, Competitive Profile Matrix, IFE Matrix, and a clear statement of mission provide the basic information needed to formulate competitive strategies successfully. The process of performing an internal audit represents an opportunity for managers and employees throughout the organization to participate in determining the future of the firm. Involvement in the process can energize and mobilize managers and employees.

We invite you to visit the DAVID page on the Prentice Hall Web site at
www.prenhall.com/davidsm
for this chapter's World Wide Web exercises.

TAKE IT TO THE NET

KEY TERMS AND CONCEPTS

ISSUES FOR REVIEW AND DISCUSSION

1. Explain why prioritizing the relative importance of strengths and weaknesses to include in an IFE Matrix is an important strategic-management activity.

2. How can delegation of authority contribute to effective strategic management?

3. Diagram a formal organizational chart that reflects the following positions: a president, two executive officers, four middle managers, and eighteen lower-level managers. Now, diagram three overlapping and hypothetical informal group structures. How can this information be helpful to a strategist in formulating and implementing strategy?

4. How could a strategist's attitude toward social responsibility affect a firm's strategy? What is your attitude toward social responsibility?

5. Which of the three basic functions of finance/accounting do you feel is most important in a small electronics manufacturing concern? Justify your position.

6. Do you think aggregate R&D expenditures for American firms will increase or decrease next year? Why?

7. Explain how you would motivate managers and employees to implement a major new strategy.

8. Why do you think production/operations managers often are not directly involved in strategy-formulation activities? Why can this be a major organizational weakness?

9. Give two examples of staffing strengths and two examples of staffing weaknesses of an organization with which you are familiar.

10. Would you ever pay out dividends when your firm's annual net profit is negative? Why? What effect could this have on a firm's strategies?

11. If a firm has zero debt in its capital structure, is that always an organizational strength? Why or why not?

12. Describe the production/operations system in a police department.

13. After conducting an internal audit, a firm discovers a total of 100 strengths and 100 weaknesses. What procedures then could be used to determine the most important of these? Why is it important to reduce the total number of key factors?

14. Select one of the suggested readings at the end of this chapter. Look up that article and give a 5-minute oral report to the class summarizing the article and your views on the topic.

15. Why do you believe cultural products affect all the functions of business?

16. Do you think cultural products affect strategy formulation, implementation, or evaluation the most? Why?

17. Identify cultural products at your college or university. Do these products, viewed collectively or separately, represent a strength or weakness for the organization?

18. Describe the computer information system at your college or university.

19. Explain the difference between data and information in terms of each being useful to strategists.

20. What are the most important characteristics of an effective computer information system?

NOTES

1. Robert Grant, "The Resource-Based Theory of Competitive Advantage: Implications for Strategy Formulation," *California Management Review* (Spring 1991): 116.

2. Reprinted by permission of the publisher from "Integrating Strength-Weakness Analysis into Strategic Planning," by William King, *Journal of Business Research II*, no. 4: p. 481. Copyright 1983 by Elsevier Science Publishing Co., Inc.

3. Igor Ansoff, "Strategic Management of Technology," *Journal of Business Strategy* 7, no. 3 (Winter 1987): 38.

4. Claude George, Jr., *The History of Management Thought*, 2nd ed. (Englewood Cliffs, N.J.: Prentice-Hall, 1972): 174.

5. Edgar Schein, *Organizational Culture and Leadership* (San Francisco: Jossey-Bass, 1985): 9.

6. John Lorsch, "Managing Culture: The Invisible Barrier to Strategic Change," *California Management Review* 28, no. 2 (1986): 95–109.

7. Y. Allarie and M. Firsirotu, "How to Implement Radical Strategies in Large Organizations," *Sloan Management Review* (Spring 1985): 19.

8. Adam Smith, *Wealth of Nations* (New York: Modern Library, 1937): 3–4.

9. Richard Daft, *Management*, 3rd ed. (Orlando, Fla.: Dryden Press, 1993): 512.

10. Shelley Kirkpatrick and Edwin Locke, "Leadership: Do Traits Matter?" *Academy of Management Executive* 5, no. 2 (May 1991): 48.

11. Peter Drucker, *Management Tasks, Responsibilities, and Practice* (New York: Harper & Row, 1973): 463.

12. Brian Dumaine, "What the Leaders of Tomorrow See," *Fortune* (July 3, 1989): 51.

13. J. M. Bryson and P. Bromiley, "Critical Factors Affecting the Planning and Implementation of Major Products," *Strategic Management Journal* 14, no. 5 (July 1993): 319.

14. Robert Waterman, Jr., "The Renewal Factor," *Business Week* (September 14, 1987): 104.

15. J. Evans and B. Bergman, *Marketing* (New York: Macmillan, 1982): 17.

16. John Wilke and Bob Ortega, "Anheuser's Sales Practices Under Probe," *The Wall Street Journal* (October 3, 1997): A2.

17. Quoted in Robert Waterman, Jr., "The Renewal Factor," *Business Week* (September 14, 1987): 108.

18. J. Van Horne, *Financial Management and Policy* (Englewood Cliffs, N.J.: Prentice-Hall, 1974): 10.

19. W. Boulton and B. Saladin, "Let's Make Production-Operations Management Top Priority for Strategic Planning in the 1980s," *Managerial Planning* 32, no. 1 (July–August 1983): 19.

20. Vida Scarpello, William Boulton, and Charles Hofer, "Reintegrating R&D into Business Strategy," *Journal of Business Strategy* 6, no. 4 (Spring 1986): 50.

21. Philip Rouseel, Kamal Saad, and Tamara Erickson, "The Evolution of Third Generation R&D," *Planning Review* 19, no. 2 (March–April 1991): 18–26.

22. Scarpello, Boulton, and Hofer, 50, 51.

23. Hugh Watson and Kelly Rainer, Jr., "A Manager's Guide to Executive Support Systems," *Business Horizons* (March–April 1991): 49.

24. Robert Mockler, "A Catalog of Commercially Available Software for Strategic Planning," *Planning Review* 19, no. 3 (May/June 1991): 28. Also, John Sterling, "Strategic Management Software Review," *Planning Review* (January–February 1992): 29–33.

CURRENT READINGS

Bamberger, Peter and Avi Fiegenbaum. "The Role of Strategic Reference Points in Explaining the Nature and Consequences of Human Resource Strategy." *Academy of Management Review* 21, no. 4 (October 1996): 926–958.

Brynjolfsson, Erik, Amy Austin Renshaw, and Marshall Van Alstyne. "The Matrix of Change." *Sloan Management Review* 38, no. 2 (Winter 1997):37–54.

Christensen, C. M. and J. L. Bower. "Customer Power, Strategic Investment, and the Failure of Leading Firms." *Strategic Management Journal* 17, no. 3 (March 1996): 197–218.

Cohen, Susan G. and Diane E. Bailey. "What Makes Teams Work: Group Effectiveness Research from the Shop Floor to the Executive Suite." *Journal of Management* 23, no. 3 (1997): 239–290.

Deadrick, Diana L., R. Bruce McAfee, and Myron Glassman. "Customers for Life: Does It Fit Your Culture?" *Business Horizons* 40, no. 4 (July–August 1997): 11–16.

Denison, Daniel R. "What IS the Difference Between Organizational Culture and Organizational Climate? A Native's Point of View on a Decade of Paradigm Wars." *Academy of Management Review* 21, no. 3 (July 1996): 619–654.

Doka, Kenneth J. "Dealing with Diversity: The Coming Challenge to American Business." *Business Horizons* 39, no. 3 (May–June 1996): 67–71.

Geletkanycz, M.A. "The Salience of 'Culture's Consequences': The Effects of Cultural Values on Top Executive Commitment to the Status Quo." *Strategic Management Journal* 18, no. 8 (September 1997): 615–634.

Grundy, Tony. "Human Resource Management—A Strategic Approach." *Long Range Planning* 30, no. 4 (August 1997): 507–517.

Heracleous, Loizos and Brian Langham. "Strategic Change and Organizational Culture at Hay Management Consultants." *Long Range Planning* 29, no. 4 (August 1996): 485–494.

Joachimsthaler, Erich and David A. Baker. "Building Brands Without Mass Media." *Harvard Business Review* (January–February 1997): 39–52.

Marino, Kenneth E. "Developing Consensus on Firm Competencies and Capabilities." *Academy of Management Executive* 10, no. 3 (August 1996): 40–51.

Meenaghan, Tony. "Ambush Marketing—A Threat to Corporate Sponsorship." *Sloan Management Review* 38, no. 1 (Fall 1996): 103–113.

Nemetz, Patricia L. and Sandra L. Christensen. "The Challenge of Cultural Diversity: Harnessing a Diversity of Views to Understand Multiculturalism." *Academy of Management Journal*, 21, no. 2 (April 1996): 434–462.

Ryan, Chuck and Walter E. Riggs. "Redefining the Product Life Cycle: The Five-Element Product Wave." *Business Horizons* 39, no. 5 (September–October 1996): 33–40.

Rindfleisch, Aric. "Marketing as Warfare: Reassessing a Dominent Metaphor." *Business Horizons* 39, no. 5 (September–October 1996): 3–10.

Stimpert, J. L. and I. M. Duhaime. "In the Eyes of the Beholder: Conceptualizations of Relatedness Held by the Managers of Large Diversified Firms." *Strategic Management Journal* 18, no. 2 (February 1997): 111–126.

Stuart, T. E. and J. M. Podolny. "Local Search and the Evolution of Technological Capabilities." *Strategic Management Journal* 17, Special Issue (Summer 1996): 21–38.

Waddock, S. A. and S. B. Graves. "The Corporate Social Performance—Financial Performance Link." *Strategic Management Journal* 18, no. 4 (April 1997): 303–320.

EXPERIENTIAL EXERCISES

Experiential Exercise 5A

PERFORMING A FINANCIAL RATIO ANALYSIS FOR HERSHEY FOODS

PURPOSE

Financial ratio analysis is one of the best techniques for identifying and evaluating internal strengths and weaknesses. Potential investors and current shareholders look closely at firms' financial ratios, making detailed comparisons to industry averages and to previous periods of time. Financial ratio analyses provide vital input information for developing an IFE Matrix.

INSTRUCTIONS

Step 1 On a separate sheet of paper, number from 1 to 20. Referring to Hershey's income statement and balance sheet (pp. 34–35), calculate 20 financial ratios for 1997 for the company. Use Table 5–4 as a reference.

Step 2 Go to your college library and find industry average financial ratios for the confectionery industry. Record the industry average values in a second column on your paper.

Step 3 In a third column, indicate whether you consider each ratio to be a strength, a weakness, or a neutral factor for Hershey.

Experiential Exercise 5B

CONSTRUCTING AN IFE MATRIX FOR HERSHEY FOODS

PURPOSE

This exercise will give you experience developing an IFE Matrix. Identifying and prioritizing factors to include in an IFE Matrix fosters communication among functional and divisional managers. Preparing an IFE Matrix allows human resource, marketing, production/operations, finance/accounting, R&D, and computer information systems managers to vocalize their concerns and thoughts regarding the business condition of the firm. This results in an improved collective understanding of the business.

INSTRUCTIONS

Step 1 Join with two other individuals to form a three-person team. Develop a team IFE Matrix for Hershey Foods.

Step 2 Compare your team's IFE Matrix to other teams' IFE Matrices. Discuss any major differences.

Step 3 What strategies do you think would allow Hershey to capitalize on its major strengths? What strategies would allow Hershey to improve upon its major weaknesses?

CONSTRUCTING AN IFE MATRIX FOR MY UNIVERSITY

PURPOSE

This exercise gives you the opportunity to evaluate your university's major strengths and weaknesses. As will become clearer in the next chapter, an organization's strategies are largely based upon striving to take advantage of strengths and improving upon weaknesses.

INSTRUCTIONS

Step 1 Join with two other individuals to form a three-person team. Develop a team IFE Matrix for your university. You may use the strength/weaknesses determined in Experiential Exercise 1D.

Step 2 Go to the board and diagram your team's IFE Matrix.

Step 3 Compare your team's IFE Matrix to other teams' IFE Matrices. Discuss any major differences.

Step 4 What strategies do you think would allow your university to capitalize on its major strengths? What strategies would allow your university to improve upon its major weaknesses?

CHAPTER 6

Strategy Analysis and Choice

CHAPTER OUTLINE

◆ **THE NATURE OF STRATEGY ANALYSIS AND CHOICE**

◆ **LONG-TERM OBJECTIVES**

◆ **A COMPREHENSIVE STRATEGY-FORMULATION FRAMEWORK**

◆ **THE INPUT STAGE**

◆ **THE MATCHING STAGE**

◆ **THE DECISION STAGE**

◆ **CULTURAL ASPECTS OF STRATEGY CHOICE**

◆ **THE POLITICS OF STRATEGY CHOICE**

◆ **THE ROLE OF A BOARD OF DIRECTORS**

■ EXPERIENTIAL EXERCISE 6A
Developing a TOWS Matrix for Hershey Foods

■ EXPERIENTIAL EXERCISE 6B
Developing a SPACE Matrix for Hershey Foods

■ EXPERIENTIAL EXERCISE 6C
Developing a BCG Matrix for Hershey Foods

■ EXPERIENTIAL EXERCISE 6D
Developing a QSPM for Hershey Foods

■ EXPERIENTIAL EXERCISE 6E
Formulating Individual Strategies

■ EXPERIENTIAL EXERCISE 6F
The Mach Test

■ EXPERIENTIAL EXERCISE 6G
Developing a BCG Matrix for My University

■ EXPERIENTIAL EXERCISE 6H
The Role of Boards of Directors

■ EXPERIENTIAL EXERCISE 6I
Locating Companies in a Grand Strategy Matrix

CHAPTER OBJECTIVES

After studying this chapter, you should be able to do the following:

1. Describe a three-stage framework for choosing among alternative strategies.

2. Explain how to develop a TOWS Matrix, SPACE Matrix, BCG Matrix, IE Matrix, and QSPM.

3. Identify important behavioral, political, ethical, and social responsibility considerations in strategy analysis and choice.

4. Discuss the role of intuition in strategic analysis and choice.

5. Discuss the role of organizational culture in strategic analysis and choice.

6. Discuss the role of a board of directors in choosing among alternative strategies.

Strategic management is not a box of tricks or a bundle of techniques. It is analytical thinking and commitment of resources to action. But quantification alone is not planning. Some of the most important issues in strategic management cannot be quantified at all.—PETER DRUCKER

Objectives are not commands; they are commitments. They do not determine the future; they are the means to mobilize resources and energies of an organization for the making of the future.—PETER DRUCKER

Life is full of lousy options.—GENERAL P. X. KELLEY

When a crisis forces choosing among alternatives, most people will choose the worse possible one.—RUDIN'S LAW

Strategy isn't something you can nail together in slap-dash fashion by sitting around a conference table.—TERRY HALLER

Planning is often doomed before it ever starts, either because too much is expected of it or because not enough is put into it.—T. J. CARTWRIGHT

To acquire or not to acquire, that is the question.—ROBERT J. TERRY

Corporate boards need to work to stay away from the traps that force every member to go along with the majority. Devil's advocates represent one easy-to-implement solution.—CHARLES SCHWENK

Whether it's broke or not, fix it—make it better. Not just products, but the whole company if necessary.—BILL SAPORITO

Strategic analysis and choice largely involves making subjective decisions based on objective information. This chapter introduces important concepts that can help strategists generate feasible alternatives, evaluate those alternatives, and choose a specific course of action. Behavioral aspects of strategy formulation are described, including politics, culture, ethics, and social responsibility considerations. Modern tools for formulating strategies are described, and the appropriate role of a board of directors is discussed.

THE NATURE OF STRATEGY ANALYSIS AND CHOICE

As indicated by Figure 6.1, this chapter focuses on establishing long-term objectives, generating alternative strategies, and selecting strategies to pursue. Strategy analysis and choice seeks to determine alternative courses of action that could best enable the firm to achieve its mission and objectives. The firm's present strategies, objectives, and mission, coupled with the external and internal audit information, provide a basis for generating and evaluating feasible alternative strategies.

Unless a desperate situation faces the firm, alternative strategies will likely represent incremental steps to move the firm from its present position to a desired future position. For example, AT&T has a strategy to acquire other firms in the communication industry, perhaps even GTE Corporation, to combat increased competition from the recent Worldcom/MCI merger. Alternative strategies do not come out of the wild blue yonder; they are derived from the firm's mission, objectives, external audit, and internal audit; they are consistent with, or build upon, past strategies that have worked well!

THE PROCESS OF GENERATING AND SELECTING STRATEGIES

Strategists never consider all feasible alternatives that could benefit the firm, because there are an infinite number of possible actions and an infinite number of ways to implement those actions. Therefore, a manageable set of the most attractive alternative strategies must be developed. The advantages, disadvantages, trade-offs, costs, and benefits of these strategies should be determined. This section discusses the process that many firms use to determine an appropriate set of alternative strategies.

Identifying and evaluating alternative strategies should involve many of the managers and employees who earlier assembled the organizational mission statement, performed the external audit, and conducted the internal audit. Representatives from each department and division of the firm should be included in this process, as was the case in previous strategy-formulation activities. Recall that involvement provides the best opportunity for managers and employees to gain an understanding of what the firm is doing and why, and to become committed to helping the firm accomplish its objectives.

All participants in the strategy analysis and choice activity should have the firm's external and internal audit information by their sides. This information, coupled with the firm's mission statement, will help participants crystallize in their own minds particular strategies that they believe could benefit the firm most. Creativity should be encouraged in this thought process.

Alternative strategies proposed by participants should be considered and discussed in a meeting or series of meetings. Proposed strategies should be listed in writing. When all feasible strategies identified by participants are given and understood, the strategies should be ranked in order of attractiveness by all participants, with 1 = *should not be implemented*, 2 = *possibly should be implemented*, 3 = *probably should be implemented*, and 4 = *definitely should be implemented*. This process will result in a prioritized list of best strategies that reflects the collective wisdom of the group.

FIGURE 6–1
A Comprehensive Strategic-Management Model

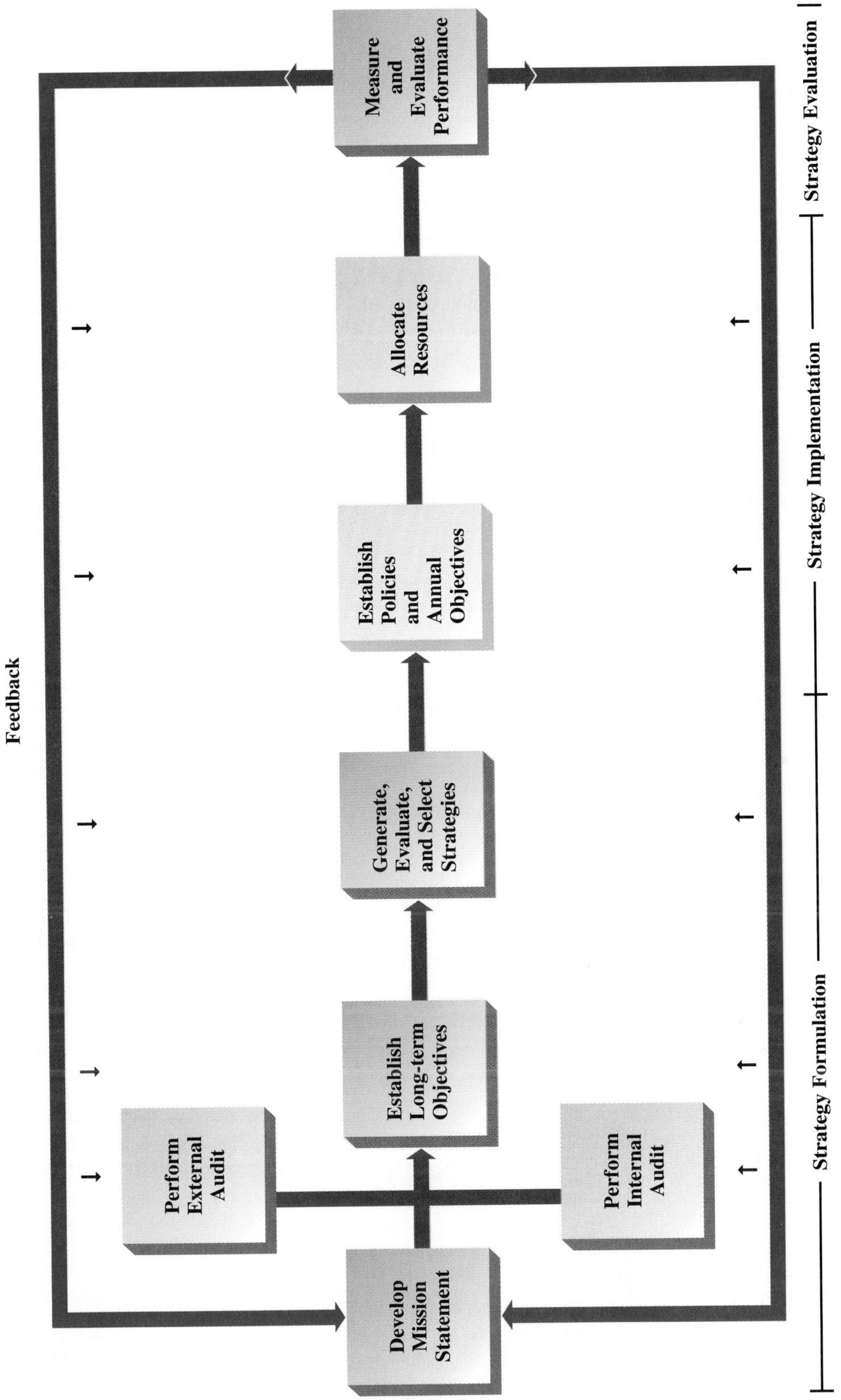

Feedback

Develop Mission Statement					
Perform External Audit	Establish Long-term Objectives	Generate, Evaluate, and Select Strategies	Establish Policies and Annual Objectives	Allocate Resources	Measure and Evaluate Performance
Perform Internal Audit					

| Strategy Formulation | Strategy Implementation | Strategy Evaluation |

As indicated in the Natural Environment Perspective, the success of some strategies can depend on environmental attitudes.

LONG-TERM OBJECTIVES

Long-term objectives represent the results expected from pursuing certain strategies. Strategies represent the actions to be taken to accomplish long-term objectives. The time frame for objectives and strategies should be consistent, usually from two to five years.

THE NATURE OF LONG-TERM OBJECTIVES   Objectives should be quantitative, measurable, realistic, understandable, challenging, hierarchical, obtainable, and congruent among organizational units. Each objective should also be associated with a time line. Objectives are commonly stated in terms such as growth in assets, growth in

NATURAL ENVIRONMENT
Formulating Strategies Based on Environmental Attitudes

Americans can be grouped into categories based on their attitudes, actions, and concern toward natural environment deterioration and preservation.

CHARACTERISTICS	HIGH CONCERN FOR THE NATURAL ENVIRONMENT	LOW CONCERN FOR THE NATURAL ENVIRONMENT
Sex		
Male	34%	55%
Female	66	45
Education		
Less than High School	11	30
High School Graduate	39	39
Some College	22	20
College Graduate Or More	28	11
Occupation		
Executive/Professional	25	11
White Collar	18	15
Blue Collar	19	36
Marital Status		
Married	69	59
Not Married	30	41
Political/Social Ideology		
Conservative	43	36
Middle of the Road	26	41
Liberal	28	16
Region		
Northeast	31	17
Midwest	27	22
South	18	48
West	24	13
Median Income (in thousands)	$32.1	$21.2

Note in the table that persons most concerned about the natural environment tend to be female, have higher household income, and live in the Midwest or Northeast. These persons especially engage in activities such as not purchasing products from companies that are environmentally irresponsible, avoiding purchasing aerosol products, recycling paper and bottles, using biodegradable products, and contributing money to environmental groups. This information can be helpful to companies in formulating strategies such as market development (where to locate new facilities), product development (manufacturing new equipment or developing green products), and market penetration (whom to focus advertising efforts upon).

Source: Adapted from the Roper Organization, 205 East 42nd Street, New York, NY 10017. Also from Joe Schwartz and Thomas Miller, "The Earth's Best Friends," American Demographics (February 1991): 28.

sales, profitability, market share, degree and nature of diversification, degree and nature of vertical integration, earnings per share, and social responsibility. Clearly established objectives offer many benefits. They provide direction, allow synergy, aid in evaluation, establish priorities, reduce uncertainty, minimize conflicts, stimulate exertion, and aid in both the allocation of resources and the design of jobs.

Long-term objectives are needed at the corporate, divisional, and functional levels in an organization. They are an important measure of managerial performance. Many practitioners and academicians attribute a significant part of U.S. industry's competitive decline to the short-term, rather than long-term, strategy orientation of managers in the United States. Arthur D. Little argues that bonuses or merit pay for managers today must be based to a greater extent on long-term objectives and strategies. A general framework for relating objectives to performance evaluation is provided in Table 6–1. A particular organization could tailor these guidelines to meet its own needs, but incentives should be attached to both long-term and annual objectives.

Clearly stated and communicated objectives are vital to success for many reasons. First, objectives help stakeholders understand their role in an organization's future. They also provide a basis for consistent decision making by managers whose values and attitudes differ. By reaching a consensus on objectives during strategy-formulation activities, an organization can minimize potential conflicts later during implementation. Objectives set forth organizational priorities and stimulate exertion and accomplishment. They serve as standards by which individuals, groups, departments, divisions, and entire organizations can be evaluated. Objectives provide the basis for designing jobs and organizing activities to be performed in an organization. They also provide direction and allow for organizational synergy.

Without long-term objectives, an organization would drift aimlessly toward some unknown end! It is hard to imagine an organization or individual being successful without clear objectives. Success only rarely occurs by accident; rather, it is the result of hard work directed toward achieving certain objectives.

NOT MANAGING BY OBJECTIVES   An unknown educator once said, "If you think education is expensive, try ignorance." The idea behind this saying also applies to establishing objectives. Strategists should avoid the following alternative ways to "not managing by objectives."

◆ Managing by Extrapolation—adheres to the principle "If it ain't broke, don't fix it." The idea is to keep on doing about the same things in the same ways because things are going well.

◆ Managing by Crisis—based on the belief that the true measure of a really good strategist is the ability to solve problems. Because there are plenty of crises and problems to go around for every person and every organization, strategists ought to bring their time and creative energy to bear on solving the most pressing problems of the day. Managing by crisis is actually a form of reacting rather than acting and of letting events dictate the whats and whens of management decisions.

ORGANIZATIONAL LEVEL	BASIS FOR ANNUAL BONUS OR MERIT PAY
Corporate	75% based on long-term objectives 25% based on annual objectives
Division	50% based on long-term objectives 50% based on annual objectives
Function	25% based on long-term objectives 75% based on annual objectives

TABLE 6–1
Varying Performance Measures by Organizational Level

◆ Managing by Subjectives—built on the idea that there is no general plan for which way to go and what to do; just do the best you can to accomplish what you think should be done. In short, "Do your own thing, the best way you know how" (sometimes referred to as *the mystery approach to decision making* because subordinates are left to figure out what is happening and why).

◆ Managing by Hope—based on the fact that the future is laden with great uncertainty, and that if we try and do not succeed, then we hope our second (or third) attempt will succeed. Decisions are predicted on the hope that they will work and that good times are just around the corner, especially if luck and good fortune are on our side.[1]

A COMPREHENSIVE STRATEGY-FORMULATION FRAMEWORK

Important strategy-formulation techniques can be integrated into a three-stage decision-making framework, as shown in Figure 6–2. The tools presented in this framework are applicable to all sizes and types of organizations and can help strategists identify, evaluate, and select strategies.

Stage 1 of the formulation framework consists of the EFE Matrix, the IFE Matrix, and the Competitive Profile Matrix. Called the *Input Stage*, Stage 1 summarizes the basic input information needed to formulate strategies. Stage 2, called the *Matching Stage*, focuses upon generating feasible alternative strategies by aligning key external and internal factors. Stage 2 techniques include the Threats-Opportunities-Weaknesses-Strengths (TOWS) Matrix, the Strategic Position and Action Evaluation (SPACE) Matrix, the Boston Consulting Group (BCG) Matrix, the Internal-External (IE) Matrix, and the Grand Strategy Matrix. Stage 3, called the *Decision Stage*, involves a single technique, the Quantitative Strategic Planning Matrix (QSPM). A QSPM uses input information from Stage 1 to objectively evaluate feasible alternative strategies identified in Stage 2. A QSPM reveals the relative attractiveness of alternative strategies and thus provides an objective basis for selecting specific strategies.

FIGURE 6–2
The Strategy-Formulation Analytical Framework

STAGE 1: THE INPUT STAGE		
External Factor Evaluation (EFE) Matrix	Competitive Profile Matrix	Internal Factor Evaluation (IFE) Matrix

STAGE 2: THE MATCHING STAGE				
Threats-Opportunities-Weaknesses-Strengths (TOWS) Matrix	Strategic Position and Action Evaluation (SPACE) Matrix	Boston Consulting Group (BCG) Matrix	Internal-External (IE) Matrix	Grand Strategy Matrix

STAGE 3: THE DECISION STAGE
Quantitative Strategic Planning Matrix (QSPM)

All nine techniques included in the *strategy-formulation framework* require integration of intuition and analysis. Autonomous divisions in an organization commonly use strategy-formulation techniques to develop strategies and objectives. Divisional analyses provide a basis for identifying, evaluating, and selecting among alternative corporate-level strategies.

Strategists themselves, not analytic tools, are always responsible and accountable for strategic decisions. Lenz emphasized that the shift from a words-oriented to a numbers-oriented planning process can give rise to a false sense of certainty; it can reduce dialogue, discussion, and argument as a means to explore understandings, test assumptions and foster organizational learning.[2] Strategists therefore must be wary of this possibility and use analytical tools to facilitate, rather than diminish, communication. Without objective information and analysis, personal biases, politics, emotions, personalities, and *halo error* (the tendency to put too much weight on a single factor) unfortunately may play a dominant role in the strategy-formulation process.

THE INPUT STAGE

Procedures for developing an EFE Matrix, an IFE Matrix, and a Competitive Profile Matrix were presented in the previous two chapters. The information derived from these three matrices provides basic input information for the matching and decision stage matrices described later in this chapter.

The input tools require strategists to quantify subjectivity during early stages of the strategy-formulation process. Making small decisions in the input matrices regarding the relative importance of external and internal factors allows strategists to generate and evaluate alternative strategies more effectively. Good intuitive judgment is always needed in determining appropriate weights and ratings.

THE MATCHING STAGE

Strategy is sometimes defined as the match an organization makes between its internal resources and skills and the opportunities and risks created by its external factors.[3] The matching stage of the strategy-formulation framework consists of five techniques that can be used in any sequence: the TOWS Matrix, the SPACE Matrix, the BCG Matrix, the IE Matrix, and the Grand Strategy Matrix. These tools rely upon information derived from the input stage to match external opportunities and threats with internal strengths and weaknesses. *Matching* external and internal critical success factors is the key to effectively generating feasible alternative strategies! For example, a firm with excess working capital (an internal strength) could take advantage of the cablevision industry's 20 percent annual growth rate (an external opportunity) by acquiring a firm in the cablevision industry. This example portrays simple one-to-one matching. In most situations, external and internal relationships are more complex, and the matching requires multiple alignments for each strategy generated. The basic concept of matching is illustrated in Table 6–2.

Any organization, whether military, product-oriented, service-oriented, governmental, or even athletic, must develop and execute good strategies to win. A good offense without a good defense, or vice versa, usually leads to defeat. Developing strategies that use strengths to capitalize on opportunities could be considered an offense, whereas strategies designed to improve upon weaknesses while avoiding threats could be termed defensive. Every organization has some external opportunities and threats and internal strengths and

TABLE 6–2
Matching Key External and Internal Factors to Formulate Alternative Strategies

KEY INTERNAL FACTOR		KEY EXTERNAL FACTOR		RESULTANT STRATEGY
Excess working capacity (an internal strength)	+	20% annual growth in the cablevision industry (an external opportunity)	=	Acquire Visioncable, Inc.
Insufficient capacity (an internal weakness)	+	Exit of two major foreign competitors from the industry (an external opportunity)	=	Pursue horizontal integration by buying competitors' facilities
Strong R & D expertise (an internal strength)	+	Decreasing numbers of young adults (an external threat)	=	Develop new products for older adults
Poor employee morale (an internal weakness)	+	Strong union activity (an external threat)	=	Develop a new employee benefits package

weaknesses that can be aligned to formulate feasible alternative strategies. As indicated in the Information Technology Perspective, falling prices for wireless communication is an opportunity facing business firms.

THE THREATS-OPPORTUNITIES-WEAKNESSES-STRENGTHS (TOWS) MATRIX

The *Threats-Opportunities-Weaknesses-Strengths (TOWS) Matrix* is an important matching tool that helps managers develop four types of strategies: SO Strategies, WO Strategies, ST Strategies, and WT Strategies.[4] Matching key external and internal factors is the most difficult part of developing a TOWS Matrix and requires good judgment, and there is no one best set of matches. Note in Table 6–2 that the first, second, third, and fourth strategies are SO, WO, ST, and WT Strategies, respectively.

SO Strategies use a firm's internal strengths to take advantage of external opportunities. All managers would like their organizations to be in a position where internal strengths can be used to take advantage of external trends and events. Organizations generally will pursue WO, ST, or WT Strategies in order to get into a situation where they can apply SO Strategies. When a firm has major weaknesses, it will strive to overcome them and make them strengths. When an organization faces major threats, it will seek to avoid them in order to concentrate on opportunities. As indicated in the Information Technology Perspective,

INFORMATION TECHNOLOGY

Are You or Your Firm Wireless?

Wireless communication is becoming more the norm than the exception for many individuals and businesses. The number of wireless users in the United States is expected to increase from 48.9 million in 1997 to over 100 million in 2001, as the average price per minute of use falls from 15 cents to 8 cents. Today, the following wireless services are widely used:

- Digital satellite television
- Satellite location tracking
- Cellular phones
- Digital smart phones that combine cellular phone, two-way-radio, paging, and Internet
- Hand-held wireless computers
- Fixed-wireless local telephone service
- Wireless computer modems
- Wireless local-area computer networks
- Wireless cable television
- Infrared wireless devices and sensors

Soon, the following additional wireless communication services will be available:

- Satellite data broadcasting
- Satellite cellular-phone service
- Satellite high-speed Internet service
- Satellite sensing
- Digital television with Internet
- Wideband digital networks
- Wireless home security

Source: Adapted from Bill Hill, "The Communications Battleground," The Wall Street Journal (September 11, 1997): R4.

immense opportunities are available to many firms today from wireless communication advances in technology.

WO Strategies aim at improving internal weaknesses by taking advantage of external opportunities. Sometimes key external opportunities exist, but a firm has internal weaknesses that prevent it from exploiting those opportunities. For example, there may be a high demand for electronic devices to control the amount and timing of fuel injection in automobile engines (opportunity), but a certain auto parts manufacturer may lack the technology required for producing these devices (weakness). One possible WO Strategy would be to acquire this technology by forming a joint venture with a firm having competency in this area. An alternative WO Strategy would be to hire and train people with the required technical capabilities.

ST Strategies use a firm's strengths to avoid or reduce the impact of external threats. This does not mean that a strong organization should always meet threats in the external environment head-on. A recent example of ST Strategy occurred when Texas Instruments used an excellent legal department (a strength) to collect nearly $700 million in damages and royalties from nine Japanese and Korean firms that infringed on patents for semiconductor memory chips (threat). Rival firms that copy ideas, innovations, and patented products are a major threat in many industries. This is a major problem for U.S. firms selling products in China.

WT Strategies are defensive tactics directed at reducing internal weaknesses and avoiding environmental threats. An organization faced with numerous external threats and internal weaknesses may indeed be in a precarious position. In fact, such a firm may have to fight for its survival, merge, retrench, declare bankruptcy, or choose liquidation.

A schematic representation of the TOWS Matrix is provided in Figure 6–3. Note that a TOWS Matrix is composed of nine cells. As shown, there are four key factor cells, four

GLOBAL PERSPECTIVE
Is Africa Open for Business?

Still mired in poverty, corruption, dictatorships, and ethnic violence, Africa receives less than 5 percent of the world's net private capital flows. However, some African nations have established democratic governments, stamped out inflation, and are beginning to attract business. *The Wall Street Journal* suggests that the five best African areas to launch new investments are South Africa, Ghana, Uganda, Botswana, and the Ivory Coast. Comments on the latter four areas are given below:

GHANA

With $1.3 billion in foreign private investment in 1996, Ghana has become a peaceful, democratic, financial mecca in Africa. The country's gross domestic product grew 5.2 percent in 1996 and another 5 percent in 1997. Ghana offers low tariffs, low taxes, and low wages. The only real negative about Ghana is that inflation is about 35 percent annually.

UGANDA

Now a peaceful country, Uganda is a model of prudence, reform, and openness. Uganda's gross domestic product growth in 1997 reached 7 percent and is projected to do the same in fiscal 1998. Foreign private investment in Uganda grew from $3 million in 1992 to $148 million in 1996.

BOTSWANA

About the size of France and located near South Africa, Botswana is a peaceful nation of 1.3 million people. Rich in diamonds and having an excellent infrastructure, Botswana recently attracted large Hyundai Motor and AB Volvo plants. Botswana offers firms low wages, political stability, low taxes, and a convenient close export market in South Africa. Foreign private investment in Botswana reached $68 million in 1996.

IVORY COAST

The port city of Abidjan will host the eight-country West African stock exchange set to open in 1998. Many foreign companies now are investing in the Ivory Coast's cocoa, oil, telecommunications, power, and other sectors. Foreign private investment in the Ivory Coast was negative $192 million in 1996, but analysts expect positive flows in 1997 and thereafter.

Source: Adapted from Michael Phillips, "Into Africa," The Wall Street Journal (September 18, 1997): R6.

strategy cells, and one cell that is always left blank (the upper left cell). The four strategy cells, labeled *SO, WO, ST,* and *WT*, are developed after completing four key factor cells, labeled *S, W, O,* and *T*. There are eight steps involved in constructing a TOWS Matrix:

1. List the firm's key external opportunities.
2. List the firm's key external threats.
3. List the firm's key internal strengths.
4. List the firm's key internal weaknesses.
5. Match internal strengths with external opportunities and record the resultant SO Strategies in the appropriate cell.
6. Match internal weaknesses with external opportunities and record the resultant WO Strategies.
7. Match internal strengths with external threats and record the resultant ST Strategies.

FIGURE 6–3
The TOWS Matrix

	STRENGTHS—S	**WEAKNESSES—W**
Always leave blank	1. 2. 3. 4. 5. 6. 7. 8. 9. 10. List strengths	1. 2. 3. 4. 5. 6. 7. 8. 9. 10. List weaknesses
OPPORTUNITIES—O 1. 2. 3. 4. 5. List opportunities 6. 7. 8. 9. 10.	**SO STRATEGIES** 1. 2. 3. 4. Use strengths to take 5. advantage of opportunities 6. 7. 8. 9. 10.	**WO STRATEGIES** 1. 2. 3. 4. Overcome weaknesses by 5. taking advantage of 6. opportunities 7. 8. 9. 10.
THREATS—T 1. 2. 3. 4. List threats 5. 6. 7. 8. 9. 10.	**ST STRATEGIES** 1. 2. 3. 4. Use strengths to avoid 5. threats 6. 7. 8. 9. 10.	**WT STRATEGIES** 1. 2. 3. 4. Minimize weaknesses and 5. avoid threats 6. 7. 8. 9. 10.

8. Match internal weaknesses with external threats and record the resultant WT Strategies.

The purpose of each Stage 2 matching tool is to generate feasible alternative strategies, not to select or determine which strategies are best! Not all of the strategies developed in the TOWS Matrix, therefore, will be selected for implementation. A sample TOWS Matrix for Cineplex Odeon, the large cinema company, is provided in Figure 6–4.

The strategy-formulation guidelines provided in Chapter 2 can enhance the process of matching key external and internal factors. For example, when an organization has both the

FIGURE 6–4
Cineplex Odeon TOWS Matrix

	STRENGTHS—S	WEAKNESSES—W
	1. Located in large population centers	1. Poor labor relations
	2. Positive cash flow 3 years running	2. Current ratio of 0.25
	3. Double the industry concession sales rate	3. Flat operating cost through falling revenue
	4. Many cost-cutting measures in place	4. Triple the G&A expenses of Carmike
	5. Upgraded audio in many places	5. Significant losses in the United States
	6. Profitable in Canada	6. Management concentrating on market share
		7. Restrictive covenants set by lenders
OPPORTUNITIES—O	**SO STRATEGIES**	**WO STRATEGIES**
1. Approached by most major chains for potential merger	1. Open theaters in Eastern Europe (S1, O2, O5)	1. Pursue merger with American Cinemas (O1, O2, W3, W4, W5, W6)
2. Opening economies in Eastern Europe		
3. Rebounding attendance (up 6.4%)		
4. Videotape industry worth estimated $18 billion vs. $6.4 billion for movie theaters		
5. Foreign per capita income growth outpacing the United States		
THREATS—T	**ST STRATEGIES**	**WT STRATEGIES**
1. 80% of all households own VCRs	1. Open 50 video rental stores in 10 markets (S1, S6, T1, T3, T5, O4)	1. Reduce corporate overhead (W3, W4, T3, T5, T6)
2. Aging population	2. Construct 20 multidimensional entertainment complexes (S1, T3, T5, T6)	2. Divest U.S. operations (T6, W2, W3, W4, W5, W6)
3. Dependence on successful movies		
4. Switch from bid to allocation for licenses		
5. Seasonality for movie releases		
6. Increased competition in exhibition		

capital and human resources needed to distribute its own products (internal strength) and distributors are unreliable, costly, or incapable of meeting the firm's needs (external threat), then forward integration can be an attractive ST Strategy. When a firm has excess production capacity (internal weakness) and its basic industry is experiencing declining annual sales and profits (external threat), then concentric diversification can be an effective WT Strategy. It is important to use specific, rather than general, strategy terms when developing a TOWS Matrix. In addition, it is important to include the "S1,O2"-type notation after each strategy in the TOWS Matrix. This notation reveals the rationale for each alternative strategy.

THE STRATEGIC POSITION AND ACTION EVALUATION (SPACE) MATRIX

The Strategic Position and Action Evaluation (SPACE) Matrix, another important Stage 2 *matching* tool, is illustrated in Figure 6–5. Its four-quadrant framework indicates whether aggressive, conservative, defensive, or competitive strategies are most appropriate for a given organization. The axes of the SPACE Matrix represent two internal dimensions (*financial strength* [FS] and *competitive advantage* [CA]) and two external dimensions (*environmental stability* [ES] and *industry strength* [IS]). These four factors are the most important determinants of an organization's overall strategic position.[5]

Depending upon the type of organization, numerous variables could make up each of the dimensions represented on the axes of the SPACE Matrix. Factors earlier included in the firm's EFE and IFE matrices should be considered in developing a SPACE Matrix. Other variables commonly included are given in Table 6–3. For example, return on investment, leverage, liquidity, working capital, and cash flow commonly are considered determining factors of an organization's financial strength. Like the TOWS Matrix, the SPACE Matrix should be tailored to the particular organization being studied and based on factual information as much as possible.

FIGURE 6–5
The SPACE Matrix

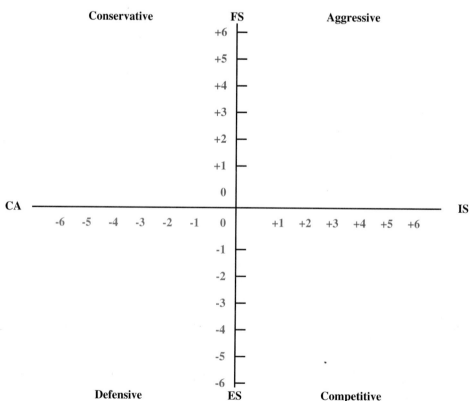

Source: H. Rowe, R. Mason, and K. Dickel, *Strategic Management and Business Policy: A Methodological Approach* (Reading, Massachusetts: Addison-Wesley Publishing Co. Inc., © 1982):155. Reprinted with permission of the publisher.

INTERNAL STRATEGIC POSITION	EXTERNAL STRATEGIC POSITION
FINANCIAL STRENGTH (FS)	*ENVIRONMENTAL STABILITY (ES)*
Return on investment	Technological changes
Leverage	Rate of inflation
Liquidity	Demand variability
Working capital	Price range of competing products
Cash flow	Barriers to entry into market
Ease of exit from market	Competitive pressure
Risk involved in business	Price elasticity of demand
COMPETITIVE ADVANTAGE (CA)	*INDUSTRY STRENGTH (IS)*
Market share	Growth potential
Product quality	Profit potential
Product life cycle	Financial stability
Customer loyalty	Technological know-how
Competition's capacity utilization	Resource utilization
Technological know-how	Capital intensity
Control over suppliers and distributors	Ease of entry into market
	Productivity, capacity utilization

TABLE 6–3
Example Factors That Make Up the SPACE Matrix Axes

Source: H. Rowe, R. Mason, and K. Dickel, *Strategic Management and Business Policy: A Methodological Approach* (Reading, Massachusetts: Addison-Wesley Publishing Co. Inc., © 1982): 155–156. Reprinted with permission of the publisher.

The steps required to develop a SPACE Matrix are as follows:

1. Select a set of variables to define financial strength (FS), competitive advantage (CA), environmental stability (ES), and industry strength (IS).

2. Assign a numerical value ranging from +1 (worst) to +6 (best) to each of the variables that make up the FS and IS dimensions. Assign a numerical value ranging from −1 (best) to −6 (worst) to each of the variables that make up the ES and CA dimensions.

3. Compute an average score for FS, CA, IS, and ES by summing the values given to the variables of each dimension and dividing by the number of variables included in the respective dimension.

4. Plot the average scores for FS, IS, ES, and CA on the appropriate axis in the SPACE Matrix.

5. Add the two scores on the *x*-axis and plot the resultant point on *X*. Add the two scores on the *y*-axis and plot the resultant point on *Y*. Plot the intersection of the new *xy* point.

6. Draw a *directional vector* from the origin of the SPACE Matrix through the new intersection point. This vector reveals the type of strategies recommended for the organization: aggressive, competitive, defensive, or conservative.

Some examples of strategy profiles that can emerge from a SPACE analysis are shown in Figure 6–6. The directional vector associated with each profile suggests the type of strategies to pursue: aggressive, conservative, defensive, or competitive. When a firm's directional vector is located in the *aggressive quadrant* (upper right quadrant) of the SPACE Matrix, an organization is in an excellent position to use its internal strengths to (1) take advantage of external opportunities, (2) overcome internal weaknesses, and (3) avoid external threats. Therefore, market penetration, market development, product development, backward integration, forward integration, horizontal integration, conglomerate diversification, concentric diversification, horizontal diversification, or a combination strategy all can be feasible, depending on the specific circumstances that face the firm.

FIGURE 6–6
Example Strategy Profiles

Aggressive Profiles

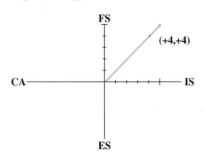

A financially strong firm that has achieved major competitive advantages in a growing and stable industry

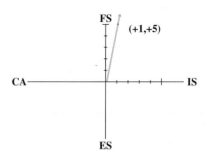

A firm whose financial strength is a dominating factor in the industry

Conservative Profiles

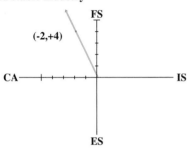

A firm that has achieved financial strength in a stable industry that is not growing; the firm has no major competitive advantages

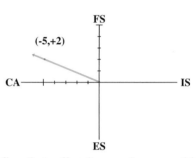

A firm that suffers from major competitive disadvantages in an industry that is technologically stable but declining in sales

Competitive Profiles

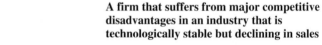

A firm with major competitive advantages in a high-growth industry

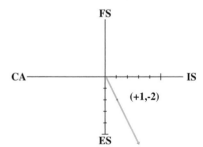

An organization that is competing fairly well in an unstable industry

Defensive Profiles

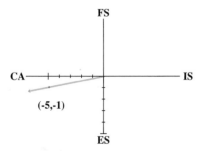

A firm that has a very weak competitive position in a negative growth, stable industry

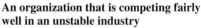

A financially troubled firm in a very unstable industry

Source: H. Rowe, R. Mason, and K. Dickel, *Strategic Management and Business Policy: A Methodological Approach* (Reading, Massachusetts: Addison-Wesley Publishing Co. Inc. © 1982): 155. Reprinted with permission of the publisher.

The directional vector may appear in the *conservative quadrant* (upper left quadrant) of the SPACE Matrix, which implies staying close to the firm's basic competencies and not taking excessive risks. Conservative strategies most often include market penetration, market development, product development, and concentric diversification. The directional vector may be located in the lower left or *defensive quadrant* of the SPACE Matrix, which suggests that the firm should focus on rectifying internal weaknesses and avoiding external threats. Defensive strategies include retrenchment, divestiture, liquidation, and concentric diversification. Finally, the directional vector may be located in the lower right or *competitive quadrant* of the SPACE Matrix, indicating competitive strategies. Competitive strategies include backward, forward, and horizonal integration; market penetration; market development; product development; and joint venture.

SPACE Matrix analysis for a bank is provided in Table 6–4. Note that competitive strategies are recommended.

THE BOSTON CONSULTING GROUP (BCG) MATRIX Autonomous divisions (or profit centers) of an organization make up what is called a *business portfolio.* When a firm's divisions compete in different industries, a separate strategy often must be

TABLE 6–4
A SPACE Matrix for a Bank

FINANCIAL STRENGTH	RATINGS
The bank's primary capital ratio is 7.23 percent, which is 1.23 percentage points over the generally required ratio of 6 percent.	1.0
The bank's return on assets is negative 0.77, compared to a bank industry average ratio of positive 0.70.	1.0
The bank's net income was $183 million, down 9 percent from a year earlier.	3.0
The bank's revenues increased 7 percent to $3.46 billion.	4.0
	9.0

INDUSTRY STRENGTH	
Deregulation provides geographic and product freedom.	4.0
Deregulation increases competition in the banking industry.	2.0
Pennsylvania's interstate banking law allows the bank to acquire other banks in New Jersey, Ohio, Kentucky, the District of Columbia, and West Virginia.	4.0
	10.0

ENVIRONMENTAL STABILITY	
Less-developed countries are experiencing high inflation and political instability.	−4.0
Headquartered in Pittsburgh, the bank historically has been heavily dependent on the steel, oil, and gas industries. These industries are depressed.	−5.0
Banking deregulation has created instability throughout the industry.	−4.0
	−13.0

COMPETITIVE ADVANTAGE	
The bank provides data processing services for more than 450 institutions in 38 states.	−2.0
Superregional banks, international banks, and nonbanks are becoming increasingly competitive.	−5.0
The bank has a large customer base.	−2.0
	−9.0

CONCLUSION

ES Average is −13.0 ÷ 3 = −4.33   IS Average is +10.0 ÷ 3 = 3.33
CA Average is −9.0 ÷ 3 = −3.00   FS Average is +9.0 ÷ 4 = 2.25
Directional Vector Coordinates: *x*-axis: −3.00 + (+3.33) = +0.33
                                               y-axis: −4.33 + (+2.25) = −2.08
The bank should pursue Competitive Strategies.

developed for each business. The *Boston Consulting Group (BCG) Matrix* and the *Internal-External (IE) Matrix* are designed specifically to enhance a multidivisional firm's efforts to formulate strategies.

The BCG Matrix graphically portrays differences among divisions in terms of relative market share position and industry growth rate. The BCG Matrix allows a multidivisional organization to manage its portfolio of businesses by examining the relative market share position and the industry growth rate of each division relative to all other divisions in the organization. *Relative market share position* is defined as the ratio of a division's own market share in a particular industry to the market share held by the largest rival firm in that industry. For example, in Table 6–5, the relative market share of Miller Lite in 1996 would be 8.5/19.5 = .44.

Relative market share position is given on the *x*-axis of the BCG Matrix. The midpoint on the *x*-axis usually is set at .50, corresponding to a division that has half the market share of the leading firm in the industry. The *y*-axis represents the industry growth rate in sales, measured in percentage terms. The growth rate percentages on the *y*-axis could range from −20 to +20 percent, with 0.0 being the midpoint. These numerical ranges on the *x*- and *y*-axes often are used, but other numerical values could be established as deemed appropriate for particular organizations.

An example of a BCG Matrix appears in Figure 6–7. Each circle represents a separate division. The size of the circle corresponds to the proportion of corporate revenue generated by that business unit, and the pie slice indicates the proportion of corporate profits generated by that division. Divisions located in Quadrant I of the BCG Matrix are called Question Marks, those located in Quadrant II are called Stars, those located in Quadrant III are called Cash Cows, and those divisions located in Quadrant IV are called Dogs.

TABLE 6–5
Top 10 Beer Brands—1996
(Ranked by unit sales)

		SALES (MIL. BARRELS)			MARKET SHARE (%)		
BRAND	**BREWER**	**1990**	**1995**	**1996**	**1990**	**1995**	**1996**
1. Budweiser	Anheuser-Busch Inc.	47.9	37.2	36.5	24.8	20.0	19.5
2. Bud Light	Anheuser-Busch Inc.	11.8	17.9	20.2	6.1	9.6	10.8
3. Miller Lite	Miller Brewing Co.	19.9	15.8	15.9	10.3	8.5	8.5
4. Coors Light	Adolph Coors	11.6	12.9	13.3	6.0	7.0	7.1
5. Busch	Anheuser-Busch Inc.	9.4	8.1	7.9	4.9	4.4	4.2
6. Natural Light	Anheuser-Busch Inc.	3.0	7.1	6.8	1.6	3.8	3.6
7. Miller Genuine Draft	Miller Brewing Co.	5.8	5.8	5.6	3.0	3.1	3.0
8. Miller High Life	Miller Brewing Co.	6.0	4.4	4.4	3.1	2.4	2.4
9. Busch Light Draft	Anheuser-Busch Inc.	1.9	4.2	4.4	1.0	2.3	2.4
10. Milwaukee's Best	Miller Brewing Co.	6.6	4.7	4.3	3.4	2.5	2.3
Total Top 10		123.9	118.1	119.3	64.2	63.6	63.8
All others		69.2	67.5	67.8	35.8	36.4	36.2
Total		193.1	185.6	187.1	100.0	100.0	100.0

Source: IMPACT DATABANK.

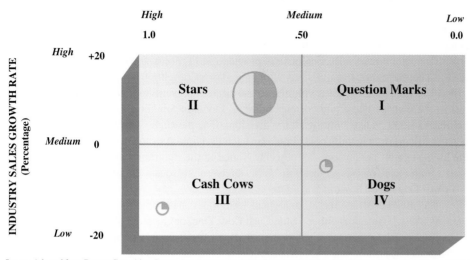

RELATIVE MARKET SHARE POSITION

Source: Adapted from Boston Consulting Group, *Perspectives on Experience* (Boston, MA.: The Boston Consulting Group, 1974).

◆ Question Marks—Divisions in Quadrant I have a low relative market share position, yet compete in a high-growth industry. Generally these firms' cash needs are high and their cash generation is low. These businesses are called *Question Marks* because the organization must decide whether to strengthen them by pursuing an intensive strategy (market penetration, market development, or product development) or to sell them.

◆ Stars—Quadrant II businesses (often called *Stars*) represent the organization's best long-run opportunities for growth and profitability. Divisions with a high relative market share and a high industry growth rate should receive substantial investment to maintain or strengthen their dominant positions. Forward, backward, and horizontal integration; market penetration; market development; product development; and joint ventures are appropriate strategies for these divisions to consider.

◆ Cash Cows—Divisions positioned in Quadrant III have a high relative market share position but compete in a low-growth industry. Called *Cash Cows* because they generate cash in excess of their needs, they often are milked. Many of today's Cash Cows were yesterday's Stars. Cash Cow divisions should be managed to maintain their strong position for as long as possible. Product development or concentric diversification may be attractive strategies for strong Cash Cows. However, as a Cash Cow division becomes weak, retrenchment or divestiture can become more appropriate.

◆ Dogs—Quadrant IV divisions of the organization have a low relative market share position and compete in a slow- or no-market-growth industry; they are *Dogs* in the firm's portfolio. Because of their weak internal and external position, these businesses often are liquidated, divested, or trimmed down through retrenchment. When a division first becomes a Dog, retrenchment can be the best strategy to pursue because many Dogs have bounced back, after strenuous asset and cost reduction, to become viable, profitable divisions.

The major benefit of the BCG Matrix is that it draws attention to the cash flow, investment characteristics, and needs of an organization's various divisions. The divisions of many firms evolve over time: Dogs become Question Marks, Question Marks become Stars, Stars become Cash Cows, and Cash Cows become Dogs in an ongoing counterclockwise motion. Less frequently, Stars become Question Marks, Question Marks become Dogs, Dogs become Cash Cows, and Cash Cows become Stars (in a clockwise motion). In some organizations no cyclical motion is apparent. Over time, organizations should strive to achieve a portfolio of divisions that are Stars.

One example of a BCG Matrix is provided in Figure 6–8, which illustrates an organization composed of five divisions with annual sales ranging from $5,000 to $60,000. Division I has the greatest sales volume, so the circle representing that division is the largest one in the matrix. The circle corresponding to Division 5 is the smallest because its sales volume ($5,000) is least among all the divisions. The pie slices within the circles reveal the percent of corporate profits contributed by each division. As shown, Division 1 contributes the highest profit percentage, 39 percent. Notice in the diagram that Division 1 is considered a Star, Division 2 is a Question Mark, Division 3 also is a Question Mark, Division 4 is a Cash Cow, and Division 5 is a Dog.

The BCG Matrix, like all analytical techniques, has some limitations. For example, viewing every business as either a Star, Cash Cow, Dog, or Question Mark is an oversimplification; many businesses fall right in the middle of the BCG Matrix and thus are not easily classified. Furthermore, the BCG Matrix does not reflect whether or not various divisions or their industries are growing over time; that is, the matrix has no temporal qualities, but rather is a snapshot of an organization at a given point in time. Finally, other variables besides relative market share position and industry growth rate in sales, such as size of the market and competitive advantages, are important in making strategic decisions about various divisions.

THE INTERNAL-EXTERNAL (IE) MATRIX The *Internal-External (IE) Matrix* positions an organization's various divisions in a nine-cell display illustrated in Figure 6–9. The IE Matrix is similar to the BCG Matrix in that both tools involve plotting organization divisions in a schematic diagram; this is why they are both called portfolio matrices. Also, the

FIGURE 6–8
An Example BCG Matrix

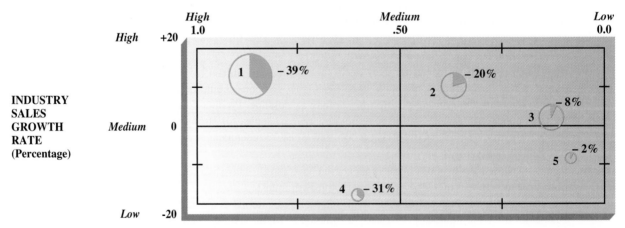

RELATIVE MARKET SHARE POSITION IN THE INDUSTRY

Division	Revenues	Percent Revenues	Profits	Percent Profits	Percent Market Share	Percent Growth Rate
1	$60,000	37	$10,000	39	80	+15
2	40,000	24	5,000	20	40	+10
3	40,000	24	2,000	8	10	1
4	20,000	12	8,000	31	60	-20
5	5,000	3	500	2	5	-10
Total	$165,000	100	$25,500	100		

FIGURE 6–9
The Internal-External (IE) Matrix

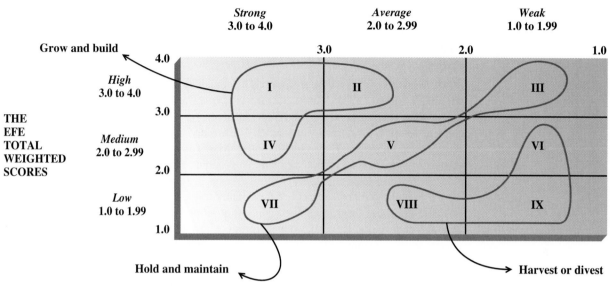

Note: The IE Matrix was developed from the General Electric (GE) Business Screen Matrix. For a description of the GE Matrix, see Michael Allen, "Diagramming GE's Planning for What's WATT" in *Corporate Planning: Techniques and Applications*, eds. R. Allio and M. Pennington (New York: AMACOM, 1979).

size of each circle represents the percentage sales contribution of each division, and pie slices reveal the percentage profit contribution of each division in both the BCG and IE Matrix.

But there are some important differences between the BCG Matrix and IE Matrix. First, the axes are different. Also, the IE Matrix requires more information about the divisions than the BCG Matrix. Further, the strategic implications of each matrix are different. For these reasons, strategists in multidivisional firms often develop both the BCG Matrix and the IE Matrix in formulating alternative strategies. A common practice is to develop a BCG Matrix and an IE Matrix for the present and then develop projected matrices to reflect expectations of the future. This before-and-after analysis forecasts the expected effect of strategic decisions on an organization's portfolio of divisions.

The IE Matrix is based on two key dimensions: the IFE total weighted scores on the *x*-axis and the EFE total weighted scores on the *y*-axis. Recall that each division of an organization should construct an IFE Matrix and an EFE Matrix for its part of the organization. The total weighted scores derived from the divisions allow construction of the corporate-level IE Matrix. On the *x*-axis of the IE Matrix, an IFE total weighted score of 1.0 to 1.99 represents a weak internal position; a score of 2.0 to 2.99 is considered average; and a score of 3.0 to 4.0 is strong. Similarly, on the *y*-axis, an EFE total weighted score of 1.0 to 1.99 is considered low; a score of 2.0 to 2.99 is medium; and a score of 3.0 to 4.0 is high.

The IE Matrix can be divided into three major regions that have different strategy implications. First, the prescription for divisions that fall into cells I, II, or IV can be described as *grow and build*. Intensive (market penetration, market development, and product development) or integrative (backward integration, forward integration, and horizontal integration) strategies can be most appropriate for these divisions. Second, divisions that fall into cells III, V, or VII can be managed best with *hold and maintain* strategies; market penetration and product development are two commonly employed strategies for these types of divisions. Third, a common prescription for divisions that fall into cells VI, VIII, or IX is *harvest or divest*. Successful organizations are able to achieve a portfolio of businesses positioned in or around cell I in the IE Matrix.

An example of a completed IE Matrix is given in Figure 6–10, which depicts an organization composed of four divisions. As indicated by the positioning of the circles, *grow and build* strategies are appropriate for Division 1, Division 2, and Division 3. Division 4 is a candidate for *harvest or divest*. Division 2 contributes the greatest percentage of company sales and thus is represented by the largest circle. Division 1 contributes the greatest proportion of total profits; it has the largest-percentage pie slice.

THE GRAND STRATEGY MATRIX   In addition to the TOWS Matrix, SPACE Matrix, BCG Matrix, and IE Matrix, the *Grand Strategy Matrix* has become a popular tool for formulating alternative strategies. All organizations can be positioned in one of the Grand Strategy Matrix's four strategy quadrants. A firm's divisions likewise could be positioned. As illustrated in Figure 6–11, the Grand Strategy Matrix is based on two evaluative dimensions: competitive position and market growth. Appropriate strategies for an organization to consider are listed in sequential order of attractiveness in each quadrant of the matrix.

Firms located in Quadrant I of the Grand Strategy Matrix are in an excellent strategic position. For these firms, continued concentration on current markets (market penetration and market development) and products (product development) are appropriate strategies. It is unwise for a Quadrant I firm to shift notably from its established competitive advantages. When a Quadrant I organization has excessive resources, then backward, forward, or horizontal integration may be effective strategies. When a Quadrant I firm is too heavily committed to a single product, then concentric diversification may reduce the risks associated with a narrow product line. Quadrant I firms can afford to take advantage of external opportunities in many areas: they can take risks aggressively when necessary.

FIGURE 6–10
An Example IE Matrix

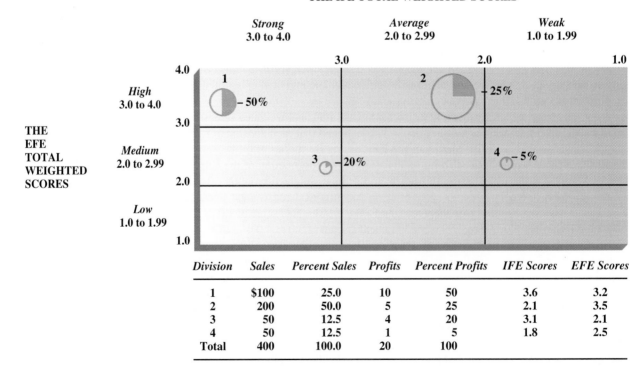

Division	Sales	Percent Sales	Profits	Percent Profits	IFE Scores	EFE Scores
1	$100	25.0	10	50	3.6	3.2
2	200	50.0	5	25	2.1	3.5
3	50	12.5	4	20	3.1	2.1
4	50	12.5	1	5	1.8	2.5
Total	400	100.0	20	100		

FIGURE 6–11
The Grand Strategy Matrix

RAPID MARKET GROWTH

Quadrant II

1. **Market development**
2. **Market penetration**
3. **Product development**
4. **Horizontal integration**
5. **Divestiture**
6. **Liquidation**

Quadrant I

1. **Market development**
2. **Market penetration**
3. **Product development**
4. **Forward integration**
5. **Backward integration**
6. **Horizontal integration**
7. **Concentric diversification**

WEAK COMPETITIVE POSITION

STRONG COMPETITIVE POSITION

Quadrant III

1. **Retrenchment**
2. **Concentric diversification**
3. **Horizontal diversification**
4. **Conglomerate diversification**
5. **Divestiture**
6. **Liquidation**

Quadrant IV

1. **Concentric diversification**
2. **Horizontal diversification**
3. **Conglomerate diversification**
4. **Joint ventures**

SLOW MARKET GROWTH

Source: Adapted from Roland Christensen, Norman Berg, and Malcolm Salter, *Policy Formulation and Administration* (Homewood, Ill.: Richard D. Irwin, 1976): 16–18.

Firms positioned in Quadrant II need to evaluate their present approach to the marketplace seriously. Although their industry is growing, they are unable to compete effectively, and they need to determine why the firm's current approach is ineffectual and how the company can best change to improve its competitiveness. Because Quadrant II firms are in a rapid-market-growth industry, an intensive strategy (as opposed to integrative or diversification) is usually the first option that should be considered. However, if the firm is lacking a distinctive competence or competitive advantage, then horizontal integration is often a desirable alternative. As a last result, divestiture or liquidation should be considered. Divestiture can provide funds needed to acquire other businesses or buy back shares of stock.

Quadrant III organizations compete in slow-growth industries and have weak competitive positions. These firms must make some drastic changes quickly to avoid further demise and possible liquidation. Extensive cost and asset reduction (retrenchment) should be pursued first. An alternative strategy is to shift resources away from the current business into different areas. If all else fails, the final options for Quadrant III businesses are divestiture or liquidation.

Finally, Quadrant IV businesses have a strong competitive position but are in a slow-growth industry. These firms have the strength to launch diversified programs into more promising growth areas. Quadrant IV firms have characteristically high cash flow levels and limited internal growth needs and often can pursue concentric, horizontal, or conglomerate diversification successfully. Quadrant IV firms also may pursue joint ventures.

THE DECISION STAGE

Analysis and intuition provide a basis for making strategy-formulation decisions. The matching techniques just discussed reveal feasible alternative strategies. Many of these strategies will likely have been proposed by managers and employees participating in the strategy analysis and choice activity. Any additional strategies resulting from the matching analyses could be discussed and added to the list of feasible alternative options. As indicated earlier in this chapter, participants could rate these strategies on a 1 to 4 scale so that a prioritized list of the best strategies could be achieved.

THE QUANTITATIVE STRATEGIC PLANNING MATRIX (QSPM) Other than ranking strategies to achieve the prioritized list, there is only one analytical technique in the literature designed to determine the relative attractiveness of feasible alternative actions. This technique is the *Quantitative Strategic Planning Matrix (QSPM)*, which comprises Stage 3 of the strategy-formulation analytical framework.[6] This technique objectively indicates which alternative strategies are best. The QSPM uses input from Stage 1 analyses and matching results from Stage 2 analyses to decide objectively among alternative strategies. That is, the EFE Matrix, IFE Matrix, and Competitive Profile Matrix that make up Stage 1, coupled with the TOWS Matrix, SPACE Analysis, BCG Matrix, IE Matrix, and Grand Strategy Matrix that make up Stage 2, provide the needed information for setting up the QSPM (Stage 3). The QSPM is a tool that allows strategists to evaluate alternative strategies objectively, based on previously identified external and internal critical success factors. Like other strategy-formulation analytical tools, the QSPM requires good intuitive judgment.

The basic format of the QSPM is illustrated in Table 6–6. Note that the left column of a QSPM consists of key external and internal factors (from Stage 1), and the top row consists of feasible alternative strategies (from Stage 2). Specifically, the left column of a QSPM consists of information obtained directly from the EFE Matrix and IFE Matrix. In a column adjacent to the critical success factors, the respective weights received by each factor in the EFE Matrix and the IFE Matrix are recorded.

TABLE 6–6
The Quantitative Strategic Planning Matrix—QSPM

		STRATEGIC ALTERNATIVES		
KEY FACTORS	**WEIGHT**	**STRATEGY 1**	**STRATEGY 2**	**STRATEGY 3**
KEY EXTERNAL FACTORS				
Economy				
Political/Legal/Governmental				
Social/Cultural/Demographic/Environmental				
Technological				
Competitive				
KEY INTERNAL FACTORS				
Management				
Marketing				
Finance/Accounting				
Production/Operations				
Research and Development				
Computer Information Systems				

The top row of a QSPM consists of alternative strategies derived from the TOWS Matrix, SPACE Matrix, BCG Matrix, IE Matrix, and Grand Strategy Matrix. These matching tools usually generate similar feasible alternatives. However, not every strategy suggested by the matching techniques has to be evaluated in a QSPM. Strategists should use good intuitive judgment in selecting strategies to include in a QSPM.

Conceptually, the QSPM determines the relative attractiveness of various strategies based on the extent to which key external and internal critical success factors are capitalized upon or improved. The relative attractiveness of each strategy within a set of alternatives is computed by determining the cumulative impact of each external and internal critical success factor. Any number of sets of alternative strategies can be included in the QSPM, and any number of strategies can make up a given set, but only strategies within a given set are evaluated relative to each other. For example, one set of strategies may include concentric, horizontal, and conglomerate diversification, whereas another set may include issuing stock and selling a division to raise needed capital. These two sets of strategies are totally different, and the QSPM evaluates strategies only within sets. Note in Table 6–6 that three strategies are included and they make up just one set.

A QSPM for a food company is provided in Table 6–7. This example illustrates all the components of the QSPM: Key Factors, Strategic Alternatives, Weights, Attractiveness Scores, Total Attractiveness Scores, and the Sum Total Attractiveness Score. The three new terms just introduced—(1) Attractiveness Scores, (2) Total Attractiveness Scores, and (3) the Sum Total Attractiveness Score—are defined and explained below as the six steps required to develop a QSPM are discussed.

Step 1 **List the firm's key external opportunities/threats and internal strengths/weaknesses in the left column of the QSPM.** This information should be taken directly from the EFE Matrix and IFE Matrix. A minimum of 10 external critical success factors and 10 internal critical success factors should be included in the QSPM.

Step 2 **Assign weights to each external and internal critical success factor.** These weights are identical to those in the EFE Matrix and the IFE Matrix. The weights are presented in a straight column just to the right of the external and internal critical success factors.

Step 3 **Examine the Stage 2 (matching) matrices and identify alternative strategies that the organization should consider implementing.** Record these strategies in the top row of the QSPM. Group the strategies into mutually exclusive sets if possible.

Step 4 **Determine the Attractiveness Scores (AS),** defined as numerical values that indicate the relative attractiveness of each strategy in a given set of alternatives. *Attractiveness Scores* are determined by examining each external or internal critical success factor, one at a time, and asking the question, "Does this factor affect the choice of strategies being made?" If the answer to this question is *yes*, then the strategies should be compared relative to that key factor. Specifically, Attractiveness Scores should be assigned to each strategy to indicate the relative attractiveness of one strategy over others, considering the particular factor. The range for Attractiveness Scores is 1 = *not attractive*, 2 = *somewhat attractive*, 3 = *reasonably attractive*, and 4 = *highly attractive*. If the answer to the above question is *no*, indicating that the respective critical success factor has no effect upon the specific choice being made, then do not assign Attractiveness Scores to the strategies in that set.

Step 5 **Compute the Total Attractiveness Scores.** *Total Attractiveness Scores* are defined as the product of multiplying the weights (Step 2) by the Attractiveness Scores (Step 4) in each row. The Total Attractiveness Scores indicate the relative attractiveness

TABLE 6–7
A QSPM for Campbell Soup Company

		STRATEGIC ALTERNATIVES			
		JOINT VENTURE IN EUROPE		JOINT VENTURE IN ASIA	
CRITICAL SUCCESS FACTORS	**WEIGHT**	**AS**	**TAS**	**AS**	**TAS**
OPPORTUNITIES					
1. One European currency—Euro	.10	4	.40	2	.20
2. Rising health consciousness in selecting foods	.15	4	.60	3	.45
3. Free market economies arising in Asia	.10	2	.20	4	.40
4. Demand for soups increasing 10 percent annually	.15	3	.45	4	.60
5. NAFTA	.05	–	–	–	–
THREATS					
1. Food revenues increasing only 1 percent annually	.10	3	.30	4	.40
2. ConAgra's Banquet TV Dinners lead market with 27.4 percent share	.05	–	–	–	–
3. Unstable economies in Asia	.10	4	.40	1	.10
4. Tin cans are not biodegradable	.05	–	–	–	–
5. Low value of the dollar	.15	4	.60	2	.30
	1.0				
STRENGTHS					
1. Profits rose 30 percent	.10	4	.40	2	.20
2. New North American division	.10	–	–	–	–
3. New health-conscious soups are successful	.10	4	.40	2	.20
4. Swanson TV dinners' market share has increased to 25.1 percent	.05	4	.20	3	.15
5. One-fifth of all managers' bonuses is based on overall corporate performance	.05	–	–	–	–
6. Capacity utilization increased from 60 percent to 80 percent	.15	3	.45	4	.60
WEAKNESSES					
1. Pepperidge Farm sales have declined 7 percent	.05	–	–	–	–
2. Restructuring cost $302 million	.05	–	–	–	–
3. The company's European operation is losing money	.15	2	.30	4	.60
4. The company is slow in globalizing	.15	4	.60	3	.45
5. Pretax profit margin of 8.4 percent is only one-half industry average	.05	–	–	–	–
SUM TOTAL ATTRACTIVENESS SCORE	1.0		5.30		4.65

AS = Attractiveness Score; TAS = Total Attractiveness Score
Attractiveness Score: 1 = not acceptable; 2 = possibly acceptable; 3 = probably acceptable; 4 = most acceptable.

of each alternative strategy, considering only the impact of the adjacent external or internal critical success factor. The higher the Total Attractiveness Score, the more attractive the strategic alternative (considering only the adjacent critical success factor).

Step 6   **Compute the Sum Total Attractiveness Score.** Add Total Attractiveness Scores in each strategy column of the QSPM. The *Sum Total Attractiveness Scores* reveal which strategy is most attractive in each set of alternatives. Higher scores indicate more attractive strategies, considering all the relevant external and internal factors that could affect the strategic decisions. The magnitude of the difference between the Sum Total Attractiveness Scores in a given set of strategic alternatives indicates the relative desirability of one strategy over another.

In Table 6–7, two alternative strategies—establishing a joint venture in Europe and establishing a joint venture in Asia—are being considered by Campbell Soup.

Note that NAFTA has no impact on the choice being made between the two strategies, so a dash (–) appears several times across that row. Several other factors also have no effect on the choice being made, so dashes are recorded in those rows as well. If a particular factor affects one strategy but not the other, it affects the choice being made, so attractiveness scores should be recorded. The sum total attractiveness score of 5.30 in Table 6.7 indicates that the joint venture in Europe is a more attractive strategy when compared to the joint venture in Asia.

You should have a rationale for each AS score assigned. In Table 6–7, the rationale for the AS scores in the first row is that the unification of Western Europe creates more stable business conditions in Europe than in Asia. The AS score of 4 for the joint venture in Europe and 2 for the joint venture in Asia indicates that the European venture is most acceptable and the Asian venture is possibly acceptable, considering only the first critical success factor. AS scores, therefore, are not mere guesses; they should be rational, defensible, and reasonable. Avoid giving each strategy the same AS score.

POSITIVE FEATURES AND LIMITATIONS OF THE QSPM A positive feature of the QSPM is that sets of strategies can be examined sequentially or simultaneously. For example, corporate-level strategies could be evaluated first, followed by division-level strategies, and then function-level strategies. There is no limit to the number of strategies that can be evaluated or the number of sets of strategies that can be examined at once using the QSPM.

Another positive feature of the QSPM is that it requires strategists to integrate pertinent external and internal factors into the decision process. Developing a QSPM makes it less likely that key factors will be overlooked or weighted inappropriately. A QSPM draws attention to important relationships that affect strategy decisions. Although developing a QSPM requires a number of subjective decisions, making small decisions along the way enhances the probability that the final strategic decisions will be best for the organization. A QSPM can be adapted for use by small and large for-profit and nonprofit organizations and can be applied to virtually any type of organization. A QSPM especially can enhance strategic choice in multinational firms because many key factors and strategies can be considered at once. It also has been applied successfully by a number of small businesses.[7]

The QSPM is not without some limitations. First, it always requires intuitive judgments and educated assumptions. The ratings and attractiveness scores require judgmental decisions, even though they should be based on objective information. Discussion among strategists, managers, and employees throughout the strategy-formulation process, including development of a QSPM, is constructive and improves strategic decisions. Constructive discussion during strategy analysis and choice may arise because of genuine differences of interpretation of information and varying opinions. Another limitation of the QSPM is that it can be only as good as the prerequisite information and matching analyses upon which it is based.

CULTURAL ASPECTS OF STRATEGY CHOICE

All organizations have a culture. *Culture* includes the set of shared values, beliefs, attitudes, customs, norms, personalities, heroes, and heroines that describe a firm. Culture is the unique way an organization does business. It is the human dimension that creates solidarity and meaning, and inspires commitment and productivity in an organization when strategy changes are made. All human beings have a basic need to make sense of their world, to feel in control, and to make meaning. When events threaten meaning, individuals react defensively. Managers and employees even may sabotage new strategies in an effort to recapture the status quo.

It is beneficial to view strategic management from a cultural perspective because success often rests upon the degree of support that strategies receive from a firm's culture.

If a firm's strategies are supported by cultural products such as values, beliefs, rites, rituals, ceremonies, stories, symbols, language, heroes, and heroines then managers often can implement changes swiftly and easily. However, if a supportive culture does not exist and is not cultivated, then strategy changes may be ineffective or even counterproductive. A firm's culture can become antagonistic to new strategies, and the result of that antagonism may be confusion and disarray.

Strategies that require fewer cultural changes may be more attractive because extensive changes can take considerable time and effort. Whenever two firms merge, culture-strategy linkages become especially important to evaluate and consider. For example, Boeing actively is integrating the culture of McDonnell Douglas with its own, and Westinghouse is trying to integrate its culture with CBS, Inc.

When two or three companies from different countries form a joint venture, such as the recent venture among Honeywell, NEC Corporation of Japan, and Compagnie des Machines Bull of France, merging corporate cultures can be a problem. Jerome Meyer, a Honeywell executive, is president and CEO of the new organization, the first multinational computer company. "We've not had an alliance of these dimensions before, with its geographic diversity and cultural conflict," said Michael Geran, an analyst with E. F. Hutton. "The skill to run it will be a tremendous challenge." He predicted that Meyer would become primarily "a referee."

Culture provides an explanation for the difficulties a firm encounters when it attempts to shift its strategic direction, as the following statement explains:

> Not only has the "right" corporate culture become the essence and foundation of corporate excellence, but success or failure of needed corporate reforms hinges on management's sagacity and ability to change the firm's driving culture in time and in tune with required changes in strategies.[8]

THE POLITICS OF STRATEGY CHOICE

All organizations are political. Unless managed, political maneuvering consumes valuable time, subverts organizational objectives, diverts human energy, and results in the loss of some valuable employees. Sometimes political biases and personal preferences get unduly embedded in strategy choice decisions. Internal politics affect the choice of strategies in all organizations. The hierarchy of command in an organization, combined with the career aspirations of different people and the need to allocate scarce resources, guarantees the formation of coalitions of individuals who strive to take care of themselves first and the organization second, third, or fourth. Coalitions of individuals often form around key strategy issues that face an enterprise. A major responsibility of strategists is to guide the development of coalitions, to nurture an overall team concept, and to gain the support of key individuals and groups of individuals.

In the absence of objective analyses, strategy decisions too often are based on the politics of the moment. With development of improved strategy-formation tools, political factors become less important in making strategic decisions. In the absence of objectivity, political factors sometimes dictate strategies, and this is unfortunate. Managing political relationships is an integral part of building enthusiasm and esprit de corps in an organization. Don Beeman and Tom Sharkey offer the following guidelines for minimizing the negative aspects of organizational politics:

1. Make clear the bases and processes for performance evaluation.
2. Differentiate rewards among high and low performers.

3. Make sure rewards are as immediately and directly related to performance as possible.

4. Minimize resource competition among managers.

5. Replace resource competition among managers.

6. Where highly cohesive political empires exist, break them apart by removing or splitting the most dysfunctional subgroups.

7. Be keenly sensitive to managers whose mode of operation is personalization of political patronage. Approach these persons with a directive to "stop political maneuvering." If it continues, remove them from the position and preferably the company.[9]

A classic study of strategic management in nine large corporations examined the political tactics of successful and unsuccessful strategists.[10] Successful strategists were found to let weakly supported ideas and proposals die through inaction and to establish additional hurdles or tests for strongly supported ideas considered unacceptable but not openly opposed. Successful strategists kept a low political profile on unacceptable proposals and strived to let most negative decisions come from subordinates or a group consensus, thereby reserving their personal vetoes for big issues and crucial moments. Successful strategists did a lot of chatting and informal questioning to stay abreast of how things were progressing and to know when to intervene. They led strategy but did not dictate it. They gave few orders, announced few decisions, depended heavily on informal questioning, and sought to probe and clarify until a consensus emerged.

Successful strategists generously and visibly rewarded key thrusts that succeeded. They assigned responsibility for major new thrusts to *champions*, the individuals most strongly identified with the idea or product and whose futures were linked to its success. They stayed alert to the symbolic impact of their own actions and statements so as not to send false signals that could stimulate movements in unwanted directions.

Successful strategists ensured that all major power bases within an organization were represented in, or had access to, top management. They interjected new faces and new views into considerations of major changes. (This is important because new employees and managers generally have more enthusiasm and drive than employees who have been with the firm a long time. New employees do not see the world the same old way nor act as screens against changes.) Successful strategists minimized their own political exposure on highly controversial issues and in circumstances where major opposition from key power centers was likely. In combination, these findings provide a basis for managing political relationships in an organization.

Because strategies must be effective in the marketplace and capable of gaining internal commitment, the following tactics used by politicians for centuries can aid strategists:

◆ *Equifinality*: It is often possible to achieve similar results using different means or paths. Strategists should recognize that achieving a successful outcome is more important than imposing the method of achieving it. It may be possible to generate new alternatives that give equal results but with far greater potential for gaining commitment.

◆ *Satisfying*: Achieving satisfactory results with an acceptable strategy is far better than failing to achieve optimal results with an unpopular strategy.

◆ *Generalization*: Shifting focus from specific issues to more general ones may increase strategists' options for gaining organizational commitment.

◆ *Focus on Higher-Order Issues*: By raising an issue to a higher level, many short-term interests can be postponed in favor of long-term interests. For instance, by focusing on issues of survival, the auto and steel industries were able to persuade unions to make concessions on wage increases.

◆ *Provide Political Access on Important Issues*: Strategy and policy decisions with significant negative consequences for middle managers will motivate intervention behavior from them. If middle managers do not have an opportunity to take a position on such decisions in appropriate political forums, they are capable of successfully resisting the decisions after they are made. Providing such political access provides strategists with information that otherwise might not be available and that could be useful in managing intervention behavior.[11]

THE ROLE OF A BOARD OF DIRECTORS

The widespread lack of involvement by *boards of directors* in the strategic-management process is changing in America. Historically, boards of directors mostly have been insiders who would not second-guess top executives on strategic issues. It generally has been understood that strategists are responsible and accountable for implementing strategy, so they, not board members, should formulate strategy. Consequently, chief executive officers usually avoided discussions of overall strategy with directors because the results of those discussions often restricted their freedom of action. The judgments of board members seldom were used on acquisitions, divestitures, large capital investments, and other strategic matters. Often, the board would meet only annually to fulfill its minimum legal requirements; in many organizations, boards served merely a traditional legitimizing role.

Today, boards of directors are composed mostly of outsiders who are becoming more involved in organizations' strategic management. The trend in America is toward smaller boards, now averaging 12 members rather than 18 as they did a few years ago. Smaller boards can discuss issues more easily; individuals in small groups take responsibility more personally. The percentage of minority individuals serving on the boards of directors of *Fortune* 1,000 companies doubled between 1992 and 1997. Although 85 percent of the 7,041 directors of Fortune 1,000 boards are white males, the percentage continues to fall. African American membership on these boards now is nearly 3 percent while women make up nearly 9 percent. Most shareholders realize that women and minorities strengthen a board and a company by bringing in new perspectives and preventing "CEO clones."

Just as directors are beginning to place more emphasis on staying informed about an organization's health and operations, they also are taking a more active role in ensuring that publicly issued documents are accurate representations of a firm's status. It is becoming widely recognized that a board of directors has legal responsibilities to stockholders and society for all company activities, for corporate performance, and for ensuring that a firm has an effective strategy. Failure to accept responsibility for auditing or evaluating a firm's strategy is considered a serious breach of a director's duties. Stockholders, government agencies, and customers are filing legal suits against directors for fraud, omissions, inaccurate disclosures, lack of due diligence, and culpable ignorance about a firm's operations with increasing frequency. Liability insurance for directors has become exceptionally expensive and has caused numerous directors to resign.

Boards of directors in corporate America today seriously are evaluating strategic plans, evaluating the top management team, and assuming responsibility for management succession. TIAA-CREF, the nation's largest pension fund, now regularly evaluates governance practices at more than 1,500 companies in which it owns a stake. *Business Week*'s first annual board of director's evaluation[12] posited that good boards of directors actively perform the following responsibilities:

- Evaluate the CEO annually.
- Link the CEO's pay to specific goals.
- Evaluate long-range strategy.
- Evaluate board members' performance through a governance committee.
- Compensate board members only in company stock.
- Require each director to own a large amount of company stock.
- Ensure no more than two board members are insiders (work for the company).
- Require directors to retire at age 70.
- Place the entire board up for election every year.
- Limit the number of other boards a member can serve on.
- Ban directors who draw consulting fees or other monies from the company.
- Ban interlocking directorships.

Business Week's top 10 boards for 1996 were those of the following:

1. Campbell Soup
2. General Electric
3. IBM
4. Compaq Computer
5. Colgate Palmolive
6. Chrysler
7. Johnson & Johnson
8. Merck
9. Hercules
10. Exxon

Business Week's 10 lowest-rated boards of directors for 1996 were those of the following:

1. Archer Daniels Midland
2. Champion International
3. H. J. Heinz
4. Rollins Environmental
5. Nationsbank
6. AT&T
7. Kmart
8. Unisys
9. Ethyl
10. Fleming Companies

Two rulings particulary affected the role of boards of directors in the strategy-formulation process. First, the Supreme Court of Delaware ruled that the directors of the Trans Union Corporation violated the interests of shareholders when they hastily accepted a takeover bid from the Marmon Group; that ruling eroded the so-called business judgment rule, which protects directors from liability as long as their decisions represent a good-faith effort to serve the best interests of the corporation. One clear signal from the Trans Union case is that haste can be costly for board members.

In another landmark ruling that illustrates how boards of directors increasingly are being held responsible for the overall performance of organizations, the Federal Deposit Insurance Corporation forced Continental Illinois to accept the resignations of 10 of the troubled bank's outside directors. The impact of increasing legal pressures on board members is that directors are demanding greater and more regular access to financial performance information.

Some boardroom reforms that are lessening the likelihood of lawsuits today include increasing the percentage of outsiders on the board, separating the positions of CEO and chairperson, requiring directors to hold substantial amounts of stock in the firm, and decreasing the board size. Outsiders now outnumber insiders at 90 percent of all American firms' boards, and the average number of outsiders is three times that of insiders.

A direct response of increased pressure on directors to stay informed and execute their responsibilities is that audit committees are becoming commonplace. A board of directors should conduct an annual strategy audit in much the same fashion that it reviews the annual financial audit. In performing such an audit, a board could work jointly with operating management and/or seek outside counsel.

The trend among corporations toward decreased diversification, increased takeover activity, increased legal pressures, multidivisional structures, and multinational operations augments the problem of keeping directors informed. Boards should play a role beyond that of performing a strategic audit. They should provide greater input and advice in the strategy-formulation process to ensure that strategists are providing for the long-term needs of the firm. This is being done through the formation of three particular board committees: nominating committees to propose candidates for the board and senior officers of the firm; compensation committees to evaluate the performance of top executives and determine the terms and conditions of their employment; and public policy committees to give board-level attention to company policies and performance on subjects of concern such as business ethics, consumer affairs, and political activities.

Nearly 41 percent of all firms that have a board of directors have developed a mission statement for the board.[13] A board of directors' mission statement outlines the purpose and intent of the board and defines to whom, or for what, the board is held accountable. A board mission statement also indicates company expectations about the quality of preparation for and the process for conducting board meetings. Overall, the mission of boards of directors must be expanded. Companies should assign managers to join directors on board committees, rather than limit the board's contact with only a few top managers. Directors must assume a more activist stance in management development, rather than just react to management initiatives.

Powerful boards of directors are associated with high organizational performance. Powerful boards participate in corporate decisions more fully, share their experiences with the CEO regarding certain strategies, and are actively involved in industry analysis. Firms can develop more powerful boards by regularly reviewing board committee activities, evaluating board meetings, and involving the board more extensively in strategic issues. More companies are paying board members partly or totally in stock, which gives outside directors more reason to identify with the shareholders they represent rather than with the CEO they oversee.

CONCLUSION

The essence of strategy formulation is an assessment of whether an organization is doing the right things and how it can be more effective in what it does. Every organization should be wary of becoming a prisoner of its own strategy, because even the best strategies become obsolete sooner or later. Regular reappraisal of strategy helps management avoid complacency. Objectives and strategies should be consciously developed and coordinated and should not merely evolve out of day-to-day operating decisions.

An organization with no sense of direction and no coherent strategy precipitates its own demise. When an organization does not know where it wants to go, it usually ends up some place it does not want to be! Every organization needs to consciously establish and communicate clear objectives and strategies.

Modern strategy-formulation tools and concepts are described in this chapter and integrated into a practical three-stage framework. Tools such as the TOWS Matrix, SPACE Matrix, BCG Matrix, IE Matrix, and QSPM can enhance significantly the quality of strategic decisions, but they should never be used to dictate the choice of strategies. Behavioral, cultural, and political aspects of strategy generation and selection are always important to consider and manage. Due to increased legal pressure from outside groups, boards of directors are assuming a more active role in strategy analysis and choice. This is a positive trend for organizations.

We invite you to visit the DAVID page on the Prentice Hall Web site at
www.prenhall.com/
for this chapter's World Wide Web exercise.

**TAKE
IT TO
THE NET**

KEY TERMS AND CONCEPTS

Aggressive Quadrant	(p. 185)	Dogs	(p. 189)	SO Strategies	(p. 180)
Attractiveness Scores (AS)	(p. 195)	Environmental Stability (ES)	(p. 184)	ST Strategies	(p. 181)
Boards of Directors	(p. 200)	Financial Strength (FS)	(p. 184)	Stars	(p. 189)
Boston Consulting Group (BCG) Matrix	(p. 188)	Grand Strategy Matrix	(p. 192)	Strategic Position and Action Evaluation (SPACE) Matrix	(p. 184)
		Halo Error	(p. 179)		
Business Portfolio	(p. 187)	Industry Strength (IS)	(p. 184)	Strategy-Formulation Framework	(p. 179)
Cash Cows	(p. 189)	Input Stage	(p. 178)		
Champions	(p. 199)	Internal-External (IE) Matrix	(p. 190)	Sum Total Attractiveness Scores	(p. 196)
Competitive Advantage (CA)	(p. 184)	Long-Term Objectives	(p. 176)	Threats-Opportunities-Weaknesses-Strengths (TOWS) Matrix	(p. 180)
Competitive Quadrant	(p. 187)	Matching	(p. 179)		
Conservative Quadrant	(p. 187)	Matching Stage	(p. 178)		
Culture	(p. 197)	Quantitative Strategic Planning Matrix (QSPM)	(p. 194)	Total Attractiveness Scores (TAS)	(p. 195)
Decision Stage	(p. 178)			WO Strategies	(p. 181)
Defensive Quadrant	(p. 187)	Question Marks	(p. 189)	WT Strategies	(p. 181)
Directional Vector	(p. 185)	Relative Market Share Position	(p. 188)		

ISSUES FOR REVIEW AND DISCUSSION

1. How would application of the strategy-formulation framework differ from a small to a large organization?

2. What types of strategies would you recommend for an organization that achieves total weighted scores of 3.6 on the IFE and 1.2 on the EFE Matrix?

3. Given the following information, develop a SPACE Matrix for the XYZ Corporation: FS = +2; ES = −6; CA = −2; IS = +4.

4. Given the information in the table below, develop a BCG Matrix and an IE Matrix:

Divisions	1	2	3
Profits	$10	$15	$25
Sales	$100	$50	$100
Relative Market Share	0.2	0.5	0.8
Industry Growth Rate	+.20	+.10	−.10
IFE Total Weighted Scores	1.6	3.1	2.2
EFE Total Weighted Scores	2.5	1.8	3.3

5. Explain the steps involved in developing a QSPM.

6. How would you develop a set of objectives for your school of business?

7. What do you think is the appropriate role of a board of directors in strategic management? Why?

8. Discuss the limitations of various strategy-formulation analytical techniques.

9. Explain why cultural factors should be an important consideration in analyzing and choosing among alternative strategies.

10. How are the TOWS Matrix, SPACE Matrix, BCG Matrix, IE Matrix, and Grand Strategy Matrix similar? How are they different?

11. How would profit and nonprofit organizations differ in their applications of the strategy-formulation framework?

12. Select an article from the suggested readings at the end of this chapter and prepare a report on that article for your class.

NOTES

1. Steven C. Brandt, *Strategic Planning in Emerging Companies* (Reading, Massachusetts: Addison-Wesley, 1981). Reprinted with permission of the publisher.

2. R. T. Lenz, "Managing the Evolution of the Strategic Planning Process," *Business Horizons* 30, no. 1 (January–February 1987): 37.

3. Robert Grant, "The Resource-Based Theory of Competitive Advantage: Implications for Strategy Formulation," *California Management Review* (Spring 1991): 114.

4. Heinz Weihrich, "The TOWS Matrix: A Tool for Situational Analysis," *Long Range Planning* 15, no. 2 (April 1982): 61.

5. H. Rowe, R. Mason, and K. Dickel, *Strategic Management and Business Policy: A Methodological Approach* (Reading, Massachusetts: Addison-Wesley Publishing Co. Inc., 1982): 155–156. Reprinted with permission of the publisher.

6. Fred David, "The Strategic Planning Matrix—A Quantitative Approach," *Long Range Planning* 19, no. 5 (October 1986): 102. Andre Gib and Robert Margulies, "Making Competitive Intelligence Relevant to the User," *Planning Review* 19, no. 3 (May/June 1991): 21.

7. Fred David, "Computer-Assisted Strategic Planning in Small Businesses," *Journal of Systems Management* 36, no. 7 (July 1985): 24–34.

8. Y. Allarie and M. Firsirotu, "How to Implement Radical Strategies in Large Organizations," *Sloan Management Review* 26, no. 3 (Spring 1985): 19. Another excellent article is P. Shrivastava, "Integrating Strategy Formulation with Organizational Culture," *Journal of Business Strategy* 5, no. 3 (Winter 1985): 103–111.

9. Don Beeman and Thomas Sharkey, "The Use and Abuse of Corporate Politics," *Business Horizons* 30, no. 2 (March–April 1987): 30.

10. James Brian Quinn, *Strategies for Change: Logical Incrementalism* (Homewood, Ill.: Richard D. Irwin, 1980): 128–145. These political tactics are listed in A. Thompson and A. Strickland, *Strategic Management: Concepts and Cases* (Plano, Texas: Business Publications, 1984): 261.

11. William Guth and Ian MacMillan, "Strategy Implementation Versus Middle Management Self-Interest," *Strategic Management Journal* 7, no. 4 (July–August 1986): 321.

12. "Best and Worst Corporate Boards of Directors," *Business Week* (November 25, 1996): 82–98.

13. Ada Demb, Danielle Chouet, Tom Lossius, and Fred Neubauer, "Defining the Role of the Board," *Long Range Planning* 22, no. 1 (February 1989): 61–68.

CURRENT READINGS

Barker, V. L. III and I. M. Duhaime. "Strategic Change in the Turnaround Process: Theory and Empirical Evidence." *Strategic Management Journal* 18, no. 1 (January 1997): 13–38.

Chakravarthy, Bala. "A New Strategy Framework for Coping with Turbulence." *Sloan Management Review* 38, no. 2 (Winter 1997): 69–82.

Daily, Catherine M. and Charles Schwenk. "Chief Executive Officers, Top Management Teams, and Boards of Directors: Congruent or Countervailing Forces?" *Journal of Management* 22, no. 2 (1996): 185–208.

Dodllinger, M. J., P. A. Golden, and T. Saxton. "The Effect of Reputation on the Decision to Joint Venture." *Strategic Management Journal* 18, no. 2 (February 1997): 127–140.

Ferris, Gerald R., Dwight D. Frink, Dharm P. S. Bhawuk, Jing Zhou, and David C. Gilmore. "Reactions of Diverse Groups to Politics in the Workplace." *Journal of Management* 22, no. 1 (1996): 23–44.

Fischer, Frank, reviewed by. *Resistance and Power in Organizations*, edited by John Jermier, David Knights, and Walter Nord. *Academy of Management Review* 22, no. 2 (April 1997): 564–567.

Gould, Des. "Developing Directors Through Personal Coaching." *Long Range Planning* 30, no. 1 (February 1997): 29–37.

Higgins, James M. "Innovate or Evaporate: Creative Techniques for Strategists." *Long Range Planning* 29, no. 3 (June 1996): 370–380.

Hill, Terry and Roy Westbrook. "SWOT Analysis: It's Time for a Product Recall." *Long Range Planning* 30, no. 1 (February 1997): 46–52.

Iansiti, Marco and Jonathan West. "Technology Integration: Turning Great Research into Great Products." *Harvard Business Review* (May–June 1997): 69–82.

Johnson, Jonathan L., Catherine M. Daily, and Alan E. Ellstrand. "Boards of Directors: A Review and Research Agenda." *Journal of Management* 22, no. 3 (1996): 409–438.

O'Neal, Don and Howard Thomas. "Developing the Strategic Board." *Long Range Planning* 29, no. 3 (June 1996): 314–327.

Pennington, Ashly and Timothy Morris. "Power and Control in Professional Partnerships." *Long Range Planning* 29, no. 6 (December 1996): 842–849.

Seward, J. K. and J. P. Walsh. "The Governance and Control of Voluntary Corporate Spin-Offs." *Strategic Management Journal* 17, no. 1 (January 1996): 25–40.

Slevin, Dennis P. and Jeffrey G. Covin. "Strategy Formation Patterns, Performance, and the Significance of Context." *Journal of Management* 23, no. 2 (1997): 189–199.

Sundaramurthy, C. "Corporate Governance Within the Context of Anti-Takeover Provisions." *Strategic Management Journal* 17, no. 5 (May 1996): 377–394.

Sundaramurthy, C., J. M. Mahoney, and J. T. Mahoney. "Board Structure, Anti-Takeover Provisions, and Stockholder Wealth." *Strategic Management Journal* 18, no. 3 (March 1997): 231–246.

Sundaramurthy, Chamu, Paula Rechner, and Weiren Wang. "Governance Antecedents of Board Entrenchment: The Case of Classified Board Provisions." *Journal of Management* 22, no. 5 (1996): 783–793.

Zajac, Edward J. and James D. Westphal. "Who Shall Succeed? How CEO/Board Preferences and Power Affect the Choice of New CEOs." *Academy of Management Journal* 39, no. 1 (February 1996): 64–90.

EXPERIENTIAL EXERCISES

DEVELOPING A TOWS MATRIX FOR HERSHEY FOODS

PURPOSE

The most widely used strategy-formulation technique among American firms is the TOWS Matrix. This exercise requires development of a TOWS Matrix for Hershey. Matching key external and internal factors in a TOWS Matrix requires good intuitive and conceptual skills. You will improve with practice in developing a TOWS Matrix.

INSTRUCTIONS

Recall from Experiential Exercise 1A that you already may have determined Hershey's external opportunities/threats and internal strengths/weaknesses. This information could be used in completing this exercise. Follow the steps outlined below:

Step 1 On a separate sheet of paper, construct a large nine-cell diagram that will represent your TOWS Matrix. Label the cells appropriately.

Step 2 Record Hershey's opportunities/threats and strengths/weaknesses appropriately in your diagram.

Step 3 Match external and internal factors to generate feasible alternative strategies for Hershey. Record SO, WO, ST, and WT Strategies in appropriate cells of the TOWS Matrix. Use the proper notation to indicate the rationale for the strategies. You do not necessarily have to have strategies in all four strategy cells.

Step 4 Compare your TOWS Matrix to another student's TOWS Matrix. Discuss any major differences.

DEVELOPING A SPACE MATRIX FOR HERSHEY FOODS

PURPOSE

Should Hershey pursue aggressive, conservative, competitive, or defensive strategies? Develop a SPACE Matrix for Hershey to answer this question. Elaborate on the strategic implications of your directional vector. Be specific in terms of strategies that could benefit Hershey.

INSTRUCTIONS

Step 1 Join with two other persons in class and develop a joint SPACE Matrix for Hershey.

Step 2 Diagram your SPACE Matrix on the board. Compare your matrix with other teams' matrices.

Step 3 Discuss the implications of your SPACE Matrix.

DEVELOPING A BCG MATRIX FOR HERSHEY FOODS

PURPOSE

Portfolio matrices are widely used by multidivisional organizations to help identify and select strategies to pursue. A BCG analysis identifies particular divisions that should receive fewer resources than others. It may identify some divisions to be divested. This exercise can give you practice developing a BCG Matrix.

INSTRUCTIONS

Step 1 Place the following five column headings at the top of a separate sheet of paper: Divisions, Revenues, Profits, Relative Market Share Position, Industry Growth Rate.

Step 2 Complete a BCG Matrix for Hershey.

Step 3 Compare your BCG Matrix to other students' matrices. Discuss any major differences.

DEVELOPING A QSPM FOR HERSHEY FOODS

PURPOSE

This exercise can give you practice developing a Quantitative Strategic Planning Matrix to determine the relative attractiveness of various strategic alternatives.

INSTRUCTIONS

Step 1 Join with two other students in class to develop a joint QSPM for Hershey.

Step 2 Go to the blackboard and record your strategies and their Sum Total Attractiveness Scores. Compare your team's strategies and sum total attractiveness scores to those of other teams.

Step 3 Discuss any major differences.

FORMULATING INDIVIDUAL STRATEGIES

PURPOSE

Individuals and organizations are alike in many ways. Each has competitors and each should plan for the future. Every individual and organization faces some external opportunities and threats and has some internal strengths and weaknesses. Both individuals and organizations establish objectives and allocate resources. These and other similarities make it possible for individuals to use many strategic-management concepts and tools. This exercise is designed to demonstrate how the TOWS Matrix can be used by individuals to plan their futures. As one nears completion of a college degree and begins interviewing for jobs, planning can be particularly important.

INSTRUCTIONS

On a separate sheet of paper, construct a TOWS Matrix. Include what you consider to be your major external opportunities, your major external threats, your major strengths, and your major weaknesses. An internal weakness may be a low grade point average. An external opportunity may be that your university offers a graduate program that interests you. Match key external and internal factors by recording in the appropriate cell of the matrix alternative strategies or actions that would allow you to capitalize upon your strengths, overcome your weaknesses, take advantage of your external opportunities, and minimize the impact of external threats. Be sure to use the appropriate matching notation in the strategy cells of the matrix. Because every individual (and organization) is unique, there is no one right answer to this exercise.

Experiential Exercise 6F

THE MACH TEST

PURPOSE

The purpose of this exercise is to enhance your understanding and awareness of the impact that behavioral and political factors can have on strategy analysis and choice.

INSTRUCTIONS

Step 1 On a separate sheet of paper, number from 1 to 10. For each of the 10 statements given below, record a *1*, *2*, *3*, *4*, or *5* to indicate your attitude, where

1 = I disagree a lot.
2 = I disagree a little.
3 = My attitude is neutral.
4 = I agree a little.
5 = I agree a lot.

1. The best way to handle people is to tell them what they want to hear.
2. When you ask someone to do something for you, it is best to give the real reason for wanting it, rather than a reason that might carry more weight.
3. Anyone who completely trusts anyone else is asking for trouble.
4. It is hard to get ahead without cutting corners here and there.
5. It is safest to assume that all people have a vicious streak, and it will come out when they are given a chance.
6. One should take action only when it is morally right.
7. Most people are basically good and kind.
8. There is no excuse for lying to someone else.
9. Most people forget more easily the death of their father than the loss of their property.
10. Generally speaking, people won't work hard unless they're forced to do so.

Step 2 Add up the numbers you recorded beside statements 1, 3, 4, 5, 9, and 10. This sum is Subtotal One. For the other four statements, reverse the numbers you recorded, so a *5* becomes a *1*, *4* becomes 2, 2 becomes *4*, 1 becomes *5*, and *3* remains *3*. Then add those four numbers to get Subtotal Two. Finally, add Subtotal One and Subtotal Two to get your Final Score.

YOUR FINAL SCORE

Your Final Score is your Machiavellian Score. Machiavellian principles are defined in a dictionary as "manipulative, dishonest, deceiving, and favoring political expediency over morality." These tactics are not desirable, are not ethical, and are not recommended in the strategic-management process! You may, however, encounter some highly Machiavellian individuals in your career, so beware. It is important for strategists not to manipulate others in the pursuit of organizational objectives. Individuals today recognize and resent manipulative tactics more than ever before. J.R. Ewing (on a television show in the 1980s, *Dallas*) was a good example of someone who was a high Mach (score over 30). The National Opinion Research Center used this short quiz in a random sample of American adults and found the national average Final Score to be 25.[1] The higher your score, the more Machiavellian (manipulative) you tend to be. The following scale is descriptive of individual scores on this test:

- ◆ Below 16: Never uses manipulation as a tool.
- ◆ 16 to 20: Rarely uses manipulation as a tool.
- ◆ 21 to 25: Sometimes uses manipulation as a tool.
- ◆ 26 to 30: Often uses manipulation as a tool.
- ◆ Over 30: Always uses manipulation as a tool.

TEST DEVELOPMENT

The Mach (Machiavellian) test was developed by Dr. Richard Christie, whose research suggests the following tendencies:

1. Men generally are more Machiavellian than women.
2. There is no significant difference between high Machs and low Machs on measures of intelligence or ability.
3. Although high Machs are detached from others, they are detached in a pathological sense.
4. Machiavellian Scores are not statistically related to authoritarian values.
5. High Machs tend to be in professions that emphasize the control and manipulation of individuals; for example, law, psychiatry, and behavioral science.
6. Machiavellianism is not significantly related to major demographic characteristics such as educational level or marital status.
7. High Machs tend to come from a city or have urban backgrounds.
8. Older adults tend to have lower Mach scores than younger adults.[2]

A classic book on power relationships, *The Prince*, was written by Niccolo Machiavelli. Several excerpts from *The Prince* are given below:

Men must either be cajoled or crushed, for they will revenge themselves for slight wrongs, while for grave ones they cannot. The injury therefore that you do to a man should be such that you need not fear his revenge.

We must bear in mind . . . that there is nothing more difficult and dangerous, or more doubtful of success, than an attempt to introduce a new order of things in any state. The innovator has for enemies all those who derived advantages from the old order of things, while those who expect to be benefitted by the new institution will be but lukewarm defenders.

A wise prince, therefore, will steadily pursue such a course that the citizens of his state will always and under all circumstances feel the need for his authority, and will therefore always prove faithful to him.

A prince should seem to be merciful, faithful, humane, religious, and upright, and should even be so in reality; but he should have his mind so trained that, when occasion requires it, he may know how to change to the opposite.[3]

NOTES

1. Richard Christie and Florence Geis, *Studies in Machiavellianism* (Orlando, Florida: Academic Press, 1970). Material in this exercise adapted with permission of the authors and the Academic Press.
2. Ibid., 82–83.
3. Niccolo Machiavelli, *The Prince* (New York: The Washington Press, 1963).

Experiential Exercise 6G

DEVELOPING A BCG MATRIX FOR MY UNIVERSITY

PURPOSE

A BCG Matrix is useful to develop for many nonprofit organizations, including colleges and universities. Of course, there are no profits for each division or department and in some cases no revenues. However, you can be creative in performing a BCG Matrix. For example, the pie slice in the circles can represent the number of majors receiving jobs upon graduation, or the number of faculty teaching in that area, or some other variable that you believe is important to consider. The size of the circles can represent the number of students majoring in particular departments or areas.

INSTRUCTIONS

Step 1 On a separate sheet of paper, develop a BCG Matrix for your university. Include all academic schools, departments, or colleges.

Step 2 Diagram your BCG Matrix on the blackboard.

Step 3 Discuss differences among the BCG Matrices on the board.

Experiential Exercise 6H

THE ROLE OF BOARDS OF DIRECTORS

PURPOSE

This exercise will give you a better understanding of the role of boards of directors in formulating, implementing, and evaluating strategies.

INSTRUCTIONS

Identify a person in your community who serves on a board of directors. Make an appointment to interview that person and seek answers to the questions given below. Summarize your findings in a five-minute oral report to the class.

On what board are you a member?

How often does the board meet?

How long have you served on the board?

What role does the board play in this company?

How has the role of the board changed in recent years?

What changes would you like to see in the role of the board?

To what extent do you prepare for the board meeting?

To what extent are you involved in strategic management of the firm?

Experiential Exercise 6I

LOCATING COMPANIES IN A GRAND STRATEGY MATRIX

PURPOSE

The Grand Strategy Matrix is a popular tool for formulating alternative strategies. All organizations can be positioned in one of the Grand Strategy Matrix's four strategy quadrants. The divisions of a firm likewise could be positioned. The Grand Strategy Matrix is based on two evaluative dimensions: competitive position and market growth. Appropriate strategies for an organization to consider are listed in sequential order of attractiveness in each quadrant of the matrix. This exercise gives you experience using a Grand Strategy Matrix.

INSTRUCTIONS

Using the year-end 1997 financial information given below, prepare a Grand Strategy Matrix on a separate sheet of paper. Write the respective company names in the appropriate quadrant of the matrix. Based on this analysis, what strategies are recommended for each company?

COMPANY	COMPANY SALES/PROFIT GROWTH (%)	INDUSTRY	INDUSTRY SALES/PROFITS GROWTH (%)
Eaton	+9/+33	Automotive Parts	+11/+27
General Signal	−5/−2	Automotive Parts	+11/+27
Pennzoil	+7/+35	Oil, Gas, & Coal	0/+13
Chevron	−7/+25	Oil, Gas, & Coal	0/+13
Microsoft	+39/+57	Computer Software	+19/+39
Novell	−27/Neg	Computer Software	+19/+39
Boise Cascade	+8/Neg	Forest Products	0/Neg
Bowater	−14/Neg	Forest Products	0/Neg

PART 3

STRATEGY IMPLEMENTATION

CHAPTER 7

Implementing Strategies: Management Issues

CHAPTER OBJECTIVES

After studying this chapter, you should be able to do the following:

1. Explain why strategy implementation is more difficult than strategy formulation.

2. Discuss the importance of annual objectives and policies in achieving organizational commitment for strategies to be implemented.

3. Explain why organizational structure is so important in strategy implementation.

4. Compare and contrast restructuring and reengineering.

5. Describe the relationships between production/operations and strategy implementation.

6. Explain how a firm can effectively link performance and pay to strategies.

7. Discuss employee stock ownership plans (ESOPs) as a strategic-management concept.

8. Describe how to modify an organizational culture to support new strategies.

You want your people to run the business as if it were their own.—WILLIAM FULMER

The ideal organizational structure is a place where ideas filter up as well as down, where the merit of ideas carries more weight than their source, and where participation and shared objectives are valued more than executive orders.—EDSON SPENCER

A management truism says structure follows strategy. However, this truism is often ignored. Too many organizations attempt to carry out a new strategy with an old structure.—DALE McCONKEY

Poor Ike; when he was a general, he gave an order and it was carried out. Now, he's going to sit in that office and give an order and not a damn thing is going to happen.—HARRY TRUMAN

Changing your pay plan is a big risk, but not changing it could be a bigger one.—NANCY PERRY

In Japan, workers receive an average 25 percent of total pay in the form of a flexible bonus. In America, the average is still only 1 percent.—NANCY PERRY

Of course, objectives are not a railroad timetable. They can be compared to a compass bearing by which a ship navigates. A compass bearing is firm, but in actual navigation, a ship may veer off its course for many miles. Without a compass bearing, a ship would neither find its port nor be able to estimate the time required to get there.—PETER DRUCKER

The best game plan in the world never blocked or tackled anybody.—VINCE LOMBARDI

In most organizations, the top performers are paid too little and the worst performers too much.
—CASS BETTINGER

The strategic-management process does not end when the firm decides what strategy or strategies to pursue. There must be a translation of strategic thought into strategic action. This translation is much easier if managers and employees of the firm understand the business, feel a part of the company, and through involvement in strategy-formulation activities have become committed to helping the organization succeed. Without understanding and commitment, strategy-implementation efforts face major problems.

Implementing strategy affects an organization from top to bottom; it impacts all the functional and divisional areas of a business. It is beyond the purpose and scope of this text to examine all the business administration concepts and tools important in strategy implementation. This chapter focuses on management issues most central to implementing strategies in the year 2000, and Chapter 8 focuses on marketing, finance/accounting, R&D, and computer information systems issues.

THE NATURE OF STRATEGY IMPLEMENTATION

The strategy-implementation stage of strategic management stands out in Figure 7–1. Successful strategy formulation does not guarantee successful strategy implementation. It is always more difficult to do something (strategy implementation) than to say you are going to do it (strategy formulation)! Although inextricably linked, strategy implementation is fundamentally different from strategy formulation. Strategy formulation and implementation can be contrasted in the following ways:

- Strategy formulation is positioning forces before the action.
- Strategy implementation is managing forces during the action.
- Strategy formulation focuses on effectiveness.
- Strategy implementation focuses on efficiency.
- Strategy formulation is primarily an intellectual process.
- Strategy implementation is primarily an operational process.
- Strategy formulation requires good intuitive and analytical skills.
- Strategy implementation requires special motivation and leadership skills.
- Strategy formulation requires coordination among a few individuals.
- Strategy implementation requires coordination among many persons.

Strategy-formulation concepts and tools do not differ greatly for small, large, for-profit, or nonprofit organizations. However, strategy implementation varies substantially among different types and sizes of organizations. Implementing strategies requires such actions as altering sales territories, adding new departments, closing facilities, hiring new employees, changing an organization's pricing strategy, developing financial budgets, developing new employee benefits, establishing cost-control procedures, changing advertising strategies, building new facilities, training new employees, transferring managers among divisions, and building a better computer information system. These types of activities obviously differ greatly between manufacturing, service, and governmental organizations.

MANAGEMENT PERSPECTIVES   In all but the smallest organizations, the transition from strategy formulation to strategy implementation requires a shift in responsibility from strategists to divisional and functional managers. Implementation problems can arise because of this shift in responsibility, especially if strategy-formulation decisions come as a surprise to middle- and lower-level managers. Managers and employees are motivated more by perceived self-interests than by organizational interests,

FIGURE 7–1
A Comprehensive Strategic-Management Model

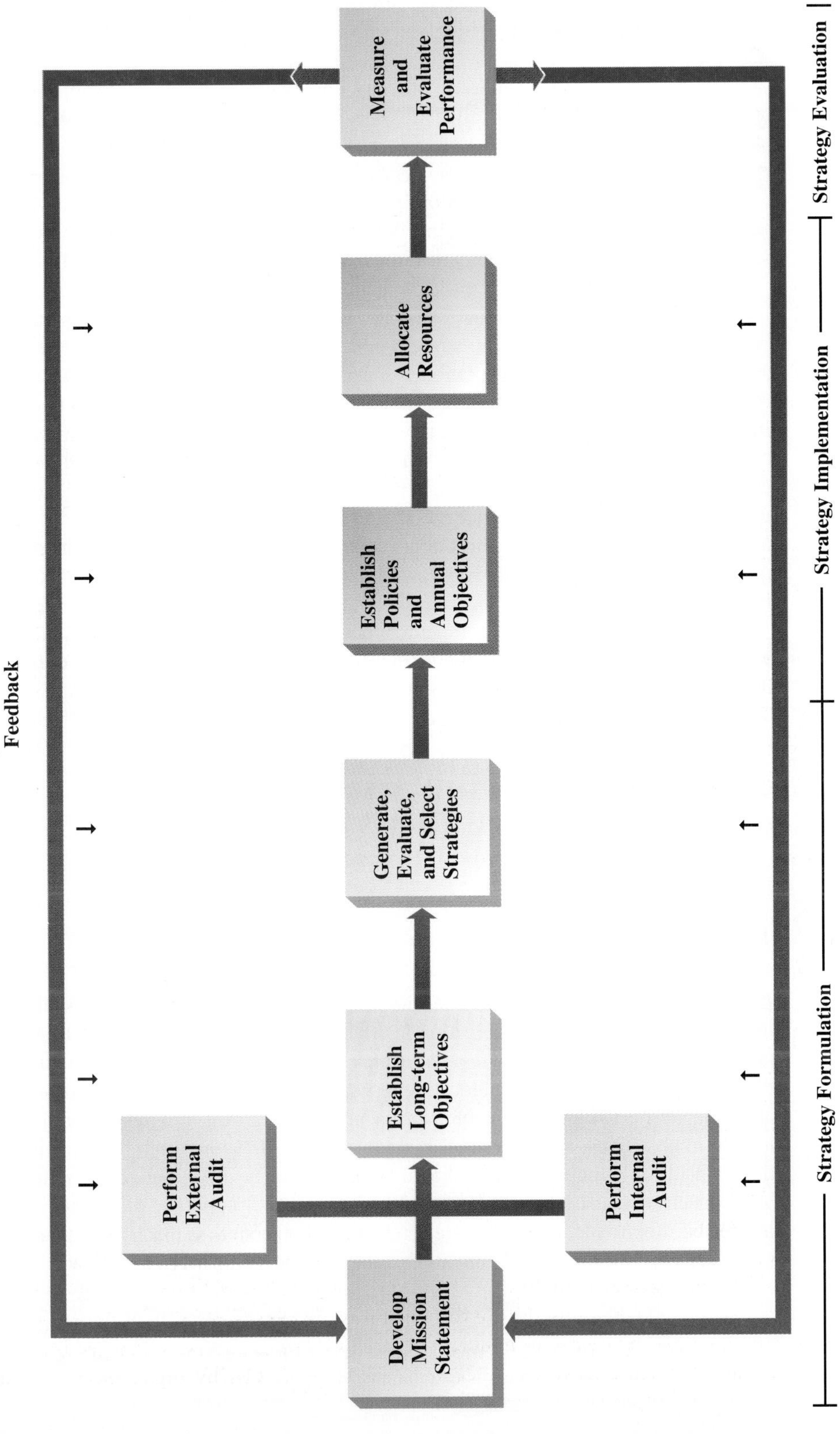

unless the two coincide. Therefore, it is essential that divisional and functional managers be involved as much as possible in strategy-formulation activities. Of equal importance, strategists should be involved as much as possible in strategy-implementation activities.

Management issues central to strategy implementation include establishing annual objectives, devising policies, allocating resources, altering an existing organizational structure, restructuring and reengineering, revising reward and incentive plans, minimizing resistance to change, matching managers with strategy, developing a strategy-supportive culture, adapting production/operations processes, developing an effective human resource function and, if necessary, downsizing. Management changes are necessarily more extensive when strategies to be implemented move a firm in a major new direction.

Managers and employees throughout an organization should participate early and directly in strategy-implementation decisions. Their role in strategy implementation should build upon prior involvement in strategy-formulation activities. Strategists' genuine personal commitment to implementation is a necessary and powerful motivational force for managers and employees. Too often, strategists are too busy to actively support strategy-implementation efforts, and their lack of interest can be detrimental to organizational success. The rationale for objectives and strategies should be understood and clearly communicated throughout an organization. Major competitors' accomplishments, products, plans, actions, and performance should be apparent to all organizational members. Major external opportunities and threats should be clear, and managers' and employees' questions should be answered. Top-down flow of communication is essential for developing bottom-up support.

Firms need to develop a competitor focus at all hierarchical levels by gathering and widely distributing competitive intelligence; every employee should be able to benchmark her or his efforts against best-in-class competitors so that the challenge becomes personal. This is a challenge for strategists of the firm. Firms should provide training for both managers and employees to ensure they have and maintain the skills necessary to be world-class performers.

ANNUAL OBJECTIVES

Establishing annual objectives is a decentralized activity that directly involves all managers in an organization. Active participation in establishing annual objectives can lead to acceptance and commitment. *Annual objectives* are essential for strategy implementation because they (1) represent the basis for allocating resources; (2) are a primary mechanism for evaluating managers; (3) are the major instrument for monitoring progress toward achieving long-term objectives; and (4) establish organizational, divisional, and departmental priorities. Considerable time and effort should be devoted to ensuring that annual objectives are well conceived, consistent with long-term objectives, and supportive of strategies to be implemented. Approving, revising, or rejecting annual objectives is much more than a rubber-stamp activity. The purpose of annual objectives can be summarized as follows:

> Annual objectives serve as guidelines for action, directing and channeling efforts and activities of organization members. They provide a source of legitimacy in an enterprise by justifying activities to stakeholders. They serve as standards of performance. They serve as an important source of employee motivation and identification. They give incentives for managers and employees to perform. They provide a basis for organizational design.[1]

INFORMATION TECHNOLOGY

How Extensively Is the Internet Used in Asia?

When it comes to using the Internet, Asia is light-years behind the United States and far behind Europe. "Even in Japan, the Internet is still in the experimental stage," says Mitsuru Shinozaki, Internet specialist at Keidanren. The following regional problems severely restrict use of the Internet for commercial or personal use throughout Asia:

1. Poor telecommunications infrastructure. Most countries, including China and India, have less than one telephone line per 100 people, compared to nearly 60 per 100 people in the United States.

2. A myriad of complex written and spoken languages. Asian languages mostly use non-Roman characters, and the Internet cannot handle them without special software.

3. There are dozens of highly diverse national boundaries, standards, and cultures.

4. There are relatively few desktop computers, and most of these are not regularly used for commerce. There are relatively few computer-literate businesspeople.

5. Most Asian cultures shun any type of electronic form of payment.

6. There are exceptionally high telecommunications and Internet connection charges.

Since creation of the Japanese version of Windows 95, personal computer shipments grew from 5.3 million in 1996 to 18.6 million in 1998. Use of the Internet tripled during this time in Japan, even though most customers and other businesses still will not use the Internet. The few Japanese companies that today have Web sites, such as Nippon Telephone & Telegraph; Fujitsu Ltd.; and Mitsubishi Motors Corp., direct customers off-line to complete purchases.

In Malaysia, Singapore, and Thailand, progress is rapidly being made to develop the infrastructure to support the Internet. China and India are working hard in this regard too, but these countries are still Third World in every aspect of the Internet, especially when compared to the United States.

Source: Adapted from Jack Gee, "Parlez-Vous Internet," Industry Week (April 21, 1997): 78–82.

Clearly stated and communicated objectives are critical to success in all types and sizes of firms. Annual objectives, stated in terms of profitability, growth, and market share by business segment, geographic area, customer groups, and product are common in organizations. Figure 7–2 illustrates how the Stamus Company could establish annual objectives based on long-term objectives. Table 7–1 reveals associated revenue figures that correspond to the objectives outlined in Figure 7–2. Note that, according to plan, the Stamus Company will slightly exceed its long-term objective of doubling company revenues between 1998 and the year 2000.

Figure 7–2 also reflects how a hierarchy of annual objectives can be established based on an organization's structure. Objectives should be consistent across hierarchical levels and form a network of supportive aims. *Horizontal consistency of objectives* is as important as *vertical consistency*. For instance, it would not be effective for manufacturing to achieve more than its annual objective of units produced if marketing could not sell the additional units.

Annual objectives should be measurable, consistent, reasonable, challenging, clear, communicated throughout the organization, characterized by an appropriate time dimension, and accompanied by commensurate rewards and sanctions. Too often, objectives are stated in generalities, with little operational usefulness. Annual objectives such as "to improve communication" or "to improve performance" are not clear, specific, or measurable. Objectives should state quantity, quality, cost, and time and also be verifiable. Terms such as "maximize," "minimize," "as soon as possible," and "adequate" should be avoided.

	1998	1999	2000
Division I Revenues	1.0	1.400	1.960
Division II Revenues	0.5	0.700	0.980
Division III Revenues	0.5	0.750	1.125
Total Company Revenues	2.0	2.850	4.065

TABLE 7-1
The Stamus Company's Revenue Expectations (in millions of dollars)

FIGURE 7–2
The Stamus Company's Hierarchy of Aims

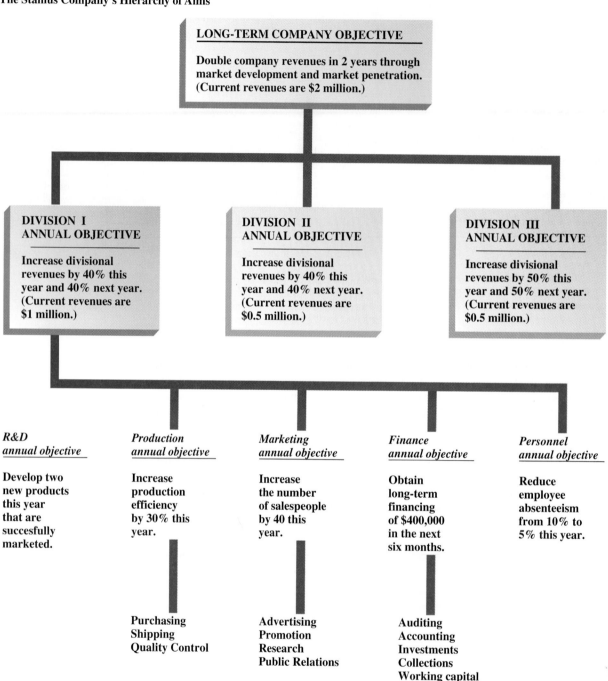

Annual objectives should be compatible with employees' and managers' values and should be supported by clearly stated policies. More of something is not always better! Improved quality or reduced cost may, for example, be more important than quantity. It is important to tie rewards and sanctions to annual objectives so that employees and managers understand that achieving objectives is critical to successful strategy implementation.

Clear annual objectives do not guarantee successful strategy implementation but they do increase the likelihood that personal and organizational aims can be accomplished. Overemphasis on achieving objectives can result in undesirable conduct, such as faking the numbers, distorting the records, and letting objectives become ends in themselves. Managers must be alert to these potential problems.

POLICIES

Changes in a firm's strategic direction do not occur automatically. On a day-to-day basis, policies are needed to make a strategy work. Policies facilitate solving recurring problems and guide the implementation of strategy. Broadly defined, *policy* refers to specific guide-lines, methods, procedures, rules, forms, and administrative practices established to support and encourage work toward stated goals. Policies are instruments for strategy implementation. Policies set boundaries, constraints, and limits on the kinds of administrative actions that can be taken to reward and sanction behavior; they clarify what can and cannot be done in pursuit of an organization's objectives. For example, Carnival's new *Paradise* ship launched in the fall 1998 has a no-smoking policy anywhere, anytime aboard ship. It is the first cruise ship to comprehensively ban smoking. Another example of corporate policy relates to surfing the Web while at work. About 40 percent of companies today do not have a formal policy preventing employees from surfing the Internet, but software is being marketed now that allows firms to monitor how, when, where, and how long various employees use the Internet at work.

Policies let both employees and managers know what is expected of them, thereby increasing the likelihood that strategies will be implemented successfully. They provide a basis for management control, allow coordination across organizational units, and reduce the amount of time managers spend making decisions. Policies also clarify what work is to be done by whom. They promote delegation of decision making to appropriate managerial levels where various problems usually arise. Many organizations have a policy manual that serves to guide and direct behavior. About 80 percent of all corporations in the United States have instituted no-smoking policies. This is not true, however, in other countries. About 4.6 trillion cigarettes are smoked annually worldwide. Countries with the highest number of cigarettes smoked per capita are listed below (U.S. rate is 1,836):

South Korea	4,153
Japan	2,739
Hungary	2,689
Greece	2,648
Poland	2,534
Romania	2,172

Policies can apply to all divisions and departments (for example, "We are an equal opportunity employer"). Some policies apply to a single department ("Employees in this department must take at least one training and development course each year"). Whatever their scope and form, policies serve as a mechanism for implementing strategies and obtaining objectives. Policies should be stated in writing whenever possible. They represent the means for carrying out strategic decisions. Examples of policies that support a company strategy, a divisional objective, and a departmental objective are given in Table 7–2.

TABLE 7–2
A Hierarchy of Policies

Company Strategy: Acquire a chain of retail stores to meet our sales growth and profitability objectives.
Supporting policies:

1. "All stores will be open from 8 A.M. to 8 P.M. Monday through Saturday." (This policy could increase retail sales if stores currently are open only 40 hours a week.)
2. "All stores must submit a Monthly Control Data Report." (This policy could reduce expense-to-sales ratios.)
3. "All stores must support company advertising by contributing 5 percent of their total monthly revenues for this purpose." (This policy could allow the company to establish a national reputation.)
4. "All stores must adhere to the uniform pricing guidelines set forth in the Company Handbook." (This policy could help assure customers that the company offers a consistent product in terms of price and quality in all its stores.)

Divisional Objective: Increase the division's revenues from $10 million in 1998 to $15 million in 2000.
Supporting policies:

1. "Beginning in January 1999, this division's salespersons must file a weekly activity report that includes the number of calls made, the number of miles traveled, the number of units sold, the dollar volume sold, and the number of new accounts opened." (This policy could ensure that salespersons do not place too great an emphasis in certain areas.)
2. "Beginning in January 1999, this division will return to its employees 5 percent of its gross revenues in the form of a Christmas bonus." (This policy could increase employee productivity.)
3. "Beginning in January 1999, inventory levels carried in warehouses will be decreased by 30 percent in accordance with a Just-in-Time manufacturing approach." (This policy could reduce production expenses and thus free funds for increased marketing efforts.)

Production Department Objective: Increase production from 20,000 units in 1998 to 30,000 units in 2000.
Supporting policies:

1. "Beginning in January 1999, employees will have the option of working up to 20 hours of overtime per week." (This policy could minimize the need to hire additional employees.)
2. "Beginning in January 1999, perfect attendance awards in the amount of $100 will be given to all employees who do not miss a workday in a given year." (This policy could decrease absenteeism and increase productivity.)
3. "Beginning in January 1999, new equipment must be leased rather than purchased." (This policy could reduce tax liabilities and thus allow more funds to be invested in modernizing production processes.)

Some example issues that may require a management policy are as follows:

◆ To offer extensive or limited management development workshops and seminars
◆ To centralize or decentralize employee-training activities
◆ To recruit through employment agencies, college campuses, and/or newspapers
◆ To promote from within or hire from the outside
◆ To promote on the basis of merit or on the basis of seniority
◆ To tie executive compensation to long-term and/or annual objectives
◆ To offer numerous or few employee benefits
◆ To negotiate directly or indirectly with labor unions
◆ To delegate authority for large expenditures or to retain this authority centrally
◆ To allow much, some, or no overtime work
◆ To establish a high- or low-safety stock of inventory
◆ To use one or more suppliers
◆ To buy, lease, or rent new production equipment
◆ To stress quality control greatly or not
◆ To establish many or only a few production standards
◆ To operate one, two, or three shifts
◆ To discourage using insider information for personal gain
◆ To discourage sexual harassment

◆ To discourage smoking at work
◆ To discourage insider trading
◆ To discourage moonlighting

RESOURCE ALLOCATION

Resource allocation is a central management activity that allows for strategy execution. In organizations that do not use a strategic-management approach to decision making, resource allocation is often based on political or personal factors. Strategic management enables resources to be allocated according to priorities established by annual objectives. Nothing could be more detrimental to strategic management and to organizational success than for resources to be allocated in ways not consistent with priorities indicated by approved annual objectives.

All organizations have at least four types of resources that can be used to achieve desired objectives: financial resources, physical resources, human resources, and technological resources. Allocating resources to particular divisions and departments does not mean that strategies will be successfully implemented. A number of factors commonly prohibit effective resource allocation, including an overprotection of resources, too great an emphasis on short-run financial criteria, organizational politics, vague strategy targets, a reluctance to take risks, and a lack of sufficient knowledge.

Below the corporate level, there often exists an absence of systematic thinking about resources allocated and strategies of the firm. Yavitz and Newman explained why:

> Managers normally have many more tasks than they can do. Managers must allocate time and resources among these tasks. Pressure builds up. Expenses are too high. The CEO wants a good financial report for the third quarter. Strategy formulation and implementation activities often get deferred. Today's problems soak up available energies and resources. Scrambled accounts and budgets fail to reveal the shift in allocation away from strategic needs to currently squeaking wheels.[2]

The real value of any resource allocation program lies in the resulting accomplishment of an organization's objectives. Effective resource allocation does not guarantee successful strategy implementation because programs, personnel, controls, and commitment must breathe life into the resources provided. Strategic management itself is sometimes referred to as a "resource allocation process."

MANAGING CONFLICT

Interdependency of objectives and competition for limited resources often leads to conflict. *Conflict* can be defined as a disagreement between two or more parties on one or more issues. Establishing annual objectives can lead to conflict because individuals have different expectations and perceptions, schedules create pressure, personalities are incompatible, and misunderstandings between line and staff occur. For example, a collection manager's objective of reducing bad debts by 50 percent in a given year may conflict with a divisional objective to increase sales by 20 percent.

Establishing objectives can lead to conflict because managers and strategists must make trade-offs, such as whether to emphasize short-term profits or long-term growth, profit margin or market share, market penetration or market development, growth or stability, high risk or low risk, and social responsiveness or profit maximization. Conflict is unavoidable in organizations, so it is important that conflict be managed and resolved before dysfunctional consequences affect organizational performance. Conflict is not always bad. An absence of conflict can signal indifference and apathy. Conflict can serve to energize opposing groups into action and may help managers identify problems.

Various approaches for managing and resolving conflict can be classified into three categories: avoidance, defusion, and confrontation. *Avoidance* includes such actions as ignoring the problem in hopes that the conflict will resolve itself or physically separating the conflicting individuals (or groups). *Defusion* can include playing down differences between conflicting parties while accentuating similarities and common interests, compromising so that there is neither a clear winner nor loser, resorting to majority rule, appealing to a higher authority, or redesigning present positions. *Confrontation* is exemplified by exchanging members of conflicting parties so that each can gain an appreciation of the other's point of view, or holding a meeting at which conflicting parties present their views and work through their differences.

MATCHING STRUCTURE WITH STRATEGY

Changes in strategy often require changes in the way an organization is structured for two major reasons. First, structure largely dictates how objectives and policies will be established. For example, objectives and policies established under a geographic organizational structure are couched in geographic terms. Objectives and policies are stated largely in terms of products in an organization whose structure is based on product groups. The structural format for developing objectives and policies can significantly impact all other strategy-implementation activities.

The second major reason why changes in strategy often require changes in structure is that structure dictates how resources will be allocated. If an organization is structured based on customer groups, then resources will be allocated in that manner. Similarly, if an organization's structure is set up along functional business lines, then resources are allocated by functional areas. Unless new or revised strategies place emphasis in the same areas as old strategies, structural reorientation commonly becomes a part of strategy implementation.

Changes in strategy lead to changes in organizational structure. Structure should be designed to facilitate the strategic pursuit of a firm and, therefore, follows strategy. Without a strategy or reasons for being (mission), designing an effective structure is difficult. Chandler found a particular structure sequence to be often repeated as organizations grow and change strategy over time; this sequence is depicted in Figure 7–3.

There is no one optimal organizational design or structure for a given strategy or type of organization. What is appropriate for one organization may not be appropriate for a similar firm, although successful firms in a given industry do tend to organize themselves in a similar way. For example, consumer goods companies tend to emulate the divisional structure-by-product form of organization. Small firms tend to be functionally structured (centralized). Medium-size firms tend to be divisionally structured (decentralized). Large firms tend to use an SBU (strategic business unit) or matrix structure. As organizations grow, their structures generally change from simple to complex as a result of concatenation, or the linking together of several basic strategies.

Numerous external and internal forces affect an organization; no firm could change its structure in response to every one of these forces, because to do so would lead to chaos. However, when a firm changes its strategy, the existing organizational structure may become ineffective. Symptoms of an ineffective organizational structure include too many levels of management, too many meetings attended by too many people, too much

FIGURE 7–3
**Chandler's Strategy-
Structure Relationship**

Source: Adapted from Alfred Chandler, *Strategy and Structure* (Cambridge, Massachusetts: MIT Press, 1962).

attention being directed toward solving interdepartmental conflicts, too large a span of control, and too many unachieved objectives. Changes in structure can facilitate strategy-implementation efforts, but changes in structure should not be expected to make a bad strategy good, to make bad managers good, or to make bad products sell.

Structure undeniably can and does influence strategy. Strategies formulated must be workable, so if a certain new strategy required massive structural changes it would not be an attractive choice. In this way, structure can shape the choice of strategies. But a more important concern is determining what types of structural changes are needed to implement new strategies and how these changes can best be accomplished. We examine this issue by focusing on seven basic types of organizational structure: functional, divisional by geographic area, divisional by product, divisional by customer, divisional by process, strategic business unit (SBU), and matrix.

THE FUNCTIONAL STRUCTURE   The most widely used structure is the functional or centralized type because this structure is the simplest and least expensive of the seven alternatives. A *functional structure* groups tasks and activities by business function such as production/operations, marketing, finance/accounting, research and development, and computer information systems. A university may structure its activities by major functions that include academic affairs, student services, alumni relations, athletics, maintenance, and accounting. Besides being simple and inexpensive, a functional structure also promotes specialization of labor, encourages efficiency, minimizes the need for an elaborate control system, and allows rapid decision making. Some disadvantages of a functional structure are that it forces accountability to the top, minimizes career development opportunities, and is sometimes characterized by low employee morale, line/staff conflicts, poor delegation of authority, and inadequate planning for products and markets.

The 1980s and 1990s witnessed most large companies abandoning the functional structure in favor of decentralization and improved accountability. A company that still adheres to a functional design, however, is Food Lion, Inc., as shown in Figure 7–4.

THE DIVISIONAL STRUCTURE   The *divisional* or *decentralized structure* is the second most common type used by American businesses. As a small organization grows, it has more difficulty managing different products and services in different markets. Some form of divisional structure generally becomes necessary to motivate employees, control operations, and compete successfully in diverse locations. The divisional structure can be organized in one of four ways: by geographic area, by product or service, by customer, or by process. With a divisional structure, functional activities are performed both centrally and in each separate division.

FIGURE 7–4
Food Lion's Organizational Chart

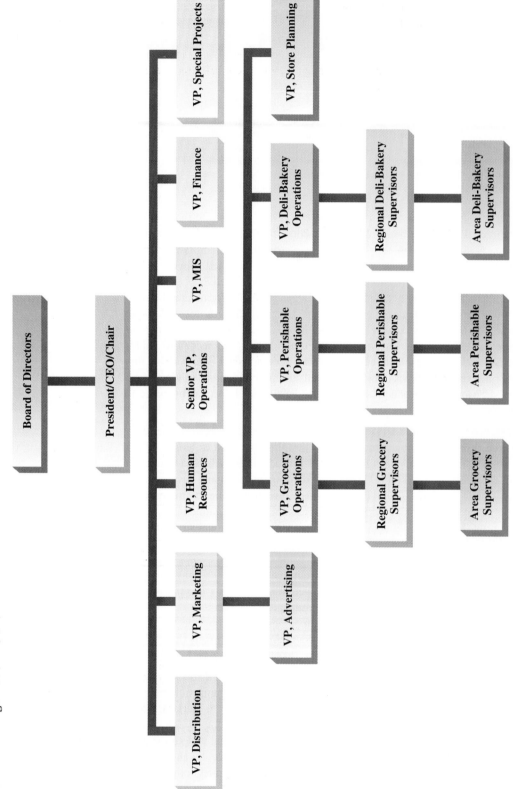

A divisional structure has some clear advantages. First and perhaps foremost, accountability is clear. That is, divisional managers can be held responsible for sales and profit levels. Because a divisional structure is based on extensive delegation of authority, managers and employees can easily see the results of their good or bad performances. As a result, employee morale is generally higher in a divisional structure than it is in a centralized structure. Other advantages of the divisional design are that it creates career development opportunities for managers, allows local control of local situations, leads to a competitive climate within an organization, and allows new businesses and products to be added easily. AT&T recently restructured by breaking large businesses into smaller, focused units, totaling 24 divisions and 19 subsidiaries.

The divisional design is not without some limitations, however. Perhaps the most important limitation is that a divisional structure is costly, for a number of reasons. First, each division requires functional specialists who must be paid. Second, there exists some duplication of staff services, facilities, and personnel; for instance, functional specialists are also needed centrally (at headquarters) to coordinate divisional activities. Third, managers must be well qualified because the divisional design forces delegation of authority; better-qualified individuals require higher salaries. A divisional structure can also be costly because it requires an elaborate, headquarters-driven control system. Finally, certain regions, products, or customers may sometimes receive special treatment, and it may be difficult to maintain consistent, companywide practices. Nonetheless, for most large organizations and many small firms, the advantages of a divisional structure more than offset the potential limitations.

A *divisional structure by geographic area* is appropriate for organizations whose strategies need to be tailored to fit the particular needs and characteristics of customers in different geographic areas. This type of structure can be most appropriate for organizations that have similar branch facilities located in widely dispersed areas. A divisional structure by geographic area allows local participation in decision making and improved coordination within a region. ABB (Asia Brown Bover, Ltd.) reorganized its management structure into three large geographic regions: Europe, the Americas, and Asia-Pacific. Percy Barnevik, ABB's chief executive officer, says the growing unification of Europe requires that the continent be treated as one market, and the opening up of markets under the North American Free Trade Agreement made establishment of one region for the Americas a logical step. Treating the Asia-Pacific region as one division ensures focused attention in the area of the world with the greatest growth potential.

The *divisional structure by product* is most effective for implementing strategies when specific products or services need special emphasis. Also, this type of structure is widely used when an organization offers only a few products or services, or when an organization's products or services differ substantially. The divisional structure allows strict control and attention to product lines, but it may also require a more skilled management force and reduced top management control. General Motors, DuPont, and Procter & Gamble use a divisional structure by product to implement strategies. Huffy, the largest bicycle company in the world, is another firm that is highly decentralized based on a divisional-by-product structure. Based in Ohio, Huffy's divisions are the Bicycle division, the Gerry Baby Products division, the Huffy Sports division, YLC Enterprises, and Washington Inventory Service. Harry Shaw, Huffy's chairman, believes decentralization is one of the keys to Huffy's success.

When a few major customers are of paramount importance and many different services are provided to these customers, then a *divisional structure by customer* can be the most effective way to implement strategies. This structure allows an organization to cater effectively to the requirements of clearly defined customer groups. For example, book publishing companies often organize their activities around customer groups such as colleges, secondary schools, and private commercial schools. Some airline companies have two major customer divisions: passengers and freight or cargo services. Merrill Lynch is organized into separate divisions that cater to different groups of customers, including wealthy individuals, institutional investors, and small corporations.

A *divisional structure by process* is similar to a functional structure, because activities are organized according to the way work is actually performed. However, a key difference between these two designs is that functional departments are not accountable for profits or revenues, whereas divisional process departments are evaluated on these criteria. An example of a divisional structure by process is a manufacturing business organized into six divisions: electrical work, glass cutting, welding, grinding, painting, and foundry work. In this case, all operations related to these specific processes would be grouped under the separate divisions. Each process (division) would be responsible for generating revenues and profits. The divisional structure by process can be particularly effective in achieving objectives when distinct production processes represent the thrust of competitiveness in an industry.

THE STRATEGIC BUSINESS UNIT (SBU) STRUCTURE   As the number, size, and diversity of divisions in an organization increase, controlling and evaluating divisional operations become increasingly difficult for strategists. Increases in sales often are not accompanied by similar increases in profitability. The span of control becomes too large at top levels of the firm. For example, in a large conglomerate organization composed of 90 divisions, the chief executive officer could have difficulty even remembering the first names of divisional presidents. In multidivisional organizations an SBU structure can greatly facilitate strategy-implementation efforts.

The *SBU structure* groups similar divisions into strategic business units and delegates authority and responsibility for each unit to a senior executive who reports directly to the chief executive officer. This change in structure can facilitate strategy implementation by improving coordination between similar divisions and channeling accountability to distinct business units. In the 90-division conglomerate just mentioned, the 90 divisions could perhaps be regrouped into 10 SBUs according to certain common characteristics such as competing in the same industry, being located in the same area, or having the same customers.

Two disadvantages of an SBU structure are that it requires an additional layer of management, which increases salary expenses, and the role of the group vice-president is often ambiguous. However, these limitations often do not outweigh the advantages of improved coordination and accountability. Atlantic Richfield and Fairchild Industries are examples of firms that successfully use an SBU-type structure.

THE MATRIX STRUCTURE   A *matrix structure* is the most complex of all designs because it depends upon both vertical and horizontal flows of authority and communication (hence the term *matrix*). In contrast, functional and divisional structures depend primarily on vertical flows of authority and communication. A matrix structure can result in higher overhead because it creates more management positions. Other characteristics of a matrix structure that contribute to overall complexity include dual lines of budget authority (a violation of the unity-of-command principle), dual sources of reward and punishment, shared authority, dual reporting channels, and a need for an extensive and effective communication system.

Despite its complexity, the matrix structure is widely used in many industries, including construction, health care, research, and defense. Some advantages of a matrix structure are that project objectives are clear, there are many channels of communication, workers can see visible results of their work, and shutting down a project can be accomplished relatively easily.

In order for a matrix structure to be effective, organizations need participative planning, training, clear mutual understanding of roles and responsibilities, excellent internal communication, and mutual trust and confidence. The matrix structure is being used more frequently by American businesses because firms are pursuing strategies that add new products, customer groups, and technology to their range of activities. Out of these changes are coming product managers, functional managers, and geographic-area managers, all of whom have important strategic responsibilities. When several variables, such as product, customer, technology, geography, functional area, and line of business, have roughly equal strategic priorities, a matrix organization can be an effective structural form.

RESTRUCTURING AND REENGINEERING

Restructuring and reengineering are becoming commonplace on the corporate landscape across the United States and Europe. *Restructuring*—also called *downsizing, rightsizing,* or *delayering*—involves reducing the size of the firm in terms of number of employees, number of divisions or units, and number of hierarchical levels in the firm's organizational structure. This reduction in size is intended to improve both efficiency and effectiveness. Restructuring is concerned primarily with shareholder well-being rather than employee well-being.

Unforgiving competition from leaner U.S. firms is forcing many European companies to downsize, laying off managers and employees. This was almost unheard of prior to the mid-1990s because European labor unions and laws required lengthy negotiations or huge severance checks before workers could be terminated. Unlike in the United States, labor union executives sit on most boards of directors of large European firms.

Job security in European companies is slowly moving toward a U.S. scenario in which firms lay off almost at will. From banks in Milan to factories in Mannhelm, European employers are starting to show people the door in an effort to streamline operations, increase efficiency, and compete against already slim and trim U.S. firms. Massive U.S.-style layoffs are still rare in Europe, but unemployment rates throughout the continent are rising quite rapidly. European firms still prefer to downsize by attrition and retirement rather than by blanket layoffs due to culture, laws, and unions. Electrolux, based in Switzerland, plans to cut 12,000 jobs and close 25 plants during 1998 and 1999.

In contrast, *reengineering* is concerned more with employee and customer well-being than shareholder well-being. Reengineering—also called process management, process innovation, or process redesign—involves reconfiguring or redesigning work, jobs, and processes for the purpose of improving cost, quality, service, and speed. Reengineering does not usually affect the organizational structure or chart, nor does it imply job loss or employee layoffs. Whereas restructuring is concerned with eliminating or establishing, shrinking or enlarging, and moving organizational departments and divisions, the focus of reengineering is changing the way work is actually carried out.

Reengineering is characterized by many tactical (short-term, business function–specific) decisions, whereas restructuring is characterized by strategic (long-term, affecting all business functions) decisions.

RESTRUCTURING   Firms often employ restructuring when various ratios appear out of line with competitors as determined through benchmarking exercises. *Benchmarking* simply involves comparing a firm against the best firms in the industry on a wide variety of performance-related criteria. Some benchmarking ratios commonly used in rationalizing the need for restructuring are headcount-to-sales-volume, or corporate-staff-to-operating-employees, or span-of-control figures.

The primary benefit sought from restructuring is cost reduction. For some highly bureaucratic firms, restructuring can actually rescue the firm from global competition and demise. But the downside of restructuring can be reduced employee commitment, creativity, and innovation that accompanies the uncertainty and trauma associated with pending and actual employee layoffs.

Another downside of restructuring is that more people today do not aspire to become managers, and many present-day managers are trying to get off the management track.[3] Sentiment against joining management ranks is higher today than ever. About 80 percent of employees say they want nothing to do with management, a major shift from just a decade ago when 60 to 70 percent hoped to become managers. Managing others historically led to enhanced career mobility, financial rewards, and executive perks; but in today's global, more competitive, restructured arena, managerial jobs demand more hours and headaches with fewer financial rewards. Managers today manage more people spread over different locations, travel more, manage diverse functions, and are change agents even when they have nothing to do with the creation of the plan or even disagree with its approach. Employers today are looking for people who can do things, not for people who make other people do things. Restructuring in many firms has made a manager's job an invisible, thankless role. More workers today are self-managed, entrepreneurs, intrepreneurs, or team-managed. Managers today need to be counselors, motivators, financial advisors, and psychologists. They also run the risk of becoming technologically behind in their areas of expertise. "Dilbert" cartoons commonly portray managers as enemies or as morons.

An example of company restructuring is ITT Corporation, which is splitting itself into three companies—ITT Educational Services, World Directories, and ITT Destinations. ITT's restructuring includes taking on $2 billion in new debt and buying back 30 million shares of its own stock in order to deter Hilton Hotels from acquiring the company in a hostile takeover.

REENGINEERING   The argument for a firm engaging in reengineering usually goes as follows: Many companies historically have been organized vertically by business function. This arrangement has led over time to managers' and employees' mind-sets being defined by their particular functions rather than by overall customer service, product quality, or corporate performance. The logic is that all firms tend to bureaucratize over time. As routines become entrenched, turf becomes delineated and defended, and politics takes precedence over performance. Walls that exist in the physical workplace can be reflections of "mental" walls.

In reengineering, a firm uses information technology to break down functional barriers and create a work system based on business processes, products, or outputs rather than on functions or inputs. Cornerstones of reengineering are decentralization, reciprocal interdependence, and information sharing. A firm that exemplifies complete information sharing is Springfield ReManufacturing Corporation, which provides to all employees a weekly income statement of the firm, as well as extensive information on other companies' performances.

There are numerous examples of firms that benefited in the 1990s from reengineering—including Union Carbide, which reduced its fixed costs by $400 million; Taco Bell, which raised its restaurant peak capacity from $400 per hour to $1,500 per hour; and AT&T which created a new business telephone system called PBX.

A benefit of reengineering is that it offers employees the opportunity to see more clearly how their particular jobs impact the final product or service being marketed by the firm. However, reengineering also can raise manager and employee anxiety which, unless calmed, can lead to corporate trauma.

LINKING PERFORMANCE AND PAY TO STRATEGIES

Most companies today are practicing some form of pay-for-performance for employees and managers other than top executives. The average employee performance bonus is 6.8

percent of pay for individual performance, 5.5 percent of pay for group productivity, and 6.4 percent of pay for companywide profitability.

Staff control of pay systems often prevents line managers from using financial compensation as a strategic tool. Flexibility regarding managerial and employee compensation is needed to allow short-term shifts in compensation that can stimulate efforts to achieve long-term objectives. NBC recently unveiled a new method for paying its affiliated stations. The compensation formula is 50 percent based on audience viewing of shows from 4 P.M. to 8 P.M. and 50 percent based on how many adults aged 25 to 54 watch NBC over the course of a day.

How can an organization's reward system be more closely linked to strategic performance? How can decisions on salary increases, promotions, merit pay, and bonuses be more closely aligned to support the long-term strategic objectives of the organization? There are no widely accepted answers to these questions, but a dual bonus system based on both annual objectives and long-term objectives is becoming common. The percentage of a manager's annual bonus attributable to short-term versus long-term results should vary by hierarchical level in the organization. A chief executive officer's annual bonus could, for example, be determined on a 75 percent short-term and 25 percent long-term basis. It is important that bonuses not be based solely on short-term results because such a system ignores long-term company strategies and objectives.

DuPont Canada has a 16 percent return-on-equity objective. If this objective is met, the company's 4,000 employees receive a "performance sharing cash award" equal to 4 percent of pay. If return-on-equity falls below 11 percent, employees get nothing. If return-on-equity exceeds 28 percent, workers receive a 10 percent bonus.

Profit sharing is another widely used form of incentive compensation. More than 30 percent of American companies have profit sharing plans, but critics emphasize that too many factors affect profits for this to be a good criterion. Taxes, pricing, or an acquisition would wipe out profits, for example. Also, firms try to minimize profits in a sense to reduce taxes.

Still another criterion widely used to link performance and pay to strategies is gain sharing. *Gain sharing* requires employees or departments to establish performance targets; if actual results exceed objectives, all members get bonuses. More than 26 percent of American companies use some form of gain sharing; about 75 percent of gain sharing plans have been adopted since 1980. Carrier, a subsidiary of United Technologies, has had excellent success with gain sharing in its six plants in Syracuse, New York; Firestone's tire plant in Wilson, North Carolina, has experienced similar success with gain sharing.

Criteria such as sales, profit, production efficiency, quality, and safety could also serve as bases for an effective *bonus system*. If an organization meets certain understood, agreed-upon profit objectives, every member of the enterprise should share in the harvest. A bonus system can be an effective tool for motivating individuals to support strategy-implementation efforts. BankAmerica, for example, recently overhauled its incentive system to link pay to sales of the bank's most profitable products and services. Branch managers receive a base salary plus a bonus based on the number of new customers and on sales of bank products. Every employee in each branch is also eligible for a bonus if the branch exceeds its goals. Thomas Peterson, a top BankAmerica executive, says, "We want to make people responsible for meeting their goals, so we pay incentives on sales, not on controlling costs or on being sure the parking lot is swept."

Five tests are often used to determine whether a performance-pay plan will benefit an organization:

1. *Does the plan capture attention?* Are people talking more about their activities and taking pride in early successes under the plan?

2. *Do employees understand the plan?* Can participants explain how it works and what they need to do to earn the incentive?

3. *Is the plan improving communications?* Do employees know more than they used to about the company's mission, plans, and objectives?

4. *Does the plan pay out when it should?* Are incentives being paid for desired results—and being withheld when objectives are not met?

5. *Is the company or unit performing better?* Are profits up? Has market share grown? Have gains resulted in part from the incentives?[4]

In addition to a dual bonus system, a combination of reward strategy incentives such as salary raises, stock options, fringe benefits, promotions, praise, recognition, criticism, fear, increased job autonomy, and awards can be used to encourage managers and employees to push hard for successful strategic implementation. The range of options for getting people, departments, and divisions to actively support strategy-implementation activities in a particular organization is almost limitless. Merck, for example, recently gave each of its 37,000 employees a 10-year option to buy 100 shares of Merck stock at a set price of $127. Steven Darien, Merck's vice-president of human resources, says, "We needed to find ways to get everyone in the workforce on board in terms of our goals and objectives. Company executives will begin meeting with all Merck workers to explore ways in which employees can contribute more."

Increasing criticism aimed at chief executive officers for their high pay has resulted in executive compensation being linked to performance of their firm more closely than ever before. CEO Deryck Maughan of Salomon saw an 87 percent drop in his pay when

GLOBAL PERSPECTIVE
How Much Are U.S. CEOs Paid versus the World?

The average CEO in the United States gets paid nearly double what the average CEO gets paid in Canada, Japan, and the United Kingdom and nearly a third more than the average CEO in Germany, Hong Kong, and France.

The difference, however, lies not in salary per se but rather in stock options and bonuses, which are rare abroad but commonplace here. Foreign countries, however, are beginning to approve stock options for their CEOs in order to be competitive. Japan approved stock options in July 1997 and Germany in January 1998. Warrant bonds, similar to stock options, are being approved by foreign multinational firms.

TOP-PAID U.S. CEOS IN 1996 AND 1997

	1996			1997	
CEO	**COMPANY**	**TOTAL PAY (MILLIONS)**	**CEO**	**COMPANY**	**TOTAL PAY (MILLIONS)**
Millard Drexler	The Gap	$104.8	Sanford Wells	Travelers Group	$230.7
Lawrence Coss	Green Tree Financial	102.4	Roberto Goizueta	Coca-Cola	111.8
			Richard Scrushy	HealthSouth	106.7
Andrew Grove	Intel	97.9	Ray Irani	Occidental Petroleum	101.5
Sanford Wells	Travelers Group	91.6			
Theodore Waitt	Gateway 2000	81.3	Eugene Isenberg	Nabors Industries	84.5
Anthony O'Reilly	H. J. Heinz	64.6	Joseph Costello	Cadence Design Systems	66.8
Stephen Hibert	Conseco	51.4			
John Reed	Citicorp	46.2	Andrew Grove	Intel	52.2
Daniel Smith	Cascade Communications	35.6	Charles McCall	HBO & Company	51.4
			Philip Purcell	Morgan Stanley Dean Witter	50.8
Casey Cowell	U.S. Robotics	33.9			
			Robert Shapiro	Monsanto	49.3

Source: Adapted from "Executive Pay," Business Week (April 20, 1998):64.

his firm incurred a $963 million in pretax losses. CEO Charles Sanford of Bankers Trust saw a 57 percent drop in his pay as his firm's return-on-equity dropped nearly half to 13.5 percent. Although the linkage between CEO pay and corporate performance is getting closer, CEO pay in the United States still can be astronomical, as indicated in the Global Perspective. A close pay-performance linkage does not imply less pay. In fact, the opposite is true when the firm does well.

MANAGING RESISTANCE TO CHANGE

No organization or individual can escape change. But the thought of change raises anxieties because people fear economic loss, inconvenience, uncertainty, and a break in normal social patterns. Almost any change in structure, technology, people, or strategies has the potential to disrupt comfortable interaction patterns. For this reason, people resist change. The strategic-management process itself can impose major changes on individuals and processes. Reorienting an organization to get people to think and act strategically is not an easy task.

> The level of familiarity with strategic thinking in the U.S. is high, but acceptance is low. U.S. management has to undergo a cultural change, and it's difficult to force people to change their thinking; it's like ordering them to use personal computers. One obstacle is that top executives are often too busy fighting fires to devote time to developing managers who can think strategically. Yet, the best-run companies recognize the need to develop managers who can fashion and implement strategy.[5]

Resistance to change can be considered the single greatest threat to successful strategy implementation. Resistance in the form of sabotaging production machines, absenteeism, filing unfounded grievances, and an unwillingness to cooperate regularly occurs in organizations. People often resist strategy implementation because they do not understand what is happening or why changes are taking place. In that case, employees may simply need accurate information. Successful strategy implementation hinges upon managers' ability to develop an organizational climate conducive to change. Change must be viewed as an opportunity rather than as a threat by managers and employees.

Resistance to change can emerge at any stage or level of the strategy-implementation process. Although there are various approaches for implementing changes, three commonly used strategies are a force change strategy, an educative change strategy, and a rational or self-interest change strategy. A *force change strategy* involves giving orders and enforcing those orders; this strategy has the advantage of being fast, but it is plagued by low commitment and high resistance. The *educative change strategy* is one that presents information to convince people of the need for change; the disadvantage of an educative change strategy is that implementation becomes slow and difficult. However, this type of strategy evokes greater commitment and less resistance than does the force strategy. Finally, a *rational* or *self-interest change strategy* is one that attempts to convince individuals that the change is to their personal advantage. When this appeal is successful, strategy implementation can be relatively easy. However, implementation changes are seldom to everyone's advantage.

The rational change strategy is the most desirable, so this approach is examined a bit further. Managers can improve the likelihood of successfully implementing change by carefully designing change efforts. Jack Duncan described a rational or self-interest change strategy as consisting of four steps. First, employees are invited to participate in the process of change and the details of transition; participation allows everyone to give opinions, to feel a part of the change process, and to identify their own self-interests regarding the recommended change. Second, some motivation or incentive to change is required;

self-interest can be the most important motivator. Third, communication is needed so that people can understand the purpose for the changes. Giving and receiving feedback is the fourth step; everyone enjoys knowing how things are going and how much progress is being made.[6]

Igor Ansoff summarized the need for strategists to manage resistance to change as follows:

> Observation of the historical transitions from one orientation to another shows that, if left unmanaged, the process becomes conflict-laden, prolonged, and costly in both human and financial terms. Management of resistance involves anticipating the focus of resistance and its intensity. Second, it involves eliminating unnecessary resistance caused by misperceptions and insecurities. Third, it involves mustering the power base necessary to assure support for the change. Fourth, it involves planning the process of change. Finally, it involves monitoring and controlling resistance during the process of change. . . .[7]

Due to diverse external and internal forces, change is a fact of life in organizations. The rate, speed, magnitude, and direction of changes vary over time by industry and organization. Strategists should strive to create a work environment in which change is recognized as necessary and beneficial so that individuals can adapt to change more easily. Adopting a strategic-management approach to decision making can itself require major changes in the philosophy and operations of a firm.

Strategists can take a number of positive actions to minimize managers' and employees' resistance to change. For example, individuals who will be affected by a change should be involved in the decision to make the change and in decisions about how to implement change. Strategists should anticipate changes and develop and offer training and development workshops so managers and employees can adapt to those changes. They also need to communicate the need for changes effectively. The strategic-management process can be described as a process of managing change. Robert Waterman describes how successful organizations involve individuals to facilitate change:

> Implementation starts with, not after, the decision. When Ford Motor Company embarked on the program to build the highly successful Taurus, management gave up the usual, sequential design process. Instead they showed the tentative design to the workforce and asked their help in devising a car that would be easy to build. Team Taurus came up with no less than 1,401 items suggested by Ford employees. What a contrast from the secrecy that characterized the industry before! When people are treated as the main engine rather than interchangeable parts, motivation, creativity, quality, and commitment to implementation go up.[8]

MANAGING THE NATURAL ENVIRONMENT

Monsanto, a large U.S. chemical company, is an excellent example of a firm that protects the natural environment. Monsanto's motto is "Zero Spills, Zero Releases, Zero Incidents, and Zero Excuses." As indicated in the Natural Environment Perspective, there needs to be more Monsanto-type companies in Asia, a continent that became more polluted in the 1990s.

The 1990s may well be remembered as the decade of the environment. Earth itself has become a stakeholder for all business firms. Consumer interest in businesses' preserving nature's ecological balance and fostering a clean, healthy environment is high and growing. Evidence of this growing interest is that circulation of the top three natural environmental magazines, *Audubon*, *Greenpeace*, and *Sierra*, is soaring. Advertising revenues from these three magazines increased nearly 25 percent annually in the 1990s, when the magazine industry in general experienced slow or no growth in advertising revenues. This consumer interest is spurring companies to reconcile environmental and economic considerations.

The ecological challenge facing all organizations requires managers to formulate strategies that preserve and conserve natural resources and control pollution. Special natural environmental issues include ozone depletion, global warming, depletion of rain forests, destruction of animal habitats, protecting endangered species, developing biodegradable products and packages, waste management, clean air, clean water, erosion, destruction of natural resources, and pollution control. Firms increasingly are developing green product lines that are biodegradable and/or are made from recycled products. Green products sell well.

The Environmental Protection Agency recently reported that U.S. citizens and organizations spend more than about $200 billion annually on pollution abatement. Environmental concerns touch all aspects of a business's operations, including workplace risk exposures, packaging, waste reduction, energy use, alternative fuels, environmental cost accounting, and recycling practices. As indicated in the Natural Environment Perspective, preserving the natural environment makes good business sense.

Managing as if the earth matters requires an understanding of how international trade, competitiveness, and global resources are connected. Managing environmental affairs can no longer be simply a technical function performed by specialists in a firm; more emphasis must be placed on developing an environmental perspective among all employees and managers of the firm. Many companies are moving environmental affairs from the staff side of the organization to the line side, to make the corporate environmental group report directly to the chief operating officer.

Societies have been plagued by environmental disasters to such an extent recently that firms failing to recognize the importance of environmental issues and challenges could suffer severe consequences. Managing environmental affairs can no longer be an incidental or secondary function of company operations. Product design, manufacturing, and ultimate disposal should not merely reflect environmental considerations, but be driven by

NATURAL ENVIRONMENT
Does Asia Smell Bad?

"Since I left Taiwan 10 years ago to study in the United States, the quality of life, the air, and the water is 10 times worse. It's not worth it to have our economy grow so rapidly and have our environment ruined," says Jeff Chiang. In Kaohsiung, Taiwan, you can light the groundwater with a match at times. This is true in many Asian cities. Many large bodies of water in Asia are nearly biologically dead, including the Black Sea, the Caspian Sea, and Lake Baikal, the largest body of fresh water in the world.

Every uptick in economic expansion that has brought prosperity to Asia has come with a surge in smoke, hazardous waste, and garbage. The unrelenting push for growth has led numerous Asian countries to destroy their green landscapes, so celebrated in paintings, and their sacred rivers, so adored in poetry.

Most steel towns of China have sulfurous black skies. China is home to four of the world's 10 dirtiest cities, including Shenyang. Children going to school in Bangkok lose 10 IQ points to lead exposure. Leaded gasoline became illegal in Thailand only in 1997. The soil around Korean petrochemical plants is contaminated.

Asians are coming to realize that preserving the natural environment is much more than just a quality-of-life issue; it is an economic one. Pollution inhibits economic development. Improving the natural environment is an important theme for many political candidates in Asia in 1998.

Asian countries purchased over $7 billion in air pollution equipment in 1997. U.S. companies lag behind the world in exporting pollution control equipment, exporting just 6 percent of their output in environmental protection products, compared to 20 percent for both German and Japanese firms. Global opportunities for U.S. environmental firms are tremendous.

Source: Adapted from Susan Moffat, "Asia Stinks," Fortune (December 9, 1996): 121–132.

them. Firms that manage environmental affairs will enhance relations with consumers, regulators, vendors, and other industry players—substantially improving their prospects of success.

Firms should formulate and implement strategies from an environmental perspective. Environmental strategies could include developing or acquiring green businesses, divesting or altering environment-damaging businesses, striving to become a low-cost producer through waste minimization and energy conservation, and pursuing a differentiation strategy through green product features. In addition to creating strategies, firms could include an environmental representative on the board of directors, conduct regular environmental audits, implement bonuses for favorable environmental results, become involved in environmental issues and programs, incorporate environmental values in mission statements, establish environmentally oriented objectives, acquire environmental skills, and provide environmental training programs for company employees and managers.

CREATING A STRATEGY-SUPPORTIVE CULTURE

Strategists should strive to preserve, emphasize, and build upon aspects of an existing *culture* that support proposed new strategies. Aspects of an existing culture that are antagonistic to a proposed strategy should be identified and changed. Substantial research indicates that new strategies are often market-driven and dictated by competitive forces. For this reason, changing a firm's culture to fit a new strategy is usually more effective than changing a strategy to fit an existing culture. Numerous techniques are available to alter an organization's culture, including recruitment, training, transfer, promotion, restructure of an organization's design, role modeling, and positive reinforcement.

Jack Duncan described *triangulation* as an effective, multi-method technique for studying and altering a firm's culture.[9] Triangulation includes the combined use of obtrusive observation, self-administered questionnaires, and personal interviews to determine the nature of a firm's culture. The process of triangulation reveals needed changes in a firm's culture that could benefit strategy.

Schein indicated that the following elements are most useful in linking culture to strategy:

1. Formal statements of organizational philosophy, charters, creeds, materials used for recruitment and selection, and socialization
2. Designing of physical spaces, facades, buildings
3. Deliberate role modeling, teaching, and coaching by leaders
4. Explicit reward and status system, promotion criteria
5. Stories, legends, myths, and parables about key people and events
6. What leaders pay attention to, measure, and control
7. Leader reactions to critical incidents and organizational crises
8. How the organization is designed and structured
9. Organizational systems and procedures
10. Criteria used for recruitment, selection, promotion, leveling off, retirement, and "excommunication" of people.[10]

In the personal and religious side of life, the impact of loss and change is easy to see.[11] Memories of loss and change often haunt individuals and organizations for years. Ibsen wrote, "Rob the average man of his life illusion and you rob him of his happiness at the same stroke."[12] When attachments to a culture are severed in an organization's attempt to change direction, employees and managers often experience deep feelings of grief. This phenomenon commonly occurs when external conditions dictate the need for a new strategy. Managers and employees often struggle to find meaning in a situation that changed many years before. Some people find comfort in memories; others find solace in the present. Weak linkages between strategic management and organizational culture can jeopardize performance and success. Deal and Kennedy emphasized that making strategic changes in an organization always threatens a culture:

> . . . people form strong attachments to heroes, legends, the rituals of daily life, the hoopla of extravaganza and ceremonies, and all the symbols of the workplace. Change strips relationships and leaves employees confused, insecure, and often angry. Unless something can be done to provide support for transitions from old to new, the force of a culture can neutralize and emasculate strategy changes.[13]

The old corporate culture at AT&T consisted of lifetime careers, intense loyalty to the company, up-from-the-ranks management succession, dedication to the service ethos, and management by consensus. As AT&T moved from a regulated monopoly to a highly competitive environment in the 1980s, the company made numerous changes to create a culture that supported the new strategy; it redesigned its organizational structure, articulated its value system explicitly, provided management training to modify behavior in support of new values, revised recruiting aims and practices, and modified old symbols. AT&T abandoned its familiar logo, a bell with a circle, and adopted a new logo, a globe encircled by electronic communications, that symbolizes its new strategies to compete with Sprint and MCI.

PRODUCTION/OPERATIONS CONCERNS WHEN IMPLEMENTING STRATEGIES

Production/operations capabilities, limitations, and policies can significantly enhance or inhibit attainment of objectives. Production processes typically constitute more than 70 percent of a firm's total assets. A major part of the strategy-implementation process takes place at the production site. Production-related decisions on plant size, plant location, product design, choice of equipment, kind of tooling, size of inventory, inventory control, quality control, cost control, use of standards, job specialization, employee training, equipment and resource utilization, shipping and packaging, and technological innovation can have a dramatic impact on the success or failure of strategy-implementation efforts.

> There was a time when people were "factors of production," managed little differently from machines or capital. No more. The best people will not tolerate it. And if that way of managing ever generated productivity, it has the reverse effect today. While capital and machines either are or can be managed toward sameness, people are individuals. They must be managed that way. When companies encourage individual expression, it is difficult for them not to be successful (renew). The only true source of success in a company is the individual.[14]

Examples of adjustments in production systems that could be required to implement various strategies are provided in Table 7–3 for both for-profit and nonprofit organizations. For instance, note that when a bank formulates and selects a strategy to add 10 new branches, a production-related implementation concern is site location. As indicated in the Natural Environment Perspective, pollution control someday may become an important concern in production decisions for companies with operations in Asia.

TABLE 7–3
Production Management and Strategy Implementation

TYPE OF ORGANIZATION	STRATEGY BEING IMPLEMENTED	PRODUCTION SYSTEM ADJUSTMENTS
Hospital	Adding a cancer center (Product Development)	Purchase specialized equipment and add specialized people.
Bank	Adding 10 new branches (Market Development)	Perform site location analysis.
Beer brewery	Purchasing a barley farm operation (Backward Integration)	Revise the inventory control system.
Steel manufacturer	Acquiring a fast-food chain (Conglomerate Diversification)	Improve the quality control system.
Computer company	Purchasing a retail distribution chain (Forward Integration)	Alter the shipping, packaging, and transportation systems.

Just in Time (*JIT*) production approaches have withstood the test of time. JIT significantly reduces the costs of implementing strategies. With JIT, parts and materials are delivered to a production site just as they are needed, rather than being stockpiled as a hedge against later deliveries. Harley-Davidson reports that at one plant alone, JIT freed $22 million previously tied up in inventory and greatly reduced reorder lead time. *Industry Week* made the following observation about JIT:

> Most of the nation's 1,000 largest industrial companies are experimenting with, or preparing to implement, "Just in Time" manufacturing schemes. Suppliers who can't, or won't, play by the new rules are finding themselves on the sidelines. "Just in Case" just isn't good enough any more.[15]

Factors that should be studied before locating production facilities include the availability of major resources, the prevailing wage rates in the area, transportation costs related to shipping and receiving, the location of major markets, political risks in the area or country, and the availability of trainable employees.

For high-technology companies, production costs may not be as important as production flexibility because major product changes can be needed often. Industries such as biogenetics and plastics rely on production systems that must be flexible enough to allow frequent changes and rapid introduction of new products. An article in *Harvard Business Review* explained why some organizations get into trouble:

> They too slowly realize that a change in product strategy alters the tasks of a production system. These tasks, which can be stated in terms of requirements for cost, product flexibility, volume flexibility, product performance, and product consistency, determine which manufacturing policies are appropriate. As strategies shift over time, so must production policies covering the location and scale of manufacturing facilities, the choice of manufacturing process, the degree of vertical integration of each manufacturing facility, the use of R&D units, the control of the production system, and the licensing of technology.[16]

A common management practice, cross-training of employees, can facilitate strategy implementation and can yield many benefits. Employees gain a better understanding of the whole business and can contribute better ideas in planning sessions. Production/operations managers need to realize, however, that cross-training employees can create problems related to the following issues:

1. It can thrust managers into roles that emphasize counseling and coaching over directing and enforcing.
2. It can necessitate substantial investments in training and incentives.
3. It can be very time-consuming.
4. Skilled workers may resent unskilled workers who learn their jobs.
5. Older employees may not want to learn new skills.

HUMAN RESOURCE CONCERNS WHEN IMPLEMENTING STRATEGIES

The job of human resource manager is changing rapidly as companies downsize and reorganize in the 1990s. Strategic responsibilities of the human resource manager include assessing the staffing needs and costs for alternative strategies proposed during strategy formulation and developing a staffing plan for effectively implementing strategies. This plan must consider how best to manage spiraling health care insurance costs. Employers' health coverage expenses consume an average 26 percent of firms' net profits, even though most companies now require employees to pay part of their health insurance premiums. The plan must also include how to motivate employees and managers during a time when layoffs are common and workloads are high.

The human resource department must develop performance incentives that clearly link performance and pay to strategies. The process of empowering managers and employees through involvement in strategic-management activities yields the greatest benefits when all organizational members understand clearly how they will benefit personally if the firm does well. Linking company and personal benefits is a major new strategic responsibility of human resource managers. Other new responsibilities for human resource managers may include establishing and administering an *employee stock ownership plan* (*ESOP*), instituting an effective child care policy, and providing leadership for managers and employees to balance work and family.

A well-designed strategic-management system can fail if insufficient attention is given to the human resource dimension. Human resource problems that arise when businesses implement strategies can usually be traced to one of three causes: (1) disruption of social and political structures, (2) failure to match individuals' aptitudes with implementation tasks, and (3) inadequate top management support for implementation activities.[17]

Strategy implementation poses a threat to many managers and employees in an organization. New power and status relationships are anticipated and realized. New formal and informal groups' values, beliefs, and priorities may be largely unknown. Managers and employees may become engaged in resistance behavior as their roles, prerogatives, and power in the firm change. Disruption of social and political structures that accompany strategy execution must be anticipated and considered during strategy formulation and managed during strategy implementation.

A concern in matching managers with strategy is that jobs have specific and relatively static responsibilities, although people are dynamic in their personal development. Commonly used methods that match managers with strategies to be implemented include transferring managers, developing leadership workshops, offering career development activities, promotions, job enlargement, and job enrichment.

A number of other guidelines can help ensure that human relationships facilitate rather than disrupt strategy-implementation efforts. Specifically, managers should do a lot of chatting and informal questioning to stay abreast of how things are progressing and to know when to intervene. Managers can build support for strategy-implementation efforts by giving few orders, announcing few decisions, depending heavily on informal questioning, and seeking to probe and clarify until a consensus emerges. Key thrusts that succeed should be rewarded generously and visibly. A sense of humor is important, too. According to Adia Personnel Services, 72 percent of personnel executives nationwide say that humor is appropriate in discussions with colleagues; 63 percent say humor is appropriate in job interviews; 58 percent say humor is appropriate in performance reviews; and 53 percent say humor is appropriate in tense meetings.

It is suprising that so often during strategy formulation, individual values, skills, and abilities needed for successful strategy implementation are not considered. It is rare that a firm selecting new strategies or significantly altering existing strategies possesses the right line and staff personnel in the right positions for successful strategy implementation. The need to match individual aptitudes with strategy-implementation tasks should be considered in strategy choice.

Inadequate support from strategists for implementation activities often undermines organizational success. Chief executive officers, small business owners, and government agency heads must be personally committed to strategy implementation and express this commitment in highly visible ways. Strategists' formal statements about the importance of strategic management must be consistent with actual support and rewards given for activities completed and objectives reached. Otherwise, stress created by inconsistency can cause uncertainty among managers and employees at all levels.

Perhaps the best method for preventing and overcoming human resource problems in strategic management is to actively involve as many managers and employees as possible in the process. Although time-consuming, this approach builds understanding, trust, commitment, and ownership and reduces resentment and hostility. The true potential of strategy formulation and implementation resides in people.

EMPLOYEE STOCK OWNERSHIP PLANS (ESOPS)

An ESOP is a tax-qualified, defined-contribution, employee-benefit plan whereby employees purchase stock of the company through borrowed money or cash contributions. ESOPs empower employees to work as owners; this is a primary reason why the number of ESOPs grew dramatically throughout the 1980s and 1990s to more than 10,000 plans covering more than 15 million employees. ESOPs now control more than $80 billion in corporate stock in the United States.

Besides reducing worker alienation and stimulating productivity, ESOPs allow firms other benefits, such as substantial tax savings. Principal, interest, and dividend payments on ESOP-funded debt are tax-deductible. Banks lend money to ESOPs at interest rates below prime. This money can be repaid in pretax dollars, lowering the debt service as much as 30 percent in some cases.

If an ESOP owns more than 50 percent of the firm, those who lend money to the ESOP are taxed on only 50 percent of the income received on the loans. ESOPs are not for every firm, however, because the initial legal, accounting, actuarial, and appraisal fees to set up an ESOP are about $50,000 for a small or mid-sized firm, with annual administration expenses of about $15,000. Analysts say ESOPs also do not work well in firms that have fluctuating payrolls and profits. Human resource managers in many firms conduct preliminary research to determine the desirability of an ESOP, and then facilitate its establishment and administration if benefits outweigh the costs.

To establish an ESOP, a firm sets up a trust fund and purchases shares of its stock, which are allocated to individual employee accounts. All full-time employees over age 21 usually participate in the plan. Allocations of stock to the trust are made on the basis of relative pay, seniority, or some other formula. When an ESOP borrows money to purchase stock, the debt is guaranteed by the company and thus appears on the firm's balance sheet. On average, ESOP employees get $1,300 worth of stock per year, but cannot take physical possession of the shares until they quit, retire, or die. The median level of employee ownership in ESOP plans is 30 to 40 percent, although the range is from about 10 to 100 percent.

Research confirms that ESOPs can have a dramatic positive effect on employee motivation and corporate performance, especially if ownership is coupled with expanded employee participation and involvement in decision making. Market surveys indicate that customers prefer to do business with firms that are employee-owned.

Many companies are following the lead of Polaroid, which established an ESOP as a tactic for preventing a hostile takeover. Polaroid's CEO MacAllister Booth says, "Twenty years from now we'll find that employees have a sizable stake in every major American corporation." (It is interesting to note here that Polaroid is chartered in the state of Delaware, which requires corporate suitors to acquire 85 percent of a target company's shares to complete a merger; over 50 percent of all American corporations are incorporated in Delaware for this reason.) Wyatt Cafeterias, a Southwestern U.S. operator of 120 cafeterias, also adopted the ESOP concept to prevent a hostile takeover. Employee productivity at Wyatt greatly increased since the ESOP began, as illustrated in the following quote:

> The key employee in our entire organization is the person serving the customer on the cafeteria line. In the past, because of high employee turnover and entry-level wages for many line jobs, these employees received far less attention and recognition than managers. We now tell the tea cart server, "You own the place. Don't wait for the manager to tell you how to do your job better or how to provide better service. You take care of it." Sure, we're looking for productivity increases, but since we began pushing decisions down to the level of people who deal directly with customers, we've discovered an awesome side effect—suddenly the work crews have this "happy to be here" attitude that the customers really love.[18]

Companies such as Avis, Procter & Gamble, BellSouth, ITT, Xerox, Delta, Austin Industries, Health Trust, The Parsons Corporation, Dyncorp, and Charter Medical have established ESOPs to assist strategists in divesting divisions, going private, and consummating leveraged buyouts. ESOPs can be found today in all kinds of firms, from small retailers to large manufacturers. Employees can own any amount from 1 percent to 100 percent of the company. Nearly all ESOPs are established in healthy firms, not failing firms.

BALANCING WORK LIFE AND HOME LIFE Work/family strategies have become so popular among companies in the 1990s that the strategies now represent a competitive advantage for those firms that offer such benefits as elder care assistance, flexible scheduling, job sharing, adoption benefits, an on-site summer camp, employee help lines, pet care, and even lawn service referrals. New corporate titles such as Work/Life Coordinator and Director of Diversity are becoming common. *Business Week* and the Center on Work and Family at Boston University have for the first time begun rating companies on their family-friendly strategies. The 10 U.S. companies that received the highest ratings for providing work-family benefits are given below in rank order:[19]

	1996	1997
1.	DuPont	MBNA America Bank
2.	Eddie Bauer	Motorola
3.	Eli Lilly	Barnett Banks
4.	First Tennessee Bank	Hewlett-Packard
5.	Hewlett-Packard	Unum Life Insurance
6.	Marriott International	Lincoln National
7.	MBNA America Bank	Merrill Lynch
8.	Merrill Lynch	DuPont
9.	Motorola	TRW
10.	Unum Life Insurance	Cigna

Human resource managers need to foster more effective balancing of professional and private lives because nearly 60 million people in the United States are now part of two-career families. A corporate objective to become more lean and mean must today include consideration for the fact that a good home life contributes immensely to a good work life.

> You can count on baby boomers to force the issue of family versus work onto the corporate agenda. Fully 73 percent of all women age 25 to 34 now work for pay, as do half of all women with babies under a year old. For them and their husbands, child care, flexible hours, and job sharing are pressing concerns.[20]

The work/family issue is no longer just a women's problem. Some specific measures that firms are taking to address this issue are providing spouse relocation assistance as an employee benefit, providing company resources for family recreational and educational use, establishing employee country clubs such as those at IBM and Bethlehem Steel, and creating family/work interaction opportunities. A recent study by Joseph Pleck of Wheaton College found that in companies that do not offer paternity leave for fathers as a benefit, most men take short informal paternity leaves anyway by combining vacation time and sick days.

Some organizations have developed family days, when family members are invited into the workplace, taken on plant or office tours, dined by management, and given a chance to see exactly what other family members do each day. Family days are inexpensive and increase the employee's pride in working for the organization. Flexible working hours during the week are another human resource response to the need for individuals to balance work life and home life. The work/family topic is being made part of the agenda at meetings and thus is becoming discussable in many organizations.

Research indicates that employees who are dissatisfied with child care arrangements are most likely to be absent or unproductive.[21] Lack of adequate child care in a community can be a deterrent in recruiting and retaining good managers and employees. Some benefits of on-site child care facilities are improved employee relations, reduced absenteeism and turnover, increased productivity, enhanced recruitment, and improved community relations.

A recent survey of women managers revealed that one-third would leave their present employer for another employer offering child care assistance. The Conference Board recently reported that more than 500 firms in the United States had created on-site or near-site child care centers for their employees, including Merck, Campbell Soup, Hoffman–La Roche, Stride-Rite, Johnson Wax, CIGNA, Champion International, Walt Disney World, and Playboy Resorts.

Other common child care service arrangements include employer-sponsored day care, child care information, and referral services. IBM, Steelcase, Honeywell, Citibank, 3M, and Southland have established contracts with third-party child care information and referral services.

The nation's largest employer-sponsored day care center is operated by Intermedics, a Texas-based medical instruments firm. Employee turnover declined 23 percent the first year Intermedics instituted the center. Due to the high cost of child care, numerous firms are forming partnerships to build and manage child care facilities. The largest collaboration so far is the new $2 million, 194-child day care center in Charlotte, financed and operated by IBM, American Express, Allstate, Duke Power, and University Research Park. The teacher-child ratio at this center is 50 percent lower than required by North Carolina law. Other large partnership child care centers have recently been built in Minneapolis, Rochester, Dallas–Fort Worth, and New York City. In Virginia, 22 companies recently pooled $100,000 to establish a parent-run child care cooperative. Other companies that effectively address child care concerns of managers and employees include Clorox and Nyloncraft. Even small businesses are beginning to offer child care benefits for employees.

Some small firms that now offer an on-site day care center for employees' children include Bowles Corporation in North Ferrisburg, Vermont; Byrne Electrical Specialists in Rockford, Michigan; Chalet Dental Clinic in Yakima, Washington; and Stackpole Ltd. in Brownsville, Tennessee.

CORPORATE FITNESS PROGRAMS   At least 10,000 U.S. employers now offer programs to improve or maintain their employees' health, such as programs to stop smoking, reduce cholesterol, promote regular exercise, and control high blood pressure. Another 1,000 American firms offer on-site, fully equipped fitness centers to promote good employee health. Perhaps the leader in this area is Johnson & Johnson, which provides an 11,000-square-foot fitness center, aerobics and other exercise classes, seminars on AIDS and alcohol abuse, and an indoor track. J & J's program is called Live for Life.

CONCLUSION

Successful strategy formulation does not at all guarantee successful strategy implementation. Although inextricably interdependent, strategy formulation and strategy implementation are characteristically different. In a single word, strategy implementation means *change*. It is widely agreed that "the real work begins after strategies are formulated." Successful strategy implementation requires support, discipline, motivation, and hard work from all managers and employees. It is sometimes frightening to think that a single individual can sabotage strategy-implementation efforts irreparably.

Formulating the right strategies is not enough, because managers and employees must be motivated to implement those strategies. Management issues considered central to strategy implementation include matching organizational structure with strategy, linking performance and pay to strategies, creating an organizational climate conducive to change, managing political relationships, creating a strategy-supportive culture, adapting production/operations processes, and managing human resources. Establishing annual objectives, devising policies, and allocating resources are central strategy-implementation activities common to all organizations. Depending on the size and type of organization, other management issues could be equally important to successful strategy implementation.

We invite you to visit the DAVID page on the Prentice Hall Web site at
www.prenhall.com/davidsm
for this chapter's World Wide Web exercises.

KEY TERMS AND CONCEPTS

Annual Objectives	(p. 218)	Downsizing	(p. 229)	Profit Sharing	(p. 231)
Avoidance	(p. 224)	Educative Change Strategy	(p. 233)	Rational Change Strategy	(p. 233)
Benchmarking	(p. 229)	Employee Stock Ownership	(p. 239)	Reengineering	(p. 229)
Bonus System	(p. 231)	Plan (ESOP)		Resistance to Change	(p. 233)
Conflict	(p. 223)	Establishing Annual Objectives	(p. 218)	Resource Allocation	(p. 223)
Confrontation	(p. 224)	Force Change Strategy	(p. 233)	Restructuring	(p. 229)
Culture	(p. 236)	Functional Structure	(p. 225)	Rightsizing	(p. 229)
Defusion	(p. 224)	Gain Sharing	(p. 231)	Self-Interest Change Strategy	(p. 233)
Delayering	(p. 229)	Horizontal Consistency of	(p. 219)	Strategic Business Unit (SBU)	(p. 228)
Decentralized Structure	(p. 225)	Objectives		Structure	
Divisional Structure by		Just in Time	(p. 238)	Triangulation	(p. 236)
Geographic Area, Product,	(p. 227)	Matrix Structure	(p. 228)	Vertical Consistency of	(p. 219)
Customer, or Process	(p. 228)	Policy	(p. 221)	Objectives	

ISSUES FOR REVIEW AND DISCUSSION

1. Allocating resources can be a political and an ad hoc activity in firms that do not use strategic management. Why is this true? Does adopting strategic management ensure easy resource allocation? Why?

2. Compare strategy formulation with strategy implementation in terms of each being an art or a science.

3. Describe the relationship between annual objectives and policies.

4. Identify a long-term objective and two supporting annual objectives for a familiar organization.

5. Identify and discuss three policies that apply to your present business policy class.

6. Explain the following statement: Horizontal consistency of goals is as important as vertical consistency.

7. Describe several reasons why conflict may occur during objective-setting activities.

8. In your opinion, what approaches to conflict resolution would be best for resolving a disagreement between a personnel manager and a sales manager over the firing of a particular salesperson? Why?

9. Describe the organizational culture of your college or university.

10. Explain why organizational structure is so important in strategy implementation.

11. In your opinion, how many separate divisions could an organization reasonably have without using an SBU-type organizational structure? Why?

12. Would you recommend a divisional structure by geographic area, product, customer, or process for a medium-sized bank in your local area? Why?

13. What are the advantages and disadvantages of decentralizing the wage and salary function of an organization? How could this be accomplished?

14. Consider a college organization with which you are familiar. How did management issues affect strategy implementation in that organization?

15. As production manager of a local newspaper, what problems would you anticipate in implementing a strategy to increase the average number of pages in the paper by 40 percent?

16. Read an article from the suggested readings at the end of this chapter and give a summary report to the class revealing your thoughts on the topic.

17. Do you believe expenditures for child care or fitness facilities are warranted from a cost/benefit perspective? Why or why not?

18. Explain why successful strategy implementation often hinges on whether the strategy-formulation process empowers managers and employees.

NOTES

1. A. G. Bedeian and W. F. Glueck, *Management*, 3rd. ed. (Chicago: The Dryden Press, 1983): 212.

2. Boris Yavits and William Newman, *Strategy in Action: The Execution, Politics, and Payoff of Business Planning* (New York: The Free Press, 1982): 195.

3. "Want to Be a Manager? Many People Say No, Calling Job Miserable," *The Wall Street Journal* (April 4, 1997): 1. Also, Stephanie Armour, "Management Loses Its Allure," *USA Today* (October 10, 1997): 1B.

4. Yavits and Newman, 58.

5. Perry Pascarella, "The Toughest Turnaround of All," *Industry Week* (April 2, 1984): 33. Reprinted with permission from *Industry Week*, April 2, 1984. Copyright Renton Publishing Inc., Cleveland, Ohio.

6. Jack Duncan, *Management* (New York: Random House, 1983): 381–390.

7. H. Igor Ansoff, "Strategic Management of Technology," *Journal of Business Strategy* 7, no. 3 (Winter 1987): 38.

8. Robert Waterman, Jr., "How the Best Get Better," *Business Week* (September 14, 1987): 104.

9. Jack Duncan, "Organizational Culture: Getting a Fix on an Elusive Concept," *Academy of Management Executive*, no. 3 (August 1989): 229.

10. E. H. Schein, "The Role of the Founder in Creating Organizational Culture," *Organizational Dynamics* (Summer 1983): 13–28.

11. T. Deal and A. Kennedy, "Culture: A New Look Through Old Lenses," *Journal of Applied Behavioral Science* 19, no. 4 (1983): 498–504.

12. H. Ibsen, "The Wild Duck," in O. G. Brochett and L. Brochett (eds.), *Plays for the Theater* (New York: Holt, Rinehart & Winston, 1967). Also, R. Pascale, "The Paradox of 'Corporate Culture': Reconciling Ourselves to Socialization," *California Management Review* 28, 2 (1985): 26, 37–40.

13. T. Deal and A. Kennedy, *Corporate Cultures: The Rites and Rituals of Corporate Life* (Reading, Massachusetts: Addison-Wesley, 1982).

14. Robert Waterman, Jr., "The Renewal Factor," *Business Week* (September 14, 1987): 100.

15. "Just in Time: Putting the Squeeze on Suppliers," *Industry Week* (July 9, 1984): 59.

16. Robert Stobaugh and Piero Telesio, "Match Manufacturing Policies and Product Strategy," *Harvard Business Review* 61, no. 2 (March–April 1983): 113.

17. R. T. Lenz and Marjorie Lyles, "Managing Human Resource Problems in Strategy Planning Systems," *Journal of Business Strategy* 60, no. 4 (Spring 1986): 58.

18. J. Warren Henry, "ESOPs with Productivity Payoffs," *Journal of Business Strategy* (July–August 1989): 33.

19. "Balancing Work and Family," *Business Week* (September 16, 1996): 74–80. Also, Keith Hammonds, "Work and Family," *Business Week* (September 15, 1997): 96–99.

20. Ronald Henkoff, "Is Greed Dead?" *Fortune* (August 14, 1989): 49.

21. Richard Levine, "Childcare: Inching up the Corporate Agenda," *Management Review* 78, no. 1 (January 1989): 43.

CURRENT READINGS

Amason, Allen C. "Distinguishing the Effects of Functional and Dysfunctional Conflict on Strategic Decision Making: Resolving a Paradox for Top Management Teams." *Academy of Management Journal* 39, no. 1 (February 1996): 123–148.

Bruton, Garry D., J. Kay Keels, and Christopher L. Shook. "Downsizing the Firm: Answering the Strategic Questions." *Academy of Management Executive* 10, no. 2 (May 1996): 38–45.

Brynjolfsson, Erik, Amy Austin, and Renshaw and Marshall Van Alstyne. "The Matrix of Change." *Sloan Management Review* 38, no. 2 (Winter 1997): 37–54.

Dutton, J. E., S. J. Ashford, R. M. O'Neill, E. Hayes, and E. E. Wierba. "Reading the Wind: How Middle Managers Assess the Context for Selling Issues to Top Managers." *Strategic Management Journal* 18, no. 5 (May 1997): 407–417.

Eisenhardt, Kathleen M., Jean L. Kahwajy, and L. J. Bourgeois III. "Conflict and Strategic Choice: How Top Management Teams Disagree." *California Management Review* 39, no. 2 (Winter 1997): 42–62.

Ettorre, Barbara. "The Empowerment Gap: Hype vs. Reality." *Management Review* (July–August 1997): 10–14.

Gomez-Mejia, Luis and Robert M. Wiserman. "Reframing Executive Compensation: An Assessment and Outlook." *Journal of Management* 23, no. 3 (1997): 291–374.

Gould, R. Morgan. "Getting from Strategy to Action: Processes for Continuous Change." *Long Range Planning* 29, no. 3 (June 1996): 278–289.

Hatfield, D. E., J. P. Liebeskind, and T. C. Opler. "The Effects of Corporate Restructuring on Aggregate Industry Specialization." *Strategic Management Journal* 17, no. 1 (January 1996): 55–72.

Heifetz, Ronald A. and Donald L. Laurie. "The Work of Leadership." *Harvard Business Review* (January–February 1997): 124–134.

Huselid, Mark A., Susan E. Jackson, and Randall S. Schuler. "Technical and Strategic Human Resource Management Effectiveness as Determinants of Firm Peformance." *Academy of Management Journal* 40, no. 1 (February 1997). 171–188.

Imberman, Woodruff. "Gainsharing: A Lemon or Lemonade?" *Business Horizons* 39, no. 1 (January–February 1996): 36–40.

Kubasek, Nancy. "Following Canada's Lead: Preventing Prosecution for Environmental Crimes." *Business Horizons* 39, no. 5 (September–October 1996): 64–70.

London, Manuel. "Redeployment and Continuous Learning in the 21st Century: Hard Lessons and Positive Examples from the Downsizing Era." *Academy of Management Executive* 10, no. 4 (November 1996): 67–79.

Mabert, Vincent A. and Roger W. Schmenner. "Assessing the Roller Coaster of Downsizing." *Business Horizons* 40, no. 4 (July–August 1997): 45–53.

Magnan, M. L. and S. St-Onge. "Bank Performance and Executive Compensation: A Managerial Discretion Perspective." *Strategic Management Journal* 18, no. 7 (August 1997): 573–582.

Majchrzak, Ann and Qianwei Wang. "Breaking the Functional Mind-Set in Process Organizations." *Harvard Business Review* (September–October 1996): 92–101.

Malone, Thomas W. "Is Empowerment Just a Fad? Control, Decision Making, and IT." *Sloan Management Review* 38, no. 2 (Winter 1997): 23–36.

Markides, Constantinos C. and Peter J. Williamson. "Corporate Diversification and Organizational Structure: A Resource-Based View." *Academy of Management Journal* 39, no. 2 (April 1996): 340–367.

Maxwell, John W. "What To Do When Win-Win Won't Work: Environmental Strategies for Costly Regulation." *Business Horizons* 39, no. 5 (September–October 1996): 60–63.

McMaster, Mike. "Foresight: Exploring the Structure of the Future." *Long Range Planning* 29, no. 2 (April 1996): 149–155.

Montemayor, Edilberto F. "Congruence Between Pay Policy and Competitive Strategy in High-Performing Firms." *Journal of Management* 22, no. 6 (1996): 889–912.

Reichers, Arnon E., John P. Wanous, and James T. Austin. "Understanding and Managing Cynicism About Organizational Change." *Academy of Management Executive* 11, no. 1 (February 1997): 48–59.

Roth, Kendall and Sharon O'Donnell. "Foreign Subsidiary Compensation Strategy: An Agency Theory Perspective" *Academy of Management Journal* 39, no. 3 (June 1996): 678–703.

Shi, J. Stephen and Jane M. Kane. "Green Issues." *Business Horizons* 39, no. 1 (January–February 1996): 65–70.

Smith, K. G., C. M. Grimm, G. Young, and S. Wally. "Strategic Groups and Rivalrous Firm Behavior: Towards a Reconciliation." *Strategic Management Journal* 18, no. 2 (February 1997): 149–158.

Sparrowe, Raymond T. and Robert C. Liden. "Process and Structure in Leader-Member Exchange." *Academy of Management Review* 22, no. 2 (April 1997): 522–552.

Strebel, Paul. "Why Do Employees Resist Change?" *Harvard Business Review* (May–June 1996): 86–94.

Taylor, Sully, Schon Beechler, and Nancy Napier. "Toward an Integrative Model of Strategic International Human Resource Management." *Academy of Management Review* 21, no. 4 (October 1996): 959–985.

Ward, Peter T., Deborah J. Bickford, and G. Keong Leong. "Configurations of Manufacturing Strategy, Business Strategy, Environment and Structure." *Journal of Management* 22, no. 4 (1996): 597–607.

EXPERIENTIAL EXERCISES

REVISING HERSHEY'S ORGANIZATIONAL CHART

PURPOSE

Developing and altering organizational charts is an important skill for strategists to possess. This exercise can improve your skill in altering an organization's hierarchical structure in response to new strategies being formulated.

INSTRUCTIONS

Step 1 Turn back to Hershey's organizational chart given in the Cohesion Case (p. 33).

Step 2 On a separate sheet of paper, diagram an organizational chart that you believe would best suit Hershey's needs if the company decided to form a divisional structure by product.

Step 3 Provide as much detail in your chart as possible, including the names of individuals and the titles of positions.

MATCHING MANAGERS WITH STRATEGY

PURPOSE

For many years, strategists believed that good managers could adapt to handle any situation. Consequently, strategists rarely replaced or transferred managers as the need arose to implement new strategies. Today, this situation is changing. Research supports the notion that certain management characteristics are needed for certain strategic situations.[1] Chase Manhattan Bank, Heublein, Texas Instruments, Corning Glass, and General Electric are examples of companies that match managers to strategic requirements.

This exercise can improve your awareness and understanding of particular managerial characteristics that have been found to be most desirable for implementing certain types of strategies. Having the right managers in the right jobs can determine the success or failure of strategy-implementation efforts. This exercise is based on a framework that has proved to be useful in "matching managers to strategy."[2]

INSTRUCTIONS

Your task is to match specific managerial characteristics with particular generic strategies. Four broad types of strategies are examined:

1. Retrenchment/Turnaround
2. Intensive (market penetration, market development, and product development)
3. Liquidation/Divestiture
4. Integration (backward, forward, and horizontal)

Five managerial characteristics have been found to be associated with each of these strategies. On a separate sheet of paper, list the four types of strategies. Beside each strategy, record the appropriate letter of the five managerial characteristics that you believe are most needed to successfully implement those strategies. Each of the managerial characteristics in the following list should be used only once in completing this exercise.

A. Is technically knowledgeable—"knows the business"

B. Is "callous"—tough-minded, determined, willing to be the bad guy

C. Is "take charge"–oriented—strong leader

D. Is a good negotiator

E. Wants to be respected, not necessarily liked

F. Has good analytical ability

G. Is low glory-seeking—willing to do dirty jobs; does not want glamour

H. Has excellent staffing skills

I. Handles pressure well

J. Is a risk taker

K. Has good relationship-building skills

L. Has good organizational and team-building skills

M. Is oriented to getting out the most efficiency, not growth

N. Anticipates problems—"problem finder"

O. Has strong analytical and diagnostic skills, especially financial

P. Is an excellent business strategist

Q. Has good communication skills

R. Has personal magnetism

S. Is highly analytical—focuses on costs/benefits, does not easily accept current ways of doing things

T. Has good interpersonal influence

NOTES

1. Marc Gerstein and Heather Reisman, "Strategic Selection: Matching Executives to Business Conditions," *Sloan Management Review* 24, no. 2 (Winter 1983): 33–47.

2. Ibid., 37.

Experiential Exercise 7C

DO ORGANIZATIONS REALLY ESTABLISH OBJECTIVES?

PURPOSE

Objectives provide direction, allow synergy, aid in evaluation, establish priorities, reduce uncertainty, minimize conflicts, stimulate exertion, and aid in both the allocation of resources and the design of jobs. This exercise will enhance your understanding of how organizations use or misuse objectives.

INSTRUCTIONS

Step 1 Join with one other person in class to form a two-person team.

Step 2 Contact by telephone the owner or manager of an organization in your city or town. Request a 30-minute personal interview or meeting with that person for the purpose of discussing "business objectives." During your meeting, seek answers to the following questions:

1. Do you believe it is important for a business to establish and clearly communicate long-term and annual objectives? Why or why not?
2. Does your organization establish objectives? If yes, what type and how many? How are the objectives communicated to individuals? Are your firm's objectives in written form or simply communicated orally?
3. To what extent are managers and employees involved in the process of establishing objectives?
4. How often are your business objectives revised and by what process?

Step 3 Take good notes during the interview. Let one person be the note taker and one person do most of the talking. Have your notes typed up and ready to turn in to your professor.

Step 4 Prepare a five-minute oral presentation for the class, reporting the results of your interview. Turn in your typed report.

Experiential Exercise 7D

UNDERSTANDING MY UNIVERSITY'S CULTURE

PURPOSE

It is something of an art to uncover the basic values and beliefs that are buried deeply in an organization's rich collection of stories, language, heroes, heroines, and rituals, yet culture can be the most important factor in implementing strategies.

INSTRUCTIONS

Step 1 On a separate sheet of paper, list the following terms: hero/heroine, belief, metaphor, language, value, symbol, story, legend, saga, folktale, myth, ceremonial, rite, and ritual.

Step 2 For your college or university, give examples of each term. If necessary, speak with faculty, staff, alumni, administration, or fellow students of the institution to identify examples of each term. Refer back to p. 236 for definitions of the terms if needed.

Step 3 Report your findings to the class. Tell the class how you feel regarding cultural products being consciously used to help implement strategies.

CHAPTER 8

Implementing Strategies: Marketing, Finance/ Accounting, R&D, and CIS Issues

CHAPTER OUTLINE

- ◆ **THE NATURE OF STRATEGY IMPLEMENTATION**
- ◆ **MARKETING ISSUES**
- ◆ **FINANCE/ACCOUNTING ISSUES**
- ◆ **RESEARCH AND DEVELOPMENT (R&D) ISSUES**
- ◆ **COMPUTER INFORMATION SYSTEMS (CIS) ISSUES**

- ■ EXPERIENTIAL EXERCISE 8A
  Developing a Product Positioning Map for Hershey Foods

- ■ EXPERIENTIAL EXERCISE 8B
  Performing an EPS/EBIT Analysis for Hershey Foods

- ■ EXPERIENTIAL EXERCISE 8C
  Preparing Pro Forma Financial Statements for Hershey Foods

- ■ EXPERIENTIAL EXERCISE 8D
  Determining the Cash Value of Hershey Foods

- ■ EXPERIENTIAL EXERCISE 8E
  Developing a Product Positioning Map for My University

- ■ EXPERIENTIAL EXERCISE 8F
  Do Banks Require Pro Forma Statements?

CHAPTER OBJECTIVES

After studying this chapter, you should be able to do the following:

1. Explain market segmentation and product positioning as strategy-implementation tools.

2. Discuss procedures for determining the worth of a business.

3. Explain why pro forma financial analysis is a central strategy-implementation tool.

4. Explain how to evaluate the attractiveness of debt versus stock as a source of capital to implement strategies.

5. Discuss the nature and role of research and development in strategy implementation.

6. Explain how computer information systems can determine the success of strategy-implementation efforts.

The greatest strategy is doomed if it's implemented badly.—BERNARD REIMANN

Organizations should approach all tasks with the idea that they can be accomplished in a superior fashion.—THOMAS WATSON, JR.

There is no "perfect" strategic decision. One always has to pay a price. One always has to balance conflicting objectives, conflicting opinions, and conflicting priorities. The best strategic decision is only an approximation—and a risk.—PETER DRUCKER

The real question isn't how well you're doing today against your own history, but how you're doing against your competitors.—DONALD KRESS

Effective organizational responses are retarded not so much by failing to recognize what needs to be done, but by not doing what ought to be done.—JOHN KEANE

As market windows open and close more quickly, it is important that R&D be tied more closely to corporate strategy.—WILLIAM SPENSER

Most of the time, strategists should not be formulating strategy at all; they should be getting on with implementing strategies they already have.—HENRY MINTZBERG

The best plan is only a plan, that is, good intentions. Unless commitment is made, there are only promises and hopes, but no plan.—PETER DRUCKER

Strategies have no chance of being implemented successfully in organizations that do not market goods and services well, in firms that cannot raise needed working capital, in firms that produce technologically inferior products, or in firms that have a weak information system. This chapter examines marketing, finance/accounting, R&D, and computer information systems (CIS) issues that are central to effective strategy implementation. Special topics include market segmentation, market positioning, evaluating the worth of a business, determining to what extent debt and/or stock should be used as a source of capital, developing pro forma financial statements, contracting R&D outside the firm, and creating an information support system. Manager and employee involvement and participation are essential for success in marketing, finance/accounting, R&D, and CIS activities.

THE NATURE OF STRATEGY IMPLEMENTATION

The quarterback can call the best play possible in the huddle, but that does not mean the play will go for a touchdown. The team may even lose yardage unless the play is executed (implemented) well. Less than 10 percent of strategies formulated are successfully implemented! There are many reasons for this low success rate, including failing to segment markets appropriately, paying too much for a new acquisition, falling behind competitors in R&D, and not recognizing the benefit of computers in managing information.

Strategy implementation directly affects the lives of plant managers, division managers, department managers, sales managers, product managers, project managers, personnel managers, staff managers, supervisors, and all employees. In some situations, individuals may not have participated in the strategy-formulation process at all and may not appreciate, understand, or even accept the work and thought that went into strategy formulation. There may even be foot dragging or resistance on their part. Managers and employees who do not understand the business and are not committed to the business may attempt to sabotage strategy-implementation efforts in hopes that the organization will return to its old ways. The strategy-implementation stage of the strategic-management process is emphasized in Figure 8–1.

MARKETING ISSUES

Countless marketing variables affect the success or failure of strategy implementation, and the scope of this text does not allow addressing all those issues. However, two variables are of central importance to strategy implementation: *market segmentation* and *product positioning*. Market segmentation and product positioning rank as marketing's most important contributions to strategic management. Some examples of marketing decisions that may require policies are as follows:

1. To use exclusive dealerships or multiple channels of distribution
2. To use heavy, light, or no TV advertising
3. To limit (or not) the share of business done with a single customer
4. To be a price leader or a price follower
5. To offer a complete or limited warranty
6. To reward salespeople based on straight salary, straight commission, or a combination salary/commission

FIGURE 8–1
A Comprehensive Strategic-Management Model

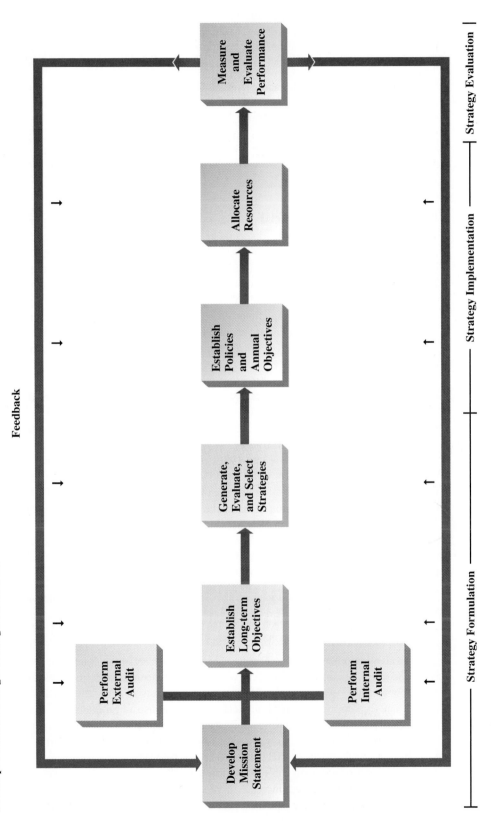

TABLE 8–1
The Marketing Mix
Component Factors

PRODUCT	PLACE	PROMOTION	PRICE
Quality	Distribution channels	Advertising	Level
Features and options	Distribution coverage	Personal selling	Discounts and
Style	Outlet location	Sales promotion	allowances
Brand name	Sales territories	Publicity	Payment terms
Packaging	Inventory levels and		
Product line	locations		
Warranty	Transportation carriers		
Service level			
Other services			

Source: E. Jerome McCarthy, *Basic Marketing: A Managerial Approach*, 9th ed. (Homewood, Illinois: Richard D. Irwin, Inc., 1987): 37–44.

MARKET SEGMENTATION   Market segmentation is widely used in implementing strategies, especially for small and specialized firms. Market segmentation can be defined as the subdividing of a market into distinct subsets of customers according to needs and buying habits. Market segmentation is an important variable in strategy implementation for at least three major reasons. First, strategies such as market development, product development, market penetration, and diversification require increased sales through new markets and products. To implement these strategies successfully, new or improved market-segmentation approaches are required. Second, market segmentation allows a firm to operate with limited resources because mass production, mass distribution, and mass advertising are not required. Market segmentation can enable a small firm to compete successfully with a large firm by maximizing per-unit profits and per-segment sales. Finally, market segmentation decisions directly affect *marketing mix variables*: product, place, promotion, and price, as indicated in Table 8–1. For example, SnackWells, a pioneer in reduced-fat snacks, has shifted its advertising emphasis from low-fat to great taste as part of its new market segmentation strategy.

Perhaps the most dramatic late-1990s market segmentation strategy was the targeting of regional tastes. Firms from McDonald's to General Motors are increasingly modifying their products to meet different regional preferences within the United States. Campbell's has a spicier version of its nacho cheese soup for the Southwest, and Burger King offers breakfast burritos in New Mexico but not in South Carolina.

Geographic and demographic bases for segmenting markets are the most commonly employed, as illustrated in Table 8–2. Beer producers, for example, have generally divided the light beer market into three segments:

> The light beer market can be meaningfully separated into three motivation segments: those who are calorie-conscious, those who prefer less alcohol, and those who prefer a lighter taste. In fact, it is possible for one person to consume light beer on three separate occasions for three different reasons. The situation may therefore dictate the segment the consumer falls into.[1]

Evaluating potential market segments requires strategists to determine the characteristics and needs of consumers, analyze consumer similarities and differences, and develop consumer group profiles. Segmenting consumer markets is generally much simpler and easier than segmenting industrial markets, because industrial products, such as electronic circuits and forklifts, have multiple applications and appeal to diverse customer groups.

Advertising strategy follows market segmentation. In 1997, U.S. firms spent over $186 billion on advertising, a 6.2 percent increase over a banner advertising year in 1996. Advertising expenditures on cable television rose 18 percent in 1997 to over $5.3 billion, in contrast to only a 2 percent increase in ad spending on network television. Airlines and cigarette makers, on average, spent 20 percent less in 1997 than in 1996, while computer,

VARIABLE	TYPICAL BREAKDOWNS
GEOGRAPHIC	
Region	Pacific, Mountain, West North Central, West South Central, East North Central, East South Central, South Atlantic, Middle Atlantic, New England
County Size	A, B, C, D
City Size	Under 5,000; 5,000–20,000; 20,000–50,000; 50,000–100,000; 100,000–250,000; 250,000–500,000; 500,000–1,000,000; 1,000,000–4,000,000; 4,000,000 or over
Density	Urban, suburban, rural
Climate	Northern, southern
DEMOGRAPHIC	
Age	Under 6, 6–11, 12–19, 20–34, 35–49, 50–64, 65+
Sex	Male, female
Family Size	1–2, 3–4, 5+
Family Life Cycle	Young, single; young, married, no children; young, married, youngest child under 6; young, married, youngest child 6 or over; older, married, with children; older, married, no children under 18; older, single; other
Income	Under $10,000; $10,001–$15,000; $15,001–$20,000; $20,001–$30,000; $30,001–$50,000; $50,001–$70,000; $70,001–$100,000; over $100,000
Occupation	Professional and technical; managers, officials, and proprietors; clerical, sales; craftsmen, foremen; operatives; farmers; retired; students; housewives; unemployed
Education	Grade school or less; some high school; high school graduate; some college; college graduate
Religion	Catholic, Protestant, Jewish, other
Race	White, Asian, Hispanic, African American
Nationality	American, British, French, German, Scandinavian, Italian, Latin American, Middle Eastern, Japanese
PSYCHOGRAPHIC	
Social Class	Lower lowers, upper lowers, lower middles, upper middles, lower uppers, upper uppers
Personality	Compulsive, gregarious, authoritarian, ambitious
BEHAVIORAL	
Use Occasion	Regular occasion, special occasion
Benefits Sought	Quality, service, economy
User Status	Nonuser, ex-user, potential user, first-time user, regular user
Usage Rate	Light user, medium user, heavy user
Loyalty Status	None, medium, strong, absolute
Readiness Stage	Unaware, aware, informed, interested, desirous, intending to buy
Attitude Toward Product	Enthusiastic, positive, indifferent, negative, hostile

TABLE 8–2
Alternative Bases for Market Segmentation

Source: Adapted from Philip Kotler, *Marketing Management: Analysis, Planning and Control*, © 1984: 256. Adapted by permission of Prentice-Hall, Inc., Englewood Cliffs, New Jersey.

liquor, and stock brokerage firms spent 20 percent more. Companies such as Pizza Hut and McDonald's have recently used advertisements that feature their own employees. (These ads have not worked well.) Pizza Hut has a 23 percent market share of the $21 billion restaurant pizza market, followed by Domino's with 11 percent and Little Caesars with 8.5 percent.

Market segmentation matrices and decision trees can facilitate implementing strategies effectively. An example of a matrix for segmenting the lawn fertilizer market is provided in Figure 8–2. Similar matrices could be developed for almost any market, product, or service. Market segmentation strategies in the high-tech arcade business in the United

FIGURE 8–2
Tools for Segmenting the Lawn Fertilizer Market

Heavy users	**High income**	Central city
		Suburban
		Rural
	Low income	Central city
		Suburban
		Rural
Light users	**High income**	Central city
		Suburban
		Rural
	Low income	Central city
		Suburban
		Rural
Nonusers	**High income**	Central city
		Suburban
		Rural
	Low income	Central city
		Suburban
		Rural

Source: Fred Winter, "Market Segmentation: A Tactical Approach," *Business Horizons* (January–February 1984): 60, 61.

States has resulted in dominance by three major firms: GameWorks, which relies on repeat business from local teens and young adults; Dave & Buster's, which attracts a slightly older crowd of local residents; and DisneyQuest, which focuses on families and tourists.

Segmentation is a key to matching supply and demand, which is one of the thorniest problems in customer service. Segmentation often reveals that large, random fluctuations in demand actually consist of several small, predictable, and manageable patterns. Matching supply and demand allows factories to produce desirable levels without extra shifts, overtime, and subcontracting. Matching supply and demand also minimizes the number and severity of stockouts. The demand for hotel rooms, for example, can be dependent on foreign tourists, businesspersons, and vacationers. Focusing on these three market segments separately, however, can allow hotel firms to predict overall supply and demand more effectively.

Banks now are segmenting markets to increase effectiveness. "You're dead in the water if you aren't segmenting the market," says Anne Moore, president of a bank consulting firm in Atlanta.

PRODUCT POSITIONING   After segmenting markets so that the firm can target particular customer groups, the next step is to find out what customers want and expect. This takes analysis and research. A severe mistake is to assume the firm knows what customers want and expect. Countless research studies reveal large differences between how customers define service and rank the importance of different service activities and how producers view services. Many firms have become successful by filling the gap between what customers and producers see as good service. What the customer believes is good service is paramount, not what the producer believes service should be.

Identifying target customers upon whom to focus marketing efforts sets the stage for deciding how to meet the needs and wants of particular consumer groups. Product positioning is widely used for this purpose. Positioning entails developing schematic representations that reflect how your products or services compare to competitors' on dimensions most important to success in the industry. The following steps are required in product positioning:

1. Select key criteria that effectively differentiate products or services in the industry.

2. Diagram a two-dimensional product positioning map with specified criteria on each axis.

3. Plot major competitors' products or services in the resultant four-quadrant matrix.

4. Identify areas in the positioning map where the company's products or services could be most competitive in the given target market. Look for vacant areas (niches).

5. Develop a marketing plan to position the company's products or services appropriately.

Because just two criteria can be examined on a single product positioning map, multiple maps are often developed to assess various approaches to strategy implementation. Multidimensional scaling could be used to examine three or more criteria simultaneously, but this technique requires computer assistance and is beyond the scope of this text. Some examples of product positioning maps are illustrated in Figure 8–3.

Some rules of thumb for using product positioning as a strategy-implementation tool are the following:

1. Look for the hole or *vacant niche*. The best strategic opportunity might be an unserved segment.

2. Don't squat between segments. Any advantage from squatting (such as a larger target market) is offset by a failure to satisfy one segment. In decision-theory terms, the intent here is to avoid suboptimization by trying to serve more than one objective function.

3. Don't serve two segments with the same strategy. Usually, a strategy successful with one segment cannot be directly transferred to another segment.

4. Don't position yourself in the middle of the map. The middle usually means a strategy that is not clearly perceived to have any distinguishing characteristics. This rule can vary with the number of competitors. For example, when there are only two competitors, as in U.S. presidential elections, the middle becomes the preferred strategic position.[2]

An effective product positioning strategy meets two criteria: (1) it uniquely distinguishes a company from the competition, and (2) it leads customers to expect slightly less service than a company can deliver. Firms should not create expectations that exceed the service the firm can or will deliver. Network Equipment Technology is an example of a company that keeps customer expectations slightly below perceived performance. This is a constant challenge for marketers. Firms need to inform customers about what to expect and then exceed the promise. Underpromise and then overdeliver!

FINANCE/ACCOUNTING ISSUES

In this section, we examine several finance/accounting concepts considered to be central to strategy implementation: acquiring needed capital, developing pro forma financial statements, preparing financial budgets, and evaluating the worth of a business. Some examples of decisions that may require finance/accounting policies are:

1. To raise capital with short-term debt, long-term debt, preferred stock, or common stock.

2. To lease or buy fixed assets.

FIGURE 8–3
Examples of Product Positioning Maps

A. **A PRODUCT POSITIONING MAP FOR BANKS**

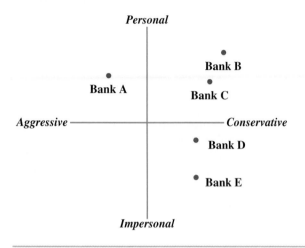

B. **A PRODUCT POSITIONING MAP FOR PERSONAL COMPUTERS**

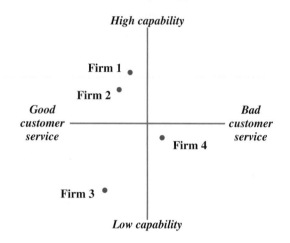

C. **A PRODUCT POSITIONING MAP FOR MENSWEAR RETAIL STORES**

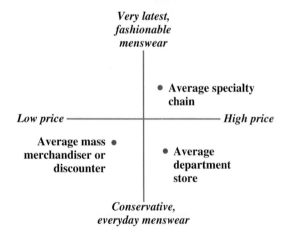

D. **A PRODUCT POSITIONING MAP FOR THE RENTAL CAR MARKET**

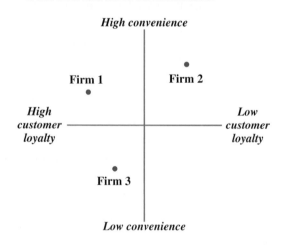

3. To determine an appropriate dividend payout ratio.
4. To use LIFO, FIFO, or a market-value accounting approach.
5. To extend the time of accounts receivable.
6. To establish a certain percentage discount on accounts within a specified period of time.
7. To determine the amount of cash that should be kept on hand.

ACQUIRING CAPITAL TO IMPLEMENT STRATEGIES Successful strategy implementation often requires additional capital. As indicated in the Global Perspective, countries and continents are like companies in that they actively strive to attract investment capital.

GLOBAL PERSPECTIVE

Which Areas of the World Attract the Most Foreign Capital (1996)?

As global competition for foreign investment dollars intensifies, China, Mexico, Indonesia, and Malaysia are winning while Russia, Hungary, Turkey, and Chile are losers. The following data (in billions of dollars) reveals regions and nations of the world that attracted the most capital investment dollars in 1996.

Source: Adapted from Urban Lehner, "Money Hungry," The Wall Street Journal (September 18, 1997): R4.

REGIONS			
East Asia/Pacific	$108.7	Indonesia	17.9
Latin America/Caribbean	74.3	Malaysia	16.0
Europe/Central Asia	31.2	Brazil	14.7
Sub-Saharan Africa	11.8	Thailand	13.3
South Asia	10.7	Argentina	11.3
Middle East/North Africa	6.9	India	8.0
		Turkey	4.7
NATIONS		Chile	4.6
China	$52.0	Russia	3.6
Mexico	28.1	Hungary	2.5

Besides net profit from operations and the sale of assets, two basic sources of capital for an organization are debt and equity. Determining an appropriate mix of debt and equity in a firm's capital structure can be vital to successful strategy implementation. An *Earnings Per Share/Earnings Before Interest and Taxes (EPS/EBIT) analysis* is the most widely used technique for determining whether debt, stock, or a combination of debt and stock is the best alternative for raising capital to implement strategies. This technique involves an examination of the impact that debt versus stock financing has on earnings per share under various assumptions as to EBIT.

Theoretically, an enterprise should have enough debt in its capital structure to boost its return on investment by applying debt to products and projects earning more than the cost of the debt. In low earning periods, too much debt in the capital structure of an organization can endanger stockholders' return and jeopardize company survival. Fixed debt obligations generally must be met, regardless of circumstances. This does not mean that stock issuances are always better than debt for raising capital. Some special concerns with stock issuances are dilution of ownership, effect on stock price, and the need to share future earnings with all new shareholders.

In the 1990s, interest rates were low, yet stock issuances remained very popular for the purpose of paying off corporate debt. Kmart is one firm that issued new stock worth over $1 billion to reduce its debt. Sony Corporation also raised nearly $3 billion by selling new shares of stock to reduce the company's debt. The lingerie maker Warnaco Group, which accounts for 30 percent of the women's bra market in the United States, recently sold 6 million shares to the public to reduce its debt.

Without going into detail on other institutional and legal issues related to the debt versus stock decision, EPS/EBIT may be best explained by working through an example. Let's say the Brown Company needs to raise $1 million to finance implementation of a market-development strategy. The company's common stock currently sells for $50 per share, and 100,000 shares are outstanding. The prime interest rate is 10 percent and the company's tax rate is 50 percent. The company's earnings before interest and taxes next year are expected to be $2 million if a recession occurs, $4 million if the economy stays as is, and $8 million if the economy significantly improves. EPS/EBIT analysis can be used to determine if all stock, all debt, or some combination of stock and debt is the best capital financing alternative. The EPS/EBIT analysis for this example is provided in Table 8–3.

As indicated by the EPS values of 9.5, 19.50, and 39.50 in Table 8–3, debt is the best financing alternative for the Brown Company if a recession, boom, or normal year is expected. An EPS/EBIT chart can be constructed to determine the break-even point, where one financing alternative becomes more attractive than another. Figure 8–4 indicates that issuing common stock is the least attractive financing alternative for the Brown Company.

EPS/EBIT analysis is a valuable tool for making capital financing decisions needed to implement strategies, but several considerations should be made whenever using this technique. First, profit levels may be higher for stock or debt alternatives when EPS levels are lower. For example, looking only at the earnings after taxes (EAT) values in Table 8–3, the common stock option is the best alternative, regardless of economic conditions. If the Brown Company's mission includes strict profit maximization, as opposed to the maximization of stockholders' wealth or some other criterion, then stock rather than debt is the best choice of financing.

Another consideration when using EPS/EBIT analysis is flexibility. As an organization's capital structure changes, so does its flexibility for considering future capital needs. Using all debt or all stock to raise capital in the present may impose fixed obligations, restrictive covenants, or other constraints that could severely reduce a firm's ability to raise additional capital in the future. Control is also a concern. When additional stock is issued to finance strategy implementation, ownership and control of the enterprise are diluted. This can be a serious concern in today's business environment of hostile takeovers, mergers, and acquisitions. Also, dilution of ownership can be an overriding concern in closely held corporations where stock issuances affect the decision-making power of majority stockholders. For example, the Smucker family owns 30 percent of the stock in Smucker's, a well-known jam and jelly company. When Smucker's acquired Dickson Family, Inc., the company used mostly debt rather than stock in order not to dilute the family ownership.

When using EPS/EBIT analysis, timing in relation to movements of stock prices, interest rates, and bond prices becomes important. In times of depressed stock prices, debt may prove to be the most suitable alternative from both a cost and a demand standpoint. However, when cost of capital (interest rates) is high, stock issuances become more attractive. In fact, even when interest rates are low, as in 1998, stock issuances can be very popular. The explosion of new mergers and acquisitions in the 1990s was fueled by equity at a time when stock prices were high. Using stock for acquisitions rather than debt enhances a

TABLE 8–3
EPS/EBIT Analysis for the Brown Company (in millions)

	COMMON STOCK FINANCING			DEBT FINANCING			COMBINATION FINANCING		
	RECESSION	**NORMAL**	**BOOM**	**RECESSION**	**NORMAL**	**BOOM**	**RECESSION**	**NORMAL**	**BOOM**
EBIT	$2.0	$ 4.0	$ 8.0	$2.0	$ 4.0	$ 8.0	$2.0	$ 4.0	$ 8.0
Interest[a]	0	0	0	.10	.10	.10	.05	.05	.05
EBT	2.0	4.0	8.0	1.9	3.9	7.9	1.95	3.95	7.95
Taxes	1.0	2.0	4.0	.95	1.95	3.95	.975	1.975	3.975
EAT	1.0	2.0	4.0	.95	1.95	3.95	.975	1.975	3.975
#Shares[b]	.12	.12	.12	.10	.10	.10	.11	.11	.11
EPS[c]	8.33	16.66	33.33	9.5	19.50	39.50	8.86	17.95	36.14

[a]The annual interest charge on $1 million at 10% is $100,000 and on $0.5 million is $50,000. This row is in $, not %.
[b]To raise all of the needed $1 million with stock, 20,000 new shares must be issued, raising the total to 120,000 shares outstanding. To raise one-half of the needed $1 million with stock, 10,000 new shares must be issued, raising the total to 110,000 shares outstanding.
[c]EPS = Earnings After Taxes (EAT) divided by shares (number of shares outstanding).

FIGURE 8–4

An EPS/EBIT Chart for the Brown Company

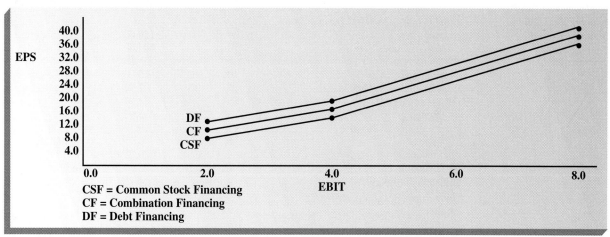

firm's reported earnings because, unlike debt acquirers, stock acquirers do not have to deduct goodwill from their earnings for years to come.

PRO FORMA FINANCIAL STATEMENTS *Pro forma (projected) financial statement analysis* is a central strategy-implementation technique because it allows an organization to examine the expected results of various actions and approaches. This type of analysis can be used to forecast the impact of various implementation decisions (for example, to increase promotion expenditures by 50 percent to support a market-development strategy, to increase salaries by 25 percent to support a market-penetration strategy, to increase research and development expenditures by 70 percent to support product development, or to sell $1 million of common stock to raise capital for diversification). Nearly all financial institutions require at least three years of projected financial statements whenever a business seeks capital. A pro forma income statement and balance sheet allow an organization to compute projected financial ratios under various strategy-implementation scenarios. When compared to prior years and to industry averages, financial ratios provide valuable insights into the feasibility of various strategy-implementation approaches.

A 1998 pro forma income statement and balance sheet for the Litten Company are provided in Table 8–4. The pro forma statements for Litten are based on five assumptions: (1) The company needs to raise $45 million to finance expansion into foreign markets; (2) $30 million of this total will be raised through increased debt and $15 million through common stock; (3) sales are expected to increase 50 percent; (4) three new facilities, costing a total of $30 million, will be constructed in foreign markets; and (5) land for the new facilities is already owned by the company. Note in Table 8–4 that Litten's strategies and their implementation are expected to result in a sales increase from $100 million to $150 million and in a net increase in income from $6 million to $9.75 million, in the forecasted year.

There are six steps in performing pro forma financial analysis:

1. Prepare the pro forma income statement before the balance sheet. Start by forecasting sales as accurately as possible.

2. Use the percentage-of-sales method to project cost of goods sold (CGS) and the expense items in the income statement. For example, if CGS is 70 percent of sales in the prior year (as it is in Table 8–4), then use that same percentage to calculate CGS in the future year—unless there is a reason to use a different

TABLE 8–4
A Pro Forma Income
Statement and Balance
Sheet for the Litten
Company (in millions)

	PRIOR YEAR 1998	PROJECTED YEAR 1999	REMARKS
PRO FORMA INCOME STATEMENT			
Sales	100	150.00	50% increase
Cost of Goods Sold	70	105.00	70% of sales
Gross Margin	30	45.00	
Selling Expense	10	15.00	10% of sales
Administrative Expense	5	7.50	5% of sales
Earnings Before Interest and Taxes	15	22.50	
Interest	3	3.00	
Earnings Before Taxes	12	19.50	
Taxes	6	9.75	50% rate
Net Income	6	9.75	
Dividends	2	5.00	
Retained Earnings	4	4.75	
PRO FORMA BALANCE SHEET			
Assets			
Cash	5	7.75	Plug figure
Accounts Receivable	2	4.00	Incr. 100%
Inventory	20	45.00	
Total Current Assets	27	56.75	
Land	15	15.00	
Plant and Equipment	50	80.00	Add 3 new plants at $10 million each
Less Depreciation	10	20.00	
Net Plant and Equipment	40	60.00	
Total Fixed Assets	55	75.00	
Total Assets	82	131.75	
Liabilities			
Accounts Payable	10	10.00	
Notes Payable	10	10.00	
Total Current Liabilities	20	20.00	
Long-term Debt	40	70.00	Borrowed $30 million
Additional Paid-in Capital	20	35.00	Issued 100,000 shares at $150 each
Retained Earnings	2	6.75	2 + 4.75
Total Liabilities and Net Worth	82	131.75	

percentage. Items such as interest, dividends, and taxes must be treated independently and cannot be forecasted using the percentage-of-sales method.

3. Calculate the projected net income.

4. Subtract from the net income any dividends to be paid and add the remaining net income to Retained Earnings. Reflect the Retained Earnings total on both the income statement and balance sheet because this item is the key link between the two projected statements.

5. Project the balance sheet items, beginning with retained earnings and then forecasting stockholders' equity, long-term liabilities, current liabilities, total liabilities, total assets, fixed assets, and current assets (in that order). Use the cash account as the plug figure; that is, use the cash account to make the assets total the liabilities and net worth. Then, make appropriate adjustments. For example, if the cash needed to balance the statements is too small (or too large), make appropriate changes to borrow more (or less) money than planned.

6. List comments (remarks) on the projected statements. Any time a significant change is made in an item from a prior year to the projected year, an explanation (remark) should be provided. Remarks are essential because otherwise pro formas are meaningless.

FINANCIAL BUDGETS   A *financial budget* is a document that details how funds will be obtained and spent for a specified period of time. Annual budgets are most common, although the period of time for a budget can range from one day to more than 10 years. Fundamentally, financial budgeting is a method for specifying what must be done to complete strategy implementation successfully. Financial budgeting should not be thought of as a tool for limiting expenditures but rather as a method for obtaining the most productive and profitable use of an organization's resources. Financial budgets can be viewed as the planned allocation of a firm's resources based on forecasts of the future.

There are almost as many different types of financial budgets as there are types of organizations. Some common types of budgets include cash budgets, operating budgets, sales budgets, profit budgets, factory budgets, capital budgets, expense budgets, divisional budgets, variable budgets, flexible budgets, and fixed budgets. When an organization is experiencing financial difficulties, budgets are especially important in guiding strategy implementation.

Perhaps the most common type of financial budget is the *cash budget*. The Financial Accounting Standards Board has mandated that every publicly held company in the United States must issue an annual cash-flow statement in addition to the usual financial reports. The statement includes all receipts and disbursements of cash in operations, investments, and financing. It supplements the Statement on Changes in Financial Position formerly included in the annual reports of all publicly held companies. A cash budget for the year 2000 for the Toddler Toy Company is provided in Table 8–5. Note that Toddler is not expecting to have surplus cash until November of 2000.

Financial budgets have some limitations. First, budgetary programs can become so detailed that they are cumbersome and overly expensive. Overbudgeting or underbudgeting can cause problems. Second, financial budgets can become a substitute for objectives.

TABLE 8–5
A Six-Month Cash Budget for the Toddler Toy Company in 2000

CASH BUDGET (IN THOUSANDS)	JULY	AUG	SEPT.	OCT.	NOV.	DEC.	JAN.
Receipts							
Collections	$12,000	$21,000	$31,000	$35,000	$22,000	$18,000	$11,000
Payments							
Purchases	14,000	21,000	28,000	14,000	14,000	7,000	
Wages and Salaries	1,500	2,000	2,500	1,500	1,500	1,000	
Rent	500	500	500	500	500	500	
Other Expenses	200	300	400	200	200	100	
Taxes	–	8,000	–	–	–	–	
Payment on Machine	–	–	10,000	–	–	–	
Total Payments	$16,200	$31,800	$41,400	$16,200	$16,200	$ 8,600	
Net Cash Gain (Loss) During Month	–4,200	–10,800	–10,400	18,800	5,800	9,400	
Cash at Start of Month If No							
Borrowing Is Done	6,000	1,800	–9,000	–19,400	–600	5,200	
Cumulative Cash (Cash at start plus							
gains or minus losses)	1,800	–9,000	–19,400	–600	5,200	14,600	
Less Desired Level of Cash	–5,000	–5,000	–5,000	–5,000	–5,000	–5,000	
Total Loans Outstanding to							
Maintain $5,000 Cash Balance	$3,200	$14,000	$24,400	$ 5,600	–	–	
Surplus Cash	–	–	–	–	$ 200	$ 9,600	

A budget is a tool and not an end in itself. Third, budgets can hide inefficiencies if based solely on precedent rather than periodic evaluation of circumstances and standards. Finally, budgets are sometimes used as instruments of tyranny that result in frustration, resentment, absenteeism, and high turnover. To minimize the effect of this last concern, managers should increase the participation of subordinates in preparing budgets.

EVALUATING THE WORTH OF A BUSINESS   Evaluating the worth of a business is central to strategy implementation because integrative, intensive, and diversification strategies are often implemented by acquiring other firms. Other strategies, such as retrenchment and divestiture, may result in the sale of a division of an organization or of the firm itself. Approximately 20,000 transactions occur each year in which businesses are bought or sold in the United States. In all these cases, it is necessary to establish the financial worth or cash value of a business to successfully implement strategies.

All the various methods for determining a business's worth can be grouped into three main approaches: what a firm owns, what a firm earns, or what a firm will bring in the market. But it is important to realize that valuation is not an exact science. The valuation of a firm's worth is based on financial facts, but common sense and intuitive judgment must enter into the process. It is difficult to assign a monetary value to factors—such as a loyal customer base, a history of growth, legal suits pending, dedicated employees, a favorable lease, a bad credit rating, or good patents—that may not be reflected in a firm's financial statements. Also, different valuation methods will yield different totals for a firm's worth, and no prescribed approach is best for a certain situation. Evaluating the worth of a business truly requires both qualitative and quantitative skills.

The first approach in evaluating the worth of a business is determining its net worth or stockholders' equity. Net worth represents the sum of common stock, additional paid-in capital, and retained earnings. After calculating net worth, add or subtract an appropriate amount for goodwill (such as high customer loyalty) and overvalued or undervalued assets. This total provides a reasonable estimate of a firm's monetary value. If a firm has goodwill, it will be listed on the balance sheet, perhaps as "intangibles."

The second approach to measuring the value of a firm grows out of the belief that the worth of any business should be based largely on the future benefits its owners may derive through net profits. A conservative rule of thumb is to establish a business's worth as five times the firm's current annual profit. A five-year average profit level could also be used. When using this approach, remember that firms normally suppress earnings in their financial statements to minimize taxes.

The third approach, letting the market determine a business's worth, involves three methods. First, base the firm's worth on the selling price of a similar company. A potential problem, however, is that sometimes comparable figures are not easy to locate, even though substantial information on firms that buy or sell to other firms is available in major libraries. The second approach is called the *price-earnings ratio method.* To use this method, divide the market price of the firm's common stock by the annual earnings per share and multiply this number by the firm's average net income for the past five years. The third approach can be called the *outstanding shares method.* To use this method, simply multiply the number of shares outstanding by the market price per share and add a premium. The premium is simply a per share dollar amount that a person or firm is willing to pay to control (acquire) the other company.

Business evaluations are becoming routine in many situations. Businesses have many strategy-implementation reasons for determining their worth in addition to preparing to be sold or to buy other companies. Employee plans, taxes, retirement, mergers, acquisitions, expansion plans, banking relationships, death of a principal, divorce, partnership agreements, and IRS audits are other reasons for a periodic valuation. It is just good business to have a reasonable understanding of what your firm is worth. This knowledge protects the interests of all parties involved.

DECIDING WHETHER TO GO PUBLIC   Going public means selling off a percentage of your company to others in order to raise capital; consequently, it dilutes the owners' control of the firm. Going public is not recommended for companies with less than $10 million in sales because the initial costs can be too high for the firm to generate sufficient cash flow to make going public worthwhile. One dollar in four is the average total cost paid to lawyers, accountants, and underwriters when an initial stock issuance is under $1 million; one dollar in 20 will go to cover these costs for issuances over $20 million.

In addition to initial costs involved with a stock offering, there are costs and obligations associated with reporting and management in a publicly held firm. For firms with more than $10 million in sales, going public can provide major advantages: It can allow the firm to raise capital to develop new products, build plants, expand, grow, and market products and services more effectively.

Before going public, a firm must have quality management with a proven track record for achieving quality earnings and positive cash flow. The company also should enjoy growing demand for its products. Sales growth of about 5 or 6 percent a year is good for a private firm, but shareholders expect public companies to grow around 10 to 15 percent per year.

RESEARCH AND DEVELOPMENT (R&D) ISSUES

Research and development (R&D) personnel can play an integral part in strategy implementation. These individuals are generally charged with developing new products and improving old products in a way that will allow effective strategy implementation. R&D employees and managers perform tasks that include transferring complex technology, adjusting processes to local raw materials, adapting processes to local markets, and altering products to particular tastes and specifications. Strategies such as product development, market penetration, and concentric diversification require that new products be successfully developed and that old products be significantly improved. But the level of management support for R&D is often constrained by resource availability:

> If U.S. business is to maintain its position in the global business environment, then R&D support will have to become a major U.S. commitment. U.S. managers cannot continue to ignore it or take funds away from it for short-term profits and still have long-term strategic options. If one runs away from more aggressive product and process strategies, one should not be surprised by the fact that competitive advantages are lost to foreign competitors.[3]

Technological improvements that affect consumer and industrial products and services shorten product life cycles. Companies in virtually every industry are relying on the development of new products and services to fuel profitability and growth. Table 8–6 provides a breakdown of R&D expenditures in 1996 for the 10 American companies that spent the most on R&D. American companies in 1997 spent about $192 billion on R&D, a 4.3 percent increase from the $184 billion in 1996. Many companies are spending much more on R&D than the average. For example, Microsoft spent 300 percent more on R&D in 1997 than in 1996 in its effort to reinvent and enhance the personal computer experience. Daniel Ling of Microsoft says, "Transferring technology into development is always a challenge, always difficult, and always requires a lot of work."

Surveys suggest that the most successful organizations use an R&D strategy that ties external opportunities to internal strength and is linked with objectives. Well-formulated

TABLE 8–6
**Ranking the Top 10
American Companies in
R&D Spending in 1996**

	COMPANY	IN TOTAL DOLLARS (MILLIONS)	INCREASE (DECREASE) FROM PRIOR YEAR	R&D/ SALES
1.	General Motors	$8,900	8.5%	5.6%
2.	Ford Motor	6,821	3.0	4.6
3.	IBM	3,934	16.2	5.2
4.	Hewlett-Packard	2,718	18.1	7.1
5.	Motorola	2,394	9.0	8.6
6.	Lucent Technologies	2,056	(23.7)	13.0
7.	TRW	1,981	5.3	20.1
8.	Johnson & Johnson	1,905	16.6	8.8
9.	Intel	1,808	39.5	8.7
10.	Pfizer	1,684	16.8	14.9

R&D policies match market opportunities with internal capabilities and provide an initial screen to all ideas generated. R&D policies can enhance strategy-implementation efforts to:

1. Emphasize product or process improvements.
2. Stress basic or applied research.
3. Be leaders or followers in R&D.
4. Develop robotics or manual-type processes.
5. Spend a high, average, or low amount of money on R&D.
6. Perform R&D within the firm or to contract R&D to outside firms.
7. Use university researchers or private sector researchers.

There must be effective interactions between R&D departments and other functional departments in implementing different types of generic business strategies. Conflicts between marketing, finance/accounting, R&D, and information systems departments can be minimized with clear policies and objectives. Table 8–7 gives some examples of R&D activities that could be required for successful implementation of various strategies.

Many firms wrestle with the decision to acquire R&D expertise from external firms or to develop R&D expertise internally. The following guidelines can be used to help make this decision:

1. If the rate of technical progress is slow, the rate of market growth is moderate, and there are significant barriers to possible new entrants, then in-house R&D is the preferred solution. The reason is that R&D, if successful, will result in a temporary product or process monopoly that the company can exploit.

2. If technology is changing rapidly and the market is growing slowly, then a major effort in R&D may be very risky, because it may lead to development of an ultimately obsolete technology or one for which there is no market.

3. If technology is changing slowly but the market is growing fast, there generally is not enough time for in-house development. The prescribed approach is to obtain R&D expertise on an exclusive or nonexclusive basis from an outside firm.

4. If both technical progress and market growth are fast, R&D expertise should be obtained through acquisition of a well-established firm in the industry.[4]

There are at least three major R&D approaches for implementing strategies. The first strategy is to be the first firm to market new technological products. This is a glamorous and exciting strategy but also a dangerous one. Firms such as 3M, Polaroid, and General Electric have been successful with this approach, but many other pioneering firms have

TABLE 8–7

Research and Development Involvement in Selected Strategy-Implementation Situations

TYPE OF ORGANIZATION	STRATEGY BEING IMPLEMENTED	R&D ACTIVITY
Pharmaceutical company	Product development	Develop a procedure for testing the effects of a new drug on different subgroups.
Boat manufacturer	Concentric diversification	Develop a procedure to test the performance of various keel designs under various conditions.
Plastic container manufacturer	Market penetration	Develop a biodegradable container.
Electronics company	Market development	Develop a telecommunications system in a foreign country.

fallen, with rival firms seizing the initiative. Two firms also using this first R&D strategy are Global Ozone Solutions and American Thermalfo; these firms manufacture machines that extract ozone-depleting chlorofluorocarbons, or CFCs, from the air. As indicated in the Natural Environment Perspective, equipment like this is needed in Southeast Asia.

A second R&D approach is to be an innovative imitator of successful products, thus minimizing the risks and costs of start-up. This approach entails allowing a pioneer firm to develop the first version of the new product and to demonstrate that a market exists. Then, laggard firms develop a similar product. This strategy requires excellent R&D personnel and an excellent marketing department.

A third R&D strategy is to be a low-cost producer by mass-producing products similar to but less expensive than products recently introduced. Far Eastern countries used this approach effectively during the 1980s to crush the $8 billion U.S. consumer electronics industry. As a new product is accepted by customers, price becomes increasingly important in the buying decision. Also, mass marketing replaces personal selling as the dominant selling strategy. This R&D strategy requires substantial investment in plant and equipment, but fewer expenditures in R&D than the two approaches described earlier.

NATURAL ENVIRONMENT

Do Smoke and Smog Still Cover Southeast Asia?

During the latter months of 1997, smoke and smog from forest fires and industrial polluters covered most of Indonesia, Malaysia, and the Philippines. The real cause of this problem is politics. Indonesia, for example, is a country run like an empire, by soldiers and civil servants dispatched throughout its 13,000 islands from the main island of Java. Their job is to keep peace while providing basic services, but at the same time facilitating exploitation of Indonesia's enormous natural resources. Over recent years, the capital of Jakarta has funded huge expansion of plantation output of timber, palm oil, and rubber. Direct costs to burn these areas are far lower than

other methods of clearing land so widespread burning is common. Indonesia's environmental ministry says its budget is too small to police fire setting.

Lack of concern for polluting the natural environmental in Southeast Asia and resultant smoke and fog have caused numerous airplane crashes, ship collisions, and medical emergencies. Whole cities of people walk around with breathing masks. Passenger airliners have crashed. Pollution is a reason often given for the falling value of Southeast Asian currencies. As shown, during the second half of 1997, Asian currencies fell against the U.S. dollar:

Thailand (baht)	35%
Indonesia (rupiah)	23
Malaysia (ringgit)	17
Philippines (peso)	15
Japan (yen)	6
Singapore (dollar)	6

Source: Adapted from Peter Waldman, "Southeast Asian Smog Is Tied to Politics," The Wall Street Journal (September 30, 1997): A10. Also, James Cox, "Asian Currencies and Stock Markets Continue Fall," USA Today (September 2, 1997): 10A.

R&D activities among American firms need to be more closely aligned to business objectives. There needs to be expanded communication between R&D managers and strategists. Corporations are experimenting with various methods to achieve this improved communication climate, including different roles and reporting arrangements for managers and new methods to reduce the time it takes research ideas to become reality.[5]

Perhaps the most current trend in R&D management has been lifting the veil of secrecy whereby firms, even major competitors, are joining forces to develop new products. Collaboration is on the rise due to new competitive pressures, rising research costs, increasing regulatory issues, and accelerated product development schedules. Companies not only are working more closely with each other on R&D, but they are also turning to consortia at universities for their R&D needs. More than 600 research consortia are now in operation in the United States. Lifting of R&D secrecy among many firms through collaboration has allowed marketing of new technologies and products even before they were available for sale.

COMPUTER INFORMATION SYSTEMS (CIS) ISSUES

Although no firm would use the same marketing or management approach for 20 years, many companies have 20-year-old *computer information systems* that threaten their very existence. Developing new user applications often takes a backseat to keeping an old system running. Countless firms still do not use the Internet. This unfortunate situation is happening at a time when the quantity and quality of information available to firms and their competitors is increasing exponentially.

Firms that gather, assimilate, and evaluate external and internal information most effectively are gaining competitive advantages over other firms. Recognizing the importance of having an effective computer information system will not be an option in the future; it will be a requirement. Information is the basis for understanding in a firm. Robert Kavner, president of AT&T Data Systems Group, says, "Modern corporations are organizing around information flow. With the growth of communications networks such as the Internet, the barriers of time and place have been breached. By mirroring people's work needs and habits, networked computing systems have made new modes of work possible."

It is estimated that the quantity of human knowledge is doubling every decade. In many industries, information is becoming the most important factor differentiating successful and unsuccessful firms. The process of strategic management is facilitated immensely in firms that have an effective information system. Many companies are establishing a new approach to information systems, one that blends the technical knowledge of the computer experts with the vision of senior management. Some guidelines that allow computer information systems to enhance strategy implementation are as follows:

1. Computer hardware and software should facilitate global information consistency.
2. All component parts should be accessible through a common order-processing system.
3. All divisions should be self-sufficient yet compatible in their information systems capabilities.
4. A basic purpose of information systems is to support cross-functional integration of the business functions.
5. Integration of voice and data communications is a goal of information systems.

INFORMATION TECHNOLOGY

How Harmful Are Hackers?

The Gap, Playboy Enterprises, Hitachi America, PeopleSoft, and Twentieth Century Fox average over 30 computer intrusion attempts daily. Thousands of companies today are plagued by computer hackers who include disgruntled employees, competitors, bored teens, sociopaths, thieves, spies, and hired agents. Computer vulnerability is a giant, expensive headache. Over 40 percent of U.S. corporations reported severe computer break-ins in 1996 and spent over $6 billion that year to safeguard their computers. These firms lost more than $10 billion due to computer hackers.

The FBI reports that 95 percent of computer break-ins go undetected and fewer than 15 percent are reported to law enforcement agencies. The FBI's senior expert on computer crime, Dennis Hughes, says "Hackers are driving us nuts. Everyone is getting hacked into. It's out of control." Hackers can download computer break-in programs free off the Internet, and hacker magazines provide easy, step-by-step tips. Hackers can read a computer screen from over a mile away, can intercept all passwords and e-mail messages, steal trade secrets and patents, and read all confidential messages such as bids on projects and new strategy initiatives.

To minimize the hacker threat, companies today must purchase expensive encryption software to scramble the traffic that flows through their computer networks; companies much teach all employees to be security-conscious; companies must construct several, not just one, complex computer firewalls to deter hackers. Hacker technology is getting exotic and developing faster than safeguards. Companies naive to the computer hacker threat are grossly negligent and vulnerable.

Even the U.S. federal government is becoming more worried about cyberterror. Research costs on cyberspace security related to the federal government are expected to reach $1 billion per year by 2004. Thomas Marsh, chair of President Clinton's Commission on Critical Infrastructure Protection, says, "Vulnerability is serious and increasing." Former senator Sam Nunn, also on the commission, says, "The only issue of equal or greater concern today is nuclear, chemical, or biological weapon proliferation."

Source: Adapted from Richard Behar, "Who's Reading Your E-Mail?" Fortune (February 3, 1997): 57–70. Also, M.J. Zuckerman, "Clinton to Get Cyberterror Plan," USA Today (October 9, 1997): 1A.

6. Data and information obtained within the firm should be available to any department or person in the firm who can demonstrate a need for it, except for reasons of security or integrity of the database.

7. Information systems design should stress effectiveness in the business environment rather than efficiency in the technical environment.[6]

Information collection, retrieval, and storage can be used to create competitive advantages in ways such as cross-selling to customers, monitoring suppliers, keeping managers and employees informed, coordinating activities among divisions, and managing funds. Like inventory and human resources, information is becoming recognized as a valuable organizational asset that can be controlled and managed. Firms that implement strategies using the best information will reap competitive advantages in the 1990s. John Young, president and CEO of Hewlett-Packard, says, "There really isn't any right amount to spend on information systems. Many management teams spend too much time thinking about how to beat down the information system's cost, instead of thinking about how to get more value out of the information they could have available and how to link that to strategic goals of the company."

A good information system can allow a firm to reduce costs. For example, on-line orders from salespersons to production facilities can shorten materials ordering time and reduce inventory costs. Direct communications between suppliers, manufacturers, marketers, and customers can link elements of the value chain together as though they were one organization. Improved quality and service often result from an improved information system.

As indicated in the Information Technology Perspective, firms must increasingly be concerned about computer hackers and take specific measures to secure and safeguard corporate communications, files, orders, and business conducted over the Internet.

Dun & Bradstreet is an example of a company that has an excellent information system. Every D & B customer and client in the world has a separate nine-digit number. The database of information associated with each number has become so widely used that it is like a business social security number. D & B reaps great competitive advantages from its information system.

CONCLUSION

Successful strategy implementation depends upon cooperation among all functional and divisional managers in an organization. Marketing departments are commonly charged with implementing strategies that require significant increases in sales revenues in new areas and with new or improved products. Finance and accounting managers must devise effective strategy-implementation approaches at low cost and minimum risk to that firm. R&D managers have to transfer complex technologies or develop new technologies to successfully implement strategies. Information systems managers are being called upon more and more to provide leadership and training for all individuals in the firm. The nature and role of marketing, finance/accounting, R&D, and computer information systems activities, coupled with management activities described in Chapter 7, largely determine organizational success.

TAKE IT TO THE NET   We invite you to visit the DAVID page on the Prentice Hall Web site at **www.prenhall.com/davidsm** for this chapter's World Wide Web exercises.

KEY TERMS AND CONCEPTS

Cash Budget	(p. 263)	Marketing Mix Variables	(p. 254)	Product Positioning	(p. 252)
Computer Information Systems	(p. 268)	Outstanding Shares Method	(p. 264)	Research and Development	(p. 265)
EPS/EBIT Analysis	(p. 259)	Price-Earnings Ratio Method	(p. 264)	Vacant Niche	(p. 257)
Financial Budget	(p. 263)	Pro Forma Financial Statement	(p. 261)		
Market Segmentation	(p. 252)	Analysis			

ISSUES FOR REVIEW AND DISCUSSION

1. Suppose your company has just acquired a firm that produces battery-operated lawn mowers, and strategists want to implement a market-penetration strategy. How would you segment the market for this product? Justify your answer.

2. Explain how you would estimate the total worth of a business.

3. Diagram and label clearly a product positioning map that includes six fast-food restaurant chains.

4. Explain why EPS/EBIT analysis is a central strategy-implementation technique.

5. How would the R&D role in strategy implementation differ in small versus large organizations?

6. Discuss the limitations of EPS/EBIT analysis.

7. Explain how marketing, finance/accounting, R&D, and computer information systems managers' involvement in strategy formulation can enhance strategy implementation.

8. Consider the following statement: "Retained earnings on the balance sheet are not monies available to finance strategy implementation." It is true or false? Explain.

9. Explain why pro forma financial statement analysis is considered both a strategy-formulation and a strategy-implementation tool.

10. Describe some marketing, finance/accounting, R&D, and computer information systems activities that a small

restaurant chain might undertake to expand into a neighboring state.

11. Select one of the suggested readings at the end of this chapter, find that article in your college library, and summarize it in a five-minute oral report for the class.

12. Discuss the computer information systems at your college or university.

NOTES

1. Fred Winter, "Market Segmentation: A Tactical Approach," *Business Horizons* 27, no. 1 (January–February 1984): 59.

2. Ralph Biggadike, "The Contributions of Marketing to Strategic Management," *Academy of Management Review* 6, no. 4 (October 1981): 627.

3. Vida Scarpello, William Boulton, and Charles Hofer, "Reintegrating R&D into Business Strategy," *Journal of Business Strategy* 6, no. 4 (Spring 1986): 55.

4. Pier Abetti, "Technology: A Key Strategic Resource," *Management Review* 78, no. 2 (February 1989): 38.

5. William Spencer and Deborah Triant, "Strengthening the Link Between R&D and Corporate Strategy," *Journal of Business Strategy* 10, no. 1 (January/February 1989): 42.

6. Thomas Davenport, Michael Hammer, and Tauno Metsisto, "How Executives Can Shape Their Company's Information Systems," *Harvard Business Review* 67, no. 2 (March–April 1989): 131.

CURRENT READINGS

Argyres, N. "Capabilites, Technological Diversification and Divisionalization." *Strategic Management Journal* 17, no. 5 (May 1996): 395–410.

Berthon, Pierre, Leyland Pitt, and Richard T. Watson. "Marketing Communication and the World Wide Web." *Business Horizons* 39, no. 5 (September-October 1996): 24–32.

Datta, Y. "Market Segmentation: An Integrated Framework." *Long Range Planning* 29 no. 6 (December 1996): 797–811.

Hattan, Mary Louise and Kenneth J. Hatten. "Information Systems Strategy: Long Overdue—and Still Not Here." *Long Range Planning* 30, no. 2 (April 1997): 254–266.

Kochhar, R. "Explaining Firm Capital Structure: The Role of Agency Theory vs. Transaction Cost Economics." *Strategic Management Journal* 17, no. 9 (November 1996): 713–728.

Kuemmerle, Walter. "Building Effective R&D Capabilities Abroad." *Harvard Business Review* (March–April 1997): 61–72.

Lawler, John J. and Robin Elliot. "Artificial Intelligence in HRM: An Experimental Study of an Expert System." *Journal of Management* 22, no. 1 (1996): 85–112.

Mentzas, Gregory. "Implementing an IS Strategy—A Team Approach." *Long Range Planning* 30, no. 1 (February 1997): 84–95.

Sakakibara, M. "Heterogeneity of Firm Capabilities and Cooperative Research and Development: An Empirical Examiniation of Motives." *Strategic Management Journal* 18, Special Issue (Summer 1997): 143–164.

Segars, Albert H. and Varun Grover. "Designing Companywide Information Systems: Risk Factors and Coping Strategies." *Long Range Planning* 29, no. 3 (June 1996): 381–392.

Shanklin, William L. and David A. Griffith. "Crafting Strategies for Global Marketing in the New Millennium." *Business Horizons* 39, no. 5 (September–October 1996): 11–16.

Stone, Merlin, Neil Woodcock, and Muriel Wilson. "Managing the Change from Marketing Planning to Customer Relationship Management." *Long Range Planning* 29, no. 5 (October 1996): 675–683.

Tufano, Peter. "How Financial Engineering Can Advance Corporate Strategy." *Harvard Business Review* (January–February 1996): 136–146.

Venkatraman, N. "Beyond Outsourcing: Managing IT Resources as a Value Center." *Sloan Management Review* 38, no. 3 (Spring 1997): 51–64.

Wright, P. and S.P. Ferris. "Agency Conflict and Corporate Strategy: The Effect of Divestment on Corporate Value." *Strategic Management Journal* 18, no. 1 (January 1997): 77–87.

EXPERIENTIAL EXERCISES

DEVELOPING A PRODUCT POSITIONING MAP FOR HERSHEY FOODS

PURPOSE

Organizations continually monitor how their products and services are positioned relative to competitors. This information is especially useful for marketing managers, but is also used by other managers and strategists.

INSTRUCTIONS

Step 1 On a separate sheet of paper, develop a product positioning map for Hershey. Include Nestlé, Mars, and Hershey in your map.

Step 2 Go to the blackboard and diagram your product positioning map.

Step 3 Compare your product positioning map with those diagrammed by other students. Discuss any major differences.

PERFORMING AN EPS/EBIT ANALYSIS FOR HERSHEY FOODS

PURPOSE

An EPS/EBIT analysis is one of the most widely used techniques for determining the extent that debt and/or stock should be used to finance strategies to be implemented. This exercise can give you practice performing EPS/EBIT analysis.

INSTRUCTIONS

Let's say Hershey needs to raise $2 billion to introduce Hershey products in 20 new countries around the world in 1999. Determine whether Hershey should have used all debt, all stock, or a 50-50 combination of debt and stock to finance this market-development strategy. Assume a 39 percent tax rate and a 16 percent interest rate. Hershey's stock price is $70 per share. Hershey pays an annual dividend of $0.84 per share of common stock. The EBIT range for 1999 is between $300 and $500 million. A total of 149 million shares of common stock are outstanding. Develop an EPS/EBIT chart to reflect your analysis.

PREPARING PRO FORMA FINANCIAL STATEMENTS FOR HERSHEY FOODS

PURPOSE

This exercise is designed to give you experience preparing pro forma financial statements. Pro forma analysis is a central strategy-implementation technique because it allows managers to anticipate and evaluate the expected results of various strategy-implementation approaches.

INSTRUCTIONS

Step 1 Work with a classmate. Develop a 1998 pro forma income statement and balance sheet for Hershey. Assume that Hershey plans to raise $100 million in 1998 to introduce Hershey products in 20 new countries and plans to obtain 50 percent financing from a bank and 50 percent financing from a stock issuance. Make other assumptions as needed, and state them clearly in written form.

Step 2 Compute Hershey's current ratio, debt-to-equity ratio, and return-on-investment ratio for 1995, 1996, and 1997. How do your 1998 projected ratios compare to the 1996 and 1997 ratios? Why is it important to make this comparison?

Step 3 Bring your pro forma statements to class and discuss any problems or questions you encountered.

Step 4 Compare your pro forma statements to the statements of other students. What major differences exist between your analysis and the work of other students?

DETERMINING THE CASH VALUE OF HERSHEY FOODS

PURPOSE

It is simply good business practice to periodically determine the financial worth or cash value of your company. This exercise gives you practice determining the total worth of a company using several methods. Use 1997 as the sample year.

INSTRUCTIONS

Step 1 Calculate the financial worth of Hershey based on three methods: (1) the net worth or stockholders' equity, (2) the future value of Hershey's earnings, and (3) the price-earnings ratio.

Step 2 In a dollar amount, how much is Hershey worth?

Step 3 Compare your analyses and conclusions with those of other students.

Experiential Exercise 8E

DEVELOPING A PRODUCT POSITIONING MAP FOR MY UNIVERSITY

PURPOSE

The purpose of this exercise is to give you practice developing product positioning maps. Nonprofit organizations, such as universities, increasingly are using product positioning maps to determine effective ways to implement strategies.

INSTRUCTIONS

Step 1 Join with two other persons in class to form a group of three.

Step 2 Jointly prepare a product positioning map that includes your institution and four other colleges or universities in your state.

Step 3 Go to the blackboard and diagram your product positioning map.

Step 4 Discuss differences among the maps diagrammed on the board.

DO BANKS REQUIRE PRO FORMA STATEMENTS?

PURPOSE

The purpose of this exercise is to explore the practical importance and use of projected financial statements in the banking business.

INSTRUCTIONS

Contact two local bankers by phone and seek answers to the questions listed below. Record the answers you receive and report your findings to the class.

1. Does your bank require projected financial statements as part of a business loan application?

2. How does your bank use projected financial statements when they are part of a business loan application?

3. What special advice do you give potential business borrowers in preparing projected financial statements?

PART 4

STRATEGY
EVALUATION

CHAPTER 9

Strategy Review, Evaluation, and Control

CHAPTER OUTLINE

◆ THE NATURE OF STRATEGY
EVALUATION

◆ A STRATEGY-EVALUATION
FRAMEWORK

◆ PUBLISHED SOURCES OF
STRATEGY-EVALUATION
INFORMATION

◆ CHARACTERISTICS OF AN
EFFECTIVE EVALUATION SYSTEM

◆ CONTINGENCY PLANNING

◆ AUDITING

◆ USING COMPUTERS TO EVALUATE
STRATEGIES

◆ GUIDELINES FOR EFFECTIVE
STRATEGIC MANAGEMENT

■ EXPERIENTIAL EXERCISE 9A
Preparing a Strategy-Evaluation Report for
Hershey Foods

■ EXPERIENTIAL EXERCISE 9B
Evaluating My University's Strategies

■ EXPERIENTIAL EXERCISE 9C
Who Prepares an Environmental Audit?

CHAPTER OBJECTIVES

After studying this chapter, you should be able to do the following:

1. Describe a practical framework for evaluating
strategies.

2. Explain why strategy evaluation is complex, sensitive, and yet essential for organizational success.

3. Discuss the importance of contingency planning
in strategy evaluation.

4. Discuss the role of auditing in strategy evaluation.

5. Explain how computers can aid in evaluating
strategies.

*C*omplicated controls do not work. They confuse. They misdirect attention from what is to be controlled to the mechanics and methodology of the control.—SEYMOUR TILLES

*S*trategic thinking lives through dialogue or dies through writer's cramp.—DAVID MOORE

*A*lthough Plan A may be selected as the most realistic . . . the other major alternatives should not be forgotten. They may well serve as contingency plans.—DALE MCCONKEY

*O*rganizations are most vulnerable when they are at the peak of their success.—R. T. LENZ

*A*s spans of control widen, computers will become even more necessary.—BRIAN DUMAINE

*S*trategy evaluation must make it as easy as possible for managers to revise their plans and reach quick agreement on the changes.—DALE MCCONKEY

*W*hile strategy is a word that is usually associated with the future, its link to the past is no less central. Life is lived forward but understood backward. Managers may live strategy in the future, but they understand it through the past.—HENRY MINTZBERG

*U*nless strategy evaluation is performed seriously and systematically, and unless strategists are willing to act on the results, energy will be used up defending yesterday. No one will have the time, resources, or will to work on exploiting today, let alone to work on making tomorrow.—PETER DRUCKER

I have a duty to the soldiers, their parents, and the country to remove immediately any commander who does not satisfy the highest performance demands. It is a mistake to put a person in a command that is not the right command. It is therefore my job to think through where that person belongs.
—GEORGE C. MARSHALL

The best-formulated and -implemented strategies become obsolete as a firm's external and internal environments change. It is essential, therefore, that strategists systematically review, evaluate, and control the execution of strategies. This chapter presents a framework that can guide managers' efforts to evaluate strategic-management activities, to make sure they are working, and to make timely changes. Computer information systems being used to evaluate strategies are discussed. Guidelines are presented for formulating, implementing, and evaluating strategies.

THE NATURE OF STRATEGY EVALUATION

The strategic-management process results in decisions that can have significant, long-lasting consequences. Erroneous strategic decisions can inflict severe penalties and can be exceedingly difficult, if not impossible, to reverse. Most strategists agree, therefore, that strategy evaluation is vital to an organization's well-being; timely evaluations can alert management to problems or potential problems before a situation becomes critical. Strategy evaluation includes three basic activities: (1) examining the underlying bases of a firm's strategy, (2) comparing expected results with actual results, and (3) taking corrective actions to ensure that performance conforms to plans. The strategy-evaluation stage of the strategic-management process is illustrated in Figure 9–1.

Adequate and timely feedback is the cornerstone of effective strategy evaluation. Strategy evaluation can be no better than the information on which it operates. Too much pressure from top managers may result in lower managers contriving numbers they think will be satisfactory.

Strategy evaluation can be a complex and sensitive undertaking. Too much emphasis on evaluating strategies may be expensive and counterproductive. No one likes to be evaluated too closely! The more managers attempt to evaluate the behavior of others, the less control they have. Yet, too little or no evaluation can create even worse problems. Strategy evaluation is essential to ensure that stated objectives are being achieved.

In many organizations, strategy evaluation is simply an appraisal of how well an organization has performed. Have the firm's assets increased? Has there been an increase in profitability? Have sales increased? Have productivity levels increased? Have profit margin, return on investment, and earnings-per-share ratios increased? Some firms argue that their strategy must have been correct if the answers to these types of questions are affirmative. Well, the strategy or strategies may have been correct, but this type of reasoning can be misleading, because strategy evaluation must have both a long-run and short-run focus. Strategies often do not affect short-term operating results until it is too late to make needed changes.

It is impossible to demonstrate conclusively that a particular strategy is optimal or even to guarantee that it will work. One can, however, evaluate it for critical flaws. Richard Rumelt offered four criteria that could be used to evaluate a strategy: consistency, consonance, feasibility, and advantage. Described in Table 9–1, *consonance* and *advantage* are mostly based on a firm's external assessment, whereas *consistency* and *feasibility* are largely based on an internal assessment.

Strategy evaluation is important because organizations face dynamic environments in which key external and internal factors often change quickly and dramatically. Success today is no guarantee for success tomorrow! An organization should never be lulled into complacency with success. Countless firms have thrived one year only to struggle for survival the following year. For example, Waste Management's profits dropped in 1997 to negative $1.27 billion. Other companies that experienced net profit losses in excess of

FIGURE 9–1
A Comprehensive Strategic-Management Model

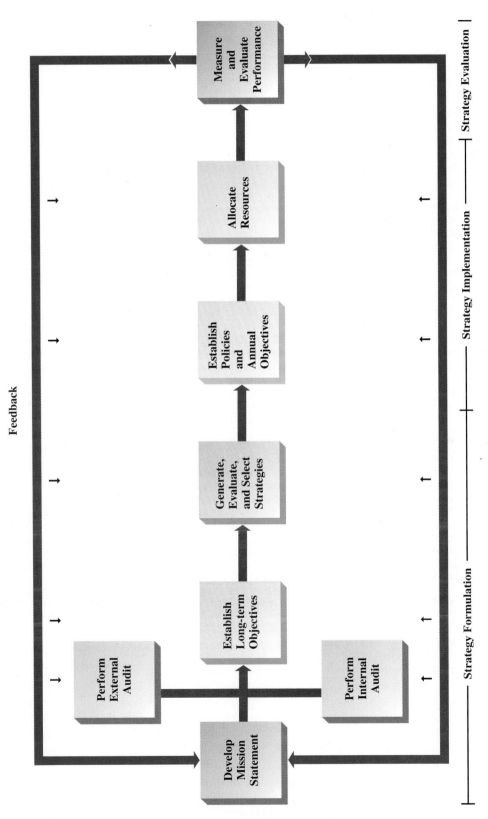

TABLE 9–1
Rumelt's Criteria for Evaluating Strategies

CONSISTENCY

A strategy should not present inconsistent goals and policies. Organizational conflict and interdepartmental bickering are often symptoms of a managerial disorder, but these problems may also be a sign of strategic inconsistency. There are three guidelines to help determine if organizational problems are due to inconsistencies in strategy:

• If managerial problems continue despite changes in personnel and if they tend to be issue-based rather than people-based, then strategies may be inconsistent.
• If success for one organizational department means, or is interpreted to mean, failure for another department, then strategies may be inconsistent.
• If policy problems and issues continue to be brought to the top for resolution, then strategies may be inconsistent.

CONSONANCE

Consonance refers to the need for strategists to examine *sets of trends* as well as individual trends in evaluating strategies. A strategy must represent an adaptive response to the external environment and to the critical changes occurring within it. One difficulty in matching a firm's key internal and external factors in the formulation of strategy is that most trends are the result of interactions among other trends. For example, the day care explosion came about as a combined result of many trends that included a rise in the average level of education, increased inflation, and an increase in women in the workforce. Although single economic or demographic trends might appear steady for many years, there are waves of change going on at the interaction level.

FEASIBILITY

A strategy must neither overtax available resources nor create unsolvable subproblems. The final broad test of strategy is its feasibility; that is, can the strategy be attempted within the physical, human, and financial resources of the enterprise? The financial resources of a business are the easiest to quantify and are normally the first limitation against which strategy is evaluated. It is sometimes forgotten, however, that innovative approaches to financing are often possible. Devices such as captive subsidiaries, sale-leaseback arrangements, and tying plant mortgages to long-term contracts have all been used effectively to help win key positions in suddenly expanding industries. A less quantifiable, but actually more rigid, limitation on strategic choice is that imposed by individual and organizational capabilities. In evaluating a strategy, it is important to examine whether an organization has demonstrated in the past that it possesses the abilities, competencies, skills, and talents needed to carry out a given strategy.

ADVANTAGE

A strategy must provide for the creation and/or maintenance of a competitive advantage in a selected area of activity. Competitive advantages normally are the result of superiority in one of three areas: 1) resources, 2) skills, or 3) position. The idea that the positioning of one's resources can enhance their combined effectiveness is familiar to military theorists, chess players, and diplomats. Position can also play a crucial role in an organization's strategy. Once gained, a good position is defensible—meaning that it is so costly to capture that rivals are deterred from full-scale attacks. Positional advantage tends to be self-sustaining as long as the key internal and environmental factors that underlie it remain stable. This is why entrenched firms can be almost impossible to unseat, even if their raw skill levels are only average. Although not all positional advantages are associated with size, it is true that larger organizations tend to operate in markets and use procedures that turn their size into advantage, while smaller firms seek product/market positions that exploit other types of advantage. The principal characteristics of good position is that it permits the firm to obtain advantage from policies that would not similarly benefit rivals without the same position. Therefore, in evaluating strategy, organizations should examine the nature of positional advantages associated with a given strategy.

Source: Adapted from Richard Rumelt, "The Evaluation of Business Strategy," in W. F. Glueck, ed., *Business Policy and Strategic Management* (New York: McGraw-Hill, 1980): 359–367.

$800 million in 1997 were Quaker Oaks, Apple Computer, Unisys, and Dow Jones. Organizational trouble can come swiftly, as further evidenced by the examples described in Table 9–2.

Strategy evaluation is becoming increasingly difficult with the passage of time, for many reasons. Domestic and world economies were more stable in years past, product life cycles were longer, product development cycles were longer, technological advancement was slower, change occurred less often, there were fewer competitors, foreign companies were weak, and there were more regulated industries. Other reasons why strategy evaluation is more difficult today include the following trends:

1. A dramatic increase in the environment's complexity
2. The increasing difficulty of predicting the future with accuracy

A few large Fortune 500 companies that experienced more than a 15 percent decline in revenues for 1997 are:

Bradlees
Coastal
Mobil
LAM Research
WHX
Apple Computer

These large companies experienced more than a 50 percent decline in profits in 1997:

Whitman	Gateway 2000
Arco Chemical	Ceridian
Value City Department Stores	3Com
Sonoco Products	Bowater
Amerada Hess	Fort James
Occidental Petroleum	Willamette Industries
CVS	Enron
International Multifoods	United Stationers
Smart & Final	Cendant
Columbia/HCA Healthcare	Lucent Technologies
Trigon Healthcare	Frontier
Tupperware	SBC Communications
Alumax	Cilcorp
Engelhard	Florida Progress
Advanta	

3. The increasing number of variables

4. The rapid rate of obsolescence of even the best plans

5. The increase in the number of both domestic and world events affecting organizations

6. The decreasing time span for which planning can be done with any degree of certainty[1]

A fundamental problem facing managers today is how to effectively control employees in light of modern organizational demands for greater flexibility, innovation, creativity, and initiative from employees.[2] How can managers today ensure that empowered employees acting in an entrepreneurial manner do not put the well-being of the business at risk? Recall that Kidder, Peabody, & Company lost $350 million when one of their traders allegedly booked fictitious profits; Sears, Roebuck and Company took a $60 million charge against earnings after admitting that its automobile service businesses were performing unnecessary repairs. The costs to companies such as these in terms of damaged reputations, fines, missed opportunities, and diversion of management's attention are enormous.

When empowered employees are held accountable for and pressured to achieve specific goals and are given wide latitude in their actions to achieve them, there can be dysfunctional behavior. For example, Nordstrom, the upscale fashion retailer known for outstanding customer services, recently was subjected to lawsuits and fines when employees underreported hours worked in order to increase their sales per hour—the company's primary performance criterion. Nordstrom's customer service and earnings were enhanced until the misconduct was reported, at which time severe penalties were levied against the firm.

THE PROCESS OF EVALUATING STRATEGIES   Strategy evaluation is necessary for all sizes and kinds of organizations. Strategy evaluation should initiate managerial questioning of expectations and assumptions, should trigger a review of objectives and values, and should stimulate creativity in generating alternatives and formulating criteria of evaluation.[3] Regardless of the size of the organization, a certain amount of *management by wandering around* at all levels is essential to effective strategy evaluation. Strategy-evaluation activities should be performed on a continuing basis, rather than at the end of specified periods of time or just after problems occur. Waiting until the end of the year, for example, could result in a firm closing the barn door after the horses have already escaped.

Evaluating strategies on a continuous rather than a periodic basis allows benchmarks of progress to be established and more effectively monitored. Some strategies take years to implement; consequently, associated results may not become apparent for years. Successful strategists combine patience with a willingness to take corrective actions promptly when necessary. There always comes a time when corrective actions are needed in an organization! Centuries ago, a writer (perhaps Solomon) made the following observations about change:

> There is a time for everything,
> A time to be born and a time to die,
> A time to plant and a time to uproot,
> A time to kill and a time to heal,
> A time to tear down and a time to build,
> A time to weep and a time to laugh,
> A time to mourn and a time to dance,
> A time to scatter stones and a time to gather them,
> A time to embrace and a time to refrain,
> A time to search and a time to give up,
> A time to keep and a time to throw away,
> A time to tear and a time to mend,
> A time to be silent and a time to speak,
> A time to love and a time to hate,
> A time for war and a time for peace.[4]

In a study that examined the timing of strategy evaluation in many organizations, Lindsay and Rue hypothesized that strategy-evaluation activities would be conducted more frequently as environmental complexity and instability increased.[5] However, the researchers found a surprising inverse relationship between planning review frequency and organizational environment. Top managers in dynamic environments performed strategy-evaluation activities less frequently than those in stable environments. Lindsay and Rue concluded that forecasting is more difficult under complex and unstable environmental conditions, so strategists may see less need for frequent evaluation of their long-range plans. Evidence for this conclusion was stronger for large firms than for small ones.

Managers and employees of the firm should be continually aware of progress being made toward achieving the firm's objectives. As critical success factors change, organizational members should be involved in determining appropriate corrective actions. If assumptions and expectations deviate significantly from forecasts, then the firm should renew strategy-formulation activities, perhaps sooner than planned. In strategy evaluation, like strategy formulation and strategy implementation, people make the difference. Through involvement in the process of evaluating strategies, managers and employees become committed to keeping the firm moving steadily toward achieving objectives.

A STRATEGY-EVALUATION FRAMEWORK

Table 9–3 summarizes strategy-evaluation activities in terms of key questions that should be addressed, alternative answers to those questions, and appropriate actions for an organization to take. Notice that corrective actions are almost always needed except when (1) external and internal factors have not significantly changed and (2) the firm is progressing satisfactorily toward achieving stated objectives. Relationships among strategy-evaluation activities are illustrated in Figure 9–2.

REVIEWING BASES OF STRATEGY   As shown in Figure 9–2, *reviewing the underlying bases of an organization's strategy* could be approached by developing a revised EFE Matrix and IFE Matrix. A *revised IFE Matrix* should focus on changes in the organization's management, marketing, finance/accounting, production/operations, R&D, and computer information systems strengths and weaknesses. A *revised EFE Matrix* should indicate how effective a firm's strategies have been in response to key opportunities and threats. This analysis could also address such questions as the following:

1. How have competitors reacted to our strategies?
2. How have competitors' strategies changed?
3. Have major competitors' strengths and weaknesses changed?
4. Why are competitors making certain strategic changes?
5. Why are some competitors' strategies more successful than others?
6. How satisfied are our competitors with their present market positions and profitability?
7. How far can our major competitors be pushed before retaliating?
8. How could we more effectively cooperate with our competitors?

Numerous external and internal factors can prohibit firms from achieving long-term and annual objectives. Externally, actions by competitors, changes in demand, changes in technology, economic changes, demographic shifts, and governmental actions may prohibit objectives from being accomplished. Internally, ineffective strategies may have been chosen or implementation activities may have been poor. Objectives may have been too optimistic. Thus, failure to achieve objectives may not be the result of unsatisfactory work by managers and employees. All organizational members need to know this to encourage

TABLE 9–3
A Strategy-Evaluation Assessment Matrix

HAVE MAJOR CHANGES OCCURRED IN THE FIRM'S INTERNAL STRATEGIC POSITION?	HAVE MAJOR CHANGES OCCURRED IN THE FIRM'S EXTERNAL STRATEGIC POSITION?	HAS THE FIRM PROGRESSED SATISFACTORILY TOWARD ACHIEVING ITS STATED OBJECTIVES?	RESULT
No	No	No	Take corrective actions
Yes	Yes	Yes	Take corrective actions
Yes	Yes	No	Take corrective actions
Yes	No	Yes	Take corrective actions
Yes	No	No	Take corrective actions
No	Yes	Yes	Take corrective actions
No	Yes	No	Take corrective actions
No	No	Yes	Continue present strategic course

FIGURE 9–2
A Strategy-Evaluation Framework

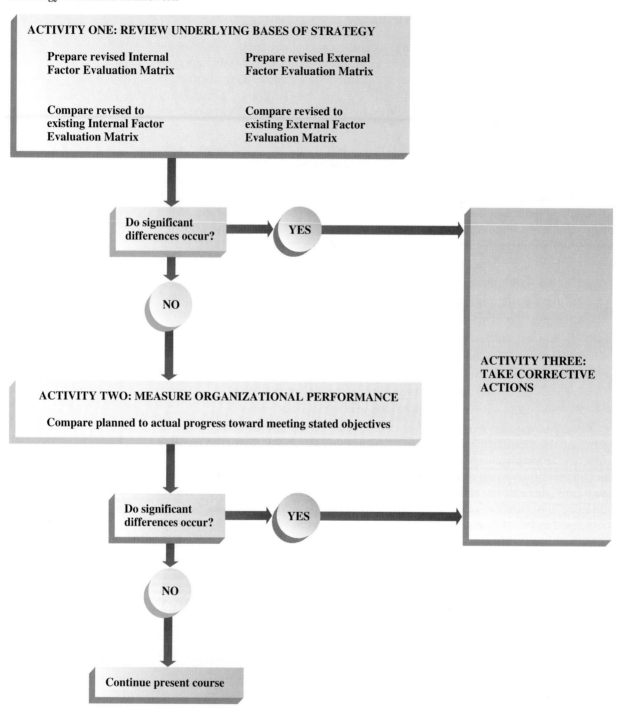

ACTIVITY ONE: REVIEW UNDERLYING BASES OF STRATEGY

Prepare revised Internal
Factor Evaluation Matrix

Prepare revised External
Factor Evaluation Matrix

Compare revised to
existing Internal Factor
Evaluation Matrix

Compare revised to
existing External Factor
Evaluation Matrix

Do significant
differences occur?

YES

NO

ACTIVITY TWO: MEASURE ORGANIZATIONAL PERFORMANCE

Compare planned to actual progress toward meeting stated objectives

Do significant
differences occur?

YES

NO

Continue present course

**ACTIVITY THREE:
TAKE CORRECTIVE
ACTIONS**

their support for strategy-evaluation activities. Organizations desperately need to know as soon as possible when their strategies are not effective. Sometimes managers and employees on the front line discover this well before strategists.

External opportunities and threats and internal strengths and weaknesses that represent the bases of current strategies should continually be monitored for change. It is not really a question of whether these factors will change, but rather when they will change and in what ways. Some key questions to address in evaluating strategies are given here.

1. Are our internal strengths still strengths?
2. Have we added other internal strengths? If so, what are they?
3. Are our internal weaknesses still weaknesses?
4. Do we now have other internal weaknesses? If so, what are they?
5. Are our external opportunities still opportunities?
6. Are there now other external opportunities? If so, what are they?
7. Are our external threats still threats?
8. Are there now other external threats? If so, what are they?
9. Are we vulnerable to a hostile takeover?

MEASURING ORGANIZATIONAL PERFORMANCE Another important strategy-evaluation activity is *measuring organizational performance*. This activity includes comparing expected results to actual results, investigating deviations from plans, evaluating individual performance, and examining progress being made toward meeting stated objectives. Both long-term and annual objectives are commonly used in this process. Criteria for evaluating strategies should be measurable and easily verifiable. Criteria that predict results may be more important than those that reveal what already has happened. For example, rather than simply being informed that sales last quarter were 20 percent under what was expected, strategists need to know that sales next quarter may be 20 percent below standard unless some action is taken to counter the trend. Really effective control requires accurate forecasting.

Failure to make satisfactory progress toward accomplishing long-term or annual objectives signals a need for corrective actions. Many factors, such as unreasonable policies, unexpected turns in the economy, unreliable suppliers or distributors, or ineffective strategies, can result in unsatisfactory progress toward meeting objectives. Problems can result from ineffectiveness (not doing the right things) or inefficiency (doing the right things poorly).

Determining which objectives are most important in the evaluation of strategies can be difficult. Strategy evaluation is based on both quantitative and qualitative criteria. Selecting the exact set of criteria for evaluating strategies depends on a particular organization's size, industry, strategies, and management philosophy. An organization pursuing a retrenchment strategy, for example, could have an entirely different set of evaluative criteria from an organization pursuing a market-development strategy. Quantitative criteria commonly used to evaluate strategies are financial ratios, which strategists use to make three critical comparisons: (1) comparing the firm's performance over different time periods, (2) comparing the firm's performance to competitors', and (3) comparing the firm's performance to industry averages. Some key financial ratios that are particularly useful as criteria for strategy evaluation are as follows:

1. Return on investment
2. Return on equity
3. Profit margin
4. Market share
5. Debt to equity
6. Earnings per share
7. Sales growth
8. Asset growth

But there are some potential problems associated with using quantitative criteria for evaluating strategies. First, most quantitative criteria are geared to annual objectives rather than long-term objectives. Also, different accounting methods can provide different results on many quantitative criteria. Third, intuitive judgments are almost always involved in deriving quantitative criteria. For these and other reasons, qualitative criteria are also important in evaluating strategies. Human factors such as high absenteeism and turnover rates, poor production quality and quantity rates, or low employee satisfaction can be underlying causes of declining performance. Marketing, finance/accounting, R&D, or computer information systems factors can also cause financial problems. Seymour Tilles identified six qualitative questions that are useful in evaluating strategies:

1. Is the strategy internally consistent?
2. Is the strategy consistent with the environment?
3. Is the strategy appropriate in view of available resources?
4. Does the strategy involve an acceptable degree of risk?
5. Does the strategy have an appropriate time framework?
6. Is the strategy workable?[6]

Some additional key questions that reveal the need for qualitative or intuitive judgments in strategy evaluation are as follows:

1. How good is the firm's balance of investments between high-risk and low-risk projects?
2. How good is the firm's balance of investments between long-term and short-term projects?
3. How good is the firm's balance of investments between slow-growing markets and fast-growing markets?
4. How good is the firm's balance of investments among different divisions?
5. To what extent are the firm's alternative strategies socially responsible?
6. What are the relationships among the firm's key internal and external strategic factors?
7. How are major competitors likely to respond to particular strategies?

TAKING CORRECTIVE ACTIONS   The final strategy-evaluation activity, *taking corrective actions*, requires making changes to reposition a firm competitively for the future. As indicated in the Global Perspective, expanding into Hong Kong is a popular action or strategy used by many firms. Other examples of changes that may be needed are altering an organization's structure, replacing one or more key individuals, selling a division, or revising a business mission. Other changes could include establishing or revising objectives, devising new policies, issuing stock to raise capital, adding additional salespersons, allocating resources differently, or developing new performance incentives. Taking corrective actions does not necessarily mean that existing strategies will be abandoned or even that new strategies must be formulated.

> The probabilities and possibilities for incorrect or inappropriate actions increase geometrically with an arithmetic increase in personnel. Any person directing an overall undertaking must check on the actions of the participants as well as the results, that they have achieved. If either the actions or results do not comply with preconceived or planned achievements, then corrective actions are needed.[7]

No organization can survive as an island; no organization can escape change. Taking corrective actions is necessary to keep an organization on track toward achieving stated objectives. In his thought-provoking books, *Future Shock* and *The Third Wave*, Alvin Toffler argued that business environments are becoming so dynamic and complex that they threaten people and organizations with *future shock*, which occurs when the nature, types, and speed of changes overpower an individual's or organization's ability and capacity to adapt. Strategy evaluation enhances an organization's ability to adapt successfully to changing circumstances. Brown and Agnew referred to this notion as *corporate agility*.[8]

GLOBAL PERSPECTIVE
Is Hong Kong the Winner?

Many Asian cities desire and even claim to have Asia's leading financial center, but Hong Kong is the clear winner. Hong Kong offers companies a free and open economy, the largest stock market in Asia except Tokyo, low tax rates, an advanced telecommunications system, an abundant supply of educated and experienced bi- and trilingual workers and professionals, a beautiful deepwater seaport, and close proximity to many other large Asian cities. Tokyo, despite its size and huge economy, remains comparably disadvantaged with English not being widely spoken, a long distance to other large Asian cities, and high operating costs. Other Asian cities such as Bangkok, Jakarta, Singapore, Shanghai, and Manila talk of financial leadership, but traffic jams, poor telephone service and infrastructure, and other problems make them no Hong Kong.

Evidence of Hong Kong's financial dominance is evidenced in the following list of new company equity issues in Asian cities and countries in 1996. This list reveals where new companies are locating in the Far East.

Source: Adapted from Sara Webb, "Still on Top," The Wall Street Journal (September 18, 1997): R18.

NATION OR CITY	NUMBER OF ISSUES	VALUE (IN MILLIONS)
Hong Kong	97	$ 8,312
Indonesia	69	6,159
Japan	20	4,869
Australia	16	4,592
Malaysia	136	4,039
Singapore	52	3,545
China	38	2,428
India	12	2,076
Taiwan	43	2,051
Philippines	33	1,893
South Korea	11	1,261
Thailand	41	1,050

As indicated in the Natural Environment Perspective, utilities across the United States increasingly are having to report where their power is derived so consumers can distinguish between polluters and nonpolluters.

Taking corrective actions raises employees' and managers' anxieties. Research suggests that participation in strategy-evaluation activities is one of the best ways to overcome individuals' resistance to change. According to Erez and Kanfer, individuals accept change best when they have a cognitive understanding of the changes, a sense of control over the situation, and an awareness that necessary actions are going to be taken to implement the changes.[9]

Strategy evaluation can lead to strategy-formulation changes, strategy-implementation changes, both formulation and implementation changes, or no changes at all. Strategists cannot escape having to revise strategies and implementation approaches sooner or later. Hussey and Langham offered the following insight on taking corrective actions:

> Resistance to change is often emotionally based and not easily overcome by rational argument. Resistance may be based on such feelings as loss of status, implied criticism of present competence, fear of failure in the new situation, annoyance at not being consulted, lack of understanding of the need for change, or insecurity in changing from well-known and fixed methods. It is necessary, therefore, to overcome such resistance by creating situations of participation and full explanation when changes are envisaged.[10]

Corrective actions should place an organization in a better position to capitalize upon internal strengths; to take advantage of key external opportunities; to avoid, reduce, or mitigate external threats; and to improve internal weaknesses. Corrective actions should have a proper time horizon and an appropriate amount of risk. They should be internally consistent and socially responsible. Perhaps most importantly, corrective actions strengthen an

NATURAL ENVIRONMENT
How Much Will You Pay for Green Electricity?

Since January 1, 1998, residential and industrial customers in California and parts of New England are able to choose their supplier of electricity just as everyone today may select their long-distance telephone carrier. More states are following suit as utility deregulation expands nationwide. The Environmental Protection Agency and others want to require all utilities in all states to disclose where their power is derived because 36 percent of all U.S. emissions of carbon dioxide, the dominant greenhouse gas, is produced by electric utilities. The Federal Trade Commission is consider-

ing a proposal to require all utilities to disclose on their bills a breakdown of their generation mix and a list of any resultant air pollutants.

Utilities are finding that environmentalism sells and that customers are, in fact, willing to pay more for power derived from noncoal sources. Branding the power generated as "green" will soon become the major meaningful differentiator in the whole energy sector, according to many analysts. California is finding that households and businesses are willing to pay, on average, $5.50 extra a month for electric-

ity generated from a mix of geothermal and hydroelectric facilities rather than from coal-burning sources. A few New England utility companies now offering environmentally correct electricity include AllEnergy, Enova Energy, Northfield Mountain Energy, and Working Assets Green Power, Inc.

Source: Adapted from "For Sale: Environmentally Correct Electricity," The Wall Street Journal (July 23, 1997): B1, B5.

organization's competitive position in its basic industry. Continuous strategy evaluation keeps strategists close to the pulse of an organization and provides information needed for an effective strategic-management system. Carter Bayles described the benefits of strategy evaluation as follows:

> Evaluation activities may renew confidence in the current business strategy or point to the need for actions to correct some weaknesses, such as erosion of product superiority or technological edge. In many cases, the benefits of strategy evaluation are much more far-reaching, for the outcome of the process may be a fundamentally new strategy that will lead, even in a business that is already turning a respectable profit, to substantially increased earnings. It is this possibility that justifies strategy evaluation, for the payoff can be very large.[11]

PUBLISHED SOURCES OF STRATEGY-EVALUATION INFORMATION

A number of publications are helpful in evaluating a firm's strategies. For example, in its May and June issue each year, *Fortune* identifies and evaluates the Fortune 1,000 (the largest manufacturers) and the Fortune 50 (the largest retailers, transportation companies, utilities, banks, insurance companies, and diversified financial corporations in the United States). In these issues *Fortune* also ranks the best and worst performers on various factors such as return on investment, sales volume, and profitability.

Fortune annually evaluates organizations in 25 industries. Eight key attributes serve as evaluative criteria: quality of management; innovativeness; quality of products or services; long-term investment value; financial soundness; community and environmental responsibility; ability to attract, develop, and keep talented people; and use of corporate assets. *Fortune's* 1997 evaluation in Table 9–4 reveals the firms considered best in their respective industries.[12]

Fortune and the Hay Group published the first-ever global list of the world's most admired companies in late 1997.[13] Some foreign companies that rank best in their industry over all U.S. competitors are the last three entries noted in Table 9–4.

COMPANY	INDUSTRY
J.P. Morgan	Money Center Banks
Golden West Financial	Savings Institutions
Merrill Lynch	Securities
Northwestern Mutual Life	Insurance: Life, Health
Berkshire Hathaway	Insurance: Property, Casualty
Norwest	Superregional Banks
American Express	Consumer Credit
Boeing	Aerospace
Southwest Airlines	Airlines
United Parcel Service	Mail, Package & Freight Delivery
Caterpillar	Industrial & Farm Equipment
Ryder System	Trucking
Toyota Motor Sales U.S.A.	Motor Vehicles & Parts
Norfolk Southern	Railroads
Nike	Apparel
Cardinal Health	Wholesalers
Herman Miller	Furniture
Nestlé USA	Food
Walgreen	Food & Drug Stores
Wal-Mart Stores	General Merchandise
Gillette	Soaps, Cosmetics
United Health Care	Health Care
Manpower	Temporary Help
Coca-Cola	Beverages
Fortune Brands	Tobacco
FPL Group	Electric & Gas Utilities
Burlington Resources	Mining, Crude Oil
Shell Oil	Petroleum Refining
Enron	Pipelines
USA Waste Services	Waste Management
Fluor	Engineering, Construction
Tyco International	Metal Products
Alcoa	Metals
Corning	Building Materials, Glass
Merck	Pharmaceuticals
Unifi	Textiles
Goodyear Tire & Rubber	Rubber & Plastic Products
DuPont	Chemicals
Kimberly-Clark	Forest & Paper Products
Omnicon Group	Advertising, Marketing
Tribune	Publishing, Printing
Walt Disney	Entertainment
Mirage Resorts	Hotels, Casinos, Resorts
Brunswick	Recreational Equipment
First Data	Computer & Data Services
Hewlett-Packard	Computers & Office Equipment
3M	Scientific & Photo Equipment
SBC Communications	Telecommunications
General Electric	Electronical Equipment
EMC	Computer Peripherals
Microsoft	Computer Software
Cicso Systems	Electrical Networks
Intel	Semiconductors
British Airways	Airlines
Toyota Motor	Motor Vehicles and Parts
Royal Dutch/Shell	Petroleum Refining

TABLE 9–4
Fortune's **1997 Top Industry Performers**

Source: Edward Robinson, "America's Most Admired Companies," *Fortune* (March 3, 1997): 68–75.

Another excellent evaluation of corporations in America, "The Annual Report on American Industry," is published annually in the January issue of *Forbes*. It provides a detailed and comprehensive evaluation of hundreds of American companies in many different industries. *Business Week*, *Industry Week*, and *Dun's Business Month* also periodically publish detailed evaluations of American businesses and industries. Although published sources of strategy-evaluation information focus primarily on large, publicly held businesses, the comparative ratios and related information are widely used to evaluate small businesses and privately owned firms as well.

CHARACTERISTICS OF AN EFFECTIVE EVALUATION SYSTEM

Strategy evaluation must meet several basic requirements to be effective. First, strategy-evaluation activities must be economical; too much information can be just as bad as too little information; and too many controls can do more harm than good. Strategy-evaluation activities also should be meaningful; they should specifically relate to a firm's objectives. They should provide managers with useful information about tasks over which they have control and influence. Strategy-evaluation activities should provide timely information; on occasion and in some areas, managers may need information daily. For example, when a firm has diversified by acquiring another firm, evaluative information may be needed frequently. However, in an R&D department, daily or even weekly evaluative information could be dysfunctional. Approximate information that is timely is generally more desirable as a basis for strategy evaluation than accurate information that does not depict the present. Frequent measurement and rapid reporting may frustrate control rather than give better control. The time dimension of control must coincide with the time span of the event being measured.

Strategy evaluation should be designed to provide a true picture of what is happening. For example, in a severe economic downturn, productivity and profitability ratios may drop alarmingly, although employees and managers are actually working harder. Strategy evaluations should portray this type of situation fairly. Information derived from the strategy-evaluation process should facilitate action and should be directed to those individuals in the organization who need to take action based on it. Managers commonly ignore evaluative reports that are provided for informational purposes only; not all managers need to receive all reports. Controls need to be action-oriented rather than information-oriented.

The strategy-evaluation process should not dominate decisions; it should foster mutual understanding, trust, and common sense! No department should fail to cooperate with another in evaluating strategies. Strategy evaluations should be simple, not too cumbersome, and not too restrictive. Complex strategy-evaluation systems often confuse people and accomplish little. The test of an effective evaluation system is its usefulness, not its complexity.

Large organizations require a more elaborate and detailed strategy-evaluation system because it is more difficult to coordinate efforts among different divisions and functional areas. Managers in small companies often communicate with each other and their employees daily and do not need extensive evaluative reporting systems. Familiarity with local environments usually makes gathering and evaluating information much easier for small organizations than for large businesses. But the key to an effective strategy-evaluation system may be the ability to convince participants that failure to accomplish certain objectives within a prescribed time is not necessarily a reflection of their performance.

There is no one ideal strategy-evaluation system. The unique characteristics of an organization, including its size, management style, purpose, problems, and strengths, can determine a strategy-evaluation and control system's final design. Robert Waterman offered the following observation about successful organizations' strategy-evaluation and control systems:

> Successful companies treat facts as friends and controls as liberating. Morgan Guaranty and Wells Fargo not only survive but thrive in the troubled waters of bank deregulation, because their strategy evaluation and control systems are sound, their risk is contained, and they know themselves and the competitive situation so well. Successful companies have a voracious hunger for facts. They see information where others see only data. They love comparisons, rankings, anything that removes decision-making from the realm of mere opinion. Successful companies maintain tight, accurate financial controls. Their people don't regard controls as an imposition of autocracy, but as the benign checks and balances that allow them to be creative and free.[14]

CONTINGENCY PLANNING

A basic premise of good strategic management is that firms plan ways to deal with unfavorable and favorable events before they occur. Too many organizations prepare contingency plans just for unfavorable events; this is a mistake, because both minimizing threats and capitalizing on opportunities can improve a firm's competitive position.

Regardless of how carefully strategies are formulated, implemented, and evaluated, unforeseen events such as strikes, boycotts, natural disasters, arrival of foreign competitors, and government actions can make a strategy obsolete. To minimize the impact of potential threats, organizations should develop contingency plans as part of the strategy-evaluation process. *Contingency plans* can be defined as alternative plans that can be put into effect if certain key events do not occur as expected. Only high-priority areas require the insurance of contingency plans. Strategists cannot and should not try to cover all bases by planning for all possible contingencies. But in any case, contingency plans should be as simple as possible.

Some contingency plans commonly established by firms include the following:

1. If a major competitor withdraws from particular markets as intelligence reports indicate, what actions should our firm take?

2. If our sales objectives are not reached, what actions should our firm take to avoid profit losses?

3. If demand for our new product exceeds plans, what actions should our firm take to meet the higher demand?

4. If certain disasters occur—such as loss of computer capabilities; a hostile takeover attempt; loss of patent protection; or destruction of manufacturing facilities due to earthquakes, tornados, or hurricanes—what actions should our firm take?

5. If a new technological advancement makes our new product obsolete sooner than expected, what actions should our firm take?

Too many organizations discard alternative strategies not selected for implementation although the work devoted to analyzing these options would render valuable information. Alternative strategies not selected for implementation can serve as contingency plans in case the strategy or strategies selected do not work.

When strategy-evaluation activities reveal the need for a major change quickly, an appropriate contingency plan can be executed in a timely way. Contingency plans can promote a strategist's ability to respond quickly to key changes in the internal and external bases of an organization's current strategy. For example, if underlying assumptions about the economy turn out to be wrong and contingency plans are ready, then managers can make appropriate changes promptly.

In some cases, external or internal conditions present unexpected opportunities. When such opportunities occur, contingency plans could allow an organization to capitalize on them quickly. Linneman and Chandran reported that contingency planning gave users such as DuPont, Dow Chemical, Consolidated Foods, and Emerson Electric three major benefits: It permitted quick response to change, it prevented panic in crisis situations, and it made managers more adaptable by encouraging them to appreciate just how variable the future can be. They suggested that effective contingency planning involves a seven-step process as follows:

1. Identify both beneficial and unfavorable events that could possibly derail the strategy or strategies.
2. Specify trigger points. Calculate about when contingent events are likely to occur.
3. Assess the impact of each contingent event. Estimate the potential benefit or harm of each contingent event.
4. Develop contingency plans. Be sure that contingency plans are compatible with current strategy and are economically feasible.
5. Assess the counterimpact of each contingency plan. That is, estimate how much each contingency plan will capitalize on or cancel out its associated contingent event. Doing this will quantify the potential value of each contingency plan.
6. Determine early warning signals for key contingent events. Monitor the early warning signals.
7. For contingent events with reliable early warning signals, develop advance action plans to take advantage of the available lead time.[15]

AUDITING

A frequently used tool in strategy evaluation is the audit. *Auditing* is defined by the American Accounting Association (AAA) as "a systematic process of objectively obtaining and evaluating evidence regarding assertions about economic actions and events to ascertain

TABLE 9–5
Key Strategy-Evaluation Questions

1. Do you feel that the strategic-management system exists to provide service to you in your day-to-day work? How has it helped you in this respect?
2. Has the strategic-management system provided the service that you feel was promised at the start of its design and implementation? In which areas has it failed and exceeded, in your opinion?
3. Do you consider that the strategic-management system has been implemented with due regard to costs and benefits? Are there any areas in which you consider the costs to be excessive?
4. Do you feel comfortable using the system? Could more attention have been paid to matching the output of the system to your needs and, if so, in what areas?
5. Is the system flexible enough in your opinion? If not, where should changes be made?
6. Do you still keep a personal store of information in a notebook or elsewhere? If so, will you share that information with the system? Do you see any benefits in so doing?
7. Is the strategic-management system still evolving? Can you influence this evolution and, if not, why not?
8. Does the system provide timely, relevant, and accurate information? Are there any areas of deficiency?
9. Do you think that the strategic-management system makes too much use of complex procedures and models? Can you suggest areas in which less complicated techniques might be used to advantage?
10. Do you consider that there has been sufficient attention paid to the confidentiality and security of the information in the system? Can you suggest areas for improvement of these aspects of its operation?

Source: Adapted from K. J. Radford, *Information Systems for Strategic Decisions.* © 1978: 220–221. Adapted by permission of Prentice-Hall, Inc., Englewood Cliffs, New Jersey. Also, Lloyd Byars, *Strategic Management* (New York: Harper & Row, 1984): 237.

TABLE 9–6
The Planning Process Audit

1. To what extent do you feel top management has been committed to the pursuit of stated corporate strategy?
2. To what extent do you feel committed to the pursuit of stated corporate strategy?
3. Has top management's decision making been consistent with stated corporate strategy?
4. Has decision making been more or less centralized than anticipated?
5. Do you feel you have received sufficient resource support (financial and human) to pursue your stated plans?
6. Do everyday, operational plans seem to support the overall corporate strategy?
7. How would you rate the extent and quality of the coordination of plans among functional areas/departments/divisions?
8. How would you rate the extent and quality of the communication of plans to lower organizational levels?
9. Does the reward system (pay, promotions, etc.) seem to be tied to your planning efforts?
10. Do the written plans seem to adequately represent the actual goals toward which managers seem to be working?
11. How complex is the present planning process?
12. How formal is the present planning process?
13. Do you feel you have the right types and amounts of external information to fulfill your planning responsibilities?
14. Do you feel you have the right types and amounts of internal information to fulfill your planning responsibilities? If not, what other internal information do you feel you need?
15. Would any other training help you do a better job of planning? If yes, what other specific training would help?
16. What are the major problems of the current planning system?
17. How might the planning process be improved upon?

Source: C. Aaron Kelly, "Auditing the Planning Process," *Managerial Planning* 32, no. 4 (January–February 1984): 13. Used with permission.

the degree of correspondence between those assertions and established criteria, and communicating the results to interested users."[16] People who perform audits can be divided into three groups: independent auditors, government auditors, and internal auditors. Independent auditors basically are certified public accountants (CPAs) who provide their services to organizations for a fee; they examine the financial statements of an organization to determine whether they have been prepared according to generally accepted accounting principles (GAAP) and whether they fairly represent the activities of the firm. Independent auditors use a set of standards called generally accepted auditing standards (GAAS). Public accounting firms often have a consulting arm that provides strategy-evaluation services.

Two government agencies—the General Accounting Office (GAO) and the Internal Revenue Service (IRS)—employ government auditors responsible for making sure that organizations comply with federal laws, statutes, and policies. GAO and IRS auditors can audit any public or private organization. The third group of auditors are employees within an organization who are responsible for safeguarding company assets, for assessing the efficiency of company operations, and for ensuring that generally accepted business procedures are practiced. To evaluate the effectiveness of an organization's strategic-management system, internal auditors often seek answers to the questions posed in Table 9–5. C. Aaron Kelly developed the *Planning Process Audit* presented in Table 9–6.

THE ENVIRONMENTAL AUDIT For an increasing number of firms, overseeing environmental affairs is no longer a technical function performed by specialists; it rather has become an important strategic-management concern. Product design, manufacturing, transportation, customer use, packaging, product disposal, and corporate rewards and sanctions should reflect environmental considerations. Firms that effectively manage environmental affairs are benefiting from constructive relations with employees, consumers, suppliers, and distributors.

Shimell emphasized the need for organizations to conduct environmental audits of their operations and to develop a Corporate Environmental Policy (CEP).[17] Shimell contended that an environmental audit should be as rigorous as a financial audit and should include training workshops in which staff can help design and implement the policy. The CEP should be budgeted and requisite funds allocated to ensure that it is not a public relations facade. A Statement of Environmental Policy should be published periodically to inform shareholders and the public of environmental actions taken by the firm.

Instituting an environmental audit can include moving environmental affairs from the staff side of the organization to the line side. Some firms are also introducing environmental criteria and objectives in their performance appraisal instruments and systems. Conoco, for example, ties compensation of all its top managers to environmental action plans. Occidental Chemical includes environmental responsibilities in all its job descriptions for positions.

USING COMPUTERS TO EVALUATE STRATEGIES

When properly designed, installed, and operated, a computer network can efficiently acquire information promptly and accurately. Networks can allow diverse strategy-evaluation reports to be generated for—and responded to by—different levels and types of managers. For example, strategists will want reports concerned with whether the mission, objectives, and strategies of the enterprise are being achieved. Middle managers could require strategy-implementation information such as whether construction of a new facility is on schedule or a product's development is proceeding as expected. Lower-level managers could need evaluation reports that focus on operational concerns such as absenteeism and turnover rates, productivity rates, and the number and nature of grievances.

Business today has become so competitive that strategists are being forced to extend planning horizons and to make decisions under greater degrees of uncertainty. As a result, more information has to be obtained and assimilated to formulate, implement, and evaluate strategic decisions. In any competitive situation, the side with the best intelligence (information) usually wins; computers enable managers to evaluate vast amounts of information quickly and accurately. Use of the Internet, World Wide Web, e-mail, and search engines can make the difference today between a firm that is up-to-date or out-of-date in the currentness of information the firm uses to make strategic decisions. As indicated in the Information Technology Perspective, breaches in computer security must be a concern for businesses.

A limitation of computer-based systems to evaluate and monitor strategy execution is that personal values, attitudes, morals, preferences, politics, personalities, and emotions are not programmable. This limitation accents the need to view computers as tools, rather than as actual decision-making devices. Computers can significantly enhance the process of effectively integrating intuition and analysis in strategy evaluation. The General Accounting Office of the United States Government offered the following conclusions regarding the appropriate role of computers in strategy evaluation:

> The aim is to enhance and extend judgment. Computers should be looked upon not as a provider of solutions, but rather as a framework which permits science and judgment to be brought together and made explicit. It is the explicitness of this structure, the decision-maker's ability to probe, modify, and examine "What if?" alternatives, that is of value in extending judgment.[18]

INFORMATION TECHNOLOGY

How Widespread Are Computer Security Breaches?

Nearly 50 percent of American companies experienced security breaches in 1997, up from 37 percent in 1996. Prevalence of security breaches among U.S. firms can be categorized as follows:

Virus contamination	27%
Notebook thefts	24
Insider abuse of Internet access	13
Fraud	6.9
Unauthorized access by insider	6.7
Theft of proprietary information	5.8
Financial fraud	5.3
Sabotage	4.5
System penetration by outsiders	3.5
Wiretapping	1.4
Eavesdropping	1.1

Despite the computer security threat, U.S. businesses are rapidly increasing their commerce over the Internet. General Electric, for example, recently moved its 40,000 customers from electronic data interchange (EDI) transactions to the Internet. Boeing recently established its Boeing Part Page, a Web site that enables all its customers to order parts and get price quotations over the Internet.

In response to the computer security threat, an abundance of new technology and tools are now available to secure Web sites and lessen the threat of computer security breaches. The tools include firewalls, digital IDs, certifica-

tion, encryption, scrambling, and digital dollars. A growing number of companies are hiring a full-time computer security person. Computer security is a profession that is growing about 20 percent per year in the United States.

Source: Adapted from Laton McCartney, "A Safety Net," Industry Week (April 21, 1997): 74–81.

GUIDELINES FOR EFFECTIVE STRATEGIC MANAGEMENT

Failing to follow certain guidelines in conducting strategic management can foster criticisms of the process and create problems for the organization. An integral part of strategy evaluation must be to evaluate the quality of the strategic-management process. Issues such as "Is strategic management in our firm a people process or paper process?" should be addressed.

> Even the most technically perfect strategic plan will serve little purpose if it is not implemented. Many organizations tend to spend an inordinate amount of time, money, and effort on developing the strategic plan, treating the means and circumstances under which it will be implemented as afterthoughts! Change comes through implementation and evaluation, not through the plan. A technically imperfect plan that is implemented well will achieve more than the perfect plan that never gets off the paper on which it is typed.[19]

Strategic management must not become a self-perpetuating bureaucratic mechanism. Rather, it must be a self-reflective learning process that familiarizes managers and employees in the organization with key strategic issues and feasible alternatives for resolving those issues. Strategic management must not become ritualistic, stilted, orchestrated, or too formal, predictable, and rigid. Words supported by numbers, rather than numbers supported by words, should represent the medium for explaining strategic issues and organizational responses. A key role of strategists is to facilitate continuous organizational learning and change. Robert Waterman emphasized this, saying:

Successful companies know how to keep things moving. If they share a habit pattern, it's the habit of habit breaking. Sometimes they seem to like change for its own sake. IBM's chief executive John Akers says, "IBM never reorganizes except for a good business reason, but if they haven't reorganized in a while, that's a good business reason." Successful companies are deliberate bureaucracy-busters. They delight in smashing pettifogging encumbrances that Harry Quadracci calls "playing office."[20]

R. T. Lenz offered some important guidelines for effective strategic management:

Keep the strategic-management process as simple and nonroutine as possible. Eliminate jargon and arcane planning language. Remember, strategic management is a process for fostering learning and action, not merely a formal system for control. To avoid routinized behavior, vary assignments, team membership, meeting formats, and the planning calendar. The process should not be totally predictable, and settings must be changed to stimulate creativity. Emphasize word-oriented plans with numbers as back-up material. If managers cannot express their strategy in a paragraph or so, they either do not have one or do not understand it. Stimulate thinking and action that challenge the assumptions underlying current corporate strategy. Welcome bad news. If strategy is not working, managers desperately need to know it. Further, no pertinent information should be classified as inadmissable merely because it cannot be quantified. Build a corporate culture in which the role of strategic management and its essential purposes are understood. Do not permit "technicians" to co-opt the process. It is ultimately a process for learning and action. Speak of it in these terms. Attend to psychological, social, and political dimensions, as well as the information infrastructure and administrative procedures supporting it.[21]

An important guideline for effective strategic management is open-mindedness. A willingness and eagerness to consider new information, new viewpoints, new ideas, and new possibilities is essential; all organizational members must share a spirit of inquiry and learning. Strategists such as chief executive officers, presidents, owners of small businesses, and heads of government agencies must commit themselves to listen to and understand managers' positions well enough to be able to restate those positions to the managers' satisfaction. In addition, managers and employees throughout the firm should be able to describe the strategists' positions to the satisfaction of the strategists. This degree of discipline will promote understanding and learning.

No organization has unlimited resources. No firm can take on an unlimited amount of debt or issue an unlimited amount of stock to raise capital. Therefore, no organization can pursue all the strategies that potentially could benefit the firm. Strategic decisions thus always have to be made to eliminate some courses of action and to allocate organizational resources among others. Most organizations can afford to pursue only a few corporate-level strategies at any given time. It is a critical mistake for managers to pursue too many strategies at the same time, thereby spreading the firm's resources so thin that all strategies are jeopardized. Joseph Charyk, CEO of The Communication Satellite Corporation (Comsat), said, "We have to face the cold fact that Comsat may not be able to do all it wants. We must make hard choices on which ventures to keep and which to fold."

Strategic decisions require trade-offs such as long-range versus short-range considerations or maximizing profits versus increasing shareholders' wealth. There are ethics issues too. Strategy trade-offs require subjective judgments and preferences. In many cases, a lack of objectivity in formulating strategy results in a loss of competitive posture and profitability. Most organizations today recognize that strategic-management concepts and techniques can enhance the effectiveness of decisions. Subjective factors such as attitudes toward risk, concern for social responsibility, and organizational culture will always affect strategy-formulation decisions, but organizations need to be as objective as possible in considering qualitative factors.

CONCLUSION

This chapter presents a strategy-evaluation framework that can facilitate accomplishment of annual and long-term objectives. Effective strategy evaluation allows an organization to capitalize on internal strengths as they develop, to exploit external opportunities as they emerge, to recognize and defend against threats, and to mitigate internal weaknesses before they become detrimental.

Strategists in successful organizations take the time to formulate, implement, and then evaluate strategies deliberately and systematically. Good strategists move their organization forward with purpose and direction, continually evaluating and improving the firm's external and internal strategic position. Strategy evaluation allows an organization to shape its own future rather than allowing it to be constantly shaped by remote forces that have little or no vested interest in the well-being of the enterprise.

Although not a guarantee for success, strategic management allows organizations to make effective long-term decisions, to execute those decisions efficiently, and to take corrective actions as needed to ensure success. Computer networks and the Internet help to coordinate strategic-management activities and to ensure that decisions are based on good information. A key to effective strategy evaluation and to successful strategic management is an integration of intuition and analysis.

A potentially fatal problem is the tendency for analytical and intuitive issues to polarize. This polarization leads to strategy evaluation that is dominated by either analysis or intuition, or to strategy evaluation that is discontinuous, with a lack of coordination among analytical and intuitive issues.[22]

Strategists in successful organizations realize that strategic management is first and foremost a people process. It is an excellent vehicle for fostering organizational communication. People are what make the difference in organizations.

The real key to effective strategic management is to accept the premise that the planning process is more important than the written plan, that the manager is continuously planning and does not stop planning when the written plan is finished. The written plan is only a snapshot as of the moment it is approved. If the manager is not planning on a continuous basis—planning, measuring, and revising—the written plan can become obsolete the day it is finished. This obsolescence becomes more of a certainty as the increasingly rapid rate of change makes the business environment more uncertain.[23]

We invite you to visit the DAVID page on the Prentice Hall Web site at
www.prenhall.com/davidsm
for this chapter's World Wide Web exercises.

TAKE
IT TO
THE NET

KEY TERMS AND CONCEPTS

ISSUES FOR REVIEW AND DISCUSSION

1. Why has strategy evaluation become so important in business today?

2. BellSouth Services is considering putting divisional EFE and IFE matrices on-line for continual updating. How would this affect strategy evaluation?

3. What types of quantitative and qualitative criteria do you think David Glass, CEO of Wal-Mart, uses to evaluate the company's strategy?

4. As owner of a local, independent supermarket, explain how you would evaluate the firm's strategy.

5. Under what conditions are corrective actions not required in the strategy-evaluation process?

6. Identify types of organizations that may need to evaluate strategy more frequently than others. Justify your choices.

7. As executive director of the state forestry commission, in what way and how frequently would you evaluate the organization's strategies?

8. Identify some key financial ratios that would be important in evaluating a bank's strategy.

9. As owner of a chain of hardware stores, describe how you would approach contingency planning.

10. Strategy evaluation allows an organization to take a proactive stance toward shaping its own future. Discuss the meaning of this statement.

11. Select an article listed in the suggested readings for this chapter. Give a five-minute oral report to the class summarizing the article and your thoughts on the particular topic.

12. Identify guidelines that you think are most important for using strategic management effectively in organizations. Justify your answer.

NOTES

1. Dale McConkey, "Planning in a Changing Environment," *Business Horizons* (September–October 1988): 64.

2. Robert Simons, "Control in an Age of Empowerment," *Harvard Business Review* (March–April 1995): 80.

3. Dale Zand, "Reviewing the Policy Process," *California Management Review* 21, no. 1 (Fall 1978): 37.

4. Eccles. 3: 1–8.

5. W. Lindsay and L. Rue, "Impact of the Organization Environment on the Long-Range Planning Process: A Contingency View," *Academy of Management Journal* 23, no. 3 (September 1980): 402.

6. Seymour Tilles, "How to Evaluate Corporate Strategy," *Harvard Business Review* 41 (July–August 1963): 111–21.

7. Claude George, Jr., *The History of Management Thought* (Englewood Cliffs, New Jersey: Prentice-Hall, 1968), 165–66.

8. John Brown and Neil Agnew, "Corporate Agility," *Business Horizons* 25, no. 2 (March–April 1982): 29.

9. M. Erez and F. Kanfer, "The Role of Goal Acceptance in Goal Setting and Task Performance," *Academy of Management Review* 8, no. 3 (July 1983): 457.

10. D. Hussey and M. Langham, *Corporate Planning: The Human Factor* (Oxford, England: Pergamon Press, 1979): 138.

11. Carter Bayles, "Strategic Control: The President's Paradox," *Business Horizons* 20, no. 4 (August 1977): 18.

12. Edward Robinson and Thomas Stewart, "America's Most Admired Companies," *Fortune* (March 2, 1998): 70–107.

13. Anne Fisher, "The World's Most Admired Companies," *Fortune* (October 27, 1997): 120.

14. Robert Waterman, Jr., "How the Best Get Better," *Business Week* (September 14, 1987): 105.

15. Robert Linneman and Rajan Chandran, "Contingency Planning: A Key to Swift Managerial Action in the Uncertain Tomorrow," *Managerial Planning* 29, no. 4 (January–February 1981): 23–27.

16. American Accounting Association, *Report of Committee on Basic Auditing Concepts* (1971): 15–74.

17. Pamela Shimell, "Corporate Environmental Policy in Practice," *Long Range Planning* 24, no. 3 (June 1991): 10.

18. GAO *Report* PAD—80–21, 17.

19. McConkey, 66.

20. Robert H. Waterman, Jr., *The Renewal Factor: How the Best Get and Keep the Competitive Edge* (New York: Bantam, 1987).

21. R. T. Lenz, "Managing the Evolution of the Strategic Planning Process," *Business Horizons* 30, no. 1 (January–February 1987): 39.

22. Michael McGinnis, "The Key to Strategic Planning: Integrating Analysis and Intuition," *Sloan Management Review* 26, no. 1 (Fall 1984): 49.

23. McConkey, 72.

CURRENT READINGS

Atkinson, Anthony A., John H. Waterhouse, and Robert B. Wells. "A Stakeholder Approach to Strategic Performance Measurement." *Sloan Management Review* 38, no. 3 (Spring 1997): 25–38.

Banker, R. D., H. H. Chang, and S. K. Majumdar. "A Framework for Analyzing Changes in Strategic Performance." *Strategic Management Journal* 17, no. 9 (November 1996): 693–712.

Hamilton, Robert D. III, Virginia A. Taylor, and Roger J. Kashlak. "Designing a Control System for a Multinational Subsidiary." *Long Range Planning* 29, no. 6 (December 1996): 857–868.

Hitt, Michael A., Robert E. Hoskisson, Richard A. Johnson, and Douglas D. Moesel. "The Market for Corporate Control and Firm Innovation." *Academy of Management Journal* 39, no. 5 (October 1996): 1084–1119.

Kroll, M., P. Wright, L. Toombs, and H. Leavell. "Forms of Control: A Critical Determinant of Acquisition Performance and CEO Rewards." *Strategic Management Journal* 18, no. 2 (February 1997): 85–96.

Lassar, W. M. and J. L. Kerr. "Strategy and Control in Supplier-Distributor Relationships: An Agency Perspective." *Strategic Management Journal* 17, no. 8 (October 1996): 613–632.

Leifer, Richard and Peter K. Mills. "An Information Processing Approach for Deciding upon Control Strategies and Reducing Control Loss in Emerging Organizations." *Journal of Management* 22, no. 1 (1996): 113–138.

Muralidharan, Raman. "Strategic Control for Fast-Moving Markets: Updating the Strategy and Monitoring Performance." *Long Range Planning* 30, no. 1 (February 1997): 64–73.

Noda, T. and J. L. Bower. "Strategy Making as Iterated Processes of Resource Allocation." *Strategic Management Journal* 17, Special Issue (Summer 1996): 159–192.

Slater, Stanley F., Eric M. Olson, and Venkateshwar K. Reddy. "Strategy-Based Performance Measurement." *Business Horizons* 40, no. 4 (July–August 1997): 37–44.

EXPERIENTIAL EXERCISES

Experiential Exercise 9A

PREPARING A STRATEGY-EVALUATION REPORT FOR HERSHEY FOODS

PURPOSE

This exercise can give you experience locating strategy-evaluation information in your college library. Published sources of information can significantly enhance the strategy-evaluation process. Performance information on competitors, for example, can help put into perspective a firm's own performance.

INSTRUCTIONS

Step 1 Use *F & S Index of Corporations and Industries, Business Periodicals Index,* and *The Wall Street Journal Index* in your college library to locate strategy-evaluation information on Hershey, Mars, and Nestlé. Read 5 to 10 articles written in the last 6 months that discuss these firms or the confectionery industry.

Step 2 Summarize your research findings by preparing a strategy-evaluation report for your instructor. Include in your report a summary of Hershey's strategies and performance in 1998 and a summary of your conclusions regarding the effectiveness of Hershey's strategies.

Step 3 Based on your analysis, do you feel Hershey is pursuing effective strategies? What recommendations would you offer Kenneth Wolfe, Hershey's chief executive officer?

Experiential Exercise 9B

EVALUATING MY UNIVERSITY'S STRATEGIES

PURPOSE

An important part of evaluating strategies is determining the nature and extent of changes in an organization's external opportunities/threats and internal strengths/weaknesses. Changes in these underlying critical success factors can indicate a need to change or modify the firm's strategies.

INSTRUCTIONS

As a class, discuss positive and negative changes in your university's external and internal factors during your college career. Begin by listing on the board new or emerging opportunities and threats. Then identify strengths and weaknesses that have changed significantly during your college career. In light of the external and internal changes identified, discuss whether your university's strategies need modifying. Are there any new strategies that you would recommend? Make a list to recommend to your department chair, dean, or chancellor.

WHO PREPARES AN ENVIRONMENTAL AUDIT?

PURPOSE

The purpose of this activity is to determine the nature and prevalence of environmental audits among companies in your state.

INSTRUCTIONS

Contact by phone at least five different plant managers or owners of large businesses in your area. Seek answers to the questions listed below. Present your findings in a written report to your instructor.

1. Does your company conduct an environmental audit? If yes, please describe the nature and scope of the audit.

2. Are environmental criteria included in the performance evaluation of managers? If yes, please specify the criteria.

3. Are environmental affairs more a technical function or a management function in your company?

4. Does your firm offer any environmental workshops for employees? If yes, please describe them.

PART 5

GLOBAL ISSUES IN STRATEGIC MANAGEMENT

CHAPTER 10

International Strategic Management

CHAPTER OUTLINE

- THE NATURE OF GLOBAL COMPETITION
- CULTURES AROUND THE WORLD
- THE GLOBAL CHALLENGE
- MEXICO
- RUSSIA
- CHINA
- JAPAN
- THE EUROPEAN UNION

- GUIDELINES FOR SUCCESS AS A GLOBAL COMPETITOR

- EXPERIENTIAL EXERCISE 10A
  Determining the Competitive Environment for Hershey's Products in Other Countries

- EXPERIENTIAL EXERCISE 10B
  Determining My University's Recruiting Efforts in Foreign Countries

- EXPERIENTIAL EXERCISE 10C
  Lessons in Doing Business Globally

CHAPTER OBJECTIVES

After studying this chapter, you should be able to do the following:

1. Describe the effects of a world economy and global competitors on strategic management.

2. Discuss the nature and strategic implications of diverse cultures around the world.

3. Discuss ramifications of the North American Free Trade Agreement (NAFTA).

4. Discuss changes in Japan as they affect strategy decisions.

5. Discuss changes in Mexico as they affect strategy decisions.

6. Discuss changes in Russia as they affect strategy decisions.

7. Discuss changes in Europe as they affect strategy decisions.

8. Discuss changes in China as they affect strategy decisions.

9. Provide guidelines for firms interested in initiating, continuing, or expanding international operations.

In the 1990s, globalization will mature from a buzzword to a pervasive reality. Companies will have to meet global standards for quality, design, pricing, and service.—BRIAN DUMAINE

Market research is unfamiliar. The closest thing to a market survey that many East Europeans have experienced is a government interrogation.—JOHN QUELCH

Sad but true, U.S. businesspeople have the lowest foreign language proficiency of any major trading nation. U.S. business schools do not emphasize foreign languages, and students traditionally avoid them.—RONALD DULEK

Japan is not going to change. We love to work hard and Americans don't. . . . The result is that we'll continue to work hard and amass huge surpluses of money. We'll buy up your land and you'll live there and pay rent.—WATARU HIRAIZUMI

The inclination of Japanese, Taiwanese, and Korean workers to sacrifice themselves for the good of the firm, in ways that we may find strange, surely bears some relation to their performance and rising competitiveness.—PHILIP WEST

For Americans in the Southwest U.S., the major foreign country that affects business operations is clear. It's Mexico.—KEN THURSTON

One can master a few phrases of Chinese or Japanese, learn that Seoul is west of Tokyo, buy the proper gifts, learn to eat with chopsticks, and still be far from understanding what is really going on in the Far East.—PHILIP WEST

Americans can be more successful if they recognize that foreign managers see them differently than they see themselves.—ARTHUR WHITEHILL

This chapter focuses on international strategic-management issues. Each day, U.S. businesses enter global markets and rival foreign firms enter U.S. markets. One-third of all college students in the United States who receive advanced degrees in science, math, and engineering are foreign citizens.

> Recently, I heard a story about former President George Bush being in a coma for three years and waking to find Dan Quayle standing at his bedside. Upon seeing the vice-president, the president began asking questions. "How long have I been asleep?" The president then inquires about the state of the U.S. economy. To his surprise, Quayle tells him that the budget and the trade deficits have been reduced to zero. Then, the president asks about inflation, which he figures must be at an all-time high. Again, to his surprise, Quayle says that inflation is not a problem. Having his doubts, the president asks for specifics. "How much," he asks "does a first-class stamp cost?" "Very reasonable," Quayle responds, "only 30 yen."[1]

THE NATURE OF GLOBAL COMPETITION

For centuries before Columbus discovered America and surely for centuries to come, businesses have searched and will continue to search for new opportunities beyond their national boundaries. There has never been a more internationalized and economically competitive society than today's. Some American industries, such as textiles, semiconductors, and consumer electronics, are in complete disarray as a result of the international challenge.

Organizations that conduct business operations across national borders are called *international firms* or *multinational corporations*. The term *parent company* refers to a firm investing in international operations, while *host country* is the country where that business is conducted. As illustrated in Figure 10–1, the strategic-management process is conceptually the same for multinational firms as for purely domestic firms; however, the process is more complex for international firms due to the presence of more variables and relationships. Social, cultural, demographic, environmental, political, governmental, legal, technological, and competitive opportunities and threats that face a multinational corporation are almost limitless, and the number and complexity of these factors increase dramatically with the number of products produced and the number of geographic areas served.

More time and effort are required to identify and evaluate external trends and events in multinational corporations. Geographical distance, cultural and national differences, and variations in business practices often make communication between domestic headquarters and overseas operations difficult. Strategy implementation can be more difficult because different cultures have different norms, values, and work ethics.

The fall of communism and advancements in telecommunications are drawing countries, cultures, and organizations worldwide closer together. Foreign revenue as a percent of total company revenues already exceeds 50 percent in hundreds of U.S. firms, including Exxon, Gillette, Dow Chemical, Citicorp, Colgate-Palmolive, and Texaco. Joint ventures and partnerships between domestic and foreign firms are becoming the rule rather than the exception!

World trade centers are proliferating in the United States and abroad because of growing interest in foreign trade. Trade centers were built in Cedar Rapids, Iowa; Santa Ana, California; Hartford, Connecticut; Pomona, California; Long Beach, California; St. Paul, Minnesota; Toledo, Ohio; and Wichita, Kansas. These new world trade centers offer many specialized services, such as assisting small businesses in exporting or importing, and housing foreign banks, export firms, and law offices.

Fully 95 percent of the world's population lives outside the United States, and this group is growing 70 percent faster than the American population! The lineup of competitors

FIGURE 10–1
A Comprehensive Strategic-Management Model

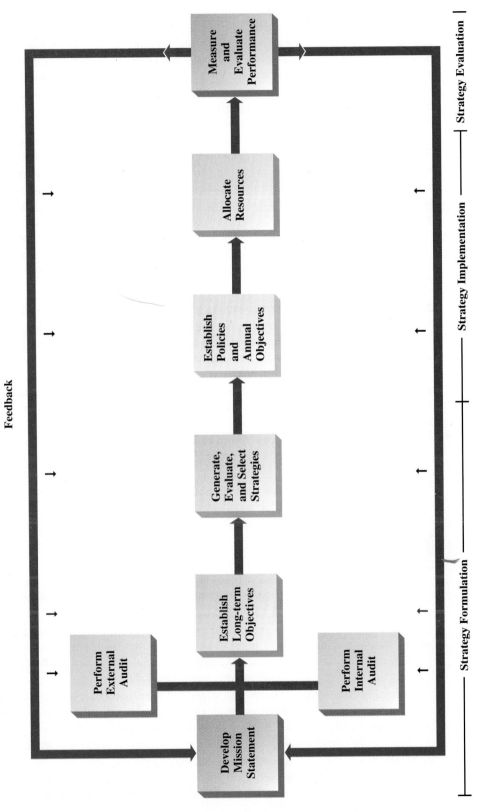

in virtually all industries today is global. Six of the world's 10 largest public companies (in annual revenues) are based in Japan, including Mitsubishi, the largest corporation in the world. Global competition is more than a management fad. General Motors, Ford, and Chrysler compete with Toyota, Daimler Benz, and Hyundai. General Electric and Westinghouse battle Siemens and Mitsubishi. Caterpillar and Deere compete with Komatsu. Goodyear battles Michelin, Bridgestone, and Pirelli. Boeing competes with Airbus. Only a few U.S. industries, such as furniture, printing, retailing, consumer packaged goods, and retail banking, are not yet greatly challenged by foreign competitors. But many products and components in these industries too are now manufactured in foreign countries.

International operations can be as simple as exporting a product to a single foreign country, or as complex as operating manufacturing, distribution, and marketing facilities in many countries. U.S. firms are acquiring foreign companies and forming joint ventures with foreign firms, and foreign firms are acquiring U.S. companies and forming joint ventures with U.S. firms. This trend is accelerating dramatically. AT&T's former Chief Executive Officer, Robert Allen, said, "The phrase *global markets* is not empty rhetoric. Foreign competitors are here. And we must be there." Many U.S. firms have been spoiled by the breadth and plenty of home markets and remain ignorant of foreign languages and culture. Even Hershey Foods derives less than 10 percent of its total revenues from outside the United States.

ADVANTAGES AND DISADVANTAGES OF INTERNATIONAL OPERATIONS

Firms have numerous reasons to formulate and implement strategies that initiate, continue, or expand involvement in business operations across national borders. Perhaps the greatest advantage is that firms can gain new customers for their products and services, thus increasing revenues. Growth in revenues and profits is a common organizational objective and often an expectation of shareholders because it is a measure of organizational success.

In addition to seeking growth, firms have the following potentially advantageous reasons to initiate, continue, and expand international operations:

1. Foreign operations can absorb excess capacity, reduce unit costs, and spread economic risks over a wider number of markets.

2. Foreign operations can allow firms to establish low-cost production facilities in locations close to raw materials and/or cheap labor.

3. Competitors in foreign markets may not exist, or competition may be less intense than in domestic markets.

4. Foreign operations may result in reduced tariffs, lower taxes, and favorable political treatment in other countries.

5. Joint ventures can enable firms to learn the technology, culture, and business practices of other people and to make contacts with potential customers, suppliers, creditors, and distributors in foreign countries.

There are also numerous potential disadvantages of initiating, continuing, or expanding business across national borders. One risk is that foreign operations could be seized by nationalistic factions, which occurred in Kuwait during the Gulf War and in Indonesia more recently. Other disadvantages include the following:

1. Firms confront different and often little-understood social, cultural, demographic, environmental, political, governmental, legal, technological, economic, and competitive forces when doing business internationally. These forces can make communication difficult between the parent firm and subsidiaries.

2. Weaknesses of competitors in foreign lands are often overestimated, and strengths are often underestimated. Keeping informed about the number and nature of competitors is more difficult when doing business internationally.

3. Language, culture, and value systems differ among countries, and this can create barriers to communication and problems managing people.

4. Gaining an understanding of regional organizations such as the European Economic Community, the Latin American Free Trade Area, the International Bank for Reconstruction and Development, and the International Finance Corporation is difficult and often required in doing business internationally.

5. Dealing with two or more monetary systems can complicate international business operations.

CULTURES AROUND THE WORLD

To successfully compete in world markets, U.S. managers must obtain a better knowledge of historical, cultural, and religious forces that motivate and drive people in other countries. In Japan, for example, business relations operate within the context of *Wa*, which stresses group harmony and social cohesion. In China, business behavior revolves around *guanxi*, or personal relations. In Korea, activities involve concern for *inhwa*, or harmony based on respect of hierarchical relationships, including obedience to authority.[2]

In Europe, it is generally true that the farther north on the continent, the more participatory the management style. Most European workers are unionized and enjoy more frequent vacations and holidays than U.S. workers. A 90-minute lunch break plus 20-minute morning and afternoon breaks are common in European firms. Guaranteed permanent employment is commonly a part of employment contracts in Europe. In socialist countries such as France, Belgium, and the United Kingdom, the only ground for immediate dismissal from work is a criminal offense. A six-month trial period at the beginning of employment is usually part of the contract with a European firm. Many Europeans resent pay-for-performance, commission salaries, and objective measurement and reward systems. This is true especially of workers in southern Europe. Many Europeans also find the notion of team spirit difficult to grasp because the unionized environment has dichotomized worker-management relations throughout Europe.

A weakness that U.S. firms have in competing with Pacific Rim firms is a lack of understanding of Far Eastern cultures, including how Asians think and behave. Spoken Chinese, for example, has more in common with spoken English than with spoken Japanese or Korean. Managers around the world face the responsibility of having to exert authority while at the same time trying to be liked by subordinates. U.S. managers consistently put more weight on being friendly and liked, whereas Asian and European managers exercise authority often without this concern. Americans tend to use first names instantly in business dealings with foreigners, but foreigners find this presumptuous. In Japan, for example, first names are used only among family members and intimate friends; even long-time business associates and coworkers shy away from the use of first names. Other cultural differences or pitfalls that U.S. managers need to know are given in Table 10–1.

AMERICAN VERSUS FOREIGN CULTURES   U.S. managers have a low tolerance for silence, whereas Asian managers view extended periods of silence as important for organizing and evaluating one's thoughts. U.S. managers are much more action-oriented than their counterparts around the world; they rush to appointments, conferences, and meetings, and then feel the day has been productive. But for foreign managers, resting, listening, meditating, and thinking is considered productive. Sitting through a conference without talking is unproductive in the United States, but it is viewed as positive in Japan if one's silence helps preserve unity.

TABLE 10–1
Cultural Pitfalls That
You Need To Know

Waving is a serious insult in Greece and Nigeria, particularly if the hand is near someone's face.

Making a "goodbye" wave in Europe can mean "no," but means "come here" in Peru.

In China, last names are written first.

A man named Carlos Lopez-Garcia should be addressed as Mr. Lopez in Latin America, but as Mr. Garcia in Brazil.

Breakfast meetings are considered uncivilized in most foreign countries.

Latin Americans average being 20 minutes late to business appointments.

Direct eye contact is impolite in Japan.

Don't cross your legs in Arab or many Asian countries—it's rude to show the sole of your shoe.

In Brazil, touching your thumb and first finger—an American "OK" sign—is the equivalent of raising your middle finger.

Nodding or tossing your head back in southern Italy, Malta, Greece, and Tunisia means "no." In India, this body motion means "yes."

Snapping your fingers is vulgar in France and Belgium.

Folding your arms across your chest is a sign of annoyance in Finland.

In China, leave some food on your plate to show that your host was so generous that you couldn't finish.

Do not eat with your left hand when dining with clients from Malaysia or India.

One form of communication works the same worldwide. It's the smile, so take that along wherever you go.

U.S. managers also put greater emphasis on short-term results than foreign managers. In marketing, for example, Japanese managers strive to achieve "everlasting customers," whereas many Americans strive to make a one-time sale. Marketing managers in Japan see making a sale as the beginning, not the end, of the selling process. This is an important distinction. Japanese managers often criticize U.S. managers for worrying more about shareholders, whom they do not know, than employees, whom they do know. Americans refer to "hourly employees," whereas Japanese refer to "lifetime employees." As indicated in the Global Perspective, even the varying pervasiveness of the Internet into homes and businesses of various countries may have an effect on the constantly evolving culture of different people.

Rose Knotts recently summarized some important cultural differences between U.S. and foreign managers:[3]

1. Americans place an exceptionally high priority on time, viewing time as an asset. Many foreigners place more worth on relationships. This difference results in foreign managers often viewing U.S. managers as "more interested in business than people."

2. Personal touching and distance norms differ around the world. Americans generally stand about 3 feet from each other in carrying on business conversations, but Arabs and Africans stand about one foot apart. Touching another person with the left hand in business dealings is taboo in some countries. American managers need to learn the personal space rules of foreign managers with whom they interact in business.

3. People in some cultures do not place the same significance on material wealth as American managers often do. Lists of the "largest corporations" and "highest-paid" executives abound in the United States. "More is better" and "bigger is better" in the United States, but not everywhere. This can be a consideration in trying to motivate individuals in other countries.

4. Family roles and relationships vary in different countries. For example, males are valued more than females in some cultures, and peer pressure, work situations, and business interactions reinforce this phenomenon.

GLOBAL PERSPECTIVE
Which Countries Have the Greatest Internet Access?

The following information reveals the extent of Internet access at home and at work among people in 22 different countries.

Source: Adapted from Bodil Jones, "Who's on the Net?" Management Review (September 1997): 6.

Country	Access at Home	Access at Work
United States	27%	25%
Sweden	10	21
Hong Kong	16	20
Australia	14	19
Finland	7	17
Canada	15	14
Netherlands	6	10
Switzerland	6	10
Mexico	2	9
Great Britain	6	8
Germany	5	6
Chile	3	6
Japan	3	6
Cyprus	3	4
Spain	3	4
Greece	2	4
Belgium	1	4
France	2	3
Italy	1	3
Peru	1	3
Turkey	0	3
Portugal	2	2

5. Language differs dramatically across countries, even countries where people speak the same language. Words and expressions commonly used in one country may be greedy or disrespectful in another.

6. Business and daily life in some societies is governed by religious factors. Prayer times, holidays, daily events, and dietary restrictions, for example, need to be respected by American managers not familiar with these practices in some countries.

7. Time spent with the family and quality of relationships are more important in some cultures than the personal achievement and accomplishments espoused by the traditional American manager. For example, where a person is in the hierarchy of a firm's organizational structure, how large the firm is, and where the firm is located are much more important factors to American managers than to many foreign managers.

8. Many cultures around the world value modesty, team spirit, collectivity, and patience much more than the competitiveness and individualism which are so important in America.

9. Punctuality is a valued personal trait when conducting business in America, but it is not revered in many of the world's societies. Eating habits also differ

dramatically across cultures. For example, belching is acceptable in many countries as evidence of satisfaction with the food that has been prepared. Chinese cultures consider it good manners to sample a portion of each food served.

10. To prevent social blunders when meeting with managers from other lands, one must learn and respect the rules of etiquette of others. Sitting on a toilet seat is viewed as unsanitary in most countries, but not the United States. Leaving food or drink after dining is considered impolite in some countries. Bowing instead of shaking hands is customary in many countries. Many cultures view Americans as unsanitary for locating toilet and bathing facilities in the same area, while Americans view people of some cultures as unsanitary for not taking a bath or shower every day.

11. Americans often do business with individuals they do not know, but this practice is not accepted in many other cultures. In Mexico and Japan, for example, an amicable relationship is often mandatory before conducting business.

In many countries, effective managers are those who are best at negotiating with government bureaucrats rather than those who inspire workers. Many U.S. managers are uncomfortable with nepotism and bribery, which are common in many countries. In almost every country except the United States, bribery is tax-deductible.

The United States has gained a reputation for defending women from sexual harassment and minorities from discrimination, but not all countries embrace the same values. For example, in the Czech Republic, it is considered a compliment when the boss openly flirts with his female secretary and invites her to dinner. U.S. managers in the Czech Republic who do not flirt seem cold and uncaring to some employees.

American managers in China have to be careful about how they arrange office furniture because Chinese workers believe in *feng shui*, the practice of harnessing natural forces. American managers in Japan have to be careful about *nemaswashio* whereby Japanese workers expect supervisors to alert them privately of changes rather than informing them in a meeting. Japanese managers have little appreciation for versatility, expecting all managers to be the same. In Japan, "If a nail sticks out, you hit it into the wall," says Brad Lashbrook, an international consultant for Wilson Learning.

Probably the biggest obstacle to the effectiveness of U.S. managers, or managers from any country working in another, is the fact that it is almost impossible to change the attitude of a foreign workforce. "The system drives you; you cannot fight the system or culture," says Bill Parker, president of Phillips Petroleum in Norway.

THE GLOBAL CHALLENGE

Foreign competitors are battering U.S. firms in many industries. In its simplest sense, the international challenge faced by U.S. business is twofold: (1) how to gain and maintain exports to other nations and (2) how to defend domestic markets against imported goods. Few companies can afford to ignore the presence of international competition. Firms that seem insulated and comfortable today may be vulnerable tomorrow; for example, foreign banks do not yet compete or operate in most of the United States.

America's economy is becoming much less American. A world economy and monetary system is emerging. Corporations in every corner of the globe are taking advantage of the opportunity to share in the benefits of worldwide economic development. Markets are shifting rapidly and in many cases converging in tastes, trends, and prices. Innovative transport systems are accelerating the transfer of technology, and shifts in the nature and location of production systems are reducing the response time to changing market conditions.

More and more countries around the world are welcoming foreign investment and capital. As a result, labor markets have steadily become more international. East Asian countries have become market leaders in labor-intensive industries, Brazil offers abundant natural resources and rapidly developing markets, and Germany offers skilled labor and technology. The drive to improve the efficiency of global business operations is leading to greater functional specialization. This is not limited to a search for the familiar low-cost labor in Latin America or Asia. Other considerations include the cost of energy, availability of resources, inflation rates, existing tax rates, and the nature of trade regulations. Yang Shangkun insists that China's door is still open to foreign capital and technology, despite the continued strength of the Communist Party.

The ability to identify and evaluate strategic opportunities and threats in an international environment is a prerequisite competency for strategists. The nuances of competing in international markets are seemingly infinite. Language, culture, politics, attitudes, and economies differ significantly across countries. The availability, depth, and reliability of economic and marketing information in different countries vary extensively, as do industrial structures, business practices, and the number and nature of regional organizations. Differences between domestic and multinational operations that affect strategic management are summarized in Table 10–2.

TABLE 10–2
Differences Between U.S. and Multinational Operations that Affect Strategic Management

FACTOR	U.S. OPERATIONS	INTERNATIONAL OPERATIONS
Language	English used almost universally	Local language must be used in many situations
Culture	Relatively homogeneous	Quite diverse, both between countries and within a country
Politics	Stable and relatively unimportant	Often volatile and of decisive importance
Economy	Relatively uniform	Wide variations among countries and between regions within countries
Government interference	Minimal and reasonably predictable	Extensive and subject to rapid change
Labor	Skilled labor available	Skilled labor often scarce, requiring training or redesign of production methods
Financing	Well-developed financial markets	Poorly developed financial markets Capital flows subject to government control
Market research	Data easy to collect	Data difficult and expensive to collect
Advertising	Many media available; few restrictions	Media limited; many restrictions; low literacy rates rule out print media in some countries
Money	U.S. dollar used	Must change from one currency to another; changing exchange rates and government restrictions are problems
Transportation/ Communication	Among the best in the world	Often inadequate
Control	Always a problem; centralized control will work	A worse problem. Centralized control won't work. Must walk a tightrope between overcentralizing and losing control through too much decentralizing
Contracts	Once signed, are binding on both parties, even if one party makes a bad deal	Can be voided and renegotiated if one party becomes dissatisfied
Labor relations	Collective bargaining; can lay off workers easily	Often cannot lay off workers; may have mandatory worker participation in management; workers may seek change through political process rather than collective bargaining
Trade barriers	Nonexistent	Extensive and very important

Source: R. G. Murdick, R. C. Moor, R. H. Eckhouse, and T. W. Zimmerer, *Business Policy: A Framework for Analysis*, 4th ed. (Columbus, Ohio: Grid Publishing Company, 1984): 275.

THE IMPACT OF DIVERSE INDUSTRIAL POLICIES   Some *industrial policies* include providing government subsidies, promoting exports, restructuring industries, nationalizing businesses, imposing regulations, changing tax laws, instituting pollution standards, and establishing import quotas. The vicissitudes of foreign affairs make identifying and selecting among alternative strategies more challenging for multinational corporations (MNCs) than for their domestic counterparts.

> Strategic management has proven to be a valuable tool in the successful firm's repertoire. Firms traveling on the path of international business face more risks than their domestic counterparts, but also may reap greater rewards. Properly done, strategic management offers these firms a map to guide them on their journey through the perilous paths of international business.[4]

Perhaps the greatest threat to domestic firms engaged in international operations is the national and international debt situation. When countries become excessively leveraged, they frequently turn to slashing imports and boosting exports to generate trade surpluses capable of servicing their debt. Faced with these policies, domestic firms producing for export markets can often no longer import essential inputs. When a debtor country is successful in boosting its exports, domestic firms often encounter a protectionist backlash in foreign countries.

Multinational business strategists can contribute to the solution of economic trade problems and improve their firms' competitive positions by maintaining and strengthening communication channels with domestic and foreign governments. Strategists are commonly on the front line of trade and financial crises around the world, so they often have direct knowledge of the gravity and interrelated nature of particular problems. Strategists should relay this knowledge and experience to political leaders. A steady stream of counsel and advice from international business strategists to policymakers and lawmakers is needed.

Strategists in multinational corporations need an understanding of foreign governments' industrial policies. Industrial policies differ from country to country as governments take different actions to develop their own economies. For example, cooperation between business and government in Japan is so good that some experts doubt whether a clear distinction exists there between government and business; some even use the term "Japan, Inc." when referring to the Japanese government and particularly the Ministry for International Trade and Industry (MITI).

Multinational corporations face unique and diverse risks such as expropriation of assets, currency losses through exchange rate fluctuations, unfavorable foreign court interpretations of contracts and agreements, social/political disturbances, import/export restrictions, tariffs, and trade barriers. Strategists in MNCs are often confronted with the need to be globally competitive and nationally responsive at the same time. With the rise in world commerce, government and regulatory bodies are more closely monitoring foreign business practices. The United States Foreign Corrupt Practices Act, for example, defines corrupt practices in many areas of business. A sensitive issue is that some MNCs sometimes violate legal and ethical standards of the home country, but not of the host country.

Before entering international markets, firms should scan relevant journals and patent reports, seek the advice of academic and research organizations, participate in international trade fairs, form partnerships, and conduct extensive research to broaden their contacts and diminish the risk of doing business in new markets. Firms can also reduce the risks of doing business internationally by obtaining insurance from the United States government's Overseas Private Investment Corporation (OPIC).

GLOBALIZATION   Globalization is a process of worldwide integration of strategy formulation, implementation, and evaluation activities. Strategic decisions are made based on their impact upon global profitability of the firm, rather than on just domestic or other individual country considerations. A global strategy seeks to meet the needs of customers

FIGURE 10–2
The Typical Evolution of an MNC

Begin Export Operations	*Conduct Licensing Activities*	*Add Foreign Sales Representatives*	*Build Foreign Manufacturing Facilities*	*Establish a Foreign Division of the Firm*	*Establish Several Foreign Business Units*	*An MNC*

Source: Adapted from C. A. Bartlett, "How Multinational Organizations Evolve," *Journal of Business Strategy* (Summer 1982): 20–32. Also, D. Shanks, "Strategic Planning for Global Competition," *Journal of Business Strategy* (Winter 1985): 83.

worldwide with the highest value at the lowest cost. This may mean locating production in countries with the lowest labor costs or abundant natural resources, locating research and complex engineering centerswhere skilled scientists and engineers can be found, and locating marketing activities close to the markets to be served. A global strategy includes designing, producing, and marketing products with global needs in mind, instead of considering individual countries alone. A global strategy integrates actions against competitors into a worldwide plan.

Globalization of industries is occurring for many reasons, including a worldwide trend toward similar consumption patterns, the emergence of global buyers and sellers, and instant transmission of money and information across continents. The European Economic Community (EEC), religions, the Olympics, the World Bank, world trade centers, the Red Cross, the Internet, environmental conferences, telecommunications, and economic summits all contribute to global interdependencies and the emerging global marketplace.

David Shanks, manager of the Strategic Management Unit of Arthur D. Little, suggested that three major factors are driving many domestic firms into international operations: (1) the maturing economies of industrialized nations, (2) the emergence of new geographic markets and business arenas, and (3) the globalization of financial systems.[5] The typical evolution of a domestic firm into a multinational corporation is illustrated in Figure 10–2.

It is clear that different industries become global for different reasons. Convergence of income levels and standardization is what made designer clothing a universal product. The need to amortize massive R&D investments over many markets is a major reason why the aircraft manufacturing industry became global. Monitoring globalization in one's industry is an important strategic-management activity. Knowing how to use that information for one's competitive advantage is even more important. For example, firms may look around the world for the best technology and select one that has the most promise for the largest number of markets. When firms design a product, they design it to be marketable in as many countries as possible. When firms manufacture a product, they select the lowest cost source, which may be Japan for semiconductors, Sri Lanka for textiles, Malaysia for simple electronics, and Europe for precision machinery. MNCs design manufacturing systems to accommodate world markets. One of the riskiest strategies for a domestic firm is to remain solely a domestic firm in an industry that is rapidly becoming global.

MEXICO

POLITICS   Mexico is a much better place for doing business in 1998 than in 1994 when Ernesto Zedillo, holding a Ph.D. from Yale, first was elected president. Zedillo and his government have made significant political, social, and economic progress in Mexico. He has basically reinvented Mexico's economic model with a focus on export-led growth, higher savings rates, and careful management of finances. Direct foreign investment into Mexico is forecasted to rise to $10.8 billion in the year 2000. Mexico's gross domestic product grew nearly 9 percent in 1997, the fastest annual growth rate in 20 years. Wages, inflation, and the value of the peso are under control.

Passage of the North American Free Trade Agreement (NAFTA) and the resultant lower tariffs have spurred trade between the United States and Mexico. NAFTA enabled Mexico to export its way out of the severe 1994 peso crisis. In January 1998, Mexico passed Japan as the second-largest market for U.S. products, trailing only Canada. Passage of NAFTA did not, as Ross Perot predicted, "create a giant sucking sound as U.S. jobs move south." U.S. unemployment rates remain low.

In the 1997 regional Mexican elections, a mayor of Mexico City was elected for the first time rather than being appointed by the president. The winner was Cuauhtemoc Cardenas, a leftist Democratic Revolutionary Party candidate who likely will challenge Zedillo for the presidency in the year 2000. Receiving only 21 percent of the mayoral vote, the old, autocratic Institutional Revolutionary Party (PRI) appears to be losing power after ruling Mexico from 1924 to 1994. PRI, which opposes privatization of industries, rigs elections, buys politicians, owns law enforcement officers, hires gangs of murderers, and supports drug traffickers, is losing power in Mexico.

President Zedillo, a member of the conservative middle-class National Action Party, is dedicated to fighting the drug trade, privatizing industry, reducing corruption, promoting democracy, and improving the natural environment. Zedillo is good for Mexico and offers hope. But his government has much work to be done before he runs for reelection in the year 2000. Nearly 80 percent of Mexico's wealth rests with 30 families. About 20 percent of the population lives on roughly a dollar per day income. About 60 percent of Mexican workers take home less than $140 per month. The minimum wage is still 80 cents per hour. Unemployment rates and interest rates are high. Banks are reluctant to make loans because consumer and business delinquency rates are high.

Shipment of illegal drugs to the United States via Mexico has climbed every year and now exceeds $120 billion per year. This level is more than twice the value of Mexico's legal exports. Over 20 percent of the Mexican population in rural areas is actually employed by drug traffickers, who have built schools and hospitals for their workers and invested in local banks. The U.S. Drug Enforcement Administration estimates that 75 percent of all drugs entering the United States from South America now come through Mexico, up from 25 percent in the 1980s. Pornography, prostitution, drug addiction, drug trafficking, illegal immigration, and pollution still are severe problems for business and society.

THE U.S.–MEXICAN BORDER   Stretching 2,100 miles from the Pacific Ocean to the Gulf of Mexico, this 180-mile wide strip of land is North America's fastest-growing region. With 11 million people and $150 billion in output, this region is an economy larger than Poland. For the 6.1 million residents on the U.S. side, the average hourly wage plus benefits is $7.71, but for the 5.1 million residents on the Mexican side, the average is $1.36. The First and Third Worlds meet along this border, which features shantytowns just down the street from luxury residential neighborhoods.

There are now over 1,500 *maquiladoras*, assembly plants on the Mexican side of the border. Many analysts contend that the *maquiladoras* are a vital key to continued U.S. global competitiveness. Mexico now ranks only behind China as global investors' favorite location for establishing business in the developing world. Amidst the swelter of economic activity, deep disparities and contrasts are likely to persist. But the two sides of the border are now so interdependent that they can only move forward together.

Tijuana, 15 minutes from San Diego, is the television-manufacturing capital of the world. Plants of Sony, Samsung, Matsushita, and others produce 14 million units annually.

Per capita income in San Diego is $25,000; in Tijuana, $3,200. Tijuana's *maquiladoras* employed 118,000 in 1996, up 28 percent from the prior year.

Cuidad Juarez, midway between the Pacific Ocean and the Gulf of Mexico and just 15 minutes from El Paso, has 235 factories employing 178,000, the largest concentration of *maquiladoras* anywhere along the border. General Motors alone has 17 auto parts plants. But explosive industrial growth and uncontrolled urban expansion have far surpassed municipal services such as sewers and street paving. Juarez and El Paso share the worst air pollution anywhere on the border.

Nuevo Laredo, 15 minutes from Laredo, Texas, is home to the largest rail and truck crossings of the Rio Grande River from Mexico into the United States. More than 4,000 loaded trucks cross the Rio Grande at Nuevo Laredo, which is home to Wal-Mart's largest distribution center.

CULTURE   Mexico always has been and still is an authoritarian society in terms of schools, churches, businesses, and families. Employers seek workers who are agreeable, respectful, and obedient, rather than innovative, creative, and independent. Mexican workers tend to be activity-oriented rather than problem solvers. When visitors walk into a Mexican business, they are impressed by the cordial friendly atmosphere. This is almost always true because Mexicans desire harmony rather than conflict; desire for harmony is an overriding social fabric in worker-manager relations. There is a much lower tolerance for adversarial relations or friction at work in Mexico as compared to the United States.

Mexican employers are paternalistic, providing workers with more than a paycheck, but in return, they expect allegiance. Weekly food baskets, free meals, free bus service, and free day care are often a part of compensation. The ideal working conditions for a Mexican worker is the family model, with everyone working together, doing their share, according to their designated roles. Mexican workers do not expect or desire a work environment where self-expression and initiative are encouraged. Whereas U.S. business embodies individualism, achievement, competition, curiosity, pragmatism, informality, spontaneity, and doing more than expected on the job, Mexican businesses stress collectivism, continuity, cooperation, belongingness, formality, and doing exactly what you're told.

In Mexico, business associates only rarely entertain at their home, a place reserved exclusively for close friends and family. Business meetings and entertaining are nearly always done at a restaurant. Preserving one's honor, saving face, and looking important is also exceptionally important in Mexico. This is why Mexicans do not accept criticism and change easily; many find it humiliating to acknowledge having made a mistake. A meeting among employees and managers in a business located in Mexico is a forum for giving orders and directions rather than for discussing problems or participating in decision making. Mexican workers desire to be closely supervised, cared for, and corrected in a civil manner. Opinions expressed by employees are often regarded as back talk in Mexico. Mexican supervisors are viewed as weak if they explain the rationale for their orders to workers.

Mexicans do not feel compelled to follow rules that are not associated with a particular person in authority they know well or work for. Thus, signs to wear ear plugs or safety glasses, or attendance or seniority policies, and even one-way street signs are often ignored. Whereas Americans follow the rules, Mexicans often do not.

Life is slower in Mexico than in the United States. People do not wear watches. The first priority is often assigned to the last request, rather than the first. Telephone systems break down. Banks may suddenly not have pesos. Phone repair can take months. Electricity for an entire plant or town can be down for hours or even days. Business and government offices open and close at different hours. Buses and taxis may be hours off schedule.

Meeting times for appointments are not rigid. Tardiness is common everywhere. Doing business effectively in Mexico requires knowledge of the Mexican way of life, culture, beliefs, and customs.

As noted, Mexican minimum wage is 80 cents per hour. Easier access to Mexico's abundant, low-cost, high-quality labor has spurred U.S. firms to locate manufacturing facilities in Mexico. Jerry Perlman, former president and chairman of Zenith Electronics Corporation, said, "If we didn't have support operations in Mexico, our annual operating costs would be $350 million to $400 million higher, and we'd be out of business." Despite low wages in Mexico, Mexicans are acquiring a global reputation for quality work, as evidenced by Ford Motor Company's $1 billion Hermosillo plant, which recently tied the Daimler-Benz plant in Germany for the auto industry's first-place award for lowest production defects.

NEW BUSINESS OPPORTUNITIES   Mexico's a good place for business for many reasons, including the fact that Mexicans are a hard-working people; 12-hour workdays are common. Also, the corporate income tax rate in Mexico is 35 percent, there are no taxes on dividends, local governments do not tax corporate income, there are no constraints on dividend and capital repatriation, and franchisers are allowed unlimited repatriation of royalties. Also, the fisheries, petrochemicals, and trucking industries have been deregulated, and more than 100 state businesses from airlines to petrochemicals have been privatized. By law, Mexican children must attend school for 10 years, and 88 percent of the citizenry is literate.

U.S. electronics and garment companies have established *maquiladoras* on the U.S.–Mexico border. AT&T, for example, moved its cordless-phone repair operation to Mexico from Singapore. DuPont Company and SCI Systems also are expanding their facilities in Guadalajara. Wal-Mart opened five warehouse clubs, called Club Aurrera, in a joint venture with Cifra, Mexico's largest retailer. Sears, Roebuck is spending $150 million to open new stores in Mexico. Southwestern Bell Corporation of St. Louis acquired Telefonos de Mexico, the state phone monopoly, and PepsiCo acquired Gamesa, the huge snack food firm. Unilever Group acquired part of Conasupo, the Mexican commodities company. Nissan plans a $1 billion expansion of its assembly plant in Aguascalientes. Compaq Computer, Lotus Development Corporation, and Microsoft have opened large subsidiaries in Mexico City.

RUSSIA

President Boris Yelsin has notified his country and the world that he will not seek reelection in the year 2000. Candidates are already jockeying to succeed him. Three frontrunners are former Prime Minister Viktor Chernomyrdin; First Deputy Prime Minister Boris Nemtsov; and Alexander Lebed, a former general. There could be political and economic turmoil in Russia leading up to this election.

Since the breakup of the Soviet Union in 1991, Russia and 11 other countries have made uneven progress toward economic reform, free markets, and openness to foreign investment and trade. Each of the countries is pursuing a political and economic reform agenda, although the pace of implementation varies significantly. The majority of these economies are now experiencing declining output, rising unemployment, difficult inflationary battles, and rapidly decaying infrastructures.

CORRUPTION   In recent years, Russia privatized nearly 200,000 businesses that employed 70 percent of the nation's workforce. Privatizing simply meant giving the firm to its workers. Being untrained and unorganized, these workers most often, in turn, gave the firm to the top directors, who have largely become rich barons. Nearly 90 percent of Russian employees still live below the poverty level. "Imagine if Lee Iacocca had thought about nothing all day but how to steal from Chrysler," says Mikhail Harshan. "This is the situation in 99 percent of Russian businesses." Many Russians eat cabbage, bread, and potatoes at nearly every meal; most live in crowded apartments sharing bedrooms and bathrooms with other families.

The climate for business in Russia worsened from 1996 to 1998 due to further director stealing, the war in Chechnya, continued devaluation of the ruble, high unemployment, high inflation, skyrocketing taxes, and increased crime. Russian tax laws are among the world's most punitive and confusing, so firms keep business off the books to avoid paying out about 90 percent of profits to the government. Tax receipts by the Russian government are far lower than expected or needed to run the country.

It is almost impossible today to run a business in Russia legally. Racketeering, money laundering, financial scams, and organized criminal activity plague business. President Boris Yeltsin's greatest failure is the state's forced criminalization of the economy. More than 500 businesspeople are murdered annually, such as American businessman Paul Tatum, murdered in Moscow after disputes with the city over control of his Radisson Slavjanskaya Hotel. Over 40,000 Russian enterprises are connected in some way to organized crime. Ten of Russia's 25 largest banks are operated by organized crime bosses. There are daily reports of business disputes being settled fatally. A U.S. businessman disappeared in Moscow in mid-1997 while two Philip Morris employees and their families narrowly escaped with their lives.

Even President Yeltsin's executive branch of the government is now described as crooked, unpredictable, and capricious in dealing with businesses. But Yeltsin's capitalism and free economy is now so firmly entrenched in Russia that there is little fear of a return to the old communism.

The risk of business investments in Russia decreases from south to north and west to east. Thus, investments in Siberia and along the Pacific coast are more stable and much less corrupt than those near Moscow or the Russian areas bordering Europe. Because the ruble is virtually of no value in Russia, companies need to pay their workers with something besides money, such as apartments, health care, and medical and food products. Bartering is an excellent way to motivate Russian workers.

Russia's economic problems are evidenced in the fact that the number of domestic airline passengers plunged for the sixth straight year in 1996 to 26.9 million, from a peak of 90.7 million in 1990. U.S. companies investing in Russia today speak of getting a toehold there, not a foothold. It is just too risky.

A $1.5 billion agreement between the Russian government and Exxon over oil drilling was shockingly abandoned by Russia in late 1997 because Exxon was meticulous in following the letter of the law.

THE RUSSIAN CULTURE   In America, unsuccessful business entrepreneurs are viewed negatively as failures, whereas successful small business owners enjoy high esteem and respect. In Russia, however, there is substantial social pressure against becoming a successful entrepreneur. Being a winner in Russia makes you the object of envy and resentment, a member of the elite rather than of the masses. Personal ambition and success are often met with vindictiveness and derision. Initiative is met with indifference at best and punishment at worst. In the face of public ridicule and organized crime, however, thousands of Russians, particularly young persons, are opening all kinds of businesses. Public scorn and their own guilt from violating the values they were raised with do not deter many. Because Russian society scorns success, publicizing achievements, material possessions, awards, or privileges earned by Russian workers is not an effective motivation tool for those workers.

The Russian people are best known for their drive, boundless energy, tenacity, hard work, and perseverance in spite of immense obstacles. This is as true today as ever. The notion that the average Russian is stupid or lazy is nonsense; Russians on average are more educated than their American counterparts and bounce up more readily from failure.

In the United States, business ethics and personal ethics are essentially the same. Deception is deception and a lie is a lie whether in business or personal affairs in America. However, in Russia, business and personal ethics are separate. To deceive someone, bribe someone, or lie to someone to promote a business transaction is ethical in Russia, but to deceive a friend or trusted colleague is unethical. There are countless examples of foreign firms being cheated by Russian business partners. The implication of this fact for American businesses is to forge strong personal relationships with their Russian business partners whenever possible; spend time with the Russians eating, relaxing, and exercising; and in the absence of a personal relationship, be exceptionally cautious with agreements, partnerships, payments, and granting credit.

The Russian people have great faith, confidence, and respect for American products and services. Russians generally have low self-confidence. American ideas, technology, and production practices are viewed by Russians as a panacea that can save them from a gloomy existence. For example, their squeaky telephone system and lack of fax machines make them feel deprived. This mind-set presents great opportunity in Russia for American products of all kinds.

Russia has historically been an autocratic state. This cultural factor is evident in business; Russian managers generally exercise power without ever being challenged by subordinates. Delegation of authority and responsibility is difficult and often nonexistent in Russian businesses. The American participative management style is not well received in Russia.

A crackdown on religion is underway in Russia. In 1997, the government considered a law to recognize only Russian Orthodoxy, Judaism, Islam, and Buddhism as indigenous religions. All other faiths and churches, including all Christian demoninations, would have to apply each year for permission to practice in Russia. Permission simply may not be granted. President Yeltsin opposes the antireligion movement and new law, but is losing the battle to prevent religious persecution—especially directed at Christians—throughout the country. The lower house of Russia's parliament, the State Duma, is dominated by Communists who favor antireligion and resist further economic reforms.

TRADE   The major barriers to increased U.S. exports to Russia are a substantial value-added tax, high import duties, and onerous Russian excise levies. In addition, the government has imposed strict quality and safety standards on the majority of goods entering Russia. However, Russian standards authorities have permitted only a tightly circumscribed number of groups to perform this testing in the United States. The customs clearance process at Russian borders points is frequently cumbersome and unpredictable. Local transportation problems also complicate the process of getting goods to the Russian market.

The 10 best prospects for U.S. exports to Russia are telecommunications equipment, computers and computer peripherals, pollution control equipment, oil and gas field machinery, construction equipment, medical equipment, electric power systems equipment, automotive parts and services, building products, and food processing and packaging equipment. The increasing ability of local organizations to pay for substantive improvements in Russia's deteriorated infrastructure also will stimulate imports of more U.S. products.

In terms of population, Russia is larger than all the other former Soviet bloc countries combined and is the fifth-largest country in the world. Russia has more oil reserves than

Saudi Arabia, vast quantities of timber and gold, and first-rate scientists. Russia spans 11 time zones. Donald Kendall, former CEO of PepsiCo, said the Soviet disintegration "means chaos in the short term but immense business opportunities in the long term. If U.S. companies wait until all the problems are solved, somebody else will get the business."

SMALL BUSINESS Many American entrepreneurs have gotten ideas for launching businesses in Russia by living in Russia and seeing for themselves how bad the services are. Stories abound about such woes as sheets coming back from the laundry with holes in them, shirts coming back from the dry cleaners missing buttons, scratchy copies of movie videos, and the widespread rudeness of shop employees. Even searching for a good meal is difficult. Lisa Dobbs, a trained French chef and wife of a foreign correspondent turned good food into a money-making enterprise. She called a Western news organization and offered to cook lunch and dinner every day for its Moscow employees. It accepted. Soon she formed Moscow Catering Co./ Kalitnikovski Produkti. Today, the catering firm has 18 employees and is swamped with orders. It recently began selling prepared food.

American entrepreneurs in Russia face numerous roadblocks. Just registering one's company with the Russian government can take 6 months. Most renovated commercial real estate in Moscow is too expensive for small firms, forcing them to settle in dingy, overcrowded office buildings.

But the opportunities for foreign entrepreneurs in Russia are huge. After-tax profits can be repatriated without restriction. Many entrepreneurs initially in business to meet the needs of foreigners are finding that demand from Russians drives growth.

Today, entrepreneurs in Russia are offering everything from catering services to video rentals to fitness centers. "There's a lot of money to be made," says Michael L. Oster, managing director of Oster & Co., a Moscow real estate and development firm. "Basically, there's still a need for just about everything." The potential for political unrest in Russia is troubling to businesspeople in that country, but the opportunities for entrepreneurs are limitless.

MONEY Russia now recognizes individual rights, including equality, privacy, freedom of speech, conscience, and free choice of work. However, these newly won freedoms have contributed to skyrocketing prices and consumer discontent. A major problem facing Russia is economic disarray. The ruble is grossly overvalued at the official exchange rate of $1.79, but the black market rate is 3 cents. Companies doing business with Russian firms must hedge against the drop of the ruble's dollar value. Many companies will not do business with the former Soviets until the ruble is converted to a gold standard like all major currencies of the world because the two-tier exchange rate is unwieldy.

JOINT VENTURES A joint venture strategy offers an excellent way to enter the Russian market. Joint ventures create a mechanism to generate hard currency, which is important due to problems valuing the ruble. Russia's joint venture law has been revised to allow foreigners to own up to 99 percent of the venture and to allow a foreigner to serve as chief executive officer.

The list of U.S. companies that have active joint ventures with Russia include Archer-Daniels-Midland, Chevron, Combustion Engineering, Dresser Industries, Hewlett-Packard, Honeywell, Johnson & Johnson, MCI, Marriott, McDonald's, Ogilvy & Mather, Radisson, RJR/Nabisco, and Young & Rubicam. In the aerospace industry, Russian firms are cooperating with Germany's Messerschmitt Company; in computers, with IBM; in manufacturing, with Combustion Engineering, Honeywell, and Siemens; in nuclear power, with Asea, Brown Boveri, and Siemens; and in telecommunications, with Nokia. PepsiCo, Inc., recently formed a joint venture with Moscow Metropolitan to sell PepsiCo food products in Moscow's subway stations.

Most analysts believe Russia will become a market that many U.S. firms will want to enter. Those firms that start mastering the complexities early and keep informed about the latest developments may likely gain the biggest rewards. Thousands of businesses in Russia have been given financial independence and broad management autonomy. Poor telecommunications equipment, however, often isolates foreign managers in Russia from the parent company. Russia's telephone system is comparable to the U.S. phone system of the 1930s.

GUIDELINES FOR STRATEGIC VENTURES The following guidelines are appropriate when considering a strategic venture into Russia. First, avoid regions with ethnic conflicts and violence. Also, make sure the potential partner has a proper charter that has been amended to permit joint venture participation. Be aware that businesspeople in these lands have little knowledge of marketing, contract law, corporate law, fax machines, voice mail, and other business practices that Westerners take for granted.

Business contracts with Russian firms should address natural environment issues because Westerners often get the blame for air and water pollution problems and habitat destruction. Work out a clear means of converting rubles to dollars before entering a proposed joint venture because neither Russian banks nor authorities can be counted on to facilitate foreign firms' getting dollar profits out of a business. Recognize that chronic shortages of raw materials hamper business in Russia, so make sure an adequate supply of competitively priced, good-quality raw materials is reliably available. Finally, make sure the business contract limits the circumstances in which expropriation would be legal. Specify a lump sum in dollars if expropriation should occur unexpectedly, and obtain expropriation insurance before signing the agreement.

A number of organizations in Russia assist foreign companies interested in initiating, continuing, or expanding business operations there. Some of these organizations are Amtorg, the Consultation Center of the Chamber of Commerce and Industry, Inpred, Interfact, and the U.S. Commercial Office (USCO). Inpred, for example, is a consulting firm in Russia that helps Western managers operate within regulations. Inpred also helps foreign firms locate partners in the republics and develop contracts, and contacts officials to set up meetings between Russian and foreign businesspersons. USCO annually sponsors about 25 trade fairs and exhibitions that introduce foreign companies and individuals to the new Russian markets, customers, buyers, and sellers.

CHINA

DEMOGRAPHICS As indicated in Table 10–3, China is almost exactly the same size as the United States, but differs in many other respects. The world's tallest building is the new 1,518-foot Shanghai World Financial Center in Shanghai, China, replacing the Petronas Towers in Juala Lumpur, Malaysia. Hong Kong was peacefully annexed, and long-time Communist dictator President Deng Xiaoping died and was replaced without incident. The Shanghai building and recent events symbolize the great economic progress China made from 1996 to 1998.

One of last remaining tenets of Marxism, the taboo against private ownership of large industrial enterprises, has been abandoned in China. President Jiang Zemin encourages all types of state- and locally owned companies to issue shares of stock to diversify their ownership. State-owned enterprises accounted for 62 percent of industrial production in 1986 but today account for only 35 percent. China today is powered by small private businesses, foreign-owned companies, joint ventures, agricultural collectives, and profitable village- and township-owned businesses.

	U.S.	CHINA	HONG KONG
Area (in thousands of sq. miles)	3,679	3,696	.415
Population (in millions)	265	1,200	6.3
Average urban population growth rate (1990–1994)	1.3%	4.1%	1.7%
Labor force (in millions, 1994)	131	715	3
Life expectancy	77	69	78
% of people with access to safe water	100	67	100
% of people with access to sanitation	95	24	85
% adult illiteracy	4	19	8
Infant mortality (per 1,000 live births)	8	30	5
Exports (in billions), 1996	$625	$151	$140
Imports (in billions), 1996	$795	$139	$153

TABLE 10–3
Comparing the United States, China, and Hong Kong

Source: Adapted from Marcus Brauchli and Joseph Kahn, "Hong Kong Yields China Both Victory and Challenge," *The Wall Street Journal* (July 1, 1997): 10.

POLITICS   Under the leadership of President Jiang Zemin, China is making rapid progress toward becoming a stable, economic trading partner in Asia. China is moving forward quickly with privatization, deregulation, reform through stock issuances to workers, stock listings, divestitures, mergers, bankruptcies, and sale of the country's 370,000 state-run enterprises. More than half of these enterprises are losing money, which undermines the health of state banks and overall reform. About half of the 113 million workers employed by these enterprises are not needed and do not work, yet still receive full benefits.

China still has more than 120 television manufacturers, 700 beer companies, and 30,000 rubber belt makers. But the state is encouraging merger and consolidation, which is transforming the economic landscape. There were 1,100 Chinese company mergers in 1997, up 33 percent from 1996. Jiang's plan is to create large, private, efficient, Chinese companies that can compete effectively and globally.

Jiang is also focusing on improving health care, pensions, education, unemployment, and poverty relief by strengthening the rule of law, promoting greater separation of government and business, and guaranteeing human rights. In 1998, China extended direct elections from villages to townships. Jiang has cut the number of specialized economic departments to ease bureaucratic meddling in business.

Jiang, however, is tightening control over the press and publishing and upholds the ruling role of the Communist Party. The Chinese government will retain control over only about 1,000 enterprises, including all those involved in infrastructure, telecommunications, certain raw materials, and the military. Labor protests in China climbed 50 percent to 3,000 in 1996 as unemployment rates climbed to 15 percent. Another 1,400 protests were reported in the first half of 1997. But what is different this time compared to 1989 when China smashed similar demonstrations in Tiananmen Square is that appeasement and conciliation, not violence, is used to end the protests. Beijing has evolved a policy of engaging protesters in dialogue and trying to mediate.

China still only takes in about 12 percent of gross domestic product in taxes, about one-third the level of most developed countries. This leaves the country strapped for cash in providing even the most basic social needs. For example, China spent only 3.8 percent of its GDP on health care, compared with about 10 percent in developed countries. Instead, state-controlled banks and companies had to take care of society's needs, which bankrupted more than half of these institutions. However, China is releasing state companies from the burden of providing health care, pensions, and housing by setting up national health and retirement systems.

Jiang Zemin's reform agenda consists of five key strategies:

1. **Restructure state enterprises.** Convert state enterprises into corporations owned by shareholders.
2. **Strengthen financial markets.** Expand capital markets by authorizing hundreds of new stock listings annually.
3. **Sell state assets.** Require all but 1,000 of China's 305,000 state enterprises to sell to shareholders or go bankrupt.
4. **Build social services.** Build low-cost housing, set up pension programs, and retrain workers to relieve burderns on state enterprises.
5. **Reduce Tariffs.** Reduce tariffs from 17 percent in 1997 to 15 percent in 2000 as part of a bid to join the World Trade Organization.[6]

OPPORTUNITIES U.S. firms increasingly are doing business in China as market reforms create a more businesslike arena daily. Foreign direct investment in China reached a massive $47 billion in 1996 and another $40 billion in 1997. This placed China second behind the United States, with annual $85 billion, as the most desirable country in the world for foreign investment.

China has set aside $3.6 billion annually to clear bad debts of state-run enterprises to help them plan to merge, divest, or declare bankruptcy. China's massive privatization program enables foreign firms to acquire state-run enterprises at bargain prices and thus gain a foothold in the Chinese market. Motorola, for example, had $3.4 billion in sales in 1996 from Hong Kong and China. Asia accounted for 21 percent of Intel's revenue in 1996, compared to 11 percent in 1995, primarily due to skyrocketing personal computer sales in China. IBM's sales within China are growing 50 percent annually, to more than $700 million in 1997.

In an effort to appease opponents of China entering the World Trade Organization (WTO), China in late 1997 reduced its average tariff rates by 26 percent, from 23 percent to 17 percent, on 4,800 items shipped in and out of the country. These cuts have accelerated national economic growth even more. If China is admitted soon, as expected, into the WTO, this should further accelerate economic development and trade. The major reason why the United States has historically not supported China's acceptance into WTO has been that country's human rights violations.

China Telecom, a state company, eclipsed AT&T as the world's largest provider of mobile phone services. China lays enough phone cable each year to rewire California. In late 1997, China added its 100 millionth phone line. China plans to spend $60 billion on telecommunications infrastructure through the year 2000, almost all through state-owned businesses. Telecommunications is a top priority in China.

China is modernizing its stock and bond markets so that companies can depend less on banks for financing.

Evidence of the success of China's market reforms is the government's attitude toward Hong Kong. As promised, China is operating Hong Kong as a separate democratic state with freedom of religion, press, and speech, and a fair legal system. Hong Kong is the centerpiece of China's efforts to reform, privatize, and expand imports and exports worldwide. The map in Figure 10–3 illustrates Hong Kong's strategic location for China. With its 6.3 million people, magnificent harbor, financial wealth, 500 banks from 43 countries, the world's eighth-largest stock market, and minimum taxation, Hong Kong serves as the gateway to fast-growing China. U.S. companies alone have 178 regional headquarters in Hong Kong and $10.5 billion in direct investment.

China's approach toward Taiwan has even changed from adversarial and confrontational to diplomatically appealing to Taiwanese to observe the Hong Kong experience and

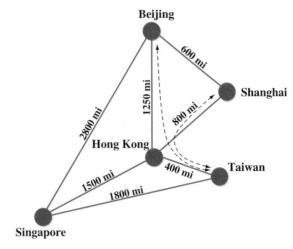

FIGURE 10–3
Hong Kong's Strategic Location

consider reuniting with mainland China. Taiwan's President Lee Teng-Hui says unification depends on assurances of democracy; China may soon grant these as needed.

There is a growing list of U.S. success stories in China. Holiday Inn has a 448-room hotel in Lhasa, Tibet. Boeing is selling 14 percent of its production to Chinese airlines. Ford and Chrysler are making money manufacturing automobiles or component parts. Playboy Enterprises operates nearly 200 sportswear boutiques in Chinese stores. Nike, Compaq Computer, Hughes, General Electric, and Weyerhaeuser are making money in their operations in China.

RISKS IN DOING BUSINESS   Risks that still restrain firms from initiating business with China include the following:

◆ Poor infrastructure

◆ Disregard for the natural environment

◆ Absence of a legal system

◆ Rampant corruption

◆ Lack of freedom of press, speech, and religion

◆ Severe human rights violations

◆ Little respect for patents, copyrights, brands, and logos

◆ Counterfeiting, fraud, and pirating of products

◆ Little respect for legal contracts

◆ No generally accepted accounting principles

McDonald's, for instance, was recently evicted from its site in Beijing after operating its largest store in the world for only two of 20 years on its lease agreement. DuPont's herbicide Londax that kills weeds in rice fields was recently pirated and manufactured extensively in China. Scores of U.S. firms such as BellSouth have lost millions of dollars in China due to "illegal business actions." You can walk into any store in Beijing and buy a pirated copy of Microsoft's Windows 95 software.

At least 20 percent of credit loans in China are nonperforming; China's banking system is in shambles. Fully 75 percent of domestic credit goes to ailing state-run businesses that generate only 1 percent of industrial production. Managers of state-run enterprises are not very ethical either, often stealing money from the business.

Technological research is almost nonexistent in China. China's factories operate with ancient equipment, old-fashioned production methods, and little regard for the needs of the marketplace. Quality control is poor, and there basically are no books or records. Ninety percent of people in China live below the poverty level; 10 percent are very rich. Urban unemployment has grown to 15 percent, but may be even higher if idle farmers and furloughed workers are included. Retail prices grew only 3 percent in 1997, after hitting 24 percent in 1994. Concern about deflation or recession is real as China posts big trade surpluses and foreign reserves exceed $121 billion. A major reason for falling prices is increased competition, but this is putting many state-run enterprises out of business. Exports from China are rising rapidly but imports into China are falling. Private factories in China are now laying off workers faster than even the state-owned companies. State-owned enterprises have fired or drastically cut the pay of more than 10 million workers annually in recent years.

The minimum wage in China is 12 cents per hour but many firms pay even less. Chinese workers usually have no health care and no compensation for injury. Few factories have fire extinguishers. Bribes are often paid to officials to avoid fines and shutdowns. Labor unions are illegal and nonexistent in China. Child labor is commonplace. Political and religious oppression and imprisonment occur. Levi Strauss has pulled all its business operations out of China in protest to its human rights violations.

STRATEGY   *Business Week* offers the following formula for success in doing business with China:

> Pick partners wisely. Avoid forming ventures with inefficient state-owned enterprises. Search for entrepreneurial companies owned by local governments, or go it alone. Insist on management control.

> Focus on fundamentals. Capitalize on China rapidly becoming a market economy by executing the basics, such as marketing, distribution, and service.

> Guard know-how. Do not hand over state-of-the-art technology just to get an agreement. Aggressively fight theft of intellectual property because China wants to shed its bad reputation in this regard.

> Fly low. Begin with a series of small ventures rather than big, costly, high-profile projects that often get snarled in bureaucratic red tape and politics.[7]

JAPAN

Keizo Obuchi was elected in July 1998 as Japan's prime minister. Obuchi's program of deregulating Japanese industries and restoring consumer confidence in Japanese financial markets is aggressively underway. But much work is needed.

The Japanese economy is experiencing its most serious slowdown since the early 1970s. The Japanese yen fell 50 percent against the dollar from 1996 to 1998. The Nikkei stock index tumbled from its December 1989 peak of 38,915 to 18,000 in late 1997. Property values in Japan declined 60 percent between 1990 and 1997. These declines decimated individual interest in investing money in Japanese securities or property. Individuals in Japan hold $10 trillion in personal financial assets, but less than 3 percent of that is in mutual funds, compared to the U.S. individuals' average 14 percent of savings in mutual funds. Japanese individuals' investment in stocks has dropped to 10 percent of savings compared to 36 percent on average for Americans. Nearly all Japanese individual savings are now kept in post office or insurance accounts drawing less than 1 percent in annual interest.[8] Industries have huge amounts of excess capital.

The decline in asset values left Japanese banks with substantial nonperforming loans and precarious balance sheets. As a result, bank lending has been weak despite low interest rates. Residential housing construction has benefited from low interest rates and falling

NATURAL ENVIRONMENT

How Much Carbon Dioxide Is Your Firm Emitting?

Global warming isn't just a fear. It's a fact. Carbon dioxide is the major culprit and the most common air pollutant. Plants, of course, breathe in carbon dioxide, which is the reason why widespread cutting of trees and rain forests as well as clearing of land and harvesting kelp in the oceans are so detrimental to the natural environment. The following statistics reveal annual carbon-dioxide emissions for various countries worldwide. Note that the United States is guiltiest.

	TOTAL TONS (MILLIONS)	TONS PER CAPITA
United States	5,475	20.52
China	3,196	2.68
Russia	1,820	12.26
Japan	1,126	9.03
India	910	0.90
Germany	833	10.24
United Kingdom	539	9.29
Ukraine	437	8.48
Canada	433	14.83
Italy	411	7.19
South Korea	370	8.33
Mexico	359	3.93

Continents and countries' relative share of harmful CO_2 emissions is given below:

Eastern Europe and former Soviet Union	27%
United States	22%
Western Europe	17%
Other Asian countries	13%
China	11%
Latin America	4%
Africa	3%

Source: *Adapted from "Clear Skies Are Goal as Pollution Is Turning into a Commodity,"* The Wall Street Journal *(October 3, 1997): A4.*

land prices, but constraints on government-supported housing finance may temper this growth. Commercial construction has declined throughout the downturn, although public construction projects initiated as part of four government stimulus packages have compensated somewhat.

Private consumption has given a boost to slowly rising economic activity. Income tax rebates and low inflation have helped bolster consumer expenditures. Business's policy of keeping layoffs to a minimum during economic slowdowns has also helped consumption levels remain steady. The Japanese are the world's best consumers. With only 2 percent of the global population, the Japanese consume two-thirds of the world's branded products.[9]

Japan's labor markets are very weak. At 3.3 percent, unemployment is high by Japanese standards. Recruitment of new college graduates is depressed, and many firms have so much redundant employment that no hiring will occur until at least 2000.

TRADE TRENDS   Japan is the world's third-largest merchandise exporter and importer (behind the United States and Germany). Machinery and equipment make up about 75 percent of Japan's exports.

The United States is by far Japan's single largest trading partner. The United States has about a 23 percent share of Japan's import market, and 30 percent of Japanese exports go to the United States. Japan has been the second-largest market for U.S. products for many years. About 70 percent of U.S. exports to Japan are manufactured goods. By comparison, about 84 percent of U.S. exports to the rest of the world are manufactured. In addition, a relatively large share of U.S. exports to Japan consists of intracompany shipments from Japanese subsidiaries in the United States to their parent firms in Japan.

TRADE CLIMATE   Japan's large trade surpluses with the United States and other industrial nations have resulted in almost continuous trade friction between Japan and these countries over the last two decades. Japan's trade surplus with the United States has bulged to more than $4 billion monthly. Consequently, the primary goal of U.S. trade policy with Japan has been to open the Japanese market to imports and foreign investment. Informal obstacles have largely prevented manufactured goods, especially high-technology products, from entering Japan's markets. These barriers include administrative guidance; opaque customs procedures, testing standards, and certification requirements; restrictive public procurement and industrial promotion policies; intellectual property regulations; and impenetrable local distribution channels.

Some deregulation has opened Japan's markets in recent years, but its trade structure remains substantially different from that of any other industrial country. Japanese exports are mainly manufactured goods, and its imports are raw materials, food, and industrial components. Most of Japan's imported goods come from its foreign subsidiaries. Deregulation and other market-opening measures that have resulted from U.S. policy initiatives may lead to some change to this trade pattern during the remainder of this century.

Although no larger in size than California, Japan supports a population five times that of California's. Japan is changing rapidly. Masakagu Yamazaki uses the term "flexible individualism" to summarize the changes occurring in Japanese society and business. Workaholic attitudes in Japan are being replaced by greater emphasis on leisure activities and consumption of leisure products and services. Rising incomes, an aging population, and more women in the workforce are increasing the demand for services in all sectors of the Japanese economy. Japanese people save much more of their income than Americans, averaging 17 percent versus 4 percent, but prices in Japan are among the highest in the world. An apple costs $2 and dinner for four can cost $600.

A comparison of educational levels of Japanese and American young people appears in Table 10–4. Teachers in Japan enjoy much more respect, status, job security, and higher pay than their counterparts in America. Japanese teachers visit their students' homes, are available after school to assist students, and supervise learning on vacation days. Education is compulsory for children ages 6 to 15 in Japan, and 95 percent of 5-year-olds and 70 percent of 4-year-olds go to kindergarten. The school year is 240 days, and many children spend Sunday and holidays being tutored or studying. Some of the forces behind the educational system in Japan are relative homogeneity in the population, an occupational system in which selection and promotion are based on educational credentials, a relatively equal distribution of educational opportunities across the population, steep competition for entry into prestigious universities, and devotion of families to enhancing the life chances of children. Many analysts contend that as we approach the year 2000 and beyond, countries around the world will be as competitive as their underlying education systems. U.S. firms could be at a disadvantage compared to Japanese firms if this holds true because the analysts are primarily referring to secondary education, literacy rates, and average education level of the populace.

Japanese women increasingly are pursuing careers outside the home, a practice that was taboo until the mid-1980s. However, women still hold only 1 percent of managerial positions in Japan despite their making up 40 percent of Japan's workforce. The 1986 Japanese law banning sex discrimination at work established no penalties for violations. Most Japanese men and women still believe that when a woman marries, taking care of her husband and children should be her priority. The Japanese government is encouraging companies to promote more women into managerial positions, but the managerial job in Japan typically requires late hours, afterwork drinking sessions with colleagues, and a pledge of allegiance to the company until retirement. Many Japanese women do not aspire to that lifestyle, so women on the career track in Japan still remain an oddity.

	AMERICANS	JAPANESE
Literacy rate	80.0%	99.0%
High school completion rate	72.2%	90.0%
Length of school year	180 days	240 days
High school seniors spending less than 5 hours per week on homework	76.0%	35.0%
Financing of education:		
National	6.2%	47.3%
State	49.0%	28.1%
Local	44.8%	24.6%
Teacher salaries	Determined locally	By national law, teachers are paid 10% more than the top civil servant.

TABLE 10–4
The Educational Levels of Young Japanese and Young Americans Compared

Sources: U.S. Department of Education and Japanese Ministry of Education.

Research and development has become a basic mission of the Japanese government and nearly all Japanese firms. It is a mission of the whole country. Japan plans to develop a futuristic space shuttle, a colony of space platforms, and an orbiting factory for manufacturing made-in-space products. Aerospace companies in the United States and worldwide consider the Japanese market to be a great opportunity and are developing strategies to capitalize on Japan's commitment to commercialize space.

Some U.S. companies have done especially well in Japanese markets, including Coca-Cola, Schick, Wella, Vicks, Scott, Del Monte, Kraft, Campbell, Unilever, Twinings, Kellogg, Borden, Ragu, and Oscar Mayer. These are all household names in Japan. Schick razor blades have 70 percent of the safety-blade market there, McDonald's has 30 percent of the fast-food hamburger market, Coca-Cola has 50 percent of the market for carbonated soft drinks, Pampers has 22 percent of the disposable-diaper market, and Kodak has 15 percent of the amateur color film market. IBM has 40 percent of the market for computers, and Caterpillar has 43 percent of the market for bulldozers.

JAPANESE MANAGEMENT STYLE　The Japanese place great importance upon group loyalty and consensus, a concept called *Wa*. Nearly all corporate activities in Japan encourage Wa among managers and employees. Wa requires that all members of a group agree and cooperate; this results in constant discussion and compromise. Japanese managers evaluate the potential attractiveness of alternative business decisions in terms of the long-term effect on the group's Wa. This is why silence, used for pondering alternatives, can be a plus in a formal Japanese meeting. Discussions potentially disruptive to Wa are generally conducted in very informal settings, such as at a bar, so as to minimize harm to the group's Wa. Entertaining is an important business activity in Japan because it strengthens Wa. Formal meetings are often conducted in informal settings. When confronted with disturbing questions or opinions, Japanese managers tend to remain silent, whereas Americans tend to respond directly, defending themselves through explanation and argument.

Most Japanese managers are reserved, quiet, distant, introspective, and other-oriented, whereas most U.S. managers are talkative, insensitive, impulsive, direct, and individual-oriented. Americans often perceive Japanese managers as wasting time and carrying on pointless conversations, whereas U.S. managers often use blunt criticism, ask prying questions, and make quick decisions. These kinds of cultural differences have disrupted many potentially productive Japanese-American business endeavors. Viewing the Japanese communication style as a prototype for all Asian and Oriental cultures is a related stereotype that must be avoided.

Americans have more freedom to control their own fate than do the Japanese. Life is much different in the United States than in Japan; the United States offers more upward mobility to its people. This is a great strength of the United States. Sherman explained:

> America is not like Japan and can never be. America's strength is the opposite: It opens its doors and brings the world's disorder in. It tolerates social change that would tear most other societies apart. This openness encourages Americans to adapt as individuals rather than as a group. Americans go west to California to get a new start; they move east to Manhattan to try to make the big time; they move to Vermont or to a farm to get close to the soil. They break away from their parents' religions or values or class; they rediscover their ethnicity. They go to night school; they change their names.[10]

GLOBAL EXPANSION   Japan is shifting from a strategy of exports to direct investment in the United States and Europe. Japan surpassed the United Kingdom in 1992 as the largest direct investor in the United States. The number of Americans working for Japanese subsidiaries in the United States now exceeds 500,000. The 10 largest Japanese employers in the United States in rank order are Matsushita Electric, Sony, Toyota, Honda, Hitachi, Toshiba, Nissan, NEC, Mitsubishi, and Fujitsu. However, over 50 percent of Japanese companies operating in the United States today face worker lawsuits on race, color, religion, age, sex, and equal employment.

The Japanese are expected to continue investing heavily in Great Britain because the British welcome the Japanese, although other European countries are divided in their attitudes toward Japan. More than 40 percent of all Japanese investment in Europe is in Britain. The Confederation of British Industry predicts that by the year 2000, an astonishing 16 percent of British factory workers will have Japanese bosses.

There are only three major industries—pharmaceuticals, chemicals, and telecommunications equipment—in which European companies are more competitive than Japanese companies. Five of the top 10 construction firms in the world are Japanese: Shimizu, Kajima, Jaisei, Takenaka, and Ohbayashi. Until European countries develop a more unified approach towards Japanese investment, England could be "exporting" Japanese products to Europe in great quantities.

During the 1990–1994 era, Japan's direct investment strategy focused largely on the United States and Europe. However, during the 1995–1999 era, Japan's focus shifted to Asia for several reasons: First, Japan wants to capitalize on Asian countries' growing markets and rapidly developing economies. Japan wants to lessen its dependence on the United States. Finally, Japan wants to be in a position to determine its own destiny in light of China's explosive growth and expansionist policies.

Asians now buy more Japanese exports than the United States, and Japanese firms are plowing these profits back into Asia. Shintaro Ishihara says, "Japan is a nation of Asian people with Asian blood. It seems natural that we recognize that we exist first for Asia." Japan's emphasis on new trade, investment, financial, and technological moves are in Asia.

To support their country's re-Asianization policy, the Japanese people are putting greater emphasis on learning the languages, foods, and cultural habits of their Asian neighbors from Manchuria to Indonesia. Japanese firms are building plants, forming alliances, and making business friends extensively in Korea, Vietnam, Thailand, Indonesia, Malaysia, Philippines, India, Taiwan, and China. Already the world's largest aid donor, Japan has targeted Asian countries as its primary recipient in order to bolster its Asian influence. Indonesia is Japan's largest aid recipient, followed by China, the Philippines, India, and Thailand. There is a growing acceptance of Japanese culture throughout Asia. Projections are for Japan's U.S. investment to decline to just over $30 billion.

LIFETIME EMPLOYMENT   The principle of lifetime employment is as strong as ever in Japan, despite Westerners' view that this policy will wilt under global competition.

Japanese law makes it illegal to fire employees, so firms cannot cut labor costs when demand falls. But this single disadvantage of a lifetime employment policy is counterbalanced by numerous advantages. For example, Japanese workers even view productivity-enhancing technologies and automation as positive because there is no downside risk of them losing their jobs. With the lifetime employment policy, Japanese firms undertake expensive training programs without fear that any workers will take their skills to rival firms. U.S. firms are only one-seventh as likely as Japanese firms to offer new employees formal training.

Another benefit of the lifetime employment is the long-term accountability built into the system; this enhances managerial decision making. Labor unions in Japan work for the business; a strike may last an hour at most. CEOs in Japan are salaried employees compensated at levels of 10 times that of lower-level managers; this compares to U.S. CEOs being paid on average 100 times the salary of lower-level managers. Stock options for CEOs are prohibited in Japan. Japanese workers are paid and promoted according to seniority rather than competence. This system promotes teamwork and eliminates a possible source of friction and jealousy among workers. Because older workers and managers are not going to be leapfrogged in promotion, they mentor and help younger, inexperienced workers and managers much more readily than in the United States. Workers in Japanese firms function as part of a clearly identified team, and assignments are given to the team rather than to individuals. Offenders of team norms risk being ostracized by the group. Lifetime employment in Japan has a bright and stable future. It is a policy that U.S. firms should consider implementing.

THE EUROPEAN UNION

Europe is one of the most open markets for U.S. companies, which are in a position to benefit from an integrated and borderless European Union (EU) and a new single currency. In order to capitalize fully, however, they must be allowed to participate in the coming wave of privatizations. In addition, U.S. exports are threatened by new product standards and rules on testing and certification, growing incompatibility in business regulations, and remaining barriers in such areas as telecommunications, heavy electrical equipment, and audiovisual services. Eliminating these obstacles is a primary trade objective of the U.S. government. U.S. companies also stand to benefit from increased marketing efforts in the EU, particularly in Germany and Italy. In 1995, U.S. firms had a 13.2 percent share of United Kingdom imports, but only a 6.5 percent in the rest of the EU. Each percentage point rise in the U.S. share of the EU market signifies a $13 billion increase in the value of U.S. exports.

Since World War II, Western European countries have had distinct national markets in which governments protected their own businesses and imposed stiff tariffs on outside firms. Jealousy, regulation, diverse economic conditions, and tensions among nations have characterized Europe for years. Viewed as separate entities, European countries have not represented a sufficiently large customer base to warrant many international companies establishing business operations in Europe. Consequently, Europe has been economically stagnant since World War II, especially compared with the United States and the Far East. For several years during the 1980s, the combined results of the largest 100 companies in Europe, excluding the oil companies, showed a profit level of zero percent. Unemployment in Europe still remains high and companies generally are not competitive in world markets.

There are also still wide differences in product tastes across European countries. For example, the French want top-loading washing machines, whereas the British want front-loading washers. The Portuguese eat only 4 pounds of beef per capita each year, whereas the French eat 13.2 pounds. Germans eat 3.8 pounds of poultry each year, whereas the Spanish eat 8.8 pounds. Electrical outlets in Britain are different from those in Holland.

With the exception of a few industries such as chemicals, most sectors of the European economy are marked by chronic overcapacity and high fixed costs, such as steel, detergents, pharmaceuticals, transportation, and banking. There is no reason why Europe's $2 billion turbine generator business should support 10 producers. Similar overcapacity problems plague other industries, such as locomotive manufacturing. European companies are moving quickly, however, to correct the overcapacity problems, and survivors will likely emerge as strong competitors in world markets. Differences among European countries are narrowing due to a massive increase in the flow of people and information across national borders, and European companies are moving rapidly to develop and market products that will be well received all over Europe. The Europlug, for example, has recently been developed and marketed in Europe as the electrical plug that "will work everywhere."

UNIFICATION AND THE EURO Unification of Western Europe and the approaching adoption of a single currency are perhaps the single most important world events affecting business strategies in the 1990s. Fifteen countries speaking with one voice is more attractive to multinational corporations than 15 countries speaking with 15 voices. A proliferation of cross-border mergers, acquisitions, and alliances in Europe is creating a new generation of European firms large enough to take on U.S. and Japanese companies. In some industries, such as packaging and electric generating equipment, European firms have already replaced American firms as world leaders.

Unification of Western Europe and the planned adoption of the euro have reduced or eliminated trade barriers between European countries; people, goods, services, and capital now flow freely across national boundaries. European banks can operate in different countries without prohibitive barriers. Trucks pass freely between national borders instead of having to wait for hours at places such as the Mount Blanc tunnel between France and Italy, where custom agents used to check documents and cargo. The Eurotunnel under the English Channel is spurring business between England and Europe. The estimated annual savings to European companies from the unification is $75 billion to $90 billion.

Unification also brought common licensing of food and beverage products in Europe, common radio and television signals, common health and safety standards, elimination of duplication in distribution systems, and standardization of product lines. It has also prompted increased competitor analysis and alliances, decentralization of businesses, new marketing efforts, new strategies, more emphasis on service, improved telecommunications and information flow, and increased momentum for a single monetary system evolving in Europe.

Perhaps the most far-reaching feature of European unification is the planned establishment of a single financial market. The January 1, 1999, scheduled introduction of a single European currency, the euro, is expected to accelerate European downsizing.

Much stronger competitors in Europe have emerged from unification, and consumers throughout Europe are benefiting from lower prices and better choices. However, European companies still pay the world's highest wages and generally have trouble offering goods at globally competitive prices. The social welfare system in Europe is especially costly to firms. Most European workers and managers enjoy lifetime employment guarantees. There is a fear throughout Europe that rising unemployment, already at 10.5 percent, may bring back overregulation and protectionism, which would hurt firms' efforts to become more globally competitive.

European industries expected to represent the greatest threat to U.S. firms in the near future are publishing, communications equipment, pharmaceuticals, and civilian aerospace. Representing a lesser but still significant threat to U.S. firms will be European banks and producers of food, beverages, computers, electronics, and autos. U.S. industries that appear for the moment to be least affected by European unification are retailing, trucking, airlines, and insurance.

MERGERS AND ACQUISITIONS   Because Brussels is headquarters of the European Union, significant business and economic activity has shifted there from other national capitals in Europe. A wave of mergers and acquisitions is sweeping Europe as companies try to consolidate strength in core markets. For example, Banco de Bilbao and Banco Vizcaya, Spain's third- and sixth-largest banks, recently combined to form the only Spanish bank to rank among the top 30 in Europe. Consolidations in the paper industry have resulted in strong competitors such as Stora Kopparbergs Bergslags and Svanska Cellusosa in Sweden and Finnpap and Kymmene in Finland. Nestlé in Switzerland has acquired a number of other food companies in both Europe and the United States. Two large accounting firms in England, Coopers & Lybrand and Deloitte & Touche Tohmatsu, recently merged, creating the largest accounting firm in Europe. Eurocom S.A., France's largest advertising agency, merged with Roux, Seguela, Cayzac & Goudard, creating by far the largest ad agency in Europe.

Some examples of European firms that have acquired U.S. firms are Pechiney of France, which acquired Triangle Industries; Grand Metropolitan of Britain, which acquired Pillsbury, Burger King, and Green Giant; Hoechst of Germany, which acquired Celanese; and Nestlé of Switzerland, which acquired Carnation.

Japanese firms are also making large acquisitions in Western Europe. For example, Fujitsu acquired Britain's last true computer maker, ICL. Mitsubishi Electric has a stated goal to increase its investment in Europe by as much as 30 percent a year. Olivetti in Italy depends on Canon and Sanyo for office equipment, and Fiat depends on Hitachi for construction gear. Nissan, Toyota, and Honda are all building manufacturing plants in Britain and expect to raise overall Japanese market share of automobiles in Britain from 12 percent to 17 percent by 1998.

After Great Britain, the European country receiving the next most extensive Japanese investment is Germany; Germany already imports 40 percent of all Japanese exports to Europe. Dusseldorf, Germany, has Europe's largest number of Japanese residents—over 7,000. Mitsubishi Electric and Toshiba are leading an array of Japanese firms planning investment of over $400 million annually in the Dusseldorf region alone.

GUIDELINES FOR SUCCESS AS A GLOBAL COMPETITOR

As indicated in the Information Technology Perspective, use of the Internet can be an effective and efficient way to enhance business globally. Another guideline for success as a global competitor is to make full use of STAT-USA on the World Wide Web. Updated monthly, this is the U.S. government's premier Internet publisher of business information.

Robert Allio offered seven guidelines for winning global battles for customer loyalty and market share:

1. Get to new global markets first. Trying to gain market share from well-entrenched competitors is exceptionally difficult.
2. Counterattack at home. Parent firms often finance expansion into host countries with profits generated at home. Competitor cash flow can be reduced by attacking them at home. An example is the 3M attack on Japanese markets for audiotape and videotape.
3. Invest in new technology. Successful firms in the 1990s are going to utilize the most efficient technology.

4. Consider alternative sourcing. Locate manufacturing facilities in low labor cost areas of the world. An example of this is Dominion Textile of Canada's building a denim manufacturing facility in Tunisia.

5. Install the right managerial system. Ensure that managers in foreign markets understand the nuances of culture and language in host countries.

6. Take early losses if necessary. Sacrifice short-term profits for long-term rewards. An example is Japanese firms' taking losses for 7 years in order to capture the European motorcycle market.

7. Join forces with competitors. Collaborate with competitors who have expertise in other parts of the value chain. Examples are Chrysler's deal with Mitsubishi and AT&T's linkup with Olivetti.[11]

Jeremy Main said there is no universal formula for going global, but any company serious about joining the race should do most or all of the following:

1. Make yourself at home in all three of the world's most important markets—North America, Europe, and Asia.

2. Develop new products for the whole world.

3. Replace profit centers based on countries or regions with ones based on product lines.

4. "Glocalize," as the Japanese call it: Make global decisions on strategic questions about products, capital, and research, but let local units decide tactical questions about packaging, marketing, and advertising.

5. Overcome parochial attitudes, such as the not-invented-here syndrome. Train people to think internationally, send them off on frequent trips, and give them the latest communications technology, such as teleconferencing.

6. Open the senior ranks to foreign employees.

7. Do whatever seems best wherever it seems best, even if people at home lose jobs or responsibilities.

8. In markets that you cannot penetrate on your own, find allies.[12]

INFORMATION TECHNOLOGY

Why Pay for Long-Distance Telephone Calls?

Computers enable persons to write each other by e-mail and even to have a voice conversation with another computer user. In late 1997, companies such as IDT unveiled Net2Phone Direct, which allows a person or business to dial an 800 or local access number, and have a voice conversation with another person by phone with the medium for transmission being the Internet rather than a phone company. The cost is 8 cents a minute within the United States, 18 cents to London, and 29 cents to Japan, all much cheaper than traditional long-distance calling. So whatever your corporate expense for long-distance phone calls may be, they probably are an inefficient use of company resources.

Large phone companies such as AT&T and MCI all but ignored developments in Internet telephony during the 1990s, but now are scrambling to reposition themselves. MCI, for example, has a calling plan that charges residential customers just 5 cents a minute for long-distance calls made on Sundays with no registration needed. Sprint now allows "registered" customers to make free long-distance calls on Monday nights (7–11 P.M.) during the National Football League season. AT&T still commands 50 percent to 60 percent of the consumer telephone market, followed by MCI with 15 percent to 20 percent and Sprint with about 10 percent, but smaller firms such as IDT and various Internet providers are gaining market share.

Source: Adapted from Kevin Maney, "Internet Long-Distance No Longer Needs a PC," USA Today (September 8, 1997): B1, B6.

David Garfield, former president of Ingersoll-Rand Company, offered three strategy suggestions to make domestic firms more competitive internationally:

1. The best defense is a good offense. Companies need to fight tooth and claw for exports and battle foreign competition on foreign ground wherever possible. This is preferable to competing intensely in domestic markets.

2. Investments that will improve competitive advantage should receive priority attention. Domestic firms should strive to reduce labor costs, lower overhead, compress production cycles, and improve the quality of products and services.

3. Domestic industries and firms need to help one another. They should give preference to American suppliers and distributors; they should encourage one another to take action to improve competitiveness in technology, quality, service, and cost.[13]

CONCLUSION

Success in business increasingly depends upon offering products and services that are competitive on a world basis, not just on a local basis. If the price and quality of a firm's products and services are not competitive with those available elsewhere in the world, the firm may soon face extinction. Global markets have become a reality in all but the most remote areas of the world. Certainly throughout the United States, even in small towns, firms feel the pressure of world competitors. Nearly half of all the automobiles sold in the United States, for example, are made in Japan and Germany.

Culture, industrial policies, joint venturing, and exporting are important in the strategic-management process of international firms. As world economies and consumption patterns become increasingly similar and interrelated, political and economic changes represent major opportunities for, and threats to, U.S. firms. To be successful in the late1990s, businesses must offer products and services that exhibit a price/quality relationship competitive with similar products and services available worldwide.

We invite you to visit the DAVID page on the Prentice Hall Web site at
www.prenhall.com/davidsm
for this chapter's World Wide Web exercises.

KEY TERMS AND CONCEPTS

European Economic Community	(p. 311)	Host Country	(p. 308)	Multinational Corporations	(p. 308)
European Union (EU)	(p. 333)	Industrial Policies	(p. 316)	Parent Company	(p. 308)
Global Markets	(p. 310)	International Firms	(p. 308)	Wa	(p. 331)

ISSUES FOR REVIEW AND DISCUSSION

1. Compare and contrast American culture with other cultures worldwide. How do differences in culture affect strategic management?

2. Explain why consumption patterns are becoming similar worldwide. What are the strategic implications of this trend?

3. What are the advantages and disadvantages of beginning export operations in a foreign country?

4. Why do you believe the airline industry is only slowly becoming global?

5. What recommendations do you have for firms wanting to do business with Russia?

6. What strategies are most commonly being pursued by Japanese firms? Why?

7. How does unification of Western Europe affect the strategies of U.S. firms?

8. What guidelines for success as a global competitor do you believe are most important?

9. Select one of the readings at the end of this chapter and prepare a 3-minute report to the class on this topic.

10. Do you believe *Guanxi*, *Inhwa*, or *Wa* would help facilitate strategic management in an organization? Why?

11. Compare and contrast the trade climate in Mexico, China, Japan, Russia, and the European Union.

12. Compare and contrast the political climate in Mexico, China, Japan, Russia, and the European Union.

13. Compare and contrast the culture in Mexico, China, Japan, Russia, and the European Union.

NOTES

1. Gephardt, Richard A. "U.S.–Japanese Trade Relations," *Vital Speeches of the Day* LV, no. 15 (May 15, 1989).

2. Jon Alston, "Wa, Guanxi, and Inhwa: Managerial Principles in Japan, China and Korea," *Business Horizons* 32, no. 2 (March–April 1989): 26.

3. Rose Knotts, "Cross-Cultural Management: Transformations and Adaptations," *Business Horizons* (January–February 1989): 29–33.

4. Ellen Fingerhut and Daryl Hatano, "Principles of Strategic Planning Applied to International Corporations," *Managerial Planning* 31, no. 5 (September–October 1983): 4–14. Also, Narendra Sethi, "Strategic Planning Systems for Multinational Companies," *Long Range Planning* 15, no. 3 (June 1982): 80–9.

5. David Shanks, "Strategic Planning for Global Competition," *Journal of Business Strategy* 5, no. 3 (Winter 1985): 80.

6. Mark Clifford, "Can China Reform Its Economy?" *Business Week* (September 29, 1997): 117–124.

7. "How You Can Win in China?" *Business Week* (May 26, 1997): 65.

8. Brian Fowler, "Japan Business Survey," *The Wall Street Journal* (September 29, 1997): B11.

9. Fowler., B12.

10. Stratford Sherman, "How to Beat the Japanese," *Fortune* (April 10, 1989): 145.

11. Robert Allio, "Formulating Global Strategy," *Planning Review* 17, no. 2 (March–April 1989): 27.

12. Jeremy Main, "How to Go Global—And Why," *Fortune* (August 28, 1989): 76.

13. David Garfield, "The International Challenge to U.S. Business," *Journal of Business Strategy* 5, no. 4 (Spring 1985): 28, 29.

CURRENT READINGS

Barkema, H. G., J. H. J. Bell, and J. M. Pennings. "Foreign Entry, Cultural Barriers, and Learning." *Strategic Management Journal* 17, no. 2 (February 1996): 151–161.

Barnes, John W., Matthew H. Crook, Taira Koybaeva, and Edwin R. Stafford. "Why Our Russian Alliances Fail." *Long Range Planning* 30, no. 4 (August 1997): 540–550.

Baron, David P. "Integrated Strategy, Trade Policy, and Global Competition." *California Management Review* 39, no. 2 (Winter 1997): 145–155.

Birkinshaw, J. "Entrepreneurship in Multinational Corporations: The Characteristics of Subsidiary Initiatives." *Strategic Management Journal* 18, no. 3 (March 1997): 207–230.

Chae, Myung-Su and John S. Hill. "The Hazards of Strategic Planning for Global Markets." *Long Range Planning* 29, no. 6 (December 1996): 880–891.

Filatotchev, Igor, Robert E. Hoskisson, Trevor Buck, and Mike Wright. "Corporate Restructuring in Russian Privatizations: Implications for U.S. Investors." *California Management Review* 38, no. 2 (Winter 1996): 87–105.

Foster, M. J. "South China: Are the Rewards Still Worth the Risks?" *Long Range Planning* 30, no. 4 (August 1997): 585–593.

Gouttefarde, Claire. "American Values in the French Workplace." *Business Horizons* 39, no. 2 (March–April 1996): 60–69.

Gowan, Mary, Santiago Ibarreche, and Charles Lackey. "Doing the Right Things in Mexico." *Academy of Management Executive* 10, no. 1 (February 1996): 74–81.

Greer, Charles R. and Gregory K. Stephens. "Employee Relations Issues for U.S. Companies in Mexico." *California Management Review* 38, no. 3 (Spring 1996): 121–145.

Hitt, M. A., M. T. Dacin, B. B. Tyler, and D. Park. "Understanding the Differences in Korean and U.S. Executives' Strategic Orientations." *Strategic Management Journal* 18, no. 2 (February 1997): 159–169.

Krug, J. A. and W. H. Hegarty. "Postacquisition Turnover Among U.S. Top Management Teams: An Analysis of the Effects of Foreign vs. Domestic Acquisitions of U.S. Targets." *Strategic Management Journal* 18, no. 8 (September 1997): 667–677.

Lomi, Alessandro and Erik R. Larsen. "Interacting Locally and Evolving Globally: A Computational Approach to the Dynamics of Organizational Population." *Academy of Management Journal* 39, no. 5 (October 1996): 1084–1119.

Lovelock, Christopher H. and George S. Yip. "Developing Global Strategies for Service Businesses." *California Management Review* 38, no. 2 (Winter 1996): 64–86.

Luo, Yadong. "Evaluating the Performance of Strategic Alliances in China." *Long Range Planning* 29, no. 4 (August 1996): 534–542.

Magretta, Joan. "Growth Through Global Sustainability: An Interview with Monsanto's CEO, Robert B. Shapiro." *Harvard Business Review* (January–February 1997): 78–90.

Northcott, Jim. "Mapping the Future for Countries." *Long Range Planning* 29, no. 2 (April 1996): 203–207.

Peng, Mike W. and Peggy Sue Heath. "The Growth of the Firm in Planned Economies in Transition: Institutions, Organizations, and Strategic Choice." *Academy of Management Review* 21, no. 2 (April 1996): 492–528.

Pincus, Laura B. and James A. Belohlav. "Legal Issues in Multinational Business Strategy: To Play the Game, You Have to Know the Rules." *Academy of Management Executive* 10, no. 3 (August 1996): 52–61.

Puffer, Sheila M., Daniel J. McCarthy, and Anatoly V. Zhuplev. "Meeting of the Mind-sets in a Changing Russia." *Business Horizons* 39, no. 6 (November–December 1996): 52–60.

Reuer, J. J. and K. D. Miller. "Agency Costs and the Performance Implications of International Joint Venture Internalization." *Strategic Management Journal* 18, no. 6 (June 1997): 425–438.

Sambharya, R. B. "Foreign Experience of Top Management Teams and International Diversification Strategies of U.S. Multinational Corporations." *Strategic Management Journal* 17, no. 9 (November 1996): 739–749.

Schuler, Randall S., Susan E. Jackson, Ellen Jackofsky, and John W. Slocum, Jr. "Managing Human Resources in Mexico: A Cultural Understanding." *Business Horizons* 39, no. 3 (May–June 1996): 55–61.

Serapio, Manuel G., Jr., and Wayne F. Cascio. "End-Games in International Alliances." *Academy of Management Executive* 10, no. 1 (February 1996): 62–73.

Smith, Esmond D., Jr., and Cuong Pham. "Doing Business in Vietnam: A Cultural Guide." *Business Horizons* 39, no. 3 (May–June 1996): 47–51.

Stewart, Rosemary. "German Management: A Challenge to Anglo-American Managerial Assumptions." *Business Horizons* 39, no. 3 (May–June 1996): 52–54.

Tallman, Stephen and Jiatao Li. "Effects of International Diversity and Product Diversity on the Performance of Multinational Firms." *Academy of Management Journal* 39, no. 1 (February 1996): 179–196.

Tezuka, Hiroyuki. "Success as the Source of Failure? Competition and Cooperation in the Japanese Economy." *Sloan Management Review* 38, no. 2 (Winter 1997): 83–93.

Vanhonacker, Wilfried. "Entering China: An Unconventional Approach." *Harvard Business Review* (March–April 1997): 130–141.

Very, P., M. Lubatkin, R. Calori and J. Veiga. "Relative Standing and the Performance of Recently Acquired European Firms." *Strategic Management Journal* 18, no. 8 (September 1997): 593–614.

Werther, William B., Jr. "Toward Global Convergence." *Business Horizons* 39, no. 1 (January–February 1996): 3–9.

Williamson, Peter J. "Asia's New Game." *Harvard Business Review* (September–October 1997): 55–65.

EXPERIENTIAL EXERCISES

Experiential Exercise 10A

DETERMINING THE COMPETITIVE ENVIRONMENT FOR HERSHEY'S PRODUCTS IN OTHER COUNTRIES

PURPOSE

Organizations are exploring potential markets in other countries. The purpose of this exercise is to assess the relative attractiveness of various foreign countries for distributing and possibly manufacturing Hershey products.

INSTRUCTIONS

Step 1 Select a European, Asian, African, South American, or Central American country of your choice.

Step 2 Go to your college library. Research your chosen country to identify social, cultural, demographic, geographic, political, legal, governmental, economic, technological, and competitive forces or trends that affect the candy and pasta market there. Decide whether you would recommend that Hershey begin or increase export operations or manufacturing operations in that country.

Step 3 Prepare a three-page typed report to Hershey's president of international operations, Patrice Le Maire. Give the results of your research and your specific recommendations to your professor.

Experiential Exercise 10B

DETERMINING MY UNIVERSITY'S RECRUITING EFFORTS IN FOREIGN COUNTRIES

PURPOSE

A competitive climate is emerging among colleges and universities around the world. Colleges and universities in Europe and Japan are increasingly recruiting American students to offset declining enrollments. Foreign students already make up more than one-third of the student body at many American universities. The purpose of this exercise is to identify particular colleges and universities in foreign countries that represent a competitive threat to American institutions of higher learning.

INSTRUCTIONS

Step 1 Select a foreign country. Conduct research to determine the number and nature of colleges and universities in that country. What are the major institutions in that country? What programs are those institutions recognized for offering? What percentage of undergraduate and graduate students attending those institutions are American? Do those institutions actively recruit American students?

Step 2 Prepare a report for the president or chancellor of your college or university that summarizes your research findings. Present your report to your professor.

LESSONS IN DOING BUSINESS GLOBALLY

PURPOSE

The purpose of this exercise is to discover some important lessons learned by local businesses who do business internationally.

INSTRUCTIONS

Contact several local business leaders by phone. Find at least three firms that engage in international or export operations. Ask the businessperson to give you several important lessons his or her firm has learned in doing business globally. Record the lessons on paper and report your findings to the class.

Name Index

SUBJECT INDEX

COMPANY INDEX

CASES

Retailing—Industry Note

Comprising businesses selling merchandise for personal or household use, retail trade is a significant part of the U.S. economy. Collectively, retail businesses racked up $2.2 trillion in 1997 sales per the latest available annual data; that is, retail sales amounted to 27 percent of the U.S. gross domestic product (GDP).

Government statistics break retail trade into two segments: nondurable and durable goods. (The retail category excludes services.) Durable goods are sold by distributors, such as building materials stores, automotive dealers, and furniture stores, and some general merchandisers. Nondurable goods generally are sold by department and general merchandise stores, apparel and accessory stores, food and drug stores, and restaurants. This survey will focus on department stores and mass merchandiser retailers that largely sell nondurable goods.

In 1997, sales of nondurables totaled $1.5 trillion and accounted for about 30 percent of personal consumption expenditures. Other 1997 personal consumption dollars went toward the purchase of services, a category that includes everything from medical care to hairstyling. Total spending on services, nondurables, and durables accounted for a hefty 60 percent of U.S. GDP in 1997.

SERVICE-SECTOR JOB ENGINE

With over 1.6 million establishments from automobile dealers and gas stations to apparel or grocery stores, retailing is also important to the U.S. economy as a major employer. Retailing employs more than 20 million Americans—18 percent of the nation's work force, or nearly one out of every five American workers.

Top Ten Department Stores

	Fiscal Year End	Revenues (Bil. $)
J. C. Penney	Jan. '97	22.7
Federated Dept. Stores	Jan. '97	15.2
May Dept. Stores	Jan. '97	12.0
Dillard, Inc.	Jan. '97	6.4
Nordstrom	Jan. '97	4.5
Dayton Hudson	Jan. '97	3.1
Mercantile Dept. Stores	Jan. '97	3.0
Neiman-Marcus	Jul. '97	1.9
Saks Holdings	Jan. '97	1.9
Proffitt's	Jan. '97	1.9

Source: Company reports.

Source: Adapted from Industry Surveys by permission of Standard & Poors, a division of McGraw-Hill Companies.

Although most people think of retailing as being dominated by the behemoth chains such as Wal-Mart and Sears, it can be considered a mom-and-pop business. Almost 88 percent of all retail companies employ fewer than 20 workers, according to the National Retail Federation, and 95 percent of all retailers operate just one store. However, the bigger businesses do garner the sales. Wal-Mart's domestic operations had estimated revenues of over $100 billion in the fiscal year that ends January 1998.

THE BIG GET BIGGER

The consolidation that has characterized department store retailing over the past 2 decades continues unabated. The top ten department store chains now account for almost one-third of U.S. department store sales.

Sears Roebuck, with a strong name franchise and a loyal customer base, remains the largest full-price general merchandise chain in the United States with $38 billion in annual revenues in 1997. However, the general merchandise sector's growth and scale is now dominated by three discount chains: Wal-Mart, Kmart, and Target (a division of Dayton Hudson Corp.).

Wal-Mart, the 800-pound gorilla, alone now accounts for 17 percent of U.S. general merchandise, apparel, and furniture sales (GAF). The bruising competition in this sector has eased as many small regional players, such as Bradlee's, Jamesway, and Caldor, have either liquidated or filed for bankruptcy reorganization. At press time, Venture Stores, Inc., a 93-unit Midwestern discount chain, filed for Chapter 11 bankruptcy protection, following a failed 22-month effort to turn business around.

The warehouse club industry, also in the discount sector, has filled customers' needs for appliances, housewares, cleaning supplies, and the like, all at rock-bottom prices. SAM'S Clubs (a division of Wal-Mart), Costco, and BJ's have grown dramatically over the past decade. Others, such as Dollar General Corp. and Family Dollar, have found a successful formula selling a limited assortment of low-end merchandise in small towns, mostly across the South and the Midwest.

RATIONALIZING ASSETS

In a mature industry such as retailing, staying competitive requires squeezing out excess costs. As a result, retailers in general—and department stores and general merchandisers in particular—are examining every aspect of their businesses. Each unit must be able to justify its existence by meeting company standards for profitability and return on investment.

When the retail environment is one of increasing revenues and profitability, a company's strategic flaws, mistakes, or errors in judgment can be hidden for a time. However, these foibles eventually will surface when growth is no longer sufficient to cover them.

In late January 1998, J. C. Penney took Wall Street by surprise with the announcement that it planned to close 75 of its 1,500 department stores. In past years, Woolworth Corp. and Kmart underwent even more radical surgery.

■ **J. C. Penny.** Since the fiscal year ended January 1995, this company has suffered declining earnings as a result of high costs and weak sales in an overcrowded

Top Discount Chains Estimated Sales for Fiscal Year Ending Jan. 1998

	Sales (Bil. $)	No. of Stores
Wal-Mart	89	1,904
Kmart	35	2,136
Target	20	797

Source: S&P estimates based on 11 months of data from company reports.

retail market. Penney plans to address these problems by eliminating 1,700 management positions and by closing 75 stores that do not meet the company's performance standards. These cuts will save the company an estimated $105 million annually. To cover the costs involved, the company will take a charge of $190 million in the fourth quarter of the fiscal year ending January 1998.

■ **Woolworth Corp.** As its sales grew during the heady 1980s, Woolworth aggressively expanded operations. The company took advantage of low-cost real estate by opening a plethora of new specialty stores. But as sales slowed and competition increased, these units became unprofitable.

To return to profitability in the 1990s, Woolworth's management has been closing or selling divisions and shuttering hundreds of stores. From 1994 through 1996, it eliminated 1,443 nonproductive stores.

In early 1997, Woolworth announced its exit from the U.S. general merchandise business. In the fiscal year ending January 1997, the company's general merchandise division reported an operating loss of $37 million on sales of $1 billion. This company, whose origins go back to the five-and-dime variety store format that Woolworth pioneered in 1879, is now a specialty retailer mainly in the apparel and athletic shoe business.

■ **Kmart.** This company erred by underestimating its competitors' strength. As Wal-Mart and Target have garnered more sales from shoppers, Kmart's market share has eroded.

With its sales per square foot declining and profitability eroding, Kmart took a restructuring charge of $862 million in 1994. In 1995, a new management team bit the bullet, marking down huge excess inventory and closing unprofitable stores. Although Kmart returned to profitability in 1996 and has remained in the black through 1997, the jury is still out on its longer-term viability.

INTERNET SHOPPING MAY SURGE

It's impossible to talk about the future of retailing without considering the impact that the Internet will have on retailing as we know it. Forrester Research, Inc., estimates that the Internet accounts for $518 million of the $2.3 trillion spent within the retail industry. However, it expects that number to grow to $6.6 billion by 2000. Some experts go so far as to predict that malls will be nearly obsolete by 2010, with some 55 percent of retail purchases being made via the Internet.

Projected On-Line Shopping Revenues

(in millions of dollars)	1996	1997	1998	1999	2000
Computer products	140	323	701	1,228	2,105
Travel	126	276	572	961	1,579
Entertainment	85	194	420	733	1,250
Apparel	46	89	163	234	322
Gifts & flowers	45	103	222	386	658
Food & drink	39	78	149	227	336
Other	37	75	144	221	329
Total	518	1,138	2,371	3,990	6,579

Source: Forrester Research Inc.

The industry most likely to be affected first by the Internet is the home shopping industry, which accounts for about $60 billion in retail sales, including catalogues, TV shopping, and computer shopping. Cataloguers will save money on shipping catalogues and printing costs and be able to refresh their on-line catalogues with relative ease.

Since 1990, catalogue sales have grown about 10 percent a year, much faster than total retail sales. This suggests that people are too pressed for time and find catalogue shopping easier and more convenient than fighting through the traffic to get to the malls. We can only surmise that as our society becomes increasingly computer-literate, people will be more than happy to log on to the computer to save themselves a trip to the mall.

At present, the items selling best on the Internet include books, flowers, CDs, computers, and some basic clothing items. One popular site is Amazon.com, offering 1.1 million books on-line and selling hardcover and paperback bestsellers at 40 percent discounts. Recently, Barnes & Noble started a Web site, and Borders and Crown Books are not far behind. Flowers also have been strong sellers. 1-800-Flowers, which started selling flowers on-line in 1992, and PCFlowers possibly have made the biggest dent in traditional retail avenues. Currently, about one-fourth of all flowers sold within the United States are sold over the Internet. CDNow's Internet site offers more than 166,000 CD titles and consumers can receive their orders within 24 hours. Among computer vendors, Dell and Gateway 2000 have successful Web sites. In fact, Dell estimates that it sells about $1 million worth of computer products each day via the Internet.

Catalogue companies have a natural advantage in selling through the Internet because their businesses already are set up as mail- and phone-order services and their distribution systems already are in place. Companies such as Land's End; L.L. Bean; and The Sharper Image already have started Web sites. Whereas Land's End uses its Web site to sell old inventory at discount prices, L.L. Bean has taken the approach of putting its entire catalogue on the Internet. The Sharper Image allows patrons to tailor their visits to see only products that they are interested in purchasing.

The Internet has many advantages over traditional shopping venues. For one, it potentially offers a broader assortment of products than any mall could match. It's also more convenient than driving through traffic, finding a parking space, finding your purchase, and waiting to pay for it. The Internet also may mean lower prices for the consumer. Even if delivery is included, the price should be lower than at a retail store due to lower overhead: The cost of maintaining a Web site is minimal versus a stores costs.

The driving force behind the use of the Internet for purchases will be access. IDC estimates that there were 246 million Americans in 1996, of which 12 million were Internet users. It expects Internet usage to ramp up to 53 million Americans by 2000. One development that may make Internet access much greater is interactive television. Television sets are in 98 percent of U.S. homes and the technology to deliver Internet access over cable is much faster than over the current telephone line. The introductory price points are much cheaper, too, at about $300 versus a low-cost computer of $1,000.

It's difficult to predict how likely people will be to use the Internet for shopping. We do not foresee the closure of malls all across America, but the Internet may make sizable inroads in the way we currently shop. A recent study by MasterCard International found that 46 percent of computer users said that they would shop less by mail and telephone if they shopped on-line.

RETAILERS TEST THE INTERNET WATERS

In this era of slow sales growth and higher labor costs, retailers' resolutions for the new year will have to focus not just on minding the store, but also on containing costs. As long as inflation is low and competition keen, raising prices is not a viable option. And the major cost reductions from consolidating divisions and implementing new technology are behind. At the same time, however, department stores and general merchandisers realize that low costs alone are not sufficient. Boosting sales is also essential.

With more people surfing the Internet—some 49 million regularly used the Internet in 1997, up from 36.9 million in 1996—and increased Internet shopping, retailers are setting up Web sites in order to sell in cyberspace. The convenience, selection, and competitive pricing of this new mode of shopping are attracting customers. Indeed, the growth trend of on-line retailing is parallel to that of catalogue retailing a decade ago.

According to estimates by Jupiter Communications, a New York City–based provider of consumer on-line research, overall Internet retailing totaled $1.1 billion in 1997, more than triple 1996's sales. On-line retailing is such a hot topic that the National Retail Federation focused an entire session on the subject at its annual convention in January 1998.

The popularity of shopping on the Web apparently gained some steam this past holiday. America Online estimated that the 114 vendors on its network doubled their Christmas sales in 1997 to $150 million.

It's not just retailers like 1-800-Flowers that are setting up Web sites, but traditional retailers as well. The Gap, for instance, offers a limited selection of basic merchandise such as khakis, T-shirts, and jeans. J. Crew touted 20 percent discounts to on-line shoppers.

Retailers are a long way from shuttering their stores in favor of selling exclusively via the Internet. However, we anticipate that more retailers will add Web sites, while others already on the Web will expand their product offerings.

OUTLOOK FOR '98

Market saturation and a paucity of pent-up demand will slow top-line sales gains in 1998. Most consumers today have closets filled with clothing and are focusing their energies on activities other than shopping.

It's not consumers' lack of money that has led us to temper our spending outlook for 1998. In fact, personal income is rising and consumers are upbeat. The University of Michigan survey of consumer confidence in December hit its highest point since 1965. S&P is projecting a 5.2 percent increase in personal income in 1998, on top of 1997's 5.8 percent rise.

Some of these extra household dollars may be saved, and we are estimating an increase in the savings rate to 4.3 percent, from 3.8 percent in 1997. This, and the moderation in spending during the fourth quarter, have softened our outlook for 1998.

The Limited, Inc.—1998

M. Jill Austin

www.limited.com
stock symbol LTD

The Limited, Inc., (614-479-7000) headquartered in Columbus, Ohio, is the largest women's apparel specialty store and mail order retailer in the United States. Net sales from 1996 to 1997 increased 6 percent to $9.19 billion whereas net income decreased 50 percent to $217 million. An additional 117,000 square feet of selling space was deleted during 1997 for a total of 28.4 million square feet of selling space for all Limited stores. Stores now number 5,640.

For over 30 years, Limited stores have achieved success by breaking "the rules" in the specialty retailing industry. Instead of offering a wide variety of types of clothing, the stores offer a limited assortment of women's sportswear in large quantities and a variety of colors. The company emphasizes rapid turnover of inventory so only the newest in fashion is in the stores at all times. The Limited, Inc., has 12 retail store divisions targeted to specific groups of shoppers: The Limited, Express, Henri Bendel, Victoria's Secret Stores, Abercrombie & Fitch, Abercrombie (Kids), Lerner New York, Lane Bryant, Structure, The Limited Too, Bath & Body Works, and Galyan's Trading Co.

Leslie Wexner, chair of The Limited, understands that the 1990s have been a time of transition for the company. He says, "Success doesn't beget success. Success begets failure because the more that you know a thing works, the less likely you are to think that it won't work. When you've had a long string of victories, it's harder to foresee your own vulnerabilities." In 1996, Wexner's Limited saw its vulnerabilities. To respond to the significant sales problems at Express, Wexner says, "we are fundamentally reinventing the business: sweeping change, greater discipline, more centralization, and a plan to build brands, not just business." This transition in thinking will require each division to define clearly its fashion, advertising, price, and market position and will require cooperation, not competition, among the division leaders.

HISTORY

Leslie Wexner's mother and father both worked in retailing. His father worked for the Miller Wall specialty chain and his mother was a buyer for Lazarus. When Wexner was 14, his parents opened their own specialty apparel store in Columbus, Ohio. After college and one year in law school, Wexner returned to work in his parents' store until he decided what he wanted to do with his life. He planned that his work in retail would be temporary, but he says he "got hooked."

In 1963, Leslie Wexner borrowed $10,000 from an aunt and a bank to open The Limited's first store. During its first year in operation, this store achieved sales of $157,000.

His strategy was to provide a "limited" assortment of quality, fashionable sportswear at medium prices. The "limited" concept worked well and by the late 1970s, Wexner began a twofold strategy of market development and product development. New stores were opened and acquired to appeal to women of different ages, sizes, and budget limits.

In the 1980s, Wexner attempted to acquire department store chains such as Federated Department Stores; R.H. Macy; and Carter Hawley Hale (CHH). Probably the greatest disappointment in Wexner's acquisition attempts was the failed attempt to acquire CHH. Wexner submitted an offer to buy CHH for $1.1 billion. At the time of the offer, CHH consisted of 124 department stores, 117 specialty stores, and 841 bookstores. Some of the store names associated with CHH at the time included Thalhimers, Neiman-Marcus, Broadway, and Bergdorf Goodman. The Limited acquired about 700,000 shares of CHH stock at the time of its offer. In response to The Limited's takeover attempt, General Cinema acquired $300 million of CHH stock and CHH began buying its own stock. The Securities and Exchange Commission stepped in to stop both The Limited and CHH from unfairly attempting to control the takeover situation. These legal developments stalled Wexner's takeover attempt. After the CHH takeover attempt failed in 1986, Wexner began thinking more about internal growth than about new acquisitions. After CHH filed for Chapter 11 bankruptcy, Wexner said about CHH, "we wouldn't take it for free."

Throughout the 1980s, Wexner acquired a variety of businesses including Lane Bryant, Victoria's Secret, Sizes Unlimited, Lerner New York, Henri Bendel, and Abercrombie & Fitch. Each of these stores was in financial trouble when acquired by Wexner. Wexner also started several store divisions during the 1980s. These include Express, Structure, Limited Too, and Cacique (sold in 1997). Penhaligon's was acquired in 1990 (sold in 1997) and Galyan's Trading Company was acquired in 1995. Bath & Body Works was started by The Limited, Inc., in 1990. The growth of The Limited, Inc., is shown in Exhibit 1.

EXHIBIT 1:   The Limited's Stores

	End of Year			Change From	
	Goal 1998	1997	1996	1998-97	1997-96
The Limited					
Stores	570	629	663	(59)	(34)
Selling Square Ft.	3,398,000	3,790,000	3,977,000	(392,000)	(187,000)
Express					
Stores	712	753	753	(41)	0
Selling Square Ft.	4,481,000	4,739,000	4,726,000	(258,000)	13,000
Lerner New York					
Stores	668	746	784	(78)	(38)
Selling Square Ft.	5,041,000	5,698,000	5,984,000	(657,000)	(286,000)

continued

EXHIBIT 1: *continued*

	End of Year			Change From	
	Goal 1998	*1997*	*1996*	*1998-97*	*1997-96*
Victoria's Secret Stores					
Stores	874	789	736	85	53
Selling Square Ft.	3,795,000	3,555,000	3,326,000	240,000	229,000
Lane Bryant					
Stores	760	773	832	(13)	(59)
Selling Square Ft.	3,666,000	3,735,000	3,980,000	(69,000)	(245,000)
Henri Bendel					
Stores	1	6	6	(5)	0
Selling Square Ft.	35,000	113,000	113,000	(78,000)	0
Abercrombie & Fitch					
Stores	186	156	127	30	29
Selling Square Ft.	1,453,000	1,234,000	1,006,000	219,000	228,000
Abercrombie (Kids)					
Stores	13	0	0	13	0
Selling Square Ft.	42,000	0	0	42,000	0
Structure					
Stores	545	544	542	1	2
Selling Square Ft.	2,161,000	2,143,000	2,117,000	18,000	26,000
Limited Too					
Stores	317	312	308	5	4
Selling Square Ft.	1,002,000	979,000	967,000	23,000	12,000
Bath & Body Works					
Stores	1,101	921	750	180	171
Selling Square Ft.	2,183,000	1,773,000	1,354,000	410,000	419,000
Galyan's Trading Co.					
Stores	15	11	9	4	2
Selling Square Ft.	1,026,000	641,000	488,000	385,000	153,000
Total Retail Businesses					
Stores	5,762	5,640	5,510	122	130
Selling Square Ft.	28,283,000	28,400,000	28,038,000	(117,000)	362,000

Source: www.freeedgar.com

PRESENT CONDITIONS

The Limited, Inc., continues to be successful, in spite of significant problems in its Express division. In 1997, the company opened 315 new stores and closed 304 stores. Growth continued in the company's men's, personal care, lingerie, and children's businesses.

The Limited, Inc., operates as four separate business groups: Women's Brands; Emerging Brands; Intimate Brands, Inc. (IBI); and Abercrombie & Fitch. Stores included in each business group and net sales for each are shown in Exhibit 2.

The Women's Brands and Emerging Brands Group are wholly company owned. In 1995, The Limited offered 16.9 percent of IBI stock in a public offering. The company retains ownership of 83 percent of shares (210 million). In 1996, 16 percent of Abercrombie & Fitch stock was sold at public offering, with The Limited, Inc., controlling 84 percent of shares (43 million).

According to Wexner, "The strategic business plan that we set in motion in 1995, a plan that essentially reinvented our core businesses and operations, is working. It's

EXHIBIT 2: Net Sales and Income for The Limited, Inc., Divisions

($ in millions)	1997	1996	1995
Women's Brands			
Express	1,189	1,386	1,445
Lerner New York	946	1,045	1,005
Lane Bryant	907	905	903
The Limited	776	855	850
Henri Bendel	83	91	91
Total Women's Brands	3,901	4,282	4,294
Emerging Brands			
Structure	660	660	576
The Limited Too	322	259	214
Galyan's Trading Co.	160	108	45
Other	6	4	0
Total Emerging Brands	1,148	1,031	835
Intimate Brands, Inc.			
Victoria's Secret Stores	1,702	1,450	1,286
Victoria's Secret Catalogue	734	684	661
Bath & Body Works	1,057	753	475
Cacique	95	88	80
Other	30	22	15
Total Intimate Brands, Inc.	3,618	2,997	2,517
Abercrombie & Fitch	522	335	235
Total Net Sales	9,189	8,645	7,881

continued

EXHIBIT 2: *continued*

($ in millions)	1997	1996	1995
Operating Income			
Women's Brands	(268)	64	54
Emerging Brands			
and Other	159	68	149
Intimate Brands	505	458	386
Abercrombie & Fitch	84	46	24
Total Operating Income	480	636	613

Source: www.freeedgar.com

having an impact at nearly every level, within the operating businesses and in the support group." Almost all of the business divisions showed good financial results in 1996.

Wexner was disappointed in the performance of Express in 1996 and 1997. Previously, Express had been one of the "stars" of the company. The store became successful as a retailer geared toward fashion-conscious young women, but the division abandoned its trendy fashions in favor of more traditional clothing geared toward older customers in the early 1990s. Sales problems at Express became critical for The Limited, Inc., in 1996. The year was so bad for Express that performance at that division negated the sales/profits gains made in the other divisions. Wexner believes these problems can be corrected if Express will refocus on its core customer. Michael Weiss, the former president of Express, left his position as leader of The Limited's women's apparel group to assist Express with its refocus efforts. However, Express sales dropped another 14 percent in 1997.

BUSINESS STRUCTURE

The Limited, Inc., includes 12 different store types, one mail order division, and six facilitating-type operations. These divisions are described briefly here.

Limited Stores

This is the flagship division of the organization. Originally, merchandise in these stores was targeted to women between the ages of 16 and 25, but that orientation changed to women in their thirties and forties several years ago. Limited Stores recently shifted its orientation to women in their twenties and thirties who want "casual American fashion." These stores focus on the sale of medium-priced fashion clothing and accessories. The company began opening larger-format Limited stores in 1990, and older stores were renovated to provide additional selling space. Most of the 629 Limited stores (as of year-end 1997) are located in regional shopping centers or malls across the United States.

Express

Express was redesigned in the early 1990s to have a more sophisticated European image instead of the neon-lit high-tech store of the mid-1980s. The company now describes its Express stores as providing "hot new fashion to young women in their early twenties." Merchandise includes "young and spirited fashions of good taste and quality." A private label brand created for Express is called Compagnie Internationale. Express added petite sizes in 1995. The 753 Express stores in operation as of year-end 1997 were located mostly in shopping malls.

Lerner New York

This division sells fashionable women's sportswear for "value-minded customers." The store created a brand called NY & Co. There were 746 Lerner stores in operation as of year-end 1997 in malls and shopping centers across the United States.

Victoria's Secret Stores

Victoria's Secret Stores are the dominant intimate apparel store in the world, presently selling more lingerie than industry competitors Vanity Fair and Maidenform. The stores were redecorated in the early 1990s in a "Victorian Parlor" style. Victoria's Secret bath and fragrance products are an increasingly important portion of store sales. The division's newest product is hosiery. There were 789 Victoria's Secret stores in the United States as of year-end 1997.

Lane Bryant

Lane Bryant had been in operation for 80 years and was actually larger than The Limited, Inc., at the time it was purchased by The Limited in 1982. Lane Bryant's market is primarily women between 30 and 50. The store specializes in the sale of medium-priced clothing, intimate apparel, and accessories for the "special-sized woman" (sizes 14 and up). Nearly all Lane Bryant stores originally were located in regional shopping centers, but Wexner has shifted Lane Bryant stores to mall locations near the other Limited stores. There were 773 Lane Bryant stores as of year-end 1997.

Henri Bendel

In 1985, The Limited purchased this upscale fashion store. The store offers the best in clothing and accessories from international designers. Prices are designed for "today's modern woman in her mid-thirties in a higher-income household." This is the only upscale store owned by The Limited. There were six Henri Bendel stores as of year-end 1997.

Abercrombie & Fitch

The Limited purchased Abercrombie & Fitch in 1988 from Oshman's Sporting Goods for $45 million. The company sells high-quality, traditional sportswear for the "young, hip customer." The Limited operated 156 Abercrombie & Fitch stores as of year-end 1997.

Abercrombie (Kids)

Abercrombie (Kids) is The Limited, Inc.'s newest division. Thirteen new stores averaging 3,230 square feet each are planned to open in 1998.

Structure

The Limited, Inc., began testing the market for men's fashions by offering "Express for Men" in Express stores beginning in 1987. Sixty-nine Structure stores were opened in 1989 and by the end of 1997 there were 544 stores. Structure stocks good-quality, affordable clothing in the latest styles. The target customer is in his mid-twenties and "urban, active, young, and creative." Structure stores generally open into Express stores so that customers can shop in both stores without having to exit to the mall area.

Limited Too

The market for girls' clothing (sizes 6–14) was tested by The Limited in the late 1980s when the Limited Too brand was offered in The Limited's flagship store. Sixty-two stores were opened during 1989, and by the end of 1997 there were 312 Limited Too Stores. Clothing sold in Limited Too stores is stylish—the newest in colors, prints, and fabrics—and moderately priced. Clothing is offered for girls to age 14.

Bath & Body Works

In response to demand by consumers for natural personal-care products, The Limited opened six Bath & Body Works stores in 1990. These stores have a natural market atmosphere and sell a variety of personal care products. There were 921 Bath & Body Works stores as of year-end 1997.

Galyan's Trading Company

In 1995, The Limited, Inc., acquired six Galyan's stores for $18 million in cash and stock. The company had a total of 11 stores by year-end 1997. The company says Galyan's is "the coolest destination in retailing for sports enthusiasts and 'wannabes' of all ages." A new distribution center for Galyan's was opened in 1997.

Victoria's Secret Catalogue

This division is one of the fastest-growing mail order operations in the United States. Since its purchase by The Limited in 1982, the catalogue has steadily increased its operations. Now Victoria's Secret Catalogue is the dominant catalogue for lingerie in the world. The Limited spent $10.7 million in 1994 to purchase a telemarketing center in Ohio so that Victoria's Secret Catalogue operations could be expanded. The division has three successful specialty catalogues: "Swim," "Country," and "City." A new catalogue introduced in 1996 was "Christmas Dreams and Fantasies." In 1996, the division established a phone center in Japan so that this market could be established for mail order sales.

Mast Industries

The business of this division is to arrange for the manufacture and import of women's clothing from around the world, and to wholesale this merchandise to The Limited's stores and to other companies. This division delivers more than 100 million garments to The Limited, Inc., each year.

Limited Distribution Services

The Limited's distribution center is located in Columbus, Ohio. The center now has seven buildings and about 4.2 million square feet. This includes a 760,000-square-foot fulfillment center and office complex for Victoria's Secret Catalogue that was completed in 1992. The Limited also owns a mail order center of approximately 750,000 square feet in Indianapolis, Indiana.

Limited Store Planning

This division is responsible for designing store layout and developing merchandising techniques for all of The Limited's retail store divisions.

Limited Real Estate

This division handles store leases for the retail divisions. In 1991, the real estate division began a process of remodeling many stores and opening new larger-format stores (6 million square feet of selling space) for a total selling space at the end of 1991 of 20.3 million square feet. By the end of 1994, the total selling space of Limited Stores was almost 25.6 million square feet. Total selling space was 28.4 million square feet by the end of 1997.

Alliance Data Services

This division handles consumer credit for both the retail and mail order divisions. Activities of Allied Data Services include billing, credit assessment, credit card receivables, and credit collection.

Gryphon Development L.P.

This division, acquired by The Limited in 1992, develops and supplies fragrances for Bath & Body Works, Victoria's Secret Stores, Victoria's Secret Catalogue, and Abercrombie & Fitch. More than 1,000 different products have been developed by this division.

COMPETITION

The retail sale of women's clothing is a very competitive business. Competitors of The Limited, Inc., include nationally, regionally, and locally owned department stores; specialty stores; and mail order catalogue businesses. Some of The Limited's major competitors are The Gap, Casual Corner, Federated Department Stores, Dayton Hudson, Dillard, May Department Stores, Charming Shoppes, Nordstrom, Sears, and J. C. Penney.

According to *Stores*, The Limited, Inc., was the number-one apparel chain in the United States during 1995 and 1996. (The top 10 apparel chains are shown in Exhibit 3.) Other specialty retailers who were in the top 10 for sales volume in 1995 and 1996 include TJX Cos., The Gap, Eddie Bauer, and Talbot's.

Two of The Limited's major competitors are discussed below.

The Gap, Inc.

At the end of May 1997, The Gap, Inc., had 1,916 apparel stores in operation in the United States. The Gap has several divisions that compete directly with The Limited stores. The Gap, Inc., (956 stores) sells casual sportswear items for both men and

EXHIBIT 3: Top 10 Apparel Chains

($ in millions)

Chain	1996 Sales	1995 Sales	Percent Change
The Limited, Inc.	$8,644	$7,881	9.7
TJX Cos.	6,689	4,447	50.4
The Gap, Inc.	5,284	4,395	20.2
Woolworth	3,750	3,600	4.2
Intimate Brands	2,997	2,517	19.1
Ross Stores	1,689	1,426	18.5
Burlington Coat	1,610	1,597	0.9
American Retail	1,300	1,250	4.0
Eddie Bauer	1,200	1,134	5.7
Talbot's	1,018	981	3.8

Source: www.freeedgar.com

EXHIBIT 4: Financial Information for The Gap, Inc.

($ in millions except per share amount)	1996	1995	1994	1993
Gross Revenue	$5,284.4	$4,395.6	$3,722.9	$3,295.7
Net Income	452.9	352.0	320.2	258.4
Long-Term Debt	0	75.0	0	75.0
Net Worth	1,654.5	1,640.5	1,375.2	1,126.5
Earnings Per Share	1.60	1.23	1.10	.89

Source: www.freeedgar.com

women. GapKids (522 stores) sells children's sportswear. Banana Republic (230 stores) sells upscale casual wear. Old Navy Clothing Company, the company's fastest-growing division (208 stores), sells budget-priced casual clothing. The Gap, Inc., also operates 209 GapKids, Gap, and Banana Republic stores in Canada, the United Kingdom, France, Germany, and Japan. Financial information for The Gap, Inc., is shown in Exhibit 4.

The Gap, Inc., recently changed its merchandise mix by offering more women's clothing and accessories and allotting less store space for casual wear such as jeans. In addition, more clothing in the stores is designed to be gender-specific; fewer items are unisex sizes and styles. The Gap also has worked to define the target market of its stores as The Limited has done, and company CEO Mickey Drexler talks in terms of identifying Gap stores as "brands."

TJX Companies

TJX Companies is the largest off-price apparel chain in the United States. At the end of August 1997, TJX Companies had 1,141 apparel stores in operation worldwide. The apparel division includes T.J. Maxx (578 stores); Marshalls (453 stores); Winners Apparel Ltd. (68 stores); Home Goods (21 stores); and T.K. Maxx (21 stores located in the United Kingdom). The company acquired Marshalls in 1995. Financial information for TJX Companies is shown in Exhibit 5.

EXHIBIT 5: Financial Information for TJX Companies

($ in millions except per share amount)	1997	1996	1995	1994	1993
Gross Revenue	$7,389.1	$6,689.4	$4,447.5	$3,842.8	$3,626.6
Net Income	306.6	213.8	84.0	82.6	127.1
Long-Term Debt	221.0	244.4	690.7	239.5	210.9
Net Worth	1,164.1	1,127.2	764.6	607.0	590.9
Earnings Per Share	1.92	1.18	.51	.52	.81

Source: www.freeedgar.com

Target customers for TJX include middle-income women between the ages of 25 and 50. Most TJX stores are located in strip shopping centers.

DEMOGRAPHIC AND SOCIETAL TRENDS

Some analysts suggest that as the baby boomers reach their forties and fifties, retailers and manufacturers of women's apparel have not provided for this group's needs. This large market group for women's apparel has found only youthful fashions and fads available for purchase. As a result, large numbers of customers began staying away from the stores entirely or purchasing fewer clothing items. Also, older shoppers (the fastest-growing demographic group) are complaining that retailers cater to younger tastes. Many baby-boomer women, who make up about half of all U.S. working women, have little time for shopping. When they do have free time, they do not equate shopping with pleasure and prefer to relax at home. Many of the women in the baby boom group spend their disposable income on items for their children and not clothing for themselves. In addition, many baby boomers have placed retirement savings, college tuition, and mortgage payments at a higher priority than spending for apparel.

However, men (of all ages) are becoming much more fashion-conscious. Men do more of their own shopping and they make more clothing purchases on impulse than in the past.

Currently, there is a "mini–baby boom" and many of today's new parents are older and have more disposable income than did new parents in the past. Also, the grandparents of children today are more likely to be affluent. Even though these trends ordinarily would indicate a good future for apparel retailing, there is a strong simultaneous trend away from the conspicuous consumption days of the 1980s. Retailers in the apparel industry are thus likely to struggle.

ECONOMIC CONDITIONS

The U.S. economy continues to remain strong, employment levels are high, income levels are increasing, and inflation is under control. However, consumer debt is high and personal bankruptcies (1.1 million) were at an all-time high at the end of 1996. Consumers are likely to defer purchasing items such as clothing so they can pay off credit card debt. The gap between rich and poor continues to increase. By the year 2000, it is estimated that the number of households with annual incomes of $15,000 or less (in 1984 dollars) will increase to about 36 percent of U.S. families, or about 40 million families. The number of downscale shoppers is increasing. Because many adults owe significant debt for cars and homes and are unable to spend much money for apparel, they often purchase clothing at outlet malls or discount stores. Occasionally, however, the downscale shopper may want to indulge him- or herself by purchasing fashion items from specialty stores.

Specialty retailers may have to take more gambles to gain a competitive advantage in this volatile industry. Specialty retailers have gained a competitive advantage in the past by guessing a fashion trend early and purchasing inventory to provide that trend to customers. If a specialty retailer purchases inventory for a fashion trend but cannot turn over the inventory, the store loses profit and cannot afford to take more risks. However, if they do not gamble by trying to keep up with fashion trends, it is impossible to make a profit when the economy turns around because the merchandise will be out-of-date.

INTERNAL FACTORS FOR THE LIMITED, INC.

Marketing

Wexner believes that his company is "reinventing the specialty store business." Because the 12 Limited retail store divisions sell different styles of clothing and related goods in a variety of price ranges, Wexner has created the impact of a department store in many malls by locating the stores in close proximity. Wexner has begun to think of his divisions of stores as a collection of "brands" rather than as groups of stores. He says, "When you think of yourself as a brand, you think more broadly. You think of the efficacy of the brand, the reputation, the integrity, the channels of distribution, whether that be in a store, a catalogue, on television, or overseas." Brand building includes defining each store's image, fashion, advertising, price, and market position. In the past, Limited divisions copied each other's designs so that the only differences in some divisions were the prices charged. Design teams are now assigned to each business, and the fashions are designed around narrowly defined brand positions for each division. Leslie Wexner believes this is "good for now. Even better for the long run."

The Limited has spent very little on advertising campaigns in the past. Instead, the company relied on walk-in traffic in malls to sell their products. Wexner says that the company actually spends a significant amount of money on advertising because it sends out hundreds of millions of catalogues per year and has over 5,600 storefronts which three million potential customers pass each day. Occasionally in the past, the company included small advertisements in "mall shopper" magazines. The company launched a national advertising campaign for the first time in November 1989. The $10 million campaign included advertisements in *Vogue, Vanity Fair,* and other women's magazines and was an attempt to increase brand recognition for the company's private labels. During the fall of 1994, the company advertised in 12 major U.S. markets that it had made mistakes in product selection during the early 1990s, and urged consumers to visit a Limited, Inc., store to see changes that had been made. The company now places some advertising on television and in magazines.

The Limited's distribution center is located in Columbus, Ohio. Over 60 percent of the U.S. population is located within a 500-mile radius of Columbus, so Wexner feels this is an ideal location for a distribution center. Another advantage of the Columbus location is its nearness to New York City, the port where incoming merchandise produced in foreign countries is received by Mast Industries. All merchandise arriving in New York is shipped directly to the distribution center for allocation among The Limited's stores. A computerized distribution system aids distributors in their selections for each store's inventory. This system allows The Limited to monitor inventory levels, the merchandise mix, and the sales pattern at each store so that appropriate adjustments can be made as needed. A new $42.1 million Bath & Body Works distribution center was opened in July 1997 in Columbus, Ohio.

Production

The Limited, Inc., does not produce its own clothing, but it has a division that contracts for the manufacture of clothing. Mast Industries specializes in contracting for production of high-quality, low-cost products. Much of the merchandise imported by Mast is marked with one of The Limited's own labels: The Limited, Compagnie Internationale, Structure, Victoria's Secret, Limited Too, and NY & Co. Leslie Wexner believes that having private-label brands allows The Limited to keep merchandise inventory current and unique.

The Limited can also maintain control over its clothing supply through Mast Industries. Mast is able to make copies of new trends in apparel and have these products on store shelves before the original design is produced for sale. Company managers try to maintain a 1,000-hour turnaround time between recognizing a new style and delivering the merchandise to stores. Mast can send high-resolution computer images of clothing designs by satellite to Far Eastern manufacturers. In addition, computer information that is collected from all individual stores is used to determine what needs to be produced in the Far East the next day. In a few days, the newly produced items arrive at the Columbus distribution center and are sent to the stores.

In 1996, Mast purchased merchandise from approximately 5,200 different suppliers, but no more than 5 percent of The Limited's inventory was purchased from any single manufacturer. About half of the Limited's inventory is produced outside the United States. By 1995, the company was working with more than 1,600 different factories. The coordination of work with so many factories made it difficult to ensure consistent quality. Two changes were made in 1995 in an effort to make sure the company's products were of consistent quality: Presidents of the store divisions were given the responsibility for ensuring quality in their divisions, and individual store managers were no longer allowed to make significant sourcing decisions on their own. The Limited flagship store was the pilot for another new approach to production in 1996. The Limited Stores reduced the number of its major manufacturers from 60 to 20 and quality control was rigidly monitored. It is expected that other store divisions will adopt this strategy.

Management

Leslie Wexner has been a guiding force for the company since its beginning. His risk-taking style has concerned some investors, but his ability to create new marketing concepts has made The Limited, Inc., the envy of other specialty retailers. Some critics suggest that Wexner is great at starting businesses, but has not been effective as a day-to-day leader of the established businesses. His tendency was to micro-manage store divisions and as recently as 1992, Wexner had 24 people reporting directly to him.

The company now uses a centralized process for planning that Wexner leads. This approach to leadership allows Wexner to remain involved in each store division without his involvement in every detail of division operations. After the company began its approach of considering store divisions as "brands," Wexner started meeting with the top managers (president, marketing director, chief financial officer, head merchant, and head designer) of each store division on a monthly basis to make sure there is "agreement and alignment around core elements of the brand." Wexner now says, "I don't believe we've ever had a stronger group of leaders. They are good business executives and passionate retailers who complement their businesses and their organizations. They are energized and badly want to win, as I do."

Financial Condition

The Limited's income statements and balance sheets are provided in Exhibit 6 and Exhibit 7, respectively. These statements reveal significant changes in levels for sales, income, assets, and shareholders' equity. A consolidated statement of The Limited's shareholders' equity is given in Exhibit 8.

EXHIBIT 6: Income Statements for The Limited, Inc.

($ in millions except per share amounts)	1997	1996	1995	1994	1993
Net Sales	$ 9,188.8	$8,644.8	$7,881.4	$7,320.8	$7,245.1
Cost of Goods Sold, Occupancy and Buying Costs	(6,370.8)	6,148.2	5,793.9	5,206.4	5,286.3
Gross Income	2,818.0	2,496.6	2,087.5	2,114.4	1,958.8
General, Administrative, and Store Operating Expenses	(2,124.7)	1,848.5	1,475.5	1,315.4	1,259.9
Special and Nonrecurring Items, Net	(213.2)	12.0	1.3	0	2.6
Operating Income	480.1	636.1	613.3	799.0	701.5
Interest Expense	(68.8)	75.4	77.5	65.4	(63.9)
Other Income (Expense), Net	36.9	41.9	21.6	10.7	7.3
Minority Interest	(56.5)	45.6	22.4	0	0
Gain in Connection with Initial Public Offerings	8.6	118.2	649.5	0	0
Income Before Taxes	400.4	675.2	1,184.5	744.3	645.0
Provision for Income Taxes	183.0	241.0	223.0	296.0	254.0
Net Income	217.4	434.2	961.5	448.3	391.0
Net Income Per Share	.79	1.54	2.68	1.25	1.08

Source: www.freeedgar.com

EXHIBIT 7: Balance Sheet for The Limited, Inc.

($ in millions)	1997	1996	1995	1994	1993
Assets					
Current Assets					
Cash and Equivalents	746.4	312.8	1,645.7	242.8	320.6
Accounts Receivable	83.4	69.3	77.5	1,292.4	1,056.9
Inventories	1,002.7	1,007.3	959.0	870.4	733.7
Store Supplies	99.2	90.4	81.8	0	0
Other	99.5	65.3	70.3	142.0	109.5
Total Current Assets	2,031.2	1,545.1	2,834.3	2,547.6	2,220.7
Property and Equipment	1,520.0	1,828.9	1,741.5	1,692.1	1,666.6
Restricted Cash	351.6	351.6	351.6	0	0
Deferred Income Taxes	56.6	0	0	0	0
Other Assets	341.5	394.4	339.2	330.3	247.9
Total Assets	4,300.9	4,120.0	5,266.6	4,570.0	4,135.2
Liabilities and Shareholders' Equity					
Current Liabilities					
Accounts Payable	300.7	307.8	280.7	275.3	250.4
Accrued Expenses	676.7	481.8	388.8	372.7	347.9
Certificates of Deposit		0	0	25.2	15.7
Income Taxes Payable	116.0	117.3	145.9	124.4	93.5
Deferred Income Taxes		0	0	0	0
Total Current Liabilities	1,093.4	906.9	815.4	797.6	707.5
Long-Term Debt	650.0	650.0	650.0	650.0	650.0
Deferred Income Taxes	0	169.9	152.1	306.1	275.1
Other Long-Term Liabilities	58.8	51.7	50.8	55.4	61.3
Minority Interest	102.1	67.3	45.7	0	0
Contingent Stock Redemption					
Agreement	351.6	351.6	351.6	0	0
Shareholders' Equity					
Common Stock	180.4	180.3	180.4	189.7	189.7
Paid-In Capital	148.0	142.9	137.1	132.9	128.9
Retained Earnings	3,613.2	3,526.2	3,200.3	2,716.5	2,397.1
Less Treasury Stock, at Cost	(1,896.6)	(1,926.9)	(316.8)	(278.2)	(274.5)
Total Shareholders' Equity	2,045.0	1,922.6	3,201.0	2,761.0	2,441.3
Total Liabilities and Shareholders' Equity	4,300.9	4,120.0	5,266.6	4,570.1	4,135.1

Source: www.freeedgar.com

EXHIBIT 8: The Limited, Inc., Consolidated Statement of Shareholders' Equity

($ in millions)

	Number of Shares Outstanding	Par Value	Paid-in Capital	Retained Earnings
1993	$357,801	$189.7	$128.9	$2,397.1
1994	357,604	189.7	132.9	2,716.5
1995	355,366	180.3	137.1	3,200.3
1996	271,071	180.3	142.9	3,526.2
1997	272,800	180.3	148.0	3,613.2

Source: www.freeedgar.com

THE YEAR 1997

Net sales for The Limited increased 6.2 percent in 1997 to $9.2 billion but net income declined 49.9 percent to $217 million. Express's sales for 1997 declined 14 percent while Lerner New York, Lane Bryant, The Limited, and Henri Bendel sales each declined 9 percent in 1997. The Limited's other divisions did very well in 1997, especially Abercrombie & Fitch with a 56 percent increase in sales, Bath & Body Works with a 40 percent increase, and Limited Too with a 24 percent increase. During 1997, The Limited reduced the total number of stores in several of its divisions, including 38 fewer Lerner stores, 59 fewer Lane Bryant stores, and 34 fewer The Limited stores.

The Limited, Inc.'s comparable store sales percentages are given in Exhibit 9. These numbers reflect per store average change in sales, rather than total division change in sales. Note that Express and Henri Bendel stores on average did poorly in 1997.

EXHIBIT 9: The Limited, Inc., Comparable Store Sale Percentages

	1997	1996	1995
Comparable Store Sales:			
Express	(15%)	(6%)	(2%)
Lerner New York	(5%)	8%	(1%)
Lane Bryant	1%	0%	(8%)
The Limited	(7%)	3%	(4%)
Henri Bendel	(13%)	(5%)	6%
Total Women's Brands	(8%)	0%	(3%)
Structure	(3%)	7%	(9%)
Limited Too	20%	8%	(4%)
Galyan's Trading Co. (since 7/2/96)	0%	12%	0
Total Emerging Brands	6%	7%	(8%)
Victoria's Secret Stores	11%	5%	(1%)
Bath & Body Works	11%	11%	21%
Cacique	10%	8%	(20%)
Total Intimate Brands	11%	8%	1%

continued

EXHIBIT 9: *continued*

	1997	1996	1995	% Change 1997–96	% Change 1996–95
Abercrombie & Fitch	21%	13%	5%		
Total Comparable Store Sales Increase (Decrease)	0%	3%	(2%)		
Store Data:					
Retail Sales Increase Attributable to New and Remodeled Stores	6%	8%	9%		
Retail Sales per Average Selling Square Foot	$295	$285	$272	4%	5%
Retail Sales per Average Store (thousands)	$1,478	$1,453	$1,419	2%	2%
Average Store Size at End of Year (selling square feet)	5,035	5,043	5,172	0	(2%)
Retail Selling Square Feet at End of Year (thousands)	28,400	28,405	27,403	0	4%
Number of Stores:					
Beginning of Year	5,633	5,298	4,867		
Opened	315	470	504		
Acquired (Sold)	(4)	0	6		
Closed	(304)	(135)	(79)		
End of Year	5,640	5,633	5,298		

Source: www.freeedgar.com

FUTURE OUTLOOK

Wexner says he is "determined to build a company of powerful, differentiated retail brands that maintain and strengthen our position as the world's dominant specialty retailer." His standard is that if a division does not have potential to earn at least $1 billion in sales in the United States, The Limited, Inc., should get out of that business. If a new concept works, Wexner is aggressive. He says, "Invent the concept. Prove it. Move forward fast." Some critics suggest that Wexner has the talent to identify unserved markets and create a marketing concept around those markets, but that he has not yet demonstrated the skill at reinventing mature businesses. Wexner responds, "My view is that whether you are turning around a business—that is, reconceptualizing it—or whether you are starting from scratch, your vision of what you are driving toward is the same." Wexner's goals for 1998 for The Limited are provided in Exhibit 1.

The potential for serious problems exist for Wexner. Some of these include (1) the possibility of downturns at the growth-oriented lingerie and personal-care divisions; (2) another downturn in the women's apparel industry; (3) investor disenchantment because of Wexner's risk-taking attitude; (4) a saturation of Limited stores in U.S. malls; and (5) difficulty finding reliable foreign suppliers.

Wexner is philosophical about the ability of The Limited to compete in the specialty apparel industry of the future. He says "The key challenge facing us in the nineties and the twenty-first century is the same one that faces us every day: to keep taking the risk of change. Sometimes when you're trying to improve, you break something that is already fixed. But unless you change, and take the risk of failure, you limit your opportunities for success. That's why questioning, probing, and reinventing are so important. That is how we redefined the specialty store business several times . . . and how we will continue to reinvent ourselves in the future."

REFERENCES

Caminiti, Susan, "In Search of the '90s Consumer," *Fortune* (September 21, 1992).

Caminiti, Susan, "Can the Limited Fix Itself?" *Fortune* (October 17, 1994).

Gill, Penny, "Les Wexner: Unlimited Success Story," *Stores* (January 1993).

Jaffe, Thomas, "One Last Throw," *Forbes* (December 18, 1995).

Jaffe, Thomas and Esther W. Book, "A Thin Coat of Whitewash?" *Forbes* (April 8, 1996).

Machan, Dyan, "Knowing Your Limits," *Forbes* (June 5, 1995).

The Limited, Inc., *Annual Report* (1994).

The Limited, Inc., *Annual Report* (1996).

"Top 20 Apparel Chains," *Stores* (July 1997).

Wal·Mart Stores, Inc.—1998

Amit Shah
Tyra Phipps

www.wal-mart.com
stock symbol WMT

Headquartered in Bentonville, Arkansas, Wal-Mart (501-273-4000) saw its sales rise from $104.8 billion in 1997 to $117.9 billion in fiscal 1998. Net income rose from $3.1 billion to $3.6 billion during that period. For more than a decade, Wal-Mart has been growing by leaps and bounds, rolling over large competitors such as Kmart and thousands of small businesses. Financial statements are shown in Exhibits 1 and 2.

In 1995, Wal-Mart ended a five-year battle with local leaders of Bennington, Vermont, to open its first store in that state and thereby lay claim to having stores in all 50 states (see Exhibit 3). The Bennington store was Wal-Mart's 2,158th store. To get approval for this store, Wal-Mart abandoned its usual format of a 200,000-square-foot store near a major highway exit and instead located in a downtown building of just 50,000 square feet. Environmentalists in Vermont say the rural character of the state is endangered by "sprawl-mart development." Other chains such as Ames and Kmart had operated in Vermont for years, so some residents were mystified by the controversy. Wal-Mart had three stores in Vermont by the end of fiscal 1997.

Wal-Mart does not have a formal mission statement. When asked about Wal-Mart's lack of a mission, Public Relations Coordinator Kim Ellis replied, "We believe that our customers are most interested in other aspects of our business, and we are focused on meeting their basic consumer needs. If in fact we did have a formal mission statement, it would be something like this: 'to provide quality products at an everyday low price and with extended customer service . . . always.'"

HISTORY

No word better applies to Wal-Mart than "growth." In 1945, Sam Walton opened his first Ben Franklin franchise in Newport, Arkansas. Based in rural Bentonville, Arkansas, Walton; his wife, Helen; and his brother, Bud, operated the nation's most successful Ben Franklin franchises. "We were a small chain," said Walton of his 16-store operation. "Things were running so smoothly we even had time for our families." What more could a man want? A great deal, as it turned out.

Sam and Bud Walton could see that the variety store was dying gradually because supermarkets and discounters were developing. Far from being secure, Walton knew that he was under siege. He decided to counterattack. He first tried to convince the top management of Ben Franklin to enter discounting. After their refusal, Sam Walton made a quick trip around the country in search of ideas. He then began opening his own discount stores in such small Arkansas towns as Bentonville and Rogers.

This case was prepared by Professors Amit Shah and Tyra Phipps of Frostburg State University as a basis for class discussion. It is not intended to illustrate either effective or ineffective handling of an administrative situation. Copyright © 1999 by Prentice Hall, Inc. ISBN 0-13-11124-4.

EXHIBIT 1: Consolidated Statements of Income

(amounts in millions except per share data)	Fiscal years ended January 31,		
	1998	1997	1996
Revenues:			
Net sales	$117,958	$104,859	$93,627
Other income—net	1,341	1,319	1,146
	119,299	106,178	94,773
Costs and Expenses:			
Cost of sales	93,438	83,510	74,505
Operating, selling and general and administrative expenses	19,358	16,946	15,021
Interest Costs:			
Debt	555	629	692
Capital leases	229	216	196
Income Before Income Taxes, Minority Interest and Equity in Unconsolidated Subsidiaries	5,719	4,877	4,359
Provision for Income Taxes			
Current	2,095	1,974	1,530
Deferred	20	(180)	76
	2,115	1,794	1,606
Income Before Minority Interest and Equity in Unconsolidated Subsidiaries	3,604	3,083	2,753
Minority Interest and Equity in Unconsolidated Subsidiaries	(78)	(27)	(13)
Net Income	3,526	3,056	2,740
Net Income Per Share	1.56	1.33	1.19

Source: www.freeedgar.com

EXHIBIT 2: Consolidated Balance Sheets

(amounts in millions)	January 31,	
	1998	1997
Assets		
Current Assets:		
Cash and cash equivalents	$ 1,447	$ 883
Receivables	976	845
Inventories		
At replacement cost	16,845	16,193
Less LIFO reserve	348	296
Inventories at LIFO cost	16,497	15,897
Prepaid expenses and other	432	368
Total Current Assets	19,352	17,993

continued

EXHIBIT 2: *continued*

	January 31,	
(amounts in millions)	1998	1997
Property, Plant and Equipment, at Cost:		
Land	$ 4,691	$ 3,689
Building and improvements	14,646	12,724
Fixtures and equipment	7,636	6,390
Transportation equipment	403	379
	27,376	23,182
Less accumulated depreciation	5,907	4,849
Net property, plant and equipment	21,469	18,333
Property Under Capital Lease:		
Property under capital lease	3,040	2,782
Less accumulated amortization	903	791
Net property under capital leases	2,137	1,991
Other Assets and Deferred Charges	2,426	1,287
Total Assets	45,384	39,604
Liabilities and Shareholders' Equity		
Current Liabilities:		
Accounts payable	9,126	7,628
Accrued liabilities	3,628	2,413
Accrued income taxes	565	298
Long-term debt due within one year	1,039	523
Obligations under capital leases due		
within one year	102	95
Total Current Liabilities	14,460	10,957
Long-Term Debt	7,191	7,709
Long-Term Obligations Under Capital Leases	2,483	2,307
Deferred Income Taxes and Other	809	463
Minority Interest	1,938	1,025
Shareholders' Equity		
Preferred stock ($.10 par value; 100 shares		
authorized, none issued)		
Common stock ($.10 par value; 5,500 shares		
authorized, 2,241 and 2,285 issued and		
outstanding in 1998 and 1997, respectively)	224	228
Capital in excess of par value	585	547
Retained earnings	18,167	16,768
Foreign currency translation adjustment	(473)	(400)
Total Shareholders' Equity	18,503	17,143
Total Liabilities and Shareholders' Equity	45,384	39,604

Source: www.freeedgar.com

EXHIBIT 3: Wal-Mart Fiscal 1998 End of Year Store Counts

	Discount Stores	Supercenters	SAM'S Clubs
Alabama	50	27	8
Alaska	3	0	3
Arizona	34	0	7
Arkansas	50	27	4
California	100	0	24
Colorado	31	5	10
Connecticut	14	0	3
Delaware	2	1	1
Florida	102	33	31
Georgia	62	25	16
Hawaii	5	0	1
Idaho	9	0	1
Illinois	95	11	24
Indiana	60	15	14
Iowa	43	2	7
Kansas	40	8	5
Kentucky	45	23	5
Louisiana	56	19	9
Maine	19	0	3
Maryland	22	1	10
Massachusetts	27	0	3
Michigan	45	0	21
Minnesota	34	0	9
Mississippi	42	14	4
Missouri	79	30	12
Montana	9	0	1
Nebraska	13	5	3
Nevada	13	0	2
New Hampshire	17	0	4
New Jersey	16	0	6
New Mexico	16	3	3
New York	51	5	18
North Carolina	78	8	14
North Dakota	8	0	2
Ohio	77	4	23
Oklahoma	57	21	6
Oregon	23	0	0
Pennsylvania	49	12	18
Rhode Island	6	0	1
South Carolina	41	12	9
South Dakota	8	0	2
Tennessee	57	30	11
Texas	169	72	52
Utah	14	0	5
Vermont	3	0	0
Virginia	31	21	10
Washington	20	0	2
West Virginia	12	6	3
Wisconsin	55	1	11
Wyoming	9	0	2
U.S. Total	1,921	441	443

continued

EXHIBIT 3:   *continued*

	Discount Stores	Supercenters	SAM'S Clubs
Alberta	16	0	0
British Columbia	12	0	0
Manitoba	9	0	0
New Brunswick	4	0	0
Newfoundland	7	0	0
Nova Scotia	7	0	0
NW Territories	1	0	0
Ontario	52	0	0
Quebec	28	0	0
Saskatchewan	8	0	0
Canada Total	144	0	0
Argentina	0	6	3
Brazil	0	5	3
Mexico	347[a]	27	28
Puerto Rico	9	0	5
China	0	2	1
Germany	0	21	0
International Total	500	61	40
Grand Total	2,421	502	483

Source: www.freeedgar.com
[a]includes 3 Superamas, 25 Bodegas, 4 Aurreras, 67 Vips, and 7 Suburbias.

The company opened its first discount department store, Wal-Mart, in November 1962. The early stores had bare tile floors and pipe racks. Wal-Mart did not begin to revamp its image significantly until the mid-1970s, and growth in the early years was slow. However, once the company went public in 1970, sales began to increase rapidly. Wal-Mart's stock doubled in value in 1997 alone.

Such retailers as Target, Venture, and Kmart provided the examples that Wal-Mart sought to emulate in its growth. The old Wal-Mart store colors, dark blue and white (too harsh), were dumped in favor of a three-tone combination of light beige, soft blue, and burnt orange. Carpeting, which long had been discarded on apparel sales floors, was put back. New racks were put into use that displayed the entire garment instead of only an edge.

In 1987, Wal-Mart implemented two new concepts: (1) hypermarkets, 200,000-square-foot stores that sell everything, including food, and (2) supercenters, scaled-down supermarkets. Also in 1987, Walton named David Glass as the new chief executive officer while he remained chair of the board. Glass is president and CEO today (see Exhibit 4).

In 1990, Wal-Mart completed the acquisition of 14 centers of McLane Company, a national distribution system in 11 states providing over 12,500 types of grocery and nongrocery products. Also in 1990, Wal-Mart sold its 14 Dot Discount Drug Stores. SAM'S Clubs that year integrated the 28 wholesale clubs of The Whole Club, Inc., of Indianapolis, Indiana, into its operations.

EXHIBIT 4: Wal-Mart's Organizational Chart

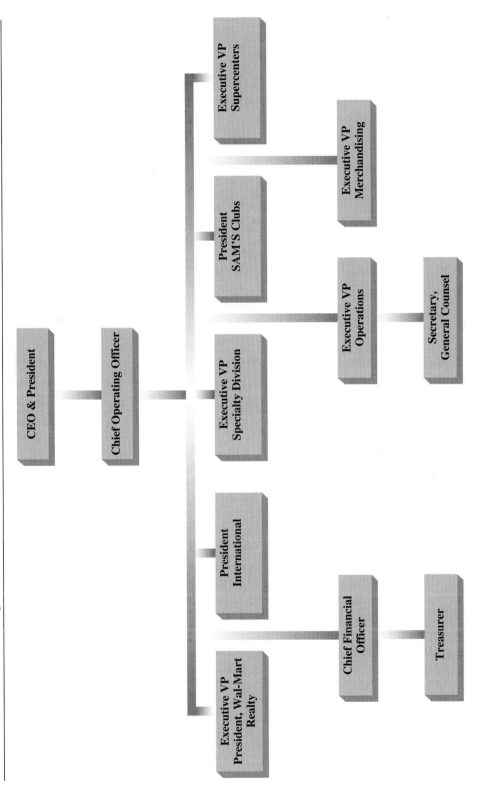

Wal-Mart unveiled in mid-1993 its first environmental demonstration store, a 121,294-square-foot facility in Lawrence, Kansas. This store is designed so that a second floor could be added to allow conversion to apartments if Wal-Mart vacates. The store is exceptionally energy-efficient but costs 20 percent more than the average Wal-Mart, which costs about $2.4 million or $20 a square foot. The environmental store features on-site recycling, native plants that make up the landscaping, and solar-powered lights. Planning for this store began in 1990 when Hillary Rodham Clinton served on Wal-Mart's board of directors. Wal-Mart constructed a second environmental demonstration store in Moore, Oklahoma. Companywide, Wal-Mart recycles over 700,000 tons of cardboard, paper, and plastic each year.

Exhibits 5 and 6 provide selected financial information for Wal-Mart in fiscal 1998.

EXHIBIT 5: Wal-Mart Divisions' Financial Data *(in millions of dollars)*

(Fiscal year ended January 31, 1998)	*Wal-Mart Stores*	*SAM'S Clubs*	*International*	*Other*	*Consolidated*
Revenues from external customers	$83,820	$20,668	$7,517	$ 5,953	$117,958
Intercompany real estate charge (income)	1,375	349		(1,724)	
Depreciation and amortization	674	104	118	738	1,634
Operating income	5,833	616	262	(208)	6,503
Interest expense					784
Income before income taxes and minority interest					5,719
Total assets	$22,002	$ 3,864	$7,390	$12,128	$ 45,384

Source: www.freeedgar.com

EXHIBIT 6: Wal-Mart Sales Data for Fiscal Year Ended January 31, 1998

Category	*Percentage of Sales*
Hard goods	23
Soft goods/domestics	21
Grocery, candy, and tobacco	14
Pharmaceuticals	9
Records and electronics	9
Sporting goods and toys	8
Health and beauty aids	7
Stationery	5
Shoes	2
Jewelry	2

Source: www.freeedgar.com

Sam Walton died in 1992. Bud Walton died in 1995. Wal-Mart's 1995 Annual Report was dedicated to Bud. Sam Walton once said about Bud: "Of course, my number-one retail partner has been my brother, Bud. Bud's wise counsel and guidance kept us from many a mistake. Often, Bud would advise taking a different direction or maybe changing the timing. I soon learned to listen to him because he has exceptional judgment and a great deal of common sense."

DIVISIONS

Wal-Mart Stores

Most Wal-Mart stores are located in towns of 5,000 to 25,000. On occasion, smaller stores are built in communities of less than 5,000. As indicated in Exhibit 7, Wal-Mart opened 37 Wal-Mart stores, 97 Supercenters, and 8 SAM'S Clubs in fiscal 1998. Most of Wal-Mart's 1998 $117 billion in sales came from Wal-Mart stores and Supercenters. International sales grew to approximately 6.3 percent of the total sales in fiscal 1998, up from 4.8 percent in fiscal 1997. SAM'S Club percentage of total sales decreased from 18.9 percent in fiscal 1997 to 17.5 percent in fiscal 1998.

Wal-Mart grouped its smaller discount stores, such as the one in Bennington, Vermont, into a new Hometown USA program. This allows the company to give special attention to customers in smaller markets in rural America. Hometown USA consists of the stores that are under 50,000 square feet and under one regional manager. The idea is to enable these stores to develop locally and with a different mix from the large prototypes. Although these stores represent Wal-Mart's heritage, they had become lost in the shuffle as the company opened 120,000- to 150,000-square-foot stores.

Wal-Mart stores generally have 36 departments and offer a wide variety of merchandise, including apparel for women, girls, men, boys, and infants. Each store also carries curtains, fabrics and notions, shoes, housewares, hardware, electronics, home supplies, sporting goods, toys, cameras and supplies, health and beauty aids, pharmaceuticals, and jewelry. Nationally advertised merchandise accounts for a majority of sales in the stores. Wal-Mart has begun marketing limited lines of merchandise under

EXHIBIT 7: Wal-Mart's Store Count Data

Fiscal Year Ended Jan. 31,	Wal-Mart Discount Stores				Wal-Mart Supercenters		SAM'S Clubs		
	Opened	Closed	Conversions	Total	Opened	Total	Opened	Closed	Total
Balance Forward	—	—	—	1,714	—	10	—	—	208
1993	159	1	24	1,848	24	34	48	0	256
1994	141	2	37	1,950	38	72	162	1	417
1995	109	5	69	1,985	75	147	21	12	426
1996	92	2	80	1,995	92	239	9	2	433
1997	59	2	92	1,960	105	344	9	6	436
1998	37	1	75	1,921	97	441	8	1	443

Source: www.freeedgar.com

the brand name SAM'S American Choice. The merchandise is selected carefully to ensure quality and must be made in the United States. Wal-Mart is developing new apparel lines such as the Kathie Lee career sportswear and dress collection, Basic Equipment sportswear, and McKids children's clothing.

Except for extended hours during certain holiday seasons, most Wal-Mart stores are open from 9:00 A.M. to 9:00 P.M. six days a week, and from 12:30 P.M. to 5:30 P.M. on Sundays, with the remainder of the stores closed on Sundays. Some Wal-Mart stores and most of the Supercenter stores are open 24 hours each day. Wal-Mart tries to meet or undersell local competition but maintains uniform prices, except when lower prices are necessary to meet local competition. Wal-Mart stores maintain a "satisfaction guaranteed" program to promote customer goodwill and acceptance.

McLane's

McLane's is the nation's largest distributor of food and merchandise to convenience stores. McLane's offers a wide variety of grocery and nongrocery products, including perishable and nonperishable items. The nongrocery products consist primarily of tobacco products, hard goods, health and beauty aids, toys, and stationery. McLane's is a wholesale distributor which sells merchandise to a variety of retailers, including the Wal-Mart stores, SAM'S Clubs, and Supercenters.

SAM'S Clubs

SAM'S Clubs are membership-only, cash-and-carry operations. A financial service credit card program (Discover Card) is available in all clubs. Qualified members include businesses and those individuals who are members of certain qualifying organizations, such as government and state employees and credit union members. Both business and individual members have an annual membership fee of $25 for the primary membership card.

SAM'S offers bulk displays of name-brand hard good merchandise, some soft goods, and institution-size grocery items. Each SAM'S also carries jewelry, sporting goods, toys, tires, stationery, and books. SAM'S now has 131 clubs with fresh-food departments such as bakery, meat, and produce.

SAM'S is a $20 billion business that is starting to grow again. The clubs were never designed to sell merchandise categories, but rather items, and because the number of items is limited to about 2,000 for the wholesale part of the business, which is 60 percent to 65 percent of sales, and to 1,000 to 1,500 for personal and individual use, it is very important for the items to be appropriate for the location. Also, the items have to come and go seasonally, so continuity by category is not appropriate. Thus, there is a problem for buyers who have to be item merchants and compete for space in the clubs.

Operating hours vary among SAM'S, but generally are Monday through Friday from 10:00 A.M. to 8:30 P.M. Most SAM'S are open on the weekend from 9:30 A.M. to 7:00 P.M. on Saturday and from 12:00 noon to 6:00 P.M. on Sunday. SAM'S attempts to maximize sales volume and inventory turnover while minimizing expenses.

During fiscal 1998, Wal-Mart opened 8 new SAM'S Clubs. This division of Wal-Mart lags behind other divisions in financial performance, but the company feels the warehouse club business has promise.

Supercenters

Wal-Mart's Supercenters combine groceries with general merchandise, giving customers one-stop shopping. Wal-Mart opened 97 Supercenters during fiscal 1998, bringing the total of Supercenters to 441 in the United States as shown in Exhibit 7.

The number of Supercenters grew from just five in 1991 to six in 1992, 30 in 1993, 68 in 1994, 143 in 1995, and 235 in 1996.

Supercenters constitute the company's fastest-growing division, and management is extremely pleased with them. Currently, the limitation is distribution, and Wal-Mart is working hard to expand its captive food distribution capabilities. Most of the Supercenters are replacements of Wal-Mart stores, so they had a jumpstart on the general merchandise side of the store, while food has tended to build a little bit more slowly. However, the company has gained market share faster than planned. Wal-Mart likes to locate Supercenters near the strongest food retailers so those facilities will "either get better or be run out of town."

The Wal-Mart Supercenter is the most important retail concept on the landscape at this time. As with the discount stores, their real competitive impact does not come the year they open, but in the third year, because they have a maturation curve that's more like a Wal-Mart store than a food store. Also, the one-stop convenience aspect of the stores has such broad appeal that it is drawing a larger customer audience on a regular basis. Supercenters are continuing to get better in many categories and are attracting a higher-income audience, in addition to their traditional customers. Supercenters provide mart carts and are on one floor, so the stores are handicapped-accessible. The company's broad assortments and everyday low prices are very compelling; extensive advertising is not needed. This represents an enormous saving over the competition. Furthermore, as Supercenters move into food distribution, they gain a major cost advantage over Super Kmart and Super Target.

International

In 1994, Wal-Mart acquired 122 Canadian Woolco stores. Wal-Mart revamped these stores in less than a year. Wal-Mart Canada already has become that nation's number-one discount chain, and is on the verge of becoming Canada's largest retailer of any sort. As indicated in Exhibit 3, the company today has 144 Wal-Mart stores in Canada, 347 in Mexico, and nine in Puerto Rico. Note that Wal-Mart also operated 61 Supercenters and 40 SAM'S Clubs outside the United States as fiscal 1998 ended. The world's largest Wal-Mart is in Mexico City.

Wal-Mart considers its Hong Kong stores as training centers for the company's expansion into China. Wal-Mart Chair Rob Walton, Sam's oldest son, is leading the company's efforts to open stores in China.

Wal-Mart recently announced plans to purchase a majority interest in Cifra SA, its joint venture partner in Mexico. This move marks Wal-Mart's first direct investment in any of its foreign partners and reflects the chain's increasing efforts to expand its international business.

With more than 50,000 associates and over 300 locations outside the United States, Wal-Mart already is serving some 5 million customers every week.

According to Bob L. Martin, president of the International Division, "We are a global brand name. To customers everywhere it means low cost, best value, greatest selection of quality merchandise, and the highest standards of customer service. But the fact that International has grown to $5 billion in sales in less than five years gives us an idea of how great the potential is."

Community involvement, responding to local needs, merchandise preferences, and buying locally are all hallmarks of the international Wal-Marts, just as they are in the United States.

Distribution Centers

Wal-Mart has 30 distribution centers nationwide, including six centers in Arkansas; four in Texas; and two each in California, Indiana, Pennsylvania, and South Carolina. Wal-Mart's distribution operations are highly automated. A typical Wal-Mart Discount Store has more than 70,000 standard items in stock. Supercenters carry more than 20,000 additional grocery items, a lot of them perishable, so they have to be ordered frequently. Associates use hand-held computers, linked by a radio-frequency network to in-store terminals, to scan items electronically and check on their availability in other area stores. To place orders, each store wires merchandise requests to the warehouses, which in turn either ship immediately or reorder. Wal-Mart computers are linked directly with over 200 vendors, so deliveries are faster. Wal-Mart has one of the world's largest private satellite communication systems to control distribution. Wal-Mart has installed point-of-sale bar-code scanning in all of its stores.

Wal-Mart owns a fleet of truck-tractors that can deliver goods to any store in 38 to 48 hours from the time the order is placed. After trucks drop off merchandise, they frequently pick up merchandise from manufacturers on the way back to the distribution center. This back-haul rate averages over 60 percent and is yet another way Wal-Mart cuts costs.

With an annual technology and communication budget of $500 million and an information systems staff of 1,200, Wal-Mart leads the industry in information technology. This means Wal-Mart is dedicated to providing its associates with the technological tools to work smarter every day. "With this technology, we're getting better, quicker, and more accurate information to manage and control every aspect of our business," said Randy Mott, senior vice-president and chief information officer.

OPERATIONS

Wal-Mart's expense structure, measured as a percentage of sales, continues to be among the lowest in the industry. Although Walton watched expenses, he rewarded sales managers handsomely. Sales figures are available to every employee at Wal-Mart. Monthly figures for each department are ranked and made available throughout the organization. Employees who do better than average get rewarded with raises, bonuses, and a pat on the back. Poor performers only rarely are fired, although demotions are possible.

All employees (called "associates") have a stake in the financial performance of the company. Store managers earn as much as $100,000 to $150,000 per year. Even part-time clerks qualify for profit-sharing and stock-purchase plans. Millionaires among Wal-Mart's middle managers are not uncommon. Executives frequently solicit ideas for improving the organization from employees and often put them into use.

With Wal-Mart stock selling at 20 to 30 times earnings—an almost incredible price—Sam Walton presided over a sizable fortune before his death. Wal-Mart stock is still 39 percent held by the Walton family. Family holdings are worth nearly $8 billion.

Continuing a Walton tradition, Wal-Mart invites over 100 analysts and institutional investors to the fieldhouse at the University of Arkansas for its annual meeting in mid-June. During the day-and-a-half session, investors can meet top executives as well as Wal-Mart district managers, buyers, and 200,000 hourly salespeople. Investors see a give-and-take meeting between buyers and district managers.

Employee Benefits

Wal-Mart management takes pride in the ongoing development of its people. Training is seen as critical to outstanding performance, and new programs are implemented often in all areas of the company. The combination of grass-roots meetings, the open-door policy, videos, printed material, classroom and home study, year-end management meetings, and on-the-job training has enabled employees to prepare themselves for advancement and added responsibilities.

Wal-Mart managers stay current with new developments and needed changes. Executives spend one week per year in hourly jobs in various stores. Sam Walton himself once traveled at least 3 days per week, visiting competitors' stores, and attending the opening of new stores (leading the Wal-Mart cheer, "Give me a W, give me a A . . .").

Wal-Mart encourages employee stock purchases; about 8 percent of Wal-Mart stock is owned by employees. Under the Stock Purchase Plan, stock may be bought by two different methods. First, an amount is deducted from each employee's check with a maximum of $62.50 per check. An additional 15 percent of the amount deducted is contributed by Wal-Mart (up to $1,800 of annual stock purchases). Second, a lump-sum purchase is allowed in April up to $1,500, with an additional 15 percent added by the company. Wal-Mart also offers an associate stock-ownership plan, and approximately 4,000 management associates have stock options.

Wal-Mart has a corporate profit-sharing plan. The purposes of the profit-sharing plan are to furnish an incentive for increased efficiency, to provide progressive recognition of service, and to encourage careers with the company for Wal-Mart associates. This is a trustee-administered plan, which means the company's contributions are made only out of net profits and are held by a trustee. The company from time to time contributes 10 percent of net profits to the trust.

Company contributions can be withdrawn only on termination. If employment with the company is terminated because of retirement, death, or permanent disability, the company contribution is fully vested (meaning the entire amount is nonforfeitable). If termination of employment occurs for any other reason, the amount that is nonforfeitable depends on the number of years of service with the company. After completion of the third year of service with the company, 20 percent of each participant's account is nonforfeitable for each subsequent year of service. After seven years of service, a participant's account is 100 percent vested.

Predatory Pricing

Three independent pharmacies in Conway, Arkansas, filed a suit claiming Wal-Mart deliberately was pricing products below cost to kill competition. Wal-Mart argued that it priced products below cost not to harm competitors but to meet or beat rivals' prices. Chancery Court Judge David L. Reynolds on October 11, 1996, found Wal-Mart guilty of predatory pricing and ordered the company to pay the pharmacies $286,407 in damages. The judge also forbade Wal-Mart from selling products below cost in Conway in the future. Competitors who had been stung by Wal-Mart's pricing policies watched the case closely.

The ruling in Arkansas marked the first time Wal-Mart failed to settle a predatory pricing case out of court. If upheld, the decision could prompt similar lawsuits elsewhere.

Wal-Mart intends to appeal the ruling to the Arkansas Supreme Court. "Wal-Mart is extremely disappointed," said Robert K. Rhoads, the retailer's attorney. "If this decision is allowed to stand, the result will be higher prices—not just for Wal-Mart customers but customers of every retail store, large and small, in Arkansas."

Diversity Among Employees

Sam Walton was admittedly old-fashioned in many respects. Wal-Mart store policies reflect many of his values. For example, store policies forbid employees from dating other employees without prior approval of the executive committee. Also, women in management positions are rare. Annual manager meetings include sessions for wives to speak out on the problems of living with a Wal-Mart manager. No women are in the ranks of Wal-Mart's top management. Walton also resisted placing women on the board of directors. Only 12 women have made it to the ranks of buyers (they are 12 percent of all buyers). Wal-Mart is an EEOC/AA employer but has managed to get away with apparently discriminatory policies.

Wal-Mart has instituted several initiatives to increase the recruitment and promotion of women and minorities including:

- a mentoring program encompassing more than 750 women and minority managers,
- a women's leadership group, in partnership with Herman Miller and Service-Master, to develop opportunities for high-potential female managers, and
- store internships during the summer for college students between their junior and senior years, with 70 percent being women or minorities.

Philanthropy

Education is a primary beneficiary of Wal-Mart charitable giving. Examples include:

- Each store awards a $1,000 college scholarship to a qualifying high school senior. More than $11 million in scholarships have been awarded since the program's inception.
- A major commitment to the United Negro College Fund. In 1997, Wal-Mart pledged $1 million to UNCF over a four-year period.
- Sponsorship of the Competitive Edge Scholarship Fund. In 1993, Wal-Mart teamed up with participating vendor-partners to start the fund, which makes four-year scholarships—each worth $20,000—available to students pursuing technology-related college degrees.
- Since 1993, Wal-Mart and SAM'S Clubs associates have raised more than $52 million in support of local United Way agencies.
- Wal-Mart Stores, Inc., is the number-one sponsor for the Children's Miracle Network Telethon. Associates from all U.S. divisions of the company helped raise more than $71 million for CMN since 1988. In calendar year 1996,

Wal-Mart donated $14.3 million, or 10 percent of the $143 million raised in the entire CMN campaign.

- In 1994, the 7,784 local charitable projects selected by associates received $6,572,531 of matching grant funds from the Wal-Mart Foundation.

Marketing

The discount retailing business is seasonal to a certain extent. Generally, the highest volume of sales and net income occurs in the fourth fiscal quarter and the lowest volume occurs during the first fiscal quarter. Wal-Mart draws customers into the store by radio and television advertising, monthly circulars, and weekly newspaper ads. Television advertising is used to convey an image of everyday low prices and quality merchandise. Radio is used to a lesser degree to promote specific products that usually are in high demand. Newspaper and monthly circulars are major contributors to the program, emphasizing deeply discounted items, and are effective at luring customers into the store.

Efforts also are made to discount corporate overhead. Visitors often mistake corporate headquarters for a warehouse because of its limited decorating and "show." Wal-Mart executives share hotel rooms when traveling to reduce expenses. The company avoids spending money on consultants and marketing experts. Instead, decisions are made based on intuitive judgments of managers and employees and on the assessment of strategies of other retail chains.

Wal-Mart censors some products. The company has banned recordings and removed magazines based on lyrics and graphics, and has stopped marketing teen rock magazines. Wal-Mart advertises a "Buy American" policy in an effort to keep production at home. Consequently, Wal-Mart buyers constantly are seeking vendors in grassroots America. In Tulsa, Zebco responded to Wal-Mart's challenge by bucking the trend toward overseas fishing tackle manufacturing. Zebco created more than 200 U.S. jobs to assemble rods and manufacture bait and cast reels. The company's bait and cast reels are the first to be manufactured in the United States in 30 years.

Innovations

Wal-Mart's Innovation Network (WIN) is one of two related services that provide entrepreneurs with a point of entry into Wal-Mart's mammoth distribution system. "The key to our approach is our use of consistent standards and open criteria," explains Gerald Udell, a professor at Southwest Missouri State University and the executive director of its Center for Business and Economic Development. Udell conceived, designed, and now administers the two Wal-Mart entrepreneurial support efforts, WIN and the Support American Made program. These programs already have helped over 3,000 inventors and entrepreneurs by evaluating products and prototypes for possible distribution by the chain.

For a $175 fee, entrepreneurs can submit their products and detailed company information to a team of analysts. Within two months, applicants receive a detailed evaluation of their company and products. These programs are aimed at explaining reasons that Wal-Mart does business with some and not with others. Instead of giving a simple no, they explain how to get a yes.

In conjunction with Chase Manhattan Bank, Wal-Mart introduced its Wal-Mart MasterCard. There is no annual fee and a low 14.48 percent APR fixed rate for purchases. On transferred balances, the APR rate is 9.9 percent.

COMPETITORS

Kmart is the second-largest U.S. retailer. However, compared to Wal-Mart, the scope of Kmart's problem becomes evident. Even though each company operates roughly the same number of stores, Wal-Mart's sales are roughly three times Kmart's sales of almost $34.4 billion. Wal-Mart's discount stores are larger than Kmart's and produce sales of about $300 per square foot, or twice the amount of Kmart's.

Should Wal-Mart, the price leader in discounting, choose to sacrifice $0.10 to $0.15 of its earnings per share, it virtually could ensure that Kmart would not operate above the break-even point.

Kmart is in a capital-intensive battle with Wal-Mart, whose annual capital expenditures are nearly four times that of Kmart's. Kmart's capital resources for this battle are limited, and if its earnings fail to improve, it cannot stay in this capital-intensive race for long. When Kmart cut its dividend rate in half, management took a step in the right direction to conserving its financial resources. The new CEO's recommendation regarding the dividend payout will be a litmus test of the urgency with which management intends to apply the company's assets toward turning around the Kmart discount stores.

Supercenters are revolutionizing the discount store battlefield, just as tanks redefined trench warfare. Wal-Mart started 1995 with 68 Supercenters, but by 2000, it will operate 800 to 900, and each will shatter the profit potential of at least one older Kmart discount store. This is the dusk of the discount-store era, and improvements in the merchandising and systems of Kmart's discount stores might do little to forestall their decline.

Kmart has slowed its rollout of its Super Kmart Centers to allow more time to develop the staff and skills needed for these stores to achieve an adequate return. By the time the rollout reaccelerates, Wal-Mart probably will be operating 500 Supercenters, and retailing will have changed greatly.

On a positive note, Kmart's board has been strengthened by new appointments and is steering the company; new management provides a fresh perspective for the company; new strategies are being implemented; same-store sales are strong; expenses are being reduced; and earnings should rise in 1998. Kmart's earnings rose dramatically to $249 million in 1997.

J.C. Penny and Sears responded to the reality of retail competition several years ago by offering consumers better values than before. They have succeeded in lifting their sales, in both dollars and units. Kmart planned to take market share from them, but was blocked. As this escape route from direct competition with Wal-Mart closes, Kmart must protect itself and fight an uneven battle with Wal-Mart and with another strong firm, Target. Dayton Hudson added 60 new Target stores in 1997 alone for a total of 796 stores.

FUTURE STRATEGIES

What strategies would you recommend to CEO David Glass? How aggressively should Wal-Mart expand internationally, and where? Should Wal-Mart get a foothold in Europe before competitors seize the initiative? Should Wal-Mart expand further in

Mexico, the United States, or Canada? Should Wal-Mart make further acquisitions such as their Woolco acquisition in Canada? Is Wal-Mart's rate of growth of Supercenters too fast? What can Wal-Mart do to improve its SAM's Clubs operations?

REFERENCES

www.freeedgar.com

www.wal-mart.com

Dayton Hudson Corporation—1998

Henry Beam

www.dhc.com
stock symbol DH

Dayton Hudson Corporation (612-370-6736/6948) is the country's fourth-largest general merchandise retailer, behind Wal-Mart, Sears, and Kmart. It is one of the few large American corporations with a female chief executive officer for a division. Headquartered in Minneapolis, Minnesota, Dayton Hudson caters to all income groups through three operating divisions: Mervyn's, the Department Store Division (DSD), and Target. Dayton Hudson's department stores are strong in the upper Midwest, controlling significant shares of the market in Detroit (Hudson's), Chicago (Marshall Field's), and Minneapolis (Dayton's). Target's upscale, general merchandise discount stores are spread across the country and account for over half of the company's sales and profits. Mervyn's, with stores primarily in California and the Midwest, caters to lower- to middle-income shoppers but is not doing well.

The department stores and Mervyn's usually are located in major malls. In contrast, Target stores are located in shopping centers. Sometimes a Target store will be located near a Mervyn's or a Dayton Hudson department store, or both. In Kalamazoo, Michigan, the largest mall has a Hudson's and a Mervyn's, and less than a mile away there is a Target store in a shopping center. Despite such closeness of locations, Dayton Hudson has made little attempt to associate the divisions with each other in the eyes of consumers, many of whom aren't aware the three divisions are part of the same corporation.

HISTORY

The Panic of 1873 left young Joseph Hudson bankrupt. After he had paid off his debts at 60 cents on the dollar, he saved enough to open a men's clothing store 18 years later in Detroit. Among his merchandising innovations were return privileges and price marking in place of bargaining. By 1891, Hudson's was the largest retailer of men's clothing in America. Remarkably, Hudson looked up all his creditors from 1873 and repaid them all in full with interest. When Hudson died in 1928, his four nephews took over and expanded the business. In 1928, Hudson's built a new building on Woodward Avenue in downtown Detroit. It eventually grew to 25 stories with 49 acres of floor space and exuded quality throughout. The Woodward Avenue store was closed in 1982 due to the steady economic decline which took place in downtown Detroit starting in the late 1950s, but the Woodward name still can be found in Hudson's stores. A department in larger Hudson's stores is called Woodward Shops and sells women's finer apparel.

This case was prepared by Professor Henry Beam of Western Michigan University as a basis for class discussion. It is not intended to illustrate either effective or ineffective handling of an administrative situation. Copyright © 1999 by Prentice Hall, Inc. ISBN 0-13-011126-0.

In 1903, George Dayton, a former banker, opened his Dayton Dry Goods store in a spot in Minneapolis where there was high foot traffic. Like Hudson, Dayton offered return privileges and liberal credit. His store grew to a full-line department store 12 stories tall. After World War II, both companies saw that the future of retailing lay in the suburbs. In 1954, Hudson's built Northland at the northwest edge of Detroit, then the largest shopping center in the United States. Dayton's built the world's first fully enclosed shopping mall, Southdale, in Minneapolis in 1956. In an attempt to diversify, Dayton's opened its first Target discount store in 1962. Dayton's went public in 1966, and in 1969 it bought the family-owned Hudson's for stock, forming Dayton Hudson Corporation. In 1978, the company bought the California-based Mervyn's retail chain of 47 stores which had been started by Mervyn Morris in 1949.

The company bought Marshall Field's department stores in 1990, taking on a billion dollars of debt in the process. Marshall Field's grew out of a dry-goods business started in Chicago in 1852 by Potter Palmer. Marshall Field bought the store in 1865, the last year of the Civil War, and built it into one of Chicago's biggest retailers. His motto, "Give the lady what she wants," was a precursor of customer-oriented retailing. The original Marshall Field's store, located in the Loop in downtown Chicago, was remodeled in 1992. It is one of the company's fastest-growing stores as well as its largest. Selected information on the stores in the three divisions is given in Exhibit 1 through Exhibit 4.

EXHIBIT 1:   Dayton Hudson Corporation 1997 Results

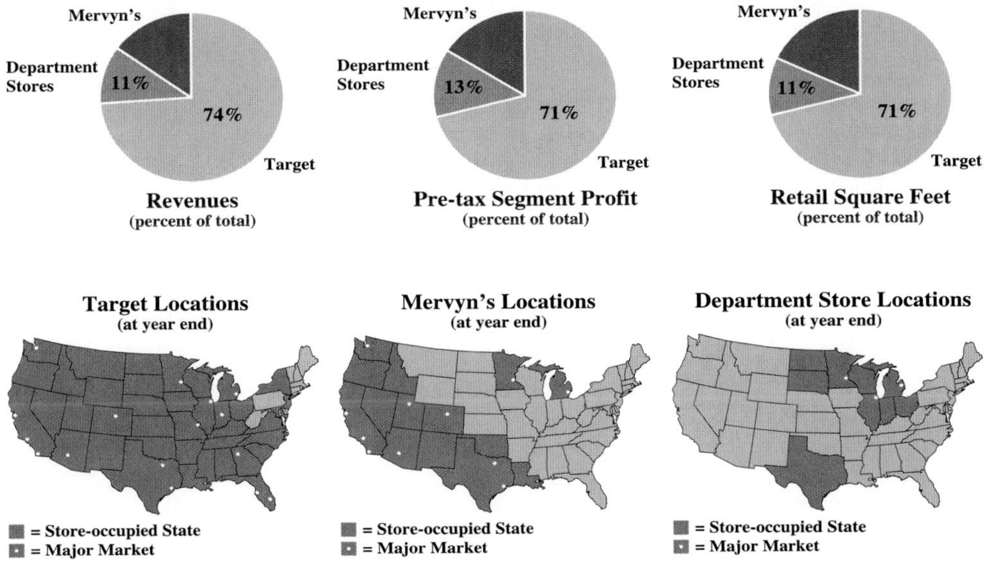

Source: Dayton Hudson Corporation, *Annual Report* (1997): 16.

STRUCTURE

Dayton Hudson's executive office provides leadership for all divisions and establishes the values under which those divisions operate. A lean corporate staff serves a support function for senior corporate management and the divisions. Each of the three operating divisions has its own CEO and president and is run like its own business. Though their organizations are separate and their strategies are distinct, the divisions are encouraged to share advances in technology and management approaches in order to achieve efficiencies that can be gained by coordinating or combining activities.

Target Division

The Target division consisted of 796 stores in 39 states coast-to-coast at the end of 1997. Selected data for the Target division is given in Exhibit 2. Target is an upscale discount store that provides good-quality, family-oriented merchandise at attractive prices in a clean, spacious, and customer-friendly environment. Its stores generally are located in small, freestanding malls. Eight regional distribution centers process 90 percent of all freight for the stores. The objective of the distribution centers is to provide next-day service to all locations. Target's performance has been strong and consistent across most merchandise categories and geographical regions during the last several years. Target invites evaluation from its customers, whom it calls guests, on "Be Our Guest Commentator" forms that are available at checkout counters.

Target's micro-marketing program helped improve its merchandise assortments on a store-by-store basis. "Micro-marketing" is Target's system for tailoring merchandise assortments to customers' needs in individual stores or markets, based on regional, climatic, demographic, and ethnic factors. This permits stores as close as 15 miles apart to offer different merchandise mixes. The typical Target customer is between 25 to 44 years old, married with children, and in a two-wage-earner family. Target advertises primarily through multipage inserts placed in local newspapers.

Target plans to open stores primarily in California, New York, New Jersey, North Carolina, and Virginia. Target's growth will continue to be in adjacent territories to minimize transportation costs and to obtain maximum benefit from advertising. These areas will continue to be a primary focus for the division's short-term growth. While the cost of a store site in these regions is generally higher, so is the sales potential in these densely populated markets. Over the past five years, Target's square footage has grown at a compound annual rate of 10 percent and is expected to continue to grow at that rate for the next few years. In 1997, Target opened 60 new stores.

EXHIBIT 2: Selected Data for Target Division

(millions of dollars)	1997	1996	1995	1994	1993	1992
Revenues	$20,368	$17,853	$15,807	$13,600	$11,743	$10,393
Operating profit	1,287	1,042	719	732	662	574
Stores	796	736	670	611	554	506
Square feet (000s)	87,158	79,360	71,108	64,446	58,087	52,211

Source: Dayton Hudson Corporation, Annual Report (1992, 1993, 1994, 1995, 1996, 1997).

In 1995, Target opened its first two supercenter stores (SuperTargets). The stores are about 180,000 square feet in size, with a fourth of the space devoted to grocery items. Certain categories, such as health and beauty aids and paper products, link the grocery and general merchandise areas and facilitate cross-over shopping. Target plans to build 20 additional supercenters in the next few years.

Mervyn's Division

Mervyn's consisted of 269 stores at the end of 1997 located primarily in the Northwest, West, and Southwest, down from 300 stores in 1996. Selected data for Mervyn's is given in Exhibit 3. It is a moderately priced family department store chain emphasizing brand name and private label casual apparel and home soft goods. Mervyn's typical customer is 25 to 44 years old, female, married with children, and working outside the home.

Performance in recent years has been disappointing. Revenues declined 3.2 percent in 1997. Mervyn's clothing line was considered to be bland and narrow. Further, the economy in California, where nearly half of Mervyn's stores are located, has been weak. The division instituted an aggressive effort to upgrade the merchandising to its core customers, women. Mervyn's reintroduced dresses in 1993 (after dropping them for two years), a change that generated more than $90 million in sales the next year. In 1995, Mervyn's embarked on a new strategy that included holding more promotions, increasing the focus on national brands sold at promotional prices, refining merchandise assortments, and using a California theme with its merchandise and advertising. Mervyn's merchandise selection is narrower and more focused, giving shoppers a higher probability of finding the right size, color, and style. Like Target, Mervyn's advertises through multipage inserts in local newspapers. Mervyn's sold all its stores in Georgia and Florida in 1997 and 1998.

Department Store Division

The Department Store Division (DSD) consisted of 65 Dayton's, Hudson's, and Marshall Field's stores in eight Midwestern states at the end of 1997. About half of these stores are located in the Chicago, Detroit, and Minneapolis/St. Paul metropolitan areas. Historically, they emphasized fashion leadership, quality merchandise, and superior customer service. The stores offered strong national brands with competitive prices in men's and women's apparel, accessories, and home furnishings.

EXHIBIT 3: Selected Data for Mervyn's Division

(millions of dollars)	1997	1996	1995	1994	1993	1992
Revenues	$ 4,227	$ 4,369	$ 4,516	$ 4,561	$ 4,436	$ 4,510
Operating profit	280	153	100	206	179	284
Stores	269	300	295	286	276	265
Square feet (000s)	21,810	24,518	24,113	23,130	22,273	21,305

Source: Dayton Hudson Corporation, Annual Report (1992, 1993, 1994, 1995, 1996, 1997).

EXHIBIT 4:   Selected Data for the Department Store Division

(millions of dollars)	1997	1996	1995	1994	1993	1992
Revenues	$ 3,161	$ 3,149	$ 3,193	$ 3,150	$ 3,054	$ 3,024
Operating profit	240	108	184	270	268	228
Stores	65	65	64	63	63	63
Square feet (000s)	14,090	14,111	13,870	13,824	13,824	13,846

Source: Dayton Hudson Corporation, *Annual Report* (1992, 1993, 1994, 1995, 1996, 1997).

The department stores use a more conservative promotional strategy, significantly reducing the frequency and duration of storewide sales events. The division's comparable-store sales results were adversely affected by the reduced promotional volume during the year. Advertising was heavily oriented to full-color tabloids available in the stores and distributed by direct mail. Selected data for the DSD is given in Exhibit 4. Note that DSD revenues remained constant but operating profit jumped 59 percent in 1997. The DSD completed the sale of all its Texas stores in 1997. The typical customer for the department stores is married, a median age of 43, with a median family income of $50,000. Over half have earned a college degree and two-thirds hold white-collar positions.

The DSD had been a primary force behind the successful Workday Casual program, which consisted of seminars, mannequins, signs, advertising, and direct mail explaining appropriate apparel for the new dress-down work environment suggested for one or two days of the week. According to a study commissioned by Levi Strauss & Company, a major maker of casual wear, casual dress is now the norm at least one day a week for 90 percent of United States office workers. Employees say casual dress encourages a more collegial working environment, reduces status differentials between managers and workers, and saves money on dry cleaning. Reflecting the current interest in golf, the departments stores now feature The Players Shop, a complete golfwear department designed to outfit golfers.

In 1996, Stephen Watson, 51, president of Dayton Hudson Corporation and chair and CEO of the DSD for the previous 10 years, abruptly was replaced by Linda Ahlers, 45. Ahlers had held top merchandising positions at Target, where she started her career in 1977. Under Ahlers, the division continued its emphasis on selling more upscale merchandise, improving the look of the stores, and boosting customer service. In 1996, Hudson's opened a large new store that occupies 300,000 square feet spread over three stories in the Somerset North Mall located north of Detroit. In addition to building new stores, the division is also starting to renovate some of its older stores in such locations as Toledo, Ohio, and Fort Wayne, Indiana.

COMPETITION

Because its three divisions, taken together, compete across all major merchandising categories, Dayton Hudson faces a wide range of competitors. The largest division, Target, competes directly with Kmart and Wal-Mart. Like Target, both Kmart and Wal-Mart began their discount store operations in 1962.

Kmart

Kmart is the nation's second-largest retailer, behind Wal-Mart. It traces its roots to the S.S. Kresge Company, incorporated in 1912, which was originally a dime store chain and headquartered in Detroit, Michigan. By the 1950s, Kresge had become one of the largest general retailers in the nation with stores primarily in urban locations. The first Kmart was opened in a suburb of Detroit after an extensive study of changes in retailing made in 1958 by its future CEO, Harry B. Cunningham. The Kmart large-store format was so successful that the company concentrated on it, rapidly opening Kmarts from coast to coast. It closed dime stores as they became unprofitable and changed the company name to Kmart in 1977.

Kmart passed Sears in retail revenue in 1990 to briefly become the nation's largest retailer. Both were overtaken the next year by the rapidly growing Wal-Mart. Kmart's stores generally were perceived as older, smaller, and less attractive than Wal-Mart's stores. Kmart attempted to grow through acquisitions in the 1980s, but met with minimal success. It purchased Walden Book Company and Builders Square in 1984, Pay-Less Drug Stores Northwest in 1985, and Office Max in 1991. Based in Cleveland, Ohio, Office Max offered office supplies at warehouse prices. Builders Square offers a wide variety of building supplies at discount prices in a warehouse format. Kmart entered the warehouse club business in 1988 with the acquisition of Pace warehouse clubs. Warehouse clubs sell a limited line of merchandise in large lots at very low prices on a cash-and-carry basis. Their primary appeal is to small businesses and families on a tight budget.

During the 1990s, Kmart fell on increasingly hard times even as it tried to upgrade the image of its stores and the quality of its merchandise. It sold its Pace membership warehouse clubs to Wal-Mart in 1994. Tired of ten successive quarters of disappointing earnings, Kmart's board dismissed CEO Joseph Antonini, a former store manager and a career Kmart employee, in March 1995, and replaced him with Floyd Hall, a former head of Dayton Hudson's Target division. By the end of 1995, Kmart had divested the remainder of its acquisitions, except its Builders Square home improvement chain, which remains for sale. Most of the proceeds of $3.5 billion were used to reduce debt. A darling of Wall Street during most of the 1960s and 1970s, Kmart stock sank to $6 per share by the end of 1995, a 13-year low, as rumors spread that it might file for Chapter 11 bankruptcy. In December 1995, Kmart suspended its dividend.

Kmart's net income increased dramatically to $249 million in 1997 as indicated in Exhibit 5. Note that Kmart closed all of its international stores in 1997.

Wal-Mart

Wal-Mart Stores is one of the best-known success stories in America. Sam Walton opened his first Wal-Mart store in Rogers, Arkansas, in 1962. Growth was slow at first. By the time Wal-Mart went public in 1970, it only had 18 stores, all in small towns in the South, and sales of $44 million. Growth accelerated during the 1970s. Wal-Mart established highly automated distribution centers to reduce shipping time, and implemented an advanced computer system to track inventory and speed up checkout and reordering. Wal-Mart's motto, "We sell for less, satisfaction guaranteed," is displayed in each of its stores. Wal-Mart has a liberal merchandise return policy and matches the prices in competitors' advertisements.

EXHIBIT 5:   Kmart's Financial Summary

(millions of dollars, except per share data)	1997	1996	1995
Summary of Operations			
Sales	$32,183	$31,437	$31,713
Cost of sales, buying and occupancy	25,152	24,390	24,675
Selling, general and administrative expenses	6,136	6,274	6,876
Interest expense, net	363	453	434
Continuing income (loss) before income taxes	418	330	(313)
Net income (loss) from continuing operations	249	231	(230)
Net income (loss)	249	(220)	(571)
Per Share of Common Stock			
Basic continuing income (loss)	.51	.48	(.51)
Diluted continuing income (loss)	.51	.48	(.51)
Dividends declared	0	0	.36
Book value	11.15	10.51	10.99
Financial Data			
Working capital	4,202	4,131	5,558
Total assets	13,558	14,286	15,033
Long-term debt	1,725	2,121	3,922
Long-term capital lease obligations	1,179	1,478	1,586
Trust convertible preferred securities	981	980	0
Capital expenditures	678	343	540
Depreciation and amortization	660	654	685
Ending market capitalization—common stock	5,469	5,418	2,858
Inventory turnover	3.5	3.5	3.4
Current ratio	2.3	2.1	2.9
Long-term debt to capitalization	32.4%	37.2%	51.1%
Ratio of income from continuing operations to fixed charges	1.5	1.4	0
Basic weighted average shares outstanding (millions)	487	484	460
Diluted weighted average shares outstanding (millions)	492	486	460
Number of Stores			
United States	2,136	2,134	2,161
International and other	0	127	149
Total stores	2,136	2,261	2,310
U.S. Kmart store sales per comparable selling square foot	$ 211	$ 201	$ 195
U.S. Kmart selling square footage (millions)	151	156	160

Source: www.freeedgar.com

EXHIBIT 6: Wal-Mart Selected Financial Data

(millions of dollars, except earnings per share, and stores)	1998	1997	1996	1995
Sales	$117,958	$104,859	$93,627	$82,494
Net income	3,604	3,056	2,740	2,681
Earnings per share	1.56	1.33	1.19	1.17
Long-term debt	7,191	7,709	8,508	9,709
Shareholders' equity	18,503	17,143	14,756	12,726
Stores	3,406	3,054	2,943	2,759

Source: Wal-Mart, *Annual Report* (1995, 1996, 1997, 1998).

In 1983, Wal-Mart entered the warehouse business with its SAM'S Clubs. By 1997, Wal-Mart was the industry leader in the United States with 443 SAM'S Clubs' sales of nearly $21 billion. Its only significant competitor in warehouse clubs is Costco Companies, which has roughly the same level of sales as SAM'S.

At the end of fiscal 1998, Wal-Mart was the world's largest retailer, operating 1,921 Wal-Mart discount stores, 441 supercenters, and 443 SAM'S Clubs in the United States. It also had 601 foreign stores, mostly in Canada and Mexico. The average community served has about 15,000 people in it.

Supercenters accounted for about 68 percent of Wal-Mart's expansion in 1997. At an average size of about 180,000 square feet, these stores are more than twice as large as the company's traditional discount stores. Sales per square foot are significantly higher at the supercenters than at the Wal-Mart units that only sell general merchandise. In 1996, Wal-Mart opened three SAM'S Clubs and a Wal-Mart in China. Selected data for Wal-Mart is given in Exhibit 6.

Target, Mervyn's, and the Department Store Division also compete to some extent with large national retailers, such as Penney's, Sears, and Montgomery Ward, and with regional department store chains, such as Kohl's in the Midwest, Dillard Department Stores in the South, and May Department Stores in the East.

FINANCIAL ASPECTS

Financial data on Dayton Hudson is given in Exhibits 7, 8, and 9. Advertising costs, which are included in selling, publicity, and administrative expenses, were $679 million, $634 million, and $670 million for 1997, 1996, and 1995, respectively. Capital expenditures for 1997 were $1.35 billion, up from $1.31 billion in 1996. Of this, 85 percent went to Target, 5 percent to Mervyn's, and 10 percent to the DSD. About 71 percent of capital expenditures went to open new stores. During 1997, Target opened 60 new stores, Mervyn's closed 31 stores, and the DSD held constant its 65 stores.

Each division has its own credit card. The transactions are handled through Dayton Hudson's wholly owned Retailer's National Bank, chartered in 1994. The divisions will also take other credit cards, such as Visa and MasterCard.

EXHIBIT 7: Dayton Hudson Corporation Consolidated Results of Operations

(millions of dollars, except per share data)	1997	1996	1995
Revenues	$27,757	$25,371	$23,516
Costs and Expenses			
Cost of retail sales, buying and occupancy	20,320	18,628	17,527
Selling, publicity and administrative	4,532	4,289	4,043
Depreciation and amortization	693	650	594
Interest expense, net	416	442	442
Taxes other than income taxes	470	445	409
Real estate repositioning charge	0	134	0
Total Costs and Expenses	26,431	24,588	23,015
Earnings before income taxes and extraordinary charges	1,326	783	501
Provision for income taxes	524	309	190
Net Earnings Before Extraordinary Charges	802	474	311
Extraordinary charges from purchase and redemption of debt, net of tax	51	11	0
Net Earnings	751	463	311
Basic Earnings Per Share			
Earnings before extraordinary charges	1.80	1.05	.67
Extraordinary charges	(.12)	(.03)	0
Basic Earnings Per Share	1.68	1.02	.67
Diluted Earnings Per Share			
Earnings before extraordinary charges	1.70	1.00	.65
Extraordinary charges	(.11)	(.03)	0
Diluted Earnings Per Share	1.59	.97	.65
Average Common Shares Outstanding (millions)			
Basic	436.1	433.3	431.0
Diluted	463.7	460.9	458.3

Source: www.freeedgar.com

CORPORATE SOCIAL RESPONSIBILITY

Every year since 1946, Dayton Hudson has contributed 5 percent of its pretax profits to philanthropic purposes. (By contrast, most large corporations in the United States contribute about 1 percent.) In 1997, the three operating divisions and the Dayton Hudson Foundation (funded by the corporation) gave about $25 million, which included corporate contributions, to 300 United Way organizations in 39 states. Employees donated another $12 million, bringing the total 1997 contribution to United Way by Dayton Hudson and its employees to about $37 million.

   Major contributions were made to programs and projects that strengthen families, promote the economic independence of individuals, or help neighborhoods respond to key social and economic concerns. Target is the lead sponsor to help restore the Washington Monument, one of our nation's oldest landmarks. CEO Robert Ulrich commented, "The Washington Monument has served as the backdrop for significant events throughout American history. That's why Target Stores is proud to have led the fundraising effort. In just 14 months, we've met our $5 million goal, ensuring the monument

EXHIBIT 8: Dayton Hudson Corporation Consolidated Statements of Financial Position

(millions of dollars)	January 31, 1998	February 1, 1997	February 3, 1996
Assets			
Current Assets			
Cash and cash equivalents	$ 211	$ 201	$ 175
Retained securitized receivables	1,555	1,720	1,510
Merchandise inventories	3,251	3,031	3,018
Other	544	488	252
Total Current Assets	5,561	5,440	4,955
Property and Equipment			
Land	1,712	1,557	1,496
Buildings and improvements	6,497	5,943	5,812
Fixtures and equipment	2,915	2,652	2,482
Construction-in-progress	389	317	434
Accumulated depreciation	(3,388)	(3,002)	(2,930)
Property and Equipment, net	8,125	7,467	7,294
Other	505	482	321
Total Assets	14,191	13,389	12,570
Liabilities and Shareholders' Investment			
Current Liabilities			
Accounts payable	2,727	2,528	2,247
Accrued liabilities	1,346	1,168	957
Income taxes payable	210	182	137
Current portion of long-term debt and notes payable	273	233	182
Total Current Liabilities	4,556	4,111	3,523
Long-Term Debt	4,425	4,808	4,959
Deferred Income Taxes and Other	720	630	623
Convertible Preferred Stock, Net	30	50	62
Shareholder's Investment			
Convertible preferred stock	280	271	257
Common stock	73	72	72
Additional paid-in-capital	196	146	110
Retained earnings	3,930	3,348	3,044
Loan to ESOP	(19)	(47)	(80)
Total Shareholders' Investment	4,460	3,790	3,403
Total Liabilities and Shareholders' Investment	14,191	13,389	12,570

Source: www.freeedgar.com

EXHIBIT 9: **Dayton Hudson Corporation Notes to Consolidated Financial Statements**

Business Segment Comparisons (millions of dollars)	1997	1996	1995[a]	1994
Revenues				
Target	$20,368	$17,853	$15,807	$13,600
Mervyn's	4,227	4,369	4,516	4,561
Department Store Division	3,162	3,149	3,193	3,150
Total revenues	27,757	25,371	23,516	21,311
Pre-tax segment profit				
Target	1,287	1,048	721	732
Mervyn's	280	272	117	198
Department Store Division	240	151	192	259
Total pre-tax segment profit	1,807	1,471	1,030	1,189
LIFO provision (expense)/credit	(6)	(9)	(17)	19
Real estate repositioning charge	0	(134)	0	0
Securitization adjustements:				
Interest equivalent	(33)	(25)	(10)	0
SFAS 125 gain	45	0	0	0
Interest expense, net	(416)	(442)	(442)	(426)
Corporate and other	(71)	(78)	(60)	(68)
Earnings before income taxes and extraordinary charges	1,326	783	501	714
Assets				
Target	9,487	8,257	7,330	6,247
Mervyn's	2,281	2,658	2,776	2,917
Department Store Division	2,188	2,296	2,309	2,392
Corporate and other	235	178	155	141
Total assets	14,191	13,389	12,570	11,697
Depreciation and amortization				
Target	437	377	328	294
Mervyn's	126	151	150	145
Department Store Division	128	119	113	108
Corporate and other	2	3	3	1
Total depreciation and amortization	693	650	594	548
Capital expenditures				
Target	1,155	1,048	1,067	842
Mervyn's	72	79	273	146
Department Store Division	124	173	161	96
Corporate and other	3	1	21	11
Total capital expenditures	1,354	1,301	1,522	1,095

[a]consisted of 53 weeks.

Source: www.freeedgar.com

will stand for generations to come." Dayton Hudson was included in the 1993 edition of *The 100 Best Companies to Work for in America.*

MANAGEMENT

College graduates long have considered jobs in retailing to be inferior to jobs in manufacturing or the professions and seldom gave them serious consideration for anything more than part-time jobs. But opportunities have shifted. High-paying union jobs decreased rapidly in the past decade and there are too many lawyers. Thus jobs in retailing, in which a store manager can make $75,000 or more after five years, are becoming much more attractive to young people. Further, given the explosive growth of the discounters, thousands of new managers must be hired or promoted each year to run the new stores. However, the work is hard and lacks glamour. Given the high turnover among part-time workers and the constant promotion of assistant managers to other stores, store managers must spend long hours interviewing and training new workers. Workweeks average 60 hours and relocations are frequent. Nevertheless, the discounters offer many young people one of today's best chances for rapid advancement and high salaries.

ROBERT ULRICH, CHAIR AND CEO

Robert Ulrich was named chair of Dayton Hudson, effective July 1, 1994, when his predecessor, Kenneth Macke, unexpectedly announced his retirement at the age of 55 after 33 years with the company. Ulrich earned a B.A. degree from the University of Michigan and completed the Stanford Executive Program at the Stanford University Graduate School of Business. He started as a merchandise trainee at Dayton's Department Store Company in 1967 and was named executive vice-president of Dayton's in 1981. In May 1984, he became president of the combined Dayton Hudson Department Store Company and was promoted to Target president in 1984. In 1987, he was promoted to Target chair and was named to the Dayton Hudson board in 1994. He retained his position as Target's CEO and president when he became chair of Dayton Hudson. Ulrich is a devotee of the arts and serves on the board of the Minneapolis Institute of Arts. Dayton Hudson's directors and officers are listed in Exhibit 10.

In his first year as chair, Ulrich embarked on a program of stripping out layers of management, such as vice-chairpersonships, and tightening lines of control and communications. In August 1995, he eliminated the position of group vice-president of Dayton Hudson and fired two senior vice-presidents. He kept his office at Target rather than move to corporate headquarters, affirming Target's central role in the corporate hierarchy.

Ulrich's first letter to shareholders as chairman explained his philosophy for managing Dayton Hudson:

> During 1994, we began to leverage the size and strength of the entire corporation against the operating objectives of each of our three retail operations. We're doing this by creating a "boundaryless" organization where "speed is life." What is powerful about the approach is its simplicity. It means taking all the tools we have across the corporation and concentrating them on our primary purpose—serving guests by providing them with the merchandise they

EXHIBIT 10:   Dayton Hudson Corporation's Organizational Chart

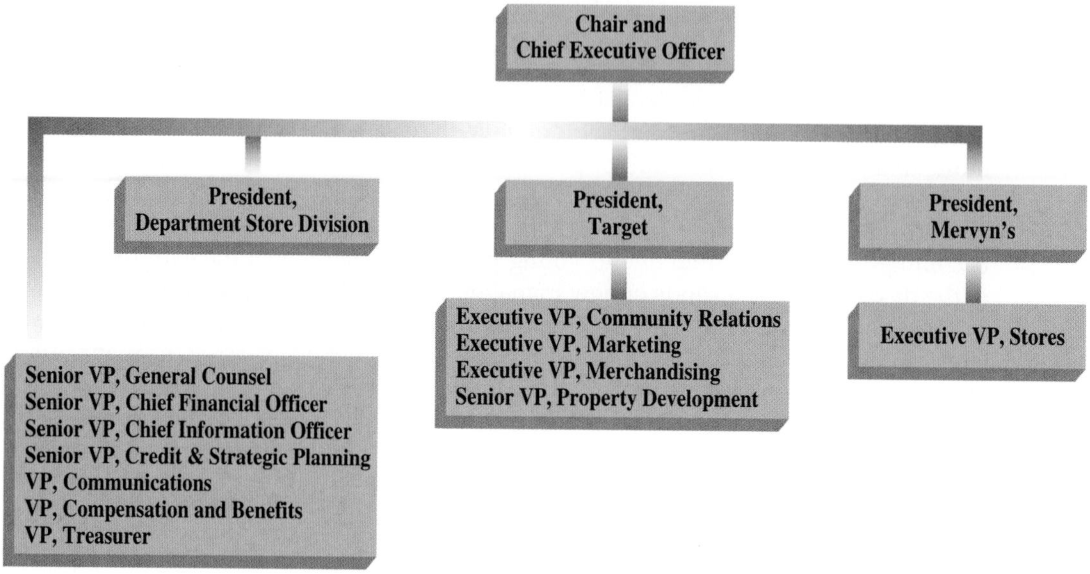

Source: Dayton Hudson, *Annual Report* (1997): 39.

want. It means sharing resources and expertise between divisions. It means taking advantage of the natural increase in speed that comes from eliminating organizational boundaries and layers. It means looking at every idea that works in one of our divisions to see if it would work just as well in another.

Ulrich was named Discounter of the Year at the 1995 Supplier Performance Awards by Retail Category for his achievements as chair of Target and its parent company, Dayton Hudson. Ulrich had been named Discounter of the Year twice before.

THE FUTURE

The first page of the 1994 *Annual Report* told what Dayton Hudson expected to accomplish in the future:

> We are committed to serving our guests better than the competition with trend-right, high-quality merchandise at very competitive prices. We are committed to being a low-cost, high-quality distributor of merchandise through "boundaryless" functioning—through leveraged resources, expertise, and economies across divisions. Our primary objective is to maximize shareholder value over time. We believe we will achieve a compound annual fully diluted earnings per share growth of 15 percent over time, while maintaining a prudent and flexible capital structure.

The primary vehicle for achieving these goals is the Target division, which is scheduled to continue receiving the major share of capital expenditures for the next several years.

According to *The Wall Street Journal*, J.C. Penney Company made a private, unsolicited bid of at least $6.5 billion for the company but was rebuffed. Despite some talk on Wall Street that Dayton Hudson would be better off if it divested itself of Mervyn's or the Department Store Division, Robert Ulrich remains committed to making the three divisions work together effectively to attain these goals.

QUESTIONS

Should Dayton-Hudson sell its Mervyn's unit?

Should Dayton-Hudson sell its Department Store Division?

How should Dayton-Hudson go about paying down its large amount of long-term debt?

Is Dayton-Hudson's policy of donating 5 percent of pretax earnings to worthwhile social causes consistent with its primary goal of maximizing shareholder value over time?

Develop a five-year strategic plan for Dayton Hudson that will permit earnings per share to increase 15 percent a year.

REFERENCES

Halverson, Richard. "Robert Ulrich—Discounter of the Year." *Discount Store News* (September 18, 1995).

Helliker, Kevin. "Sold on the Job: Retail Chains Offer a Lot of Opportunity, Young Managers Find." *The Wall Street Journal* (August 25, 1995): A1.

Lee, Louise and Robert Berner. "Penney Discloses Failed Attempt to Buy Dayton for Over $6.5 Billion." *The Wall Street Journal* (April 26, 1996): A3.

Levering, Robert and Milton Moskowitz. *The 100 Best Companies to Work for in America.* (New York: Currency/Doubleday, 1993).

Mahoney, Tom and Leonard Sloane. *The Great Merchants.* (New York: Harper & Row, 1966).

Gaming—Industry Note

The gaming industry faces only moderate revenue growth in 1998, partly because the pace of new casino approvals has slowed. We estimate that U.S. casino revenues will total about $23 billion in 1998, compared with the $22 billion estimated for 1997. (S & P's numbers for casino revenues include estimates for Native American casinos and certain others that are not publicly disclosed.) This 4 percent rise would be substantially smaller than the double-digit increases generated earlier in the decade, when there was a big boost from the development of new gaming markets such as Illinois and Mississippi.

With the U.S. unemployment rate at relatively low levels and a hike in the federal minimum wage having gone into effect in 1997, we expect that labor cost pressures will increase in 1998 for operators of lodging and gaming facilities.

Consolidation may result in cost savings for the lodging industry, however. Hotel companies are seeing a sizable amount of acquisition activity, both on a corporate and an individual property basis. In our view, the corporate mergers largely reflect managements' recognition of opportunities to generate earnings growth through operating synergies and cost reductions. As for the purchase of single hotels, it is often more economical to buy an existing property than to build a new one.

AS CASINO INDUSTRY GROWS, CHALLENGES LIE AHEAD

Revenues continue to rise in the gaming industry, but conditions for longer-term growth in the United States have weakened. No new states have approved non-Native American casinos since Indiana legalized gambling in mid-1993. Although the development of glamorous and distinctive new facilities should boost the number of gambling visitors to existing markets, the industry's ability to generate sustained double-digit revenue growth will likely depend on geographic expansion. For many Americans, a visit to a casino still requires a long-distance trip by plane, train, car, or bus.

Current geographic growth prospects don't seem strong; ironically, the healthy U.S. economy is partly to blame for this. With more people employed and improved economic conditions in various parts of the country, states and localities have less incentive to look at gaming as a prospective new source of taxes, tourism, and jobs. Proposals to approve gaming were included on various states' election ballots in November 1996. The most significant approvals included a favorable vote in Michigan to allow up to three casinos in Detroit, as well as various local approvals of casinos in Louisiana.

Another challenge for gaming industry participants is the growth of computer-based home gambling through mediums such as the Internet; such activity is reportedly already underway. The long-term future of Internet-based gambling will depend on various factors, including the extent to which it is controlled or deterred by regulation. The summer 1996 issue of *Hospitality and Leisure Executive Report* notes, "The U.S.

Note: Adapted from *Industry Survey* by permission of Standard & Poor's, a division of the McGraw-Hill Companies.
Source: Standard & Poor's, "Lodging & Gaming," *Industry Survey* (January 15, 1998): 1–15.

Justice Department contends that any type of casino or gaming wager by an American citizen on the Internet or through interstate telephone lines is illegal." However, full enforcement of this prohibition could be difficult, given the huge number of Internet sites that would have to be monitored. Also, much of the Internet-based gambling may be initiated from sites outside U.S. boundaries.

S&P estimates that U.S. gaming revenues (or "winnings") from casinos were up about 5 percent in 1997 from 1996, helped by a growing contribution from boats in Indiana and the full-year inclusion of a second casino on Native American land in Connecticut. Growth was more modest, however, in the established gaming markets: Atlantic City's revenue growth was limited to 3 percent; and in Nevada, casino winnings increased an estimated 4 percent.

In 1998, with less stimulus from new facilities coming on stream, we expect that U.S. casino winnings, including those from Native American-owned casinos, will rise 4 percent, to about $23 billion. Much of the new industry capacity expected to come on-stream in 1998, including two large new casino/hotels (in Las Vegas and Mississippi) developed by Mirage Resorts, is not expected to open until the fourth quarter.

Not Just the Odds

Looking ahead, we expect that the casino companies with the best opportunities for earnings growth will be those that can successfully develop distinctive new facilities at a reasonable cost. In general, the opening of new themed projects should boost consumer spending and provide additional incentives for both first-time and repeat visits by prospective gamblers.

Nonetheless, as some consumers continue to find casinos objectionable—or at least not their cup of tea—the gaming companies have a limited, albeit growing, pool of potential customers. Although casino odds favor the house, this hasn't always been enough for gaming facilities to be successful. Ultimately, each company's winnings from gaming tables, slot machines, and other sources must cover the sometimes sizable costs of developing facilities and attracting customers.

If They Build It, Will Someone Come?

The slowdown in gaming approvals in new states has contributed to a flurry of proposals for new casino projects in the established Las Vegas and Atlantic City markets. If all proposed projects were actually built—which we assume is unlikely—the amount spent on new casino/hotels or expansions in those markets between 1998 and 2002 would total more than $7 billion.

In both Atlantic City and some of the newer gaming markets—such as the riverboat states—efforts are being made to attract more overnight visitors. Such consumers are likely to be more well-heeled and are apt to spend more money than the day-trippers who typically frequent those markets. In particular, hotels are increasingly being developed for casino boat projects, and both infrastructure improvements and new casino/hotel facilities are planned for Atlantic City.

None of these markets, however, is even close to rivaling Las Vegas, where a convenient and busy airport, a growing number of high-profile attractions, and millions of convention visitors have helped to make the desert city one of the country's prime overnight destinations.

Seeing Las Vegas

Las Vegas remains the largest U.S. gaming market, helped by a highly developed infrastructure. The city's McCarran Airport is likely to handle more than 30 million passengers again in 1997, and the Las Vegas area now has more than 100,000 hotel rooms available for visitors.

In the first eight months of 1997, Las Vegas had 20.6 million visitors, up 3.8 percent from the year before, according to the Las Vegas Convention & Visitors Authority (LVCVA). Convention attendance was up 3 percent, year to year, to 2.4 million for the eight-month period, but with 10 percent more rooms available, the average hotel room occupancy level dipped to 88.2 percent from 91.8 percent.

In the Las Vegas Strip area, where most of the city's highest-profile facilities are located, we suspect that a broadened customer base for gambling has led to a decline in per capita spending among visitors at the casinos. In downtown Las Vegas, visitation levels may have been bolstered in recent years by an overhead light display called the Fremont Street Experience, which debuted in December 1995.

In Las Vegas, the trend toward large new, themed gaming facilities is continuing. Planned building projects include:

- **Bellagio.** Mirage Resorts is developing this 3,005-room casino/hotel project, which is expected to open in late 1998. The project, with an estimated price tag of about $1.4 billion, is intended to draw a somewhat more affluent clientele than the company's flagship Mirage casino/hotel, which debuted in 1989.

- **Paris.** Hilton Hotels is building a 3,000-room Parisian-themed casino/hotel slated to open in mid-1999. This project, part of Hilton's December 1996 acquisition of casino company Bally Entertainment, will cost an estimated $750 million.

- **Project Paradise.** In the spring of 1997, Circus Circus Enterprises began construction of a new casino/hotel resort initially known as Project Paradise. Located at the southern end of the Las Vegas Strip, this would be Circus Circus's fifth casino/hotel on the Strip, including the jointly owned Monte Carlo. In December 1996, Circus Circus imploded the Hacienda Hotel and Casino to make way for construction of its new casino/hotel, which is expected to have at least 3,000 hotel rooms. Also, in late 1996 and early 1997, Circus Circus added about 3,000 hotel rooms at two of its existing Las Vegas Strip facilities.

- **Venetian Casino Resort.** The Las Vegas Sands, Inc., is planning a casino/hotel project that would have about 3,000 suites and some 116,000 square feet of gaming space. Ground has already been broken for this facility, which is slated to open in April 1999.

- **Planet Hollywood.** A joint venture casino/hotel project, which would feature the movie-related theme of Planet Hollywood's restaurant business, is planned for the site of the current Aladdin casino/hotel. The approximately $250 million project would open in 1999.

Investing in New Jersey

In Atlantic City, where there are 12 casino/hotels, we expect gaming revenues in 1998 to approximate 1997's estimated $3.9 billion.

In Atlantic City's Marina section, three new casino/hotels have been proposed at the site of a former city landfill. Under the plan, ownership of the land, known as the H-Tract, would be transferred to Mirage Resorts, currently one of the largest casino operators in Las Vegas. Mirage has been absent as a casino operator in Atlantic City since the late 1980s, when it sold its Grand casino/hotel to Bally's.

However, development on the H-Tract appears to depend on improvements in nearby transportation facilities, including construction of a tunnel. Mirage would potentially pay a portion of the costs for the road system upgrade and provide funds to clean up the former landfill site. Development on the H-Tract could include a wholly owned Mirage project, a casino/hotel developed by Circus Circus Enterprises, and a third facility that would be a joint venture of Mirage and Boyd Corp. We don't expect any of these projects to open before 1999. The H-Tract facilities would join two casino/hotels already in the Marina section—Harrah's and Trump's Castle—for which expansions either recently opened or are planned.

In Atlantic City's Boardwalk area, various new facilities either recently opened or are planned. For example, in July 1997, Bally's Park Place opened a large new Western-themed annex, making Bally's the third Atlantic City facility with more than 100,000 square feet of casino space; the other two are Trump Plaza and Trump Taj Mahal. The Boardwalk area currently has ten casinos operating.

Rolling on the River

Riverboat gambling has mushroomed in popularity in the past decade as additional states—Illinois, Indiana, Iowa, Louisiana, Mississippi, and Missouri—have approved the practice. (Some of these "riverboats," however, are actually immobile barges, and some operate on lakes or on Mississippi's Gulf Coast.)

■ **Mississippi.** Mississippi is the highest-revenue "riverboat" casino state; 1997 gaming revenues totaled an estimated $1.9 billion, up approximately 6 percent from the year before. A further 6 percent rise is projected for 1998. As of late 1997, there were about 29 water-based casinos operating in the state, which imposes no limit on the number of licenses that can be granted. However, growing competition has contributed to the closing of approximately 10 gaming facilities since the first casino opened there in August 1992.

Future expansion is expected to include a 1,775-room casino/hotel developed by Mirage Resorts in Biloxi. The project, expected to cost about $550 million, is likely to open in 1998's second half.

Also, more hotel rooms have been added in the northern Mississippi gaming market, near Memphis, Tennessee; this should encourage longer-term visits. In 1996 and 1997, Grand Casinos, Inc., opened more than 700 rooms at its property there, and Circus Circus Enterprises added 1,200 hotel rooms in late 1997.

■ **Louisiana.** Only 15 riverboat gaming licenses are permitted in this state, with no more than six to a parish (equivalent to a county). In 1997, gaming revenues from the 14 boats in operation totaled an estimated $1.2 billion, up only about 3 percent from the year before. One of the 14 casino boats—Hilton's New Orleans facility—closed in October 1997.

In April 1996, Louisiana lawmakers approved legislation mandating statewide local elections on a parish-by-parish basis to determine whether gaming should be permitted in each parish. Later in the year, it appeared that all parishes with existing gaming riverboats had approved the presence of such casinos.

An issue which is still not fully resolved is the future of a large land-based casino in New Orleans. A temporary facility there closed in November 1995 after only five months of operation. Revenue levels had been disappointing, and the project entered bankruptcy proceedings. If bondholders and state, local, and court officials provide various approvals, however, the project may still be revived.

- **Illinois.** This state has nine gaming boat projects operating. Since April 1996, Chicago-area casinos have been facing new competition from gaming facilities in nearby northern Indiana. Partly as a result, 1997 casino boat winnings in Illinois fell an estimated 8 percent, year to year, to $1.03 billion, following a decline of approximately 4 percent in 1996. In 1998, we look for a further decline of about 5 percent.

  The profit picture for some Illinois gaming operators is also likely to be hurt by higher gaming taxes, with the maximum state tax rate on casino revenues rising to 35 percent, while the minimum drops to 15 percent. Previously, there was a single tax rate of 20 percent.

- **Missouri.** Casino operators in this state are restricted by a $500 loss limit per visitor. However, Missouri gaming revenues totaled an estimated $740 million in 1997, up approximately 30 percent from 1996's level, boosted by the opening of new facilities. As of October 1997, there were about 11 water-based gaming projects open in the state, including five which each had a pair of casinos. Recent expansion includes the March 1997 opening of a four-boat joint venture of Harrah's and Players International in the St. Louis suburb of Maryland Heights. This venture, which we're treating as two projects, includes 120,000 square feet of gaming space and a 291-room hotel.

  Unless the loss limit is removed, however, it wouldn't be surprising if one or more of the Missouri casino boats soon closed.

- **Indiana.** This state allows 11 gaming licenses, and as of November 1997, eight casino boats were open. In 1997, Indiana casino winnings totaled an estimated $700 million, up sharply from approximately $370 million in 1996, when there were fewer boats in operation. The state's first casino boat opened in December 1995, in Evansville. Other locations now include Gary (with two), Hammond, Rising Sun, East Chicago, and Lawrenceburg.

Native American Casinos See New Growth

In some states, there continues to be development of new casinos owned by various Native American tribes. Though not publicly owned, some are managed by publicly owned companies. In October 1996, Connecticut's second Native American casino opened on Mohegan land in the central part of the state. In 1997, we expect that the Mohegan and Mashantucket Pequot casinos in Connecticut had combined casino revenues of more than $1 billion, including about $935 million from slot machines.

Other Types of Gambling

Gambling in the United States extends far beyond casinos and video gaming terminals. For example, 37 states and the District of Columbia have lotteries, more than two-thirds have horse racing, several allow jai alai, and nearly all permit bingo, according to *International Gaming & Wagering Business (IG & WB)*. The magazine estimates that in 1996, casino activity (including facilities on Native American land) accounted for 50 percent of the $47.7 billion lost by gamblers in a variety of legal U.S. activities.

Among all noncasino forms of gambling, state lotteries were the single biggest moneymaker. Although delivering billions of dollars in prizes, lotteries accounted for 34 percent of all gambling dollars lost, leaving players $16.2 billion in the red, according to *IG & WB*. After paying out prizes, the largest state lotteries—such as those in New York and Florida—still each have annual net revenues of more than $1 billion. Each of the ten most populous states in the United States now has a lottery. Texas, which adopted a lottery in 1992, was the last of these to start operations.

Among other forms of legal gambling, pari-mutuel wagering (horses, greyhounds, and jai alai) lightened gamblers' wallets by a total of $3.7 billion in 1996. Charitable games, including bingo, brought in about $2.4 billion.

Gaming trends

Gaming companies are witnessing the following trends:

- **Growing revenue contributions from slot machines.** In general, it's easier for new gamblers to feed slot machines than to learn the nuances of various table games. Because the gaming industry is seeking to broaden its customer base, casino companies are generally allotting more space to slot machines. They're also encouraging slot usage through the placement of video machines and the promotion of large jackpots. In 1997, slot machines generated about 69 percent of winnings for Atlantic City casinos, compared with just 50 percent in the mid-1980s.

- **In newer gaming jurisdictions, an increased emphasis on attracting overnight customers.** Initially, most of the new casinos in the riverboat states opened without any attached hotel facilities. As a result, many of their visitors tended to be day-trippers and people who lived nearby. Now, state and local officials are looking for greater investment in lodging facilities; they hope this will encourage longer-term visits from out-of-towners and help the local economies. The casino companies also see advantages, because overnight visitors are likely to spend more on a per capita basis than are day-trippers.

Circus Circus Enterprises, Inc.—1998

John Ross III
Mike Keeffe
Bill Middlebrook

www.circuscircus.org
stock symbol CIR

> We possess the resources to accomplish the big projects: the know-how, the financial power, and the places to invest. The renovation of our existing projects will soon be behind us, which last year represented the broadest scope of construction ever taken on by a gaming company. Now we are well-positioned to originate new projects. Getting big projects right is the route to future wealth in gaming; big successful projects tend to provide long staying power in our business. When the counting is over, we think our customers and investors will hold the winning hand.
>
> —Circus Circus Entertainment, Inc., *Annual Report* (1997): 2.

Big projects and a winning hand. Circus Circus (707-734-0410) does seem to have both. And big projects they are, with huge pink-and-white-striped concrete circus tents, a 600-foot-long riverboat replica, a giant castle, and a great pyramid. Its latest project, Project Paradise, will include a 3,744-room hotel/casino and a 10-acre aquatic environment with beaches, a snorkeling reef, and a swim-up shark exhibit. But Circus Circus's net income dropped 28 percent in fiscal 1996 and another 12 percent in fiscal 1997.

Circus Circus Enterprises, Inc., (hereafter Circus) describes itself as in the business of entertainment, and has been one of the innovators in the theme resort concept popular in casino gaming. Their areas of operation are the glitzy vacation and convention meccas of Nevada's Las Vegas, Reno, and Laughlin, as well as other locations in the United States and abroad. Historically, Circus's marketing of its products was called "right out of the bargain basement" and catered to "low rollers." Circus has continually broadened its market and now aims more at the middle-income gambler, family-oriented vacationer, and upscale traveler and player.

Circus was purchased in 1974 for $50,000 as a small and unprofitable casino operation by partners William G. Bennett, an aggressive cost-cutter who ran furniture stores before entering the gaming industry in 1965, and William N. Pennington (see Exhibit 1 for board of directors and top managers). The partners were able to rejuvenate Circus

This case was prepared by Professors John K. Ross III, Michael J. Keeffe, and Bill J. Middlebrook of Southwest Texas State University. The case was prepared for classroom purposes only, and is not designed to show effective or ineffective handling of administrative situations. Copyright © 1999 by Prentice Hall, Inc. ISBN 0-13-11128-7.

EXHIBIT 1: Circus Circus Enterprises, Inc., Directors and Officers

Directors

Name	Age	Title
Clyde T. Turner	60	Chair of the Board and CEO, Circus Circus Enterprises
Michael S. Ensign	60	Vice-Chair of the Board and COO, Circus Circus Enterprises
Glenn Schaeffer	44	President and CFO, Circus Circus Enterprises
William A. Richardson	51	Executive Vice-President, Circus Circus Enterprises
Richard P. Banis	53	Former President and COO, Circus Circus Enterprises
Arthur H. Bilger	45	Former President and COO, New World Communications Group International
Richard A. Etter	59	Former Chair and CEO, Bank of America—Nevada
Michael D. McKee	52	Executive Vice-President, The Irving Company

Officers

Clyde T. Turner	Chair of the Board and Chief Executive Officer
Michael S. Ensign	Vice-Chair of the Board and Chief Operating Officer
Glenn Schaeffer	President, Chief Financial Officer, and Treasurer
William A. Richardson	Executive Vice-President
Tony Alamo	Senior Vice-President, Operations
Gregg Solomon	Senior Vice-President, Operations
Kurt D. Sullivan	Senior Vice-President, Operations
Steve Greathouse	Senior Vice-President, Operations
Yvett Landau	Vice-President, General Counsel, and Secretary
Les Martin	Vice-President and Chief Accounting Officer

Source: Circus Circus Enterprises, Inc., *Annual Report* (1997); Circus Circus Enterprises, Inc., Proxy Statement, June 24, 1997; Circus Circus Enterprises, Inc., news release (August 13, 1997).

with fresh marketing, went public with a stock offering in October 1983, and experienced rapid growth and high profitability over time. Between 1993 and 1997, the average return on invested capital was 16.5 percent and Circus generated over $1 billion in free cash flow. Today, Circus is one of the major players in the Las Vegas, Reno, and Laughlin markets in terms of square footage of casino space and number of hotel rooms, despite the incredible growth in these markets. Circus's casino gaming

EXHIBIT 2: Circus Circus Enterprises, Inc., Sources of Revenues as a Percentage of Net Revenues

Fiscal Year Ending January 31,	1998	1997	1996	1995
Casinos	46.7	49.2	51.2	52.3
Food & Beverage	15.9	15.8	15.5	16.2
Hotel	24.4	22.0	21.4	19.9
Other	10.5	11.0	12.2	14.2
Unconsolidated	7.3	6.5	3.5	.5
Less: Complimentary Allowances	4.8	4.5	3.8	3.1

Source: Circus Circus Enterprises, Inc., 10-K (January 31, 1997).

operations provide slightly less than one-half of total revenues (see Exhibit 2). During fiscal 1997, Circus's casino revenues declined nearly 4 percent to $632 million while the room revenues increased 12.4 percent.

CIRCUS CIRCUS OPERATIONS

Circus defines entertainment as pure play and fun, and it goes out of the way to see that customers have plenty of opportunity for both. Each Circus location has a distinctive personality. Circus Circus—Las Vegas is the world of the Big Top, where live circus acts perform free every 30 minutes. Kids may cluster around video games while the adults migrate to nickel slot machines and dollar game tables. Located at the north end of the Las Vegas Strip, Circus Circus—Las Vegas sits on 69 acres of land with 3,744 hotel rooms; shopping areas; two specialty restaurants; a buffet with seating for 1,200; fast-food shops; cocktail lounges; video arcades; 109,000 square feet of casino space; and the Grand Slam Canyon, a 5-acre glass-enclosed theme park with a four-loop roller coaster. Approximately 380 guests may stay at nearby Circusland RV Park.

The Luxor, an Egyptian-themed hotel and casino complex, opened on October 15, 1993, as 10,000 people entered to play at the 2,245 slot and video poker games and 106 game tables in the 120,000-square-foot casino in the hotel atrium (reported to be the world's largest). By the end of the opening weekend, 40,000 people per day were visiting the 30-story bronze pyramid that encases the hotel and entertainment facilities.

The Luxor features a 30-story pyramid and two new 22-story hotel towers. It includes 492 suites and is connected to Excalibur, another Circus property, by a climate-controlled skyway with moving walkways. Situated at the south end of the Las Vegas Strip on a 64-acre site adjacent to Excalibur, the Luxor features a food and entertainment area on three levels beneath the hotel atrium. The pyramid's hotel rooms can be reached from the four corners of the building by state-of-the-art "inclinators" which travel at a 39-degree angle. Parking is available for 3,200 vehicles, including a covered garage which contains approximately 1,800 spaces.

During 1997, the Luxor underwent major renovation costing $323.3 million. The resulting complex contains 4,425 hotel rooms; extensively renovated casino space; an additional 20,000 square feet of convention area; an 800-seat buffet; a series of IMAX® attractions; five theme restaurants; seven cocktail lounges; and a variety of specialty shops. Circus expects to draw significant walk-in traffic to the newly refurbished Luxor and is one of the principal components of what Circus calls its "Masterplan Mile."

Located next to the Luxor, Excalibur is one of the first sights travelers see as they exit Interstate Highway 15 (management was confident that the sight of a giant, colorful medieval castle would make a lasting impression on mainstream tourists and vacationing families arriving in Las Vegas). Guests cross a drawbridge, with moat, onto a cobblestone walkway that multicolored spires, turrets, and battlements loom above. The castle walls are four 28-story hotel towers containing a total of 4,000 rooms. Inside is a medieval world complete with a Fantasy Faire inhabited by strolling jugglers, fire eaters, and acrobats, as well as a Royal Village complete with peasants, serfs, ladies-in-waiting, and medieval theme shops. The 110,000-square-foot casino has 2,471 slot machines, 80 game tables, a sports book, and a poker and keno area. There are 12 restaurants jointly capable of feeding more than 20,000 people daily, a 1,000-seat amphitheater, and 4,000 parking spaces. Excalibur, which opened in June 1990, was built for $294 million and primarily financed with internally generated funds.

Situated between the two anchors on the Las Vegas Strip are two smaller casinos owned and operated by Circus. The Silver City Casino and Slots-A-Fun primarily depend on the foot traffic along the Strip for their gambling patrons. Combined, they offer almost 1,000 slot machines and 45 gaming tables on 34,900 square feet of casino floor.

Circus owns and operates 13 properties in Nevada, one in Mississippi, and one in Illinois (see Exhibit 3).

All of Circus's operations do well in the city of Las Vegas, although 1997 operational earnings for the Luxor and Circus Circus—Las Vegas were off 38 percent from the previous year. Management credits the disruption in services due to renovations for this decline. However, Circus's combined hotel room occupancy rates remain above 90 percent due, in part, to low room rates ($45 to $69 at Circus Circus—Las Vegas) and popular buffets. Each of the major properties contain large, inexpensive buffets that management believes make staying with Circus more attractive.

The company's other big top facility is Circus Circus—Reno. With the addition of Skyway Tower in 1985, this big top now offers a total of 1,605 hotel rooms; 60,000 square feet of casino space; a buffet that can seat 700 people; shops; video arcades; cocktail lounges; midway games; and circus acts. Circus Circus—Reno had several marginal years, but has become one of the leaders in the Reno market. For fiscal year 1997, competition from the Silver Legacy (50 percent owned by Circus) as well as flooding, storms, and renovation reduced operating income some $13.6 million from the previous year.

The Colorado Belle and The Edgewater Hotel are located 90 miles south of Las Vegas in Laughlin, Nevada, on the banks of the Colorado River. The Colorado Belle, opened in 1987, features a huge paddle-wheel riverboat replica, a buffet, cocktail lounges, and shops. The Edgewater, acquired in 1983, has a Southwestern motif; a 44,000-square-foot casino; a bowling center; a buffet; and cocktail lounges. Combined, these two properties contain almost 2,700 rooms and 108,000 square feet of casino space. These two operations contributed 12 percent of the company's revenues in the year ended January 31, 1997, down from 21 percent in 1994. Additionally, these properties saw a decrease of 17 percent in operating revenue from the previous year. The extensive proliferation of casinos throughout the region, primarily on Native American land, and the development of megaresorts in Las Vegas have seriously eroded outlying markets such as Laughlin.

EXHIBIT 3:   Circus Circus Entertainment, Inc., Properties, 1998

Location/Property	Hotel Rooms	Casino Square Footage	Slots[a]	Gaming Tables	Parking Spaces
Las Vegas, Nevada					
Circus Circus	3,744	109,000	2,429	75	4,700
Luxor	4,425	120,000	2,119	106	3,200
Excalibur	4,000	110,000	2,471	80	4,000
Silver City	0	18,200	448	19	350
Slots-A-Fun	0	16,700	540	26	0
Reno, Nevada					
Circus Circus	1,605	60,000	1,791	65	3,000
Laughlin, Nevada					
Colorado Belle	1,226	64,000	1,254	40	1,700
Edgewater	1,450	44,000	1,286	42	2,300
Jean, Nevada					
Gold Strike	813	37,000	1,080	22	2,100
Nevada Landing	303	36,000	1,050	21	1,400
Henderson, Nevada					
Railroad Pass	120	21,000	406	9	600
Tunica, Mississippi					
Gold Strike	1,066	48,000	1,231	46	1,400
Joint Ventures					
Las Vegas, Nevada					
Monte Carlo	3,002	90,000	2,161	95	4,000
Elgin, Illinois					
Grand Victoria	0	36,000	977	56	2,000
Reno, Nevada					
Silver Legacy	1,711	85,000	2,277	83	1,800

[a]Includes slot machines and other coin-operated devices.
Source: www.freeedgar.com

Three properties purchased in 1995 and located in Jean and Henderson, Nevada, are recent investments by Circus. The Gold Strike and Nevada Landing service the I-15 market between Las Vegas and southern California. These properties have 73,000 square feet of casino space; 2,130 slot machines; and 43 gaming tables combined. Each has limited hotel space (1,116 rooms total) and depends heavily on I-15 traffic. The Railroad Pass is considered a local casino and is dependent on Henderson residents as its market. This smaller casino contains only 406 slot machines and 9 gaming tables.

Circus's dockside casino located in Tunica, Mississippi, opened in 1994 on 24 acres of land located along the Mississippi River approximately 20 miles south of Memphis. In 1997, operating income declined by more than 50 percent due to the increase in competition and lack of hotel rooms. Circus decided to renovate the property and add a 1,066-room tower hotel. The casino was rethemed to be more upscale and renamed the Gold Strike Casino Resort. Total cost for all remodeling is estimated at $125 million.

Joint Ventures

Circus is currently engaged in three joint ventures through the wholly owned subsidiary Circus Participant. In Las Vegas, Circus joined with Mirage Resorts to build and operate the Monte Carlo, a hotel/casino with 3,002 rooms designed along the lines of the grand casinos of the Mediterranean. It is located on 46 acres (with 600 feet on the Las Vegas Strip) between the New York–New York Casino and the soon-to-be-completed Bellagio, with all three casinos to be connected by monorail. The Monte Carlo features a 90,000-square-foot casino containing 2,161 slot machines and 95 gaming tables, as well as a 550-seat bingo parlor; high-tech arcade rides; restaurants; buffets; a microbrewery; approximately 15,000 square feet of meeting and convention space; and a 1,200-seat theater. Opened on June 21, 1996, the Monte Carlo generated $14.6 million as Circus's share in operating income for the first 7 months of operation.

In Elgin, Illinois, Circus is in a 50 percent partnership with Hyatt Development Corporation in The Grand Victoria. Styled to resemble a Victorian riverboat, this floating casino and land-based entertainment complex includes some 36,000 square feet of casino space containing 977 slot machines and 56 gaming tables. The adjacent land-based complex contains two movie theaters; a 240-seat buffet; restaurants; and parking for approximately 2,000 vehicles. Built for $112 million, The Grand Victoria returned to Circus $44 million in operating income in 1996.

The third joint venture is a 50 percent partnership with Eldorado Limited in the Silver Legacy. Opened in 1995, this casino is located between Circus Circus—Reno and the Eldorado Hotel and Casino on two city blocks in downtown Reno, Nevada. The Silver Legacy has 1,711 hotel rooms; 85,000 square feet of casino space; 2,277 slot machines; and 83 gaming tables. Management seems to believe that the Silver Legacy holds promise; however, the Reno market is suffering and the opening of the Silver Legacy cannibalized the Circus Circus—Reno market.

Circus engaged in a fourth joint venture to penetrate the Canadian market, but on January 23, 1997, announced it had been bought out by Hilton Hotels Corporation, one of three partners in the venture.

Circus has achieved success through an aggressive growth strategy and a corporate structure designed to enhance that growth. A strong cash position, innovative ideas, and attention to cost control has allowed Circus to satisfy the bottom line during a period when competitors were typically taking on large debt obligations to finance new projects (see Exhibits 4, 5, 6, and 7). Yet, the market is changing. Gambling of all kinds has spread across the country; no longer does the average individual need to go the Las Vegas or New Jersey. Instead, gambling can be found as close as the local quick market (lottery), bingo hall, many Native American reservations, the Mississippi River, and other sites. There are now almost 300 casinos in Las Vegas alone, 60 in Colorado, and 160 in California. In order to maintain a competitive edge, Circus continues to invest heavily in renovation of existing properties (a strategy common to the entertainment/amusement industry) and to develop new projects.

EXHIBIT 4: Circus Circus Entertainment, Inc., Selected Financial Information

	FY 98	FY 97	FY 96	FY 95	FY 94	FY 93	FY 92	FY 91
Earnings per share	.95	.99	1.33	1.59	1.34	2.05	1.84	1.39
Current ratio	.86	1.17	1.30	1.35	.95	.90	1.14	.88
Total liabilities / Total assets	.66	.62	.44	.54	.57	.48	.58	.77
Operating profit margin	.17	.17	.19	.22	.21	.24	.24	.22

Source: Circus Circus Enterprises, Inc., *Annual Reports* and 10Ks, 1991–1997; www.freeedgar.com.

EXHIBIT 5: Circus Circus Entertainment, Inc., 12-Year Summary

For fiscal year ending January 31,	Revenues (in 000)	Net Income (in 000)
1998	$1,354,487	$ 89,908
1997	1,334,250	100,733
1996	1,299,596	128,898
1995	1,170,182	136,286
1994	954,923	116,189
1993	843,025	117,322
1992	806,023	103,348
1991	692,052	76,292
1990	522,376	76,064
1989	511,960	81,714
1988	458,856	55,900
1987	373,967	28,198
1986	306,993	37,375

Source: Circus Circus Enterprises, Inc., *Annual Reports* and 10Ks, 1991–1997; www.freeedgar.com.

EXHIBIT 6: Circus Circus Enterprises, Inc., Annual Income (in thousands)

Fiscal year ending	1/31/98	1/31/97	1/31/96	1/31/95
Revenues				
Casino	$ 632,122	$ 655,902	$ 664,772	$ 612,115
Rooms	330,644	294,241	278,807	232,346
Food and beverage	215,584	210,384	201,385	189,664
Other	142,407	146,554	158,534	166,295
Earnings of unconsolidated affiliates	98,977	86,646	45,485	5,459
	1,419,734	1,393,727	1,348,983	1,205,879
Less complimentary allowances	(65,247)	(59,477)	(49,387)	(35,697)
Net revenue	1,354,487	1,334,250	1,299,596	1,170,182
Costs and Expenses				
Casino	316,902	302,096	275,680	246,416
Rooms	122,934	116,508	110,362	94,257

continued

EXHIBIT 6: *continued*

Fiscal year ending	1/31/98	1/31/97	1/31/96	1/31/95
Food and beverage	199,955	200,722	188,712	177,136
Other operating expenses	90,187	90,601	92,631	107,297
General and administrative	232,536	227,348	215,083	183,175
Depreciation and amortization	117,474	95,414	93,938	81,109
Preopening expense	3,447	0	0	3,012
Abandonment loss	0	48,309	45,148	0
	1,083,435	1,080,998	1,021,554	892,402
Operating profit before corporate expense	271,052	223,252	278,042	277,780
Corporate expense	34,552	31,083	26,669	21,773
Income from operations	236,500	222,169	251,373	256,007
Other Income (expense)				
Interest, dividends and other income (Loss)	9,779	5,077	4,022	225
Interest income and guarantee fees from unconsolidated affiliate	6,041	6,865	7,517	992
Interest expense	(88,847)	(54,681)	(51,537)	(42,734)
Interest expense from unconsolidated affiliate	(15,551)	(15,567)	(5,616)	0
	(88,578)	(58,306)	(45,614)	(41,517)
Income before provision for income tax	147,922	163,863	205,759	214,490
Provision for income tax	58,014	63,130	76,861	78,204
Net income	89,908	100,733	128,898	136,286
Earnings per share				
Income before extraordinary loss	.95	.99	1.33	1.59
Net income per share	.94	.99	1.33	1.59

Source: Circus Circus Enterprises, Inc., *Annual Reports* and 10Ks, 1993–1997; www.freeedgar.com.

EXHIBIT 7: **Circus Circus Enterprises, Inc., Consolidated Balance Sheets (in thousands)**

Fiscal year ending	1/31/98	1/31/97	1/31/96	1/31/95
Assets				
Cash and cash equivalents	$ 58,631	$ 69,516	$ 62,704	$ 53,764
Accounts Receivable	21,714	34,434	16,527	8,931
Income tax receivable	11,926	7,735	—	—
Inventories	22,440	19,371	20,459	22,660
Prepaid expenses	20,281	19,951	19,418	20,103
Deferred income tax	7,871	8,577	7,272	5,463
Total Current	*142,863*	*151,849*	*124,380*	*110,921*
Property, equipment, and leasehold interests, at cost, net	2,466,848	1,920,032	1,474,684	1,239,062
Other assets				
Excess of purchase price over fair market value of net assets aquired, net	375,375	385,583	394,518	9,836
Notes receivable	1,075	36,443	27,508	68,083
Investments in unconsolidated affiliates	255,392	214,123	173,270	74,840

continued

EXHIBIT 7: *continued*

	1/31/98	*1/31/97*	*1/31/96*	*1/31/95*
Deferred charges and other assets	21,995	21,081	17,533	9,806
Total other assets	*653,837*	*657,230*	*612,829*	*162,565*
Total Assets	*3,263,548*	*2,729,111*	*2,213,503*	*1,512,548*

Liabilities and Stockholders' Equity

Current liabilities				
Current portion of long-term debt	3,071	379	863	106
Accounts and contracts payable				
Trade	22,103	22,658	16,824	12,102
Construction	40,670	21,144	0	1,101
Accrued Liabilities				
Salaries, wages and vacations	36,107	31,847	30,866	24,946
Progressive jackpots	7,511	6,799	8,151	7,447
Advance room deposits	6,217	7,383	7,517	8,701
Interest payable	17,828	9,004	3,169	2,331
Other	33,451	30,554	28,142	25,274
Total current liabilities	166,958	129,768	95,532	82,008
Long-term debt	1,788,818	1,405,897	715,214	632,652
Other liabilities				
Deferred income tax	175,934	152,635	148,096	110,776
Other long-term liabilities	8,089	6,439	9,319	988
Total other liabilities	184,023	159,074	157,415	111,764
Total liabilities	2,139,799	1,694,739	968,161	826,424
Redeemable preferred stock	0	17,631	18,530	—
Temporary equity	0	44,950	—	—
Commitments and contingent liabilities				
Stockholders' equity				
Common stock $.01–2/3 par value				
Authorized—450,000,000 shares				
Issued—113,609,008 and				
112,808,337 shares	1,893	1,880	1,880	1,607
Additional paid-in capital	558,658	498,893	527,205	124,960
Retained earnings	1,074,271	984,363	883,630	754,732
Treasury stock (18,496,125 and				
18,749,209 shares), at cost	(511,073)	(513,345)	(185,903)	(195,175)
Total stockholders' equity	1,123,749	971,791	1,226,812	686,124
Total liabilities and stockholders' equity	3,263,548	2,729,111	2,213,503	1,512,548

Note: — indicates information not available.
Source: Circus Circus Enterprises, Inc., *Annual Reports* and 10Ks, 1993–1997; www.freeedgar.com.

New Ventures

Circus currently has three new projects planned for opening within the near future. The largest project, named Project Paradise, is scheduled for completion in late 1998 or early 1999, and is estimated to cost $800 million (excluding land). Circus owns a contiguous mile of the southern end of the Las Vegas Strip, which it calls its "Masterplan Mile," where the Excalibur and Luxor resorts are situated. Located next to the Luxor, Project Paradise will aim for the upscale traveler and player and will be styled as a South Seas adventure. The resort will contain a 42-story hotel/casino with over 3,744 rooms and a

10-acre aquatic environment. The aquatic environment will contain a surfing beach, swim-up shark tank, and snorkeling reef. A separate Four Seasons Resort with some 400 rooms will complement Project Paradise. Circus anticipates that the remainder of its "Masterplan Mile" eventually will be composed of at least one additional casino/ resort and a number of stand-alone hotels and amusement centers.

Circus also plans two other casino projects, provided all the necessary licenses and agreements can be obtained. Along the Mississippi Gulf, Circus plans to construct a casino/resort containing 1,500 rooms at an estimated cost of $225 million. Circus has agreed with Mirage to develop a 150-acre site in the Marina district in Atlantic City at an unspecified time, anticipated to cost between $600 and $800 million.

Most of Circus's projects are tailored to attract mainstream tourists and family vacationers. However, several joint ventures and some components of the "Masterplan Mile" also will attract the upscale customer.

THE GAMING INDUSTRY

By 1997, the gaming industry had captured a large amount of the vacation/leisure time dollars spent in the United States. Gamblers lost over $44.3 billion on legal wagering in 1995 (up from $29.9 billion in 1992) at racetracks, bingo parlors, lotteries, and casinos. These figures do not include dollars spent on lodging, food, transportation, and other related expenditures associated with visits to gaming facilities. Casino gambling accounts for 76 percent of all legal gambling expenditures, far ahead of second-place Native American reservation gambling at 8.9 percent and lotteries at 7.1 percent. The popularity of casino gambling may be credited to a more frequent and somewhat higher payout as compared to lotteries and racetracks; however, recycled winnings restore a high return to casino operators.

Geographic expansion has slowed considerably as no additional states have approved casino-type gambling since 1993. Growth has occurred in developed locations, with Las Vegas and Atlantic City leading the way.

Las Vegas remains the largest U.S. gaming market and one of the largest convention markets with more than 100,000 hotel rooms hosting more than 29.6 million visitors in 1996, up 2.2 percent over 1995. Casino operators are building to take advantage of this continued growth. Recent projects include the Monte Carlo ($350 million), New York–New York ($350 million), Bellagio ($1.4 billion), Hilton Hotels ($750 million), and Project Paradise ($800 million). Additionally, Harrah's is adding a 986-room tower with 46 suites and remodeling 500 current rooms, and Caesar's Palace plans to add 2,000 rooms. According to the Las Vegas Convention and Visitor Authority, Las Vegas is a destination market, with most visitors planning their trip more than a week in advance (81 percent), arriving by car (47 percent) or airplane (42 percent), and staying in a hotel (72 percent). Gamblers typically are return visitors (77 percent), averaging 2.2 trips per year and like playing the slots (65 percent).

For Atlantic City, besides the geographical separation, the primary differences in the two markets reflect the different types of consumers frequenting these markets. While Las Vegas attracts overnight resort-seeking vacationers, Atlantic City's clientele are predominantly day-trippers traveling by automobile or bus. Atlantic City gaming revenues are expected to continue to grow, perhaps to $4 billion in 1997 split among the 12 currently operating casino/hotels. Growth in the Atlantic City area will be concentrated in the Marina section; Mirage Resorts has an agreement with the city to develop

150 acres of the marina as a destination resort. This development will include a resort wholly owned by Mirage, a casino/hotel developed by Circus, and a joint venture complex developed by Mirage and Boyd Corp. Currently in Atlantic City, Donald Trump's gaming empire of Trump's Castle, Trump Plaza, and Trump Taj Mahal holds a total market share of 30 percent. The next closest in market share is Caesar's (10.3 percent), Tropicana and Bally's (9.2 percent each), and Showboat (9.0 percent).

There remains a number of smaller markets located around the United States, primarily in Mississippi, Louisiana, Illinois, Missouri, and Indiana. Each state has imposed various restrictions on the development of casino operations. In some cases, for example Illinois, where there are only ten gaming licenses available, this has severely restricted the growth opportunities and hurt revenues. In Mississippi and Louisiana, revenues are up 8 percent and 15 percent respectively in riverboat operations. Native American casinos continue to be developed on federally controlled Native American land. These casinos are not publicly held but do tend to be managed by publicly held corporations. These other locations present a mix of opportunities and generally constitute only a small portion of overall gaming revenues.

MAJOR INDUSTRY PLAYERS

Over the past several years there have been numerous changes as mergers and acquisitions reshaped the gaming industry. As of year-end 1997, the industry was a combination of corporations engaged solely in gaming and multinational conglomerates. The largest competitors, in terms of revenue, combined multiple industries to generate both large revenues and substantial profits (see Exhibit 8). However, those engaged primarily in gaming also could be extremely profitable.

ITT Corporation

As one of the world's largest hotel and gaming corporations, ITT owns the Sheraton, The Luxury Collection, the Four Points Hotels, and Caesar's, as well as communications and educational services. In 1996, ITT hosted approximately 50 million customer nights in locations worldwide. Gaming operations are located in Las Vegas; Atlantic

EXHIBIT 8: Major U.S. Gaming, Lottery & Pari-mutuel Companies, 1996 Revenues and Net Income (in millions)

	1996 Revenues	*1996 Net Income*
ITT	$6,597.0	$249.0
Hilton Hotels	3,940.0	156.0
Harrah's Entertainment	1,586.0	98.9
Mirage Resorts	1,358.3	206.0
Circus Circus	1,247.0	100.7
Trump Hotel and Casino, Inc.	976.3	(4.9)
MGM Grand	804.8	74.5
Aztar	777.5	20.6
International Game Technology	733.5	118.0

Source: Individual companies annual reports and 10Ks, 1996.

City; Halifax and Sydney, Nova Scotia; Lake Tahoe, Nevada; Tunica, Mississippi; Lima, Peru; Cairo, Egypt; Canada; and Australia. In 1996, ITT had net income of $249 million on revenues of $6.6 billion. In June 1996, ITT announced plans to join with Planet Hollywood to develop casino/hotels with the Planet Hollywood theme in both Las Vegas and Atlantic City. However, these plans may be deferred as ITT fends off an acquisition bid from Hilton Hotels.

Hilton Hotels

Hilton owns or leases and operates 29 hotels, and manages 42 hotels partially or wholly owned by others. Twelve of the hotels are also casinos, six of which are located in Nevada; two in Atlantic City; with the other four in Australia, Turkey, and Uruguay. In 1996, Hilton had net income of $156 million on $3.9 billion in revenues. Although continuing with expansion at current properties, Hilton seems to want to expand through acquisition. In 1997, Hilton tried to acquire ITT Corporation in a combination of cash and stock transactions estimated at $6.5 billion. After ITT rejected the offer, Hilton management chose to pursue the takeover on a hostile basis. The cost of such a takeover attempt could be extremely expensive for both corporations.

Harrah's Entertainment, Inc.

Harrah's is primarily engaged in the gaming industry with Nevada casino/hotels in Reno, Lake Tahoe, Las Vegas, and Laughlin; and a casino/hotel in Atlantic City, New Jersey. It has riverboats or dockside casinos in Joliet, Illinois; Vicksburg and Tunica, Mississippi; Shreveport, Louisiana; and St. Louis and North Kansas City, Missouri. It manages limited-stakes casinos in Colorado, three casinos on Native American land, and one casino in Auckland, New Zealand. In 1996, Harrah's operated a total of over 700,000 square feet of casino space with more than 19,000 slot machines and over 900 game tables. With this and almost 6,500 hotel rooms, the corporation had a net income of $99 million on nearly $1.6 billion in revenues.

Mirage Resorts, Inc.

Mirage's gaming operations are currently located in Nevada. It owns and operates the Golden Nugget—Downtown, Las Vegas; the Mirage on the Strip in Las Vegas; Treasure Island—Reno; and the Golden Nugget—Laughlin. Additionally, Mirage is a 50 percent owner of the Monte Carlo with Circus Circus. Net income for Mirage Resorts in 1996 was $206 million on revenues of almost $1.4 billion. Current expansion plans include the development of the Bellagio in Las Vegas ($1.4 billion estimated cost) and the Beau Rivage in Biloxi, Mississippi ($550 million estimated cost). These two properties would add a total of 265,900 square feet of casino space, 252 gaming tables, and 4,746 slot machines to the current Mirage inventory. An additional project is the development of the Marina area in Atlantic City, New Jersey, in partnership with Boyd Gaming.

MGM Grand Hotel and Casino

This hotel/casino is located on approximately 113 acres at the northeast corner of Las Vegas Boulevard. The casino is one of the largest in the world with 3,708 slot machines and 163 game tables in approximately 171,500 square feet. Current plans call for extensive renovation costing $250 million. Through a wholly owned subsidiary, MGM owns and operates the MGM Grand Diamond Beach Hotel and a hotel/casino resort in Darwin, Australia. Additionally, MGM and Primadonna Resorts, Inc., each own 50 percent of New York–New York Hotel and Casino, a $460 million architecturally distinctive, themed destination resort which opened on January 3, 1997, across the street from the MGM Grand. MGM also intends to construct and operate a destination hotel/casino, entertainment, and retail facility in Atlantic City on approximately 35 acres of land on the Atlantic City Boardwalk. In 1996, MGM reported a net income of $74.5 million on $804.8 million revenues.

THE LEGAL ENVIRONMENT

Within the gaming industry, all operators must consider compliance with extensive gaming regulations as a primary concern. Each state or country has its own specific regulations and regulatory boards requiring extensive reporting and licensing requirements. For example, in Las Vegas, gambling operations are subject to regulatory control by the Nevada State Gaming Control Board, the Clark County Nevada Gaming and Liquor Licensing Board, and city government regulations. The laws, regulations, and supervisory procedures of virtually all gaming authorities are based upon public policy primarily concerned with (a) preventing unsavory or unsuitable persons from having a direct or indirect involvement with gaming at any time or in any capacity and (b) establishing and maintaining responsible accounting practices and procedures. Additional regulations typically cover the maintenance of effective controls over the financial practices of licensees (including the establishment of minimum procedures for internal fiscal affairs and the safeguarding of assets and revenues, provisions for reliable record keeping and the filing of periodic reports, and the prevention of cheating and fraudulent practices) and securing state and local revenues through taxation and licensing fees. All gaming companies must submit detailed operating and financial reports to authorities. Nearly all financial transactions—including loans, leases, and the sale of securities—must be reported. Some financial activities are subject to approval by regulatory agencies. As Circus moves into other locations outside of Nevada, it will need to adhere to local regulations.

FUTURE CONSIDERATIONS

Circus Circus states that it is "in the business of entertainment, with . . . core strength in casino gaming," and that it intends to focus its efforts on Las Vegas, Atlantic City, and the state of Mississippi. Circus further states that the "future product in gaming, to be sure, is the entertainment resort."

Circus was one of the innovators of the gaming resort concept and continues to be a leader in the field. However, the entertainment resort industry operates differently than the traditional casino gaming industry. In the past, consumers visited a casino to experience the thrill of gambling. Now, they not only gamble, but they also expect to be dazzled by enormous entertainment complexes that cost billions of dollars to build. Competition continues to increase although growth rates have slowed.

For years, analysts have questioned the ability of the gaming industry to continue high growth in established markets as the industry matures. Through the 1970s and 1980s, the gaming industry experienced rapid growth. Through the 1990s, the industry began to experience a shakeout of marginal competitors and a consolidation phase. Circus Circus has been successful through this turmoil, but now faces the task of maintaining high growth in a more mature industry.

REFERENCES

"Circus Circus Announces Promotion." *PR Newswire* (June 10, 1997).

"Lodging and Gaming." Standard and Poor's, *Industry Survey* (June 19, 1997).

"Casinos Move into New Areas." Standard and Poor's, *Industry Survey* (March 11, 1993).

Circus Circus Enterprises, Inc. *Annual Report to Shareholders* (1989).

Circus Circus Enterprises, Inc. *Annual Report to Shareholders* (1990).

Circus Circus Enterprises, Inc. *Annual Report to Shareholders* (1993).

Circus Circus Enterprises, Inc. *Annual Report to Shareholders* (1994).

Circus Circus Enterprises, Inc. *Annual Report to Shareholders* (1995).

Circus Circus Enterprises, Inc. *Annual Report to Shareholders* (1996).

Circus Circus Enterprises, Inc. *Annual Report to Shareholders* (1997).

Circus Circus Enterprises, Inc. *Annual Report to Shareholders* (1998).

Corning, Blair. "Luxor: Egypt Opens in Vegas." *San Antonio Express News* (October 24, 1993).

Lalli, Sergio. "Excalibur Awaiteth." *Hotel and Motel Management* (June 11, 1990).

"Economic Impacts of Casino Gaming in the United States." Author Anderson, American Gaming Association (May 1997).

Harrah's Entertainment, Inc. "Harrah's Survey of Casino Entertainment" (1996).

"ITT Board Rejects Hilton's Offer as Inadequate, Reaffirms Belief that ITT's Comprehensive Plan Is in the Best Interest of ITT Shareholders" (August 14, 1997).

www.freeedgar.com

Harrah's Entertainment, Inc.—1998

Fred David

www.harrahs.com
stock symbol HET

Headquartered in Memphis, Tennessee, Harrah's Entertainment, Inc., (901-762-8600) is one of the leading casino entertainment companies in the United States, currently operating facilities in 14 different markets. Harrah's casino business commenced operations nearly 60 years ago and is unique in its broad geographic diversification. Harrah's operates casino/hotels in the five traditional U.S. gaming markets of Nevada's Reno, Lake Tahoe, Las Vegas, and Laughlin and of New Jersey's Atlantic City. It operates riverboat casinos in Joliet, Illinois, and in North Kansas City and St. Louis in Missouri. Harrah's also operates dockside casinos in both Vicksburg and Tunica, Mississippi, and in Shreveport, Louisiana. Harrah's manages limited-stakes casinos in Central City and Black Hawk, Colorado, as well as casinos on two Native American reservations—one near Phoenix, Arizona, and the other north of Seattle, Washington. In 1996, the company commenced operations of a land-based casino in Auckland, New Zealand.

Harrah's operating profits per division are given in Exhibit 1.

Harrah's 1997 gaming volume percentage by region are given in Exhibit 2.

EXHIBIT 1: Harrah's Entertainment, Inc., Operating Profit

(in millions of dollars)

Division	1997	1996	1995
Riverboat	$124	$141	$172
Atlantic City	73	75	86
Southern Nevada	42	68	73
Northern Nevada	45	60	66
Native American/Limited Stakes	10	7	8
New Orleans	0	0	(28)

Source: Harrah's Entertainment, Inc., *Annual Report* (1997): 26–29.

This case was prepared by Professor Fred David of Francis Marion University as a basis for class discussion. It is not intended to illustrate either effective or ineffective handling of an administrative situation. Copyright © 1999 by Prentice Hall, Inc. ISBN 0-13-11120-1.

EXHIBIT 2: Harrah's Entertainment, Inc., 1997 Gaming Volume Percentage by State, New Zealand

Region	Percentage	Region	Percentage
Nevada	27.5	Mississippi	8.2
New Jersey	16.5	New Zealand	6.6
Missouri	14.1	Arizona	5.6
Louisiana	10.2	North Carolina	1.1
Illinois	9.5	Washington	0.6

Source: Harrah's Entertainment, Inc., Annual Report (1997): 22.

Harrah's mission statement, as given on page 1 of the company's 1997 *Annual Report*, is as follows:

> Our vision at Harrah's Entertainment, Inc., is to offer exciting environments and to be legendary at creating smiles, laughter, and lasting memories with every guest we entertain.

SOUTHERN NEVADA DIVISION

Consisting of Las Vegas and Laughlin, Harrah's Southern Nevada Division experienced a 38.4 percent decline in operating profits from $68 million in 1996 to $42 million in 1997, as indicated in Exhibit 3.

Las Vegas

Newly renovated, Harrah's—Las Vegas is located on approximately 17.3 acres on the Las Vegas Strip and consists of a 15-floor hotel tower, a 23-floor hotel tower, and a 35-story hotel tower. The hotel features 1,651 guest rooms and 46 suites. Adjacent low-rise buildings house the casino and the 15,000-square-foot convention center. The casino occupies approximately 79,800 square feet and has 1,980 slot machines and 85 game tables. Also on site are five restaurants, the 525-seat Commander's Theatre, a 367-seat cabaret, an arcade, a health club, and a heated pool.

EXHIBIT 3: Harrah's Entertainment, Inc., Southern Nevada Division Revenues, Operating Profit and Margin, 1995–1997

	(in millions)			Percentage of Difference	
	1997	1996	1995	97 v. 96	96 v. 95
Casino revenues	$191.0	$190.8	$198.3	0.1	(3.8)
Total revenues	288.2	289.8	297.2	(0.6)	(2.5)
Operating profit	41.9	68.0	72.8	(38.4)	(6.6)
Operating margin	14.5%	23.5%	24.5%	(9.0)	(1.0)

Source: Harrah's Entertainment, Inc., Annual Report (1997): 27.

The 1997 $200 million expansion of Harrah's—Las Vegas included a new 35-story hotel tower with 986 rooms and 46 suites; 22,200 additional square feet of casino space; three new restaurant facilities; and a complete renovation of the facade of the casino located on the Strip. The casino's primary feeder markets for the Southern Nevada Division are the Midwest, California, and Canada.

Laughlin

Harrah's Laughlin, Nevada, facility is located on a 44.9-acre site in a natural cove on the Colorado River and features a hotel with 1,635 standard rooms and 21 suites; a 90-seat cabaret; five restaurants; and two snack bars, including a McDonald's and a Baskin Robbins which are operated by nonaffiliated companies. Harrah's—Laughlin has approximately 47,000 square feet of casino space; 1,366 slot machines; 41 game tables; and approximately 7,000 square feet of convention center space. In 1996, a 378-seat showroom and a 3,164-seat outdoor amphitheater were constructed at the property. Other amenities include a health club, swimming pools, an arcade, and retail shops. It is the only property in Laughlin with a developed beachfront on the river. The casino's primary feeder markets are the Los Angeles and Phoenix areas, where a combined total of more than 17 million people reside.

NORTHERN NEVADA DIVISION

Consisting of Lake Tahoe and Reno, Harrah's Northern Nevada Division experienced a 25.6 percent decline in operating profits from $60 million in 1996 to $45 million in 1997, as indicated in Exhibit 4.

Lake Tahoe

Harrah's—Lake Tahoe is situated on 22.9 acres near Lake Tahoe and consists of an 18-story tower and an adjoining low-rise building which has a 16,500-square-foot convention center; approximately 63,200 square feet of casino space; 1,871 slot machines; and 109 game tables. The casino/hotel, with 79 suites and 453 luxury rooms, has seven restaurants, three snack bars, the 688-seat South Shore Showroom, a health club, retail shops, a heated pool, and an arcade.

EXHIBIT 4:   Harrah's Entertainment, Inc., Northern Nevada Division Revenues, Operating Profit and Margin, 1995–1997

	(in millions)			Percentage of Difference	
	1997	1996	1995	97 v. 96	96 v. 95
Casino revenues	$217.3	$226.5	$243.6	(4.1)	(7.0)
Total revenues	287.8	299.2	315.6	(3.8)	(5.2)
Operating profit	44.5	59.8	66.4	(25.6)	(9.9)
Operating margin	15.5%	20.0%	21.0%	(4.5)	(1.0)

Source: Harrah's Entertainment, Inc., *Annual Report* (1997): 27.

Harrah's also operates Bill's Lake Tahoe Casino, which is located on a 2.1-acre site adjacent to Harrah's—Lake Tahoe. The casino has approximately 18,000 square feet of space, with 590 slot machines and 20 game tables, and two casual on-premise restaurants, Bennigan's and McDonald's, operated by nonaffiliated restaurant companies. Most customers visiting Harrah's Northern Nevada casinos are from California and the Pacific Northwest.

Reno

Harrah's—Reno, situated on approximately 3.7 acres, consists of a casino/hotel complex with a 24-story structure; an approximately 14,500-square-foot convention center; and 57,000 square feet of casino space with 1,613 slot machines and 76 game tables. The facilities include a Harrah's hotel with 557 rooms and 8 suites, the 420-seat Sammy's Showroom, a 37-seat cabaret, a pool, a health club, and an arcade. The property has one snack bar and seven restaurants, including a Planet Hollywood restaurant and lounge and a McDonald's, operated by nonaffiliated restaurant companies. Harrah's operates a 408-room, 26-story Hampton Inn hotel adjacent to Harrah's—Reno. The hotel, which is operated by Harrah's pursuant to a license agreement from Promus Hotels, Inc. (a subsidiary of PHC), provides high-quality, moderately priced guest rooms to accommodate Harrah's guests. Customers visiting Harrah's—Reno mainly are from northern California, the Pacific Northwest, and Canada.

MANAGED CASINOS ON NATIVE AMERICAN LANDS

Harrah's manages three casinos on Native American lands. Harrah's continues to pursue additional development opportunities for casinos on Native American land and opened a casino in Cherokee, North Carolina, in November 1997. The facility contains approximately 60,000 square feet of casino space.

In early 1997, Harrah's received National Indian Gaming Commission approval of development and negotiated management agreements with the Prairie Band of Potawatomi Indians for a development near Topeka, Kansas. Plans call for the construction of a $37 million casino facility which will include approximately 27,000 square feet of casino space. This facility is expected to be completed by the end of 1997.

Harrah's—Phoenix Ak-Chin casino is owned by the Ak-Chin Indian Community and is located on approximately 20 acres of land on the community's reservation, about 25 miles south of Phoenix, Arizona. The casino includes 38,000 square feet of casino space with 475 slot machines; 41 poker tables; bingo and keno playing space; two restaurants; an entertainment lounge; 3,250 square feet of meeting room space; and a retail shop. The primary markets for the casino are Phoenix and Tucson.

ATLANTIC CITY

Harrah's Atlantic City, New Jersey, Division experienced a 2.3 percent decline in operating profits from $75 million in 1996 to $73 million in 1997, as shown in Exhibit 5.

The Harrah's—Atlantic City casino/hotel is situated on 24.17 acres in the Marina area of Atlantic City and has approximately 80,600 square feet of casino space with 2,507 slot machines and 96 game tables. It consists of dual 16-story hotel towers with

---

EXHIBIT 5: Harrah's Entertainment, Inc., Atlantic City Revenues, Operating Profit and Margin, 1995–1997

	(in millions)			*Percentage of Difference*	
	1997	*1996*	*1995*	*97 v. 96*	*96 v. 95*
Casino revenues	$314.9	$310.1	$314.7	1.5	(1.5)
Total revenues	349.5	338.6	341.5	3.2	(0.8)
Operating profit	73.3	75.0	85.6	(2.3)	(12.4)
Operating margin	21.0%	22.2%	25.1%	(1.2)	(2.9)

Source: Harrah's Entertainment, Inc., *Annual Report* (1997): 27.

251 suites and 509 rooms, and adjoining low-rise buildings which house the casino space and the 26,100-square-foot convention center. The facilities include seven restaurants; an 820-seat showroom; a health club with swimming pool; a teen center with video games; child care facilities; and parking for 2,395 cars, including a substantial portion in a parking garage. The property also has a 72-slip marina. Harrah's also owns approximately 8.45 acres of land adjacent to Harrah's—Atlantic City and 170 acres of wetlands in the Marina area. Most of the casino's customers arrive by car from within a 150-mile radius which includes Philadelphia, New York, and northern New Jersey.

NEW ZEALAND

Sky City, a casino entertainment facility in Auckland, New Zealand, opened in February 1996. The project is owned by Sky City Limited, a publicly traded New Zealand corporation in which Harrah's ownership is 12.5 percent. The facility is located on 3.1 acres of land and has approximately 45,000 square feet of casino space; 1,050 slot machines; and 100 game tables. A special attraction of the facility is a 1,066-foot Sky Tower, which opened in 1997. The Sky Tower, the tallest structure in the Southern Hemisphere, features one open-air and two enclosed observation decks as well as a revolving bar and restaurant.

RIVERBOAT CASINOS

Harrah's Riverboat Division experienced a 12 percent decline in operating profits from $141 million in 1996 to $124 million in 1997, as indicated in Exhibit 6.

Joliet

Harrah's—Joliet is located in downtown Joliet, Illinois, on the Des Plaines River. The two riverboat casinos, the Harrah's *Northern Star,* a modern 210-foot yacht, and the *Southern Star II,* a 210-foot riverboat, offer a combined total of 37,000 square feet of casino space with 56 game tables and 988 slot machines. Each riverboat can accommodate approximately 825 guests per cruise. Harrah's—Joliet offers a total of 18 cruises per day. The Chicago metropolitan area is the primary market for Harrah's—Joliet as Joliet is only 30 miles from downtown Chicago. Harrah's—Joliet revenues declined 15.5 percent in 1997.

EXHIBIT 6: Harrah's Entertainment, Inc., Riverboat Casinos Revenues, Operating Profit and Margin, 1995–1997

	(in millions)			Percentage of Difference	
	1997	1996	1995	97 v. 96	96 v. 95
Casino revenues	$614.8	$596.0	$557.2	3.2	7.0
Total revenues	656.2	629.1	593.5	4.3	6.0
Operating profit	124.2	141.2	172.2	(12.0)	(18.0)
Operating margin	18.9%	22.4%	29.0%	(3.5)	(6.6)

Source: Harrah's Entertainment, Inc., *Annual Report* (1997): 26.

Tunica

Harrah's—Tunica Mardi Gras Casino is a stationary riverboat casino complex which opened in April 1996. It is situated on 88 acres of land in Tunica, Mississippi, approximately 30 miles south of downtown Memphis, Tennessee. The facilities include approximately 50,000 square feet of casino space with 1,166 slot machines and 51 game tables; three restaurants; a child care facility; an arcade; a retail shop; a 13,500-square-foot entertainment/ballroom area; and customer parking for 2,560 cars. The Harrah's hotel, which features 181 rooms, 18 suites, and exercise facilities, opened in June 1996. Tunica revenues increased 5.9 percent in 1997 over 1996.

Vicksburg

Harrah's—Vicksburg reported 1997 revenues and operating profit which were virtually even with the prior year. This is a dockside casino entertainment complex on approximately 10.3 acres in Vicksburg, Mississippi. The complex, which is located downtown on the Yazoo Diversion Canal of the Mississippi River, includes a 297-foot stationary riverboat casino designed in the spirit of a traditional 1800s riverboat and has approximately 11,800 square feet of casino space; 605 slot machines; and 31 game tables. The casino is docked next to Harrah's shoreside complex which features two restaurants, a snack bar/lounge, child care facilities, an arcade, a retail outlet, and more. Adjacent to the riverboat is a Harrah's hotel, with 109 rooms and eight suites. The casino's primary markets are western and central Mississippi and eastern Louisiana.

Shreveport

Harrah's—Shreveport is a dockside riverboat casino in downtown Shreveport, Louisiana, which includes a 254-foot nineteenth century–design paddle-wheel riverboat, the *ShreveStar*, with 28,000 square feet of gaming space; 1,033 slot machines; and 42 game tables. A pavilion, on 11.2 acres of land, adjoins the casino on the banks of the Red River and includes two restaurants and a 4,100-square-foot area for private parties and group functions. Customers visiting this casino usually are from northwestern Louisiana and east Texas, including the Dallas–Fort Worth area. Harrah's—Shreveport's 1997 revenues declined 1.9 percent although operating profit increased 2.5 percent.

North Kansas City

Harrah's owns and operates riverboat casino facilities situated on 55 acres of land in North Kansas City, Missouri. Operating profits for this facility declined 24.9 percent in 1997 on the heels of a 17.5 percent drop in 1996. The facilities include a 295-foot classic sternwheeler-designed stationary riverboat, the *North Star,* with approximately 31,600 square feet of casino space; 1,043 slot machines; and 53 game tables. In May 1996, the company opened a second casino at the North Kansas City property, the *Mardi Gras,* which is constructed on a floating stationary barge. At year end, with both boats operational, the facilities offered a combined total of approximately 62,100 square feet of casino space; 1,938 slot machines; and 98 game tables.

Shoreside facilities were expanded in 1996 and at year end included a pavilion that housed three restaurants and 10,000 square feet of meeting space. In March 1996, construction was completed on a three-story 1,060-car parking garage and new surface parking. Total on-site parking, including valet parking, is now available for 2,738 cars. In December 1996, the $78 million expansion of the Harrah's—North Kansas City facilities was completed with the opening of a Harrah's hotel which features 181 rooms and 19 suites. Additional property amenities include two snack bars, an arcade, a swimming pool, and an exercise room. The casino's primary feeder market is the Kansas City area.

St. Louis

Harrah's newest riverboat casino project, Harrah's—St. Louis Riverport, reported an operating loss of $1.4 million for 1997. With Players International, Inc., Harrah's is part of a riverboat casino project along the Missouri River in Maryland Heights, Missouri, in northwest St. Louis County, 16 miles from downtown St. Louis. The partnership formed by Harrah's and Players leases space to both Harrah's and Players in which both operate their separately branded casinos and specialty restaurants. Each company operates two riverboat casinos. Harrah's riverboats have approximately 26,000 square feet of gaming space each, with a total of approximately 1,230 slot machines and 80 game tables. A shoreside pavilion houses three restaurants, a snack bar, an entertainment lounge, and retail space. Additional amenities are a special events center and child care facilities. Also included in the shoreside facilities is a seven-story, 291-room Harrah's hotel; an 1,850-car parking garage; and additional parking for 3,000 cars. Harrah's manages the shoreside pavilion, hotel, and parking areas for a fee. Approximately 74 acres of land being used for the development are owned by Harrah's and leased to the partnership. Approximately 140 acres of additional land included in the development are owned by the partnership.

THE FUTURE

Harrah's obviously is spending a lot of money in a lot of places to capitalize on society's increasing acceptance of gaming. But company revenues and profits are not rising nearly enough to justify operating expenses (see Exhibit 7) and in many locations are falling. The company reports only a 1.5 percent increase of assets in 1997 over 1996 (see Exhibit 8). Harrah's is in need of a clear strategic plan. More customers are turning to the Internet to gamble rather than visiting gaming facilities. Analysts warn that Internet gambling volume will accelerate annually and significantly erode Harrah's and other casino organizations' revenues.

What specific recommendations do you have for Harrah's new chair, president, and CEO Philip Satre? (See Exhibit 9.) Prepare a three-year strategic plan for Harrah's.

EXHIBIT 7:   Harrah's Entertainment, Inc., Consolidated Balance Sheets

	Year Ended December 31,		
(in thousands, except per share amounts)	*1997*	*1996*	*1995*
Revenues			
Casino	$1,338,003	$1,323,466	$1,313,910
Food and beverage	196,765	188,081	181,312
Rooms	128,354	115,456	109,036
Management fees	24,566	16,227	12,762
Other	78,954	78,729	115,87
Less: casino promotional allowances	(147,432)	(135,939)	(154,102)
Total revenues	1,619,210	1,586,020	1,578,795
Operating expenses			
Direct			
Casino	685,942	649,720	620,438
Food and beverage	103,604	95,909	91,495
Rooms	39,719	35,460	32,915
Depreciation of buildings, riverboats and equipment	103,670	92,130	80,416
Development costs	10,524	12,021	17,428
Write-downs and reserves	13,806	52,188	93,348
Project opening costs	17,631	5,907	450
Other	385,630	358,000	353,318
Total operating expenses	1,360,526	1,301,335	1,289,808
Operating profit	258,684	284,685	288,987
Corporate expense	(27,155)	(34,348)	(30,347)
Equity in income (losses) of nonconsolidated affiliates	(11,05)	1,182	(49,245)
Venture restructuring costs	(6,94)	(14,601)	0
Income from operations	213,532	236,918	209,395
Interest expense, net of interest capitalized	(79,071)	(69,968)	(73,890)
Gains on sales of equity interests in New Zealand subsidiary	37,388	0	11,773
Other income, including interest income	11,799	5,160	4,305
Income before income taxes and minority interests	183,648	172,110	151,583
Provision for income taxes	(68,746)	(67,316)	(60,677)
Minority interests	(7,380)	(5,897)	(12,096)
Income from continuing operations	107,522	98,897	78,810
Discontinued operations			
Earnings from hotel operations, net of tax provision of $15,434	0	0	21,230
Spin-off transaction expenses, net of tax benefit of $5,134	0	0	(21,194)

continued

EXHIBIT 7: *continued*

(in thousands, except per share amounts)	Year Ended December 31,		
	1997	*1996*	*1995*
Income before extraordinary loss	107,522	98,897	78,846
Extraordinary loss, net of tax benefit of $4,477	(8,134)	0	0
Net income	99,388	98,897	78,846
Earnings (loss) per share-basic			
Continuing operations	1.07	0.96	0.77
Discontinued operations			
Earnings from hotel operations, net	0	0	0.21
Spin-off transaction expenses, net	0	0	(0.21)
Extraordinary loss, net	(0.08)	0	0
Net income	0.99	0.96	0.77
Earnings (loss) per share-diluted			
Continuing operations	1.06	0.95	0.76
Discontinued operations			
Earnings from hotel operations, net	0	0	0.21
Spin-off transaction expenses, net	0	0	(0.21)
Extraordinary loss, net	(0.08)	0	0
Net income	0.98	0.95	0.76
Weighted average common shares outstanding	100,618	102,598	102,341
Weighted average common and common equivalent shares outstanding	101,254	103,736	103,188

Source: Harrah's Entertainment, Inc.; www.freedgar.com.

EXHIBIT 8:   Harrah's Entertainment, Inc., Consolidated Balance Sheets

(in thousands, except per share amounts)	Year Ended December 31,		
	1997	*1996*	*1995*
Assets			
Current assets			
Cash and cash equivalents	$ 116,443	$ 105,594	$ 96,345
Receivables, less allowance for doubtful accounts of $11,462 and $14,064	43,767	41,203	37,751
Deferred income taxes	17,436	25,551	21,425
Prepayments and other	21,653	18,401	21,275
Inventories	13,011	10,838	12,040
Total current assets	212,310	201,587	188,836
Land, buildings, riverboats and equipment			
Land and land improvements	218,703	232,721	232,616
Buildings, riverboats and improvements	1,334,279	1,248,792	1,054,758
Furniture, fixtures and equipment	600,358	496,447	436,340
	2,153,340	1,977,960	1,723,714
Less: accumulated depreciation	(675,286)	(588,066)	(518,824)
	1,478,054	1,389,894	1,204,890
			continued

EXHIBIT 8: *continued*

(in thousands, except share amounts)	Year Ended December 31,		
	1997	1996	1995
Investments in and advances to nonconsolidated affiliates	152,401	215,539	71,939
Deferred income tax benefits	0	0	4,532
Deferred costs and other	162,741	167,053	166,537
	$2,005,506	$1,974,073	$1,636,734
Liabilities and Stockholders' Equity			
Current liabilities			
Accounts payable	45,233	44,934	46,178
Construction payables	7,186	17,975	4,718
Accrued expenses	156,694	139,892	148,632
Current portion of long-term debt	1,837	1,841	2,038
Total current liabilities	210,950	204,642	201,566
Long-term debt	924,397	889,538	753,705
Deferred credits and other	98,177	97,740	72,006
Deferred income taxes	22,361	45,443	0
	1,255,885	1,237,363	1,027,277
Minority interests	14,118	16,964	23,908
Commitments and contingencies			
Stockholders' equity			
Common stock, $0.10 par value, authorized–360,000,000 shares, outstanding–101,035,898 and 102,969,699 shares (net of 3,001,568 and 771,571 shares held in treasury)	10,104	10,297	10,267
Capital surplus	388,925	385,941	362,783
Retained earnings	349,386	290,797	204,838
Unrealized gain on marketable equity securities	2,884	51,394	10,552
Deferred compensation related to restricted stock	(15,796)	(18,683)	(2,891)
	735,503	719,746	585,549
	$2,005,506	$1,974,073	$1,636,734

Source: Harrah's Entertainment, Inc.; www.freedgar.com.

Fred David

EXHIBIT 9: Harrah's Entertainment, Inc., Organizational Chart

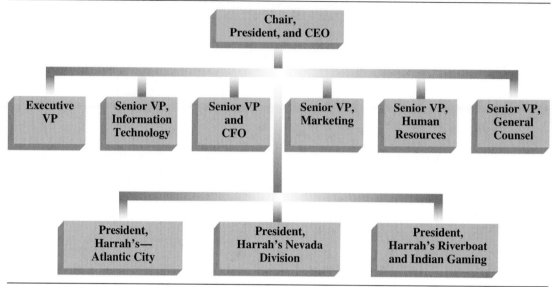

Source: www.freeedgar.com

Banking—Industry Note

In a move that would have been unthinkable a few years ago, Citicorp and Travelers Corp. shocked the banking and insurance industries in April 1998 with an agreement to merge. By far the largest merger to date in the financial or any other industry, the deal immediately sparked debate about its likely impacts on customers, competition, and regulation of both the industries involved.

The merger was a surprise, not only for its sheer size (the combined company will have nearly $700 billion in assets) but also for the unlikely melding of two distinct industry participants: a bank-holding company and an insurance company. In fact, it may have created a new industry group—one with just a single participant so far. Because such a new institution has no industry peers, analysts have had trouble determining what valuation to place on it.

At the core of the matter, the merger creates a company completely at odds with current bank regulations: a bank with the ability to offer proprietary insurance and underwriting products and an insurance company free to cross-market traditional banking products. Although the usual talk of dilution, cost cutting, and cross-selling opportunities were of interest, the merger was about substantially more—a major repositioning of how banks do business. Management's plan to create the "model financial institution of the future," as the merger was advertised, no doubt will have repercussions.

TIME IS OF THE ESSENCE

Under current regulations, the combination would have a somewhat lengthy, but limited, period of time to prove its success. The deal is structured as Travelers Group acquiring Citicorp and then applying for a new bank-holding company charter, which would give the new entity a two-year exemption from laws preventing banks from underwriting insurance. In addition, three one-year extensions would be available, leaving the potential of a full five years for the combined company to exist under present rules governing bank-holding companies. The calculated risk, however, is that meaningful financial reform legislation embracing the combination of banks, insurance companies, and securities firms will come to pass within this five-year time horizon.

Time may be an important consideration because creating a company with $125 million in market capitalization is no small task. As a new industry behemoth, the combined company—to be called Citigroup—also will have a tremendous advantage in garnering initial market share in its quest to become a one-size-fits-all financial services firm. That could create substantial pressure for others—even those who don't believe that this marriage will succeed—to make strategic moves sooner rather than later.

Note: Adapted from *Industry Survey* by permission of Standard & Poor's, a division of the McGraw-Hill Companies.
Source: Standard & Poor's, "Banking," *Industry Survey* (June 11, 1998): 1–17.

Ironically, it has been bank and insurance industry lobbyists who prevented large-scale regulatory changes from occurring already: In this turf war, neither side has been willing to cede much power to the other. Some banks oppose provisions of the proposed rules that effectively would grant insurance and securities regulators new authority over banking products. One way or another, the merger of two industry titans makes it apparent that legislators will need to work faster on financial services modernization reform.

The reasons for reform are now compelling—much more so than was the case a decade ago when meaningful financial services reform first came on the scene. Banks contend that they need broader powers so they can better compete with foreign banks, many of which already can own insurance and brokerage companies. Banks also make a good case that customers would benefit from the ability to buy products through one source instead of several. The continued globalization of economies makes it imperative that United States–based banks have the tools they need to be competitive with other multinational institutions.

Earnings Hit Another Record in 1997

According to data provided by the Federal Deposit Insurance Corporation (FDIC), earnings for the 9,143 reporting commercial banks in the United States totaled $59.24 billion in 1997, up from the record high of $52.36 billion achieved in 1996. This year-to-year gain was attributable to higher net interest income and noninterest income, which more than offset greater loan loss provisions and noninterest expenses. More than two-thirds of all commercial banks reported higher earnings in 1997 compared with 1996. However, the percentage of unprofitable institutions rose slightly to 4.51 percent, from 4.24 percent a year earlier.

Banks' net interest income in 1997 advanced 7.2 percent, year to year, benefiting from a 9.2 percent increase in earning assets. This was partly offset by a narrower net interest margin: 4.21 percent, versus 4.27 percent in 1996. The commercial and industrial segment led loan growth, with a 12.2 percent rise; this was followed by loans secured by real estate, with a 9.2 percent gain, and farm loans, up 8.6 percent. Loans to individuals declined 0.2 percent.

Loan loss provisions increased 21.5 percent to $19.8 billion in 1997 and were only somewhat higher than net charge-offs of $18.3 billion. As bank managements have become more comfortable with reserve levels, they have been less willing to make provisions much in excess of charge-offs or to build reserves further.

Noninterest income in 1997 rose 11.7 percent, year to year, helped by higher income from trust activities and other fee-related sources. Noninterest expense, up 5.8 percent, reflected higher costs for personnel and infrastructure as well as technology and Year 2000 issues.

Net charge-offs increased to 0.63 percent of total loans and leases in 1997, from 0.58 percent the year before. Loans to individuals had the highest charge-off rate, at 2.70 percent of total loans; this included a 5.11 percent rate for credit card loans. In contrast, loans for real estate had the lowest charge-off rate, at 0.06 percent.

U.S. banks' return on assets was 1.23 percent in 1997, up modestly from 1.19 percent the year before. Return on equity increased to 14.70 percent, from 14.46 percent in 1996.

The number of problem institutions (defined as those having financial, operational, or managerial weaknesses that threaten their continued financial viability) declined further, to 71 institutions with $5 billion in assets as of December 31, 1997. A year earlier, there were 82 such institutions, also with $5 billion in assets.

Profit Outlook Still Favorable

Many of the same factors that brought bank earnings to record levels in 1997 remain intact. Specifically, strong capital levels, healthy loan loss reserves, respectable loan growth, diversification into additional fee-based businesses, and expansion and cost cutting through consolidation are expected to continue to boost earnings. Stable interest rate policy by the Federal Reserve and a still-relaxed regulatory environment will provide a continuation of the important underpinnings that have served the industry well in recent years.

Our forecast calls for aggregate bank earnings to rise by 11 percent to 12 percent, year to year, in 1998. The projected gain is somewhat below 1997's 13 percent rise, due in part to reduced expectations for overall economic growth. S&P's Economics Department currently is projecting real GDP growth of 3.2 percent in 1998, down from 3.8 percent in 1997. Similarly, growth in personal income is likely to be held to 5.4 percent in 1998, versus the 5.8 percent advance seen in 1997.

Within our 1998 forecast, we expect about one-third of commercial banks to achieve earnings growth surpassing 12 percent. Such banks are likely to have regional service territories with better-than-average employment and income growth, strong efficiency ratios, and a greater proportion of revenues being derived from activities other than traditional lending.

Federal Reserve Policy on Hold for Now

Having engineered one of the longest periods of economic expansion yet seen (seven years and counting), the Federal Reserve appears more or less willing to sit back and watch its handiwork while waiting to see if growth and/or inflation pick up meaningful steam. Although economic growth (as measured by real GDP) accelerated in 1997 (3.8 percent, versus 2.8 percent in 1996), inflation remains tepid and the Fed is mindful of the potential softening that recent turmoil in Asia could have on U.S. growth. The Fed's most recent move, a March 1997 increase in the Fed funds rate, was characterized by most as a preemptive strike against inflation and appears to have done its job.

Although the Fed has been content to hold interest rates steady since then, it indicated more of a bias toward tightening—i.e., an interest rate increase—at its most recent policy meeting in mid-May 1998. With Asia's impact on the U.S. economy still uncertain, however, any move by the Fed likely would be small.

The importance of this era's stable Fed interest rate policy cannot be overstated. Not that many years ago, investors were making fairly substantial bets on the expected direction and magnitude of Federal Reserve rate movements. In today's environment, interest rate–sensitive securities, including bank stocks, are trading more on fundamentals than on anticipation of Fed moves.

Stable short-term interest rate policy benefits banks in several ways. New loan demand, for example, is more predictable, and banks do not have to devise strategies to cope with sharp changes in future interest rate levels and their impact on the lending business. In addition, less emphasis can be placed on interest rate risk management, allowing bank managements to be more focused on growth opportunities. The environment also portends less volatility in businesses other than lending.

Although short-term interest rates have been steady, long-term rates have dropped considerably since mid-1997. This has created a unique situation for banks. A surge of refinancings as homeowners rush to take advantage of lower mortgage rates could have several effects on bank earnings. Refinancing at lower rates reduces the total level of interest income generated by mortgage loans, but the impact is mitigated as banks fund the new loans at lower rates.

Separately, banks should expect a short-term surge in fees related to refinancing, such as fees for applications, credit checks, etc. A less noticeable, but still important, impact is on credit quality. Following a refinancing, customers' mortgage payments are lower and thus more affordable. This means that customers are more likely to be able to make their monthly debt servicing obligations and fewer will default.

Consumer Credit Quality: Disaster Not Likely

Concerns about consumer credit quality have diminished in the past six months. Several developments have contributed to this improvement. First, low unemployment levels and rising wages have helped the average consumer borrower. Second, rises in delinquencies through the first half of 1997 caused banks to rethink marketing strategies and focus on a higher-credit borrower, albeit at the expense of better growth rates in lending volume.

Despite the uptick in delinquencies in the early part of 1997, banks actually have done quite well at keeping delinquencies at manageable levels. Current delinquency rates range from 3.5 percent to 5 percent, compared with rates of 6 percent and higher during past credit quality downturns.

The credit quality picture also appears to be strongly influenced by regional economies. The Southeast, for example, fares best, with most of that region's states carrying noncurrent loan rates (loans past due 90 days or more as a percentage of total loans) of less than 1 percent. The Northeast, by contrast, has noncurrent loan rates of up to 2.1 percent. Reasons for the difference include economic growth, which factors in the employment level and the pace of income growth, and the underwriting prudence of individual bank managements competing in those states.

The latest concerns over credit quality should come as no surprise. Banks typically chase the sectors with the most abundant growth rates. As a result, every few years, banks face credit quality concerns because of overlending to a certain category of borrowers. In the early to mid-1980s, loans to less-developed countries were the culprit. In the late 1980s, loans to the North American commercial real estate market caused huge write-offs.

Will recent weakness in the credit quality of consumer loans prove to be the undoing of banks' earnings progress in the 1990s? Most likely, no. Historically, damaging errors in underwriting practices stemmed mainly from a large dollar volume of loans to a limited number of borrowers. Thus, problems for a few large borrowers in a particular sector had a substantial impact on overall credit quality.

In the case of consumer lending, the opposite is true. Consumer lending is the product of many borrowers and small dollar volume loans. In addition, consumer loans carry wide margins, which lets the category remain profitable enough to absorb credit losses and still contribute meaningfully to a bank's earnings. In addition, banks remain well reserved for credit card losses. Most commercial and industrial loans, in contrast, are typically at the prime rate or slightly above; the narrower margins they generate may not compensate adequately for risk.

Of course, banks' ability to avoid future credit quality downturns depends largely on overall economic conditions. As long as the Fed succeeds in keeping economic growth stable enough to prevent wide swings in economic activity, the banking system should have no major problem with loan losses.

Money Centers Fret Over Asia

Some money center banks were stung by trading-related losses in the fourth quarter of 1997 following financial turmoil in Asia. According to the Office of the Comptroller of the Currency, revenues from securities trading fell 52 percent, year to year, to $1.2 billion in the fourth quarter. Some offsets, however, were seen in foreign exchange revenue, which increased $211 million to $1.3 billion on volatility-related volume.

Credit losses on derivatives, while relatively well contained in the quarter, are growing. Although a total of 459 banks hold derivatives, just eight (mostly the large money centers) account for some 95 percent of the national amount of derivatives in the banking system.

Although money center bank stock prices were hit particularly hard in the wake of Asia's debacle, most analysts viewed the matter in context and were not willing to make the leap that long-term structural problems may be forming in the world's financial trading system. Losses appeared to have been well controlled, and banks immediately began proclaiming that their hedging techniques had worked to minimize losses or that measures had been put in place to limit further losses should such an event occur again.

First-half 1998 results no doubt will show the intermediate-term impact on bank earnings. Expectations are for relatively weak revenues from trading, foreign exchange, and lending volume as Asian companies assess the future of their domestic economies. In the meantime, banks appear willing to allow the region to regain its footing; some even are looking at the area's weakened financial condition as an opportunity to acquire foreign assets inexpensively.

The Search for Revenue Growth Continues

Banks have worked hard on the expense side of the equation over the last few years, and their efforts are commendable. "Rationalizing the branch network" and "streamlining the workforce" have been popular phrases used in bank restructurings. Bank mergers also have been used as a convenient cost-cutting method when overlap in administrative activities and branch territory provided opportunities to consolidate functions. In the aggregate, efficiency ratios at commercial bank-holding companies have never been better.

As a result of this success, however, efficiency ratios may be approaching optimum levels. As efficiency improves, the number of ways to reduce costs declines. Another popular earnings booster has been share repurchase programs. But as bank stock prices rise, managements are increasingly reluctant to buy back their own company's shares at valuations not seen before.

Many banks have turned their full attention toward revenue growth, but they continue to face new challenges. In 1994 and 1995, banks found heady growth in the consumer lending arena, particularly in credit cards. Consumers' propensity to borrow and spend led to a rapid buildup in consumer loan portfolios and rising credit card fee income for banks. But given recent saturation in the credit card market and banks' own efforts to rein in growth and shore up credit quality, banks now must develop new revenue sources.

Noninterest income continues to remain a favorite avenue for revenue growth. Many banks, particularly the largest and those with the broadest product mixes, steadily have been increasing the proportion of revenues derived from noninterest income, including mortgage banking fees, trust income, securities processing, and brokerage income.

The emphasis on noninterest income is a positive trend for several reasons. The growth rate of such revenues is typically much more stable than the traditional lending business, which waxes and wanes with the interest rate cycle. In addition, because noninterest income sources don't adhere to typical loan growth cycles, they can provide an important offset in case the pace of loan growth slows. Moreover, such fee-based revenues don't carry the associated burden of credit costs, as loans do. In the event of an economic downturn, the trend favoring noninterest income sources should help banks maintain earnings momentum.

Compared with the banking systems of most developed countries, the U.S. industry is highly fragmented. In terms of pricing and service, thousands of smaller players try to compete on equal footing with industry leaders. Yet because the largest banks often extend their reach into smaller communities, small banks, which may not offer as wide an array of banking products, are finding it tougher to attract and retain customers.

In the past several years, the pace of consolidation among banking institutions has accelerated. Efforts to increase efficiency, service levels, and product depth are behind much of the merger trend. According to the Federal Deposit Insurance Corp. (FDIC), the number of FDIC-insured banks slipped from 14,628 in 1975 to approximately 14,500 in 1984, and fell to 10,451 in 1994; 9,940 in 1995; 9,528 in 1996; and 9,143 in 1997. Industry consolidation is expected to continue.

As of year-end 1997, 66 banks had assets of more than $10 billion each; their aggregate assets were $3.12 trillion (equal to 60 percent of total industry assets of $5 trillion). At that time, 367 banks had assets of more than $1 billion (80 percent of industry assets). In 1994, there were 392 banks with assets of more than $1 billion, representing 75 percent of total commercial banking assets, according to the FDIC.

At the end of 1997, nine banks had assets of more than $100 billion each. The five largest bank-holding companies in the United States, ranked by assets, were Chase Manhattan Corp. ($366 billion); Citicorp ($311 billion); NationsBank ($265 billion); J.P. Morgan & Co. ($262 billion); and BankAmerica ($260 billion).

Competitive Strategies: Retail and Commercial

Most banks in the United States are small entities competing in limited markets for local business. These banks often compete for retail business against money center banks and large regional banks operating in their territories.

Retail banking remains a service-oriented business. To make banking more pleasant and convenient for customers, today's banks are investing in new technology. Automatic teller machines (ATMs) are widespread. Many bank branches operate drive-through windows, and home banking services are being marketed heavily.

Largest U.S. Bank-Holding Companies

(in millions of dollars)

	Total Assets		
Company	12/31/96	12/31/97	Percentage of Change
1. Chase Manhattan	336,099	365,521	8.8
2. Citicorp	281,018	310,897	10.6
3. NationsBank	226,994	264,562	16.6
4. J.P. Morgan	222,026	262,159	18.1
5. BankAmerica	250,753	260,159	3.8
6. First Union	151,847	157,274	3.6
7. Bankers Trust	120,235	140,102	16.5
8. Banc One	112,154	115,901	3.4
9. First Chicago	104,619	114,096	9.1
10. Wells Fargo	108,888	98,456	(9.6)

Source: American Banker.

Competition has heated up in the retail market as some banks have expanded and achieved economies of scale through acquisitions. Interstate banks have the servicing advantages of larger ATM networks and more product offerings, such as mutual funds, insurance, and a broader variety of loan products.

The large money center banks compete in the national market for the business of large corporations. They strive to obtain wholesale business in the international markets, although Citicorp is the only U.S. money center with operations that are truly global in scope. Bankers Trust and J.P. Morgan don't have any consumer operations, and there isn't much overlap in the geographic territories of the other three money center banks (BankAmerica, Chase Manhattan, and First Chicago). Money centers do compete against one another in certain categories, however, such as the so-called middle market, which encompasses corporations with revenues of $100 million to $500 million.

Industry competition has continued to heighten as the consolidation wave has reached every corner of the financial services industry. Consolidation has forced banks to rethink their corporate strategies in many areas, including geographic expansion, pricing of products and services, and ways to optimize efficiency. Merged companies often set lofty performance goals for themselves relating to improved earnings growth, better return on assets and equity, and enhanced efficiency levels, all of which heat up competition.

Increasingly, commercial banks also must compete with other kinds of financial institutions, such as credit card companies and other specialized consumer lending organizations. Some banks have been buying these institutions to acquire their large customer bases, strong marketing skills, and efficiency levels. Banc One's mid-1997 acquisition of credit card issuer First USA is a good example of how former competitors can link together to form industry powerhouses.

Top 10 Earners in Banking

(in millions of dollars, ranked by 1997 net income)

| | Net Income | | Profitability Ratios | | | |
| | | | Return on Assets | | Return on Equity | |
Company	1996	1997	1996	1997	1996	1997
1. Chase Manhattan	2,461.0	3,708.0	0.77	1.05	12.48	18.73
2. Citicorp	3,788.0	3,591.0	1.40	1.22	20.40	18.10
3. BankAmerica	2,873.0	3,210.0	1.19	1.26	15.00	16.69
4. NationsBank	2,375.0	3,077.0	1.18	1.26	17.95	15.26
5. First Union	1,499.0	1,896.0	1.31	1.39	18.85	18.90
6. First Chicago	1,436.0	1,525.0	1.28	1.41	17.00	18.60
7. J.P. Morgan	1,574.1	1,465.0	0.73	0.58	14.90	13.40
8. Norwest Corp.	1,153.9	1,351.0	1.51	1.65	21.90	22.10
9. Banc One	1,672.8	1,305.7	1.59	1.16	17.83	13.33
10. Fleet Financial Group	1,138.8	1,303.0	1.37	1.59	17.43	18.10

Source: American Banker.

Banc One Corporation—1998

Jack Goebel

www.bankone.com
stock symbol ONE

Banc One, according to a recent Towers Perrin Banking Survey, received the highest rating of all banks when two questions were asked of analysts and chief executive officers: "Which financial institution does a superior job of attracting, motivating, and retaining the right people?" and "If you could bank with any institution other than your own, where would you bank?"

Over the last 10 years, Banc One has recorded the highest average return on assets and the second-highest return on equity of the 25 largest U.S. banking organizations. *EuroMoney* magazine recently ranked Banc One as number 6 among the world's 100 best banks. There was only one other U.S. bank in the top ten, J. P. Morgan, which ranked number 1. However, Banc One's net income declined 21.9 percent in 1997 to $1.3 billion as indicated in Exhibit 1.

Headquartered in Columbus, Ohio, Banc One (614-248-5944) is a bank-holding corporation for 72 affiliate banks. (The corporation uses the spelling *Banc* because Ohio and several other states forbid using the word *bank* in a bank-holding company's name.) It also operates several additional corporations that engage in data processing, venture capital, investment and merchant banking, trusts, stock brokerage, investment management, equipment leasing, mortgage banking, credit card administration, consumer finance, and insurance.

As of December 31, 1997, Banc One's affiliate banks had over 1,300 banking offices located in Arizona, Colorado, Illinois, Indiana, Kentucky, Louisiana, Ohio, Oklahoma, Texas, Utah, West Virginia, and Wisconsin. It has full-service branches in each of these states. Banc One and its consolidated subsidiaries have approximately 56,600 full-time-equivalent employees. Banc One is the fourth-largest bank-holding company in the United States, with more than $115.9 billion in assets.

Banc One celebrated its thirtieth anniversary in 1998 as a multibank-holding company. The corporation's deposits in 1997 exceeded $77 billion, up 4.3 percent over 1996. Banc One's return on average common equity declined to 13.3 percent in 1997 from 17.8 percent the previous year. In 1997, Banc One acquired First USA to become the third-largest credit card company in the United States. In 1997, Banc One also acquired Liberty Bancorp in Oklahoma City and First Commerce in New Orleans.

This case was prepared by Professor Jack Goebel of Francis Marion University as a basis for class discussion. It is not intended to illustrate either effective or ineffective handling of an administrative situation. Copyright © 1999 by Prentice Hall, Inc. ISBN 0-13-011133-3.

EXHIBIT 1: Banc One's Overview of Operations

	1997	1996	Percentage of Change
Per common share			
Net income, diluted	$ 1.99	$ 2.52	(21.0)
Cash dividends declared	1.38	1.24	11.3
Book value	15.89	16.93	(6.1)
For the year (in millions)			
Total revenue	13,219.1	12,099.1	9.3
Net income	1,305.7	1,672.8	(21.9)
Weighted average common shares outstanding, diluted (millions)	655.7	664.3	
At year-end			
Total managed assets	147,035.3	134,724.5	9.1
Assets	115,901.3	112,153.5	3.3
Deposits	77,414.3	74,223.0	4.3
Total loans and leases	82,052.8	79,389.7	3.4
Total equity	$ 10,376.0	$ 9,868.0	5.1
Common stockholders of record	105,631	97,074	
Employees (full-time equivalent)	56,600	54,400	

Net income for 1997 was $1,305.7 million, or $1.99 per share, down $367.1 million from $1,672.8 million, or $2.52 per share, in 1996. Lower net income in 1997 was primarily the result of $328.8 million in after-tax restructuring and merger-related charges recorded in connection with the acquisition of First USA, Inc., and other strategic initiatives.

Return on average assets and return on average common equity for 1997 were 1.16 percent and 13.33 percent, respectively, compared with 1.59 percent and 17.83 percent, respectively, for 1996. Excluding the impact of the restructuring and merger-related charges, return on average assets and return on average common equity for 1997 remained strong at 1.46 percent and 16.72 percent, respectively.

Key highlights for 1997, compared with 1996, include the following:

- Gross revenue grew 9.3 percent, reflecting both strong loan growth and increased loan processing and servicing income resulting primarily from the impact of credit card activities.

- Managed assets grew 9.1 percent, reflecting a 17.2 percent growth in average managed credit card loans.

- The managed net interest margin increased to 6.26 percent from 6.06 percent.

- Capital levels remained strong, with ending equity to total assets of 8.95 percent, compared with 8.80 percent a year ago.

Source: Adapted from Banc One, *Annual Report* (1997): 1, 27.

Chair and CEO John B. McCoy is the third member of the McCoy family to lead Banc One. John H. McCoy, his grandfather, served as president and guided the corporation during its early years. John G. McCoy, his father, joined the bank in 1937 and did much to build Banc One, then called City National Bank. After John H.'s death in 1958, John G. became president and CEO; upon John G.'s retirement in 1984, John B. became president and eventually chair in 1987.

John B. McCoy is people-oriented and genuinely interested in watching people grow. However, when queried about his thoughts regarding people who made mistakes, the outspoken McCoy responded, "You learn from mistakes, not from successes, so hold up your hand and tell us. . . . But if you have a problem, and don't tell, and it's a disaster, it's your ass. . . ."

INFORMATION SHARING

A key to Banc One's ability to control and evaluate its decentralized operation is through a Management Information and Control System (MICS). When an affiliate is brought into Banc One's structure, MICS is installed to gather and evaluate the affiliate's data and report the data in the same manner for each entity. Individual and comparative financial results are provided. To ensure that information is timely, monthly updates and forecasts are prepared by local staff. In essence, affiliates share and compare data. The ultimate objective is "to be able to measure every aspect of our business across the company in exactly the same way for comparison purposes," said McCoy. Just as MICS measures every aspect of the affiliates' financial performance, similar systems are being developed to continually report sales and profitability of all products within each defined market. Accordingly, bank personnel in each of the offices can concentrate on fulfilling the financial needs of their customers with a broader menu of products and services. These changes require a level of selling skills not normally associated with the banking industry. Consequently, extensive sales training is now a significant element in personnel training and development.

With many firms attempting to cut costs by outsourcing some of their operational activities, CEO McCoy continues to improve and develop new technologies within the Banc One system. For example, through a seven-year alliance with Electronic Data Systems (EDS) in Dallas, Banc One installed parts of its Strategic Banking System (SBS) in its affiliates. SBS is a state-of-the-art, total-bank-operating system keyed to the customer, thus providing to each affiliate bank a total financial picture of customer relationships. SBS integrates Banc One's product profitability and household demographic systems and gives Banc One personnel (e.g., customer service representatives, loan officers, and new account managers) immediate access to relevant information for additional sales. McCoy described an example of building a loyal customer base: "If Mrs. Smith walks into a branch to make a checking deposit, a message will come up on the screen that prompts our service representative to offer her a credit card with a $5,000 limit. Because she's a longtime customer, a message will appear with an offer to waive the service fee for three years." Development costs for SBS exceeded $100 million, but EDS incurred the greater part of the cost and risk in developing SBS. EDS, however, retains the right to sell the system to other banks.

Perhaps most telling is Banc One's commitment over the past 28 years to allocate annually three percent of its profits to technology research and development. Banc One is known as the technology bank. As a Kidder Peabody vice president commented, "I've never heard a bank say they were determined to spend a certain amount of their income stream on R&D and have it turn out to such advantage."

CEO McCoy works at keeping things simple and predictable. Among his rules are to keep management in place when a bank is taken over because managers know the market better than anyone else, consolidate back-office functions, and never buy a bank more than one-third the size of the corporation. "That way, if the deal turns out to be a bust," he says, "it won't drag down the entire bank."

CREDIT QUALITY

Banc One's 1997 Annual Report noted that nonperforming assets as a percent of total loans were at .49 percent compared with .47 percent in 1996; Banc One ended 1997 with $409 million in nonperforming loans. Another $150 million in loans were delinquent 90 days or more, so the total of severely problematic loans was $559 million for 1997. This was up from $484 million in 1996.

Banc One expects to continue to concentrate on retail and on small- and middle-market business lending in the market areas served by its affiliates. "We do not actively seek large, national credit relationships and consequently have only 16 relationships in excess of $50 million," says McCoy. Further, Banc One's marketing emphasis in credit cards has shifted to higher-quality cards. The bank recognizes that gross yields may decline but anticipates that corresponding lower loss rates and lower delinquency ratios will result in higher profit margins.

BRANCH DELIVERY SYSTEM

While the long-term future of branch banking may be questionable, Banc One still considers the branch banking network a critical element in its ability to retain and attract new customers. Banc One takes the position that the branch banking office will continue to be transformed to meet the changing needs of its customers. This transformation includes increasing ease of access and focused product offerings. "Ease of access" means closer proximity or expanded hours of operation, and "focused products" suggests that all products may not be offered at every branch location. For instance, Banc One offices in grocery stores have high check-cashing activity but little loan activity. Thus, branches should be configured to provide relevant transaction services.

Banc One has been experimenting with seven-day-a-week banking in selected markets. About half of the 300 offices offering seven-day-a-week service are freestanding, and the remainder are located in supermarkets, hospitals, employment centers, recreational areas, retail stores, manufacturing plants, retirement homes, and distribution centers. In addition, Banc One has a branch office on almost every college campus in the markets they serve. The strategy is to develop a constant stream of new customers and convince them to continue to bank with Banc One as they start their careers.

A uniform Banc One product line now is offered in all markets. The uniform products are designed to offer more options, including lower fees for self-service customers, and to provide customers across the country with consistent features and benefits. In addition, customers will be able to access their accounts from any location.

Customers already can access their accounts at any time of the day or night, thanks to the creation of two national call centers in 1996. One is located in Houston, Texas, and the other in Tempe, Arizona. Both provide 24-hour customer service every day of the year. The centers replaced the 21 locations of the former retail system.

Banc One's focus is fine-tuning its delivery system for nontraditional banking services through existing banking offices. These services are offered through the "personal investment centers" (PICS) marketing umbrella. The PICS are focal points for product information and for closing sales. They are staffed with licensed professionals who can offer an expanded product line to branch banking customers. The approximately 800 PICS in existing bank offices offer the full range of nontraditional bank financial services in close proximity to products offered through the traditional branch network. The nontraditional services include brokerage services, bank-managed and other mutual funds, and selected insurance products.

Banc One and affiliates have amassed a branching network augmented by ATMs that places the bank's distribution system as one of the largest in the nation.

STRUCTURE

Banc One Corporation is structured into four strategic business units (SBUs): Banc One Commercial Banking Group, Banc One Retail Group, Finance One Group, and Banc One Capital Holdings Group.

Banc One Commercial Banking Group

Bank One Commercial Banking Group focuses on providing customers a broad spectrum of loan and lease products.

Banc One Retail Group

Banc One Retail Group is the only banking organization in the United States to have ATMs in all 50 states.

Now a part of the Retail Group, First USA, Inc., was a financial services company specializing in the bank card business and was the fourth-largest among domestic Visa and MasterCard issuers, with $22.4 billion in managed receivables and 16 million cardholders. The combination of First USA's operations with Banc One's 16 million cardholders and $12.6 billion in managed receivables produced the nation's third-largest card operation; it had 40.5 million cardholders and assets of $40.8 billion at year-end 1997.

Finance One Group

Finance One Group has the nation's fastest-growing, largest, and most profitable non-bank finance companies. Finance One has developed profitable markets far beyond the 12 states where Banc One offices are located. Finance One does business nationwide, managing $28 billion in assets with more than 3,000 employees in 33 states.

Finance One's Consumer Financial Services Division, with $7.2 billion in assets, focuses primarily on home improvement and education loans.

Finance One's Indirect Financial Services Division provides financing services to dealers, including loans and leases to their customers, as well as financing of their inventories. The division manages $17.6 billion of assets. The majority of these assets are auto-related but also include loans originated through marine, recreational vehicle, aircraft, and home improvement dealers.

Finance One's Commercial Financial Services Division principally is involved in leasing equipment to middle-market customers, large corporations, and municipalities. The division manages over $2.8 billion in assets.

Finance One's Banc One Mortgage Corporation focuses on refinancing homes and had a portfolio of more than $20 billion at year-end 1997.

Banc One Capital Holdings Group

Banc One Corporation long has been noted for its expertise in retail and middle-market banking. Recent initiatives in nitch markets include middle-market corporate banking; merchant and investment banking; mortgage banking; and bank card, trust, and cash management services. These markets are being developed to complement the affiliate network and distribution system.

Banc One Capital Corporation has demonstrated an ability to assist corporate bankers in expanding rather than replacing their relationships. Banc One Capital Corporation staff has grown from 25 in 1989 to more than 300 as of 1997.

A part of this Group, The One Group® Family of Mutual Funds continued its growth and reputation as one of the premier mutual fund families in the nation. In 1996, The One Group grew to $15.4 billion in assets managed, an increase of 41 percent from 1995. This outstanding growth was due to a 275 percent increase in sales of The One Group by the retail distribution channel.

AFFILIATION PHILOSOPHY

The Federal Deposit Insurance Corporation indicates that it is likely that the pace of consolidation in the banking industry will continue into the next century. Banc One expects the consolidation trend to continue and to be a participant. Although there were over 9,300 banks in the United States in late 1997, the top 25 controlled 60 percent of the assets and had 50 percent of the deposits.

Banc One offers the observation that many banks it will acquire over the next several years will have been active acquirers in their own right in the recent past. With full interstate banking initiated, this process likely will accelerate. It is reasonable to assume that less than 50 banks will control more than three-fourths of all the banking assets in the country.

Banc One plans to continue building banking franchises in each of the markets it serves. Its clear objective is to be one of the top three banking companies in terms of market share in all significant markets served by the corporation. It continues to affiliate with banks in geographic areas where it can meet that goal. Banc One plans to continue expansion both in new areas as well as filling in markets where it currently has banks. Thus, Banc One's affiliation philosophy remains unchanged. It plans to build the franchise "one bank at a time" and evolve the affiliation procedure to the point that it adds to both earnings and shareholder value. Banc One will affiliate with banks in attractive markets and will continue to promote considerable autonomy and provide centralized support for operations and technology, thus enhancing the affiliates' ability to serve customers.

Banc One seeks to establish a "meaningful presence"—defined as the first, second, or third share of the market—in the major markets that it serves. Consistent with this strategy, Banc One sold an affiliate bank with assets of $124 million in Fresno, California, which Banc One acquired in its 1994 affiliation with Arizona's Valley National Corporation. Banc One also sold its four banks in Michigan to Citizens Banking Corporation. The Michigan banks were acquired in 1987 and 1988 and ranked eleventh in the state with assets of $672 million.

THE FUTURE

As indicated in Exhibit 2, Banc One's net income per share and total book value declined sharply in 1997, yet Banc One's long-term borrowings nearly doubled to $11 billion. See Exhibit 3 and 4 for other financial data. Some analysts contend that Banc One's structure as described herein and newly formed in 1997 is ineffective.

Prepare a three-year strategic plan for Banc One. Include specific recommendations regarding Banc One's expansion into nontraditional bank financial services. Do you feel that Banc One's vision statement (see Exhibit 5), organizational structure, and operating philosophy will be adequate to sustain a multibillion-dollar corporate giant well into the future? Include an acquisition plan in your recommendations to CEO McCoy.

EXHIBIT 2: **Banc One Corporation, Five-Year Performance Summary**[a]
(unaudited)

(millions, except ratios and per share data)	1997	1996	1995	1994	1993	Annual Growth 1997/96	Comp. Growth 5 years
Income and expense:							
Total gross revenue	$ 13,219.1	$ 12,099.1	$10,363.3	$ 8,761.5	$ 8,194.1	9.26%	10.05%
Net interest income[b]	5,446.0	5,201.8	4,330.6	4,499.0	4,560.1	4.69	5.23
Noninterest income	3,835.9	3,362.9	2,775.4	1,851.9	1,788.7	14.07	18.52
Noninterest expense	6,048.8	5,062.0	4,326.9	4,164.3	3,894.9	19.49	10.43
Net income	1,305.7	1,672.8	1,445.2	1,188.1	1,272.0	(21.95)	6.60
Per common share data:							
Net income, basic	2.04	2.60	2.26	1.82	2.05	(21.54)	5.24
Net income, diluted	1.99	2.52	2.20	1.80	2.04	(21.03)	4.99
Cash dividends declared	1.38	1.24	1.13	1.03	.88	11.29	13.27
Book value	15.89	16.93	15.54	15.01	13.90	(6.14)	.25
Balance sheet:							
Loans and leases	82,052.8	79,389.7	68,417.9	65,483.5	59,102.0	3.35	9.17
Managed loans and leases	115,548.8	103,434.5	88,003.6	76,901.0	63,610.5	11.71	16.07
Deposits	77,414.3	74,223.0	69,273.4	70,836.8	68,236.0	4.30	2.90
Long-term borrowings	11,066.4	6,827.8	4,330.5	2,938.6	2,292.2	62.08	42.72
Total assets	115,901.3	112,153.5	97,888.8	95,283.4	89,496.9	3.34	6.63
Operating ratios:							
Return on average assets	1.16%	1.59%	1.54%	1.28%	1.53%		
Net interest margin[b, c]	5.41	5.45	5.08	5.33	6.11		
Noninterest income to expense[d]	62.47	66.10	64.19	50.87	45.62		
Efficiency ratio[e]	65.57	59.22	60.87	62.93	61.46		

[a] All share and per share amounts have been restated to reflect common stock dividends.
[b] Fully taxable equivalent basis (FTE).
[c] As a percent of average earning assets.
[d] Excluding securities transactions.
[e] Noninterest expense divided by net interest income (FTE) plus noninterest income excluding securities transactions.

continued

EXHIBIT 2: *continued*

(millions, except ratios and per share data)	1997	1996	1995	1994	1993	Annual Growth 1997/96	Comp. Growth 5 years
Equity ratios:							
Return on average common equity	13.33%	17.83%	17.26%	14.73%	18.17%		
Average common equity to average assets	8.64	8.85	8.81	8.56	8.31		
Long-term borrowings to common equity	108.06	70.67	49.20	36.72	30.57		
Credit quality:							
Net charge-offs to average loans and leases^f	1.35	1.08	.71	.57	.79		
Ending allowance to loans and leases^f	1.62	1.51	1.47	1.47	1.74		
Nonperforming assets to total loans and leases^f	.56	.54	.62	.71	1.06		
Loans delinquent 90 days or more to total loans and leases^f	.66	.60	.44	.30	.39		
Common stock data:							
Average shares outstanding, basic	632.4	632.5	626.2	639.9	610.8		
Average shares outstanding, diluted	655.7	664.3	657.1	658.8	624.0		
Common shares traded, as originally reported	475.1	227.8	179.0	242.7	163.3		
Stock price, year-end	$49.37	$39.09	$31.10	$20.97	$29.40	26.30%	9.10%
Stock splits and dividends	0	10%	0	10%	5:4		
Dividend payout ratio	61.35%	37.96%	39.59%	44.46%	34.17%		

^{f} Includes loans held for sale.
Source: Banc One Corporation, *Annual Report* (1997): 24.

EXHIBIT 3: Consolidated Balance Sheet at December 31, 1997, and 1996

(millions, except per share amounts)	December 31, 1997	December 31, 1996
Assets:		
Cash and due from banks	$ 7,727.4	$ 6,524.4
Short-term investments	838.3	680.7
Loans held for sale	2,362.0	1,473.8
Securities:		
Securities held to maturity	785.3	4,397.9
Securities available for sale	14,467.9	14,733.8
Total securities (fair value approximates $15,268.0 and $19,163.2 at December 31, 1997, and 1996, respectively)	15,253.2	19,131.7
Loans and leases (net of unearned income of $2,013.7 and $1,383.3 and allowance for credit losses of $1,325.9 and $1,197.7 at December 31, 1997, and 1996, respectively)	80,726.9	78,192.0
Other assets:		
Bank premises and equipment, net	1,882.2	1,799.2
Interest earned, not collected	821.3	782.1
Other real estate owned	66.6	53.0
Excess of cost over net assets of affiliates purchased	741.8	508.4
Other	5,481.6	3,008.2
Total other assets	8,993.5	6,150.9
Total assets	$115,901.3	$112,153.5
Liabilities:		
Deposits:		
Noninterest-bearing	$ 18,444.2	$ 16,340.6
Interest-bearing	58,970.1	57,882.4
Total deposits	77,414.3	74,223.0
Federal funds purchased and repurchase agreements	10,708.2	12,858.5
Other short-term borrowings	3,095.7	5,466.9
Long-term debt	11,066.4	6,827.8
Accrued interest payable	489.7	468.6
Other liabilities	2,751.0	2,440.7
Total liabilities	105,525.3	102,285.5
Commitments and contingencies		
Stockholders' equity:		
Preferred stock, 35,000,000 shares authorized:		
Series C convertible, no par value, 2,707,917 and 4,140,314 shares issued and outstanding at December 31, 1997, and 1996, respectively	135.4	207.0
Convertible preferred stock of pooled affiliate, 5,750,000 shares issued and outstanding at December 31, 1996		.1
Common stock, no par value, $5 stated value, 950,000,000 shares and 600,000,000 shares authorized at December 31, 1997, and 1996, respectively; 645,956,436 and 576,517,822 shares issued at December 31, 1997, and 1996, respectively (December 31, 1997, shares reflect the 10% stock dividend payable.)	3,229.8	2,882.6
Capital in excess of aggregate stated value	6,718.7	4,346.4
Retained earnings	239.8	2,625.1
Net unrealized holding gains on securities available for sale, net of tax	121.0	19.9

continued

EXHIBIT 3: *continued*

(millions, except per share amounts)	December 31, 1997	December 31, 1996
Treasury stock (1,421,331 and 5,829,915 shares, at December 31, 1997, and 1996, respectively), at cost	(68.7)	(213.1)
Total stockholders' equity	10,376.0	9,868.0
Total liabilities and stockholders' equity	$115,901.3	$112,153.5

Source: Adapted from Banc One Corporation, *Annual Report* (1997): 53.

EXHIBIT 4: Consolidated Statement of Income, 1995–1997

(millions, except per share amounts)	1997	1996	1995
Interest income:			
Loans and leases	$8,128.7	$7,437.9	$6,393.0
Securities:			
Taxable	986.0	1,127.2	973.4
Tax-exempt	80.2	94.9	116.7
Loans held for sale	139.2	39.5	32.9
Other	49.1	36.7	71.9
Total interest income	9,383.2	8,736.2	7,587.9
Interest expense:			
Deposits:			
Demand, savings and money market deposits	1,124.4	1,006.2	922.3
Time deposits	1,420.7	1,454.0	1,504.1
Borrowings	1,445.8	1,137.4	910.4
Total interest expense	3,990.9	3,597.6	3,336.8
Net interest income	5,392.3	5,138.6	4,251.1
Provision for credit losses	1,211.1	942.7	526.1
Net interest income after provision for credit losses	4,181.2	4,195.9	3,725.0
Noninterest income:			
Investment management and advisory activities	315.5	279.1	239.4
Service charges on deposit accounts	702.4	654.1	544.7
Loan processing and servicing income	1,802.2	1,453.3	1,425.6
Securities gains (losses)	57.0	16.7	(2.0)
Other	958.8	959.7	567.7
Total noninterest income	3,835.9	3,362.9	2,775.4
Noninterest expense:			
Salary and related costs	2,367.5	2,204.6	1,875.6
Net occupancy expense, exclusive of depreciation	209.9	192.1	175.1
Equipment expense	133.7	125.2	110.5
Depreciation and amortization	458.3	447.5	367.4
Outside services and processing	859.1	674.2	528.3
Marketing and development	712.9	445.9	424.9
Communication and transportation	427.6	378.4	324.7

continued

EXHIBIT 4: *continued*

(millions, except per share amounts)	1997	1996	1995
Other	542.5	594.1	520.4
Restructuring charges	337.3	0	0
Total noninterest expense	6,048.8	5,062.0	4,326.9
Income before income taxes	1,968.3	2,496.8	2,173.5
Provision for income taxes	662.6	824.0	728.3
Net income	1,305.7	1,672.8	1,445.2
Net income per common share (amounts reflect the 10% common stock dividend):			
Net income per common share, basic	2.04	2.60	2.26
Net income per common share, diluted	1.99	2.52	2.20

Source: Adapted from Banc One Corporation, *Annual Report* (1997): 54.

EXHIBIT 5:   Vision Statement

Corporate Vision

**"We will settle for nothing less than to be a national leader in
providing financial services to the people and businesses of America.
We are committed to the relentless pursuit of ideas that enable
those we serve to prosper and achieve their goals."**

The Guiding Principles
We are driven by:

The Customer
*To do what's right for
the customer.*

Extraordinary Goals
Aim for the "impossible" – exceed the expected.

A Commitment to Our People
*Having the best, making them
the best through support,
recognition and reward.*

Teamwork
*Every individual wins when
Banc One wins.*

Simplicity
*To succeed, we must be easy
to do business with.*

Ethics
*Integrity. Honesty. Respect
for the individual.*

Source: Banc One Corporation, *Annual Report* (1997): inside front cover.

Citicorp—1998

Fred David

www.citicorp.com
stock symbol CCI

Citicorp (212-559-4822) is a bank-holding company and the sole shareholder of Citibank, N.A., the largest bank in the United States. Citibank has more credit card customers around the world (56 million) than any other bank. Citibank has relationships with one in five U.S. households (Citicorp 1997 *Annual Report*, p. 11). Citibank recently purchased AT&T's Universal Card business and is placing minibranches in Blockbuster Video stores. Citicorp had 93,700 employees at year-end 1997, including 54,800 persons outside of the United States. These employees work in over 3,000 locations in 98 countries and territories worldwide.

Citibank truly is the most global bank in the world, having significant banking market share and offices in 19 Latin American countries that generated $1.7 billion in Global Consumer Banking division revenues in 1997; in 13 European countries that generated $2.9 billion; in 10 Central and Eastern Europe, Middle East, and African countries that generated $0.3 billion; and in 13 Asia Pacific countries that generated $2.1 billion. Citibank's North American Global Consumer revenues were $8.0 billion in 1997 as indicated in Exhibit 1. But Citicorp generates more revenues and more net income from its other division—Global Corporate Banking. As indicated in Exhibit 2, Citicorp's Global Corporate Banking revenues outside of North America were highest in Latin America, Europe, and Japan.

But all is not well with Citicorp, whose return on total stockholders' equity dropped from 18.95 in 1996 to 17.10 in 1997, and whose total net income dropped from $3.8 billion to $3.6 billion. Citicorp's net income to average assets fell from 1.40 in 1996 to 1.22 in 1997 as indicated in Exhibit 3. Economic trouble in Asia in late 1997 and 1998 are hurting Citicorp's net income further.

EXHIBIT 1:   Global Consumer Locations, Revenues, Loans, Accounts, and Branches—1997

(in billions of dollars for revenue and loans)	Countries	Revenue	Loans	Accounts	Branches
North America[a]	2	$8.0	$87.8	35.6	380
Europe	13	$2.9	$16.7	8.1	464
Latin America	19	$1.7	$ 9.3	4.9	166
Central and Eastern Europe, Middle East, Africa	10	$0.3	$ 1.4	1.3	21
Asia Pacific[b]	13	$2.1	$23.2	6.2	93

[a] Revenues and loans are adjusted for the effect of credit card receivables securitization.
[b] Includes Japan.
Source: www.freeedgar.com

This case was prepared by Professor Fred David of Francis Marion University, as a basis for class discussion. It is not intended to illustrate either effective or ineffective handling of an administrative situation. Copyright © 1999 by Prentice Hall, Inc. ISBN 0-13-011135-X.

EXHIBIT 2: Global Corporate Banking Revenues, by Product, Region

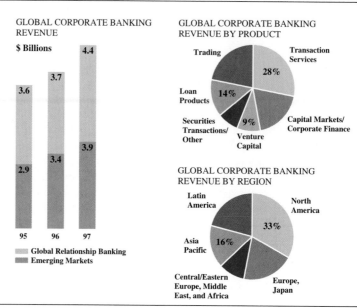

GLOBAL CORPORATE BANKING REVENUE

GLOBAL CORPORATE BANKING REVENUE BY PRODUCT

GLOBAL CORPORATE BANKING REVENUE BY REGION

Source: www.freeedgar.com

EXHIBIT 3: Citicorp in Brief

(in millions of dollars except per share data)	1997	1996	1995	1994	1993
Net Income—Before Accounting Changes	$ 3,591	$ 3,788	$ 3,464	$ 3,422	$ 1,919
Net Income—After Accounting Changes	3,591	3,788	3,464	3,366	2,219
NET INCOME PER SHARE					
Basic					
Before Accounting Changes	$ 7.53	$ 7.73	$ 7.60	$ 7.84	$ 4.26
After Accounting Changes	7.53	7.73	7.60	7.69	5.05
Diluted					
Before Accounting Changes	7.33	7.43	6.50	6.40	3.54
After Accounting Changes	7.33	7.43	6.50	6.29	4.13
Dividends Declared Per Common Share	2.10	1.80	1.20	0.45	0
As a Percentage of Income, Assuming Dilution, After Accounting Changes	28.65%	24.23%	18.46%	7.15%	0
AT YEAR END					
Total Loans, Net of Unearned Income and Allowance for Credit Losses	$178,197	$169,109	$160,274	$147,265	$134,588
Total Assets	310,897	281,018	256,853	250,489	216,574
Total Deposits	199,121	184,955	167,131	155,726	145,089
Long-Term Debt	19,785	18,850	18,488	17,894	18,160
Common Stockholders' Equity	19,293	18,644	16,510	13,582	10,066
Total Stockholders' Equity	21,196	20,722	19,581	17,769	13,953

continued

EXHIBIT 3: *continued*

(in millions of dollars except per share data)	1997	1996	1995	1994	1993
Tier 1 Capital	21,096	19,796	18,915	16,919	13,388
Total Capital (Tier 1 and Tier 2)	31,156	28,870	27,725	26,119	23,152
FINANCIAL RATIOS					
Net Income to Average Assets	1.22	1.40	1.29	1.29	0.97
Return on Common Stockholders' Equity	18.11	20.35	20.80	25.81	21.06
Return on Total Stockholders' Equity	17.10	18.95	18.33	21.43	17.72
Average Common Stockholders' Equity to Average Assets	6.46	6.60	5.59	4.47	3.95
Average Total Stockholders' Equity to Average Assets	7.12	7.40	7.03	6.02	5.48
Common Stockholders' Equity to Assets	6.21	6.63	6.43	5.42	4.65
Total Stockholders' Equity to Assets	6.82	7.37	7.62	7.09	6.44
Tier 1 Capital Ratio	8.34	8.39	8.41	7.80	6.62
Total Capital Ratio (Tier 1 and Tier 2)	12.31	12.23	12.33	12.04	11.45
Leverage Ratio	7.01	7.42	7.45	6.67	6.15
SHARE DATA					
Year End Stock Price	$ 126⁷⁄₁₆	$ 103	$ 67¼	$ 41³⁄₈	$ 36⁷⁄₈
Common Equity Per Share	42.50	40.25	38.64	34.38	26.04
EARNINGS ANALYSIS					
Total Revenue	$ 21,616	$ 20,196	$ 18,678	$ 16,748	$ 16,075
Effect of Credit Card Securitization Activity	1,713	1,392	917	934	1,282
Net Cost to Carry	(5)	(46)	23	89	252
Capital Building Transactions	0	0	0	(80)	2
ADJUSTED REVENUE	23,324	21,542	19,618	17,691	17,611
Total Operating Expense	13,987	12,197	11,102	10,256	10,615
Net OREO Benefits (Costs)	72	44	105	(9)	(245)
Restructuring Charges	(889)	0	0	0	(425)
ADJUSTED OPERATING EXPENSE	13,170	12,241	11,207	10,247	9,945
OPERATING MARGIN	10,154	9,301	8,411	7,444	7,666
Global Consumer Credit Costs	3,538	3,115	2,473	2,338	2,740
Global Corporate Banking Credit (Bene-fits) Costs	(95)	(87)	72	239	1,036
OPERATING MARGIN LESS CREDIT COSTS	6,711	6,273	5,866	4,867	3,890
Additional Provision	100	200	281	336	603
Restructuring Charges	889	0	0	0	425
Capital Building Transactions	0	0	0	80	(2)
INCOME BEFORE TAXES AND CUMULATIVE EFFECTS OF ACCOUNTING CHANGES	5,722	6,073	5,585	4,611	2,860
Income Taxes	2,131	2,285	2,121	1,189	941
INCOME BEFORE CUMULATIVE EFFECTS OF ACCOUNTING CHANGES	3,591	3,788	3,464	3,422	1,919
Cumulative Effects of Accounting Changes	0	0	0	(56)	300
Net Income	$ 3,591	$ 3,788	$ 3,464	$ 3,366	$ 2,219

Source: www.freeedgar.com

STRUCTURE

Citicorp is structured into two major groups—Global Consumer and Global Corporate Banking.

Citicorp's Global Consumer Division

Citicorp's Global Consumer division focuses on serving individuals through credit and charge cards and traditional banking operations. This division earned $1.6 billion in 1997, down 6 percent from 1996, excluding restructuring charges. Net income for this division fell from $2.0 billion in 1996 to $1.6 billion in 1997 as indicated in Exhibit 4.

EXHIBIT 4: Citicorp's Financial Summary

Business Focus	Net Income (Loss) $ millions			Average Assets $ billions			Return on Assets		
	1997	1996	1995	1997	1996	1995	1997	1996	1995
Global Consumer	$1,553	$2,028	$1,963	$132	$126	$120	1.18%	1.61%	1.64%
Global Corporate Banking	2,390	2,161	1,760	156	139	144	1.53	1.55	1.22
Core Businesses	3,943	4,189	3,723	288	265	264	1.37	1.58	1.41
Corporate Items	(352)	(401)	(259)	7	5	5	NM	NM	NM
Total Citicorp	$3,591	$3,788	$3,464	$295	$270	$269	1.22	1.40	1.29
Supplemental Information Global Consumer									
Citibanking	$ 478	$ 723	$ 573	$ 85	$ 83	$ 80	0.56%	0.87%	0.72%
Cards	764	1,024	1,164	31	27	25	2.46	3.79	4.66
Private Bank	311	281	226	16	16	15	1.94	1.76	1.51
Total	$1,553	$2,028	$1,963	$132	$126	$120	1.18	1.61	1.64
Global Consumer Businesses in:									
Emerging Markets	$ 819	$ 933	$ 801	$ 42	$ 38	$ 35	1.95%	2.46%	2.29%
Developed Markets	734	1,095	1,162	90	88	85	0.82	1.24	1.37
Total	$1,553	$2,028	$1,963	$132	$126	$120	1.18	1.61	1.64
Global Corporate Banking Emerging Markets	$1,559	$1,436	$1,132	$ 72	$ 60	$ 50	2.17%	2.39%	2.26%
Global Relationship Banking	831	725	628	84	79	94	0.99	0.92	0.67
Total	$2,390	$2,161	$1,760	$156	$139	$144	1.53	1.55	1.22

Source: www.freeedgar.com

Citicorp's Global Consumer division total revenues are provided in Exhibit 5. Note that total revenues increased slightly in 1997 but operating expenses increased dramatically. This division of Citicorp is further divided into three operating units—Citibanking, Cards, and Private Bank. Citibanking is the company's worldwide branch network and electronic delivery systems. Cards are the company's massive credit card operations and sales. Private Bank provides personalized wealth management services for the high net-worth clients. Exhibits 6, 7, and 8 summarize Citibanking, Cards, and Private Bank operations respectively for 1997 and the two years prior. Note that for 1997, Citibanking's net income dropped to $478 million from $723 million the prior year, while Cards' net income declined to $764 million from $1 billion the prior year, and Private Bank's net income increased to $311 million from $281 million.

EXHIBIT 5: Global Consumer's Financial Summary

(in millions of dollars)	1997	1996[a]	1995[a]
Total Revenue	$12,350	$12,113	$11,436
Effect of Credit Card Securitization Activity	1,713	1,392	917
Net Cost to Carry Cash-Basis Loans and OREO	(2)	(10)	12
ADJUSTED REVENUE	14,061	13,495	12,365
Total Operating Expense	8,271	7,302	6,816
Net OREO Benefits (Costs)[b]	4	(5)	0
Restructuring Charge	(580)	0	0
ADJUSTED OPERATING EXPENSE	7,695	7,297	6,816
Operating Margin	6,366	6,198	5,549
Net Write-offs	1,831	1,728	1,544
Effect of Credit Card Securitization Activity	1,713	1,392	917
Net Cost to Carry and Net OREO (Benefits) Costs	(6)	(5)	12
CREDIT COSTS	3,538	3,115	2,473
OPERATING MARGIN LESS CREDIT COSTS	2,828	3,083	3,076
Additional Provision	100	200	200
Restructuring Charge	580	0	0
INCOME BEFORE TAXES	2,148	2,883	2,876
Income Taxes	595	855	913
NET INCOME	$ 1,553	$ 2,028	$ 1,963
Average Assets (in billions of dollars)	$ 132	$ 126	$ 120
Return on Assets	1.18%	1.61%	1.64%
Excluding Restructuring Charge			
Income	$ 1,904	$ 2,028	$ 1,963
Return on Assets	1.44%	1.61%	1.64%

[a] Reclassified to conform to the 1997 presentation.
[b] Includes amounts related to writedowns, gains and losses on sales, and direct expense related to OREO for certain real estate lending activities.
Source: www.freeedgar.com

EXHIBIT 6:   Global Consumer Citibanking's Financial Summary

(in millions of dollars)	1997	1996[a]	1995[a]
Total Revenue	$6,030	$5,796	$5,441
Total Operating Expense	4,790	4,129	3,831
Restructuring Charge	(457)	0	0
ADJUSTED OPERATING EXPENSE	4,333	4,129	3,831
Operating Margin	1,697	1,667	1,610
Credit Costs	567	634	706
OPERATING MARGIN LESS CREDIT COSTS	1,130	1,033	904
Additional Provision	0	4	42
Restructuring Charge	457	0	0
INCOME BEFORE TAXES	673	1,029	862
Income Taxes	195	306	289
NET INCOME	$ 478	$ 723	$ 573
Average Assets (in billions of dollars)	$85	$83	$80
Return on Assets	0.56%	0.87%	0.72%
Excluding Restructuring Charge			
Income	$ 753	$ 723	$ 573
Return on Assets	0.89%	0.87%	0.72%

[a] Reclassified to conform to the 1997 presentation.

EXHIBIT 7:   Global Consumer Cards' Financial Summary

(in millions of dollars)	1997	1996[a]	1995[a]
Total Revenue	$5,190	$5,274	$5,066
Effect of Credit Card Securitization Activity	1,713	1,392	917
ADJUSTED REVENUE	6,903	6,666	5,983
Total Operating Expense	2,729	2,482	2,352
Restructuring Charge	(95)	0	0
ADJUSTED OPERATING EXPENSE	2,634	2,482	2,352
Operating Margin	4,269	4,184	3,631
Net Write-offs	1,277	1,090	814
Effect of Credit Card Securitization Activity	1,713	1,392	917
CREDIT COSTS	2,990	2,482	1,731
OPERATING MARGIN LESS CREDIT COSTS	1,279	1,702	1,900
Additional Provision	100	196	158
Restructuring Charge	95	0	0
Income Before Taxes	1,084	1,506	1,742
Income Taxes	320	482	578
NET INCOME	$ 764	$1,024	$1,164
Average Assets (in billions of dollars)	$ 31	$ 27	$ 25
Return on Assets	2.46%	3.79%	4.66%

continued

EXHIBIT 7: *continued*

(in millions of dollars)	1997	1996[a]	1995[a]
Excluding Restructuring Charge			
Income	$ 822	$1,024	$1,164
Return on Assets[b]	2.65%	3.79%	4.66%

[a] Reclassified to conform to the 1997 presentation.
[b] Adjusted for the effect of credit card securitization, the return on managed assets for worldwide Cards was 1.45% in 1997, 1.92% in 1996, and 2.40% in 1995.
Source: www.freeedgar.com

EXHIBIT 8: Global Consumer Private Bank's Financial Summary

(in millions of dollars)	1997	1996[a]	1995[a]
Total Revenue	$1,130	$1,043	$929
Net Cost to Carry Cash-Basis Loans and OREO	(2)	(10)	12
ADJUSTED REVENUE	1,128	1,033	941
Total Operating Expense	752	691	633
Net OREO Benefits (Costs)[b]	4	(5)	0
Restructuring Charge	(28)	0	0
ADJUSTED OPERATING EXPENSE	728	686	633
Operating Margin	400	347	308
Net (Recoveries) Write-offs	(13)	4	24
Net Cost to Carry and Net OREO (Benefits) Costs	(6)	(5)	12
CREDIT (BENEFITS) COSTS	(19)	(1)	36
OPERATING MARGIN LESS CREDIT COSTS	419	348	272
Restructuring Charge	28	0	0
INCOME BEFORE TAXES	391	348	272
Income Taxes	80	67	46
NET INCOME	$ 311	$ 281	$226
Average Assets (in billions of dollars)	$ 16	$ 16	$ 15
Return on Assets	1.94%	1.76%	1.51%
Excluding Restructuring Charge			
Income	$ 329	$ 281	$226
Return on Assets	2.06%	1.76%	1.51%

[a] Reclassified to conform to the 1997 presentation.
[b] Includes amounts related to writedowns, gains and losses on sales, and direct expense related to OREO for certain real estate lending activities.
Source: www.freeedgar.com

Citicorp's Global Consumer division also reports revenues and income geographically, with Developed Markets referring to North America, Europe, and Japan, whereas Emerging Markets refers to all other geographic areas of the world. Exhibit 9 reveals 1997 financial data geographically as generated by the Global Consumer division of Citicorp. Note that Global Consumer's total net income declined dramatically in Developed Markets and declined less in Emerging Markets.

EXHIBIT 9:   Global Consumer Businesses in Developed and Emerging Markets

(in millions of dollars)	Developed Markets[a]			Emerging Markets[a]		
	1997	1996[b]	1995[b]	1997	1996[b]	1995[b]
Total Revenue	$8,540	$8,478	$8,318	$3,810	$3,635	$3,118
Effect of Credit Card Securitization Activity	1,713	1,392	917	0	0	0
Net Cost to Carry Cash-Basis Loans and OREO	(2)	(10)	12	0	0	0
ADJUSTED REVENUE	10,251	9,860	9,247	3,810	3,635	3,118
Total Operating Expense	5,880	5,242	5,093	2,391	2,060	1,723
Net OREO Benefits (Costs)[c]	4	(5)	0	0	0	0
Restructuring Charge	(449)	0	0	(131)	0	0
ADJUSTED OPERATING EXPENSE	5,435	5,237	5,093	2,260	2,060	1,723
Operating Margin	4,816	4,623	4,154	1,550	1,575	1,395
Net Write-offs	1,463	1,371	1,247	368	357	297
Effect of Credit Card Securitization Activity	1,713	1,392	917	0	0	0
Net Cost to Carry and Net OREO Costs	(6)	(5)	12	0	0	0
CREDIT COSTS	3,170	2,758	2,176	368	357	297
OPERATING MARGIN LESS CREDIT COSTS	1,646	1,865	1,978	1,182	1,218	1,098
Additional Provision	49	185	170	51	15	30
Restructuring Charge	449	0	0	131	0	0
INCOME BEFORE TAXES	1,148	1,680	1,808	1,000	1,203	1,068
Income Taxes	414	585	646	181	270	267
NET INCOME	$ 734	$1,095	$1,162	$ 819	$ 933	$ 801
Average Assets (in billions of dollars)	$ 90	$ 88	$ 85	$ 42	$ 38	$ 35
Return on Assets	0.82%	1.24%	1.37%	1.95%	2.46%	2.29%
Excluding Restructuring Charge						
Income	$1,003	$1,095	$1,162	$ 901	$ 933	$ 801
Return on Assets	1.11%	1.24%	1.37%	2.15%	2.46%	2.29%

[a] Developed markets comprise activities in North America, Europe, and Japan. Emerging markets comprises activities in all other geographic areas.
[b] Reclassified to conform to the 1997 presentation.
[c] Includes amounts related to writedowns, gains and losses on sales, and direct expense related to OREO for certain real estate lending activities.
Source: www.freeedgar.com

Citicorp's Global Corporate Banking Division

Citicorp's Global Corporate Banking division focuses on serving corporations, financial institutions, governments, investors, and others with banking products. This division had revenues of $8.3 billion in 1997, up $1.1 billion or 16 percent over 1996 levels. This division's net income increased from $2.2 billion in 1996 to $2.4 billion in 1997.

Exhibit 10 summarizes Citicorp's Global Corporate Banking division financial results for 1997 and the two years prior. Note that this division's return on assets dropped to 1.53 percent from 1.55 percent a year earlier. This division of Citicorp is not further divided except into Developed Markets and Emerging Markets. Exhibit 11 summarizes the Global Corporate Banking division operations in Emerging Markets in 1997.

EXHIBIT 10: Global Corporate Banking Financial Summary

(in millions of dollars)	1997	1996[a]	1995[a]
Total Revenue	$8,272	$7,188	$6,522
Net Cost to Carry Cash-Basis Loans and OREO	(3)	(36)	11
ADJUSTED REVENUE	8,269	7,152	6,533
Total Operating Expense	5,213	4,418	3,946
Net OREO Benefits	68	49	105
Restructuring Charge	(281)	0	0
ADJUSTED OPERATING EXPENSE	5,000	4,467	4,051
Operating Margin	3,269	2,685	2,482
Net (Recoveries) Write-offs	(24)	(2)	166
Net Cost to Carry and Net OREO Benefits	(71)	(85)	(94)
CREDIT (BENEFITS) COSTS	(95)	(87)	72
OPERATING MARGIN LESS CREDIT (BENEFITS) COSTS	3,364	2,772	2,410
Additional Provision	0	0	81
Restructuring Charge	281	0	0
INCOME BEFORE TAXES	3,083	2,772	2,329
Income Taxes	693	611	569
NET INCOME	$2,390	$2,161	$1,760
Average Assets (in billions of dollars)	$ 156	$ 139	$ 144
Return on Assets	1.53%	1.55%	1.22%
Excluding Restructuring Charge			
Income	$2,558	$2,161	$1,760
Return on Assets	1.64%	1.55%	1.22%

[a] Reclassified to conform to the 1997 presentation.
Source: www.freeedgar.com

EXHIBIT 11: Global Corporate Banking Emerging Markets Financial Data

(in millions of dollars)	1997	1996[a]	1995[a]
Total Revenue	$3,888	$3,444	$2,895
Net Cost to Carry Cash-Basis Loans and OREO	15	3	14
ADJUSTED REVENUE	3,903	3,447	2,909
Total Operating Expense	2,018	1,696	1,393
Net OREO Benefits	0	4	7
Restructuring Charge	(54)	0	0
ADJUSTED OPERATING EXPENSE	1,964	1,700	1,400
Operating Margin	1,939	1,747	1,509
Net Write-offs (Recoveries)	56	(3)	26
Net Cost to Carry and Net OREO Costs (Benefits)	15	(1)	7
CREDIT COSTS (BENEFITS)	71	(4)	33
OPERATING MARGIN LESS CREDIT COSTS (BENEFITS)	1,868	1,751	1,476
Additional Provision	0	0	(19)
Restructuring Charge	54	0	0
INCOME BEFORE TAXES	1,814	1,751	1,495
Income Taxes	255	315	363
NET INCOME	$1,559	$1,436	$1,132
Average Assets (in billions of dollars)	$ 72	$ 60	$ 50
Return on Assets	2.17%	2.39%	2.26%
Excluding Restructuring Charge			
Income	$1,591	$1,436	$1,132
Return on Assets	2.21%	2.39%	2.26%

[a] Reclassified to conform to the 1997 presentation.
Source: www.freeedgar.com

FINANCIAL SUMMARY

Citicorp's consolidated statement of income and consolidated balance sheet is provided in Exhibits 12 and 13. Note that total net income declined to $3.6 billion. Even consumer loans declined in 1997 to $108 billion from $111 billion in 1996, while the company's long-term debt increased to $19.8 billion.

CONCLUSION

Citicorp wants to expand aggressively around the world through acquisition and merger. The banking industry domestically is consolidating rapidly. The Eurodollar is expected to become a reality in Europe soon and Citicorp wants to provide global banking leadership for this event. Citicorp expects Asian economies to rebound in 1998 and 1999 and would like to be positioned to provide banking leadership in these parts of the world as well.

Prepare a three-year strategic plan for Chief Executive Officer John Reed. Include two large competitor banks that you feel Citicorp should try to acquire to keep pace with banking consolidation nationally and, indeed, globally.

EXHIBIT 12: Consolidated Statement of Income

(in millions of dollars except per share amounts)	1997	1996	1995
Interest Revenue			
Loans, including Fees	$18,967	$18,509	$17,808
Deposits with Banks	995	858	770
Federal Funds Sold and Securities Purchased Under Resale Agreements	872	902	1,056
Securities, including Dividends	2,197	1,770	1,544
Trading Account Assets	1,012	1,310	1,785
Loans Held For Sale	440	0	0
	24,483	23,349	22,963
Interest Expense			
Deposits	9,613	8,974	8,902
Trading Account Liabilities	310	313	300
Purchased Funds and Other Borrowings	1,814	1,775	2,379
Long-Term Debt	1,344	1,347	1,431
	13,081	12,409	13,012
NET INTEREST REVENUE	11,402	10,940	9,951
PROVISION FOR CREDIT LOSSES	1,907	1,926	1,991
NET INTEREST REVENUE AFTER PROVISION FOR CREDIT LOSSES	9,495	9,014	7,960
Fees, Commissions, and Other Revenue			
Fees and Commissions	5,817	5,469	5,165
Foreign Exchange	1,486	864	1,053
Trading Account	241	637	559
Securities Transactions	668	210	132
Other Revenue	2,002	2,076	1,818
	10,214	9,256	8,727
Operating Expense			
Salaries	5,286	4,880	4,445
Employee Benefits	1,331	1,364	1,281
Total Employee Expense	6,617	6,244	5,726
Net Premises and Equipment Expense	1,961	1,843	1,698
Restructuring Charge	889	0	0
Other Expense	4,520	4,110	3,678
	13,987	12,197	11,102
INCOME BEFORE TAXES	5,722	6,073	5,585
INCOME TAXES	2,131	2,285	2,121
NET INCOME	$ 3,591	$ 3,788	$ 3,464
INCOME APPLICABLE TO COMMON STOCK	$ 3,451	$ 3,631	$ 3,126
Earnings Per Share			
BASIC	$ 7.53	$ 7.73	$ 7.60
DILUTED	$ 7.33	$ 7.43	$ 6.50

Source: www.freeedgar.com

EXHIBIT 13:   Consolidated Balance Sheet

(in millions of dollars)	December 31, 1997	December 31, 1996
ASSETS		
Cash and Due from Banks	$ 8,585	$ 6,905
Deposits at Interest with Banks	13,049	11,648
Securities, at Fair Value		
Available for Sale	30,762	26,062
Venture Capital	2,599	2,124
Trading Account Assets	40,356	30,785
Loans Held for Sale	3,515	—
Federal Funds Sold and Securities Purchased		
Under Resale Agreements	10,233	11,133
Loans, Net		
Consumer	108,066	111,847
Commercial	75,947	62,765
Loans, Net of Unearned Income	184,013	174,612
Allowance for Credit Losses	(5,816)	(5,503)
Total Loans, Net	178,197	169,109
Customers' Acceptance Liability	1,726	2,077
Premises and Equipment, Net	4,474	4,667
Interest and Fees Receivable	3,288	3,068
Other Assets	14,113	13,440
TOTAL	$310,897	$281,018
LIABILITIES		
Non-Interest-Bearing Deposits in U.S. Offices	$ 16,901	$ 14,867
Interest-Bearing Deposits in U.S. Offices	40,361	40,254
Non-Interest-Bearing Deposits in Offices Outside the U.S.	9,627	9,891
Interest-Bearing Deposits in Offices Outside the U.S.	132,232	119,943
Total Deposits	199,121	184,955
Trading Account Liabilities	30,986	22,003
Purchased Funds and Other Borrowings	21,231	18,191
Acceptances Outstanding	1,826	2,104
Accrued Taxes and Other Expense	6,464	5,992
Other Liabilities	10,288	8,201
Long-Term Debt	19,785	18,850
STOCKHOLDERS' EQUITY		
Preferred Stock (Without par value)	1,903	2,078
Common Stock ($1.00 par value)	506	506
Issued Shares: 506,298,235 in each period		
Surplus	6,501	6,595
Retained Earnings	16,789	14,303
Net Unrealized Gains—Securities Available for Sale	535	676
Foreign Currency Translation	(626)	(486)
Common Stock in Treasury, at Cost	(4,412)	(2,950)
Shares: 52,355,947 in 1997 and 43,081,217 in 1996		
Total Stockholders' Equity	21,196	20,722
TOTAL	$310,897	$281,018

Source: www.freeedgar.com

Audubon Zoo—1997

Caroline Fisher
Claire J. Anderson

www.auduboninstitute.org

Audubon Zoo (504-861-2537) was the focus of national concern in the early 1970s following the publication of well-documented stories of animals kept in conditions which were variously termed an "animal ghetto,"[1] "the New Orleans antiquarium," and even "an animal concentration camp."[2] In 1971, the Bureau of Governmental Research recommended a $5.6 million zoo improvement plan to the Audubon Park Commission and the City Council of New Orleans. The local *Times-Picayune* commented on the new zoo: "It's not going to be quite like the 'Planet of the Apes' situation in which the apes caged and studied human beings but something along those broad general lines."[3] The new zoo confined people to bridges and walkways while the animals roamed amidst grass, shrubs, trees, pools, and fake rocks. The gracefully curving pathways, generously lined with luxuriant plantings, gave the visitor a sense of being alone in a wilderness, although crowds of visitors might be only a few yards away.

Although the physical surroundings were vastly improved, operating a successful zoo would take much more than that. Could the Audubon Zoo develop a strategy that would help it grow and become profitable? How would the economic and political climate affect its efforts? The New Orleans web site at www.neworleans.net offers up-to-date information about the demographic area surrounding Audubon Zoo.

BEGINNINGS

The Audubon Park Commission launched a $5.6 million development program, based on the Bureau of Governmental Research plan for the zoo in 1972. After voters passed a bond issue and a property tax dedicated to the zoo by an overwhelming majority that November, serious discussions began about what should be done. The New Orleans City Planning Commission finally approved the master plan for the Audubon Park Zoo later that year. But the institution of the master plan was far from smooth.

Over two dozen special-interest groups ultimately were involved in choosing whether to renovate/expand the existing facilities or move to another site. Expansion became a major community controversy. Some residents opposed zoo expansion, fearing "loss of green space" would affect the secluded character of the neighborhood. Others opposed the loss of what they saw as an attractive and educational facility.

Most of the opposition came from the zoo's affluent neighbors. Zoo Director John Moore ascribed the criticism to "a select few people who have the money and power to make a lot of noise." He went on to say, "[T]he real basis behind the problem is that the neighbors who live around the edge of the park have a selfish concern because they want the park as their private back yard."[4] Legal battles over the expansion plans continued until early 1976. Then, the 4th Circuit Court of Appeals ruled that the expansion was legal.[5] An out-of-court agreement with the zoo's neighbors followed shortly.

Expansion of the Audubon Park Zoo took it from 14 to 58 acres. The zoo was laid out in geographic sections: the Asian Domain, World of Primates, World's Grasslands, Savannah, North American Prairie, South American Pampas, and Louisiana Swamp, according to the Zoo Master Plan developed by the Bureau of Governmental Research. Additional exhibits included the Wisner Discovery Zoo, Sea Lion exhibit, and Flight Cage. See Exhibit 1 for a map of the zoo.

The main outward purpose of the Audubon Park Zoo is entertainment. Many promotional efforts of the zoo are aimed at creating an image of the zoo as an entertaining place to go. Such a campaign is necessary to attract visitors to the zoo. Behind the scenes, the zoo preserves and breeds many animal species, conducts research, and educates the public. The mission statement of the Audubon Institute, the parent organization of the zoo, is given in Exhibit 2.

A chronology of major events in the life of the Audubon Zoo is given in Exhibit 3. One of the first significant changes made was the institution of an admission charge in 1972. Admission to the zoo had been free to anyone prior to the adoption of the renovation plan. Ostensibly, the initial purpose behind instituting the admission charge was to prevent vandalism,[6] but the need for additional income also was apparent. Despite the institution of and increases in admission charges, admissions increased dramatically in the next two decades (see Exhibit 4).

Admission Policy

The commission recommended the institution of an admission charge. Arguments generally advanced against such a charge held that it results in an overall decline in attendance and a reduction of nongate revenues. Proponents held that gate charges control vandalism, produce greater revenues, and result in increased public awareness and appreciation of the facility. In the early 1970s, no major international zoo failed to charge admission, and 73 percent of the 125 United States zoos charged admission.

The commission argued that there is no such thing as a free zoo; someone must pay. If the zoo is tax-supported, then locals carry a disproportionate share of the cost. At the time, neighboring Jefferson Parish was growing steadily in size and surely would bring a large, nonpaying constitution to the new zoo. Further, as most zoos are tourist attractions, tourists should pay because they contribute little to the local tax revenues.

The average yearly attendance for a zoo may be estimated using projected population figures multiplied by a "visitor generating factor." The average visitor generating factor of 14 zoos similar in size and climate to the Audubon Zoo was 1.34, with a rather wide range from a low of .58 in the cities of Phoenix and Miami to a high of 2.80 in Jackson, Mississippi.

EXHIBIT 1:   Audubon Zoo

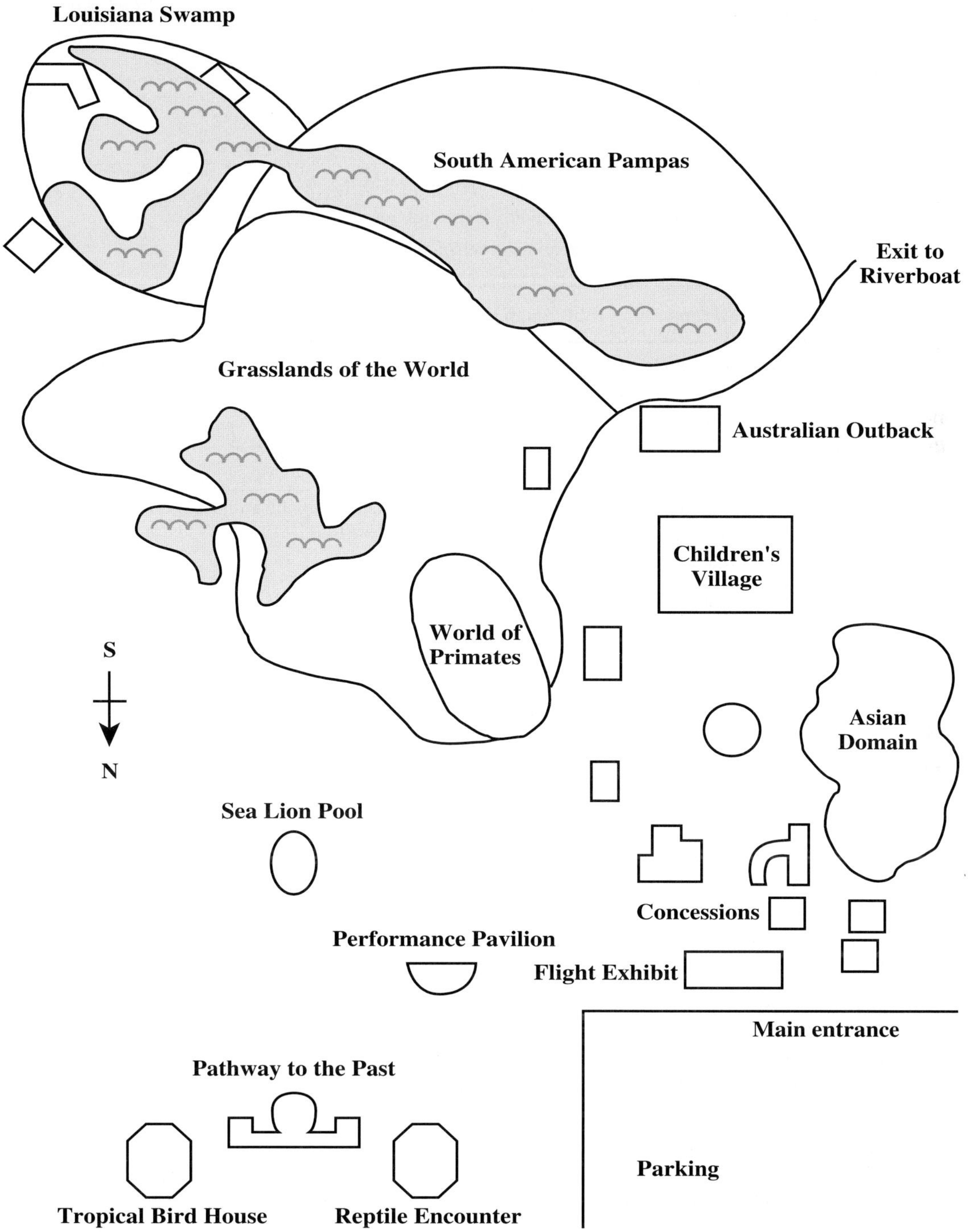

Louisiana Swamp

South American Pampas

Exit to Riverboat

Grasslands of the World

Australian Outback

Children's Village

S

World of Primates

Asian Domain

N

Sea Lion Pool

Concessions

Performance Pavilion

Flight Exhibit

Main entrance

Pathway to the Past

Parking

Tropical Bird House   **Reptile Encounter**

Source: Audubon Zoo Institute, 1997.

EXHIBIT 2:   Audubon Institute Mission Statement

The Audubon Institute is a family of museums and parks dedicated to nature and unified with a purpose of celebrating life through nature. Its mission is to:

- provide a guest experience of outstanding quality;
- exhibit the diversity of wildlife;
- preserve native Louisiana habitats;
- educate our diverse audience about the natural world;
- enhance the care and survival of wildlife through research and conservation;
- provide opportunities for recreation in natural settings;
- operate a financially self-sufficient collection of facilities; and
- weave quality entertainment through the guest experiences.

Source: The Audubon Institute, 1997.

EXHIBIT 3:   Chronology of Events for the Zoo

1972	Voters approved a referendum to provide tax dollars to renovate and expand the zoo. The first Zoo-To-Do was held. An admission charge was instituted.
1974	Friends of the Zoo formed to increase support of the zoo.
1975	Renovations began with $25 million public and private funds; 14 acres to be expanded to 58 acres.
1976	The Friends of the Zoo assumed responsibility for concessions.
1977	Ron Forman took over as park and zoo director.
1980	Last animal removed from antiquated cage—a turning point in zoo history.
1981	Contract signed allowing New Orleans Steamboat Company to bring passengers from downtown to the park.
1981	Zoo accredited, and delegates from the American Association of Zoological Parks Aquariums ranked the Audubon Zoo as one of the top three zoos of its size in America.
1985	The zoo was designated as a Rescue Center for Endangered and Threatened Plants.
1986	Voters approved a $25 million bond issue for the Aquarium.
1988	The Friends of the Zoo became The Audubon Institute.
1990	The Aquarium of the Americas (Phase I) opened in September.
1993	The Freeport-McMoRan Audubon Species Survival Center (FMASSC) was dedicated in December.
1994	The Audubon Institute assumed responsibility of the Louisiana Nature and Science Center through a merger with the Society for Environmental Education.
1995	The Entergy IMAX® Theatre (Phase II) opened in early October.
1996	The Audubon Institute for Research of Endangered Species (ACRES) opened.
1996	*Butterflies in Flight* exhibit opened with free-flying tropical butterflies and birds sharing the same garden as they do in nature.
1997	*Komodo Dragons* exhibit opened.

Source: The Audubon Institute, 1997.

EXHIBIT 4: Admissions for Zoo

Year	Number of Paid Admissions	Number of Member Admissions
1975	324,000	N/A
1980	707,000	N/A
1985	856,064	145,020
1990	725,469	219,668
1991	634,396	191,771
1992	699,772	176,936
1993	727,775	187,225
1994	637,007	182,993
1995	820,597	175,432
1996	782,804	149,419
1997	833,819[a]	120,550

Admission Charges

Year	Adult	Child/Senior
1975	$ .75	$ .25
1980	2.00	1.00
1985	4.50	2.00
1990	6.50	3.00
1991	7.00	3.25
1992	7.00	3.25
1993	7.50	3.50
1994	7.75	3.75
1995	7.75	3.75
1996	8.00	4.00
1997	8.00	4.00

[a] projected; N/A—Not applicable
Source: The Audubon Institute, 1997.

BUILDING REVENUES

The Friends of the Zoo was formed in 1974 and incorporated in 1975 with 400 original members. The stated purpose of the Friends was to increase support and awareness of the Audubon Park Zoo. Initially, the Friends of the Zoo tried to increase interest and commitment to the zoo, but its activities increased over the following years to involvement in funding, operating, and governing the zoo.

The Friends of the Zoo has a 24-member governing board. Yearly elections are held for six members of the board who serve four-year terms. The board oversees policies of the zoo and sets guidelines for memberships, concessions, fund raising, and marketing. However, actual policy making and operations are controlled by the Audubon Park Commission, which sets zoo hours, admission prices, and so forth.

Through its volunteer programs, Friends of the Zoo staff many of the zoo's programs. Volunteers from members of the Friends of the Zoo serve as "edZOOcators"; as education volunteers who were specially trained to conduct interpretive education programs; and as "Zoo Area Patrollers," who provide general information about geographic areas of the zoo and help with crowd control. Other volunteers assist in the Commissary, Animal Health Care Center, and Wild Bird Rehabilitation Center, or help with such endeavors as membership, public relations, graphics, clerical work, research, and horticulture.

Fund Raising

The Audubon Park Zoo and the Friends of the Zoo raise funds through five major types of activities: Friends of the Zoo membership, concessions, Adopt An Animal, Zoo-To-Do, and capital fund drives. Zoo managers from around the country come to the Audubon Park Zoo for tips on fund raising.

Membership

Membership in the Friends of the Zoo is open to anyone. The membership fees increased over the years, as summarized in Exhibit 5. The number of members increased steadily, from the original 400 members in 1974 to 38,000 members in 1990, but after the formation of the Friends of the Aquarium in 1990, declined to 28,000 in 1992. In 1994, the 1-2-3 Program was started whereby people could become members of the zoo, the aquarium, the Learning Center, any combination of two, or all three. Exhibit 6 shows the resulting membership patterns.

Membership allows free entry to the Audubon Park Zoo and many other zoos around the United States. Participation in Zoobilation (annual members-only evenings at the zoo) and the many volunteer programs described earlier are other benefits of membership.

Increasing membership had required a special approach to marketing the zoo. Chip Weigand, director of marketing for the zoo, stated,

> . . . [I]n marketing memberships we try to encourage repeat visitations, the feeling that one can visit as often as one wants, the idea that the zoo changes from visit to visit, and that there are good reasons to make one large payment or donation for a membership card, rather than paying for each visit. . . . [T]he overwhelming factor is a good zoo that people want to visit often, so that a membership makes good economical sense.

Results of research conducted on visitors to the zoo are contained in Exhibit 7. Customer satisfaction was found to be high in all areas. The average age of the visitors is 40, and the visitors' favorite exhibits are the Primates, Swampland, and Asian Domain.

In 1985, the zoo announced a new membership group designed for businesses, the Audubon Zoo Curator Club, with four categories of membership: Bronze, $250; Silver, $500; Gold, $1,000; and Platinum, $2,500 and more.

EXHIBIT 5:   Zoo Memberships and Fees

Year	Family Fee	Individual Fee	Total Memberships
1980	$20	$10	7,000
1985	40	20	27,000
1990	49	29	38,154
1991	49	30	30,171
1992	49	30	30,015
1993	55	35	30,208
1994	59	39	22,507
1995	59	39	25,082
1996	59	39	26,632
1997	59	39	26,716

Source: The Audubon Institute, 1997.

EXHIBIT 6:   1-2-3 Program Memberships and Fees

	1996	1995	1994
Number of Family Memberships:			
Zoo only	8,669	8,767	12,425
Aqua only	789	983	2,236
LNC only	46	156	634
Zoo/Aqua	10,939	10,299	9,043
Zoo/LNC	77	76	111
Aqua/LNC	16	30	45
All 3	7,092	7,535	3,569
Total	27,628	27,846	30,063
Fee per Number of Locations Joined:			
1 location	$ 59	$ 59	$ 59
2 locations	89	89	89
3 locations	109	109	109

Source: The Audubon Institute, 1997.

EXHIBIT 7:   Audubon Zoo Visitor Exit Surveys, 1996

	1st Quarter	2nd Quarter
Satisfaction with Zoo		
value	4.6[a]	4.6
appeal	4.6	4.6
overall visit	4.7	4.8
educational experience	4.6	4.7
entertainment experience	4.8	4.5
Satisfaction with Zoo Staff		
exhibit staff courtesy	4.8	4.1
exhibit staff knowledge	4.8	4.4
gift shop courtesy	4.5	4.2
food courtesy	4.4	4.4
ticket office courtesy	4.6	4.4
Satisfaction with Facilities		
cleanliness	4.5	4.4
gift shop	4.3	4.0
parking	4.6	4.5
signs (inside)	4.6	4.6
signs (outside)	4.1	4.0
grounds	4.7	4.6
crowd size	4.4	4.4
food service	4.4	4.4

[a]Scale of 1–5 with 5 being highest
Source: The Audubon Institute, 1996.

Concessions

The Friends of the Zoo took over the Audubon Park Zoo concessions for refreshments and gifts in 1976, through a public bidding process. Concessions were run by volunteer members of the Friends of the Zoo, and all profits went directly to the zoo. Prior to 1976, concession rentals brought in $15,000 in a good year. Profits from operation of concessions by the Friends of the Zoo were $400,000 a year by 1980 and almost $700,000 in 1988. In 1993, the Friends of the Zoo considered leasing the concessions to a third-party vendor. This option was explored and partially occurred when the Audubon Institute allowed a McDonald's to be built on zoo premises in 1994.

Adopt An Animal

Zoo Parents pay a fee to "adopt" an animal, the fee varying with the animal chosen. Zoo Parents members' names are listed on a large sign inside the zoo. They also have their own celebration, Zoo Parents Day, held at the zoo every year.

Zoo-To-Do

Zoo-To-Do is a black-tie fund raiser held annually with live music, food and drink, and souvenirs such as posters or ceramic necklaces. Admission tickets, limited to 3,000 annually, are priced starting at $150 per person. A raffle is conducted in conjunction with the Zoo-To-Do, with raffle items varying from an opportunity to be Zoo Curator for the day to the use of a Mercedes-Benz for a year. Despite the rather stiff price, the Zoo-To-Do is a popular sellout every year. Local restaurants and other businesses donate most of the necessary supplies, decreasing the cost of the affair. In 1985, the Zoo-To-Do raised almost $500,000 in one night, more money than any other nonmedical fund raiser in the country.[7] The Zoo-To-Do continues to sell out annually and remains a major fund raiser as well as a great public relations event for the zoo.

Capital Fund Drives

The Audubon Zoo Development Fund was established in 1973. Corporate/industrial support of the zoo is very strong—many corporations underwrite construction of zoo displays and facilities. A sponsorship is considered to be for the life of the exhibit. The development department operates on a 12 percent overhead rate, which means 88 cents of every dollar raised goes towards the projects. The ability of the Audubon Institute (formed in 1988) to obtain corporate sponsorship is unprecedented and has achieved national recognition by other zoos.

Advertising

The Audubon Zoo launched impressive marketing campaigns in the 1980s. The zoo received ADDY awards from the New Orleans Advertising Club year after year.[8] In 1986, the film *Urban Eden*, produced by Alford Advertising and Buckholtz Productions, Inc., in New Orleans, finished first among 40 entries in the documentary films, public relations category of the 8th Annual Houston International Film Festival. The first-place Gold Award recognized the film for vividly portraying Audubon Zoo as a conservation, rather than a confinement, environment.

EXHIBIT 8: 1996 Marketing Budget

Advertising (includes media purchase, media production, agency fees)	$250,000
Events	183,000
News releases/Press kits	20,000
Research	3,000
Postage/Freight	16,000
Professional services, services, supplies, other	45,000
Total	517,000

Source: The Audubon Institute, 1997.

During the same year, local television affiliates of the ABC, CBS, and NBC networks produced independent TV spots using the theme "One of the World's Greatest Zoos Is in Your Own Back Yard . . . Audubon Zoo!" Along with some innovative views of the Audubon Zoo being in someone's "backyard," local news anchor personalities enjoyed "monkeying around" with the animals and the zoo enjoyed some welcome free exposure.[9]

In 1996, the marketing budget was over $500,000, including $250,000 for advertising and $183,000 for special events. Not included in this budget was developmental fund raising or membership. The marketing budget is shown in Exhibit 8.

The American Association of Zoological Parks and Aquariums reported that most zoos find the majority of their visitors live within a single population center in close proximity to the park.[10] Thus, in order to sustain attendance over the years, zoos must attract the same amount of visitors repeatedly. A large number of the Audubon Zoo's promotional programs and special events are aimed at just that.

Progress first was slow among non-natives. For example, Simon & Schuster, a reputable publishing firm, in its 218-page *Frommer's 1983-84 Guide to New Orleans* managed only a 3-word allusion to a "very nice zoo." A 1984 study found that only 36 percent of the visitors were tourists, and even this number probably was influenced to some extent by an overflow from the World's Fair.

Promotional Programs

The Audubon Park Zoo and the Friends of the Zoo conduct a number of very successful promotional programs. The effect is a calendar of events and celebrations that attract a variety of people to the zoo (and raise additional revenue). Exhibit 9 lists the major annual promotional programs conducted by the zoo.

EXHIBIT 9: Selected Audubon Park Zoo Promotional Programs

MONTH	ACTIVITY
March	Louisiana Black Heritage Festival. A 2-day celebration of Louisiana's African American history and its contributions through food, music, and arts and crafts.
March	Earth Fest. The environment and our planet are the focus of this fun-filled and educational event. Recycling, conservation displays, and puppet shows.
April	Jazz Search. This entertainment series is aimed at finding the best new talent in the area with the winners to be featured at the New Orleans's Jazz & Heritage Festival.

continued

EXHIBIT 9: *continued*

April	Zoo-To-Do for Kids. At this "pint-sized" version of the Zoo-To-Do, fun and games abound for kids.
May	Zoo-To-Do. Annual black-tie fund raiser featuring over 100 of New Orleans's finest restaurants and three music stages.
May	Mothers Day event held.
August	Lego Invitational. Architectural firms turn thousands upon thousands of Lego pieces into their own original creations.
October	Louisiana Swamp Festival. Cajun food, music, and crafts highlight this 4-day salute to Louisiana's bayou country; features hands-on contact with live swamp animals.
October	Boo at the Zoo. This annual Halloween extravaganza features games, special entertainment, trick or treat, a haunted house, and the Zoo's Spook Train.

Source: The Audubon Institute, 1997.

In addition to annual promotions, the zoo schedules concerts of well-known musicians—such as Irma Thomas, Pete Fountain, The Monkeys, and Manhattan Transfer—and other special events throughout the year. As a result, a variety of events occurs each month.

Many educational activities are conducted all year long. These include a Junior Zoo Keeper program for seventh and eighth graders; an intern program for high school and college students; and a ZOOmobile which takes live animals to such locations as special education classes, hospitals, and retirement homes. Learning Adventures for adults, children, and families are creatively designed and titled (e.g., Twilight Treks, Love After Hours, Families Great and Small, Critter Care, and Investigating Inverts).

Attracting Visitors

A riverboat ride on the romantic, paddle-wheel *Cotton Blossom* takes visitors from downtown to the zoo. Originally, the trip began at a dock in the French Quarter, but now it initiates at a dock immediately adjacent to New Orleans's newest attraction, the Riverwalk on the site of the 1984 Louisiana World Exposition. Not only is the riverboat ride great fun, but it also lures tourists and conventioneers from the downtown attractions of the French Quarter and the Riverwalk to the zoo, some 6 miles upstream. A further allure of the riverboat ride is the return trip on the New Orleans Streetcar, one of the few remaining trolley cars in the United States. The Zoo Cruise not only draws more visitors, but also generates additional revenue through landing fees paid by the New Orleans Steamboat Company, and keeps traffic out of uptown New Orleans.[11]

STAFF

The Zoo Director

Ron Forman, the Audubon Zoo director, was called a "zoomaster extraordinaire" and was described by the press as a "cross between Doctor Doolittle and the Wizard of Oz"; as a "practical visionary"; and as "serious, but with a sense of humor."[12] A native New Orleanian, Forman quit an MBA program to join the city government as an administrative assistant and found himself doing a business analysis project on the Audubon Park. Once the city was committed to a new zoo, Forman was placed on board as an assistant to the zoo director, John Moore. In early 1977, Moore gave up the battle between the "animal people"[13] and the "people people,"[13] and Forman took over as park and zoo director.

Forman was said to bring an MBA-meets-menagerie style to the zoo, which was responsible for transforming itself from a public burden into an almost completely self-sustaining operation. The result not only benefited the citizens of the city, but also added a major tourist attraction to the economically troubled city of the 1980s and 1990s.

The zoo's ability to generate operating funds has been ascribed to the dedication of the Friends of the Zoo, continuing increases in attendance, and creative special events and programs. A history of adequate operating funds allows the zoo to guarantee capital donors that their gifts will be used to build and maintain top-notch exhibits. A comparison of the 1995 and 1996 combined statements of operating income and expenses for the Audubon Institute is in Exhibit 10.

EXHIBIT 10:   Audubon Institute Statement of Operating Income and Expenses

(in thousands of dollars)	1996 Audubon Park & Zoo	1996 Total	1995 Audubon Park & Zoo	1995 Total
Operating Revenues				
Admissions	$3,071	$14,403	$2,932	$11,003
Food Services & Gift Shop	2,086	4,937	2,176	4,739
Membership Support	1,199	2,191	1,225	2,191
Recreational & Educational	969	1,138	1,250	1,919
Other	118	370	255	456
Total Revenues	7,443	22,947	7,838	20,308
Operating Expenses				
Curatorial	2,180	6,004	2,165	3,804
Maintenance & Facilities	2,108	5,187	1,889	4,406
Food Service & Gift Shop	1,318	2,695	1,523	2,722
Membership	441	745	491	790
Recreational & Educational	856	1,515	903	2,597
Marketing	933	2,792	699	1,527
Visitor Services & Volunteers	362	1,045	363	956
Administration	1,491	3,217	1,246	2,772
Fringe Benefits	765	1,692	816	1,533
Total Operating Expenses	10,454	24,891	10,095	21,107
Income (Loss) from Operations	(3,011)	(1,944)	(2,257)	(799)
Nonoperating Items				
Debt Service Funded by Operations	(25)	(1,696)	0	(1,207)
Dedicated Tax Millage	274	1,705	252	1,467
Interest/Endowment Income	40	1,054	40	877
Transfers	2,100	0	1,965	0
Fundraising transfer to Operations	660	1,326	0	465
Total	3,049	2,389	2,257	1,602
Excess (Deficit) of Revenue over Expenditures	38	445	(0)	803

Source: The Audubon Institute, *Annual Report* (1995); and *Annual Report* (1996).

EXHIBIT 11: Audubon Institute Employees and Volunteers as of 12-31-1996

Location	Employees	Volunteers	Hours
ACRES/FMASSC	12	0	0
Aquarium	278	356	60,518
Nature Center	38	91	14,855
Zoo	342	772	115,403

Source: The Audubon Institute, *Annual Report* (1996).

Employees

The zoo uses two classes of employees—civil service through the Audubon Park Commission, and non–civil service. The civil service employees include the curators and zoo keepers. They fall under the jurisdiction of the city civil service system, but are paid out of the budget of the Friends of the Zoo. Employees who work in public relations, advertising, concessions, fund raising, and so forth are hired through the Friends of the Zoo and are non–civil service. The zoo also depends upon a cadre of volunteers to keep it functioning smoothly. See Exhibit 11 for the breakdown between employees and volunteers in 1996.

A visitor to the new Audubon Zoo quickly can see why New Orleanians are so proud of their zoo. In a city termed among the dirtiest in the nation, the zoo is virtually spotless. This is a result of adequate staffing and the clear pride of both those who work at and those who visit the zoo. One of the first points made by volunteers guiding school groups is that anyone seeing a piece of trash on the ground must pick it up.[14] A 1986 city poll showed that 93 percent of the citizens surveyed gave the zoo a high approval rating—rare for a public facility.

Kudos come from groups outside the local area as well. Delegates from the American Association of Zoological Parks and Aquariums ranked the Audubon Zoo as one of the three top zoos of its size in America. In 1982, the American Association of Nurserymen gave the zoo a Special Judges Award for its use of plant materials. In 1985, the Audubon Park Zoo received the Phoenix Award from the Society of American Travel Writers for its achievements in conservation, preservation, and beautification.

Zoo Director Forman demonstrates that zoos have almost unlimited potential. His wealth of ideas is important because expanded facilities and programs are required to maintain attendance at any public attraction. Forman realizes that the zoo continually must be in a state of progression or change. Thus, he initiated a series of temporary exhibits ranging from *Earth Stalkers* (a dinosaur exhibit) to *Butterflies in Flight*. The most ambitious of Forman's ideas was that the city establish an aquarium and riverfront park.

EXPANSION OF THE AUDUBON INSTITUTE

The success of the new zoo inspired Forman and the Friends of the Zoo to explore future projects targeted at both area residents and tourists. In 1988, the Friends of the Zoo changed its name to the Audubon Institute to reflect its growing interest in activities beyond the zoo alone. The Audubon Institute planned to promote the development of facilities other than the zoo and to manage those facilities once they were established. The Audubon Institute sought to remain committed to preserving endangered wildlife and offering educational opportunities through development of such projects.

The Aquarium of the Americas

In 1986, Forman and a group of supporters proposed the development of an aquarium and riverfront park to the New Orleans City Council. In November 1986, the electorate approved it by a 70 percent margin—one of the largest margins the city ever gave to a tax proposal. Forman hailed the vote of confidence as a mandate to build a world-class aquarium that would produce new jobs, stimulate the local economy, and create an educational resource for the children of the city.[15]

The Aquarium of the Americas opened in 1990. The $40 million project, consisting of the 14-acre Woldenberg Park and the aquarium itself, provides a logical pedestrian link between the major attractions of the Riverwalk and the Jax Brewery, two shopping centers in the French Quarter. The facility is 110,000 square feet in size and includes five permanent exhibits: *Caribbean Reef, Amazon Rainforest, Mississippi River, Gulf of Mexico,* and *Living in Water.* Management of the aquarium is by the Audubon Institute.

A feasibility study prepared by Harrison Price Company[16] projected a probable 863,000 visitors by the year 1991, with 75 percent of the visitors coming from outside the metropolitan area. That attendance figure was reached in only 4 months and 6 days from the grand opening. Through 1992, attendance remained strong (1,407,051 visitors), after a slight drop from the initial grand opening figure. However, attendance in 1993 dropped by nearly 100,000 and in 1994 by a further 150,000. Yet, the aquarium still remains a profitable attraction, bringing in almost $2 million in operating revenues in 1996.

As he has advocated for the zoo, Forman keeps the aquarium constantly changing. He initiated several temporary exhibits, including the most popular, SHARKS! In 1995, the Aquarium of the Americas reached the 7 million attendance mark.[17]

Construction on the $25 million Phase II of the aquarium began in 1995 and was completed for the opening in 1996. The aquarium now includes a 10,000-square-foot Changing Exhibit Gallery with new tanks that afford 360-degree viewing, new species, and a variety of hands-on activities.

Preservation Projects

The Institute finished construction of the highly anticipated Entergy IMAX® Theatre in 1995 as part of Phase II. It was expected to receive 650,000 visitors and to earn a profit of $700,000 in its first year.[18] The IMAX Theatre, the largest of its kind in the Gulf area, has 354 seats and nearly a six-story-high screen. The Institute chose *The Living Sea,* an exotic journey through coral reefs and the depths of the Central Pacific, as its initial offering, and changes films every 3 to 5 months. It showed its first 3-D film in 1996. Admission cost $6.50 for adults and $4.50 for children in 1996, but a combo ticket for the IMAX Theatre and the aquarium is offered at a reduced price of $14 for adults and $9 for children.

Freeport-McMoRan Audubon Species Survival Center

The Institute designated the Westbank of New Orleans as the most appropriate site for their preservation projects. In 1993, the Freeport-McMoRan Audubon Species Survival Center was dedicated in conjunction with the U.S. Fish and Wildlife Service. The center provides endangered animals a refuge where they can breed and eventually boost their numbers. Located on a 1,200-acre site, the center initially housed the Mississippi sandhill crane and the Baird's tapir, and added other species as the center expanded.

Audubon Center for Research of Endangered Species

The Audubon Institute next constructed the Audubon Center for Research of Endangered Species to study advanced breeding techniques, animal behavior, and nutrition. In 1996 the institute opened a 36,000-square-foot building, which includes labs for reproduction, molecular genetics, cryogenics, and veterinary care. U.S. Sen. J. Bennett Johnston secured $19 million in federal funds for the Research Center, the first breeding center of its kind. The third part of the project is the Audubon Wilderness Park, which features an orientation center and hiking trails.

Louisiana Nature and Science Center

The institute reaffirmed its commitment to education and entertainment with the acquisition of the Louisiana Nature and Science Center. The Audubon Institute merged with the Society for Environmental Education in 1994 and assumed control of the 86-acre site. The stated purpose of the center is to provide ecological and environmental science programs to the entire community.

Parks

Over the years, the Audubon Institute acquired control over three park areas. Its original park, Audubon Park, is in the heart of uptown New Orleans, running from St. Charles Avenue to the Mississippi River. This 400-acre park includes over 4,000 live oak trees, gardens, lagoons, recreation areas, and a golf course.

The Woldenberg Riverfront Park is on the Mississippi River in the French Quarter. The Aquarium of the Americas and the IMAX Theatre are in this park. The park's 17 acres are landscaped with trees, shrubs, and brick pathways. Its Hibernia Pavilion is used for frequent open-air concerts, and its Great Lawn is the site of a variety of festivals.

The last addition to the Audubon Institute's parks is Wilderness Park, which opened in 1996. Wilderness Park's 129 acres feature an orientation center, hiking trails, and picnic areas (open to groups by advance booking). An interpretive center and naturalists facilitate the Audubon Institute's educational goals by teaching visitors to help south Louisiana's unique environment.

Riverfront 2000, proposed by Forman in the late 1980s, is almost fully achieved now, with the realization of the above-mentioned projects and facilities. However, Riverfront 2000 also had proposed constructing an insectarium in 1997 and a natural history museum soon after.

THE FUTURE

Although the Institute initiated many new and successful projects, the zoo was by no means relegated to the back burner. The zoo has its own plans for the future. A new animal hospital on zoo grounds was dedicated in 1996. Forman and his zoo staff continue to upgrade and create new exhibits. Plans involve the creation of a *Mezoamerica* exhibit in 1997, a Diefenthal Earth Lab, and a new *Elephant* exhibit.

EXHIBIT 12: A Few Facts about the New Orleans MSA

Population	1,317,600
Households	482,800
Median Household EBI	$27,968
Average Temperature	70 degrees Fahrenheit
Average Annual Rainfall	63 inches
Average Elevation	5 feet below sea level
Area	363.5 square miles
	199.4 square miles of land

Major Economic Activities: Tourism (10.1 million visitor per year); Oil and Gas Industry

Taxes:

State Sales Tax	4.0 percent
Parish (County) Sales Tax	5.0 percent (Orleans)
	4.0 percent (Jefferson)
State Income Tax	2.1–2.6 percent on first $20,000
	3.0–3.5 percent on next $30,000
	6.0 percent on $51,000 and over

Parish Property Tax of 126.15 mills (Orleans) is based on 10 percent of appraised value over $75,000 homestead exemption.

Source: Sales and Marketing Management, 1996; New Orleans Metropolitan Conventions and Visitations Bureau.

Forman holds the future of the zoo and the Audubon Institute in a tremendously optimistic light, considering the forces opposing them. The institute faces a rather weak New Orleans economic situation. (See Exhibit 12 for facts regarding the New Orleans area.) In addition, it operates in a city where many attractions compete for the leisure dollar of natives and tourists. It has to vie with the French Quarter, Dixieland Jazz, casinos, the Superdome, and the greatest attraction of all, Mardi Gras. Forman believes his once weak and now powerful Audubon Institute possesses the necessary message and facilities to forge successfully into the next millennium.

REFERENCES

1. Millie Ball, "The New Zoo of '82," *Dixie Magazine, Sunday Times Picayune* (June 24, 1979).
2. *Times-Picayune* (March 30, 1975).
3. *Times Picayune* (January 20, 1976).
4. *Times Picayune* (April 29, 1972).
5. *Jefferson Business* (August 1985).
6. Ibid.
7. *Advertising Age* (March 17, 1986).
8. Karen Sausmann (ed.), *Zoological Park and Aquarium Fundamentals* (Wheeling, W. Va: American Association of Zoological Park Zoological Parks and Aquariums, 1982): 111.

9. *Times Picayune* (November 30, 1981).

10. Steve Brooks, "Don't Say `No Can Do' to Audubon Zoo Chief," *Jefferson Business* (May 5, 1986).

11. Ross Yuchey, "No Longer Is Heard a Discouraging Word at the Audubon Zoo," *New Orleans* (August 1980): 53.

12. Ibid, 49.

13. *At the Zoo* (Winter 1987).

14. Feasibility Analysis and Conceptual Planning for a Major Aquarium Attraction, prepared for the City of New Orleans (March 1985).

15. Audubon Institute, *The Audubon Family Tree* (Summer 1995).

16. Audubon Institute, *Annual Report* (1993): [page number]; *Annual Report* (1994).

17. Stewart Yerton, "Force of Nature," *Times-Picayune* (October 1, 1995).

18. Paul A. Greenberg, "Forman: Education Main Audubon Institute Mission," *IMAX Theatre, The Times-Picayune.*

Riverbanks Zoological Park and Botanical Garden—1997

Carolyn R. Stokes

www.riverbanks.org

The Riverbanks Zoo and Garden (803-779-8717) is a 170-acre park located on the Lower Saluda River in Columbia, the capital of South Carolina. The complex is composed of the Riverbanks Zoo, with over 2,000 animals in natural habits, and the 70-acre Riverbanks Botanical Garden, which maintains woodlands, gardens, historic ruins, plant collections, and visitor facilities. The Riverbanks Zoo and Garden is a major attraction in the Southeast. Riverbank's admission receipts increased 1.4 percent for 1997 over 1996.

Riverbanks is recognized as one of the best zoos in America for conservation efforts and recreational activities, and has received numerous awards. Riverbanks is recognized as one of the top five zoos in North America with respect to support for the American Zoo and Aquarium Association (AZA) programs. The Aquarium Reptile Complex was named one of the top three new exhibits in the country by AZA in 1990. The zoo has received recognition for its captive breeding accomplishments. The zoo received the prestigious Governor's Cup Award from the South Carolina Chamber of Commerce in 1989 as the state's leading attraction, and in 1989 and 1993 was named the outstanding travel attraction of the year by the Southeast Tourism Association. In 1990, when more than 1 million people visited the zoo, Riverbanks was recognized as one of the 20 most-visited zoos in the United States. Riverbanks in the 1990s has approximately 850,000 visitors annually (see Exhibit 1) with 25 percent coming from outside the state.

Executive Director Palmer Krantz continues to move Riverbanks into the future, further developing current attractions and activities and adding new ones. The zoo is adding new animals and renovating, refurbishing, or supplying new habitats to some current residents. The Garden is planting new species and enhancing environments of some current species. Riverbanks is adding new attractions such as Jewels of the Sky and expanding others, such as the Lights Before Christmas display. All of these activities are in keeping with the mission (see Exhibit 2) of the Riverbanks Zoological Park and Botanical Garden, "to foster an appreciation and concern for all living things."

This case was prepared by Carolyn R. Stokes of Francis Marion University, as a basis for class discussion. It is not intended to illustrate either effective or ineffective handling of an administrative situation. Copyright © 1999 by Prentice Hall, Inc. ISBN 0-13-011139-2.

Carolyn R. Stokes

EXHIBIT 1: Riverbanks Zoo Attendance Analysis for the Month of June, 1997

Attendance

	June 1997	June 1996
Paid Attendance:		
Regular	35,992	39,784
Group	13,785	13,703
Total Paid	49,777	53,487
Free Attendance:		
Lex./Rich. School Groups	1,150	1,479
Riverbanks Society	23,322	22,053
Prepaid & Complimentary	3,597	4,144
Promotional—Free Friday's	816	0
Children under Three	6,028	6,143
Total Free	34,913	33,829
TOTAL MONTHLY ATTENDANCE	84,690	87,316

Attendance Statistics

	June 1997	June 1996	Budgeted for June
Number of Saturdays in the Month	4	5	4
Number of Sundays in the Month	5	5	5
Average Attend. on: Saturdays	4,355	5,296	5,111
Sundays	4,169	3,538	3,538
Weekdays	1,707	2,157	2,306
Inclement Weather Days:			
Saturdays	2	0	0
Sundays	0	0	0
Weekdays	0	0	0

Notes: 1) Inclement weather is defined as rain or daily high temp. 100F or above and below 50F, as recorded at the Zoo.
2) Average attendance excludes inclement weather days.
3) Weekday averages exclude holidays.

134

EXHIBIT 2: Riverbanks Mission Statement

It is our mission to foster appreciation and concern for all living things.
We are dedicated to providing:

- the highest standards of care for our animal and plant collections
- a diverse educational and high-quality recreational experience for all Riverbanks visitors
- all the resources at our disposal for the conservation of the earth's flora and fauna

DEVELOPMENT

For many years, citizens in Richland and Lexington Counties expressed concern over the need for a zoo in the community. In 1969, the General Assembly of South Carolina created Riverbanks with a Riverbanks Park Commission. Individuals, businesses, and local governments recognized the need and provided the necessary financial support and work for the establishment of Riverbanks. With government and private sectors working together, the zoo opened its gates to the public in 1974, and was named the most outstanding tax-supported attraction by the South Carolina Chamber of Commerce. In 1976, the private sector established the Riverbanks Society, a nonprofit organization dedicated to the support of Riverbanks and the preservation of the earth's flora and fauna. In 1981, Riverbanks was designated as a recipient of country tax millage from Richland and Lexington Counties, further solidifying the financial governmental support base.

In 1983, the Education Center opened to facilitate zoo educational programs to fulfill further the mission of Riverbanks by assisting in the understanding of and appreciation for animals. In 1988, the Farm was added to allow visitors the opportunity to see and learn more about farm animals. In 1988, the Kenya Cafe and the Elephant's Trunk Gift Shop were built to allow visitors better opportunities for refreshment and zoo-related gift purchases. In 1989, the award-winning Aquarium Reptile Complex was opened. In 1992, the zoo's African Plains section had a major renovation. The following year, Riverbanks Animal Health Center opened to fulfill further the mission of Riverbanks by providing a high level of health care. The Animal Health Center has facilities, equipment, and staff for varying levels of care, including surgery.

In 1993, construction on the Botanical Garden began on property joined to the zoo grounds by a new bridge over the Lower Saluda River. The new Botanical Garden on the left bank of the Saluda opened in 1995, with the name changing to the Riverbanks Zoological Park and Botanical Garden in 1995.

Riverbanks is governed by the Riverbanks Parks Commission, supported by the Riverbanks Society, and managed by the Riverbanks staff under the leadership of Palmer E. Krantz III, the executive director. Riverbanks is accredited by the American Association of Zoological Parks and Aquariums, and is a member of the American Association of Botanical Gardens and Arboreta. With about 122 employees and $5 million in annual revenues (see Exhibit 3), Riverbanks Zoological Park and Botanical Garden is one of the leading zoos in the country.

Carolyn R. Stokes

EXHIBIT 3: **Riverbanks Park Commission—General Fund Statement of Revenues, Expenditures and Changes in Fund Balance, For the Fiscal Year Ended June 30, 1997**

	1997	1996
Revenues		
Earned Revenues:		
Admissions Net Revenue	$1,924,982	$1,901,223
Ogden Concession Fees	593,264	521,341
Riverbanks Society Contribution	376,176	377,371
Other Revenues	548,216	446,570
Total Earned Revenues	3,442,638	3,246,505
Governmental Support:		
Richland County	801,007	666,000
Lexington County	642,000	492,373
State of South Carolina	182,989	182,989
Total Governmental Support	1,525,996	1,341,362
Total Revenues	4,968,634	4,587,867
Expenditures		
Administrative	773,575	674,022
Animal Care	1,602,207	1,475,968
Botanical	835,845	803,331
Education	156,227	150,075
Facility Management (including utilities)	1,393,808	1,338,994
Marketing	510,416	401,897
Total Expenditures	5,272,078	4,844,287
Excess (deficit) of Revenue over Expend.	(303,444)	(259,420)
Fund Equity—Beginning of Period	689,586	938,687
Fund Equity—End of Period	386,142	679,267

RIVERBANKS ZOO

The zoo uses a modern approach to exhibit design by housing wild animals in naturalistic settings preferable for both animal residents and human visitors. The naturalistic settings at Riverbanks enable animals to enjoy living more as they would in the wild, and visitors get to see the animals in a more realistic environment. At the Farm, some domesticated animals are exhibited in a barn and related settings so visitors can view them as they would on a working farm. The zoo is home to more than 2,000 animals, including 300 birds; 300 reptiles and amphibians; and 1,300 fish and invertebrates.

Major zoo attractions include the Aquarium Reptile Complex, an African Plains section, a Large Mammal Area, and a Birdhouse. The Aquarium Reptile Complex (ARC), with a 55,000-gallon aquarium, has four galleries featuring animals from South Carolina, the Desert, the Tropics, and the Pacific Ocean. The complex is innovative in the unique blending of the features of a reptile habitat with those of an aquarium.

The zoo's African Plains section features giraffes, zebras, and ostriches in a savannah setting complete with moats. The Large Mammal Area features elephants, tigers, lions, and polar bears. The 20,000-square-foot Birdhouse has a range of environments suitable for the various species in residence. At scheduled times during the day, there is a rainstorm in the Birdhouse.

Riverbanks Farm features a barn and barnyards with animals such as goats, cows, pigs, chickens, Belgian horses, and honey bees. Here, visitors can view chickens hatching from eggs and Riverbanks staff milking a cow. Visitors can view the feedings of many animals in all sections of the zoo.

In line with the mission of Riverbanks, the zoo participates in the Species Survival Plans (SSPs) of the AZA to ensure the survival of endangered species. Many zoos participate in the program. For example, in Texas, the Houston Zoological Gardens hatched two critically endangered species, the prairie chicken and the Hawaiian thrush. Riverbanks focuses on 23 endangered species, including the golden lion tamarin, Siberian tiger, palm cockatoo, Chinese alligator, and Bali mynah. Riverbanks has received awards for successfully breeding back howlers and white-faced sakis. Riverbanks has the honor of being the first zoo to breed in captivity two rare birds, the toco toucan and the crimson seedcracker, and the first zoo in the Western Hemisphere to breed milky eagle owls, blue-billed weavers, and cinereous vultures. Riverbanks has the only pair of cinereous vultures raising their own.

In 1996 through 1997, Riverbanks established a research department and hired a reproductive physiologist. Riverbanks's new COnservation REsearch Program (CORE) is generating reproductive databases of rare species to be used internationally in zoological and scientific communities. Riverbanks's serious interest in conservation research is demonstrated by its decision to host the first Southeastern Conservation Research Consortium. The conference will provide a forum to foster conservation-oriented collaborations among zoological institutions, wildlife agencies, and academic institutions. The consortium, conducted on June 4–6, 1998, gave presentations, panel discussions, tours, and special activities designed to promote conservation research. With its new research department, Riverbanks moves further toward the fulfillment of its mission.

THE BOTANICAL GARDEN

The Botanical Garden envisioned during the Riverbanks planning stages became feasible in the early 1990s. In 1993, following successful fund-raising programs, construction began, and on June 10, 1995, the Riverbanks Botanical Garden opened to the public. Visitors pass through the main entrance, proceed through a portion of the zoo, and then walk or ride a tram across a new bridge over the Saluda River on the way to the Botanical Garden. They enter through the Visitors Center, which provides guests with a shop for garden-related products, a cafe, a gallery, and multipurpose spaces for functions. Guests exit the rear of the Visitors Center into a walled garden with cascade and pinwheel fountains, and find exotic annuals, perennials, and bulbs complementing the permanent shrubbery and trees.

Beside the Garden is an amphitheater. It is terraced and grass-carpeted for seating, and has a large domed stage for cultural events such as a zoo ballet and educational programs. At the rear of the garden is the entrance to the woods, which has a walking trail. Here, visitors enjoy scenic river views and see the ruins of an historic mill. On the trail, visitors can view many trees, plants, flowers, and animals indigenous to the upper and lower parts of the state. The scenic trail in 1996 was featured on a program of *Nature Scene,* a nationally broadcast series originating at the educational television station in South Carolina.

In the Garden, a woodland log cabin was completed in 1998. This rough-hewn cabin located near the mill ruins will have exhibits to assist viewers in the interpretation of the mill ruins and the flora and fauna of the area. There will be an outdoor classroom for educational programs.

The Garden is a leading source of horticultural and botanical information in the area. Through a cooperative effort with Clemson Extension Service, the public can access information by talking with an extension agent or by using the Internet in the Visitors Center. The Garden also provides facilities for related activities. For example, the Bonsai show, held in the Visitors Center, permitted guests to see miniature trees and learn how to grow them.

A new entrance to the Garden is expected to open in 1999. This planned second entrance to the Riverbanks Zoological Park and Botanical Garden will be on the Lexington County side of the property. This west-side entrance should facilitate entrance to and increase the attendance of Riverbanks.

SPECIAL ATTRACTIONS

In 1987, Riverbanks began an event, Lights Before Christmas, with the holiday lighting of about 25 percent of the zoo. Now, 80 percent of the zoo is beautified in December with colorful lights along walkways, in trees, on shrubbery, and in other locations. At the entrance, visitors are greeted with lighted trees containing large stars and the sound of Christmas music. There are colorful lighted images of different animals, including a bear, lion, horse, deer, frog, rhino, pig, and fox. Some of the animals appear to be in motion. For example, there appears to be an elephant spraying water over his back and an ostrich running through the woods. Visitors on their way to the bridge pass under an arch artfully decorated with colorful lights, and can view numerous decorated trees and shrubs, as well as a group of frog figures that appear to be playing. On the sides of the bridge are images of icicles and stars. On the west river bank, visitors can view lovely images of colorful butterflies and flowers.

Riverbanks is one of a number of zoos that present attractions of this kind. The Winnipeg, Canada, Assiniboine Park Zoo, one of the coldest zoos in the world, features The Lights of the Wild and reindeer sleigh rides. The Fort Worth, Texas, zoo presents a Zoobilee of Lights that increases December attendance to 75,000.

In 1997, Riverbanks's Lights Before Christmas attracted over 70,000 visitors during the 28 evenings of the lights. Winter attractions are especially important to Riverbanks because two-thirds of its annual attendance of 850,000 occurs between April and August. Riverbanks's Lights Before Christmas 1997 attendance revenue was approximately $145,000. This event also generates revenue from concessions and additional memberships purchased.

With a million lights designed to depict animal and garden scenes, Riverbanks's Lights Before Christmas was named one of the Top Twenty Events in the Southeast by the Southeast Tourism Society, and as one of the Top 100 Events in North America by the American Bus Association in 1997.

EDUCATION DEPARTMENT

The Education Department, established in 1993, works to interpret animal exhibits and plants for visitors and to assist them in learning about the animal and plant worlds. Its primary facility is the Education Center, which has two classrooms, an auditorium, and a library. Other facilities available at Riverbanks for education programs include a classroom in the Aquarium Reptile Complex, another in the Riverbanks Farm, and the amphitheater outside the Botanical Garden. An outdoor classroom has been completed in the Garden Woodlands.

During the week, Riverbanks offers classes to groups ranging from preschool to college. On weekends and in the summer, Riverbanks offers classes and programs for students, scouts, teachers, and families. Programs include the Zoo Camp for overnight events, a one-week day camp for kindergarteners, and Wildlife in the Zoo for elementary school gifted classes. Annually, over 45,000 people participate in the educational programs.

FINANCING

The original construction, major renovations and expansions, and the annual operating budget have been funded by individuals, businesses, and government. The Riverbanks Zoological Park and Botanical Garden has an annual operating budget of over $5 million. Revenues from admissions and concession fees provide approximately 60 percent of the resources; funds from Richland and Lexington Counties and the state, as well as federal and city grants, provide approximately 30 percent; and the Riverbanks Society provides approximately 10 percent. Nationally, government provides approximately 54 percent of the support for zoos.

Riverbanks, a nonprofit organization, uses fund accounting to report its financial position and results of operations. The balance sheets for the year ending June 30, 1997, can be seen in Exhibit 4.

Operating revenues rose from $4.5 million in 1996 to $4.9 million in 1997. Riverbanks has received approval of a $15 million proposal from Richland and Lexington Counties for some renovations and expansions, including a new gorilla exhibit by the river, a new elephant exhibit, a new birdhouse, and other projects.

Admission revenues are impacted by weather conditions because most of the attractions are outdoor. Riverbanks earns admissions revenue directly from visitors who pay per visit or indirectly from Riverbanks Society members who pay per year for one of the different memberships. General admission fees are $5.75 for adults and $3.25 for children ages 3 to 12 but drop to $4.75 and $2.75, respectively, every Tuesday (see Exhibit 5). Discounts are available for groups, special activities, or special days. Free classes are provided for Lexington and Richland County schools. Charges for special activities vary.

EXHIBIT 4: Riverbanks Park Commission—General Fund Comparative Balance Sheets as of June 30, 1997 and 1996

	June 30 1997	June 30 1996	Changes
Assets			
Cash on Hand, On Deposit & Invested in REPO	$432,935	$1,011,456	($578,521)
Accounts Receivable—General	124,215	116,285	7,930
Accounts Receivable—Other Governments	58,000	0	58,000
Accounts Receivable—Ticket Sales	7,418	3,629	3,789
Accounts Receivable—Consignment Tickets	1,401	2,491	(1,090)
Accounts Receivable—Riverbanks Society	27,189	45,259	(18,070)
Pledge Receivable—BB&T	30,000	0	30,000
Due From Capital Fund	151,636	2,418	149,218
Inventory—For Resale - Merchandise	0	0	0
Inventories—General Supplies & Animal Feed	25,941	20,421	5,520
Total Assets	858,733	1,201,959	(343,226)
Liabilities and Fund Equity			
Current Liabilities			
Accounts Payable	126,318	322,000	(195,682)
Accrued Salaries Payable	108,249	102,709	5,540
Payroll Taxes Accrued and Withheld	841	4,270	(3,429)
Admissions, Sales and Use Taxes Payable	11,339	11,316	23
Deferred Revenue—Consign, Tickets & Mkt.	92,345	82,396	9,949
Loan Payable—Trams and Carousel	133,500	0	133,500
Total Liabilities	472,592	522,691	(50,099)
Fund Equity			
Reserved for:			
Inventories—General Supplies & Animal Feed	25,941	20,421	5,520
Operating Cushion	400,000	400,000	0
Major Repairs and Renovation	34,318	290,597	(256,279)
Unreserved, Undesignated (Deficit)	(74,117)	(31,750)	(42,367)
Total Fund Equity	386,142	679,268	(293,126)
Total Liabilities and Fund Equity	858,733	1,201,959	(343,226)

EXHIBIT 5: Riverbanks Park Commission Riverbanks Zoo—General Fund Budget

Attendance and Admissions Revenue Projection	*Fiscal Year 1997–98*		
	Budgeted 1997–98 Attendance	*Admission Fees*	*Budgeted Revenue 1997–98*
Admission category:			
Adults	194,650	$5.75	$1,119,238
Children	77,350	3.25	251,388
Family Day adults (every Tuesday)	19,550	4.75	92,863
Family Day children (every Tuesday)	7,650	2.75	21,038
Students	15,300	4.50	68,850
Senior citizens	13,600	4.25	57,800
Christmas Lights—adult	29,750	4.00	119,000
Christmas Lights—child	9,350	2.75	25,713
Group—adults	55,250	4.00	221,000
Group—children	91,800	2.75	252,450
Children under 3	49,300	0.00	0
Society	178,500	0.00	0
Free school groups—Rich/Lex Counties	39,950	0.00	0
Other—comp., promo., free Fridays, etc.	68,000	0.00	0
Total Attendance and Revenue	850,000		2,229,338
Less 5% admissions tax			106,159
Budgeted Admissions Revenue 1997–1998			2,123,179

RIVERBANKS SOCIETY

The Riverbanks Society, which grew out of the private sector that provided much-needed support prior to the opening of Riverbanks, provides funds for operations, construction and renovations, new exhibits, and special activities. In each of the past 3 years, its total annual contributions exceeded $600,000. The society contributed $377,371 in direct support in 1996 and $376,176 in 1997.

Many of the exhibits and portions of the garden were provided by individual donations. For example, the Old Rose Garden located in the Botanical Garden and the Galapagos tortoise exhibit in the zoo were fully funded by private contributions, as were other projects in previous years. A new, endangered-species carousel, funded by a local business, will be the focal point of Flamingo Plaza when construction is completed in the summer of 1998. The carousel will have replicas of 22 endangered species that children can ride, and a scenic mural of other endangered species in their natural habitats.

The Riverbanks Society offers reasonable membership fees that allow admission for individuals or family members for one year. The society offers individuals and families a variety of memberships costing from $25 to $100 for standard membership, and from $250 to $1,000 for Gold Card membership. Types of memberships and associated benefits are shown in Exhibit 6. Society members enjoy benefits in addition to those in the exhibit. Riverbanks sends society members a bimonthly newsletter and a quarterly magazine. Riverbanks staff conduct tours of Africa and other countries for Riverbanks Society members.

EXHIBIT 6:   Riverbanks Society Memberships

Standard Memberships

Individual—$25
  Free admission for one adult named on card plus four guest passes

Dual—$32
  Free admission for two adults from the same household named on card, or free admission for one adult named on card and one guest at any time, plus four guest passes

Family/Grandparent—$42
  Free admission for two adults from the same household named on card and all children 18 and under living in same household, or grandchildren 18 and under living anywhere, plus 10 guest passes

Family Plus—$56
  Free admission for four adults from the same household named on card and all children 18 and under living in same household, or grandchildren 18 and under living anywhere, plus 10 guest passes

Patron—$100
  Free admission for four adults named on card and all children 18 and under living in the same household, or grandchildren 18 and under living anywhere, plus 15 guest passes

Gold Card Memberships

Curators' Circle—$250
  Free admission for four adults named on the card and all children 18 and under living in the same household, or grandchildren 18 and under living anywhere, and 15 guest passes. Special added benefits: limited access to the garden through the west gate entrance; Curators' tour with society director; invitation to an annual Gold Card reception; Gold Card previews

Director's Circle—$500
  Same benefits as Curators' Circle and 20 passes. Special added benefits: duplicate membership cards; Riverbanks gift

Benefactor—$1,000
  Same benefits as Director's Circle and 25 guest passes. Special added benefits: VIP zoo & garden tour; invitation to benefactors' events

THE FUTURE

The Riverbanks Zoological Park and Botanical Garden, an institution offering many opportunities for recreation and education, should have a bright future. Riverbanks's staff continues to receive support from the public and private sector. The Research Consortium scheduled for 1998 should enhance Riverbanks's reputation and research programs. The Education Center should continue to grow with more possible avenues in the garden. The Botanical Garden should attract more visitors as it further develops and as the proposed extra entrance point is completed.

REFERENCE

[1] www.riverbanks.org/grpsales.htm

Dakota, Minnesota & Eastern Railroad Corporation—1997

Paul R. Reed

Carol J. Cumber

www.dmerail.com

Kevin V. Schieffer caught himself shaking his head as he thought back over his first 6 months as president and chief executive officer of the Dakota, Minnesota & Eastern Railroad (DM&E). Replacing J. C. "Pete" McIntyre, who led the railroad through the first 10 years of its existence, was a tough job. McIntyre had indicated early in 1996 that he wanted to step down before the end of the year. The changeover occurred that November, with McIntyre agreeing to serve as chair of the board for the next two years.

The year ended on a somewhat favorable note with 1996 revenues reaching a record $56.6 million, although net income fell to $3.0 million versus $3.4 million in 1995. The new year came in like the proverbial lion with record low temperatures and the worst blizzards in memory. This was followed by massive spring melt and torrential rain. The effect on DM&E was disastrous. The railroad literally was shut down for most of January and various portions closed intermittently through the next 4 months. The important lines to Aberdeen and Mansfield, South Dakota, remained under water and were not expected to reopen until late in the year. All of this placed DM&E in a fairly precarious financial position. Revenues were down while operating expenses, including snow removal and flood damage, were up dramatically. Schieffer knew that the next several months would be all-important to DM&E. Some remedial steps already had been taken, but much remained. When and how the railroad would right itself would occupy Schieffer's thoughts for some time.

THE BEGINNINGS

During the 1970s, the 1980s, and well into the 1990s, the railroad industry in the upper Midwest had felt drastic changes stemming from the deregulation of both trucking and railroads, the decline of heavy industry, the loss of local railroad business, the growth of coal traffic, and mergers. During this period, many lines merged; were downsized; or disappeared with pieces purchased by former competitors, short line railroad holding companies, or, in many cases, entrepreneurs desiring to operate their own railroads.

Most of the trackage of what is now DM&E (see Exhibit 1) had been unprofitable for the Chicago and Northwestern Railroad (C&NW) for several years. In 1983 and again in 1985, C&NW petitioned to abandon the line from 5 miles west of Pierre to

This case was prepared by Professor Paul R. Reed of Sam Houston State University and Professor Carol J. Cumber of South Dakota State University as a basis for class discussion. It is not intended to illustrate either effective or ineffective handling of an administrative situation. Copyright © 1999 by Prentice Hall, Inc. ISBN 0-13-011141-4.

EXHIBIT 1:   Dakota, Minnesota & Eastern Railroad System map, May 1997

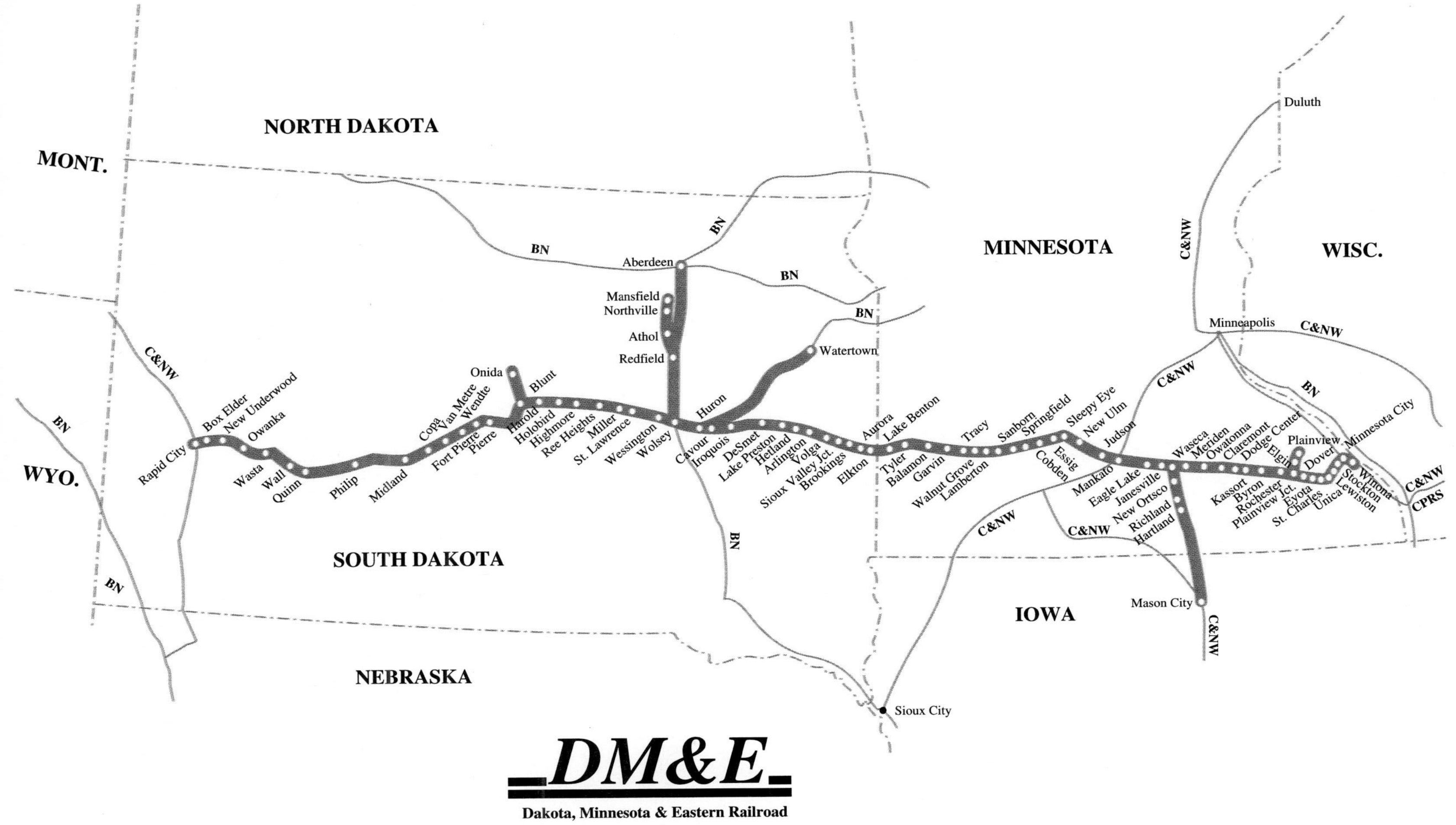

DM&E

Dakota, Minnesota & Eastern Railroad

Source: Dakota, Minnesota & Eastern Railroad Corporation (1997).

Rapid City. That action would have left South Dakota with no centrally located east-west rail transportation. C&NW's request was met with unusually strong opposition from both the state and U.S. Sen. Larry Pressler (R-South Dakota). Realizing that abandonment was no longer a wise move, C&NW came to a sales agreement with a group of investors in 1986. The $26 million purchase gave the buyers 826 miles of badly worn track and permission to operate over an additional 139 miles. Included were 18 locomotives with an average age of 35 years as well as maintenance and repair equipment. C&NW retained ownership of the tracks at DM&E's main traffic interchanges at Winona and Mankato, Minnesota; Mason City, Iowa; and Rapid City, South Dakota. No freight cars were included in the sale; in fact, DM&E would pay monetary penalties unless 89 percent of its originated traffic was loaded in C&NW freight cars. These restrictions took years of negotiating to remove.

INTERNAL ENVIRONMENT

Description of the Railroad

The 1,098-mile DM&E is headquartered in Brookings, South Dakota, and operates mainly in South Dakota and Minnesota, although a 69-mile branch line serves Mason City, Iowa. The 203-mile north-south "Colony Line" purchased in 1996 gives the railroad a few miles of track in Wyoming and Nebraska. Exhibit 2 shows the Winona–Rapid City main line and branch lines to Colony and Mason City that carry the greatest freight tonnage. It also indicates that most traffic is eastbound. Westbound trains consist mostly of empty cars being returned for loading. Track conditions on most of the line prevent freight train speeds in excess of 25 mph, although there is a 94-mile section of completely rebuilt track that can support speeds of 49 mph. Approximately 220 miles of track is limited to speeds of 10 mph.

DM&E serves the main line with a minimum 6-day-per-week commercial (scheduled) train service between Rapid City and Winona. A similar schedule handles freight between Minnesota's Waseca and Albert Lea and South Dakota's Rapid City and Belle Fourche. During peak months (June to October), one or two grain trains per 7-day week often are scheduled. Branch lines use trains on an as-needed basis. Local freights provide service to many on-line customers, thus relieving commercial trains from making numerous stops between Rapid City and Winona.

Freight cars are sorted and blocked at division points in Minnesota at Waseca and in South Dakota at Huron and Rapid City. DM&E turns over much of its traffic to the Union Pacific (UP) at Mankato, Albert Lea, and Winona. Increasing amounts of interchange business is done between DM&E and Canadian Pacific near Winona. Burlington Northern Santa Fe (BNSF) participates with DM&E on considerable business at Wolsey, South Dakota, and Crawford, Nebraska. Exhibit 3 indicates the population sizes of the largest cities along DM&E's routes and the ownership of the trackage.

The company owns and operates a car and locomotive repair facility at Huron, where it performs major repairs and overhauls on its 70 locomotives. Similar services are provided to freight cars at Huron, Rapid City, and Waseca. All active locomotives have been rebuilt or received major overhauls since 1987. The availability rate for locomotives is over 90 percent and approaches 100 percent during the winter months when many units are stored due to lower traffic requirements. During the summer-fall season, DM&E occasionally leases a few locomotives to handle increased traffic.

EXHIBIT 2: Dakota, Minnesota & Eastern Railroad Corporation, 1996 Freight Density Map Shown in Million Gross Tons per Mile (no scale)

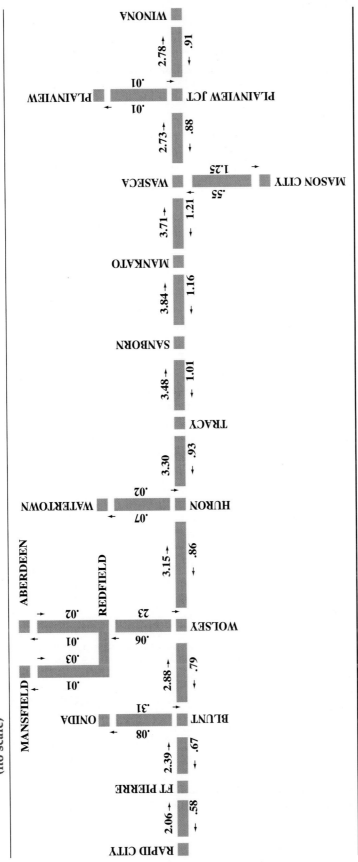

Source: Dakota, Minnesota & Eastern Railroad Corporation.

EXHIBIT 3: Largest Cities and Track Ownership

State	City	Size	Track Ownership
Minnesota	Winona	47,828	DM&E & UP
	Rochester	70,745	DM&E
	Owatonna	19,386	UP
	Waseca	18,079	DM&E
	Mankato	31,477	UP
Iowa	Mason City	29,040	UP
South Dakota	Brookings	16,270	DM&E
	Huron	12,448	BNSF & DM&E
	Watertown	17,592	BNSF & DM&E
	Aberdeen	24,927	BNSF & DM&E
	Pierre	12,926	DM&E
	Rapid City	54,523	DM&E

Source: U.S. Bureau of the Census (1990).

Grain and grain-derived products make up 43.5 percent of DM&E's carloads. Grain shipments include wheat from South Dakota, as well as corn and soybeans from eastern South Dakota and the western two-thirds of Minnesota. The second major item of traffic is bentonite clay (used in foundry operations, oil drilling, iron ore pelletizing, and cat litter). Other major traffic items include cement, wood chips, lumber, and kaolin clay (used in manufacturing cement). Exhibit 4 shows the traffic mix.

EXHIBIT 4: Dakota, Minnesota & Eastern Railroad, Carloading by Category (1991–1996)

Categories of Traffic	1991	1992	1993	1994	1995	1996
wheat	10,532	9,883	11,319	10,353	9,085	11,338
bentonite clay	9,054	9,666	9,545	10,737	10,729	12,554
wood chips	3,232	3,353	2,369	2,359	2,466	2,406
corn	8,045	8,469	4,281	4,601	7,894	8,561
cement	2,171	2,853	2,581	2,514	1,993	3,344
industrial sand	2,369	3,407	3,040	3,276	2,338	766
lumber/boards	656	546	458	454	647	691
soybeans	2,766	2,973	1,921	2,275	2,133	3,436
kaolin clay	1,036	1,295	2,321	466	2,144	2,220
soybean oil	1,969	1,971	2,231	2,005	1,756	1,826
wheat flour	974	930	891	1,124	1,301	1,169
other	8,658	9,814	9,813	10,429	10,721	12,085
Total	51,462	55,160	51,040	50,593	53,207	60,396

Source: Dakota, Minnesota & Eastern Railroad Corporation (1997).

Mission

The mission of DM&E is to meet customers' expectations with scheduled freight service that is consistent and reliable; to achieve timely turnaround of equipment; to improve the safety and quality of the workplace for employees; and to develop growth opportunities for the company, its employees, and customers.

Senior Management

DM&E maintains a lean organization throughout its entire structure. Half of senior management is relatively new and, as a group, appears fairly young, well qualified, and highly motivated.

Schieffer, president and chief executive officer, is a lawyer by profession who has a long association with DM&E. As a member of Sen. Pressler's staff, he was involved on the spin-off of DM&E from C&NW and later was active in getting bentonite and other Colony Line traffic rerouted to DM&E. Entering private practice in 1993, he became DM&E's attorney and was instrumental in renegotiating many of the onerous restrictions made during DM&E's inception. He negotiated the 1996 purchase of the Colony Line and related agreements to include elimination of the requirements to use C&NW (now Union Pacific) freight cars.

Lynn A. Anderson, vice-president, marketing, strategic planning, and public affairs, is responsible for marketing, pricing, and sales. He serves as liaison to various federal, state, and local governments. Anderson spent 15 years with C&NW, rising to the position of general manager of grain marketing and pricing. He was directly involved in the formation of DM&E in 1986.

Kurt V. Feaster, vice-president, finance, is responsible for all accounting and financial matters, including implementing budget policies and financial planning for all departments. Before joining DM&E in 1992, he was chief financial officer first at the Montana Rail Link and later at the Wheeling and Lake Erie Railway.

Vernon L. Colbert, chief transportation officer, has responsibility for scheduling; car utilization; the Customer Service Center; train operations; dispatching; personnel (engineers, conductors, and brakemen); and division point operations. Colbert spent 32 years with BNSF, where he worked his way up from station agent to superintendent of operations. He joined DM&E in 1997.

Douglas G. DeBerg, chief engineer, is responsible for upgrading and maintaining the railroad infrastructure including track, bridges, signals, and buildings. He spent over 30 years working in various engineering capacities for five different railroads. He joined DM&E in 1995.

Daniel L. Goodwin, chief mechanical officer, oversees operational maintenance, major rebuilding, and repair of locomotives and freight cars. He spent over 26 years with three different railroads, last serving as superintendent for the Wheeling and Lake Erie Railway. He joined DM&E in 1997.

Corporate Philosophy

DM&E has made a long-term commitment to provide consistent and reliable freight service and to not diversify into nonrail efforts. Overall, DM&E believes in strengthening its position as a rail freight carrier in the upper Midwest by making its existing system more efficient and better at serving its present territory. Accordingly, DM&E

increased revenues by enlarging its market share of freight shipped by existing customers, by regaining customers who had shifted to trucks when the railroad was operated by previous owners, by serving new shippers in its territory, and by improving relations with other railroads. At present, the railroad continues to employ a strategy of strengthening its existing traffic base and increasing its market share within the territory it serves rather than expanding much beyond South Dakota and Minnesota. DM&E also has shown great interest in better controlling its main traffic interchanges. The Colony Line purchase eliminated Rapid City as an interchange problem. Problems with Union Pacific interchanges have been greatly alleviated. A long-term goal is ownership of UP's Winona freight yard, which would permit direct interchange with Mississippi River barge traffic and improve the interchange with the Canadian Pacific.

Marketing

DM&E aggressively sought traffic from both large and small shippers. It initiated long-term agreements with large shippers to stabilize its traffic base and gave 8 or 10 percent discounts to grain shippers to make unit train shipments of 25 cars or more. DM&E enticed agricultural customers with pricing and service packages that provide access to markets in Texas, the eastern United States, the Pacific coast, and the Gulf Coast via the Mississippi River. DM&E's computerized Customer Service Center enables better communication with customers on car supply, transit times, loss or damage, billing, car tracing, switching, weighing, and diversion issues.

Anderson's department continually looks for new customers and markets for current ones. DM&E took advantage of the Winona end of track on the Mississippi River by developing a rail-barge service that opened up new markets to shippers and receivers at prices that took advantage of cheaper barge rates. Shipping in the opposite direction, DM&E has been dispatching unit grain trains of 54 or 108 cars to the Pacific Northwest via BNSF. DM&E ships wheat trains to flour mills across the nation. DM&E has been successful in gaining some new industry along its lines. For example, a new soybean processing facility in Volga, South Dakota, is generating over 1,500 cars per year and plans to increase output by 50 percent.

DM&E's innovative efforts, however, often are offset by nature. The wet spring of 1995 reduced wheat production, so DM&E moved 1,200 fewer carloads of wheat than it had planned. (Corn and soybean production were not affected by the weather.) The "mild" 1995–1996 winter and a favorable spring resulted in an excellent year for all crops. High production along with record or near-record prices for corn and wheat resulted in DM&E's moving 4,200 more carloads of grain than in 1995. The harsh weather conditions in the 1996–1997 winter and spring caused winter wheat production to be down 29 percent from the previous year. Wheat business was expected to be down again in 1997, attributed to late planting due to spring flooding and lower prices paid to farmers. In spite of some hail damage, the 1997 outlook for corn and beans was good.[1]

Transportation

Providing accident-free, consistent, and reliable service that meets customer needs is a never-ending challenge to DM&E's Colbert and his Transportation Department. Poor track, lack of adequate sidings to permit train passings, locomotive and train crew shortages, lack of crew training and rail knowledge, crew failure to follow rules, and the weather too often equated to slow transit time, high operating costs, train accidents, unsatisfied customers, and low employee morale.

DM&E inherited trackage that, in the main, had not received adequate maintenance in 20 to 30 years. A great portion of the line west of Pierre, for example, is the original 72-pound (per yard) rail laid in the early 1900s. Eighty-odd years of traffic have made the track and the supporting grade increasingly unable to support 100-ton railcars moving at speeds much above 10 mph.

Lack of adequate sidings (6,000 ft.) often causes one DM&E train to wait several hours to avoid meeting a train coming from the opposite direction. Additional time is lost when there is a shortage of rested train crews or a lack of locomotives. Inadequate operating and safety training, lack of rules, and noncompliance with those rules that exist have caused derailments, personal injury, and unnecessary operating expenses.

The weather adds its toll. A wintertime Rapid City–Winona trip may take more than 100 hours rather than the ideal 60 hours. Heavy rains result in unstable track which, already impaired by deferred or improper maintenance, ultimately causes a high percent of the derailments that have cost DM&E $3.5 million annually for the past 3 years.

The above factors cause train crew overtime, extra crews, higher freight car rental expenses, accident costs, damage costs, increased insurance rates, increased locomotive fuel expenses, maintenance expenses, and customer and employee dissatisfaction. These items can add several million dollars to operating expenses. Colbert and his staff continually fight to improve service while lowering costs. Actions implemented since his arrival in 1997 include the following:

- formation of cross-functional quality circle–type teams to open lines of communication throughout the railroad. Teams meet monthly to identify and solve problems. Day-to-day issues are solved locally, and larger issues are presented by a team member to department heads on a regular basis. Teams receive adoption/rejection feedback from management with full explanations.

- institution of drug and alcohol testing, and training in and testing on DM&E policy and rules.

- improvement in reporting of and accountability for accidents. This includes studying locomotive recorders (similar to flight recorders) to determine crew actions prior to and at the time of derailments. Thorough investigations are the rule and people are held accountable for their actions.

- increased supervision of crew performance and retraining when needed. The emphasis here is developmental rather than punitive.

Colbert also placed all trains on a schedule in an effort to improve consistency and reliability. It is hoped that this will improve customer satisfaction while enabling DM&E's marketing, engineering, and mechanical departments to better plan and coordinate activities. The main line commercial trains had been on time approximately 15 percent of the time. All departments are working to reach Schieffer's consistency goal of 90 percent.

One of the major products of faster train service is the reduction of the average car cycle (the number of days that cars are on DM&E rails from when they are received empty from another railroad to when they are returned as a load to a connecting line). The average time is approximately 12 days. For every one of those days, DM&E is paying car-hire expense ($18 a day) for cars from other railroads, and lease, capital cost, and interest on its own 3,000 cars.[2] DM&E has monthly payments of $1 million on its lease cars, and unutilized cars contribute nothing to paying this expense.

Colbert leads a team of 84 locomotive engineers, 70 conductors, and a management and operational staff of 24. DM&E trains its own conductors and has a 70-day cross-training program, in conjunction with the Canadian Pacific Railroad, whereby senior conductors may qualify as engineers. This dual qualification adds job stability by permitting conductors to serve as engineers during peak seasons and to return to their former duties during slack times. An increased number of operating crews and the addition of newer and more powerful locomotives should give DM&E needed flexibility in train makeup and scheduling.

Engineering

This department has the herculean task of maintaining track, bridges, and other physical sites in a safe condition commensurate with DM&E's requirements. Responsibilities for DeBerg and his staff include cross-tie replacement; rail replacement; rock ballasting; surfacing (cleaning, leveling, and smoothing of track); and subgrade and bridge improvements.

As mentioned earlier, DM&E inherited a poorly maintained railroad. Added to these woes was the discovery that the native clay (Pierre shale) subgrade on the Pierre–Rapid City section would prove very unstable during periods of heavy rain. When water is trapped between the wet clay and the track structure, the wet clay could be unable to support the weight of 100-ton car trains. The end result frequently is that water, clay, ballast, and so forth are squeezed to both sides of the railbed and the track sinks. Some of these soft spot areas extend 500 feet. Unseasonably wet weather in 4 of the last 5 years played havoc with the Pierre–Rapid City tracks. DM&E has tried many methods throughout the years to correct this problem and has experienced varying degrees of success. The installation of 35 miles of waterproof fabric between the ballast and the clay was deemed a failure. The installation of perforated lateral or longitudinal drain pipes to remove trapped pockets of water met with success when there was natural drainage away from the track structure; in cases where there wasn't, the trapped water created new soft spot areas. DeBerg began experimenting with a composition of lime and fly ash (coal ashes) mixed with earth to strengthen unstable soils. Early results were encouraging.

DM&E spent in excess of $88 million on track and bridge–related capital projects by the end of 1996. Over 72 percent of this was from cash generated from operations, and the remainder came from federal and state loans and grants as well as loans from customers. DM&E also performs normal maintenance and maintenance-support activities that are not included in capital expenditures. Exhibit 5 shows capital expenditures for 1987–1996.

Budgeted capital track expenditures for 1997 approximated $10 million. Included were installation of 70,000 cross ties, rock ballasting and surfacing 450 miles of track,

EXHIBIT 5:   **Dakota, Minnesota & Eastern Railroad Corporation, Capital Expenditures Funding Sources**

(in millions of dollars)	1994	1995	1996	TOTAL
CAPITAL EXPENDITURES:				
SD Track-West of Pierre	$2,019	$3,066	$ 2,852	$20,867
SD Track-East of Pierre	2,216	3,220	26,536	43,380
Total SD Track	*4,235*	*6,286*	*29,388*	*64,247*
MN Track	4,350	2,346	1,315	24,128
Total All Track	*8,585*	*8,632*	*30,703*	*88,375*
Locomotive	2,869	6,220	990	15,695
All Other	934	1,855	2,196	8,398
Total	*12,388*	*16,707*	*33,889*	*112,468*
FUNDED BY:				
FRA[a] Grant for track improvements in SD	66	0	0	861
FRA Grant for SD Road Crossings & Signals	401	155	455	3,887
SD Bond/RECD Loan	0	0	21,114	21,114
Funds Secured from SD Customers	0	106	289	865
FRA Loan for track improvements expended in SD	0	0	0	7,650
FRA Grant for track improvements in MN	55	0	0	1,119
FRA Grant for MN Road Crossings & Signals	439	309	232	3,704
MN State Loan	1,229	0	0	7,195
Funds Secured from MN Customers	200	301	386	1,963
DM&E Cash	9,998	15,836	11,413	64,110
Total	*12,388*	*16,707*	*33,889*	*112,468*

[a] Federal Railroad Administration (FRA), a subdepartment of U.S. Department of Transportation.
Source: Dakota, Minnesota & Eastern Railroad Corporation.

upgrading bridges, and replacing several wooden bridges with culvert and earthen fill. Other projects involve building up and smoothing rail ends and joints, continuing rail testing, and replacing and upgrading rail yards. Also added was the initiation of a "trailer" vehicle, operated by a track inspector who follows trains looking for damage to track or structures. Deficiencies noted are reported by radio so crews and material can be dispatched to the scene for repairs. This program has prevented many likely derailments.

The Engineering Department includes 33 employees who are spaced equally along the 11 sections of the 1,098-mile rail. Each three-person team is responsible for maintaining a safe railroad across its section. The department's other 37 nonmanagement employees install and maintain signals, repair bridges, inspect track, and operate a variety of equipment. This base workforce is augmented by temporary hires during the spring and summer. Also, the railroad uses contractors for all major capital projects, such as the state's rebuilding of 94 miles of track in South Dakota between Wolsey and Pierre with new 115-pound continuously welded rail.

Mechanical

This department is tasked with repairing and maintaining DM&E's 70 locomotives and 3,000 freight cars (up from 59 and 300, respectively, in 1995) and repairing cars owned by other railroads that are on DM&E track. Goodwin's department has the equipment and expertise to perform almost any type of repair or maintenance work. The fact that locomotive availability remains 95 percent or higher with units averaging 30 years in age is a testament in itself. Goodwin has emphasized purchasing newer and more powerful locomotives so eventually most trains can be pulled by two locomotives. He is a personable leader and is a strong advocate of the recently adopted quality circle program.

Human Resources

The Human Resource Department (HR) led by Jan Todd is relatively new. Hiring and training are done at the department level, whereas pay, benefits, performance appraisal, and administrative record keeping are performed by HR, which takes a back seat to no functions at DM&E. Schieffer continually stresses the importance of all employees both as people and as the real cause of the railroad's success. Most key managers seem to echo this philosophy, though a few seem to have difficulty adjusting from the too-typical railroad confrontational leadership style.

Workforce Concerns

Communications

Schieffer and his principal staff make every effort to spend as much time out on the line as possible. Agenda items include quality-of-life issues and the four operational goals of improved transit times, consistency and reliability, car cycle times, and safety.[3] The institution of cross-functional quality circles is one of many empowerment activities utilized to improve communications, employee involvement, and team spirit. Face-to-face communication is supplemented by a quarterly newsletter, *DM&E Enroute*, which keeps employees, customers, and supporters informed of current operations and future plans. There is an open invitation to employees to phone Schieffer direct or, in his absence, to leave a message. A growing number of employees have a positive attitude towards these efforts, although some feel they need more one-to-one contact; another group wonders whether they are really listened to; and others say that quality circles is just another program bound to fail.

Stability

DM&E recognizes the importance of job security to employee morale, turnover, and possible increased productivity. The use of temporary employees and contract labor greatly minimizes layoffs in the seasonal transportation, engineering, and mechanical departments. In addition, cross-training affords flexibility needed to efficiently move employees where needed.

Pay

DM&E pays its craft, clerical, and nonunion employees very competitively versus local rates. DM&E has admitted from the beginning that it could not match the train crew

EXHIBIT 6: Sample Benefit Comparison

Benefit	DM&E	Unionized Railroad Plan
life insurance	$50,000	$10,000
accidental AD&D	$50,000	$8,000
401(k)	yes	not provided
profit sharing	yes	not provided
maximum medical	$1,000,000	$500,000
deductible	$100 each individual	$100 each individual
maximum out-of-pocket	$500 individual, $1,000 family	$2,000 each person covered

Source: Dakota, Minnesota & Eastern Railroad Corporation, Benefit Brochures.

pay of unionized Class I railroads. Rates of pay are 15 to 25 percent below comparable wages on the Burlington Northern Sante Fe Railroad. Extensive overtime on DM&E, profit sharing for nonunion personnel, and year-round employment (Class I railroads often have winter layoffs) undoubtedly narrows this gap. DM&E also has used bonus and merit pay to further reward nonunion employees. Bonuses in 1995 and 1996 averaged 3 percent.

Benefits

The benefit package offered DM&E employees equals or exceeds those provided by the major union railroads. Exhibit 6 gives a sample comparison.

Unions

DM&E remained nonunion until June 1990 when train crew, railcar repair staff, and electricians began being represented by the United Transportation Union. Unions tried to organize train dispatchers in 1991, mechanical employees in 1995, and engineering employees in 1997. The unions lost all three elections, although the engineering election was rescheduled due to a technical error on the part of the National Labor Relations Board.

Summary of Financial Performance 1995–1997

DM&E has continued to improve its operating revenue since start-up and particularly from 1992 to date. The railroad generated $45.7 million in operating revenues in 1995 and traffic volume was 53.2 thousand carloads. Operating revenues for 1996 were $55.6 million and traffic volume was 60.4 thousand carloads, a 23.7 percent increase in revenues and a 13.5 percent increase in carloads. During the first 5 months of 1997, operating revenues were $4.3 million under budget due primarily to extremely harsh winter weather and spring flooding problems.

Revenues

Traffic volume in 1995 and 1996 decreased in three of 12 commodity groups but had an overall increase of 8.3 percent. The largest increases were in shipments of bentonite clay, wheat, cement, corn, and soybeans. Decreases in shipments of wheat flour and wood chips were attributable to weather and market conditions. A major carload loss in low-revenue-producing industrial sand was due to competition.

Operating Expenses

These expenses rose 27.7 percent between 1995 and 1996. Increased traffic and related activities increased expenses in seven of eight categories. The decrease in the accident damage, injury, and insurance category was an encouraging sign. Expenses during the first 5 months of 1997 exceeded the budget by $2.6 million and resulted in a $3.1 million operating loss for the period. Exhibit 7 presents 1995–1996 income and earnings data.

EXHIBIT 7: Dakota, Minnesota & Eastern Railroad Corporation, Statements of Income and Retained Earnings

	Years Ended December 31,	
	1996	*1995*
Revenue		
Freight	55,648,725	44,782,303
Other	913,832	944,115
Total revenue	56,562,557	45,726,418
Operating Expenses		
Transportation:		
Car hire	9,134,599	5,734,443
Fuel	5,769,317	4,006,205
Salaries, benefits, rent, and other	10,274,690	7,513,630
	25,178,606	17,254,278
Accident damage, injury, and insurance	3,870,039	4,323,784
Maintenance of equipment	3,474,778	2,282,938
Maintenance of way	5,276,503	4,174,736
General and administrative	4,189,941	4,016,464
Depreciation and amortization	5,455,831	5,075,024
Total operating expenses	47,445,698	37,127,224
Operating Income	9,116,859	8,599,194
Other income, net	1,214,643	619,023
Interest expense	(5,760,438)	(3,794,587)
Income Before Income Tax Expense	4,571,064	5,423,630
Income tax expense	1,746,120	2,033,861
Net Income	2,824,944	3,389,769
Preferred Stock Dividend	(112,000)	(112,000)
Increase in Preferred Stock Value	(75,000)	(75,000)
Retained Earnings at Beginning of Year	15,875,694	12,672,925
Retained Earnings at End of Year	18,513,638	15,875,694

Source: Dakota, Minnesota & Eastern Railroad Corporation.

Liquidity and Capital Resources

Cash generated from operations is DM&E's primary source of liquidity and is used principally to fund working capital for debt service and capital expenditures. This latter category includes cost of track improvements, locomotive and railcar purchase, technology enhancement, and motor vehicle and other equipment purchase. See Exhibit 8 for 1995–1996 cash flow data.

EXHIBIT 8: Dakota, Minnesota & Eastern Railroad Corporation, Statements of Cash Flows

	Years Ended December 31,	
	1996	1995
Cash Flows from Operating Activities		
Net income	2,824,944	3,389,769
Adjustments to reconcile net income to net cash provided by operating activities:		
Depreciation and amortization	5,455,831	5,075,024
(Gain) loss on sale of assets	(207,080)	35,138
Deferred income taxes	1,547,102	2,069,801
Deferred interest on debt	116,836	122,838
Changes in current assets and liabilities:		
Accounts receivable	2,236,433	(2,188,122)
Other current assets	(12,028,789)	(4,528,531)
Accounts and notes payable	1,920,673	719,865
Accrued expenses and income taxes payable	(1,486,498)	3,966,514
Changes in other liabilities	(193,710)	(61,146)
Net cash provided by operating activities	185,742	8,601,150
Cash Flows from Investing Activities		
Capital expenditures	(17,929,156)	(16,707,492)
Colony Line acquisition	(10,453,313)	0
Restricted cash	(3,927,065)	0
Proceeds from sale of land and property	3,873,343	332,004
Deferred costs	(557,442)	0
Net cash used in investing activities	(28,993,633)	(16,375,488)
Cash Flows from Financing Activities		
Borrowings on revolving loan facility	25,470,000	5,169,069
Repayments of revolving loan facility	(29,399,069)	(3,890,000)
Proceeds from issuance of long-term debt	37,863,569	4,060,500
Repayments of long-term debt	(7,498,291)	(1,042,167)
Government grants	1,222,521	1,845,433
Exercise of stock warrants	86,250	0
Deferred costs	(1,815,009)	(421,496)
Net cash provided by financing activities	25,929,971	5,721,339
Net Decrease in Cash and Cash Equivalents	(2,877,920)	(2,052,999)
Cash and Cash Equivalents at Beginning of Year	3,263,499	5,316,498
Cash and Cash Equivalents at End of Year	385,579	3,263,499

Source: Dakota, Minnesota & Eastern Railroad Corporation.

Liabilities

DM&E was highly leveraged at start-up and has been forced continually to ask for federal, state, and local financing to assist in roadbed maintenance and major construction. Long-term debt includes loans for Wolsey–Pierre, South Dakota, rail replacement; purchase of the Colony Line; costs of track rehabilitation; and payments for older, more expensive debt. Major off balance sheet commitments are for operating leases on locomotives, freight cars, and other equipment. These commitments total over $120 million. Debt covenants require that certain financial ratios be maintained. Due to severe weather, DM&E was in technical violation of certain covenants as of March 31, 1997. A major portion of a private equity placement of $7 million to existing shareholders increased liquidity sufficiently to satisfy a major lender concern and to cure the technical default. Other covenant violations were waived temporarily or amended and the railroad felt it would be able to maintain compliance through the remainder of 1997. See Exhibit 9 for balance sheet information for 1995 and 1996.

EXHIBIT 9: Dakota, Minnesota & Eastern Railroad Corporation, Balance Sheets

	Years Ended December 31,	
	1996	1995
Assets		
Current Assets		
Cash and cash equivalents	385,579	3,263,499
Accounts receivable	6,936,246	9,172,679
Insurance claims and other receivables	2,106,974	1,976,999
Material and supplies	2,790,726	5,634,284
Prepaid expenses	840,828	690,204
Tax refund receivable	466,180	139,198
Deferred income taxes	581,500	376,247
Total current assets	14,108,033	21,253,110
Property, Plant, and Equipment, net	106,283,187	73,242,973
Restricted Cash	3,927,065	0
Deferred Costs	4,338,446	2,237,409
	128,656,731	96,733,492
Liabilities and Shareholders' Equity		
Current Liabilities		
Accounts payable	3,929,602	1,804,689
Revolving loan facility	0	3,929,069
Note payable	178,084	382,324
Accrued expenses	11,458,870	12,479,188
Current maturities of long-term debt	1,160,559	1,282,186
Total current liabilities	16,727,115	19,877,456
Long-Term Debt, excluding current maturities	73,197,622	42,710,717

continued

EXHIBIT 9: *continued*

	1996	*1995*
Other Liabilities	196,633	273,507
Deferred Income Taxes	14,572,017	12,819,662
Total liabilities	104,693,387	75,681,342
Commitments and Contingencies		
Shareholders' Equity		
Redeemable Series A preferred stock—$1.00 par value, 10,000 shares authorized and outstanding	2,773,000	2,586,000
Common stock—$0.01 par value, 1,000,000 shares authorized and 750,000 and 725,000 shares outstanding, respectively	7,500	7,250
Paid-in capital—common stock	2,836,426	2,750,426
Retained earnings	18,513,638	15,875,694
Treasury stock—at cost, 24,000 shares	(167,220)	(167,220)
Total shareholders' equity	23,963,344	21,052,150
	128,656,731	96,733,492

Source: Dakota, Minnesota & Eastern Railroad Corporation.

EXTERNAL ENVIRONMENT

Competition

DM&E's operations are subject to competition from railroads and trucks.

Rail

There are several short line and three major railroads that have lines that connect with or are near DM&E's service area.

- Canadian Pacific Railroad (CP). CP is deemed to be friendly. The only connection with DM&E is near Winona, Minnesota. Interchange traffic has grown from a few cars 2 years ago to several thousand cars annually.

- Union Pacific (UP). UP is more friendly than its C&NW predecessor. It strives to be more cooperative with interchange traffic at Minnesota's Mankato, Albert Lea, and Winona. It also owns the freight yard in Winona where much of DM&E traffic originates and terminates. DM&E has an ongoing offer to purchase this freight yard but UP has shown no interest.

- Burlington Northern Sante Fe (BNSF). This railroad has played a sort of Jekyll-and-Hyde role with DM&E. It has been very cooperative in providing DM&E grain traffic with direct access to the Gulf, the Pacific Northwest, and the Midwest; on the other hand, it has offered below-cost rates to try to siphon bentonite traffic from DM&E to its parallel line farther west. DM&E responded by lowering its own rates and increasing service. BNSF has made minimal effort to repair the joint DM&E–BNSF South Dakota line running between Wolsey and Aberdeen which is still under water. Thus, DM&E is blocked from the south while the BNSF can directly service or provide customers near access from the north.

- Short Lines. The short line railroads in the area provide no impact on DM&E.

Trucks

This mode of transportation carries a greater share of intercity traffic than do railroads. Their innate flexibility, relatively low capital requirements, and huge network of tax-supported highways give them great advantage in smaller volume and under-500-mile shipments. Railroads are very competitive in bulk shipments over long distances. Inter-modal shipments (trucks or containers on rail flatcars) often offer the advantages of both modes to shippers. Although DM&E has considered intermodal shipments in the past, management feels that the slow track speed over much of their line limits the economic feasibility of this mode of transportation. DM&E faces the strongest truck competition in Minnesota.

Weather

DM&E's location in the upper Midwest always will subject the railroad to weather extremes. Although the flood of 1993 caused extensive crop damage, the moderate temperatures and rainfall in 1994 resulted in bumper crops in both South Dakota and Minnesota. The spring of 1995 was the wettest on record for South Dakota. The 1996–1997 winter was called the worst ever by veteran railroaders. North Dakota, South Dakota, and western Minnesota were declared federal disaster areas then. DM&E suffered through substantial snowfall; bitterly cold temperatures that sent wind chills as low as 80 degrees below zero; and snow drifts of 20 feet or higher, with several over a half-mile long. The severe winter weather combined with the washouts in the spring cost the railroad more than $3 million. (This estimate breaks down to $1.8 million for snow removal and $1.3 million for flood-related damage.) DM&E is anticipating approximately $1.9 million in federal aid to assist in the repair of flood-damaged rail lines.

Legal/Political Arena

Both South Dakota and Minnesota have a history of support for the rail industry in general and DM&E in particular. Exhibit 5 shows that DM&E has been a recipient of $46.4 million in grants or loans either directly from both states or indirectly through state-influenced Federal Railroad Administration grants. State governors and legislators have been instrumental in getting federal disaster assistance to help repair damage caused by the elements. The South Dakota government was heavily involved in the formation of DM&E; its purchase of the Colony Line; and the financing, along with a federal agency, of $21 million to rebuild 94 miles of South Dakota track between Wolsey and Pierre.

PLANNING THE FUTURE

Schieffer's day soon filled with the normal business of a busy executive. He spent several hours gathering and dispersing information, making decisions, and checking on the progress of previous ones. It was late afternoon before he got back to his earlier thoughts of the railroad's near- and long-term future. The railroad had been following basically a market penetration strategy since start-up, and Anderson and his marketing people had developed some innovative services during that time. First priority, in the short run, had to be getting back on track. What could be done to improve the steps taken already? Had they overlooked anything? In the background was the desire to buy UP's Winona rail yard. BNSF's lease of the South Dakota–owned Sioux City–Aberdeen line would be up in 4 or 5 years. Even if these possibilities came to fruition, would DM&E's future be guaranteed? Maybe a more daring option was in order? The rich, low-sulfur coal fields of Wyoming lay 200 or so miles west of the Colony Line. Extending DM&E's tracks to those mines and rebuilding the current main line to hold heavy coal trains would cost in the 10 figures! Both UP and BNSF undoubtedly would be furious at someone breaking their transportation monopoly. Yet, DM&E could offer the shortest route to Chicago and the upper Midwest, and shipping coal by barge down the Mississippi was also an option. "Well, Rome wasn't built in a day," Schieffer muttered to himself as he reached for his briefcase and car keys.

REFERENCES

[1] "Business Trails '96 Pace," *DM&E Enroute* (July 1997): 3.

[2] "Employee Meeting Highlights," *DM&E Enroute* (February 1997): 4a.

[3] Ibid: 4a.

RailTex, Inc.—1998

Paul R. Reed
Ronald L. Earl
Donald Bumpass

www.railtex.com
stock symbol RTEX

As the 737 began its long descent into the San Antonio, Texas, airport, Bruce Flohr checked his watch and concluded that the flight would arrive at the gate 15 to 20 minutes late. Still, he would have plenty of time to get to the RailTex, Inc., headquarters (210-841-7600) in San Antonio, Texas, and get briefings from his principal staff. Although Flohr's visit with some of the Wall Street "gurus" went well, he still felt ill at ease. The railroad industry had never been as volatile as during the last few years, and RailTex would have to work even harder to maintain its position as one of the leading operators of short line freight railroads in North America.

RailTex continued to prosper in 1997, posting record carloadings, operating revenues, operating income, net income, and earnings per basic common share. Carloadings increased 36 percent to 488,264; operating revenues grew 23 percent to $148.8 million; operating income increased 4 percent to $23 million; net income rose 6 percent to $10.6 million; and earnings per basic common share increased 6 percent to $1.16. See financial and operations data in Exhibits 1, 2, 3, and 4.

The Beginnings

Flohr started RailTex as an open-top hopper freight car leasing company in 1977. The company's target market was quarry operators who needed this type of car to haul sand, gravel, and rock for construction sites. By 1989, the leasing business had grown to 630 railcars and annual revenues of $8 million. RailTex branched into the short line railroad business in 1984 when it acquired a ten-year lease from the city of San Diego, California, to operate the 145-mile-long San Diego & Imperial Valley Railroad. Flohr and his RailTex team immediately turned the perennial loser into a profit maker by reducing operating costs and greatly increasing the marketing effort. Annual traffic grew from 1,600 to 6,000 carloads within three years. Similar success followed as RailTex increased its short line holdings to nine by 1989. At this juncture, it became obvious to Flohr that the successful leasing and short line branches of the company were demanding capital far in excess of RailTex's ability to raise it. Major railroad downsizing and resultant short line spin-offs appeared to offer the brightest future for the company, so RailTex sold off the car-leasing portion of the firm and used the proceeds from that sale to reduce debt and provide funding for rail line acquisition. RailTex continued to expand its short line empire in the 1990s.

This case was prepared by Professors Paul R. Reed, Ronald L. Earl, and Donald Bumpass of Sam Houston State University as a basis for class discussion. It is not intended to illustrate either effective or ineffective handling of an administrative situation. Copyright © 1999 by Prentice Hall, Inc. ISBN 0-13-011143-0.

EXHIBIT 1: RailTex, Inc., and Subsidiaries, Consolidated Statements of Income

(in thousands of dollars, except per share amounts)	Years Ended December 31,		
	1997	1996	1995
Operating Revenues	$148,791	$121,106	$107,841
Operating Revenues:			
Transportation	54,361	39,006	33,523
General and administrative	26,367	20,948	21,250
Equipment	17,954	15,718	15,828
Maintenance of way	14,168	13,246	11,208
Depreciation and amortization	12,940	10,147	8,237
Special Charge	0	0	2,140
Total operating expenses	125,790	99,065	92,186
Operating Income	23,001	22,041	15,655
Interest Expense	(10,527)	(6,893)	(5,696)
Other Income, net	4,198	1,521	1,715
Income Before Income Taxes	16,672	16,669	11,674
Income Taxes	(6,048)	(6,708)	(4,776)
Net Income	$10,624	$9,961	$6,898
Basic Earnings per Share	$1.16	$1.09	$0.79
Weighted Average Number of Basic Shares of Common Stock Outstanding	9,153	9,112	8,699
Diluted Earnings per Share	$1.15	$1.08	$0.78
Weighted Average Number of Diluted Shares of Common Stock Outstanding	9,222	9,231	8,897

Source: RailTex, Inc., and Subsidiaries, *Annual Report* (1997): 29.

EXHIBIT 2:   RailTex, Inc., and Subsidiaries, Consolidated Statements of Cash Flows

	For the Years Ended December 31,		
(in thousands of dollars)	*1997*	*1996*	*1995*
Operating Activities:			
Net income	$10,624	$9,961	$6,898
Adjustments to reconcile net income to net cash provided by operating activities:			
Depreciation and amortization	12,940	10,147	8,237
Special Charge	0	0	2,140
Deferred income taxes	2,182	3,424	1,371
Provision for losses on accounts receivable	638	783	544
Amortization of deferred financing costs	384	348	345
Gain on sale of assets	(6,771)	(1,280)	(1,599)
Write down of investments	2,100	0	0
Other	(275)	0	0
Changes in current assets and liabilities affecting operations—			
Accounts receivable	(5,975)	(6,950)	(7,817)
Prepaid expenses	(59)	51	(177)
Accounts payable and accrued liabilities	10,109	7,035	7,824
Net cash provided by operating activities	25,897	23,519	17,766
Investing Activities:			
Purchase of property and equipment	(35,507)	(21,393)	(23,975)
Proceeds from sale of property and equipment	7,327	2,354	2,320
Purchase of new properties and related equipment and other costs	(25,978)	(16,682)	(40,200)
Purchase of investments in Brazilian railroad companies and related costs	(1,362)	(21,775)	0
Sale of preferred shares in Brazilian railroad company	2,758	0	0
Organization and acquisition costs	(97)	(88)	(484)
(Increase) decrease in other assets	(152)	(917)	25
Net cash used in investing activities	(53,011)	(58,501)	(62,314)
Financing Activities:			
Short-term notes payable, net	218	(937)	27
Proceeds from long-term debt	75,000	41,569	100,343
Principal payments on long-term debt and capital leases	(53,398)	(5,197)	(81,144)
Net increase in working capital facility	4,000	0	0
Deferred financing costs	(369)	(465)	(521)
Issuance of common stock	74	25	25,749
Net cash provided by financing activities	25,525	34,995	44,454
Effect of Exchange Rate Changes on Cash	51	(35)	57
Net Change in Cash and Cash Equivalents	(1,538)	(22)	(37)
Cash and Cash Equivalents, beginning of year	2,108	2,130	2,167
Cash and Cash Equivalents, end of year	$570	$2,108	$2,130

Source: RailTex, Inc., and Subsidiaries, *Annual Report* (1997): 32.

EXHIBIT 3: RailTex, Inc., and Subsidiaries, Consolidated Balance Sheets

	December 31,	
(in thousands of dollars, except per share amounts)	*1997*	*1996*
ASSETS		
Current Assets:		
Cash and cash equivalents	$570	$2,108
Accounts receivable, less doubtful receivables of $1,563 in 1997; $612 in 1996	32,171	26,834
Prepaid expenses	2,527	2,468
Deferred tax assets, net	1,777	1,141
Total current assets	37,045	32,551
Property and Equipment, net	259,444	209,420
Other Assets:		
Investments in Brazilian railroad companies	17,809	21,380
Other, net	5,610	6,119
Total other assets	23,419	27,499
Total assets	319,908	269,470
LIABILITIES AND SHAREHOLDERS' EQUITY		
Current Liabilities:		
Short-term notes payable	384	352
Current portion of long-term debt	7,763	6,361
Accounts payable	18,829	14,624
Accrued liabilities	17,434	11,445
Total current liabilities	44,410	32,782
Deferred Income Taxes, Net	20,521	17,703
Long-Term Debt	112,893	87,343
Senior Notes Payable	00	50,985
Senior Subordinated Notes Payable	5,000	5,000
Other Liabilities	3,826	3,939
Total liabilities	186,650	146,767
Commitments and Contingencies		
Shareholders' Equity:		
Preferred Stock; $1.00 par value; 10 million shares authorized; no shares issued or outstanding	0	0
Common stock; $.10 par value; 30 million shares authorized; issued and outstanding 9,160,924 in 1997; 9,124,290 in 1996	916	912
Paid-in capital	83,799	83,629
Retained earnings	48,901	38,277
Cumulative translation adjustment	(358)	(115)
Total shareholders' equity	133,258	122,703
Total liabilities and shareholders' equity	319,908	269,470

Source: RailTex, Inc., and Subsidiaries, *Annual Report* (1997): 30.

EXHIBIT 4: RailTex, Inc., and Subsidiaries, Selected Consolidated Financial and Operating Data

	Years Ended December 31,				
(in thousands of dollars, except per share and operating data)	1997	1996	1995	1994	1993
Summary of Income Statement Data:					
Operating revenues	$148,791	$121,106	$107,841	$74,528	$59,849
Operating expenses	(125,790)	(99,065)	(90,046)	(61,351)	(49,534)
Operating income before Special Charge	23,001	22,041	17,795	13,177	10,315
Special Charge[a]	0	0	(2,140)	0	0
Operating income	23,001	22,041	15,655	13,177	10,315
Interest expense	(10,527)	(6,893)	(5,696)	(2,965)	(4,719)
Other income, net	4,198	1,521	1,715	1,287	504
Income before taxes	16,672	16,669	11,674	11,499	6,100
Income taxes	(6,048)	(6,708)	(4,776)	(4,618)	(2,467)
Net income	$10,624	$9,961	$6,898	$6,881	$3,633
Per Share Data[b]:					
Basic earnings per share	$1.16	$1.09	$0.79	$0.96	$0.73
Weighted average number of basic shares of Common Stock (in thousands)	9,153	9,112	8,699	7,157	4,991
Diluted earnings per share	$1.15	$1.08	$0.78	$0.88	$0.65
Weighted average number of diluted shares of Common Stock (in thousands)	9,222	9,231	8,897	7,820	5,621
Operating Data:					
Total track mileage[c]	3,884	3,431	3,390	2,713	2,496
Total carloads	488,264	359,669	318,187	253,163	222,909
Total employees[c]	873	720	681	505	402
Operating revenues per mile[c]	38,309	35,298	31,812	27,471	23,978
Operating revenues per carload	305	337	339	294	268
Operating revenues per employee	170,436	168,203	158,357	147,580	148,878
Carloads per mile[c]	126	105	94	93	89
Carloads per employee[c]	559	500	467	501	555
Labor ratio[d]	30.9%	28.9%	30.3%	29.1%	30.6%
Operating ratio before Special Charge[e]	84.5%	81.8%	83.5%	82.3%	82.8%
Operating ratio after Special Charge[e]	84.5%	81.8%	85.5%	82.3%	82.8%
Balance Sheet Data as of Period End:					
Total assets	319,908	269,470	204,982	139,656	113,303
Long-term debt	125,656	98,704	58,911	43,389	29,310
Shareholders' equity	133,258	122,703	112,602	72,382	65,671

[a] A result of the disposition of a railroad.
[b] The Company adopted Statement of Financial Accounting Standards No. 128, "Earnings Per Share," effective December 15, 1997, and as a result reported earnings per share for 1993, 1994, 1995, and 1996 were restated.
[c] Total track mileage and total employees are calculated based on weighted monthly averages over the respective periods.
[d] Labor ratio equals labor expenses divided by operating revenues.
[e] Operating ratio equals operating expenses divided by operating revenues.
Source: Adapted from RailTex, Inc., and Subsidiaries, Annual Report (1997): 18.

INTERNAL ENVIRONMENT

Description of the Company

The RailTex vision statement reads:

> We are a growing, international, rail-oriented, logistics company that is customer focused, locally managed and centrally supported. We value quality of life, character, personal initiative, creativity, team work, and perseverance. We are highly motivated, innovative, and multi-skilled. We are trained to understand and empowered to rapidly respond to our customers' needs in a safe, effective, and efficient manner. Our success in converting opportunities into realities benefits our co-workers, customers, shareholders, and the communities we serve.

Through its subsidiaries, RailTex operates 29 short line railroads in the United States, Canada, and Mexico. These lines total 3,915 miles and vary in length from 14 to 527 miles. Traffic on individual railroads runs from a few hundred to approximately 50,000 carloads annually. RailTex also owns a 10 percent equity interest in a 4,400-mile railroad in central and eastern Brazil and a 6 percent equity interest in a 4,200-mile railroad in southern Brazil. Both railroads had been operating at a loss due to bloated payrolls, poor track and equipment maintenance, and inefficient operating procedures. RailTex personnel were instrumental in the turnaround of both lines. Payroll was halved and steps were instituted to correct other deficiencies. Flohr feels the Brazilian properties will add greatly to RailTex's bottom line within a few years.

The majority of RailTex track is maintained to support train speeds of 25 mph or less. This is in keeping with the relatively short distance that its trains travel and with the delivery and pickup nature of its business. On those rail lines where time is a factor, RailTex maintains track that can support speeds up to 40 or 60 mph. This flexible philosophy often enables RailTex to have lower capital expenditures for track maintenance than the previous owners had. Regular track maintenance is performed by RailTex employees and major renovations usually are contracted out. Most of this labor is not unionized and wages are, accordingly, lower.

The company owned 266 locomotives and leased 15 others as of year-end, 1997. The locomotives have an average age of 32 years and most have been rebuilt or overhauled within the last several years. Unit availability averaged 90 percent in 1997, but it should be noted that not all of RailTex's locomotives can operate at peak efficiency. Such a situation is not unusual for short lines. RailTex personnel perform normal maintenance and midlevel overhaul and a large part of major overhaul is contracted out. RailTex owns or leases 1,234 freight cars of various categories and has a rent sharing agreement with owners of 2,571 additional cars that are used by on-line shippers.

Lumber and forest products, coal, and chemicals made up 45.5 percent of RailTex's revenues in 1997. Some of its railroads have a diversified traffic mix and others ship only one or two commodities. In time, RailTex hopes to reduce its heavy reliance on a few types of traffic by acquiring railroads that ship other commodities. Exhibit 5 shows freight revenues and carloads by commodity group.

EXHIBIT 5: RailTex, Inc., Freight Revenues and Carloads Comparison by Commodity Group

	Freight Revenues			
	1997		1996	
	(dollars in thousands)			
Commodity Group	*Dollars*	*% of Total*	*Dollars*	*% of Total*
Lumber and forest products	$24,155	18.9%	$21,811	21.2%
Coal	18,937	14.8	16,240	15.8
Chemicals	15,120	11.8	11,484	11.1
Scrap paper and paper products	12,113	9.5	9,758	9.5
Farm Products	10,269	8.0	8,986	8.7
Scrap metal and metal products	10,107	7.9	7,419	7.2
Food products	6,461	5.0	5,944	5.8
Nonmetallic ores	6,346	5.0	6,898	6.7
Autos and auto parts	5,385	4.2	478	0.5
Petroleum products	5,375	4.2	4,767	4.6
Mineral and stone	5,228	4.1	5,008	4.9
Railroad equipment	3,900	3.0	1,374	1.3
Other	4,618	3.6	2,850	2.7
	$128,014	100.0%	$103,017	100.0%

| | Carloads | | | | Average Freight Revenues Per Carload[a] | |
| | 1997 | | 1996 | | | |
Commodity Group	*Number*	*% of Total*	*Number*	*% of Total*	*1997*	*1996*
Lumber and forest products	63,903	13.1%	57,456	16.0%	$378	$380
Coal	99,322	20.3	84,957	23.6	191	191
Chemicals	47,066	9.6	33,221	9.2	321	346
Scrap paper and paper products	33,996	7.0	24,075	6.7	356	405
Farm Products	40,276	8.2	34,767	9.7	255	258
Scrap metal and metal products	37,354	7.7	23,231	6.5	271	319
Food products	24,625	5.0	22,049	6.1	262	270
Nonmetallic ores	35,511	7.3	36,365	10.1	179	190
Autos and auto parts	31,003	6.3	738	0.2	174	647
Petroleum products	14,162	2.9	11,623	3.2	380	410
Mineral and stone	15,457	3.2	14,306	4.0	338	350
Railroad equipment	24,901	5.1	7,284	2.0	157	189
Other	20,688	4.3	9,597	2.7	223	297
	488,264	100.0%	359,669	100.0%	$262	$286

[a]Calculated as freight revenues divided by car loads.
Source: RailTex, Inc., Form 10-5 (1997): 20.

Management

Flohr has been chair of the board and chief executive officer since he founded RailTex in 1977. Flohr has 32 years of railroad experience and held top leadership positions in the Federal Railroad Administration and the Southern Pacific Transportation Company. He is a founder and past chair of the Regional Railroads of America, and is a director of the Association of American Railroads. Flohr has been described as the "classic entrepreneurial visionary." He restructured the company and his role in it as the organization expanded in size and complexity. Flohr believes in empowering subordinates and is a relations-type leader.

Staff Support, Compensation

Flohr has stressed a decentralized management structure by placing a general manager (GM) in charge of each railroad who is responsible for pricing, staffing, purchasing, marketing, and operations. Every railroad has a corporate approved annual plan which is updated quarterly and reviewed monthly.

GMs report to a regional general manager (RGM). (The three RailTex regions are Mississippi River—East, Mississippi River—West, and Canada.) The three RGMs have their offices at corporate headquarters and serve not only as supervisors but as points of contact, expediters, advisors, and mentors, but final decisions are still in the purview of the GMs.

Corporate staff supports the short lines by developing policies in such functional areas as safety, maintenance, fuel purchase, human resources, accounting, and government regulation compliance, as well as by providing financial and strategic planning guidance. The corporate marketing staff assists at and coordinates sales calls, provides industrial development expertise, and offers formal marketing training.

Each railroad's workforce varies in size and composition. The smallest railroad has four employees and the largest has 108. The majority of lines have a manager in charge of train operations, a marketing director, and one or more clerks. Every railroad has a transportation specialist (transpec) who operates the locomotive and switches cars. Flexibility is the key on the short line and cross-training of employees is a must. Transpecs make minor engine or railcar repairs, grab a broom, wield a paint brush, and do other jobs as necessary. All employees are expected to pitch in when and where needed. This willingness to do the "extra" enhances teamwork and morale, and eliminates the need to hire individuals to perform narrowly defined jobs, as often is done on unionized railroads.

At corporate headquarters, employees below executive and senior management levels receive quarterly profit sharing based on a percentage of their aggregate salaries. The Executive Incentive Plan pertains to managers, GMs, and above. From 20 to 40 percent of their annual compensation is at "risk" based upon goal attainment, and the remainder of their salaries is fixed. In addition, stock options and other long-term incentives are available if various performance targets are met or exceeded.

Growth Strategy

Corporate strategy is twofold. The first is to increase the number of short lines in the RailTex portfolio while maintaining diversity of railroad geographic location, types of commodities hauled, customers served, and connecting railroads. For example, operating too many railroads in one area could overexpose the company to a regional recession, and relying too heavily on hauling coal could subject the firm to the uncertainties of environmental legislation and the weather.

The second strategy is to grow each railroad from within. Improving service to current customers while increasing marketing efforts to attract new and former rail users adds to the revenue side of the operation. At the same time, operating efficiency and a flexible workforce have a positive impact on expenses. Annual increases in the number of carloads and resultant operating revenue growth are a perennial occurrence on the vast majority of RailTex properties. Operating expenses, in general, increase along with higher operating revenues but at a lesser rate. The result is an improved bottom line.

Acquisition Technique

RailTex owns 19 North American rail lines, leases four, both owns and leases four others, and operates two under contract. (The four lines added in 1996 and the two lines added during the first six months of 1997 were by purchase.) Normally, RailTex bids against other short line line operators for available properties. The selling railroad makes its selection based on such factors as the price it will receive from the buyer and the price per carload it will pay the new operator for interchanged traffic. Other important factors for the divesting line to consider are the prospective operator's experience and ability to close the financial transaction and begin immediate operations.

RailTex has a competitive advantage over many of its short line competitors due to its ability to finance acquisitions quickly with borrowings under a $75 million revolving line of credit and a $25 million Canadian revolving credit line.

New properties are integrated into RailTex by a "Go Team," headed by the RGM, of selected marketing, support, and operational personnel from headquarters and the other RailTex railroads. The Go Team arrives on site while the former owner is still operating the line. Visits with customers and familiarization with the property have top priority. After a few days, RailTex's policies and procedures are put in place and the Go Team begins operating the line until the newly appointed GM has time to hire and train a permanent workforce. Assembling a workforce is often difficult, particularly if the divesting line's employees are unionized. Many elect to transfer to other union jobs rather than join RailTex. The Go Team usually completes its work in a few weeks and its members return to their regular jobs. The Go Team innovation helps the new line begin operations with minimum interruption and service delay. Some glitches occur, however, such as railcars put in wrong sidings, missed connections, and other mishaps. Safety is always paramount.

Marketing

Marketing plays a key role in RailTex's combination strategies of acquisition and internal growth of "same railroad," i.e., increased revenues on railroads owned more than one year. The company's marketing efforts are aimed at satisfying the business needs of its more than 940 customers. The company often increases scheduled train service or dispatches extra trains in the event of a customer emergency. It also helps customers negotiate price and service levels with connecting railroads, and secures various types of railcars to assist customers in their operations. Such arrangements can be made by equipment purchase, lease, or rental. See Exhibit 6 for listing of railroads with which RailTex may interchange traffic.

EXHIBIT 6: RailTex, Inc., and Subsidiaries, Interchanged Traffic

| | 1997 | | 1996 | |
Connecting Carrier	Freight Revenues	Carloads	Freight Revenues	Carloads
Union Pacific Corporation	31.8%	27.8%	37.3%	38.2%
Canadian National Railways	19.8	19.3	20.5	13.9
CSX Transportation, Inc.	18.9	22.1	16.2	19.1
Consolidated Rail Corporation	10.6	8.6	8.4	6.8
Norfolk Southern Railway Company	8.0	10.7	6.2	9.8
Burlington Northern Sante Fe Railway Company	3.7	2.4	4.7	3.3
All other railroads	7.2	9.1	6.7	8.9
Total interchanged traffic	100.0%	100.0%	100.0%	100.0%

Source: RailTex, Inc., and Subsidiaries, *Annual Report* (1997): 8.

The GM is responsible for the railroad's marketing effort. These managers are assisted not only by local and corporate marketing personnel but also by their entire staff. All employees have business cards. Transpecs, for example, are encouraged to identify and, if possible, satisfy customer needs as they pick up and deliver railcars on site. Items beyond their control are passed on to the appropriate individual for action.

Each railroad marketing director/salesperson job has been restructured to eliminate most duties in the nonmarketing areas. Much of their time is now devoted to making customer contacts and identify potential customers within 50 miles of the rail line. Off-line businesses are made aware of the cost and service advantages of using a combination of rail/truck transportation. Marketer compensation has become more commission-based and bonuses are tied to revenue growth. A semiannual performance quality survey measures customer satisfaction. The response rate has increased to 90 percent and a 6 on a 7-point Likert scale is the target for this customer critical success factor.

Human Resources Management

The Human Resources Management (HRM) function at RailTex is in transition. There is a greater interest in corporatewide policies and procedures to guide the field operations. Hiring and on-the-job training are done at the department/railroad level, and pay, benefits, performance appraisal development, and record keeping are done in San Antonio. RailTex continually stresses the importance of employees as people and as the real cause of the company's success. This philosophy seems to permeate the organization.

Communications

Good communications are a must for the geographically spread RailTex operations. The company appears to utilize a wide variety of techniques to communicate with its various constituencies. Headquarters employees attend monthly breakfast meetings, and the RGMs and other corporate officials hold frequent "town hall meetings" out on the rail lines. Face-to-face communications is supplemented by the HRM-slanted bimonthly *RailTex Express* employee newsletter, as well as by the *RailTex Quarterly*, which provides a wider message to employees and customers. The company provides a toll-free fax number for current and potential shareholders to obtain the latest news releases. The company also utilizes and responds to employee attitude surveys and an anonymous question-and-answer section of *RailTex Express*. RailTex also encourages employees to use the phone to find answers, and provides a corporate "Yellow Pages" with processes alphabetized and described and the individual(s) responsible.

Training

Acquiring or updating skills, abilities, and knowledge is a must for all RailTex employees. Flohr has attended executive management courses at Stanford. GMs attend biannual in-house seminars on managerial techniques. New GMs receive training at headquarters and in the field, such as at the Hazardous Materials School in Pueblo, Colorado. Headquarters hosts 1-week ground schools for new transpecs. Many other training programs are scheduled when needed, such as a recent headquarters conference for future leaders. On-the-job training is ubiquitous out on the railroads, with RailTex providing support such as videos and other training aids on request. Safety is the topic that dominates most employee instruction.

Pay

RailTex pays its craft, clerical, and nonunion employees very competitively versus local rates. Individual pay within job categories is a function of location, performance, and revenue/profit. Rates of pay are 15 to 25 percent below wages for comparable union jobs. Profit sharing at RailTex normally reduces this disparity by half or more.

Benefits

The benefits package offered by RailTex equals or exceeds those provided by the major union railroads. Exhibit 7 gives a sample comparison.

Unions

Union activity has not been a major issue at RailTex. Currently, the 37 operations employees from three of RailTex's U.S. railroads are represented by the United Transportation Union (UTU). The collective bargaining agreement negotiations are still going on between the UTU and each railroad. The 14 employees of one Canadian RailTex

EXHIBIT 7:   Sample Benefit Comparison

Benefit	RailTex	Unionized National Railroad Plan
Life insurance	$50,000	$10,000
Accidental D&D	$50,000	$8,000
401(k)	yes	not provided
Profit sharing	yes	not provided
Maximum medical	$1,000,000	$500,000
Deductible	$100 each individual $300 family	$100 each individual $200 family
Maximum out-of-pocket	$500 individual $1,000 family	$2,000 each person covered

Source: RailTex, Inc., Benefit Brochure.

property are represented by the Brotherhood of Locomotive Engineers. A major issue for both unions was the lack of similarity of wage rates when compared to equally skilled union employees on adjacent rail lines. An arbitration panel ruled the wage rate should be local nonrailroad union prevailing wage, not the connecting large railroad wage scale.

Although future union activity is uncertain, it appears that unionization presently is a minor threat to the company. The 51 unionized employees represent only 6 percent of the RailTex workforce. The revenue and operating income contributions of these four unionized lines to RailTex are relatively small.

THE FUTURE

As the 737 touched down, Flohr began summing up his thoughts of the last several minutes. RailTex had been following basically a horizontal integration/market penetration combination strategy since start-up. Line acquisition had slowed since the 1993 purchases of four large lines (averaging 300 miles) and four smaller lines (averaging 24 miles). "Same railroad" growth also had slowed. Had these lines "topped out" or would a greater marketing effort be needed? What of other strategies, such as product development or market development? Trackside warehouses which offer transload facilities between rail and truck appeared promising and would enable RailTex to serve new customers 50 to 75 miles from its rail lines. Funding decisions were intertwined in all of this. Debt to equity was already .1 above the industry average, and stock prices in the $18 to $19 range didn't encourage another secondary offering. Flohr concluded that he and the new vice-president for business development and acquisitions would have much to talk about during the next several days. The old adrenaline kicked up a notch as the plane came to the gate.

REFERENCES

Interviews with President Bruce M. Flohr, RailTex, Inc., February-June 1997.

"RailTex, Inc.," *Basic Report*, A. G. Edwards & Sons Inc., June 18, 1996, p. 1.

"RailTex, Inc. (A), Case 9-395-033," *Harvard Business School*, March 95, p. 8.

"Indiana & Ohio," *CTC Board*, June 1997, pp. 52-53.

Greyhound Lines, Inc.—1998

James Harbin

www.greyhound.com
stock symbol BUS

Headquartered in Dallas, Texas, Greyhound (214-789-7000) is the only nationwide provider of scheduled intercity bus transportation services in the United States. The company's primary business consists of scheduled passenger service, package express service, and food services at certain terminals which accounted for 85.4 percent, 4.6 percent, and 2.8 percent, respectively, of the company's total operating revenues for 1997. (See Exhibit 1.) The company's operations include a nationwide network of terminal and maintenance facilities; a fleet of approximately 2,400 buses; and approximately 1,600 sales outlets. In 1997, Greyhound carried 20.7 million passengers to destinations all across America. Greyhound ended the year 1997 with a net loss of $16.9 million, the third consecutive year loss.

Everyone understands that annual reports are stated in positive terms. A critic of Greyhound could say that although total operating revenues of $771 million in 1997 indeed were 10 percent better than 1996 (see Exhibit 2), they were only 1 percent better than 1992. Total assets increased from $500 million in 1996 to $566 million in 1997 (see Exhibit 3).

There are those who believe that for Greyhound, there is a light at the end of the tunnel rather than a rapidly approaching train—or plane. Greyhound is the sole remaining national bus company. By virtue of having a monopoly, one would think that, with sufficient demand, a company could squeeze out a profit.

PREVIOUS MANAGEMENT AND PAST MISTAKES

Reengineering—or Digging a Hole?

Frank Schmieder, a former investment banker who had worked 2 years for Greyhound, took over as CEO in 1991 just before the company declared bankruptcy. Employees saw Schmieder as an intelligent, although volatile, boss, and union leaders saw him as an affable negotiator who occasionally rode the bus and ate in terminal lunchrooms. The creditors who had appointed him as CEO were impressed by his cost-cutting fever. That fever was shared by his 46-year-old lieutenant, M. Michael Doyle, who came to Greyhound in 1987 from a finance post at Philips Petroleum Company. A brusque, compact, numbers-oriented executive, Doyle sometimes was intimidating.

Although neither man had much transportation experience, they hammered together a reorganization plan that called for relentless cutting of workers, routes, services, and buses. The bus fleet was reduced from 3,700 to 2,400. All that cutting, combined with a

---

EXHIBIT 1: Greyhound Lines, Inc., and Subsidiaries, Results of Operations

The following table sets forth the Company's results of operations as a percentage of total operating revenue for 1997, 1996 and 1995:

	Years Ended December 31,		
	1997	*1996*	*1995*
Operating Revenues			
Transportation Services			
Regular route	85.4%	85.3%	85.3%
Package express	4.6	4.8	5.4
Food services	2.8	3.0	3.0
Other operating revenues	7.2	6.9	6.3
Total Operating Revenues	100.0	100.0	100.0
Operating Expenses			
Maintenance	10.0	10.5	10.4
Transportation	24.3	24.4	23.9
Agents' commissions and station costs	18.3	18.8	19.1
Marketing, advertising, and traffic	3.5	3.7	3.9
Insurance and safety	5.9	5.9	8.0
General and administrative	11.8	11.5	11.0
Depreciation and amortization	4.0	4.4	4.7
Operating taxes and licenses	6.7	7.1	7.3
Operating rents	7.7	7.7	7.3
Cost of goods sold—Food services	1.7	1.9	1.9
Other operating expenses	1.3	1.1	1.1
Total Operating Expenses	95.2	97.0	98.6
Operating Income	4.8	3.0	1.4
Interest Expense	3.6	3.9	4.0
Income Tax Provision	0.1	0	0.1
Net Income (Loss) before Extraordinary Items	1.1	(0.9)	(2.7)

The following table sets forth certain operating data for the Company for 1997, 1996, and 1995. Certain statistics have been adjusted and restated from those previously published to provide consistent comparisons.

	Years Ended December 31,		
	1997	*1996*	*1995*
Regular Service Miles (000's)	285,749	265,259	256,683
Total Bus Miles (000's)	291,597	270,187	259,746
Passenger Miles (000's)	6,977,301	6,243,262	6,033,780
Passengers Carried (000's)	20,735	18,348	17,548
Average Trip Length (passenger miles/passengers carried)	336	340	344
Load (avg. number of passengers per regular service mile)	24.4	23.5	23.5
Load Factor (percentage of available seats filled)	53.1%	51.2%	51.1%
Yield (regular route revenue/passenger mile)	$0.0944	$0.0957	$0.0929
Total Revenue per Total Bus Mile	2.64	2.59	2.53
Operating Income per Total Bus Mile	0.13	0.08	0.04
Cost per Total Bus Mile:			
Maintenance	$0.264	$0.272	$0.264
Transportation	0.642	0.633	0.604

Source: Greyhound Lines, Inc., and Subsidiaries, *Annual Report* (1997): 20.

EXHIBIT 2: Greyhound Lines, Inc. and Subsidiaries, Consolidated Statements of Operations

	Years Ended December 31,		
(in thousands of dollars, except per share amounts)	*1997*	*1996*	*1995*
Operating Revenues			
Transportation services			
Regular route	658,396	597,779	560,239
Package express	35,676	33,527	35,690
Food services	21,411	21,363	19,440
Other operating revenues	55,639	48,189	41,752
Total Operating Revenues	771,122	700,858	657,121
Operating Expenses			
Maintenance	77,022	73,441	68,540
Transportation	187,311	170,979	156,878
Agents' commissions and station costs	141,100	131,715	125,650
Marketing, advertising, and traffic	26,860	25,811	25,513
Insurance and safety	45,860	41,088	52,820
General and administrative	90,752	80,496	72,105
Depreciation and amortization	31,259	30,683	31,010
Operating taxes and licenses	51,511	49,831	48,186
Operating rents	59,105	53,993	47,884
Cost of goods sold—Food services	13,289	13,774	12,597
Other operating expenses	9,947	8,243	6,575
Total Operating Expenses	734,016	680,054	647,758
Operating Income	37,106	20,804	9,363
Interest Expense	27,657	27,346	26,807
Net Income (Loss) before Income Taxes	9,449	(6,542)	(17,444)
Income Tax Provision	1,051	62	374
Net Income (Loss) before Extraordinary Item	8,398	(6,604)	(17,818)
Extraordinary Item	25,323	0	0
Net Loss	(16,925)	(6,604)	(17,818)
Preferred Dividends	3,648	0	0
Net Loss Attributable to Common Stockholders	(20,573)	(6,604)	(17,818)
Net Income (Loss) Attributable to Common Stockholders before Extraordinary Item	4,750	(6,604)	(17,818)
Net Income (Loss) per Share of Common Stock:			
Basic			
Net Income (Loss) Attributable to Common Stockholders before Extraordinary Item	0.08	(0.11)	(0.33)
Extraordinary Item	(0.43)	0	0
Net Loss Attributable to Common Stockholders	(0.35)	(0.11)	(0.33)
Diluted			
Net Income (Loss) Attributable to Common Stockholders before Extraordinary Item	0.08	(0.11)	(0.33)
Extraordinary Item	(0.42)	0	0
Net Loss Attributable to Common Stockholders	(0.34)	(0.11)	(0.33)

Source: Greyhound Lines, Inc., and Subsidiaries, *Annual Report* (1997): 33.

EXHIBIT 3: Greyhound Lines, Inc., and Subsidiaries, Consolidated Statements of Financial Position

	December 31,	
(in thousands of dollars, except per share amounts)	*1997*	*1996*
Current Assets		
Cash and cash equivalents	2,052	898
Accounts receivable, less allowance for doubtful accounts of $268 and $241	35,364	32,844
Inventories	4,658	3,840
Prepaid expenses	4,949	8,179
Assets held for sale	3,889	4,224
Other current assets	9,694	11,329
Total Current Assets	60,606	61,314
Prepaid Pension Plans	25,378	24,927
Property, Plant and Equipment, net of accumulated depreciation of $124,374 and $101,901	341,292	314,454
Investments in Unconsolidatd Affiliates	6,076	2,437
Insurance and Security Deposits	72,693	76,180
Goodwill, net of accumulated amortization of $499 and $0	30,215	0
Intangible Assets, net of accumulated amortization of $22,188 and $19,105	30,333	20,970
Total Assets	566,593	500,282
Current Liabilities		
Accounts payable	32,731	23,900
Accrued liabilities	62,237	53,500
Unredeemed tickets	10,325	9,523
Current portion of reserve for injuries and damages	21,374	19,864
Current maturities of long-term debt	4,469	11,662
Total Current Liabilities	131,136	118,449
Reserve for Injuries and Damages	36,591	40,099
Long-Term Debt	207,953	192,581
Other Liabilities	11,314	8,272
Total Liabilities	386,994	359,401
Commitments and Contingencies		
Stockholders' Equity		
Preferred Stock (10,000,000 shares authorized; par value $.01)		
8½% Convertible Exchangeable Preferred Stock (2,760,000 shares authorized and 2,400,000 shares issued as of December 31, 1997; aggregate liquidation preference $60,000)	60,000	0
Series A Junior Preferred Stock (1,500,000 and 500,000 shares authorized as of December 31, 1997, and 1996; par value $.01; none issued)	0	0
Common Stock (100,000,000 shares authorized; 59,437,514 and 58,469,469 shares issued as of December 31, 1997, and 1996, respectively; par value $.01)	594	585
Capital in Excess of Par Value	229,365	229,104
Retained Deficit	(101,809)	(81,237)
Less: Unfunded Accumulated Pension Obligation	(7,513)	(6,533)
Less: Treasury Stock, at cost (109,192 shares)	(1,038)	(1,038)
Total Stockholders' Equity	179,599	140,881
Total Liabilities and Stockholders' Equity	566,593	500,282

Source: Adapted from Greyhound Lines, Inc., and Subsidiaries, *Annual Report* (1997): 32.

plan to computerize everything from passenger reservations to fleet scheduling, won Wall Street's approval. Within a month of Greyhound's emergence from Chapter 11, its newly issued stock was trading at $13.50 a share, compared with the $4.00 to $7.50 expected by its own advisers.

At headquarters, some employees had to search vacant offices to get office supplies. Some drivers said they had to break speed limits to meet the new schedules. Ridership began to slide in 1992. Yet, industry analysts remained bullish as cost cutting led to a year-end profit of $11 million on revenues of $683 million. This was Greyhound's first profitable year since 1989.

Meanwhile, at the local level, turnover approached 100 percent at some terminals; 30 percent was not unusual. In survey after survey, customers listed discourtesy as a major problem. Some terminal workers were observed making fun of customers and ignoring them. Under the new cost-cutting policy of not handling customers' baggage, bags were often found piled up and left unprotected.

A Reservation System Called TRIPS

In April 1993, with management's promise that TRIPS would be the key unlocking Greyhound's turnaround, the company rolled out a prospectus for a $90 million stock offering. Doyle, as chief financial officer, and several other top Greyhound executives heavily promoted the offering.

There were some serious reservations within the company concerning this new computerized reservation system. Even the vice-president in charge of developing TRIPS, Thomas Thompson, tried to warn Doyle of anticipated problems through written reports at one particular meeting. His objections, as he recalls, were quickly rejected by Doyle, who declared, "We made these commitments, and, by God, we're going to live up to them" and ruled out any further discussion of dissent.

Several employees believed that most of the critical reports on TRIPS were destroyed and any mention of the critical reports was purged from many Greyhound agendas, calendars, and computer files. However, Doyle says he never ordered or knew of the destruction of any TRIPS-related documents. "I don't believe that I ever cut anybody off," he said. "Ultimately, [TRIPS] was a group decision."

The prospectus for the $90 million stock offering pledged that TRIPS would improve customer service, make ticket buying convenient, and allow customers to reserve space on specific trips. Some Greyhound executives were incredulous; their passengers were accustomed to arriving at a terminal, buying a ticket, and catching a bus. Some wondered how many of its low-income passengers would have credit cards or even telephones to make use of the system. But their concerns were drowned out by financial necessity and the perception, one former executive says, "that the messenger got shot."

By June 1993, Greyhound stock was more than $20 a share. It had been about $12 at the beginning of the year. In late July 1993, the company fully activated both the telephone information service and TRIPS. The combination of terminal agents and more than 400 telephone operators taking reservations were far more than the TRIPS computers could handle. "It was like turning on a spigot to get a drink and getting a fire hose." Thompson recalled.

Historically, Greyhound's phone calls averaged 60,000 a day. The toll-free TRIPS line received an estimated 800,000 calls. At the same time, a new discount fare was introduced. The TRIPS computers were backed up so badly that on some days it took

45 seconds to respond to a single keystroke and 5 minutes to print a ticket. TRIPS crashed so often in some locations that agents were writing ticket manually. Lines of frustrated customers snaked around bus terminals.

Although volume was a major culprit, the amount of training (40 hours per employee) and the undereducation and low morale of TRIPS's Greyhound employees also contributed to problems. The sheer complexity of TRIPS was another contributor. Greyhound technicians estimated that they would need a system capable of managing as many as 1,800 vehicle stops a day. Greyhound had given the 40-or-so people developing the system a $6 million start-up budget and little more than a year to complete it. By comparison, American Airlines, with a small army of technicians, spent 3 decades and several hundred million dollars perfecting its Sabre reservation system.

Meanwhile: Back at Corporate Headquarters

During this period of 1991 to 1994, while Greyhound progressed on its goals of (1) reducing the annual operating budget by $100 million, (2) reducing the bus fleet by half, (3) reducing the workforce by a fifth, and (4) replacing many full-time positions with part-timers, Schmieder's salary rose 57 percent to $526,000 and Doyle's rose nearly 65 percent to $265,000. Greyhound first-line employees earned about $6 an hour with no chance of promotion, and the average Greyhound customer earned less than $17,000 a year.

Greyhound had purchased its last remaining direct competitor, Trailways, in 1987 for $86 million, but sold it in 1991 for $5.25 million to reduce the company's bank debt.

There were many extravagant expenditures as perceived by some within the company. A move into a new trendy headquarters; $90,000 monthly interior design bills; expensive new furniture; lavish donations; season tickets for professional sports teams; and plush travel accounts for top executives were some of the more extravagant items. In addition, consultants were called in to the tune of a $5,000 monthly retainer for one; $375-an-hour one-on-one sessions for another; and $175,000 a month for another. There were two $560,000 seminars, one in Los Angeles, and one in Atlanta, for Greyhound employees.

Just-in-Time Selling

With its stock trading at $21.75 on August 4, 1993 (largely on the promise of TRIPS and the reengineering), Doyle sold 15,000 shares that he had purchased 2 months earlier for $9.81. In June, he had exercised options to buy and sell 22,642 Greyhound shares on similar terms. In the first 2 weeks of August 1993, Schmieder exercised options and sold 13,600 shares for an indicated profit of $155,000. During the same period, two other Greyhound executives sold a total of 21,300 shares at similar profits.

On September 23, nearly 2 months after the TRIPS trouble began, Greyhound stunned Wall Street by announcing that ridership had plunged 12 percent in August and that 1993 earnings would trail expectations. Greyhound stock tumbled 24 percent, to $11.75 a share, in a single day. That same day, the company released a press report blaming the ridership fall on an uncertain economy. There was no mention of TRIPS.

In late January 1995, Greyhound announced that the Securities and Exchange Commission (SEC) was investigating possible securities law violations by the company. Greyhound said the SEC was investigating possible insider trading and the adequacy of the company's internal accounting procedures. They further said the SEC was examining the adequacy of public disclosures related to both the troubled 1993 introduction of TRIPS and the company's disappointing earnings that same year.

Under pressure from Greyhound's board of directors, Schmieder resigned in mid-summer 1994. Doyle resigned shortly after that.

CURRENT MANAGEMENT AND CURRENT STRATEGIES

Craig Lentzsch, a former Greyhound executive, was appointed president and CEO in November 1994. Lentzsch, a 48-year-old Wharton Business School graduate, was known for his grasp of the technical side of the industry. He had worked for Greyhound as vice-chair in the late 1980s, and prior to that had worked in strategic planning for then-rival Trailways Lines, Inc.

The Turnaround Strategy 1994–1997

A key to Greyhound's turnaround involved a "back-to-basics" strategy. Lentzsch described one of the very first things Greyhound did: "We started answering the damn telephone." Before his arrival, a potential bus customer had to call four or five times before getting through to a sales representative. "The prior management had cut costs so deeply that they didn't have enough people answering the telephone," Lentzsch said. "And if you did get through, you often were told the bus was full. How much of that misery are you going to put up with?"

The management team before Lentzsch had decided that a bus line should be run the way an airline was. That decision lead to the introduction of TRIPS, which meant that customers needed to make reservations weeks in advance and buses were supposed to roll out full or close to it. The problem with this approach was not so much that bus customers didn't make reservations—some did—but that they didn't show up and get on the bus.

"Over 80 percent of those who made reservations were no-shows," said Jack Haugsland, chief operating officer. "About 75 percent of our customers buy tickets with cash 3 hours before the bus leaves the station." Because of the large percentage of no-shows, many walk-up customers without reservations were turned away. It was a classic example, said Greyhound's new chief financial officer, of a company not understanding its customers. "Our customer base is last-minute buyers," he said.

One of the first things management did was dismantle the "airline" model which relied on reservations. It was replaced with a much simpler one: If you want to travel by bus, you show up at the terminal, and within a reasonable period of time you will get a seat on the bus at an affordable price. Greyhound today does not take reservations.

Another new strategy is the switch from a capacity-constrained system such as the airlines use to a capacity-flexible system. For example, if a bus scheduled to leave at 10 A.M. is full, an additional bus will be rolled out. Because buses are a lot cheaper than planes, a bus company can afford to have extra buses in the wings, especially for peak travel periods in summer months and for the Thanksgiving and Christmas holidays (see Exhibit 4).

A third new strategy was revamping the pricing structure. Previous management had raised the prices of the "walk-in" tickets as high as possible and lowered those of the advance-purchase tickets, thereby pricing many of their core customers, last-minute walk-ins, out of the market. Greyhound dropped its prices significantly, turning to an "everyday low pricing" year-round strategy in an attempt to make bus travel more affordable.

EXHIBIT 4: Seasonal Travel Demand and Cash Flow

The company's business is seasonal in nature and generally follows the pattern of the travel industry as a whole, with peaks during the summer months and the Thanksgiving and Christmas holiday periods. As a result, cash flows are seasonal in nature with a disproportionate amount of the annual cash flows being generated during the peak travel periods. The following table sets forth certain operating data by quarter for 1997 and 1996:

	Year Ended December 31, 1997				
(in millions of dollars, except per share amounts)	First Quarter	Second Quarter	Third Quarter [b]	Fourth Quarter [b]	Total [b]
Total Operating Revenues	161.1	181.5	228.5	200.0	771.1
EBITDA [a]	(2.0)	10.2	39.4	20.8	68.4
Operating Income (Loss)	(9.5)	2.8	31.5	12.3	37.1
Net Income (Loss) before Extraordinary Item	(17.2)	(4.9)	23.5	3.3	4.7
Net Income (Loss) per Share of Common Stock:[c] Basic					
Net Income (Loss) Attributable to Common Shareholders before Extraordinary Item	(0.29)	(0.08)	0.40	0.06	0.08
Diluted					
Net Income (Loss) Attributable to Common Shareholders before Extraordinary Item	(0.29)	(0.08)	0.34	0.05	0.08

	Year Ended December 31, 1996				
(in millions of dollars, except per share amounts)	First Quarter	Second Quarter	Third Quarter	Fourth Quarter	Total
Total Operating Revenues	141.6	172.3	208.1	178.9	700.9
EBITDA [a]	(7.3)	8.5	34.1	16.2	51.5
Operating Income (Loss)	(14.9)	1.2	26.4	8.1	20.8
Net Income (Loss) before Extraordinary Item	(21.5)	(5.5)	19.4	1.0	(6.6)
Net Income (Loss) per Share of Common Stock:[c] Basic					
Net Income (Loss) Attributable to Common Shareholders before Extraordinary Item	(0.37)	(0.10)	0.33	0.02	(0.11)
Diluted					
Net Income (Loss) Attributable to Common Shareholders before Extraordinary Item	(0.37)	(0.10)	0.33	0.02	(0.11)

[a] Represents earnings before interest, taxes, depreciation and amortization, and extraordinary items.
[b] Third quarter and fourth quarter 1997 include results of operations for Carolina and Valley, which were acquired during the third quarter of 1997.
[c] Note that the earnings per share for the year will not be equal to the summation of the individual quarters due to earnings per share utilizing weighted average shares, which would be different for the year compared to the quarters.
Source: Greyhound Lines, Inc., and Subsidiaries, *Annual Report* (1997): 28.

Greyhound reopened several hundred previously dropped rural stops, thereby offering service that other forms of transportation no longer provided.

Greyhound is exploiting opportunities as alliance partners with air, rail, and other regional bus lines in providing reliable mixed-mode transportation. With the NAFTA agreement in place, and research studies estimates that the Mexican market is worth approximately $200 million a year and is growing at 20 percent annually, opportunities exist for partnerships with Mexican bus lines. In the summer of 1997, Greyhound acquired a 49 percent stake in Crucero, a Mexican transportation concern that provides bus service along an 800-mile route between Los Angeles and Ciudad Obregon, a city in the border state of Sonora.

By obtaining a new credit line, convincing bondholders to trade for equity, and raising $35 million in a 1994 rights offering that priced shares at $2.15, Greyhound was able to buy several hundred new buses (reducing the average age of their fleet from 9.5 years in 1993 to 6 years in 1996) and several new terminals in better areas of cities. During the first half of 1998, Greyhound purchased 163 new buses.

Previous management did not think that package express was worth much effort. The new team believes the potential is there for increased business. At one time, this portion of the business was lucrative, generating revenue in the $90 million range, or about 15 percent of total revenue. Because Greyhound puts packages on buses already carrying passengers, that's mostly gravy.

The company also plans on generating additional revenue by selling advertising on the outside and inside of their buses. Certain niche opportunities such as casino trips and college markets also are being pursued.

1997 Results

The year 1997 may prove to have been a critical one for Greyhound. Total revenues were up. Passenger count was up. Revenue per bus mile was up, and operating income increased more than 50 percent over the year before. During 1995 and 1996, Greyhound undertook the rebuilding of its infrastructure with new buses, increased telephone capacity, more drivers, and an improved field staff in an attempt to win back old customers and gain new ones.

Total operating revenues increased $70.2 million, or 10 percent, to $771.1 million for 1997 compared to 1996. Transportation services revenues in 1997 increased $62.7 million, or over 9.9 percent, over 1996.

Food service revenues increased $48 thousand, or 0.2 percent, to $21.4 million in 1997. Other operating revenue, consisting primarily of revenue from charter and in-terminal sales and services, increased $7.4 million, or 15.4 percent, to $55.6 million.

The company anticipates continuing significant capital expenditures which include acquiring buses, making improvements to its terminals, and maintaining and upgrading its computer systems. The company's experience indicates that as the age of its bus fleet increases, the dependability and quality of service declines. It is Greyhound's hope that these capital improvements will lead to better customer service. Capital expenditures for 1997 totaled $38.6 million (see Exhibit 5), including the acquisitions of four new bus terminals, but excluding bus acquisitions. The company ordered 100 new buses having an estimated aggregate purchase price of up to $26 million in 1997, a majority of which was financed through capital or operating leases.

EXHIBIT 5:   Greyhound Lines, Inc., Bus Acquisitions and Other Capital Expenditures for 1997, 1996, and 1995

	1997	1996	1995
Bus Acquisitions			
Buses acquired through operating leases [a]	190	132	73
Buses acquired through capital leases [a]	0	77	0
Buses purchased through cash flows or borrowings [b]	20	35	102
Total buses acquired	210	244	175
Capital Expenditures (in millions of dollars)			
Bus purchases, net of sale proceeds [c]	$5.7	$(6.7)	$24.3
Real estate purchases	11.5	12.0	3.4
Other, net of sale proceeds	21.4	16.4	6.3
Total capital expenditures, net of sale proceeds	$38.6	$21.7	$34.0

[a] Includes buses that were purchased in the year indicated and that subsequently were sold and leased back by the Company in such year. Excludes buses that were purchased in a prior year and sold and leased back by the Company in the year indicated.
[b] Includes buses that were purchased in the year indicated and that were sold and leased back by the Company in a subsequent year. Excludes buses that were purchased in the year indicated and that subsequently were sold and leased back by the Company in such year.
[c] Consists of the purchase price of buses purchased in the year indicated, including the purchase price of buses that subsequently were sold and leased back by the Company, minus the net proceeds to the Company from all sale-leaseback transactions and other sales of buses during such year.
Source: Adapted from Greyhound Lines, Inc., and Subsidiaries, *Annual Report* (1997): 25.

A LIGHT OR A TRAIN (OR PLANE) AT THE END OF THE TUNNEL?

The Case for a Light

There are several reasons for guarded optimism at Greyhound. Internally, they now have a driver for the company with industry and Greyhound experience (see Exhibit 6). If Greyhound can quit shooting itself in the foot, it may be able to survive and even prosper.

Greyhound serves a diverse customer base, consisting primarily of low- to middle-income passengers from a wide variety of ethnic backgrounds. Management believes that the demographic groups that make up the core of the company's customer base are growing at rates faster than the U.S. population as a whole. Greyhound believes that it is uniquely positioned to serve this broad and growing market because (1) its operating costs, which are lower on an available-seat-mile basis than other modes of intercity transportation, enable it to offer passengers everyday low prices, (2) it offers the only means of regularly scheduled intercity transportation in many of its markets, and (3) it provides additional capacity during peak travel periods to accommodate passengers who lack the flexibility to shift their travel to off-peak periods.

First and foremost, Greyhound must convince more travelers to take the bus. The company is regaining lost ridership by paying attention to basic blocking and tackling with its return to its "Take the bus and leave the driving to us" strategy. Pricing its services more realistically certainly will help entice riders.

EXHIBIT 6: Greyhound's Organizational Chart—Functional Design

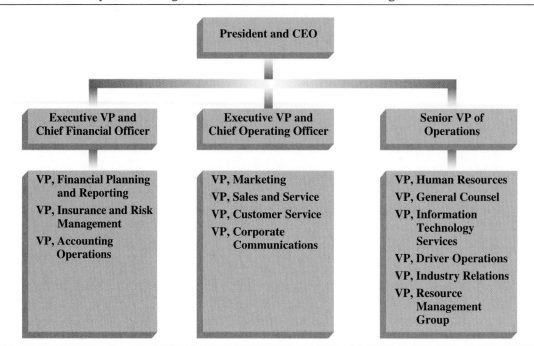

Source: Greyhound Lines, Inc., and Subsidiaries, *Annual Report* (1997): 15.

Greyhound's strong brand name is synonymous with bus travel. Its icon of a running greyhound dog may be one of the United States' most recognizable, at least for past generations.

Its national network may yet prevail against discount airlines. As excess capacity is taken out of service, airlines may have to increase their prices. Bus travel should benefit if fewer people can afford to fly. Amtrak cutbacks and concerns about commuter airline safety also should place more passengers on buses.

Analysts estimate that currently there is a pool of about 4 million people who ride the bus nationwide. As baby boomers age and new Asian and Mexican immigrants enter the United States and then disperse, the pool will grow to about 6 million over the next three to five years.

A large number of companies in the United States do well serving less-affluent Americans. There are 20 to 25 million households in the United States representing 60 to 70 million people who do not have bank accounts. Ever wonder why in the front of nearly every phone book there are instructions and locations for telephone customers to pay their bills in person? It is to serve a growing group, composed mostly of low-wage blue-collar workers, the unemployed, recent immigrants, and retirees. These are some of Greyhound's prime target markets.

The Case for a Train (or Plane)

On the other hand, the future for Greyhound looks anything but bright. Is the glass half-full or half-empty? Increased automobile ownership and discount airlines have reduced the bus industry's share of interstate travel to an estimated 6 percent, down from 30 percent in 1960. The entire industry carries only about 35 million passengers annually. This is compared to more than 430 million air travelers. These trends do not bode well for Greyhound.

Bus ridership suffers from an image problem. Many assume that only the poor board buses. While the poor do ride the bus, more than 50 percent of Greyhound's revenue comes from middle-income America.

Many Americans see little glamour or rationale for riding a bus and passing through dismal terminals. Many travelers no more think of taking a bus than taking a horse. Unlike generations of Americans in the 1930s, 1940s, and 1950s, many have never been on a bus, not counting school buses. When it's time to travel, they either drive or fly.

Carnival Corporation—1998

Dr. Mike Keeffe
Dr. John K. Ross III
Dr. Bill Middlebrook

www.carnival.com
stock symbol CCL

Carnival Corporation (305-599-2600; 800-438-6744) is considered the leader and innovator in the cruise travel industry. From inauspicious beginnings, Carnival grew from two converted ocean liners to an organization with two cruise divisions (and a joint venture to operate a third cruise line) and a chain of Alaskan hotels and tour coaches. Corporate revenues for fiscal 1997 reached $2.4 billion with net income of $666 million. Carnival was the first in the cruise industry to carry over 1 million passengers in a single year and the first cruise line to carry 5 million passengers. Currently, its market share of the cruise travel industry stands at almost 30 percent.

Carnival Corporation CEO and Chair Micky Arison and Carnival Cruise Lines President Bob Dickinson are prepared to maintain Carnival's reputation as the leader and innovator in the industry. They have assembled one of the newest fleets catering to cruisers with the introduction of several superliners built specifically for the Caribbean and Alaskan cruise markets, with four more superliners to be delivered by the year 2000. Additionally, the company expanded its Holland America Lines fleet to cater to experienced cruisers and has plans to add three more ships to its fleet in the premium cruise segment. Strategically, Carnival Corporation seems to have made the right moves at the right times, sometimes in direct contradiction to industry analysts and cruise trends.

Cruise Lines International Association (CLIA), an industry trade group, has tracked the growth of the cruise industry for over 25 years. CLIA reports that in 1970, approximately 500,000 passengers took cruises for three consecutive nights or more, reaching over 5 million passengers in 1997, an average annual compound growth rate of approximately 9.2 percent. CLIA notes that at the end of 1996, the industry had 129 ships in service with an aggregate berth capacity of 110,000. CLIA estimates that the number of passengers carried in North America increased from 4.38 million in 1995 to 4.6 million in 1996, or by approximately 5 percent. In 1997, there were 135 vessels with an aggregate capacity of 124,000 berths operating in the North American market.

Carnival Corporation estimates that less than 10 percent of the North American population has ever cruised. Various cruise operators, including Carnival Corporation, have based their expansion and capital spending programs on the possibility of capturing part of the 90 percent of the North American population who have yet to take a cruise vacation.

This case was prepared by Dr. Mike Keeffe, Dr. John K. Ross III, and Dr. Bill Middlebrook of Southwest Texas State University, as a basis for class discussion. It is not intended to illustrate either effective or ineffective handling of an administrative situation. Copyright © 1999 by Prentice Hall, Inc. ISBN 0-13-011147-3.

THE EVOLUTION OF CRUISING

With the replacement of ocean liners by aircraft in the 1960s as the primary means of transoceanic travel, the opportunity for developing the modern cruise industry was created. Ships no longer required to ferry passengers from destination to destination became available to investors with visions of a new vacation alternative to complement the increasing affluence of Americans. Cruising, once in the purview of only the rich and leisure class, was targeted to the middle class, with service and amenities similar to the grand days of first-class ocean travel.

According to Robert Meyers, editor and publisher of *Cruise Travel* magazine, the increasing popularity of taking a cruise as a vacation can be traced to two serendipitously timed events. First, television's *Love Boat* series dispelled many myths associated with cruising and depicted people of all ages and backgrounds enjoying the cruise experience. This show was among the top 10 shows on television for many years according to Nielsen ratings, and provided extensive publicity for cruise operators. Second, the increasing affluence of Americans and the increased participation of women in the workforce gave couples and families more disposable income for discretionary purposes, especially vacations. As the myths were dispelled and disposable income grew, younger couples and families "turned on" to the benefits of cruising as a vacation alternative, creating a large new target market for the cruise product and accelerated the growth in the number of Americans taking cruises as a vacation.

CARNIVAL HISTORY

In 1972, Ted Arison, backed by American Travel Services, Inc. (ATSI), purchased an aging ocean liner from Canadian Pacific Empress Lines for $6.5 million. The new ATSI subsidiary, Carnival Cruise Line, refurbished the vessel from bow to stern and renamed it the *Mardi Gras* to capture the party spirit. (Also included in the deal was another ship later renamed the *Carnivale*.) The company's start-up was not promising, however, as on the first voyage the *Mardi Gras*, with over 300 invited travel agents aboard, ran aground in Miami Harbor. The ship was slow and guzzled expensive fuel, limiting the number of ports of call and lengthening the minimum stay of passengers on the ship just to break even. To complement the *Mardi Gras* and the *Carnivale*, Arison then bought another old ocean vessel from Union Castle Lines and named it the *Festivale*. To attract customers, Arison began adding on-board diversions such as planned activities, a casino, nightclubs, discos, and other forms of entertainment designed to enhance the shipboard experience.

Carnival lost money for the next three years and in late 1974, Arison bought out the Carnival Cruise subsidiary of ATSI, for $1 cash and the assumption of $5 million in debt. One month later, the *Mardi Gras* began showing a profit and through the remainder of 1975 operated at more than 100 percent capacity. (Normal ship capacity is determined by the number of fixed berths available. Ships, like hotels, can operate beyond this fixed capacity by using rollaway beds, pullmans, and upper bunks.) Arison (then chair); Dickinson (then vice-president of sales and marketing); and Arison's son, Micky (then president of Carnival), began to alter the approach to cruise vacations. Carnival went after first-time and younger cruisers with a moderately priced vacation package that included airfare to the port of embarkation and back home after the cruise. Per diem rates were very competitive with other vacation packages and Carnival offered passage to multiple exotic Caribbean ports, several meals served daily with premier restaurant service, and all forms of entertainment and activities included in the base fare. The only things not included in the fare were items of a personal nature; liquor purchases; gambling; and tips for the cabin steward, table waiter, and bus staff. Carnival continued to add to the shipboard experience with a greater variety of activities, nightclubs, and other forms of entertainment and varied ports of call to increase its attractiveness to potential customers. It was the first modern cruise operator to use multimedia advertising promotions and established the theme of "Fun Ship" cruises, primarily promoting the ship as the destination and ports of call as secondary. Carnival told the public that it was throwing a shipboard party and everyone was invited. Today, the "Fun Ship" theme still permeates all Carnival Cruise ships.

Throughout the 1980s, Carnival was able to maintain a growth rate of approximately 30 percent, about three times that of the industry as a whole, and between 1982 and 1988 its ships sailed with an average of 104 percent capacity (currently, it operates at 104 percent to 105 percent capacity, depending on the season). Targeting younger, first-time passengers by promoting the ship as a destination proved to be extremely successful. Carnival's 1987 customer profile showed that 30 percent of the passengers were between the ages of 25 and 39 with household incomes of $25,000 to $50,000.

In 1987, Ted Arison sold 20 percent of his shares in Carnival Cruise Lines and immediately generated over $400 million for further expansion. In 1988, Carnival acquired the Holland America Line which had four cruise ships with a total of 4,500 berths. Holland America was positioned to the higher-income travelers with cruise prices averaging 25 to 35 percent more than similar Carnival cruises. The deal also included two Holland America subsidiaries, Windstar Sail Cruises and Holland America Westours. This success, and the foresight of management, allowed Carnival to begin an aggressive superliner-building campaign for its core subsidiary. By 1989, the cruise segments of Carnival Corporation carried over 750,000 passengers in one year, a first in the cruise industry.

Ted Arison relinquished the role of chair to his son, Micky, in 1990, a time when the explosive growth of the 1980s began to subside. Higher fuel prices and increased airline costs began to affect the industry as a whole, and the Persian Gulf War caused many cruise operators to divert ships from European and Indian ports to the Caribbean area of operations, increasing the number of ships competing directly with Carnival. Carnival's stock price fell from $25 in June of 1990 to $13 late in the year. The company also incurred a $25.5 million loss during fiscal 1990 for the operation of the Crystal Palace Resort and Casino. In 1991 Carnival reached a settlement with the Bahamian government (effective March 1, 1992) to surrender the 672-room Riveria Towers to the Hotel Corporation of the Bahamas in exchange for the cancellation of some debt incurred in constructing and developing the resort. The corporation took a $135 million write-off on the Crystal Palace for that year.

The early 1990s, even with industry-wide demand slowing, were still a very exciting time. Carnival took delivery of its first two superliners, the *Fantasy* (1990) and the *Ecstasy* (1991), which were to further penetrate the 3- and 4-day cruise market and supplement the 7-day market. In early 1991, Carnival took delivery of the third superliner, *Sensation*, and later in the year contracted for the fourth superliner to be named the *Fascination* (inaugural sailing 1994).

In 1991, Carnival attempted to acquire Premier Cruise Lines, then the official cruise line for Walt Disney World in Orlando, Florida, for approximately $372 million. The deal was never consummated because the involved parties could not agree on price. In

1992, Carnival acquired 50 percent of Seabourn, gaining the cruise operations of K/S Seabourn Cruise Lines, and formed a partnership with Atle Byrnestad. Seabourn serves the ultraluxury market with destinations in South America, the Mediterranean, Southeast Asia, and the Baltics.

The 1993–1995 period saw the addition of the superliner *Imagination* for Carnival Cruise Lines and the *Ryndam* for Holland America Lines. In 1994, the company discontinued operations of Fiestamarina Lines which attempted to serve Spanish-speaking clientele. Fiestamarina was beset with marketing and operational problems and never reached continuous operations. Many industry analysts and observers were surprised at the failure of Carnival to successfully develop this market. In 1995, Carnival sold a 49 percent interest in the Epirotiki Line, a Greek cruise operator, for $25 million and purchased $101 million (face amount) of senior secured notes of Kloster Cruise Limited, the parent of competitor Norwegian Cruise Lines, for $81 million. Kloster was having financial difficulties and Carnival could not obtain common stock of the company in a negotiated agreement.

Carnival Corporation is expanding through internally generated growth as evidenced by the number of new ships on order (see Exhibit 1). Additionally, Carnival seems to be willing to continue with its external expansion through acquisitions if the right opportunities arise.

In June 1997, Royal Caribbean made a bid to buy Celebrity Cruise Lines for $500 million and assumption of $800 million of debt. Within a week, Carnival responded by submitting a counteroffer to Celebrity for $510 million and the assumption of debt, and two days later, it raised its bid to $525 million. However, Royal Caribbean seems to have had the inside track and announced on June 30, 1997, its final merger arrangements with Celebrity. As a result, Carnival's competitor has 17 ships with approximately 30,000 berths.

The Cruise Product

Ted and Micky Arison envisioned a product of classical cruise elegance with modern convenience at a price comparable to land-based vacation packages sold by travel agents. Carnival's all-inclusive package, when compared to resorts or a theme park

EXHIBIT 1: Carnival and Holland America Ships under Construction

Vessel	Expected Delivery	Passenger Capacity[a]
Carnival Cruise Lines		
Elation	2/98	2,040
Paradise	11/98	2,040
Carnival Triumph	6/99	2,640
Carnival Victory	7/00	2,640
Total Carnival Cruise Lines		9,360
Holland America Line		
HAL Newbuild I	2/99	1,440
HAL Newbuild II	9/99	1,440
Total Holland America Line		4,200
Total all vessels passenger capacity		13,560

[a]In accordance with industry practice, all capacities indicated within this document are calculated based on two passengers per cabin even though some cabins can accommodate three or four passengers.
Source: Adapted from Carnival Corporation, *Annual Report* (1997).

such as Walt Disney World, often is priced below these destinations, especially when Carnival's array of activities, entertainment, and meals is considered.

A typical vacation on a Carnival cruise ship starts when the bags are tagged for the ship at the airport. Upon arriving at the port of embarkation, passengers are ferried by air-conditioned buses to the ship for boarding, and luggage is delivered by the cruise ship staff to each passenger's cabin. Waiters dot the ship offering tropical drinks to the backdrop of a Caribbean rhythm while the cruise staff orients passengers to the various decks, cabins, and public rooms. In a few hours (most ships sail in the early evening), dinner is served in the main dining rooms where the wine selection rivals that of the finest restaurants and the variety of main dishes is designed to suit every palate. Diners can always order double portions if they decide not to save room for the variety of desserts and after-dinner specialties.

After dinner, cruisers can choose between many forms of entertainment, including live music, dancing, nightclubs, and a selection of movies, and then attend the midnight buffet. (Most ships have five or more distinct nightclubs.) During the night, a daily program of activities is delivered to each passenger's cabin. The biggest decisions to be made for the duration of the vacation will be what to do (or not to do), what to eat and when (usually eight separate serving times, not including the 24-hour room service), and when to sleep. Service in all areas from dining to housekeeping is upscale and immediate. The service is so good that a common shipboard joke is that if you leave your bed during the night to visit the head (sea talk for bathroom), your cabin steward will have made the bed and placed chocolates on the pillow by the time you return.

After the cruise, passengers are transported back to the airport in air-conditioned buses for the flight home. Representatives of the cruise line are at the airport to help cruisers meet their scheduled flights. When all amenities are considered, most vacation packages would be hard-pressed to match Carnival's per diem prices that range from $125 to $250 per person, depending on accommodations. (Holland America and Seabourn per diems average $300 per person.) Occasional specials allow for even lower prices.

CARNIVAL OPERATIONS

Carnival Corporation, headquartered in Miami, Florida, is composed of Carnival Cruise Lines; Holland America Lines (which includes Windstar Sail Cruises, Holland America Westours, and Westmark Hotels); and a joint venture with Atle Byrnestad to operate Seabourn Cruise Lines. Its ships are subject to inspection by the U.S. Coast Guard for compliance with the Convention for the Safety of Life at Sea, which requires specific structural requirements for safety of passengers at sea, and by the U.S. Public Health Service for sanitary standards. The company also is regulated in some aspects by the Federal Maritime Commission.

At its helm, Carnival Corporation is led by CEO and Chair Micky Arison. Carnival Cruise Lines president and chief operating officer is Bob Dickinson. A. Kirk Lanterman is president and CEO of Holland America Lines. Carnival Corporation's organizational chart is presented in Exhibit 2.

The company's product positioning stems from its belief that the cruise market actually comprises three primary segments with different passenger demographics,

EXHIBIT 2:   Carnival Corporation Organizational Chart

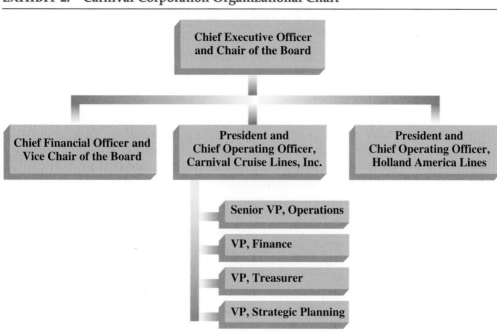

Source: Carnival Corporation, *Annual Report* 1997.

passenger characteristics, and growth requirements. The three segments are the contemporary, premium, and luxury segments. The contemporary segment is served by Carnival ships for cruises that are seven days or shorter in length and feature a casual ambiance. The premium segment, served by Holland America, serves the seven-day-and-longer market and appeals to more affluent consumers. The luxury segment, which is considerably smaller than the other segments, caters to experienced cruisers for seven-day-and-longer sailings and is served by Seabourn. Specialty sailing cruises are provided by Windstar Sail Cruises, a subsidiary of Holland America.

Corporate structure is built around the profit center concept and is updated periodically for control and coordination purposes. The cruise subsidiaries of Carnival give the corporation a presence in most of the major cruise segments and provide for worldwide operations.

Carnival has always placed a high priority on marketing in an attempt to promote cruises as an alternative to land-based vacations. Education and the creation of awareness are critical to corporate marketing efforts. Carnival was the first cruise line to successfully break away from traditional print media and use television to reach a broader market. Even though other lines have followed Carnival's lead in selecting promotional media and are near in total advertising expenditures, the organization still leads all cruise competitors in advertising and marketing expenditures.

Carnival wants to remain the leader and innovator in the cruise industry and intends to do this with sophisticated promotional efforts and by gaining loyalty from former cruisers, by refurbishing ships, varying activities and ports of call, and being innovative in all aspects of ship operations. Management intends to build on the theme of the ship as a destination given their historical success with this promotional effort. The company capitalizes and amortizes direct-response advertising and expenses other advertising costs as incurred. Advertising expenses totaled $109 million in 1996, $98 million in 1995, and $85 million in 1994.

FINANCIAL PERFORMANCE

Carnival retains Price Waterhouse as independent accountants and the Barnett Bank Trust Company—North America as its registrar and stock transfer agent. Its Class A Common Stock trades on the New York Stock Exchange. In December 1996, Carnival amended the terms of its revolving credit facility primarily to combine two facilities into a single $1 billion unsecured revolving credit facility due 2001.

The consolidated financial statements for Carnival are shown in Exhibits 3, 4, and 5, and selected financial data are presented in Exhibit 6.

Customer cruise deposits, which represent unearned revenue, are included in the balance sheet when received and are recognized as cruise revenues on completion of the voyage. Customers are required to pay the full cruise fare (minus deposit) 60 days in advance, with the fares being recognized as cruise revenue on completion of the voyage.

Property and equipment on the financial statements is stated at cost. Depreciation and amortization is calculated using the straight-line method over the following estimated useful lives: vessels 25 to 30 years, buildings 20 to 40 years, equipment 2 to 20 years, and leasehold improvements at the shorter of the term of lease or related asset

EXHIBIT 3: Carnival Corporation, Consolidated Statements of Operations

	Years Ended November 30,		
(in thousands of dollars, except per share data)	*1997*	*1996*	*1995*
Revenues	$2,447,468	$2,212,572	$1,998,150
Costs and Expenses			
Operating expenses	1,322,669	1,241,269	1,131,113
Selling and administrative	296,533	274,855	248,566
Depreciation and amortization	167,287	144,987	128,433
Total	1,786,489	1,661,111	1,508,112
Operating Income before Income from Affiliated Operations	660,979	551,461	490,038
Income from Affiliated Operations, Net	53,091	45,967	
Operating Income	714,070	597,428	490,038
Nonoperating Income (Expense)			
Interest income	8,675	18,597	14,403
Interest expense, net of capitalized interest	(55,898)	(64,092)	(63,080)
Other income	5,436	23,414	19,104
Income tax expense	(6,233)	(9,045)	(9,374)
Total	(48,020)	(31,126)	(38,947)
Net Income	666,050	566,302	451,091
Earnings Per Share	2.23	1.95	1.59

Source: Carnival Corporation, *Annual Report* (1997): 18.

EXHIBIT 4: Carnival Corporation, Consolidated Balance Sheets

(in thousands of dollars, except per share data)	Years Ended November 30, 1997	1996
Assets		
Current Assets		
Cash and cash equivalents	$ 139,989	$ 111,629
Short-term investments	9,738	12,486
Accounts receivable	57,090	38,109
Consumable inventories, at average cost	54,970	53,281
Prepaid expenses and other	74,238	75,428
Total current assets	336,025	290,933
Property and Equipment, Net	4,327,413	4,099,038
Other Assets		
Investments in and advances to affiliates	479,329	430,330
Goodwill, less accumulated amortization of $62,256 and $55,274	212,607	219,589
Other assets	71,401	61,998
Total Assets	5,426,775	5,101,888
Liabilities and Shareholders' Equity		
Current Liabilities		
Current portion of long-term debt	59,620	66,369
Accounts payable	106,783	84,748
Accrued liabilities	154,253	126,511
Customer deposits	420,908	352,698
Dividends payable	44,578	32,416
Total current liabilities	786,142	662,742
Long-Term Debt	1,015,294	1,277,529
Convertible Notes		39,103
Deferred Income and Other Long-Term Liabilities	20,241	91,630
Commitments and Contingencies		
Shareholders' Equity		
Class A Common Stock; $.01 par value; one vote per share; 399,500 shares authorized; 297,204 and 239,733 shares issued and outstanding	2,972	2,397
Class B Common Stock; $.01 par value; five votes per share; 100,500 shares authorized; zero and 54,957 shares issued and outstanding	0	550
Paid-in capital	866,097	819,610
Retained earnings	2,731,213	2,207,781
Other	4,816	546
Total shareholders' equity	3,605,098	3,030,884
Total Liabilities and Shareholders' Equity	5,426,775	5,101,888

Source: Adapted from Carnival Corporation, *Annual Report* (1997): 17.

EXHIBIT 5: Carnival Corporation, Consolidated Statements of Cash Flows

	Years Ended November 30,		
(in thousands of dollars)	*1997*	*1996*	*1995*
Operating Activities			
Net income	$ 666,050	$ 566,302	$ 451,091
Adjustments to reconcile net income to net cash provided from operating activities			
Depreciation and amortization	167,287	144,987	128,433
Income from affiliates in excess of dividends received	(46,569)	(43,224)	
Other	2,540	19,639	7,681
Changes in operating assets and liabilities			
Decrease (increase) in			
Receivables	(21,229)	(4,432)	(12,655)
Consumable inventories	(1,689)	(4,461)	(3,698)
Prepaid expenses and other	903	(4,919)	(20,849)
Increase (decrease) in			
Accounts payable	22,035	(5,489)	3,487
Accrued liabilities	20,042	13,028	(1,385)
Customer deposits	68,210	60,092	35,101
Net cash provided from operating activities	877,580	741,523	587,206
Investing Activities			
Decrease in short-term investments, net	2,748	37,710	19,720
Additions to property and equipment, net	(497,657)	(901,905)	(485,097)
Proceeds from sale of fixed assets	17,401	94,291	1,196
Proceeds from litigation settlements applied to cost of ships	0	43,050	19,426
Purchase of equity interests in affiliates	(38,378)	(163,112)	0
Other reductions in (additions to) investments in and advances to affiliates	39,540	(23,903)	11,783
Decrease (increase) in other assets	21,805	94,644	(95,108)
Net cash used for investing activities	(454,901)	(819,225)	(528,080)
Financing Activities			
Proceeds from issuance of common stock	5,162	3,728	49,032
Principal payments of long-term debt	(424,391)	(735,246)	(406,600)
Dividends paid	(130,456)	(103,877)	(85,098)
Proceeds from long-term debt	155,366	971,361	382,800
Net cash (used for) provided from financing activities	(394,319)	135,966	(59,866)
Net increase (decrease) in cash and cash equivalents	28,360	58,264	(740)
Cash and cash equivalents at beginning of year	111,629	53,365	54,105
Cash and cash equivalents at end of year	139,989	111,629	53,365

Source: Carnival Corporation, *Annual Report* (1997): 19.

EXHIBIT 6:   Carnival Corporation, Selected Financial Data by Segment

	Years Ended November 30,		
(in thousands of dollars)	*1997*	*1996*	*1995*
Revenues			
Cruise	$2,257,567	$2,003,458	$1,800,775
Tour	242,646	263,356	241,909
Intersegment revenues	(52,745)	(54,242)	(44,534)
Total	2,447,468	2,212,572	1,998,150
Gross Operating profit			
Cruise	1,072,758	913,880	810,736
Tour	52,041	57,423	56,301
Total	1,124,799	971,303	867,037
Depreciation and Amortization			
Cruise	157,454	135,694	119,381
Tour	8,862	8,317	8,129
Corporate	971	976	923
Total	167,287	144,987	128,433
Operating Income			
Cruise	656,009	535,814	470,592
Tour	13,262	21,252	24,168
Corporate	44,799	40,362	(4,722)
Total	714,070	597,428	490,038
Identifiable Assets			
Cruise	4,744,140	4,514,675	3,910,243
Tour	163,941	150,851	138,313
Corporate	518,694	436,362	56,931
Total	5,426,775	5,101,888	4,105,487
Capital Expenditures			
Cruise	414,963	841,871	456,920
Tour	42,507	14,964	8,747
Corporate	40,187	1,810	
Total	497,657	858,645	465,667

Source: Carnival Corporation, *Annual Report* (1997): 27.

life. Goodwill of $275 million resulting from the acquisition of HAL Antillen, N.V. (Holland America Lines) is being amortized using the straight-line method over 40 years.

In 1996, Carnival reached an agreement with the trustees of Wartsila and creditors for the bankruptcy which resulted in a cash payment of approximately $80 million, of which $5 million was used to pay certain costs, $32 million was recorded as other income, and $43 million was used to reduce the cost basis of certain ships which had been affected by the bankruptcy.

According to the Internal Revenue Code of 1986, Carnival is considered a controlled foreign corporation (CFC) because 50 percent of its stock is held by individuals who are residents of foreign countries and because its countries of incorporation exempt shipping operations of U.S. persons from income tax. Because of its CFC status, Carnival expects that all of its income (with the exception of U.S. source income from the transportation, hotel, and tour businesses of Holland America) will be exempt from U.S. federal income taxes at the corporate level.

The primary financial consideration of importance to Carnival management is the control of costs, both fixed and variable, for the maintenance of a healthy profit margin. Carnival has the lowest break-even point of any organization in the cruise industry (ships break even at approximately 60 percent of capacity) due to operational experience and economies of scale. Unfortunately, fixed costs (including depreciation, fuel, insurance, port charges, and crew costs), which represent more than 33 percent of the company's operating expenses, cannot be reduced significantly in relation to decreases in passenger loads and aggregate passenger ticket revenue. (Major expense items are airfare (25 to 30 percent), travel agent fees (10 percent), and labor (13 to 15 percent). Increases in these costs negatively could affect the profitability of the organization.

PRINCIPAL SUBSIDIARIES

Carnival Cruise Lines, Inc.

Carnival Cruise Lines, Inc., is a Panamanian corporation and its subsidiaries are incorporated in Panama, the Netherlands Antilles, the British Virgin Islands, Liberia, and the Bahamas. At the end of fiscal 1997, Carnival operated 22 ships, principally in the Caribbean, and had an assortment of ports of call serving the 3-, 4-, and 7-day cruise markets (see Exhibit 7).

Each ship is a floating resort including a full maritime staff, shopkeepers, casino operators, entertainers, and complete hotel staff. Approximately 14 percent of corporate revenue is generated from shipboard casino operations, liquor sales, and gift shop items. At various ports of call, passengers can take advantage of tours, shore excursions, and duty-free shopping at their own expense.

Shipboard operations are designed to provide maximum entertainment, activities, and service. The size of the company and the similarity in design of the new cruise ships has allowed Carnival to achieve various economies of scale, and management is very cost-conscious.

Although Carnival Cruise Lines is increasing its presence in the shorter-cruise markets, its general marketing strategy is to use 3-, 4-, or 7-day moderately priced cruises to fit the time and budget constraints of the middle class. Including port charges, shorter

EXHIBIT 7: The Ships of Carnival Corporation

Name	Registry	Service cap[a]	Gross tons	Length/ Width	Areas of operation
Carnival Cruise Lines					
Destiny	Panama	2,642	101,000	893/116	Caribbean
Inspiration	Panama	2,040	70,367	855/104	Caribbean
Imagination	Panama	2,040	70,367	855/104	Caribbean
Fascination	Panama	2,040	70,367	855/104	Caribbean
Sensation	Panama	2,040	70,367	855/104	Caribbean
Ecstasy	Liberia	2,040	70,367	855/104	Caribbean
Fantasy	Liberia	2,044	70,367	855/104	Bahamas
Celebration	Liberia	1,486	47,262	738/92	Caribbean
Jubilee	Panama	1,486	47,262	738/92	Mexican Riviera
Holiday	Panama	1,452	46,052	727/92	Mexican Riviera
Tropicale[b]	Liberia	1,022	36,674	660/85	Alaska, Caribbean
Total Carnival Ships Capacity	20,332				
Holland America Lines					
Veendam	Bahamas	1,266	55,451	720/101	Alaska, Caribbean
Ryndam	Netherlands	1,266	55,451	720/101	Alaska, Caribbean
Maasdam	Netherlands	1,266	55,451	720/101	Europe, Caribbean
Statendam	Netherlands	1,266	55,451	720/101	Alaska, Caribbean
Westerdam	Netherlands	1,494	53,872	798/95	Canada, Caribbean
Noordam	Netherlands	1,214	33,930	704/89	Alaska, Caribbean
Nieuw Amsterdam	Netherlands	1,214	33,930	704/89	Alaska, Caribbean
Rotterdam V[b]	Netherlands	1,075	37,783	749/94	Alaska, Worldwide
Total HAL Ships Capacity	10,061				
Windstar Cruises					
Wind Spirit	Bahamas	148	5,736	440/52	Caribbean, Mediterranean
Wind Song	Bahamas	148	5,703	440/52	South Pacific
Wind Star	Bahamas	148	5,703	440/52	Caribbean, Mediterranean
Total Windstar Ships Capacity	444				
Total Capacity	30,837				

[a]In accordance with industry practice, passenger capacity is calculated based on two passengers per cabin even though some cabins can accommodate three or four passengers.
[b]In November 1996, Carnival's cruise ship *Tropicale* was sold to the joint venture with HMM and the company chartered the vessel back until the vessel enters service with the joint venture in late 1998. Holland America Line's *Rotterdam V* is expected to be replaced in September 1997 by the *Rotterdam VI*, which is currently under construction.
Source: Carnival Corporation, 1997.

cruises can cost less than $500 per person (depending on accommodations) up to roughly $3,000 per person in a luxury suite on a seven-day cruise. (Per diem rates for shorter cruises are slightly higher, on average, than per diem rates for seven-day cruises.) Average rates per day are approximately $180, excluding gambling, liquor, soft drinks, and items of a personal nature. Guests are expected to tip their cabin stewards and waiters at a suggested rate of $3 per person per day and the bus staff at $1.50 per person per day.

About 99 percent of all Carnival cruises are sold through travel agents who receive a standard commission of 10 percent (15 percent in Florida). Carnival works extensively with travel agents to promote cruises as an alternative to a Disney or European vacation. In addition to training travel agents from nonaffiliated travel/vacation firms to sell cruises, a special group of Carnival employees regularly poses as prospective clients and visits travel agents. If an agent visited by one of these Carnival employees recommends a cruise before another vacation option, he or she receives $100. If a travel agent specifies a Carnival cruise before other options, he or she receives $1,000 on the spot. During fiscal 1995, Carnival took reservations from about 29,000 of the approximately 45,000 travel agencies in the United States and Canada, and no one travel agency accounted for more than 2 percent of Carnival revenues.

On-board service is labor-intensive. Carnival employs help from about 50 nations—mostly Third World countries—with reasonable returns to employees. For example, waiters on the *Jubilee* can earn approximately $18,000 to $27,000 per year (base salary and tips), significantly greater than they could earn in their home countries for similar employment. Waiters typically work 10 hours per day with approximately one day off per week for a specified contract period (usually three to nine months). Carnival records show that employees remain with the company for approximately eight years and that applicants exceed demand for all cruise positions. Nonetheless, the American Maritime union has cited Carnival (and other cruise operators) several times for exploitation of its crew.

Holland America Lines

In 1989, Carnival acquired all the outstanding stock of HAL Antillen N.V. from Holland America Lines N.V. for $625 million in cash. Carnival financed the purchase through $250 million in retained earnings (cash account) and borrowed the other $375 million from banks at .25 percent over the prime rate. Carnival received the assets and operations of the Holland America Lines, including Westours, Westmark Hotels, and Windstar Sail Cruises. Holland America currently has eight cruise ships with a capacity of 8,795 berths, and Carnival has ordered new ships to be delivered in the future.

Founded in 1873, Holland America Lines is an upscale line (it charges an average of 25 percent more than similar Carnival cruises) with principal destinations in Alaska during the summer and in the Caribbean during the fall and winter, and some worldwide cruises of up to 98 days. Holland America targets an older, more sophisticated cruiser with fewer youth-oriented activities. On Holland America ships, passengers can dance to the sounds of the Big Band era and avoid the discos of Carnival ships. Passengers on Holland America ships enjoy more service (Holland America has a higher staff-to-passenger ratio than Carnival), have more cabin and public space per person, and benefit from the "no tipping" shipboard policy. Holland America has not enjoyed the spectacular growth of Carnival cruise ships, but sustained constant growth in the 1980s and early 1990s with high occupancy. The operation of these ships and the structure of the crew is similar to the Carnival cruise ship model, and the acquisition of the line gave the Carnival Corporation a presence in the Alaskan market where it had none before.

Holland America Westours is the largest tour operator in Alaska and the Canadian Rockies and complements Holland America cruises. The transportation division of Westours includes over 290 motor coaches composed of the Gray Line of Alaska, the Gray Line of Seattle, Westours motorcoaches, the McKinley Explorer railroad coaches, and three-day tours by boat to glaciers and other points of interest. Carnival management believes that Alaskan cruises and tours should increase in the future because the aging population wants relaxing vacations with scenic beauty and because Alaska is a U.S. destination.

Westmark Hotels consists of 16 hotels in Alaska and the Yukon territories and complements cruise operations and Westours. Westmark is the largest group of hotels in the region providing moderately priced rooms for the vacationer.

Windstar Sail Cruises was acquired by Holland America Lines in 1988 and consists of three computer-controlled sailing vessels with a berth capacity of 444 each. Windstar is upscale and offers an alternative to traditional cruise liners with a more intimate, activity-oriented cruise. The ships operate primarily in the Mediterranean and the South Pacific and visit ports not accessible to large cruise ships. Although catering to a small segment of the cruise vacation industry, Windstar helps with Carnival's commitment to participate in all segments of the cruise industry.

Seabourn Cruise Lines

In April 1992, the company acquired 25 percent of the capital stock of Seabourn. As part of the transaction, the company also made a subordinated secured ten-year loan of $15 million to Seabourn and a $10 million convertible loan to Seabourn. In December 1995, the $10 million convertible loan was converted by the company into an additional 25 percent equity interest in Seabourn.

Seabourn targets the luxury market with three vessels providing 200 passengers per ship with all-suite accommodations. Seabourn cruises the Americas, Europe, Scandinavia, the Mediterranean, and the Far East.

Airtours

In April 1996, the company acquired a 29.5 percent interest in Airtours for approximately $307 million. With its subsidiaries, Airtours is the largest air-inclusive tour operator in the world and is publicly traded on the London Stock Exchange. Airtours provides air-inclusive packaged holidays to the British, Scandinavian, and North American markets. Airtours provides holidays to approximately five million people per year and owns or operates 32 hotels, two cruise ships, and 31 aircraft.

Airtours operates 18 aircraft (one additional aircraft is scheduled to enter service in the spring of 1997) exclusively for its U.K. tour operators, providing a large proportion of their flying requirements. In addition, Airtours's subsidiary Premiair operates a fleet of 13 aircraft (one additional aircraft is scheduled to enter service with Premiair in the spring of 1997), which provides most of the flying requirements for Airtours's Scandinavian tour operators.

Airtours owns or operates 32 hotels (a total of 6,500 rooms) which provide rooms to Airtours's tour operators principally in the Mediterranean and the Canary Islands. In addition, Airtours has a 50 percent interest in Tenerife Sol, a joint venture with Sol Hotels Group of Spain, which owns and operates three Canary Islands hotels providing a total of 1,300 rooms.

Through its subsidiary Sun Cruises, Airtours owns and operates two cruise ships. Both the 800-berth MS *Seawing* and the 1,062-berth MS *Carousel* commenced operations in 1995. Recently, Airtours acquired a third ship, the MS *Sundream*, which is the sister ship of the MS *Carousel*. The MS *Sundream* commenced operations in 1997. The ships operate in the Mediterranean, the Caribbean, and around the Canary Islands, and reservations are handled exclusively by Airtours's tour operators.

Joint Venture with Hyundai Merchant Marine Co., Ltd.

In 1996, the Carnival and Hyundai Merchant Marine Co., Ltd., signed an agreement to form a 50-50 joint venture to develop the Asian cruise vacation market. Each contributed $4.8 million as the initial capital of the joint venture. In addition, Carnival sold the cruise ship *Tropicale* to the joint venture for approximately $95.5 million cash. Carnival has chartered the vessel from the joint venture until the joint venture is ready to begin cruise operations in the Asian market in late 1998. The joint venture borrowed the $95.5 million purchase price from a financial institution and Carnival and HMM each guaranteed 50 percent of the borrowed funds.

FUTURE CONSIDERATIONS

Carnival's management will continue to monitor several strategic factors and issues for the next few years. The industry itself should see further consolidation through mergers and buyouts, and the expansion of industry negatively could affect the profitability of various cruise operators. Another factor of concern to management is how to reach the large North American market.

With the industry maturing, cruise competitors have become more sophisticated in their marketing efforts, and price competition is the norm in most cruise segments. (For a partial listing of major industry competitors, see Exhibit 8.) Royal Caribbean Cruise Lines has instituted a major shipbuilding program and is successfully challenging Carnival Cruise Lines in the contemporary segment. Walt Disney Company entered the cruise market with two 80,000-ton cruise liners in 1997, impacting significantly the family cruise vacation segment.

The increasing industry capacity is also a source of concern to cruise operators. The slow growth in industry demand is occurring during a period when industry berth capacity continues to grow. The entry of Disney and the ships already on order by current operators will increase industry berth capacity by over 10,000 per year for the next three years, a significant increase. The danger lies in cruise operators using the "price weapon" in their marketing campaigns to fill cabins. If cruise operators cannot make a reasonable return on investment, they will have to reduce operating costs, affecting quality of services, to remain profitable. This will increase the likelihood of further industry acquisitions, mergers, and consolidation. A worst-case scenario is the financial failure of weaker lines.

Still, Carnival's management believes that demand should increase during the remainder of the 1990s. Reaching more of the North American target market would improve industry profitability. Industry analysts state the problem is that an assessment of market potential is only an educated guess. What if the current demand figures are reflective of the future?

EXHIBIT 8: Carnival Corporation's Major Competitors—1996

Celebrity Cruises, 5200 Blue Lagoon Drive, Miami, FL 33126
Celebrity Cruises operates four modern cruise ships on 4-, 7-, and 10-day cruises to Bermuda, the Caribbean, the Panama Canal, and Alaska. Celebrity attracts first-time cruisers as well as seasoned cruisers. Purchased by Royal Caribbean on July 30, 1997.

Costa Cruise Lines, World Trade Center, 80m Southwest 8th Street, Miami, FL 33131
Costa promotes itself as the Italian cruise line offering a strictly Italian experience. Costa has six refurbished ships and two modern cruise liners that offer Caribbean and Mediterranean cruises for 7 days or longer. Costa's mix of ships and destinations appeals to a wide spectrum of people: first-time cruisers, young adults, and seasoned cruise passengers.

Norwegian Cruise Lines, 95 Merrick Way, Coral Gables, FL 33134
Norwegian Cruise Lines, formally Norwegian Caribbean Lines, was the first to base a modern fleet of cruise ships in the Port of Miami. It operates six modern cruise liners on 3-, 4-, and 7-day Eastern and Western Caribbean cruises and cruises to Bermuda. A wide variety of activities and entertainment attracts a diverse array of customers.

Premier Cruise Lines, P.O. Box 573, Cape Canaveral, FL 32930
A former subsidiary of the Greyhound Corporation, Premier operates two refurbished cruise ships and was the official cruise line of Walt Disney World. Premier offers 3- or 4-day Caribbean cruises. Premier attracts families with children as well as traditional cruise passengers.

Princess Cruises, 10100 Santa Monica Boulevard, Los Angeles, CA 90067
Princess Cruises, with its fleet of nine "Love Boats," offers 7-day and extended cruises to the Caribbean, Alaska, Canada, Africa, the Far East, South America, and Europe. Princesses's primary market is the upscale experienced traveler over age 50, according to Mike Hannan, senior vice-president for marketing services. Princess ships have an ambiance best described as casual elegance, and are famous for their Italian-style dining rooms and on-board entertainment.

Royal Caribbean Cruise Lines, 1050 Caribbean Way, Miami, FL 33132
RCCL's nine ships consistently have been given high marks by passengers and travel agents over the past 21 years. RCCL's ships are built for the contemporary market, are large and modern, and offer 3-, 4-, and 7-day as well as extended cruises. RCCL prides itself on service and exceptional cuisine. With the purchase of Celebrity, RCCL became the largest cruise line in the world.

Other Industry Competitors (Partial List)

American Hawaii Cruises	1 ship—Hawaiian Islands
Club Med	2 ships—Europe, Caribbean
Commodore Cruise Line	1 ship—Caribbean
Cunard Line	8 ships—Caribbean, Worldwide
Dolphin Cruise Line	3 ships—Caribbean, Bermuda
Radisson Seven Seas Cruises	3 ships—Worldwide
Royal Olympic Cruises	6 ships—Caribbean, Worldwide
Royal Cruise Line	4 ships—Caribbean, Alaska, Worldwide

Source: Cruise Lines International Association, 1996.

Southwest Airlines Co.—1998

Amit Shah
Charles R. Sterrett

www.iflyswa.com
stock symbol LUV

For five consecutive years (1991 through 1996), the Department of Transportation (DOT) Air Travel Consumer Report listed Southwest Airlines (214-792-5155) as having the best on-time performance, best baggage handling, and fewest customer complaints of all the major carriers. In a highly competitive industry, all carriers continually strive to be first place in any of the categories of the DOT report; Southwest is the only airline ever to hold the triple crown for its annual performance. No other airline has earned the triple crown for even one month! In addition to this achievement, Southwest continues to operate profitably; it made $317.7 million in net income on $3.8 billion in 1997 revenues. In an industry which historically is awash in red ink and in which airlines continually go in and out of bankruptcy or fail, Southwest has an enviable record of 24 consecutive years of operating at a profit. How has it accomplished this record of success?

In their best-selling book, *Nuts,* Kevin and Jackie Freiburg point to a company with people who are committed to working hard and having fun and who avoid following industry trends. The Freiburgs note that Southwest, based in Dallas, Texas, is a company which likes to keep prices at rock bottom; believes the customer comes second; runs recruiting ads that say, "Work at a place where wearing pants is optional"; paints its $30 million assets to look like killer whales and state flags; avoids trendy management programs; avoids formal, documented strategic planning; spends more time at planning parties than in writing policies; and once settled a legal dispute by arm wrestling.

HISTORY AND GROWTH OF SOUTHWEST AIRLINES

According to Southwest folklore, the airline was conceived in 1967 on a napkin when Rollin King, an investment advisor, met with his lawyer, Herb Kelleher, to discuss his idea for a low-fare, no-frills airline to fly between three of the major cities in Texas. At that time, King ran an unprofitable air charter service between small Texas cities. One day, his banker, John Parker, suggested that King concentrate on flying between the three biggest cities in the state. Parker suggested that the market was open for exploitation because he could never get a seat on the airlines currently flying between those cities, and besides, the fares were too high. King knew his current airline couldn't compete, so he decided to start a bigger one. He put together a plan and a feasibility study, and went to see Kelleher. In that meeting, King scribbled three lines on a cocktail napkin; labeled the points Houston, Dallas, and San Antonio; and muttered, "Herb, let's start our own airline." Kelleher loosened his tie and knitted his brow before replying, "Rollin, you're crazy. Let's do it!" Kelleher completed the necessary paperwork to create Air Southwest Co. (later Southwest Airline Co.). Then, the two filed for approval, and on February 20, 1968, the Texas Aeronautical Commission approved their plans to fly between the three cities.

The very next day, the upstart airline ran into stiff opposition from several of the major carriers then doing business in Texas. On February 21, 1968, these carriers—Braniff, Texas International, and Continental—blocked approval with a temporary restraining order. They argued that Texas didn't need another carrier. For the next three years, Southwest was unable to proceed while it fought legal battles with these airlines over the right to offer flights between the three cities. In 1971, however, Southwest won the right to fly and began to offer service with a total of four planes and about 200 employees. The efforts to quash the airline led to the unbridled enthusiasm for the airline by King, Kelleher, and the other employees which became an important part of Southwest's culture.

The outlook for Southwest was bleak, however. The legal battles left the airline flat broke and deep in debt. In its first year of operation, it lost $3.7 million, and it did not earn a profit for the next year and a half. But in 1973, it turned its first profit and never looked back. By 1978, it was one of the most profitable airlines in the country.

In its early years, Southwest faced other legal battles. For example, in 1974, a new airport opened to serve the greater Dallas–Fort Worth area, but it was further from downtown Dallas than Love Field. Southwest was using Love Field and wanted to continue to do so. But competitors wanted Southwest to move to the new airport to share in the costs, and they began to pressure Congress to pass a law barring flights from Love Field to any airport outside of the state of Texas. Southwest was able to negotiate a compromise, known as the Wright amendment, that allowed Southwest to fly to airports (including Love Field) in the four states bordering Texas. The Wright amendment forced Southwest into a key part of its strategy, to become an interstate carrier.

Southwest grew steadily, and by 1975 had expanded it operations to eight more cities in Texas. By the end of the 1970s, it dominated the Texas market. Its major appeal was to passengers who wanted low prices and frequent departures. In the 1980s, Southwest continued to expand and by 1993, it was serving 34 cities in 15 states. Southwest slowly, but methodically, moved across the Southwestern states, into California, the Midwest, and the Northwest. Its latest targets are Florida, where it serves four cities, and the East Coast, where it presently serves only Baltimore, Maryland, and Providence, Rhode Island. With its low prices and no-frills approach, it quickly dominated the markets it entered. In some markets, after Southwest entered, competitors soon withdrew, allowing the airline to expand even faster than projected. For example, when Southwest entered the California market in 1990, it quickly became the second-largest player, with over 20 percent of the intrastate market. Several competitors soon abandoned the Los Angeles–San Francisco route when they were unable to match Southwest's $59 one-way fare. Before Southwest entered this market, fares had been as high as $186 one-way.

California offers a good example of the real dilemma facing competing carriers, who often referred to Southwest as a "500-pound cockroach, too big to stamp out." While airfares were dropping, passenger traffic increased dramatically. But competitors such as American and US Airways were losing money on several key route segments, even though they cut service drastically. In late 1994, United began to fight back by launching a low-cost, high-frequency shuttle service on the West Coast. But it found that even a shuttle could not win against Southwest in a head-to-head battle. So United repositioned its shuttle away from Southwest's routes and even abandoned some routes altogether. According to the DOT, eight airlines surrendered West Coast routes to Southwest while one-way fares fell by over 30 percent to an average of $60 and traffic increased by almost 60 percent. The major problem for the larger airlines was that many of these West Coast routes were critical for feeding traffic into their highly profitable transcontinental and transpacific routes, and Southwest was cutting into that market.

Southwest is currently the fifth-largest domestic carrier in terms of customers boarded. The airline has transformed itself from a regional carrier operating out of Dallas into a truly national carrier. As of October 1997, the airline served 51 cities in 25 states and operated more than 2,200 flights a day with a fleet of 251 Boeing 737s. For the first half of 1997, Southwest flew 13,547 million revenue passenger miles (RPMs) compared with 12,646 million RPMs for the same period of 1996. But most remarkable is 24 years in a row of profitable operations, with total revenue in 1997 of $3.8 billion, an increase of 12 percent over 1996. Operating income in 1997 rose by 49 percent over 1996. Net income rose by 53 percent from $207.3 million in 1996 to $317.7 million in 1997. Financial statements are shown in Exhibits 1 and 2.

MANAGEMENT

While Southwest was going through its traumatic beginnings, King and Kelleher realized they needed someone to run the company. King hired Lamar Muse, an executive with airline experience, as CEO. Muse raised funding to keep the airline going and hired an experienced management team as company officers. He was able to purchase three brand-new Boeing 737s at bargain-basement prices because Boeing had overproduced in a period when airlines were in a slump. Muse led the airline in its climb to profitability but, in a dispute with the board, he was ousted in 1978. With Muse out, Kelleher moved into the top position and has run the airline ever since. Exhibit 3 shows the organizational chart of the company.

Kelleher is as well known for his zany antics as for his fun-loving, seemingly carefree style of management. For example, in 1992, he made headlines with an event called "Malice in Dallas," which was the result of a dispute over Southwest's "Just Plane Smart" slogan. Stevens Aviation, a small airline sales company in South Carolina, was using the slogan "Plane Smart" and claimed Southwest was infringing on its territory. Rather than go to court over the trademark, Stevens's chair suggested an arm wrestling match. Kelleher readily agreed, lost amid much fanfare, and was carried out on a stretcher while a "trainer" fed him shots of whiskey. Stevens let him use the slogan anyway, and both companies benefited from the bonanza of publicity surrounding the event. Kelleher is the guy who dressed up as the Easter Bunny, Elvis, and other costumed characters for some of the company's many parties, but he is also the shrewd businessperson who led the airline to 24 profitable years. His skills have made him one of America's most admired CEOs. If Herb Kelleher is crazy, as some claim, perhaps the CEO of Southwest is crazy like a fox.

EXHIBIT 1: Southwest Airlines Co., Consolidated Statement of Income

(in thousands of dollars, except per share amounts)	Years Ended December 31,		
	1997	1996	1995
Operating Revenues			
Passenger	$3,639,193	$3,269,238	$2,760,756
Freight	94,758	80,005	65,825
Other	82,870	56,927	46,170
Total operating revenues	3,816,821	3,406,170	2,872,751
Operating Expenses			
Salaries, wages, and benefits	1,136,542	999,719	867,984
Fuel and oil	494,952	484,673	365,670
Maintenance materials and repairs	256,501	253,521	217,259
Agency commissions	157,211	140,940	123,380
Aircraft rentals	201,954	190,663	169,461
Landing fees and other rentals	208,845	187,600	160,322
Depreciation	195,568	183,470	156,771
Other operating expenses	646,012	614,749	498,373
Total operating expenses	3,292,585	3,055,335	2,559,220
Operating Income	524,236	350,835	313,531
Other Expenses (Income):			
Interest expense	63,454	59,269	58,810
Capitalized interest	(19,779)	(22,267)	(31,371)
Interest income	(36,616)	(25,797)	(20,095)
Nonoperating (gains) losses, net	221	(1,732)	1,047
Total other expenses	7,280	9,473	8,391
Income before Income Taxes	516,956	341,362	305,140
Provision for Income Taxes	199,184	134,025	122,514
Net Income	317,772	207,337	182,626
Net Income per Share, Basic	1.45	.95	.85
Net Income per Share, Diluted	1.40	.92	.82

Source: Adapted from Southwest Airlines Co., *Annual Report* (1997): F7.

EXHIBIT 2: Southwest Airlines Co., Consolidated Balance Sheet

(in thousands of dollars, except per share amounts)	December 31, 1997	1996
Assets		
Current assets		
Cash and cash equivalents	623,343	581,841
Accounts receivable	76,530	73,440
Inventories of parts and supplies, at cost	52,376	51,094
Deferred income taxes	18,843	11,560
Prepaid expenses and other current assets	35,324	33,055
Total current assets	806,416	750,990
Property and equipment, at cost		
Flight equipment	3,987,493	3,435,304
Ground property and equipment	601,957	523,958
Deposits on flight equipment purchase contracts	221,874	198,366
Less allowance for depreciation	(1,375,631)	(1,188,405)
Other assets	4,051	3,266
Total assets	4,246,160	3,723,479
Liabilities and Stockholders' Equity		
Current liabilities		
Accounts payable	160,891	214,232
Accrued liabilities	426,950	368,625
Air traffic liability	153,341	158,098
Current maturities of long-term debt	121,324	12,327
Other current liabilities	6,007	12,122
Total current liabilities	868,513	765,404
Long-term debt less current maturities	628,106	650,226
Deferred income taxes	438,981	349,987
Deferred gains from sale and leaseback of aircraft	256,255	274,891
Other deferred liabilities	45,287	34,659
Commitments and contingencies		
Stockholders' equity		
Common stock, $1.00 par value: 680,000,000 shares authorized; 221,207,083 and 145,112,090 shares issued and outstanding in 1997 and 1996, respectively	221,207	145,112
Capital in excess of par value	155,696	181,650
Retained earnings	1,632,115	1,321,550
Total stockholders' equity	2,009,018	1,648,312
Total liabilities and stockholders' equity	4,246,160	3,723,479

Source: Adapted from Southwest Airlines Co., *Annual Report* (1997): F6.

EXHIBIT 3: Southwest Airlines Co., Organization Chart

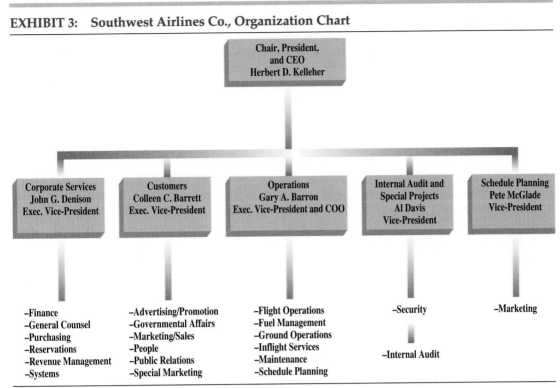

Source: Southwest Airlines Co., March 1997.

Even though the airline has grown to over 20,000 employees, Southwest's management team drives home the feeling that all of its people are part of one big family. Southwest's Culture Committee is headed by Colleen Barrett, Kelleher's former legal secretary and now an executive vice-president, the highest-ranking woman in the airline industry. Barrett regularly visits each of the company's stations to reiterate the airline's history and motivate employees. As keeper of the company's culture, Barrett has devised unique ways to preserve Southwest's underdog background and can-do spirit. She constantly reinforces the company's message that employees should be treated the way customers are and continually celebrates workers who go above and beyond the call of duty. Barrett also commemorates all employee birthdays and special events with cards signed, "Herb and Colleen." Employees know the culture and expect each other to live up to it.

STRATEGY

Southwest's operation under Kelleher has a number of characteristics that seem to contribute to its success. It always has been able to seize quickly a strategic opportunity whenever it arises. Other key factors are its conservative growth pattern, cost-containment policy, and the commitment of its employees.

Kelleher always resisted attempts to expand too rapidly. His philosophy was to expand only when there were resources available to go into a new location with 10 to

12 flights per day—not just one or two. He also resisted the temptation to begin transcontinental operations or to get into a head-to-head battle with the major carriers on long-distance routes. But even with a conservative approach, Southwest expanded at a vigorous pace. Its debt has remained the lowest among U.S. carriers and, with an A-rating, Southwest has the highest Standard and Poor's credit rating in the industry.

Southwest made its mark by concentrating on flying large numbers of passengers on high-frequency short hops (usually one hour or less) at bargain fares. Southwest avoided the hub-and-spoke operations of its larger rivals, taking its passengers directly from city to city. Southwest also tends to avoid the more congested major airports in favor of smaller satellite fields. Kelleher revealed the niche strategy of Southwest in noting that when other airlines set up hub-and-spoke systems in which passengers are shunted to a few major hubs where they are transferred to other planes going to their destinations, "we wound up with a unique market niche: We are the world's only short-haul, high-frequency, low-fare, point-to-point carrier. . . . We wound up with a market segment that is peculiarly ours, and everything about the airline has been adapted to serving that market segment in the most efficient and economical way possible."

Southwest continues to be the lowest-cost airline in its markets. Even when trying to match Southwest's cut-rate fares, the larger carriers could not do so without incurring substantial losses. Southwest's operating costs per available seat mile (the number of seats multiplied by the distance flown) average 15 to 25 percent below its rivals. One of the major factors in this enviable record was that all of its planes used to be of a single type—Boeing 737s—which dramatically lowered the company's costs of training, maintenance, and inventory. Because all Southwest crews knew the 737 inside and out, they could substitute personnel rapidly from one flight to another in an emergency. In addition, Southwest recognized that planes only earn money while they are in the air, so the company worked hard to achieve a faster turnaround time on the ground. Most airlines take up to one hour to unload passengers, clean and service a plane, and board new passengers. Southwest has a turnaround time for most flights of 20 minutes or less. Thorough knowledge of the 737 helped in this achievement.

Southwest also cut costs in the customer service area as well. Because its flights are usually one hour or less, it does not offer meals—only peanuts and drinks. Boarding passes are reusable plastic cards, and boarding time is saved because Southwest has no assigned seating. The airline does not subscribe to any centralized reservation service. It will not even transfer baggage to other carriers—that is the passengers' responsibility. Even with this frugality, passengers do not seem to object because the price is right.

Southwest has achieved a team spirit which others can only envy. One of the reasons for this is that the company truly believes that employees come first, not the customers. Southwest is known for providing employees with tremendous amounts of information which will enable them to better understand the company, its mission, its customers, and its competition. Southwest believes that information is power. It is the resource that enables employees to do their jobs better. Armed with this knowledge, they are able to serve the customers better, and customers who deal with Southwest rarely get the runaround.

Even though unionized, Southwest was able to negotiate flexible work rules that enabled it to meet its rapid turnaround schedules. It's not unusual for pilots to help flight attendants clean the airplanes or to help the ground crew load baggage. Consequently, employee productivity is very high and the airline is able to maintain a lean staff. In good times, Kelleher resisted the temptation to overhire and so avoided layoffs during lean times. Southwest has laid off only three people in 24 years, and immediately hired them back. This employee-retention policy has contributed to employees' feeling of security and a fierce sense of loyalty. The people of Southwest see themselves as crusaders whose mission is to give ordinary people the opportunity to fly.

Maximizing profitability is a major goal at Southwest. This leads to a drive to keep cost low and quality high. Southwest adheres to Peters and Waterman's concept of "stick with the knitting." The airline's ideal products are safe, frequent, low-cost flights that get passengers to their destination on time—and often closer to their destination than the major airlines which use the larger airports further from the cities. Southwest uses Dallas's Love Field, Houston's Hobby Airport, and Chicago's Midway Airport, which are closer to their respective downtowns, are less congested, and are, therefore, more convenient for the business traveler. This also helps Southwest's on-time performance.

In its marketing approach, Southwest always tried to set itself apart from the rest of the industry. It also played up its fun-loving, rebel reputation. In the early years when the big airlines were trying to run Southwest out of business by undercutting its low fares, Southwest made its customers an unprecedented offer. In response to a Braniff ad offering a $13 fare between Houston and Dallas, Southwest placed an ad that read, "Nobody's going to shoot Southwest Airlines out of the sky for a lousy $13." It then offered passengers the opportunity to purchase a ticket from Southwest for the same price, which was half the normal fare, or to buy a full-fare ticket for $26 and receive a bottle of premium whiskey along with it. The response was unprecedented. Southwest's planes were full and, for a short time, Southwest was one of the top liquor distributors in the state of Texas.

Southwest's ads always try to convince the customer that what the airline offers them is of real value to them. Southwest also believes it is in the business of making flying fun and, with its ads, wants customers to know that when they fly Southwest, they'll have an experience unlike any other. Southwest promises safe, reliable, frequent, low-cost air transportation topped off with outstanding service. By keeping its promises, Southwest earned high credibility in every market it serves.

COMPETITORS

Three of Southwest's major competitors are United Airlines, Delta Air Lines, and America West Airlines. United, with over 90,000 employees, is one of Southwest's most formidable competitors. United, the number-two U.S. airline, flies over 500 aircraft to about 140 locations in the United States and overseas. In addition, it operates the United Express which feeds passengers from regional carriers into the United system, and its United shuttle provides over 450 short-haul flights between 20 cities in the Western states. The latter service is one that often puts United into direct competition with Southwest.

Delta, the third-largest U.S. carrier, has over 63,000 employees and fiscal 1997 sales of $13.6 billion. Delta flies to about 190 U.S. and foreign locations, and is particularly strong throughout much of the southern United States where two of its major hubs—Atlanta and Dallas–Fort Worth—are located. Delta also has built up a low-fare regional carrier service and has acquired a minority stake in three regional airlines which can feed passengers into its several hubs. Delta has begun to focus much of its attention on its transatlantic operations, but remains a strong U.S. competitor and is intent on attracting more business traffic.

America West, the smallest of Southwest's competitors, has about 9,600 employees and earned fiscal 1996 sales of $1.7 billion. The airline serves 49 cities in the United States and a total of seven locations in Mexico and Canada. America West has strong positions in its hubs, Phoenix and Las Vegas. However, many of its locations put it into direct competition with Southwest. With Continental and Mesa airlines, which have small stakes in America West, America West has formed alliances which give it access to another 35 destinations.

All of the competitors have come into head-to-head competition with Southwest on several occasions. Southwest always welcomed competition and firmly believes it can come out ahead in any of those situations. Kelleher, when asked about his thoughts on facing a competitor such as the United shuttle, stated, "I think it's good to have some real competitive activity that gets your people stirred up and renews their vigor and their energy and their desire to win. I think the United's shuttle assault on Southwest Airlines, which was a very direct assault, drew our people closer together and made them better as a consequence."

THE FUTURE

Today, Southwest provides service to only 51 cities, so there are tremendous opportunities for expansion. The problem: Where to go next? Over 100 cities have asked the airline to begin service in their communities because of the positive impact the company has when it begins operations in a new location. The introduction of Southwest's low fares and frequent flights opens up the market and gives many more people the freedom to fly.

Southwest continues to forge ahead in other ways as well. The airline introduced a new aircraft to the fleet in October 1997: the Boeing 737-700. Southwest was the launch customer for this aircraft, which is able to fly high, fast, and far and still be fuel-efficient. Southwest has purchased 60 of these aircraft, which require less maintenance time than the traditional 737s.

In 1997, Southwest Airlines added a 24-hour emergency medical service for its customers for in-flight medical emergencies. The airline now has emergency room physicians on call 24 hours a day through a service called MedLink. MedLink can put a physician in contact with Southwest's flight attendants during a medical emergency. The physician can make diagnoses, advise treatments, and issue medical recommendations, including whether or not an emergency landing should be made. Southwest is the first major airline to make the medical service accessible by in-flight telephone.

Throughout its history, Southwest consistently followed a clearly defined purpose and a well-thought-out strategy: to make a profit, achieve job security for every employee, and make flying affordable for more people. Can Southwest continue to maintain this strategy? Will its position remain unassailable by competitors? Will it continue to operate as only a short-haul carrier? In its 1997 annual report, Southwest announced new nonstop flights from Nashville to Los Angeles and to Oakland—well beyond the typical one-hour flight. What are the implications of expanding to longer-haul operations? Will Southwest begin to lose the distinguishing characteristics that were the hallmarks of its success? And how about international routes, especially to Canada or Mexico? Southwest certainly has come a long way from the little company with three aircraft that began operations in 1971. What's next?

Central United Methodist Church—1998

Robert T. Barrett

The family came into the Fellowship Hall and noticed an excited mass of people. The group of four waited in line to receive their food, picked up drinks, and moved on to look for places to sit. All places were either taken or "reserved" by regulars at the dinner. The family of four ate their food while standing in the hallway, left before the programs began, and decided to join another church.

Central United Methodist Church (803-662-3218), located at the heart of downtown Florence, South Carolina, is a vibrant and growing church. The Wednesday night supper program, centered around family ministries, is so popular that it has outgrown Fellowship Hall. The ministerial staff, church leaders, and other church members are concerned and do not want to lose other potential members just because of inadequate space.

MISSION STATEMENTS

Following is the mission statement for United Methodist Church:

> The mission of the Church is to make disciples of Jesus Christ. Local churches provide the most significant arena through which disciple making occurs. This statement was taken from the Disciplines of the United Methodist Church.

Following is the mission statement for Central United Methodist Church:

> It is our mission to proclaim the good news of Jesus Christ in deeds as well as words. It is our purpose to make the proclamation to the people of our local congregation, our immediate community, and to those beyond our sight. It is our plan to carry out the Mission through our local congregation, through the United Methodist Connection, and through ecumenical relationships.

PAST AND PRESENT

Central United Methodist Church was established in the late 1800s and moved to its present site at the corner of Irby and Cheves Streets in 1913. Through a variety of land and property acquisitions since 1913, Central's main campus has grown to include approximately 200 feet of frontage on Irby Street and 300 feet of frontage on Cheves

Street. With the downtown location, a limited number of acquisition possibilities remain available to Central. In the mid-1900s, Central had the opportunity to purchase a house adjacent to church property for $30,000, but turned it down. The owner then sold the property to a group who developed a hotel and cafeteria there. After the venture failed, the church bought the property in 1980 for $100,000. In 1984, Central purchased an adjacent building which currently serves as the primary facility for the youth ministry as well as the location of five Sunday School classes. Central continues to seek more property for building and parking.

Exhibit 1 shows the membership levels for Central over the past eight years, along with average attendance levels for Sunday morning worship (two services) and Sunday School. Of this membership, approximately 23 percent are less than 10 years of age (young people on rolls prior to formally joining the church in seventh grade are considered "preparatory members"), approximately 12 percent are in the 11-to-20-year-old bracket, approximately 16 percent are in the 21-to-30-year-old bracket, approximately 14 percent are in the 30-to-40-year-old bracket, approximately 12 percent are in both the 41-to-50 and the 51-to-60-year-old brackets, and the remaining 11 percent are in the 61-year-old-and-over brackets. Over 60 percent of the membership is less than age 40, with 35 percent of this group classified as children and youth. Another breakdown of church membership shows that approximately 60 percent of the membership are married, with a bulk of the remaining 40 percent in the children and youth age brackets: This reflects the commitment of the membership to strong family values. In a time of declining memberships in churches across the country, Central has been able to maintain membership and participation levels.

Exhibit 2 gives the value of property owned and debt owed by Central over the past eight years. The value of church property has grown while debt service has continued to decline over recent years.

Exhibit 3 gives information on contributions to the operating budget, the building fund, and to a category labeled Building Fund Extra for designated project gifts. Contributions have increased steadily over the past eight years. Church budgets in excess of $800,000 have been overpledged (and collected) for the past three years. The annual budget for 1997 along with a proposed 1998 budget are given in Exhibit 4.

EXHIBIT 1: Central United Methodist Church Membership and Attendance Levels

Year	Church Membership	Average Attendance	Sunday School Membership	Average Attendance
1996	1,863	589	572	322
1995	1,866	590	1,416	380
1994	1,855	551	1,376	331
1993	1,826	535	1,206	323
1992	1,801	522	1,111	308
1991	1,797	523	1,088	338
1990	1,795	540	1,091	336
1989	1,800	534	1,048	342

Source: Central United Methodist Church document.

EXHIBIT 2: Central United Methodist Church Assets and Debt

Year	Value of Church Campus Property	Parsonage and Furniture	Other Assets	Debt
1996	$8,223,700	$432,700	$476,997	$103,100
1995	8,223,700	432,700	476,997	188,000
1994	8,223,700	432,500	535,625	206,105
1993	6,944,000	213,500	320,000	388,271
1992	7,492,875	313,000	380,000	458,166
1991	7,492,875	313,000	380,000	467,532
1990	7,492,875	313,000	380,000	427,348
1989	6,107,068	314,000	380,000	526,000

Source: Central United Methodist Church document.

EXHIBIT 3: Central United Methodist Church Contributions

Year	Operating Budget	Building Fund	Building Fund Extra
1996	$830,009.91	$145,231.33	$ 6,464.75
1995	734,799.03	131,661.41	7,251.00
1994	691,713.08	133,602.07	26,527.24
1993	631,750.74	125,171.98	1,589.50
1992	587,278.22	110,831.43	2,204.50
1991	561,148.50	115,747.47	3,810.77
1990	518,341.80	120,976.75	8,635.50
1989	499,069.64	102,735.34	38,221.41

Source: Central United Methodist Church documents.

EXHIBIT 4: Central United Methodist Church, Detailed Analysis of Proposed Budget

	Account Expenses	1997 Annual Budget	1998 Proposed Budget
Salaries			
005001	Pastor	$ 60,939.00	$ 62,939.00
005002	Associate pastor	35,554.00	25,600.00
005003	Director of Children's Ministry	12,426.00	12,826.00
005004	Music director and organist	38,431.00	39,631.00
005005	Assistant music director	4,952.00	5,102.00
005006	Church secretary	16,074.00	16,556.00
005007	Financial secretary	18,639.00	19,199.00
005008	Church visitor	5,296.00	5,482.00
005009	Hostess	3,047.00	3,127.00
005010	R & M personnel	11,363.00	11,703.00
005011	Custodian	10,489.00	11,248.00
005012	Custodian	10,400.00	11,248.00
005013	Custodian/maid	10,400.00	11,462.00
005014	Salary contingency	5,000.00	5,000.00
005015	Office assistant/receptionist	6,934.00	6,925.00
005016	Building and property superintendent	8,998.00	16,625.00
005018	Music assistant—children	.00	3,200.00
005019	Director of handbells	.00	2,000.00

continued

EXHIBIT 4: *continued*

	Account Expenses	1997 Annual Budget	1998 Proposed Budget
005290	Nursery workers salaries	9,812.00	9,812.00
005805	Day camp staff (7)	12,200.00	12,200.00
005807	Camp director	7,850.00	8,090.00
05003A	Director of Adult Ministry	12,426.00	12,826.00
05003Y	Director of Youth Ministry	.00	12,826.00
05012S	Working janitor supervisor	5,627.00	.00
Total Salaries		306,857.00	325,627.00

Allowances

005101	Pastor reimbursement	3,500.00	3,500.00
005102	Associate minister reimbursement	2,880.00	3,500.00
		6,380.00	7,000.00

Travel Allowance

005103	Director, Children Ministry	900.00	900.00
005104	Church visitor	1,200.00	1,200.00
005808	Camp director	150.00	150.00
05103A	Director, Adult Ministry	900.00	900.00
05103Y	Director, Youth	.00	900.00
		3,150.00	4,050.00

Continuing Education

005110	Pastor	400.00	400.00
005111	Associate minister	600.00	600.00
005112	Director, Children Ministry	600.00	600.00
005113	Music Director/Organist	800.00	800.00
005114	Director, Children's Choir	.00	200.00
005115	Office staff	900.00	900.00
005116	Handbell director	.00	200.00
05112A	Director, Adult Ministry	600.00	600.00
05112Y	Director, Youth Ministry	.00	600.00
		3,900.00	4,900.00

Social Security

005122	Lay employees social security	16,093.00	18,033.00
		16,093.00	18,033.00

Hospitalization

005130	Pastor	1,500.00	1,500.00
005131	Associate minister	1,500.00	1,500.00
005133	Music director/Organist	1,500.00	1,500.00
005134	Lay employees	.00	.00
		4,500.00	4,500.00

Utilities

005140	Pastor	3,400.00	3,400.00
005141	Associate minister	3,400.00	3,400.00
		6,800.00	6,800.00

Pension

005161	Pastor	.00	.00
005162	Associate minister	.00	.00
005164	Music director/Organist	3,821.00	3,869.00
005165	Building/property superintendent	585.00	665.00
005166	DCE Children	497.00	549.00
005167	DCE Adult	497.00	549.00
005168	Janitor—Johnny	437.00	450.00
005169	Church secretary	643.00	662.00
005170	Receptionist	277.00	277.00

continued

EXHIBIT 4: *continued*

	Account Expenses	1997 Annual Budget	1998 Proposed Budget
005171	Financial secretary	746.00	768.00
005172	Custodian—Mary Mc	.00	458.00
05166Y	Director of Youth	.00	549.00
		7,503.00	8,796.00
Total Allowances		48,326.00	54,079.00

Councils

Children's Council Activities

005201	UMC—Human sexuality program	500.00	.00
005202	Sunday School promotion	300.00	200.00
005203	Sunday School Christmas program	250.00	250.00
005204	Sunday School teacher appreciation	400.00	400.00
005205	Vacation Bible school	2,500.00	2,500.00
005209	Leadership training/support	600.00	600.00
005210	UMC—Drug education program	.00	.00
005211	Summer Children's Ministry	500.00	600.00
005212	Wed. night children's program	800.00	700.00
005213	Children's events	500.00	600.00
005214	Parenting class	.00	400.00
		6,350.00	6,250.00

Youth Council Activities

005222	Confirmation	400.00	400.00
005223	Senior recognition	450.00	450.00
005224	Puppet ministry	100.00	.00
005225	Methodist Youth Fellowship	2,000.00	2,000.00
005227	Sunday School social	600.00	600.00
005229	Leadership training/support	2,500.00	2,500.00
005265	Youth miscellaneous	300.00	500.00
		6,350.00	6,450.00

Adults Council Activities

005230	College age	500.00	500.00
005231	Single Ministry	250.00	250.00
005232	Adult teacher appreciation	200.00	400.00
005234	Leadership training/support	500.00	500.00
005237	Sandwich generation	.00	200.00
		1,450.00	1,850.00

Senior Adult Council

005294	Senior Adult postage	.00	100.00
005295	Young at Hearts	1,000.00	1,200.00
005296	Joy Singles	250.00	250.00
005297	Trips/travel (Senior Adult)	200.00	200.00
005298	Senior Adult Ministries	100.00	100.00
005299	Leadership training/support	500.00	500.00
		2,050.00	2,350.00

Family Life Council

005240	Wednesday night programs	500.00	800.00
005244	Leadership training/support	500.00	500.00
005246	Decorations	.00	200.00
005282	Summer suppers	.00	500.00
005283	Wednesday night suppers	500.00	500.00
005284	Family, picnic/summer	800.00	300.00
005285	5th Sunday events	400.00	400.00
		2,700.00	3,200.00

continued

EXHIBIT 4: *continued*

Account Expenses	*1997 Annual Budget*	*1998 Proposed Budget*
Children's Supplies/Equipment		
005250 Paper, glue, markers, etc.	1,000.00	1,000.00
005251 Nursery	600.00	600.00
005252 Preschool and toddlers	500.00	400.00
005253 Elementary (6–12 yrs.)	600.00	600.00
005255 Sunday School classroom equipment	200.00	200.00
	2,900.00	2,800.00
General Administration		
005291 Literature (Sunday School curricula)	9,500.00	9,500.00
005292 Library	500.00	500.00
	10,000.00	10,000.00
Recreation Committee		
005226 Athletics	3,000.00	.00
005235 Adult golf tournament	600.00	600.00
005270 Basketball equipment	.00	300.00
005271 Basketball fees	.00	2,500.00
005276 Recreation breakfast	.00	200.00
	3,600.00	3,600.00
Scouting		
005236 Boy Scouts	1,300.00	900.00
005238 Girl Scouts	.00	300.00
	1,300.00	1,200.00
Total Councils	36,700.00	37,700.00
Outreach Committee		
005208 Sunshine class	900.00	900.00
005302 Missionary to Brazil	3,750.00	3,750.00
005304 Golden Cross	250.00	250.00
005306 School of Mission training	200.00	200.00
005307 Operating budget	500.00	500.00
005309 Work teams	500.00	500.00
005310 Lighthouse Ministries	6,000.00	6,000.00
005501 Meals on wheels	600.00	600.00
005502 Incidentals/home supplies	500.00	500.00
Total Outreach Committee	13,200.00	13,200.00
Worship Committee		
005401 Altar Guild budget	1,250.00	1,250.00
005402 Music operating budget	5,000.00	5,000.00
005403 Music instrument tuning	2,000.00	1,600.00
005406 Organ R & M escrow	.00	1,000.00
005407 Christmas tree	200.00	200.00
005408 Operating and special needs	2,000.00	1,000.00
005409 Children's choir miscellaneous	.00	2,000.00
Total Worship Committee	10,450.00	12,050.00
Stewardship		
005606 Centralight newsletter	3,000.00	3,000.00
006001 Stewardship campaign	2,000.00	2,000.00
Total Stewardship	5,000.00	5,000.00
Evangelism Committee		
005600 Leadership development	.00	1,500.00

continued

EXHIBIT 4: *continued*

Account Expenses		*1997 Annual Budget*	*1998 Proposed Budget*
005601	Evangelism operating budget	1,700.00	3,000.00
005602	Upper rooms	1,000.00	1,000.00
005603	Radio ministry	3,900.00	3,900.00
005604	Lenten services	1,400.00	1,500.00
005605	Training supplies	500.00	500.00
005607	Evangelism miscellaneous	300.00	500.00
005608	Special services	1,000.00	1,000.00
005609	Advertisement—radio spots	1,500.00	2,000.00
05605B	Visitors' brochure	2,000.00	1,000.00
Total Evangelism Committee		13,300.00	15,900.00
Church Property			
005701	Repairs and maintenance	6,500.00	6,500.00
005703	Parsonage furnishings, R&M	3,000.00	3,000.00
005704	Church furnishings	2,000.00	2,000.00
005706	Insurance/Workers' Compensation	18,000.00	18,000.00
005707	Janitorial supplies/equipment	5,000.00	5,000.00
005708	Kitchen supplies	2,500.00	2,500.00
005709	Office machines/R&M/contracts	4,000.00	7,000.00
005711	Maintenance contract/repair	15,000.00	15,000.00
005712	R & M escrow fund (3%)	23,901.00	25,255.00
005730	Utilities	70,000.00	73,000.00
005731	Telephone information service	1,000.00	1,000.00
005735	Bus/van maintenance	3,200.00	3,200.00
005740	Camp repairs and maintenance	5,180.00	5,180.00
005741	Camp R & M escrow	2,500.00	2,500.00
005742	Camp utilities	3,380.00	3,380.00
005743	Camp pool R & M	4,780.00	4,780.00
005750	Facility/janitorial fees	.00	.00
Total Church Property		169,941.00	177,295.00
Camp Sexton Committee			
058151	Publicity	500.00	500.00
058152	Trail improvement	200.00	200.00
058153	Day camp instructional supplies	1,400.00	1,000.00
058154	Day camp bus	2,300.00	2,300.00
058155	Church van—fuel	100.00	100.00
058156	Day camp food	1,300.00	1,700.00
058158	Day camp—T-shirts	500.00	500.00
581515	Income (user and camper fees)	.00	.00
Total Camp Sexton Committee		6,300.00	6,300.00
Conference			
005901	District parsonage/office	3,104.00	3,426.00
005902	Episcopal Fund	4,005.00	4,004.00
005903	District superintendent compensation	7,012.00	7,301.00
005904	Pension fund	33,378.00	37,638.00
005905	Equitable compensation fund	1,934.00	2,199.00
005906	Conference insurance	30,179.00	30,507.00
005907	Senior college scholarship	11,132.00	11,590.00
005908	Camps/retreats Ministry	3,168.00	3,298.00
005909	Congregational development	8,003.00	8,333.00
005910	Methodist Homes residents assistant	5,169.00	5,382.00

continued

EXHIBIT 4:   *continued*

	Account Expenses	1997 Annual Budget	1998 Proposed Budget
005911	Spartanburg Methodist College	4,304.00	4,482.00
005912	Campus Ministry	3,321.00	3,357.00
005913	World Service and Conference	28,889.00	30,008.00
005914	District administration	5,801.00	5,668.00
005915	Ministerial education	6,552.00	6,632.00
005916	General Conference administration	1,130.00	1,157.00
005918	Focus 2000/Mission initiative	398.00	305.00
005919	Black college fund	2,727.00	2,762.00
005920	Conference administration	4,762.00	6,916.00
005921	Jurisdiction mission/ministry	735.00	1,521.00
005922	African university fund	632.00	641.00
005924	Interdenominational cooperation	301.00	409.00
005925	Lake Junaluska mission	900.00	900.00
Total Conference		167,536.00	178,436.00
Miscellaneous			
005404	Offering envelopes	1,200.00	1,200.00
005405	Bulletins	16,500.00	16,500.00
006002	Postage	8,900.00	8,900.00
006003	Office/computer supplies	10,000.00	11,000.00
006005	Annual Conference	1,800.00	1,200.00
006006	Student aid	600.00	600.00
006007	Contingency	4,000.00	4,000.00
006010	Designated gifts	.00	.00
Total Miscellaneous		43,000.00	43,400.00
Total Expenses		820,610.00	868,987.00

Source: Central United Methodist Church (1998).

Florence, South Carolina

Founded in 1850, Florence remains a railroad city. Florence is located in a region of South Carolina called the Pee Dee, named after a tribe of Native Americans who inhabited the area. The local Chamber of Commerce touts Florence as the trade, industrial, medical, transportation, cultural, financial, and educational center of the Pee Dee. Located where interstate highways I-95 and I-20 intersect, Florence sees many travelers headed north to New York, south to Florida, east to Myrtle Beach, and west to the Appalachian Mountains.

The city of Florence has more than 33,000 residents, projected to double by the year 2010. Florence County has 122,000 residents, and projects growth to 130,000 by 2010. Florence has churches of all denominations. Within three miles of the downtown location of Central United Methodist Church are Baptist, Presbyterian, Lutheran, Episcopal, and other Methodist churches. In the city of Florence, there are five Methodist churches. Many other churches have chosen to locate in areas on the outskirts of town. Thus, as the population of Florence grows, there is increased "competition" for parishioners.

Church Staff and Volunteer Structure

Central United Methodist Church is served by a staff of 23 persons. The senior pastor acts as the chief administrative officer of this staff. Other primary staff members include one associate minister, a minister of music, a part-time director of children's ministries, a part-time director of adult ministries, and a part-time director of youth ministries. Clerical and custodian assistants make up most of the remaining staff positions. The church has adopted a successful strategy of using part-time staff, and the benefits are apparent in efficiencies and quality of service. This strategy allows the church to hire a person who is skilled in a particular function for the limited amount of time needed for that job.

As with most churches, much of the church's work is carried out by volunteers. The committee structure which helps to govern and carry out church programs is headed by the Administrative Board. Major subdivisions reporting to the Administrative Board are the Council on Ministries, the Finance Committee, and the Pastor Parish Committee. The Council on Ministries is the major programming arm of the church with 12 councils and committees in charge of the variety of church programs. These volunteer groups include the Children's Council, Youth Council, Adult Council, Senior Adult Council, Family Life Council, Recreation Committee, Scouting Committee, Outreach Committee, Worship Committee, Stewardship Committee, Evangelism Committee, and Camp Sexton Committee.

Church Property

Central United Methodist Church owns property in the downtown Florence location at Cheves and Irby Streets, a large tract of land just outside of Florence named Camp Sexton after the donor, and a Boy Scout Hut a few miles from the main church property. Most church programs are held at the downtown location, detailed below. A summer camp for children is held for several weeks at Camp Sexton. Camp Sexton hosts special programs during the year and a Sunday afternoon swim session for church members during the summer. The church-sponsored Boy Scout troop meets weekly in the Boy Scout Hut.

The church sanctuary seats approximately 400 people. The sanctuary overflows for performances of the Masterworks Choir, the Christmas Eve services, Easter and Mother's Day Sunday services, and large funerals and weddings.

Every classroom on the property is filled with a Sunday School class. Classes are held in the library, the Fellowship Hall, and the youth lounge. Many of the classrooms have been deemed inadequate for their specific purpose, particularly for small children's classrooms and nurseries. Sunday School classes for adults typically develop around age groupings. As the church grows, there will likely be a need for additional Sunday School classes.

As the example at the beginning of this case pointed out, the Fellowship Hall, which is the only large multipurpose space on the church campus, may not be of appropriate size to accommodate the larger programs of the church. The enormous popularity of the Wednesday night supper program has placed attendance for this program beyond the physical capacity of the Fellowship Hall, which can comfortably seat about 250 people at the most. Other church programs which use a large space include wedding receptions, Sunday School promotions, district youth rallies, and church charge conferences. Other programs, such as state conference-wide meetings, could utilize a larger space if one were available.

LONG RANGE PLANNING COMMITTEE

The Fellowship Hall capacity problem was one in a number of concerns facing Central United Methodist Church as it continued to expand its ministry (see Exhibit 5 organizational chart). In 1991, the Administrative Board of the church formed the Long Range

EXHIBIT 5: Central United Methodist Church—Organizational Chart

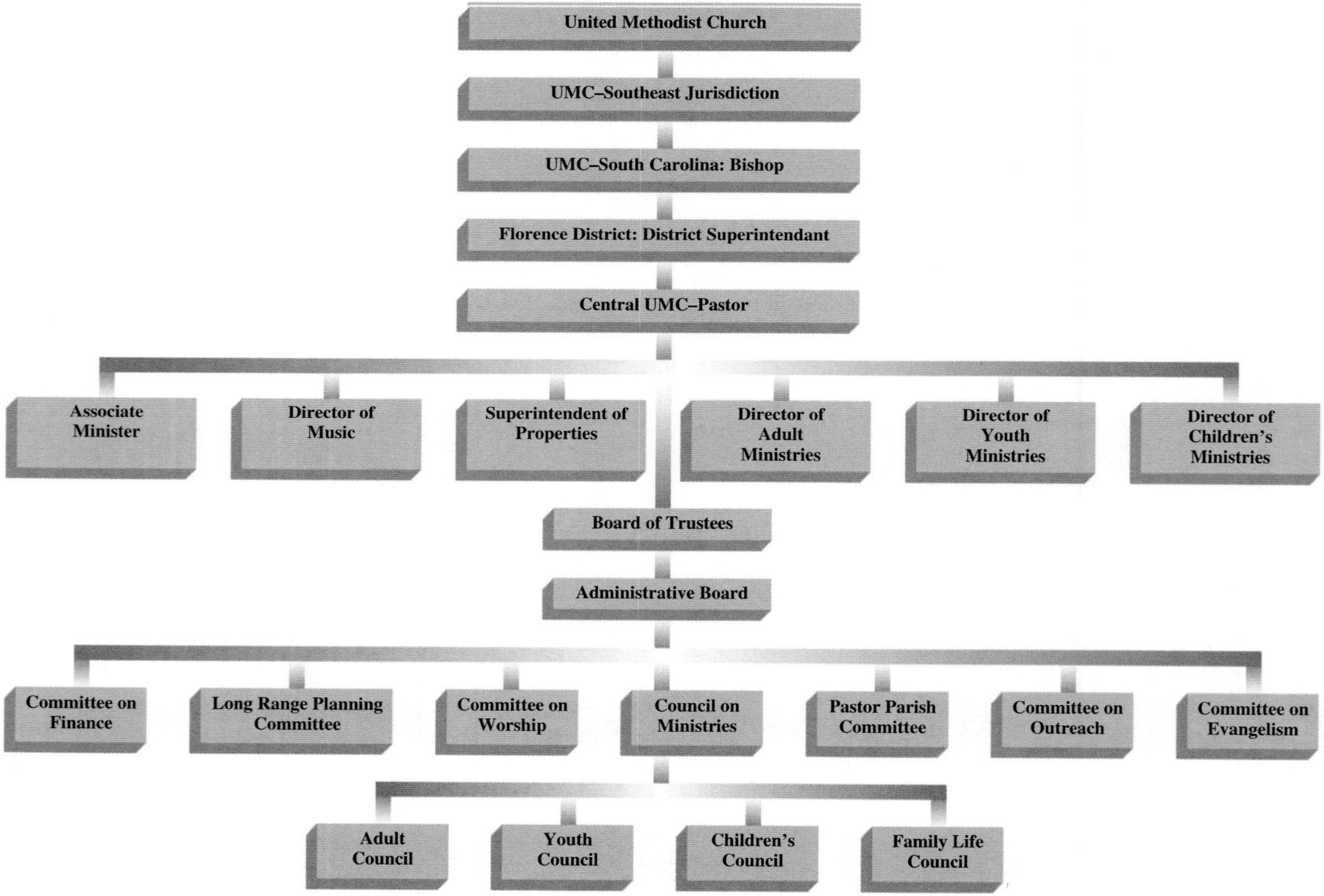

Source: Central United Methodist Church document.

Planning Committee to review existing programs of the church, evaluate the adequacy of the facilities to carry out these programs, evaluate staffing levels which support current programs, and to project future needs. It was felt that when these needs were identified, a direction could be established as to how to meet them. The committee consisted of church members from a wide range of ages (from youth representatives to retirement age members), time in church (from less than five years to over 50 years as a member of Central), and vocation (for example, housewives/mothers, teachers, engineers, and lawyers).

The committee met monthly, beginning with research of the literature on church development, discussions of church trends in our society, and analysis of how these trends apply to Central. The committee received reports from all programs of the church and interviewed all professional and volunteer leaders responsible for the programs in an effort to understand the existing programs and their projected needs. The committee made a physical inspection of all properties and facilities of the church. The committee developed and distributed a questionnaire to get direct input from the congregation during the planning process. Open meetings were held to gather additional information from members of the congregation.

One of the staff reports, given by the minister of music, highlighted some of the needs of the sanctuary. Based on recommendations made by an expert on acoustics, the minister of music recommended some major modifications to the sanctuary which would enhance the sound quality there. In addition, new carpet, repairs to the dome ceiling, and patching and painting of the walls were needed.

The Long Range Planning Committee identified three levels of facility needs for the church which the committee referred to as Urgent Needs, Immediate Needs, and Future Needs. In addition, a list of General Needs was defined by the committee.

Specific Facility Needs or Improvements

Urgent

- Sanctuary repair/renovation with full consideration of the recommendations of the acoustical study, and to specifically include:
  - Floor/carpet repair/replacement/refinishing
  - Upgrade sound system including radio broadcasting and tape recording
  - Interior painting and entrance paving
  - Chancel alterations

Immediate

- Four preschool classrooms in accordance with appropriate state regulations (e.g., first-floor location)
- Four classrooms for other age groups (adults, older children)
- Multiple-use social and recreational facility with adjacent kitchen (500–600 seats)
- Increased administrative office space
- Covered entrance for passenger delivery by automobile or bus
- Designated Girl Scout meeting/equipment storage area
- Medium-size meeting room with adjacent kitchen (125–200 seats) for formal functions (possibly existing)

Future

- Sanctuary improvements to increase openness for greeting and gathering, especially in inclement weather; improve traffic flow within and between buildings (sanctuary, nursery, classrooms); improve chancel area; and consider enlargement
- Covered walkways connecting buildings
- Improved restroom facilities for sanctuary and education building (enlarged capacity, better location/distribution for convenience, improved plumbing and appearance, and additional number)
- All-weather facility (e.g., a lodge) at Camp Sexton

General Needs

- Long-term (10–25 years) facility development and land use plan should be developed by professional planner/architect
- Adoption of policy to rigidly adhere to this plan when considering and authorizing renovation or construction of all facilities, including those provided as memorials and honorariums
- Develop plan for funding construction or renovation of facilities which relies more on establishment of a building fund before construction and less on loans

Final Report

The final report of the Long Range Planning Committee is due before the Administrative Board. The board would like recommendations for long-range planning as well as suggestions for immediate changes needed.

Using specifics laid out by the Long Range Planning Committee and suggestions made by other church committees, the board has named the following goals for the coming year.

GOALS FOR 1998

1. Increase congregational participation in ministries of outreach.
   - Lighthouse Ministry (helping the local poor)
   - Mission team—local or foreign
   - Community service—facilities, other
   - Camp Sexton
   - Brazil missionary
   - Connectional or Conference Missions
2. Increase the number of and enrich the quality of disciples.
   - Spiritual development
   - Reach out through media
   - Stewardship of resources

- Activate inactive members
- Reach out to unchurched people in all programs
- Special evangelical event

3. Upgrade and expand facilities.
- Continue development of Long Range Land Use Plan
- Develop schematics and capital fund plan for first phase of renovation and construction

Elkins Lake Baptist Church—1997

Paul Reed
Christie Haney
Sharese Whitecotton
Ronald Earl

Pastor Ken Hugghins stared at the shelves of books which literally had taken over three walls of his office. He thought back to 1990 when he became pastor of Elkins Lake Baptist Church (ELBC) (409-295-7694). The church had grown steadily, from 487 members in 1990 to 776 members in 1996. Now, several concerns were paramount as he led the church to plan for the future. Could the membership continue to fund the needed facilities for the ministry and could growth continue? Was the church doing all it could to reach a greater number of young families with both churched and unchurched backgrounds? Would senior members be willing to support and help with new programs? How would membership react to the new facility and would it allow them to remain close? Would expanding the facilities allow ELBC the resources to increase membership activities?

The questions seemed to multiply as quickly as the books on the pastor's shelves. No doubt, many of the printed resources Pastor Hugghins had collected contained helpful information, but the answers to the kinds of questions filling his mind were to be found in places far beyond his bookshelves.

EXTERNAL ENVIRONMENT

History

On Easter Sunday, 1970, an informal worship service was held in the Elkins Lake Subdivision Clubhouse. Reverend W. Y. Pond, Jr., of First Baptist Church, Huntsville, Texas, had been asked by the subdivision management to offer an early worship service for its personnel who worked on Sunday. In the following months, interest and attendance grew, and the idea of organizing a new Baptist church developed.

On April 4, 1971, Dr. Jerry Dawson, interim pastor, led the regular attendees to charter Elkins Lake Baptist Church. The charter membership numbered 52 persons. Six men were elected to serve as deacons.

This case was prepared by Professors Paul Reed, Christie Haney, Sharese Whitecotton, and Ronald Earl of Sam Houston State University as a basis for class discussion. It is not intended to illustrate either effective or ineffective handling of an administrative situation. Copyright © 1999 by Prentice Hall, Inc. ISBN 0-13-011154-6.

By January 1972, ELBC was financially strong enough to hire Wilbur J. McDaniel as a full-time pastor. Pastor McDaniel led the congregation in planning, locating, and constructing its own building on 10 acres that fronted the east access road which paralleled Interstate 45. This site was chosen because of anticipated future residential development in the surrounding areas, including the Elkins Lake subdivision. A group of retired builders, sponsored by the denomination, provided volunteer labor for the construction of a sanctuary, offices, and classrooms, which encompassed 5,400 square feet. Membership provided the funds necessary for building materials.

In 1978, the physical plant was doubled to 10,800 square feet. Additional classrooms, an expanded fellowship hall, and kitchen were added to the site with membership funding. Eight years later, the members of ELBC voted to spend $225,000 for property on Highway 19, approximately a mile north of the church site, in hopes of eventually relocating the church closer to central Huntsville. The money was obtained from the church's building fund and a loan secured from a local bank. However, the combination of a large and sophisticated building plan, a $1.8 million design requiring 46,000 square feet, and the recession of the late 1980s temporarily stalled the church's relocation plans.

The year 1990 brought a transition in pastoral leadership. Once again, the church focused its efforts on relocation and paid off the loan on the proposed property. The church had the timber on the property cut and sold, and put the proceeds into the building fund.

By 1991, new growth again created the need for additional space. The sanctuary was expanded by removing a wall in the foyer and gained seating for 60 more people. Two portable buildings for Sunday school classes and other activities were placed on the property. Parking was expanded at that time, as well.

By the spring of 1994, the congregation had grown too large to attend a single Sunday morning worship service together. This situation was solved temporarily by assigning a different group of members each Sunday to view the service via television. This proved less than satisfactory, and the congregation decided to have two Sunday services, the first at 8:30 A.M. and the second at 10:50 A.M. This alleviated the overcrowding and allowed the members and visitors to attend the early service and use the majority of the day for other activities. Although both services were held continually throughout the year, the 8:30 A.M. worship service was only lightly attended. Pastor Hugghins grew concerned that if ELBC continued to grow, the second worship service again would be overcrowded. At the time, he stated, "I am concerned about the separation of the congregation and wonder how long they will be satisfied with two worship services." He also was troubled because another church in the area that had two Sunday services for a long period of time consequently had divided, with one group forming its own church.

In the fall of 1994, after hearing some cost estimates for its proposed building plans, the church determined it was too expensive. The building committee then created a multiphase rebuilding design and presented it to the congregation for approval. After some discussion, the revised plan, consisting of 17,798 square feet, was approved as Phase I of the entire rebuilding plan. In December 1995, ground was broken and Phase I of the multiphase plan was started. In March 1996, construction began. The building was funded by a bank loan for $620,000 which was backed by pledges from the church members. (The 15-year loan has a balloon payment in 1999.)

The church also approached the membership about a separate bond program to secure $160,000 from the membership; the members will be paid back from the sale of the old church and property. At present, the old church and property have been on the market for nine months.

March 1997 brought Phase I to a close and opened the doors of a new building for services. Phase I delivered 6,527 square feet of sanctuary space; 1,890 square feet for offices and the library; 7,067 square feet of classrooms; and 2,314 square feet for the kitchen, bathrooms, and miscellaneous space. The old site's temporary buildings were moved to the new site for classroom space until the other phases are complete; in the meantime, some classes are held in the sanctuary. With the additional space, the two separate Sunday morning services were no longer needed. An alternative worship service schedule combined both services, and started at 10:20 A.M. and ended at 11:30 A.M. Dr. Hugghins jokingly remarked, "This new schedule allows us to beat the Methodists to lunch."

Local Area

Huntsville is located on Interstate 45 approximately 70 miles north of Houston and 170 miles south of the Dallas–Fort Worth area. An east Texas county seat, Huntsville has Sam Houston State University (SHSU), the headquarters of the Texas Department of Criminal Justice (TDCJ), and four prison units within its city limits. Counting local citizens, inmates of the four prison units, and all university students residing in Huntsville, the city's population in 1996 was 34,592. TDCJ employs approximately 3,000 people to staff its administrative headquarters and the four prisons. The university has approximately 12,500 students and 2,200 faculty and staff members. The Huntsville population is supported by these institutions or by small service and light industry firms in the community. Less than 30 percent of the residents are members of a local church.

The economic conditions of Huntsville are stable and appear to be growing slightly. The 1996 unemployment rate was 3.3 percent with little fluctuation. The total number of Huntsville residents employed in 1996 was 21,309. A 1995 tax survey stated nearby Houston's gross tax rate as 0.665, but Huntsville's gross tax rate was 0.384.

Overall, the Huntsville area, in relation to its size, has a fairly large amount of criminal activity, which is directly related to the high use of alcohol and recreational drugs. In 1996, of the 1,251 misdemeanor offenses committed, 59.1 percent were alcohol- or drug-related. Recreational and social activities are limited in number due to the locality and size of the community.

On the immediate west side of the city are three residential communities, the largest being the Elkins Lake Subdivision. "Elkins," as it is called, originally was developed to serve as a retirement community for those who wished to live in a rural setting but have all the amenities of a big city (Houston) nearby. Elkins contains about 850 homes and is centered around three lakes and a challenging 18-hole golf course. During the past 5 years, the average age of the Elkins resident decreased as more working families with children purchased property. Now, only half the Elkins residents are retired. The remaining adult residents are employed full-time and range from 30 to 50 years of age.

At its new location, ELBC is not visible from either Interstate 45 or Highway 19. The two-lane Highway 19 is not completely developed and is not used to full capacity at this time.

Competition

There are a total of 76 churches of assorted denominations located in Walker County. ELBC, which is affiliated with the Southern Baptist Convention, faces competition from five other Southern Baptist Churches in Huntsville. Three of these churches are located in central Huntsville, and ELBC and the other two are on the perimeter of town. (See Exhibit 1.) Assorted data on membership trends, receipts, expenditures, debts, salaries, and property values of the Huntsville Southern Baptist churches are shown in Exhibits 2 through 11.

EXHIBIT 1: Southern Baptist Church Locations, Huntsville, Texas, Area

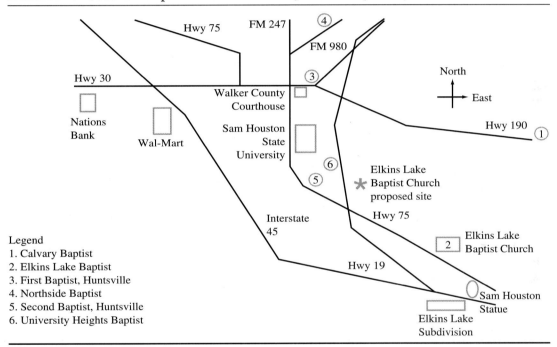

Legend
1. Calvary Baptist
2. Elkins Lake Baptist
3. First Baptist, Huntsville
4. Northside Baptist
5. Second Baptist, Huntsville
6. University Heights Baptist

EXHIBIT 2: Walker County Southern Baptist Churches, Membership

| | Church Membership | | | | |
Church	1996	1995	1994	1993	1992
Calvary Baptist	779	665	674	646	606
Elkins Lake Baptist	776	719	708	651	575
First Baptist	2,481	2,496	2,468	2,415	2,361
Northside Baptist	949	825	635	532	440
Second Baptist	NA	983	986	1,006	1,088
University Heights Baptist	1,602	1,554	1,515	1,677	1,590

Source: Tyron Evergreen Baptist Association.

EXHIBIT 3:   Walker County Southern Baptist Churches, Membership

	Members Lost Within Past Year				
Church	1996	1995	1994	1993	1992
Calvary Baptist	16	27	30	33	20
Elkins Lake Baptist	11	33	16	34	32
First Baptist	73	61	53	60	63
Northside Baptist	10	11	14	11	19
Second Baptist	NA	15	34	52	84
University Heights Baptist	41	42	57	33	48

Source: Tyron Evergreen Baptist Association.

EXHIBIT 4:   Walker County Southern Baptist Churches, Attendance

	AM Worship Service Attendance				
Church	1996	1995	1994	1993	1992
Calvary Baptist	170	132	170	300	385
Elkins Lake Baptist	207	210	278	192	200
First Baptist	384	417	464	474	447
Northside Baptist	375	325	275	225	225
Second Baptist	NA	84	80	95	297
University Heights Baptist	600	500	500	500	650

Source: Tyron Evergreen Baptist Association.

EXHIBIT 5:   Walker County Southern Baptist Churches, Sunday School

	Sunday School Enrollment				
Church	1996	1995	1994	1993	1992
Calvary Baptist	213	223	297	351	279
Elkins Lake Baptist	393	421	424	398	404
First Baptist	1,034	1,094	1,139	1,066	1,022
Northside Baptist	290	292	260	176	182
Second Baptist	NA	109	131	128	394
University Heights Baptist	942	940	942	1,064	1,056

Source: Tyron Evergreen Baptist Association.

EXHIBIT 6:   Walker County Southern Baptist Churches, Sunday School

	Total Young Adult Sunday School Enrollment				
Church	1996	1995	1994	1993	1992
Calvary Baptist	34	57	47	42	26
Elkins Lake Baptist	90	77	117	51	36
First Baptist	300	292	237	156	141
Northside Baptist	49	57	56	12	32
Second Baptist	NA	8	0	12	66
University Heights Baptist	275	143	155	119	118

Source: Tyron Evergreen Baptist Association.

EXHIBIT 7: Walker County Southern Baptist Churches, Receipts

Church	Church Receipts				
	1996	1995	1994	1993	1992
Calvary Baptist	$210,151	$233,732	$248,724	$202,314	$168,916
Elkins Lake Baptist	544,993	363,556	323,451	248,589	269,564
First Baptist	812,551	788,394	776,039	672,594	763,755
Northside Baptist	301,737	249,936	221,000	181,280	149,838
Second Baptist	NA	110,195	159,632	115,963	234,671
University Heights Baptist	915,62	660,947	453,675	407,454	425,346

Source: Tyron Evergreen Baptist Association.

EXHIBIT 8: Walker County Southern Baptist Churches, Expenditures

Church	Total Local Expenditures				
	1996	1995	1994	1993	1992
Calvary Baptist	$165,338	$172,956	$215,380	$203,407	$618,278
Elkins Lake Baptist	236,873	195,243	172,442	163,805	240,305
First Baptist	619,762	688,989	675,128	415,638	600,027
Northside Baptist	289,840	204,623	149,753	135,900	51,304
Second Baptist	NA	104,857	88,293	76,708	234,667
University Heights Baptist	402,456	546,376	299,088	306,001	336,343

Source: Tyron Evergreen Baptist Association.

EXHIBIT 9: Walker County Southern Baptist Churches, Debt

Church	Total Church Debt				
	1996	1995	1994	1993	1992
Calvary Baptist	$312,573	328,951	$344,500	$359,020	$363,000
Elkins Lake Baptist	222,000	69,543	77,943	87,842	98,724
First Baptist	745,500	830,124	880,092	545,493	573,278
Northside Baptist	88,774	113,010	200,000	3,000	14,000
Second Baptist	NA	0	0	0	0
University Heights Baptist	79,000	17,948	14,090	28,846	30,075

Source: Tyron Evergreen Baptist Association.

EXHIBIT 10: Walker County Southern Baptist Churches, Salaries

Church	Church Staff Salaries				
	1996	1995	1994	1993	1992
Calvary Baptist	NA	$ 91,420	$ 86,529	$ 96,376	$105,715
Elkins Lake Baptist	NA	133,523	126,215	124,446	116,128
First Baptist	NA	218,560	222,756	235,610	230,216
Northside Baptist	NA	41,482	28,529	23,800	32,416
Second Baptist	NA	79,447	67,980	57,792	110,697
University Heights Baptist	NA	234,029	129,611	210,711	173,340

Source: Tyron Evergreen Baptist Association.

EXHIBIT 11: Walker County Southern Baptist Churches, Property

Church	Value of Church Property				
	1996	1995	1994	1993	1992
Calvary Baptist	$ 650,000	$ 650,000	$ 650,000	$ 650,000	$ 650,000
Elkins Lake Baptist	1,600,000	800,000	800,000	800,000	800,000
First Baptist	4,472,909	4,600,000	4,600,000	4,472,909	472,909
Northside Baptist	1,500,000	1,500,000	1,500,000	265,000	265,000
Second Baptist	NA	1,275,000	1,275,000	1,275,000	1,275,000
University Heights Baptist	2,800,000	1,700,000	1,700,000	1,700,000	2,025,000

Source: Tyron Evergreen Baptist Association.

INTERNAL ENVIRONMENT

Elkins Lake Baptist Church was incorporated under the state laws of Texas and operates under a constitution and bylaws. It closely follows the Southern Baptist doctrine.

Personnel and Organized Committees

Since 1990, the church has employed Dr. Hugghins as full-time pastor. The two other full-time employees are an education director and a secretary. The eight paid part-time employees are a music director, a secretary, a pianist, an organist, a custodian, and three nursery aides.

ELBC relies heavily on volunteers from the congregation to organize and conduct the daily operations of business. Workers may be true volunteers or recruits for specific tasks. The volunteers were very important to the entire process of building the new facilities. Members with specific expertise were put on the corresponding committees so the entire building process could benefit from their knowledge. A strong worker base is provided by not only employed members but also retired members who lend active leadership and participation.

There is currently no formal personnel policy manual for staff, and Dr. Hugghins does not feel a need for one at this time. The church has written job descriptions and standards but does not conduct formal performance appraisals; Pastor Hugghins remarks, "It's not a priority right now." All raises are discussed and decided by the personnel committee. There are formal guidelines for committees, but no similar guidelines for volunteer positions such as the Sunday School teacher. Training is provided when deemed necessary for all workers. ELBC does not wish to become too policy-oriented.

Some of the regular volunteers include three individuals responsible for the nursery on Sunday, one person for the library, and two in charge of the sound system. In addition, there are four members in charge of Wednesday night meals and 10 members who take care of maintenance of the buildings and grounds. Member volunteers staff 19 committees with various functions that are essential to the church's day-to-day operations. A chair is appointed to each committee, whose recommendations require a vote during congregational business meetings.

The church's financial affairs are directed by the treasurer and the finance/budget committee. The budget for each year is established through a process in which the various committees and the pastor present their respective needs and expenditures for the coming year. Also, revenue projections are adjusted for attendance trends. After the budget is finalized, it is presented to the membership for vote during a Sunday morning worship service. Quarterly, the church has a business meeting led by the pastor, in which present and future financial matters are discussed and voted upon. (Financial statements for 1992 through 1996 are shown in Exhibit 12.)

Although ELBC has numerous committees, it does not have a long-range planning committee. The pastor would like to form a building committee to look at and discuss the other phases of the facilities, but nothing has come of this idea yet. Presently, the church has no written goals that extend beyond one year. The church leadership does not consider this to be a problem because they believe that a clear consensus exists as to the direction that the church is and should be taking.

The pastor looks to a panel of deacons for general policy guidance, but in fact he receives great latitude in exercising control over church affairs. There are 18 deacons who serve for a three-year period. The deacons are on a rotating schedule and volunteer their time as well. The pastor and the deacons use a participative management style. Normally, the pastor confers with the deacons before recommending a change to the membership, who finalize the decision by a vote. For example, if Pastor Hugghins feels the church is in need of a new van, he discusses the proposal with the transportation committee and deacons and, with their approval, brings it before the congregation for final consent.

EXHIBIT 12:   ELBC Financial Statement as of December 31

	1996	1995	1994	1993	1992
Summary of Accounts					
Bank balance					
Checking	$ 30,538.53	$ 5,000.00	$ 10,766.98	$ 5,511.85	$ 5,511.85
Building Fund	56,369.11	94,121.75	28,922.64	36,534.00	23,535.00
Certificate of deposit	30,000.00	79,709.69	32,500.00	.00	.00
Total receipts year					
to date	346,074.95	357,174.69	317,229.84	255,922.20	234,784.19
Projected budget needs	320,382.00	278,388.91	227,148.00	270,286.00	262,447.00
Percentage of collections					
over expenses	108.02%	117.61%	114.46%	94.69%	89.46%
Expenditures					
100 Missions	61,200.89	54,447.24	55,384.95	42,621.61	38,438.19
200 Personnel	159,583.76	136,255.08	145,417.99	135,252.01	131,918.34
300 Music Ministry	3,564.91	3,205.11	3,902.41	2,608.54	3,275.90
400 Education Ministry	10,826.83	8,594.52	11,255.26	8,821.71	8,916.51
500 College and Youth	2,841.46	1,054.77	3,783.22	2,743.78	1,747.35
600 Church					
administration	20,874.27	15,666.26	15,318.49	14,061.80	14,000.49
700 Building and					
equipment	30,313.02	28,110.57	23,856.98	24,599.36	21,446.34
800 Debt retirement	18,715.32	17,186.55	18,863.10	18,732.00	18,688.00
900 Miscellaneous	458.02	227.80	431.83	412.80	204.27
Total Expenditures	308,378.48	264,747.90	278,214.23	249,853.61	238,635.39

Source: Elkins Lake Baptist Church.

The Pastor's Outlook

Pastor Hugghins believes the church body needs to be well informed and involved in order to create a sense of ownership even as the church grows larger. He states, "I believe in delegating considerable authority to the other staff members because of my busy schedule. This ensures that the church will continue to operate smoothly in my absence." Dr. Hugghins recognizes that his main duties are to be both a teacher and a motivator from the pulpit, and an encourager and supporter for the members whenever needed. This includes counseling in times of illness, crisis, and life-style transitions. Needless to say, his cellular phone is always ringing.

Pastor Hugghins considers the current target market of the church to be primarily middle- to upper-class families, consisting mostly of white individuals age 50 and above. He would like to broaden the membership base by continuing to place emphasis on targeting younger families, as is evident by the types of programs presently being implemented. Although ELBC has experienced a steady increase in membership, there has been a decrease in attendance.

One problem that Dr. Hugghins has experienced when dealing with change is that some people are resistant to new members and their new ideas. To this, Pastor Hugghins remarks, "This ain't your granddaddy's Oldsmobile."

Part of ELBC's growth may be attributed to Huntsville's growing population. The new building seems so enormous compared to the old that some members have expressed fear of losing touch with one another. One senior member stated, "There are a lot of new families now and I think the new facilities have helped. I don't know the new members yet; I just know they are new because I've never seen them before." Both members and visitors have commented that the new church's decor lacks the "traditional Southern Baptist touch." The new facilities do not have the stained glass or pews which are usually standard for Southern Baptist churches. Instead, there are portable interlocking chairs that are removed for the Wednesday night worship service.

Dr. Hugghins feels ELBC serves a variety of people with a variety of needs. Some of ELBC's programs include connection with the Baptist Student Union on the campus of SHSU, a fellowship supper held each Wednesday night before the worship service, a marriage enrichment series, and a parenting series.

Outreach Programs

ELBC has developed several outreach programs to attract new membership, especially young families and children. Pastor Hugghins considers the active and visible ministries with leadership from the congregation to be a real asset of the church. A Sunday morning Bible study is conducted at the Elkins Lake Country Club for those individuals wishing a more interactive worship session. Approximately 25 individuals regularly attend what Dr. Hugghins refers to as an "informal Bible study." The attendees are of various denominations, not just Southern Baptist.

On Sunday evenings, there are small discussion and Bible studies groups on various topics relating to religion and everyday challenges. Girls in Action, Royal Ambassadors, and Mission Friends are programs designed for the youth of the church to cultivate mission awareness. In addition, the church has several choirs to serve various interests of the congregation.

ELBC is represented at SHSU's freshman orientation each fall to make the incoming students aware of its presence. ELBC is also affiliated with the Walker County Jail and the Gulf Coast Trade Center, which is a facility for the rehabilitation for juvenile delinquents. In addition, the church is affiliated with various missions such as the Mexican Mission to reach the Hispanic population in the area. All of these outreach programs are staffed by church volunteers. Two couples from ELBC lead a nursing home ministry.

Although there are presently many opportunities for ministry, the pastor feels that there remains a need for more ministries aimed toward young adults. "One program I would like to see implemented is a small group study for adults from age 20 to age 50," he says. Other Baptist churches which have developed this program feel it creates more intimate relationships, improves communication between adults, and helps participants learn about Christianity; they also become more active in the church and its programs. Pastor Hugghins believes this type of program also would attract more young adults to leadership positions within the church and continuously bring in new, innovative ideas. A second program the pastor wishes to start is support groups for widows, victims of domestic violence, children of alcoholics, and others. He hopes such support groups will bring the congregation closer together and create a more family-like atmosphere within the church.

The church also sponsors two scholarships for a summer mission intern program. The pastor sees these missions as friendly and open to people of all faith backgrounds and believes they convey a real spirit of cooperation and acceptance to new visitors.

Marketing

Pastor Hugghins is quite proud of ELBC's marketing efforts, which consist of a radio broadcast of the Sunday morning worship service, newspaper advertisements, two 30-second radio broadcast advertisements during each Huntsville High School home football game, and seasonal radio greetings during the Christmas season. The newspaper advertisements range in price from $85 to $125 per advertisement. The announcements at the home games cost approximately $800 per year. The radio services for the church cost $4,500 per year. ELBC is also promoted by the Baptist Student Union on the campus of SHSU by flyers publicizing special events and announcements concerning activities at the church.

On one side of its two entrances, ELBC has a textured concrete sign that is four feet high and five feet wide and contains only the church name. Worship times are not stated on the sign. Yet, the sign is hard to read because it is all one color.

Preparing for Future Growth

Southern Baptists long have held to the strategy of growing through Sunday School. Therefore, great emphasis usually is placed in properly designing and utilizing educational space. Two rules of thumb normally are used in planning educational space. The first is to provide approximately 45 square feet of floor space per person. The second is that a church should not maintain an average of Sunday School attendance in excess of 80 percent of its own design capacity. The "80% Rule" also holds true for worship services. (See Exhibit 13.) Some authorities believe that if a growing church fills its auditorium on average to more than 80 percent of its capacity, the overcrowdedness (over a 2-to-3-year period) will tend to limit the growth.

EXHIBIT 13: Attendance Averaged by Month for ELBC

Month and Year	Average Persons Attending	Number of Persons Above 80%
January 1996	244	+52
February 1996	240	+48
March 1996	224	+32
April 1996	263	+71
May 1996	232	+40
June 1996	210	+18
July 1996	210	+18
August 1996	238	+46
September 1996	262	+70
October 1996	240	+48
November 1996	214	+22
December 1996	216	+24
January 1997	204	+12
February 1997	235	+43
March 1997	308	−108
April 1997	274	−142
May 1997	251	−165
June 1997	255	−161

Source: Elkins Lake Baptist Church, *The Window.*

There also are two standards practiced in site planning. These include having two acres per 400 attendees and one parking space per three members. ELBC's 22.5-acre site is limited in parking due to the unexpected growth of the church. Currently, ELBC's parking area can accommodate 170 cars.

A large portion of the property remains wooded, and a sizeable pond is located next to the present facility. Dr. Hugghins would like to take advantage of the acreage by offering various activities on the property. He feels it is important to have a children's playground built on the premises. Also, he states, "I would like to see day camps or maybe even sports camps held on the property as well."

Dr. Hugghins would like to implement Sunday "movie nights,"which occasionally could replace the traditional evening services, and believes the church should take advantage of SHSU's cable television channel. He would like to create a Web page and use audiovisual aides during worship; "blended worship" has proven successful for other churches of various denominations in reaching all generations.

Dr. Hugghins began to think about questions that he should present to the various committees in regard to the future of the church. What considerations should be taken into account by ELBC when contemplating its future? Would the continued reaching out to younger citizens split the church membership into groups of young and old? Are the steps taken by ELBC to accommodate growth in membership adequate? Would the continued focus on rapid growth leave the long-time members feeling distanced from the original "feeling" of the church? How soon would ELBC reach capacity for church services, Sunday School, and parking if it does not continue with the multiphase plan? Would a "blended worship" service work for ELBC?

REFERENCES

Elkins Lake Baptist Church, *Constitution and Bylaws.*

Elkins Lake Baptist Church, *The Window* (1996, 1997).

Huntsville–Walker County Chamber of Commerce, *Community/Economic Profile for 1996* (1997) [Online] http://chamber.huntsville.tx.us/economy.html

Judicial District Community Supervision and Corrections Department, *Fiscal Year 1996 Annual Report.*

Minutes of the Tyron Evergreen Baptist Association of Texas, 91st Annual Session, Conroe, Texas (1992).

Minutes of the Tyron Evergreen Baptist Association of Texas, 92nd Annual Session, Conroe, Texas (1993).

Minutes of the Tyron Evergreen Baptist Association of Texas, 93rd Annual Session, Conroe, Texas (1994).

Minutes of the Tyron Evergreen Baptist Association of Texas, 94th Annual Session, Conroe, Texas (1995).

Minutes of the Tyron Evergreen Baptist Association of Texas, 95th Annual Session, Conroe, Texas (1996).

Grace Lutheran Church—1997

Carol J. Cumber
Paul R. Reed

Pastor John Anders walked slowly from his desk to the lone office window, making last-minute mental notes for the upcoming meeting he was to chair. The room was neat and welcoming, a reflection of the man himself. Gazing out the window, his eyes swept past the trees and well-tended lawn of Grace Lutheran Church, and paused at the education wing and enlarged fellowship hall that were part of the church's latest expansion. He was new to Grace Lutheran, having accepted the call less than 1 year ago. He was the senior pastor and had the longer tenure; Associate Pastor Linda Nelson arrived only the previous month. Yet here he was, leading his congregation in the time-consuming, often difficult process of long-term strategic planning. A committee of 50 had been formed to undertake this endeavor. They seemed up to the task, willing to put in the long hours to help guide Grace Lutheran's future. They were using Kennon L. Callahan's book, *Twelve Keys to an Effective Church*, as a guide. The book included a workbook to help organize the committee's work into 12 fields of examination. It was hoped this work would result in not only a realistic assessment of Grace Lutheran's present standing and stature, but also a "game plan" for the future. To keep the committee on task, members were asked to limit their planning discussion to the areas listed in the workbook.

Returning to his desk, Pastor Anders sat back and thought about the selection of Callahan's book. Although there were many strategic-management texts on the market, relatively few dealt specifically with church planning. He was pleased with the text and workbook chosen, but had some nagging doubts about the book's "fit" with his church. After all, even though the author offered the 12 keys as appropriate planning tools for many religious organizations, the book obviously was written with the Methodist denomination in mind. Although Methodists and Lutherans both were Protestant religions and quite similar in philosophy and theology, they were different in worship styles. In terms of comparison, Lutherans structured their services in a more formal, liturgical fashion whereas the preaching in a Methodist church was less biblical and theological. Both emphasized the concept of grace, but Lutherans relied more on formal prayer. Would Callahan's book be general enough to benefit this Lutheran congregation?

The time had come to go to the church hall and start the planning session. As he entered the room, he was pleased to hear the buzz of excited conversation. Even though it was 6:30 on a Friday evening, the room was filled with planning committee members who smiled and greeted him as he entered. Responding with a smile of his own, he thought, "This is a good start."

This case was prepared by Professors Carol J. Cumber of South Dakota State University and Paul R. Reed of Sam Houston State University as a basis for class discussion. It is not intended to illustrate either effective or ineffective handling of an administrative situation. Copyright © 1999 by Prentice Hall, Inc. ISBN 0-13-011157-0.

EXTERNAL ENVIRONMENT

Grace Lutheran Church is located in Waterford, a county seat in eastern South Dakota with a population of approximately 17,000. It is a stable community that has grown about 10 percent per decade. The residents take to heart their motto, "Waterford Is Someplace Special." The community is clean and attractive, with tree-lined streets and numerous well-tended parks, including the popular South Dakota Gardens and Arboretum with its 70 acres of perennial, annual, and woody ornamental trees, shrubs, and flowers. The town offers many activities for its youth, including organized sports; cultural activities; and day trips for skiing, hiking, and fishing.

Waterford takes pride in hosting one of the top-rated arts festivals in the nation. One July weekend every summer, the Waterford Summer Arts Festival attracts more than 70,000 people to sample diverse food, entertainment, and offerings from over 200 artists. Cultural opportunities are many for a town this size, thanks in part to a strong arts council, two state museums, and a state university.

Boasting a low unemployment rate (1.5 percent in 1996), Waterford has experienced stable economic growth, attributed primarily to activities in retail and wholesale trade, manufacturing, agriculture, and services (most notably for the state university). As is common in the northern plains states, limitations in both the diversity of employment opportunities and the potential for career growth resulted in the chronic problem of emigration of the state's college-educated young adults.

Employed residents enjoy an average commute time of only nine minutes. As there is easy access to an interstate and two much larger commercial areas less than one hour away, expanding the retail trade in Waterford is a continuing challenge. Yet, the downtown stays healthy; store occupants are primarily antique shops, restaurants, service organizations, and niche retail shops. However, after new Kmart and Wal-Mart discount stores were built next to the interstate, the two malls on the edge of town experienced an exodus of retail shops and are severely underutilized.

Median household income is $34,351, which is higher than the national median of $32,264, and considerably higher than the state average of $29,733. Single-family residences predominate, although the number of apartments, duplexes, and condominiums is increasing. Waterford has one of the lowest crime rates in the nation, and consistently places among the safest cities in the state.

Within the community are 32 religious organizations (29 Protestant, two Catholic, and one Islamic). Of this total, five are Lutheran, with Grace Lutheran and Atonement Lutheran the only churches in town affiliated with the Evangelical Lutheran Church of America (ELCA).

HISTORY, BACKGROUND, AND STAFFING

Grace Lutheran Church is a relatively young church, formed in 1963 by 40 families with Pastor Joseph Johnsby as founding pastor. It was an amiable parting from Atonement Lutheran Church, which had grown to the point that a new ELCA-affiliated church was not only feasible but also desirable. In its 34-year history, Grace Lutheran has been served by six pastors. Its synodical roots were the American Lutheran Church, which in 1988 merged with the American Evangelical Lutheran Church and the Lutheran Church of America to become the Evangelical Lutheran Church of

America. This consortium of Lutheran churches includes 5.2 million members in 11,023 congregations and 65 synods throughout the country. Grace Lutheran Church is a member of a bishop-led state synod that consists of eight conferences. The presiding bishop is headquartered in Chicago. Although the individual churches operate within an overall ELCA constitution, there is a great deal of independence for mission statement development and implementation among the churches. Discussion of church issues typically starts at the conference level and includes a democratic voting process within the membership. Financial support of the Evangelical Lutheran Church of America by affiliated churches is expected. Individual churches determine their contribution amount; there is no set fee. Grace Lutheran includes its support of ELCA in its formal budget.

Grace Lutheran flourished, and now includes 1,365 baptized members. Over the past 10 years, membership grew (see Exhibit 1), and the church added space in 1979 and 1991 to accommodate the growth. Atonement Lutheran Church, the other ELCA-affiliated Lutheran church in Waterford, remains the larger of the two, with a baptized membership of 2,495. Although there has been a national trend of membership decline in traditional Protestant churches, with resulting population pyramids skewed heavily toward the elderly, Grace Lutheran is encouraged that its own membership population pyramid reveals 10–14 year olds as the largest population percentile group (see Exhibit 2).

Grace Lutheran offers two worship services each Sunday morning, enhanced by an organ; one of four choirs (Chancel, Gospel, Hi-School, and Youth); and a brass quintet. A religious education program begins at age three, and approximately 275 children are enrolled in Sunday School. Other than the confirmation program, educational and social group options for teens are limited and not well attended. Adult opportunities include an adult forum, Bible study groups, church circles, and Lutheran Men in Mission.

Grace Lutheran employs two full-time pastors. Although new to the congregation, both were well received by the members. The pastors appear eager to develop the long-term planning which both believe is necessary to move Grace Lutheran securely into the next century.

EXHIBIT 1:   Grace Lutheran Church Membership: 1984–1996

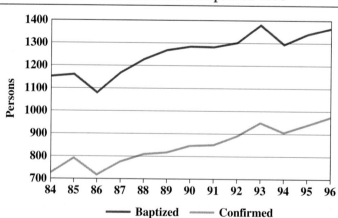

Source: Grace Lutheran Church Records.

EXHIBIT 2:   Grace Lutheran Church Membership Distribution

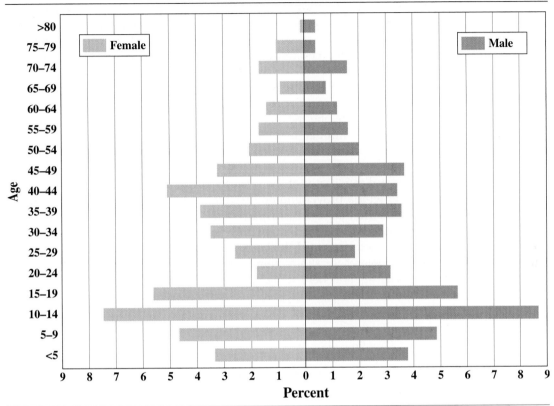

Source: Grace Lutheran Church Records.

Senior Pastor Anders has responsibilities in the staffing and administration areas, and Associate Pastor Nelson is responsible for youth and social activities. Jointly, they are involved with pastoral care, worship, music, education, membership participation, and the standing boards.

Pastors Anders and Nelson are both native South Dakotans, and came to Grace Lutheran after previously serving at only one church. Baptized members at their former churches were 402 and 250, respectively.

Additional paid staff include a secretary, custodian, organist, choir director, and financial secretary. As is common in religious organizations, a great deal of education and committee work is completed by volunteers.

STRATEGIC PLANNING

Although there was a small committee to plan building and structural projects, church members had never completed an overall strategic plan that included programmatic planning. The advent of new pastoral leadership convinced them the time was right. Whereas the strategic planning process was new to Pastor Anders, several committee members, because of their professional positions in the community, were experienced in it. The members weren't embracing strategic planning in response to any major problems. Indeed, a factor in Pastor Anders's accepting the call to Grace Lutheran Church was the apparent willingness of its members to be proactive and to look to the future, build on their strengths, and accept change. He didn't believe he'd have to deal with traditional parishioners' frequent complaint, "But that's not how we did it in the past."

As Pastor Anders looked around the room full of strategic planning committee members, he was filled with appreciation for their willingness to work hard. Through a process which culminated in the inclusion of both volunteers and specially solicited members, the resulting committee had elected chairpeople for the group. The group had already met in subcommittees, and now gathered to report its findings in 12 key areas of their church.

As coordinator and moderator of the strategic planning committee, Pastor Anders opened the meeting with a prayer and an ice-breaker. He wanted to begin the discussion on a positive note. To that end, he displayed an overhead transparency detailing an outline for the evening's discussion. Following the Callahan book's instruction to focus on strengths, the overhead repeated the book's explicit discouragement of any discussion of weakness, problems, or shortcomings. Additionally, there was to be no discussion of threats. "The agenda here tonight," Pastor Anders said, "is to identify our strengths to exploit and to develop objectives." With that in mind, the business of the evening began.

Key Characteristics for Planning

One of the purposes of the workbook for *Twelve Keys to an Effective Church* was to help members organize their church by key characteristics for planning purposes. Subcommittees responsible for exploring each key characteristic made a brief presentation to the full committee. Their reports were as follows:

1. Specific, Concrete Missional Objectives

Due to terminology confusion, this subcommittee's members had difficulties following the workbook. What did "missional" mean? Did it mean a mission statement, or did it mean missional, as in missionary outreach? If they strictly followed the workbook's criteria, they had to give their church a very poor evaluation. Anecdotally, they believed outreach to be one of their church's strengths. The actions, however, tended to be by individuals; they were not formal actions "officially" listed as missional. The subcommittee's members concluded that "missional objectives" was one area in which Lutherans differed from the Methodist author of *Twelve Keys to an Effective Church*.

Grace Lutheran has a written mission statement. As is common in organizations, although Grace Lutheran has a formal, published mission statement, its contents were unknown to many of its members. This mission statement is as follows:

> We, as members of Grace Lutheran Church, are God's children, saved by grace through Jesus Christ, blessed with different abilities, and all part of one body. God has called us through the Holy Spirit and empowered us to live in Christian love and to proclaim the Gospel message. We accept and confess the Creeds, together with Luther's Small Catechism and Augsburg Confession.

Our mission includes the following:

- to thank, praise, serve, and obey God;
- to pray and to include the Lord in all aspects of our lives;
- to participate in congregational worship and fellowship;
- to teach God's Word;
- to administer and partake of the Sacraments;
- to be God's witnesses to one another, to the Waterford community, and beyond;
- to forgive as He has forgiven us;
- to give our time, talents, and earnings in response to His love;
- to reach out to those in need;
- and above all, to love one another and celebrate with joy and hope our oneness in Christ.

2. Pastoral and Lay Visitation

Pastors Anders and Nelson listened attentively to the discussion regarding expectations of visitation. Participants were enthusiastic regarding the pastors' efforts. They suggested that congregational needs should be formally prioritized, with crisis calls taking top priority, and that an ongoing visitation program should be developed as the pastors' tenure increases. It was recognized that it would be unrealistic to expect both pastors to have developed a visitation program already. Participation by lay church members in terms of "taking care of their own" in times of need was thought to be exemplary.

3. Corporate, Dynamic Worship

Participants struggled with the workbook's requirement to evaluate themselves regarding "warmth and winsomeness" of the congregation and church services. Although no one specifically greeted new members and visitors, which was required for a high score in the workbook, they felt strongly that all members played that role. With seating rating in the "comfortably full" range, well-tended structural facilities, a good music program, and strong sermons, they were well satisfied in this area.

4. Significant Relational Groups

The intent of relational groups is on fellowship, not tasks. The groups include WELCA, which are women's groups involving Bible study, friendship, and service at weddings and funerals; Lutheran Men in Mission, a men's group for Bible study; Quilters, a group that jointly makes quilts to send to Lutheran World Relief; Search, an in-depth Bible study group for men and women; and various choir groups. Almost all participants in these groups are at least 30 years old.

5. Strong Leadership Resources

Grace Lutheran is governed by a Congregational Council which normally meets once a month. The council consists of eight elected members with three-year, staggered terms, and the executive committee of president, vice-president, secretary, and treasurer. The

EXHIBIT 3:   Grace Lutheran Overall Leadership Core

	Number of Members
Standing Boards	56
Liaisons to Council	8
Officers	4
Sunday School Teachers	100
Memorial Trust Committee	5
Women's Circles	20
Bible Study	12
Confirmation Teachers	15
Youth Group Directors	6
Worship/Music	25
Altar Guild	4
Women's Guild Officers	4

Source: Grace Lutheran Strategic Planning Meeting, April 1997.

Congregational Council has final authority in most areas. Exceptions include constitutional issues mandating congregational vote, most notably annual budgetary changes in excess of 5 percent.

The leadership core at Grace Lutheran (see Exhibit 3) totals 259 out of an estimated total active membership of 700 (approximately one-third the full membership), and is skewed toward professionals.

There are eight standing boards who report to the Congregational Council:

Board of Christian Education   This board is responsible for developing, promoting, and administering educational opportunities for people of all ages.

Board of Church and Community   Its purpose is to educate the congregation and to increase its awareness of and empathy for those outside the congregation. This education is seen as the foundation for promoting involvement in specific social, economic, and political needs. The board's vision statement includes offering financial, emotional, and spiritual support to those in need, not only in the community but also nationally and internationally.

Board of Church Finance   Members' responsibilities include accounting of income and expenditures, development of proposed budgets (with input from other boards and committees), and financial management of fund drives.

Board of Membership Participation   Its duties include coordinating and encouraging congregational participation. The board's focus is on new members, visitation of members, recreational and special events, and meals for members in need. Additional responsibilities include keeping membership lists current, posting newspaper recognition of members on bulletin board displays, and maintaining a photograph and video history of church activities.

Board of Operations and Maintenance   This board oversees the proper functioning and care of the properties and equipment of the congregation. Responsibilities include dealing with inventory, equipment and property maintenance and purchase, insurance review and purchase, and availability of facilities for events.

Board of Purpose and Planning   Its primary function is assisting the congregation in its efforts to fulfill its mission and purposes, to anticipate future trends and developments, and to encourage a process of developing and responding to initiatives. Its members annually assess the church's mission statement and evaluate the congregation's progress toward its fulfillment. They submit suggestions based upon their evaluations to the Congregational Council, which governs Grace Lutheran.

Board of Worship and Music   Its members recognize that although the clergy are primarily the worship leaders, the act of worship is the responsibility of all gathered together. To this end, they assist the pastors with Sunday services and additional communion services. Their duties include preparation of the worship area, assistance with various liturgies, and scheduling all vocal and instrumental music.

Board of Youth Ministry   Its specific responsibilities include overseeing all youth groups' activities in an attempt to alternate between faith development, stewardship (service), fun, and fellowship. Youth groups include the Minor League (grades 3–5), Friendship League (grades 6–8), and Hi-League (grades 9–12), and typically meet once or twice a month.

6. Streamlined Structure and Solid, Participatory Decision Making

It was agreed that the leaders made good decisions, but there was concern that there were so many boards that their decisions aren't streamlined enough. The committee also questioned whether formal conflict resolution procedures should be developed.

7. Several Competent Programs and Activities

Once again, members had difficulty fitting their church to the book's criteria. It was hard to identify programs that had "communitywide competency and respect." Additionally, Grace Lutheran has no evaluation procedures for its programs. Again, they observed that although Grace Lutheran offered many individual activities, none were described as "official" church functions. Marketing has never been emphasized at Grace Lutheran, leaving members to wonder whether that should change. Advertising has been limited to publishing the worship schedule in the local paper's "church page."

8. Open Accessibility

Accessibility was viewed in terms of location of the church, ingress and egress to the church site, and accessibility to space and facilities. Participants concluded that the church ranked high because of its total accessibility to the handicapped and because of the ease of entering and exiting the church lot and facility, although they found crowding in the entrance areas, especially in the winter when members had to deal with storing heavy jackets and boots. Also under consideration was "people" accessibility—to the pastors and key leaders; participants concluded that there is high accessibility to them.

9. High Visibility

Grace Lutheran is located on a minor thoroughfare street close to the major thoroughfare 22nd Avenue. Sunnydale Community Church, directly to the east, has superior visibility and location. It is common to hear directions to Grace Lutheran in terms of "It's right next to Sunnydale." There are no signs at 22nd Avenue advertising Grace Lutheran. Participants concluded that this was not a problem, for Waterford is still small enough for everyone to know where Grace Lutheran is located. They acknowledged, however, that very little marketing was done to keep their church in people's minds.

10. Adequate Parking, Land, and Landscaping

Even though 60 to 65 percent of members attend the first service, parking was found to be adequate if both lot and street parking were utilized. If growth continues, there is the potential for 50 additional parking spaces at the expense of green space. Participants disagreed with the workbook's requirement of computing "annual giving value" of each parking space by dividing total parking spaces into total church income, and so ignored this section. The aesthetic value of the church property was praised. It is well cared for, with timely maintenance and a large, tastefully landscaped green area (see Exhibit 4).

EXHIBIT 4: Grace Lutheran Church Site Diagram

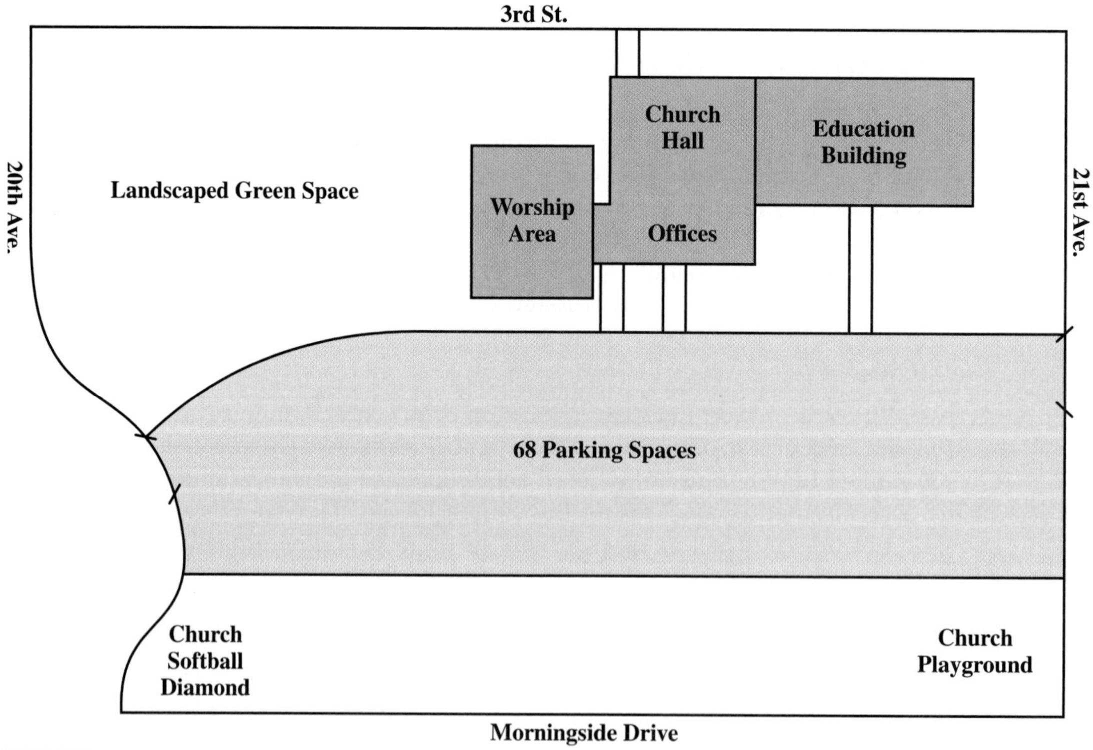

Source: Grace Lutheran Church, Internal Reports.

244

11. Adequate Space and Facilities

Discussion centered on whether major uses of space maximize the utilization of facilities. The church hall is considered adequate. Although there are separate education facilities, the space is limited. The nursery, while considered necessary, is difficult to staff, for it is small and poorly ventilated. It has adequate supplies for toddlers but no cribs or changing tables.

The worship area is comfortably filled, but members complain of inadequate lighting and a poor-quality sound system. There is a lack of space in front for special programs and no stage for performances. The church hosts a number of community organization meetings, such as support groups, Boy and Girl Scouts, the literary council, preschool screening, and so forth. Members are aware that their facility lacks showers for the basketball players. Storage space is considered adequate except in the office area.

12. Solid Financial Resources

Grace Lutheran has a history of meeting its budget. Ironically, the times it failed to do so were during the building campaigns for the 1979 and 1991 expansions. Even though donations were expected to be over and above the normal contribution, it didn't turn out that way. In comparison with nine other congregations in South Dakota with similar Sunday attendance figures, Grace Lutheran is second in both income and indebtedness (see Exhibit 5).

At $291 per year, Grace Lutheran's contributions per confirmed member are below the national ELCA average of $368. As South Dakota regularly ranks well below the national average for per capita income, this is not surprising. Noteworthy is that Grace Lutheran's contribution rate is above the state average of $274.

A recently hired financial secretary assists in budget development. Budget projections come from the standing boards to the financial committee. The proposed budgets must be approved by the Congregation Council and, ultimately, the full congregation. Grace Lutheran's net worth was calculated as $869,319 for 1996; $860,898 for 1995; and $805,066 for 1994 (see Exhibit 6).

There is concern that although currently in a stable financial position, the church is not setting aside enough money to pay off its bonds (see Exhibit 7). It is predicted that if proactive financial planning is not completed, Grace Lutheran will need to borrow funds in three years not only to finance new undertakings that may result from its strategic planning, but also to cover basic expenses (see Exhibit 8 on pages 247–251).

EXHIBIT 5: **Grace Lutheran in Comparison to 10 Congregations in South Dakota, (in terms of 300–400 per Sunday attendance)**

Rank	
2	Indebtedness
2	Income
4	Baptized Members
4	Benevolence Giving
4	Operations and Expenses
7	Attendance

Source: ELCA Headquarters, Chicago, Ill.

EXHIBIT 6: Grace Lutheran Church, Assets and Liabilities

	1996	1995	1994
Assets			
Cash on hand	$ .00	$ .00	$ .00
Savings account	61,424.44	27,183.00	34,595.00
Stocks (market value)	1,370.70	1,102.50	848.00
Land, building (1990 appraisal)	1,180,000.00	1,180,000.00	1,180,000.00
Total	1,242,795.14	1,208,285.50	1,215,443.00
Liabilities			
Restricted accounts, savings	45,759.09	539.32	28,933.00
Bonds	115,200.00	116,200.00	157,000.00
Mortgage	212,516.58	230,647.69	224,444.00
Total	373,475.67	347,387.01	410,377.00
Net Worth	869,319.47	860,898.49	805,066.00

Source: Grace Lutheran Church, Internal Reports.

EXHIBIT 7: Grace Lutheran Church, Bond Payment Schedule

Date	Savings Accrued for Payment[a]	Bond Payment Due	Net Difference
April 1997	$33,405	$ 0	$33,405
July 1998	45,905	$29,700	16,205
July 1999	26,205	15,500	10,705
February 2000	16,538	10,000	6,538
June 2000	9,870	22,500	−12,630
December 2000	5,833	500	5,333
July 2001	10,333	16,000	−5,667
July 2003	20,000	20,500	−500
July 2004	10,000	500	9,500

Source: Ascension Lutheran Board of Church Finance, April 1997.
[a]Based upon current budget requiring $833/month deposit into savings for bond payment, plus accrued interest.

EXHIBIT 8:   Grace Lutheran Church Treasurer's Reports, 1994–1996

1996

	Original Budget	Actual Ytd	% Actual to Budget
Income			
General offering	$265,500.00	$267,811.59	100.5
Loose offering	5,000.00	4,336.42	86.7
Sunday School offering (75%)	1,000.00	1,024.34	102.4
Building gifts/miscellaneous	2,000.00	815.46	40.8
Total Income	274,500.00	273,987.81	99.8
Expenses			
Mission Outreach			
ELCA/SD Synod	29,865.00	29,865.00	100.0
University Lutheran Center	2,000.00	2,003.00	100.2
Indian Concerns/Lutepisc	1,100.00	1,133.00	103.0
World Mission/Refugee	2,000.00	2,000.00	100.0
Seminary Scholarship	800.00	800.00	100.0
St. Dysmas Prison Congregation	350.00	350.00	100.0
Friendship Circle	200.00	200.00	100.0
Boy Scout Troop 29	50.00	50.00	100.0
Medary Conference	50.00	50.00	100.0
Subtotal	36,415.00	36,415.00	100.1
Salary/Fringe Benefits			
Senior pastor—salary/housing	35,091.50	34,933.99	99.6
Senior pastor—pension/insurance	10,083.00	9,851.08	97.7
Associate pastor—salary/housing: pulpit	2,400.00	800.00	33.3
Associate pastor—pension/insurance: mileage	696.00	246.90	35.5
Intern pastor	5,045.00	4,552.96	90.2
Secretary—salary	16,995.00	18,604.45	109.5
Secretary sub—salary	780.00	612.00	78.5
Custodian—salary	8,180.00	9,388.72	114.8
Custodian sub—salary	123.00	38.50	31.3
Organist—salary	4,674.00	4,704.00	100.6
Organist sub—salary	200.00	200.00	100.0
Chancel choir director—salary	1,219.00	1,219.00	100.0
Choir director subs—salary	200.00	0.00	0.0
NLK Choir director—salary	270.00	0.00	0.0
Joy Choir director—salary	270.00	0.00	0.0
Youth Choir accompanists	225.00	0.00	0.0
Social security/insurance	3,794.00	4,064.95	107.1
Moving/interview expenses	5,000.00	4,320.73	86.4
Senior pastor—medical reimbursement	538.50	538.50	100.0
Subtotal	95,784.00	94,075.78	98.2
Ministry Support			
Senior pastor—travel	2,500.00	1,247.34	49.9

continued

EXHIBIT 8:   *continued*

	1996		
	Original Budget	*Actual Ytd*	*% Actual to Budget*
Associate pastor—travel	$ 1,000.00	$ 572.46	57.2
Intern pastor—travel	500.00	64.38	12.9
Senior pastor—continuing education	500.00	450.00	90.0
Associate pastor—continuing education	500.00	163.06	32.6
Professional supply	150.00	145.17	96.8
Office supply	7,135.00	7,135.00	100.0
Delegate expenses	250.00	538.00	215.2
The Lutheran	1,475.00	1,574.65	106.8
Subtotal	14,010.00	11,890.06	84.9
Church Boards			
Christian Education	7,865.00	5,896.33	76.7
Church and Community	50.00	89.32	178.6
Church Finance	3,225.00	3,159.52	98.0
Membership Participation	600.00	600.00	100.0
Operations and Maintenance	13,600.00	11,440.57	84.1
Purpose and Planning	25.00	25.00	100.0
Worship and Music	4,200.00	4,200.00	100.0
Youth Ministry	2,300.00	1,901.93	82.7
Subtotal	31,865.00	17,312.67	85.7
Debt Obligation			
Mortgage	36,480.00	36,480.00	100.0
Bond interest payment	7,480.00	7,476.78	100.0
Bond repayment	10,000.00	10,000.00	100.0
Subtotal	53,960.00	53,956.78	100.0
Special Needs			
Professional bookkeeper	6,000.00	1,486.30	24.8
Pastor salary contingency	14,646.00	15,480.00	105.7
Shingle sanctuary roof	12,000.00	10,276.00	85.6
Contingency fund	10,000.00	1,567.45	15.7
Year-end transfer to savings	0.00	21,491.77	
Subtotal	42,646.00	50,301.52	118.0
Total Expenses	274,500.00	273,987.81	99.8

	1995		
	Original Budget	*Actual Ytd*	*% Actual to Budget*
Income			
General offering	$258,500.00	$259,149.47	100.3
Loose offering	5,000.00	3,976.30	79.5
Sunday School	1,000.00	1,135.50	113.6

continued

EXHIBIT 8: *continued*

	1995		
	Original Budget	Actual Ytd	% Actual to Budget
Building gifts/miscellaneous	$ 2,000.00	$ 476.00	23.8
Total Income	266,500.00	264,737.27	99.3
Expenses			
Mission Outreach			
ELCA/SD Synod	26,961.00	26,928.00	99.9
University Lutheran Center	2,000.00	2,000.00	100.0
Indian Concerns/Lutepisc	1,100.00	1,030.99	93.7
World Mission/Refugee	300.00	300.00	100.0
Congregation Behind Prison Walls	350.00	350.00	100.0
Friendship Circle	200.00	200.00	100.0
Medary Conference	50.00	47.45	94.9
Seminary Scholarship	800.00	641.00	80.1
Boy Scout Troop 29	50.00	50.00	100.0
Subtotal	31,811.00	31,547.44	100.0
Salary/Fringe			
Senior pastor—salary/housing	40,930.00	39,205.52	95.8
Senior pastor—pension/insurance	12,480.00	9,400.68	75.3
Associate pastor—salary/housing	33,880.00	34,267.50	101.1
Associate pastor—pension/insurance	6,950.00	7,174.52	103.2
Intern pastor	3,258.00	3,504.83	107.6
Secretary—salary	17,220.00	17,105.75	99.3
Custodian—salary	8,100.00	7,657.12	94.5
Organist—salary	4,474.00	3,940.34	88.1
Choir director—salary	1,519.00	1,528.40	100.6
Social security/insurance	3,714.00	3,510.13	94.5
Subtotal	132,525.00	127,294.79	96.1
Ministry Support			
Travel	4,000.00	3,344.71	83.6
Continuing education	1,000.00	996.67	99.7
Professional supply	150.00	117.92	78.6
Pulpit supply	130.00	0.00	0.0
Office supply	5,870.00	5,387.59	91.8
Delegate expenses	250.00	208.00	83.2
The Lutheran	1,295.00	1,208.40	94.0
Subtotal	12,685.00	11,263.29	88.8
Church Boards			
Worship and Music	3,800.00	3,607.22	94.9
Christian Education	7,585.00	6,022.85	79.4
Membership Participation	1,575.00	1,792.66	113.8
Church Finance	3,125.00	3,205.72	102.6
Purpose and Planning	25.00	18.40	73.6
Church and Community	250.00	250.00	100.0

continued

EXHIBIT 8: *continued*

1995

	Original Budget	Actual Ytd	% Actual to Budget
Youth Ministry	$ 2,000.00	$ 2,182.01	109.1
Operations and Maintenance	11,300.00	12,242.19	108.3
Subtotal	29,660.00	19,071.05	98.1
Debt Obligation			
Mortgage	36,480.00	36,480.00	100.0
Bond interest payment	9,750.00	9,348.41	95.9
Bond repayment	13,589.00	19,482.29	143.4
Subtotal	59,819.00	65,310.70	109.2
Total Expenses	260,500.00	264,737.27	99.3

1994

	Original Budget	Actual Ytd	% Actual to Budget
Income			
General offering	$249,200.00	$251,476.00	100.9
Loose offering	6,200.00	4,629.05	74.7
Sunday School	1,000.00	1,093.31	109.3
Building gifts/miscellaneous	3,880.00	1,218.44	31.4
Total Income	260,280.00	258,416.80	99.3
Expenses			
Mission Outreach			
ELCA/SD Synod	25,420.00	25,420.00	100.0
University Lutheran Center	2,000.00	2,000.00	100.0
Indian Concerns/Lutepisc	1,100.00	1,120.00	101.8
World Mission/Refugee	300.00	296.31	98.8
Congregation Behind Prison Walls	300.00	300.00	100.0
Friendship Circle	200.00	200.00	100.0
Medary Conference	50.00	50.00	100.0
Subtotal	29,370.00	29,386.31	100.1
Salary/Fringe Benefits			
Senior pastor—salary/housing	40,330.00	40,330.00	100.0
Senior pastor—pension/insurance	12,460.00	12,505.39	100.4
Associate pastor—salary/housing	33,080.00	33,080.00	100.0
Associate pastor—pension/insurance	6,750.00	6,797.02	100.7
Secretary—salary	15,970.00	16,209.14	101.5
Custodian—salary	7,000.00	6,066.75	86.7
Social security/insurance	2,910.00	3,092.19	106.3

continued

EXHIBIT 8: *continued*

	1994		
	Original Budget	*Actual Ytd*	*% Actual to Budget*
Summer intern	$ 2,280.00	$ 2,280.00	10.0
Subtotal	120,780.00	120,350.49	100.0
Ministry Support			
Travel	4,000.00	4,000.00	100.0
Continuing education	1,000.00	1,000.00	100.0
Delegate expense	250.00	230.62	92.2
Pulpit supply	130.00	0.00	0.0
Office supply	5,800.00	5,014.45	86.5
Professional supply	150.00	126.98	84.7
Subtotal	11,330.00	10,372.05	91.5
Church Boards			
Worship and Music	4,000.00	4,000.00	103.3
Christian Education	8,455.00	7,577.28	89.6
Membership Participation	1,850.00	1,533.05	82.9
Church Finance	3,000.00	3,025.87	100.9
Purpose and Planning	25.00	27.63	110.5
Church and Community	250.00	168.40	67.4
Youth Ministry	2,025.00	1,586.98	78.4
Operations and Maintenance	11,200.00	11,401.45	101.8
Subtotal	35,820.00	34,631.26	96.7
Debt Obligation			
Mortgage	36,480.00	36,480.00	100.0
Bond interest payment	11,000.00	11,181.90	101.7
Bond repayment	15,500.00	16,004.79	103.3
Subtotal	62,980.00	63,666.69	101.1
Total Expenses	260,280.00	258,416.80	99.3

Source: Grace Lutheran Church, Internal Reports.

CONCLUSION

Pastor Anders watched the strategic planning committee members as they participated with Pastor Nelson in a closing prayer. He was proud of them and of their hard
work, good ideas, and obvious commitment to this large undertaking. After bidding
them goodnight, he walked slowly back to his office, thinking to himself, "So much
discussion, so many ideas! Now we need to prioritize and decide where Grace Lutheran goes from here."

REFERENCES

Waterford, South Dakota Community Information & Demographics. 1997. Waterford, South Dakota Chamber of Commerce.

Callahan, Kennon L. 1983. *Twelve Keys to an Effective Church.* San Francisco: Harper Collins.

Constitution for Grace Lutheran Church. 1994. Grace Lutheran Church, Waterford, SD.

Experience Waterford. 1997. Waterford Area Chamber of Commerce & Visitors Bureau.

Median Household Income for 1994. United States Bureau of the Census.

Our Towns. 1997. The Waterford Register, January 30.

Profile of Our Congregation. 1996. Grace Lutheran Church, Waterford, SD.

1996 Annual Report. Grace Lutheran Church, Annual Meeting January 28, 1997.

The Classic Car Club of America, Inc.—1997

Matthew C. Sonfield

www.classiccarclub.org

The Classic Car Club of America, Inc. (CCCA) (847-390-0443) was formed in 1952 by a small group of enthusiasts interested in the luxury cars of the late 1920s and 1930s. CCCA designated certain high-priced, high-quality, and limited-production cars as "Classic Cars," and chose the period of 1925 to 1942 as the "Classic Era." CCCA members felt that cars built prior to 1925 had not reached technical maturity, and that the quality of most so-called luxury cars built after World War II had succumbed to the economic pressures of mass production. Some pictures of Classic Cars are provided in Exhibit 1.

EXHIBIT 1:   Classic Cars

1926 Duesenberg (above); 1934 Rolls Royce (top right); 1941 Packard (right).
Source: The Classic Car Club of America, Inc.

Over the years, CCCA modified and expanded its list of recognized Classics, and extended the time period to 1948 to include certain pre–World War II models that continued in production for a few years after the war. All Classics were of considerably higher price and quality than the mass-production cars of the 1925–1948 era, and most had original prices ranging from $2,000 to $5,000. (This was a considerable amount of money at that time; in 1930, a Ford Model A—*not* a Classic—sold new for about $450.) Some of the most luxurious Classic cars, such as the American Duesenberg, the English Rolls-Royce, the French Hispano-Suiza, and the Italian Isotta-Fraschini, sold new in the $10,000-to-$20,000 range! Exhibit 2 lists those cars recognized as Classics by the CCCA in 1997.

EXHIBIT 2: CCCA-Recognized Classic Cars

A.C.	Excelsior*	Minerva*
Adler*	Farman*	N.A.G.*
Alfa Romeo	Fiat*	Nash*
Alvis*	FN*	Packard*
Amilcar*	Franklin*	Peerless
Armstrong-Siddeley*	Frazier-Nash*	Peugot*
Aston Martin*	Hispano-Suiza*	Pierce-Arrow
Auburn*	Horch	Railton*
Austro-Daimler	Hotchkiss*	Raymond Mays*
Ballot*	Hudson*	Renault*
Bentley	Humber*	Reo*
Benz*	Invicta	Revere
Blackhawk	Isotta-Fraschini	Riley*
B.M.W.*	Itala	Roamer*
Brewster*	Jaguar*	Rochet Schneider*
Brough Superior*	Jensen*	Rohr*
Bucciali*	Jordan*	Rolls-Royce
Bugatti	Julian*	Ruxton
Buick*	Kissell*	Squire
Cadillac*	Lagonda*	S.S. and S.S. Jaguar*
Chenard-Walcker*	Lanchester*	Stearns-Knight
Chrysler*	Lancia*	Stevens-Duryea
Cord	La Salle*	Steyr*
Cunningham	Lincoln*	Studebaker*
Dagmar*	Lincoln Continental	Stutz
Daimler*	Locomobile*	Sunbeam*
Darracq*	Marmon*	Talbot*
Delage*	Maserati*	Talbot-Lago*
Delahaye*	Maybach	Tatra*
Delaunay Belleville*	McFarlan	Triumph*
Doble	Mercedes	Vauxhall*
Dorris	Mercedes-Benz*	Voisin
Duesenberg	Mercer	Wills St. Claire
Du Pont	M.G.*	Willys-Knight*

*Indicates that only certain models of this make are considered Classic. Some other 1925–1948 custom-bodied cars not listed above may be approved as Classic upon individual application.
Source: The Classic Car Club of America, Inc.

THE COLLECTOR CAR HOBBY

The "collector car" hobby in the United States is a broad and wide-reaching activity. Basically, a "collector car" is any automobile owned for purposes other than normal transportation. The most widely read collector car hobby magazine, *Hemmings Motor News*, had a circulation of about 264,000 in June 1997. Another magazine, *Car Collector*, estimates that nearly 1 million Americans are engaged in the old-car hobby. A figure of 350,000 to 500,000 is a conservative estimate of the number of Americans involved with collector cars.

"Collector car" is a loose term that covers turn-of-the-century "horseless carriages" and current but limited-production cars such as Italian super-sports cars. Naturally, owners of collector cars enjoy the company of other persons with similar interests, thus a wide variety of car clubs exist to suit almost any particular segment of this vast hobby. The largest of these clubs, the Antique Automobile Club of America, caters to owners of virtually any car 25 years old or older and has a membership of more than 55,000. CCCA has a more restricted focus and fewer members.

CCCA ORGANIZATION AND ACTIVITIES

When the CCCA's fiscal year ended on October 31, 1996, the club had 5,647 members. (Exhibit 3 gives a comparison of membership figures for recent years.) The categories and dues of members are as follows:

Active (regular membership—$40/year)

Associate (for spouse of active member, no publications—$7/year)

Life (after 10 years, one-time fee of $800)

Life Associate (for spouse of Life member—$80)

Honorary (famous car designers, etc.)

CCCA members receive a variety of benefits from their membership. One is the quarterly magazine, *The Classic Car*. High in quality and highly respected by automotive historians, it features color photos of Classics on the front and back covers and 48 or more pages of articles and black-and-white photos of Classics within. Members get

EXHIBIT 3: Selected CCCA Membership Data (for Oct. 31 fiscal year endings)

	1996	*1995*	*1994*	*1993*	*1992*	*1991*
Active Members	4,307	4,310	4,333	4,179	4,184	4,156
Associate Members	1,068	1,035	1,046	1,005	1,012	977
Life Members	201	197	198	199	195	188
Life Associate Members	66	63	59	59	60	59
Honorary Members	5	5	5	5	5	6
Total	5,647	5,610	5,641	5,447	5,456	5,386

Source: The Classic Car Club of America, Inc.

CCCA's *Bulletin*, published eight times a year, which carries club and hobby news; technical columns; and members' and commercial ads for Classic cars, parts, and related items. Members also receive the club's annual *Handbook and Directory*, which contains the CCCA bylaws, judging rules, requirements for regions, as well as a current listing of members and the Classic cars they own. CCCA solicits commercial car-related advertisements for the *Handbook and Directory*, and its cost is largely paid for by these advertisements. Advertisements also cover some of the costs of *The Classic Car* and *Bulletin*.

The CCCA sponsors three types of national events each year. The Annual Meeting in January includes business meetings and a car-judging meet and is held in a different location in the United States each year. In April and July, a series of Grand Classic judging meets are held in 10 to 12 locations around the country, with a total of 400 to 600 Classics being exhibited and judged. At CCCA judging meets, cars are rated by a point system which takes into account the quality and authenticity of restoration and the general condition of the car, both mechanically and cosmetically. CCCA judging meets are usually not publicized to the general public, and access to view the cars is generally restricted to club members and their guests only.

Each year the club sponsors several Classic CARavans in various parts of the United States and Canada. The CARavan is a tour in which members in as many as 100 Classic cars join together in a weeklong (occasionally longer) planned itinerary.

The Annual Meeting, Grand Classics judging meets, and CARavans are designed to be financially self-supporting, with attending members paying fees that cover the costs of the events. Some CCCA members volunteer as technical advisors to other members. The club makes available for sale to members certain club-related products such as hats, ties, shirts, and umbrellas with a Classic Car design.

The club is managed by a 15-member board of directors, with a president, vice-presidents, treasurer, and secretary. All are club member volunteers (from all over the United States) who have shown a willingness and ability to help run the CCCA and who are elected by the total membership to three-year terms of office. They are not reimbursed for their expenses, which include attending eight board meetings each year, most of which are held at club headquarters in Des Plaines, Illinois (a site chosen for its central location within the United States and its proximity to Chicago's main airport). Another member volunteers as executive administrator and oversees the club's secretary and daily operations. The only paid employees of the club are the full-time office secretary and the part-time publications editor. CCCA's organization chart is shown in Exhibit 4.

In addition to paying dues and belonging to the national CCCA, the majority of members also pay dues and belong to a local CCCA region. In 1997, there were 32 regions throughout the United States (see Exhibit 5). Each region sponsors a variety of local activities for members and their Classics and publishes its own magazine or newsletter. Many of the regions also derive revenues from the sale of Classic Car replacement parts or service items offered to all members of the national club.

Legally separate from the CCCA and its regions is the Classic Car Club of America Museum. It occupies space as part of a larger old-car museum in Hickory Corners, Michigan, and displays a variety of donated Classic cars. The CCCA Museum, unlike the CCCA itself, is eligible to receive tax-deductible gifts of money and property (such as cars). Although the CCCA has granted the museum the right to use the CCCA name, the museum has a separate board of trustees and is run independently of the club. Because of this legal separation, the club's directors do not have the authority to make

EXHIBIT 4:   1997 CCCA Organization Chart

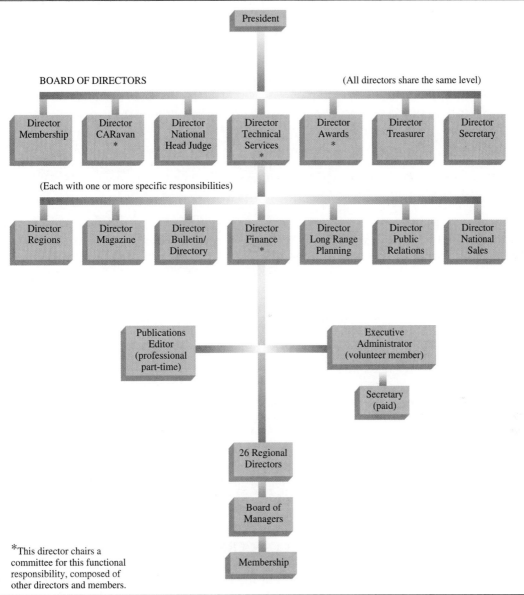

Source: The Classic Car Club of America, Inc.

EXHIBIT 5:   Boundaries of Regions of Classic Car Club of America

Source: The Classic Car Club of America, Inc.

strategic decisions for the museum, nor can the museum's performance and finances benefit the club.

MEMBERSHIP EXPANSION CONCERNS

Although the officers and directors of the CCCA believe the club to be strong, both financially and in its value to its members, they realize that a variety of concerns about the future exist.

One concern is the continuing effect of inflation upon the club's ability to maintain its current level of services and benefits to the membership. In particular, the costs of publications and headquarters office administration have risen considerably over the years. The board of directors responded both by watching costs carefully and by raising annual dues several times (from $10 in the 1960s to the current $40 per year), but it recognizes that certain cost increases are unavoidable and that raising dues too high may result in a loss of members. (Financial statements are provided in Exhibits 6 and 7.)

EXHIBIT 6: CCCA Financial Statements (Cash Flow Basis) Income Statement

	Year Ended October 31,			
	1996	*1995*	*1994*	*1993*
Receipts				
Active Dues (Dues Received for Current Fiscal Year)	$ 55,033	$ 66,094	$ 44,913	$ 46,879
Prepaid Active Dues (Dues Received for Next Fiscal Year)	85,134	75,174	62,524	87,382
Associate Dues	2,280	2,460	1,645	1,960
Prepaid Associate Dues	3,395	3,107	2,662	3,540
Life Membership	0	4,740	750	1,260
Publications Sales	1,726	1,907	1,344	2,683
Bulletin Advertising	23,236	14,552	10,990	11,176
Magazine Advertising	2,300	1,234	2,250	1,815
Directory Advertising	14,200	12,550	9,289	10,010
Awards (Member Registration Fees for Meets, etc.)	9,883	11,415	10,720	15,975
CARavan	33,676	30,550	22,700	32,400
National Sales Items (Badges, Jewelry, Ties, etc.)	4,850	5,002	4,759	4,358
Interest Earned	11,539	19,262	15,282	12,531
Regional Insurance (Reimbursement from Regions)	4,420	2,835	3,865	2,100
Miscellaneous and Foreign Exchange	1,433	1,246	997	941
Total Receipts	$253,105	$252,128	$194,690	$235,010
Disbursements				
Bulletin	$ 55,648	$ 49,157	$ 39,152	$ 19,538
Magazine	61,599	57,698	51,566	47,972
Directory	15,674	15,053	12,803	1,784
Awards (Judging, Meetings, Trophies, etc.)	10,908	17,882	21,190	4,038
General Administration (Supplies, Equipment, Postage, etc.)	21,731	5,152	3,405	11,801
Office (Wages, Rent, Condo Expenses, Real Estate Taxes)	32,729	51,186	52,970	27,750
CARavan	15,979	11,262	16,025	46,924
National Sales Items	781	7,286	1,569	2,623
Membership (Recruitment, Renewals)	5,983	3,739	6,203	7,246
Regional Insurance	4,832	4,832	4,832	2,800
Regional Relations	0	0	0	27
Computer Expenses	3,988	0	28,760	9,339
Miscellaneous and Foreign Exchange	5,956	6,475	10,449	456
Taxes	1,550	(279)	2,351	1,377
Total Disbursements	$237,358	$229,443	$251,275	$183,675
Excess Receipts over Disbursements	$ 15,747	$ 22,685	($ 56,585)	$ 51,335

Note: Certain unusual one-time receipts and disbursements omitted.
Source: The Classic Car Club of America, Inc.

EXHIBIT 7: CCCA Balance Sheet

	For October 31,		
	1996	1995	1994
Assets			
Bank Balance	$ 28,970	$ 43,038	$104,432
Investments (at cost: money market funds, C.D.'s, etc.)	256,743	210,717	209,191
(includes life membership fund)	64,746	0	0
Office Condominium	84,968	75,000	0
Total Assets	370,681	328,755	313,623
Liabilities (none)	0	0	0
Owners' Equity	370,681	328,755	313,623
Total Liabilities and Owners' Equity	370,681	328,755	313,623

Source: The Classic Car Club of America, Inc.

One way to overcome this problem is to increase the number of members and thus create greater revenues for the club. The number of members who pay full dues has increased only moderately over the years. The directors know that many Classic owners do not belong to the CCCA. While CCCA members accounted for ownership of about 8,000 Classics in 1997, no one really knows how many Classics exist or how many of their owners are not in the club. Club efforts in recent years to increase membership have been targeted at these Classic-owning non-CCCA members. CCCA sent letters to past members who failed to renew their CCCA membership (about 5 percent to 10 percent each year); region officers contacted local non-CCCA members known to own Classics; mailings were made to Classic-owning persons found in directories of other old-car clubs; articles about CCCA activities as well as a few paid advertisements were placed in various old-car hobby magazines; and membership ads were placed in single-marque car clubs (such as the Packard Club) in return for allowing those clubs to place their membership ads in the CCCA's publications.

Some CCCA members do not own Classics although most do, for much of the pleasure of belonging to the club derives from participating in the various activities with a Classic car. Although enthusiasts who do not own their own Classics might be an appropriate target for CCCA membership recruitment efforts, CCCA's primary focus is on persons who currently own Classic cars.

The membership recruitment efforts have only been moderately successful. Although new members have offset the annual 5 to 10 percent attrition rate, total membership has risen only slightly in recent years. Unless the listing of recognized Classics is expanded, the number of Classic Cars in existence is fixed, and with it, by and large, the number of Classic owners eligible for CCCA membership.

There are varying opinions within the CCCA with regard to expanding the current listing of Classic Cars, and there are two directions for such an expansion. One way is to add further makes and/or models within the current 1925–1948 limit. Another way is to add cars built before 1925 or after 1948.

No new makes of cars have been added in recent years, but several times the board voted to add additional models of existing Classic makes to the CCCA's 1925–1948 listing (for example, by adding a Packard model line slightly lower in original price to an already listed model line of the same year). The additions draw a mixed reaction from the membership. Some members felt that such additions dilute the meaning of "Classic," while most members seemed either to support the directors' decisions or have no strong opinion.

More controversial is the issue of expanding the listing to before 1925 or after 1948. Very few members support going earlier than 1925, and a sizable minority of members make several arguments for a post-1948 expansion. They say that some high-quality cars were built after 1948 and should be considered "Classic." They argue that the club currently is not attracting young members (only 13 percent of CCCA members are under 45) because younger people are less able to afford a Classic and are unable to "identify" with a 1925–1948 car as they can with a car of the 1950s or 1960s. It is true that many current CCCA members own Classics because of nostalgia for cars of their youth.

On the other hand, most members of the board, along with a clear majority of the membership, argue against the expansion of the list of Classics past 1948. The primary argument is that a Classic Car is more than just a high-quality luxury car; rather, it is the product of a "Classic Era" when the truly wealthy lived a life-style separate from the rest of the population, and when an elite group of auto makers and custom body craftspeople were willing and able to produce cars resonant with the upper-class life-style. By the end of World War II, it is argued within CCCA, social and economic changes ended this life-style, and economic pressures closed down the custom body builders and most of the independent luxury car makers; the remaining luxury cars generally became only bigger, heavier, and better-appointed versions of other cars made by multiline manufacturers. Thus, expanding beyond 1948 would alter the basic focus, purpose, and "philosophy" of the club, and it is this narrow focus that differentiates the CCCA from other clubs and makes it so attractive and important to its members. Furthermore, it is argued, although a few truly special car models were made after 1948, the quantities produced were very small, and the addition of these cars to the CCCA listing would bring in very few new members.

There is also a concern about the use of members' Classics and the nature of CCCA activities. In 1952, when the club was founded, most people viewed Classics as simply "old cars" which generally could be bought for a few hundred to a few thousand dollars. All prices rose significantly in the 1970s and 1980s (but leveled off or dropped a little in the 1990s). Today, many view Classics as major investment items, and professional dealers and auctions are significant factors in the marketplace. Current prices of Classics vary greatly, depending upon the make of car, its condition, and type of body. Although some less exotic and unrestored Classic models can be found for under $15,000, most sell for $20,000 to $75,000, and the most desirable Classics (convertible models with custom bodies, 12- and 16-cylinder engines, etc.) can sell for $100,000 and more. (A very small number of especially exotic and desirable Classics have sold in the $250,000 to $1,000,000 range, and a 1929 Bugatti Royale reportedly sold in 1987 for over $9.8 million!) Furthermore, judging meets have become very serious events, with high scores adding significantly to a Classic's sales value. Thus many highly desirable and/or top-scoring Classics are now hardly driven at all, and are transported in enclosed trailers to and from judging meets. Although most Classic owners still enjoy driving their cars, and the CARavans are popular, some members yearn for the "old days" when there was less emphasis on judging and on a car's value and when CCCA members would drive and park their Classics anywhere.

Still another concern of some members is the possibility of a greater stress in future years on the conservation of gasoline in this country. If the country should focus more seriously on its high usage of gasoline, how would the public view Classic Cars and the collector car hobby in general? Would the ownership and driving of cars for nontransportation purposes be considered unpatriotic or wasteful?

FUTURE DIRECTION OF THE CCCA

In response to these various concerns, the CCCA board established a Long Range Planning Committee to study issues relating to the future of the club and to make recommendations to the board. In 1983 and again in 1991, CCCA sent all members a questionnaire along with their membership renewal material. The response rate was excellent. Exhibit 8 presents the 1991 questionnaire and a tabulation of those responses which were quantifiable, along with a comparison to the 1983 survey responses.

Some issues seemed more important than others, and deserved the board's more immediate attention. Although the survey clarified some of the opinions of the membership, the board did not view this survey as a ballot, nor did it feel obligated to follow the majority preference in every area. The CCCA board continued to study these and other issues.

The officers and directors of the club simply wanted to do a good job. Their fellow members had elected them to keep the club strong and to improve it further. They wanted to be proactive as well as reactive; they wanted to be imaginative in their strategic-management activities and to respond to concerns and issues already raised.

Together for their regular board meeting, the 15 officers and directors of the CCCA asked themselves the following questions:

1. What are the various criteria we should consider when making strategic decisions for the club? How do we balance financial and nonfinancial objectives? Which are primary and which are secondary?

2. How important are, and how should we deal with, rising costs to the club?

3. If we are forced to choose between raising dues or lowering the services provided to the members, which takes priority?

4. Is expansion of the listing of recognized Classics desirable?

5. Which is preferable: adding cars within the 1925–1948 time period or adding cars of earlier or later years? What are the pros and cons of these alternatives?

6. How important is it to increase the number of members in the club? What are some alternative ways to increase membership?

7. How can younger people be attracted to the CCCA? How important is this? What are some specific strategies to accomplish this?

8. Are there other possible sources of revenue to the club? What might some be?

9. Were important questions not included in the previous membership surveys that should be included in a future survey?

10. Are there other long-range issues or concerns that the club has not yet addressed?

EXHIBIT 8: Classic Car Club of America 1991 Questionnaire Response Survey, with 1983 Comparative Responses as Available and Applicable (all percents based on those answering)

---

1. I have been a member of the CCCA:

   1991   8% less than 2 years   19% 2–5 years   20% 5–10 years   53% more than 10 years

   (1983) 11% less than 2 years   20% 2–5 years   18% 5–10 years   51% more than 10 years

2. My age is:

   1991   0% under 25   3% 25–34   10% 35–44   24% 45–54   32% 55–64   31% 65 or over

   (1983) 1% under 25   3% 25–34   17% 35–44   30% 45–54   28% 55–64   22% 65 or over

3. My age when joining CCCA was:

   1991   7% under 25   19% 25–34   26% 35–44   26% 45–54   17% 55–64   5% 65 or over

   (1983) not asked

4. I live in the _____ Region. (Not tabulated in this summary.)

5. I am a member of a CCCA region:

   1991   76% yes   24% no

   (1983) 69% yes   31% no

   If yes, which region: 15% Michigan, 13% So. Cal., 6.4% Pac. NW, others less than 6%.

   If not, why not? Of those responding here (54% of those who answered "no"): 30% indicated distance, 21% no time, 13% no Classic or not running, 8% not invited or didn't know about it, 9% not interested, 3% lack of activities, and 16% miscellaneous of less than 2% each.

6. I have attended:

1991	(1983)	
74%	(64%)	One or more Grand Classics
27%	(19%)	One or more National CCCA CARavans
34%	(24%)	One or more Annual Meetings
65%	(52%)	One or more Regional events
13%	—	None of the above

7. I belong to how many other car clubs:

	Average	0	1	2	3	4	5	6–9	10 or more
1991	3	8%	18%	22%	19%	12%	9%	11%	2%
(1983)	3	9%	19%	23%	17%	12%	7%	11%	2%

   I am more active in some of these clubs than I am in CCCA:

   1991   42% yes   58% no

   (1983) 44% yes   56% no

   If yes, why? Of those responding here (84% of those who answered "yes"): 22% prefer a one-marque club, 21% indicated distance, 16% interested in other clubs, 10% also interested in nonclassics, 10% want more activities, 8% don't own Classic or not running, and 13% miscellaneous of 3% or less.

8. Compared to other clubs, the CCCA is:

   1991   32% the best   47% better than most   20% average   1% poor

   (1983) 31% the best   47% better than most   21% average   1% poor

9. Compared to other clubs, the value I receive for my CCCA dues is:

   1991   29% the best   42% better than most   28% average   1% poor

   (1983) 27% the best   40% better than most   31% average   3% poor

10. Overall, I rate *The Classic Car Magazine*:

    1991   74% excellent   23% good   3% fair   0% poor

    (1983) 74% excellent   24% good   1% fair   0% poor

continued

263

EXHIBIT 8: *continued*

11. Overall, I rate the *CCCA Bulletin:*

1991	55% excellent	39% good	6% fair	0% poor
(1983)	35% excellent	51% good	13% fair	1% poor

12. With regard to the CCCA listing of recognized Classic cars:

1991	(1983)	
63%	(69%)	I basically think the current listing is good.
32%	(28%)	I think the listing should be expanded.
5%	(3%)	I think the listing should be reduced.

Of those commenting (31%) and desiring change: 26% accept newer cars, 18% accept others in Classic era, 7% accept older cars, 11% eliminate some current Classics, 7% 1925–1948 year span, and 31% other of less than 5% each.

13. With regard to the scoring currently used and at Grand Classics and Annual Meetings:

1991	(1983)	
82%	(86%)	I basically think the current system is good.
18%	(14%)	I think the system could be improved. If so, how?

Of those commenting (only 10%): 19% judging/scoring, 10% more points, 10% drive cars before judging, 8% recognize original cars, 11% better judges, etc., and 42% misc. of 5% or less.

14. Overall I would rate the Grand Classics as:

1991	46% excellent	32% good	3% fair	1% poor	18% don't know
(1983)	50% excellent	30% good	2% fair	1% poor	17% don't know

or 100% basis without "don't know"

1991	56% excellent	39% good	4% fair	1% poor	_____
(1983)	61% excellent	36% good	2% fair	1% poor	_____

15. Overall I would rate the Annual Meetings as:

1991	21% excellent	23% good	2% fair	0% poor	54% don't know
(1983)	15% excellent	22% good	5% fair	0% poor	59% don't know

or 100% basis without "don't know"

1991	46% excellent	50% good	4% fair	0% poor	_____
(1983)	35% excellent	53% good	12% fair	0% poor	_____

16. Overall I would rate the CARavans as:

1991	32% excellent	11% good	1% fair	0% poor	56% don't know
(1983)	28% excellent	16% good	2% fair	0% poor	54% don't know

or 100% basis without "don't know"

1991	73% excellent	25% good	2% fair	0% poor	_____
(1983)	61% excellent	35% good	3% fair	1% poor	_____

17. The CCCA has not associated itself with automobile auctions. How do you feel about this policy?

[1991]	62% strongly agree	21% agree	4% disagree	3% strongly disagree	9% don't know

or 100% basis without "don't know"

[1991]	69% strongly agree	23% agree	4% disagree	3% strongly disagree

This question was not asked in 1983.

18. I completed the previous CCCA questionnaire sent to members in 1983:

23% yes	37% no	40% don't know

or 100% basis without "don't know"

38% yes	62% no

continued

EXHIBIT 8: *continued*

19. If there is one thing I'd recommend the CCCA *not change*, it would be:
    Of those commenting (24%): 26% 1925–1948 year span, 20% publications, 9% quality of cars considered Classic, 8% CARavans, 6% happy with club, 5% Grand Classics, 4% judging/scoring, and 22% other of 3% or less.

20. If there is one thing I'd recommend the CCCA change, it would be:
    Of those commenting (25%): 13% accept newer cars, 7% judging/scoring, 6% accept other cars in the Classic era, 4% encourage younger people, 4% CARavans, and 66% miscellaneous 3% or less.

21. I think the CCCA could be improved by: (only 15% commenting)
    An emphasis on encouraging younger members. A desire to see newer cars accepted, and general happiness with the Club. Many miscellaneous comments too numerous to list.

22. Other comments (only 18% responding)
    Principally a general satisfaction with the Club.
    Encourage younger people.
    Many miscellaneous comments too numerous to list.

Source: The Classic Car Club of America, Inc. Used with permission.

Harley-Davidson, Inc.—1998

Charles B. Shrader
Fred R. David
Timothy T. Dannels

www.harley-davidson.com
stock symbol HDI

> Our competitors try to imitate our motorcycles, but they can't copy the intangibles that make owning a Harley-Davidson a life-fulfilling experience. We determine what's original and authentic. They're duplicating hardware, but they can only copy where we've been. They have no idea where we're going.
>
> —*1996 Annual Report*

Net sales for 1997 of $1,762.6 million were $231.4 million, or 15.1 percent, higher than net sales for 1996. Net income and diluted earnings per share from continuing operations were $174.1 million and $1.13, respectively, for 1997 as compared with $143.4 million and $.94, respectively, for 1996. The gain on disposition and diluted earnings per share from discontinued operations was $22.6 million and $.15, respectively, for 1996.

The company increased its quarterly dividend payment in June 1997 from $.03 per share, to $.035 per share, which resulted in a total year payout of $.135 per share.

Jeffrey L. Bleustein, president and CEO of Harley-Davidson Inc. (414-342-4680), sat back in his chair in his Milwaukee, Wisconsin, office and pondered his company's situation. Bleustein had been with Harley since 1975. He was one of the original group of managers who purchased Harley from AMF and turned around the company in the 1980s. He experienced firsthand the pressures Japanese competition placed on the company. And he had successfully employed his skills as a mechanical engineer and mathematician to build Harley into a world-class manufacturer.

In 1997, he faced new challenges. Demand for Harleys was greater than supply. The company was going to open two new plants, one in Milwaukee and one in Kansas City, but would that be enough? Was Harley inviting new competitors into the business by not responding to customer demand? Were the new Harley look-alike bikes built by the Japanese going to steal away market share? Should he worry about the new U.S. competitors—Polaris, Excelsior, and Indian? Could these new companies also capitalize on the baby boom generation and wave of nostalgia in the motorcycle market which had

This case was prepared by Professor Charles B. Shrader of Iowa State University, Professor Fred R. David of Francis Marion University, and Professor Timothy T. Dannels of Iowa State University as a basis for class discussion. It is not intended to illustrate either effective or ineffective handling of an administrative situation. Copyright © 1999 by Prentice Hall, Inc. ISBN 0-13-011163-5.

EXHIBIT 1: Harley-Davidson, Inc., Motorcycle Unit Shipments and Net Sales

	1997	1996	Increase	%Change
Motorcycle units (excluding Buell)	132,285	118,771	13,514	11.4%
Net sales (in millions):				
Motorcycles (excluding Buell)	$1,382.8	$1,199.2	$183.6	15.3
Motorcycle Parts and Accessories	241.9	211.2	30.7	14.5
General Merchandise	95.1	90.7	4.4	4.8
Other	42.8	30.1	12.7	42.2
Total Motorcycles and Related Products	1,762.6	1,531.2	231.4	15.1

Source: Harley-Davidson, Inc., Annual Report (1997): 41.

served Harley so well? He wondered whether these developments posed any real threat to Harley's preeminent position in the super-heavyweight motorcycle segment. Harley had divested itself in 1996 of Holiday Rambler, a recreational vehicle maker, to focus on motorcycles; it was a move Bleustein thought should strengthen Harley. He also knew that his company had an aggressive strategic plan to increase motorcycle production to 200,000 units by Harley's one-hundredth anniversary in 2003. But would these strategic moves be sufficient? As he eased further into his chair, he thought of the many rides he had taken and the numerous rallies he had attended. His company was indeed close to its customers. Harley's quality was superb and demand was sky-high. Bleustein concluded there probably would be smooth riding for Harley on through 2003.

HISTORY

The Harley-Davidson story began in 1903 when William Harley, aged 21 and a draftsman at a Milwaukee manufacturing firm, designed and built a motorcycle with the help of three Davidson brothers: Arthur, a pattern maker; Walter, a railroad mechanic; and William, a toolmaker. At first, Harley and the brothers tinkered with ideas, motors, and old bicycle frames. Legend has it that they fashioned their first carburetor from a tin can. They made a three-horsepower, 25-cubic-inch engine and successfully road tested the first motored cycle.

Operating out of a shed in the Davidson family's backyard, the men built and sold three motorcycles. Production was expanded to eight in 1904, and in 1906, the company's first building was erected on the current site of the main offices in Milwaukee, Wisconsin. Harley-Davidson Motor Company was incorporated in 1907, and Arthur set off to recruit dealers in New England and the South. William completed a degree in engineering, specializing in internal combustion engines, and quickly applied his expertise in the company; he developed the first V-twin engine in 1909. He followed this with a major breakthrough in 1912—the first commercially successful motorcycle clutch. This made possible the use of a roller chain to power the motorcycle. The company offered its first three-speed transmission in 1915.

During the early 1900s, the United States experienced rapid growth in the motorcycle industry, with firms such as Excelsior, Indian, Merkel, Thor, and Yale growing and competing. Most of the early U.S. motorcycle companies turned out shoddy, unreliable products. But this was not considered to be true of Harley-Davidson and Indian cycles. Early continued success in racing and endurance made Harley a favorite among motorcyclists. The company's V-twin engines became known for power and reliability.

During World War I, Harley-Davidson supplied the military with motorcycles and became the largest motorcycle company in the world in 1918. The company built a 300,000-square-foot plant in Milwaukee in 1922. In 1949, Harley first faced international competition from British motorcycles, such as Nortons and Triumphs, which handled better and were cheaper, lighter, and just as fast even though they had smaller engines. To counter the British threat, Harley-Davidson improved the design of its engines and increased the horsepower of its heavier cycles. The result, in 1957, was the first modern superbike—the Harley Sportster. It was also during the 1950s that Harley developed the styling that is famous to this day.

Motorcycle enthusiasts more than ever began to go with Japanese products because of their price and performance advantages. Harley even lost some loyal Harley owners and police department contracts. The company was losing ground rapidly in both technological advances and the market. Starting in 1975 and continuing through the mid-1980s, Japanese companies penetrated the big-bore, custom motorcycle market with Harley look-alikes sporting V-twin engines. The Honda Magna and Shadow, the Suzuki Intruder, and the Yamaha Virago were representative of the Japanese imitations. The Japanese captured a significant share of the large cycle segment, controlled nearly 90 percent of the total motorcycle market, and were about to put Harley out of business.

The Japanese threat became so strong and Japanese bikes were so successful that Harley requested and received tariff protection from the government in 1983. It was at this point in Harley's history that a dramatic turnaround began to take shape.

Harley-Davidson soon adopted a very efficient approach to manufacturing. Three major programs were combined to compose the manufacturing approach: materials as needed (MAN) or just-in-time inventory, statistical operator control (SOC), and employee involvement. Under the MAN system, Harley suppliers must comply with the company's quality requirements. Harley offers long-term contracts to suppliers who comply and who deliver only the exact quantity needed for a given period of time. Harley also transports materials from suppliers. When the Harley transportation company makes scheduled pickups from suppliers, Harley has greater control over the shipments and is able to cut costs.

This efficient approach to manufacturing allowed Harley to accomplish one of the most remarkable turnarounds in American corporate history. Harley went from needing tariff protection from Japanese competition in the 1980s to being a world-class manufacturer in the 1990s.

CURRENT SITUATION

Harley is now winning the battle among the heavyweight motorcycle competitors—Honda, Kawasaki, Suzuki, and Yamaha. Harley ended 1997 with a 49.1 percent share of the heavyweight motorcycle market in the United States and 15 percent internationally. However, the company has an unusual—and big—problem; because of a lack of plant capacity, Harley cannot meet demand for its motorcycles. Customers worldwide who order a new Harley must wait at least a year for delivery. Dealers are upset because they have no inventory. Consumers are upset. Harley's domestic market share was 48.2 percent in 1996 while its European market share was 6.8 percent.

EXHIBIT 2: Harley-Davidson, Inc., Consolidated Statements of Operations

| | Years ended December 31, | | |
(in thousands of dollars, except per share amounts)	1997	1996	1995
Net sales	1,762,569	1,531,227	1,350,466
Cost of goods sold	1,176,352	1,041,133	939,067
Gross profit	586,217	490,094	411,399
Operating income from financial services	12,355	7,801	3,620
Selling, administrative and engineering	(328,569)	(269,449)	(234,223)
Income from operations	270,003	228,446	180,796
Interest income	7,871	3,309	1,446
Interest expense	—	—	(1,350)
Other—net	(1,572)	(4,133)	(4,903)
Income from continuing operations before provision for income taxes	276,302	227,622	175,989
Provision for income taxes	102,232	84,213	64,939
Income from continuing operations	174,070	143,409	111,050
Discontinued operations:			
Income from operations, net of applicable income taxes	—	—	1,430
Gain on disposition of discontinued operations, net of applicable income taxes	—	22,619	—
Net income	174,070	166,028	112,480
Basic earnings per common share:			
Income from continuing operations	1.15	.95	.74
Income from discontinued operations	—	.15	.01
Net income	1.15	1.10	.75
Diluted earnings per common share:			
Income from continuing operations	1.13	.94	.73
Income from discontinued operations	—	.15	.01
Net income	1.13	1.09	.74
Cash dividends per common share	.135	.11	.09

Source: Harley-Davidson, Inc., *Annual Report* (1997): 49.

The Harley-Davidson corporate vision statement is as follows:

Harley-Davidson is an action-oriented, international company—a leader in its commitment to continuously improve the quality of profitable relationships with stakeholders (customers, employees, suppliers, shareholders, governments, and society). Harley-Davidson believes the key to success is to balance stakeholders' interests through the empowerment of all employers to focus on value-added activities.

At Harley-Davidson, we don't run our business on a quarter-to-quarter basis. We also don't run our business for Wall Street, ourselves, or even our customers. Our focus has been and will continue to be on long-term growth, which we believe is attainable only by balancing the interests of all our stakeholders. This way we all grow. Together.

EXHIBIT 3: Harley-Davidson, Inc., Consolidated Balance Sheets

	December 31,	
(in thousands of dollars, except share amounts)	*1997*	*1996*
ASSETS		
Current assets:		
Cash and cash equivalents	$147,462	$142,479
Accounts receivable, net	102,797	141,315
Finance receivables, net	293,329	183,808
Inventories	117,475	101,386
Deferred income taxes	24,941	25,999
Prepaid expenses	18,017	18,142
Total current assets	704,021	613,129
Finance receivable, net	249,346	154,264
Property, plant, and equipment, net	528,869	409,434
Deferred income taxes	3,001	4,691
Goodwill	38,707	40,900
Other assets	74,957	77,567
	1,598,901	1,299,985
LIABILITIES AND SHAREHOLDERS' EQUITY		
Current liabilities:		
Accounts payable	$106,112	$100,699
Accrued and other liabilities	164,938	142,334
Current portion of finance debt	90,638	8,065
Total current liabilities	361,688	251,098
Finance debt	280,000	250,000
Long-term liabilities	62,131	70,366
Postretirement health care benefits	68,414	65,801
COMMITMENTS AND CONTINGENCIES		
Shareholders' equity:		
Series A Junior Participating preferred stock, none issued	—	—
Common stock, 157,241,441, and 156,252,182 shares issued in 1997 and 1996, respectively	1,572	1,562
Additional paid-in capital	187,180	174,371
Retained earnings	683,824	530,782
Cumulative foreign currency translation adjustment	(2,835)	(566)
	869,741	706,149
Less:		
Treasury stock (4,916,488 and 4,914,368 shares in 1997 and 1996, respectively), at cost	(41,959)	(41,933)
Unearned compensation	(1,114)	(1,496)
Total shareholders' equity	826,668	662,720
	$1,598,901	$1,299,985

Source: Harley-Davidson, Inc., *Annual Report* (1997): 50.

Harley continues to invest heavily in research and development and in quality improvement techniques. One payoff is a computer-aided design (CAD) system that allows management to make changes in the entire product line while maintaining elements of the traditional styling. Harley is recognized as an industry leader in many aspects of production, including belt-driven technology, vibration isolation, and steering geometry.

The company is currently in the midst of the largest product development effort in its history. In 1996, it completed construction of a new Product Development Center in Milwaukee. The company developed the new facility to reduce time to market and to increase Harley's competitive advantage. The Product Development Center brings together manufacturing and product engineers, styling teams, purchasing staff, and supplier representatives.

Employee involvement at Harley means the full participation of all employees in the continuous improvement process. Decisions made in quality circles are a major source of input for quality improvement. Employees participate in meetings and have a stake in the success of the company through bonus programs which share Harley's financial rewards and through the Employee Stock Purchase Program. The employee involvement practices at Harley ensure high morale, low absenteeism, and few grievances. The goal is to continue to grow and develop people. In 1996, the company invested more in employee training than in any year in its history.

Harley's purchasing strategy includes working with suppliers that are close to Harley's own facilities. Nearly 80 percent of the company's suppliers are located within 180 miles of Milwaukee. Proximity to suppliers means that Harley can implement its MAN system and just-in-time inventory practices. Plant productivity continued to improve in the 1990s. For example, the York plant produced approximately 160 motorcycles a day in 1987 and 285 a day in 1990, and currently produces over 300 motorcycles a day. The concern for quality is transmitted to dealers as well. Harley mechanics at dealerships are expected to take a series of qualifying examinations dealing with 24 motorcycle repair categories. Exam questions deal with categories such as transmission, suspension, and electronics repair. Mechanics receive factory training and support, and dealers keep their customers apprised of how well the local mechanics are doing.

Harley-Davidson managers recognized the need to improve its ability to meet increasing demand and satisfy their customers. The year 1997 saw continued work on the strategy to increase capacity through expansion and new facilities, and to grow demand through styling, quality, and customer satisfaction. In addition to its new Milwaukee Product Development Center, the company completed a new Parts and Accessories Distribution Center in Milwaukee and broke ground for a new Sportster manufacturing facility in Kansas City (scheduled for completion in 1998). Start-up efforts for the new engine/transmission facility in the Milwaukee area continued in 1996 as well.

HARLEY DIVISIONS

Harley operates in two segments: (1) Motorcycles and Related Products and (2) Financial Services. Harley's Motorcycles and Related Products segment designs, manufactures, and sells super-heavyweight (engine displacement of 851 cc or above) touring and custom motorcycles and a broad range of related products. Harley is currently the only major American motorcycle manufacturer. The company's export bike sales were $457.8 million in 1997, an increase of 8.8 percent over 1996.

Sales and operating profits (losses) attributable to Harley's major business segments are as follows (in thousands of dollars):

Years Ended December 31,	1997	1996	1995	1994
Net sales:				
Motorcycles and Related Products	$1,762,569	$1,531,227	$1,350,466	$1,158,887
Financial Services	n/a	n/a	n/a	n/a
	$1,762,569	$1,531,227	$1,350,466	$1,158,887
Income (loss) from operations:				
Motorcycles and Related Products	$265,486	$228,093	$184,475	$163,510
Financial Services	12,355	7,801	3,620	—
General corporate expenses	(7,838)	(7,448)	(7,299)	(9,948)
	$270,003	$228,446	$180,796	$153,562

Source: Harley-Davidson, Inc., *Annual Report* (1997): 41.

Motorcycles and Related Products and Activities

Motorcycles

Harley's motorcycles emphasize traditional styling, design simplicity, durability, ease of service, and evolutionary change. Studies indicate that the typical Harley motorcycle owner is a male in his mid-forties, with a household income of approximately $68,000, who purchases a motorcycle for recreational rather than transportation purposes, and who is an experienced motorcycle rider. Over two-thirds of Harley's sales are to buyers with at least 1 year of college, and 34 percent have a college degree. About 9 percent of Harley sales are to females.

The super-heavyweight class of motorcycles comprises four types: standard, which emphasizes simplicity and cost; performance, which emphasizes racing and speed; touring, which emphasizes comfort and amenities for long-distance travel; and custom, which emphasizes styling and individual owner preferences. Touring and custom models are the only class of super-heavyweight motorcycle that Harley manufactures. Harley sells 20 models of touring and custom super-heavyweight motorcycles, with suggested 1997 retail prices ranging from $5,200 to $19,300. The touring segment of the super-heavyweight market was pioneered by Harley and includes motorcycles equipped for long-distance touring, with fairings, windshields, saddlebags, and Tour Pak. The custom segment of the market includes motorcycles featuring the distinctive styling associated with certain classic Harley-Davidson motorcycles. These motorcycles are highly customized through the use of trim and accessories. Harley's motorcycles are based on variations of five basic chassis designs and are powered by three air-cooled, twin-cylinder engines of "V" configuration that have displacement of 883 cc; 1,200 cc; and 1,340 cc. Harley manufactures its own engines and frames.

The top of Harley's custom product line typically is priced at approximately twice that of its competitors' custom motorcycles. The custom portion of the Harley product line represents the highest unit volumes and continues to command a price premium because of its features, styling, and high resale value. Harley's smallest displacement custom motorcycle (the 883 cc Sportster) is directly price competitive with comparable motorcycles. Surveys of retail purchasers indicate that, historically, over 80 percent of the purchasers of the Sportster model have owned competitors' motorcycles or are new to the sport of motorcycling.

Motorcycle Products

Harley's Motorcycle Products business consists primarily of parts, accessories, and rider apparel. The major product categories for motorcycle parts are replacement parts, mechanical accessories, rider accessories (Motor Clothes), and specially formulated oil and other lubricants. Harley's replacement parts include original equipment parts, generally made in the United States, and a less expensive line of imported parts introduced to compete against foreign-source aftermarket suppliers. Harley provides a variety of services to its dealers and retail customers, including optional extended-service contracts, insurance programs, service training schools, delivery of its motorcycles, motorcycling vacations, memberships in an owners' club, and customized software packages. Harley has had recent success with its program emphasizing modern store design and display techniques in the merchandising of parts and accessories by its dealers. Currently, more than 370 domestic and 90 international dealerships have completed or are in the process of finishing store design renovation projects. Net sales for parts and accessories were 13.7 percent, 13.7 percent, and 14.2 percent of net sales in the motorcycles segment during 1997, 1996, and 1995, respectively.

Licensing

In recent years, Harley endeavored to create an awareness of the brand among the nonriding public by licensing the trademark "Harley-Davidson" through production and sales of a broad range of consumer items, including T-shirts and other clothing, trading cards, jewelry, small leather goods, and toys. Although the majority of licensing activity occurs in the United States, Harley has expanded into international markets. This licensing activity provides Harley with a valuable source of advertising. Licensing also has proven to be an effective means of enhancing Harley's image with consumers and provides an important tool for policing the unauthorized use of Harley's trademarks. Royalty revenues from licensing were about $24 million, $19 million, and $24 million during 1997, 1996, and 1995, respectively.

Marketing and Distribution

Harley's basic channel of distribution for its motorcycles and related products in the United States is approximately 600 independently owned full-service dealerships. With respect to sales of new motorcycles, approximately 75 percent of the dealerships sell Harley motorcycles exclusively. All dealerships carry Harley's replacement parts and aftermarket accessories and service Harley motorcycles.

Harley divides its marketing efforts among dealer promotions, customer events, magazine and direct mail advertising, public relations, and cooperative programs with dealers. The company also sponsors racing activities and special promotional events, and participates in all major motorcycle consumer shows and rallies. To encourage Harley owners to become more actively involved in the sport of motorcycling, Harley formed a riders club in 1983. The Harley Owners Group (HOG) currently has more than 380,000

EXHIBIT 4: Harley-Davidson, Inc., Revenues and Assets by Geographic Location

	Years ended December 31,		
(in thousands of dollars)	*1997*	*1996*	*1995*
Revenues[a]:			
United States	$1,304,748	$1,110,527	$949,415
Canada	62,717	58,053	48,046
Germany	81,541	82,800	102,638
Japan	90,243	79,401	69,350
Other foreign countries	223,320	200,446	181,017
	1,762,569	1,531,227	1,350,466
Long-lived assets[b]:			
United States	607,363	492,054	353,801
Other foreign countries	7,073	7,508	5,325
	614,436	499,562	359,126

[a]Revenues are attributed to geographic regions based on location of customer.
[b]Long-lived assets include all long-term assets except those specifically excluded under SFAS No. 131 such as deferred income taxes and financial instruments, including finance receivables.
Source: Harley-Davidson, Inc., *Annual Report* (1997): 68.

members worldwide and is the industry's largest company-sponsored enthusiast organization. Harley's expenditures on domestic marketing, selling, and advertising were $85.2 million, $75.4 million, and $71.5 million during 1997, 1996, and 1995, respectively.

International Sales

International sales were $458 million in 1997 and $421 million in 1996. Harley believes that the international heavyweight market (engine displacements of 651 cc and above) is growing and is significantly larger than the U.S. heavyweight market. Harley has wholly owned subsidiaries in Germany, Japan, and the United Kingdom. The German subsidiary also serves Austria and France. The combined foreign subsidiaries have a network of 577 independent dealers in 55 countries, of which approximately 43 percent sell Harley motorcycles exclusively. Japan, Germany, and Canada, in that order, are Harley's largest export markets and account for 51 percent of export sales.

Competition

The United States and international super-heavyweight/heavyweight motorcycle markets are highly competitive. Harley's competitors, Yamaha, Honda, Suzuki, and Kawasaki, have financial and marketing resources greater than Harley's as well as large overall sales volumes and a more diversified product line. Custom and touring motorcycles are generally the most expensive and most profitable vehicles in the market. Resale prices of Harley-Davidson motorcycles, as a percentage of price when new, are significantly higher than resale prices of motorcycles sold by the competitors. The primary reason for this is that production of Harley bikes is more than a year behind demand.

Polaris Industries has expanded its current business by entering the motorcycle market. Their first bike, the "Victory" cruiser motorcycle, is scheduled to be introduced to the public in the spring of 1998. Polaris, the world's largest producer of snowmobiles (annual sales of $826 million), is the first major U.S. competitive threat that Harley faces. Polaris has competed successfully with Honda, Yamaha, Kawasaki, and Suzuki in their current product lines, and has the manufacturing, engineering, and marketing expertise to potentially compete—and excel—in the motorcycle market. As part of its diversification strategy, Polaris will strive to capitalize on its brand name to attract and maintain loyal customers in the motorcycle market.

The "Victory" will be a heavyweight cruiser priced thousands of dollars less than the average Harley. Polaris will use its recreational vehicle experience and marketing expertise to target U.S. motorcycle riders who own Japanese bikes. Polaris's goal is to grow the motorcycle market and capture customers before they move to the super-heavyweight segment.

While Polaris is planning to attack Harley at the low end of the heavyweight market segment, a new company is positioning to attack at the high end. In early 1996, the Excelsior-Henderson Motorcycle Manufacturing Company was reborn. Excelsior motorcycles once held a prestigious place in the U.S. market. Early American heroes such as Henry Ford and Charles Lindbergh rode Excelsiors. The original company did not survive the Great Depression and terminated operations in 1931. Excelsiors were known only to motorcycle enthusiasts until two brothers, Dave and Dan Hanlon of Belle Plaine, Minnesota, decided to resurrect the Excelsior brand name. The Hanlons have taken the company public and received a $7 million low-interest loan from the state of Minnesota to get started. They plan to offer their "Super X" motorcycle to those who are seeking something different. At $17,500, the Super X will cost more than a comparable Harley. The Hanlons claim the Super X will have a better engine, suspension, and better brakes than Harleys, and hope to build 400 Super Xs by the end of 1998.

In addition to these two new competitors, several other U.S. and Japanese companies have entered the foray as well. Honda and the other Japanese companies introduced new Harley look-alike bikes in the early 1990s. BMW announced plans to build a heavyweight cruiser. And several entrepreneurs tried, albeit unsuccessfully, to restart Indian, a defunct U.S. company that stopped making motorcycles in 1953. On top of all this, companies such as American Eagle and Titan were buying Harleys, customizing them, and then selling them at prices in the $27,000 range. Any success by Polaris and the other new companies would steal market share from Harley and might also trigger entry of other firms into the motorcycle industry.

Harley estimates its worldwide competitive position to be as follows:

651+ cc Motorcycles Registration Data (*units in thousands*)

	1997	1996	1995	1994
North America				
Total registrations	205.4	178.5	163.1	150.4
Harley-Davidson registrations	99.3	85.1	77.0	69.5
Harley-Davidson market share percentage	48.3%	47.7%	47.2%	46.2%
Europe				
Total registrations	250.3	224.7	207.2	201.9
Harley-Davidson registrations	15.3	15.3	15.4	14.4
Harley-Davidson market share percentage	6.1%	6.8%	7.4%	7.1%
Asia/Pacific				
Total registrations	58.9	37.4	39.4	39.1
Harley-Davidson registrations	9.7	8.2	7.9	7.6
Harley-Davidson market share percentage	16.5%	21.9%	20.1%	19.4%

Source: Harley-Davidson, Inc., *Annual Report* (1997): 39.

Eaglemark Financial Services

Headquartered in Plano, Texas, Eaglemark was established to provide financing for Harley dealers and owners in the U.S. and Canada. Operating under the name "Harley Credit and Insurance," the company built on the loyalty customers have for the brand name. Eaglemark entered the European market in 1998 in a joint venture with Transamerica Distribution Finance Corporation, to provide financing for Harley's European dealers.

Eaglemark emphasizes fast personal service, competitive terms, and real value to its customers. Services for customers include motorcycle leasing, motorcycle installment loans, credit cards (the Harley Credit Card), insurance (casualty/auto/accident/home/health), and extended service contracts. Services for dealers include inventory floor planning, financing, insurance, and access to a credit card processing network.

Eaglemark aims to provide Harley customers with a complementary set of financial services associated with the Harley name. During 1997, 95 percent of Harley's dealers in the United States and Canada used Eaglemark's services. In 1997, Eaglemark financed 19 percent of new Harleys sold in the United States, up from 17 percent in 1996.

FINANCIAL PERFORMANCE

Harley's financial performance improved steadily from 1988 to 1996. Harley reduced its long-term debt from $168 million in 1988 to $29 million in 1994. Harley reported worldwide net sales of $1.35 billion in 1995 and $1.53 billion in 1996. Net profit for Harley was $184.5 million and $228.1 million in 1995 and 1996, respectively, and profit margins were 13.7 percent and 14.9 percent in the same two years. Worldwide motorcycle demand continues to outpace production, and dealers throughout the world remain on an allocation program that limits the number of motorcycles that can be ordered. Harley expects worldwide demand to continue to outpace production for the next several years.

Harley has held more than 60 percent of the super-heavyweight segment (engine displacement of 851 cc or above) of the domestic motorcycle segment during the past several years. Although definitive market share information does not exist for many of the smaller foreign markets, it is estimated that Harley holds approximately 13 percent of the heavyweight segment (engine displacement of 751 cc or above) of the foreign markets in which it competes. Outside of the United States, super-heavyweight segment data is generally not available.

Total international revenues in the Motorcycles and Related Products segment increased to $458 million during 1997 (over $421 million in 1996 and $401 million in 1995). During 1997, 1996, and 1995, these sales accounted for 26 percent, 27 percent, and 30 percent, respectively, of Harley's motorcycle sales. At year-end 1997, Harley had 305 dealers in 30 European, Middle East, or African countries and 179 dealers in 8 Asian/Pacific countries. Harley had 17 dealers in Latin America.

Harley reported 1997 sales of motorcycle parts and accessories of $241.9 million, a 14.5 percent revenue increase over 1996. Sales of Harley's motor clothes line of rider accessories increased 4.8 percent in 1997 to $42.8 million.

The Motorcycles and Related Products segment reported net income of $265 million in 1997, a 16.4 percent increase over 1996.

The operating income of the Financial Services segment was $12.35 million in 1997, up from $7.8 million in 1996 and $3.6 million in 1995.

Motorcycle production volumes are expected to increase for the next several years. Harley surpassed its goal of producing/shipping 100,000 units in 1995—they actually shipped over 105,000 units. Harley also surpassed its 1996 goal of 115,000 units by shipping over 119,000 units. Output for 1997 was 137,000 units.

THE HARLEY IMAGE

Few motorcycle companies can elicit the name recognition and brand loyalty of Harley-Davidson. Harley's appeal is based on the thrill and prestige of owning and riding the king of big bikes. Harley's are known as sturdy, powerful, macho bikes that are not for wimps or kids, but are true bikes for the open road.

Part of the Harley image is built on an appreciation of tradition. Harley bikes are considered to be of classic design. The teardrop gas tanks, the "soft-tail" suspensions, and the low, uneven rumble of Harley engines are believed to be the substance of fundamental motorcycling. The company has a knack for combining the old and the new. For example, Harley recently offered a bike with a "springer" front-end fork. The spring fork had not been offered on Harley motorcycles since 1949. Harley made major technological improvements in the fork but maintained the original look and offered it on a limited-edition model. The springer fork was made to appeal to someone who wanted traditional style and custom design as well as modern advancements.

A worrisome problem with the Harley image, on the other hand, is the perceived connection between Harleys and "outlaw" groups. The negative image associated with the Road Warrior films affected sales in some areas to such a degree that the company initiated a public relations campaign. The campaign gently attacks the biker image by directing the majority of advertising at young professionals. The message is that Harley-Davidson represents fun, recreation, and reliability. The company trumpets that famous professionals (such as the former baseball star Reggie Jackson) ride Harleys, and advertisements picturing these celebrities atop their "hogs" further help the company's image. The campaign seems to work. More doctors, lawyers, and dentists have begun to purchase Harleys.

A related image problem for Harley is that it cannot attract very many women customers. Harleys are very big and heavy. The Harley low-rider series attracts some women customers because the bikes are lower and easier to get on. Notwithstanding this partial success, some Japanese companies introduced smaller, lighter, low-riding, inexpensive Harley look-alikes in a straightforward attempt to attract women buyers. Honda's Rebel (250 cc) and Yamaha's Route 66 (V-twin, 250 cc) are two such bikes that have become fairly successful with women who participate in the sport of motorcycling.

Perhaps the most objective indicator of the strength of the image came from an unlikely source—Japan itself. The Japanese have made numerous attempts to copy Harley-Davidson's designs. For example, Suzuki went to great lengths to hide the radiator of the Intruder (1,400 cc) because Harleys are air-cooled. Yamaha's Virago (1,100 cc) and Kawasaki's Vulcan (1,500 cc) were V-twin street bikes conspicuously styled in the

EXHIBIT 5: Harley-Davidson, Inc.

	Years ended December 31,		
(in thousands of dollars)	1997	1996	1995
Net sales:			
Motorcycles and Related Products	$1,762,569	$1,531,227	$1,350,466
Financial Services[a]	n/a	n/a	n/a
	$1,762,569	$1,531,227	$1,350,466
Income from operations:			
Motorcycles and Related Products	$265,486	$228,093	$184,475
Financial Services[a]	12,355	7,801	3,620
General corporate expenses	(7,838)	(7,448)	(7,299)
	$270,003	$228,446	$180,796

	Motorcycles and Related Products	Transportation Vehicles[b]	Financial Services[a]	Corporate	Consolidated
1997					
Identifiable assets	$856,779	n/a	$598,514	$143,608	$1,598,901
Depreciation and amortization	66,426	n/a	3,489	263	70,178
Net capital expenditures	183,194	n/a	2,834	143	186,171
1996					
Identifiable assets	$770,271	n/a	$387,666	$142,048	$1,299,985
Depreciation and amortization	51,657	n/a	3,367	258	55,282
Net capital expenditures	176,771	n/a	1,994	6	178,771
1995					
Identifiable assets	$575,118	$111,556	$269,461	$24,535	$980,670
Depreciation and amortization	41,754	n/a	320	255	42,329
Net capital expenditures	112,579	n/a	221	185	112,985

Source: Harley-Davidson, Inc., *Annual Report* (1997): 68.

[a] The results of operations for the majority-owned financial services subsidiary are included as Operating income from financial services in the statements of operations.

[b] The results of operations for the Transportation Vehicles segment are classified as discontinued operations in the statements of operations.

Harley tradition. Nevertheless, some analysts feel that Japanese imitations only serve to strengthen the mystique of the original. The more the Japanese try to make look-alike bikes, the more the real thing increases in value.

Quality Products and Customer Price/Value Perception

Harley motorcycles elicit an emotional response from their makers as well as their owners. One important thing about Harley bikes is that each one is slightly different from another. Even two bikes of the same model year will have some variation, some small difference in the chrome, handlebars, grips, or something that will make it unique to its owner. Therefore, Harleys are in effect "mass-customized." This phenomena creates a great deal of loyalty on the part of owners and makers.

Harley's big bikes are not the lowest-priced bikes on the market but they retain their value. Many bikes even increase in value over time and, in general, demand is greater than supply. Dealers sell the motorcycles years in advance of having them in stock. A $500 to $1,000 deposit is necessary to place an order. And it is rumored that customers sometimes speculate and make money selling their orders to the higher bidders.

Aggressive Marketing

Harley is promoting its motorcycles, accessories, and motor clothes in a more aggressive fashion than in the past. The company's ads are taking on a more humorous and engaging tone. One ad exclaims, "Thank God they don't leak oil anymore!" Another ad, for the new "Cow Glide," states, "It tends to mosey."

The Harley Owners Groups or HOG clubs begun in 1983 and, promoted by the company, are growing by leaps and bounds. The clubs allow owners to get together to have fun. The Stamford, Connecticut, HOG chapter has a home page on the Internet that lists national HOG events including rallies, motorcycle shows, and chapter meetings. HOG membership in 1997 was 380,000 members, and there are 988 chapters in 105 countries.

The company has also upgraded the retail stores, they are nicer than the traditional bike shop, with unique floor design and extended shopping hours. Factory floor workers are sent out to meet with customers on demonstration rides. The demonstration ride promotional program is expensive, but Harley feels that it is a very worthwhile and personal way to stay in touch with the customer. In addition, Harley is marketing a line of toys and plans to become more heavily involved in racing, both in the attempt to appeal to different potential customers of all ages.

Yet, Harley jealously maintains loyalty to its core customer. Ninety-eight percent of Harley motorcycles are sold to men. Bleustein notes that, "we want to reach out to new customers but not lose sight of our roots and where we came from."

STRATEGIC MANAGEMENT—"PLAN 2003"

Harley's strategic-management plan, "Plan 2003," covers growing its motorcycle business, developing its employees, and enhancing its abilities to satisfy loyal customers. The company has the following objectives:

- Establish Harley-Davidson as a leader in employee development and participation.
- Grow and maintain demand for over 200,000 motorcycle units by 2003.
- Continue to provide exceptional styling, performance, quality and reliability, customer service, and affordable prices.
- Meet future demand by expanding existing distribution and manufacturing capacity and adding new production and retail distribution points.
- Improve information services through integration of information technologies—enable all stakeholders to easily do business with Harley.
- Drive financial results to levels comparable with other high-performance companies.

Charles B. Shrader/Fred R. David/Timothy T. Dannels

HARLEY'S FUTURE

Harley is one of only a few firms apologizing to its dealers for not being able to meet demand. Virtually no Harley dealers in the United States or overseas have any retail inventory of Harley bikes. Consumers must get on one- to two-year waiting lists to purchase new Harleys. The company must expand capacity, and the major questions are where, how, and when. Harley plans to reach its 200,000 annual motorcycle output goal in 2003 by expanding production and building new facilities.

1. How should Harley handle the increased pressure of competitive threat? Can Harley continue to survive on image? Do the foreign manufacturers have the ability to dampen Harley's growth in the United States and globally? Does Polaris (or any other domestic firm) have the potential to cut into Harley's market share?

2. Was the sale of Holiday Rambler a sound strategic move for Harley? Discuss the strategic implications of the decision to sell. Is Eaglemark a good "fit" for Harley's long-term strategic goals?

3. How does Harley ensure success in the future? What contingency plans, if any, must it be prepared to implement?

4. Evaluate Harley's current strategic plan and develop/recommend a strategic plan for the future.

Winnebago Industries, Incorporated—1998

John G. Marcis
Fred R. David

www.winnebagoind.com
stock symbol WGO

Saving money is nice, but it is not the real reason people travel in a motor home. Motor homing is just plain fun. Motor homers are an adventurous lot—they like to go, see, and do. Florida residents have replaced Californians as the most active motor home campers. New Yorkers are third on the "most-on-the-go" list. Recreational vehicle (RV) owners say that they not only save money when camping but also can avoid the bother of having to stop for restaurants and bathrooms.

Motor home traveling is purported to be much less expensive than traveling by car or plane and staying in motels. Motor homers stop when there is something to see and do. They often spend summers where it is cool and winters where it is warm. In fact, industry advertisements tout the RV life-style with the slogan, "Wherever you go, you're always at home."

Winnebago Industries, Incorporated, is a leading manufacturer of motor homes. Company revenues for 1997 dropped to $436 million from $483 million the prior year. The company uses state-of-art computer-aided design and manufacturing systems on automotive-styled assembly lines. Although Winnebago competes with Fleetwood and Coachmen, the name *Winnebago* is considered synonymous with the term *motor home*.

Winnebago was founded in 1958 and has always been headquartered in Forest City, Iowa (515-582-3535). The company's common stock is listed on the New York, Chicago, and Pacific Stock Exchanges. Options for Winnebago's common stock are traded on the Chicago Board Options Exchange. Corporate press releases are available at www.prnewswire.com/cnoc/exec/menu/105967.

Winnebago Industries is a financially stable company. The firm owns its land, buildings, and equipment, and has no long-term debt. The firm has an enviable cash balance, which provides the company with the opportunity for future growth. The company is devoted to focusing resources on building RVs, increasing its share of the RV market, and enhancing profitability.

Early Motor Homing

The first motor home was built in 1915 to take people from the Atlantic Coast to San Francisco. It had wooden wheels and hard rubber tires. It was promoted as having all the comforts of an ocean cruiser. By the 1920s, the house car had become a fixture in the United States

This case was prepared by Professors John G. Marcis and Fred R. David of Francis Marion University as a basis for class discussion. It is not intended to illustrate either effective or ineffective handling of an administrative situation. Copyright © 1999 by Prentice Hall, Inc. ISBN 0-13-011166-X.

and a symbol of freedom. All kinds of house cars could be seen traveling across America's dirt roads. They ranged from what looked like large moving cigars to two-story houses with porches on wheels. But these house cars featured poor weight distribution, poor insulation, and poor economy. From the 1930s to the 1950s, they gave way in popularity to the trailer.

In the mid-1950s, motor homes were called motorized trailers. They were over-weight, underpowered, and poorly insulated, but still a vast improvement over the house cars of the 1920s. In the 1960s, motor homing became much more popular, largely as a result of the innovations of Winnebago. From Forest City, Iowa, where the company was founded in 1958, Winnebago set the pace for new development of motor homes. The Winnebago name became a household word. Buyers of motor homes were asked, "When will your Winnebago be delivered?"

INTERNAL ENVIRONMENT

Corporate Mission Statement

Winnebago's motto is "Quality Is a Journey—Not a Destination." From the beginning, the company recognized the critical roles played by employees, customers, and dealers in the total quality process. The significance of quality to the firm is evidenced by its mission statement, statement of values, and its statement of guiding principles (see Exhibit 1).

Production Facilities

Winnebago has major production facilities in Forest City, Iowa. These facilities take up over 1.4 million square feet and contain the company's manufacturing, maintenance, product testing, and service operations. The company also has 698,000 square feet of warehouse and executive office space in Forest City. Winnebago leases one manufacturing facility and one storage facility (74,000 square feet and 10,000 square feet, respectively) in Hampton, Iowa; a manufacturing facility (17,200 square feet) in Lorimor, Iowa; and a manufacturing facility (40,000 square feet) in Garner, Iowa, which is sub-leased to Northern Iowa Electronics (NIE). All Forest City facilities are located on approximately 784 acres of land owned by Winnebago.

Winnebago has four 1,000-foot assembly lines for producing motor homes. Winnebago's statistical process control has enhanced the quality of its van products. As a motor home flows down the assembly line, quality control is carefully monitored. Units are taken randomly from the line for a thorough examination. The performance of every RV is tested before it is delivered to a dealer's lot. The company makes sure that all of its motor home components meet or exceed federal and durability standards. Some of the tests routinely performed include lamination strength, appliance performance, chip resistance, vibration, drop, salt spray, and crash tests.

Research and Development

Winnebago uses computer technology to design its motor homes. The company has a state-of-the-art computer-aided design/computer-aided manufacturing (CAD/CAM) system. This system aids in producing low-cost sheet metal parts, new paint lines for steel and aluminum parts, and modifications of assembly equipment.

EXHIBIT 1: Winnebago Industries, Inc., Mission Statement

Winnebago Industries, Inc., is a leading international manufacturer of recreation vehicles (RVs) and related products and services. Our mission is to continually improve our products and services to meet or exceed the expectations of our customers. We emphasize employee teamwork and involvement in identifying and implementing programs to save time and lower production costs while maintaining the highest quality values. These strategies allow us to prosper as a business with a high degree of integrity and to provide a reasonable return for our shareholders, the ultimate owners of our business.

VALUES

How we accomplish our mission is as important as the mission itself. Fundamental to the success of the Company are these basic values we describe as the four P's:

People—Our employees are the source of our vast strength. They provide our corporate intelligence and determine our reputation and vitality. Involvement and teamwork are our core human values.

Products—Our products are the end result of our teamwork's combined efforts, and they should be the best in meeting or exceeding our customers' expectations worldwide. As our products are viewed, so are we viewed.

Plant—Our facilities are the most technologically advanced in the RV industry. We continue to review facility improvements that will increase the utilization of our plant capacity and enable us to build the best quality product for the investment.

Profitability—Profitability is the ultimate measure of how efficiently we provide our customers with the best products for their needs. Profitability is required to survive and grow. As our respect and position within the marketplace grows, so will our profit.

GUIDING PRINCIPLES

Quality comes first—To achieve customer satisfaction, the quality of our products and services must be our number-one priority.

Customers are central to our existence—Our work must be done with our customers in mind, providing products and services that meet or exceed the expectations of our customers. We must not only satisfy our customers, we must also surprise and delight them.

Continuous improvement is essential to our success—We must strive for excellence in everything we do: in our products, in their safety and value, as well as in our services, our human relations, our competitiveness, and our profitability.

Employee involvement is our way of life—We are a team. We must treat each other with trust and respect.

Dealers and suppliers are our partners—The Company must maintain mutually beneficial relationships with dealers, suppliers, and our other business associates.

Integrity is never compromised—The Company must pursue conduct worldwide in a manner that is socially responsible and that commands respect for its integrity and for its positive contributions to society. Our doors are open to all men and women alike without discrimination and without regard to ethnic origin or personal beliefs.

Source: Winnebago Industries, Inc., *Annual Report* (1997).

EXHIBIT 2: Winnebago Industries, Inc., Net Revenues by Major Product Class

(in thousands of dollars)	Fiscal year ended[a]				
	August 30, 1997	August 31, 1996	August 26, 1995	August 27, 1994	August 28, 1993
Motor homes (Class A & C)	381,191	432,212	402,435	385,319	326,861
Other recreation vehicle revenues[b]	19,771	17,166	19,513	21,903	17,655
Other manufactured products revenues[c]	35,750	34,020	36,961	25,184	20,344
Total manufactured products revenues	436,712	483,398	458,909	432,406	364,860
Finance revenues[d]	1,420	1,406	1,220	831	595
Total net revenues	438,132	484,804	460,129	433,237	365,455

[a]The fiscal year ended August 31, 1996, contained 53 weeks; all other fiscal years in the table contained 52 weeks. All years are appropriately restated to exclude the Company's discontinued Cycle-Sat subsidiary's revenues from satellite courier and tape duplication services and discontinued NIE subsidiary's revenues from contract assembly of a variety of electronic products.
[b]Primarily EuroVan Campers, recreation vehicle–related parts, recreation vehicle service revenue, and van conversions.
[c]Primarily sales of extruded aluminum, commercial vehicles, and component products for other manufacturers.
[d]WAC revenues from dealer financing.

Source: www.freeedgar.com

Winnebago's 40,000-square-foot product testing facility houses some of the most sophisticated technology used in the RV industry, such as a high- and low-temperature chamber for subjecting parts to extreme temperatures and high stress.

Product Line

In the second quarter of 1997, the board of directors elected Ronald D. Buckmeier as vice-president of product development. The product development team implemented a process to develop new products and maximize production efficiencies. The new system involves a cross-functional approach for the design and manufacture of RVs and streamlines the production process. Intensive product development allowed Winnebago Industries to bring to the 1998 market the most extensive new product lineup in the firm's history (see Exhibit 2).

Winnebago manufactures three kinds of recreational vehicles: the Class A Motor Home, Class B Van Camper, and Class C Motor Home.

Class A motor homes are constructed on a chassis that already has the engine and drive components. They range in length from 23 to 37 feet and in price from $32,000 to over $219,000. Class A motor homes traditionally include the Winnebago Adventurer, Winnebago Brave, and Winnebago Warrior; the Itasca Suncruiser and Itasca Sunrise; the Vectra and Vectra Grand Tour; and the Luxor. In 1998, the Minnie With Body Slide-out and the Sunflower were introduced to the Winnebago line. The Winnebago Brave and Itasca Sunrise models are the company's top-selling vehicles, although the Winnebago Adventurer and Itasca Suncruiser are popular. Sales of Winnebago's Class A motor homes have decreased for three consecutive years (see Exhibit 3). Unit sales of these motor homes were 6,820 (in 1994); 5,993 (in 1995); 5,893 (in 1996); and 4,834 (in 1997). Significant product development in 1997 led to wide-body construction and slideout floor plans on over one-half of the 1998 models.

EXHIBIT 3:   Winnebago Industries, Inc., Unit Sales of Recreation Vehicles

Year Ended	August 30, 1997	August 31, 1996	August 26, 1995	August 27, 1994	August 28, 1993
Class A	4,834	5,893	5,993	6,820	6,095
Class C	2,724	2,857	2,853	1,862	1,988
Total Motor Homes	7,558	8,750	8,846	8,682	8,093
Class B Conversions	1,205	857	1,014	376	0

Note: The fiscal year ended August 31, 1996 contained 53 weeks; all other fiscal years in the table contained 52 weeks.
Source: www.freeedgar.com

Winnebago's Class B Van Campers actually are conventional vans manufactured by Ford, General Motors, and Chrysler that are custom-tailored by Winnebago with special interiors, exteriors, windows, and vents. In many American households, van campers are replacing the family car as the vehicle of choice. These vehicles can turn a long family trip from an ordeal into a pleasant adventure. Winnebago manufactures the EuroVan Camper conversion for Volkswagen of America and Volkswagen of Canada. Class B Van Campers are 17 feet in length. Unit sales decreased from 1,014 in 1995 to 857 in 1996, and then rebounded to 1,205 in 1997.

Class C motor homes are constructed on a van chassis; the driver's compartment is accessible to the living area. These motor homes are compact and easy to drive. They range from 21 to 29 feet in length and have five popular floor plans. Typical options of a Class C vehicle include 6 feet of head room, shower, stove, sink, refrigerator, and two double beds. Winnebago's Minnie Winnie vehicle is the most popular Class C motor home in the country. The company's Itasca Sundancer and Itasca Spirit also are popular. Sales of Winnebago's Class C motor homes declined in 1997 to 2,724 vehicles from 2,857 in 1996.

Marketing

Consumer research reveals that demographics for motor home buyers are undergoing changes. Traditionally, buyers are "woofies" ("well-off older folks," defined as people over 50 years of age with discretionary income available) with time to enjoy leisure travel and outdoor recreation. Since 1990, more baby boomers, aged 37 to 51 as of 1997, have been purchasing vehicles for weekend and vacation travel.

The peak selling season for RVs historically is spring and summer. Class A and Class C motor homes are marketed under the Winnebago and Itasca brand names and are sold through a network of approximately 360 dealers. Most of the dealers are in the United States and a few are in Canada and other foreign countries. Ten dealers account for more than 25 percent of Winnebago's motor home sales, and one dealer accounts for 7.2 percent of motor home sales. Most Winnebago dealers also are dealers for automobiles and other motor home lines, but all dealers must provide complete service for Winnebago RVs. Sales agreements with dealers are renewed on an annual or biannual basis.

Winnebago has 29 field sales and service personnel to aid its dealers. The company promotes its products through advertisements in national RV magazines, cable television, radio, newspapers, and trade shows. A substantial portion of Winnebago's sales of RVs to dealers is made on cash terms. Most dealers are financed on a "floor plan" basis under which a bank or finance company lends the dealer all of the purchase price, collateralized by a lien, or title to, the merchandise purchased. Winnebago, on request of the lending institution, will execute a repurchase agreement. These agreements provide that in the event of dealer default, Winnebago will repurchase the financed merchandise.

Numerous Winnebago caravans are arranged each year to travel across the United States, Mexico, and Canada. With over 60,000 members since 1972, the Winnebago International Travelers' Club is one of the world's largest motor home associations. Members organize national, state, and local Winnebago rallies; have a monthly newspaper; and offer discounts at KOA campsites nationwide.

Service

Winnebago Industries believes it has the most comprehensive service program in the RV industry. This provides the firm with a critical market advantage when selling its motor homes. With the purchase of any new Class A or Class C motor home (except the Rialta), Winnebago offers a comprehensive one-year / 15,000-mile warranty on sidewalls and slideout room assemblies, and a ten-year fiberglass roof warranty. Winnebago offers a two-year / 24,000-mile warranty on the Rialta, its front wheel drive Class C motor home. Winnebago also instituted a toll-free hotline to respond to inquiries from prospective customers and to expedite and resolve warranty issues. Every owner of a new Winnebago motor home receives free roadside assistance for 12 months.

The Winnebago Logo and Licensing

Eighty percent of American adults recognize the Winnebago name. Nine licensees currently pay royalties to Winnebago for using the company's name on products ranging from camping equipment to clothing. Presently, more than 2,000 retail outlets carry one or more products bearing the Winnebago logo.

Although licensing of the Winnebago name began in 1982, revenues to date have not been significant. There are now Winnebago bass and fishing boats, marine flotation devices, backpacks, sports bags, travel bags, slacks, shorts, shirts, vests, jackets, gloves, socks, hats, stoves, lanterns, grills, sleeping bags, air mattresses, tents, screenhouses, and suitcases. Winnebago's Scout one sleeping bag, Chieftain IV tent, Double Diamond air mattress, and other products have been advertised in many magazines. Winnebago has a series of recreational vehicle trading cards.

A separate owners' club also has been created for race enthusiasts. Winnebago and the National Association for Stock Car Auto Racing (NASCAR) have an agreement that makes Winnebago "The Official Motor Home of NASCAR," and Winnebago is the official motor home of the Texas Motor Speedway and the Phoenix International Raceway.

WINNEBAGO: 1958 THROUGH 1997

Winnebago's phenomenal growth during the 1960s came to an end in 1970. That year was marked by a recession, and Winnebago's stock plunged nearly 60 percent before recovering. The OPEC oil embargoes of 1973 and 1974 had disastrous effects on Winnebago because gas either was unavailable or became unaffordable to many families. The company's net income averaged less than 1 percent of sales between 1973 and 1978. From a level of $229 million in 1978, Winnebago's sales dropped to $92 million in 1979.

A troubled board of directors called John Hanson, founder of the company, out of retirement in March 1979, and reelected him chair of the board and president of Winnebago. To resolve Winnebago's problems, Hanson reduced the number of employees from 4,000 to 800 in less than 9 months. He initiated the development of a propane conversion system for motor homes. This system allows users to power their vehicles with less costly propane, which eliminates worries about the supply and cost of gasoline. Hanson also pioneered the development of a lightweight, fuel-efficient motor home powered by a revolutionary heavy-duty diesel engine.

In 1992, Winnebago's sales increased 32 percent, but net income was a negative $10.6 million. Several new products were introduced, including the new bus-styled Vectra. The company created a new subsidiary in 1992, Winnebago Industries Europe, headquartered in Cologne, Germany, to expand operations internationally.

In June 1996, Hanson died at the age of 83. Fred G. Dohrmann, the company's CEO, added the title of chair. Dohrmann had guided Winnebago through an industry-wide slump in the late 1980s and early 1990s.

In a series of strategic moves, Winnebago refocused its core business operation by divesting itself of business and corporate assets that were not directly related to domestic production, sales, and financing of RVs.

In August 1996, the board of directors decided to sell Cycle-Sat, Incorporated, a telecommunications service firm that uses satellite, fiber-optic, and digital technologies. (As a result of this sale, Winnebago recorded a net gain of almost $16.5 million during the first quarter of 1997.) During the fourth quarter of fiscal 1996, the board of directors voted to discontinue financial support of the buyer of its former North Iowa Electronics business.

Fiscal year 1996 was a record year for revenues and the fourth consecutive year of improved operating performance for the company. Revenues from manufactured products increased about 5 percent from the previous year, although net income decreased by more than one-half ($27,756,000 to $12,385,000). Net income per share decreased from $1.10 to $0.49 (see Exhibit 4).

In August 1997, the board of directors approved the sale of its European division, Winnebago Industries Europe, as well as Outdoor America, a mall in Temple, Texas. As a result of these transactions, Winnebago recorded a tax credit of approximately $3.7 million in the fourth quarter of 1997.

Operating results for fiscal 1997 were adversely impacted by soft market conditions for motor homes in the last half of the year. Winnebago therefore increased its promotional program to stimulate wholesale and retail activity.

Revenues for fiscal 1997 were $438.1 million, compared to revenues of $484.8 million for the previous fiscal year. Net income for fiscal 1997 was $23 million, or $0.91 per share, compared to almost $12.4 million, or $0.49 per share, for the previous year. For other financial information, see Exhibit 5.

In December 1997, Dohrmann, a 23-year employee of the firm, announced his plans to retire in April 1998.

The board of directors elected Bruce D. Hertzke to the position of chair and CEO upon Dohrmann's retirement. Hertzke had joined Winnebago in 1971 as an hourly production employee and worked in various production and engineering supervisory positions since then.

EXHIBIT 4: Winnebago Industries, Inc., Consolidated Statements of Operations

	Year Ended		
(in thousands of dollars, except per share data)	August 30, 1997	August 31, 1996	August 26, 1995
Continuing Operations			
Revenues			
Manufactured products	436,712	483,398	458,909
Finance	1,420	1,406	1,220
Total net revenues	438,132	484,804	460,129
Costs and expenses			
Cost of manufactured products	385,540	417,231	397,870
Selling and delivery	27,131	25,290	25,416
General and administrative	20,313	21,574	18,951
Total costs and expenses	432,984	464,095	442,237
Operating income	5,148	20,709	17,892
Financial income	1,844	354	2,114
Income from continuing operations before income taxes	6,992	21,063	20,006
Provision (credit) for taxes	416	6,639	(7,912)
Income from continuing operations	6,576	14,424	27,918
Discontinued operations			
Income (loss) from operations of discontinued Cycle-Sat subsidiary (less applicable income tax provisions and (credits) of $261, and $88, respectively)	0	593	(162)
Gain on sale of Cycle-Sat subsidiary (less applicable income tax provision of $13,339)	16,472	0	0
Loss from the disposal of discontinued operations (less applicable income tax credits of $1,157)	0	(2,632)	0
Net income	23,048	12,385	27,756
Income (loss) per share:			
Income from continuing operations	.26	.57	1.11
Discontinued operations	.65	(.08)	(.01)
Net income	$.91	$.49	$1.10
Weighted average number of shares of stock (in thousands)	25,435	25,349	25,286

Source: www.freeedgar.com

EXHIBIT 5: Winnebago Industries, Inc., Balance Sheet

	Fiscal Year Ended	
(in thousands of dollars)	August 30, 1997	August 31, 1996
Assets		
Current assets		
Cash and cash equivalents	32,130	797
Marketable securities	0	4,316
Receivables, less allowance for doubtful accounts ($1,429 and $702 respectively)	31,322	30,029
Dealer financing receivables, less allowance for doubtful accounts ($155 and $197, respectively)	13,336	11,491
		continued

EXHIBIT 5: *continued*

(in thousands of dollars)	Fiscal Year Ended	
	August 30, 1997	August 31, 1996
Inventories	53,584	63,103
Prepaid expenses	5,872	3,253
Deferred income taxes	4,917	6,343
Current assets of discontinued operations	0	7,285
Total current assets	141,161	126,617
Property and equipment, at cost		
Land	1,167	1,501
Buildings	42,455	43,952
Machinery and equipment	66,142	67,456
Transportation equipment	5,004	7,878
	114,768	120,787
Less accumulated depreciation	81,175	80,858
Total property and equipment, net	33,593	39,929
Long-term notes receivable, less allowances ($1,465 and $797, respectively)	5,692	3,918
Investment in life insurance	17,641	16,821
Deferred income taxes, net	14,900	14,548
Other assets	488	3,906
Long-term assets of discontinued operations	0	14,857
Total assets	213,475	220,596
Liabilities and Stockholders' Equity		
Current liabilities		
Current maturities of long-term debt	695	1,866
Accounts payable trade	20,471	20,232
Current liabilities of discontinued operations	0	17,532
Provision for loss on disposal of electronic component assembly segment	0	4,074
Accrued expenses		
Insurance	2,687	2,947
Product warranties	3,329	3,489
Vacation liability	3,012	3,116
Promotional	2,508	2,193
Other	8,524	9,013
Total current liabilities	41,226	64,462
Long-term debt	0	1,692
Postretirement health care and deferred compensation benefits	48,367	46,937
Minority interest in discontinued operations	0	2,194
Contingent liabilities and commitments		
Stockholders' Equity		
Capital stock common, par value $.50; authorized 60,000,000 shares	12,927	12,920
Additional paid-in capital	23,109	23,723
Reinvested earnings	92,179	74,221
	128,215	110,864
Less treasury stock, at cost	4,333	5,553
Total stockholders' equity	123,882	105,311
Total liabilities and stockholders' equity	213,475	220,596

Source: www.freeedgar.com

289

EXTERNAL ENVIRONMENT

Winnebago's motor homes can attract a low-frills buyer desiring the most stripped-down RV, the person with expensive tastes desiring the ultimate in RV luxury, and everyone in between. RVs can be purchased or rented. Many families unable to buy a mobile home rent one to take on vacation. As the baby boomers age and approach retirement, many of them will consider selling their primary residence, purchasing and moving into a motor home, and traveling to any point they desire in North America. It is estimated that from now until 2005, an average of 4,400 Americans a day will turn 50.

The motel and hotel industries have been experiencing an oversupply of available rooms, which has resulted in low room rates. Compared to the cost of owning/renting and operating an RV, the costs of staying in a motor home versus a motel are about the same if not a bit lower in favor of the motel. Motor home sales historically increase whenever travel, tourism, and vacationing gain in popularity. The converse is also true.

Lower fuel prices; low interest and inflation rates; and a robust, fully employed economy spur motor home sales. However, Winnebago did not prosper during the favorable economic conditions in 1997.

There are about 122,000 campsites in U.S. state parks, including 4,500 maintained by the U.S. Forest Service and 100 in the National Parks System. In addition, there are more than 15,000 private campgrounds and over 1,620 county parks. Winnebagos can access nearly all of these sites.

COMPETITORS

Twelve firms account for 80 percent of the RV industry's volume. Among the largest publicly held are Fleetwood Enterprises, Winnebago Industries, Coachmen Industries, Rexhall Industries, Mallard Coach, Kit Manufacturing, Harley-Davidson, and Skyline Corporation. Of all the competitors, Fleetwood Enterprises is first in sales, followed by Coachmen and then Winnebago. The following is a list of major motor home competitors:

Company	Headquarters Location
Fleetwood Enterprises, Inc.	Riverside, CA
Coachmen Industries, Inc.	Elkhart, IN
Mark III Industries, Inc.	Ocala, FL
Jayco, Inc.	Middlebury, IN
Glaval Corp.	Elkhart, IN
Newmar Corp.	Nappanee, IN
Monaco Coach Corp.	Junction City, OR
Tiffin Motor Homes, Inc.	Red Bay, AL

Fleetwood

Fleetwood Enterprises is the nation's largest producer of both RVs and manufactured housing. It holds 30 percent of the RV market. The RV line includes conventional Class A motor homes, chopped-van Class C motor homes, travel trailers, fifth-wheel travel trailers, folding camping trailers, and truck campers. Motor homes represent 62 percent of Fleetwood's sales and mobile home sales account for 38 percent of revenues.

Fleetwood's folding campers sell under the name Coleman (the famous brand that Fleetwood acquired in 1989); motor homes sell under the names Pace Arrow, Southwind, Cambria, Limited, Flair, Jamboree, and Tioga; and travel trailers sell as Avion, Prowler, Terry, and Wilderness brands. For Fleetwood, the payoff is more presence and enhanced sales.

Fleetwood recently acquired a Germany-based luxury motor home manufacturer named Nielsmen and Bischoff. This acquisition paves the way for expanded distribution of Fleetwood recreational vehicles in Europe. Fleetwood is adding 20 percent more production capacity to its base of 27 plants in order to meet rising demand in both its motor homes and mobile homes.

THE FUTURE

How does the opening of markets in Eastern Europe and the countries that belonged to the former Soviet Union affect Winnebago? Are these the types of markets in which Winnebago should invest some of its limited capital? What emphasis should the firm place on international operation in the future?

(in thousands of dollars)	Recreation Vehicles and Other Manufactured Products	Financing	General Corporate	Total
1997				
Net revenues from continuing operations	436,712	1,420	0	438,132
Operating income (loss) from continuing operations	6,976	736	(2,564)	5,148
Identifiable assets	136,810	16,912	59,753	213,475
Depreciation and amortization	5,797	9	662	6,468
Capital expenditures	3,982	35	421	4,438

Summary information for WIE is as follows: Net revenues—$9,655. Operating loss—$(6,375). The Company sold WIE during August 1997. As a result of the sale, the Company recorded a capital loss for tax purposes resulting in a tax credit of approximately $3,700,000 due to this loss. These amounts are included in the Recreation Vehicles and Other Manufactured Products segment above.

	Recreation Vehicles and Other Manufactured Products	Financing	General Corporate	Total
1996				
Net revenues from continuing operations	483,398	1,406	0	484,804
Operating income (loss) from continuing operations	23,169	1,518	(3,978)	20,709
Identifiable assets	154,238	15,250	51,108	220,596
Depreciation and amortization	5,790	7	3,903	9,700
Capital expenditures	6,754	0	3,709	10,463

Summary information for WIE is as follows: Net revenues—$13,773. Operating loss—$(238). Identifiable assets—$10,388. These amounts are included in the Recreation Vehicles and Other Manufactured Products segment above.

continued

John G. Marcis/Fred R. David

continued

(in thousands of dollars)	Recreation Vehicles and Other Manufactured Products	Financing	General Corporate	Total
1995				
Net revenues from continuing operations	458,909	1,220	0	460,129
Operating income (loss) from continuing operations	19,053	989	(2,150)	17,892
Identifiable assets	135,036	12,690	63,904	211,630
Depreciation and amortization	5,292	12	3,559	8,863
Capital expenditures	7,977	16	1,355	9,348

Summary information for WIE is as follows: Net revenues—$8,834. Operating loss—$(1,209). Identifiable assets—$9,426. These amounts are included in the Recreation Vehicles and Other Manufactured Products segment above.

Source: www.freeedgar.com

Personal Care Products—Industry Note

Faced with a mature domestic market, U.S. personal products manufacturers long have looked to international markets to expand their operations. The currency fluctuations inherent in this strategy always have been viewed as a normal part of doing business. And overall, the fluctuations balance out, as a weak currency in one market typically has been offset by a strong one in another.

Over the past 2 years, however, the unprecedented strength of the U.S. dollar has resulted in an unusual cycle in which many currencies, including the Japanese yen and the German mark, have fallen against the dollar. For companies with a broad global presence, this situation has the potential to wipe out foreign earnings gains when they are translated back into U.S. dollars. Moreover, the ongoing economic slump in Japan and recent currency devaluations in Southeast Asia are likely to put a crimp in the consumer multinationals' ambitious growth plans for the near future.

ASIAN FLU INFECTS WORLD MARKETS

On July 2, 1997, Thailand announced that it would no longer peg its currency, the baht, to the U.S. dollar. One by one, other Southeast Asian countries—including Malaysia, Indonesia, Singapore, the Philippines, and South Korea—followed suit. The actions toppled currencies and stock markets across the region and led to fears of decelerating growth rates or even economic collapse. The troubles reached a peak in late October 1997 when the Hong Kong market, faced with similar currency pressures, tumbled by nearly a third.

Prior to this turmoil, the region's economic growth rate was running at about twice that of the rest of the world. For all its rapid growth over the past decade, however, the region's total gross domestic product (GDP) is estimated at only some $800 billion. Although these economies are far smaller than those of Japan or Western Europe, consumer products companies have viewed them as a vital stepping stone to reaching the world's most populous continent and countries such as India and China.

For the near term, weak economic conditions in Southeast Asia are likely to restrict sales of household nondurable products because consumers will tend to pull back from expensive imported products. Furthermore, weaker local currencies mean that a U.S. company must either raise prices in local currencies to cover dollar costs, which makes

Source: Adapted from *Industry Surveys* by permission of Standard & Poor's, a division of the McGraw-Hill Companies. Standard & Poor's, "Household Nondurables," *Industry Surveys* (25 December 1997): 1–7.

them less competitive and further hurts sales growth, or eat the loss from currency translations when converting those sales back into dollars.

Obviously, the higher the percentage of sales a company derives from Asia, the more it will feel the pinch. Companies such as Gillette, Unilever, and Procter & Gamble Co., which derive a large portion of their sales from these markets, are likely to feel a heavier impact.

Latin America not immune

The meltdown in Asian stocks is likely to have repercussions on the world's other major emerging growth arena: Latin America. On October 30, 1997, Brazil moved to increase its interest rates sharply in order to fend off currency speculators who believe Brazil's currency, the real, is overvalued. The impact of higher local interest rates and a hike in the external cost of capital is expected to dampen economic activity in Latin America's largest economy. This turmoil is also likely to have a spillover effect on Brazil's main trading partner, Argentina, which has also seen upward spikes in interest rates in recent weeks.

This is bad news for consumer products companies that increasingly have come to depend on Latin America as a source of dynamic growth. In recent years, U.S. exports to Latin America have been growing at twice the rate of any other region in the world.

Regions' underlying growth should resurface

In the near term, recapitalizing these regions' financial systems likely will result in higher taxes, tighter money, and slower growth. Yet Standard & Poor's believes that the long-term macroeconomic outlook in Latin America and Asia continues to be positive. Economic reforms, corporate restructurings, high population growth, and favorable demographics should continue to spur strong economic growth in both regions for some time to come.

In addition, there is a silver lining for some of the larger consumer companies. Companies that buy goods assembled in Southeast Asia or have a manufacturing plant in the region will pay lower prices for raw materials and overhead as a result of the devaluation. Avon and Colgate, for instance, both operate manufacturing plants in the region, which will help cushion the blow on the revenue side.

Foreign Sales of Major Household and Personal Goods Companies 1994–1996

	1996		1995		1994	
Company	Foreign Sales (in millions of dollars)	Percentage of Total Sales	Foreign Sales (in millions of dollars)	Percentage of Total Sales	Foreign Sales (in millions of dollars)	Percentage of Total Sales
Alberto-Culver	442	28	361	27	297	24
Avon	3,142	65	2,907	65	2,731	64
Clorox	303	14	181	9	NA	NA
Colgate-Palmolive	2,738	31	2,474	30	2,400	32
Gillette	3,588	37	2,650	30	2,539	32
Procter & Gamble	18,151	51	17,249	52	15,221	50
Unilever	41,164	79	40,303	81	36,301	80

NA: Not available.
Source: Annual reports.

MASSIVE COST CUTTING BOOSTS INDUSTRY PROFITS

Back in the United States, household nondurables companies are faced with a very competitive marketplace that offers little room for price increases. Factors such as increasingly discerning consumers, competition from private label products, pricing pressures from megaretailers, and slowly rising raw material prices are forcing household and personal products manufacturers to hold down their costs in order to sustain profit margins. In recent years, leading companies have embarked on huge restructuring programs aimed at streamlining manufacturing processes and consolidating overhead, while still retaining the resources needed to create new products and to expand in the world's growth areas. Some of the more substantial programs are described below.

Avon announces makeover

In October 1997, Avon Products, Inc., announced a restructuring program that will touch virtually every aspect of its business. As part of its major overhaul, the company will attack inefficiencies in the supply chain for a smoother order and merchandise flow between its many divisions and offices, upgrade systems to allow sharing of information, reduce the number of products it carries by about 30 percent, and reposition its global brands.

By 2000, the company hopes to save approximately $400 million in costs, of which $200 million will be reinvested into advertising and promotions to support new and existing global brands. Avon's goal is to improve gross margins by one point annually beginning in 1998, increase sales by 8 percent to 10 percent a year, and raise earnings by 16 percent to 18 percent a year.

Brand globalization

As part of their global strategy, manufacturers have been emphasizing the development of "universal" brands, formulas, and packaging. This strategy usually reduces both manufacturing costs and the amount of capital that companies need to tie up in multiple kinds of inventory.

Brand globalization can take several forms. In many cases, companies simply take products that have large shares in existing markets and introduce them in new ones. Although consumer needs may vary from one country to another, the way a company understands and meets those needs can be more or less consistent across national boundaries. That's why companies can reapply technologies, advertising ideas, and consumer insights to various geographical areas.

A well-known company's world leadership and brand reputation can offer a distinct advantage when it attempts to move core brands into new countries. These companies also are able to transfer a successful new product launch from one country into another. Colgate's baking soda toothpaste, for example, was so successful in the United States that the company introduced it in 44 other countries.

The main goal is to have global brands that are uniformly strong in the various regions in which they are sold. Although Avon has sold its products in international markets for more than 40 years, only recently has it been developing a stable of "global brands" with a consistent concept and image that will appeal to customers around the world.

Having global brands also enables a manufacturer to save money by having "focused factories," that is, one factory that produces a particular product and ships it throughout its entire worldwide distribution system.

Sales and Profit Growth of Major Household and Personal Goods Companies, 1994–1996

Company	Net Sales (in millions of dollars)			Operating Profit (in millions of dollars)		
	1996	1995	1994	1996	1995	1994
Alberto-Culver	1,590.4	1,358.2	1,216.1	122.1	104.5	88.0
Avon	4,814.2	4,492.1	4,266.5	510.4	465.0	433.8
Clorox	2,217.8	1,984.2	1,836.9	416.0	370.4	337.9
Colgate-Palmolive	8,749.0	8,358.2	7,587.9	954.6	824.0	879.9
Dial	1,406.4	1,365.2	1,511.4	70.4	–23.7	160.0
Gillette	9,697.7	8,834.5	7,935.1	1,525.0	1,700.0	1,458.0
Procter & Gamble	35,284.0	33,482.0	30,385.0	4,022.0	3,307.0	294.0
Unilever	52,069.9	49,640.6	45,396.6	4,464.7	3,979.2	3,864.1

Source: Company reports.

STRONG PROFIT GAINS IN 1997—DESPITE ANEMIC SALES

During the first 9 months of 1997, net profits for the household products group rose about 13 percent to 15 percent, year to year, favorably influenced by volume growth, cost-cutting programs, and productivity gains. The most notable negative influence on industry profitability came from the effect of the strong dollar on international currency translations. Pockets of economic weakness, particularly in Japan and Brazil, masked strong gains elsewhere and tempered overall growth.

Underneath the strong profit gains, however, was a relatively weak sales environment. For manufacturers of household and personal products, a key issue is pricing. According to industry sources, prices for most household and personal products have risen only about 1 percent annually, on average, over the past five years, significantly below the overall rate of inflation. Therefore, companies have tried to drive top-line growth by creating new products and entering new markets.

For full-year 1997, Standard & Poor's expects sales to rise at a low single-digit rate and profits to rise in the 12 percent to 14 percent range, year to year. Raw material prices are likely to remain stable, and manufacturers should continue to reap the benefits of operating efficiencies achieved through past restructuring programs.

What's ahead for 1998?

Standard & Poor's expects the leading household and personal care products manufacturers to show steady operating earnings growth of approximately 10 percent to 12 percent in 1998. The major factors in this positive outlook are projected sale gains in the mid-single digits and modest margin improvement as a result of recent corporate restructurings and cost control initiatives. Overall unit volume should rise approximately 5 percent to 9 percent from that of 1997.

Much of the revenue growth is likely to come from expansion into international markets, modest volume gains in the United States, and contributions from acquisitions. With no letup seen in the competitive environment, it's unlikely that price increases will make a meaningful contribution.

INDUSTRY TRENDS

Demographic changes, both in the United States and internationally, are reshaping the household nondurables industry. In the United States, the slow rate of population growth and the graying of America are having a profound affect on the way companies do business. To achieve success in the highly competitive household products and personal care industries, companies need to understand these basic trends.

Population growth and shifting demand

The U.S. population totaled nearly an estimated 268 million as of September 1997. From an average annual increase of 1.7 percent in 1950s, population growth slowed to less than 1 percent a year in the 1980s. So far in the 1990s, annual gains have been slightly above 1 percent. This slow growth is likely to result in a substantial deceleration in demand for consumer goods in the coming years. Even more important, however, is how the population is dispersed.

A long-term trend affecting the U.S. market is the aging of the population. The main impetus is the advancing population bulge of baby boomers, the segment of the population born between 1946 and 1964. There are currently about 75 million baby boomers, accounting for about 30 percent of the population. With the first wave of baby boomers now passing the half-century mark, they're reaching an age when their consumption patterns are likely to change radically from a focus on goods to an emphasis on services in such areas as health care, finance, and leisure.

This aging population balloon has been a driving force for manufacturers in their creation of new products. For instance, Colgate-Palmolive addressed the needs of an aging population with its new Colgate Total toothpaste, the first toothpaste approved to fight gingivitis, a common gum problem among older consumers.

The baby boom generation is also characterized by a keen sensitivity to their looks and a notorious need for instant self-gratification. Eye creams, in particular, sell well as women start noticing fine lines. Hair color is also an important product. Procter &

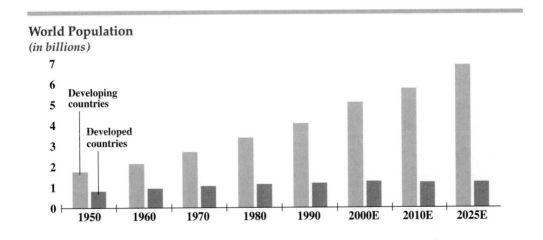

World Population
(in billions)

E: Estimated
Source: U.S. Department of Commerce; Population Reference Bureau.

Gamble's new beta-hydroxy addition to its Oil of Olay line, called the Age Defying Series, is targeted to women over 30 and addresses the group's quest for eternal youth.

World's Most Populous Countries
(estimated, in millions)

Rank	Country	1996 Population	Rank	Country	2025 Population
1	China	1,236.7	1	China	1,569.6
2	India	969.7	2	India	1,384.6
3	United States	267.7	3	United States	335.1
4	Indonesia	204.3	4	Indonesia	276.4
5	Brazil	160.3	5	Pakistan	232.9
6	Russia	147.3	6	Nigeria	231.6
7	Pakistan	137.8	7	Brazil	212.9
8	Japan	126.1	8	Bangladesh	180.3
9	Bangladesh	122.2	9	Mexico	140.8
10	Nigeria	107.1	10	Russia	131.4

Source: Population Reference Bureau.

Avon Products, Inc.—1998

Jim Camerius

www.avon.com
stock symbol AVP

"We've proven that broader access to Avon products works in many markets around the world," said James Preston, chair and chief executive officer of Avon Products, Inc. (212-546-6015). "We need to extend that idea to win over the potential American customers who don't shop Avon because they don't like the one-on-one sales approach," he added. In late 1997, upon announcing that Avon soon would test the strategy of selling through retail outlets as part of a new marketing program, he said, "The more we can get our face and name out there, the better it is for our representatives." Avon's sales for 1997 increased 5.5 percent to almost $5.1 billion and net income increased 6.6 percent to nearly $339 million (see Exhibits 1 and 2).

THE COMPANY AND ITS PRODUCTS

At year-end 1997, Avon Products, Inc., was the world's largest direct selling organization and merchandiser of beauty and beauty-related products. From corporate offices in New York City, Avon marketed product lines to women in 134 countries through 2.5 million independent sales representatives who sold primarily on a door-to-door basis. Total U.S. sales in 1997 were $1.7 billion, about one-third of Avon's total sales. The company's worldwide workforce of 34,995 employees staffed divisions of product management, manufacturing, and sales and service.

Avon's line includes approximately 600 products such as skin care items; makeup; perfume fragrances for men and women; and toiletries for bath, hair care, personal care, hand and body care, and sun care. Popular brand names include Skin-So-Soft, a product in the bath products area, which benefited from wide publicity concerning alternative uses; Moisture Therapy; and Imari fragrance. With Avon Color, a line of more than 350 shades of lip, eye, face, and nail colors, the company assures customers that Avon has just the right shade for them and that their total "look" can be coordinated. Avon's Anew Perfecting Complex for Face was judged one of the most successful skin care products in company history.

Internationally, the company's product line is marketed primarily at moderate price points. The marketing strategy emphasizes department store quality at discount store prices. Global marketing efforts result in a number of highly successful brands in the areas of cosmetics, skin care, and fragrance.

This case was prepared by Professor Jim Camerius of Northern Michigan University as a basis for class discussion. It is not intended to illustrate either effective or ineffective handling of an administrative situation. Copyright © 1999 by Prentice Hall, Inc. ISBN 0-13-011168-6.

EXHIBIT 1: Avon Products, Inc., Balance Sheet

(in millions, except per share data)	December 31, 1997	1996
Assets		
Current assets		
Cash, including cash equivalents of $60.0 and $87.9	$ 141.9	$ 184.5
Accounts receivable (less allowance for doubtful accounts of $35.5 and $36.4)	444.8	437.0
Inventories	564.8	530.0
Prepaid expenses and other	192.5	198.1
Total current assets	1,344.0	1,349.6
Property, plant and equipment, at cost		
Land	48.6	51.5
Buildings and improvements	567.0	564.5
Equipment	666.0	608.9
	1,281.6	1,224.9
Less accumulated depreciation	670.6	658.3
	611.0	566.6
Other assets	317.9	306.2
Total assets	2,272.9	2,222.4
Liabilities and Shareholders' Equity		
Current liabilities		
Debt maturing within one year	132.1	97.1
Accounts payable	476.0	469.3
Accrued compensation	111.3	142.4
Other accrued liabilities	268.9	238.7
Sales and other taxes	101.0	124.6
Income taxes	266.6	319.2
Total current liabilities	1,355.9	1,391.3
Long-term debt	102.2	104.5
Employee benefit plans	367.6	384.8
Deferred income taxes	31.2	33.9
Other liabilities (including minority interests of $37.5 and $41.1)	131.0	66.2
Commitments and contingencies		
Shareholders' equity		
Common stock, par value $.25—authorized: 400,000,000 shares; issued 174,711,173 and 173,957,379 shares	43.7	43.5
Additional paid-in capital	733.1	693.6
Retained earnings	660.9	488.8
Translation adjustments	(270.3)	(210.7)
Treasury stock, at cost—42,897,463 and 41,137,297 shares	(882.4)	(773.5)
Total shareholders' equity	285.0	241.7
Total liabilities and shareholders' equity	$2,272.9	$2,222.4

Source: www. freeedgar.com

EXHIBIT 2:   Avon Products, Inc., Income Statement

(in millions, except share data)	Years ended December 31,		
	1997	1996	1995
Net sales	$5,079.4	$4,814.2	$4,492.1
Cost of sales	2,051.0	1,921.2	1,769.0
Marketing, distribution and administrative expenses	2,484.3	2,348.2	2,215.6
Interest expense	41.8	40.0	41.3
Interest income	(16.7)	(14.5)	(19.4)
Other (income) expense, net	(15.9)	8.9	20.6
Total costs, expenses and other	4,544.5	4,303.8	4,027.1
Income from continuing operations before taxes and minority interest	534.9	510.4	465.0
Income taxes	197.9	191.4	176.4
Income from continuing operations before minority interest	337.0	319.0	288.6
Minority interest	1.8	(1.1)	(2.5)
Income from continuing operations	338.8	317.9	286.1
Loss on disposals, net of taxes	0	0	(29.6)
Net income	338.8	317.9	256.5
Earnings per share:			
Basic:			
Continuing operations	2.56	2.38	2.10
Discontinued operations	0	0	(.22)
Net income	2.56	2.38	1.88
Diluted:			
Continuing operations	2.54	2.36	2.09
Discontinued operations	0	0	(.22)
Net income	2.54	2.36	1.87

Source: www.freeedgar.com

Avon is also the world's largest manufacturer and distributor of fashion jewelry, and markets an extensive line of gifts and collectibles. A fashion apparel catalogue, "Avon Style," was added in 1994.

For 1997, high-margin cosmetics, fragrance, and toiletries products account for 60.9 percent of total sales; gift and decorative, 20.7 percent; apparel, 11.1 percent; and fashion jewelry and accessories, 7.2 percent respectively.

THE EARLY YEARS

In the late 1800s, David McConnell, a door-to-door book salesman, had an idea he believed would encourage women to buy his books. Following a common trade practice of the period, he gave prospective customers a gift of perfume to arouse their interest. Before long, he discovered that the perfume was more popular than the books. He formed a new firm, which he called the California Perfume Company. "I started in a space scarcely larger than an ordinary kitchen pantry," McConnell noted in 1900. "My ambition was to manufacture a line of goods superior to any other and take those goods through canvassing agents directly from the laboratory to the consumer."

EXHIBIT 3:   The Principles that Guide Avon

1. To provide individuals an opportunity to earn in support of their well-being and happiness;
2. To serve families throughout the world with products of the highest quality backed by a guarantee of satisfaction;
3. To render a service to customers that is outstanding in its helpfulness and courtesy;
4. To give full recognition to employees and representatives, on whose contributions Avon depends;
5. To share with others the rewards of growth and success;
6. To meet fully the obligations of corporate citizenship by contributing to the well-being of society and the environment in which it functions; and
7. To maintain and cherish the friendly spirit of Avon.

Source: Avon Products, Inc., *Avon Representative Success Book.*

McConnell based his business upon products sold directly to the consumer, an image of the company that captured the beauty and excitement of the state of California, and a national network of sales agents he had organized during his years as a bookseller.

A series of corporate principles developed by McConnell continue to influence decision making for the company. These principles are shown in Exhibit 3.

As the firm grew, so did the product line. In 1920, the company introduced a line of products called Avon that consisted of a toothbrush, cleanser, and vanity set. The Avon name was inspired by the area around the company's laboratory at Suffern, New York, which McConnell thought resembled the countryside of William Shakespeare's home, Stratford-on-Avon, England. The name of the line became so popular that in 1929, the company officially became Avon. By 1929, the company was selling low-cost home care and beauty products door-to-door and through catalogues in all 48 states.

In the early 1950s, the sales representatives' territories were reduced in size, a strategy that led to quadrupling the sales force and increasing sales sixfold over the next 12 years. Avon advertisements appeared on television for the first time during this period. The famous slogan, "Avon Calling," was first televised in 1954.

In 1960, total sales were $1.5 million, an 18 percent increase over the previous year; international sales were $8.2 million; and the company consisted of 6,800 employees and 125,000 sales representatives. By 1969, total sales had grown to $558.6 million; international sales were $193.1 million; and the firm had 20,800 employees and over 400,000 sales representatives. Manufacturing plants, distribution centers, and sales branches were opened throughout the world as part of an expansion program.

The 1970s presented Avon management with some of its greatest challenges. The strength of the U.S. dollar reduced the company's international profits; recession and inflation affected sales of some products; in 1975, some 25,000 Avon sales representatives quit due to decreased earning opportunities. Avon products were outpaced by offerings of retail cosmetic firms that appealed to women whose new attitudes favored more exciting product lines. The traditional direct sales approach was nearly toppled during this period by social changes that management had not anticipated, such as the growth in the number of working women. Direct sales firms were hurt in two ways: fewer women were at home for door-to-door salespeople to call on and fewer women wanted to make money in their spare time selling cosmetics to their neighbors. These trends continue.

The 1980s were difficult. Hostile takeover attempts plagued the firm during the period. Avon sales volume in the United States and international markets showed little or no growth. Profit margins on many products declined due to price discounting by competitors. Turnover rates of sales representatives increased. Corporate debt, although recently reduced, was perceived as "staggering."

DIVERSIFICATION THROUGH ACQUISITION

In 1979, Avon purchased Tiffany & Company, a prestigious jeweler, for $104 million. The Tiffany purchase set the tone for the next decade: diversification through acquisition. This included an ill-fated billion-dollar plunge into the home health care industry and a later entry into the prestige fragrance industry through the 1987 acquisition of Giorgio, Inc., of Beverly Hills, California.

Several attempts made by other firms, such as Amway Corporation and Mary Kay Cosmetics, to take over Avon during the 1980s interfered with management's ability to plan effectively for the future. Although Avon Chair Hicks Waldron established a five-year plan in 1985 to restore profit growth to the firm's basic businesses, Avon's corporate earnings continued to stagnate. Tiffany & Company was sold in 1984 to an investment group led by Tiffany management. The Giorgio unit was sold to outside interests in August 1994.

Selective, relatively small acquisitions in the core direct selling/direct marketing areas of expertise were seen by management in the 1990s as one way to accelerate overall growth of the firm.

A 1996 purchase of Justine Pty. Ltd., a South African direct seller of cosmetics, provided a potential entry point to other markets in sub-Saharan Africa.

Avon acquired Discovery Toys, Inc., in January 1997. The firm was a privately held direct seller of educational products for children and a leader in its products category. Discovery Toys's sales force and product line both were considered by Preston to be complementary to Avon's existing businesses. It was operated as a separate unit. Management felt that it could accelerate the sales growth of the Discovery unit by leveraging Avon expertise in worldwide markets.

The Avon organization chart is shown in Exhibit 4.

VISION STATEMENT

Avon's research department had informed management that corporate problems centered around image and market access. Out of high-level management discussions emerged a new vision for the firm, a new marketing orientation, and a new approach to strategic development.

To inspire a new global direction, management developed the Avon vision statement: "To be the company that best understands and satisfies the product, service, and self-fulfillment needs of women, globally."

> We are, uniquely among major corporations, a woman's company. We sell our products to, for, and through women. We understand their needs and preferences better than most. This understanding should guide our basic business and influence our choice of new business opportunities. We need to become, and are becoming, more customer-oriented and more market-driven.

EXHIBIT 4:   Avon Products, Inc., Organization Chart 1997

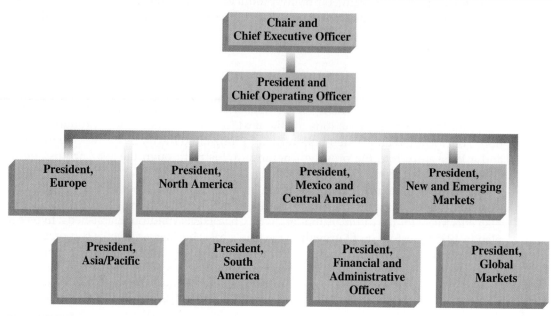

Staff Officers:

Finance
General Auditor
President, Betterware Co.
Treasurer
Corporate Communications
Chief Information
Controller
General Counsel
Investor Relations
Scientific Officer
Human Resources and Corporate Affairs

Source: Avon Products, Inc.

Each one of the 18 words in the vision statement has considerable meaning. The three most important elements, however, are the focus on women, on being global, and on the additional opportunities for Avon in self-fulfillment.

COMPETITION

The direct selling industry consists of a few large, well-established firms and many small organizations that sell about every product imaginable including toys, animal food, collectibles, plant care products, clothing, computer software, and financial services. Avon is substantially larger in terms of sales representatives, sales volume, and resources than Mary Kay Cosmetics, Inc., its nearest direct competitor.

Mary Kay, with corporate headquarters in Dallas, Texas, experienced spectacular sales growth in its early years and was suffering some of the same problems that were affecting the entire direct selling industry. The original corporate sales concept was based on a marketing plan for sales associates to sell the company's products at home demonstration shows. The company had problems replenishing the sales force on a continuing basis with new recruits, as many women sought full-time positions in other areas. According to Richard Bartlett, president of Mary Kay, "Senior management will have to react to a changing environment by being much more flexible, by being able to come out with new products, by introducing new innovations, and by developing new strategies."

Several other firms (such as Procter & Gamble Co.; Unilever NV; and Revlon, Inc.) that sell cosmetics and personal care products primarily through department stores and mass merchandisers are considered important competitors in the marketplace.

The changing nature of science and technology is a strategic concern in the external environment. Orth Laboratories's Retin-A treatment for acne that doubles as an antiwrinkle cream is evidence of this change. New drug applications for six to eight other retinoids are known to be under way with anti-aging claims. At the same time, greater understanding of skin physiology enables the development of more advanced traditional skin care products, including those that legitimately can make counterirritant claims and those that can protect users from environmental damage, such as from the sun.

INTERNATIONAL MARKETING AND EXPANSION

Avon in 1997 derived 65.9 percent of its sales and 67.9 percent of net income from operations of its international subsidiaries. Total international sales in 1997 were $3.35 billion, compared to Avon U.S. sales of $1.7 billion. Total 1997 international pretax income was $465.9 million compared to Avon U.S. pretax income of $219.8 million.

The international operations of the company are divided into four geographic regions: (1) the Americas, which include Canada, Central America, and South America; (2) Avon U.S., Avon's largest established market; (3) Pacific Region, which includes the Philippines, Thailand, Japan, New Zealand, Australia, and China; and (4) the European Region, which comprises the United Kingdom, Central Europe, and Russia. (See Exhibits 5 and 6.)

Geographic Growth

The first area is geographic growth. Enormous growth opportunities exist in countries with huge populations such as China, Indonesia, and India. For Eastern Europe, management is excited about the potential in Poland, Czechoslovakia, and Hungary. In the Pacific Rim area, countries such as Vietnam, Cambodia, and Laos are targeted as market opportunities.

Emerging and Developing Markets

The second area of growth is the emerging and developing markets of Latin America, the Pacific Rim, and other areas. In those markets, the retail infrastructure is undeveloped, especially in the interiors of those countries. Avon representatives provide consumers with an opportunity to buy a wide range of quality products at acceptable prices. In some developing markets, where access to brand label goods is particularly

EXHIBIT 5: Avon's Sales and Income by Region

| (in millions of dollars) | Years ended December 31, | | | | | |
| | 1997 | | 1996 | | 1995 | |
	Net Sales	Pretax Income	Net Sales	Pretax Income	Net Sales	Pretax Income
United States	$1,732.9	$219.8	$1,672.5	$227.3	$1,584.8	$211.6
International						
Americas	1,752.6	310.8	1,609.9	291.9	1,466.9	265.8
Pacific	782.4	55.9	751.1	73.6	712.0	67.5
Europe	811.5	99.2	780.7	54.4	728.4	41.7
Total International	3,346.5	465.9	3,141.7	419.9	2,907.3	375.0
Total from operations	$5,079.4	685.7	$4,814.2	647.2	$4,492.1	586.6
Corporate expenses	(104.3)		(95.4)		(74.6)	
Interest expense	(41.8)		(40.0)		(41.3)	
Other expense, net	(4.7)		(1.4)		(5.7)	
Total	$ 534.9		$ 510.4		$ 465.0	

Source: www.freeedgar.com

EXHIBIT 6: Avon's Identifiable Assets by Geographic Area

(in millions of dollars)	1997	1996	1995
United States	$ 528.9	$ 470.2	$ 449.2
International			
Americas	583.5	548.8	498.4
Pacific	378.4	383.5	375.5
Europe	363.5	377.4	339.7
Total International	1,325.4	1,309.7	1,213.6
Corporate and other	418.6	442.5	390.0
Total	$2,272.9	$2,222.4	$2,052.8

Source: www.freeedgar.com

prized, Avon's direct selling method opened up an extraordinary earnings opportunity for Avon representatives. In China, for example, a six-month inventory of lotion sold out in only two weeks. In Poland, Avon offers customers access to cosmetics and personal care items never before available to them. In one corporate study, it was determined that Polish women are willing to spend a considerable portion of their discretionary income on Avon products. China, Russia, and Central/Eastern Europe, including Poland, are considered by management to be Avon's primary opportunities for growth in 1997.

Developed Industrial Markets

The third area of international growth is the United States and other developed industrial areas such as Canada, Western Europe, Japan, and Australia. However, the old system isn't going to prosper without major change. In established markets, the single most compelling issue is erosion of the core customer base. The number of people buying from Avon in markets like the United States has dwindled by 2 to 3 percent per year for about 12 years. "We applied all the tried-and-true stimuli to our direct selling system: changes in recruiting, incentives, commissions, brochures, and more," said Preston. "We had some success. But we didn't stop the decline of customer purchasing activity." Management feels growth will come by updating the direct selling channel. Avon management considers Japan to be one of the most significant trouble spots for the firm. The sluggish Japanese economy, intense pricing pressure, and operating issues contribute to Avon Japan's disappointing performance.

NEW GLOBAL MARKETING STRATEGIES

Satisfying the subtleties and intricacies of customer demand around the world means that the firm's business would vary from country to country and market to market. In the United States, for example, Avon tested Avon Select, a direct marketing program, to enable customers to buy Avon products in various settings. Customers could order products by four methods: through their Avon representative, by mail through special catalogues, by the 1-800-FOR-AVON telephone, or by fax. In 1996, Avon set up a home page on the Internet to provide consumers with information about Avon and to help potential customers get in touch with an Avon representative.

Similar opportunities are available worldwide. In Taiwan, for instance, Avon products are sold by representatives in some 2,000 storefronts, where orders can be placed via fax for next-day delivery. Also in Taiwan, Avon sells products in the cosmetic aisles of outlets that are similar to American drugstores. In Malaysia, Avon has 145 franchised boutiques that provide half of the company's Malaysian sales. In all cases, new programs are designed to complement the existing network of sales representatives. The company also spends 2 to 3 percent of annual sales revenues on image-enhancing advertising and promotion programs worldwide to make customers aware of Avon products and the purchase options available.

The traditional door-to-door method, with the Avon lady as the homemaker's friend and beauty consultant, made the company the world's largest cosmetics firm and the number-one direct seller. The approach is viewed as expensive (the salesperson receives a 20 to 50 percent commission) and there are problems associated with hiring, training, managing, and motivating the sales force.

Retail stores offer a fixed location and a controlled environment but have the potential of conflicting with direct selling methods. In early 1997, in an effort to discontinue salespeople who were buying at reduced prices only for themselves, Avon eliminated deep discounts on certain promotional items. The move prompted an estimated loss of 25,000 Avon sales representatives, about 6 percent of the U.S. sales force. Susan Kropf, Avon U.S. president, said that the policy change confused many representatives, including those who weren't affected by the change. "There are some lessons learned," she noted in retrospect. "Any major field changes we may undertake . . . will be pretested, very simple to understand, and communicated with painstaking care."

In an effort to keep the sales force content, management is considering a concept which proved successful in Asia: give sales representatives a cut of the new business either through franchising opportunities or by giving referrals of customers who shop at the stores. Avon tested letting consumers shop in its Tampa and San Francisco "express centers," which previously were used only by representatives to pick up products for their customers. The first "consumer-oriented" express center opened in Washington, D.C., in January 1998. Management is considering a range of options, including company-owned stores, franchises, and shopping mall kiosks.

Avon is testing a direct mail catalogue, whereby customers can bypass the Avon representative and place orders themselves. Success of a mail order catalogue will depend greatly upon Avon's ability to manage its mailing and customer lists, control inventory carefully, offer quality merchandise, and project a distinctive customer-benefiting image. In a limited test of a catalogue, Avon reached a "more upscale customer" who placed an average order of $40, more than double that of the order typically placed through the Avon sales brochure.

MANAGING FOR THE NEXT MILLENNIUM

In early 1997, CEO Preston identified four areas to "manage for the next millennium": global marketing, global management, global customer growth, and global corporate responsibility.

Global Marketing

A global product council plays an integral role in launching global brands and communicating Avon's beauty image. The Avon Global Product Council consists of 35 of the company's most experienced marketers from all over the world and represents countries that account for over 85 percent of Avon's total sales. The council ensures that all global brands share consistency of formulation, packaging, and imagery.

In its strategic marketing process, Avon provides fewer brands to more markets. Avon's global brands include Anew, Avon Color, Revival, Rare Gold, Natori, and Millennia. Anew is an alpha-hydroxy acid product that was reformulated and repackaged into an anti-aging skin care line. Avon Color is viewed as the company's premier global cosmetics line. Revival, Rare Gold, Natori, and Millennia are global fragrances. The fragrance Josie debuted in 1997, named in honor of world-renowned designer Josie Natori. Other global brands include Avon Basics, which is a line of vitamin-enriched basic skin care products, and Avon Skin Care, which is a line of cleansers, toners, and unique complexes for adding moisture to the skin. To support the global brands, Avon annually publishes more than 750 million brochures in over a dozen languages, and provides media kits with photographs of models and products, typefaces, and advertising samples.

Global Management

The global management program emphasizes the quality of the company's executives. The approach calls for a strong management team. As the company's newer markets such as China, Russia, and Central Europe expand and as Avon enters more countries such as the Ukraine, Romania, and Vietnam, the need for experienced direct selling managers is critical. Avon created leadership development and cross-functional train-ing programs for high-potential managers throughout the company. The company needs seasoned executives with direct selling experience who can assume key manage-ment positions anywhere in the world.

Global Customer Growth

Customer growth has become a central focus of the entire company. Avon research studies show that both established and developing markets offer potential for increas-ing the customer base, particularly among women who think favorably about Avon but don't have easy access to the company's products. Avon is tapping this potential mar-ket by launching a variety of customer growth programs around the world.

Global Corporate Responsibility

Avon envisions itself as a company committed to responding to the needs of women globally. Avon management is committed to implementing programs in areas such as health and empowerment to help women lead healthier and more fulfilling lives.

THE FUTURE

In the fall of 1997, Preston announced a cost-cutting plan predicted to result in $150 to $200 million in charges against earnings over a two-year period, but expected to increase overall profitability by about $200 million by the year 2000. The plan includes testing alternative methods of distribution, increased funding of advertising and mar-keting programs, and a reduction in the number of products in the product line by 30 percent. Preston feels that a reduced product line will allow the firm to put more resources behind fewer products and to save millions of dollars on the costs of ingredi-ents, warehouse space, and distribution. Fewer products will also mean savings in pro-motion efforts and fewer pages in the sales brochure.

Revlon, Inc.—1998

M. Jill Austin
Melodie R. Phillips

www.revlon.com
stock symbol REV

Revlon (212-593-4300 or 212-527-4000) established itself as a leader in its industry by focusing its energies on product and technology development. Successes have been documented not only through tremendous growth in domestic product introductions and sales, but also in the continued development of international markets. Net sales for 1997 increased 10.2 percent to $2.39 billion (compared to $2.17 billion in 1996) and operating income increased 6 percent in 1997 to $213.3 million. Chair Jerry Levin stated that the company "revolutionized the entire industry, creating whole new categories of products and convincing consumers to change where they shop." (See Exhibit 1 for Organizational Chart.)

Product categories for the company include skin care, cosmetics, personal care, fragrance, and professional products. Some of the company's most recognized brand names include Revlon, Ultima II, ColorStay, Almay, Charlie, Flex, Mitchum, and Jean Nate. Successful products developed by the company in the mid-1990s include ColorStay lip color, Revlon Age Defying makeup, ColorStay eye and face makeup, Charlie White fragrance, Almay Clear Complexion makeup, and Lasting fragrance. Exhibit 2 shows the company products in each business category.

The company is moving into an era of "transforming the beauty industry," says Levin, through the Revlon vision to "provide glamour, excitement, and innovation to consumers through high-quality products at affordable prices." Revlon aims to emerge as the dominant cosmetics and personal care firm through the twenty-first century. Levin calls the company's current era "the beginning of a long and exciting journey."

PAST AND PRESENT

History

Revlon, Inc., was formed with a $300 investment in 1932 by brothers Charles and Joseph Revson with Charles Lachmann. Lachmann was a nail polish supplier who is most notably remembered for his contribution of the *l* in the Revlon name. In the early years, Revson developed a near-monopoly on beauty parlor sales by selling his nail polish door-to-door at salons. He expanded into the lipstick market with the slogan "Matching Lips and Fingertips." Some of the landmark advertising campaigns directed

This case was prepared by Professors M. Jill Austin and Melodie R. Phillips of Middle Tennessee State University as a basis for class discussion. It is not intended to illustrate either effective or ineffective handling of an administrative situation. Copyright © 1999 by Prentice Hall, Inc. ISBN 0-13-011160-0.

EXHIBIT 1: Revlon, Inc., Organizational Chart

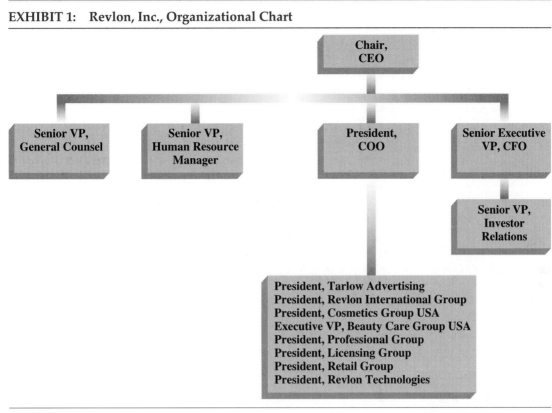

Source: Revlon, Inc., *Annual Report* (1997).

by Revson included "Fatal Apple" and "Fire and Ice." Revson was a hard taskmaster, expecting of his workers the same whole-life devotion which he gave to Revlon. He sometimes held meetings until two o'clock in the morning, called employees at home to discuss business, cursed out employees, and pretended to fall asleep during some presentations. Charles Revson was the primary force behind the success of Revlon until his death in 1968.

The company started with only one product, nail enamel. Revlon nail enamel was manufactured with pigments instead of the dyes that typically were used in this type of manufacturing. This approach allowed Revlon to market a large number of color options to consumers relatively quickly. It took the three company founders just six years to transform their small nail enamel company into a multimillion-dollar organization. This successful collaboration launched one of the most recognizable brands and companies in the world.

Originally, Revlon offered its nail enamels through a limited distribution system in which professional salons carried the products. However, as the 1930s progressed, the products were distributed widely in select drug stores and department stores. As the world entered WWII, Revlon contributed to the war effort by providing first aid kits and dye markers for the U.S. Navy. After the war, Revlon expanded its product lines with the introduction of manicure and pedicure instruments (a natural complement to the nail enamel products). Revlon management recognized global demand potential,

EXHIBIT 2: Revlon, Inc., Products and Business Categories

Cosmetics	Skin Care	Fragrances	Personal Care	Professional
REVLON	**REVLON**	**REVLON**	**REVLON**	**REVLON**
Revlon	Moon Dance	Charlie	Flex	Revlon Professional
ColorStay	Revlon Results	Charlie Red	Flex Balsam	Roux Fanci-full
Revlon Age Defying	Eterna 27	Charlie White	Outrageous	Realistic
Super Lustrous		Charlie Sunshine	Aquamarine	Crème of Nature
Moon Drops	**ALMAY**	Cherish	Mitchum	Arosci
Velvet Touch	Time-Off	Fire & Ice	Lady Mitchum	Sensor Perm
New Complexion	Moisture Balance	Fire & Ice Cool	Hi & Dry	Perfect Perm
Touch & Glow	Moisture Renew	Lasting	Colorsilk	Fermadyl
Lashful	Almay Clear Com-	StreetWear Scents	Frost & Glow	Perfect Touch
Lengthwise	plexion Treatment	Jontue	Revlon Shadings	Salon Perfection
Naturally Glamorous		Ciara	Jean Nate	Revlonissimo
Custom Eyes	**ULTIMA II**		Roux Fanci-full	Voila
Softstroke Timeliner	Ultima II	**ULTIMA II**	Realistic	True Cystem
StreetWear	Interactives	Madly	Crème of Nature	Young Color
Revlon Implements	CHR	UII	Herba Rich	Creative Nail Design
			Fabu-laxer	Contours
ALMAY	**SIGNIFICANT**	**SIGNIFICANT**		American Crew
Almay	**REGIONAL BRANDS**	**REGIONAL BRANDS**	**ALMAY**	R Pro
Time-Off	Jeanne Gatineau	Floid	Almay	
Almay Clear Com-	Natural Honey	Versace		**SIGNIFICANT**
plexion Makeup		Charlie Gold	**SIGNIFICANT**	**REGIONAL BRANDS**
Amazing		Myrurgia	**REGIONAL BRANDS**	Colomer
One Coat			Bozzano	Intercosmo
			Juvena	Personal Bio Point
ULTIMA II			Geniol	Natural Wonder
Ultima II			Golorama	Llongueras
Wonderwear			Llongueras	
The Nakeds			Bain de Soleil	
			ZP-11	
SIGNIFICANT				
REGIONAL BRANDS				
Colorama				
Juvena				
Jeanne Gatineau				

Source: Revlon, Inc., *Annual Report* (1996).

and began offering company products in a number of new markets. Stock was first offered in the company in 1955. The 1960s were associated with the "American Look" campaign designed to introduce the all-American girl to the world cosmetics market via well-known U.S. models. Further identifying with the changing role of women in the market and society, the Charlie fragrance line was introduced in the early 1970s. Sales for this extremely popular line surpassed $1 billion by 1977.

After the death of Charles Revson, Michel Bergerac took control of the company. He built up the pharmaceutical side of the business. By 1985, two-thirds of Revlon's sales were health care products such as Tums and Oxy acne medications and the company was losing ground in cosmetics. Millionaire Ronald Perelman made five offers to purchase Revlon and eventually took over the company for $1.8 billion in a leveraged buyout. Perelman returned the company to its roots and sold off the health care products. He refocused the company as an internationally known manufacturer and seller of cosmetics and fragrances. Perelman took the company private in 1987 by buying the stock from all of the public shareholders. A subsidiary of MacAndrews & Forbes still holds 83 percent of the outstanding shares of Revlon and Perelman is chair and chief executive officer of that subsidiary.

The Present

Revlon continues to focus on developing products to reach existing customers and to attract new customer groups in both domestic and international markets. Research and development expenses were $26.3 million in 1996. The company was taken public in 1996 and is traded on the New York Stock Exchange. Revlon currently has the number-one market position in lip makeup and nail enamel, and the number-two position in face makeup. Revlon's success has been greatly influenced by its continuous and ongoing efforts in the areas of product development. The company recently launched a line of multivitamins, a line of cosmetics for Hispanic and light-skinned African American women, and hair color products called ColorStay. Steven Perelman, vice-president of fragrance marketing, has focused the company's fragrance growth on three brands—Fire and Ice, Charlie, and Cherish.

In an effort to ensure that the company maintains control of its product developments, Revlon sued L'Oreal and Maybelline in 1996 for copyright infringement of the Revlon patent used in two of its lipsticks. Revlon also has legal action pending against Urban Decay, a small California nail company that claimed trademark infringement by Revlon with its StreetWear line. Urban Decay claimed that Revlon copied two color options offered by Urban Decay, and Revlon responded with a lawsuit of its own claiming that it had not infringed on any trademarks.

Building an international presence is central to Revlon's growth program. Alex Kumar, president of Revlon International, says, "Globalization is a dynamic idea-sharing process that enables us to leverage the best ideas and practices of Revlon businesses all over the world." International markets accounted for 39 percent of Revlon's net sales in 1997, down from 42 percent in 1996. The completion of acquisitions in South America increased distribution and manufacturing capabilities in these markets. In September 1996, Revlon gained approval to manufacture, distribute, and market Revlon products in China and the first manufactured goods rolled off the production line that December. The company acquired Bionature S.A., a South American manufacturer of hair and personal care products in 1997.

EXTERNAL FACTORS

Demographic and Societal Trends

The cosmetics and personal care industry is impacted by two major changes in the demographic composition of the U.S. population: the aging population and the change in proportions of racial and ethnic populations. Aging baby boomers make up a significant proportion of the adult U.S. population. The 77 million Americans born between 1946 and 1964 are a significant market for the cosmetics/personal care industry. The number of Americans between the ages of 35 and 54 grew by nearly 18 million from 1985 to 1995. Many baby boomers have high levels of disposable income and are brand-loyal consumers. In addition, it appears that baby boomers' consumption patterns and rates did not change as they aged. The number of people in the mature market (aged 55 and older) also continues to increase. Many of these consumers are wealthier and more willing to spend than ever before. Additionally, women in the mature age group remain active in the workforce for longer periods of time than in the past. The aging of the population has been coupled with a mini baby boom.

The ethnic/racial makeup of the American population is shifting. While African Americans represent the largest minority segment (36 million by 2000), the Hispanic American segment is the fastest-growing segment and is projected to be the largest minority segment in the United States by the year 2010 with approximately 40.5 million individuals. The result is that the non-Hispanic white share of the U.S. population is expected to decline to 68 percent by the year 2010. The Asian American population in the United States is also growing rapidly.

Other social concerns that may impact the industry include consumers' concerns about product safety and the use of testing products on animals by cosmetics companies. Increasingly, cosmetics/personal care is not an industry for women only; men purchase personal care products such as skin creams and many men are trying cosmetics in an effort to improve their appearances.

Economic Trends and Issues

U.S. economic growth has been good since the early 1990s. Although the free-spending 1980s are over, middle-income consumers continue to see growth in salaries and disposable income. American consumers now have significant credit card debt. Because of this debt, consumers may elect not to purchase some expensive nonessential products. In addition, many baby boomers are saving for their retirements and their children's college educations, and/or are caring for their parents. They may be unwilling to spend significant dollars on items such as expensive cosmetics.

International economics provides unique challenges for companies in the cosmetics/skin care industry. Many emerging economies in Asia and Eastern Europe are eager to have mass marketers enter operations in their countries, but operating situations generally are uncertain. The European and Latin American countries have not enjoyed the same level of prosperity during the last decade as the United States has. Countries such as Brazil and Mexico have experienced hyperinflation for several years. High inflation, the strength of the dollar in international markets, and the fluctuation of foreign currency exchange rates all pose difficulties for companies operating in international markets.

Competition

Competition is intense in the cosmetics/skin care industry. In the past, the retail cosmetics industry was dominated by sales of cosmetics in specialty stores and department stores where beauty consultants provided service. Today, large numbers of women prefer purchasing these items at drug stores, supermarkets, and volume retailers such as Kmart and Wal-Mart and from door-to-door sellers such as Avon. The major competitors listed in the Fortune 500 for Revlon include Procter & Gamble; Avon Products; Estee Lauder Companies, Inc.; Alberto-Culver Company; and International Flavors & Fragrances, Inc. The cosmetics and skin care industry is a $66 billion business worldwide.

Other competitors include small companies such as Urban Decay; specialty stores such as Bath and Body Works, Bath and Body Shop, and H20; and retailers selling their own brands such as Benneton, Banana Republic, and Victoria's Secret. Competition for the African American market is increasing with brands such as Fashion Flair and new cosmetics lines launched by Iman and Patti LaBelle. A discussion of major competitors of Revlon, Inc., follows.

Procter and Gamble

Procter & Gamble (P&G) is a multinational company offering products in a wide range of categories including personal care, cosmetics, fragrances, hair care, and skin care. Some of the P&G products not in the cosmetics/skin care industry include diapers, baking mixes, bleach, dish care products, juice, laundry products, oral care products, and peanut butter. The company operates in more than 70 countries.

Revlon faces competition from P&G in a number of product categories. P&G offers hair care products through its Pantene, Vidal Sassoon, and Ivory brands. P&G skin care lines include Oil of Olay, Noxzema, and Clearasil. Fragrance lines sold by P&G include Giorgio, Hugo Boss, Old Spice, Venezia, and Wings. The P&G cosmetics line includes Cover Girl and Max Factor. Procter and Gamble posted sales of $7.1 billion in the beauty care division in 1997. Selected financial information for P&G is shown in Exhibit 3.

L'Oreal/Maybelline

L'Oreal is the world's largest cosmetics firm. In 1996, L'Oreal acquired Maybelline, one of its leading competitors, for $660 million in an attempt to strengthen its position in the U.S. market. L'Oreal previously held only a 7.5 percent share of the market, but the

EXHIBIT 3:   Financial Information for Procter & Gamble

(in millions of dollars)	1997	1996
Net Sales	$35,764	$35,284
Operating Income	5,488	4,815
Net Earnings	3,415	3,046
Total Debt	27,544	27,730
Long-Term Debt	4,143	4,670

Source: www.freeedgar.com

Maybelline acquisition gave L'Oreal the number-two position in cosmetics in the United States. Maybelline added an established firm with substantial market share. L'Oreal competes with Revlon in cosmetics (with L'Oreal and Maybelline products), hair care (with L'Oreal products), and fragrances markets. L'Oreal is a privately held company, with 49 percent of its stock held by the Swiss firm, Nestlé.

Unilever N.V.

Unilever is an Anglo-Dutch firm that until recently was noted as a manufacturer of soap/detergent products and food products. The company also manufactures personal care products. Some of the Unilever brands include skin care (Ponds, Vaseline, Pears, and Hazeline); hair care (Organics, Sunsilk, Clinic, and Gloria); perfume (Brute, Impulse, Denim, Axe/Lynx, and Rexoral/Reward); and prestige fragrance lines (Elizabeth Arden, Calvin Klein, Elizabeth Taylor, Karl Lagerfeld, and Chloe). Unilever now markets seven of the top ten fragrance products in the United States, including Obsession, White Diamonds, Passion, Black Pearls, and Eternity.

The company is a world leader in prestige fragrances and leads the hair care market in Africa, the Middle East, Latin America, and Asia/Pacific. Its skin care products lead the market in North America, Africa, Latin America, Asia/Pacific, and the Middle East.

Avon Products, Inc.

Avon is the number-one direct seller of cosmetics and beauty products in the world. Its direct sales force numbers 2.3 million people. Some brand names for Avon products include its cosmetics line Avon Color, fragrances Josie and Natori, and toiletries Skin-So-Soft. The company also sells jewelry and gift items. Avon has subsidiaries in 41 countries and distributes its products in 89 countries. Avon posted sales of $5.1 billion dollars in 1997. Selected financial information is provided in Exhibit 4.

Estee Lauder

The Estee Lauder Companies, Inc., manufactures and markets cosmetics, fragrances, and skin care products. Some of the company's cosmetics/skin care brands include Estee Lauder and Clinique. Fragrances are sold under the brands Beautiful and White Linen. In addition, Estee Lauder holds the worldwide license for Tommy Hilfiger fragrances and cosmetics. In 1997, the company acquired jane, a cosmetics line targeted

EXHIBIT 4: Financial Information for Avon Products, Inc.

(in millions of dollars)	1997	1996	1995
Net Sales	$5,079.4	$4,814.2	$4,492.1
Gross Profit	3,028.4	2,893.0	2,723.1
Net Income	338.8	317.9	256.5
Total Assets	2,272.9	2,222.4	2,052.8
Long-Term Debt	102.2	104.5	114.2

Source: www.freeedgar.com

EXHIBIT 5: Financial Information for Estee Lauder Companies, Inc.

(in millions of dollars)	1997	1996	1995
Net Sales	$3,381.6	$3,194.5	$2,899.1
Gross Profit	—	2,463.5	2,224.3
Operating Income	—	310.3	230.9
Net Earnings	1,976.0	160.4	121.2
Total Assets	1,873.1	1,821.6	1,721.7
Total Debt		127.5	194.0
Advertising and promotion expenditures	976.2	921.2	847.7

Source: www.esteelauder.com

toward young women. The company also has an investment in MAC (Make-Up Art Cosmetics, Limited). Selected financial information for Estee Lauder is shown in Exhibit 5.

INTERNAL FACTORS

Organization/Management

Revlon actively engages in cross-training and collaborative efforts. The working environment is one of cultivating new ideas from a variety of sources. Employees are encouraged to present new ideas and contribute to the marketing savvy and vision that has led Revlon to its many successes. According to Levin, the company's work environment is "fast-moving, action-oriented, and thrives on challenge. We champion collaboration and team management."

Around 1990, Levin led the company in recruiting a strong team of experienced managers who would work to achieve leadership in the cosmetics/skin care industry. It was about this same time that Revlon developed its vision statement to "provide glamour, excitement, and innovation to consumers through high-quality products at affordable prices." The company set up the Revlon Learning Center and developed training programs to communicate its strategic principles to employees. Training provided a means for ensuring an effective teamwork approach. In 1994, Revlon established annual Charlie Awards to recognize employees whose accomplishments significantly impacted Revlon.

Marketing

Revlon follows the philosophy that a company succeeds in the cosmetic/skin care industry not just by creating a commotion about its products, but also through creating a commotion around them. Kroger and Revlon recently announced a joint promotions effort to provide in-store beauty seminars that will highlight new Revlon products and provide makeup artists to show customers how to use them. *The Revlon Report*, a consumer guide that includes fashion and color trend information and new products features, is distributed in 30 countries. Promotional expenditures for Revlon now approach $150 million annually, reflecting the company's commitment to keeping the brand and its spokespersons in the minds of consumers. Revlon has increased advertising and consumer promotions spending by a compounded annual growth rate of 19 percent since 1993.

Advertising continues to be one of the primary areas of promotions spending by Revlon and primary spokesperson Cindy Crawford is one of the most recognizable faces in the cosmetics world. Her clean-cut, all-American image helped propel Revlon's image and brands to the top of the cosmetics industry. Television and print advertisements also feature Halle Berry, Daisy Fuentes, and Melanie Griffith.

Product development and innovation is another key marketing factor for Revlon. According to Katherine Dwyer, president of Revlon Cosmetics USA, "Innovation is sustainable. It's a continuous process that starts with listening to consumers and having the desire to fulfill their needs. Innovative product ideas are the fusion of information, imagination, and technology. Combine these, and you've got a winner." Revlon has introduced new and exciting products to the marketplace. Some of these new products include the Age Defying and Almay lines and StreetWear. Several varieties of Charlie fragrances (original, white, and red) have proven moderately successful and additional products are being added. Products are in development for Hispanic American and light-skinned African American women.

Production

Globalization of manufacturing and distribution efforts enabled the consolidation of production facilities, increased operating efficiency, and better use of capital assets. Production facilities were reduced in number and centralized to cover core regions. Planning for long-term growth includes a focus on and utilization of top-notch production facilities and distribution systems.

The Revlon Site Distribution Center in Phoenix, Arizona, handles components, raw materials, and finished stocks of cosmetics and personal care products. The distribution center maintains a 99 percent accuracy rating in both inventory and order filling.

Financial Conditions

Significant financial issues impact the company's operations. Long-term debt in 1997 increased to $1.46 billion from $1.35 billion in 1996. This debt, payable by March 1998, represents several years of debt problems for Revlon.

Revlon's statements of operations, balance sheets, and results of operations are provided in Exhibits 6, 7, and 8. These statements reveal increasing levels for sales, but mixed financial results in other areas.

THE FUTURE

CEO George Fellows believes that "We have in place all of the elements that are essential to the sustained growth of our business and to the expansion of the company's leadership on a global scale. I am confident that in the years ahead, the people of Revlon will achieve even stronger results than they have since the transformation of the company began just a few years ago."

EXHIBIT 6:   Revlon, Inc., and Subsidiaries, Consolidated Statements of Operations

(in millions of dollars, except per share data)	1997	1996	1995
	Year Ended December 31,		
Net sales	$ 2,390.9	$ 2,169.5	$ 1,940.0
Cost of Sales	832.1	726.5	653.0
Gross profit	1,558.8	1,443.0	1,287.0
Selling, general and administrative expenses	1,337.9	1,242.4	1,141.4
Business consolidation costs and other, net	7.6	0	0
Operating income	213.3	200.6	145.6
Other expenses (income):			
Interest expense	136.2	133.4	142.6
Interest and net investment income	(3.0)	(3.4)	(4.9)
Gain on sale of subsidiary stock	(6.0)	0	0
Amortization of debt issuance costs	6.7	8.3	11.0
Foreign currency losses, net	6.4	5.7	10.9
Miscellaneous, net	5.1	6.3	1.8
Other expenses, net	145.4	150.3	161.4
Income (loss) before income taxes	67.9	50.3	(15.8)
Provision for income taxes	9.4	25.5	25.4
Income (loss) before extraordinary items	58.5	24.8	(41.2)
Extraordinary items—early extinguishment of debt	(14.9)	(6.6)	0
Net income (loss)	43.6	18.2	(41.2)
Basic income (loss) per common share:			
Income (loss) before extraordinary items	1.14	0.50	(0.97)
Extraordinary items	(0.29)	(0.13)	0
Net income (loss) per common share	0.85	0.37	(0.97)
Diluted income (loss) per common share:			
Income (loss) before extraordinary items	1.14	0.50	(0.97)
Extraordinary items	(0.29)	(0.13)	0
Net income (loss) per common share	0.85	0.37	(0.97)
Weighted average common shares outstanding:			
Basic	51,131,440	49,687,500	42,500,000
Dilutive	51,544,318	49,818,792	42,500,000

Source: Revlon, Inc., *Annual Report* (1997): 38.

EXHIBIT 7: Revlon, Inc., and Subsidiaries, Consolidated Balance Sheets

(in millions of dollars, except per share data)	December 31, 1997	1996	1995
Assets			
Current assets:			
Cash and cash equivalents	$ 42.8	$ 38.6	$ 36.3
Trade receivables, less allowances of $25.9; $24.9; and $23.7, respectively	493.9	426.8	363.1
Inventories	349.3	281.1	277.8
Prepaid expenses and other	97.5	74.5	62.4
Total current assets	983.5	821.0	739.6
Property, plant and equipment, Net	378.2	381.1	367.1
Other assets	143.7	139.2	142.9
Intangible assets, net	329.2	280.6	285.7
Total assets	$1,834.6	$1,621.9	$1,535.3
Liabilities and Stockholders' Deficiency			
Current Liabilities:			
Short-term borrowings—third parties	42.7	27.1	22.7
Current portion of long-term debt—third parties	5.5	8.8	9.2
Accounts payable	195.5	161.9	151.6
Accrued expenses and other	366.1	366.2	370.6
Total current liabilities	609.8	564.0	554.1
Long-term debt—third parties	1,427.8	1,321.8	1,426.2
Long-term debt—affiliates	30.9	30.4	41.3
Other long-term liabilities	224.6	202.8	215.7
Stockholders' deficiency:			
Preferred stock, par value $.01 per share; 20,000,000 shares authorized, 546 shares of Series A Preferred Stock issued and outstanding	54.6	54.6	54.6
Class B Common Stock, par value $.01 per share; 200,000,000 shares authorized, 31,250,000 issued and outstanding	0.3	0.3	0.3
Class A Common Stock, par value $.01 per share; 350,000,000 shares authorized, 19,886,575; 19,875,000; and 11,250,000 issued and outstanding, respectively	0.2	0.2	0.1
Capital deficiency	(231.1)	(231.6)	(416.8)
Accumulated deficit since June 24, 1992	(258.8)	(302.4)	(318.2)
Adjustment for minimum pension liability	(4.5)	(12.4)	(17.0)
Currency translation adjustment	(19.2)	(5.8)	(5.0)
Total stockholders' deficiency	(458.5)	(497.1)	(702.0)
Total liabilities and stockholders' deficiency	$1,834.6	$1,621.9	$1,535.3

Source: Adapted from Revlon, Inc., *Annual Report* (1996) (1997).

EXHIBIT 8:   Revlon, Inc., and Subsidiaries, Results of Operations:

	Year Ended December 31,		
	1997	1996	1995
Income (loss) before income taxes:			
Domestic	$ 83.4	$ 9.8	$ (39.4)
Foreign	(15.5)	40.5	23.6
	67.9	50.3	(15.8)
Net sales:			
United States	1,452.5	1,259.7	1,115.4
International	938.4	909.8	824.6
	2,390.9	2,169.5	1,940.0
Cost of sales	34.8%	33.5%	33.7%
Gross profit	65.2	66.5	66.3
Selling, general and administrative expenses	56.0	57.3	58.8
Business consolidation costs and other, net	0.3	0	0
Operating income	8.9	9.2	7.5

Source: Adapted from Revlon, Inc., *Annual Report* (1997): 27, 55.

Global dominance by Revlon continues to be a strong focus of corporate planners. Revlon currently is pursuing operations in Russia, India, and China through the acquisition or completion of manufacturing and distribution facilities. European and Japanese markets continue to be receptive to the mass market introduction of Revlon products through drug stores and other mass volume retailers. Revlon is the leading brand of cosmetics in South Africa and regional brands are gaining ground rapidly in South American markets such as Brazil.

Promotion remains a critical component of the success of Revlon. Strategies designed to appeal to younger consumers are currently under way, including a Web site that offers a virtual makeover. This allows consumers to test new products and color options before they purchase them. This form of promotion is considerably less expensive than mass market advertising and it has tremendous potential in reaching large numbers of customers.

As Revlon, Inc., deals with its debt problems and tries to continue its strategy of innovation, product development, and globalization, several issues must be considered:

1. Should Revlon continue its efforts in international markets?

2. Should Revlon diversify its operations or develop joint ventures with other cosmetics companies?

3. What role does innovation play in the strategic planning of Revlon, Inc? Which specific types of innovation might Revlon use?

4. What is the role "branding" should play in future growth strategies of Revlon?

5. How will competitive reactions impact Revlon's future plans?

6. What is the impact of social trends and economic trends on companies in the cosmetics/skin care industry?

7. What plans should Revlon, Inc., develop to pay off long-term debt?

REFERENCES

1. Field, Karen Auguston, "Who Says Automation Isn't Flexible?" *Modern Materials Handling* (June 1997).

2. "George Fellows Named Revlon CEO, Succeeding Jerry W. Levin," *PR Newswire* (January 30, 1997).

3. Parker-Pope, Tara, "For Revlon, Skin Care is the New Frontier," *The Wall Street Journal* (April 9, 1997).

4. Parker-Pope, Tara and Gregory Zuckerman, "Revlon's Stock Gains on Perelman Plan for Refinancing $1.15 Billion in Debt," *The Wall Street Journal* (February 24, 1997).

5. Revlon, Inc., *Annual Report* (1996).

6. "Revlon Takes Court Action Over Longlasting Lip Colour from L'Oreal and Maybelline," *Cosmetics International* (May 25, 1996).

7. Sandler, Linda and Yumiko Ono, "Revlon's Makeup Fails to Hide Some Frowns as Investors Wonder if Perelman Will Pay Debt," *The Wall Street Journal* (December 2, 1997).

8. Sloan, Pat. "Revlon, Combe to Invest $60 Mil in Hair-Color Push," *Advertising Age* (May 19, 1997).

9. "The Branding of Beauty," *The Economist* (October 21, 1995).

10. Wilke, Michael, "Revlon's New Line of Vitamins Eyes Niche for Women," *Advertising Age* (January 1, 1996).

11. www.avon.com.

12. www.esteelauder.com.

13. www.fortune500.com.

14. www.pg.com.

15. www.revlon.com.

16. www.unilever.com.

Tobacco—Industry Note

TOBACCO COMPANIES' PROFIT DECREASES

Results for U.S. tobacco companies were generally underwhelming in 1997. Increased cigarette selling prices were offset by significant legal settlement costs, slowing profits in nontobacco operations, and adverse foreign currency exchange translations.

Profits for global tobacco operations of Philip Morris Co. (PM) decreased 5 percent during 1997. These were hurt mainly by $1.5 billion of litigation settlement costs, reflecting the industry's settlements with Mississippi, Florida, and Texas, as well as unfavorable foreign currency exchange rates.

PM's nontobacco operations, which account for about 40 percent of the company's total, rose by 9 percent in 1997. This improvement reflected modest growth for PM's food and beer operations, and gains on the sale of "unstrategic" businesses—specifically, a real estate subsidiary and a Brazilian ice cream business.

R.J. Reynolds Tobacco Company, a unit of RJR Nabisco Holdings, recorded a 23 percent decline in its total tobacco profits in 1997. RJR Nabisco was hurt mainly by $359 million in litigation settlement costs (also reflecting the industry's settlements in Mississippi, Florida, and Texas). Additionally, it was affected by unfavorable currency exchange translations and an intentional halt in shipments to certain trade groups in order to reduce their excessive inventory levels.

UST, Inc., the dominant U.S. producer of moist smokeless tobacco products, recorded a 5 percent decrease in operating profits during 1997, hurt by a 2 percent fall in smokeless tobacco unit volumes and an unfavorable shift in product mix toward low-priced products.

Earnings per share for the tobacco companies were also penalized by a temporary halt in their share repurchases since mid-1997. A collective decision was made to put the funds toward potential national settlement payment reserves.

LEAF FARMERS

The value of U.S. tobacco leaf and product exports in the fiscal year ended June 1997 was $6.7 billion—$66 million higher than the previous year. Cigarette price increases accounted for a large portion of the gain.

During the fiscal year ended June 1997, about two-thirds of U.S. grown tobacco leaf was used for U.S. manufacture; the remainder was exported. The value of the exported leaf exceeded the value of imported tobacco leaf during the fiscal year by nearly $500 million. The total tobacco balance of trade (leaf and cigarettes) was positive, at $5.2 billion.

Source: Adapted from *Industry Surveys* by permission of Standard & Poor's, a division of McGraw-Hill Companies. *Standard & Poor's,* "Alcoholic Beverages & Tobacco," *Industry Surveys* (5 March 1998): 4–13.

Domestic Cigarette Producers' Market Shares (in percent)

Company	1994	1995	1996	E1997
Philip Morris	44.8	46.1	47.8	49.1
RJR Nabisco	26.7	25.7	24.6	24.2
B&W/American Brands	18.7	18.0	17.2	16.1
Lorillard	7.5	8.0	8.4	8.7
Other	2.3	2.2	2.0	1.9
Total	100.0	100.0	100.0	100.0

E: Estimated by S&P.
Source: Philip Morris Inc.

The domestic cigarette industry, which accounts for roughly 95 percent of U.S. tobacco product sales, is a virtual oligopoly. The three leading cigarette producers control approximately 90 percent of domestic sales: PM (with a leading 49 percent market share in 1997, according to S&P estimates); RJR Nabisco (24 percent); and Brown & Williamson (16 percent).

Since 1983, PM has been the nation's largest tobacco company. In 1997, its U.S. cigarette shipments totaled 11.8 billion packs (each containing 20 cigarettes), an increase of 2 percent from 1996. A wholly owned subsidiary of the Philip Morris Companies Inc., PM sells Marlboro, Benson & Hedges, Merit, Virginia Slims, and Parliament as its major premium brands. Its principal discount brands are Basic and Cambridge.

PM's Marlboro is the largest-selling cigarette brand in the United States. In 1997, shipments totaled 8.2 billion packs, up 5 percent from 1996. This equaled 34 percent of the U.S. market, up from 33 percent in 1996.

The nation's second-largest tobacco company is RJR, a wholly owned subsidiary of RJR Nabisco Holdings Corp. RJR's largest-selling premium cigarette brands in the United States are Winston, Salem, and Camel, and its principal discount brands are Doral, Monarch, and Vantage.

Besides cigarettes, moist smokeless tobacco is the only other major category within the domestic tobacco industry. A growing $1.4 billion business, this category is controlled by UST, Inc. UST commanded about a 77 percent market share in 1997, down from about 85 percent in 1993, according to S&P estimates.

HOW THE INDUSTRY OPERATES

The American cigarette industry is wide-reaching, mature, and consolidated.

The use of tobacco has been traced to the indigenous peoples of North America, who were growing and using tobacco by the time Europeans had begun exploring the continent in the sixteenth century.

Once immigrants began to settle on the continent's east coast, they employed the land's rich soil, temperate climate, vast amounts of arable land, and its abundance of cheap and slave labor in the cultivation of crops—including tobacco. By the mid-1800s, the United States had become the world's heaviest per capita growers and users of tobacco.

However, although tobacco was a big trading product in the 1800s, Americans who did use tobacco at this time either chewed it or smoked it in a pipe. A domestic commercial industry for tobacco products didn't evolve for many years; brand-name goods had not been created yet.

In the early 1900s, the U.S. tobacco industry began to develop into a significant industry. With the U.S. population growing rapidly and with life-styles becoming more time-constrained, cigarette smoking gradually became the preferred way to enjoy tobacco; cigar smoking and tobacco chewing became unacceptable in many places. Mass-produced branded consumer goods were becoming popular, which also helped the cigarette industry grow. In addition, cigarette-making machines were widely introduced to manufacturers, letting the industry meet the nation's growing demand for cigarettes.

The Industry Today

By 1996, the U.S. tobacco industry was an approximately $46 billion industry. Cigarettes accounted for nearly 95 percent of total sales that year; the remaining 5 percent was for cigars, moist smokeless tobacco, chewing tobacco, and snuff.

It is estimated that U.S. cigarette consumption declined by about 2 percent in 1997, falling to approximately 23.8 billion packs. Higher selling prices and growing restrictions on where people can smoke have dampened consumption. These factors also have reduced demand for smoking tobacco used in pipes and in roll-your-own cigarettes in recent years.

Although consumption on a pound basis has declined steadily for all tobacco products over the past decade, there nevertheless have been areas of growth in this highly mature industry.

Cigar Sales on the Upswing

Of all the major tobacco product categories, cigars have experienced the fastest unit growth in recent years. Attributable in part by an upturn in luxury goods in general, total U.S. consumption of cigars is estimated by the U.S. Department of Agriculture

Tobacco Products—U.S. per Capita Consumption

Year	Cigarettes[a]	Large Cigars & Cigarillos[b]	Smoking Tobacco[b]	Chewing Tobacco[b]	Snuff[a]	Total Tobacco Products[a]
	Units		Pounds			
P 1996	2,482	32.7	0.1	0.6	0.31	4.70
R 1995	2,505	27.5	0.1	0.7	0.31	4.70
R 1994	2,524	25.3	0.2	0.7	0.32	4.90
R 1993	2,543	23.4	0.2	0.7	0.30	5.37
1992	2,641	24.5	0.2	0.8	0.29	5.30
1991	2,720	25.1	0.2	0.8	0.28	5.54
1990	2,826	26.4	0.2	0.8	0.28	5.62
1989	2,926	27.9	0.2	0.8	0.27	5.68
1988	3,096	29.1	0.3	0.9	0.26	6.11
1987	3,197	31.7	0.3	0.9	0.25	6.30

[a]Consumption per capita, 18 years and over.
[b]Consumption per male, 18 years and over.
P: Preliminary.
R: Revised.
Source: U.S. Department of Agriculture.

(USDA) to have risen by 12 percent in 1997, to 5.1 billion units. Cigar consumption has risen at an annual rate of nearly 11 percent since 1994.

Snuff is the only other product category within the U.S. tobacco industry to experience unit growth in 1997; its output is expected to increase for the ninth straight year. Production in 1997 is projected by the USDA to be nearly 64 million pounds. Of this total, about 6 percent is considered dry snuff, with the remainder moist snuff. Although dry snuff use continues to decline, consumption of moist snuff continues to grow, perhaps helped by the increased restrictions on smoking.

UST, Inc.—1998

Marilyn M. Helms
Fred R. David

stock symbol UST

UST (203-661-1100) derives more than 90 percent of its profits from the sale of Skoal and Copenhagen brands of moist snuff. It is the leader in the smokeless tobacco market, having captured about an 85 percent share based primarily in 1997 from its three top products—Copenhagen (42 percent), Skoal (39 percent), and Skoal Bandits (2 percent). UST boasts one of the highest profit margins and returns on assets in all of corporate America and has sales over $1.4 billion in 1997. Yet, growth in moist snuff volume has slowed from a high of 4 percent in the early 1990s. UST, based in Greenwich, Connecticut, derives the remainder of its earnings from pipe tobacco, pipes and pipe cleaners, and Chateau Ste. Michelle wines. (UST, Inc.—formerly U.S. Tobacco—should not be confused with UST Corp., another firm.) See Exhibits 1, 2, 3, and 4 for financial data.

EXHIBIT 1:   UST, Inc., Consolidated Statement of Earnings

	Year ended December 31,		
(in thousands, except per share amounts)	*1997*	*1996*	*1995*
Net Sales	$1,401,718	$1,371,705	$1,305,796
Costs and Expenses			
Cost of products sold	265,193	246,381	236,743
Excise taxes	26,749	26,375	25,460
Selling, advertising and administrative	398,468	348,059	335,824
Interest, net	7,451	6,364	3,179
Total Costs and Expenses	697,861	627,179	601,206
Earnings Before Income Taxes	703,857	744,526	704,590
Income Taxes	264,719	280,527	274,830
Net Earnings	439,138	463,999	429,760
Net earnings per share			
Basic	2.39	2.48	2.21
Diluted	2.37	2.44	2.17
Average number of shares			
Basic	183,931	187,386	194,374
Diluted	185,602	190,067	197,613

Source: UST, Inc., Annual Report (1997): 32.

This case was prepared by Professors Marilyn M. Helms of University of Tennessee at Chattanooga and Fred R. David of Francis Marion University as a basis for class discussion. It is not intended to illustrate either effective or ineffective handling of an administrative situation. Copyright © 1999 by Prentice Hall, Inc. ISBN 0-13-011173-2.

EXHIBIT 2: UST, Inc., Consolidated Statement of Financial Position

(in thousands of dollars)	December 31,		
	1997	1996	1995
Assets			
Current assets			
Cash and cash equivalents	6,927	54,452	69,403
Accounts receivable	67,702	77,855	69,598
Inventories	319,666	271,425	256,101
Prepaid expenses and other current assets	31,753	40,446	30,453
Deferred income taxes	15,796	6,392	9,042
Property, plant and equipment, net	326,709	300,885	294,806
Other assets	58,161	55,937	55,349
Total assets	826,714	807,392	784,752
Liabilities and Stockholders' Equity			
Current liabilities			
Short-term obligations	10,000	150,000	100,000
Accounts payable and accrued expenses	119,345	113,635	111,767
Income taxes	37,174	42,918	68,956
Total current liabilities	166,519	306,553	280,723
Long-term debt	100,000	100,000	100,000
Postretirement benefits other than pensions	73,868	70,209	65,292
Other liabilities	48,396	48,610	45,180
Total liabilities	388,783	525,372	491,195
Stockholders' equity			
Capital stock	103,307	102,077	101,040
Additional paid-in capital	474,661	414,274	373,935
Retained earnings	528,518	388,505	203,659
	1,106,486	904,856	678,634
Less cost of shares in treasury	668,555	622,836	385,077
Total stockholders' equity	437,931	282,020	293,557
Total liabilities and stockholders' equity	826,714	807,392	784,752

Source: UST, Inc., Annual Report (1997).

UST's sales for 1997 grew to $1.4 billion from $1.37 billion in the prior-year period. Net earnings, however, decreased to $439 million from $464 million in the prior-year period.

Selling and advertising expenses increased in 1997 primarily due to consumer promotions in support of moist smokeless tobacco products, including the introduction of a new product, Copenhagen Long Cut. Additional increased expenses for 1997 resulted from higher spending for the international operations primarily related to moist smokeless tobacco market development in Mexico.

In 1995, UST introduced a new product, the Skoal Flavor Packs, with a national rollout in 1996. The product is marketed to "smokers who can't smoke. " Skoal Bandits, a moist snuff, packaged in portion packs similar to small tea bags, is showing continual growth. UST also manufactures dry snuff and introduced the Skoal Long Cut brand in 1984. UST claims to be unconcerned with moves by Conwood and Helme Tobacco into the discount snuff market.

EXHIBIT 3:   UST, Inc., Consolidated Industry Segment Data

(in thousands of dollars)	Year ended December 31,		
	1997	1996	1995
Net Sales to Unaffiliated Customers			
Tobacco			
Smokeless tobacco	$1,180,535	$1,170,014	$1,119,828
Other tobacco products	7,588	8,413	8,792
	1,188,123	1,178,427	1,128,620
Wine	145,048	122,458	109,453
Other	72,534	74,508	70,742
Elimination of intersegment sales	(3,987)	(3,688)	(3,019)
Net sales	1,401,718	1,371,705	1,305,796
Operating Profit (Loss)			
Tobacco	712,204	751,115	720,965
Wine	29,178	19,875	13,493
Other	(5,680)	(500)	(5,384)
Operating profit	735,702	770,490	729,074
Corporate expenses	(24,394)	(19,600)	(21,305)
Interest, net	(7,451)	(6,364)	(3,179)
Earnings before income taxes	703,857	744,526	704,590
Identifiable Assets at December 31			
Tobacco	457,559	453,228	431,424
Wine	220,881	186,611	176,565
Other	110,609	93,875	88,847
Corporate	37,665	73,678	87,916
	826,714	807,392	784,752
Capital Expenditures (Dispositions), Net			
Tobacco	28,627	22,606	2,266
Wine	19,478	11,551	10,762
Other	7,134	3,037	2,447
Corporate	511	(445)	(1,473)
	55,750	36,749	14,002
Depreciation			
Tobacco	17,128	16,746	17,642
Wine	10,465	8,949	7,693
Other	2,096	1,911	2,386
Corporate	447	537	633
	30,136	28,143	28,354

Source: UST, Inc., *Annual Report* (1997).

Over the past ten years, UST increased its share of the moist snuff market by 57 percent. (Like Conwood, UST is taking advantage of its existing warehouse and distribution networks and has diversified into other markets. UST owns an entertainment division and purchased the Ste. Michelle Vintners, which operates wineries in Washington State and California. Each of these two sectors account for 7 percent of sales revenue.) As diversification increases, a greater decentralization of operations can be expected.

Regionally, the Southeast remains the pocket of strength for UST, with the Northeast, Southwest, and West a bit softer. Analysts anticipate a growth with the popularity

EXHIBIT 4: UST, Inc., Comparative Highlights

(in thousands of dollars, except per share amounts)	For the year ended December 31,		% Change
	1997	1996	
Financial Results			
Net sales	$1,401,718	$1,371,705	2.2%
Net earnings	439,138	463,999	(5.4)
Basic earnings per share	2.39	2.48	(3.6)
Diluted earnings per share	2.37	2.44	(2.9)
Dividends per share	1.62	1.48	9.5
Measurements			
Return on net sales	31.3%	33.8%	
Return on average assets	53.7	58.3	
Return on average stockholders' equity	122.0	161.2	
Dividends paid as a percentage of net earnings	67.9	59.8	
Percentage of total debt to stockholders' equity	25.1	88.6	
Other Data			
Average number of shares (in thousands):			
Basic	183,931	187,386	
Diluted	185,602	190,067	
Number of stockholders of record at year end	10,799	11,907	
Average number of employees	4,677	4,467	

Source: UST, Inc., *Annual Report*, (1997): 1.

of Skoal Flavor Packs. Basic earnings per share for 1977 were $2.39, a 3 percent decrease from 1996, but an 8 percent gain over 1995.

The company's drive toward increased operating efficiencies is motivated by its demanding customers. The company's new mainframe-based Sales Tracking and Reporting System (STARS) is an example of UST's response to customer demand for increased efficiency. STARS provides the company's sales and marketing personnel with instant access to product and customer information. UST's new server-based Logistics Information Tracking and Reporting System (LITARS) monitors order delivery and tracks shipments to customers. This is UST's first client/server application and it utilizes Power Builder and SQL Server software. The company's plan for implementing new technologies includes a strategic planning committee, reliance on tested technologies, and the employment of Windows-based LANS.

UST PROBLEMS AND LITIGATION

The 1997 UST Annual Report listed several allegations relating specifically to smokeless tobacco products. These actions are in varying stages of pretrial activities.

UST has also been named in another action in Illinois seeking damages and other relief brought by an individual plaintiff and purports to state a class action on behalf of himself and all other persons similarly situated, alleging that his use of UST's smokeless tobacco products resulted in his addiction to nicotine, increased use of defendant's smokeless tobacco products, and gum deterioration.

UST believes, and has been so advised by counsel handling these cases, that it has a number of meritorious defenses to all such pending litigation. All such cases are and will continue to be vigorously defended, and UST believes that the ultimate outcome of all such pending litigation will not have a material adverse effect on the company.

On April 25, 1997, a federal district court ruled that the FDA, as a matter of law, is not precluded from regulating cigarettes and smokeless tobacco as "medical devices" and implementing certain labeling and access restrictions. Further trial proceedings are still required to determine whether the FDA, based on the facts, can prove that smokeless tobacco products fit the statutory definitions and whether the FDA's restrictions are justified.

On July 3, 1997, UST was served with a summons and complaint in an action entitled *Doyle* v. *United States Tobacco Company, et al.*, (Case No. C-97-380), 33rd Judicial District Court, Parish of Allen, Louisiana. This action was brought by an individual plaintiff and purports to state a class action on behalf of himself and "all smokeless tobacco users on or before June 30, 1997." The action seeks the establishment of a medical monitoring fund; the complaint does not state a claim for compensatory damages and states that "plaintiffs represent that no individual claim within the class will exceed $75,000."

The firm has faced past fines for allegedly providing samples to minors. UST has a variety of policies and procedures to discourage the use of its products by minors. For example, salespeople are fired immediately if found providing samples of the product to minors. Also, drug stores and other retail establishments will have to comply with a new FDA rule aimed at making it more difficult for young people to start using cigarettes and smokeless tobacco. A ban on product sampling could hurt UST more than cigarette manufacturers because consumers need to learn how to dip (chew) tobacco.

Because numerous other legal actions specifically target smoking, smokeless tobacco manufacturers feel they may be a future target of increased regulation.

Brown and Williamson, makers of Kool and Capri cigarettes as well as Tube Rose and Bloodhound Smokeless Tobacco, joined with five other smokeless tobacco makers in September 1995 to try to block the Food and Drug Administration's efforts to regulate the tobacco industry.

THE SMOKELESS TOBACCO INDUSTRY

On August 28, 1996, the US Food and Drug Administration (FDA) asserted jurisdiction over cigarettes and smokeless tobacco under the Federal Food, Drug, and Cosmetics Act. Under this act, a product is a "drug" or "device" subject to FDA jurisdiction if it is "intended to affect the structure or any function of the body." The FDA determined that nicotine in cigarettes and smokeless tobacco does "affect the structure or any function of the body" because nicotine causes addiction and other pharmacological effects. The FDA then determined that these pharmacological effects are "intended" because a scientific consensus has emerged that nicotine is addictive; recent studies have shown that most consumers use cigarettes and smokeless tobacco for pharmacological purposes, including satisfying their addiction to nicotine; and newly disclosed evidence from the tobacco manufacturers has revealed that the manufacturers know that nicotine causes pharmacological effects, including addiction, and design their products to provide pharmacologically active doses of nicotine. The FDA thus concluded that cigarettes and smokeless tobacco are subject to FDA jurisdiction because they contain a "drug," nicotine, and a "device" for delivering this drug to the body.

Since 1613, when John Rolfe sent the first shipment of Virginia tobacco from Jamestown to England, growing tobacco and manufacturing its products have been among the leading industries in America. Many products are manufactured from the tobacco plant. Among these are many brands of cigarettes, cigars, snuff, chewing tobacco, pipe tobacco, and useful chemical products, including those which kill insects or fungi. Of these products, the smokeless category of the tobacco industry is a dynamic segment facing many ethical and social changes.

Today, the U.S. tobacco industry is an approximately $45 billion industry, with cigarettes accounting for nearly 95 percent of the total. The remaining 5 percent of usage is for cigars, moist smokeless tobacco, chewing tobacco, and snuff. The cigarette industry is quite mature and consolidated, with the top three producers accounting for approximately 90 percent of industry sales.

The smokeless tobacco industry (SIC Code 2131) is divided into two major areas—chewing tobacco and snuff—with each area comprising different products. The chewing tobacco area consists of loose-leaf, moist, firm plug, and twist/roll products. The snuff group consists of dry and moist, depending on the amount of moisture added to the tobacco during manufacturing.

The aggregate tobacco industry is classed with oligopolistic industries such as aluminum, paper, and automobile production. Implications for all firms in an oligopolistic industry are high capital costs and barriers to enter the industry, hazardous antitrust and legal action, fruitless price cutting, and monopolistic situations when firms join in a concerted action.

The U.S. tobacco products industry has undergone substantial consolidation over the years. Prompted mainly by the combined challenges of declining U.S. consumption trends in a highly developed marketplace and the steady rise in legal and regulatory burdens, many manufacturers either joined forces with competitors or perished. The increased scale needed to compete in the industry has erected very high barriers to entry.

The smokeless tobacco industry is highly concentrated near the tobacco producing region of the United States. The five states that have the greatest number of workers in the industry are Kentucky, Tennessee, Georgia, North Carolina, and Illinois. Georgia and Illinois have replaced Virginia and Pennsylvania as leading employers of smokeless tobacco workers. Over one-half of the employment in the industry is concentrated in Kentucky. The reasons for this geographic concentration are obvious, the first being a desire to locate factories close to raw materials. This pattern can be seen in other industries which require large quantities of bulky raw materials, such as the steel industry and the petroleum industry. Another reason is that the industry is concentrated in the area of the country which has traditionally been considered the prime market for the smokeless tobacco industry, the South.

Direct substitute products for smokeless tobacco are cigarettes and cigars. Secondary substitute products can include gum, mints, and candy. The cigarette industry dwarfs the smokeless industry, with its 1996 shipments of $34,348.2 million as opposed to $2,073.7 million for the smokeless industry.

In 1976, the cigar industry fell from its historic position as the second-largest segment of the tobacco business to third place, behind the smokeless industry. But after growing at 2.4 percent since 1976, consumption on a compound annual growth rate rose to 8.9 percent from 1991 to 1994, and then zoomed to 30.6 percent from 1994

EXHIBIT 5: Tobacco Products—U.S. Per Capita Consumption

Year	Cigarettes[a] Units	Large Cigars & Cigarillos Units	Smoking Tobacco[b] Pounds	Chewing Tobacco[b] Pounds	Snuff[a] Pounds	Total Tobacco Product[a] Pounds
1996	2490	35.0	0.15	0.63	0.31	4.90
1995	2510	27.6	0.16	0.67	0.31	4.90
1994	2527	25.3	0.16	0.67	0.32	4.90
1993	2538	23.4	0.17	0.70	0.30	5.37
1992	2641	24.1	0.18	0.75	0.29	5.30

[a]Consumption per capita, 18 years and over.
[b]Consumption per male, 18 years and over.

to 1995. Cigar sales went through the roof with a 10 percent growth in units in 1996, and the imported premium category is on pace for 1997 to double 1993's total unit volume according to *Cigar Insider,* a publication that tracks that category. The surge of interest in cigars is straining the supply chain, from tobacco growers and cigar factories to box makers and band engravers. Smoking life-style magazines *Cigar Aficionado* and *Smoke* are capitalizing on the stogie's neo-cool image and drawing in luxury-goods advertisers.

Exhibit 5 shows a breakdown on consumption by category of tobacco products.

COMPETITION

Over the past 10 years, UST increased its share of the moist snuff market by 57 percent (from 23 percent to 80 percent). Like Conwood, UST is taking advantage of its existing warehouse and distribution and has diversified into other markets. As industry diversification increases, a greater decentralization of operations can be expected to rise with more than 150 brands of smokeless tobacco products available in the domestic market. UST leads all firms in the smokeless tobacco industry with 80 percent of total smokeless tobacco sales. Conwood, which represents about 11 percent of the market, is the only company which has entries in all segments of the tobacco industry. The other smokeless segment players include Pinkerton; National Tobacco; John Middleton; JBG, Inc.; RC Owen; Red Lion International; TOP Tobacco; Nuway-Microflake; and Swisher, and each has less than 2 percent of the total market.

Conwood

Conwood's major brand of chewing tobacco is Levi Garrett. Taylor's Pride and Levi Garrett Plug are their moist plug brands. Kodiak and Hawken were moist snuff brands introduced in 1981. In 1982, the company acquired another smokeless tobacco company, Scotten Dillon, which included their major brands of Union Workman and Uncle Sam. Conwood has the highest market share of any company in the dry snuff and twist/roll categories, while in the moist snuff market, Conwood's 11 percent market share is second only to UST. Conwood takes advantage of its existing warehouse and distribution networks and has diversified into other consumer-related products such as popcorn, concession supplies, and a full line of insecticides.

Pinkerton

Pinkerton Tobacco's cash cow in the mature loose-leaf segment is the Red Man brand. Red Man is also available in a moist plug form. Both forms have dwindled from their 34 percent market share in 1981. In 1993, a new entry in the moist form, called High Country, was introduced.

While its share of the moist snuff market was less than 2 percent in 1992, Pinkerton, like other tobacco manufacturers, is considering the discount snuff market as a means of expanding sales. Pinkerton's 1994 entry into the discount moist snuff segment was Timberwolf, which is produced in two flavors (regular and wintergreen) and two cuts (long and fine). Pinkerton titles this segment EDLP ("everyday low price"). As UST introduced its individually packaged Skoal Bandits, Pinkerton entered a similar product, Renegades, into the market in 1989.

ANALYZING THE SMOKELESS TOBACCO INDUSTRY USING PORTER'S FIVE FORCES

Threat of New Competitors Entering the Industry

The threat of new competitors entering the industry is limited as the industry is in maturity. Although there is rivalry among the existing industry competitors, the high entry costs, government regulations of tobacco growing, and the high costs to establish a new consumer brand with promotion are significant entry barriers to limit competition. Processing costs are also high enough so there is little or no threat of cigarette producers changing over to smokeless products production.

The Intensity of Rivalry Among Existing Competitors

Rivalry among competitors is very intense as the smokeless tobacco producers all fight for market share. They heavily promote their products in order to retain their market share and try to steal market share from their competitors. Producers use marketing, flavorings, and continued product modifications to create product interest and awareness. They also sponsor sporting events and heavily promote samples and free products to their target markets.

The Threat of Substitute Products or Services

The threat of substitute products is very limited as only other forms of smokeless products are really direct substitutes (smokeless, chewing tobacco, and snuff formats). Cigarette smoking is not a true direct substitute and as most workplaces and businesses forbid smoking cigarettes, few smokeless users will switch forms. Most are very loyal to brands and to product categories. Other indirect substitutes are food, candy, chewing gum, and almost anything else used in or near the mouth. Caffeine and alcohol are also considered by many as possible nicotine substitutes for the energy and stimulation effects of these products.

The Bargaining Power of Buyers

Buyers of the smokeless tobacco products, while a large group, have very little bargaining power. Most are avid, addicted consumers of the products and, as substitutes are not available, will continue to pay higher prices for these products. Excise taxes or "sin taxes" placed on these products increase the prices but consumers continue to pay and have high brand loyalty. Although some consumers may switch among products as prices among competing products become significantly different, as a group smokeless users are a captive audience for the tobacco manufacturers.

Tobacco products are very inelastic. As prices increase, consumers will continue to purchase the products. Progressively higher excise taxes imposed on the products do little to reduce consumption. Because substitutes are few, consumers are willing to pay more for these addictive products. Demand is inelastic as there are few or no substitutes in the minds of the consumers of these products. Generally, customers do not readily notice higher prices and buyers are slow to change their buying habits and search for lower prices. Buyers think the higher prices are justified by quality improvements, normal inflation, and other events. Demand is more elastic in the long run than the short run for this product.

The Bargaining Power of Suppliers

The suppliers of tobacco have more bargaining power than buyers. Because tobacco is the major ingredient and a large cost item for the tobacco producer, the suppliers of these raw materials have significant bargaining power. As tobacco crops are federally regulated and limited, there is a high demand for this output.

RESOURCE UTILIZATION

The most important raw material in the processing of smokeless tobacco products is the tobacco leaf. There is no substitute raw material for the tobacco leaf. Ninety-five percent of the tobacco grown in the United States is purchased at auctions from farmers. (The remaining 5 percent is principally cigar leaf tobacco.) Tobacco leaves are bundled in piles by growers for auction and are checked by U.S. government inspectors. At an auction, the buyer must pay immediately for the product. There are no credit terms, so tobacco manufacturers have a cash outlay on the front end.

The government regulates the number of acres of tobacco that may be grown in the United States. The government will go to each farm and state to monitor tobacco acreage. For example, a 20-acre farm may be allowed only two-and-a-half acres of tobacco. This rating for the farm may not change for a long time. If the land has never had tobacco acreage assigned to it and the government wants to hold down production, regulators may not allow any to be grown until a later year. This helps keep the price reasonably high for the farmers, but it can create shortages for the smokeless tobacco manufacturers. To overcome possible shortages in the United States, tobacco companies import some tobacco. Argentina, Columbia and other South American countries provide a good grade of tobacco for production in the United States.

There is competition for the tobacco raw material. Cigarettes are made from the same type of tobacco as smokeless tobacco. This means that smokeless tobacco manufacturers must compete not only with other smokeless tobacco manufacturers in purchasing tobacco leaves, but also with the smoking tobacco manufacturers. Because there is no substitute in either industry for tobacco, manufacturers constantly must have a strategy to accommodate inventory shortages.

After tobacco is purchased at auction, it must be processed further. For smokeless tobacco, leaves are run through shredders, which strip the leaf away from the stem. The leaves are dried, then moisture is added back. After the moisture content in tobacco is at its desired level, the shredded product is packed into a wooden barrel called a hogshead. It will be stored from three to five years for curing.

Tobacco cannot be used for processing before being cured because of taste and smell. The sweating process that takes place during the curing process changes the taste and smell of the tobacco. These processes tie up money in raw materials for three to five years before the companies are able to get a return on their outlay. This delay in the use of the raw material means that producers must have good long-range planning. If they underestimate future needs, years could be required for the reestablishment of inventories.

Tobacco production in the United States has remained fairly constant for the last few years. Snuff production has shown an increase every year which indicates the rising popularity of moist snuff. Moist snuff is also more popular with manufacturers because the major ingredient in moist snuff is water. A 1-ounce package of moist snuff may only contain one-tenth of an ounce of tobacco.

The United States is the world's leading tobacco exporter as well as the largest importer. The rising share of U.S. exports partially may be explained by increasing domestic taxes, prices, and government regulation. Currently, smokeless manufacturers sell most of their chewing tobacco and snuff domestically. However, UST is spending time and resources to develop, on a long-range basis, its moist smokeless tobacco internationally, where it is believed that there is considerable potential for success. (The opening of Far Eastern markets created an explosion in cigarette exports, with more than one-third of U.S. cigarettes being shipped to Japan and Taiwan.)

ETHICAL ISSUES

As with other tobacco products, there is concern over health hazards associated with smokeless tobacco. As early as 1761, awareness of smokeless tobacco's harmful effects was known as English physician John Hill warned consumers of the dangers of tobacco's use. The American Cancer Society and the American Dental Association have opposed tobacco chewing because of teeth staining as well as gum and mouth infection, which can lead to cancer. Also, dry snuff sniffed through the nostrils is considered harmful because the nerves of smell are irritated, which lessens the ability to distinguish odors. Smokeless tobacco use increases the risk of oral cancer, which includes cancer of the cheeks and gums, by 300 percent. Elevated cholesterol levels and blood pressure are other harmful side effects. The elevated levels of blood pressure appear to be from tobacco's high sodium and sugar contents. According to the American Cancer Society, some of the major ingredients in dip and chewing tobacco are nicotine (an addictive drug), polonium 210 (nuclear waste), formaldehyde (embalming fluid), cancer-causing chemicals, and radioactive elements. These are just part of the ingredients, none of which are safe, and all cause gum disease and cancer.

A December 1995 report by the American Health Foundation claims that smokeless tobacco has a cancer-causing chemical exposure greater than cigarettes. The report may result in a financial blow for UST. Spit tobacco poses health hazards to users, contrary to popular notions that it is a safe alternative to smoking. The various forms of spit tobacco have been found to cause mouth cancer, a disease responsible for more than 8,000 casualties annually. Aside from oral cancer, spit tobacco also leads to bad breath, teeth stains, gum inflammation, and/or periodontal disease with bone loss. The concentrated nicotine absorbed orally also accelerates heart rate and increases blood pressure, and can heighten the risk of coronary artery, occlusive vasular and cerebrovascular diseases, as well as stroke.

Information found in a 1991 study conducted by researchers at the University of Minnesota at Minneapolis focused on the current situation and future of the tobacco industry. They concluded the usage of smokeless tobacco in the future is likely to precede cigarette use because cigarette smokers are more likely to change their habits to smokeless tobacco. The health problems associated with smokeless tobacco use include sickness for first-time users, cancer of the mouth and throat, leukoplakia, potential cardiovascular problems, and peptic ulcers. With the use of this variety of tobacco continuing to increase, these health problems also will increase. Thus, problems associated with cigarette usage simply will be replaced with an entire new series of problems.

A study released in 1995 by the American Health Foundation found that a single can of smokeless tobacco contains about three times the dosage of cancer-causing chemicals found in a pack of cigarettes, and the average user of smokeless tobacco consumes three cans per week. In Kansas, a team of lawyers is preparing a nationwide class action alleging that UST and others have known for years that their products are addictive and harmful. Perhaps more ominously, UST's fundamental business is changing for the worse. Analysts expect profits to increase, but much of the rise will come from higher prices.

Some evidence exists which suggests tobacco manufacturers manipulate nicotine levels in smokeless products in order to increase and maintain consumer usage of their products. The possible utilization of this addictive agent as more than just a flavoring instrument raises ethical considerations. This, along with growing health issues of smokeless tobacco, has caused increased concerns.

SMOKELESS TOBACCO EDUCATION

Discouraging the use of smokeless tobacco by youth has been espoused by many medical studies. The age of children using tobacco products continuously gets lower. A recent study showed that the education of children regarding the adverse effects of tobacco begins at age 10 and the use of smokeless tobacco begins at age 12. Researchers concluded that educational emphasis on tobacco should occur in the lower grades, more specifically the fifth grade level.

The Comprehensive Smokeless Tobacco Health Education Act of 1986 was an effort by Congress aimed at curbing the use of spit tobacco. The requirements put forth by the act are threefold: inform the public of the hazards of smokeless tobacco; label packaging and restrict advertising of smokeless tobacco products; and discourage underage sales. The third requirement was upgraded to the banning of underage smokeless tobacco sales by the passage of the ADAMHA Reorganization Act in 1992. Evidence of public concern regarding smokeless tobacco is shown in the proposed federal excise tax on moist snuff. The Health Security Act proposes a $12.86 per pound tax on moist snuff, which is a dramatic increase from former levels of just 36 cents per pound.

Increased use of smokeless products by underage consumers has been linked to open use of tobacco by sports figures. In an effort to curb the negative association between baseball and chewing tobacco, minor league professional baseball outlawed its use in 1993. Fines are imposed on any employee using smokeless tobacco on or around baseball fields. A similar ban exists in New Zealand and Australia, where law prohibits "tobacco association with sports promotion." The National Cancer Institute currently targets youth in its promotional campaign to discourage the use of smokeless tobacco products.

Lennie Dykstra follows his own advice on tobacco. This baseball player, who was known for the wad of chewing tobacco in his mouth, now advocates quitting or never starting chewing tobacco. Joe Garagiola also is waging a one-man campaign to alert today's baseball players and others as to the perils of smokeless tobacco use. The former player founded the National Spit Tobacco Education Program and has toured spring training since 1994 to get the message out. Estimates have between 38 percent and 42 percent of major leaguers chewing tobacco.

MARKETING

Since 1972, smokeless tobacco product shipments have grown 4.5 times, and are now second only to cigarettes in tobacco products. Rising consumption of moist snuff and chewing tobacco has given rise to a period of heavy promotion intended to recruit new users and increase individual companies' market shares.

Traditional users of smokeless tobacco products are miners, farmers, and factory workers. These types of workers usually are required to have both hands free, and the use of lighted materials is generally prohibited because of potentially hazardous conditions. Chewing tobacco still remains predominantly a blue-collar, rural/suburban activity, but there has been some progress to new urban, inner-city markets as a result of the country western craze.

A recent study by the Department of Health and Human Services found that 19 percent of high school males use smokeless tobacco. Usage by the under-19 sector is highest in Tennessee and Montana. The study further discovered that the Midwest surpassed the South in youth usage between 1985 and 1989. Of student athletes who used smokeless tobacco products, 57 percent played baseball and 40 percent played football.

Over the last 15 to 20 years, consumers generally have been attracted to lighter products in all consumption areas. It is this lighter, milder, sweeter-tasting appeal that smokeless tobacco producers are selling to customers, at least for growth products like loose-leaf and moist snuff. Consumers can enjoy mild tobacco taste without ever "lighting up." Nationally, states have laws limiting smoking in public areas, according to the Health and Human Resource Department. Additionally, many companies have banned smoking. All of these reasons are conducive to the purchase and use of smokeless tobacco products. In addition, smokeless tobacco manufacturers have promoted their products as the most economical form of tobacco use.

Smokeless tobacco producers now are expanding their customer base into other consumer segments, including active outdoor people, sports enthusiasts, business executives, and professional people. New, younger consumers, many of whom have never used any form of tobacco before, are being attracted to smokeless tobacco products, especially the moist snuff. These younger consumers like the moist snuff because it is more socially acceptable than chewing tobacco, and snuff can be used indoors as well as outdoors, because one does not have to "spit." Internationally, most find the practice of "dipping" and "spitting" to be "gross." It is not a social custom taken up by many people.

In addition to these new, younger consumers, users of the more traditional forms of smokeless tobacco are switching to loose-leaf and moist snuff. The attraction of loose-leaf snuff lies in its image, flavor, and convenience; it is milder and sweeter than other available products. Smokeless tobacco producers fervently are promoting the idea of good taste and striving to introduce milder, more flavorful formulations like mint, wintergreen, licorice, and raspberry. UST's new Skoal Flavor Packs masks the tobacco flavor and does not require spitting. Also, individually portioned packages, like Skoal Bandits and Renegades, appeal to consumers concerned with the appearance of smokeless tobacco inside the mouth. These products contain the tobacco in a tea bag–like wrapping which circumvents the need for loose tobacco particles in the user's mouth. It is this idea of a quality product, exemplified by freshness and taste preference, that smokeless tobacco producers feel will lead consumers to becoming brand loyalists.

Characters featured in tobacco advertising, such as Joe Camel, the Marlboro Man, attractive models, or race-car heroes typically portrayed appear credible and appealing. They could influence children regarding the decision to smoke or use smokeless tobacco products.

In 1987, a radio and television advertising ban on smokeless tobacco products took effect, and manufacturers were required to put warning labels on product packages. Also, the Federal Trade Commission proposed an amendment to the Comprehensive Smokeless Tobacco Health Education Act of 1986 to include the placement of warning labels on advertising, cars, and uniforms at car races.

Smokeless tobacco producers use various ways to promote their products. Free product sampling is widely used by manufacturers for new and existing products. Samples are distributed to consumers at sporting events such as car races, concerts, gun and boat shows, and tobacco retail shows. UST has been very successful at promoting the two largest-selling brands of moist snuff in the industry, Skoal and Copenhagen. Branded merchandise is offered by UST through its Country Western Store and its concert catalogue, through which items are sold for a combination of cash and proofs of purchase from Skoal products, include T-shirts, knives, watches, key chains, radios, Skoal silver lids, and belt buckles. UST's sales representatives capitalize on product awareness with one-on-one product sampling to put products directly in the hands of customers. These new potential customers in turn demonstrate the use of the products to their friends.

UST's leading promotion is its sponsorship of the Skoal Bandit racing team on the NASCAR Grand National Circuit. Grand National racing commands an especially avid following in the Southeast, which is one of the fastest-growing markets for smokeless tobacco. Support promotion is comprehensive, including personal appearances at shopping malls and other locations by the Skoal Bandit racing team. Similar promotional efforts are made throughout the country, throughout the year, in connection with rodeo, skiing, and other sports events on local, regional, and national levels.

The industry expects new markets to be women, as well as international consumers. Analysts also feel the portrayal of smokeless tobacco use in movies like *City Slickers* and *A League of Their Own* provides good industry exposure.

THE FUTURE

While discount smokeless tobacco products enjoy only a marginal market share, their potential appears bright. Furthermore, rising export figures present an optimistic picture for expansion for American manufacturers. Increasing negative pressure on cigarette smokers offers interesting possibilities for smokeless tobacco products. However, key questions remain. Will health claims against smokeless tobacco products and advertising restrictions and warning labels hurt UST? Will litigation against smokeless tobacco users increase? With saturated markets, how can UST increase usage throughout the United States, target women and international users, and promote the lower-priced brands?

Will private label goods hurt the premium-priced brand name Skoal and Copenhagen products? Should UST cut prices and market the products more aggressively to attract new users? With men aged 18 to 34 declining in number, how can UST maintain its growth? With U.S. population growth only rising 1 percent annually, is there any hope to expand the domestic market share? Should prices be increased? How can UST ensure the viability of new product ideas and introductions?

Where should UST target internationally—Mexico, China, Sweden, or the former Soviet Union? Should UST target college campuses to draw younger users to their sweet smokeless products and risk sanctions by regulators and antismoking activists? With the current courts' awarding damages to tobacco users diagnosed with cancer, should the tobacco industry try to develop its market in alternative products? (Note: Tobacco has alternative users in nutrition, drug production, antibiotics, antiseptics, and other areas.) Will smokeless tobacco continue to be a cash cow? Is diversification the only alternative to ensure survival? What are the disadvantages of being a niche player?

Swisher International Group, Inc.—1998

David Stanton

stock symbol SWR

What do Bill Clinton, Rush Limbaugh, Sharon Stone, Michael Jordan, Demi Moore, Arnold Schwarzenegger, and more than 6 million other Americans have in common? Cigars. For years, cigars had an image problem. Cigar smoking was a smelly, disgusting habit of crotchety old men, politicians, and corporate executives. Not anymore. Today, cigars are chic, sexy, and everywhere.

Today's cigar smoker is younger and more likely to be a woman than ever before. Men are still a large majority, but more professional women and more female celebrities are joining the men in smoking cigars. A woman who smokes a cigar is seen as fearless, independent, fun, and a bit naughty. And despite American Cancer Society warnings that cigar smoking can cause cancer of the mouth and larynx, cigar bars and tobacco shops are sprouting across the country to support a $5.1 billion cigar habit and the fastest-growing segment of the tobacco market. Driving the trend is the imported, hand-rolled cigar made from premium tobacco. As with fine liquor or wine, taste is everything and premium cigars are expensive, from $1 to $20 apiece.

Marvin Shanken's five-year-old *Cigar Aficionado* magazine has been a catalyst of the trend. Shanken, the founder of *Wine Spectator* magazine, says he decided to launch *Cigar Aficionado* on a hunch. The magazine helped begin and sustain the cigar boom by associating cigars with success and the good life. On the cover is a cigar-smoking celebrity. Inside are drooling cigar reviews, interviews with celebrities and cigar industry insiders, and articles on everything from high-end audio equipment to personal spas. Sharing space with the articles are ads for Rolex; Saks Fifth Avenue; and pricey cognac, bourbon, and single-malt scotch whisky. It is practically a how-to manual for conspicuous consumption. The magazine itself is conspicuous at 9-by-12 inches and roughly one-and-a-half pounds of slick, glossy paper. The magazine's readers have higher-than-average incomes, but cigars are not just for the wealthy. Almost anyone can afford an expensive cigar occasionally and enjoy a little piece of success.

Swisher International Group, Inc. (904-353-4311), headquartered in Jacksonville, Florida, is profiting from the cigar boom. Swisher sells more cigars than any other company in the world. It owns the most widely sold cigar brand name in the world (Swisher Sweets) and is the most diversified cigar company, with revenues spread evenly over all cigar categories, rather than on premium cigars as its competitors are. Swisher also is diversified outside the cigar business, with about 28 percent of its

This case was prepared by David Stanton of the University of South Carolina as a basis for class discussion. It is not intended to illustrate either effective or ineffective handling of an administrative situation. Copyright © 1999 by Prentice Hall, Inc. ISBN 0-13-011175-9.

revenues coming from smokeless tobacco, an even faster-growing market segment than cigars.

Swisher had a 10 percent share of the premium cigar market in 1996, but the company is better known for its cheaper, machine made, mass market large cigars. It leads in mass market large cigars (26 percent share), little cigars (41 percent share), and dry snuff (30 percent share), and has a 5 percent niche share in moist smokeless tobacco. Swisher's revenues and net income increased nicely in 1997 to $276 million and $39 million respectively.

Since 1993, there has been an ongoing industry increase in cigar sales in all categories—mass market large, mass market little, and premium. Retail sales broke the billion-dollar barrier for the first time in 1995 and approximated $1.4 billion in 1997. The growth can be attributed to more favorable exposure in the media, the increased acceptance of cigar smoking at home and in public places such as restaurants and cigar bars, and positive demographics boosted by the baby boomers who have reached the traditional cigar-smoking age.

HISTORY

Swisher was founded in Newark, Ohio, in 1861. It acquired one of its most famous brands, King Edward, in 1918, and in 1924 moved its main production facilities to Jacksonville, Florida, where it remains today. It created its signature Swisher Sweets in 1958, and was acquired by American Maize-Products Company in 1966.

In recent years, Swisher completed three major cost saving initiatives. In 1992, the company closed its dry snuff and moist snuff plant in Helmetta, New Jersey, and moved its operations to its Wheeling, West Virginia, facility. Effective June 30, 1994, Helme Tobacco Company, Swisher's wholly owned smokeless tobacco subsidiary, was merged into Swisher. Helme's executive office in Stamford, Connecticut, was closed, and the Helme and Swisher management and sales forces were consolidated. As a result of the merger, Swisher realized significant reductions in selling, general, and administrative expenses. In 1994, the company closed its Waycross, Georgia, cigar plant and consolidated all of its cigar manufacturing in its Jacksonville facility. As a result of these consolidations, Swisher incurred pretax restructuring charges totaling $14.2 million, and realized significant cost savings in its base manufacturing and selling costs, as well as its general and administrative expenses.

In February 1995, American Maize Chair of the Board William Ziegler III blocked an offer by Eridania Beghin-Say, S.A., (EBS) to purchase American Maize at $32 per share. After shareholders publicly criticized Ziegler for blocking the sale, the board of directors removed him as chair, a position he had held since 1964. Ziegler sued to block the sale and won on appeal. In the final settlement, EBS agreed to sell Swisher to Ziegler upon completion of the American Maize acquisition at $40 per share.

Through November 6, 1995, Swisher International, Inc., was a wholly owned subsidiary of American Maize. On November 6, 1995, EBS sold the common stock of Swisher International, Inc., to Swisher International Group, Inc., a holding company that was at that time a wholly owned subsidiary of Hay Island Holding Corporation, which in turn is owned and controlled by Ziegler. The purchase price was $169,773,000, composed of $39,773,000 in cash and $130,000,000 in debt.

On December 18, 1996, Swisher International Group, Inc., completed an initial public offering of 6 million shares of Class A Common Stock at $17 each. The Class A shares carry one vote each. Hay Island owns 28.1 million shares of Class B stock, which carry 10 votes each, and although Hay Island owns 82.4 percent of the shares, it controls 97.9 percent of the vote. Thus, Ziegler, through Hay Island, can control any matter that may be brought before the board for a vote. Further, any Class B shares that are sold to the public in the future will be converted automatically into Class A shares, allowing Ziegler, through Hay Island, to sell shares while retaining the votes to control the board of directors.

INTERNAL ENVIRONMENT

Operations

Swisher's manufacturing strategy is to be the low-cost producer in its industry; to produce high-quality products; and to maintain flexible manufacturing capabilities that enable it to respond to changing market demands, develop new products, and extend the product line of existing brands.

Swisher believes that its Jacksonville facility, which manufactures over 4 million cigars daily, is the most automated cigar-manufacturing facility in the United States. As a result of the emphasis on increased automation, productivity has increased and fewer machines are required to perform the same manufacturing processes. Manufacturing large quantities of certain cigar sizes enables Swisher to use high-volume, efficient equipment to manufacture them in large production runs. Swisher also manufactures its reconstituted tobacco wrapper and binder, manufactures its boxes, and packages its cigars at the Jacksonville facility.

Products

Swisher sells mass market large cigars, premium cigars, little cigars, moist and dry snuff, and loose-leaf chewing tobacco. It currently derives about half of its revenues from mass market large cigars, 12 percent from premium cigars, 10 percent from little cigars, and 28 percent from smokeless tobacco. The company has low raw material inventory requirements for cigar production due to its long-standing relationships with major tobacco suppliers.

Mass market large cigars generally are machine made and have a retail price of $1 or less per cigar. They are made with filler threshed into short uniform pieces and wrappers made from reconstituted tobacco. Swisher is expanding production at its mass market, machine made cigar manufacturing facility in Jacksonville.

Premium cigars generally are handmade and have a retail price above $1 per cigar. They are made by wrapping natural-leaf binder tobacco around long filler tobacco to create a bunch that is pressed into a mold. Then natural-leaf wrapper tobacco is hand-rolled around the bunch and the cigar is cut to length. Higher grades of tobacco are used in premium cigars, with blends varying depending on the desired characteristics. The supply of premium cigars is relatively inelastic because increases in the supply of labor and raw materials tend to trail increased demand. Higher grades of tobacco are used in premium cigars, and fine tobacco takes time to produce. First, the grower must provide a quality crop. It is an involved, labor-intensive process, subject to the vagaries of the weather. Then, the raw tobacco must be cured, fermented, and aged for several years before it is ready for use in a fine cigar. Also, it takes about a year to properly train a new cigar roller, and there is a bidding war for qualified cigar rollers. Swisher now purchases its premium cigars from contractors located in the Dominican Republic, Honduras, and Nicaragua, but the company is building its own cigar-making facility in Honduras as well as a joint venture facility in the Dominican Republic.

Little cigars are machine made, mass market cigars that weigh less than three pounds per thousand. They consist of cut filler tobacco, a filter and a wrapper made from reconstituted tobacco, and, like cigarettes, are sold in packs of 20. They are the lowest-priced products of the mass market cigar category. Swisher historically purchased little cigars from outside manufacturers, but began to manufacture them at its Jacksonville facility. The company began producing all of its little cigars itself in the fourth quarter of 1997. Swisher believes that this will increase production capacity, reduce its cost of producing little cigars, and increase its already generous margins.

Swisher's largest working capital requirements are driven by its smokeless tobacco operations. Because the tobacco for these products must be aged before being processed into finished products, Swisher must maintain sufficient raw material inventory to ensure proper aging and an adequate supply. Swisher manufactures all its smokeless tobacco products at its Wheeling, West Virginia, facility.

Moist snuff is made from Kentucky or Tennessee dark-fired tobacco that has been aged for at least 3 years and then cut, flavored, and fermented for eight weeks. After fermentation, more flavoring is added before the snuff is packaged for sale. Swisher is expanding its moist snuff manufacturing capacity.

Dry snuff is made from Kentucky, Tennessee, and Virginia dark-fired tobacco that is aged for at least 3 years. It is then fermented for approximately 30 days, dried, cut into a fine tobacco flour, and flavored before packaging.

Loose-leaf chewing tobacco is made from air-cured tobacco grown primarily in Wisconsin and Pennsylvania. It is aged for at least two years, threshed to remove stems, blended, flavored, and packaged in foil pouches. Swisher supplies many distributors with private label loose-leaf products.

Marketing and Distribution

Swisher considers itself "first and foremost" a marketing company and, indeed, Swisher appears to be the most marketing-oriented company in the industry. It built its leadership position on established brand names. Swisher Sweets is the best-selling brand in the United States and the world in both the large and little cigar categories, and Swisher estimates that its products are available in over 70 countries worldwide. During 1997, approximately 3.5 percent of the Swisher revenues were derived from export sales and royalties. Swisher employs 250 salespeople marketing its products nationally (compared to only 140 for Consolidated Cigar) and sells to more than 200,000 outlets.

The sales force has two divisions. One sells mass market cigars and smokeless tobacco; the other is a separate sales force for premium cigars.

The mass market sales force is organized into territories and calls on direct-buying accounts such as tobacco distributors, wholesale grocers, and retail chains as well as retailers who purchase from such direct buying accounts. Most of the company's sales are to tobacco distributors, including McLane Company, Inc., which accounted for approximately 12 percent, 14 percent, and 12 percent of Swisher's net sales in 1997,

1996, and 1995, respectively, and food and drug chains, such as Food Lion, Winn Dixie, Rite Aid, CVS, and Walgreens. Swisher's products ultimately are sold through grocery and drug stores, mass merchandisers, convenience stores, smokeshops, bars, restaurants, and other stores.

Direct retail account contact helps Swisher introduce new products, improve the quality and quantity of its shelf space, and improve the placement of point-of-sale materials for its products. Through this organization, Swisher has become the category manager for the "other tobacco" category with several of its big retail chain accounts, allowing the company to better market its products.

Swisher has allocated more resources to premium cigars as sales have risen. The Premium and Export Division markets its premium cigars to smoke shops, restaurants, cigar bars, golf club pro shops, and tobacco retailers.

Swisher's salespeople use laptop computers to access consumer account and product information while in the field. Swisher makes the most extensive use of Nielsen data of any company in the industry. The company uses the data to track national and regional trends in cigars and smokeless tobacco, including industry unit and market share trends. The data, in combination with market research, help the company to develop regionally targeted marketing strategies, reposition products, or develop new ones.

Swisher's marketing focuses on selected print advertising and point-of-sale promotions. The company's promotional programs primarily are geared to providing discounts, coupons, and rebate offers to its customers and to offer display fixtures to the retail stores it services.

Swisher leads the cigar market, but it trails in the larger smokeless market. However, the company has succeeded in leveraging its cigar leadership to support its smokeless brands. Salespeople use the cigars' market strength at the retail level to ensure that its smokeless tobacco products are well displayed. The smokeless products are backed with promotional pricing, merchandising materials, and extensive print advertising. Swisher's share of the smokeless market is increasing.

Swisher is the leading exporter of American-made cigars. First introduced in 1906, the King Edward brand is the most widely distributed American cigar and the leading export brand. Export sales are generated through an international network of distributors and through Swisher International, Limited, a wholly owned duty-free sales company in the United Kingdom. Swisher estimates that its products are available in over 70 countries. The company also is increasing its presence in foreign markets through licensing agreements. The company has licensed brands to manufacturers in the Netherlands, England, Germany, and the Canary Islands (for distribution to Spain). Export sales and royalties on licensed sales generate only a small portion of revenues, but the company is seeking to increase its exports and licensing agreements.

Research and Development

Swisher has a successful track record of developing and introducing new products. In 1996, new products contributed 11 percent of net sales, or $31 million, and more than 25 percent of Swisher's net sales are from products introduced in the past 10 years. In most cases, Swisher takes advantage of its position as the leader in the cigar industry when developing and introducing new products; most are different sizes, shapes, and flavors of the company's well-known existing brands, although several are substantially different products. Swisher has a sensory evaluation lab that pretests its products and can test any blend changes as well.

The company's most successful new product introduction has been little cigars. Swisher entered the little cigar market in 1986 with its new Swisher Sweets brand of little cigars. In 1997, it had a 45 percent share of the little cigar market it entered only 10 years before.

Swisher recently developed several new products under its well-known King Edward brand. In 1996, it introduced King Edward aromatic vanilla- and cherry-flavored cigars with a wood tip. In 1997, it introduced the King Edward Classic, a mid-priced large cigar with an imported, natural-leaf wrapper.

In 1996, Swisher introduced two new cigars under the Blackstone name, a new brand of cigars which are made from a pipe tobacco blend and have the aroma and flavor of pipe tobacco. The new brand has been a strong performer.

In 1997, Swisher launched Cazadores. Cazadores is the first of a new category created by Swisher: machine made, mass market premium cigars. The product is designed to capitalize on the industry shortage of premium cigars. Because Cazadores are machine made rather than hand rolled, Swisher expects to be able to meet demand. Cazadores have high-quality filler tobacco, a natural tobacco wrapper, and premium-style packaging. The new cigar is priced at around $1.50 each and packaged for individual sale in convenience stores and large retail outlets, instead of in the small cigar stores where premium cigars usually are sold. Initial reaction was favorable, with reorders exceeding projections.

In the premium cigar category, Swisher added new products to its Bering and Pleiades brands. It also introduced new brands such as Siglo 21 and Flor de Jalapa. And, in 1997, the company launched Pleiades Reserve Privee, a specially aged, "vintage" tobacco cigar line available in limited quantities.

Swisher also introduced new value-priced and private label products in its smokeless tobacco market. Silver Creek Fine Cut, Silver Creek Straight, and Silver Creek Cherry are new additions to its Silver Creek brand of moist snuff line.

Finance

When Ziegler bought Swisher International, Inc., through Swisher International Group, his Hay Island Holding Corporation's subsidiary, Swisher International Group assumed debt amounting to $130 million. When Swisher International Group went public in 1996, the net proceeds of $95.1 million went to Hay Island rather than to pay down the debt. As a result, a significant portion of cash flow from operations must be dedicated to the payment of principal of and interest on debt, thereby reducing the amount of funds available for working capital, capital expenditures, and other purposes. The terms of the credit agreement restrict Swisher's ability to declare dividends or make distributions, and the company does not anticipate that any dividends will be declared on the common stock. It currently intends to retain all earnings for use in the operations of its business.

The acquisition was accounted for as a purchase, which resulted in a new basis of accounting for periods subsequent to the acquisition date. As a result of the acquisition, Swisher's consolidated results of operations and cash flows for the year ended December 31, 1996, and for the period from November 7 to December 31, 1995, are not comparable to prior periods.

Management

Swisher is a family-owned, family-run company. William Ziegler III is chief executive officer and chair of the board. William T. Ziegler, his son, is chief operating officer and chair of the executive committee. His daughter, Cynthia Z. Brighton, is treasurer and vice-president—financial services. His son, Karl H. Ziegler, is secretary. His son, Peter M. Ziegler, is vice-president—corporate planning. His daughter, Helen Z. Benjamin, is assistant secretary. William T. Ziegler's wife, Jackqueline B. Ziegler, is vice-president—marketing development of the company's wholly owned subsidiary, Swisher International, Inc. (See Exhibit 1.)

Under the leadership of the Ziegler family, Swisher pursues manufacturing efficiencies through a "total resource management" program. It includes cross-departmental employee teams that troubleshoot manufacturing problems, and a "Big Idea" program whereby employees are awarded incentive bonuses for introducing and implementing cost-saving ideas.

The company maintains a management incentive plan to compensate employees for their contributions to revenue growth, improved operating profit, cost control, and production facility utilization. In 1997, the company paid bonuses of approximately $2.9 million under the plan for the year ended December 31, 1996.

Swisher and Hay Island entered into a management services agreement (MSA) effective January 1, 1997. The services provided by Hay Island include treasury and cash management; risk management (including obtaining liability, property, and casualty insurance); human resource management; marketing support; long-term strategic

EXHIBIT 1:   Organizational Chart for Swisher International Group, Inc.

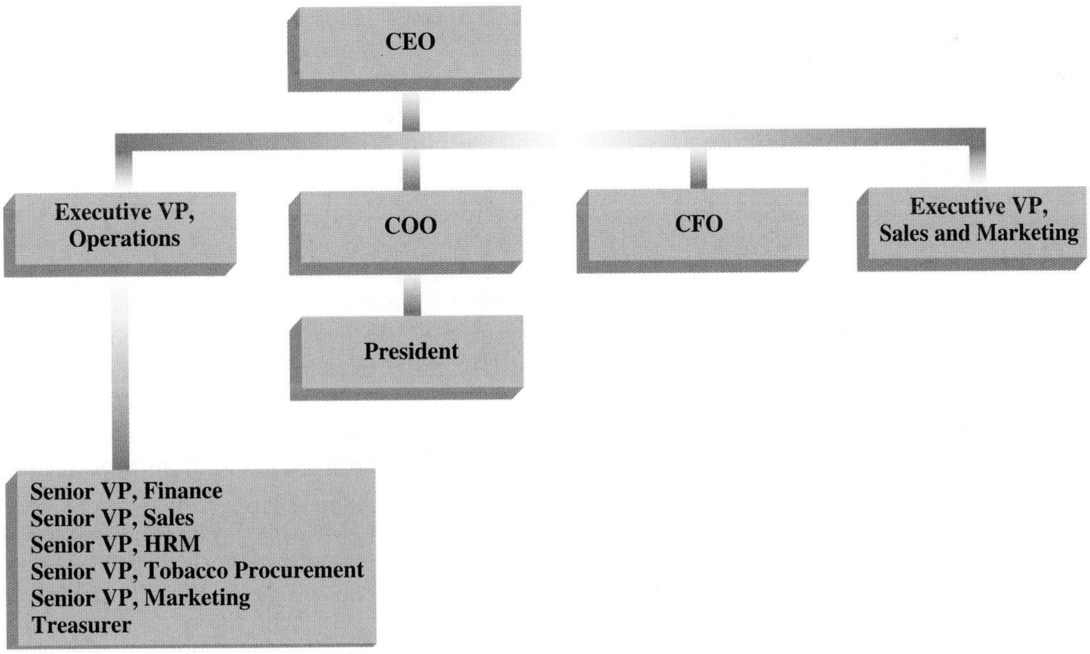

Source: Swisher International Group, Inc.

347

planning; business development; and investor relations. William Ziegler III; William T. Ziegler; Cynthia Z. Brighton; Karl H. Ziegler; Peter M. Ziegler; Helen Z. Benjamin; and Jackqueline B. Ziegler became employees of Hay Island and are compensated through the MSA.

SALES

Swisher—1996

For the year ended December 31, 1996, Swisher's net income was nearly $24.8 million, an increase of 16 percent, or almost $3.5 million, from 1995 net income of over $21 million. Net sales increased $38.8 million, or 20.8 percent, from $186.4 million in 1995 to an all-time high of $225.2 million in 1996. Most of the net income growth came from improved margins, up from 8.4 percent of net sales in 1995 to 11.0 percent of net sales in 1996.

The increase in net sales was primarily due to higher sales of cigars and, to a lesser extent, higher sales of smokeless tobacco products. Cigar sales increased due to growth in unit volumes of premium, mass market large cigars and little cigars, a shift in sales mix to higher-priced cigars, and price increases on all cigar brands. Smokeless tobacco sales increased as a result of continued volume increases, particularly in moist snuff. Selling, general, and administrative expenses increased in 1996, but at a slower rate than the increase in net sales. Operating profit rose 71 percent, from $34 million in 1995 to $58 million in 1996. Over the same period, earnings per share on a pro forma basis increased from $.45 to $.86. Swisher has the highest gross profit and pro forma operating margins in the cigar industry. Swisher's 1996 average debt balance was $122.9 million, down from $129.0 million in 1995.

Swisher's brands now account for approximately 8 percent of worldwide cigar unit sales and 31 percent of cigar unit sales in the United States. In nearly every category in 1996, Swisher exceeded industry growth rates, resulting in increased market share.

In 1996, approximately 2.8 billion mass market, machine made large cigars were sold in the United States. The category is the nation's biggest in terms of units and sales dollars, with 61 percent of unit sales and an estimated 68 percent of retail dollar sales in 1996. Swisher is the category leader, and Swisher Sweets is the dominant large cigar brand, accounting for approximately one of every four cigars sold. Swisher had a 26 percent unit market share in 1996, with net sales of $108 million. Swisher's established mass market, large cigar brands include Swisher Sweets, King Edward, Optimo, Santa Fe, Keep Moving, and El Trelles. The Swisher Sweets large cigar brand is sold in various shapes and styles, including Kings, Tip Cigarillos, Cigarillos, Perfectos, Wood Tips, Blunts, and the new Swisher Sweets Outlaws rough-cut cigar. The King Edward large cigar brand is also sold in a variety of shapes and flavors, including Wood Tips, Sweet Cherry Wood Tips, Sweet Vanilla Wood Tips, Imperials, Specials, and Tip Cigarillos.

In 1996, the U.S. market for premium cigars consisted of approximately 274 million units, or only 6 percent of the total cigar market. However, because of their higher prices, premium cigars accounted for an estimated 22 percent of total retail cigar revenues, or about $264 million. In 1996, the premium cigar market grew by a remarkable 67 percent. Swisher had a 10 percent unit market share in 1996, with net sales of $31 million, just 10 years after it entered the premium cigar business with the 1986 acquisition of the Bering brand. Swisher's established premium brands include Bering and La Primadora, and recent product introductions include Siglo 21, Sabroso, Flor de Jalapa, and La Diligencia. It also has exclusive rights to the United States distribution of the Pleiades, Casa Buena, and Carlin premium brands. In 1996, Swisher had approximately $10 million in back orders for premium cigars, an industry-wide problem caused by increased demand.

In 1996, the market for little cigars in the United States consisted of approximately 1.5 billion units sold, or 33 percent of the total cigar market. Little cigars carry the highest margins of any cigar. The U.S. mass market, little cigar category accounted for an estimated $120 million of retail sales in 1996, or 10 percent of total cigar revenues. Industry little cigar unit sales were up 6 percent from the previous year. Swisher introduced its first little cigars in 1986. By 1996, the company had a 41 percent unit market share and net sales of $22 million. The company's brands include Swisher Sweets Little Cigars and King Edward Little Cigars. Swisher Sweets Little Cigars are the largest-selling little cigars in the United States in both units and dollars. Swisher has capitalized on the success of Swisher Sweets Little Cigars by introducing menthol, light, and cherry-flavored versions. In 1996, the Swisher Sweets brand grew at nearly twice the rate of the entire little cigar category, which led to an increase in market share.

In 1996, total U.S. retail revenues for smokeless tobacco products approximated $1.4 billion. Swisher's smokeless tobacco net sales totaled $64 million in 1996.

Total U.S. moist snuff retail revenues were $1.92 billion (56.2 million pounds). While the overall moist snuff market showed modest growth of approximately 4 percent in 1996, Swisher's unit sales were up 14 percent, which led to an increase in market share. Swisher had a 4.6 percent share of the 1996 moist snuff market. Swisher's sales, as measured in pounds, increased from 1987 to 1996 at a compound annual rate of 17.8 percent, or more than three times the market growth rate of approximately 5 percent. Moist snuff represented approximately 45 percent of the company's 1996 net sales of smokeless tobacco products. Swisher's moist snuff brands include Silver Creek, Redwood, Cooper, and Gold River. In addition, the company manufactures private label brands for distributors. In 1996, the company installed new packaging equipment at its Wheeling, West Virginia, facility that lowered the cost of each pound sold.

Retail sales of dry snuff in 1996 were an estimated $76 million (4.7 million pounds). From 1985 to 1996, the dry snuff market declined at a 6.1 percent compound annual rate in terms of pounds sold. However, dry snuff still provides significant cash flow because of the industry's ability to offset the decline with price increases. Swisher had a 29.2 percent share of the 1996 market, and has maintained a relatively constant market share. Its major brands are Tops, Navy, Railroad Mills, Superior, Buttercup, Square, Society, and Honey Bee. The category, with its substantial profit margins and low marketing costs, helps generate strong cash flow for Swisher.

Swisher had a 6.7 percent share of the 1996 loose-leaf chewing tobacco market. The company's unit sales of loose-leaf chewing tobacco increased by 10.4 percent from 1995 to 1996 even as industry unit sales declined by about 3 percent. The company attributes this growth to a revised marketing strategy, new promotional pricing, and the successful introduction of product extensions, such as the new flavors of Earl Caulfield's. Mail Pouch, which celebrated its 100th anniversary in 1996, was the original loose-leaf chewing tobacco, and it is still a strong selling brand. Swisher's brands also include Lancaster Limited-Reserve Chewing Tobacco, Chattanooga Chew, and Earl Caulfield's. Swisher also supplies many distributors with private label products.

Swisher—1997

Swisher's long-term debt and common stock outstanding remained constant in 1997 while revenues and net income increased dramatically (see Exhibit 2). In 1997, the market for mass market large cigars in the United States consisted of an estimated 3.2 billion units, or 62 percent of the total cigar market. Swisher had the leading unit market share of the domestic mass market for large cigars at an estimated 26 percent.

In 1997, the market for premium cigars in the United States represented an estimated 375 million units, or almost 7 percent of the total cigar market. Swisher's unit share of the premium cigar market in 1997 was an estimated 6 percent.

In 1997, the market for little cigars in the United States represented an estimated 1.6 billion units, or 31 percent of the total cigar market. Swisher had the leading unit market share of mass market little cigars at an estimated 46 percent including Swisher Sweets, King Edward, and the new Blackstone little cigar brand.

The overall cigar market has experienced rapid growth in unit volume and dollar sales since 1993, reversing the steady decline in the market from 1973 to 1993. Led by growth in mass market large and premium cigars, the overall United States cigar market has increased at an estimated compound annual rate of 10.7 percent in unit terms, and has increased at nearly three times that rate in retail dollar sales from 1993 to 1997. Unit sales of mass market large and premium cigars have increased at estimated compound annual rates of 11.8 percent and 35.9 percent, respectively, from 1993 to 1997, while retail dollar sales of both categories have increased more rapidly due to price increases. Little cigar unit volume grew from 1985 to 1993 at a compound annual rate of 0.6 percent. From 1993 to 1997, little cigar unit volume increased at an estimated compound annual rate of 5.7 percent.

Loose leaf is the predominant product in the chewing tobacco category, with plug and twist representing less than 10 percent of the chewing tobacco volume in 1997.

Moist snuff, with estimated industry retail sales in 1997 of $2 billion (57.7 million pounds), is the largest category of smokeless tobacco in terms of retail sales. Swisher's branded moist snuff comes in various flavors, such as natural, wintergreen, cherry and spearmint, and in both fine and long cut varieties.

Retail sales of all chewing tobacco in 1997, of which over 90 percent is loose leaf, were an estimated $477 million (50.3 million pounds).

Aggregate retail sales of all dry snuff in 1997 were an estimated $76 million (4.4 million pounds). Although total unit consumption of smokeless tobacco products has remained relatively stable since the late 1980s, retail dollar sales have increased at an estimated compound annual rate of 7.9 percent from $1.0 billion in 1985 to an estimated $2.6 billion in 1997, primarily due to the growth of the moist snuff category. Consumption of moist snuff, which represents over one-half of the pounds sold in the smokeless tobacco market and an estimated 78 percent of the retail sales, has increased in terms of retail dollar sales at an estimated compound annual rate of 10.9 percent from 1985 to 1997. Loose-leaf chewing tobacco sales, in terms of pounds, declined from 1985 to 1997 at an estimated compound annual rate of 2.9 percent. However, industry retail dollar sales of all chewing tobacco (of which over 90 percent is loose-leaf) increased from $381.8 million to an estimated $477.0 million over the same period as a result of the industry's ability to increase product prices. Although the mature dry snuff market has been declining in terms of pounds sold from 1985 to 1997 at an estimated 6.2 percent compound annual rate, dry snuff has continued to provide a significant source of cash flow.

EXHIBIT 2: Swisher International Group, Inc., and Subsidiaries, Consolidated Balance Sheets

(dollars in thousands)	As of December 31, 1997	1996
Assets:		
Current assets:		
Cash and cash equivalents	$ 1,057	$ 1,744
Accounts receivable, less allowance for doubtful accounts of $1,643 and $1,783, respectively	32,348	22,365
Inventories	60,714	54,936
Deferred income taxes	1,218	1,203
Prepaid income taxes	0	323
Other current assets	3,096	2,247
Total current assets	98,433	82,818
Property, plant and equipment:		
Land	1,299	1,319
Buildings and improvements	10,812	10,054
Machinery and equipment	51,300	46,284
Construction in progress	11,998	2,848
	75,409	60,505
Less, accumulated depreciation	7,155	3,642
	68,254	56,863
Goodwill, net of accumulated amortization of $3,512 and $1,808, respectively	46,733	48,437
Investments in affiliates	13,315	0
Prepaid pension cost	4,972	4,660
Other assets	6,050	6,152
Total assets	$237,757	$198,930
Liabilities and Stockholders' Equity:		
Current liabilities:		
Current portion of long-term debt	0	17,102
Accounts payable	8,102	4,927
Accrued expenses	8,657	8,087
Due to affiliates	5,900	0
Income taxes payable	2,863	0
Total current liabilities	25,522	30,116
Long-term debt	101,092	100,583
Deferred income taxes	7,296	4,589
Accrued postretirement and postemployment benefits	14,241	13,788
Other liabilities	3,657	3,311
Total liabilities	151,808	152,387
Commitments and contingencies		
Stockholders' equity:		
Common Stock	341	341
Paid-in capital	45,428	45,428
Retained earnings	40,069	774
Cumulative translation adjustments	111	0
Total stockholders' equity	85,949	46,543
Total liabilities and stockholders' equity	$237,757	$198,930

Source: www.freeedgar.com

EXHIBIT 3: Swisher International Group, Inc., and Subsidiaries, Consolidated Statements of Income

	Successor			Predecessor
(dollars in thousands)	Year Ended December 31, 1997	Year Ended December 31, 1996	Period from November 7 to December 31, 1995	Period from January 1 to November 6, 1995
Net sales	$275,644	$225,229	$31,266	$155,120
Cost of sales	137,708	113,764	16,514	83,522
Gross profit	137,936	111,465	14,752	71,598
Selling, general and administrative expenses	64,862	61,008	7,207	40,331
Operating profit	73,074	50,457	7,545	31,267
Interest expense, net	8,049	9,505	1,670	3,437
Other expense (income), net	340	153	25	(2,360)
Income before income taxes and minority interest	64,685	40,799	5,850	30,190
Provision for income taxes	25,390	16,006	2,228	11,536
Income before minority interest	39,295	24,793	3,622	18,654
Minority interest in earnings of subsidiary	0	0	0	(967)
Net income	39,295	24,793	3,622	17,687
Earnings per share:				
Basic	1.15	.73		
Diluted	1.15	.73		
Weighted average shares outstanding:				
Basic	34,100	34,100		
Diluted	34,152	34,100		

Source: www.freeedgar.com

EXTERNAL ENVIRONMENT

Competition

Including Swisher, four manufacturers dominate the U.S. cigar industry with more than 80 percent of the market. Swisher's three significant competitors in the cigar market are Consolidated Cigar Holdings Inc.; General Cigar Holdings, Inc.; and Havatampa/Phillies Cigar Corporation. Tobacco Exporters International Limited (a subsidiary of Rothmans International) is a significant competitor in the little cigar market.

Consolidated Cigar Holdings, Inc., is the largest manufacturer and marketer of cigars sold in the United States in terms of dollar sales. Its cigar products are marketed under a number of well-known brand names at all price levels and in all segments, and the company's share of the premium cigar market is larger than Swisher's.

General Cigar Holdings, Inc., is the largest U.S. manufacturer and marketer of brand name premium cigars. Its Macanudo and Partagas brands are the two top-selling premium cigar brands sold in the United States. Approximately 80 percent of the company's premium cigar sales in fiscal 1996 were at suggested retail prices of $3 or more per unit. The company participates in the mass market cigar segment through its Garcia y Vega brand.

Havatampa/Phillies Cigar Corporation of Tampa, Florida, is the fourth-largest U.S. cigar company in sales. Havatampa makes machine made, popularly priced large and little cigars. In 1997, the world's oldest tobacco company, Spain's Tabacalera SA, announced plans to buy the cigar division of Havatampa. It also announced plans to buy two Central American producers, Tabacalera San Cristobal de Honduras S.A. and Tabacalera San Cristobal de Nicaragua SA, which together make 24 million premium cigars annually. Tabacalera also announced an agreement to buy Max Rohr Importer, Inc., a leading U.S. importer and distributor of premium cigars. The acquisitions will make Tabacalera, which has had virtually no U.S. manufacturing or retailing presence, a leading player with more than 25 percent of the U.S. market for large cigars. The company will be able to produce and sell over 1 billion cigars annually. Tabacalera, founded in 1636, calls itself the inventor of the modern cigar. With 6,650 employees, the company produces nearly 400 million cigars and 3.5 billion packs of cigarettes a year.

Swisher's major competitors in the smokeless tobacco products market are UST, Inc.; Conwood Corporation; Brown & Williamson Tobacco Company; National Tobacco Company; and Pinkerton Group, Inc. UST, which owns almost 80 percent of the moist snuff market, has taken notice of the success of Swisher's moist snuff value pricing strategy and introduced its own value brand, Red Seal.

Litigation and Regulation

The tobacco industry is experiencing significant health-related litigation. There have been no adverse decisions or judgments rendered against smokeless tobacco or cigar manufacturers, but Swisher is named in two actions brought by plaintiffs against a number of smokeless tobacco manufacturers.

In June 1997, the five largest U.S. tobacco companies announced an agreement with trial lawyers and the attorneys general of the states suing them for medicare/medicaid reimbursement. The settlement proposed new federal legislation that would force tobacco companies to pay substantial penalties and subject them to federal Food and Drug Administration (FDA) regulation. The legislation proposed by the settlement has not been introduced, but it eventually could affect Swisher's smokeless tobacco business. Press reports indicate that the legislation will be directed at manufacturers of cigarettes and smokeless tobacco. However, pressure to include cigars in the legislation has come from former Surgeon General C. Everett Koop and former FDA Commissioner David Kessler, two of the most powerful forces in the tobacco debate and advisers to President Bill Clinton on the proposed settlement.

In addition to increased litigation, the tobacco industry has been under ever-increasing regulatory pressure in recent years. Special interest groups, surgeons general, and state and federal elected officials have grown more aggressive in their efforts to reduce tobacco consumption. Much of the focus has been directed at cigarettes, although cigar and smokeless tobacco companies also have been affected.

Cigar and smokeless tobacco companies are subject to federal, state, and local taxes and regulations. Higher taxes and expansion of smoking regulations have contributed to a decline in tobacco consumption, and the trend is toward more regulation and higher taxes. Most states and many local governments now restrict or prohibit smoking in some public places, and the Balanced Budget Act adopted by Congress in 1997 increases federal excise taxes on all tobacco products. In Massachusetts, lawmakers are pushing for warning labels on cigars similar to those on cigarettes. Texas has banned all self-service tobacco displays, including those for cigars.

In 1996, the FDA published new regulations prohibiting the sale of cigarettes and smokeless tobacco products to minors and restricting marketing and manufacturing practices. The portion requiring age identification took effect in February 1997. In April 1997, a U.S. district court in North Carolina held that the FDA was authorized to regulate tobacco products, but invalidated the portions of the regulations that sought to restrict advertising and promotion. The district court's decision has been appealed to the United States Court of Appeals for the Fourth Circuit. The remaining provisions of the regulation are due to take effect in 1998. Any further provisions of these regulations that become effective could affect Swisher adversely.

CONSIDERATIONS FOR THE FUTURE

Swisher is the largest, most diversified, and most profitable cigar company in the industry. With the highest gross profit and pro forma operating margins in the cigar industry, Swisher is well positioned to continue its dynamic growth.

Cigar sales peaked at 11.2 billion units in 1973, after which volume declined for the next 20 years, reaching a low of only 3.4 billion units in 1993. The cigar market has experienced rapid growth in unit volume and dollar sales since then. From 1993 to 1996, the U.S. cigar market grew at an average annual rate of 9.8 percent in unit volume, and almost twice that rate in retail dollar sales. But even with these impressive gains, the estimated 4.4 billion cigars sold in 1996 was only about 40 percent of the 1973 peak, so there appears to be room for more growth. For now, sales growth appears to be gaining momentum. Growth was 7 percent in 1995 and 12 percent in 1996, and the industry backlog for premium cigars continues to rise. The demographics favor continued growth. Even though today's cigar smoker is often a young professional, the traditional cigar smoker is in his fifties. This age group will grow fastest in future years now that baby boomers are reaching their fifties.

Premium cigars are the fastest-growing sector of the industry, but they could prove to be the most volatile segment if the economy slows or if the current surge in the category proves to be a passing fad. Rather than relying only on growth in the premium cigar market, Swisher has achieved most of its earnings growth through market share gains. Any slowdown in the premium category will not impact Swisher's earnings as severely as it would hurt its less-diversified competitors.

Although the current trends in tobacco litigation, regulation, and consumption could cause problems for Swisher, they also may present opportunities. Government efforts are directed primarily at cigarettes, by far the largest segment of the market. To the extent that people quit smoking cigarettes in favor of other forms of tobacco use, Swisher could benefit. It remains to be seen whether that gain will prove sufficient to counteract any adverse effects of these trends.

Processed Food—Industry Note

Key themes within the U.S. food industry in 1996 were substantially higher grain prices, corporate restructurings, and business portfolio "right sizing." Standard & Poor's anticipates that the first of these themes—higher grain prices—will be less of a factor in 1997, but the latter two likely will repeat themselves. That's because both corporate restructurings and portfolio adjustments are part of the longer-term evolution of these highly mature and competitive industries, which today call for more focused company structures.

PRICEY GRAIN CUTS INDUSTRY GAIN

During 1996, the market prices of the most important grain-based crops rose sharply due to weather-ravaged lower U.S. harvests and continued strong export demand. This situation drained U.S. reserves for corn, soybeans, and wheat to perilously low levels. This, in turn, pushed up prices. The market price for corn—the nation's most important crop, as measured by its 1996 farm value of $24 billion—rose by more than 40 percent in 1996. Meanwhile, the price of soybeans (with farm value of $17 billion) rose by 24 percent and the price of wheat (with farm value of $9.6 billion) shot up by 32 percent.

These price increases put pressure on most food-related industries. Perhaps the most affected by the rise of corn prices was the agribusiness industry, due to its heavy reliance on corn and other grains to turn out products ranging from vegetable oils and flour to sweeteners. Agribusiness companies hurt by the run-up in corn and other grains included chicken processors, such as Tyson Foods and ConAgra, Inc., that use corn-based animal feeds; grain millers Archer-Daniels-Midland Co., ConAgra, and CPC International; and pet food manufacturers Ralston Purina and H.J. Heinz.

Food companies whose earnings are more reliant on the fortunes of their branded consumer products—such as Campbell Soup Co.; Kellogg Co.; and RJR Nabisco Holdings—were less affected by the rise in grain prices. For these companies, ingredients constitute a much smaller percentage of total input costs.

Assuming an average harvest in the fall of 1997 for corn, soybeans, and wheat, S&P anticipates that increased plantings of all three crops should help replenish their reserves to more normal levels. S&P believes this should lead to at least a modest reduction in their prices throughout the year.

Source: Adapted from *Industry Surveys* by permission of Standard & Poor's, a division of McGraw-Hill Companies. *Standard & Poor's,* "Foods & Nonalcoholic Beverages," *Industry Surveys* (29 May 1997): 1–17.

REPEATED RESTRUCTURINGS

Since the beginning of 1996, many of the nation's major food companies have enacted large corporate restructurings. These are generally attempts to support profit growth in an industry that throughout the 1990s has been characterized by low growth and little room for price increases.

Heinz Plays Catch-up

The most recent of these major restructurings was announced by H.J. Heinz in March 1997. Heinz said it would take a pretax charge of approximately $650 million in its fiscal fourth quarter (ended April 30, 1997) to cover all of the steps related to the restructuring. These steps include closing or selling at least 25 of its 104 plants around the world, eliminating about 6 percent of its 43,000-person workforce, and selling various "nonstrategic" businesses.

One such sale is of its Ore-Ida food service business, which has annual sales of about $500 million. Heinz also sold its poultry and ice cream operations in New Zealand in April 1997. In addition, it said that during its coming fiscal year it would sell businesses including a fats-and-oil business in South Korea and a chain of cardiofitness centers. Due to these actions, Heinz intends to generate pretax savings of approximately $120 million in its fiscal year ended April 1998, and approximately $200 million annually thereafter.

Heinz's announcement closely followed similar actions by one of its fiercest competitors. In November 1996, Campbell Soup Co. took a $160 million restructuring charge to cover the costs of plant closings, asset sales, divestitures, and organizational changes. This move called for the sale of various "nonstrategic" businesses (with approximately $500 million of Campbell's nearly $8 billion in annual sales) over the following two years. It also included the elimination of 2 percent of Campbell's North American workforce, or 650 employees; that action was to be spread out from November 1996 to the end of 1997. Together, the moves are designed to generate about $200 million in pretax savings by the end of 1998.

These restructurings stem from the need to cut costs in a very competitive marketplace that offers very little room for price increases. This situation has forced these companies to look to cost savings as never before to sustain profit margins. Given the mature state of the U.S. food industry, as well as S&P's projection of further low levels of food price inflation ahead, more restructurings within the industry are likely to continue for the foreseeable future.

FOOD COMPANIES' RESPECTABLE GAINS

Since early 1995, the most notable negative influence on industry profitability has been high prices for soybeans and grains (particularly corn and wheat). Despite this, profits for packaged food producers such as Campbell Soup, Sara Lee, and Hershey Foods enjoyed mid-teen growth. These companies' profits were favorably influenced by growth in the respective industries and productivity gains. Their vulnerability to possible spikes in grain costs is much less severe than it is for agribusiness companies, which are the major users of these commodities.

Packaged food producers are insulated from the ups and downs of agricultural commodities by many factors. For one, marketing costs for packaged food products are relatively stable and constitute a high proportion of total input costs. In addition, the packaged food producers' active use of hedging techniques helps limit their exposure to commodity price fluctuations. Finally, their increasing use of global sourcing of important raw materials helps further limit raw material shortages in a given geographic region.

A TRADE SURPLUS FOR U.S. PROCESSED FOOD

The United States is among the world's leaders in both exports and imports of processed foods and beverages. This will likely continue well into the future, given the appeal of American brand names, the growing influence of U.S. multinational firms abroad, and the leading role that the United States plays in global commerce.

The growth of U.S. processed food exports has been robust in recent years, with exports exceeding imports every year since 1992. Between 1991 and 1995, the value of exports rose by 55 percent while the value of imports grew a much slower 21 percent. According to the USDA's Economic Research Service (ERS), the United States exported $29.4 billion worth of processed foods in 1995; this exceeded imports by $4.6 billion. The ERS distinguishes processed foods from bulk agricultural products by their "value-added" content. That is, processed foods are products that have had some combination of labor, technology, and materials applied to raw commodity inputs, such as wheat and yeast, in order to transform them into items like breads or pastries.

Most of these processed foods have been characterized as "minimally processed" (as opposed to "highly processed"). Minimally processed products include fresh and frozen meats, frozen fish, soybean oil, and canned fruits and vegetables. Worldwide, the United States is dominant in these industries, reflecting the nation's efficiency in field crops and meat and poultry production.

Although "minimally processed" products will continue to account for most exports in coming years, an increasing proportion of U.S. processed food exports will be "highly processed" brand name products like Wrigley chewing gum, Kellogg cereals, and Coca-Cola soft drinks. The future growth of these products will be driven principally by rising incomes, changing demographics, and the "westernization" of eating habits in many developing countries.

A Variety of Export Destinations

The United States exports processed foods and beverages to nearly every country in the world. Relatively few countries, however, constitute the bulk of the business. Between 1989 and 1995 (latest data available), the United States exported more than $158 billion of processed foods to 233 countries, including the 15 nations of the former Soviet Union. Between 1993 and 1995, nearly half of U.S. exports of processed foods went to only three countries: Japan, Canada, and Mexico. These three nations rank among the top five destinations for U.S. processed products in each of the nine major product groups of processed foods and beverages.

More than 60 percent of Japan's imports of U.S. processed foods are from two industries: meat packing and frozen fish. Japan also imports large amounts of U.S.

frozen fruits and vegetables, prepared feeds, and poultry. The recent surge in Japanese imports of American food products has been helped by the strong currency exchange value of the yen compared with the dollar and reduced tariffs.

Canada is the second-largest importer of U.S. exports, with meat packing, frozen fish, canned fruits and vegetables, and miscellaneous products (spices, teas, and other food preparations) leading the list of industry goods shipped. Each of these industries generated more than $1 billion worth of U.S. exports to Canada from 1991 to 1995, but together they constituted only about one-third of total U.S. processed food exports to Canada. The remainder was a large and diverse mix of products, with an additional 31 industries shipping at least $100 million in processed food exports during that period.

The third-largest importer of U.S. processed foods is Mexico. The leading U.S. exports to Mexico are meat and poultry products. Although Mexican imports of U.S. processed foods have been hurt since 1995 by that country's economic hardships, long-term U.S. export prospects to Mexico remain bright.

Imports from around the World

U.S. food imports come from a wide variety of sources. Between 1993 and 1995, 51 percent of processed food imports came from just eight countries: Canada, Thailand, Mexico, France, Italy, Australia, Brazil, and New Zealand.

Canada, by far the leading exporter of processed foods to the United States, commanded a 19 percent market share during that three-year period. The dominant U.S. imports from Canada were from the same two industries that led American exports to Canada: meat packing and frozen fish, accounting for 40 percent of U.S. processed food imports from Canada between 1993 and 1995.

Thailand, the second-largest exporter of processed foods to the United States, attained only a 6 percent share of the U.S. import market during that three-year period. Most of the imported processed foods from Thailand were prepared fish, frozen fish, canned fish, and cured fish.

Outlook for U.S. Processed Food Exports

We expect the steady growth in processed food trade surplus since 1991 will extend well into the future. This will be driven principally by continued strength for minimally processed foods in developing foreign countries, particularly in Asia. It also will be driven by even stronger demand for highly processed food products.

Although the industrialized countries of Western Europe have long served as major destinations for American processed foods and beverages, trade between the United States and Western Europe hasn't grown much in recent years. Thus, the share of American exports going to Western Europe probably will slowly decline. Conversely, U.S. exports of processed food and beverages to Mexico and Canada have increased since the signing of the North American Free Trade Agreement. They're likely to continue to do so, even though exports to Mexico since 1995 have been hurt temporarily by the peso's devaluation. Further negotiations on trade agreements with other Western Hemisphere countries—notably Chile, Costa Rica, Brazil, Argentina, Uruguay, and Paraguay—could increase American exports to Latin America.

U.S. Direct Investment Abroad Growing

U.S. companies are among the largest investors in foreign food processing industries. According to the ERS, U.S. investments doubled from $15 billion to $31 billion in the five years between 1991 and 1995, increasing steadily each year. Interestingly, U.S. investments in food manufacturing abroad aren't concentrated in any particular products; they're spread across the board. Currently, about 70 percent of U.S. food industry investments are in Western Europe, Canada, and Mexico. Within Europe, the United Kingdom, Germany, the Netherlands, and France are the major recipients of U.S. foreign direct investment. Although U.S. investment is growing rapidly in some areas of Latin America and Asia, the investments are starting at a lower base.

Foreign Ownership on the Rise

In 1995, companies based in the European Union (EU) collectively held the largest investment stake in U.S. food companies, valued at $15.7 billion by the U.S. Department of Commerce. Companies based in the United Kingdom account for most of the EU investments in U.S. food makers, with $10 billion in 1995. This mostly reflects the numerous U.S. acquisitions over the years by Unilever N.V., the world's third-largest food processor after Nestlé S.A. and the Phillip Morris Cos. Unilever now owns such popular and familiar brands as Lipton tea, Ragu spaghetti sauce, and Wishbone salad dressing.

Investment in the American food-processing industry by companies based in non-EU European countries was valued at $1.8 billion in 1995. Major non-EU companies with significant American investments include Switzerland's Nestlé S.A., maker of such widely known products as Stouffer's frozen foods, Nestlé candy bars, and Carnation instant drink products. Companies based in Canada, Japan, and other Asian and Pacific Rim countries account for the remaining investment in U.S. food makers.

Campbell Soup Company—1998

Amit Shah

Fred R. David

www.campbellsoup.com
stock symbol CPB

With world headquarters in Camden, New Jersey, Campbell Soup Company (609-342-4800) had a sales increase of almost 4 percent in 1997 to $7.96 billion although earnings decreased almost 12 percent to $713 million. (See Exhibits 1 and 2 for financial data.)

EXHIBIT 1: Campbell Soup Company, Consolidated Statements of Earnings

(in millions of dollars, except per share amounts)	FY 1997 53 weeks	FY 1996 52 weeks	FY 1995 52 weeks
Net Sales	$7,964	$7,678	$7,250
Costs and expenses			
Cost of products sold	4,305	4,363	4,255
Marketing and selling expenses	1,636	1,499	1,371
Administrative expenses	324	343	326
Research and development expenses	77	84	88
Other expense	140	72	63
Restructuring charge	216	0	0
Total costs and expenses	6,698	6,361	6,103
Earnings Before Interest and Taxes	1,266	1,317	1,147
Interest expense	167	126	115
Interest income	8	6	10
Earnings before taxes	1,107	1,197	1,042
Taxes on earnings	394	395	344
Net Earnings	713	802	698
Earnings Per Share	1.51	1.61	1.40
Weighted average shares outstanding	472	498	498

Source: www.freeedgar.com

EXHIBIT 2: Campbell Soup Company, Consolidated Balance Sheets

(in millions of dollars)	Fiscal Year Ended		
	August 3, 1997	July 28, 1996	July 30, 1995
Current Assets			
Cash and cash equivalents	$ 26	$ 34	$ 53
Accounts receivable	633	618	631
Inventories	762	739	755
Other current assets	162	227	142
Total current assets	1,583	1,618	1,581
Plant assets, net of depreciation	2,560	2,681	2,584
Intangible assets, net of amortization	1,793	1,808	1,715
Other assets	523	525	435
Total assets	6,459	6,632	6,315
Current Liabilities			
Notes payable	1,506	865	865
Payable to suppliers and others	608	568	556
Accrued liabilities	642	593	545
Dividend payable	88	86	78
Accrued income taxes	137	117	120
Total current liabilities	2,981	2,229	2,164
Long-term debt	1,153	744	857
Nonpension postretirement benefits	442	452	434
Other liabilities	463	465	392
Total liabilities	5,039	3,890	3,847
Shareowners' Equity			
Preferred stock; authorized 40 shares; none issued	0	0	0
Capital stock, $.0375 par value; authorized 560 shares; issued 542 shares (1996, 1997); $.075 par value; authorized 280 shares; issued 271 shares (1996, 1995)	20	20	20
Capital surplus	338	228	165
Earnings retained in the business	3,571	3,211	2,755
Capital stock in treasury, 84 shares in 1997, 48 shares in 1996, 22 shares in 1995, at cost	(2,459)	(779)	(550)
Cumulative translation adjustments	(50)	62	78
Total shareowners' equity	1,420	2,742	2,468
Total liabilities and shareowners' equity	6,459	6,632	6,315

Source: www.freeedgar.com

Global soup volume grew 16 percent as U.S. soup volume increased 3 percent and international soup volume increased 7 percent. In 1996, Campbell derived 15 percent of its income before taxes and interest and 31 percent of its sales from outside the United States (see Exhibit 3).

CEO David Johnson wrote in Campbell's 1996 Annual Report: "There are no speed limits on the road to business excellence. We aspire to a performance profile more like the world's best consumer products companies. Competing and winning is our culture. We are proud of our traditions and determined to extend them. Our greatest weapon is people power, and for Campbell this means boundless opportunity."

Campbell Soup does not have a mission statement. However, a student recently proposed the following mission statement for Campbell:

EXHIBIT 3: Campbell Soup Company, Geographic Area Data

(in millions of dollars)	Fiscal Year Ended		
	August 3, 1997	July 28, 1996	July 30, 1995
Net Sales			
United States	$5,495	$5,332	$5,012
Europe	1,201	1,122	1,143
Australia	613	614	521
Other countries	795	733	658
Adjustments and eliminations	(140)	(123)	(84)
Consolidated	7,964	7,678	7,250
Earnings Before Taxes			
United States	1,155	1,123	957
Europe	50	71	74
Australia	26	76	81
Other countries	96	96	90
Unallocated corporate expenses	(61)	(49)	(55)
Earnings before interest and taxes	1,266	1,317	1,147
Interest, net	(159)	(120)	(105)
Consolidated	1,107	1,197	1,042
Identifiable Assets			
United States	3,913	4,144	4,171
Europe	860	817	814
Australia	919	980	773
Other countries	767	691	557
Consolidated	6,459	6,632	6,315

Source: www.freeedgar.com

Campbell Soup Company aims to offer nutritional food products to people all over the world. Our worldwide growth strategy focuses on what we do best—soup and biscuits. We are working aggressively to capture tomorrow's opportunities today.

Campbell Soup Company brand power is our pride, our inheritance, our future. With a powerhouse of trademarks that proclaims innovation, quality, and consumer trust, Campbell will leverage brand strengths to deliver profitable, sustainable volume.

Campbell will concentrate on using methods and technologies while relying on the skills and experience of our people to build and expand low-cost business systems. This will ensure gains in productivity, quality, and service to our manufacturing processes and marketing base.

We will continue to evaluate our business portfolio to ensure that our time, talent, and money are applied to areas providing maximum return on investment. The intent is to deliver consistent financial results which keep us in the top quartile versus the best companies in the food industry. We are committed to strengthen our organization, create competitive advantage, and achieve our vision, "Campbell Brands Preferred Around the World."

The three most popular Campbell soups in the United States are Chicken Noodle, Cream of Mushroom, and Tomato, respectively. The number-one top-selling Campbell soup in 1996 in other countries are listed below:

United States	Chicken Noodle
Canada	Tomato
Australia	Cream of Pumpkin
Hong Kong	Cream Style Corn with Chicken
Japan	Cream Style Corn
Mexico	Clam Chowder
United Kingdom	Cream of Mushroom Soup

TOP MANAGEMENT

Throughout the 1970s and 1980s, Campbell Soup Company was run by the founder's son, John Dorrance, Jr., who died in 1989. Disagreement then spread throughout the Dorrance family, which owns 60 percent of Campbell's stock. Campbell's CEO, Gordon McGovern, resigned soon after Dorrance's death. Then in 1990, Campbell elected a new CEO, David Johnson, who previously was CEO of Gerber Products Company.

At age 64, Johnson retired in 1997 from the active running of Campbell Soup, although he will remain chair of the board until July 1998. Johnson was the guiding force behind dramatic changes at Campbell over the past seven years; it is not surprising that many investors are concerned about the company's future in the post-Johnson era.

Dale Morrison is now president and CEO of Campbell Soup, with ten presidents of various divisions reporting to him (see Exhibit 4). CEO Morrison purchased just over $1 million of Campbell's shares around July 1, 1997. Campbell's executives are required to own at least three times their annual salary in Campbell stock. Members of Campbell's board of directors must purchase or own at least 1,000 shares of Campbell stock. These two requirements ensure that the company's top management team is totally committed to seeing the firm prosper.

ECONOMIC FACTORS

Real disposable income for U.S. citizens dropped in recent years and food as a percentage of total personal consumption expenditures also decreased. Weak economies worldwide have limited sales of Campbell's premium-priced products such as ready-to-serve soups and Pepperidge Farm cookies. The U.S. population is not growing much, so the fight for food volume growth in the U.S. market is intense. Opportunities to increase revenues are greater abroad than in the United States. In addition to higher population growth and food consumption abroad, some international markets continue to be dominated by small, regional food processors who are sometimes inefficient producers and/or marketers.

Europe is beginning to follow the U.S. trend of seeking convenience in cooking and packaging. This trend allows food companies to offer more value-added products such as soups; chicken that already has been cut into pieces, boned, and skinned; marinated

EXHIBIT 4: Campbell Soup Company Organizational Chart

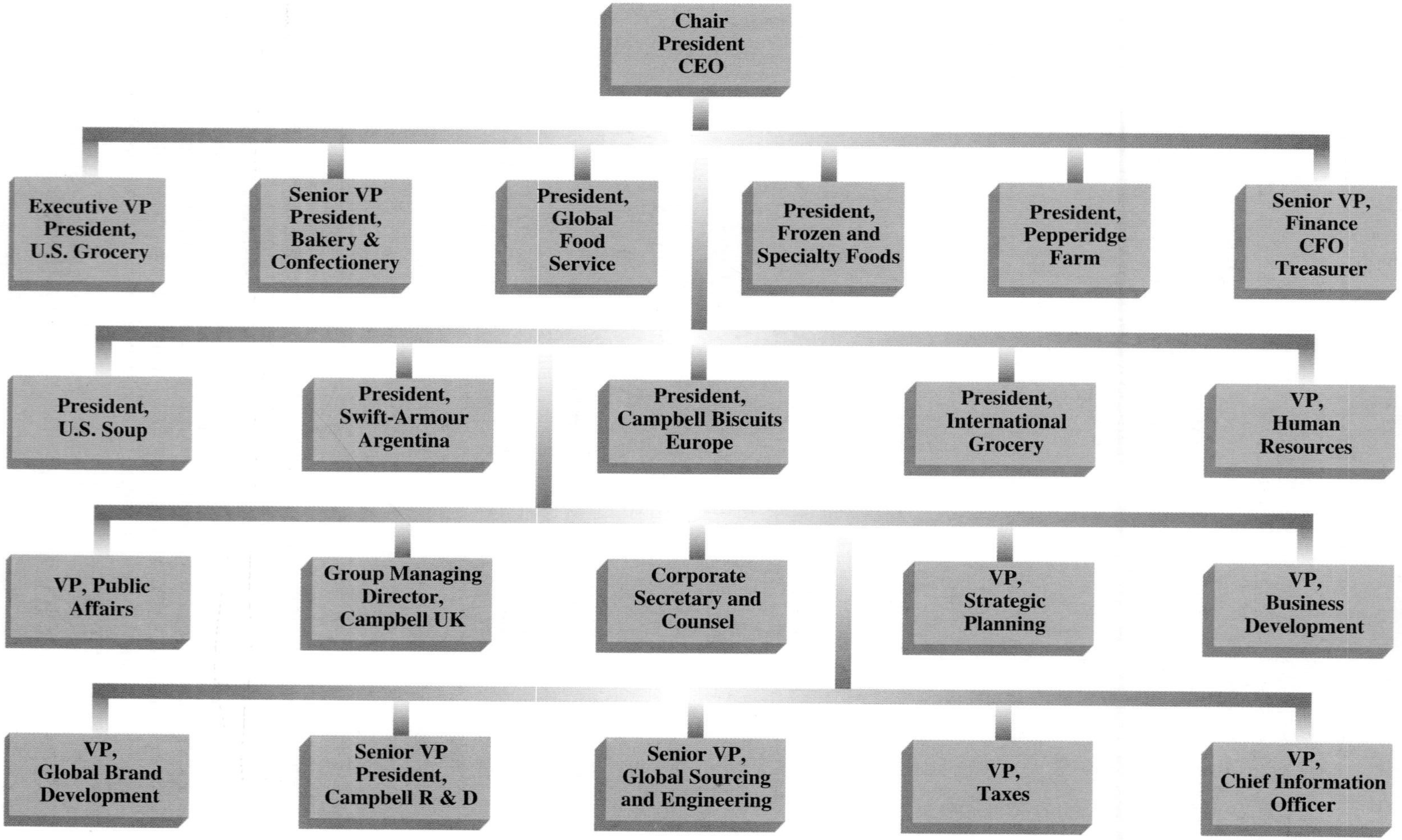

Source: Adapted from Campbell Soup Company, *Annual Report* (1997).

meats; ready-to-serve microwavable meals; single-serve portions; and cereals containing fruit and nuts.

Barriers to entry in the food industry are nearly insurmountable because it is a volume-driven business. Economies of scale for production, marketing, and distribution efficiencies are very important. There is a consolidation of food companies around the world, especially in Europe. As companies develop brand names that sell well around the world, they reap greater marketing efficiencies and profits.

There is a real fight among U.S. and European food companies for supermarket shelf space and freezer space. For frozen foods, space is particularly limited in supermarkets due to the extra cost of buying and maintaining freezers. Firms that win space have a better chance of capturing customers' attention and dollars, but at the risk of price wars. Among the grocery areas most sensitive to price wars are frozen dinners and shelf-stable items. Thus, when ConAgra obtained extra freezer space for its Healthy Choice frozen dinners, price wars broke out. Campbell's Swanson brand frozen dinners compete directly with ConAgra's Healthy Choice.

Over the past 6 years, Campbell divested 26 low-margin, nonstrategic businesses. By 1997, Campbell consolidated its frozen food operations; closed its facilities in Salisbury, Maryland, and Philadelphia, Pennsylvania; and shifted certain operations to its Omaha, Nebraska, plant. Campbell plans to divest a number of businesses over several years and to make further acquisitions.

In 1997, Morrison announced that Campbell Soup intends to spin off seven non-core businesses such as North America's number-one brands in pickles and frozen dinners, Vlasic and Swanson, and key European and Argentinean businesses. Campbell's goals are to concentrate on growing its core global businesses—soup and sauces, bakery and confectionery goods, and food service—and to capture opportunities to reduce costs in the core and noncore businesses.

BRAND POWER

Campbell aggressively extends its products using creativity and innovation. Some products, such as Pepperidge Farm gravy, "borrowed" trademarks from other Campbell products. Godiva chocolate, known for luxury and indulgence, "loaned" its name to a new line of coffees and a liqueur. Prego spaghetti sauce extended its savory benefits to a new pizza sauce line, with first-year results exceeding expectations. These brand extension successes added more than $30 million to sales.

The volume of Campbell's Home Cookin ready-to-serve soups do well, supported by the advertising slogan, "It doesn't get any better than Campbell's best." In the competitive "healthy soup" category, Campbell's Healthy Request 98-percent-fat-free, ready-to-serve varieties have a leadership position. Campbell's Double Noodle dry soup variety is increasing dry soup volume. Campbell launched a new advertising campaign entitled "Never Underestimate the Power of Soup" in 1993. Another theme, titled "Campbell's: Makes Everything M'm! M'm! Better," is successful. In June 1996, Campbell's introduced 19 new soups, the biggest launch in its history.

Campbell's bakery and confectionary business features many well-known brands. Pepperidge Farm produces cookies, frozen garlic bread, and rolls. Delacre, the pan-European brand, holds number-one market share in cookie assortments, and Arnott's, in the Pacific Rim, ranks as the world's seventh-largest and Australia's number-one biscuit (cookie and cracker) brand.

Strong volume performance was posted in 1996 by Swanson frozen dinners, led by Hungry Man entrees. In the grocery arena, Franco-American launched Spaghetti-Os pasta varieties using the cartoon character Garfield. V8 vegetable juices has a new audience with V8 Picante, a mild-flavored salsa drink; with V8 Splash, a new tropical beverage; and as the first vegetable juice in a plastic bottle. V8 holds a strong number-one category position in the United States. Meal enhancement introductions included Marie's line of Luscious Low-Fat salad dressings and Vlasic Pickles To Go single-serve pickles.

The company has done a particularly good job in fighting back the challenge from Progresso in ready-to-serve soups. Campbell met Progresso's challenge through new product introductions and the company kept promotions to a minimum, which obviously helped profitability. As a result, Campbell increased its market share lead over Progresso in the ready-to-serve segment from 13 points in 1996 to nearly 28 points in 1997.

Innovations at Campbell continues. The company is test marketing a program consisting of dietetically correct foods that are prepackaged and delivered to a customer's home on a weekly basis. This program, called Intelligent Cuisine, originally was brought to the medical profession for its input. It has enjoyed preliminary success.

GLOBAL MARKETING

Campbell is relentlessly pursuing its vision, Campbell Brands Preferred Around the World. Currently, 95 percent of Campbell soups are sold in markets with just 5 percent of the world's population.

In the United Kingdom, Campbell's condensed varieties are the fastest-growing soups. In Mexico, Campbell's new condensed soup variety has become a top seller. In Canada, Campbell's Chunky soups do well. Progress in the Australian market continues with introductions of new condensed varieties and has taken the Campbell brand from number 4 to number 1 in the vegetable category. Strong growth in Campbell's Hong Kong business led to expansion of Swanson broths into Taiwan; meanwhile, markets in Indonesia, Singapore, Malaysia, and Thailand also are growing.

Campbell introduced condensed soups and broth in China in 1993. China's 1.2 billion people consume almost six servings of soup per person per week. Campbell is exploring the possibility of manufacturing soup in China to generate additional savings and establish a base for long-term profitability throughout Asia. Since acquiring a majority ownership in Arnott's Limited in Australia, Campbell's Bakery and Confectionary group derives more than half of its sales and operating earnings from outside North America. Pepperidge Farm, which mainly targets consumers in the United States, Central America, and South America, has expanded into Canada and Mexico.

In Europe, Campbell's line of Delacre premium homemade-style cookies, Biscuits Maison de Delacre, is very popular. Its simultaneous introductions in France, Belgium, Holland, and Germany was the industry's first-ever pan-European launch in overall coordination of production, advertising, public relations, promotion, and packaging.

Campbell's Golden V8 vegetable juice was launched in Japan in 1993. The growing popularity of Mexican salsa in the United States led to the introduction of V8 Picante, a vegetable juice mixture of tomatoes, chilies, jalapeño peppers, and lime, to American consumers. In addition, V8 vegetable juice entries to Mexico and China, along with a new uniform formula for V8 in Europe, are contributing to Campbell's revenues.

INFORMATION SYSTEMS

Campbell's expenditures on research activities relating to new products and the improvement of existing products were approximately $84 million in 1996, $88 million in 1995, $78 million in 1994, and $69 million in 1993. The company conducts research at the Campbell Institute for Research and Technology in Camden, New Jersey, and in other locations in the United States and foreign countries.

Campbell concentrates on using methods, technologies, and brain power in the most efficient manner possible to eliminate non-value-added steps while improving overall processes. Campbell has upgraded its record-keeping databases to a universal system that tracks every step of the manufacturing process. The company's transition to a worldwide Campbell Integrated Manufacturing Information System (CIMIS) is the biggest and most promising computer system undertaking in its history. At Campbell's U.S. plants alone, savings from CIMIS are estimated at $22 million annually.

As one of the first companies to adopt Efficient Consumer Response, Campbell cut costs out of the supply chain. Driven by everyday low-procurement pricing, reengineered promotion programs offered incentives without adding cost. In addition, Continuous Product Replenishment (CPR) improved overall efficiencies by maximizing return on retail space and reducing inventories. In 1995, Campbell had 30 percent of its U.S. customers on CPR and aims to increase compliance. As shipments better matched consumer demand and as production peaks and valleys were eliminated, Campbell reduced manufacturing capacity. Campbell decreased inventories, excluding acquisitions, by $85 million and reduced cash invested in the soup business by 15 percent. With production peaks eliminated, Campbell restructured and downsized its manufacturing assets, improving efficiency and lowering costs.

Campbell's manufacturing and product development technologies rank among the most innovative in the industry. At the technology center in Camden, technical and manufacturing concepts are perfected before they are applied in practice at plant locations. Along with developing and applying many new technologies, such as fat-sparing and sodium-sparing techniques, the center assists Campbell in streamlining costs, improving productivity, and gaining competitive advantage.

CAMPBELL DIVISIONS

Campbell Soup is organized into four major divisions: U.S.A., Bakery & Confectionery, International Grocery, and Interdivision. The financial performance of each division for 1995 through 1997 is given in Exhibit 5.

U.S.A.

Campbell's major businesses in the United States include soup, prepared foods, pork and beans, V8, condiments, and sauces. From the days when an ad featuring the famous Campbell Kid boasted "21 kinds of soup . . . 10 cents a can," management led the way to the introductions of dry, microwavable, and ramen noodle soups.

EXHIBIT 5: Campbell Soup Company, Financial Performance by Division

(in millions of dollars, except per share amounts)	FY 1996		FY 1995	
	Sales	Earnings	Sales	Earnings
Contributions by Division:				
U.S.A.	$4,561	$1,033	$4,295	$ 885
Bakery & Confectionary	1,722	197	1,600	182
International Grocery	1,476	136	1,412	135
Interdivision	(81)	0	(57)	0
Total Sales	7,678		7,250	
Total operating earnings		1,366		1,202
Unallocated corporate expenses		(49)		(55)
Earnings Before Interest and Taxes		1,317		1,147
Interest, net		(120)		(105)
Taxes on earnings		(395)		(344)
Net Earnings		802		698
Earnings Per Share		3.22		2.80

Source: www.freeedgar.com

Americans purchase more than 3 billion cans of Campbell's soups annually, and on average have nine cans on their pantry shelves at any time during the year. Campbell Soup brands include Home Cookin, Chunky, and Healthy Request. Integral parts of the soup business are Swanson's canned chicken, beef, and vegetable broths. Campbell's share of the total prepared soup market is 56 percent, with total wet soup share at 81.8 percent. Campbell's ready-to-serve soups account for almost 10 percent of Campbell's total wet soup share. Other components of the total prepared soup market include dehydrated and ramen noodle soups in several types of packaging including pouches, single-serve cups, and block forms.

Soup sales in the United States increased 6 percent to almost $4.6 billion in 1996, with acquisitions contributing 50 percent of the sales growth. Operating earnings of U.S. operations increased 17 percent to over $1 billion. Canned soup volume increased 3 percent. Overall soup volume increased 1 percent.

Bakery and Confectionery

Campbell's Bakery and Confectionary division ranks as the fourth-largest bakery goods producer in the world and includes Arnott's Limited in Australia, Delacre and Lamy-Lutti in Europe, and Godiva Chocolatier worldwide. Products range from frozen garlic bread and rolls to Biscuits Maison, patterned after Pepperidge Farm's American Collection and Old Fashioned cookies. In 1995, Campbell acquired FSB, a supplier of sandwich buns and English-style muffins to quick-service restaurants.

Campbell brands offer a wide variety of fresh baked goods including breads, rolls, croutons, stuffing, cookies, and crackers; snack items including Arnott's macadamia nuts; and frozen foods including pastries, cakes, pizzas, danish, single-serve desserts, and muffins. The products are offered through traditional marketing outlets.

Pepperidge Farm products are offered through food service, thrift stores, and mail order distribution. Pepperidge Farm has a new $181 million bakery and biscuit plant in Denver, Pennsylvania, which is the most technologically advanced bakery in the world.

The breakthrough technology employed in this new facility provides impetus to drive profitable volume growth through new products.

Sales of this division grew 8 percent in fiscal 1996 to $1.7 billion while earnings increased 8 percent to $197 million. Pepperidge Farm, Nestlé Foods, and Hershey Foods led the way. The 1995 Greenfield Healthy Foods acquisition gave impetus to Pepperidge Farm's move into the rapidly growing market of fat-free cookies. Godiva Chocolatier reported double-digit volume growth in the United States, Europe, and Japan, and the Lamy-Lutti confectionery business reported good gains in Europe.

International Grocery

Campbell's International Grocery division consists of soup, sauces, juices, and frozen food businesses outside the United States. Sales in 1996 were almost $1.5 billion, up 5 percent from 1995 while earnings were up 1 percent to $136 million because of the decline in beef sales in Europe. The Stratford-upon-Avon Foods acquisition in the United Kingdom contributed 30 percent of the sales growth. The devaluation of the Mexican peso reduced earnings by $4 million for the year.

Campbell's international presence can be found in Great Britain, Europe, and Asia under Betis, Pleyben, Exeter, Unger, Freshbake, Groko, Logro, Beeck, Kattus, Probare, Lacroix, Granny's, Lamy-Lutti, Devos-Lemmens, Imperial, Kwatta, Tubble Gum, Laforest Perigord, Chantenac, and many other food and confectionery brands, including the world-famous Godiva chocolates.

In 1993, Campbell acquired Fray Bentos, the leading premium canned meat brand in the United Kingdom, and acquired the Spring Valley juice business in Australia. Then in 1995, Campbell acquired Homepride, a leading cooking sauce manufacturer in Britain.

Campbell Frozen and Specialty Foods has four plants located in the United Kingdom servicing the retail and food service markets. The main products are savory pastries and pies, sausages, quiche, sausage rolls, shepherd's pie, ready meals, meat products such as burgers, snacks, and small cake confectionery products. Brand names include Campbell's and Freshbake, and there are also private labels for supermarket stock.

Acquired by Campbell Soup Company in 1979, Groko, located in the Netherlands, processes and distributes frozen vegetable and potato products exclusively to major supermarket chains in Europe through independent distributors.

Campbell Asia is based in Hong Kong and oversees trading in Hong Kong, Singapore, Malaysia, Taiwan, and Korea. Sales agents and exporters handle sales to the Philippines, Guam, Indonesia, and the Pacific Islands. Campbell brands include Campbell's condensed soups, Chunky Ready-to-Serve, Swanson Broth, Swanson Condensed, Campbell's Beans, V8, V8 Tomato Juices, Franco-American pasta and gravies, Prego, and Spring Valley juices. Campbell established a biscuit headquarters in Hong Kong, where consumer trials of cookies and crackers have begun. Other test markets include Singapore, Taiwan, and Korea.

Campbell Japan is responsible for sales of Campbell products throughout Japan, with sales offices located in Tokyo, Okinawa, and Osaka. Products sold include Campbell's condensed and ready-to-serve soup, Godiva Chocolates, V8 juices, and Pepperidge Farm and Delacre biscuits.

Campbell Australia is headquartered in Melbourne, Australia, with a plant at Shepparton to serve the Pacific Basin island countries including New Zealand, Indonesia, and the Philippines. In addition to Campbell's soups, the division markets Chunky and Chunky-for-One brand soups, V8 Juice, Spring Valley fruit juices, Campbell's spaghetti sauce, tomato paste, Heat 'n' Serve canned meals, Real Stocks (liquid cooking stock), and Oriental Sauces. Baco flavored milk and Iso-Tonic sports drinks are brands featured in the Australia market. Campbell commands 26 percent of this market, and another enterprise, Melbourne Mushrooms, has 31 percent of the bulk and prepackaged fresh mushroom market.

Swift-Armour A.S.A., headquartered in Buenos Aires, with production facilities in Rosario, began operation in Argentina in 1907 and has remained a leading producer of beef products. Acquired in 1980 by Campbell Soup Company, the Swift-Armour brand is well known for its beef and other products. Since 1990, Argentina has experienced an economic boom that has benefitted long-suffering Argentines. Consumers now have more disposable income, and as a result Swift-Armour's domestic sales are up strongly. Market share for all Swift-Armour canned meat products has increased from 50 to 62 percent. The new plant at Rosario operates at 100 percent capacity. Swift-Armour's domestic product lines include canned meats, marmalades, edible fats, ketchup, canned vegetables, and canned fruits under the Swift label, and pastas and edible oils under the La Patrona brand.

Swift-Armour has an aggressive marketing campaign to introduce Campbell product lines into Argentina after market tests showed an excellent predisposition for the products among consumers. V8 juice is a new category to the Argentine market and Swift-Armour believes there is great growth potential for this beverage.

Swift-Armour is the largest beef exporter in Argentina and exports canned meat to some 50 countries. Frozen meat is exported to the United States, Italy, and Japan, and most of the beef which is processed into Campbell's soups in the United States comes from Swift-Armour. In addition, the agribusiness division manages 570,000 acres with over 100,000 head of cattle.

In 1995, Campbell acquired Pace, the leader in the fast-growing Mexican sauce category. This was the largest acquisition ever made by Campbell.

Interdivision

This division has operated at a loss. Its losses were $60 million in 1994, $57 million in 1995, and $81 million in 1996.

THE FUTURE

Identify and evaluate some other foreign food companies that Campbell could acquire, and make some specific recommendations to CEO Morrison in this regard. Should Morrison alter Campbell's organizational structure? Would a product structure (e.g., a soup division, a frozen foods division, a bakery division) be more effective than the hybrid geographic/product structure? Develop several alternative organizational charts for Morrison and specify the advantages and disadvantages of each design for the company.

Campbell will have another cache of new product offerings for fiscal 1998. New ready-to-serve soup products soon will be announced and the company likely will have an entirely new soup advertising campaign after using "Never Underestimate the Power of Soup" as the tag line for two years. Efforts in condensed soup will focus on building base business volume. Campbell also likely will have more new product introductions this year in its nonsoup grocery lines.

Let's say CEO Morrison asks you to gather information necessary to develop a five-year strategic plan. Include a mission statement for Campbell Soup Company. Include five-year pro forma financial statements to show the impact of your recommendations and an EPS/EBIT analysis to determine whether Campbell should use debt or stock to raise additional capital.

Pilgrim's Pride Corporation—1998

James L. Harbin

www.pilgrimspride.com
stock symbol CHX

Headquartered in Pittsburg, Texas, Pilgrim's Pride Corporation (903-855-1000) is engaged in the production, processing, and marketing of fresh chicken and further processed and prepared chicken products. The company offers a broad range of over 600 value-added products, such as breast fillets, nuggets, tenders, patties, and deli foods. These products, which undergo one or more further processing steps (including deboning, cutting, forming, battering, breading, and cooking) are packaged in quantities. Additionally, Pilgrim's can develop and produce new products to meet specific customers' needs.

Products are sold under the Pilgrim's Pride label to supermarkets and food service distributors such as Sysco and Kraft General Foods, which resell them to restaurants, hospitals, and the like; fast-food chains; and wholesale discount clubs. The company's primary domestic distribution is in the central, southwestern, and western United States and to the food service industry nationally.

Pilgrim's Pride is one of approximately 45 survivors out of approximately 4,000 firms in existence a few decades ago. Lonnie "Bo" Pilgrim, one of a family of seven children raised during the Great Depression, took his concern from a small farm-supply store 40 years ago to a corporation producing nearly $1.3 billion in fiscal 1997 sales (see Exhibits 1 and 2). Currently, Pilgrim's is the fifth-largest producer of poultry products in the United States and the world, and the second-largest of 25 major chicken producers in Mexico. It is the 22nd-largest egg producer in the United States. It produces more than 1.1 billion pounds of dressed poultry and 41 million dozen table eggs annually. Pilgrim's employs more than 12,000 people and has over 1,500 contract growers. Most of its facilities are in Texas, Arkansas, and Mexico.

Pilgrim's remarkable growth has taken place in a commodity industry about which, every year for the past 50 years, economists have been predicting doom and gloom. Citing industry sales as an indicator, experts also deduced that the chicken industry finally has matured. The big question facing Pilgrim's today is whether it can continue to grow through additional marketing techniques, further cost curtailment, increased integration (gaining control over supplies and distribution), and improved genetics and growing techniques while at the same time facing competitors who are larger and just as savvy.

This case was prepared by Professor James L. Harbin of Texas A & M University—Texarkana as a basis for class discussion. It is not intended to illustrate either effective or ineffective handling of an administrative situation. Copyright © 1999 by Prentice Hall, Inc. ISBN 0-13-011179-1.

EXHIBIT 1: Pilgrim's Pride Corporation, Organizational Chart

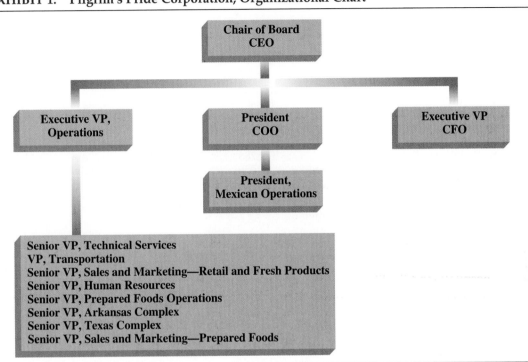

Source: Adapted from Pilgrim's Pride Corporation, *Annual Report* (1997).

BO PILGRIM'S BACKGROUND AND PHILOSOPHY

Bo Pilgrim's story is a classic one of deprivation to determination and then to success. Born in northwest Texas in 1928, he was the fourth of seven children. His father died when Bo was 9, and he left home at 12 to live with his grandmother.

His entrepreneurial spirit had early roots. One of his first goals in life, he says, was "to be able to buy a soda when I wanted it. My father would on occasion give me money for a cold drink, but only after I had finished some work he wanted done for it." He learned early that he could buy his own soft drinks. He bought sodas from his father's general merchandise store and sold them at a profit to the local factory workers. He later peddled newspapers, raised chickens and hogs, hauled gravel, picked peas and cotton, and sacked groceries—all before he turned 18.

Bo is a tireless worker at age 70. "Getting up with the chickens" would aptly describe Pilgrim's daily routines. He still works 12-hour days, which include a daily exercise regimen of treadmill work and swimming (he had a heart attack about 12 years ago). "People retire too early," said Pilgrim, "they should retire when they don't enjoy working anymore. I won't retire!"

He likens business to "a game, even a war." Commenting on how he spends his time, he noted, "I spend one-third of my working days dealing with the government, one-third with lawyers, and the remaining one-third of my time is spent constructively."

EXHIBIT 2: Pilgrim's Pride Corporation and Subsidiaries, Selected Financial Data

(in thousands of dollars, except per share data)	Fiscal Years Ended			
	Sept. 27, 1997	Sept. 28, 1996	Sept. 30, 1995	Oct. 1, 1994
Income Statement Data:				
Net Sales	$1,277,649	$1,139,310	$931,806	$922,609
Gross margin	114,497	70,640	74,144	110,827
Operating income (loss)	63,894	21,504[a]	24,930[a]	59,698
Income (loss) before income taxes and extraordinary charge	43,824	47	2,091	42,448
Income tax expense (benefit)[b]	2,788	4,551	10,058	11,390
Income (loss) before extraordinary charge	41,036	(4,504)	(7,967)	31,058
Extraordinary charge—early repayment of debt, net of tax	0	(2,780)	0	0
Net income (loss)	41,036	(7,284)	(7,967)	31,058
Per Common Share Data:				
Income (loss) before extraordinary charge	1.49	(0.16)	(0.29)	1.13
Extraordinary charge—early repayment of debt	0	(0.10)	0	0
Net income (loss)	1.49	(0.26)	(0.29)	1.13
Cash dividends	0.06	0.06	0.06	0.06
Book value[c]	6.62	5.19	5.51	5.86
Balance Sheet Summary:				
Working capital	133,542	88,455	88,395	99,724
Total assets	579,124	536,722	497,604	438,683
Notes payable and current maturities of long-term debt	11,596	35,850	18,187	4,493
Long-term debt, less current maturities	224,743	198,334	182,988	152,631
Total stockholders' equity	182,516	143,135	152,074	161,696
Key Indicators (as a percentage of net sales):				
Gross margin	9.0%	6.2%	8.0%	12.0%
Selling, general and administrative expenses	4.0%	4.3%	5.3%	5.5%
Operating income (loss)	5.0%	1.9%	2.7%	6.5%
Interest expense, net	1.7%	1.9%	1.9%	2.1%
Net income (loss)	3.2%	(0.6)%	(0.9)%	3.4%

[a]The peso decline and the related economic recession in Mexico contributed significantly to the operating losses experienced by the company's Mexican operations of $8.2 million and $17.0 million for fiscal years 1996 and 1995, respectively.

[b]The company does not include income or losses from its Mexican operations in its determination of taxable income for U.S. income tax purposes based upon its determination that such earnings will be indefinitely reinvested in Mexico.

[c]Amounts are based on end-of-period shares of common stock outstanding.

Source: Adapted from Pilgrim's Pride Corporation, *Annual Report* (1997): 14.

He commented, "Today, we don't appreciate how much we have and how easy it is to get things. I'm definitely hooked on the free enterprise system." He added, "In fact, when I visited with President Reagan a few years ago, I reminded him that the chicken and egg industry has never had any kind of subsidy. I also shared my belief that the government should not be in the business of protecting the inefficient."

On entrepreneurship, Pilgrim said, "It is more than just shooting from the hip. A company has four resources—people, dollars, time, and facilities. Our company's objective is to gain optimum use of these four through planning, building pride, and rewarding our employees."

Educated in a three-room school without electricity, Bo still believes in "old-fashioned Christian values" and the idea that "there is more to life than just making a dollar." He had three children with his wife of 40 years, and for more than 30 years he has taught a Sunday School class.

When asked about his secret of success, Bo responded, "Take your abilities, season them with experience on the job, and combine that with drive and motivation, and you will be successful. The way to make a difference in your life is to make that *mind-boggling* decision to not be average."

Most Texans know Bo as the chicken king who wears a Pilgrim's hat in his television commercials. Visitors to corporate headquarters get parking spaces marked with a picture of a chicken and the words, "Pullet her in." First-floor lobby walls are festooned with more than 300 samples of memorabilia of Pilgrim and his company—wooden thank-you plaques, framed newspaper clippings, and photographs of him with prominent politicians. In the second-floor executive office suite, representations of chickens are everywhere—ceramic chickens, oil paintings of chickens, photographs of chickens, and stuffed chickens.

History

Because commodity chicken downcycles almost bankrupted Pilgrim's twice over the years, the company has increasingly emphasized value-added and branded products, including its chill-pack and further processed and prepared food lines (see Exhibit 3). In the late 1980s, Pilgrim's spent $25 million on a facility for preparing chickens. Such products generate higher prices per pound, exhibit lower price volatility, and result in higher and more consistent profit margins than non-value-added products such as whole ice-pack chicken.

In order to crack the food service business with processed and prepared chicken, Pilgrim's priced its products below Tyson Foods, Inc., (its chief competitor) at a loss. The company also had to spend approximately $6 million to $8 million a year on advertising, promotion, and supermarket slotting allowances to entice this business.

Pilgrim's Pride lost about $50 million over three years trying to enter the prepared chicken market. In fiscal 1988, the company lost a net $8 million on $506 million in sales. Disgruntled investors dumped the stock, which had just had an initial public offering in January of 1987. The value of Bo Pilgrim's stake shrank by 76 percent, to $61 million.

Pilgrim's finally turned the corner with a strategic retreat from the supermarkets and a major advance into the food service market. Retail products now account for a mere 2 percent of Pilgrim's prepared chicken sales. In food service Pilgrim's positioned itself as an alternative to Tyson, aiming at those customers leery of being too dependent

EXHIBIT 3: **Pilgrim's Pride Corporation, Prepared Foods Product Mix Shift**
(millions of pounds)

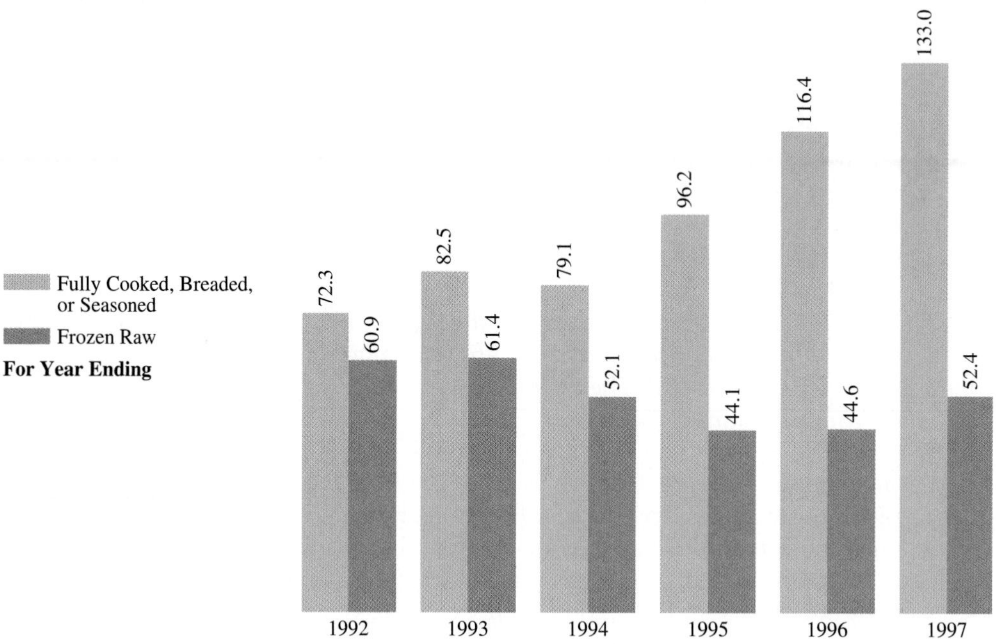

Legend:
- Fully Cooked, Breaded, or Seasoned
- Frozen Raw

For Year Ending

Year	Fully Cooked, Breaded, or Seasoned	Frozen Raw
1992	72.3	60.9
1993	82.5	61.4
1994	79.1	52.1
1995	96.2	44.1
1996	116.4	44.6
1997	133.0	52.4

Source: Pilgrim's Pride Corporation.

on one supplier. "A lot of buyers gave us information to help us duplicate the products they were buying from Tyson," Pilgrim says. With customers such as Kraft General Foods, Wendy's, and Kentucky Fried Chicken, the company now has been able to raise its prices to be in line with Tyson.

After suffering its biggest loss in the history of the company in 1992, Pilgrim's rebounded in 1993 and 1994. In fiscal 1997, the company had an all-time sales high of almost $1.3 billion, an increase of 12 percent over fiscal 1996 sales of over $1.1 billion. Pilgrim's recorded $41 million in net income in fiscal 1997, a jump of over $48 million from its $7.3 million loss the previous year.

Mission

A large group of Pilgrim employees representing all areas of the company met to brainstorm their direction, vision, and mission. Many in the group were fearful that rather than developing a mission, they might end up with a "mission statement." The difference, according to Monty Henderson, president and CEO, is "that a mission statement becomes very wordy and usually winds up as a long paragraph or two that no one—not even the authors—can remember and usually winds up in a file somewhere. A mission, by contrast, is known by everyone, practiced daily by everyone, and becomes a way of life."

After much discussion about their business, their customers, and their competition, the group came to a consensus that Pilgrim's vision is "to achieve and maintain leadership in each product and service that we provide." To achieve this, the group felt that their mission was summed up as "Our job is customer satisfaction . . . every day."

Because of increased emphasis in the international market, Pilgrim's later amended its vision to "To be a world-class chicken company—better than the best."

Marketing

Pilgrim's has a consumer-oriented market strategy. The company annually increased its marketing activities and expenditures as it developed new products and geographic markets. As a result of its marketing activities, the company achieved significant consumer awareness for the Pilgrim's Pride brand name in southwestern and western metropolitan markets. The company believes that this brand awareness is beneficial to the introduction and acceptance of new products, such as its further processed and prepared food lines.

The company utilizes television, radio, and newspaper advertising; point-of-sale and coupon promotions; and other marketing techniques to develop consumer awareness and brand loyalty for its products. Bo Pilgrim is the featured spokesperson in the company's television and radio commercials, and his likeness in a pilgrim's hat appears on all the company's branded products. Advertising slogans have included "Better from the egg to the leg," "It's a mind-boggling thing," "The honest chicken from real Pilgrim's," and "Real chickens from real Pilgrim's."

The company maintains an active program to identify consumer preferences primarily by testing new product ideas, packaging designs, and methods through taste panels and focus groups located in key geographic markets. This program led to the identification and introduction of new products such as the company's whole boneless chicken, leaner chicken, and the entire further processed and prepared foods line.

Pilgrim's has nine distribution centers. There are four in Texas, two in Arizona, one in Oklahoma, and two in Mexico.

Competition

Pilgrim's competes with other integrated chicken companies and to a lesser extent with local and regional poultry companies that are not fully integrated. Pilgrim's has been competing for retail grocery sales of chill-pack products since 1982 and fast-food product sales of whole and precut chickens since 1965. It currently supplies Church's, Kentucky Fried Chicken, Wendy's, Grandy's, and Chili's.

The primary competitive factors in the chicken industry include price, product line, and customer service. Although its products are competitively priced and generally supported with in-store promotions and discount programs, the company believes that product quality, brand awareness, and customer service are the primary methods through which it competes. Currently, Pilgrim's believes that it has only one competitor (Tyson) with a more complete line of value-added products.

Tyson, the number-one poultry processor with 1996 sales of over $6.4 billion, solidified its position in 1997 with the purchase of Hudson Foods, Inc., for $682 million. Prior to the purchase, Tyson controlled 22 percent of the market; the acquisition of Hudson added another 5 percent. Tyson's strategy has been one of many acquisitions over the past decade.

"Our marketing strategy for success is simple—segment, concentrate, dominate. We identify a promising market segment, concentrate our resources in it, and ultimately

EXHIBIT 4: Pilgrim's Pride Corporation and Subsidiaries, Operations in the United States and Mexico

(in thousands of dollars)	Years Ended		
	Sept. 27, 1997	*Sept. 28, 1996*	*Sept. 30, 1995*
Sales to unaffiliated customers:			
United States	$1,002,652	$ 911,181	$772,315
Mexico	274,997	228,129	159,491
	1,277,649	1,139,310	931,806
Operating income (loss):			
United States	29,321	29,705	41,923
Mexico	34,573	(8,201)	(16,993)
	63,894	21,504	24,930
Identifiable assets:			
United States	404,213	363,543	328,489
Mexico	174,911	173,179	169,115
	579,124	536,722	497,604

Source: Pilgrim's Pride Corporation, *Annual Report* (1997): 24.

gain for Tyson Foods a dominate share of that segment," stated a recent Tyson annual report. "Our customers include all of the nation's top 50 food service distributors, 88 of the top 100 restaurant chains, 100 of the top retail supermarket chains, and every major wholesale club."

Because of this strategy of segment, concentrate, and dominate (after several years of diversifying into beef, pork, and seafood), Tyson's decided in 1996 to dispose of its red meat business. Although the red meat division was profitable, Tyson felt that the resources necessary to become a major factor in that market would produce greater returns in their core business, chickens.

Mexico

After only a few years, Pilgrim's became the second-largest chicken producer in Mexico. Its business strategy for Mexico calls for using its U.S. management expertise to solidify its position as the most efficient operator in Mexico and, at the same time, to develop a strong consumer and trade franchise for the Pilgrim's Pride brand. Pilgrim's sales in Mexico rose to $274 million in fiscal 1997, an increase of 20 percent over $228 million in fiscal 1996 (see Exhibit 4).

With Mexico's rising population and strengthening economy, demand for chicken is expected to be strong. In 1995, Pilgrim's Pride acquired five chicken companies located near Queretaro, Mexico.

THE BROILER INDUSTRY

The domestic integrated broiler industry encompasses the breeding, growing, processing, and marketing of chicken products. The production of poultry is one of the largest agricultural industries in the United States. Prior to World War II, the broiler industry was highly fragmented with numerous small, independent breeders, growers, and processors. The industry has experienced consolidation during the last five decades and now has a relatively small number of larger, more integrated companies. Integration of the industry led to lower profit margins at each independent production stage and enhanced the need for coordination between production stages.

The broiler industry is characterized by intense price competition, resulting in an emphasis on improving genetic, nutritional, and processing technologies in an effort to minimize production costs. These factors, coupled with the feed conversion advantages of chickens, enabled the industry to enjoy consistently lower production costs per pound than other competing meats. As an example of the adoption of improved methods and technology, certain industry participants have moved toward product packaging at the plant level, including deep-chill processing as an alternative to ice-packing whole chickens and shipping in bulk form. Deep-chill processing rapidly lowers the temperature of chickens to slightly above freezing and extends freshness and shelf life.

Industry Profitability

Industry profitability is primarily a function of consumption of chicken and competing meats and the costs of feed grains. Historically, the broiler industry operated on a fairly predictable cycle of about three years; a year of good profits, followed by a year of expanded output and declining profits, followed by a year of losses and production cuts.

The chicken companies have spend much of their energy trying to escape the commodity cycle through marketing. Frank Perdue, with his classic commercials, was the first to demonstrate that a company could charge a premium for a brand name bird. Today the biggest producers all play the brand loyalty game. This leaves the chicken producers in an odd situation: They are commodities concerns trying to behave like consumer products companies. As Prudential-Bache's John McMillin foretold in the 1980s, "The 1990s chicken industry will be better capitalized, more competitive, and less profitable." The prediction came true.

Industry profitability can be significantly influenced by feed costs, which are influenced by a number of factors unrelated to the broiler industry, including legislation that provides discretion to the federal government to set price and income supports for grain. Historically, feed costs have averaged approximately 50 percent of total production costs of non-value-added products and have fluctuated substantially with the price of corn, milo, and soybean meal. By comparison, feed costs typically average approximately 25 percent of total production costs of further processed and prepared chicken products such as nuggets, fillets, and deli products, and as a result, increased emphasis on sales of such products by chicken producers reduces the sensitivity of earnings to feed cost movements.

Although feed costs may vary dramatically, the production costs of chicken are not as severely affected by changing feed ingredient prices as are the production costs of beef and pork. Chickens require approximately two pounds of dry feed to produce one pound of meat, compared to cattle and hogs, which require approximately seven to three pounds, respectively, of feed.

Industry Problems

Across the southeastern United States, where 85 percent of the country's chickens are processed, the poultry industry is brooding over a barrage of bad publicity. Chicken processing plants are said to be dirty; rotten meat is reaching the market; salmonella-tainted chickens are poisoning people; and the chicken growers who contract with the processors are being ripped off. Even Ross Perot publicly lambasted Bill Clinton's gubernatorial record by saying that the Arkansas poultry business is "not an industry of tomorrow."

Leaders of the South's largest agribusiness concede that they have a problem. In September 1993, a coalition of the Arkansas Poultry Federation, Hudson Foods, Pilgrim's Pride, and Tyson Foods ran full-page ads in several Arkansas newspapers to counter the problem. Its main caption was "Here in Arkansas, it wasn't a Goose that laid the Golden Egg. It was a Chicken." It further stated that one out of 12 working Arkansans was employed by the poultry industry; poultry was a $3 billion-plus industry in Arkansas; salaries and benefits averaged more than $25,000 per employee; and the poultry industry was the largest taxpayer in Arkansas.

The industry's biggest worry may be microscopic in physical size. Chickens in battery farms (and those in farmyards) often live in their own dung, which in turn encourages the growth of bacteria such as salmonella and campylobacter, which in turn contaminate the meat during processing. About 6 million Americans are made ill by such bacteria every year, and about 1,300 die. Scientists at the Centers for Disease Control say chickens may be the cause in up to half of those cases.

The industry's high-tech, fast-paced production lines, which process some 200,000 birds a day at a single plant, heighten fecal contamination. Bacteria often spread among birds as they speed along conveyors from hot collective baths through wet mechanical feather pickers to tanks of cold water. Partly to hold down the price of poultry, the industry has not tried to produce cleaner chickens, but instead relies on consumers to cook the meat thoroughly.

Injury and illness rates for poultry workers are double the rates of manufacturing generally, according to the Labor Department. And new technology often is used to reduce stress—for chickens, to make their meat more tender, rather than for workers. "The industry has one foot in the twenty-first century when it comes to chickens, but they left one foot back in the nineteenth century when it comes to people," stated Bob Hall, research director of the Institute for Southern Studies, a labor-funded advocacy group in Durham, North Carolina.

Conditions for the production line workers can be tough. Repetitive motion from such tasks as pulling out chicken guts can cause disabling injuries. Employees frequently spend shifts in either a freezing cooler or 95-degree heat. Conditions can be so crowded that blood from a chicken one worker handles sometimes can splash onto a coworker. The line speed—up to 90 chickens a minute—is double the rate a decade ago.

In the past 20 years, the number of major U.S. processors decreased from more than 100 to about 30. This consolidation resulted in a highly centralized and vertically integrated industry in which a half-dozen major players control over 43 percent of American production. As a result, the country has been carved up into regional buying monopolies and each region's dominant processor can dictate terms to the growers.

The processors provide growers with chicks and feed, and then slaughter and market the birds. The growers provide chicken houses, utilities, and labor. The growers receive only short-term contracts from the processors with no formal assurances of long-term business relationships.

A recent report from the Texas Commissioner of Agriculture concluded that although "the grower makes a substantial capital investment and takes most of the risk, he or she is not sharing in the success of the industry." In some cases, growers have received as little as $579 in annual income per 20,000-bird-capacity chicken house.

The processors defend their practices. Industry spokespeople point out that growers are guaranteed a price for adult chickens, typically about 3.5¢ to 4¢ a pound. Thus, the processors contend, growers are sheltered from much of the risk of the volatile chicken market. Bill Roenigk, spokesperson for the National Broiler Council, a processor trade group, says studies have shown that chicken farmers' average return on investment is 5 percent, or higher than that in many other agriculture operations.

CHANGING DEMAND AND SUPPLY

Chicken has experienced greater growth in per capita consumption than most other major meat categories over the last 20 years.

The major factors influencing this growth are consumer awareness of the health and nutritional characteristics of chicken, the price advantage of chicken relative to red meat, and the convenience of further processed and prepared chicken products. The principal health and nutritional characteristics include lower levels of fat, cholesterol, and calories per pound for chicken relative to red meat. When compared with other meats, chicken has a significant price advantage, which has increased over time.

Recent growth in the consumption of chicken has been enhanced by new product forms and packaging which increase convenience and product versatility. These products typically undergo one or more further processing steps, including deboning, forming, battering, breading, and cooking. Production of these further processed products is the fastest-growing segment of the broiler industry. The market share of the further processed product group has increased over the years.

The United States is becoming a nation of bird eaters. According to the Department of Agriculture, per capita consumption of poultry is steadily rising at the same time per capita consumption of beef is falling dramatically. Chicken is now the dominant meat consumed in the United States. For three decades, pork was king.

Many projections show chicken consumption per person in the United States (see Exhibit 5) to reach 100 pounds by 2000. In Mexico, a modernized chicken industry is emerging and will certainly fuel greater demand for this economical, healthy source of protein. Consumption is currently 38 pounds per capita in Mexico (see Exhibit 6) and is projected to grow by 10 percent per year.

Notwithstanding an occasional salmonella scare, birds are perceived as more healthful than beef. A 100-gram piece of chicken contains 3.7 grams of saturated fat, compared with 20.7 grams of saturated fat in a piece of T-bone steak weighing the same amount, according to the Agriculture Department.

Chicken companies lately have increased profit margins by producing scores of what the industry calls value-added items: chicken parts that have been boned, skinned, marinated, or otherwise processed for the convenience of consumers. Pilgrim's product mix for fiscal 1997 was 133 million pounds of fully cooked, breaded, or seasoned chicken, and just 52.4 million pounds of frozen raw chicken. Just as any fool can cook a steak, any fool now can cook a chicken breast.

The poultry sector isn't solely chicken; it also includes turkey, duck, goose, and quail. But the poultry industry in America is chicken-driven. Last year, chicken nuggets accounted for about 10 percent of total U.S. broiler output and showed chicken companies what could happen if they went beyond selling what are called, in the trade, "feathers-off, guts-out birds."

Since chicken nuggets hit the market nationally in 1982, chicken producers have been swamping supermarkets with value-added products—teriyaki tidbits, breaded

EXHIBIT 5:   United States Per Capita Consumption of Meat

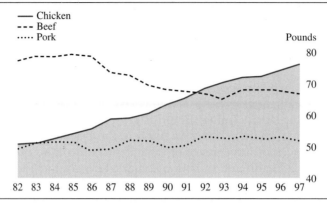

Source: USDA, cited in Pilgrim's Pride Corporation, *Annual Report* (1997): 13.

EXHIBIT 6:   Mexico Per Capita Consumption of Meat

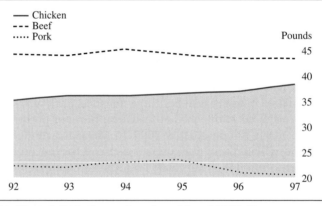

Source: USDA, cited in Pilgrim's Pride Corporation, *Annual Report* (1997): 13.

wings, whole cooked birds with salt and spices injected into their flesh—and consumers have responded. "Demand has expanded for poultry since 1983 in a way that I've never seen demand for any meat take off since World War II," noted Patrick Luby, vice-president and corporate economist at Oscar Meyer Foods Corp. in Madison, Wisconsin.

Value-added chicken should, of course, properly be called value-subtracted. It is the whole bird, not its processed parts, that offers consumers the greatest value—and that value is considerable when compared with beef and pork.

Chicken, priced pound per pound, is one-third the cost of beef and one-half the cost of pork. Non-value-added chickens are selling for less than they did in 1923, when Mrs. Wilmer Steele of Ocean View, Delaware, sold what chicken historians say was the nation's first flock of commercial broilers for 62¢ a pound. Why is chicken cheaper than the competition? The answer has to do with the fact that a chicken is highly efficient at converting feed to flesh. As noted, to produce a pound of meat, a chicken consumes less than two pounds of feed, compared with six or seven pounds for a cow and three for a pig.

Also, a chicken doesn't live long. The shorter a creature's life cycle, the quicker its generations can be manipulated genetically. Chicken breeders steadily have developed birds that grow bigger on less feed in less time. Breeders may be approaching the limits of practicality on this score; modern chickens have "put on so much weight that they have some real problems mating," said Walter Becker, professor emeritus of genetics and cell biology at Washington State University.

Furthermore, chickens don't graze. Raising cattle requires an investment in land; raising chickens doesn't. Chickens used to need to run around in the sun; otherwise, they would develop a vitamin D deficiency and rickets. But in the 1920s, poultry producers solved the vitamin D problem by adding cod-liver oil to chicken feed. Since then, they have been able to raise thousands of chickens in confinement, allowing about 0.7 square foot per bird.

THE FUTURE

During the next few years, per capita consumption of chicken could more than double throughout the world. In 1996, poultry consumption for Russia, Japan, and China was 16, 28, and 7 pounds per person, respectively. Russia's per capita consumption of poultry is about the rate at which Americans consumed chicken and turkey in 1910. Many nations simply do not have chickens. Many don't have the grain to raise chickens, therefore it is cheaper to import one pound of chicken than the two pounds of grain that it takes to produce a pound of chicken meat.

In the domestic market, fewer and fewer meals consumed at home are made from scratch. Sixty-seven percent of consumers prefer foods that are convenient and 42 percent are willing to pay more for that convenience. With 70 percent of mothers working outside of the home and 40 percent of consumers not knowing what they will eat for dinner as late as four o'clock in the afternoon, meal planning and preparation take a back seat to convenience.

Although 82 percent of consumers prepare chicken at home at least weekly, nearly 52 percent of every food dollar is spent on food prepared outside of the home. On any given day, nearly half of American adults order a meal in a restaurant or food service outlet.

All is not rosy for the chicken industry. Per capita consumption for chicken was flat in 1995, after growing for more than a decade. Record-high corn prices in recent years combined with a glut of beef and other kinds of meat negatively affected sales and profits.

Overseas markets are always unpredictable. During 1996, in response to planned U.S. sanctions on textiles and electronic goods, China threatened to impose an additional 100 percent tariff on top of its existing 45 percent levy on U.S. poultry. Russia briefly banned U.S. chicken imports in 1996 and only recently backed off a threat to impose quotas.

Concern for healthy food may be slackening. Some say nutrition is on the back burner, with taste the big thing. One analyst recently commented, "A few years back, when everyone was concerned about health and diet, the fast-food restaurants started wringing fat from hamburgers but sales dropped because they had less and less flavor. So restaurants took bacon and slapped slices of that on the sandwiches, and sales took off like gangbusters." The increasing size of hamburgers is but another sign that fat may be back.

Prepare a five-year strategic plan for Pilgrim's Pride.

H.J. Heinz Company—1998

Henry Beam
Thomas Carey

stock symbol HNZ

H.J. Heinz Company (412-456-6000/5700) is a worldwide provider of processed food products and nutritional services. Headquartered in Pittsburgh, Pennsylvania, it had 43,000 employees before its planned 6 percent reduction of its workforce, and markets over 4,000 varieties of food products in more than 200 countries. It had manufacturing facilities in 21 countries before its intended closing or selling of 25 percent of those plants. Its two best-known global brands are Heinz and Weight Watchers. Heinz reported record sales of $9.35 billion and net income of almost $302 million in the fiscal year ended April 1997. Over the years, Heinz has expanded its core businesses and continues to grow through selected acquisitions. In addition to ketchup, its original and best-known product, Heinz's product mix includes sauces, pet food, baby food, frozen dinners and desserts, snacks, pasta, tuna, nutrition drinks, and soup. Heinz's CEO has a goal "to make Heinz ketchup as ubiquitous as Coca-Cola. Everywhere fast food is sold—whether in Asia, Africa, Europe, or the Americas—Heinz ketchup will be there, too."

HISTORY

In 1869, Henry J. Heinz formed a partnership with his friend, Clarence Noble, to sell grated horseradish fresh from his family's garden in western Pennsylvania. The firm soon moved to Pittsburgh and continued to grow until the overextended enterprise was forced into bankruptcy by the banking panic of 1875. Heinz paid all related debts before founding a new business, F. & J. Heinz, with his cousin and brother that same year. In its first few years, the company produced pickles, horseradish, and what would become a world-renowned product—bottled ketchup. By 1888, Heinz gained financial control and changed the company's name to H.J. Heinz.

Heinz put his ketchup in a narrow-necked bottle for both easier pouring and reduced contact with air, which darkened the sauce. In 1895, a 17-ounce "Imperial Bottle" of ketchup was introduced with a delicately embossed symmetrical shape to appeal to higher-end hotels, restaurants, and upper-income families. A succession of prepared products followed. Heinz had discovered that most people were willing to let someone else take over a share of their kitchen operations and that a pure product of superior quality will find a ready market if properly packaged and promoted.

While traveling on a New York City elevated train in 1896, Heinz saw a shoe store sign advertising "21 styles." He liked the phrase and came up with the slogan "57 varieties" to describe what his company produced. The H.J. Heinz Company already produced more than 57 varieties, but Heinz stuck with the phrase because he liked the sound of the number 57. Heinz also designed a streetcar ad featuring the slogan. The public latched onto the slogan, which is displayed on the Heinz label to this day. In 1910, Heinz added a small dark-green pickle to the bottom of the label to further product recognition; the pickle remains an element of the Heinz label. The H.J. Heinz Company became the largest producer of ketchup, pickles, and vinegar in the nation.

After Henry Heinz died in 1919, his son, Howard, continued to grow the business internally. Later, the company was run by H. J. Heinz II from 1941 to 1966. By the end of the 1940s, Heinz and ketchup went together naturally. As stated in a 1949 issue of the *Saturday Evening Post*, "Heinz Ketchup, although not the first commercial ketchup, has led the American market for so long that it has determined the shape of almost all ketchup bottles because the public just naturally recognizes that shape as ketchup." The H.J. Heinz Company went public in 1946.

In 1958, Heinz began to make acquisitions in Europe and Mexico as well in the United States. Under R. Burt Goodin, the first nonfamily member to become president, the pace of acquisitions quickened. Dr. Anthony J. F. O'Reilly became the company's fifth president and CEO in 1979. Under his guidance, Heinz became a leader in the nutrition and wellness field with the 1978 purchase of Weight Watchers and its development into a global brand. He also created major company production bases in Spain, Portugal, and New Zealand. Significant events in Heinz's history are given in Exhibit 1. Locations of its major facilities are given in Exhibit 2.

EXHIBIT 1:   Milestones in History of the H.J. Heinz Company

1869	Henry J. Heinz and Clarence Noble start Heinz & Noble, laying the groundwork for the H.J. Heinz Company.
1876	Ketchup is added to the company's condiment line, which also includes celery sauce, pickled cucumbers, and vinegar.
1896	Henry Heinz turns more than 60 products into "57 Varieties." The number later becomes famous and virtually synonymous with the H.J. Heinz Company.
1931	Howard Heinz, Henry's son, adds two new lines: ready-to-serve quality soups and baby foods.
1946	H. J. "Jack" Heinz II, grandson of the founder, takes the company public and launches international operations in Holland, Venezuela, Japan, and Italy.
1963	Heinz acquires StarKist and "Charlie the Tuna" becomes a national media star.
1965	Heinz acquires Ore-Ida and transforms a regional business into the leading retail frozen potato brand in the United States.
1966	R. Burt Goodin, architect of the modern Heinz, becomes the first non-Heinz family member to become CEO.
1978	Heinz acquires Weight Watchers International, the largest program for weight loss in the United States.
1979	Anthony J. F. O'Reilly, 43, is named CEO. He ushers in an era of global growth, expanding into Africa, China, Russia, Eastern Europe, and the Pacific Rim.
1987	Chair Henry J. Heinz II, in his fifty-sixth year of service to Heinz, dies at the age of 78. O'Reilly is the first non-Heinz family member named chair, president, and CEO.
1994	Heinz celebrates 125th anniversary since Henry Heinz started Heinz & Noble.
1997	Heinz announces Project Millennia, the largest restructuring in its history.

Source: H. J. Heinz Company, *Annual Report* (1997).

EXHIBIT 2:   H.J. Heinz Company, Locations of Major Facilities

World Headquarters

600 Grant Street, Pittsburgh, Pennsylvania.

The Americas

Heinz U.S.A. Established 1869. Pittsburgh, Pennsylvania.
Ore-Ida Foods, Inc. Acquired 1965. Boise, Idaho.
StarKist Foods, Inc. Acquired 1963. Newport, Kentucky.
    StarKist Caribe, Inc. Acquired 1963. Mayaguez, Puerto Rico.
    StarKist Samoa, Inc. Acquired 1963. Pago Pago, American Samoa.
Weight Watchers International, Inc. Acquired 1978. Woodbury, New York.
    Cardio-Fitness Corporation. Acquired 1985. New York, New York.
    The Fitness Institute. Acquired 1988. Willowdale, Ontario, Canada.
Weight Watchers Gourmet Food Company. Established 1991. Pittsburgh, Pennsylvania.
Crestar Food Products, Inc. Acquired 1991. Brentwood, Tennessee.
H.J. Heinz Company of Canada Ltd. Established 1909. North York, Ontario, Canada.
    Omstead Foods Limited. Acquired 1991. Wheatley, Ontario, Canada.
    Shady Maple Farm Ltd. Acquired 1989. LaGuadeloupe, Quebec, Canada.
    Heinz Bakery Products. Established 1992. Mississauga, Ontario, Canada.
    Martin Pet Foods. Acquired 1996. Elmira, Ontario, Canada.
Alimentos Heinz C.A. Established 1959. Caracas, Venezuela.

Europe and Africa

H.J. Heinz Company, Limited. Established 1905. Hayes, Middlesex, England.
PLADA S.p.A. (Plasmon Dietetici Alimentari S.p.A.). Acquired 1963. Milan, Italy.
AIAL (Arimpex S.r.l. Industrie Alimentari). Acquired 1992. Commessaggio, Italy.
Dega S.r.l. Acquired 1994. Mori, Italy.
Fattoria Scaldasole S.p.A. Acquired 1996. Monguzzo, Italy.
Mareblu S.r.l. Acquired 1996. Milan, Italy.
H.J. Heinz Northern Europe. Established 1995. Hayes, Middlesex, England.
    H.J. Heinz B.V. Acquired 1958. Elst, Gelderland, Netherlands.
    H.J. Heinz Branch Belgium. Established 1984. Brussels, Belgium.
    H.J. Heinz GmbH. Established 1970. Cologne, Germany.
    H.J. Heinz S.A.R.L. Established 1979. Paris, France.
    Pioneer Food Cannery Ltd. Acquired 1995. Tema, Ghana.
    Ets. Paul Paulet S.A. Acquired 1981. Douarnenez, France.
    IDAL (Industrias de Alimentação, Lda.) Fish Division. Acquired 1988. Peniche, Portugal.
    Indian Ocean Tuna Ltd. Established 1995. Victoria, Mahe, Seychelles.
Heinz Iberica, S.A. Established 1987. Madrid, Spain.
IDAL (Industrias de Alimentação, Lda.). Acquired 1965. Lisbon, Portugal.
COPAIS Food & Beverage Company S.A. Acquired 1990. Athens, Greece.
H.J. Heinz Central Eastern Europe. Established 1994. Pittsburgh, Pennsylvania.
    Heinz Kecskeméti Konzervgyár RT. Acquired 1992. Kecskemet, Hungary.
    H.J. Heinz Company C.I.S. Established 1994. Moscow, Russia.
    Heinz Polska Sp. Established 1994. Warsaw, Poland.
    PMV / Zabreh. Acquired 1995. Zabreh, Czech Republic.
H.J. Heinz Company (Ireland) Limited. Incorporated 1966. Dublin, Ireland.
Custom Foods Limited. Established 1992. Dundalk, Ireland.
H.J. Heinz Southern Africa. Established 1995. Johannesburg, South Africa.
    H.J. Heinz (Botswana)(Proprietary) Ltd. Formed 1988. Gaborone, Botswana.
    Kgalagadi Soap Industries (Pty) Ltd. Acquired 1988. Gaborone, Botswana.
    Refined Oil Products. Formed 1987. Gaborone, Botswana.
    Olivine Industries (Private) Limited. Acquired 1982. Harare, Zimbabwe.

continued

Exhibit 2: *continued*

Chegutu Canners (Pvt) Ltd. Established 1992. Chegutu, Zimbabwe.
Heinz South Africa (Pty) Ltd. Established 1995. Johannesburg, South Africa.
Heinz Frozen Foods (Pty) Ltd. Established 1995. Klerksdorp, South Africa.
Cairo Foods Industries SAE. Established 1992. Cairo, Egypt.

The Pacific Rim and Southwest Asia

H.J. Heinz Pacific Rim. Established 1996.
H.J. Heinz Australia Ltd. Established 1935. Doveton, Victoria, Australia.
Wattie's Limited. Acquired 1992. Auckland, New Zealand.
Heinz Japan Ltd. Established 1961. Tokyo, Japan.
Heinz-UFE Ltd. Established 1984. Guangzhou, People's Republic of China.
Seoul-Heinz Ltd. Established 1986. Seoul, South Korea.
Heinz Win Chance Ltd. Established 1987. Bangkok, Thailand.
Heinz India Private Limited. Acquired 1994. Bombay, India.

Source: Adapted from H.J. Heinz Company, *Annual Report* (1997).

PRODUCTS

Heinz has organized its products into six core categories in which it seeks global leadership. A seventh category is for Heinz's other leading brands. In 1996, twenty-seven of Heinz's products and brands recorded more than $100 million in sales. Products with the leading market share position in their respective markets generate about two-thirds of the company's sales.

Food Service

Heinz is the largest prepared food supplier to the U.S. food service market, which consists of restaurants, diners, cafeterias, and other away-from-home eating places. Food service has annual sales of over $1 billion. Products include packets of ketchup, salad dressing, and frozen soup concentrate. Heinz fills 6 billion single-serve condiment pouches each year at its Mason, Ohio, factory. Heinz enhanced its position in this business by its recent purchase of Chef Francisco frozen soups and the Moore's and Domani brands of frozen onion rings, vegetables, and pastas.

Food service is growing at 6 percent annually in the United States. Today, U.S. families spend about 50¢ of every food dollar on meals outside the home, up from about 33¢ in the 1970s. Heinz expects its food service business to double in five years in Europe. It is also seeking to increase its presence in Asia.

Infant Feeding

Sales of jarred baby foods, cereals, formulas, juices, and biscuits were about $1 billion in 1997. In the United States, Heinz's market share rose to 17 percent on sales of $100 million, considerably behind industry leader Gerber but ahead of Beechnut (a division of Ralcorp Holdings). However, Heinz is the market leader outside the United States. It has over half of the infant food market in Australia, Canada, Italy, New Zealand, and the United Kingdom. In 1995, Heinz built a $20 million baby food plant in Russia and expanded its infant feeding business in Eastern Europe, Russia, India, and China.

Ketchup and Condiments

Heinz is the world's largest buyer of tomatoes, a key ingredient for its ketchup and related products, such as steak and barbecue sauce. Each year, it processes more than 2 million tons of tomatoes. It sells $1 billion of ketchup around the world (9 billion ounces) and has more than 50 percent of the domestic ketchup market. As U.S. fast-food chains grow in popularity around the world, so will Heinz ketchup and condiments. A billboard for Heinz ketchup in Moscow proclaims, "The whole world knows it."

Heinz's ketchup is facing challenges from salsa and private brands. Salsa was introduced to American consumers in 1947. It has an array of sauces that include picante, enchilada, taco, and other chili-based sauces. In the 1990s, salsa has outsold ketchup in some retail stores, indicating the changing nature of American tastes. Large food retailers such as A&P, Jewel, and Meijer's Thrifty Acres offer lower-cost, private label ketchup which competes directly with Heinz ketchup. Private label brands can be sold for less because there are no promotion or advertising costs associated with them.

Pet Food

With annual sales approaching $2 billion, Heinz Pet Products offers a broad range of cat and dog foods. Heinz's 9-Lives cat food is the market leader. In 1995, Heinz acquired Quaker Oats's pet food business for $725 million. Heinz's 9-Lives cat food (promoted by Morris the Cat) is the market leader. Its dog food brands include Kibbles 'n Bits, Gravy Train, Cycle, Ken-L Ration, and Jerky Treats. Heinz, Ralcorp, and Nestlé-Alpo each have about 20 percent of the domestic pet food business. Heinz also has about a third of the fast-growing and high-margin pet treats market.

Tuna

Tuna is a high-quality, low-cost, low-fat source of protein. Heinz wants to become "the tuna supplier to the world." It operates canneries and fishing fleets in each of the oceans where tuna swim. Heinz's StarKist division is the world's largest processor of canned tuna and holds approximately 20 percent of the $5 billion worldwide retail market and 50 percent of the $1.4 billion U.S. retail market. The U.S. market for tuna is relatively flat, while international tuna sales are growing about 6 percent per year. StarKist advertising features Charlie the Tuna and Morris the Cat. Besides its U.S. seafood business, Heinz operates modern, automated canneries in the Pacific and Indian Oceans, and in Africa and in Europe. In June 1997, Heinz acquired John West Foods Limited, the United Kingdom's leading brand of canned tuna and fish.

Weight Control

Weight Watchers International is the world's largest weight control service system with 4 million members. It produces diet foods and operates a weight control meeting business. Each week, more than 1 million people attend Weight Watchers meetings. The Weight Watchers brand offers retail frozen, refrigerated, and shelf-stable products. Its frozen desserts are the number-one brand in the supermarket. In 1994, Heinz purchased The Budget Gourmet brand of frozen meals to complement its Weight Watchers brand frozen entrees and desserts in the United States. Weight Watchers has about 50 percent of the U.S. diet food and weight control market.

In 1997, Weight Watchers was profitable in Europe. Sales in the United Kingdom increased 50 percent largely due to the introduction of a new, easy-to-follow diet. However, it was not profitable in the United States. Heinz plans to close some storefronts used for Weight Watchers meetings and hold classes in low-overhead sites such as church basements and schools.

Other Leading Brands

Products not falling into one of the six core categories are placed in a category Heinz calls other leading brands. These include retail frozen snacks and pasta in the United States and beans, pasta, and soup in the United Kingdom. Heinz also markets food products in Pacific Rim countries, including Australia and New Zealand. The other leading brands category accounted for about a quarter of Heinz's sales in 1997.

OPERATIONS

Heinz's Soup Business

Heinz is the country's largest producer of private label soup, with nearly 90 percent share of the private label market. Overall, Heinz has a 7 percent share of the total U.S. soup market. Campbell Soup Company is by far the largest producer of brand name canned soups in the United States, with a market share of nearly 75 percent of the $2.5 billion U.S. canned soup market.

Heinz made a major attempt to enter the brand name soup business in 1970, but failed because it wasn't able to adequately fund national media advertising. Instead, it decided to withdraw from the brand name soup market in United States and concentrate on its private label business. This profitable private label soup business in the United States complements Heinz's leadership position in branded soups in countries such as Canada, the U.K., Australia, and New Zealand.

Finance

Highlights of the H.J. Heinz Company's performance for the fiscal years ended in 1995 through 1997 are given in Exhibit 3. Heinz has increased its dividend every year for over 20 years. Income statement and balance sheet data are given in Exhibits 4 and 5. Heinz's fiscal years end on or after April 30. The results for the fiscal year ending April 30, 1997, include a one-time pretax restructuring charge of $647 million associated with Heinz's restructuring plan, Project Millennia, and capital gains of $85 million on sales of assets. Business segment and geographic data are given in Exhibit 6. Advertising costs for fiscal years ending in 1997, 1996, and 1995 were $346.8 million; $377.8 million; and $314.8 million, respectively.

Production

Heinz long has been proud of the quality of its products. Indeed, Henry Heinz deliberately put Heinz ketchup in a clear bottle so consumers could see that it did not contain any impurities. Heinz operates modern production facilities around the world. It recently spent $120 million to renovate and expand its manufacturing complex on Pittsburgh's north side. The facility produces soup, baby foods, and sauces, and houses

EXHIBIT 3: **H.J. Heinz Company and Subsidiaries, Summary of Operations and Other Data**

	Fiscal Year Ending		
(dollars in thousands, except per share data)	April 30, 1997	May 1, 1996	May 3, 1995
Summary of operations:			
Sales	$9,357,007	$9,112,265	$8,086,794
Cost of products sold	6,385,091	5,775,357	5,119,597
Interest expense	274,746	277,411	210,585
Provision for income taxes	177,193	364,342	346,982
Income before cumulative effect of accounting change	301,871	659,319	591,025
Net income	301,871	659,319	591,025
Income per common share before cumulative effect of accounting change	0.81	1.75	1.59
Net income per common share	0.81	1.75	1.59
Other related data:			
Dividends paid:			
Common	416,923	381,871	345,358
per share	1.13$^{1}/_{2}$	1.03$^{1}/_{2}$	0.94
Preferred	43	56	64
Average shares for earnings per share	373,703,246	377,155,837	372,806,306
Number of employees	44,700	43,300	42,200
Capital expenditures	377,457	334,787	341,788
Depreciation and amortization expense	340,490	343,809	315,267
Total assets	8,437,787	8,623,691	8,247,188
Total debt	3,447,435	3,363,828	3,401,076
Shareholders' equity	2,440,421	2,706,757	2,472,869
Pretax return on average invested capital	12.6%	21.8%	22.1%
Return on average shareholders' equity before cumulative effect of accounting change	11.7%	25.5%	24.6%
Book value per common share	6.64	7.34	6.76
Price range of common stock:			
High	44$^{7}/_{8}$	36$^{5}/_{8}$	28$^{5}/_{8}$
Low	29$^{3}/_{4}$	27$^{5}/_{8}$	21$^{1}/_{8}$

Note: The 1997 results include a pretax charge for restructuring and related costs of $647.2 million, offset by capital gains of $85.3 million from the sale of nonstrategic assets in New Zealand and the U.K.
Source: H.J. Heinz Company, *Annual Report* (1997).

EXHIBIT 4: **H.J. Heinz Company and Subsidiaries, Consolidated Statements of Income and Retained Earnings**

	Fiscal Year Ended		
(dollars in thousands, except per share data)	April 30, 1997 (52 weeks)	May 1, 1996 (52 weeks)	May 3, 1995 (53 weeks)
Consolidated statements of income:			
Sales	$9,357,007	$9,112,265	$8,086,794
Cost of products sold	6,385,091	5,775,357	5,119,597
Gross profit	2,971,916	3,336,908	2,967,197
Selling, general and administrative expenses	2,215,645	2,049,336	1,811,388
Operating income	756,271	1,287,572	1,155,809
			continued

EXHIBIT 4: *continued*

	Fiscal Year Ended		
	April 30, 1997 (52 weeks)	May 1, 1996 (52 weeks)	May 3, 1995 (53 weeks)
Interest income	39,359	44,824	36,566
Interest expense	274,746	277,411	210,585
Other expense, net	41,820	31,324	43,783
Income before income taxes	479,064	1,023,661	938,007
Provision for income taxes	177,193	364,342	346,982
Net income	301,871	659,319	591,025
Consolidated statements of retained earnings:			
Amount at beginning of year	4,156,380	3,878,988	3,633,385
Net income	301,871	659,319	591,025
Cash dividends:			
Common stock	416,923	381,871	345,358
Preferred stock	43	56	64
Amount at end of year	4,041,285	4,156,380	3,878,988
Per common share amounts:			
Net income	0.81	1.75	1.59
Cash dividends	1.13½	1.03½	0.94
Average shares for earnings per share	373,703,246	377,155,837	372,806,306

Source: H.J. Heinz Company, *Annual Report* (1997).

EXHIBIT 5: H.J. Heinz Company and Subsidiaries, Consolidated Balance Sheets

	Fiscal Year Ended	
(dollars in thousands)	April 30, 1997	May 1, 1996
Current assets:		
Cash and cash equivalents	$ 156,986	$ 90,064
Short-term investments, at cost which approximates market	31,451	18,316
Receivables (net of allowances: 1997—$18,934 and 1996—$17,298)	1,118,874	1,207,874
Inventories:		
Finished goods and work-in-process	1,040,104	1,115,367
Packaging material and ingredients	392,407	378,596
Prepaid expenses	208,246	221,669
Other current assets	65,038	14,806
Total current assets	3,013,106	3,046,692
Property, plant and equipment:		
Land	55,992	62,243
Buildings and leasehold improvements	871,417	824,308
Equipment, furniture and other	3,453,189	3,333,493
Less accumulated depreciation	1,901,378	1,603,216
Total property, plant and equipment, net	2,479,220	2,616,828
Other noncurrent assets:		
Goodwill (net of amortization: 1997—$259,019 and 1996—$211,693)	1,803,552	1,737,478
Other intangibles (net of amortization: 1997—$163,232 and 1996—$141,886)	627,096	649,048
		continued

EXHIBIT 5: *continued*

	Fiscal Year Ended	
	April 30, 1997	*May 1, 1996*
Other noncurrent assets	514,813	573,645
Total other noncurrent assets	2,945,461	2,960,171
Total assets	8,437,787	8,623,691
Current liabilities:		
Short-term debt	589,893	994,586
Portion of long-term debt due within one year	573,549	87,583
Accounts payable	865,154	870,337
Salaries and wages	64,836	72,678
Accrued marketing	164,354	146,055
Accrued restructuring costs	210,804	0
Other accrued liabilities	315,662	368,182
Income taxes	96,163	175,701
Total current liabilities	2,880,415	2,715,122
Long-term debt and other liabilities:		
Long-term debt	2,283,993	2,281,659
Deferred income taxes	265,409	319,936
Non-pension postretirement benefits	211,500	209,994
Other	356,049	390,223
Total long-term debt and other liabilities	3,116,951	3,201,812
Shareholders' equity:		
Capital stock:		
Third cumulative preferred, $1.70 first series, $10 par value	241	271
Common stock, 431,096,485 shares issued, $.25 par value	107,774	107,774
Additional capital	175,811	154,602
Retained earnings	4,041,285	4,156,380
Cumulative translation adjustments	(210,864)	(155,753)
	4,114,247	4,263,274
Less:		
Treasury shares, at cost (63,912,463 shares at April 30, 1997, and 62,498,417 shares at May 1, 1996)	1,629,501	1,500,866
Unfunded pension obligation	26,962	32,550
Unearned compensation relating to the ESOP	17,363	23,101
Total shareholders' equity	2,440,421	2,706,757
Total liabilities and shareholders' equity	8,437,787	8,623,691

Source: www.freeedgar.com

EXHIBIT 6: H.J. Heinz Company and Subsidiaries, Segment and Geographic Data (dollars in thousands)

(dollars in thousands)	Domestic	Foreign	Worldwide
for fiscal year ended April 30, 1997			
Sales	$5,169,779	$4,187,228	$9,357,007
Operating income	174,280	581,991	756,271
Operating income excluding restructuring related items[a]	704,880	613,309	1,318,189
Identifiable assets	4,474,740	3,963,047	8,437,787
Capital expenditures[b]	192,682	184,775	377,457
Depreciation and amortization expense	203,587	136,903	340,490
for fiscal year ended May 1, 1996			
Sales	5,235,847	3,876,418	9,112,265
Operating income	739,807	547,765	1,287,572
Identifiable assets	4,801,790	3,821,901	8,623,691
Capital expenditures[b]	185,874	148,913	334,787
Depreciation and amortization expense	206,912	136,897	343,809
for fiscal year ended May 3, 1995			
Sales	4,628,507	3,458,287	8,086,794
Operating income	656,897	498,912	1,155,809
Identifiable assets	4,812,122	3,435,066	8,247,188
Capital expenditures[b]	188,099	153,689	341,788
Depreciation and amortization expense	197,009	118,258	315,267

	North America	Europe	Asia/Pacific	Other
for fiscal year ended April 30, 1997				
Sales	$5,586,730	$2,281,364	$1,129,788	$359,125
Operating income	208,585	320,347	166,552	60,787
Operating income excluding restructuring related items[a]	751,685	374,202	130,515	61,787
Identifiable assets	4,941,301	2,241,006	995,762	259,718
Capital expenditures[b]	213,574	102,677	31,442	29,764
Depreciation and amortization expense	221,249	81,932	29,944	7,365
for fiscal year ended May 1, 1996				
Sales	5,598,286	2,133,690	1,085,747	294,542
Operating income	801,090	336,481	114,239	35,762
Identifiable assets	5,099,632	2,289,919	978,292	255,848
Capital expenditures[b]	195,517	65,485	40,294	33,491
Depreciation and amortization expense	224,824	72,530	30,674	15,781
for fiscal year ended May 3, 1995				
Sales	4,982,959	1,881,013	1,006,198	216,624
Operating income	715,592	282,941	121,951	35,325
Identifiable assets	5,161,418	1,979,351	919,988	186,431

continued

EXHIBIT 6: *continued*

	North America	Europe	Asia/ Pacific	Other
Capital expenditures[b]	201,912	72,384	48,435	19,057
Depreciation and amortization expense	213,243	68,122	28,214	5,688

[a]Excludes domestic and foreign charges for restructuring and related costs of $530.6 million and $116.6 million, respectively. Also excludes gains on the sale of an ice cream business in New Zealand and real estate in the U.K. of $72.1 million and $13.2 million, respectively.
[b]Excludes property, plant, and equipment acquired through acquisitions.
Note: Processed food products represent more than 90 percent of consolidated sales. There were no material amounts of sales or transfers among geographic areas and no material amounts of United States export sales.
Source: www.freeedgar.com

some of the world's most advanced food processing lines. Throughout its core businesses, Heinz seeks to build high-volume, low-cost facilities.

PUBLIC SERVICE

Throughout the world, Heinz affiliates contributed to the welfare of their communities. In 1997, the H.J. Heinz Company Foundation gave a total of $5.6 million in grants to 850 organizations. Heinz U.S.A. donated more than $330,000 to hospitals as a sponsor of the Children's Miracle Network Telethon. While owned by Heinz, Ore-Ida raised more than $100,000 for Toys for Tots. Heinz Pet Products again supported the Homeless Homer label program, which benefits homeless pets.

THE FOOD INDUSTRY

H.J. Heinz Company is one of the largest publicly held food companies in the United States, as shown in Exhibit 7. Food companies prospered during the 1980s, aided by cost reduction efficiencies, consolidation, and inflation. In the 1990s, it became apparent

EXHIBIT 7:   Top 12 Companies in the Food Processing Industry, 1996 (millions of dollars)

Company	Sales	Net Income	Major Brands/Products
Archer Daniels	$13,314	$696	Agricultural commodities
CPC	9,844	580	Mazola, Hellman's, Skippy
Campbell Soup	7,964	713	Campbell's, Pepperidge Farm, Vlasic pickles
ConAgra	24,822	545	Grocery products, Healthy Choice
General Mills	5,416	476	Wheaties, Betty Crocker, Bisquick, Hamburger Helper
Grand Metropolitan PLC	13,614	563	Pillsbury, Green Giant, Burger King
H.J. Heinz	9,357	658	Heinz ketchup, StarKist, Weight Watchers
Hershey	3,989	308	Hershey's, Reese's, pasta
Kellogg	6,677	629	Corn Flakes, Rice Krispies, Special K, Lender's Bagels
Nabisco Holdings	8,889	374	Oreo, Triscuit, Ritz, Grey Poupon, Life Savers
Quaker Oats	5,199	179	Quaker Oats, Aunt Jemima, Gatorade
Sara Lee	18,624	916	Sara Lee, Douwe Egberts, Jimmy Dean, Mr. Turkey; also consumer products

Note: Net income figures do not include special gains or restructuring charges.
Source: Value Line Investment Survey.

that inflation, a major source of earnings increases in the 1980s, had fallen to a minimal 2 to 3 percent per year. As a general rule, food companies have to work harder to increase earnings from cost or volume growth. Food companies typically employ one of the following three basic strategies.

1. Major Acquisitions

Because it is very difficult to increase market share of an established brand, some firms expand by acquiring complementary brands. Heinz made major acquisitions that complemented its pet food business (from Quaker Oats in 1995) and its food service business (from Borden in 1994).

2. Divestment

Some large, multiproduct companies improve overall efficiency by selling selected businesses. General Mills sold its seafood and restaurant businesses, leaving itself primarily in the cereal and convenience food businesses. Campbell Soup sold several businesses that had low margins in order to concentrate on its higher-margined products such as soup. In a variation of this strategy, Ralston Purina created separate stocks for its Ralston-Continental (breakfast foods) and Ralcorp (consumer foods) units.

Heinz sold peripheral businesses, such as its Hubinger corn milling unit (1991), its Italian confectionery business (1994), and its Near East specialty rice business (1994). In 1997, Heinz announced plans for Project Millenia, the largest restructuring it ever had undertaken.

3. Building on traditional strengths

Some firms acquire complementary new brands at reasonable prices and with no earnings per share dilution.

CEO O'REILLY

Heinz's CEO O'Reilly (known as Tony) was born in Ireland in 1936. O'Reilly was an outstanding rugby player as a youth, playing both at the amateur level in school and as a professional. O'Reilly felt "rugby football was the greatest tutor and best training for business I ever had. It teaches you all the basic elements that are necessary." These include discipline; teamwork; determination; collegiality; and learning to live with defeat, win with grace, and fight back from adversity. In the off-season, he earned a bachelor's of civil law degree in 1958 from University College, Dublin. In 1980, when he was already CEO of Heinz, he earned a doctoral degree from the University of Bradford, England.

After several jobs in England and Ireland, O'Reilly joined Heinz in 1969 as manager of its largest and most profitable international affiliate, Heinz United Kingdom. O'Reilly's rise at Heinz was rapid, and in 1979 he became CEO. He has a photographic memory and a legendary ability to recall facts, figures, names, dates, and people. He also has a high energy level, needing only four or five hours of sleep a night. In addition to being CEO of Heinz, O'Reilly is also chair of Waterford Wedgewood and of Independent Newspapers, Ireland's largest publishing group. Independent Newspapers publishes over 160 newspapers and magazines with a weekly circulation of over

13 million in Europe, Africa, and Australia. O'Reilly also holds several directorships. When asked how he juggled his time between so many commitments on both sides of the Atlantic Ocean, he quipped, "I don't play golf."

O'Reilly built his reputation in the United States by turning around Heinz's Ore-Ida and U.S. operations that weren't performing up to potential. In 1978, O'Reilly shook up Heinz and the food industry with the bold acquisition of Weight Watchers International for $100 million. He correctly anticipated the 1980s obsession with health and fitness, and Weight Watchers became a star performer.

When he came to the United States, O'Reilly implemented a leadership tool he still uses. At the start of each year, he wrote letters to those reporting to him, setting out his expectations for them and what he thought were the shortcomings of their performance the previous year. They were more career reviews than performance reviews. The letters revealed his management ideas ("An area senior vice-president is not a Mr. Nice Guy, but a change agent"); his sense of humor ("I am dictating this letter to you slowly because I know you can't read fast"); and his focus on the bottom line ("I have just reviewed the second quarter financials . . . to say that I am disappointed is an understatement"). O'Reilly's achievements at Heinz received wide praise in the business press in the 1980s.

In November 1996, Heinz named William R. Johnson as president, chief operating officer, and the heir apparent to run Heinz when O'Reilly retires. Johnson, 48, joined Heinz in 1982 after working for Ralston Purina and Anderson Clayton. He made his mark at Heinz by successfully cutting costs in the tuna and pet food businesses. In those jobs, he instituted "price-based costing," whereby he determined first what consumers were willing to pay, and then drove costs down to provide adequate margins at that selling price.

Compensation

In the 1990s, the press and security analysts began to give close scrutiny to the issue of executive compensation, especially stock options, which were often granted below market value. *Business Week* featured O'Reilly in its March 30, 1992, article on CEO pay after he exercised stock options worth $71.5 million, making himself the nation's highest-paid CEO. His 1991 base salary was $514,000, not high in comparison to CEOs of firms of similar size. Some of his stock options were granted as far back as 1982. O'Reilly kept the Heinz stock, making him the third-largest holder of Heinz stock.

To some business analysts, O'Reilly's exercise of stock options granted over a period of time was annual compensation. However, the Heinz board of directors felt it clearly was not. In 1990, O'Reilly signed a five-year contract that awarded him the largest single grant of stock options to that time: 6 million shares. O'Reilly insisted that what was good for him was good for Heinz shareholders. "Heinz was worth $900 million in 1980, and it's worth $10 billion today—with the same number of shares issued," he said in 1991.

In 1996, O'Reilly realized a gain of $61.5 million on the exercise of the 6 million stock options granted in 1990. The gain is equal to the fair market value on the date of exercise, less the exercise price, times the number of shares acquired. He used about $32 million of the gain to purchase 1.1 million shares of Heinz, raising his ownership of Heinz stock to 1.6 percent of the shares outstanding. The rest of the gain was used to pay taxes on the transaction. O'Reilly's 1997 salary was $777,941 and his bonus was $1.4

million. Although he did not exercise any stock options in 1997, he was granted options to buy 750,000 shares of stock at an exercise price of $31.875.

PROJECT MILLENNIA

In recent years, Heinz came under increasing criticism from stock market analysts for not doing as much as it could to increase earnings in an environment of low inflation and annual food industry growth of about 1 percent. Heinz has been one of the last of the large food companies to try to improve its profitability through restructuring.

On March 14, 1997, Heinz announced Project Millennia, the largest restructuring in its history. Under Project Millennia, Heinz will concentrate on brand building; increasing media spending by 30 percent over two years; overseas expansion; and increases in efficiency through such programs as Efficient Consumer Response, a program designed to make grocery store operations more efficient. In implementing the project, it sold the food service portion of its frozen potato business in 1997 for $500 million to McCain Foods of Canada. Heinz will close or divest about 25 percent of its plants throughout the world and invest heavily in building new ones in fast-growing markets. It will reduce its global workforce by about 2,500. Heinz expects annual cost savings of $200 million once the restructuring is complete.

O'Reilly also set ambitious new financial goals. He expects Heinz to increase sales to between $14 billion to $15 billion in 5 years and have earnings grow 10 percent to 12 percent a year. O'Reilly also promised "high-quality" earnings growth. In the past few years, analysts criticized O'Reilly for making his financial goals through one-time asset gains, favorable tax rates, and end-of-quarter promotions which increased sales but reduced margins.

O'Reilly closed his letter to shareholders in the 1997 Heinz *Annual Report* as follows:

> When I became CEO in 1979, Heinz's market capitalization was $900 million; today it is $17 billion, with fewer shares in issue. How was it done? By emphasis on big brands, by expansion into new global markets, by product innovation, by low-cost operations, by excellent management, and by focusing on shareholders, consumers, and customers. We will continue with this winning formula to generate double-digit earnings growth into the next century.

Aerospace—Industry Note

COMMERCIAL TRANSPORT AND LAUNCH MARKETS REVIVE INDUSTRY PROFITS

U.S. aerospace and defense companies continued to post strong profit gains in 1997, building on a turnaround that began in 1996. After years of drastic downsizing and consolidation that finally brought operating costs in line with revenues, the industry benefited from a sharp upturn in commercial jet production, expanded demand for regional commercial jets, the revival of the single-engine aircraft market, and increased activity in several military programs.

Industry prospects remain bright as strong profits at commercial airlines enhance the likelihood that the airlines actually will take delivery on the large orders for new aircraft placed in the past two years.

The rise in aircraft orders is supporting an industry-wide surge in production, led by a 50 percent hike in 1997 aircraft production by the Boeing Co., the dominant force in commercial jet aircraft. This jump in output by Boeing resulted from an overall plan to roughly double monthly plane production by 1998's second quarter to 43.5 planes per month, up from 21.5 at year-end 1996. Although Boeing stumbled badly during the ramp up and suffered from weak earnings, the rest of the industry prospered from the increased activity.

Boeing's difficulties arose from the pressure to double production while hiring more than 30,000 new workers. The inexperienced workforce and late deliveries by suppliers resulted in extra production costs and costly penalties for late delivery of aircraft.

At one point in the fourth quarter of 1997, production was in such disarray that Boeing stopped production of the 747 jumbo jets and the workhorse 737s. The monthlong shutdown was used to complete production projects that had been delayed and to reorganize the production lines to ensure a more orderly process when production resumed.

The shutdown and delays cost Boeing $1.3 billion in 1997. Further costs of up to $1 billion are expected in the first half of 1998 before Boeing's strained operations return to complete normalcy.

SALES UP STRONGLY IN 1997

Based on forecasts by the Aerospace Industries Association (AIA), total industry sales are believed to have totaled $129.6 billion in 1997, up 11 percent from $116.5 billion in 1996. The strong rise was attributed to increased sales of civilian aircraft, engines, and parts. And the outlook for 1998 remains bright due to a rich backlog and the prospects for improved performance by Boeing by midyear 1998. The AIA is forecasting that shipments will rise another 11 percent to as much as $144.5 billion in 1998.

Source: Adapted from *Industry Survey* by permission of Standard & Poor's, a division of McGraw-Hill Companies. *Standard & Poor's,* "Aerospace & Defense," *Industry Survey* (January 29, 1998): 1–8.

SALES OF THE AEROSPACE INDUSTRY, BY CUSTOMER

		Aerospace Products and Services				
(in millions of dollars)	Year	Government		Commercial Aerospace[a]	Non aerospace Products and Services	Total Sales
		Dept. of Defense	NASA and Other Agencies			
	1997	42,321	11,767	53,930	21,604	129,622
	R 1996	42,106	12,363	42,605	19,415	116,489
	R 1995	42,401	11,413	36,004	17,964	107,782
	1994	43,795	11,932	36,405	18,426	110,558

[a]Includes exports.
R: Revised.
Source: Aerospace Industries Association.

The AIA forecast reflects a projected $10.5 billion rise in civil aircraft deliveries to about $45 billion. However, this may be partially offset by a modest decline in sales to the U.S. Department of Defense (DOD)—the aerospace industry's largest customer— along with flat shipments to the National Aeronautics and Space Administration (NASA) and other government agencies.

With market conditions stabilizing, the industry's cost-cutting frenzy has abated. Employment levels have been rising as cutbacks in defense-related jobs have been outweighed by new opportunities in civilian applications.

Satellites, Launches Aiding Industry

The satellite business also is booming, as numerous communications satellite launches are being ordered to support development of a variety of new satellite-based services. At least six systems are now being developed that aspire to offer global wireless telephone services. Each of these systems expects to launch more than a dozen satellites, with Motorola's Iridium system planning to use a constellation of 66 satellites.

Satellites also are posing a competitive threat to cable television. The satellite TV industry is led by General Motors's Hughes division's DirecTV, which has more than 3 million U.S. subscribers in only its third year of operation. DirecTV now is being expanded into foreign markets. The strong demand for satellites is increasing the need for rockets to carry them into space, as well as for ground-based facilities to support launch operations.

The satellite boom is helping the transition of the U.S. military machine into a leading-edge commercial industry. Making the transition from military contractor to commercial entity required fundamental changes in the business practices of America's leading aerospace and defense companies. Those in the forefront of this change, such as Lockheed Martin, altered their approaches so they now function more like mass production, assembly-line businesses, discarding the previous industry-wide practices of batch or unit order production.

Uniformity in design and manufacturing is helping the U.S. industry maintain its cost-competitiveness. This is increasingly important as foreign players are emerging as a growing competitive threat, in contrast to the days when the U.S. industry largely was sheltered from competition because its primary customer was the U.S. government.

MERGER & ACQUISITIONS THE WAY TO GO, SAYS UNCLE SAM

In the wake of the Soviet Union's breakup and the end of the Cold War, the U.S. government reduced its military and defense expenditures. As a result, the government no longer can provide sufficient order volume to support more than one or two competitors in many aerospace and defense industry niches. As a result, the government's buying strategy has changed.

In the past, the U.S. government often selected two producers to share production of key programs. The proportions of total annual production favored the producer that had performed best the year before. But now that order sizes are shrinking, the government's strategy generally is to pick one supplier and utilize various incentive payments and penalties to ensure its optimal performance.

In conjunction with this change in procurement methods, the U.S. government has become openly receptive to mergers among military suppliers, especially those in direct competition with one another. Over the past two or three years, for example, Lockheed Martin (formerly Lockheed Aerospace) acquired several of the largest defense companies. Thus, in short order, it emerged as a dominant force in the defense industry. With the expected completion of a pending deal to acquire Northrop Grumman, Lockheed Martin will become an even more powerful force.

In fact, Lockheed, Boeing, and Raytheon Co. now form a triumvirate of powerful industry leaders. Each has significantly greater mass than any competitor in the next tier of aerospace companies.

As consolidation continues, the pressure increases for smaller companies to merge, find partners, or form other kinds of business relationships that will ensure long-term competitiveness. Aerospace is a capital- and technology-intensive industry; its participants must be sufficiently large to marshal the resources needed to compete effectively.

The appropriate size has been ratcheted up by the combination of decreasing defense dollars and the increasing size of the emerging industry leaders. Second-tier players must develop a critical mass or risk declining profits over time as the industry leaders seek to dominate attractive market niches.

Boeing Jumps on M&A Bandwagon . . .

The merger between Boeing and McDonnell Douglas in 1997 reflected the defense industry's new reality. Long a shrinking presence in the commercial aircraft industry, McDonnell Douglas nonetheless remained a leader in military aircraft and one of the leading military contractors. But in recent years, McDonnell Douglas lost several critical contracts for next-generation military aircraft to Lockheed Martin and Boeing.

The loss of crucial contracts meant that, despite its $49 billion backlog for delivery over the next decade, McDonnell Douglas would not participate in the next generation of military fighters. Lacking a long-term future in military or commercial aircraft, McDonnell Douglas agreed to merge with Boeing; the transaction was completed in August 1997.

After an absence of 60 years, Boeing reentered the military aircraft industry, first as a subcontractor to Lockheed on its F-22 Air Superiority Fighter jet, and then on its own in the competition for the U.S. military's Joint Strike Fighter. With its backlog approaching $90 billion in 1997, Boeing was aggressive in hiring and training employees to meet its burgeoning demand.

Boeing's acquisition spree began in 1996 when it acquired Rockwell International's space and defense businesses. Boeing's aim was to diversify beyond the volatile commercial aircraft sector that had been its main market. McDonnell Douglas was attractive because it had spare commercial aircraft production capacity at a time when that sector was in a cyclical upswing. With production problems at its main plants in the Seattle area, Boeing even now is studying how to make use of the recently acquired workforce.

. . . While Others Realign Their Businesses

Another recent major combination was the result of successive deals by Raytheon Co. to acquire the defense electronics divisions of Hughes Electronics (a wholly owned subsidiary of General Motors Corp.) and Texas Instruments for a total of $12.5 billion. Hughes itself had been an acquirer, buying a missile business from General Dynamics in 1992. The defense industry leader at that time, General Dynamics implemented a strategy to divest defense businesses for which an attractive price could be realized.

After shedding all of its businesses except military ships and military ground vehicles, General Dynamics now is building on its remaining markets with acquisitions that increase its core competencies. In 1997, it acquired two such businesses from Lockheed, which was adjusting its business mix after completing six acquisitions since 1992.

Continuing the industry's rapid pace of change, on July 3, 1997, Lockheed Martin agreed to a seventh acquisition, which will bring an eighth company along. Lockheed agreed to acquire Northrop Grumman, a distant fourth in the defense industry rankings. Northrop itself had a pending deal to acquire Logicon Inc.; if government approval is received, Lockheed will acquire both companies.

EUROPE PROTESTS BOEING–MCDONNELL DOUGLAS DEAL

To American observers, the Boeing–McDonnell Douglas merger may appear part of a natural evolution, resulting from the decline in McDonnell Douglas's commercial aircraft market share (now less than 5 percent). But for the European Union (EU), the combination posed a competitive threat to Airbus Industrie, the European consortium that designs and markets commercial aircraft manufactured by the group's four partners.

At present, Airbus is Boeing's only significant competitor in the markets for full-size narrow-body and wide-body jet aircraft that hold between 125 and 350 passengers. What concerned the EU wasn't just the proposed combination; after all, McDonnell Douglas's presence in the market served only to weaken the price structure. The consortium also was concerned about the terms of Boeing's recent contractual arrangements with three U.S. airlines. These airlines—Delta, American, and Continental Airlines—had agreed to the exclusive use of Boeing aircraft for the next 20 years, reportedly in exchange for deep price cuts.

The standardization of aircraft fleets with one manufacturer's planes is expected to help these airlines operate more efficiently by reducing parts inventories and training costs for pilots and mechanics. Such efficiencies could increase over time if Boeing standardizes its aircraft interiors so that pilots more easily can fly a variety of models. Currently, pilots must be retrained each time an airline wants to assign them to different models, especially those from different manufacturers.

Airlines have determined that while they may sacrifice bargaining power by committing to buy from a single manufacturer, operating costs will be substantially lower for a single-manufacturer fleet than for a fleet comprising planes from several manufacturers.

The EU's complaint charged that Boeing's exclusive 20-year deals violated antitrust laws by prohibiting competing manufacturers from seeking sales from the airlines involved. The EU asked U.S. government regulators, who had to approve the merger before its consummation, to consider the EU's position. The EU threatened to impose penalties on planes sold to European airlines if its demands weren't met.

As the EU Council's July 24, 1997, vote on the merger approached, positions on both sides of the Atlantic Ocean seemed to harden. Boeing refused concessions on the key issue of exclusive long-term contractual arrangements with the airlines, and Europe's Minister of Competition, Karel Van Miert, threatened stiff fines on planes sold to European airlines if the merger was ruled illegal by the EU.

Faced with this threat to Boeing, the leading U.S. exporter in the country's biggest export industry, President Clinton undertook a day of frenzied transatlantic phone calls, threatening retaliation if European nations followed through on their threats. A trade war loomed.

Boeing Blinked . . .

At the last minute, as Boeing made a crucial concessions and President Clinton lent a hand, the dispute was resolved. In the view of the EU, Boeing caved in to all of Van Miert's demands. Boeing agreed not to enforce the exclusivity provisions of the three current contracts with airlines and not to enter into such deals for ten years.

In addition, Boeing will maintain Douglas Aircraft, the commercial aircraft unit of McDonnell Douglas, as a separate legal entity, and will present an annual financial report to the EU. Boeing also agreed to license to its competitors certain key patents or technology that would have blocked their ability to compete with Boeing.

. . . Or Did It Just Wink?

Although it appears that Boeing acceded to all of the EU's demands, those concessions will have little impact on Boeing's dominance of the commercial aircraft industry. Although Boeing may not enter into exclusive contract arrangements for the next ten years, nothing would prevent airlines from buying exclusively from Boeing if it is to the airlines' advantage. Maintaining Douglas Aircraft as a separate legal entity does not prevent Boeing from melding the two companies' operations.

Licensing of technology also is not expected to be a key obstacle to Boeing, as it will receive standard licensing and royalty fees on such technology exchanges. This should permit Boeing to have a lower production cost than its competitors, who will have to pay fees in addition to production costs.

Overall, the EU's only significant victory may have been to set a precedent by forcing consideration of its opinion in a merger of two non-European companies. This well may have been the EU's real objective. The increasing globalization of numerous industries will result in mergers that will have an effect on several continents, and more conflicts are bound to arise in the future.

U.S. LEADS GLOBAL AEROSPACE INDUSTRY

Sales of the U.S. aerospace industry increased by some 11 percent to approximately $129.6 billion in 1997, compared with $116.5 billion in 1996, according to AIA estimates. The aerospace industry includes several distinct business segments: aircraft (which represent roughly half of industry sales); space (about one-fourth); missiles (6.5 percent); and related products and services (the remaining 17 percent).

Civil aircraft sales for 1997 likely accounted for more than half of the estimated $70 billion in aircraft shipments. This reflects the rise in deliveries of commercial aircraft following the rush of orders in 1996. The balance of shipments represents military aircraft. In 1996, aircraft deliveries were split about half-and-half between civilian and military, with the total rising to $60 billion from $55 billion in 1995.

Over the past 10 years, U.S. government business as a share of total industry sales dropped from about 75 percent to approximately 50 percent. By customer, we estimate that U.S. aerospace industry sales (excluding related products and services) break down as follows: 40 percent to DOD; 10 percent to NASA and other agencies; and 50 percent to other customers (foreign military and all civilian orders).

The aerospace industry is one of the largest exporters in the United States. Exports (mainly to highly developed international markets) should total approximately $50 billion in 1997. This reflects a two-year jump of about 50 percent from $33.1 billion in 1995. With imports offsetting part of the export total, net industry exports are valued at about $34 billion for 1997. Three-fourths of those exports were civil aerospace products—primarily aircraft and aircraft engines, engine parts, and spares.

BOEING CONTINUES TO DOMINATE WORLD COMMERCIAL AIRLINER MARKET

The world's primary manufacturers of large commercial jets (those with 115 to 500 seats) are the Boeing Co. (with 67 percent of unit deliveries in 1996 as restated to include McDonnell Douglas Corp.'s 11 percent share) and the European consortium Airbus Industrie (33 percent). Boeing has the broadest product line, and its 747 enjoys a monopoly in the jumbo jet category, but Airbus is aiming to introduce its own jumbo jet to compete head-to-head with Boeing over the next few years.

SALES OF THE AEROSPACE INDUSTRY, BY PRODUCT

(in millions of current dollars)

Year	Aircraft		Missiles	Space	Non aero-space	Total Aerospace Sales
	Civil	Military				
1997	38,643	30,478	8,284	30,613	21,604	129,622
R 1996	26,869	33,039	8,044	29,122	19,415	116,489
R 1995	23,965	31,082	7,386	27,385	17,964	107,782
1994	25,596	32,052	7,563	26,921	17,426	109,558

R: Revised.
Source: Aerospace Industries Association.

The regional jet transport market is served by numerous general aviation manufacturers that produce jet aircraft and turboprop aircraft ranging in size from 15 to 70 seats. Many of these general aviation manufacturers also produce business jets, small turboprop transports, and private aircraft. Manufacturers of large jets now are trying to address the upper range of the regional jet market by making smaller versions of existing jets that seat from 50 to 125 passengers.

COMMERCIAL SPACE: THE FINAL FRONTIER

Although budgets are flat, U.S. government programs still represent the lion's share of spending on space. DOD and NASA spend about $27 billion on space programs, accounting for about 70 percent of total worldwide government space spending.

Within a decade, however, commercial space could eclipse the government space sector. Propelled by rapid growth in telecommunications, broadcast, aircraft navigation, and imaging applications, the worldwide commercial space market is estimated to have totaled $10 billion in 1997.

Commercial space products are primarily satellites, satellite launchers (ELVs, or expendable launch vehicles), and supporting ground equipment. U.S.–based companies manufacture about 70 percent of satellites worldwide, led by Hughes Electronics Corp. Other U.S. satellite manufacturers include Lockheed Martin, Space Systems/ Loral (51 percent owned by Loral Space & Communications), TRW Inc. (which specializes in government satellites), and CTA Inc. (a privately owned company prominent in the emerging market for small satellites).

Another aspect of the commercial space business involves launching satellites. The creation of various satellite services companies and the development of new services (such as satellite broadcast cable television and global mobile telephone services) has generated rapid growth in satellite launch demand.

Despite its lead in satellite technology and production, the United States commands only about one-third of the worldwide launch business. U.S. competitors include Lockheed Martin; Orbital Sciences Corp.; and Boeing Space Systems. Paris-based Arianespace, an affiliate of the European Space Union and the world leader in commercial launches, has about 60 percent of the market.

NASA's space shuttle also is used to launch commercial as well as government satellites, and U.S. companies are developing next-generation reusable launch vehicles. Several commercial joint ventures have been announced between U.S. companies and those in Russia and Ukraine. Meanwhile, China, India, Israel, and other countries are developing satellite launch capabilities.

The Boeing Company—1998

Carolyn R. Stokes

Arthur Boyett

www.boeing.com
stock symbol BA

The Boeing Company (206-655-2121), headquartered in Seattle, Washington, is the largest aerospace firm in the United States as measured by total 1997 sales of $45.8 billion. Boeing is the world's leading manufacturer of commercial aircraft with 60 percent of the market, as well as the world leader in military aircraft. Boeing is one of the largest U.S. exporters with over $10 billion in sales to foreign countries. In 1996, Boeing acquired the Rockwell space and defense division, and in 1997 it merged with McDonnell Douglas to gain a greater share of the military and space market. Jetliners currently in production include the Boeing 737, 747, 757, 767, and the recently introduced 777 model, together with the newly acquired McDonnell Douglas model MD-11 trijets and MD-80 and MD-90 twinjets. The MD-95 is in the late stages of development. Boeing manufactures helicopters, military aircraft, electronic systems, and missiles; provides information services for aerospace related activities; and is a major contractors in the Space Station. But Boeing's net income for 1997 was negative $178 million.

A robust U.S. economy is good for most airline carriers, which are Boeing's primary customers. Growth in passenger traffic averaged approximately 5.5 percent over the last 5 years, leading to substantially better financial performance for airlines. Growth in freight traffic is increasing at a greater rate. Boeing predicts a cargo growth rate of 6.6 percent annually for the next 20 years. The airlines broke even in 1995 and moved upward in 1996 to record a profit. Growth continued in 1996 with many airlines enjoying substantial profits. The market for new aircraft strengthened. Boeing, led by the new CEO Philip M. Condit, had revenues for commercial aircraft of almost $27 billion as compared with nearly $20 billion in 1996 (see Exhibit 1). Newly acquired McDonnell Douglas had revenues of $13.8 billion in 1996 compared to $14.3 billion in 1995.

Because of increased demand and the growing number of orders in 1994, Boeing increased production rates on some models. By the end of 1996, Boeing was producing 21.5 jetliners per month as compared with 18.5 at the beginning of 1995. Boeing had major increases in production on the 767 and the new 777, and increased production in 1997 on all models except the 767. This change in the production schedule brought the production rate up to 40 per month by the end of 1997.

In information, defense, and space systems, Boeing recorded net earnings of $1.3 billion on sales of $18.1 billion in 1997, down from $1.4 billion in 1996 as shown in Exhibit 2. The 1996 revenues included $92 million of Rockwell revenue in the December

EXHIBIT 1: The Boeing Company, Commercial Aircraft

(dollars in millions)	1997	1996
Revenues	$26,929	$19,916
Operating profit (loss)	(1,837)	956

Source: Boeing Company and Subsidiaries, *Annual Report* (1997): 19.

EXHIBIT 2: The Boeing Company and Subsidiaries, Operations (dollars in millions)

Year ended December 31,	Net earnings (loss)			Revenues			Research and development		
	1997	1996	1995	1997	1996	1995	1997	1996	1995
Commercial Aircraft	$(1,837)	$ 956	$(1,280)	$26,929	$19,916	$17,511	$1,208	$1,156	$1,232
ISDS	1,317	1,387	1,312	18,125	14,934	14,849	716	477	442
Other	381	329	355	746	603	600	0	0	0
Unallocated expense	(216)	(54)	(703)	0	0	0	0	0	0
Earnings (loss) from operations	(355)	2,618	(316)	0	0	0	0	0	0
Other income, principally interest	428	388	280	0	0	0	0	0	0
Interest and debt expense	(513)	(393)	(376)	0	0	0	0	0	0
ShareValue Trust	99	(133)	0	0	0	0	0	0	0
Earnings (loss) before taxes	(341)	2,480	(412)	0	0	0	0	0	0
Income taxes (benefit)	(163)	662	(376)	0	0	0	0	0	0
	(178)	1,818	(36)	45,800	35,453	32,960	1,924	1,633	1,674

Year ended December 31,	Assets			Liabilities			Depreciation and amortization		
	1997	1996	1995	1997	1996	1995	1997	1996	1995
Commercial Aircraft	12,763	12,484	12,923	6,917	5,824	5,249	570	605	629
ISDS	6,597	6,785	5,243	2,379	2,361	1,290	365	299	311
Other	4,716	3,903	4,441	396	286	285	91	110	116
Unallocated	13,948	14,708	9,270	15,379	15,907	12,526	432	252	250
	38,024	37,880	31,877	25,071	24,378	19,350	1,458	1,266	1,306

Year ended December 31,	Capital expenditures, net			Contractual backlog (unaudited)		
	1997	1996	1995	1997	1996	1995
Commercial Aircraft	531	336	343	93,788	86,151	73,715
ISDS	463	304	186	27,852	28,022	21,773
Other	1	1	1	0	0	0
Unallocated	396	330	217	0	0	0
	1,391	971	747	121,640	114,173	95,488

ISDS = Information, Space and Defense Systems.
Other = Customer and Commercial Financing, Other.
Source: The Boeing Company and Subsidiaries, *Annual Report* (1997): 49.

acquisition of Rockwell aerospace and defense segments. McDonnell Douglas's defense and space division had operating profit of almost $1.2 billion on revenues of $10 billion in 1996 compared to profit of $1 billion on revenues of $10 billion in 1995. Boeing is in an aerospace environment facing rising demand for some commercial aircraft and defense products. It is gaining revenues from additional defense and space contracts obtained with its acquisition of Rockwell and its merger with McDonnell Douglas. The company needs a clear strategic plan for the future.

ROCKWELL ACQUISITION AND MCDONNELL DOUGLAS MERGER

Boeing added significantly to its holdings, its employee base, and its share of the aviation and aerospace market through two business combinations. In December 1996, Boeing acquired the aerospace and defense business of Rockwell Corporation in a transaction that was accounted for as a purchase. In August 1997, Boeing merged with McDonnell Douglas Corporation in a transaction that was accounted for as a pooling of interests.

On August 1, 1997, Boeing issued 279 million shares of its common stock to the shareholders of McDonnell Douglas in exchange for all of the McDonnell Douglas stock. Boeing recorded the combination as a pooling of interests. The assets, liabilities, and stockholders' equity of McDonnell Douglas were recorded in Boeing's accounting records at the same values at which they were being shown on the McDonnell Douglas financial statements. No goodwill was recorded. All financial statements issued by Boeing after the combination include the assets, liabilities, and operations of the combined companies.

The first official financial statement of the merged giant aerospace companies, the Boeing Form 10-Q for the quarter ended June 30, 1997, was filed after August 1, 1997, the effective date of the merger of Boeing and McDonnell Douglas. As a result, it shows two sets of financial statements: those for the Boeing Company as it existed at June 30, 1997, and those for the combined companies as they would have been had the pooling of interests taken place prior to June 30, 1997. Financial data are given in Exhibits 3, 4, and 5. Note that the increase in net assets (stockholders' equity) of Boeing between the June 30, 1997, balance sheet including McDonnell Douglas and the one without McDonnell Douglas was over $2.8 billion, the book value of McDonnell Douglas's net assets acquired.

EXHIBIT 3: The Boeing Company and Subsidiaries, Balance Sheet Comparisons, With and Without McDonnell Douglas

(dollars in millions)	Including McDonnell Douglas		Without McDonnell Douglas	
	6/30/97	12/31/96	6/30/97	12/31/96
Assets				
Cash & cash equivalents	$5,580	$ 5,469	$5,413	$4,375
Short-term investments	968	883	968	883
Accounts receivable	2,998	2,870	2,056	1,988
Current portion of customer financing	732	774	193	150
				continued

EXHIBIT 3: *continued*

(dollars in millions)	Including McDonnell Douglas		Without McDonnell Douglas	
	6/30/97	12/31/96	6/30/97	12/31/96
Deferred income taxes	986	1,362	368	745
Inventories, net of advances & progress billings	10,124	9,151	7,497	6,939
Total current assets	21,388	20,509	16,495	15,080
Customer financing	3,274	3,114	508	648
Property, plant and equipment, net	8,303	8,266	6,814	6,813
Deferred income taxes	122	143	511	415
Goodwill	2,437	2,478	2,437	2,478
Prepaid pension expense	3,295	3,014	1,910	1,708
Other assets	426	356	186	112
Total Assets	39,245	37,880	28,861	27,254

Liabilities and Shareholders' Equity

Accounts payable and other liabilities	10,855	9,901	8,383	7,306
Advances in excess of related costs	1,880	1,714	1,002	973
Income tax payable	395	474	404	350
Current portion of long-term debt	575	637	316	13
Total current liabilities	13,705	12,726	10,105	8,642
Accrued retiree health care	4,803	4,800	3,694	3,691
Long-term debt	6,405	6,789	3,619	3,980
Total liabilities	24,913	24,315	17,418	16,313
Minority interest	63	63	0	0
Shareholders' equity:				
Common shares, par value $5.00—				
1,200,000,000 shares authorized;				
Less Treasury shares, at cost				
Plus additional paid-in capital	5,791	3,962	5,549	3,752
Retained earnings	9,780	10,820	7,152	8,447
ShareValue Trust shares—26,249,537 and 26,119,702	(1258)	(1,258)	(1,258)	(1,258)
Unearned compensation	(39)	(22)		
Total shareholders' equity	14,274	13,502	11,443	10,941
Total Liabilities and Shareholders' Equity	39,250	37,880	28,861	27,254

Source: www.freeedgar.com

EXHIBIT 4: **The Boeing Company and Subsidiaries, Consolidated Statements of Net Earnings Comparisons, With and Without McDonnell Douglas**

(dollars in millions, except per share data)	Including McDonnell Douglas Six month ended June 30		Without McDonnell Douglas Six months ended June 30	
	1997	1996	1997	1996
Sales and other operating revenue	$22,670	$16,467	$16,607	$10,568
Costs and expenses	21,155	15,239	15,633	9,930
Earnings from operations	1,515	1,228	974	638

continued

EXHIBIT 4: *continued*

(dollars in millions, except per share data)	Including McDonnell Douglas Six month ended June 30		Without McDonnell Douglas Six months ended June 30	
	1997	1996	1997	1996
Other income, principally interest	215	165	165	128
Interest and debt expense	(243)	(199)	(119)	(75)
ShareValue Trust appreciation change	(2)	0	(2)	0
Earnings before federal taxes on income	1,485	1,194	1,018	691
Federal taxes on income	469	286	307	104
Net earnings	1,016	908	711	587
Earnings per share	1.05	0.93	1.02	0.85

Source: www.freeedgar.com

EXHIBIT 5: **The Boeing Company and Subsidiaries, Consolidated Statements of Financial Position**

(dollars in millions, except per share data)	December 31,	
	1997	1996
Assets		
Cash and cash equivalents	$ 4,420	$ 5,469
Short-term investments	729	883
Accounts receivable	3,121	2,870
Current portion of customer and commercial financing	261	774
Deferred income taxes	1,765	1,362
Inventories, net of advances and progress billings	8,967	9,151
Total current assets	19,263	20,509
Customer and commercial financing	4,339	3,114
Property, plant and equipment, net	8,391	8,266
Deferred income taxes	15	143
Goodwill	2,395	2,478
Prepaid pension expense	3,271	3,014
Other assets	350	356
	38,024	37,880
Liabilities and Shareholders' Equity		
Accounts payable and other liabilities	11,548	9,901
Advances in excess of related costs	1,575	1,714
Income taxes payable	298	474
Short-term debt and current portion of long-term debt	731	637
Total current liabilities	14,152	12,726
Accrued retiree health care	4,796	4,800
Long-term debt	6,123	6,852
Shareholders' equity:		
Common shares, par value $5.00— 1,200,000,000 shared authorized;		
Shares issued—1,000,029,538 and 993,347,933	5,000	4,967
Additional paid-in capital	1,090	920
Treasury shares, at cost—164,667 and 30,440	(9)	(1)

continued

EXHIBIT 5:   *continued*

(dollars in millions, except per share data)	December 31,	
	1997	*1996*
Retained earnings	8,147	8,896
Unearned compensation	(20)	(22)
ShareValue Trust shares—26,385,260 and 26,119,702	(1,255)	(1,258)
Total shareholders' equity	12,953	13,502
	38,024	37,880

Source: The Boeing Company and Subsidiaries, *Annual Report* (1997): 52.

COMMERCIAL AIRCRAFT

In 1996, airline demand for new aircraft rose. Boeing received a substantial increase in orders which led it to increase production rates. However, due to cutbacks in production in recent years and the implementation of a new manufacturing plan, Boeing is experiencing some delays in production. For example, one problem lies with titanium material required for supplier production. The forging houses that process the titanium are booked until mid-1998. Delays in this forged material created a bottleneck for production and delays of aircraft deliveries, according to Cole in the September 16, 1997, issue of the *WSJ*. However, after shutting down the production of the 747 for sense one month and slowing the production of the 737, Boeing is getting back to its earlier production schedule and expects to deliver aircraft on time. Boeing's recent commercial aircraft deliveries are shown in Exhibit 6.

Boeing delivered 374 commercial jet aircraft for 1997 compared with 269 in 1996. The backlogs, increases in current orders, and expected increases in demand generated by airline travel should push production levels for aircraft back to the 1993 level soon.

Boeing commercial airjet development has focused on the 777 and the family of 737s. United Airlines received and put into service in May 1995 the first 777 developed to meet the need for more efficient, comfortable, and high-capacity jets. The 777 seats 305 to 440 passengers and has a range of 5,300 miles. Deliveries of the 777-200 with extended range took place early in 1997. In the first quarter of 1997, United Airlines and British Airways received and put into service the increased gross weight version of the

EXHIBIT 6:   **The Boeing Company, Commercial Jet Aircraft Deliveries by Model**

1995–1997	*1997*	*1996*	*1995*
737	135	76	89
747	39	26	25
757	46	42	43
767	41	42	36
777	59	32	13
MD-80	16	12	18
MD-90	26	24	14
MD-11	12	15	18
Total	374	269	256

Source: Boeing Company and Subsidiaries, *Annual Report* (1997): 19.

777-200 referred to as the 777-200 IGW. The jetcraft, having a range of up to 7,230 nautical miles, is to be used for British Airways flights between London and the U.S. East Coast. Deliveries of the 777-300 with 20 percent additional capacity are expected in 1998. As of December 1996, Boeing had received 318 orders and 126 options for the 777s.

The smallest member of the Boeing jetliner family is the 737, the best-selling aircraft of all time with 3,604 orders and 2,840 deliveries. The 737 family, developed for short-to-medium-range flights, is being designed for greater range and speed and to meet new noise and emission standards. The 737-700 is scheduled for late 1997, the 737-800 is scheduled for early 1998, and the 737-600 is scheduled for late 1998. In 1996, Boeing announced an alliance with General Electric to build a business jet derivative of the 737-700. The Boeing Business Jet (BBJ) is scheduled to be flight tested in 1998 and delivered in 1999. As of December 1996, Boeing has received 517 orders and 287 options for 737s.

The Boeing 757 and 767 are medium-capacity, fuel-efficient twinjets that meet Federal Aviation Administration (FAA) requirements for extended-range operations. The 757 can carry 180 to 230 passengers, depending on the configuration, as far as 4,600 nautical miles. Boeing is developing a new version with 20 percent additional seating and 10 percent lower per seat operating cost. This new 757-300 is scheduled for delivery in 1999.

The 767 is larger, carrying about 260 passengers in mixed class, with a range on some versions in excess of 6,000 nautical miles. The 767-200 can carry 210 passengers a range of 7,500 miles, and the 767-300 can carry 252 passengers. A new extended-range version of the 767 was introduced early in 1997, and a planned 767-400ERX for 300 passengers is scheduled for delivery in the year 2000. Deliveries of the 757s are expected to increase from 42 in 1996 to 48 in 1997, and deliveries of the 767s are expected to increase from 42 in 1996 to 45 in 1997.

The flagship of the Boeing airplane family, the 747-400, can carry 569 passengers more than 7,000 nautical miles, and offers airline customers the lowest seat-mile costs of any aircraft in the world. The 747-400 has both an all-cargo and a combination cargo/passenger model. The Boeing 747 freight aircraft are in great demand at the Narita, the new Tokyo International Airport, which handles more than 1.5 million tons of freight, more than any other airport in the world. Almost 80 percent of the jets using Narita are Boeing 747s, according to Woolsey in the April 1997 issue of *Air Transport World*. The 747-400F gives Boeing's airline customers the capability of carrying 20 tons more payload on the routes they can fly, compared to 747-200 freighters, or carrying the same payload 800 nautical miles farther.

Changes are being made on the production of McDonnell Douglas airjets. Production of the MD-80 and MD-90 twinjets will be discontinued about 1999 when current orders are delivered. The MD-11 trijet is expected to be produced at a rate of one per month.

The European Airbus consortium remains Boeing's most formidable competitor in the commercial aircraft industry. The Airbus consortium consists of Aerospatiale SA of France, British Aerospace PLC, the aircraft unit of Daimier Benz AG of Germany, and Construcciones Aeronauticas SA of Spain. In the recent merger arrangements with McDonnell Douglas, the European Union's European Commission helped Airbus Industrie negotiate with Boeing on altering Boeing's exclusive sales agreements with U.S. major airlines. Airbus Industrie, headquartered in Toulouse, France, is much smaller than Boeing. In 1996, Airbus had $8.8 billion in revenues and 2,800 employees compared with $22.7 billion in revenues and 150,981 employees for Boeing. Airbus has been successful in negotiating contracts in competition with Boeing. For example, in April 1996, Airbus won the China Aviation Supplies contract for $1.5 billion and has orders for planes from Lufthansa. With these orders, Airbus and Boeing would be supplying approximately equal amounts of aircraft to Lufthansa, according to Taverna in the June 16, 1997, issue of *Aviation Week & Space Technology*. Airbus's primary focus is on commercial airliners, whereas Boeing is also active in defense and space systems and in pilot training.

Boeing accumulated $93.7 billion in backlog contracts in commercial aircraft by the end of 1997. In the third quarter of 1997, Boeing won a major order from Turkish Airlines in intense competition with Airbus, and won over Airbus in competition to receive a $3 billion to $4 billion sales contract with China. Boeing has about 60 percent of the Chinese aircraft business and expects Chinese travel to increase by 10 percent annually. Boeing sells commercial aircraft not only to airlines, but also to investment companies for leasing and to a tour company. A British tour company has ordered new Boeing 757-200s to enhance profits by means of its vertical integration plan, according to Proctor in the March 24, 1997, issue of *Aviation Week and Space Technology*.

In the highly competitive market for commercial aircraft, Boeing's reputation for customer service is an effective marketing tool. Boeing is providing ready access to parts and training programs using the Internet and CD-ROMs. Customers can access information on approximately 400,000 parts on the Web. Information on availability of parts, lead time, back orders, status of orders, and exchangeability of parts is now available to small and large customers. Using its Web site, initiated at the end of 1996, Boeing sold about $25 million in spare parts by the end of December 1997.

Boeing has built additional parts and service facilities to better meet customer needs. In 1994, Boeing began performing full checks on jets at a facility near the airport in Saudi Arabia. The same year, in Beijing, Boeing opened the world's largest spare parts center and assigned a senior executive as president of China operations at new headquarters in Beijing. Early in 1995, Boeing opened a new avionics service center in Singapore. By 1998, Boeing plans to open its eighth regional parts distribution center in Dubai, Arabia. Boeing maintains field representatives in 60 countries.

Boeing provides distance learning for customers in training for pilots, mechanics, and maintenance people using the latest technology. Boeing trains about 6,000 pilots and ground personnel annually for airline customers around the world at the Customer Service Training Center in Seattle, located approximately halfway between London and Tokyo.

MILITARY AND SPACE PRODUCTS

Boeing made a major advance in the defense and space segment by purchasing the Rockwell defense and space division and by finalizing a merger with McDonnell Douglas. Before these additions, Boeing's defense and space segment revenues were $18.1 billion for 1997, up slightly from $14.9 billion in 1996. Spending on defense and space had leveled at approximately $90 billion annually for the United States. Boeing expects U.S. defense and space spending to remain steady at $90 billion for the next five years.

The principal defense and space programs at Boeing include the International Space Station, B-2 bomber subcontract work, CH-47 helicopter, F-22 Advanced Tactical Fighter, E-3 AWACS and 767 AWACS, V-22 Osprey tiltrotor transport, and RAH-66 Comanche helicopter. Major space and defense projects at McDonnell Douglas include the F/A-18E/ F, the F/A-18C/D, the F-15, the T45, and the C-17 military aircraft, and the Delta II, Delta

III, and Space Stations projects in the missile and space division. Classified projects for the U.S. government also continue to contribute to defense and space segment revenues.

Boeing is a significant player in the National Aeronautical Space Administration (NASA). In 1993, Boeing was selected as NASA's prime contractor for the restructured International Space Station Alpha; today, Boeing is the prime contractor for NASA station's living and laboratory modules. Boeing is leading the team in the largest international venture in science and space ever undertaken. The project is aided by the efforts of 13 nations. The first launch of station hardware was in late 1997.

Boeing has been successful at teaming with other defense and space companies. Boeing North America, in a joint venture with Lockheed Martin, signed a six-year, $7 billion contract with NASA to consolidate shuttle ground flight and ground operations. Boeing North America has a contract for up to $1.3 billion with the U.S. Air Force to produce the Navstar Global Positioning System satellites. Boeing led a team that was awarded a $1.1 billion Airborne Laser Program Definition and Risk Reduction contract for developing a high-power laser and optical steering system.

In partnership with Lockheed Martin Corporation, Boeing continues with the development of the F-22 fighter. The first test of the new F-22 was in late 1997. The V-22 Osprey helicopter is being developed with Bell Helicopter Textronrogram. The Bell Boeing aircraft entered the $1.4 billion low-rate production in 1996. Deliveries of the V-22 designed for the Marines and Special Forces are expected to begin in 1999. This helicopter will meet the need for medium-lift requirements with exceptional mobility and rapid deployment. The CH-47 Chinook helicopter program consists of the remanufacturing of existing helicopters and the manufacturing of new Ch-47s; contracts are mostly with foreign governments. A Boeing/Sikorsky team is developing a twenty-first-century version of the RAH-66 Comanche armed reconnaissance helicopter and is currently flight testing a prototype which is the centerpiece of the U.S. Army's modernization plan.

Boeing was awarded a $660 million contract to work in competition with Lockheed Martin on the building of the Joint Strike Fighter; orders of 3,000 aircraft for the winner are expected in the next century. McDonnell Douglas also is involved in the development of this project. Early in 1992, Boeing delivered the final E-3 Airborne Warning and Control System (AWACS) aircraft built for the French and United Kingdom air forces. The AWACS system is now being offered on the military derivative 767 airplane. The Japanese government ordered two Boeing 767 AWACS in 1993 and two more in 1994, with the delivery of the first 767 AWAC to Japan in 1994. The Japanese government ordered four additional 767 AWACS with delivery expected to begin in 1998.

CONCLUSION

As indicated in Exhibit 7, Boeing's net income fell to negative $178 million in 1997, after rising dramatically in 1996. The 1997 net loss of $178 million approached the $1.2 million in net earnings of 1993. The future remains uncertain and Boeing could experience stronger competition in the commercial aircraft sector if Airbus merges with Lockheed Martin. In the face of this expected business environment, prepare a strategic plan for CEO Condit and Boeing (see Exhibit 8). Keep in mind Boeing's current mission statement (from its Annual Report): "To be the number-one aerospace company in the world and among the premier industrial concerns in terms of quality, profitability, and growth."

EXHIBIT 7: The Boeing Company and Subsidiaries, Consolidated Statements of Operations

	Year ended December 31,		
(dollars in millions, except per share data)	*1997*	*1996*	*1995*
Sales and other operating revenues	$45,800	$35,453	$32,960
Operating costs and expenses	40,644	29,383	27,370
General and administrative expense	2,187	1,819	1,794
Research and development expense	1,924	1,633	1,674
Special charges	1,400	0	2,438
Earnings (loss) from operations	(355)	2,618	(316)
Other income, principally interest	428	388	280
Interest and debt expense	(513)	(393)	(376)
ShareValue Trust	99	(133)	0
Earnings (loss) before income taxes	(341)	2,480	(412)
Income taxes (benefit)	(163)	662	(376)
Net earnings (loss)	(178)	1,818	(36)
Earnings (loss) per share			
Basic	(.18)	1.88	(.04)
Diluted	(.18)	1.85	(.04)
Cash dividends per share	.56	.55	.50

Source: The Boeing Company and Subsidiaries, *Annual Report* (1997): 51.

EXHIBIT 8: Boeing's Organizational Chart

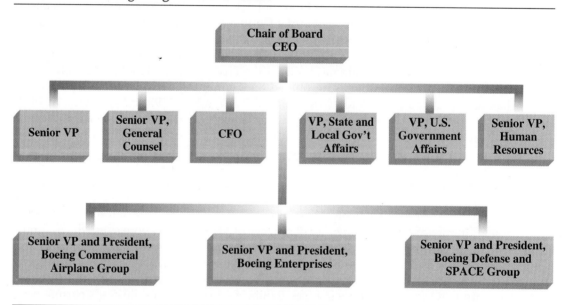

Source: Adapted from Boeing Company and Subsidiaries, *Annual Report* (1996).

Computers and Internet Providers— Industry Note

COMPUTER HARDWARE: CATCHING THE NEXT WAVE

Growth in computer hardware spending largely has been driven by business spending. First, businesses began to use the earliest computers to automate back-office operations such as accounting. Then, with the introduction of the personal computer (PC) and greater power at the desktop, front-office tasks also were automated. In each evolutionary step, as the market broadened, computer hardware revenues gained momentum.

The most recent stage in the computer hardware revolution reflects a shift to network computing. Networked computers draw in a growing base of corporate and consumer computer users and should expand the market's reach further as the world connects to the information superhighway. This growth should fuel computer hard-

Computer Industry Sales
(in thousands of units)

	1995	1996	% Change
Desktop PCs	51,493	61,088	18.6
Portable PCs	9,707	12,412	27.9
Servers	1,670	2,216	32.7
Workstations	1,371	1,823	33.0
Multiuser systems	186	224	20.4
Total	64,427	77,763	20.7

Source: Trend FOCUS, Inc.

Enterprise Platform Shifts Show Strong Demand for PC Servers
(Average number of systems per Fortune 1000 enterprise)

	1986	1988	1990	1992	1994	1996
Mainframe	4	4	5	4	4	4
Midrange	12	18	10	19	24	30
Server	8	18	22	56	173	328
PC	185	300	335	591	1,014	1,432

Source: Sentry Technology Group.

Source: Adapted from *Industry Survey* by permission of Standard & Poor's, a division of McGraw-Hill Companies. Standard & Poor's, "Computers: Hardware," *Industry Survey* (February 26, 1998): 6–9; "Computers: Consumer Services & the Internet," *Industry Survey* (February 12, 1998): 1–8.

ware spending, which can be divided into three segments: PCs (including notebooks), systems and servers (ranging up to large-scale systems such as mainframes and super-computers), and workstations. Each segment's pace of growth will differ, however, as competitors dive in to catch this next wave.

PC Segment Is Largest and Arguably the Most Competitive

The PC segment is the largest portion of computer hardware industry in terms of both units and dollars. The number of PC units shipped worldwide now total some 80 million units annually, worth an estimated $160 billion.

Growth in worldwide PC shipments averaged more than 20 percent annually between 1991 and 1995, driven largely by the increasing affordability and performance of PCs. Corporations leveraged that technology to increase productivity. Growth of approximately 15 percent is forecast through the end of the decade; it should be driven by the PC's continued price/performance improvements, Internet-driven demand, and greater PC penetration in consumer and emerging markets.

The PC segment is probably the most competitive in the computer hardware market. The top 10 worldwide vendors in 1992 accounted for roughly half the market for PCs; by 1994, however, a shakeout of second- and third-tier suppliers resulting from an aggressive pricing environment left the top ten with a 65 percent share. Further consolidation in the industry caused some industry pundits to forecast that the top five vendors could garner as much as 70 percent market share by 2000.

Compaq Computer has held the leading vendor spot for the past several years; its share of the worldwide market grew to 14 percent as of the third quarter of 1997, from 10 percent a year earlier. The four next-largest vendors, as of 1997's third quarter, were IBM Corp.; Dell Computer; Hewlett-Packard Co. (HP); and Packard Bell-NEC. Together, these top five vendors accounted for 39 percent of the market. Due to its unstable finances, longtime price leader Packard Bell was recently forced to join forces with NEC, a Japanese manufacturer.

Notably absent from the latest top five tally is Apple Computer. Reasons for this include its well-publicized internal problems, aggravated by a fiercely competitive market. As recently as mid-1994, the question was whether Apple was number one or number two in worldwide PC shipments.

Estimated Mainframe Market Share by Percentage—1996

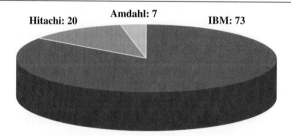

Hitachi: 20   Amdahl: 7   IBM: 73

Source: META Group.

Large, Multiuser Systems: PC Vendors Enter the Field as Categories Blur

Large or multiuser systems—including supercomputers, mainframes, minicomputers, and servers—account for about 35 percent of annual worldwide spending on computer hardware, by S&P's estimate, or around $85 billion. These platforms are in varying stages of maturity. Spending on mainframes and minicomputers has been flat to down over the past several years, reflecting sharp declines in average selling prices.

Conversely, spending on servers has grown sharply, as customers are increasingly downloading those applications traditionally found on mainframes and minicomputers to high-powered PC servers and superservers.

As increasingly powerful desktop computers have migrated upward, the lines between categories are blurring. As PC vendors are broadening their product lines with better desktop machines, PC server growth has exploded with sales of some 1.7 million units. For this low end of the server segment, Compaq dominates, with IBM and HP vying for the number 2 spot. Meanwhile, in the Unix server market (consisting of higher-end systems running the Unix operating system), HP holds the top spot, followed closely by Sun Microsystems and IBM, based on preliminary 1997 estimates for revenues of $23 billion for the total Unix server market.

In mainframes, the high end of the scale, IBM dominates. The market for mainframes is roughly $11 billion, according to 1997 estimates by the Cloverdale, California, Data Analysis Group. This market is largely measured by the annual shipped amount

Worldwide PC Market Share

(in percent, based on units shipped)	3rd Quarter 1996	3rd Quarter 1997
Compaq	10	14
IBM	9	8
Dell	4	6
Hewlett-Packard	4	6
Packard Bell-NEC	6	5
Others	67	61

Source: International Data Corp.

Worldwide PC Server Market Share

(in percent, based on units shipped)	1996	E1997
Compaq	30	28
IBM	11	13
Hewlett-Packard	12	13
Digital	4	4
Dell	3	9
Other	40	33

E: Estimated.
Source: International Data Corp.

Top Five Workstation Vendors

(ranked by unit shipments)	Unix Shipments		PC Shipments
Sun	285,815	Compaq	199,700
Hewlett-Packard	108,165	Hewlett-Packard	181,500
Silicon Graphics	83,850	Dell	127,800
IBM	71,774	IBM	106,000
Digital	33,310	Digital	56,390

Source: International Data Corp.

of MIPS—a measurement of the millions of instructions per second the machines are capable of performing. In 1996, this figure was approximately 500,000; IBM accounted for 73 percent of the market.

Workstations Face Greater Competition from Desktop

Workstations account for about 5 percent to 7 percent of worldwide computer hardware spending, or about $18 billion. The industry's fastest-growing sector in the late 1980s, workstations were unique in that they combined powerful processors, networking, and graphical user interfaces in a single compelling package for the first time, aimed at engineering, 3-D animation, and scientific applications.

Unix vendors dominated this market in the past, once accounting for some 85 percent to 90 percent of the market. Now, more powerful desktops that use Intel Corp. processors and Microsoft's Windows NT operating system are offering a cheaper alternative. According to estimates by International Data Corp. (IDC), a market research firm based in Framingham, Massachusetts, PC workstations outshipped Unix workstations for the first time in 1997. For workstation vendors, average annual unit growth should be in the high single digits through the balance of the decade, but lower prices will limit revenue growth.

INDUSTRY TRENDS

Computer hardware spending in 1996 totaled some $250 billion, accounting for 40 percent of the more than $600 billion spent on information technology (IT) that year, according to estimates by IDC.

The investment in technology grew as companies recognized the productivity benefits of this spending. In fact, the worldwide IT market was valued at just $360 billion in 1993, again based on estimates by IDC. Thus, the current figures reflect a 67 percent jump in just 3 years.

Still, the rate of that growth has slowed—spending grew 13 percent in 1996, down from 1995's 14.5 percent rate. This slowing partly reflects different spending patterns. IT now plays a greater role in defining a company's strategy for doing business, thus buying decisions now are made by senior management, not at departmental levels. Furthermore, as the size of IT investments now is greater, approval is part of most corporations' regular annual budget schedules.

The U.S. Market for Computer Hardware Is Maturing

Similar to the reduced rate of growth in overall IT spending, the pace of computer hardware growth in the United States also declined. For example, U.S. PC shipments, according to IDC, grew at 27 percent and 24 percent in 1994 and 1995, respectively. In 1996, the rate was cut to 15 percent. Most estimates for 1997 and 1998 propose PC shipments growing between 15 percent and 20 percent annually. By 2000 and 2001, most industry forecasts project shipments growing around 10 percent.

Part of this slowdown reflects the law of large numbers: Annual worldwide PC shipments now amount to 80 million units, compared with less than 40 million units in 1993, according to IDC. Still, certain industry fundamentals indicate the industry is indeed maturing. The number of new entrants appears to have slowed as existing computer hardware vendors broadened their product offerings. And although margins are higher than those in most other industries, these companies are becoming more focused on cash management and emphasizing higher asset returns.

However, the computer industry was founded on innovation. It will continue to reinvent itself as new technologies are discovered and introduced for worldwide consumption. We view the relatively lower rates of growth as a natural phenomenon; high levels of growth are simply unsustainable over long periods of time.

Competitive Pricing Here to Stay

Price competition has been the hallmark of the PC market, as PCs became more commodity-like with the standardization of their components: Microsoft's Windows operating system software is used in an estimated 83 percent of PCs worldwide, and Intel's processors are used in approximately 85 percent.

Pricing became fiercest in the PC market in 1992, when Compaq led a shakeout in second- and third-tier suppliers. Compaq is leading the charge again in 1997—dominating the sub-$1,000 PC market at the low end and challenging the price points of direct

---

Information Technology Spending by Percentage—1996

Total: $610 billion

Other 10.8
Other Asia-Pacific 7.6
U.S. 41.5
Japan 15.9
Italy 2.4
France 4.5
United Kingdom 4.8
Germany 6.9
Other Americas 2.9
Canada 2.7

Source: International Data Corp.

---

sellers such as Dell Computer at the high end. Direct sellers traditionally have been able to underprice indirect sellers such as Compaq and HP, which sell through retail channels. This was true because direct sellers achieve savings by maintaining low inventory levels; in addition, they don't have to pay the incentives or price guarantees that indirect sellers typically pay resellers. However, PC makers who sell indirectly are now using the direct sellers' techniques—such as advertising toll-free 800 numbers through which consumers can order PCs over the phone and instituting build-to-order strategies—to gain efficiencies and narrow the price gap.

THE INTERNET ENTERS THE MAINSTREAM

In just four quick years, the global system of computer networks called the Internet underwent a metamorphosis from an obscure communication system used by a limited number of academics and researchers to a massive web of more than 70 million interconnected computers encompassing users from all walks of life.

In the process, the Internet has been transformed from a static, text-based medium understandable by a very few to a graphically rich interactive medium well suited to the fast-growing commercial/consumer market. In 1998, the Internet should continue to become a larger part of the daily lives of a growing group of users drawn by its convenience and resources.

The Internet has one big advantage over traditional media: interactivity. The Web is a dynamic medium for communicating in real time. In addition, a user on the Web can influence and manipulate content.

A Web-based magazine, for example, can offer quick links to related Web sites and provide a search feature to find articles on a particular topic. Users can search indexes for older issues and communicate with columnists via e-mail.

In addition, a magazine on the Internet is not limited to a predetermined number of pages or by a weekly publication schedule. Publishers can adjust content throughout the day, without being constrained by publication dates and physical production and distribution schedules.

AOL Extends its Dominance

America Online, Inc., (AOL) recently extended its leading position in the provision of on-line services. In the third quarter of 1997, AOL passed the 10 million subscriber market, thus dwarfing its nearest competitors—Microsoft Network, Prodigy, and AT&T WorldNet—with their combined total of 3.5 million subscribers.

In September 1997, AOL acquired CompuServe Corp.'s worldwide subscriber base from WorldCom, Inc., in exchange for AOL's ANS Communications network subsidiary. In addition, AOL entered into a long-term strategic partnership with WorldCom to acquire much-needed network capacity. Upon completion of the transaction, expected by March 1998, AOL will add CompuServe's 2.6 million subscribers to its customer base.

AOL successfully leveraged its highly trafficked on-line service to generate lucrative nonsubscriber revenues through marketing agreements with established on-line retailers such as CUC International, Inc., and Amazon.com. AOL's advertising revenues more than doubled in 1997 on the strength of its huge share of on-line subscribers.

World Wide Web and E-Mail

Subscribers, in Millions	Internet Subscribers Capable of Viewing the World Wide Web	Internet Subscribers Capable of Receiving E-Mail
E 2002	149.9	178.0
E 2001	128.1	151.5
E 2000	106.2	120.0
E 1999	85.0	96.8
E 1998	63.6	70.5
E 1997	47.4	48.7
1996	35.7	35.7
1995	25.6	25.6
1994	20.0	20.0

E: Estimated.
Source: In-Stat.

As AOL's subscriber growth rate begins to slow, the company plans to benefit from the growing acceptance of electronic commerce and the maturation of on-line advertising.

INDUSTRY TRENDS

With more than 58 million adults (or three users per subscription) in the United States on-line as of the third quarter of 1997, up from 35 million at the end of 1996, the Internet is in an exceptional growth phase. This growth has pushed the capacity of existing networking infrastructure to its limits.

In addition to on-line consumers, the Internet spawned corporate intranets that use the infrastructure and standards of the Internet within enclosed company networks.

As the Internet began to mature, consolidation among Internet service providers (ISPs) began to occur. The spread and maturation of the Internet has put intense focus on security issues as users attempt to protect themselves from fraud and theft.

Estimated Number of Host Computers on the Internet

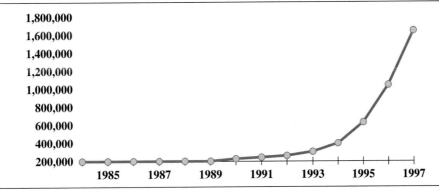

Source: Adapted from Network Wizards.

Runaway Growth

By any measure, the Internet is one of the fastest-growing commercial phenomena ever. As of early 1997, a new computer was being added to the Internet every four seconds. Currently, the global network is growing 10 percent per month, doubling in size nearly every ten months. Such exponential growth led to the expansion of the Internet from 562 connected host computers in 1983 to roughly 16.2 million computers at the end of 1997.

At any time from 1983 through 1996, half of the Internet's historical growth had occurred in the preceding 12 to 14 months. In terms of the number of host computers, the Internet was only 3 percent of its current size just six years ago.

Contributing to this growth is greater use of the World Wide Web and e-mail. By 2002, the number of Internet subscribers using the Web is expected to triple to approximately 150 million. E-mail, the primary communications medium of the Internet, does not require Web-based connectivity. E-mail use is projected to grow even more rapidly than Web use as developing nations with older infrastructures that are not compatible with the Web become a greater percentage of total e-mail users.

As a result of the Internet's historical roots in the U.S. Department of Defense, the United States accounts for approximately half of the world's total Internet users. About 132 countries currently are connected directly with the Internet. Another 52 countries can send and receive electronic mail over computer networks but do not have direct connections to the Internet.

The Internet is expected to continue growing swiftly for the near future as new countries become connected and as Internet penetration increases in developed nations.

In the United States, one of the countries with the highest number of Internet users, only about one-fifth of the population is connected, leaving plenty of room for growth. When consumers today are asked why they purchased a personal computer, the most common answer is to connect to the Internet.

ISPs Begin to Consolidate

As of November 1997, the number of ISPs totaled some 4,000, nearly triple the 1,500 that existed in mid-1996. Low barriers to entry and the ability of small ISPs to serve local service areas with affordable computer and networking hardware have driven this spectacular growth.

The nascent ISP industry can be broken into three tiers: national, regional, and local. As telecommunications service providers seek to purchase valuable equipment that connects users directly to the Internet, the national providers have been consolidating rapidly.

In September 1997, WorldCom, Inc., purchased America Online's networking business, adding to its purchase of UUnet in 1996. In mid-October 1997, ICG Communications, Inc., agreed to buy Netcom On-line Communications Service, Inc., the fifth-largest ISP. In May 1997, GTE Corp. bought BBN Corp. and renamed the Internet service GTE Internetworking.

With the advent of America Online's path-breaking pricing model—$19.95 per month for unlimited Internet access—mid-sized ISPs were forced to acquire small ISPs to achieve economies of scale and remain profitable. For example, regional ISPs Earth-Link Network, Inc., and MindSpring Enterprises have been snapping up local providers. MindSpring has acquired the rights to 19 smaller ISPs, boosting its subscriber base to more than 220,000.

Internet Service Providers (as of June 1997)

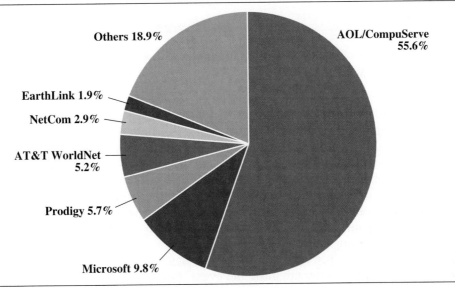

Others 18.9%

AOL/CompuServe 55.6%

EarthLink 1.9%

NetCom 2.9%

AT&T WorldNet 5.2%

Prodigy 5.7%

Microsoft 9.8%

Source: IDC/Link.

In local markets, many ISPs have begun focusing on business customers to make up for lost revenue from the less profitable consumer market. These smaller ISPs are seeking to offer value-added services, such as guaranteed connections and Web site development, to small business customers.

Apple Computer, Inc.—1998

David Stanton

www.apple.com
stock symbol AAPL

As word of the deal spread at the Macworld trade show in Boston, an important yearly pilgrimage for Macintosh fans, thousands audibly gasped. "We have to let go of the notion that in order for Apple to win, Microsoft has to lose," Apple founder Steve Jobs told the shocked crowd. "The era of setting this up as a competition between Apple and Microsoft is over as far as I'm concerned."

Not all were convinced. When Microsoft Chairman Bill Gates appeared on a giant video screen, looming over the crowd at the show to announce the Microsoft investment in Apple, thousands booed and hissed. "It was anathema," said one analyst. "It was like putting Darth Vader up at a Star Wars convention."

"I think it's just another way for Bill Gates to take over the world," said a longtime Macintosh user who attended the event. Microsoft's investing in Apple "is a bit like NASA trying to rescue Mir," said one prominent Silicon Valley investor.

Steve Jobs was back in charge of the company he cofounded more than 20 years before, acting as de facto CEO even though he had refused the official job. In the following months, he would make changes in the company even as the search for a CEO continued. The changes would include abandoning the short-lived policy of licensing Apple's operating system to third-party clone makers, buying out the license of Apple's largest clone maker, and launching a push to develop an inexpensive network computer.

HISTORY

Apple was born in 1976, when Steve Jobs and Stephen Wozniak designed the Apple I computer in the garage of Jobs's parents' home in Cupertino, California. Jobs sold his Volkswagen van and Wozniak sold his programmable calculator to finance the building of the first 50 circuit boards. The company was incorporated in 1977 and introduced a more advanced computer called the Apple II that helped to launch the era of desktop computers.

The company went public in 1980. Morgan Stanley and Co. and Hambrecht & Quist underwrote an initial public offering of 4.6 million shares of Apple common stock at a price of $22 per share. Every share was bought within minutes of the offering, making it the largest public offering since Ford went public in 1956.

In 1982, Apple became the first personal computer (PC) company to reach $1 billion in annual sales. By 1983, less than 5 years after incorporation and with the PC boom in full swing, Apple entered the Fortune 500 at number 411. The company hired former Pepsi president John Sculley as president and CEO, and established a new direction in personal computing with the introduction of the Lisa® computer. Although Lisa was not a financial success, it was a milestone product that reestablished Apple as a technological pioneer, and set the industry standard for software based on a graphical user interface. Lisa technology was the foundation for the much anticipated Macintosh® introduced in January 1984. With icons, pull-down menus, windows, and a mouse, the Macintosh, or "Mac," set a new standard for ease of use in the industry that continues today. It would take 6 more years for Microsoft to introduce a usable graphical interface for the PC.

In 1985, Jobs decided to make a play for control of the company and planned to stage a boardroom coup while Sculley was gone. Sculley learned of the coup and foiled it with the support of the board. Jobs resigned that day, leaving Sculley as the head of Apple. Jobs started a new computer company, NeXT, and Wozniak resigned to start a company to develop home video products.

By 1990, the market was saturated with PC clones of every conceivable configuration, and Apple was still the only company selling Macs. In late May, Microsoft introduced Windows 3.0, which could run on virtually all of the PC clones in the world. Apple was in trouble and considered licensing the Mac operating system (OS). There also was talk of porting the Mac OS to run on Intel-based machines.

In 1992, Apple lost a copyright ruling in its lawsuit against Microsoft, essentially ending its hopes of defeating Microsoft Windows in court. With the introduction of the Performa line, Macintosh products became available through mass merchandisers and superstores. Apple also began to sell its computers through mail order companies. The moves conceded the failure of Apple's policy of exclusive distribution through its retail dealers.

Apple introduced the Newton personal digital assistant in 1993. The hand-held computer was an expensive failure. The fallout prompted Apple to boot Sculley as CEO. President and COO Michael Spindler was named CEO. Apple reported a sharp decline in profits to $86.6 million, down from 1992's $530.4 million. The company announced layoffs of 2,500 employees, about 15 percent of its workforce.

In 1994, Apple launched a successful new line of computers called the Power Macintosh®, using a powerful microprocessor developed in alliance with IBM and Motorola. Profits rebounded to $310.2 million. Apple announced it would, for the first time, license its operating system to other computer makers.

In 1995, Apple launched a new line of laptops but had to recall them after two models burst into flames. Other companies were profiting from the PC boom, but component shortages kept Apple customers waiting. By midyear, Apple's backlog soared to $1 billion. Apple reported a larger-than-expected 48 percent drop in fourth quarter profits to $60 million despite a 20 percent rise in sales to a record $3 billion. It was a harbinger of troubles to come, although Apple finished the year with net income of $424 million.

In January 1996, Apple posted a $69 million first quarter loss, its first Christmas quarter loss. Apple also announced layoffs of 1,300 employees, 8 percent of its workforce. Apple and Sun Microsystems, Inc., discussed a merger, but talks broke down over price. Gilbert Amelio, a member of Apple's board of directors since 1994 and former CEO of National Semiconductor Corp., successfully made a bid to replace

Spindler in February 1996. The turnover was punctuated by a stunning loss of $740 million in the March 1996 quarter, with more than half of the loss from inventory write-downs. Amelio promised to make the company profitable in a year, a promise that would prove impossible to keep.

In December, Apple announced plans to acquire Steve Jobs's NeXT Software, Inc., for $400 million, reuniting the cofounder with the company. Apple plans to use NeXT's operating system to resuscitate the company's floundering efforts to develop a new generation of the Mac OS. Apple had an $816 million net loss in 1996, and nearly a $1.5 billion loss for 1997 with a revenue drop of 28 percent.

OVERVIEW

Headquartered in Cupertino, California, Apple (408-996-1010) develops, manufactures, licenses, and markets computer hardware, software, and services for business, education, consumer, entertainment, scientific, engineering, and government customers in more than 140 countries. Apple owns manufacturing facilities in Ireland and Singapore. Distribution facilities are located in the United States, Europe, Canada, Australia, Singapore, and Japan.

Apple is a company in trouble that well may have seen its best days. At one time, Apple dominated the PC market. Today, it is in trouble, saved only by the fact that Apple users are almost fanatically devoted. It has clung to an anachronistic business model. Apple is the only company in the PC market that makes both computers and the operating system to run them, whereas the market is dominated by computers that combine Intel processors with Microsoft operating systems.

When it comes to rank-and-file Apple users, though, hope springs eternal. Individual Apple users remain committed to the company even as corporate America moves to Wintel. Apple is not just a company to many of its customers. One fan operates the EvangeList, an e-mail list devoted to Apple that claims 40,000 subscribers. It and the EvangeList Web site are devoted to helping people "evangelize Apple, Macintosh, and Newton—and to make the world a better place!" Included on the site is a section on "guerrilla" tactics for individuals to promote Apple and a list of "Simple Things You Can Do to Save Apple Computer." Although that sort of fanaticism is by no means universal among Apple customers, it is unique to Apple.

The Macintosh

The Macintosh platform includes the Macintosh Performa® series for consumers, a range of PowerBook® mobile computers, and the Power Macintosh series of desktop PCs. Sales to date of Macintosh computers exceed 26 million units.

In 1997, Apple introduced a new operating system for the Macintosh PC. It is the most significant Mac OS upgrade since its introduction in 1984. Mac OS 8 is an effort by Apple to cut its OS development losses. When Microsoft's Windows® 95 was under development, Apple said it had a revolutionary new OS in the works, code-named Copland. Copland was a disaster that wasted several years of OS development and gave Microsoft a free ride in the OS competition. Copland was to have been released as Mac OS 8. The version of Mac OS 8 finally released in 1997 contains some Copland features, but it was nowhere near the promise of Copland and came a year later. The December

1996 acquisition of NeXT signaled that Apple was abandoning Copland and that its future OS development will be based on NeXT's software. Mac OS 8 is expected to generate much needed revenues for Apple as Macintosh users upgrade their software.

Claris Corporation, a wholly owned subsidiary of Apple, was the largest vendor of Macintosh software applications (based on units shipped) worldwide, and the eighth-largest vendor of PC software applications (based on revenue) worldwide. In early 1998, Apple liquidated Claris Corporation, laying off hundreds of employees.

Core Markets

Apple still holds the number-one market share in education. According to a 1995–1996 market research study by Quality Education Data, Apple's installed base of computers for kindergarten through twelfth grade in public schools was 63 percent—a 4 point increase from the previous year. Apple's dominance is threatened by more recent inroads by Mac clones and aggressive promotions of Windows-based systems from Compaq and other companies.

Apple leads one of the fastest-growing parts of the business market—business communication and publishing—in which Apple has an estimated 47 percent share of U.S. commercial publishing customers and a 26 percent share of U.S. corporate publishing customers. Apple holds an estimated 50 percent share of the engineering, scientific, and technical markets.

Apple provides leading products and technologies for creative professionals across all segments of the entertainment industry, from CD-ROM to film/video production, animation, and special effects, to music. Apple boasts leadership in key entertainment segments, such as a 70 percent market share in music production and 60 percent in video postproduction.

However, despite the company's strong position in these specialty markets, a bigger challenge remains: how to convince other businesses to stick with the Macintosh. Many companies and organizations that once standardized on the Mac platform are phasing it out in favor of Intel-based machines running Microsoft Windows. Dataquest, which tracks PC sales worldwide, says Apple's share of the worldwide market fell in 1996 to 5.2 percent from 7.9 percent.

INTERNAL OPERATIONS

Marketing and Distribution

A number of uncertainties may affect the marketing and distribution of Apple's products. Currently, the primary means of distribution is through third-party computer resellers. Such resellers include consumer channels such as mass merchandise stores, consumer electronics outlets, and computer superstores. Apple's business and financial results could be affected adversely if the financial condition of these resellers weakens or if resellers within consumer channels decide not to continue to distribute Apple's products.

Uncertainty over demand for Apple's products may cause resellers to reduce their ordering and marketing of its products. Under Apple's arrangements, resellers have the option to reduce or eliminate unfilled orders previously placed, in most instances without financial penalty. Resellers also have the option to return products to Apple without penalty within certain limits, beyond which they may be assessed fees. Apple recently

EXHIBIT 1: Apple Computer, Inc., Consolidated Statements of Operations

(in millions of dollars, except per share amounts)	Fiscal years ended September		
	1997	1996	1995
Net sales	$7,081	$9,833	$11,062
Costs and expenses:			
Cost of sales	5,713	8,865	8,204
Research and development	485	604	614
Selling, general and administrative	1,286	1,568	1,583
Special charges:			
In-process research and development	375	0	0
Restructuring costs	217	179	(23)
Termination of license agreement	75	0	0
	8,151	11,216	10,378
Operating income (loss)	(1,070)	(1,383)	684
Interest and other income (expense), net	25	88	(10)
Income (loss) before provision (benefit) for income taxes	(1,045)	(1,295)	674
Provision (benefit) for income taxes	0	(479)	250
Net income (loss)	(1,045)	(816)	424
Earnings (loss) per common and common equivalent share	$(8.29)	$(6.59)	$3.45
Common and common equivalent shares used in the calculations of earnings (loss) per share (in thousands)	126,062	123,734	123,047

Source: Apple Computer, Inc., *Annual Report* (1997): 32.

experienced a reduction in ordering from historical levels by resellers due to uncertainty concerning its condition and prospects.

Research and Development

Research and development expenditures decreased 25 percent from $604 million in the fiscal ended in September 1996 to $485 million in the fiscal ended in September 1997 (see Exhibit 1). Fiscal 1997 expenditures as a percentage of net sales came to over $8.1 billion, dwarfing the year's $7 billion in sales. Apple reported a net loss for fiscal 1997 of nearly $1.5 billion.

Finance

Apple's financial statements are provided in Exhibits 2 and 3. Note that Apple's long-term debt more than tripled from $303 million by September 1995 to $949 million by September 1996, but increased only to $951 million as of September 1997.

Management

Apple's management is unsettled. The company's chief administrative officer left in May 1997. The chief technology officer left with former CEO Amelio in July, and the heads of marketing and of research and development resigned after the shift away from OS licensing. The new board has given Jobs the freedom to make changes in the company even as the search for a new CEO continues. Jobs's presence is believed by

EXHIBIT 2:   Apple Computer, Inc., Consolidated Balance Sheets

	Fiscal year ended		
(in millions of dollars)	September 26, 1997	September 27, 1996	September 27, 1995
Assets:			
Current assets:			
Cash and cash equivalents	$1,230	$1,552	$756
Short-term investments	229	193	196
Accounts receivable, net of allowance for doubtful accounts of $99 ($91 in 1996 and $87 in 1995)	1,035	1,496	1,931
Inventories:			
Purchased parts	141	213	841
Work in process	15	43	291
Finished goods	281	406	643
	437	662	1,775
Deferred tax assets	259	342	251
Other current assets	234	270	315
Total current assets	3,424	4,515	5,224
Property, plant, and equipment:			
Land and buildings	453	480	504
Machinery and equipment	460	544	638
Office furniture and equipment	110	136	145
Leasehold improvements	172	188	205
	1,195	1,348	1,492
Accumulated depreciation and amortization	(709)	(750)	(781)
Net property, plant, and equipment	486	598	711
Other assets	323	251	296
	$4,233	$5,364	$6,231
Liabilities and Shareholders' Equity:			
Current liabilities:			
Notes payable to banks	$25	$186	$461
Accounts payable	685	791	1,165
Accrued compensation and employee benefits	99	120	131
Accrued marketing and distribution	278	257	206
Accrued warranty and related	128	181	85
Accrued restructuring costs	180	117	0
Other current liabilities	423	351	277
Total current liabilities	1,818	2,003	2,325
Long-term debt	951	949	303
Deferred tax liabilities	264	354	702
Commitments and contingencies:			
Shareholders' equity:			
Series A nonvoting convertible preferred stock, no par value; 150,000 shares authorized, issued and outstanding	150	0	NA
Common stock, no par value; 320,000,000 shares authorized; 127,949,220 shares issued and outstanding in 1997 (124,496,972 shares in 1996 and 122,921,601 shares in 1995)	498	439	398

continued

EXHIBIT 2: *continued*

	Fiscal year ended		
(in millions of dollars)	*September 26, 1997*	*September 27, 1996*	*September 27, 1995*
Retained earnings	589	1,634	2,464
Other	(37)	(15)	39
Total shareholders' equity	1,200	2,058	2,901
	$4,233	$5,364	$6,231

Source: Apple Computer, Inc., *Annual Report* (1997): 31.

EXHIBIT 3: **Apple Computer, Inc., Industry Segment and Geographic Information**

	Fiscal year ended		
(in millions of dollars)	*September 26, 1997*	*September 27, 1996*	*September 29, 1995*
Net sales to unaffiliated customers:			
United States	$3,507	$4,735	$5,791
EMEA	1,667	2,222	2,365
Japan	1,070	1,792	1,822
Asia Pacific	490	563	519
Other	347	521	565
Total net sales	7,081	9,833	11,062
Transfers between geographic areas (eliminated in consolidation):			
United States	206	517	511
EMEA	207	121	178
Japan	5	0	0
Asia Pacific	1,270	3,035	3,619
Total transfers	1,688	3,673	4,308
Operating income (loss):			
United States	(913)	(1,198)	(74)
EMEA	(129)	(186)	245
Japan	(86)	(4)	47
Asia Pacific	104	3	388
Other	(29)	0	48
Eliminations	(17)	2	30
Corporate income (expense), net	25	88	(10)
Income (loss) before provision (benefit) for income taxes	(1,045)	(1,295)	674
Identifiable assets:			
United States	1,543	1,935	2,955
EMEA	557	648	927
Japan	383	559	686
Asia Pacific	286	312	581
Other	119	171	157
Eliminations	(135)	(26)	(34)
Corporate assets	1,480	1,765	959
Total assets	$4,233	$5,364	$6,231

Source: Apple Computer, Inc., *Annual Report,* (1997): 56.

analysts to be driving away executives and hurting Apple's efforts to find a new chief executive. More executive departures and layoffs are expected to follow.

APPLE: 1997

Apple posted an unexpected $120 million loss for the first quarter of fiscal 1997 as sales of its flagship Macintosh model continued to fall sharply. Faced with shrinking revenues, the company announced plans for yet another restructuring that included layoffs of another 4,100 employees and cuts in research and development. Apple lost $708 million in the second quarter.

On June 26, Jobs anonymously dumped 1.5 million shares of Apple stock. Analysts speculated—and Jobs later confirmed—that the shares were those Jobs obtained as part of the NeXT acquisition. "I pretty much had given up hope that the Apple board was going to do anything," Jobs told *Time* magazine. "I didn't think the stock was going up."

In July, Apple began a search for a new CEO. Amelio, once dubbed the Turnaround King, left the company saddled with losses in five out of six financial quarters and an uncertain future strategy. As CEO, he garnered an estimated $13 million in salary and benefits for 1996. Jobs assumed the role of de facto CEO, fueling speculation he would take over the troubled company but, when offered the position, he declined. Weighed down by continued bad news, Apple shares slid to $12.75, a 12-year low for the shares.

On August 6, after nearly a month of uncertainty about Apple's future, Apple and Microsoft shocked the computer world when they announced that Microsoft would invest $150 million in Apple. Apple had turned to its bitterest enemy for help, symbolically declaring defeat. The next day, Apple shares rose sharply and traded briefly at $30 per share as analysts and investors applauded the deal. Not everyone was happy, but after the shock wore off, most Mac users seemed to approve of the deal.

The investment hardly will be missed from Microsoft's $9 billion cash hoard, and Apple already had large cash reserves (over $1.2 billion), but the deal provides a needed psychological boost that could keep other software companies and Mac customers from defecting. The news of Microsoft's investment in Apple and strong sales of Mac OS 8 also should help drive fall sales of Apple computers.

Apple agreed to make Microsoft's Internet Explorer program, software for browsing on the World Wide Web, the standard browser on new Macintoshes. Apple still will ship browsing software made by Microsoft rival Netscape Communications Corp., but using it will require the customer to take special steps to call it up. Microsoft pledged to continue writing its Office business software for the Macintosh, but did not commit to support future generations of Apple's operating system. Also, the agreement gives each company access to the other's patents.

Apple also announced major changes to its board of directors, with all but two of the old board's members gone. Apple's board had been criticized for failing to step in as the company foundered and for being too deferential to the company's chief executives. The new members won widespread praise.

Jobs said that a new chair will not be chosen until a new CEO is named. After a period in which Jobs acted as de facto CEO, he was named interim CEO by the board pending the completion of the search for a permanent CEO.

COMPETITION

Apple is competing in one of the fastest-changing markets in the world. Computers are becoming faster and cheaper, and the companies which are doing well are those which are able to adapt to that change. Apple is one of the few large computer companies which has fared poorly.

A few years ago, Dell Computer Corp. was in trouble. Its notebook computer sales were a flop because of poor design and low quality. Dell still tried to sell the notebook through retail outlets even though it drained profits from the company's direct sales. The company recorded a $100 million loss in one quarter.

Company founder Michael Dell ended the retail sales, fixed the problems with the notebook computers, and launched a two-pronged marketing effort to consumers and corporate customers. The consumer bought mainly on price, but the corporate buyer needed a carefully developed relationship.

Dell installs custom software and keeps track of business customers' inventory. It delivers orders quickly. And like competitors IBM and Compaq, it added a sales and engineering force devoted solely to certain large companies.

Dell also set standards in the industry for slim inventory and quick delivery. It always built computers to order, avoiding inventory costs, but in recent years it reduced component inventory by adopting just-in-time delivery, with some components delivered only minutes before they are needed.

Today, Dell is riding high. It is steadily and rapidly taking big-business market share from IBM and Compaq, in many cases forcing them to lower their prices to existing customers. Its earnings are up 86 percent on sales that are up 60 percent. The stock price tripled in eight months, making Dell's founder more wealthy than Texas oilman H. Ross Perot.

Other companies are attempting to emulate Dell's success. Packard Bell NEC, Inc., began direct sales to its corporate customers. Compaq began stockpiling components that quickly can be assembled into built-to-order computers that then are shipped to a retail outlet. IBM; Digital Equipment Corp.; and Taiwan's Acer, Inc., are sending partially assembled models into the dealer channel that can be finished once an order is taken.

Two companies illustrate the rapid growth of the non-Mac OS PC market. Microsoft Corporation is the largest software company, and Compaq Computer Corporation is the largest PC manufacturer.

In contrast to the growth of the rest of the industry, the Mac OS market is shrinking. In Apple's third quarter of fiscal 1997, the Mac OS share of the domestic computer market shrank 29 percent from the same quarter last year, to 4.6 percent of all PCs shipped in the United States.

Apple's year-on-year shipments of computers dropped more than 24 percent. But despite declining sales, Apple regained some market share lost to clone makers. The company's share of the Mac OS market increased to more than 80 percent, a gain of 12 percent from the first quarter of the calendar year, when Apple had less than 70 percent. Analysts attributed Apple's gain to aggressive pricing of its new desktop and portable systems and the education system's buying season for kindergarten through twelfth grade classroom computer resources.

In the second calendar quarter, Apple slipped to seventh place in Dataquest's ranking of the nation's largest computer makers, with 4.5 percent of the U.S. PC market. Apple in the 1996 calendar year ranked third, with 7.2 percent of the market.

In 1996, Mac OS software sales decreased 23 percent and represented just 11 percent of the application software market, down from 18 percent in 1994 and 14 percent in 1995. Sales of Windows applications increased 16.3 percent in 1996 and accounted for 81 percent of the application software sold in the United States and Canada.

Apple's response to competition has been to avoid it. With no permanent CEO in place, Jobs reversed Apple's licensing policy. Since assuming Apple leadership, Jobs has led a fight against the clone makers, whom Jobs believed were hurting sales while paying too little for their Mac OS licenses.

Apple has refused to license OS 8 to cloners, except in a few market niches such as low-cost machines. This left cloners unable to market machines with Apple's latest OS, effectively strangling the clone market. Apple also refused to certify a hardware specification it had agreed to support that would have allowed clone makers to build machines from cheaper, off-the-shelf components rather than from components designed to Apple specifications.

Apple bought out Power Computing's license to sell the Mac OS, and the company that had been the largest Mac OS clone maker will now switch to Windows-based computers. Motorola has decided to stop building clones. The non-Apple Mac OS clone market is now essentially dead except for a few niche markets.

CONCLUSION

Apple still has more than $1 billion in cash. Also, more than 1.2 million copies of Mac OS 8 have been sold since the product's retail introduction on July 26, 1997, quadrupling the company's expectations. However, the company's survival is by no means assured. The deal with Microsoft boosted the stock price, but industry analysts say Apple's long-term prospects are not significantly brighter, with or without Microsoft. The company has yet to figure out how to stop its computer sales from plunging.

Although Jobs is said to blame some of Apple's woes on competition with the clone makers, not everyone agrees, and even many of the Mac faithful believe that the end of the clone market signals doom for Apple. Another problem is Apple's computers themselves. Apple's machines are slower and more expensive than the clones, and they are more expensive than Intel-based computers.

The Mac OS's share of the overall PC market continues to decline, and the company may not be able to overcome that trend. Businesses are abandoning the platform. Apple's share of the corporate market has dropped in two years from more than 7 percent to just over 2 percent, and companies continue to replace aging Apples with Intel-based Windows computers from IBM, Compaq, and Dell.

Apple continues to do well in a few niche markets, but new customers are reluctant to make a major purchase such as a computer when the future of the company and the platform itself is at risk. The end of cloning means that the platform has no life independent of Apple and will rise or fall with the company. Apple is not in immediate jeopardy, but its future is clouded indeed.

What strategies would you recommend Apple pursue to save itself from extinction? Prepare a three-year strategic plan for the company.

America Online, Inc.—1998

David Stanton

www.aol.com
stock symbol AOL

There may be more than 100 sites on the World Wide Web devoted to everything that is wrong with America Online (703-448-8700), including sites such as "AOL Sucks," "Why and How to Leave AOL," "AOHELL," "Yeah, Yeah, Another AOL Sucks Page," and "America On Hold." Those who post to the sites generally complain about censorship, poor service, lack of security, and spam (unsolicited commercial e-mail).

So why do almost 10 million people subscribe to AOL? The many reasons include availability, simplicity, and content. AOL is available via a local telephone call to more people than any other provider. In many areas, it is the only service that has a local number, so for most AOL subscribers there are no long-distance fees.

Once you are on-line with AOL, there are many opportunities to join interest groups such as chat rooms and forums where you can discuss your interests with others. The exclusive AOL content areas, called channels, organize the vast stores of information on AOL into a digestible form. In addition to the proprietary content, AOL provides unlimited access to the Internet.

AOL is the world's most popular on-line service. The service provides subscribers with a variety of interactive features—electronic mail, Internet access, entertainment, reference, news, sports, weather, financial information and transactions, electronic shopping, and more.

AOL's primary market is the home computer user, and that market is growing. For the first time, households with children are more likely to have a PC than not. Fifty-two percent of U.S. households with children have PCs.

AOL has a commanding lead in the home market. According to a report from PCMeter, AOL is the number-one presence in cyberspace. More than 55 percent of all time spent on-line from home is spent on AOL. Of 25 top-rated sites or areas, 15 are on AOL's service. AOL leads with huge audiences for e-mail, chat, news, sports, personal finance, marketplace, and travel.

AOL's advertising revenue is growing faster than its subscriber revenue, and the company expects ad revenues to lead it into profitability. AOL's potential market for ad sales is large and growing as more people get on-line. According to the spring 1997 CommerceNet/Nielsen Internet Demographics Survey, of the 220 million people over age 16 in the United States and Canada, 23 percent, or 50.6 million people, are using the Internet in some way. Almost 75 percent of Web users search for information about products and services, and 5.6 million people have purchased on-line.

HISTORY

In 1985, Steve Case cofounded what has become America Online. Then called Quantum Computer Services, the company operated on-line services under several names before consolidating them under the America Online name and changing the name of the company to America Online, Inc., in 1991. The company went public in 1992 at $11.50 per share.

Case was the right person at the right time—the beginning of the Information Revolution. In December 1993, America Online surpassed 500,000 members. In less than 4 years, membership grew a stunning 1,800 percent to almost 10 million in fiscal 1997 (see Exhibit 1).

It happened because people discovered that computers could be used as a basic medium of communication. Before the advent of on-line services, most computers were isolated units, useful only for the work that could be done on one machine. Many were connected to local area networks (LANs) or even to larger networks, but the networks themselves were isolated from each other. However, everyone had a telephone. With a modem, a telephone line, and an on-line service such as AOL, individuals were able to form virtual communities based on mutual interests, correspond via electronic mail, and access information at remote locations via computer.

And people were willing to pay for it. At first, computer nerds and businesspeople joined AOL. As more people joined it and other services, AOL evolved into something more, with something for everybody. Anyone can find something on AOL that relates to his or her personal or business interests. At first, much of the fascination was with the medium and its novelty. Today, it's the content.

There are three major on-line services today: AOL, Netscape (formerly Prodigy and CompuServe), and the Microsoft Network. AOL, Prodigy, and CompuServe began before the Web was born and the Internet was opened to commercial use. The advent of the

EXHIBIT 1: AOL Worldwide Membership Climbs (in millions)

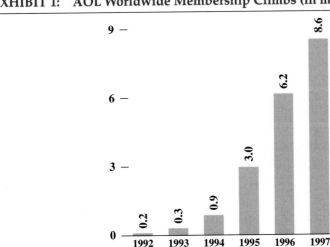

Source: America Online, Inc., *Annual Report* (1997): 9.

Internet is changing the definition of an on-line service, but in the past an on-line service was a place people visited to access the proprietary content located there, and people reached the service by dialing into the company's proprietary network. Once there, they could use and enjoy all the features of that service, but that was all.

The development of the Internet changed on-line services. The Internet became available to consumers in 1993, but its development began in the 1960s at the height of the Cold War. The Rand Corporation, a military think tank, was trying to find a way for U.S. authorities to communicate with one another after a nuclear attack. At the time, communication networks were linear, like a chain. If one link was destroyed, the whole network would be useless.

Paul Baran, one of the participants in the project, conceived the idea of a communications network that was set up more like a fishnet than a chain. This structure could allow information through the network even if a section had been destroyed.

In 1993, the first graphical software became available for navigating the new World Wide Web. Until the advent of the Web, AOL competed exclusively with other services much like itself—self-contained communities with centralized content and methods of communication. The rising popularity of the Web gave rise to a new kind of service—the Internet service provider, or ISP. ISPs provide the user with a mailbox and a way to the Internet, but do not provide the content or the software.

As the Internet grew, the quantity and diversity of the information available through it soon surpassed what the on-line services could offer, and providers soon found they had to offer Internet access if they were to compete with the ISPs. The on-line services already had dial-up networks in place, and were in many places the first to bring local-number Internet access to the consumer. Thus, the decision of the on-line services to offer Internet access contributed to its rapid growth.

The Internet has been a mixed blessing for AOL. It greatly increased the competition for market share because almost everything AOL has to offer can be found in some form on the Internet. Because of this, many AOL subscribers leave for an account with an ISP. At the same time, though, the Internet has been the main reason for the explosion in consumer interest in getting on-line, and AOL is the easiest and most popular way for novices to do that. It also is still the only way to connect in some areas without incurring expensive long-distance telephone charges.

INTERNAL OPERATIONS

Headquartered in Dulles, Virginia, AOL has operations in the United States, Canada, the United Kingdom, France, Japan, and Germany (see Exhibit 2).

AOL, Inc., is responsible for the core business functions of finance, human resources, legal affairs, corporate communications, development, and technology. AOL, Inc., also oversees the operations of the three divisions formed in 1996: AOL Networks, ANS Communications, and AOL Studios (see Exhibit 3).

AOL Networks

AOL Networks includes the flagship AOL service and AOL International Services. The division, which added more than 3 million members in 1997, is the jewel in the AOL crown.

EXHIBIT 2:   AOL International Markets, as Entered by Month, Year

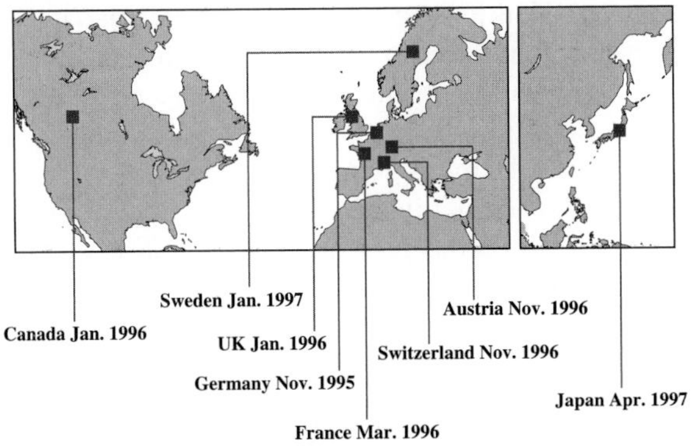

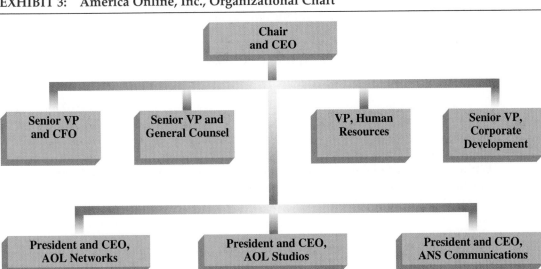

Canada Jan. 1996
Sweden Jan. 1997
UK Jan. 1996
Germany Nov. 1995
France Mar. 1996
Austria Nov. 1996
Switzerland Nov. 1996
Japan Apr. 1997

Source: Adapted from America Online, Inc., *Annual Report* (1997): 9.

EXHIBIT 3:   America Online, Inc., Organizational Chart

Chair and CEO

Senior VP and CFO

Senior VP and General Counsel

VP, Human Resources

Senior VP, Corporate Development

President and CEO, AOL Networks

President and CEO, AOL Studios

President and CEO, ANS Communications

Source: Adapted from America Online, Inc., *Annual Report* (1997).

The division is charged with creating the unique "AOL experience" through the establishment of technology and media partnerships, marketing, customer service, and product development. AOL Networks is responsible for extending the AOL brand into the mainstream market and developing new revenue streams via interactive marketing programs, advertising, and on-line transactions.

The AOL Networks division generates almost all the company's revenues. The largest source of revenues continues to be subscriber fees, which were nearly $1.5 billion in 1997. Advertising, merchandising, and transaction revenues accounted for $255 million.

ANS Communications

ANS Communications provides networking services to the world's largest dial-up network, AOL's AOLnet. AOL is its largest customer, but it also has outside corporate clients.

ANS offers services that fall into three areas: Enterprise Networking Services, Security Solutions, and Web Hosting and Applications. ANS designs, engineers, installs, manages, monitors, and maintains private corporate data networks over one of the fastest, largest TCP/IP networks in the world–ANSnet.

ANS has offices across the United States and in Europe. Through ANS Communications Europe, Ltd., and partnerships worldwide, ANS is expanding globally. ANS had non-AOL revenues of $31 million for 1997.

AOL Studios

AOL Studios is the content development business of AOL. As the Internet's leading online content programmer, it creates, markets, and distributes content on America Online and the World Wide Web. It accounts for only a small percentage of AOL's revenues, but is seen as critical to AOL's long-term success.

AOL Studios includes such AOL content ventures as investment hit Motley Fool and Digital Cities, localized content that could expand to 40 cities in 1997. The division is working on new content, which, for now, generates little revenue. The division currently is a money loser, but it is expected to generate profits from its advertising, merchandising, and transaction programs, and may get syndication fees from distributors that carry AOL Studios content. AOL Studios is expected to become a money maker by generating revenues of about $115 million in fiscal year 1998.

Marketing and Distribution

The goals of AOL's marketing programs are to attract and retain members, build brand recognition and member loyalty, and make it easy for people to try and subscribe to the AOL service. To encourage people to do so, AOL gives away an introductory package that includes the AOL software and a free 1-month trial membership.

There are many ways for people to get the introductory package. It is available at major software retailers and bookstores. It can be obtained by calling toll-free 800-4-ONLINE or by downloading it from www.aol.com. In addition, the software has been installed on most leading PCs, including those offered by IBM, Apple, Compaq, Dell, AST, Gateway 2000, HP, Packard Bell, Tandy, Toshiba, NEC, and Compudyne. It can be accessed through an icon on the Windows 95 and Apple Macintosh desktops and through Internet service providers such as the AT&T WorldNet service. It even has been distributed in boxes of Chex cereal, and it appears as a kind of bonus track on some music CDs. It is estimated that more than 100 million copies have been distributed by bulk mail.

AOL has been criticized for massive spending on some of these marketing methods, especially the "shotgun mailings" that are expensive and tend to yield higher percentages of short-term members who soon cancel their accounts. Its efforts to build its brand name include a broad array of programs and strategies, including broadcast advertising campaigns, direct mail, and magazine inserts. The company has begun to diversify its marketing methods into more targeted markets. It is also placing more emphasis on joint marketing, cross-promotion, and bundling agreements.

AOL has entered into joint marketing agreements with some media partners, affinity groups, and associations. Such agreements allow it to market directly to and cater to the needs of specific audiences. AOL has also pursued cross-promotional opportunities through existing and new partnerships. Examples include agreements with ABC Sports; CBS SportsLine; CUC International, Inc.; the Cartoon Network; Tel-Save Holdings, Inc.; and 1-800-Flowers. These agreements provide for AOL and its partners to jointly market, promote, and advertise their products and services. AOL's marketing strategy is expected to place a greater emphasis on these cost-effective agreements.

Actual distribution of the AOL service is primarily via AOLnet, which provides dial-up modem access to users through ANS and via leased third-party network access lines. Users with third-party Internet access can access the service through the Internet.

America Online offers "tiered" pricing in the United States. The flat, unlimited use rate is $19.95 per month. Those who pay in advance can opt for a 1-year unlimited usage membership for $17.95 per month. Consumers who already have Internet service through an ISP can get AOL content for $9.95 a month, and those who wish to use AOL as an Internet-only provider can do so for $10 a month. Consumers whose on-line usage is light may join AOL for $4.95 per month for 3 hours of service, with additional time costing $2.50 an hour.

Research and Development

Perhaps AOL's biggest competitive advantage has been the ease with which a novice can use its service to get on-line. As the Internet becomes more user-friendly, that competitive advantage is diminishing somewhat. In the future, AOL expects its content to be more of a selling point than its ease of use, and an important component of the company's business strategy is an increasing reliance on revenue generated by that content, including the sale of merchandise, advertising and related revenues, and transaction fees associated with electronic commerce. Because of this, the company is investing more in content development.

Greenhouse Networks is a business unit of AOL Studios. Long known as the development studio of AOL, Greenhouse Networks recently was refocused to build entertainment properties of "massive scope" not just for AOL, but for the Web, TV, print, and, it is hoped, film. Since 1994, Greenhouse has led the industry in developing more than 50 original on-line properties for America Online and the Internet.

Finance

AOL, by most measures, is a successful company. Revenues and subscriber numbers are high and rising rapidly. Its market is growing, and AOL is a household name. But the company has struggled over the years to make a profit.

In this it is hardly unusual among on-line services or Internet providers. Most companies in the business, including AOL, are sacrificing current profits for market share, hoping that the profits will come when the rapid growth in the industry levels off. Meanwhile, they are investing in marketing and increased capacity to handle the rising demand.

From 1992 to 1994, its first 3 years as a public company, AOL recorded profits ranging from $2.2 million to $6.2 million. The company lost more than $35 million in 1995, but managed to record a $29 million profit in 1996 (see Exhibit 4); however, AOL was criticized for its marketing expenses and for its financial reporting practices related to marketing. For 1997, AOL incurred a $499 million loss in net income.

EXHIBIT 4: America Online, Inc., Consolidated Statements of Operations

(amounts in thousands, except per share data)	Year ended June 30,		
	1997	1996	1995
Revenues:			
On-line service revenues	$1,429,445	$ 991,656	$344,309
Other revenues	255,783	102,198	49,981
Total revenues	1,685,228	1,093,854	394,290
Costs and expenses:			
Cost of revenues	1,040,762	638,025	232,318
Marketing			
Marketing	409,260	212,710	77,064
Write-off of deferred subscriber acquisition costs	385,221	0	0
Product development	58,208	43,164	11,669
General and administrative	193,537	110,653	42,700
Acquired research and development	0	16,981	50,335
Amortization of goodwill	6,549	7,078	1,653
Restructuring charge	48,627	0	0
Contract termination charge	24,506	0	0
Settlement charge	24,204	0	0
Total costs and expenses	2,190,874	1,028,611	415,739
Income (loss) from operations	(505,646)	65,243	(21,449)
Other income (expense), net	6,299	(2,056)	3,074
Merger expenses	0	(848)	(2,207)
Income (loss) before provision for income taxes	(499,347)	62,339	(20,582)
Provision for income taxes	0	(32,523)	(15,169)
Net income (loss)	(499,347)	29,816	(35,751)
Earnings (loss) per share:			
Net income (loss)	(5.22)	0.28	(0.51)
Weighted average shares outstanding	95,607	108,097	69,550

Source: www.freeedgar.com

AOL's reported marketing expenses grew from $5.6 million in 1992 to $212.7 million in 1996. However, controversial accounting methods masked the real cost of AOL's marketing efforts. The company had capitalized and amortized its marketing costs, normally an item that is reported as an expense. "The income statement in a company which capitalizes expenses to this extent . . . is basically meaningless," one analyst wrote.

The accounting masked the fact that AOL had actually spent $449.7 million on marketing in 1996, not the $212.7 million it reported. The company changed its reporting of marketing expenses in 1997 and took a $385 million charge to cover the change, which contributed to its 1997 loss of $499 million. The change wiped out most of AOL's net worth, plus all the profit it claimed to have made in its entire 11-year history. A member of a New York management firm commented, "When you cut through the noise, the facts are that this company has never made any money."

Management

Stephen M. Case is president, chair of the board of directors, and CEO of America Online, Inc., the largest and fastest-growing consumer on-line service in the world. In 1985, when Case cofounded the company later to become America Online, his goal was to create a mass market for on-line services by applying the classic consumer marketing experience he gained at PepsiCo and Procter & Gamble. Case oversees AOL Networks, ANS Communications, and AOL Studios.

Robert W. Pittman was appointed president and CEO of AOL Networks in November 1996. He was managing partner and CEO of Century 21 Real Estate Corp. from October 1995 to October 1996. Pittman had been president and CEO of Time Warner Enterprises and of MTV Networks, of which he was cofounder. Pittman has been a director of AOL since October 1995.

Bruce R. Bond was appointed president and CEO of ANS Communications in July 1996. He was managing director of British Telecom's National Business Communications from 1993 to May 1996. He joined British Telecom, one of the world's leading providers of integrated telecommunications services, in 1989 as director of corporate strategy after spending two years as corporate vice-president for strategic planning with U.S. West, Inc., a diversified telecommunications company. Bond also held posts in planning and marketing with AT&T Corp., a long-distance telephone carrier, and the Bell Operating Companies.

Theodore J. Leonsis was appointed president and CEO of AOL Studios in October 1996. Leonsis joined AOL in September 1994 as president of the America Online Services Company, an operating division of AOL. Leonsis previously was president of Redgate Communications Corporation, which was acquired by AOL in May 1994.

AOL: 1997

The year began with what was perhaps the most controversial episode in the short history of the company—the near-collapse of its systems under the demanding crush that flat rate pricing generated. From 1994 to 1997, the Internet grew quickly, with the numbers of sites, consumers, and providers more than doubling.

At the time, AOL and other on-line services were charging hourly rates. The ISP market, however, had established $19.95 or less as the price for a month of unlimited access to the Internet. Heavy AOL users could incur charges that were many times more than that, and AOL was losing customers to the ISPs almost as fast as it gained new ones. It finally decided to go to flat rate pricing, matching the ISP market price of $19.95 per month.

The problem was that AOL had the network capacity of an hourly service, and it failed to increase that capacity to handle the increased traffic generated by the flat rate. Usage soared under the new pricing plan but customers found it almost impossible to connect, with nearly every call resulting in a busy signal. When people did finally get through, they were reluctant to disconnect for fear they wouldn't be able to get back on, and that made the problem even worse. The increased load on AOL's system resulted in repeated blackouts and slowdowns in e-mail, Internet access, and the AOL content areas.

The problems generated enough complaints from users that attorneys general in many states threatened legal action against the company for failure to deliver the service it was selling. The company settled the dispute by offering users a free month of services, and began steadily adding capacity to its network.

After a barrage of negative publicity over busy signals, slow and unpredictable network performance, e-mail blackouts, and customer billing disputes, AOL's network overhaul is improving the situation. By July, a $350 million investment and 150,000 new modems had produced results. A study showed that AOL's first-attempt call failure rate for the evening hours was 34.7 percent—a major improvement over the situation in January, when 80 percent of users' log-on attempts in the evenings failed. AOL also was able to rent additional network capacity from third-party providers, including Sprint Communications Co.

AOL says it will continue adding 20,000 to 25,000 modems a month "for the foreseeable future." The overhaul also improved AOL's e-mail system, almost quadrupling its capacity from 4 million pieces of mail per day in the first quarter of fiscal 1997 to 15 million per day by the end of the fourth quarter (see Exhibit 5). Analysts have estimated that the final cost could exceed $500 million by the end of the company's fiscal year in June 1998.

On September 7, 1997, America Online, Inc., reached a deal to take over its biggest competitor, the faltering CompuServe, Inc., on-line service that has 2.6 million customers. Under terms of the deal, CompuServe still would exist as a separate service but would be fully operated by AOL. The deal gives AOL a combined customer base of more than 13.6 million subscribers.

The transaction, which is subject to regulatory approvals and approval by CompuServe shareholders, is expected to close on or before March 1, 1998. If approved, AOL's biggest competitor would be Microsoft Corp.'s Microsoft Network, with 2.3 million users.

EXHIBIT 5:   Fiscal 1997—Total Daily E-mail, by Quarter (in millions)

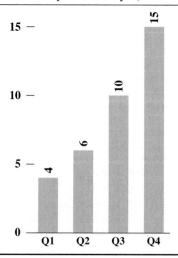

Source: America Online, Inc., *Annual Report* (1997): 9.

AOL will acquire CompuServe's Interactive Services Division under a complex deal involving telecommunications giant WorldCom, Inc. WorldCom agreed to buy CompuServe, Inc., from H&R Block, Inc., as part of a $1.2 billion stock swap. It then agreed to trade CompuServe's on-line service, including its content and subscribers, to AOL in exchange for AOL's ANS network service division.

WorldCom also agreed to give AOL $175 million in cash, which brings the total estimated value of the deal to around $425 million. The cash infusion may finally put AOL on the road to profitability.

Under the deal, WorldCom would keep CompuServe's global data network. That, combined with AOL's ANS network, would be a substantial addition to WorldCom's data networks. WorldCom also owns Fairfax-based UUNet Technologies, Inc., one of the largest Internet service providers. Under the deal, WorldCom would agree to provide network services to AOL for 5 years at discounted prices.

AOL Networks will continue to manage AOLnet, the world's largest dial-up network, through a portfolio strategy that now includes WorldCom's UUNet, in addition to GTE/BBN and Sprint. From this team of providers, AOL expects to have access to approximately 650,000 modems by the end of 1997—more than triple its modem capacity of January 1997.

The agreement should be especially useful to AOL in its efforts to expand abroad (see Exhibit 6). AOL began serious overseas marketing in 1995 in a 50-50 joint venture with Bertelsmann A.G., a German media company. Since then, the AOL Europe venture has attracted nearly 700,000 subscribers. Under the agreement, AOL Europe will gain CompuServe's 850,000 European users, making it the largest European online service.

Bertelsmann agreed to pay AOL $75 million to become an equal partner in the European CompuServe venture, and AOL and Bertelsmann each plan to spend $25 million to develop the European service. The merger would extend the AOL-Bertelsmann

EXHIBIT 6: AOL Builds International Membership (in thousands)

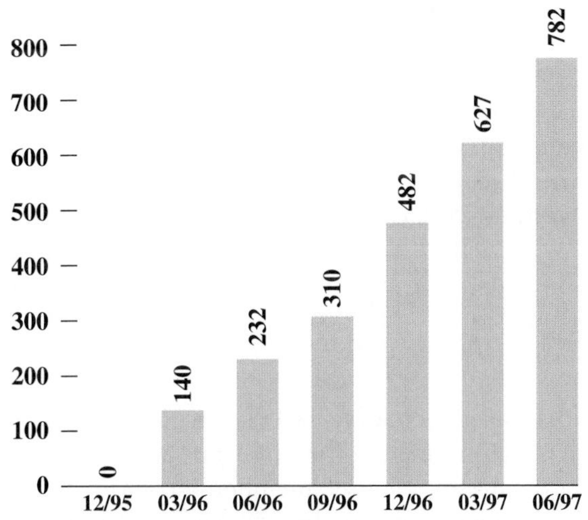

Source: America Online, Inc., *Annual Report* (1997): 9.

partnership's existing reach in Germany, the United Kingdom, France, Austria, Switzerland, and Sweden, and give the partnership access to a number of markets now served by CompuServe's Internet on-line services.

AOL would also gain more than 300,000 CompuServe members elsewhere around the world, including Japan, where AOL launched its own service in April, and Canada, where AOL has over 100,000 members. CompuServe's on-line division also has services in Asia, Latin America, and Australia.

The addition of the CompuServe subscribers will diversify AOL in important ways. The on-line business was pioneered by CompuServe in the 1980s, but by the 1990s, CompuServe was overtaken by AOL, which had more savvy marketing and a hipper image among young users. AOL is dominant in the home user market, but CompuServe has been able to carve out a niche for itself among businesses and professional users by focusing its content on business and technology. AOL has had difficulty attracting business users, but the addition of CompuServe should help AOL deliver the high-value business and professional audience to its commercial advertisers.

AOL lost $499 million in fiscal 1997. The company had revenues of nearly $1.7 billion, an increase of 54 percent over almost $1.1 billion in 1996. Expenses in 1997, however, were almost $2.2 billion, up almost 113 percent from over $1 billion in 1996.

The 1997 net loss includes charges totaling $482.5 million. The charges were $385.2 million for the write-off of deferred subscriber acquisition costs; $48.6 million for a restructuring charge; $24.2 million for legal settlements; and $24.5 million for contract termination charges.

AOL's operating margin declined in fiscal 1997, driven by the impact of the company's switch to flat rate pricing and the resulting increase in member usage. Average daily subscriber usage in the first quarter of fiscal 1997, the last quarter before the introduction of flat rate pricing, was approximately 14 minutes. In the fourth quarter of fiscal year 1997, average daily subscriber usage more than doubled to 37 minutes (see Exhibit 7). There also was a substantial decrease in the average revenue per member-hour. The company also experienced higher cost of revenues relative to total revenues.

For fiscal 1997, on-line service revenues increased from nearly $992 million to over $1.4 billion, or 44 percent over fiscal 1996 (see Exhibit 8). This increase primarily was attributable to a 53 percent increase in the quarterly average number of subscribers for fiscal 1997 compared to fiscal 1996, offset by a 6 percent decrease in the average monthly on-line service revenue per subscriber. The average monthly on-line service revenue per AOL North American subscriber decreased from $17.96 in fiscal 1996 to $16.87 in fiscal 1997.

Other revenues, consisting principally of electronic commerce and advertising revenues, as well as data network service revenues, increased by 150 percent, from $102 million in fiscal 1996 to almost $256 million in fiscal 1997. This increase primarily was attributable to an increase in electronic commerce and advertising revenues, driven by increases in the sale of merchandise and advertising on AOL's on-line service.

Merchandise sales increased by 152 percent from $43 million in fiscal 1996 to $109 million in fiscal 1997, reflecting the impact of an expanded number of products offered for sale to the company's larger membership base. Advertising and electronic commerce transaction fees increased by 558 percent, from $12 million in fiscal 1996 to $79

EXHIBIT 7: 1997—Average Member Daily Time On-line (in minutes)

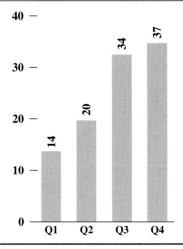

Source: America Online, Inc., *Annual Report* (1997): 9.

EXHIBIT 8: America Online, Inc., Fiscal Year 1997 Highlights

(in thousands of dollars for revenues)	Year ended June 30,		
	1997	1996	1995
Revenues			
On-line service revenues	$1,429,445	$ 991,656	$ 344,309
Other revenues	255,783	102,198	49,981
Total revenues	1,685,228	1,093,854	394,290
Operations			
Worldwide members	8,636,000	6,198,000	3,005,000
Employees	7,371	5,338	2,200
Average hours per member per month (Q4 average)	18.5	6.4	6.5
Modems in AOLnet (U.S.)	350,000	143,000	16,000
Maximum simultaneous users	384,000	120,000	59,000
Service revenue per member per month	$ 16.87	$ 17.96	$ 16.28
Electronic commerce revenue per member per month	$ 2.38	$ 0.99	$ 0.69

Source: America Online, Inc., *Annual Report* (1997): 8.

million in fiscal 1997. AOL's cobranded Visa credit card, first introduced during fiscal 1997, generated more than $18.9 million in revenues during the year.

In fiscal 1997, other revenues represented approximately 15 percent of total revenues, compared to approximately 10 percent in fiscal 1996. The company expects that the growth in other revenues, assuming such growth continues, will be the primary source of future profit growth.

COMPETITION

AOL competes in the businesses of on-line and Internet services, advertising, and electronic commerce. It competes with the traditional on-line services of the Microsoft Network and Netscape. It also competes with various national and local independent Internet service providers, such as NETCOM On-Line Communication Services. Long-distance and regional telephone and cable companies, such as AT&T, MCI, and various regional Bell operating companies also offer competing Internet service. The @Home Network and WebTV currently compete with AOL both for subscribers and for advertising and electronic commerce revenues. AOL also competes for advertising and electronic commerce revenues with major Web sites operated by search services and other companies such as Yahoo! Inc.; Netscape Communications Corporation; Infoseek Corporation; CNET, Inc.; Lycos, Inc.; and Excite, Inc., and with media companies such as The Walt Disney Company and Time Warner, Inc.

AOL's subscriber base still is growing rapidly, but more people are choosing ISPs over traditional on-line services. In 1996, more than two times as many Internet users accessed the Internet via an on-line service as went direct through an ISP. In 1997, more Internet users went through ISPs than through on-line services. The use of ISPs has grown dramatically—more than tripling to 17.6 million users.

At the same time, more Web sites are providing content similar to AOL. Yahoo! and CNET's Snap!Online sites have begun to develop the kind of destination content that distinguished AOL, and these new Web-based sites are free. If they are able to continue their content development and turn a profit from advertising and merchandising revenues, they may pose a threat in the future to the competitiveness of AOL's business model.

AOL also competes with more traditional media such as television. An America Online survey found that 37 percent of AOL subscribers watch less TV than they used to and that 22 percent view fewer videos, while only 7 percent watch more TV and only 6 percent view more videos. On a typical night, AOL has more users than CNN's Larry King has viewers.

CONCLUSION

AOL has overcome some of the problems it faced in fiscal 1996 and 1997. Access problems are now largely a thing of the past. The company announced record profits of $19.2 million, or 16 cents per share, for the first quarter of fiscal 1998, compared with a loss of $353.7 million, or $3.80 per share, in the same quarter the previous year. Revenues increased 49 percent to a record $521.6 million.

AOL also had strong subscriber growth even as it curbed its marketing expenses. In the quarter ending September 30, 1997, AOL spent $97.8 million, or 19 percent of revenues, to sign up an additional 821,000 subscribers. In the same quarter the year before, the company had spent $150.2 million, or 43 percent of revenues, to add about half as many, or 414,000. The AOL network reached a record of 520,000 simultaneous users, with peak usage tripling over the past year. The company also improved its cash and short-term investment position since the end of fiscal 1997 by $54.3 million to a total of $228.9 million.

AOL reached a milestone when it surpassed the 10 million subscriber mark. AOL's new numbers give it about 20 percent of the world's on-line population and half of the wired households in the United States, making AOL and the rest of the Internet a more viable medium for advertisers. "We've reached 10 million members, and we're gearing up to support millions more," CEO Steve Case said in a press release in late 1997.

Despite the turnaround, AOL faces a number of threats, including hackers who continue to deface its content areas, password thieves who roam chat rooms, and an ever-increasing amount of spam that annoys users and burdens AOL's e-mail system. The company has been unable to halt the illegal chat room trade in child pornography, and the news media continue to report tales of children victimized by sexual predators they met on AOL.

There are other difficulties as well. Internet access via AOL is slower than on most ISPs. AOL still suffers from e-mail outages. Its e-mail system is proprietary, so members must use AOL's software, which is much less versatile than even bare-bones commercial software or the e-mail included with Microsoft's Internet Explorer and Netscape Navigator. The same is true of AOL's USENET newsgroup software. AOL needs to improve its Internet access and allow the use of standard third-party software if it is to maintain its strong share of the growing on-line market.

This will be increasingly important as the Internet evolves. At the moment, the Internet is still in a primitive state. In the future, the amount of data transmitted will vastly increase to include high-quality video and audio transmission on a large scale. AOL is not in a position to make the kind of capital investments in equipment that the bandwidth explosion will demand. If it does not remain a profitable company, it will not be able to take advantage of the evolution of the Internet and may be left behind.

Medical Equipment—Industry Note

FROM LATEX GLOVES TO MRI IMAGERS, A COMPLEX AND DIVERSE INDUSTRY

The United States is the recognized global leader in the production of medical equipment and supplies, commanding about 42 percent of the $130 billion global market for medical devices in 1996, based on estimates from the Health Industry Manufacturers Association (HIMA). The rest of the market consisted of medical products produced in Europe (27 percent), Japan (15 percent), and other areas (16 percent).

Based on HIMA data, worldwide sales in 1996 were divided by product category as follows: surgical and medical instruments, 28 percent; hospital supplies and implantables, 26 percent; in vitro diagnostics, 18 percent; electromedical equipment, 12 percent; x-ray equipment, 10 percent; and dental equipment, 6 percent. Hospitals accounted for approximately two-fifths of worldwide industry sales, with the balance derived from physicians and dentists, nursing homes, clinics, home health care operators, and others.

Leading medical products manufacturers such as Baxter International, Johnson & Johnson, Abbott Laboratories, and Becton Dickinson offer comprehensive lines of both conventional hospital supply and high-tech products. The industry also includes a large number of small- and medium-sized companies whose economic viability often rests on the success of a relatively limited number of high-tech products. Among these firms are U.S. Surgical (which produces surgical staplers and laparoscopic instruments); St. Jude Medical (heart valves and pacemakers); Boston Scientific (minimally invasive surgical products); and Stryker Corp. (orthopedic devices).

INDUSTRY TRENDS

Demographics highly positive

The medical device industry isn't subject to the economic cycles that affect most other industries; demand for its products remains fairly constant from year to year. Nonetheless, a crop of aging baby boomers and longer average life expectancies bode well for device sales growth in the years ahead because these products are used by elderly persons in disproportionately large amounts.

Based on a new study published by the World Health Organization (WHO), the global population over age 65 is forecast to rise from 380 million in 1997 to over 690 million by the year 2025. According to projections made by the U.S. Census Bureau, the segment of the population over age 65 is expected to expand by about 16 percent from 1997 through 2010. The segment of Americans between 45 and 64 years of age is projected to increase by a whopping 48 percent over the same period.

Source: Adapted from *Industry Survey* by permission of Standard & Poor's, a division of the McGraw-Hill Companies. *Standard & Poor's,* "Healthcare: Products & Supplies," *Industry Survey* (March 19, 1998): 8–14.

Although more people than ever will be living longer, that does not mean they will be free from health problems. According to WHO, the incidence of cancer, heart disease, and other chronic diseases, which presently cause some 24 million deaths per year, is expected to increase in the years ahead. This is largely because many people have unhealthy life-styles, which include smoking, obesity, poor diet, and lack of exercise.

WHO projected a doubling in cancer cases in most countries over the next 25 years, along with a 33 percent increase in lung cancer in women and a 40 percent rise in prostate cancer in men in Europe by 2005.

The "graying of America" is especially bullish for cardiovascular products, such as pacemakers, defibrillators, and angioplasty catheters, which are used mostly on elderly patients. Orthopedic knee and hip implants and related products also are used primarily by the elderly, as are such diagnostic imaging products as magnetic resonance imaging and computed tomography machines.

Managed care continues to reshape the market

The medical device marketplace continues to evolve toward a managed care environment. In the past, nearly all device sales were generated by company salespeople who traveled the country to apprise hospitals and surgeons of their products' merits. But major purchasing decisions are now increasingly made by managers of health maintenance organizations, preferred provider organizations, large hospital consortiums, government agencies, and other large managed care buyers who wield substantial leverage in terms of product selection.

More than half of all medical device purchases in the United States now are made by managed care buyers; the proportion is expected to expand to over 75 percent within the next 5 years. Managed care providers use their collective purchasing clout to secure discounts on bulk purchases of pharmaceuticals and medical products, as well as on physician and hospital services.

Trade surplus in medical technology grows

Beefed-up foreign expansion programs by leading American medical equipment manufacturers, especially in rapidly developing Third World nations, are boosting the U.S. trade surplus in medical technology. Based on estimates made by the Commerce Department, the U.S. trade surplus in medical and dental instruments and supplies increased to $5.9 billion in 1997 from $5.2 billion in 1996. According to Commerce, exports rose 10.2 percent to $11.2 billion, while imports climbed 8.5 percent to $5.9 billion.

U.S. firms also are building manufacturing and marketing infrastructures abroad to serve local markets better and to improve manufacturing efficiency. Relocation of production and R&D facilities overseas offers many important advantages in terms of lowering production costs and being able to ship and deliver products on a more timely basis.

Easier product development is another important incentive spurring foreign expansion. New-product approval times in Europe are usually faster than in the United States, which is restrained by stringent FDA restrictions and backlogs (although this situation improved somewhat in 1997).

Although emerging markets accounted for only 15.6 percent of the $130 billion global medical technology market in 1996, they are expected to reach 17 percent of the total by 2000 and 25 percent by 2005, based on HIMA estimates. The U.S. medical technology market is expected to expand by about 7 percent a year over the 1997–1999

Worldwide Production of Medical Technology Products—1996 (in percent)

By Country, Total $129.5 billion	By Product Group

Australia 0.2   Other 8.3
Canada 1.2
Japan 14.6

Western Europe 28.4

United States 47.3

Dental equipment 6.0

X-ray equipment 10.0

Electromedical equipment 12.2

Surgical and medical instruments 28.1

In vitro diagnostics 17.5

Hospital supplies and implantables 26.2

Source: Health Industry Manufacturers Association.

period, comparable to the pace projected for the whole world. Meanwhile, the annual growth rate for 1997–1999 is expected to hit 19 percent and 12 percent in Asia and Latin America, respectively. Growth may slow to 5 percent in Europe, partially reflecting greater conservatism in government health care spending.

Notes on a specific market sector

Orthopedics

Strong demographic trends for an aging population and new products should let this market exhibit ongoing 6 percent to 7 percent compound annual growth in the years ahead. Based on estimates made by Stryker Corp., the worldwide orthopedic market totaled $9.7 billion in 1997. Shipments for 1997 by geographic markets were divided as follows: United States, 55 percent; Europe, 26 percent; Japan, 11 percent; Pacific region, 5 percent; and Latin America and Canada, 3 percent collectively.

The U.S. rehabilitation/orthopedic market was valued at $5.4 billion in 1997 by Stryker. Leading producers of conventional orthopedic equipment include the Zimmer division of Bristol-Myers Squibb; the Howmedica unit of Pfizer; DePuy (a unit of Boehringer-Mannheim); Biomet; Sulzer Bros.; Smith & Nephew; and Stryker.

Most hip and knee replacements result from osteoarthritis—a condition affecting the elderly in which joints become painful, impairing mobility—and rheumatoid arthritis, a disease that destroys cartilage at joint surfaces. Reconstructive devices such as hip and knee replacements dramatically can increase patients' quality of life by letting them regain mobility without experiencing excruciating pain. Orthopedic research in recent years led to the development of a widening array of prosthetic equipment and other related devices, including porous hips and knees that allow bone to grow directly into the metal implant.

Orthopedic Market in the United States—1997 (in percentages)

Total $5.4 billion

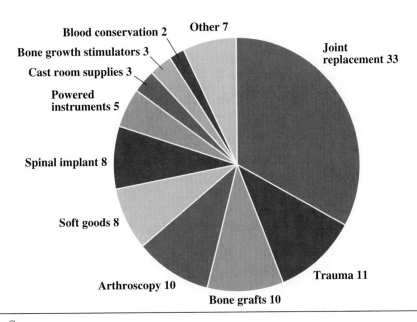

Blood conservation 2

Bone growth stimulators 3

Cast room supplies 3

Powered instruments 5

Spinal implant 8

Soft goods 8

Arthroscopy 10

Bone grafts 10

Other 7

Joint replacement 33

Trauma 11

Source: Stryker Corp.

Stryker Corporation—1998

Henry H. Beam

www.stryker.com
www.endostrykercorp.com
stock symbol SYK

Stryker Corporation (616-385-2600) is a maker of medical equipment based in Kalamazoo, Michigan. Although not yet a household name, Stryker is one of America's most consistently profitable growth companies. In 1997, Stryker posted record sales of $980 million and net earnings of $125 million. Stryker has achieved more than 20 percent annual net earnings growth every year since John Brown, its chair, president, and CEO, joined the firm in 1977. Stryker's consistent success has not gone unnoticed. On Wall Street, its stock increasingly is on the recommended list of leading brokerage firms. During a visit to Stryker's Kalamazoo facilities in 1992, President George Bush hailed the company's people as "leaders in an innovative industry that makes our country proud."

All this growth comes from making products that people hope they never have to use, but are glad to have available when they need them. Stryker develops, manufactures, and markets a wide variety of surgical products and specialty hospital beds that are sold primarily to physicians and hospitals throughout the world. Stryker is a leading producer of orthopedic implants, powered surgical implements, surgical visualization products, arthroscopic surgery systems, and specialty hospital beds. Stryker also provides outpatient physical therapy services in the United States.

In the 1950s and 1960s, Stryker's reputation was enhanced by good publicity about some of its unique products. Roy Campanella, the Brooklyn Dodgers baseball star who had been paralyzed from injuries sustained in an automobile accident in 1958, was cared for on Stryker equipment. *Life* magazine did a story about the Tennessee American Legion buying a Circ-O-Lectric Hospital Bed for Sergeant Alvin York, the World War I Medal of Honor winner who was an invalid by the early 1960s. When Senator Edward Kennedy suffered a back injury in a plane crash in 1964, he was cared for on a Stryker turning frame and later moved to a Circ-O-Lectric Hospital Bed, both of which were pictured in national magazines during his recovery. Such favorable publicity enhanced the company's image.

HISTORY

The Stryker Company takes it name from its founder, Dr. Homer Stryker, a remarkable man in many respects. After serving briefly in World War I, Dr. Stryker earned his medical degree from the University of Michigan in 1925. He chose orthopedics as his

---

This case was prepared by Professor Henry H. Beam of Western Michigan University as a basis for class discussion. It is not intended to illustrate either effective or ineffective handling of an administrative situation. Copyright © 1999 by Prentice Hall, Inc. ISBN 0-13-011180-5.

specialty and located his medical practice in Kalamazoo. Throughout his life he liked to fiddle with gadgets. During the early years of his medical practice, Dr. Stryker invented a mobile hospital bed and a cast-cutting saw. The mobile bed had a frame that pivoted from side to side so physicians could position injured patients for treatment while keeping them immobile. He won a contract to supply the Army with his beds during World War II, and soon was running a small business as well as a medical practice. The contract was terminated when the war ended in 1945, but the business continued.

Dr. Stryker wrote of his invention of the cast-cutting saw:

> In 1943, the removal of a large cast was a tedious process for me and an unpleasant one at best for the patient. In search of a better way, I observed that if a small circular blade with sharp teeth was pressed firmly against the skin, or the soft cast padding used to protect the skin, and then moved back and forth, no more than an eighth of an inch of skin would move with the saw teeth and neither the skin nor the padding would be cut.
>
> However, if I took the same blade and pressed against a plaster cast and moved it back and forth with the same stroke and pressure, it would cut the plaster. I took a 1/20th horsepower electric grinder, replaced the grinding stone with a 2-inch diameter saw blade, and designed and attached a mechanism which would convert the rotation of the saw to oscillation, with the teeth oscillating about an eighth of an inch at about 18,000 oscillations per minute. When completed, the instrument was tested by removing a cast at the hospital. I was able to remove the cast without disturbing the patient, in about one-fourth the time previously required.

This is typical of how Dr. Stryker used his creativity to improve the products that physicians used to treat their patients, which is still primarily what the company does today. The rapid acceptance of the cast cutter by physicians and of the hospital bed by the Army convinced Dr. Stryker that he had more than a part-time business on his hands. In 1946, the Orthopedic Frame Company was incorporated with Dr. Stryker as its sole shareholder. Dr. Stryker continued with his medical practice, in which he continued to develop pioneering surgical techniques. His business grew rapidly. His son, Lee, joined him in the business in 1955 after earning a bachelor's degree in business administration from Syracuse University. Lee's business sense balanced his father's desire to use the company as an outlet for his inventive talents. Both Dr. Stryker and Lee were very active in community activities.

In 1964, the company changed its name to the Stryker Corporation. New products came regularly and sales reached $4.7 million in 1966. Although Dr. Stryker's medical equipment manufacturing business would make him wealthy, he gave away hundreds of ideas and techniques free of charge to other physicians, who passed them on to their patients. Dr. Stryker retired from his company in 1969. The company continued to grow under the guidance of Lee Stryker until Lee's death in an airplane crash in July 1976. In the next year, John Brown became president of Stryker.

Brown graduated from Auburn University in 1957 with a bachelor of science degree in chemical engineering and held management positions with Ormet Corporation, Thiokol, and Bristol-Myers Squibb, where he was president of a subsidiary. At Stryker, Brown took charge of a firm with sales of $23 million and net income of $1.5 million. He swiftly took steps to decentralize the company into the autonomous divisional structure it has today. When he realized that salespeople were quitting because the compensation system had been changed from commissions to salaries and bonuses only, he restored commissions as the dominant form of compensation for salespeople. He also established goals of 20 percent growth in sales and earnings per share a year, every year. At the time, nearly 70 percent of Stryker's sales were of hospital beds. Building on the strength of the Stryker name with hospitals, Brown added hip implants and video cameras and strengthened the line of powered surgical tools. Now Stryker Surgical, which sells these products, makes up about three-fourths of the company's sales.

Stryker made its first public stock offering in 1977, when about 40 percent of the company's stock was sold to the public. Officers, directors, and members of the founding Stryker family presently own about a third of the shares. In July 1977, Stryker's stock moved from the NASDAQ Stock Market to the New York Stock Exchange.

In 1993, Stryker paid $33 million to acquire 20 percent of the outstanding shares of Matsumoto Medical Instruments of Japan. In 1994, Stryker paid $60.7 million to purchase an additional 31 percent, and in 1997, purchased another 17 percent, bringing its ownership to 68 percent. Matsumoto is the premier distributor of medical devices in Japan and the exclusive distributor of Stryker products there. Matsumoto helped Stryker achieve market leadership in hip implants, powered instruments, and endoscopic video systems in one of the world's largest and most sophisticated medical markets.

In 1996, Stryker purchased Osteo Holdings AG for $45.5 million. Osteo, which is based in Switzerland, produces a broad variety of high-quality trauma products and had 1995 sales of $23.7 million. Stryker saw the acquisition of Osteo as a way to enter the $1 billion global trauma market.

At the end of 1996, Stryker incurred a one-time $61 million net gain from the settlement of patent litigation relating to infringement by a competitor on a patented Osteonics hip implant. Stryker management also recorded $42 million in one-time charges involving the conversion of several distributors to direct sales and the write-down of assets.

As of December 31, 1997, Stryker had 5,274 employees worldwide. No employees are covered by collective bargaining agreements. The company's principal owned domestic facilities and its administrative offices are located in the adjacent southwest Michigan cities of Kalamazoo and Portage. A 190,000-square-foot facility in Portage, completed in 1992, houses manufacturing, warehousing, and distribution for surgical instrument production. Stryker also leases facilities in Allendale, New Jersey (orthopedic implant business); Santa Clara, California (endoscopic systems business); St. Louis, Missouri (medical service business); and Arroyo, Puerto Rico (assembly of disposable tubing sets and other manufacturing). Stryker's financial statements are shown in Exhibits 1 (see page 455), 2 (see page 455), and 3 (see page 457). The members of the board of directors and the top corporate officers are shown in Exhibit 4 (see page 458).

THE U.S. HEALTH CARE INDUSTRY

The U.S. health care system is highly diverse. Health care providers deliver many different kinds of services in a wide variety of settings: acute care inpatient general hospitals, specialty hospitals, free-standing ambulatory clinics and surgical centers, nursing homes, and patients' homes (via home health care services). Despite a growing proportion of elderly people in the U.S. population, hospital admission rates declined for the past decade and are expected to continue to decline in the future.

EXHIBIT 1: Stryker Corporation, Consolidated Statements of Earning

	Year ended December 31		
(in thousands, except per share amounts)	1997	1996	1995
Net sales	$980,135	$910,060	$871,952
Cost of sales	397,766	392,358	369,444
Gross profit	582,369	517,702	502,508
Operating expenses:			
Research, development, and engineering	56,895	56,870	43,771
Selling, general, and administrative	341,500	326,641	301,426
Special charges	0	41,778	0
Gain on patent judgment	0	(61,094)	0
	398,395	364,195	345,197
Operating income	183,974	153,507	157,311
Other income	10,476	6,939	5,782
Earnings before income taxes and minority interest	194,450	160,446	163,093
Income taxes	70,000	61,650	66,900
Earnings before minority interest	124,450	98,796	96,193
Minority interest	870	5,664	(9,183)
Net earnings	125,320	104,460	87,010
Net earnings per share of common stock:			
Basic	1.30	1.08	.90
Diluted	1.28	1.06	.88

Source: www.freeedgar.com

EXHIBIT 2: Stryker Corporation, Consolidated Balance Sheet

	Year ended December 31		
(in thousands, except per share amounts)	1997	1996	1995
Assets			
Cash and cash equivalents	$154,027	$175,673	$69,049
Marketable debt securities	197,041	191,900	195,599
Accounts receivable, less allowance of			
$11,700 ($9,500 in 1996 and $7,800 in 1995)	176,214	166,052	163,593
Inventories	136,246	127,387	133,619
Deferred income taxes	78,896	78,034	47,058
Prepaid expenses and other current assets	14,184	14,491	14,335
Total current assets	756,608	753,537	623,253
Property, plant, and equipment			
Land, buildings, and improvements	116,830	130,240	138,324
Machinery and equipment	183,619	159,945	147,177
	300,449	290,185	285,501
Less allowance for depreciation	136,582	117,882	102,909
	163,867	172,303	182,592
Intangibles, less accumulated amortization of			
$23,400 ($17,510 in 1996 and $11,344 in			
1995)	46,110	45,375	18,193

continued

EXHIBIT 2: *continued*

	Year ended December 31		
	1997	*1996*	*1995*
Other	18,490	22,291	30,853
	64,600	67,666	49,046
	985,075	993,506	854,891
Liabilities and Stockholders' Equity			
Current liabilities			
Accounts payable	55,034	62,433	49,029
Accrued compensation	43,927	37,693	32,447
Income taxes	36,971	56,723	25,633
Accrued expenses and other liabilities	93,452	90,489	64,277
Current maturities of long-term debt	73,627	4,403	3,052
Total current liabilities	303,011	251,741	174,438
Long-term debt, excluding current maturities	4,449	89,502	96,967
Other liabilities	29,168	36,034	24,214
Minority interest	35,672	85,868	104,993
Stockholders' equity			
Common stock, $.10 par value:			
Authorized—150,000 shares			
Outstanding—96,059 shares (96,787 in 1996 and 97,108 in 1995)	9,606	9,679	9,711
Additional paid-in capital	18	5,922	14,736
Retained earnings	612,939	514,318	419,537
Unrealized (losses) gains on securities	(376)	1,196	2,314
Foreign translation adjustments	(9,412)	(754)	7,981
Total stockholders' equity	612,775	530,361	454,279
	985,075	993,506	854,891

Source: www.freeedgar.com

In contrast, outpatient volume has increased in recent years. This is due to restricted reimbursement for inpatient care and the development of diagnostic and therapeutic procedures that do not require inpatient settings. According to the American Hospital Association, the number of outpatient surgical procedures performed at community hospitals more than tripled from 1982 through 1992, while inpatient surgeries declined by one-third over the same period.

Business conditions throughout the hospital industry are becoming tougher under the expanding influence of managed care plans such as health maintenance organizations and constrained reimbursement from both the federal government and insurance companies. The number of hospitals in the United States has been declining for nearly two decades. With about a third of all hospital beds in the United States considered to be excess capacity, the fast pace of hospital mergers is likely to continue. As purchasing decisions in the 1980s and 1990s shifted away from physicians to hospitals and managed care facilities, producers of medical equipment were forced to demonstrate the cost-effectiveness of their products. Growth was spurred by new devices that could reduce hospital stays and increase labor productivity.

EXHIBIT 3: Stryker Corporation, Sales Percentage, 1995–1997

	Percentage of Net Sales			Percentage Change	
	1997	1996	1995	1997/96	1996/95
Net sales	100.0%	100.0%	100.0%	8%	4%
Cost of sales	40.6	43.1	42.4	1	6
Gross profit	59.4	56.9	57.6	13	3
Research, development, and engineering expense	5.8	6.2	5.0	0	30
Selling, general, and administrative expense	34.8	35.9	34.6	5	8
Special charges	0	4.6	0	0	0
Gain on patent judgment	0	(6.7)	0	0	0
Operating income	18.8	16.9	18.0	20	(2)
Other income	1.0	0.7	0.7	51	20
Earnings before income taxes and minority interest	19.8	17.6	18.7	21	(2)
Income taxes	7.1	6.7	7.7	14	(8)
Earnings before minority interest	12.7	10.9	11.0	26	3
Minority interest	0.1	0.6	(1.0)	(85)	0
Net earnings	12.8	11.5	10.0	20	20

The table below sets forth domestic/international and product line sales information:

	Net Sales (in thousands)			Percentage Change	
	1997	1996	1995	1997/96	1996/95
Domestic/international sales					
Domestic	$633,252	$564,534	$477,207	12%	18%
International	346,883	345,526	394,745	0	(12)
Total net sales	980,135	910,060	871,952	8	4
Product line sales					
Stryker Surgical	740,369	669,898	608,646	11	10
Stryker Medical	207,481	196,083	158,516	6	24
Matsumoto Distributed Products	32,285	44,079	104,790	(27)	(58)
Total net sales	980,135	910,060	871,952	8	4

Source: www.freeedgar.com

The medical products and services segment of the health care industry encompasses more than 125,000 different items, ranging from gauze pads to sophisticated diagnostic machines. Stryker participates primarily in two segments of the health care industry: surgical and medical instruments, and surgical appliances and supplies.

The United States is the acknowledged global leader in the production of medical equipment and supplies, and it commands about half of the $85 billion worldwide medical goods market. Export growth in recent years benefitted from the demand for sophisticated diagnostic equipment and a growing emphasis on the provision of quality health care services worldwide.

In the United States, the Federal Drug Administration (FDA) is responsible for ensuring that all products sold comply with applicable federal safety standards. The FDA possesses the authority to recall products, temporarily suspend devices it considers high-risk, and impose penalties for violations. The FDA reviews medical devices

EXHIBIT 4: Stryker Corporation's Organizational Chart—Divisional Design

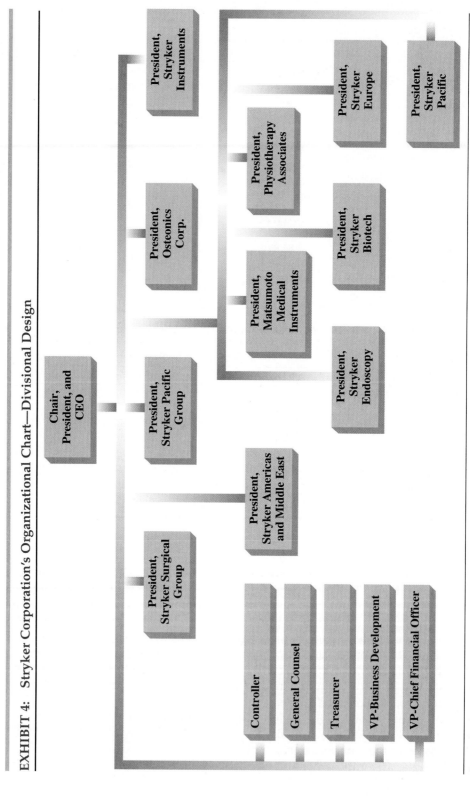

Source: Stryker Corporation; *www.freeedgar.com.*

under one of two procedures. A firm introducing a completely new device must submit a Product Marketing Application (PMA). The PMA must demonstrate the device's safety as well as its benefits. New devices that resemble products already on the market are reviewed under a less stringent procedure called "501(k) pre-market notification." In 1992, only 12 PMAs were approved, and about 2,500 new products were approved under the 501(k) procedure.

STRYKER'S ORGANIZATION

Since 1981, Stryker has been organized into three major product lines: Stryker Surgical, Stryker Medical, and Matsumoto Distributed Products.

Stryker Surgical

Stryker Surgical had sales of $740 million in 1997, which represented almost 76 percent of the company's total sales.

Endoscopy division

This division makes a broad range of medical video imaging equipment and instruments for arthroscopy and general surgery. In an endoscopic (less invasive) surgical procedure, the surgeon removes or repairs damaged tissue through several small punctures rather than an open incision. Patients experience reduced trauma and pain, less time in the hospital, and a quicker return to work. Medical costs also are less. For example, less-invasive removal of the gallbladder requires a single day in the hospital followed by a week of convalescence. Traditional gallbladder surgery, by contrast, means four to eight days in the hospital and a month's convalescence.

Imaging technology plays a crucial role in endoscopic procedures. Stryker is a leader in medical video imaging systems. Through pioneering engineering work, Stryker miniaturized a three-chip video camera (with a separate computer chip for each primary color) and was the first company to offer the surgeon a broadcast-quality image. This division had sales of $145 million in 1996.

Instruments division

This division produces a wide range of operating room equipment that is utilized primarily in orthopedic procedures, such as bone saws and drills. It is a market leader for battery-powered heavy-duty surgical instruments. Its Stryker 940 cast removal system is the newest version of Dr. Stryker's original cast cutter. To keep pace with its growing sales volume, the Instruments division expanded its manufacturing capabilities in 1994, doubling the clean room space at its Kalamazoo facility and enlarging its facilities in Arroyo, Puerto Rico, by 50 percent. This division had sales of $200 million in 1996.

Osteonics division

Osteonics produces both total and partial hip and knee implants. Every year, about 500,000 people in the United States and a comparable number abroad undergo joint replacement surgery to regain some of their previous mobility. According to Standard & Poor's, most hip and knee replacements result from osteoarthritis—a condition affecting the aged in which joints become painful and mobility is impaired—and rheumatoid arthritis, a disease that destroys cartilage at the joint's surface. In its March 19, 1998, edition of *Industry Survey,* Standard & Poor's also noted that orthopedic research in recent years led to the development of a broad array of prosthetic equipment and related devices, and that recent innovations include porous hips and knees, which allow bone to grow directly into the metal implant.

Cost considerations are an increasingly important factor in countries in which joint replacement surgery is practiced. The Osteonics division was reorganized into vertically integrated work cells with a significant gain in efficiency. The new organization helped Osteonics to increase teamwork, cut lead time, reduce inventory requirements, boost quality, and control costs. The cells also enabled Osteonics to meet its customers' needs for a rapid response in orders. This division had sales of $325 million in 1996.

Stryker Medical

Stryker Medical had sales of $207 million in 1997, which represented 21 percent of the company's total sales.

Medical division

This division produces specialty stretchers and beds, which facilitate the transportation, transfer, and treatment of patients within the hospital. Over the past seven years, this division designed a line of innovative stretchers as a result of a close analysis of hospital needs. It focused on reducing the number of patient transfers (from bed to stretcher to operating table and back again) performed in a hospital. It also produces accessories such as bedside stands and overbed tables. This division had sales of $120 million in 1996.

Physiotherapy Associates division

At the end of 1996, the Physiotherapy Associates division operated 185 outpatient rehabilitation centers in 20 states and the District of Columbia. The centers provide physical, occupational, and speech therapy to help speed a patient's return to work or full activity following orthopedic or neurological injury.

Physiotherapy Associates generally operate multiple facilities within a single area, offering patients the convenience of a choice of locations. By organizing a number of practices into a group that shares certain functions, Physiotherapy Associates is able to achieve substantial operating efficiencies. All of its facilities are leased. This division had sales of $75 million in 1996.

Matsumoto Distributed Products

Stryker sought to improve distribution of its products internationally with its investment in Matsumoto, a Japanese distributor of medical technology founded in 1913. Matsumoto's current focus is on orthopedics, ophthalmology, general surgery, and emergency care. In addition to Stryker products, Matsumoto also distributes devices from other leading American and European medical devices makers. Matsumoto's $32 million in sales represents 3 percent of Stryker's 1997 sales and almost a 37 percent decrease from Matsumoto's 1996 sales.

Shortly after Stryker took a majority ownership position in Matsumoto, several medical instrument companies stopped distributing through Matsumoto because they felt uncomfortable with Stryker's majority influence. As a result, Matsumoto saw sales of non-Stryker products fall by more than half from 1995 to 1996.

Geographic data on Stryker's sales is given in Exhibit 5. Stryker's sales and operating income by product line are shown in Exhibit 6.

COMPETITIVE POSITION

Each of Stryker's divisions competes with specialty firms and with a subsidiary of one or more large corporations. In the $400 million arthroscopy market, Stryker is one of the four leaders. Its principal competitors are Dyonics/Acufex (a subsidiary of Smith & Nephew), Wisap, Xomed, and Zimmer. Zimmer is a subsidiary of Bristol-Myers Squibb and had 1996 sales of $1.2 billion. In the $600 million laparoscopic imaging products market, Stryker is one of four market leaders. Its principal competitors are Karl Storz (a German Company), Richard Wolf, Olympus Optical (a Japanese company), and Circon.

EXHIBIT 5: Stryker Corporation, 1995–1997 Sales by Geographic Location

(in thousands of dollars)	1997	1996	1995
Net sales			
United States operations:			
Domestic	$633,252	$564,534	$477,207
Export	179,008	156,242	137,355
Foreign operations:			
Pacific	188,270	193,723	272,362
Europe	122,672	102,859	83,674
Other	16,988	15,764	13,521
Eliminations	(160,055)	(123,062)	(112,167)
Total net sales	980,135	910,060	871,952
Operating income			
United States operations	189,713	176,370	121,411
Foreign operations:			
Pacific	(6,344)	(19,824)	35,060
Europe	11,567	8,396	9,491
Other	2,510	2,561	1,954
Total foreign operations	7,733	(8,867)	46,505
Corporate expenses	(13,472)	(13,996)	(10,605)
Total operating income	183,974	153,507	157,311
Assets			
United States operations	302,855	319,481	283,471
Foreign operations:			
Pacific	188,478	228,315	273,686
Europe	131,971	118,292	65,406
Other	15,788	12,500	9,304
Corporate	345,983	314,918	223,024
Total assets	985,075	993,506	854,891

Source: www.freeedgar.com

EXHIBIT 6: Stryker Corporation, 1995–1997 Sales by Product Line

(in thousands of dollars, except per share data)

Product Line Sales (unaudited)	1997		1996		1995	
Stryker Surgical Orthopedic implants, endoscopic systems, powered surgical instruments and other operating room devices	$740,369	76%	$669,898	74%	$608,646	70%
Stryker Medical Hospital beds and stretchers and physical therapy services	207,481	21	196,083	21	158,516	18
Matsumoto Distributed Products Orthopedic, ophthalmic, and general surgery products sourced from other companies for sale in Japan	32,285	3	44,079	5	104,790	12
	980,135	100	910,060	100	871,952	100

Domestic/International Sales (unaudited)	1997		1996		1995	
Domestic	633,252	65	564,534	62	477,207	55
International	346,883	35	345,526	38	394,745	45
	980,135	100	910,060	100	871,952	100

Source: www.freeedgar.com

In the $600 million powered surgical instruments and accessories market, Stryker and Zimmer each have about 33 percent of the market, followed by Midas-Rex with 17 percent. These firms are also competitors in international markets.

Stryker is the fifth-place company in the $2 billion U.S. market for orthopedic reconstructive products, primarily hips and knees, with about 8 percent of the market. The four firms with higher market share are Zimmer; Howmedica (a subsidiary of Pfizer); DePuy (a subsidiary of Boehringer-Mannheim, a German company); and Biomet. These firms are also Stryker's principal competitors overseas.

Stryker's primary competitor in the $400 million hospital bed market is Hill-Rom, a division of Hillenbrand Industries. Its primary competitors in the specialty stretcher market are Ferno Washington, Hausted, Hill-Rom, and Midmark Corporation. In the outpatient physical therapy market, Stryker's principal competitors are independent practices and hospital-based services. HealthSouth, NovaCare/RCI, and Rehability also are competitors.

MANUFACTURING AND RESEARCH & DEVELOPMENT

Stryker's manufacturing processes consist primarily of precision machining, metal fabrication, assembly operations, and the investment (precision) casting of cobalt chrome and finishing of cobalt chrome and titanium. The principal raw materials used by the company are stainless steel, aluminum, cobalt chrome, and titanium alloys. In all, purchases from outside sources were approximately half of the company's total cost of sales in 1996.

Most of the company's products and product improvements were developed internally. The company maintains close working relationships with physicians and medical personnel in hospitals and universities who assist in product research and development. Expenditures for product research, development, and engineering were $43.8 million in 1995, and $56.9 million in both 1996 and 1997. Most of this spending was under the direct control of the operating divisions, where research and development can be highly focused on the markets Stryker serves. Stryker seeks to obtain patent protection whenever possible on its products. It currently holds over 200 patents on products it developed.

THE SALES FORCE AND 20 PERCENT GROWTH

Most of the company's products are marketed in the United States directly to more than 7,500 hospitals; to doctors; and to nonhospital health care facilities. The company maintains separate and dedicated sales forces for each of its principal product lines to provide focus and a high level of expertise to each medical specialty served. The 340-member domestic sales force is compensated in large part by commissions, which is the way CEO Brown likes it. "The beauty of commissions is there's no cap," he said. "The more the individual sells, the more he or she makes. The most ambitious and driven salespeople thrive in a commission environment." Two divisions—instruments and endoscopy—have taken a radical approach and pay their sales representatives solely on commissions and bonuses. These divisions are among the most successful. According to Ron Elenbaas, the surgical group's president, "We are trying to create a salesperson's paradise, an organization where they are respected and rewarded." In 1994, Stryker formed a new sales team to address the needs of large, national accounts. This team sells the full range of Stryker products across divisional lines.

Salespeople are made aware of how they rank among all Stryker salespeople. For example, at Stryker Surgical's national sales meetings, which usually are held at resorts, tables at the awards banquets are arranged in order of performance: the top-selling region sits nearest the stage, the worst-selling region sits farthest away. Brown likes to fuel the competitive fire in his salespeople. He sends out a monthly newsletter to top managers that ranks each division by growth and includes comments on performance, good and bad. Brown was honored as one of America's best CEOs in the September 1977 issue of *Worth*, in which he was quoted as saying, "I try to set expectations. I think I've persuaded our employees that it's a worthwhile goal. Ask any of our employees either here in Michigan or from Berlin to Osaka, and they'll tell you that what they have to do is increase sales 20 percent every year."

The company treats very well those who perform very well. Top salespeople can make as much as $200,000 a year. However, representatives who only turn in average sales don't get any praise. According to Elenbaas, "Reps may hunger for praise, but we don't praise a mediocre performance. We ignore it. Our philosophy is, it's much better to support your stars than to waste your time on people who aren't going to make it." See Exhibit 7 for the reasons given by the surgical group for its success in sales.

THE FUTURE

Stryker has prospered for 20 years under Brown's direction and the company's sales soon will exceed $1 billion per year. Despite such success, Stryker may be in danger of failing to make its target of 20 percent earnings growth every year. First, Matsumoto's

---

EXHIBIT 7:   Stryker Surgical's Five Ways to Grow 20 Percent Every Year

Stryker has delivered 20 percent revenue and earnings growth for 17 years. Among the company's most successful and entrepreneurial divisions are instruments and endoscopy, also known as the Surgical group. Here are the five keys to that group's success:

1. **Competitive compensation:** With a commissions-only pay structure, there is no ceiling on what salespeople can make. This attracts highly competitive, ambitious, and confident reps.

2. **Freedom:** There are no call reports or time-consuming paperwork. Salespeople are encouraged to do what they do best: sell. Their numbers are their call reports.

3. **Accountability:** With freedom comes responsibility. Salespeople must deliver at least 20 percent growth each year . . . or else.

4. **Celebration:** Management continually celebrates, recognizes, and rewards excellence. Top reps get weekly handwritten notes of praise; are offered seats on the group's president's council, where they can speak their minds to management about the company's strengths and weaknesses; and receive bonus checks directly from Chairman John Brown at an annual breakfast.

5. **Support:** The sales force comes first at Stryker. Marketing, sales support, and R&D will do whatever it takes to help reps make the sale and keep the customer.

Source: Stryker Corporation, *Sales and Marketing Management* (November 1994): 71.

sales in Japan don't seem likely to regain their 1995 levels for several years because other makers of medical instruments are reluctant to have their products distributed by a firm in which Stryker has majority ownership. Second, most of Stryker's major markets have shown annual growth rates of 5 percent or less over the last few years. This means Stryker's divisions need to grow more rapidly than the market segments in which they compete in order to meet the 20 percent per year growth goal. Third, mergers and acquisitions within the health care sector probably will continue at a rapid pace. This could lead to the emergence of larger and more powerful buying groups that could put increased pressure on the suppliers of medical equipment, such as Stryker, to reduce the cost of their products. Fourth, some members of the sales force may tire of the continued pressure to increase their sales 20 percent per year and look for jobs with other companies.

Stryker does have some opportunities available to help make its sales goals. One method is using its strong financial position to make selected acquisitions. Stryker entered the trauma business in 1996 with its acquisition of Osteo Holdings. The trauma market consists of products such as nails, screws, and plates designed to help physicians in stabilizing fractures, either externally or internally. The trauma market is estimated to be about $600 million in the United States and $1 billion worldwide. A second opportunity is new niche markets for Stryker Endoscopy outside arthroscopy, such as in powered instruments to ear, nose, and throat (ENT) surgeons. Few existing power tools cater to the specific demands of ENT surgeons for the approximately 500,000 procedures they perform each year. A third opportunity for growth is in adding centers to its Physiotherapy Associates division. Each center averages $400,000 in revenue per year. It is important for Stryker to take advantage of these and other opportunities available to it. As long as Brown is the CEO, everyone at Stryker will be expected to help sales and earnings increase 20 percent a year, every year.

If Stryker should become a $1 billion company, will it be realistic for Brown to expect sales and earnings per share to continue to grow at 20 percent every year? How can Stryker maintain the patient-oriented values of Dr. Homer Stryker while pursuing growth of 20 percent per year? Should salary be a component of the compensation system in all divisions? Most of Stryker's sales force primarily is trained to sell the products made by its divisions—should Stryker consider reorganizing its sales force so all its members can sell the full line of Stryker products?

Biomet, Inc.—1998

Satish P. Deshpande
Peter Schoderbek

www.biomet.com
stock symbol BMET

During fiscal year 1997, Biomet's sales increased 8 percent to $580 million. Net income and earnings per share increased by 13 percent and 15 percent to $106 million and $.94 respectively.

Biomet, Inc., (219-267-6639) is a specialty manufacturer of orthopedic products including reconstructive and trauma devices, electrical bone growth stimulators, orthopedic support devices, operating room supplies, powered surgical instruments, general surgical instruments, and arthroscopy products. Biomet has its corporate headquarters and primary manufacturing operations in Warsaw, Indiana, and facilities in 15 locations around the world. The company distributes products to over 100 countries. Biomet employs approximately 2,500 people worldwide.

Orthopedic implant manufacturers have faced increased pressure to contain their costs as hospitals seek various ways to limit expensive inventories. Burdensome regulations, expensive product liability, and managed care have driven many manufacturers into developing and manufacturing their products abroad. On the other hand, the Food and Drug Administration (FDA) has come under increasing public and political pressure to speed up the approvals of drugs and medical devices. In current Senate hearings, the FDA has been under attack for failing to provide timely access to new medical technology. Some congressional leaders are calling for privatization of the governmental agency. The Clinton administration has announced a number of steps to ease restrictions. These are positive signals for Biomet.

HISTORY

Biomet, Inc., was incorporated in 1977 in Indiana by Dane A. Miller, Ph.D.; Niles L. Noblitt; Jerry Ferguson; and Ray Harroff. Miller is president and CEO of Biomet, and Noblitt is board chair. Miller and several other key Biomet managers worked at the Zimmer division of Bristol-Myers Squibb before forming their own company. The company initially sold orthopedic support products through 10 distributors. Biomet entered the reconstructive device market in the early 1980s by offering a titanium alloy-based hip system. Biomet enhanced its reputation with technological advances in hip replacement systems as well as in a total knee replacement. Biomet was founded on the premise that major orthopedic companies, which primarily were divisions of large pharmaceutical companies, had neglected a service orientation approach to orthopedic surgeons' needs. Through a dedication to high levels of service and a variety of innovative products, Biomet penetrated the growing market for orthopedic products.

In 1984, Biomet acquired the Orthopedic Equipment Co. (OEC), a subsidiary of Diasonics, for $8.4 million when OEC had sales of $21.5 million and was twice the size of Biomet. The principal reason stated for the acquisition was to acquire OEC's large distribution network, foreign manufacturing facilities, and a complementary product line (trauma and operating room supplies). The acquisition also allowed Biomet to penetrate the European market through two manufacturing facilities in the United Kingdom. The activities of OEC, more recently, have been split among the various divisions.

In 1988, Biomet acquired Electro-Biology, Inc. (EBI), a leader in the electrical growth stimulation device field for $25.8 million. This acquisition provided Biomet with a strong presence in the electrical stimulation and external fixation markets. In 1991, a newly formed subsidiary of Biomet, Effner Biomet Corp., purchased all of the operations of Effner GmbH and its related companies. Effner is engaged in the manufacture and sale of orthopedic implants, general surgical instruments, and arthroscopy products, with the majority of sales in Germany.

Biomet also entered a joint development agreement with United States Surgical Corporation to develop, manufacture, and market bioresorbable orthopedic products. This venture has been termed Poly-Medics and concentrates on three primary areas: bone replacement and augmentation, fracture healing, and musculoskeletal soft tissue repair. Bioresorbable products essentially degrade in the body and are broken down into carbon dioxide and water. Examples of this include absorbable staples and sutures. In orthopedics, bioabsorbable materials eliminate the need for a second operation to remove metal fixation parts left in the body.

In 1992, Biomet purchased Walter Lorenz Surgical Instruments, Inc., (Lorenz Surgical) for $19 million. Lorenz Surgical, based in Jacksonville, Florida, was a leading marketer of oral-maxillofacial products used by oral surgeons. Product offerings include orthognathic instruments (used for jaw alignment), craniofacial instruments (used to treat severe skull deformities), rigid fixation systems, exodontial instruments, and a transmandibular implant system. These products principally are used to correct deformities, assist in the repair of trauma fractures, and for cosmetic applications. Lorenz Surgical is a stand-alone company which sells its products through a growing distributor network in the United States. It is also strongly positioned in key international markets.

In 1994, Biomet purchased Kirschner Medical Corporation of Maryland for $38.9 million ($13.3 million over the fair value). Kirschner, as does Biomet, produces joint replacement products for hips, knees, and shoulders, as well as fracture fixation products. Kirschner is a market leader in shoulder implants. Kirschner also produces braces, supports, splints, and cast material, and has four manufacturing plants in the United States and one in Spain. During fiscal year 1996, Kirschner's orthopedic operations were consolidated into Biomet, eliminating duplicative administrative and overhead expenses. During the same period, Biomet Europe was established to coordinate manufacturing, development, and sales activities in Europe.

In 1997, Biomet and Merck KgaA announced their intention to establish a 50-50 joint venture called Biomet-Merck for orthopedic products in Europe. Both organizations would contribute their existing European operations to the venture, whose pro forma shares for the next fiscal year are expected to be in excess of $200 million. The venture would give Biomet the exclusive right to license Merck's existing biomaterial-based orthopedic products as well as future products developed by the joint venture for sale outside of Europe.

COMPETITORS

As shown in Exhibit 1, Biomet estimates the 1997 orthopedic market in the United States to be worth $3.8 billion. Reconstructive devices make up nearly half the orthopedic market. This nearly $1.8 billion market segment includes total hip, knee, and shoulder replacements.

Exhibit 2 provides detailed information on the reconstructive market in the United States. The hip replacement market is estimated to be $780 million, and approximately 240,000 hip procedures are performed in the United States annually. Biomet has the second-largest share of the $50 million U.S. shoulder replacement market. Approximately 250,000 knee procedures are performed annually in the United States, and the market is growing between 3 percent to 5 percent every year. Other companies that sell orthopedic products include Zimmer, a division of Bristol-Myers Squibb; Howmedica, a division of Pfizer; and De Puy, owned by the Boehringer-Mannheim Corporation. Biomet, however, is the only independent publicly held company in the industry. Zimmer, the leader in the orthopedics field, has over 20 percent of the reconstructive market.

**EXHIBIT 1: Biomet Estimates of 1997 $3.8 Billion Orthopedic Market—
United States (in millions)**

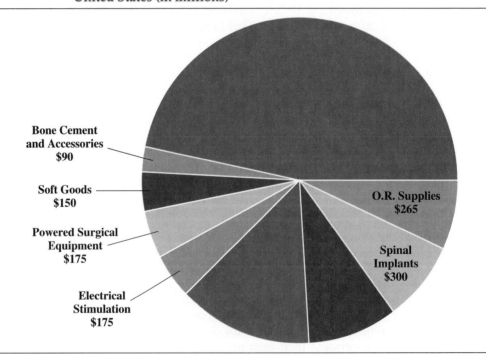

Source: Adapted from Biomet, Inc., *Annual Report* (1997).

EXHIBIT 2: 1997 Reconstructive Device Market in the United States

Major Areas	Market (in millions)	Biomet Market Share	Rank	Entire Market Growth in 1997 over 1996
Hips	$780	13% to 14%	4	1% to 2%
Shoulders	70	26% to 28%	2	4% to 6%
Knees	925	12% to 13%	4	3% to 5%

Source: Adapted from Biomet, Inc., *Annual Report* (1997).

Growth in the reconstructive market has been attributed to better products and techniques which improve surgical outcomes, cost-effective techniques, and demographics. Recent products last longer and require less time in the operating room, thereby lowering costs. People living longer accounts for the expanded patient pool. Life expectancies increased by approximately 5 percent over the past two decades. Male life expectancy increased from 67 years to 71 years, while female life expectancy increased from 74 years to 78 years. Of the estimated 37 million Americans who suffer from arthritis, approximately 14 million of them (38 percent) are between ages 45 and 64. Active life-styles, according to Biomet officials, led to joint replacement at younger ages. Likewise, the pool of people aged 75 and over is increasing. Clearly, demographics are favorable for Biomet.

The general population growth rate from 1989 to 2010 is projected to be only 14 percent. The 55- to 74-year-old sector is expected to grow 40 percent between 1997 and 2010, an increase of 16 million people. The over-75-year-old population is expected to grow by 16 percent to 18 million people over the same period. The over-65-year-old population segment accounts for more than two-thirds of total health care expenditures.

Competition in the implant market is primarily on the basis of service and product design, while competition in the sale of generic internal fixation devices tends to be more on price. Purchasing decisions for hospitals increasingly are being made through buying groups which are able to negotiate price discounts from the manufacturers.

Two factors squeezing profits for surgical implant companies are the following: 1) the higher utilization of lower-priced implants for the elderly who require less functionality and longevity of implants, and 2) surgeons are becoming more cooperative with hospital administrators in narrowing their choice of products, thereby allowing hospitals to deal with fewer manufacturers.

PRODUCTS

Biomet's products are divided into three groups: reconstructive products; Electro–Biology, Inc. (EBI); and other products. Reconstructive products include hips, knees, and shoulder replacements. EBI products include noninvasive and implantable electrical bone growth and spinal and external fixation devices. Other products include internal fixation systems surgical and nonsurgical products. It also includes Arthrotek, the company's sports medicine subsidiary. Exhibit 3 gives sales by product group for the past three fiscal years.

EXHIBIT 3:   Biomet's Sales of Reconstructive Devices

| | Years Ended May 31, | | | | | |
| | 1997 | | 1996 | | 1995 | |
(dollar amounts in thousands)	Net Sales	Percent of Net Sales	Net Sales	Percent of Net Sales	Net Sales	Percent of Net Sales
Reconstructive Products	$352,122	61	$326,834	61	$272,643	60
EBI Products	114,321	20	108,627	20	98,490	22
Other Products	113,904	19	99,698	19	81,139	18
Total	580,347	100	535,159	100	452,272	100

Source: Biomet, Inc., 10-K (1997); *Annual Report* (1997).

Reconstructive Products

Biomet's sales of reconstructive devices worldwide increased almost 8 percent during the fiscal year ended in May 1997 to over $352 million. These devices replace joints that have deteriorated either from diseases such as arthritis or through injury. Reconstructive joint surgery involves modification of the area surrounding the affected joint and insertion of one or more manufactured joint components. Biomet's primary reconstructive products concern the hip, knee, and shoulder, although the company can produce peripheral joints for the wrist, elbow, finger, or large toe. A hip prosthesis consists of a femoral head, neck, and stem manufactured in a variety of head sizes, neck lengths, stem lengths, and configurations.

Biomet's AGC Total Knee System is one of its largest-selling product groups. The product features left and right femoral components, matching tibial components, and appropriately sized patella components for resurfacing. Biomet's various major knee systems, with their variety of options, are one of the most versatile and comprehensive available in the orthopedic market.

Biomet also has a Patient-Matched Implant (PMI) services group which designs, manufactures, and delivers one-of-a-kind reconstructive and trauma devices for orthopedic surgeons. The company acquired a patent in 1990 for a process which allows a physician to create prior to surgery (through the use of computed tomography or magnetic resonance imaging data) electronic 3-D models which are then translated into a PMI design for manufacture.

Electro-Biology, Inc., Products

EBI's sales of $114 million during the fiscal year ended in May 1997 represented a 5 percent increase over the prior year. EBI's primary products include the bone healing system, the spinal fusion stimulator, and a line of external fixation devices. EBI produces noninvasive electrical stimulation devices for the treatment of recalcitrant bone fractures, a spinal fusion stimulator, and external fixation devices. Electrical stimulation devices utilize electrical current to produce a biological response at the cellular level. Electrical stimulation provides an alternative to surgery in the treatment of recalcitrant bone fractures (nonunions) and failed joint fusions.

One of EBI's major products is the EBI Bone Healing System used on fractured bones that do not heal under normal methods. A coil connected to a battery-operated treatment unit is placed on the fracture. The system produces a pulsating electromagnetic field which affects the cells. Because the system is noninvasive, it poses no surgical risks and has no known side effects. The company plans to introduce a newly designed compact version of the system during fiscal year 1998.

EBI also manufactures an implantable spinal stimulation device which serves as an adjunct to surgical spinal fusion treatment. Lumbar back pain is caused by the inability of vertebrae to provide stability for the spine. In order to provide stability, simulated bone material is grafted onto the spinal vertebrae in the problem area. In 75 percent of the cases, this material will induce bone growth and stabilize the spine. In the remaining 25 percent of the cases, spinal fusion stimulation has proven to be unsuccessful. The spinal fusion stimulator is implanted during surgery required for the bone graft and delivers electricity to the bone graft material, thereby accelerating bone growth and eventually fusing the spine. Biomet estimates the total U.S. market for electric stimulation products at about $175 million.

Until 1995, Biomet had exclusive right with Orthofix of Italy to distribute the Orthofix External Fixation System in the United States that is used in trauma situations when the bone has been fractured or crushed in many places. It essentially allows the physician to hold in place complicated fractures of long bones when casts, rods, or plates are inappropriate. This exclusive distribution right expired in 1995. Early in the fiscal year ended in May 1996, Biomet launched the Dynafix external fixation system.

In June 1997, Biomet announced that it would appeal a jury verdict that was entered against it in United States District Court for the District of New Jersey in an action brought by Orthofix SRL against EBI and Biomet concerning events related to the expiration of the distribution agreement. The jury found that in spite of Orthofix's refusal to renew the agreement, EBI's development of the Dynafix system prior to the expiration of the contract constituted a breach of the distribution agreement. The jury awarded Orthofix $49 million in compensatory damages and $100 million in punitive damages. The jury also ruled that Orthofix breached the distribution agreement and tortiously interfered with EBI's economic relations, but it awarded only nominal damages to EBI. Currently, EBI is a market leader in the $100 million domestic market for external fixation systems.

EBI also positioned itself to compete in the $300 million market for spinal implant products. The Spinelink System, which is manufactured out of titanium, with its modular link and polydirectional screws, allows a surgeon to tailor segmentational construction to the patient's anatomy.

Other Products

Biomet's sales of other products during the fiscal year ended May 1997 were almost $114 million. This was a 14 percent increase over the previous fiscal year and in great part was due to increased sales of spinal products internationally, various fixation products, Lorenz's craniomaxillofacial products, and the introduction of the Indiana Tome Carpal Tunnel Release System. Fixation products include both internal and external bone fixation devices. Internal devices include nails, plates, screws, pins, and wires designed to temporarily stabilize bone injuries. Orthopedic support devices include elbow, wrist, abdominal, thigh, and ankle supports, as well as a wide variety of knee braces.

OPERATIONS

Product Development

Biomet spent nearly $70 million on research and development in the last three years and expects the amount to increase in the future. A number of new products are scheduled for introduction during the 1998 fiscal year. This includes the Mallory-Head Modular Calar System; the Bi-Polar Shoulder System (a hemiarthroplasty system for shoulder replacement); EBI's SpineLink Spinal System (a versatile spinal implant fixation system); and the LactoSorb Craniomaxillofacial Fixation System, which features a patented copolymer that naturally resorbs within the body after healing has occurred. New product introduction will enable the company to enter new high-growth U.S. market segments, such as the estimated $300 million spinal implant market, the $50 million carpal tunnel release market, and the $100 million market for casting materials. The planned joint venture with Merck KgaA would enable the company to enter the estimated $200 million global market for bone cements and accessories.

International Operations

Biomet's total sales in the fiscal year ended May 1997 increased 8 percent to $580 million from $535 million in the previous year. Increased sales in Europe, Latin America, and certain countries in the Pacific Rim resulted from strengthened distribution channels and new product offerings. Foreign sales (sales outside the United States), as a percentage of net sales in 1997, were about 27 percent, which was a slight increase from the previous year. Foreign currency translation adjustments negatively influenced Biomet's sales by approximately $3 million in the fiscal year ended May 1997. Exhibit 4 presents industry segment and geographic information. Biomet officials feel that the proposed joint venture with Merck KgaA will provide numerous opportunities in Europe.

Team Biomet

The team concept started in Biomet in 1977 and is today an integral part of the firm's philosophy. Biomet decentralized decision making so decisions can be made at the appropriate level. Teams are composed of employees in design, manufacturing, quality, and production planning. Physically, employees are located by functional areas within the facility where routine decisions are handled. Only those decisions related to large commitments of capital expenditures or changes in strategic policies require presidential or vice-presidential signatures.

Communications between subsidiaries and departments is frequent and open. Members of management interact with the workers on a daily basis and at many corporate events which foster camaraderie. When Miller started the company with his colleagues, his goal was to create an organization that could grow unencumbered by the bureaucratic structures and conservatism that he believed stifled initiative and creativity at many large firms. Although Miller and his colleagues keep an open door for employees, they are constantly on the shop floor talking to employees in their work settings. The team concept is stressed in company brochures and meetings. There is a Biomet Team Appreciation Day as well as company picnics, Christmas parties, and other special events. The quarterly in-house publication *Bio Briefs* informs employees of corporate and product information and recognizes promotions, birthdays, births, anniversaries, and so forth.

EXHIBIT 4: Biomet, Inc., Industry Segment and Geographic Information

(dollar amounts in thousands)	1997	1996	1995
Net sales:			
North America	$468,757	$439,638	$377,923
Europe	110,039	95,521	74,349
Other	1,551	0	0
Intercompany	19,085	14,023	16,572
Eliminations	(19,085)	(14,023)	(16,572)
	580,347	535,159	452,272
Operating income:			
North America	144,536	124,667	106,954
Europe	15,131	12,613	12,073
Other	144	0	0
	159,811	137,280	119,027
Identifiable assets:			
North America	511,442	502,229	438,985
Europe	138,059	125,126	117,525
Other	7,149	0	0
Eliminations	(28,294)	(28,886)	(17,426)
	628,356	598,469	539,084

Source: Biomet, Inc., *Annual Report* (1997).

Biomet's team concept offers every employee financial incentives, including cash bonuses, company shares, and stock options. Insiders own approximately 25 percent of the outstanding stock. The team concept extends to distributors as well. In fall 1990, *Bio Briefs* carried the following letter to the president from a distributor:

> When I was with a former company, I used to imagine a company where you came to meetings to learn—not to see who had on the most expensive suit. I used to imagine a company who had an interest in me and my business—not just to see how much they could get out of me. I used to imagine a company where the owners of that company were trying to keep my customers pleased—not the people in the administrative positions of the company. I used to imagine a company where my family was important—not to see how long I could be away from them. I used to imagine a company who wanted to help me make my business do as well as possible—not just to meet my current quota.
>
> Thank you for being the company that others can only imagine.

The team concept also extends to the medical profession. When patients face unusual circumstances, Biomet officials often are called upon to design specialty products. Biomet enjoys a healthy reputation in the medical profession for its team effort. This concept is reinforced in daily operations.

Financial Information

Results in 1997 show an increase in sales of 8 percent, in net income of 13 percent, in per share earnings of almost 15 percent, and in assets of almost 5 percent. Consolidated financial information is given in Exhibits 5 and 6.

EXHIBIT 5: Biomet, Inc., Income Statements

(in thousands, except per share data)	For the years ended May 31,		
	1997	1996	1995
Net sales	$580,347	$535,159	$452,272
Cost of sales	185,795	174,364	142,143
Gross profit	394,552	360,795	310,129
Selling, general and administrative expenses	211,540	199,461	169,332
Research and development expense	23,201	24,054	21,770
Operating income	159,811	137,280	119,027
Other income, net	9,972	13,505	6,947
Interest expense	(651)	(1,116)	(1,032)
Income before income taxes	169,132	149,669	124,942
Provision for income taxes	62,678	55,563	45,742
Net Income	106,454	94,106	79,200
Earnings per share, based on the weighted average number of shares outstanding during the year	.94	.82	.69
Weighted average number of shares	113,765	115,461	115,459

Source: Biomet, Inc., *Annual Report* (1997): 26.

EXHIBIT 6: Biomet, Inc., Consolidated Balance Sheets

(in thousands, except per share data)	As of May 31,	
	1997	1996
Assets		
Current assets:		
Cash and cash equivalents	$82,034	$106,068
Investments	41,237	30,834
Accounts and notes receivable, less allowance for doubtful receivables (1997—$6,175 and 1996—$6,889)	162,135	154,055
Inventories	151,523	151,465
Prepaid expenses and other	27,311	20,494
Total current assets	464,240	462,916
Property, plant and equipment:		
Land and improvements	9,544	5,874
Buildings and improvements	53,156	48,648
Machinery and equipment	90,139	78,175
	152,839	132,697
Less, Accumulated depreciation	61,927	52,533
Property, plant and equipment, net	90,912	80,164
Investments	44,527	31,159
Intangible assets, net of accumulated amortization (1997—$12,215 and 1996—$9,973)	5,787	7,665
Excess acquisition costs over fair value of acquired net assets, net of accumulated amortization (1997—$6,979 and 1996—$4,468)	20,306	14,947
Other assets	2,584	1,618
Total assets	628,356	598,469
		continued

EXHIBIT 6: *continued*

	As of May 31,	
	1997	*1996*
Liabilities and Shareholders' Equity		
Current liabilities:		
Short-term borrowings	5,568	3,358
Accounts payable	17,140	16,667
Accrued income taxes	12,181	11,295
Accrued wages and commissions	12,232	11,460
Other accrued expenses	25,793	19,319
Total current liabilities	72,914	62,099
Deferred federal income taxes	2,229	1,509
Other liabilities	385	791
Total liabilities	75,528	64,399
Commitments and contingencies		
Shareholders' equity:		
Preferred shares, $100 par value Authorized 5 shares, none issued	0	0
Common shares, without par value: Authorized 500,000 shares; issued and outstanding 1997—$111,214 shares and 1996—115,826 shares	73,587	68,376
Additional paid-in capital	16,001	14,410
Retained earnings	472,450	458,193
Net unrealized appreciation of available-for-sale securities	1,040	584
Cumulative translation adjustment	(10,250)	(7,493)
Total shareholders' equity	552,828	534,070
Total liabilities and shareholders' equity	628,356	598,469

Source: Biomet, Inc., *Annual Report* (1997): 27.

THE FUTURE

Prepare a three-year strategic plan for CEO Miller.

Magazine Publishing—Industry Note

MAGAZINE AD PAGES UP

Thanks to a thriving national economy, magazines are enjoying a very good year in advertising. According to the Publishers Information Bureau (PIB), magazine ad pages rose 5 percent, year to year, in July 1997, marking the eighth consecutive monthly gain. For the 7 months through July, ad pages were up 5 percent from the comparable year-earlier period. Reported advertising revenues jumped 12.5 percent, year to year, in July 1997 and 12.3 percent in the seven months through July.

Nine of the top 10 magazine ad categories showed year-to-date gains through July 1997. The strongest included automotive (up 17 percent, year to year), toiletries and cosmetics (up 19 percent), drugs and remedies (up 33 percent), and apparel and foot-wear (up 18 percent). Of the top 10, only food was down (off a fractional 0.1 percent). Helped by a healthy holiday season, we expect full-year advertising to advance 13 percent. [Note: Because the PIB tallies data from roughly 200 magazines, its statistics are representative, not comprehensive.]

Magazine circulation revenues probably rose less than 2 percent for the year in 1996 and are projected to rise about 3 percent in 1997, largely reflecting higher cover prices. Single-copy sales have been soft for more than a decade, while growth in the number of subscriptions has slowed in recent years. In the first half of 1997, single-copy sales grew just 1.2 percent, year to year, for the 581 titles measured by the Audit Bureau of Circulation.

BRAND EXTENSIONS: MONEY TREES FOR MAGAZINES

Brand extensions—whereby a magazine produces goods for sale or licenses its name to manufacturers—have been around for decades. Yet magazine publishers today are expanding their branding endeavors. According to PIB, these so-called ancillary revenues make up nearly 10 percent of most magazines' total annual earnings, a contribution that is expected to rise to 20 percent by 2002. For some publishers, such as Playboy Enterprises; Meredith Corp.; and the Reader's Digest Association, these revenues already represent more than 50 percent of total corporate revenues. In today's market, opportunities for growth from branding are greater than from either advertising or circulation revenues.

Additional revenues are coming not only from product extensions but also from other ventures, such as contract (or custom) publishing and spin-off products; the latter can include special interest magazines, books, audiotapes, videocassettes, CD-ROMs, radio and cable television shows, and Web sites. Magazines also are lending their names to trade shows, tours, seminars, and conferences.

Source: Adapted from *Industry Survey* by permission of Standard & Poor's, a division of the McGraw-Hill Companies. *Standard & Poor's*, "Publishing," *Industry Survey* (October 2, 1997): 5–13.

Those in the branding game include *McCall's* (dolls); *Better Homes and Gardens* (garden centers, books, greeting cards, and more); *Outdoor Life* (a cable TV channel); *Money* (seminars); *Soap Opera Digest* (an awards show); *Traditional Home* (advertiser-sponsored show house tours); *Popular Science* (a cable TV show on The Learning Channel); *Woman's Day* (exercise videos); *Elle* (cosmetic cases); *Reader's Digest* (books, records, audiotapes, videocassettes, and more); and *Playboy* (a wide range of leisure items from apparel to laser discs).

PAPER PRICES MAY SEE MODEST INCREASES

Markets for certain papers, such as packaging and office papers, are holding steady, while other sectors, including newsprint, coated magazine stock, and most grades of book paper, remain soft. Book publishers use a wide range of paper grades, from the more expensive heavily coated papers to less expensive newsprint-grade papers. Magazines, meanwhile, use mostly No. 5 lightweight coated paper, and newspapers employ regular old newsprint.

All three publishing sectors are paying less for paper now than a year ago. After price hikes in 1994 and 1995, when paper prices peaked at more than 50 percent above previous lows, most grades of paper saw demand fall toward the end of 1995. As of January 1997, newsprint and coated paper prices were down 30 percent to 40 percent from 1995 levels. On April 1, 1997, a price hike of 7 percent was slow to take hold and another 7 percent hike, announced for July 1, 1997, did not stick.

The price of coated paper used by magazines declined roughly 35 percent on average in 1996. According to *Pulp & Paper Week,* one of the typical coated groundwood papers had a list price of between $1,220 and $1,260 per ton in January 1997, but was actually selling at $740 to $820 per ton. Transaction prices rose 5 percent to 7 percent in the first quarter of 1997 versus late 1996, and moderate increases are probable again before year-end 1997.

Although increases in advertising are pushing up demand, publishers continue to economize on paper usage wherever possible. Thus, the next upswing in paper prices should be a relatively weak one.

ELECTRONIC PUBLISHING BOOM DRAWS NEWCOMERS

According to *Editor & Publisher* magazine, there were more than 4,100 World Wide Web–based news sites at the beginning of 1997 that were operating according to professional journalistic standards. Roughly 1,600 of these Web sites were owned by print newspaper companies; 1,300 by magazine publishing companies; more than 800 by television or radio broadcasting companies; and 400 by news services that range from the major wire services to government news services.

Nontraditional publishers and other firms not formally considered publishers or news providers are now into electronic publishing as never before. Among the many dozens of news sites that have been established by nontraditional Web publishers are the following: Netscape's home page, Excite Live's NewsTracker, Infoseek's Your News, and Yahoo!'s My Personal Yahoo! news page. In many cities there are also City Guide sites that give local news and information—going-out guides, maps, and so on.

On-line profits tangled in the Web

Publishers who operate profitable Web sites are definitely in the minority. Among newspaper publishers, roughly one-third reported that they turned a profit in 1996 or expected to be profitable in 1997. The few that do make money generate only modest returns.

This should come as no surprise. Because the number of Web sites is growing faster than the number of on-line users, the many choices contribute to audience fragmentation and make it difficult to establish a large audience. The Internet Advertising Bureau, in its first year of compiling such statistics, reported that total Web advertising spending in 1996 was $267 million. That is a tidy sum, and one which will probably more than double in 1997. However, the largesse is spread among thousands of players.

Although many Web sites generate revenues, publishers freely admit that these sites aren't yet profitable. In addition to absorbing the costs of designing and setting up a site, Web publishers must pay their staff and all the other expenses related to maintaining the site, generating readership, and seeking advertising revenues. Nonetheless, publishers continue to investigate the newer media for fear of losing their core business to other publishers—including those using some kind of hybrid telephone/television/computer—in the future.

On-line publications versus print

Electronic editions of a publication often include articles published in the print version. However, most on-line publications offer features not available in the printed product. Depending on the publication and the on-line service, on-line subscribers may be able to interact with writers and editors via e-mail or electronic bulletin boards. Some host on-line conferences that give users an opportunity to chat with editors or noted personalities.

The extent to which readers of a printed publication will switch to an electronic version of the same publication is hard to predict. In one respect, on-line versions of magazines offer less than the print editions because they typically don't include all of the photographs, tables, illustrations, and other artwork found in print.

On the other hand, an electronic version may contain sound and video clips—something no print publication can match. Additionally, electronic information, which can be manipulated on a computer screen, is a valuable resource for researchers, students, writers, and others. On-line publications also have the potential to attract new readers who otherwise might never have examined the print version. Computer users are more likely than the general population to read a newspaper or magazine, and computer services give them access to media outside their regions or usual interests.

MAGAZINE SUBSCRIPTIONS RISE, NEWSSTAND SALES SLIP

Newsstand sales for the nation's major national magazines have been declining for well over a decade, with no letup in sight. Subscriptions, however, have been in a general uptrend. For consumers, subscriptions are not only less expensive per issue than single newsstand copies, but they're also a more convenient way to get a magazine.

The shortage of retail display space for the hundreds of magazines published each year has hurt single-copy sales of individual titles. Single-copy sales usually are impulse purchases. Because today's consumer makes fewer shopping trips and generally has less time to shop than in past years, there may be fewer opportunities for impulse buying. Single issues are often purchased by people with only a passing interest in a topic who don't want to be locked into a full-year subscription. In addition, the modern shopper faces more choices when spending discretionary dollars.

Although most magazines rely primarily on subscription sales, special issues can attract a larger number of nonsubscribers. *Playboy*'s Playmate of the Year issue and the swimsuit edition of *Sports Illustrated*, for example, sell well on a single-copy basis, as does the less legendary Holidays at Home issue released by *Country Home.*

These problems notwithstanding, hope springs eternal for publishers. As a result, numerous new titles hit the newsstands every year. More than 900 new magazines were introduced in 1996, up from just 265 new magazines in 1986. The topics and titles may be much the same as yesteryear's, but publishers keep up with changing tastes by issuing new magazines with new editorial slants. Efforts to distinguish new publications from the hundreds of others that crowd the newsstands also have contributed to the proliferation of niche titles. Whatever the subject, there is a magazine devoted to it: *Inline Skater, Superb Word Finds, Cigar Aficionado,* and *Shape* are but a few.

REVENUE FACTORS

Factors affecting magazine publishers' revenues include advertising, subscriptions, and single-copy sales.

Advertising rates based on circulation

Magazines usually sell three primary types of advertising: run of press, mail order, and insert. Most magazine advertising pages and revenues are derived from run of press ads, which are printed within the magazine.

Advertising rates are based on each magazine's average per issue circulation, usually stated as "cost per thousand" circulation. These rates usually must be competitive with those of comparable magazines serving the same target audience. Readers' response to advertisers' products and services, the effectiveness of the magazine's sales team, and the quality of customer service are factors affecting advertisers' demand for ad space in a particular magazine.

Circulation: building readership

Subscriptions usually are a magazine's largest source of circulation revenues. They may be generated through direct mail solicitation, agencies, insert cards, and other means. Newsstand sales, including single-copy sales at supermarkets, drugstores, and other retail outlets, are another important source of circulation revenues for most magazines.

Publishers sometimes lure subscribers with discounts from the stated cover price. Others give premiums, such as cameras, radios, watches, complimentary issues, and the like. However, these premium giveaways aren't used as frequently today as they were in the early 1980s, when they were virtually *de rigeur.* Publishers who buy their premiums wholesale claim that this marketing technique is more cost-effective than others. This may be true: A free gift often induces subscribers to pay more—up to the full cover price—for the subscription. But for a sale to qualify as valid according to

Audit Bureau of Circulation rules, the value of a premium or discount must not exceed 50 percent of the basic subscription price.

Although discounts and giveaways attract subscribers, they do not necessarily provide readers—and the number of readers is what advertisers care about. Editorial content, therefore, is crucial to maintaining a loyal readership. Readers must perceive the magazine as valuable and worth the investment of their time and money.

The trend toward increasing market segmentation can be seen clearly within magazine publishing as specialized titles and local and regional emphasis proliferate. Magazines focused on such areas as parenting, children, and city and regional life are common, as are upscale publications; magazines for the elderly (or the "mature" reader); and magazines that cover personal finance, travel, sports, and computing.

General interest magazines can benefit from the segmentation trend by producing special editions and theme sections to promote readership and advertising.

Playboy Enterprises, Inc.—1998

Kay W. Lawrimore

Fred R. David

www.playboy.com
stock symbol PLA

Headquartered in Chicago, Illinois, Playboy Enterprises, Inc., (PEI) (312-751-8000) is an international media and entertainment company that publishes *Playboy* magazine in the United States and licenses editions internationally; develops and markets other branded media products, including newsstand specials, calendars, books, CD-ROMs, and an on-line service; creates and distributes programming for television and home video; markets the Playboy trademarks on apparel, accessories, and products sold around the world; and operates a direct marketing business, including the Critics' Choice Video, Collectors' Choice Music, and Playboy catalogs.

PEI's current mission statement is given as follows:

> PEI is a preeminent international media and entertainment company with a worldwide recognized brand and many windows of opportunity to expand the Playboy franchise and develop other related entertainment franchises globally by leveraging Playboy's strengths of publishing, brand management, and marketing.

MANAGEMENT

As indicated in Exhibit 1, Christie Hefner, daughter of founder Hugh Hefner, is chair of PEI. Christie Hefner was only one year old when her father launched *Playboy* with $600 of his own cash in 1953. The company went public in 1971, with the family retaining 70 percent of the stock. In the early 1970s, the magazine sold more than 7 million copies a month. By the early 1980s, circulation was falling and Christie Hefner was named president of a company with over $35 million in cash. In 1988, she was named chair of the board and CEO. Hugh Hefner, with 71 percent of the voting stock, has maintained control of *Playboy* magazine, the cash cow for PEI. None of PEI's 700 employees are represented by collective bargaining agreements. PEI's revenues increased 7.2 percent to $296 million in the fiscal year ended June 1997.

This case was prepared by Professors Kay W. Lawrimore and Fred R. David of Francis Marion University as a basis for class discussion. It is not intended to illustrate either effective or ineffective handling of an administrative situation. Copyright © 1999 by Prentice Hall, Inc. ISBN 0-13-011194-5.

EXHIBIT 1: Playboy Enterprises, Inc., Organizational Chart

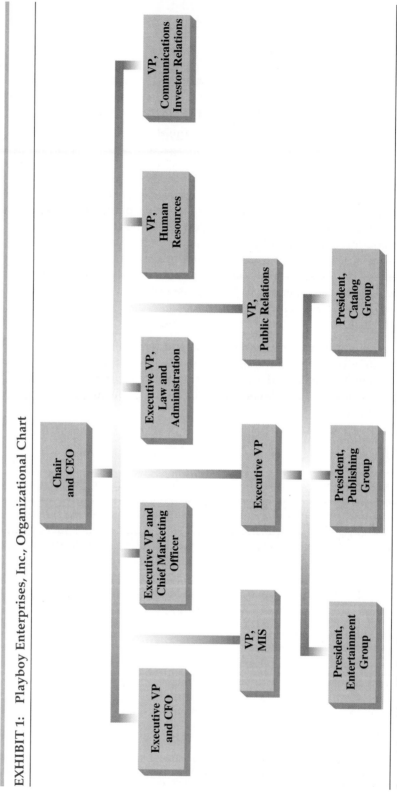

Source: Adapted from Playboy Enterprises, Inc., *Annual Report* (1997).

FINANCIAL STATUS

When Playboy Enterprises, Inc., first went public on the New York Stock Exchange in 1971, its stock certificate featured a reclining nude. Some 20,000 people purchased a single share of PEI stock just to get a copy of the certificate. Although the certificate no longer features a nude female, there are more than 20 million shares outstanding.

For the fiscal year ending in June 1997 (see Exhibit 2), PEI reported net income of almost $21.4 million, or $1.05 per share. Excluding the $6.6 million tax benefit, PEI's net income nearly quadrupled, rising from almost $4.3 million, or $.21 per share, for the fiscal year ending in June 1996. Operating income rose nearly 66 percent to $15.7 million on a 7 percent revenue increase to $296.6 million from almost $9.5 million in the fiscal year ending in June 1996. Several of PEI's businesses can experience variations in quarterly performance. As a result, PEI's performance in any quarterly period is not necessarily reflective of full-year or longer-term trends. Variations in quarterly performances are caused by revenues and profit contributions from multiyear agreements being recognized, depending upon the timing of program delivery, license period, month of issue for the magazine, amount of public interest in the pictorials, and other factors.

ORGANIZATION

PEI's four divisions are Publishing, Entertainment, Catalog, and Product Marketing.

EXHIBIT 2: Playboy Enterprises, Inc., Consolidated Statements of Operations

(in thousands, except per share amounts)	Year ended June 30,		
	1997	1996	1995
Net revenues	$296,623	$276,587	$247,249
Costs and expenses			
Cost of sales	(245,023)	(234,247)	(214,327)
Selling and administrative expenses	(35,855)	(32,847)	(29,865)
Total costs and expenses	(280,878)	(267,094)	(244,192)
Operating income	15,745	9,493	3,057
Nonoperating income (expense)			
Investment income	73	88	139
Interest expense	(427)	(680)	(708)
Other, net	(640)	(452)	(52)
Total nonoperating expense	(994)	(1,044)	(621)
Income before income taxes	14,751	8,449	2,436
Income tax benefit (expense)	6,643	(4,197)	(1,807)
Net income	21,394	4,252	629
Weighted average number of common shares outstanding	20,318	20,014	19,984
Net income per common share	$1.05	$0.21	$0.03

Source: www.freeedgar.com

Publishing

The Publishing Group includes the publication of *Playboy* magazine and related businesses. For the fiscal year ending in June 1997, the Publishing Group reported revenues of $137.7 million, a 4 percent increase from the previous year (see Exhibit 3). Operating income for 1997 was $8.4 million, a decline from $9.2 million in the fiscal year ending in June 1996.

EXHIBIT 3: PEI's Financial Data by Segment

(in thousands)	Six Months Ended 12/31/97	Fiscal Year Ended 6/30/97	Fiscal Year Ended 6/30/96	Fiscal Year Ended 6/30/95
Net Revenues				
Publishing				
Playboy magazine				
Subscription	$25,919	$52,955	$51,837	$50,531
Newsstand	11,345	21,972	24,408	24,876
Advertising	13,718	28,414	27,431	27,588
Other	(44)	1,651	1,653	1,387
Total Playboy magazine	50,938	104,992	105,329	104,382
Other domestic publishing	11,755	22,745	21,419	18,718
International publishing	5,305	9,951	6,172	4,173
Total Publishing	67,998	137,688	132,920	127,273
Entertainment				
Playboy TV				
Cable	9,560	21,165	21,149	18,938
Satellite direct-to-home	14,047	23,065	16,457	9,602
Off-network productions	1,331	3,052	1,672	420
Total Playboy TV	24,938	47,282	39,278	28,960
Domestic home video	3,247	8,515	9,370	9,517
International TV and home video	4,728	12,218	11,955	11,160
Total Playboy Businesses	32,913	68,015	60,603	49,637
AdulTVision	2,305	4,487	1,907	0
Movies and other	2,138	2,214	2,316	2,060
Total Entertainment	37,356	74,716	64,826	51,697
Product Marketing	4,199	7,968	7,125	6,844
Casino Gaming	0	0	0	0
Catalog	39,988	76,251	71,716	61,435
Total Net Revenues	149,541	296,623	276,587	247,249
Operating Income (Loss)				
Publishing	2,831	8,387	9,235	10,709
Entertainment				
Before programming expense	19,144	39,609	30,467	21,097
Programming expense	(11,153)	(21,355)	(21,263)	(20,130)
Total Entertainment	7,991	18,254	9,204	967
Product Marketing	1,614	3,512	3,692	3,428
Casino Gaming	(541)	0	0	0
Catalog	1,959	4,795	5,244	5,209
Corporate Administration and Promotion	(9,395)	(19,203)	(17,882)	(17,256)
Total Operating Income	4,459	15,745	9,493	3,057

Source: www.freeedgar.com

Playboy *Magazine*

Playboy's editorial vitality, diversity, and cultural connection are evident in the fiction, articles, investigative reporting, interviews, celebrity profiles, and entertainment and service features that are monthly staples of the publication. Regular columns on politics, books, movies, music, style, men, women, and relationships reflect contemporary social and cultural issues and further the magazine's ongoing dialogue with its readers. The magazine's revenues were $105 million in the fiscal year ending in June 1997; $105.3 million in 1996; and $104.4 million in 1995.

Playboy magazine has a worldwide monthly circulation, which includes overseas editions, of 4.5 million copies. Approximately 3.3 million copies of the U.S. edition are sold monthly. An independent audit agency, Audit Bureau of Circulations, reports the magazine's circulation rate base (the total newsstand and subscription guaranteed to advertisers) was greater than the combined rate bases of *Rolling Stone*, *Esquire*, and *GQ* (see Exhibit 4). The magazine's rate base of 3.15 is higher than the rate bases of *Newsweek*, *Cosmopolitan*, and *Business Week* but is less than *Reader's Digest* and *Time*. Mediamark Research, Inc., (MRI) data indicate the median age of male *Playboy* subscribers of 32, with a median annual household income of $41,200. MRI reports the magazine is read by one in every seven men aged 18 to 34.

During the 1960s, the magazine relied upon newsstand sales, but today about 80 percent of the total copies sold are subscription copies. Direct mail campaigns and television advertising campaigns are used to attract new subscribers. The price of a one-year subscription ranges from $19.97 to $34.96 depending on the source of the subscription and the length of time the subscription has been held. Subscription copies are distributed by second-class mail. Presorting and other methods lower the cost.

Warner Publishing Services, a national distributor with a network of approximately 300 wholesalers, distributes the magazine to newsstands and other retail outlets. The number of issues sold in the retail outlets varies from month to month, depending on the cover, the pictorials, and the editorial features. The 1995 December issue featuring Farrah Fawcett set a six-year sales record. Fiscal 1997 did not have a blockbuster issue and newsstand sales fell 10 percent. As each issue goes on sale, PEI

EXHIBIT 4: Selected U.S. Consumer Publications (1997)

	Rate Base (1)	*Ranking (2)*
Reader's Digest	15.00	1
TV Guide	13.00	2
National Geographic	8.50	3
Time	4.00	10
Playboy	3.15	12
People	3.15	12
Sports Illustrated	3.15	12
Newsweek	3.10	15
Cosmopolitan	2.25	20
Rolling Stone	1.25	45
Business Week	0.88	83
Esquire	0.65	111
GQ	0.65	111

Source: www.freeedgar.com

receives a cash advance based on estimated sales. Retail outlets return unsold issues to the wholesalers who shred the return magazines and report the returns via affidavit to Warner Publishing Services. The national distributor settles with PEI based upon the actual number sold compared to the forecasted number. The last increase in the basic U.S. newsstand cover price was in 1993. The U.S. newsstand cover price for regular issues of $4.95, and the Canadian cover price of $5.95 (in Canadian dollars) did not change during the fiscal year ended June 1997.

The U.S. National Defense Authorization Act of 1997 bans the sale or rental of sexually oriented written or videotaped material at commissaries, PXs, and ship stores. PEI considers this act unconstitutional and intends to challenge it in court, but does not consider that the law will greatly impact sales.

To attract advertisers, the U.S. *Playboy* magazine is published in 15 advertising editions: eight regional, two state, four metro, and one upper-income zip-coded edition. Advertising pages peaked at 1,434 in 1988 and declined to 660 in 1993, 595 in 1994 and 1995, and 569 pages in 1996. Retail/direct mail, tobacco, beer/wine/liquor accounted for 68 percent of the advertising pages during the fiscal year ended June 1996 (see Exhibit 5). The magazine has had difficulty attracting additional advertisers but obtained new clients such as America Online, Aramis, Calvin Klein, Gillette, HBO, Turtle Wax, Yamaha, Kawasaki, and Sega.

In 1996, the U.S. Food and Drug Administration announced a regulation restricting publication of tobacco advertisements. "Adult publications" are exempt from this regulation and PEI contends that *Playboy* qualifies as an adult publication.

The net advertising revenues of the U.S. edition of *Playboy* magazine for the fiscal years ended June 30 in 1997, 1996, 1995, 1994, and 1993 were $28.4 million, $27.4 million, $27.6 million, $28.0 million, and $30.4 million, respectively.

Quad/Graphics, Inc., in Wisconsin, prints *Playboy* magazine. Paper, the principal raw material used in the production, is purchased from several suppliers. Paper prices began impacting PEI in 1994 with a 7 percent increase. The average paper prices for the fiscal year ended June 30, 1996, were 46 percent higher than the previous year. To

EXHIBIT 5: Magazine Advertising by Category, as Percent of Total Ad Pages

Advertising Category	*Six Months Ended Dec. 31,* 1997	*Fiscal Years Ended June 30,*		
		1997	1996	1995
Tobacco	23%	21%	24%	20%
Beer/Wine/Liquor	22	24	19	18
Retail/Direct Mail	21	23	25	31
Home Electronics	9	4	1	4
Drugs/Remedies	5	3	3	4
Toiletries/Cosmetics	4	7	9	9
Jewelry/Optical/Photo	4	4	3	3
Entertainment	3	3	2	1
Automotives	3	4	8	4
Apparel/Footwear/Accessories	3	4	3	4
All Other	3	3	3	2

mitigate this increase in production costs, PEI raised the prices for newsstand issues and lowered *Playboy* magazine's circulation rate to 3.15 million.

Playboy-*Related Businesses*

Playboy-related businesses include newsstand photo specials, calendars, overseas editions of *Playboy*, a home page on the World Wide Web, multimedia products, 900-number audiotext services, *Playboy* collectible trading cards, books, and 20 percent interest in duPont Publishing, Inc.

Twenty-one newsstand specials with a cover price of $6.95 helped to offset the increase in paper costs during fiscal 1996.

Overseas editions of *Playboy* magazine sell approximately 1.2 million copies monthly. Overseas editions retain the distinctive style, look, and tone of the U.S. edition, and include the work of the specific nation's writers and artists. During 1997, PEI licensed the right to publish the magazine in Australia, Brazil, Croatia, the Czech Republic, France, Germany, Greece, Italy, Japan, Mexico, the Netherlands, Poland, Russia, Spain, and Taiwan. Brazil, Germany, and Japan accounted for approximately 55 percent of the total licensing revenues from 1996 overseas editions. In previous years, the magazine was licensed in Argentina, Turkey, and South Africa. Scandinavia is planned for 1998. The terms of licenses vary but typically are for three or five years, have a guaranteed minimum royalty, and apply a formula for computing additional royalty based upon circulation and advertising revenue. PEI has equity interest in only one country, Poland. In 1996, PEI increased the equity interest to 90 percent in the Polish edition.

Hefner says, "There is no cookie cutter for doing business overseas. In some countries, we've found the best way to get in is with small partners who are entrepreneurial." In Russia, the partner is a woman who established the first functional periodical distribution system in Russia and used the distribution system to start a daily paper, a woman's magazine, and then *Playboy*. Russian *Playboy* is a bimonthly publication which started with a circulation of 80,000 in July 1995. At $5 an issue, the magazine is considered a luxury for most Russians. Advertisers include Mercedes, GM, Pioneer, and Sony.

PEI's home pages on the World Wide Web provide four sources of revenue: advertising, shopping, subscription, and pay per view. Averaging 4.6 million hits per day in 1996, the PEI's home page is one of the most-visited sites, according to unaudited information from Nielson I/PRO. Visitors are attracted from more than 150 countries and territories. This free site generated a profit in 1996 from the sale of advertising. In the fiscal year ended June 1997, the site delivered as many as 1.7 million pages in a single day and advertising revenue almost tripled the 1996 revenue. A digital version of the Playboy catalog, Playboy Store, was added to the site in 1996 and Web site sales equaled almost 9 percent of the print catalog sales in fiscal 1997. Introduced in 1996, Playboy Cyber Club allowed members to interact with the *Playboy* magazine editors, have chat rooms, and access more than 50,000 pages on the site. Subscriptions for the Playboy Cyber Club are received from 76 countries.

PEI owns a 20 percent interest in duPont Publishing, Inc., and receives management fees. DuPont Publishing expanded to three publications in the fiscal year ended June 1997: *A Buyers Gallery of Fine Boats*, *A Buyers Gallery of Fine Homes*, and *A Buyers Gallery of Fine Automobiles*. PEI has an option to acquire the remaining 80 percent interest at a price based on fair market value as of December 31, 1999. This investment is accounted for on the equity method with PEI's share of duPont's net income or loss included in nonoperating income or expenses.

Entertainment

The entertainment division's strategy is to build a library of Playboy programming that can be packaged in multiple formats for worldwide distribution. To strengthen brand identification of Playboy programming internationally, PEI consolidated all its television services and programming under the name Playboy TV and developed a logo.

After an operating loss of $7.3 million in the fiscal year ended June 1995 and a profit of $9.2 million in the fiscal year ended June 1996, the Entertainment Group reported a profit of $18.3 million on revenue of $74.7 million in the fiscal year ended June 1997. In 1995, Hefner reported that the cable, software, and phone companies "are now coming to our door asking if they can have the rights to carry our content." The division is aggressively expanding, and in 1997, PEI invested $30.7 million in producing 166 hours of original programming and in licensing other programming for broadcast. Due to the strong demand for the movies, PEI is able to presell distribution rights.

Playboy Television

In 1982, PEI introduced Playboy Television, available only by monthly subscriptions. Fee structures vary with cable systems but PEI usually receives about 35 percent of the retail price, which ranges from $5 to $13 per month. The number of monthly subscribers has declined from approximately 205,000 as of June 30, 1994; to 201,000 as of June 30, 1995; to 192,000 monthly subscribers as of June 30, 1996; and to 156,000 as of June 30, 1997.

As pay-per-view became available, the PEI focused on this option. The retail price of pay-per-view programming is determined by cable system operators but typically ranges from $3.95 to $6.95 for a program. Fee structures vary, but the Entertainment division generally receives 40 percent of the retail price.

As of 1996, about 11.6 million cable households could purchase PEI programming on a monthly basis; 4.9 million could purchase only on a pay-per-view basis; and 6.5 million could purchase either. As of June 1997, Playboy TV was available to 11.2 million cable addressable households, a 1 percent decrease compared to 1996. Households with 24-hour availability decreased 1.1 million to 2.8 million during the fiscal year ended June 1997. PEI has contracts with 16 of the 20 largest multiple system operators (MSOs). Once the MSOs' arrangements have been made, household cable access

Cable Household Growth

	Total Cable Households	Addressable Households	Cable Addressable Households
June 30, 1995	60,350	23,450	10,600
June 30, 1996	62,850	26,400	11,300
June 30, 1997	64,000	29,350	11,200
December 31, 1997	64,500	30,700	11,600
Compound Annual Growth Rate (July 1, 1994– December 31, 1997)	2.7%	11.4%	3.7%

depends upon PEI's negotiations with cable affiliates. As of 1997, not all of the cable affiliates were offering Playboy Television.

The "going-forward rules" announced in fiscal 1995 by the Federal Communications Commission and the Telecommunications Act of 1996 negatively impacted cable access. In May 1997, the law took effect, requiring cable operators to either use additional blocking technology to ensure that the audio and video portions do not bleed or to restrict the period during which the programming is transmitted. In August 1997, Hefner said, "Preliminary results from the cable systems carrying Playboy TV confirm our estimates of an approximately $5 million annual revenue decline as a result of Section 505 of the Telecommunications Act." PEI is challenging Section 505 and is seeking a permanent injunction against its enforcement.

Via encrypted signal, PEI provides Playboy Television to home satellite dish owners. As of June 30 in 1997, 1996, 1995, and 1994, Playboy Television was available on a monthly subscription and/or pay-per-view basis to approximately 6.3 million, 4.9 million, 3.3 million and 1.9 million DTH viewers, respectively. The DTH market historically has shown higher buy rates than traditional cable markets have.

Playboy Television is the only adult service available in all three U.S. satellite businesses—SirecTV, PrimeStar, and AlphStar.

In July 1995, PEI introduced a second pay television channel, AdulTVision. This channel is offered principally on a pay-per-view basis and is available to about 5.3 million cable and satellite homes. The channel experienced an operating loss for fiscal 1996. With a 135 percent increase in revenue for fiscal 1997, a profit was reported.

Domestic Home Video

Following the style, quality, and focus of *Playboy* magazine, Playboy home videos are distributed via video, music, and other retail stores. In the fiscal year ended June 1996, PEI introduced 14 new videos with eight of these entering the top five on the sales chart. The video *The Best of Pamela Anderson* had exceptionally high sales. In the fiscal year ended June 1997, lower net sales of new releases was experienced partially due to no releases featuring celebrities. Domestic home video revenues was positively impacted in 1996 and 1997 by the 3-year distribution agreement with Uni Distribution Corporation. This agreement expires 1998.

International Television and Home Video

In 1995, PEI entered its first international television programming agreement with a joint venture agreement with Flextch plc to offer Playboy Television to the United Kingdom. After the first year, Playboy Television in England lost an estimated £2.1 million for failing to attract enough viewers. In an attempt to maximize appeal, Playboy Television shifted its target audience from couples to males and changed advertising agencies. Recognizing that the international markets differ in the restrictions of pornography (for instance, Britain and Ireland have stricter restrictions than Germany, Portugal, and Russia), Playboy Television varies its programs with the different countries. PEI plans to launch networks in Spain, Portugal, and South Korea in 1998.

PEI has expanded the international network by entering into exclusive multiyear multiproduct output agreements with overseas pay television distributors. Licenses differ, but PEI typically receives license fees for programming and for use of the logo and trademark. PEI has equity agreements with the channels in Great Britain, Japan, and Latin America.

Separate distribution agreements allow for U.S. video products, with dubbing or subtitling into local languages, to be sold in 48 countries in South America, Europe, Australia, Asia, and Africa. High sales in South Korea contribute to higher revenue and profit contribution.

Since 1979, the PEI marketing department has sponsored a Playboy jazz festival in Los Angeles. The event offers advertisers sponsorship and advertising opportunities through the festival program, free community concerts, jazz clinics, film forums, and a national public radio broadcast. Additionally, PEI has a five-city jazz tour with concerts in Denver; Atlanta; Washington, D.C.; Detroit; and Chicago. Each city offers Playboy advertisers promotional opportunities.

Casino Gambling

In fiscal 1996, PEI announced plans to reenter the casino gaming business with a consortium of Greek investors. PEI and the consortium received a 12-year exclusive gaming license on the island of Rhodes. PEI will own less than 20 percent and will receive licensing royalties on revenues of the hotel/casino. Gaming was profitable for PEI during the 1970s and 1980s. PEI intends to create an entertaining experience for adults and is exploring other locations for casinos.

Catalog

PEI's catalog business includes the *Playboy Critics' Choice Video, Collector's Choice Music,* and Playboy catalogs. PEI's catalog revenue increased 6 percent to $76.2 million in the fiscal year ended June 1997 from $71.7 million in 1996. Operating income declined 8 percent in the fiscal year ended June 1997 to $4.8 million. The cost of paper, postage, expanded mailings to prospective customers, and the one-time costs associated with moving to a new headquarters negatively impacted income.

The Playboy catalog offers fashions and accessories, home videos, gifts, calendars, art products, back issues of the magazine, and newsstand specials. The Playboy catalog is published three times annually and has an on-line version, Playboy Store. Web site sales equaled almost 9 percent of print catalog sales in the fiscal year ended June 1997 with orders from 40 countries, and 80 percent of those orders were made to first-time buyers. Plans for 1998 include expanding this interactive catalog.

Critics' Choice Video is one of the largest-circulation catalogs of prerecorded videocassettes serving the sell-through market, the fastest-growing segment of the video industry. The catalog features more than 2,000 titles, including major theatrical releases and special interest videos. The *Critic's Choice Video* catalog generates the most sales of all PEI's videos at deeply discounted prices, a competitive pricing strategy which was introduced in the second quarter of 1996 and which has continued. To differentiate itself from the mass marketers, PEI explores acquisition opportunities such as *Time Warner Viewer's Edge.* A Web site and an oversized catalog featuring 10,000 in-stock videos is planned for 1998. In the fiscal year ended June 1997, the 900 telephone service was converted to a toll-free 800 service and offers information on approximately 70,000 videos not listed in the catalogs.

The 1994 introduction of a music catalog, *Collectors' Choice Music,* generated revenues surpassing the industry norm and produced a profit for the year. This catalog features more than 1,500 titles in CD and cassette formats from a wide assortment of classical, pop, rock, rhythm and blues, jazz, and country music. It also offers an extensive library of hard-to-find recordings. This catalog is published three times annually and a Web site (www.ccmusic.com) features more than 30,000 titles.

For the *Critics's Choice Video* and *Collectors' Choice Music* catalogs, customers can inquire by telephone about the availability of any film or musical recording. All of the catalogs offer unique merchandise, such as exclusive releases that have higher profit margins. For 1997, the Catalog Group Continuous Quality Improvement Program developed improvements for processing returns and for creating a more customer-friendly phone ordering system.

Product Marketing

"We've also moved from being a passive licensing company to a more active brand management company," said Hefner in 1996.

The name *Playboy* and the rabbit head design are among the most recognized trademarks in the world. The company leverages the power of its brand recognition, design expertise, art collection, and customer base to develop and market apparel, accessories, and other products to consumers worldwide.

The value of the trademark, copyrights, and intellectual properties were protected with the judgment in a copyright infringement case between PEI and Starware Publishing Corporation. Starware thought that the images were public domain when they were downloaded. The court awarded PEI $20,000 for each image and $50,000 for trademark violations.

In fiscal 1996, approximately 75 percent of the royalties earned from licensing PEI's trademarks were derived from licensees in Asia, 10 percent from England, and 10 percent from the United States. To expand the Asia market, PEI established sales and distribution offices throughout China. In 1997, PEI began to distribute products in the 6,500 7-Eleven stores in Japan.

Special Editions, Ltd., (SEL) markets original art, limited edition prints, posters, and art products. To increase revenue, SEL is shifting from direct sales to licensing. For 1997, SEL expanded its product line to include bathroom accessories, umbrellas, and lapel pins. The trademarks and service marks of Sarah Coventry, Inc., are owned by PEI.

The Playboy and Playmate product lines consist primarily of men's and women's clothing, accessories, watches, jewelry, fragrances, small leather goods, stationery, and home fashions. In 1997, to capture the cigar craze, PEI formed an agreement with a world's top cigar producer, Consolidated Cigar Corporation. These products are marketed in North America, Europe, Asia, Australia, and South America, primarily through mass merchants and other retail outlets, by licensees under exclusive license agreements that authorize the manufacture, sale, and distribution of products in a designated territory. Royalties are based on a fixed or variable percentage of the licensee's total new sales, in some cases against a guaranteed minimum.

IMAGE

For consumers of PEI products, popularity of the Playboy name stems from its association with fun, sexiness, and quality. Aspirational, adventurous, and romantic are a few of the many characteristics that define the PEI customer. Overseas, the Playboy logo benefits from its strong identification with Western freedoms, American life-style, and a desire for "the good life." Domestically, the image of PEI contains visions of a mansion with 60 employees and $3.9 million in costs, as a place of beautiful models, parties, and nude photo shoots. However, as a result of the protests against pornography suppliers lodged by church, womens', and sex crime prevention groups in congressional hearings, many retailers won't carry *Playboy, Hustler,* and other such publications to avoid customer base erosion.

PUBLIC AFFAIRS

PEI established the Playboy Foundation in 1965 to provide financial support for organizations dedicated to protect civil rights and civil liberties, promote First Amendment rights and freedom of expression, and support research and education in human sexuality and reproductive rights. In fiscal 1996, the foundation awarded nearly $313,000 in grants and in-kind contributions to organizations working in these areas. *Playboy* magazine provides more than $783,000 in free advertising space to nonprofit groups such as the Nature Conservancy, National Veterans Legal Services Program, and Special Olympics. A basic tenet of The Playboy Philosophy is that the First Amendment is the keystone to all other rights. PEI established the Hugh M. Hefner First Amendment Awards in 1979 to honor individuals who have championed freedom of expression.

Another important component of PEI's philosophy is that the company has a responsibility to give back to its communities—"doing well by doing good." In 1985, the foundation established the Neighborhood Relations Boards, composed of nonexecutive employees who award grants to small- and medium-sized organizations that serve traditionally disadvantaged people. PEI actively encourages its employees to get involved in their communities. The foundation's Matching Gift program matches employee contributions to nonprofit organizations dollar for dollar (up to $350 per employee per year), and the Time Match program provides $2 for each hour that an employee volunteers for a nonprofit group.

THE FUTURE

PEI wants to capitalize on technology to expand revenue opportunities. A database of 12 million names has been developed and PEI wants to use it to develop new products, cross-sell products, and to attract advertisers. Should PEI create nonexclusive partnerships with technology companies? How can PEI better utilize Internet opportunities?

PEI also wants to continue its international expansion. Which new countries should be targeted by PEI for entry?

Which of PEI's four divisions should receive the greatest emphasis and resources? Should the company focus more on publishing, licensing, television, telephone, catalogs, videos, or artwork? Should the company focus on global markets or domestic markets? Should PEI focus on interactive media or direct marketing?

How can PEI improve its corporate image among critics who contend that its business is obscene, pornographic, and unethical? Do you agree with these critics?

Should PEI make a major acquisition in the near future to begin publishing other magazines, such as *Cosmopolitan*, *Woman's Day*, *Ladies' Home Journal*, *Gentleman's Quarterly*, or *Esquire*? Which of these magazines feasibly could be acquired? What should be PEI's offering price?

There are rumors that PEI itself could be the target of an acquisition soon. How much is the company worth today?

Develop a five-year strategic plan for PEI.

Athletic Footwear—Industry Note

Although a mature industry, the athletic footwear segment posted moderate growth in 1996. Sales reached $14.1 billion at the retail level, up 6 percent from 1995. At wholesale, sales totaled $9 billion, representing a 9 percent increase from 1995. Although retail dollar spending rose, unit sales remained flat, indicating rising prices in this segment. After several years of growth at more modest price points, premium-priced products outpaced the market in 1996. In fact, sales of shoes priced at more than $100 surged 34 percent in 1996, leading all footwear categories. However, premium-priced athletic shoes still account for just more than 1 percent of all footwear sales.

The growth of cross-training shoes has stunted the overall growth of the athletic footwear segment. This lets consumers purchase fewer pairs of sneakers because these cross-trainers can be used for tennis, running, aerobics, and several other activities. Sales in this segment increased 17 percent in 1996, following a 15 percent rise in 1995.

New product introductions should help rejuvenate growth in athletic footwear, as many high-profile designers—such as Tommy Hilfiger, Ralph Lauren, Calvin Klein, Donna Karan, and Nautica—all plan to launch athletic footwear lines in 1997 and early 1998. In February 1997, Tommy Hilfiger, with a license to Stride Rite, successfully launched an athletic shoe line targeted at leisure wearers. Ralph Lauren's line is expected to be introduced in the spring of 1998; it will focus on performance features. The Sporting Goods Manufacturers Association projects the wholesale athletic footwear segment to grow 8 percent in 1997 to approximately $9.7 billion.

BRANDED U.S. ATHLETIC FOOTWEAR MARKET

(in millions of dollars)

Brand	Sales			Market Share (%)		
	1994	1995	1996	1994	1995	1996
1. Nike	2,017	2,529	3,261	30.8	37.4	43.4
2. Reebok	1,410	1,405	1,210	21.5	20.8	16.1
3. Fila	291	380	575	4.4	5.6	7.7
4. Adidas	331	355	390	5.1	5.2	5.2
5. Keds	305	245	200	4.7	3.6	2.7
6. New Balance	130	151	200	2.0	2.2	2.7
7. Converse	298	208	190	4.6	3.1	2.5
8. Airwalk	102	126	158	1.6	1.9	2.1
9. LA. Gear	296	193	140	4.5	2.9	1.9
10. ASICS	187	122	131	2.9	1.8	1.7

Source: Sporting Goods Intelligence.

Source: Adapted from *Industry Survey* by permission of Standard & Poor's, a division of the McGraw-Hill Companies. *Standard & Poor's,* "Apparel & Footwear," *Industry Survey* (August 21, 1997): 3–5.

■ **The big get bigger.** While overall sales have grown modestly, sales of the biggest athletic footwear manufacturers have grown more rapidly as the industry has become more concentrated. In 1996, the strongest brand performances were Adidas, Fila, New Balance, and Nike. Each company saw its sales increase at least 20 percent worldwide, far outpacing the rest of the market. The athletic segment received a big boost in 1996 from the Olympic Games in Atlanta as most of the big brands made their presence known with promotions and endorsements.

The top four branded U.S. athletic footwear companies (Nike, Reebok, Fila, and Adidas) accounted for 72.4 percent of the market in 1996, up from 69 percent in 1995. In the spring of 1997, several companies reported signs of slowing growth in demand. However, we believe this may only be temporary, as "Olympic fever" has ebbed. Demand should pick up later in the year with the introduction of several new products, such as Fila's Grant Hill IV. These additions should spur continued growth through 1998, although it perhaps won't be as strong as the growth experienced in 1995 and 1996.

■ **Follow the leader.** Nike has been the clear industry leader for several years and now holds a commanding 43.4 percent market share. Many of the industry's trends—and the competition's success—depend on Nike's success and strategy. For example, in the spring of 1997, when Nike's sales showed signs of slowing, stock prices of the entire footwear sector (both manufacturers and retailers) fell sharply. As Nike goes, so goes the industry.

In addition, while some companies have trouble selling their products at premium price points, Nike will test the pricing boundaries this summer with the release of its $180 Penny Hardaway FoamPosit basketball shoe. This launch's success may determine the reaction of Nike's competitors, many of whom recently attempted to lower their prices in order to stimulate demand.

With the U.S. market maturing, Nike recently shifted its focus toward international markets. To make its presence felt internationally, Nike is trying to conquer the market for soccer, the world's most popular sport. The company recently spent $200 million to sponsor the Brazil national soccer team. Along with its other huge endorsement contracts—most notably basketball superstar Michael Jordan and golf phenomenon Tiger Woods—this gives Nike a competitive advantage in its industry, leaving its competitors scrambling to match its success.

■ **A league of their own.** Perhaps the most intriguing trend that should drive future growth in athletic footwear is the recent rise of women's sports. The role of women in athletics continues to grow by leaps and bounds. According to American Sports Data, Inc., a sports market research firm in Hartsdale, New York, 41 million females aged six and older frequently participated in some sport, fitness, or outdoor activity in 1996, representing a 30 percent increase from 1987. In addition, female participation in both team and individual sports rose 26 percent over the same period. More importantly, this growth seems to be accelerating; it should continue into 1998.

The excellent performances of the U.S. women's teams in soccer, gymnastics, and basketball at the 1996 Summer Olympics fueled more interest. The formation of the new Women's National Basketball Association (WNBA), officially sponsored by the National Basketball Association, will accelerate this trend. This new league's success certainly is not guaranteed; others have tried and failed. However, it has significant corporate sponsors (including General Motors, Sears, Coca-Cola, Anheuser-Busch, and, of course, Nike); a major television deal; and a huge marketing campaign. The American Basketball League, a rival to the WNBA, began its operations in 1996, but with considerably less media and corporate attention. In addition to sports leagues, magazines such as *Women's Sports Illustrated* have begun to surface.

To be successful, manufacturers need to design products that truly increase performance and make women's sports participants more comfortable. The first step is determining what women need and want. According to surveys, women have basically the same needs as men when it comes to sports footwear: They're more concerned with comfort and performance than fashion. Women won't buy products just because they're made for women; they're looking for the best performance product.

Once again, Nike is on the forefront of this trend, with the introduction of its women's basketball shoe, Air Swoopes, named after basketball player Sheryl Swoopes. Women's products currently account for just over 20 percent of Nike's U.S. sales, but the company believes that share could exceed 40 percent within five years. Other brands have followed Nike's lead with new product offerings and player endorsements.

Lady Footlocker currently is the only national women's athletic footwear chain. However, with the current explosive growth in its market, we expect competition soon.

Nike, Inc.—1998

M. Jill Austin

www.nike.com
stock symbol NKE

The athletic shoe industry and Nike (503-671-6453) have grown dramatically in the last several years, but some analysts predict that athletic shoe sales will increase only slightly in the next few years. Consumer trend watchers believe that the youth market now demands brands such as Tiva sandals and Doc Marten's work boots instead of branded athletic shoes. In addition, there is some evidence that consumers are purchasing casual shoes and moderately priced athletic shoes instead of branded athletic shoes. As a result, competition will become more intense. According to Philip Knight, CEO of Nike, Inc., global sales will ensure the continued success of Nike:

> If we do become truly global, we'll be a much better company and have a serious advantage on the competition. When that day comes, we will have an educated, integrated work force on the ground in every country, sharing a clear and current understanding with other Nike-ites worldwide. A retailer in Singapore or Shanghai will be as important as one in New York.

Nike sells athletic shoes, accessories, sports equipment, and clothing for men, women, and children. The company's products are sold to approximately 19,700 retail accounts in the United States, including department stores, footwear stores, and sporting goods stores. Nike also sells it products through independent distributors, licensees, and subsidiaries in 110 countries around the world. Approximately 31,000 international retail outlets sell Nike products. Nike operates a total of 33 distribution centers in Asia, Canada, Latin America, Europe, and Australia.

Nike, Inc., operates 84 retail stores in the United States, including 39 factory outlets, 31 Cole Haan stores, five employee-only stores, and nine NikeTown stores. The company's nine NikeTown stores are located in Portland, Oregon; Chicago; Atlanta, Georgia; New York City; Seattle; Boston; Los Angeles; San Francisco; and Orange County, California. NikeTown stores contain sports memorabilia, educational exhibits, basketball goals for use by customers, and Nike products. Nike does not plan to become a major retail force, but believes that these stores help educate consumers about the breadth of Nike products.

The Nike name and logo have such high consumer awareness that the company no longer includes the Nike name on its products; the "swoosh" logo is all that it uses. The evolution of the Nike, Inc., logo is shown in Exhibit 1. Knight hopes to maintain his company's competitive advantage through the 1990s by marketing athletic shoes, clothing, sports equipment, and accessories around the world and by making a few acquisitions that will strengthen the company's core businesses. Knight has challenged

---

EXHIBIT 1: The Evolution of the Nike Logo

| 1964 | 1971 | 1978 | 1985 | 1995 |

Source: Nike, Inc.

Nike employees to help the company become a $12 billion company by the year 2000. If Nike is to live up to its namesake, "the goddess of victory," Knight and his team will have to stay ahead of competitors in the marathon race for dominance in the athletic shoe industry.

HISTORY

Knight, a dedicated long-distance runner, developed a plan to make low-cost running shoes in Japan and to sell them in the United States as part of his work toward an M.B.A. degree at Stanford University. After graduation, Knight teamed up with Bill Bowerman, his former track coach at the University of Oregon, to make his plan a reality. Because Bowerman's hobby was making handcrafted lightweight running shoes, his expertise was very valuable to entrepreneur Knight. In 1964, Bowerman and Knight each contributed $500 and started Blue Ribbon Sports. Knight negotiated with a Japanese athletic shoe manufacturer, Onitsuka Tiger Co., to manufacture the shoes that Bowerman had designed. Blue Ribbon Sports shoes gained a cult following among serious runners because Knight distributed the shoes, called Tigers, at track meets.

In 1971, Blue Ribbon Sports received a trademark on its Swoosh logo and Knight and Bowerman introduced the brand name Nike that same year. Blue Ribbon Sports parted ways with Onitsuka Tiger in 1972 and contracted with other Asian manufacturers to produce the company's shoes. Blue Ribbon Sports officially changed its name to Nike in 1978. During the late 1970s and early 1980s, Nike researchers used their technological expertise to develop several types of athletic shoes which revolutionized the industry. The company became more successful every year with profits increasing steadily.

In 1984, after five years of 44 percent annual growth, Nike missed the emerging market for aerobic shoes. The company had concentrated its efforts on an unsuccessful line of casual shoes. Reebok took the lead in the athletic shoe industry when it began selling large numbers of its fashion-oriented aerobic shoes to women.

Nike stock prices decreased by 60 percent in 1984, and between 1983 and 1985, profits declined by 80 percent. Some analysts suggested that the decreases in stock prices and profits were the fault of managers who became complacent after the firm's early success. During the early 1980s, Knight focused his attention on international operations and left daily decision making to other managers. Other top managers

Goal
12 Billion
by
2000

switched from job to job, which led to poor coordination between the design, marketing, and production efforts of the company. An excess inventory of 22 million pairs of shoes in 1985 forced Nike to cut prices to reduce its inventory and release some of its manufacturing capacity in the Far East. Much of that capacity was picked up by Reebok. After Nike lost the top spot in the industry, it had to lay off 350 employees in 1986.

Knight took several steps to reestablish the dominance of Nike in the industry. He created small management teams to focus on narrow markets. He also put a stop to the job changing of top executives. New advertising campaigns were developed that stressed the technology of the shoes. Focus groups were used to determine customers' athletic shoe needs. The company also began to add touches of fashion, including color, to its many new products. All of these changes helped Nike regain a slight leadership position in the industry in 1988.

In 1988, Nike purchased New Hampshire–based Cole Haan for $64 million. The subsidiary has several brand names including Country, Sporting, Classic, Bragano, and Cole Haan. A new footwear category, Tensile Air was introduced in 1990. The Tensile Air is a dress shoe with the Nike air-cushioning system. Nike's casual footwear business grew 16 percent the following year, led by Cole Haan. Nike also acquired the Cole Haan Accessories Company in 1990, a distributor of high-quality belts, braces, and small leather goods. In 1990, Nike opened its first retail store called NikeTown in Portland, Oregon. Nike acquired Tetra Plastics, the manufacturer of the plastic film in Nike's air sole shoes, in 1991 for $37.5 million. Nike purchased a cap-making company called Sports Specialties in 1993. In 1994, Nike's Outdoor division added a new shoe called "Air Mada" and the Nike sport sandal became the top seller in the market. In 1995, Nike acquired Canstar Sports, Inc., the world's largest hockey equipment maker, for $395 million. Canstar, now called Bauer, Inc., manufactures in-line roller skates, ice skates, and blades; protective gear; hockey sticks; and hockey jerseys.

The company continued to make progress in the international market in the early 1990s. Nike passed the $1 billion sales mark in Europe in 1993, but international sales decreased in 1994 by 15 percent to $927.3 million. Sales reached $178 million in the Asia/ Pacific Region in 1993 and increased by 59 percent to $283.4 million in 1994. By 1997, sales in the Asia/Pacific Region were $1.25 billion and sales in Europe were $1.8 billion. Nike's total international sales increased by 27 percent to $1.7 billion in 1995, and by 49 percent to almost $3.5 billion in 1997. For fiscal year 1997, total revenues at Nike increased by 42 percent to nearly $9.2 billion and net income increased by 44 percent to $795.8 million. Knight believes the international market segment is where most future growth for Nike, Inc., will occur. Domestic and international revenues for Nike are shown in Exhibit 2.

COMPETITION

The athletic shoe industry grew $2 billion to almost $10 billion at wholesale from 1985 to 1993. However, toward the end of 1993, industry leaders began seeing reductions in orders. Nike reported a 3.6 percent sales decrease for fiscal year 1994 (ending May 31, 1994) and Reebok had a sales decline of 4.6 percent for 1993. However, sales at both companies improved the following year with Nike at nearly $4.8 billion and Reebok at nearly $3.3 billion. By 1996, Nike (nearly $6.5 billion) had almost twice the sales of Reebok (nearly $3.5 billion).

EXHIBIT 2: Domestic and International Revenues for Nike, Inc.

(dollars in millions)	1997	1996	1995
U.S. Footwear	3,770.6	2,772.5	2,309.4
U.S. Apparel	1,431.6	842.5	423.9
Total U.S.	5,201.6	3,615.0	2,733.3
International Footwear	2,391.0	1,682.3	1,244.3
International Apparel	1,089.8	651.4	472.7
Total International	3,480.8	2,333.7	1,717.0
Other Brands	504.1	521.9	310.6
Total Nike	9,186.5	6,470.6	4,760.9

Source: www.freeedgar.com

Nike and Reebok are the two major sellers of athletic shoes in the United States and in global markets. The U.S. market share for Nike and Reebok is 40 percent and 16 percent, respectively. This represents a significant change from 1994 when Nike market share was 30 percent and Reebok market share was 21 percent.

Some of the other two dozen competitors in the industry include Adidas; New Balance; K-Swiss; Fila; Asics; L.A. Gear; Keds; Converse; and British Knights. The most intense competition has been among the two industry leaders Nike and Reebok. The secret to success for these two competitors is that they contract the manufacturing of shoes to low-wage factories in Far Eastern countries. This strategy allows each company to concentrate on marketing, image, and research and development.

Reebok International, Ltd.

Reebok designs and develops athletic shoes and clothing. The company sells 175 models of shoes in 450 different color combinations for aerobics, cycling, volleyball, tennis, fitness, running, basketball, soccer, and walking and for children's footwear. The company recently diversified its offerings to include more types of casual shoes, sports clothing, and other types of athletic shoes. Some examples of these products include Reebok Outdoor shoes, City Trails (women's hiking shoes), F-16 (men's leather casual shoes), and BlackTop basketball shoes. The company owns a health club in New York City and produces exercise programs for cable television and educational films for schools. During 1992, Reebok opened retail stores called Reebok Station in Boston; Santa Monica, California; and New York City. In addition, the company owns 100 factory outlet stores and four Rockport stores.

In the early 1980s, Reebok sold aerobic shoes primarily to women, but by the mid-1980s, large numbers of men were buying Reebok shoes. Men now account for about 45 percent of Reebok sales. The company's shoes are designed to make a fashion statement and are marketed to build on this image. Reebok CEO Paul Fireman believes that "Reebok is basically about freedom of expression."

Reebok took the lead in revenues from Nike in 1987, but Nike regained it in 1990. About this time, CEO Fireman began using Nike's best strategies to compete with Nike. First, Reebok entered the Nike-dominated men's team sports market. Reebok developed a series of marketing campaigns around sports stars in an effort to increase its

EXHIBIT 3:   Selected Financial Information for Reebok

(dollars in millions except per share amount)	1996	1995
Gross Revenue	$3,478.6	$3,481.5
Net Income	139.0	209.7
Long-term Debt	854.1	254.2
Net Worth	381.2	895.3
Net Profit Margin (%)	4.0	6.0
Earnings Per Share	2.00	2.65

Source: www.freeedgar.com.

market share. Some of the sports personalities who signed marketing contracts with Reebok include Shaquille O'Neal (estimated $15 million for five years), Michael Chang, and Greg Norman. Reebok net income decreased by 11 percent in 1996, but rebounded somewhat in 1997 due to Reebok's new Ultralite and DMX2000 shoe lines. Reebok also has been successful in selling its products to international markets. In 1996, international operations were 42 percent of total sales. Selected financial information for Reebok is shown in Exhibit 3.

International Competition

Competition is increasing in Europe. Adidas, a German company, is the number-one seller of athletic shoes in Europe. Nike and Reebok are second and third, respectively. Some analysts believe that doing well in the European market is crucial to the continued success of companies in the athletic shoe industry. Nike sales in Europe, Asia, Canada, and Latin America increased to $2.3 billion in 1996 and to almost $3.5 billion in 1997. Reebok's total international revenues were almost $1.5 billion in 1996. Both Nike and Reebok hope to continue increasing their revenues in the international retail market.

Adidas, the top European-owned competitor, will be fighting to maintain its share of the market for athletic shoes. Founded in 1948, Adidas outfitted such sports stars as Al Oerter (1956 Olympics) and Kareem Abdul-Jabbar (NBA). Some of the sports stars who currently have endorsement contracts with Adidas include Steffi Graff, Kobe Bryant, Donovan Bailey, and Tracy McGrady. Disputes in this family-owned company threatened the success of the company after it gained a 70 percent market share in the United States. One brother became so angry he founded the rival company, Puma. Subsequently, Adidas's U.S. market share dropped from 70 percent to 2 percent. The family sold the company for $320 million in 1989. The new owner became involved in other issues and neglected the company. By the time the current CEO took over in 1993, Adidas was losing about $100 million per year. When asked what he knew about the athletic shoe industry, CEO Robert Louis-Dreyfus replied, "All I did was borrow what Nike and Reebok were doing. It was there for everybody to see." For example, Adidas beat Nike in a $100 million deal that allows the New York Yankees to wear the Adidas logo on team uniforms. Nike CEO Knight said, "It's becoming a very, very competitive business, and we take the threat from both Adidas and Reebok very seriously."

In the last five years, Adidas has recovered from significant financial problems and will be an important competitor in the critical European market. Several recent decisions should provide momentum for the company: Manufacturing was moved from high-cost European factories, management was downsized, and a significant amount of

EXHIBIT 4:   Selected Financial Information for Adidas

(DM in millions)	1996	1995
Net Sales	$4,709	$3,500
Operating Income	360	243
Net Income	314	245
Inventories	1,088	843
Receivables and Other		
Current Assets	818	563
Total Current Assets	1,990	1,447
Total Assets	2,456	1,777
Working Capital	555	343
Total Borrowings, Net	340	407
Total Liabilities	1,506	1,180
Shareholders' Equity	904	577

Source: www.freeedgar.com

money was allocated for marketing expenses. Adidas net income in U.S. dollars was $184 million in 1996. Steve Wynn, the president of Adidas U.S. division, said, "We have huge market share to gain in the United States. We're very focused on what we need to do right now. In 1998, you're going to see some very big improvements in our sales." Selected financial information for Adidas is shown in Exhibit 4.

CHANGES IN THE ATHLETIC SHOE INDUSTRY

The athletic shoe industry has changed tremendously since "sneakers" were invented. In 1873, the sneaker was developed from India rubber and canvas material. Dunlop became the dominant seller of sneakers in 1938. Keds and PF Fliers dominated the children's market in the 1960s. Adult standard brands such as Adidas and Converse were well accepted by sports enthusiasts for years but in the late 1960s, the industry started to change. Nike entered the market, life-styles began to change, and companies began to contract for manufacturing rather than invest in plants and equipment to manufacture their own products.

Changes in Life-style

Since the late 1970s, athletic shoe buyers have become much more brand-conscious. In addition, athletic shoes have replaced other casual shoes as the primary street shoe for many consumers. Less than 10 percent of the people who wear athletic shoes buy them for the sport for which they were intended. Some trend watchers believe that athletic shoe companies will have some difficulty selling their products to the youth market in the next few years because of young people's shift to work boots and sandals.

Large numbers of baby boomers are interested in staying fit and healthy and have changed their diet and increased their physical activity. However, of adults aged 25 to 55, only one in five exercises as much as twice a week. In the 1980s, people became obsessed with fitness, and by 1991, sales in the fitness equipment industry exceeded $30 billion. Presently only 10 percent of the U.S. adult population gets the surgeon general's recommended amount of exercise (20 minutes of vigorous exercise, three times per week).

The traditional age of those purchasing athletic shoes is changing. The number of people aged 45 and older is expected to increase by 18 million during the 1990s. The ages from 45 to 54 generally are the peak earning and spending years for adults. As more baby boomers move into this age group, they will demand more attention from consumer goods companies. More girls are involved in sports today than ever before. It is estimated that only one in 27 girls was actively involved in sports in 1971, but the number is one in three girls in 1997. These two disparate age groups present tremendous opportunities for athletic shoe makers.

Contract Manufacturing

Many athletic shoe companies contract with manufacturing companies in the Far East to produce their shoes. Countries that manufacture shoes for Nike; L.A. Gear; and Reebok include South Korea, Taiwan, China, Thailand, Malaysia, and Indonesia. The athletic shoe companies develop design specifications for the shoes in the United States and then send them to the factories to be produced.

Even with recent changes in exchange rates in these countries and tariffs of 8.5 percent to 37.5 percent, it is still cost-effective to have shoes made overseas. A shoe that costs approximately $14 to make will be sold wholesale for $25 to $30.

Among the advantages of foreign contract manufacturing are that no capital investment is required and the athletic shoe companies can operate with little long-term debt. Labor costs and benefits in the Far East are less expensive, child labor laws are nonexistent, and there are no labor unions. Yet there are several disadvantages to contract manufacturing. Some countries, such as Korea, which have produced large numbers of athletic shoes in the past, are developing the expertise and contacts to begin producing sophisticated electronics products and do not wish to continue producing athletic shoes. Some additional disadvantages of overseas production include labor unrest, political unrest, delays caused by shipping, and unreliability of quota systems (embargoes).

Legal Changes

The global marketplace has many legal restrictions that athletic shoe manufacturers must consider. The North American Free Trade Agreement (NAFTA) and the General Agreement on Tariffs and Trade (GATT) both provide better access to world trade. Companies operating in Mexico and Canada will benefit from reduced import/export duties outlined in the NAFTA agreement. GATT provides commitments for access to international markets and tariff reductions on many products. The European Union (EU) increased the power of European countries to control imports and also provided a single, coordinated market rather than many different markets in Europe. In 1995, at the request of European footwear manufacturers, the EU imposed antidumping duties on athletic footwear imported to the EU from China and Indonesia. In 1995, the United States restored diplomatic relations with Vietnam, a potential high-volume producer of athletic shoes. In June 1997, President Clinton awarded most favored nation status (MFN) to China and Congress supported the president's decision. Because China is a major source of footwear production, it is important for athletic shoe companies that MFN status for China continues. These legal changes, along with country-specific laws, will provide for many opportunities and some threats for international business operations.

NIKE INTERNAL FACTORS

Six primary internal factors for Nike include research and development, marketing, distribution, social responsibility, management style/culture, and financial returns.

Research and Development

Nike spent approximately $73.2 million on product research, development, and evaluation in 1997. R & D in the athletic shoe industry is largely design innovation and does not require a large investment in equipment. In 1980, the company formed the Nike Sport Research Laboratory (NSRL), which uses video cameras and traction-testing devices in research in children's foot morphology, "turf toe," and apparel aerodynamics. In addition, NSRL evaluates ideas developed by the Advanced Product Engineering (APE) group. APE is involved in long-term product development. Shoes are created for five years in the future. This group developed cross-training shoes, the Nike Footbridge stability device, inflatable fit systems, and the Nike 180 air-cushioning system. Researchers make shoe molds in the model shop and evaluate the shoe tension and adhesion in the testing lab.

Nike continues to rely on developments to differentiate its products from competitors. The company presently sells approximately 300 models of athletic shoes in 900 styles for 25 different sports including basketball, tennis, cross-training, baseball, hiking, cycling, cheerleading, water sports, golf, and soccer. Exhibit 5 indicates the major developments of Nike design from 1964 to the present.

Marketing

Because Nike does not actually produce shoes, the main focus of the company is creating and marketing the products. Nike positions its products as high-performance shoes. The general target market for Nike athletic shoes is males and females between eighteen and thirty-four years old. Products are revamped continually. Shoe types that sell year-round are revamped quarterly. On average, Nike begins distribution of one new shoe style every single day.

Nike advertises its products in a variety of ways and targets its ads to specific groups or types of people. Advertising expenditures were $978.2 million in 1997. The company continues to spend advertising dollars on TV ads during professional and college sports events, prime-time programs, and late-night programs. Prime-time ads are intended to reach a broad range of adults and late-night TV advertising is geared toward younger adults. Print is also very important in advertising Nike products. Print media such as *Sports Illustrated, People, Runner's World, Glamour, Self, Tennis, Money, Bicycling,* and *Weight Watchers* advertise Nike products. During the 1996 Olympics, Nike spent approximately $30 million for advertising and the sponsorship of individual athletes and teams. Nike Park, set up near the Olympic stadium, provided basketball shooting centers and a Nike store. The 1998 Winter Olympics in Japan provided Nike with a unique opportunity to gain market share in international markets and the 2000 Summer Olympics in Australia are expected to do the same. Nike has been successful in its attempts to build loyalty by licensing Nike gear to college sports teams. Approximately 50 percent of professional baseball players wear Nike shoes. Most top college football teams wear Nike shoes and 33 top college basketball and football teams wear Nike clothing. In 1997, Nike outfitted eight National Football League teams.

EXHIBIT 5: Nike, Inc., Technological Developments

Date	Development	Purpose
1964	Lightweight shoe	Reduces weight for better performance
1975	"Waffle" sole shoe	High traction, light weight
1979	Nike Air Sole	Air-cushioning system that lessens the impact of the heel on pavement to prevent injuries
1983	The Destiny	First running shoe for children
1987	Visible Air line (10 shoe models)	Gas-cushioning system designed to prevent injury (window allows consumer to see the air bag)
1987	Cross-training shoe	Suitable for several different types of sports including running, baseball, and aerobics
1988	Footbridge Stability Device	Material added to shoes to improve fit and stability of wear
1989	Air Pressure (pump shoe with a separate device to pump up the shoe)	Provides a tighter fit
1990	Air 180	Air cushioning in the heel and front of the shoe; heel cushion is 50 percent larger than previous models (consumer has a 180 degree view of the heel air bag)
	Built-in pump shoe	Provides a tighter fit, with the convenience of a built-in pump
1991	Huarache Fit	Combination of neoprene and lycra spandex that provides runners with a form-fitting, supportive, and lightweight shoe
1993	Air Max Cushioning	Provides 30 percent more cushioning
mid-1990s	Foamposite	Material that ensures no rough spots in the shoe
mid-1990s	Zoom Air Cushioning	Material that is used in midsole to absorb pounding without taking away stability or speed

Source: Nike, Inc.

Some of the celebrity spokespersons for Nike include Michael Jordan, Andre Agassi, Charles Barkley, Troy Aikman, Pete Sampras, Deion Sanders, Carl Lewis, Scottie Pippen, Cheryl Swoopes, and Tiger Woods. Michael Jordan's Nike contract has, to date, been the most lucrative endorsement contract for a professional sports player. Pete Sampras signed a reported $18 million, five-year deal in 1994 to promote Nike tennis wear. It is estimated that the company spends approximately $100 million per year on endorsement fees for sports stars. Exhibit 6 shows some of Nike's advertising campaigns.

International marketing efforts continue. Nike has operations in 110 countries on six continents. Knight said, "There's a pretty strong recognition that we'll be bigger in a couple of years outside the United States than inside." Nike is already number one in the overall footwear market in Spain, France, Belgium, Holland, Luxembourg, Finland, Italy, and the United Kingdom. Some of the new markets that are now being pursued include Chile, Peru, Bolivia, India, Mexico, South Africa, and several Eastern European

EXHIBIT 6: Nike, Inc., Advertisements

Theme	Visual Image
"Hangtime"	Air Jordan basketball shoe promotion featuring Michael Jordan and Spike Lee.
"Revolution"	Beatles song "Revolution" played and images of sports stars were shown.
"Bo Knows"	Illustrates the range of Nike shoes (20 different sport categories).
"Just Do It"	Shows people from many walks of life exercising in Nike shoes.
"Multiple Bo's"	Bo Jackson meets Sonny Bono and fourteen other Bo Jacksons who represent different sports.
"Announcers"	TV sports announcers discuss Nike shoe performance and breadth of product line. (Super Bowl XXIV)
"Rock and Roll Tennis"	Andre Agassi shows his tennis skills in rock video format.
"Instant Karma"	Print campaign targeted to women.
"I Am Not a Role Model"	Charles Barkley says sports stars are not role models, but parents should be role models.
"Aerospace Jordan"	Cartoon characters Bugs Bunny, Looney Tunes bad guy Marvin the Martian, and Michael Jordan travel to Mars. (Super Bowl XXVII)
"Running," "Go Slow," "Aerobics"	A series of three TV ads for women that stress comfort and developing a sense of self.
"The Wall"	A soccer ad that ran during the 1994 World Cup. The ad showed paintings on a wall of famous soccer players come to life.
"Air Swoopes"	An ad with Sheryl Swoopes introducing the Air Swoopes basketball shoe and announcing Nike sponsorship of the women's U.S. Olympic basketball team.
"Search and Destroy"	Olympic athletes are warriors and doing whatever is necessary to win. In the end, a runner vomits and a bloody mouthpiece sails across the Nike logo.
"Broad-Minded"	An advertisement with Tiger Woods. The statement made is "We're not just canvas and leather shoes. We're big—and broad-minded."
"Nike vs. Evil"	Eight soccer stars are pitted in a fight against the devil.

Source: Nike, Inc.

countries. In fiscal 1997, the revenues from Europe, Asia/Pacific, and Latin America/Canada were 20 percent, 13.6 percent, and 6 percent respectively of Nike's total revenues. Exhibit 7 shows the company's assets, operating income, and revenues in international and domestic markets.

Distribution

Nike opened a 630,000-square-foot apparel distribution center in Memphis in 1992 that is called Nike Next Day. Footwear is distributed from centers in Greenland, New Hampshire; Beaverton, Oregon; Wilsonville, Oregon; and Memphis, Tennessee. Nike apparel is shipped from Memphis and Greenville, North Carolina. Sports Specialty products are distributed from Irvine, California, and Cole Haan and Bauer products are distributed from Greenland, New Hampshire. The company operates a "Futures" ordering program that allows retailers to order up to six months in advance with a guarantee they will receive their orders within a certain time period and at a certain price. However, retailers can receive apparel orders the next day if they place their orders by 7:00 P.M. the day before.

EXHIBIT 7: Nike, Inc., Operations by Geographic Area

(in thousands)	Year Ended May 31,		
	1997	1996	1995
Revenues from unrelated entities:			
United States	$5,529,132	$3,964,662	$2,997,864
Europe	1,833,722	1,334,340	980,444
Asia/Pacific	1,245,217	735,094	515,652
Latin America/Canada and other	578,468	436,529	266,874
	9,186,539	6,470,625	4,760,834
Total revenues:			
United States	5,531,957	3,972,815	3,004,260
Europe	1,833,722	1,341,738	985,882
Asia/Pacific	1,245,217	735,094	515,652
Latin America/Canada and other	730,046	503,591	298,323
Less inter-geographic revenues	(154,403)	(82,613)	(43,283)
	9,186,539	6,470,625	4,760,834
Operating income:			
United States	968,993	697,094	501,685
Europe	170,612	145,722	113,800
Asia/Pacific	174,997	123,585	64,168
Latin America/Canada and other	71,342	55,851	37,721
Less corporate, interest and other income (expense) and eliminations	(90,722)	(123,162)	(67,510)
	1,295,222	899,090	649,864
Assets:			
United States	2,994,017	2,371,991	1,659,522
Europe	1,272,918	941,522	771,752
Asia/Pacific	665,776	386,485	306,390
Latin America/Canada and other	328,681	188,839	209,389
Total identifiable assets	5,261,392	3,888,837	2,947,053
Corporate cash and eliminations	99,815	62,791	195,692
Total assets	5,361,207	3,951,628	3,142,745

Source: www.freeedgar.com

Knight worries that the brand will lose its image as a superior sports shoe if international marketing is not monitored carefully. Nike purchased the distribution operations of many of its worldwide distributors in an attempt to control marketing of Nike products. Some of these "Nike-owned" countries include Singapore, Taiwan, Hong Kong, New Zealand, Korea, Japan, and Malaysia. Nike recently consolidated the operations of 31 distribution centers in the European Union into one distribution center in Belgium.

Social Responsibility

Nike received some criticism in the past few years regarding the contracting of manufacturing of its shoes. Some consumers are concerned about the exploitative practices of managers in some Asian countries. A few years ago, it was reported that 6,700 Indonesian employees worked in a plant with 100-degree temperatures and suffocating paint and glue smells. To emphasize its concerns about companies that manufacture products overseas, the Made in America Foundation urged consumers to send their "old, dirty, smelly, worn-out Nikes" to the Nike CEO. Another recent complaint was that a Nike

---

EXHIBIT 8:   Nike, Inc., Code of Conduct

Nike, Inc., is committed to the promotion of best practices and continuous improvement in:

- Occupational health and safety, compensation, hours of work, and benefits.
- Minimizing our impact on the environment.
- Management practices that recognize the dignity of the individual, the rights of the free association and collective bargaining, and the right to a workplace free of harassment, abuse, and/or corporal punishment.
- The principle that decisions on hiring, salary, benefits, advancement, termination, or retirement are based solely on the ability of an individual to do his/her job.

Source: "Nike Puts Its Code of Conduct in the Pocket of Workers," *PR Newswire* (September 17, 1997).

manager struck a Vietnamese production worker with a Nike shoe. According to President and Chief Operating Officer Thomas Clark, "since 1994, Nike has had independent auditors test factory compliance with our Code of Conduct." The Nike Code of Conduct is shown in Exhibit 8.

Former UN Ambassador Andrew Young was asked by Nike in 1997 to review labor practices in Third World factories. Ambassador Young reported that Nike was "no worse" than many other companies operating abroad and he found "no pattern of systematic abuses." Young recommended that Nike develop ways to ensure that employees have the right to file grievances and have an outside board of observers monitor the company's compliance with human rights standards. The company set up a labor practices department in 1996. Nike's labor initiatives in factories producing its products are recounted in Exhibit 9.

Nike developed several programs that show the company's concern for social responsibility issues. For example, Nike and the Boys & Girls Clubs of America began a program called the Kids Movement in 1993 to promote fitness among young people. Nike also provides funds for the Children's Television Workshop program *Ghostwriter*, a show that promotes literacy. The "Just Do It" corporate giving program provides funding for programs for young people who live in the inner cities. Nike P.L.A.Y. (Participate in the Lives of America's Youth) encourages youth to be active in sports by providing facilities and sports opportunities for youth.

N.E.A.T. (Nike Environmental Action Team) was formed in 1993. The purpose of this group is to pursue environmental initiatives by recycling old athletic shoes and by reusing them in new products. Nike recovers 100,000 pairs of shoes each month in its "Reuse-A-Shoe" program for recycling. Nike demonstrates its concern for the environment by using the recycled materials in the soles of its new shoes and providing recycled material for sports fields/tracks. Every year, Nike recycles 5 million pounds of solid wastes. Exhibit 10 shows the life of a Nike product and Nike's environmental impact.

Another issue of concern Nike has dealt with in the past few years is the pressure to hire more minority workers in leadership positions at Nike. Operation PUSH (a Chicago civil rights organization) organized a boycott of Nike in 1990 in an attempt to force the company to increase its hiring of minorities.

EXHIBIT 9:   Nike, Inc., Labor Initiatives

In response to Ambassador Young's recommendations on international labor issues, Nike:

- adopted a termination policy for contractors who violate the code of conduct.
- developed penalties for violations of the code of conduct.
- implemented training for managers.
- established training programs for U.S. managers who will work in international markets.

Examples of Nike's leadership on labor in international production facilities include the following:

- 1992—The first code of conduct in the sporting goods industry (dealing with international labor issues) was developed by Nike.
- 1994 (and following)—Independent auditors test factory compliance with the Nike code of conduct.
- 1996—A labor practices department was established by Nike. More than 1,000 production personnel in Nike contract factories work each day to monitor labor conditions.
- 1996—Nike joined President Clinton's Coalition on Fair Labor Practices. The company agreed to follow the Apparel Industry Partnership's Workplace Code of Conduct and to "help the industry eradicate sweatshops in the United States and abroad."
- 1997—Ambassador Andrew Young conducted an independent assessment of Nike labor practices.
- 1997—Nike issued a card (printed in 11 languages) to managers and workers in international production facilities.
- 1997—Eight weeks of training in 16 Asian cities was completed to reinforce the Nike code of conduct.
- 1997—Comprehension of the code was added to the corporate audit manual as a criteria for judgment.

Source: "Nike Puts Its Code of Conduct in the Pocket of Workers," *PR Newswire* (September 17, 1997).

EXHIBIT 10:   The Life of a Nike Product—Environmental Impact

1. **Research and Development**—Nike evaluates raw materials to reduce environmental impact (recycled materials, durable materials).
2. **Manufacturing**—The goal is to maximize product quality and minimize waste. The company does not dump the overflow of rubber from molds; instead they grate it into powder and mix it with new rubber so it can be used. Dangerous chemicals used in the production process have been replaced with cleaner, water-based products.
3. **Retail**—Packaging has been reduced, no glues are used in the boxes, and box content includes recycled materials.
4. **Consumers**—Nike collects used shoes through its Reuse-A-Shoe program. This reduces the number of shoes in landfills.
5. **Down-Cycling**—Old athletic shoes are ground up into three materials: lights, foam, and rubber. These materials are made into new products such as carpet padding, equestrian trails, basketball courts, running tracks, and tennis courts.

Source: Nike, Inc., Consumer Affairs, 1997.

Management Style/Culture

Knight created a strong culture at Nike, Inc., based on company loyalty and locker-room camaraderie. Most corporate employees are health-conscious young people. Forty-one percent of corporate employees are under the age of thirty. Knight trusts these employees to "Just Do It." He sometimes drops out of sight for months at a time and then reemerges with some new approach for the company. His philosophy is "Play by the rules, but be ferocious. . . . It's all right to be Goliath, but always act like David." The 74-acre corporate campus of Nike, Inc., provides a sense of the culture: It has wooded areas, running trails, a lake, and a fitness center. Knight believes that people should find a "sense of peace at work."

In 1994, Tom Clark took over as president of Nike, Inc. Clark had worked at Nike for 14 years when he was appointed by Knight to replace Richard Donahue. The characteristics that should allow Clark to be successful as president include his collaborative management style, his concern about keeping lines of communication open, and his desire to facilitate decision making. Some critics suggest that Donahue, in his four years as president, added management layers that slowed the company's reaction time. Clark said, "Collaboration is in our genes, but the days when a few decision makers can get together in the hall are over."

In an effort to involve employees in decisions that affect them, employees were asked to participate in the creation of LifeTrek, a benefit and compensation program. The categories of LifeTrek include keeping healthy, taking care of family, making life easier, taking time off, protecting people, managing money, "worktrek," and pay/performance/teamwork. Some of the specific aspects of LifeTrek include:

1. earning up to $150 in credits for living a healthy life-style (exercising, wearing a seat belt, not smoking)
2. a variety of health insurance options
3. a child education savings account (Nike matches 25 percent of savings up to $250 per year) and a Nike scholarship fund ($500 to $3,000 annually)
4. on-site fitness center
5. paid time-off bank (replaces vacation/sick leave policies). Employees accrue a certain number of days per year and can use these days for vacation, sickness, or personal days.
6. insurance for disability and life insurance
7. dependent care spending account matched by Nike for employees who earn less than $60,000 per year (Nike pays up to 30 percent of this cost)
8. profit sharing and retirement accounts
9. training and tuition assistance

These attempts by Nike to provide for all areas of life demonstrate a culture of caring for the whole life of employees.

Financial Returns

Nike, Inc., income statements and balance sheets for 1991 to 1997 are provided in Exhibits 11 and 12. These statements reveal increases for sales, income, assets, and shareholders' equity. Consolidated statements of Nike shareholders' equity are shown in Exhibit 13.

EXHIBIT 11:   Nike, Inc., Consolidated Statement of Income

(dollars in millions except per share data)	1997	1996	1995
Revenues	$9,186.5	$6,470.6	$4,760.8
Costs and Expenses:			
Costs of Sales	5,503.0	3,906.7	2,865.3
Selling and Administrative Expenses	2,303.7	1,588.6	1,209.8
Interest Expense	52.3	39.5	24.2
Other (income)/expense, net	32.3	36.7	11.7
	7,891.3	5,571.5	4,111.0
Income Before Income Taxes	1,295.2	899.1	649.9
Income Taxes	499.4	345.9	250.2
Net Income	795.8	553.2	399.7
Net Income per Common Share	2.68	3.77	5.44

Source: www.freeedgar.com

EXHIBIT 12:   Nike, Inc., Consolidated Balance Sheet

(dollars in millions)	1997	1996	1995
Assets			
Current Assets:			
Case and Equivalents	$ 445.4	$ 262.1	$ 216.1
Accounts Receivable, less allowance for doubtful accounts	1,754.1	1,346.1	1,053.2
Inventory	1,338.6	931.2	629.7
Deferred Income Taxes	135.7	93.1	72.7
Prepaid Expenses	157.1	94.4	74.2
Total Current Assets	3,830.9	2,726.9	2,045.9
Property, Plant, and Equipment	922.4	643.5	554.9
Identifiable Intangible Assets and Goodwill	464.2	474.8	495.9
Other Assets	143.7	106.4	46.0
Total Assets	5,361.2	3,951.6	3,142.7
Liabilities and Shareholders' Equity			
Current Liabilities:			
Current Portion of Long-Term Debt	2.2	7.3	31.9
Notes Payable	553.2	445.1	397.1
Accounts Payable	687.1	455.0	297.7
Accrued Liabilities	570.5	480.4	345.2
Income Taxes Payable	53.9	79.3	35.6
Total Current Liabilities	1,866.9	1,467.1	1,107.5
Long-Term Debt	296.0	9.5	10.6
Non-current Deferred Income Tax	42.1	1.9	17.8
Other Non-current Liabilities	0	41.4	41.9

continued

EXHIBIT 12: *continued*

(dollars in millions)	1997	1996	1995
Redeemable Preferred Stock	.3	.3	.3
Shareholder's Equity:			
Common Stock at Stated Value:			
Class A Convertible	.2	.2	.2
Class B Convertible	2.7	2.7	2.7
Capital in Excess of Stated Value	210.6	154.8	122.4
Foreign Currency Transaction Adjustments	(31.3)	(16.5)	1.6
Retained Earnings	2,973.7	2,290.2	1,837.8
Total Shareholders' Equity	3,155.8	2,431.4	1,964.7
Total Liabilities and Shareholders' Equity	5,361.2	3,951.6	3,142.7

Source: www.freeedgar.com

EXHIBIT 13: Nike, Inc., Consolidated Statement of Shareholders' Equity

(dollars in millions)

Date	Common Stock Class A	Class B	Capital in Excess of Stated Value	Foreign Currency Transaction Adjustment	Retained Earnings	Total
1990	.17	2.7	78.6	1.0	701.7	784.2
1991	.16	2.7	84.7	(4.4)	949.7	1,032.8
1992	.16	2.7	93.8	.7	1,234.3	1,331.7
1993	.16	2.7	108.5	(7.8)	1,542.5	1,646.0
1994	.16	2.7	108.3	(15.1)	1,644.9	1,740.9
1995	.16	2.7	122.4	1.6	1,837.8	1,964.7
1996	.16	2.7	154.8	(16.5)	2,290.2	2,431.4
1997	.15	2.7	210.7	(31.3)	2,973.7	3,155.8

Source: www.freeedgar.com

THE FUTURE

Even with limited growth and intense competition in the U.S. athletic shoe market, Nike is expected to perform well in the future. With its innovative marketing and advertising, it should remain a force in the industry. However, there is concern in the industry that consumers will become less brand-loyal and begin purchasing moderately priced athletic shoes at discount stores instead of the higher-priced Nike products. "Brands are powerful when they communicate underlying value," said Knight. "In our industry, and probably in other consumer products, consumers will not trade down if there is value and quality in the high end."

There is a tremendous opportunity in the international market for Nike. In the United States, there are 4 people for every pair of Nikes; France has 11; Japan has 50; and China has 11,821. The greatest potential growth area for Nike is in the overseas market.

Consider the following questions regarding Nike's future:

1. Is Nike trying to supply products for too many sports? Should Nike narrow its product line in athletic shoes?
2. What types of acquisitions would you suggest to Knight for Nike?
3. Should Nike begin producing some of its own products?
4. Is Nike taking the correct approach in marketing its shoes internationally?
5. What changes in product and advertising should the company pursue to appeal to the aging baby boomers? To young people?
6. How can Nike maintain a competitive advantage over Reebok?

E. L. Nickell Company—1998

Henry Beam

Thomas Carey

Shelby Nickell

The E. L. Nickell Company (616-435-2475) of Constantine, Michigan, is a privately held specialty producer of pressure vessels and shell and tube heat exchangers for the industrial refrigeration industry. E. L. Nickell Company's sales were $4.85 million in 1995, $6.10 million in 1996, and $7.1 million in 1997. The increase in sales is attributed largely to increased production of stainless steel products, especially heat exchangers. The company employs 42 full-time and three part-time workers.

HISTORY

The E. L. Nickell Company traces its origins back to World War II, when Elwood L. (E. L.) Nickell worked in Chicago for the H. A. Phillips Company, owned by his brother-in-law, Harry Phillips. The H. A. Phillips Company held patents on float valves used in commercial refrigeration systems. These were the first valves mounted internally within a refrigeration pressure vessel and are still in high demand. A pressure vessel is a special type of hollow container that is designed to hold a gas or liquid up to a specified high pressure, such as 100 pounds per square inch.

Looking ahead to the war's end, Harry could see that large cold storage distribution centers for food products soon would replace the small, in-house refrigeration units individual grocery stores traditionally used. In 1944, Harry asked E. L. whether he was interested in starting a pressure vessel business which would be the exclusive supplier of pressure vessels for his float valve business. E. L. quickly decided that being in his own business beat punching a time clock for someone else. He chose the village of Constantine, Michigan, as the location for the new business because it was situated midway between Chicago and Detroit and near major highways. Constantine is only 90 miles from Gary, Indiana, where U.S. Steel has a large facility that makes pressure vessel-quality (PVQ) steel.

Production initially took place in the basement of E. L.'s home. A few years later, the company moved into an old ice house. Ironically, the house had been built to supply ice for home refrigeration. Over the years, this facility was expanded several times. Assembly of float valves for the H. A. Phillips Company was phased out as the demand for pressure vessels grew.

This case was prepared by Professors Henry Beam and Thomas Carey of Western Michigan University and by Shelby Nickell, CEO of E. L. Nickell Company as a basis for class discussion. It is not intended to illustrate either effective or ineffective handling of an administrative situation. Copyright © 1999 by Prentice Hall, Inc. ISBN 0-13-011199-6.

Although E. L. was considered by those who knew him to be an artist as a welder, he lacked interest in the business end of the company. As a result, the company's fortunes rose and fell until his death in 1962. E. L.'s wife, Lyda, recalled that her attorney advised her to sell the business, saying, "You have no management experience, you're not an engineer, and it's a very technical business." Instead of selling, Lyda decided to run the company herself. She became president of a company with 16 employees and annual sales of $206,000.

With the exception of a woman who worked in bookkeeping, all the employees were men. For the first few months, Lyda spent half her time on her feet, learning the business from the shop floor. On weekends, she studied technical books. At first, she told herself she was saving the business for her teenage sons, Bruce and Shelby. "But as the years went by, I began to realize that I was doing the business just as much for me as I was for them—because I enjoyed the challenge of it," she recalled.

Although her formal education ended in the eighth grade, Lyda understood people; it was a talent which helped her direct the company. Reflecting on her decision to run the firm, Lyda said:

> I had no formal training, but I knew I could manage people. I knew I could do it. I knew I would have to hire the technical help, but I don't think I knew enough to be scared. The key to running a successful business is having competent employees. I have been very fortunate to have had that, and I always try to treat them the way I would want to be treated.

Over the next 30 years, the company became a leading supplier of pressure vessels for industrial refrigeration plants. In 1989, in recognition of her achievements, Lyda was chosen by the State of Michigan as one of its top 50 businesswomen.

Her older son, Bruce, served as general manager from 1972 to 1977, when he left the firm over philosophical differences with his mother. Lyda said, "When children join a family firm, there's too many times your heart does the talking instead of your head. You have to be really tough." Bruce founded and became part-owner of Zorn Industries in Elkhart, Indiana, a manufacturer of underground storage tanks. After holding a variety of jobs in different parts of the country, Shelby, Lyda's younger son, joined the family business in 1980 and became general manager. In 1986, Lyda hired her brother, George Parker, as general manager. Shelby was promoted to executive vice-president and took an extended leave of absence to finish his bachelor's degree in business administration as a nontraditional student at Western Michigan University, located about 30 miles to the north in Kalamazoo, Michigan. After receiving his B.B.A. degree in 1993, Shelby entered the M.B.A. program at Western Michigan University. He hoped his graduate studies would help him address some of the challenges faced by the company. Shelby enjoyed his studies and was an excellent student. He also liked to talk about the E. L. Nickell Company and chide his professors that very little of what they taught actually applied to his business or to small or custom businesses in general. "None of the textbooks I've read yet relate to our company," he told them. "The material in them just doesn't apply."

THE INDUSTRY

Annual sales in the industrial refrigeration industry were about $500 million in 1997, with pressure vessels accounting for about 12 percent of that amount. Eighty percent of all pressure vessels are made by large engineering firms for exclusive use in refrigeration systems they design and build themselves. Their primary customers are the military, large domestic project contractors, and the U.S. and foreign governments. The remaining 20 percent are made by small firms, such as E. L. Nickell Company, which produce only pressure vessels. These small firms sold virtually all of their vessels to small- to medium-sized contractors who included them in refrigeration systems. E. L. Nickell Company has supplied pressure vessels for large food processors (Kraft Foods), beverage producers (Coors Brewing), and cities (the City of North Falls, for its municipal ice skating rink). It built a few vessels for chemical and pharmaceutical firms (Dow Chemical Company, Pharmacia, and Upjohn Company). In the summer of 1996, E. L. Nickell Company supplied two receivers, each 10 feet in diameter and 38 feet long, to the City of Chicago for use in its multibuilding air conditioning system. This is the world's largest refrigeration system, supplying 117,500 tons of refrigeration. The system is designed to reduce the peak daytime use of electricity in Chicago by making ice at night and blowing air over the ice during the day to provide cooling to multiple downtown buildings.

E. L. Nickell's Product Lines

Pressure vessels accounted for 81 percent of units produced in 1997, while the remaining 19 percent were shell and tube heat exchangers. In a shell and tube heat exchanger, hundreds of small tubes are located within the outer pressure shell to facilitate heat transfer. The small tubes often are made of copper. Even though copper is more expensive than steel or aluminum, it is a better conductor of heat. Each unit is custom built to individual customer specifications and constructed according to strict national code standards. The company's state-of-the-art computer-aided design (CAD) capability permits it to meet performance requirements with exacting engineering standards. The design process involved both engineers and drafting personnel.

E. L. Nickell's products should not be confused with the propane tanks that are a familiar sight along rural roads. Those are standardized tanks, as are the air tanks that are used in gas stations. They represent the mass production market for pressure vessels. E. L. Nickell only makes custom pressure vessels for industrial use. According to Shelby, "Unless you look inside a cold storage warehouse or the engine room of an indoor ice skating rink, you probably will never see an E. L. Nickell tank, which uses thousands of tons of refrigeration. By way of comparison, most home refrigerators require somewhere around one-third of a ton." E. L. Nickell pressure vessels and heat exchangers usually are covered with between 4 and 6 inches of insulation, which means unless a person was on a job site during installation, he or she wouldn't be able to see the pressure vessels, anyway.

The insulation serves two purposes. First, it helps hold down operating costs because the ambient temperature in an engine room usually is quite warm. Second, it prevents external corrosion. Without insulation, the warm engine room air condenses on the cool surface of pressure vessels and causes external corrosion. Over a period of years, such corrosion could reduce the original thickness of the steel, making for an extremely dangerous situation.

It takes up to a year to design and construct a complete commercial refrigeration system. Pressure vessels are one of the last items ordered—sometimes, they aren't ordered until construction has started on the job site. This works to E. L. Nickell's advantage because it can fill custom orders quickly, working around the clock when necessary. Sometimes the pressure vessels are installed first and a building is erected around them. Installation can be expensive, involving heavy-duty cranes to lift the pressure vessels into place and as many as 100 workers on the construction site.

Once installed, an E. L. Nickell pressure vessel typically remains in place for decades without service. The tanks do not corrode internally because ammonia, the refrigerant used in industrial refrigeration systems, is noncorrosive in both liquid and gas forms. A refrigerant is a fluid that absorbs heat by evaporating at a low temperature and pressure and gives up that heat by condensing at a higher temperature and pressure. Because the tanks are made of thick steel to meet stringent pressure and temperature specifications, they, too, need little maintenance other than periodic painting. If maintenance is needed, it is preferable to do it on site due to the high cost of removing the vessel and bringing it back to Constantine.

COMPETITION

Other specialty manufacturers are located in the East, the Southwest, and on the West Coast. E. L. Nickell Company, Refrigeration Valve Specialties of Texas, and Precision Heat Exchanger of North Carolina are the only specialty manufacturers that produce both pressure vessels and heat exchangers. E. L. Nickell is the oldest and most experienced of the three firms. Even though direct competition occurs between these firms, freight costs based on distance shipped can become a significant factor in the total cost to the customer. Thus, each manufacturer has a price advantage in its own region.

Shipping costs primarily are a function of distance rather than of weight. If a small vessel has to be shipped a long distance, shipping costs could exceed the cost to make the vessel itself. As Shelby notes, "We once lost a bid for a small vessel in Seattle, Washington, to a West Coast firm. We bid $900 to make the vessel, $200 less than the other bidder, but freight to Seattle, Washington, would have been $2,800!"

Shipping is a much smaller percent of the total cost for a large pressure vessel or heat exchanger. For example, a $100,000 heat exchanger delivered to Seattle would have about $3,000 in freight costs. Thus, E. L. Nickell is able to be competitive on bids for large vessels and heat exchangers from all over the country. When all else is equal among the three firms, delivery time usually becomes the controlling factor for getting an order. Shelby notes that "in about 25 percent of order placements, customers did not even request a price quotation. They simply sent in orders with a requested delivery date."

INTERNAL ENVIRONMENT

Facilities

All products are manufactured in three company-owned facilities in Constantine. The main plant has grown substantially from E. L.'s original workshop. Occupying 30,000 square feet, the steel and concrete structure contains under a common roof separate areas for fabrication, assembly, painting, and testing. Sales, engineering, and administration are located in offices at the front of the main plant. The last major addition to the main plant was made in 1991 to facilitate construction and shipping of larger vessels. It cost $1 million and added a space 65 feet wide by 200 feet long. Loading is accomplished by driving a flat bed truck into the facility and lifting the completed pressure vessel onto it with an overhead crane.

The second building, the machine shop, is located about two blocks away. It, too, is made out of steel and concrete blocks. A massive vertical turret lathe and Blanchard surface grinder located near the entrance are used to finish heat exchanger tube sheets. Shelby purchased the vertical turret lathe secondhand many years ago for 25 cents a pound. In the rear, a computerized machining center performs precision machining operations, such as drilling holes in the tube sheets used in tube and shell heat exchangers.

The third building, a long, narrow storage facility, is located across the access road from the machine shop. Made of wood, it is too much of a fire hazard to use for fabrication operations such as flame cutting and welding. Miscellaneous items are stored here, including the heads (end caps) for pressure vessels, heat exchanger tubes, and delivery vehicles. According to Shelby, "The heads make the best outdoor barbecue grills. A lot of our employees have one at home. Usually they weld legs onto them." Heads range in weight from 25 pounds for small vessels to 7,500 pounds for the largest vessels.

The present site offers little room for expansion. It is bound by a railroad on the north side and by a designated wetlands area on the south and east sides. The Michigan Department of Natural Resources will not permit E. L. Nickell to build on designated wetlands areas. Limited expansion is possible to the west, but would take some of the area now used for a parking lot.

Production Processes

Small and large vessels are produced differently. Small vessels are cut to length from steel pipe and have an outside diameter ranging from 4 inches to 24 inches. The ends are then beveled to the proper angle for welding. In the final step, a head is attached to each end to form the completed pressure vessel.

Large vessels have a diameter greater than 24 inches. The largest vessel made by the company is 14 feet in diameter and 40 feet long. To make a large vessel, sheets of flat steel are rolled into circular forms according to the grain of the steel and welded together. Very large vessels require a dozen or more sheets of steel. A completed vessel (which can weigh up to 50 tons) can be moved only with the assistance of an overhead crane. Prices on the largest vessels range from $200,000 to $300,000, plus shipping.

All vessels have external and internal fixtures attached to them. Internal fixtures include pipes, baffles, and other specialized items, depending on the specific application. External fixtures include ladders, support saddles, insulation standoffs, the stainless steel code nameplate, and sight glasses for viewing the inside of the pressure vessel while in operation. The plant is full of portable arc welding equipment. In addition, a state-of-the-art Lincoln Electric submerged-arc welder, which cost $350,000, is located permanently in the center of the plant. In submerged-arc welding, the electric arc and the weld puddle are submerged under a pile of flux and move precisely along the seam to be welded. Before welding can start, the pressure vessel must be positioned horizontally on rollers which are affixed to a track in the building floor. Once on the rollers, the vessel can be rotated and moved forward and backward so all seams can be welded without moving the submerged-arc welder. The submerged-arc welder is idle about half the time because it takes about as much time to position and prepare a vessel for welding as it does to do the welding. Exhibit 1 shows the firm's 1997 staffing.

Dale Jones, the production manager, has been with the company for over 30 years. Shelby spoke of him with great respect:

EXHIBIT 1:   E. L. Nickell Company, Summary of Staffing, Fall 1997

Main Plant

ASME Certified Welders and Steel Fabricators (21)
Production Manager
Quality Control Manager
Quality Control Assistant
Purchasing Manager
Engineers (2)
Designers (CAD Operators)(3)
Internal Sales Personnel (3)
Bookkeeper
Clerical Personnel (2)
Administrative Assistant
Chief Operations Manager
CEO and President

Machine Shop

Machining Manager
Computer Numerical Control (CNC) Operators (3)

Source: E. L. Nickell Company.

Dale has probably forgotten more about what it takes to fabricate vessels and get shipments out the door than most people will ever know. Somehow, every month, he manages to produce and ship whatever our customers need, and on time. I've asked him if he could put his methods down in writing so that when he retires, those who will follow him could gain from his experience and knowledge. He has agreed that some of the methods he uses would be beneficial for his replacement, but that he is not sure himself, at least not on a conscious level, why he does what he does, given certain conditions. Sometimes, when I walk through the plant, I will ask him why something is being done in a particular way. He'll respond, "I don't know. It's just the way it needs to be done."

Purchasing and Inventory

Purchasing and inventory are handled on a manual basis. Stewart Nickell, the purchasing director and Shelby's first cousin, does the pricing and costing almost totally on a subjective basis. The company stocks materials in raw form.

High-grade PVQ steel plate is stocked in 8-foot widths in several lengths up to 20 feet long, and in several thicknesses between 3/16 of an inch and 4 inches. To make a pressure vessel, the plate is thermally cut to the proper length and width so it can be rolled into circles of given diameter to make up the shells for a particular vessel. The heads are purchased in the completed shape for each diameter and thickness of vessel. The company stocks several hundred different diameters and thicknesses of heads, ranging from 4 inches in diameter and 3/16 inch thick to 10 feet in diameter and 1 1/4 inches thick.

Pipe is stocked in several lengths and thicknesses for each diameter. Individual pieces are cut from these basic lengths of pipe for use as the vessel shell. Pipe is also cut to various lengths for use as connections which are fitted into the pressure vessel's

519

shell. These connections are used as the inlets and outlets which permit the ammonia refrigerant to enter and leave the vessel once it is installed in a refrigeration system. Two other very important connections are the drain, which allows for drainage in the event of a maintenance shutdown, and the pressure relief valve, which relieves pressure on the vessel in the event of accidental overpressurization.

Code Compliance

E. L. Nickell complies with the American Society of Mechanical Engineers (ASME) Code for production of its pressure vessels and with the Tubular Exchanger Manufacturers' Association for production of heat exchangers. The function of the ASME's Boiler and Pressure Vessel Committee is "to establish rules of safety governing the design, fabrication, and inspection during construction of boilers and pressure vessels, and to interpret those rules when questions arise regarding their intent." The National Board of Boiler and Pressure Vessel Inspections (NATL'B), formed in 1919, enforces the ASME Code rules.

The ASME Code contained 11 sections, each of which is applicable to particular aspects of the design and construction of pressure vessels. The E. L. Nickell Company complies with Section VIII, Division I, which covers the design and construction of pressure vessels for nonlethal, nonnuclear, and not-for-human-inhabitance uses. Not-for-human-inhabitance sites include diving bells and submarines. A company wishing to build pressure vessels in compliance with a particular section of the code has to start with that section and write its own code compliance document called the Main Document. The Main Document references the specific paragraphs in the ASME Code it intends to comply with for design calculations, material specifications, fabrication methods, inspection level, and testing criteria. It needs to identify what job positions are going to perform each type of activity relative to building pressure vessels.

Authorization to produce ASME Code pressure vessels is issued on a temporary basis for a period of three years. A complete review of an application to build pressure vessels costs about $12,000 to $15,000, all paid by the company, even if the review was unsuccessful. Shelby comments, "I can't verify any of them, but I've heard stories of people wanting to go into the ASME Codes pressure vessel business investing upward of a million dollars prior to their initial authorization review and then failing the review." The authorization review process must be repeated every three years. Even for a first-time review, documentation must be complete and facilities for fabrication in existence before NATL'B will accept an application for authorization review. E. L. Nickell also complies with other codes, including the American Welding Society Code, the Pressure Piping Code, the American Piping Institute Code, and the International Institute of Ammonia Refrigeration Standards. All welds are carefully inspected by an authorized inspector. Welds that don't meet specifications must be rewelded until they do.

Few firms attempt entry into the business because of the high capital requirements prior to the first review for authorization to produce code products. An attempt at entry occurs about once every three or four years. Most new entrants failed in their first year of operation because they entered the business on the basis of a single customer who couldn't provide enough volume to cover fixed costs.

Marketing

Although marketing is an important function in most companies, it receives almost no attention at E. L. Nickell Company. Shelby says industrial refrigeration is such a small niche market that many of the tools typically used in marketing do not apply.

We don't advertise. I don't know where we would advertise if we did. We already know almost everyone in the business, and potential new customers usually have heard about us. It's a small industry and everyone knows everyone. The E. L. Nickell Company has never performed any marketing or developed a market database. As a result, our name recognition and reputation have been created by "word of mouth" and longevity. Historically, sales personnel have not performed the function of selling. This condition is based on the fact that only on very rare occasions do we sell to the end user. By the time we become involved with providing a pressure vessel, it has already been or is being sold by a contractor or engineering firm to an end user. This means our sales personnel primarily perform a function of estimating price and delivery. Most of our orders are generated through manufacturers' representatives.

In 1997, eight regional manufacturers' representatives gave the E. L. Nickell Company's products national coverage. E. L. Nickell sells its products only in the United States. However, in the past few years, an increasing number of units have been sold and delivered to large contractors in the United States who include E. L. Nickell units in complete systems they sell and install abroad. According to Shelby, "We don't keep track of units sold for use abroad, but I guess it must be getting close to 20 percent of our business now." E. L. Nickell recently built a special heat exchanger with titanium tubes for use in a geothermal electricity generation facility in Lithuania and sold pressure vessels for use in a refrigeration facility in Poland.

Finance and Personnel

Lyda Nickell, 75, owns a majority of the shares. The remaining shares are divided between Shelby, 50, and other family members. Lyda's goal is to see sales reach $10 million in the next few years. "When we get up there, then I'll retire," she says. Fictional financial data for E. L. Nickell Company is given in Exhibits 2 and 3 only for the purpose of class discussion.

The company's personnel policies reflect Lyda's lifelong belief that people are the company's most important resource. Over the last 30 years, the company's annual turnover rate has averaged less than 1 percent. Most of E. L. Nickell's employees work there because they like the autonomy of action and the nonrepetitive nature of custom fabricating. Employees are given the parts and the construction drawing. Then they

---

EXHIBIT 2:   E. L. Nickell Company Income Statements[a]

	1996	1997
Sales	$6,102,000	$7,098,000
Cost of Goods Sold	4,765,000	5,603,000
Selling and Administrative	483,000	569,000
Gross income	854,000	926,000
Taxes	427,000	463,000
Net Income	427,000	463,000

[a] Being closely held, E.L. Nickell Company does not provide financial information to the general public. The data in these statements are fictional and are provided by the casewriters to facilitate classroom discussion of the case.

EXHIBIT 3:   E. L. Nickell Company Balance Sheets[a]

	1996	1997
Assets		
Current Assets		
Cash and equivalents	$ 180,000	$ 185,000
Accounts receivable	553,000	685,000
Inventory	330,000	425,000
Work in progress	775,000	885,000
Deferred Income Taxes	4,560	5,670
Property, Plant and Equipment (net of depreciation)	3,480,000	3,260,000
	5,322,560	5,445,670
Liabilities and Shareholders' Equity		
Accounts payable	653,000	390,750
Income taxes payable	35,700	24,060
Long-term debt	325,000	292,000
Deferred taxes	25,000	28,000
Shareholders' equity	4,283,860	4,710,860
	5,322,560	5,445,670

[a]Being closely held, E. L. Nickell Company does not provide financial information to the general public. The data in these statements are fictional and are provided by the casewriters to facilitate classroom discussion of the case.

decide for themselves the best way to construct a given pressure vessel. It is very unusual for the company to build two identical pressure vessels in the same year. Advancement occurs only when there is an opening, which can be several years in a period of nongrowth. Some people have waited several years for a particular job to open up.

Hourly compensation ranges from $8.95 per hour for a janitor trainee to $16.35 per hour for a welder at the highest skill level. Average direct labor cost is $12.91 per hour. Direct labor constitutes less than 10 percent of total costs. Seniority is not a factor in determining compensation, which is based exclusively on performance and qualifications. Employees receive annual paid vacation based on years of service. An unusual form of compensation is the birthday bonus, which is an extra week of pay during the week of the employee's birthday. The birthday bonus becomes effective in the second full year of employment. Overall, the E. L. Nickell benefits package amounts to about 37.5 percent of wages. Exhibit 4 provides economic data about St. Joseph County, in which Constantine is located. Exhibit 5 shows the firm's organization chart, which has changed little since 1980.

Community Involvement

Over the years, Shelby has taken a personal interest in the village of Constantine. A few years ago, he purchased a small parcel of land on the south bank of the St. Joseph River, which flows through Constantine. He had the land developed into a riverfront park with access for the disabled and intends to donate it to the village someday. A half-mile to the south, Shelby had some other land cleared so that it could also be developed into parkland for use by the general public. Lyda and Shelby have both served on several community boards and given money, materials, and time toward several community development projects over the years.

EXHIBIT 4:   Economic Data on St. Joseph County

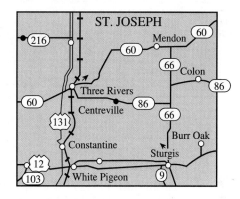

County Seat: Centreville

LOCATION SERVICES

Three Rivers Chamber of Commerce
103 S. Douglas Avenue
Three Rivers, MI 49093

Contact:	Chris Byrnes
Phone:	616/278-8193
FAX:	616/273-1832

POPULATION

1970 Census	47,392
1980 Census	56,083
1990 Census	58,913
Median Age (as of 1990)	32.8 years

LABOR FORCE (1992 average)

Total Labor Force	27,000
Employed	24,350
Total Unemployment	2,625
Unemployment Rate	9.7%
3–Year Average	10.2%

PRINCIPAL ECONOMIC BASE EMPLOYERS

Kirsch, Sturgis	818	Drapery hardware/home products
Grummon Olson, Sturgis	652	Aluminum truck bodies
Lear Siegler, Mendon	480	Plastics—auto and appliances
Ross Laboratories, Sturgis	461	Similac: hosp. dietary prod.
GM/Saginaw Div., Three Rivers	300	Steering gear parts
Burr Oak Tool & Gauge, Sturgis	280	Tools, dies, special machinery
Armstrong Intern'l, Three Rivers	199	Traps, humidifiers
Sturgis Molded Products, Sturgis	193	Injection molding
Vanguard Industries, Colon	160	Palomino campers
Continental Accessories, Sturgis	152	After-market auto products
Sturgis Iron & Metal	150	Process scrap steel
Weyerhaeuser, Three Rivers	150	Corrugated boxes
Owens–Illinois, Constantine	149	Crowns and closures
Bleyco Paper, Burr Oak	135	Wax paper processing
Sturgis Foundry, Sturgis	135	Gray iron castings
Arch Workshop, Sturgis	132	Assemble pallets, signs
LASCO Bath Fixtures, Three Rivers	130	Fiberglass tub and shower units
Johnson, Three Rivers	129	Rotary steam joints
Centurion Vehicles	120	Truck and van conversion
Rood Industries, Sturgis	115	Fabricated metal tubing
Total employees	5,040	

Source: Michigan Department of Commerce, County Profiles.

EXHIBIT 5:   E. L. Nickell Company Organizational Chart

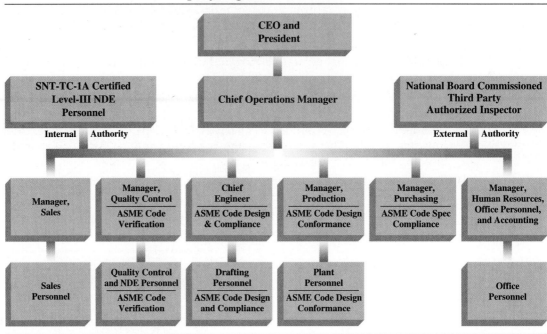

Source: E. L. Nickell Company.

THE FUTURE

In the fall of 1997, Shelby expressed concern over an unintended consequence on E. L. Nickell Company of the passage of the North American Free Trade Agreement (NAFTA) in 1995. Under NAFTA, goods such as steel that are produced in Mexico must be marked to U.S. market prices if they cross the border and are sold in the United States. However, if the steel is used to make a finished product in Mexico, then the finished product can be sold for whatever price its manufacturer desires. Mexico is the world's sixteenth-largest steel producer and the fifth-largest importer of steel to the United States behind the European Union, Canada, Brazil, and Japan. Mexico recently built the world's largest and most modern steel mill on its west coast. According to Shelby, "Because Mexican steel is sold at such low prices to Mexican producers and because Mexican labor is so cheap, firms can construct pressure vessels in Mexico, ship them to Constantine, and sell them for less than what it would cost the E. L. Nickell Company to buy the raw materials." Pressure vessels made in Mexico must meet the same code requirements as those made by E. L. Nickell; however, manufacturing facilities in Mexico do not have to comply with OSHA, EPA, and other regulations that E. L. Nickell must comply with in the United States. The Mexican government sees the export of steel as a way for it to strengthen its economy and improve the balance of trade.

Shelby must deal with questions that have to do with the day-to-day operation of E. L. Nickell Company as well as with the threat of inexpensive Mexican steel.

1. Should the company develop a database of past customers to facilitate more rapid quoting on bids for custom vessels? According to company records, when the company returns a quote within 24 hours, it receives the job 72 percent of the time. If it waits more than 24 hours, the chances of getting the job drop to 51 percent.

2. Should the company enlarge its current facility or move to a larger facility to permit operation of a second shift? Large pressure vessels are heavy and difficult to move. They reduce plant capacity because they stay in the same place in the plant until shipped.

3. Because E. L. Nickell is almost totally dependent on the industrial refrigeration industry, should it try to develop a new product in another market that would be compatible with its existing expertise?

4. If Mexico continues to subsidize the manufacture of steel without regard to safety and environmental standards, should E. L. Nickell Company build a plant on the U.S. West Coast or in Mexico?